Books by Walter Johnson

THE BATTLE AGAINST ISOLATION

WILLIAM ALLEN WHITE'S AMERICA

THE UNITED STATES: EXPERIMENT IN DEMOCRACY
(with Avery Craven)

HOW WE DRAFTED ADLAI STEVENSON

1600 PENNSYLVANIA AVENUE: PRESIDENTS AND THE PEOPLE, 1929–1959

THE FULBRIGHT PROGRAM: A HISTORY
(with Francis J. Colligan)

Edited by Walter Johnson

SELECTED LETTERS OF WILLIAM ALLEN WHITE

ROOSEVELT AND THE RUSSIANS: THE YALTA CONFERENCE
By Edward R. Stettinius, Jr.

TURBULENT ERA: A DIPLOMATIC RECORD OF FORTY YEARS, 1904–1945
By Joseph C. Grew

THE PAPERS OF ADLAI E. STEVENSON
Volume I: Beginnings of Education, 1900–1941
Volume II: Washington to Springfield, 1941–1948
Volume III: Governor of Illinois, 1949–1953
Volume IV: "Let's Talk Sense to the American People," 1952–1955
Volume V: Visit to Asia, the Middle East, and Europe —
March–August 1953
Volume VI: Toward a New America, 1955–1957
Volume VII: Continuing Education and the Unfinished Business of
American Society — 1957–1961
Volume VIII: Ambassador to the United Nations — 1961–1965

The Papers of Adlai E. Stevenson

WALTER JOHNSON, *Editor*

CAROL EVANS, *Assistant Editor*

C. ERIC SEARS, *Editorial Assistant*

The Papers o

Adlai E. Stevenson

VOLUME VIII

Ambassador to the United Nations

1961–1965

LITTLE, BROWN *and* COMPANY • *Boston* • *Toronto*

FIRST EDITION

The editors gratefully acknowledge the permission of the following authors, publishers, individuals and institutions to reprint selected materials as noted:

Basic Books, Inc., Barry Bingham, Jr., Anti-Defamation League of B'nai B'rith, Ellis O. Briggs, The Brookings Institution, the Chicago *Sun-Times*, Harlan Cleveland, Coward, McCann & Geoghegan, Inc., Mrs. John Currie, Roxane Eberlein, James T. Farrell, *Foreign Affairs*, Mrs. Felix Frankfurter, Clayton Fritchey, Richard N. Gardner, Harry Golden, Harper & Row, Publishers, Inc., The Johns Hopkins University Press, Houghton Mifflin Company, I.H.T. Corporation, Gerald Johnson, *Life*, J. B. Lippincott Company, the *London Sunday Times*, *Look*, *Los Angeles Times* Syndicate, Dwight MacDonald, Macmillan Publishing Co., Inc., John J. McCloy, Mrs. Ralph McGill, Carl McGowan, *Meet The Press*, Bill D. Moyers, *Nation*, *Newsweek*, *The New Yorker*, *New York Post*, W. W. Norton & Co., Inc., the *Observer*, Mrs. Jacqueline Kennedy Onassis, Paul, Weiss, Rifkind, Wharton & Garrison, G. P. Putnam's Sons, Dean Rusk, *San Francisco Chronicle*, the *Saturday Evening Post*, Don A. Schanche, Arthur Schlesinger, Jr., Eric Sevareid, Mrs. John Steinbeck, U Thant, *The Times*, Marietta Tree, The Viking Press Inc., Publishers, Mrs. Hope McKay Virtue, the *Village Voice*, the *Washington Post*, the *Washington Star*, David J. Webster, Willard Wirtz, the *Wisconsin State Journal*, Ralph W. Yarborough, Charles Yost.

Harcourt Brace Jovanovich, Inc., and Faber and Faber Limited for excerpts from *Murder in the Cathedral* by T. S. Eliot. Copyright 1935, by Harcourt Brace Jovanovich, Inc.; renewed 1963 by T. S. Eliot. Reprinted by permission of the publishers.

Little, Brown and Company for excerpts from *The Complete Poems of Emily Dickinson*, edited by Thomas H. Johnson. Copyright 1914, 1942 by Martha Dickinson Bianchi.

Little, Brown and Company for excerpts from *Everyone but Thee and Me* by Ogden Nash. Copyright © 1962 by Ogden Nash.

Library of Congress Cataloging in Publication Data (Revised)

Stevenson, Adlai Ewing, 1900–1965.
    The papers of Adlai E. Stevenson

    Includes bibliographical references.
    CONTENTS: v. 1. Beginnings of education, 1900–1941.—v. 2. Washington to Springfield, 1941–1948.—v. 3. Governor of Illinois, 1949–1953.—v. 4. "Let's talk sense to the American people," 1952–1955. [etc.]
    1. United States—Politics and government—1945–
2. Illinois—Politics and government—1865–1950—
Sources. 3. Stevenson, Adlai Ewing, 1900–1965.
4. Statesmen—United States—Correspondence.
I. Johnson, Walter, 1915–   ed.
E742.5.S747   973.921'092'4   73-175478
ISBN 0-316-46944-0 (v.8)

MV
*Published simultaneously in Canada
by Little, Brown & Company (Canada) Limited*

PRINTED IN THE UNITED STATES OF AMERICA

Foreword

At the memorial services to Adlai E. Stevenson on July 19, 1965, in the hall of the General Assembly of the United Nations, his longtime friend Archibald MacLeish observed:

> . . . His effectiveness here, his services to this organization and to the country to which his life was given, others have spoken of and will speak. They were great services, greatly rendered. But the most important thing about them, or so it seems to me, was their humanity. It is not, in the long history of civilization, the accomplishment which counts but the manner of the accomplishment. Works of will are notoriously short-lived and even works of intellect can fail when the intelligence is cynical or dry. It is only when the end is reached through the human heart as well as through the human mind that the accomplishment is certain to endure. And it is for that reason that Adlai Stevenson seems certain of remembrance.
>
> His great achievement was not political triumph or, indeed, triumph of any kind. His great achievement was the enrichment of his time by the nature of his relationships with his time. If his intelligence was remarkable it was remarkable, even more than for its clarity, for its modesty, its humor, its naturalness, its total lack of vanity or arrogance. If he was one of the great articulators of his time, one of the few, true voices, it was because the words he spoke were the words of his own thought, of his deepest and most personal conviction. It was himself he gave in word and thought and action, not to his friends alone but to his country, to his world. And the gift had consequences. It changed the tone and temper of political life in the United States for a genera-

tion. It humanized the quality of international dialogue throughout a great part of the world. It enlightened a dark time. . . .[1]

The Secretary-General of the United Nations, U Thant, said:

> . . . During the four and a half years that he served at the United Nations, he stood as the embodiment of dedication to the principles of the United Nations. His many speeches, which expressed so well his whole mental and intellectual approach, in the championship of fundamental rights, in defense of the dignity and worth of the human person, in support of the equal rights of nations large and small, were cheered and applauded by all sides of the house. He not only spoke with a rare gift of phrase but with such an obvious sincerity that his words carried conviction. . . .[2]

The foreign minister of India, Swaran Singh, stated on July 17, 1965: "In Stevenson's death another voice which upheld human values in this strife torn world has been stilled. His patient gentleness of approach to complex problems that divide the great countries, charm of manner and clarity of vision will be missed by all." [3]

The president of the Eighteenth General Assembly of the United Nations, Venezuelan Ambassador Dr. Carlos Sosa Rodriguez, said in the memorial ceremony on July 19:

> . . . We, his colleagues in the United Nations, have lost one of its most enlightened sons and the United Nations one of its most faithful champions.
>
> . . . Perhaps better than any other public figure, Adlai Stevenson gave the world an image of a modern and liberal North America, conscious of the outstanding role it is called upon to play in history and conscious of the enormous responsibility derived for her from her great military and economic power. It would be difficult to classify Adlai Stevenson, from the political standpoint, as a man of the right or a man of the left. Stevenson was a liberal in the true sense of the word. He was a man free of extremism, ever respectful of the opinions and viewpoints of others, but always convinced of the force of reason, not of the reason of force. His liberal spirit was reflected in all his acts as a public figure and especially in his performance as a diplomat.[4]

Max Freedman wrote in the Washington *Star*, July 15, 1965:

[1] The United States mission to the United Nations (USUN) published the speeches delivered at the memorial ceremony, as did the *Department of State Bulletin*, August 9, 1965.
[2] Ibid.
[3] New York *Times*, July 18, 1965.
[4] See note 1, above.

By the grace of his spirit and the splendor of his mind Adlai Stevenson turned the sting of defeat into a crown of glory. . . . He had a higher aim in view than his place as America's prose laureate. He wanted words on the political platform to be used as counters of truth and never as weapons of deception. He has left us his example to shame those who fall below his standards.

The Times (London) wrote:

He died full of disappointments, yet his life has left a mark that will not be eradicated. Abroad he came to represent that aspect of his country which most sustains foreign confidence in the fundamental virtue of its intentions even when its actions seem wrong. Through all the placid confidence of the Eisenhower era, and the clumsy crusades of Mr. Dulles, he reminded the world that there was another America — sensitive, self-critical, thoughtful, and visionary. At home he kept the light of intellect burning through a period when it was not fashionable to think. He restored faith in a profession which had come to be regarded as rough, and even disreputable. He came to represent for many the conscience of his country.[5]

The Toronto *Daily Star* wrote:

Adlai Stevenson was an American whom America shared with the world. For millions of people he represented what America ought to be — its intellect, its culture and wit, its wisdom, and its grace under the terrible pressure of duty.

. . . But while Adlai Stevenson never reached the power for which he yearned, his impact was enormous. His was a call for justice within America's borders and an understanding of the historic revolution that is sweeping the have-not world. He was a man of vast eloquence and he used it to become a spokesman of an enlightened United States.[6]

Walter Lippmann wrote in the New York *Herald Tribune* on July 20, 1965:

We must wonder whether we have buried with Adlai Stevenson some element of the promise of American life. For in this generation he has stood apart, not only for his deeds and his words and his wit and his lovableness, but as somehow a living specimen of the kind of American that Americans themselves, and the great mass of mankind, would like to think that Americans are.

. . . Shall we see his like again? Or was he the last of his noble breed? On this question hangs the American future. On one course

[5] Reprinted in the *Saturday Review*, August 21, 1965.
[6] Ibid.

we shall plunge ourselves into the making of a ramshackle empire in an era when no empire can long survive, and we shall wave the flag to cover our spiritual nakedness.

Or, we shall, as Adlai Stevenson would have done, remain true to our original loyalty, and transcending assertiveness, vulgar ambition, and the seductions of power, we shall make this country not only great and free but at peace with its own conscience.

Historian Henry Steele Commager wrote in the *Observer* (London), July 18, 1965:

Adlai Stevenson presents us with a spectacle rare in American, and probably in modern, history — a man whose public career was crowded into a few short years, whose every foray into large politics was marked by defeat, and who exercised immense authority wholly without power, an authority whose sanctions were entirely intellectual and moral. . . . [He] managed, by sheer force of intelligence and moral distinction, to lift the whole level of public life and discourse, and to infuse American politics with a dignity, a vitality, an excitement it had not known since the early days of the New Deal.

Robert M. Hutchins wrote in the Los Angeles *Times,* August 29, 1965:

He was sensitive, modest, honest and critical, especially of himself. In a word, he was civilized. He had a vision of a civilized world, and he thought he could do something to bring it into existence. The way he could help was to talk sense to the American people and to the world. . . . The word I cannot tolerate in regard to Adlai Stevenson is "failure." He failed of election to the Presidency. What of it? He succeeded in becoming what few Presidents have been. He was a light to the world.

Judge Carl McGowan remarked:

He was an ornament of our generation, but his greatest and most lasting gifts have been bestowed upon our children and those who come after them. He proved that one can, although denied power, make of integrity and credibility a great national asset. That is the kind of accomplishment which speaks to the young in accents their elders cannot always hear.[7]

On January 23, 1961, Adlai E. Stevenson presented his credentials as Ambassador Extraordinary and Plenipotentiary and Permanent Representative of the United States to Dag Hammarskjöld, Secretary-General

---

[7] Speech to the Law and Legal clubs of Chicago, Illinois, March 11, 1966.

of the United Nations. Stevenson had been a significant figure in the creation of the world organization.[8] He wrote:

> I thought then if they did not overload it with too many tasks, which they did, they would surely tear it apart with dissension, which they almost did, or they would drown it in words. (Why do so many people feel that to be immortal a speech must be eternal?) Returning after fifteen years I found the United Nations more overloaded, more riven by dissension, still suffocated with rhetoric, but — miraculously — mature, strong and vibrant with hope.[9]

Stevenson was the most eminent person ever to have been made a permanent representative to the UN. Not only had he been an architect of the organization, but in the years after his governorship of Illinois he had traveled to most of the countries of the world, he had studied their problems, and he had held lengthy discussions with the people in power at home or who were at the UN representing their countries during his four and a half years as ambassador.[10]

In view of his prestige and his widespread travels, Stevenson was able to have a relationship with foreign ministers, heads of government, and influential private citizens that no predecessor had ever had. As a result he was more than a product of his instructions. While he was a mouthpiece for policies determined in Washington, he was able to accomplish certain creative things because of who he was. At one point, for instance, during the UN operation in the Congo, through his friendship with banker André Meyer, of Lazard Frères and Company, pressure was put on Belgian mining interests to reduce their support of Moise Tshombe, ruler of the province of Katanga, and to inform him that secession was not acceptable.[11]

Some of the international civil servants with whom Stevenson worked from 1961 to 1965 knew him when they were young staff members at the 1945 San Francisco Conference, at the Preparatory Commission in London in the fall of 1945, and at the General Assembly meetings in 1946 and 1947. He was identified in their minds as a real father of the United Nations. He had built up trust with them through his devotion to the principles of the UN Charter. Their respect for and warmth toward him was obvious when he returned to the UN in 1961.

[8] For Stevenson's activities at the San Francisco Conference (1945), the Preparatory Commission meetings in London (1945), and the meetings of the General Assembly in 1946 and 1947, see *The Papers of Adlai E. Stevenson*, Vol. II.

[9] Adlai E. Stevenson, *Looking Outward: Years of Crisis at the United Nations*, edited with commentary by Robert L. Schiffer and Selma Schiffer, preface by John F. Kennedy (New York: Harper & Row, 1963), p. xvi.

[10] See, for instance, the chronicle of his extensive trip to Asia, the Middle East, and Europe in 1953, in *The Papers of Adlai E. Stevenson*, Vol. V.

[11] Harlan Cleveland, interview with Walter Johnson, April 30, 1973.

They understood his commitment to the idea of the United Nations, "its potentiality for peace." Ambassador Francis T. P. Plimpton, Stevenson's close friend from Harvard Law School days who had been appointed by Kennedy at Stevenson's request as deputy permanent representative to the UN, recalled: "He really was an idealist, and, while he was a perfectly good enough realist about the U.N., it was the idea of the place that captured his imagination." [12]

The crises at the United Nations during Stevenson's four and a half years were incessant. The Bay of Pigs; the Cuban missile crisis; the UN forces in the Congo, on Cyprus, on the Egyptian-Israeli border, and in Kashmir; the death of Dag Hammarskjöld and the Soviet "troika" proposal for three heads of the organization; the near bankruptcy and impasse over Article 19 of the Charter; the wrangle with Portugal over its unyielding control of African colonies; white racism in Southern Rhodesia and South Africa; and the quest for disarmament required almost constant negotiations.

Mr. Plimpton also wrote:

> As for those four and a half years at the United Nations, they were, in a way, one perpetual litigation, not between two parties but between 117, with no judge but the 117 parties themselves. . . . In that litigation, and in the accompanying interminable negotiations with all sorts of conditions of delegates from the four corners of the earth . . . [Stevenson] went straight to the essential core of the problem, refusing to get enmeshed in preliminary details; he took the long view, avoiding entanglement in tactical immediacy. . . . He was a superb private negotiator — patient, tolerant, friendly but firm, understanding of others' points of view but persistent in his own, and persuasive of his cause because persuaded by his cause.[13]

Ambassador Stevenson, as head of the United States mission to the United Nations (USUN), was not only the representative of the President of the United States at the UN. He was acutely aware that he was also UN ambassador to the American people and, as a result, made an immense number of speeches to public groups — to "the community of the concerned." [14] He was as convinced, as he had been during the 1952 campaign, that it was the duty of people in public life to contribute to

[12] Oral history interview, October 21, 1969, p. 69, in the John F. Kennedy Library.
[13] "Adlai E. Stevenson," *Harvard Law School Bulletin*, January, 1967, p. 3.
[14] Harlan Cleveland, "Crisis Diplomacy," *Foreign Affairs*, Vol. XLI, No. 4 (July, 1963), p. 639. See also Francis T. P. Plimpton, "They Sent You Our Best," in *As We Knew Adlai: The Stevenson Story by Twenty-two Friends*, edited and with preface by Edward P. Doyle, foreword by Adlai E. Stevenson III (New York: Harper & Row, 1966), p. 256.

the education of the public so that the "people will understand and will have the tools of good judgment and wise decision." [15]

Stevenson was convinced that the United Nations should be the "very center" of United States foreign policy. He was in a real sense the UN ambassador to the United States government. Holding Cabinet rank and with the assurance that he would play a key role in the formulation of foreign policy, Stevenson attempted to persuade the White House and the Department of State to make the United Nations the "very center" of foreign policy.

Stevenson's notes of his conversation with President-elect Kennedy and Secretary of State-designate Dean Rusk on December 11, 1960, read at one point: "UN center of our foreign policy." [16] Rusk wrote: "In general, his notes of the December 11 conversation are reasonably accurate." [17]

Mr. and Mrs. Edison Dick, neighbors and old friends of Stevenson, saw a great deal of him while he was deciding whether to accept appointment to the United Nations and they discussed the question with him. Mrs. Dick, after reading the notes, wrote in 1972 about the telephone conversations that it was "too far in the past for me to state positively what I remember of them," and "they are not clear-cut in my memory." However, she went on, "I know that AES felt strongly that the UN needed great strengthening and apparently felt that it should be the center of our foreign policy. I find it hard to believe that Kennedy or Rusk would agree to it as *the* center of our foreign policy — perhaps they agreed to its being a center of our foreign policy." [18]

Mrs. Ronald Tree, an old friend who served as special adviser to Stevenson at the UN, wrote that Stevenson, after deciding to accept the appointment, "began to think constructively about the conditions for the job. I think he felt in a strong position because at that point he did not care desperately about it, but knew that Kennedy needed him for domestic as well as global political reasons." But Mrs. Tree was unable to remember whether President Kennedy agreed to all the details of Steven-

15 *Major Campaign Speeches of Adlai E. Stevenson, 1952* (New York: Random House, 1953), p. xxv.

16 For these notes, see *The Papers of Adlai E. Stevenson*, Vol. VII, pp. 596–597.

17 Letter to Walter Johnson, April 11, 1972. Rusk did not comment specifically, however, on the phrase "UN center of our foreign policy."

18 Letter to Carol Evans, May 15, 1972. William McC. Blair, Jr., Stevenson's law partner and longtime aide, appointed ambassador to Denmark by Kennedy, wrote that the conversations were never discussed with him. Letter to Carol Evans, May 9, 1972. Willard Wirtz, another Stevenson law partner, appointed Under Secretary of Labor by Kennedy, wrote that Stevenson discussed the conversations with him but that he was unable to recollect the "Kennedy reactions." Wirtz added: "My fuzzy general impression is that the Governor felt that the conversations had been sufficiently more satisfactory than he expected them to be that he decided to go ahead with the Ambassadorship despite an earlier strong inclination not to do so." Letter to Carol Evans, May 9, 1972.

son's "conditions" for accepting the post.[19] Francis T. P. Plimpton wrote that Stevenson never discussed with him in detail the extent to which the President accepted these conditions.[20]

Whatever the extent of the agreement by the President to his conditions, Stevenson said to the Senate Foreign Relations Committee on January 18, 1961: "We should use it [the UN] not as a device in the cold war, not just in defensive reaction to Soviet initiatives, but affirmatively to advance its great purposes — to liberate men from the scourge of war, poverty, disease, ignorance, and oppression." [21]

As Senator J. W. Fulbright has observed, however, the United Nations was consigned after President Franklin D. Roosevelt's death to the "care of unsympathetic men of his own country." The framers of the Truman Doctrine in 1947 disdained the UN and "nurtured an intensive hostility toward Communism and the Soviet Union." Fulbright added:

> Like the Soviet Union and other great powers, we have treated the United Nations as an instrument of our policy, to be used when it is helpful but otherwise ignored . . . the United Nations has never been treated as a potential world-security community — as an institution to be developed and strengthened for the long-term purpose of protecting humanity from the destructiveness of unrestrained nationalism. The immediate, short-term advantage of the leading members has invariably been given precedence over the needs of the collectivity. That is why the United Nations has not worked.[22]

Stevenson in attempting to make the UN work, in attempting to return to the vision of the founders of the organization, ran up against the determined opposition of implacable Cold Warriors in both the Kennedy and Johnson administrations. Men like Stevenson and Chester Bowles (Under Secretary of State until he was ousted in November, 1961) in trying to persuade their government to rethink the assumptions of the Cold War, were confronted with the opposition of the Dean Achesons, the Dean Rusks, and both Presidents whose anti-Communism was the guiding spirit of United States foreign policy.[23] Bowles wrote:

[19] Letter to Carol Evans, May 8, 1972. Among the conditions were that he was to be a member of the Cabinet, with the "option to attend" National Security Council meetings when foreign policy matters were being considered, and that he "should be in mainstream of policy making. No important decisions without opportunity to express views." See *The Papers of Adlai E. Stevenson*, Vol. VII, pp. 594–598.

[20] Letter to Carol Evans, May 12, 1972.

[21] USUN press release, January 18, 1961.

[22] "Reflections: In Thrall to Fear," *New Yorker*, January 8, 1972, p. 59. See also his *The Crippled Giant: American Foreign Policy and Its Domestic Consequences* (New York: Random House, 1972).

[23] Arthur M. Schlesinger, Jr., feels this paragraph gives a misleading impression of Kennedy's foreign policy views. Schlesinger writes: "He was not at all a rigid cold

. . . The judgment on foreign policy issues of many liberals, even those with experience in foreign affairs was distorted by their determination to establish themselves as "realists." Having been charged with "woolly headedness," "softness on Communism" and similar crimes during the Republican Administration, they felt it necessary to demonstrate they were, in fact, tough characters.[24]

Bowles also wrote:

Adlai's principal opponents (and also mine) in and around the new administration were a strange collection of individuals who had attached themselves to Kennedy for a variety of reasons. Among them were Joe Alsop and Dean Acheson, the most articulate and most vindictive. Both clung to cold-war concepts and seemed to assume that somehow we could destroy distasteful ideas with bombs, and both ridiculed Adlai's and my concern about our relations with the developing nations of Africa, Latin America and Asia. Their distrust of Adlai was strongly supported by several members of Kennedy's so-called "Boston Mafia." . . .

Another faction that was close to Kennedy (although probably not as close as they claimed to be) was a small group of playboys who enjoyed basking in the prestige of Jackie and Jack, and they looked upon Adlai and me as traitors to our "Ivy League" background.[25]

Despite the assurances from two Presidents that he would play a "key role," Stevenson had little authority "within the foreign policy machine." [26] Stevenson's national and international following was such that both President Kennedy and President Johnson wanted him to remain as ambassador to the United Nations while denying him a key role in foreign policy formulation. Former Secretary of State Dean Rusk wrote:

---

warrior of the Acheson-Rusk school. Nor was he indifferent to the UN; in fact, it always seemed to me to be much more on his mind than it was on the mind of the top State Department officials (except, of course, for those for whom it was a direct responsibility). . . . JFK, in my judgment, agreed rather more with Stevenson and Bowles than he did with Rusk and Acheson; but he found it easier to do business with Rusk and Acheson than he did with Stevenson and Bowles. The man from the foreign policy establishment that met Kennedy's needs best on both scores was Harriman, who combined, so to speak, Stevenson's views with Acheson's directness and decisiveness." Letter to Walter Johnson, February 7, 1975.

24 *Promises to Keep: My Years in Public Life, 1941–1969* (New York: Harper & Row, 1971), p. 344; and see pp. 619–625 for a letter he wrote to Stevenson on July 23, 1961, analyzing the position of the "tough characters."

25 Letter to Walter Johnson, December 5, 1972.

26 Arnold Beichman, *The "Other" State Department: The United States Mission to the United Nations — Its Role in the Making of Foreign Policy* (New York: Basic Books, 1967), p. 12. However, Dean Rusk stated that Stevenson had more authority than many people thought. Letter to Walter Johnson, May 23, 1973.

As matters turned out, the participation of Adlai Stevenson in making policy varied directly with the amount of time which he was willing and able to spend in Washington. It was just not possible to play a major role from New York. He was invited to all Cabinet meetings and meetings of the National Security Council but could not always attend. When he was in town, I usually had a general tour d'horizon with him about outstanding policy questions and had a pretty good idea about his point of view. His views were not always accepted by President Kennedy or President Johnson but, in the main, the Presidents usually knew what he thought.[27]

On December 4, 1961, James Plimsoll, Australian ambassador to the United Nations, wrote his government of a conversation that he had just had with Stevenson:

Stevenson then spoke to me very frankly about his position here, which he said, had not been an easy one for him. He did not find it easy to take detailed instructions on almost everything and would have liked more freedom and to be given more discretion. On some aspects of policy such as Cuba, he had been very much in agreement with the Administration. He had however tried to perform his duties loyally even where he had disagreed with the policy decided on. "The Young President" had started off by trying to do everything himself in international affairs but he was now seeing that this was impossible and he was making greater use of others. Kennedy was now consulting Stevenson more and bringing him more into things and as a result Stevenson was a great deal happier. Stevenson had hopes as a result he could have more say on policy on a number of things he had to handle here.[28]

Arthur M. Schlesinger, Jr., a friend and admirer of both Kennedy and Stevenson, wrote that after the 1956 Democratic Convention "their relationship began to take on a slight tinge of mutual exasperation." [29]

Schlesinger, as special assistant to President Kennedy, was the White House liaison with Stevenson. The President told Schlesinger that he wished he had "more rapport" with Stevenson. Schlesinger observed that the President, "who had an essential respect and liking for Stevenson, tried, when he thought of it, to make their relationship effective." [30] Ken-

---

[27] Letter to Walter Johnson, April 11, 1972. Arthur M. Schlesinger, Jr., has also noted that in order to influence policy, Stevenson had to be present at Cabinet and National Security Council meetings, but that pressing matters at the United Nations often prevented this. *A Thousand Days: John F. Kennedy in the White House* (Boston: Houghton Mifflin, 1965), p. 464. Francis T. P. Plimpton stated: "This UN operation is a very demanding one, and the idea that you can spend one or two days a week in Washington and do the job up here is just out of the question." Oral history interview, John F. Kennedy Library, p. 6.

[28] Foreign Office records, Canberra, Australia.

[29] *A Thousand Days*, p. 9.

[30] Ibid., p. 462. Ralph Dungan, who had also been a special assistant to President Kennedy, stated that the White House spent "too much time in trying to keep Adlai happy." Interview with Walter Johnson, Princeton, New Jersey, May 25, 1969.

nedy understood Stevenson's prestige in the world and his influence on a large following in the United States, Schlesinger wrote. The President, moreover, admired Stevenson's "public presence and wit, valued his skills as diplomat and orator, and considered him . . . capable of original thought." Schlesinger added, however, that certain of Stevenson's "idiosyncrasies did try" the President. Stevenson never seemed "wholly at ease on visits to the White House," according to Schlesinger. The President believed Stevenson was unable to make up his mind, but Schlesinger remarked: "It was his manner, deliberately self-deprecatory, that conveyed an appearance of indecision which did not really exist." [31]

John Steele, Time-Life bureau chief in Washington, D.C., during the Kennedy Administration and a close friend of Stevenson's, wrote:

> Stevenson was miscast on the New Frontier. The men of John F. Kennedy were flat-stomached; Stevenson was paunchy. They talked in cryptic, often barely understandable phrases; Stevenson talked in long sentences, comma-struck with parenthetical, often qualifying phrases. He was epigrammatic, enjoyed discourse for discourse's sake. The New Frontiersmen were grim, passionate men with their own brand of acidic humor. Stevenson's eyes lit up with his own wry wit, often directed at himself and never cruelly at others. With the succeeding Johnson administration his relations were only a bit more comfortable. President Johnson's taste runs to swift analysis of a situation, often brief debate, and then crisp decision making. Stevenson worried a problem, pondered it, qualified it, then came up with a recommendation. As the President's decision-making group grew ever smaller, Stevenson was moved ever farther away from its epicenter.[32]

Many of the "bright young men" around Kennedy, Stevenson viewed as "brash and arrogant." After the Bay of Pigs, he said, "I believe in on-the-job training, but not for Presidents." The stakes were much too high and Stevenson feared that one of those "decisive" and "impulsive" young men could "bumble" the nation into a nuclear war. Once he remarked of Kennedy, "I can't say I like that young man. He is altogether too sure of himself, and he is not as likely to be right as he thinks he is." [33] Following the Bay of Pigs, Stevenson remarked to Mary McGrory after a visit to the White House, "That young man, he never says 'please' and he never says 'I'm sorry.'" [34]

Benjamin C. Bradlee asked Kennedy on March 3, 1962, whether every member of his administration was happy about Kennedy's decision to resume nuclear testing in the atmosphere. Kennedy replied: "I suppose if

[31] *A Thousand Days*, pp. 64, 462–463.
[32] *Life*, July 23, 1965, p. 3.
[33] Conversations with Mrs. John B. Currie. Mrs. Currie kept notes of her conversations with Stevenson and kindly made a transcript available to the editor.
[34] "The Perfectionist and the Press," in *As We Knew Adlai*, p. 178.

you grabbed Adlai by the nuts, he might object." Bradlee adds that Stevenson was "a man whose popularity with liberal Democrats Kennedy resented." Bradlee also describes being at the White House on November 15, 1962, when Stevenson phoned the President about a meeting he had just had with Vasily Kuznetsov on the Cuban missile crisis. Kennedy then called McGeorge Bundy. Bradlee writes: "The president referred to Stevenson in a manner that did nothing to dispel the rumors that he was less than 100 percent behind his UN ambassador." [35]

Although President Lyndon B. Johnson paid Stevenson greater deference than Kennedy had done, Johnson also excluded him from the key decision-making. Johnson once told Stevenson that whenever he wanted to see the President, he should not stand on formalities but "just come barging in through the back door of the White House." Stevenson in relating this statement to Peter Lisagor of the Washington bureau of the Chicago *Daily News* asked, "How does one barge into the back door of the White House?" [36]

In fact, Stevenson's relations with Johnson were so unsubstantial that, at the time of the U Thant peace initiative on Vietnam, Stevenson sent memoranda about the proposals to the White House because, according to Harlan Cleveland, Stevenson could not have taken them in person and have been sure to see the President.[37]

According to Francis T. P. Plimpton, Stevenson was always conscious of the "awful problem: suppose he doesn't agree. As I think he said publicly — he certainly said it privately to me — it would be practically an earthquake if he were to say, 'I disagree and I resign.' He would do that only about some sort of life and death matter. He was conscious of that awful difficulty." [38]

Two nights before he died, in a talk with his friend Eric Sevareid, of the Columbia Broadcasting System, Stevenson revealed his "profound frustration, a certain resentment that stopped just short of bitterness." He told Sevareid he simply "had to get out of the UN job." "I guess I've been too patient. I guess that's a character weakness of mine." Sevareid reported that Stevenson made no specific criticism of President Johnson. "I had the feeling that he had great respect for the President's capacities, but no warm regard for him as a person," Sevareid wrote. As to Secretary of State Rusk, Stevenson said, "Oh, . . . I just can't seem to make him out. He's so sort of wooden." [39]

---

[35] *Conversations with Kennedy* (New York: W. W. Norton, 1975), pp. 62–63, 120–121.
[36] Syndicated column, Honolulu *Star Bulletin*, August 20, 1974.
[37] Interview with Walter Johnson, April 30, 1973.
[38] Oral history interview, John F. Kennedy Library, p. 3.
[39] Francis T. P. Plimpton remarked: "I think he had a good regard for [Dean] Rusk, but he thought of him as a technician rather than as a broadminded, knowledgeable citizen of the world, so to speak." Ibid., pp. 4–5.

"The Vietnam war deeply worried him," Sevareid noted. When the conversation turned to the U Thant–Stevenson peace initiatives on Vietnam in 1964 and 1965, Stevenson maintained that these opportunities should have been pursued. Sevareid wrote: "He was accustomed to making policy, not to being told what the policy was to be and how he was to defend and explain it before the world. In particular, he could not bear having certain White House and State Department people whom he regarded as mere youngsters telling him what to do. He felt these men simply did not understand his difficulties at the UN, and he doubted their wisdom about this dangerous world." [40]

United States policy at the UN is determined in Washington, regardless of the eminence of the permanent representative. The direct telephone lines between USUN, the White House and the Department of State provide a continuous dialogue.[41] Ambassador Plimpton wrote that Stevenson's speeches were "conglomerates of State Department drafts, USUN and AES objections (sometimes substantive and always stylistic) and redrafts, occasional White House arbitration of those objections, and eventual hard-fought cease-fires and compromises." [42]

There were 99 members of the UN when Stevenson became the U.S. ambassador in 1961. Conferences, meetings and receptions were incessant. "Is it all worthwhile?" Stevenson wrote in 1963. "Of course it is — if peace is worthwhile. Making peace is not merely a matter of nations looking at each other, but of their looking together in the same direction. Each peaceful gesture, each little thing, each humble effort at pacification, accomplished at any level, brings peace closer. The journey of a thousand leagues begins with a single step." [43]

Stevenson's papers from the United Nations period are deposited in the Princeton University Library. The reader should be warned, however, that after his death a number of his papers were classified. The Historical Division of the Department of State refused the editor access to these papers. Under the Freedom of Information Act, the editor applied for a declassification review of some material. Through internal evidence in the unclassified papers and as the result of suggestions from Roxane

---

[40] "The Final Troubled Hours of Adlai Stevenson," *Look*, November 30, 1965.

[41] Almost all important calls to the President, the Secretary of State, and ambassadors were monitored by USUN, but transcripts of these calls were generally not typed up. For personal calls, Stevenson had one telephone that did not go through the USUN switchboard. Roxane Eberlein, interview with Walter Johnson, March 12, 1973.

[42] "They Sent You Our Best," in *As We Knew Adlai*, p. 261. Harlan Cleveland wrote: "Plimpton's description of AES speeches is good. But the saving grace was that Stevenson had a talent for identifying people who could produce original drafts good enough so that after his editing they sounded like Adlai Stevenson." Letter to Walter Johnson, April 30, 1973.

[43] *Looking Outward*, p. xvii.

Eberlein and John Stewart, of the John Fitzgerald Kennedy Library, it was possible for the editor to make specific requests for some documents. Had the editor been allowed to examine all the classified material, obviously he could have prepared a much more satisfactory list for declassification review. Arthur Schlesinger, Jr., authorized the John Fitzgerald Kennedy Library to make available his various memoranda to President Kennedy of talks with Stevenson. Requests to others close to Stevenson, while he was ambassador, for recommendations of documents to be requested for declassification review went unheeded.

Among the important documents declassified were: (1) Stevenson's memorandum to President Kennedy, October 12, 1961, on "Nuclear Testing and the United Nations"; (2) Stevenson's letter to President Kennedy, June 28, 1962, on disarmament, the nuclear test ban treaty, proliferation of nuclear weapons, and foreign bases; (3) Stevenson material on the Cuban missile crisis; (4) Stevenson's lengthy recommendations to President Johnson on foreign policy, November 18, 1964; (5) Stevenson's letters to President Johnson, February 16 and February 17, 1965, on his conversations with U Thant about Vietnam; (6) Stevenson's report to President Johnson, February 27, 1965, on further talks with U Thant about Vietnam; (7) Stevenson's memoranda of March 1, 1965, and April 28, 1965, about Vietnam; and (8) Stevenson's report of his final talk with U Thant, July 7, 1965.

Seven requests for declassification were refused. Since the editor never saw the documents, it is impossible to explain why the requests were refused other than the vague phrase used by the government in the refusal, the "national security." Two of these seven documents were memoranda from Arthur Schlesinger, Jr., to President Kennedy about the article by Charles Bartlett and Stewart Alsop, "The White House in the Cuban Crisis," *Saturday Evening Post,* December 8, 1962. It is difficult to believe that the "national security" can conceivably apply. If the refusal was based on concealing the fact that President Kennedy had indeed read and approved the article *before* publication, it was a fruitless gesture since other information, included in the present volume, substantiates this fact.

Not having access to the totality of the Stevenson papers may well mean that the volume contains more personal material about social activities — as important as these were to Stevenson — than a volume based on the entire collection would contain. As the volume stands now, the reader may receive the erroneous impression that social life at the UN dominated him. The concluding volume of *The Papers of Adlai E. Stevenson* is, therefore, the least satisfactory to the editor since he has been "shackled" in this way.

All the material used in this volume is in the Princeton University Library unless otherwise noted in footnote references. The speeches at the United Nations selected by the editor are from the United Nations *Official Records* of the Security Council or the General Assembly. Stevenson changed his speeches up to the point of delivery. The press releases, therefore, do not contain the changes. The *Official Records* do, however, since they are verbatim transcripts. Speeches delivered outside the UN were a more difficult problem. He apparently gave away his corrected copy at times. When the reading copy was available it was used. Otherwise, it was necessary to rely on press releases.

Speeches given outside the UN did not originate from the Department of State. Stevenson, with the assistance of Clayton Fritchey, Barbara Ward, Archibald MacLeish, Arthur Schlesinger, Jr., and others, drafted them. According to Clayton Fritchey, speeches delivered outside the UN were not cleared with the Department of State since they were "within the policy" of the government. He remembered only one example where Stevenson went beyond policy. At Fritchey's recommendation Stevenson deleted these sentences from the speech.[44]

The printed speech cannot reproduce the rhythmical flow of Stevenson's language or his pronunciation of words. The cadence and pronunciation can be heard in *Adlai E. Stevenson: The Man, the Candidate, the Statesman. A Portrait Through Excerpts from His Most Memorable Speeches,* narration by Bill Scott, produced by Audio-Stage, Inc., for the Macmillan Company, 1965.

The editor searched widely for handwritten letters and postcards. Many people were most cooperative, making all their Stevenson items available. Some preferred to send only selections from their collections. A few refused to send any material at all. Those who refused to send any handwritten material for all the eight volumes in this series include Ellen Stevenson, Dorothy Fosdick, Harriet Welling, Ruth Field, Mary Lasker, and Barbara Ward. Some letters which would cause unnecessary anguish to people still living were not included, or appropriate deletions have been made within such letters. These deletions — as well as others made because the material was redundant or trivial — are indicated by ellipses. The location of handwritten letters, postcards, or originals of typewritten letters is given in the footnote references. Stevenson's signature has been included on handwritten letters. In the case of typewritten letters it was necessary to work largely from carbon copies. When the original letter was located, and he signed it "AD" or "ADLAI," the signature has been included.

Whenever a statement in a letter was unclear, the editor, where possible, wrote to the recipient of the letter. The replies added greatly to

[44] Interview with Walter Johnson, April 6, 1973.

the editorial information contained in these volumes. This research technique, when supplemented by interviews with those people most knowledgeable about a specific situation, furnished the editor with information that would be unavailable if *The Papers of Adlai E. Stevenson* were to be published only a long time after his death.

The editor generally did not include letters written to Stevenson. Publishing letters written by people still alive or recently deceased requires obtaining formal permission — a time-consuming task. Instead, the editor has summarized the contents of an incoming letter where it was necessary to make Stevenson's reply understandable.

Under the legal agreement between Walter Johnson and Adlai E. Stevenson III, Borden Stevenson, and John Fell Stevenson, Adlai III agreed to read each volume before publication. In the event of disagreement as to the inclusion of any item of his father's papers, the matter was to be referred to Judge Carl McGowan for final — and irrevocable — decision. No disagreement with Adlai III arose.

Contents

Illustrations

Part One

1961

President Kennedy, on Adlai E. Stevenson's recommendation, appointed Francis T. P. Plimpton, Stevenson's Harvard Law School classmate, as deputy representative to the United Nations and a deputy representative in the Security Council, with the rank of ambassador extraordinary and plenipotentiary, and career diplomat Charles W. Yost also as a deputy representative in the Security Council, with the personal rank of ambassador. Philip M. Klutznick, of Chicago, was appointed representative on the Economic and Social Council, with the personal rank of ambassador, and Jonathan B. Bingham of New York (later to be a congressman) was appointed minister and representative on the Trusteeship Council. Eleanor Roosevelt was a delegate to the General Assembly. Mrs. Charles Tillett, a longtime political supporter from North Carolina, was representative on the Commission on the Status of Women. Marietta Tree, Stevenson's close friend for many years, was appointed U.S. representative to the United Nations Committee on Human Rights. Charles P. Noyes, whom Stevenson knew as a young staff member of the U.S. delegation to the 1945 San Francisco Conference where the United Nations was founded, was Stevenson's choice as counselor of the mission. Career diplomat Richard F. Pedersen was senior adviser for political affairs. Jane Dick, Stevenson's close friend since the 1920's, was appointed representative on the Social Commission. From his Chicago law office, Stevenson brought Roxane Eberlein to be one of his secretaries. Rosemary Spencer and Norma Garaventa, permanent employees at USUN, were also secretaries. In 1962 when Rosemary Spencer became protocol officer, Judy Dawidoff replaced her as secretary. Clayton Fritchey, active in both of Stevenson's presidential campaigns, was made director of public affairs. In all, Stevenson had a staff of 115 people.

In Washington, at Stevenson's recommendation, Harlan Cleveland, dean of the Maxwell School at Syracuse University, was appointed Assistant Secretary of State for International Organization Affairs. Richard N. Gardner served as one of Cleveland's deputy assistant sec-

retaries,[1] *Woodruff Wallner, a senior Foreign Service officer, was senior deputy assistant secretary. He was later succeeded by Joseph J. Sisco, a senior Foreign Service officer.*

The type of day Stevenson put in as ambassador to the United Nations was described by the New Yorker *shortly after his death.*

THE TALK OF THE TOWN [2]

Notes and Comment

One of the big "if"s in recent history is what our country might have become and how the world at large might have been affected if Adlai Ewing Stevenson had been elected President of the United States thirteen years ago. Some months back, talking about this "if" and about the various blows Mr. Stevenson had had to take, we asked one of his closest friends, Mrs. Edison Dick, who had known him for forty years, whether she felt sorry for him. "Not at all," she said. "I can feel sorry for a person who hasn't prevailed against fate, but I think he has prevailed." Over the past year, we had the deep pleasure of seeing quite a bit of Mr. Stevenson, with the intention of writing about him in these pages, and the more we saw of him, the surer we were she was right. Of course, every time we listened to him speak, and every time we read his prose, we regretted that he wasn't doing some writing in these pages himself. "I had a taste for literature and for the academic," he said to us last winter, early on a Sunday morning — a corner of time he had reserved in his back-breaking schedule for one of his talks with us — and he went on, "It's been part of the luggage I've carried in public life which doesn't yield public dividends." As always when he talked about himself, there was a lightness in the texture of his voice, and now its tone conveyed a detached, wry enjoyment of his own plight.

That morning was two days after his sixty-fifth birthday, and he had been awakened at his apartment in the Waldorf Towers — his official residence as United States Ambassador to the United Nations — at one in the morning by a caller from the State Department who wanted to tell him about the country's first major air strike in Vietnam. When we arrived for our appointment, around eight o'clock, we learned that Mr. Stevenson had been on the telephone with Government officials intermittently throughout the rest of the night. Nevertheless, he looked fresh and alert, and he was newly shaven and pink-cheeked, dressed in pin-striped navy trousers, a brown tweed jacket, a blue shirt open at the neck, and well-worn bedroom slippers. He had a new crisis on his hands, he told us. Also, he was wondering what to

---

[1] See Richard N. Gardner, *In Pursuit of World Order: US Foreign Policy and International Organizations* (New York: Praeger, 1965).

[2] From the *New Yorker*, July 24, 1965. Reprinted by permission; © 1965 The New Yorker Magazine, Inc.

do about a number of house guests — friends who had come from far points to help him celebrate his birthday. They would be getting up soon, and meanwhile he had arranged for several meetings, on the crisis, to be held later that morning at his office at the United States Mission to the United Nations. He expected to attend a hastily called meeting of the Security Council in the afternoon or evening. Notwithstanding this program, Mr. Stevenson showed no inclination to call off our talk. At the time, we were preoccupied with the broad question of what *might* have been, for him, and, as a result of having already spent a good many hours watching him and listening to him, with the further question of what might still *be*. We asked him, after one jangling telephone call, what he would like above all else to be doing at that moment. "I'd like to be out on my farm, in Libertyville, pruning trees," he said, and then, with that delightful, friendly Stevenson laugh, he added, "And I'd like an opportunity to get some rest. I've had about eleven days' vacation all told since I went into this job, four years ago. I'd like to do some reflecting and reading. I have an enormous accumulation of books I'd like to read. I'd like to be able to spend some time with my children and my grandchildren. And I'd like to travel, in a leisurely way, when I wouldn't be on exhibition and wouldn't have to perform. In the past twenty-four years — ever since I went to Washington during the war — I haven't had an opportunity to travel without having the travel coupled with ceremonies or the writing of articles or the taking of notes. But my first responsibility is to the President and to this job. I'd like to be useful as long as I can be. I've been so involved with affairs of my own generation I'd feel a little bereft if I were *not* involved. It's tempting sometimes to dream about a tranquil old age, but I think I'd be a little restive."

In the past four and a half years, in addition to attending sessions with President Kennedy's Cabinet, and then with President Johnson's, and attending meetings of the Security Council and the General Assembly and endless United Nations commissions, Mr. Stevenson had several speaking engagements a week, usually at luncheons or at dinners. (When he was not attending breakfasts, luncheons, cocktail parties, dinners, cookouts, and suppers given by other people, at least half of which were connected in one way or another with the United Nations, he usually played host at two or three of them a week himself.) One of his extracurricular appearances last August, shortly before the Democratic Convention, was at the final dinner of the annual meeting of the American Bar Association, held in the Grand Ballroom of the Waldorf-Astoria, where he was to make a speech. We met Mr. Stevenson at his apartment a few minutes before he was due at the dinner, and accompanied him to the Grand Ballroom, marvelling as we went at his fantastic energy. He appeared to be wholly absorbed in what he was about to do; there was no sign that he had walked into hundreds of other ballrooms set up for two or three thousand chicken dinners to be eaten by uncomfortably dinner-jacketed or strenuously gowned goers and doers — lawyers, engineers, actors, opera lovers, zoologists, and all the others. From the Bar Association dais, he looked into thousands of unanimated faces without mirroring anything of what he saw; his expression remained lively. An audience of lawyers, Mr. Stevenson had warned us, was by nature extremely conservative, and it seemed to us that he was relishing the challenge. The usual string orchestra, in red-and-gold uniforms, played "Some Enchanted Evening" from a balcony, and Mr. Stevenson, looking up, gave the musicians a nod. He remarked to one of the lawyers on the dais that a pre-dinner highball might be a good idea, and the lawyer offered him what he described as his own "slightly used bourbon." Mr. Stevenson smiled gratefully and took it. Then, as his custom was at dinners of this kind, he put on his horn-rimmed glasses and started studying the speech he had written and making improvements in it. As usual, there were interruptions for autographs, for the introduction of wives, and for announcements from citizens that they had voted for him in 1952 and/or 1956 — information that was frequently offered in a near-recriminatory key, because, in a success-happy age, he had not won.

In addressing the A.B.A., Mr. Stevenson tried to make his gray, largely humorless audience laugh, and he succeeded. "I've been paying dues to the A.B.A. for forty years," he began, before starting to read his prepared speech. "Now I have the privilege of making a speech. Without compensation, of course. [Laughter] There's something about a Presidential election year that makes even retired politicians restless. [Laughter] At the United Nations, I sometimes yearn for the peace and tranquillity of a political campaign. Everybody wants to talk to me about politics, evidently forgetting that I am now a statesman. [Laughter]" With his audience warmed up and at least somewhat relaxed, Mr. Stevenson said what he had come to say. The pronouncements of Barry Goldwater were much in the minds of Americans that August, and Mr. Stevenson made it clear that he, too, was thinking about them. "I have thought that the strength of the American political system lay precisely in its lack of extreme contrasts, in its rejection of dogma, in the fact that rigid ideology really has no relevance to our great political parties," he said. "And this system has remained intact for more than a century — the most stable, durable, and adaptable system the world has ever seen. But now, as society and the world become more complex, some people want to repeal the whole thing. They seem to yearn for the old simplicity, for the shorthand analysis, for the black-and-white choice, for the cheap-and-easy answer, for the child's guide to good and evil. The very color and diversity of our pluralistic society seem to confuse them; they want it plain and unitary." The lawyers sat there. Quite evidently, they were not on fire. But Mr. Stevenson wound up with undiminished passion and undiminished devotion to what he wanted to tell them. "The greatness of the issues calls out for greatness in ourselves, to vindicate democracy, to speak for freedom, and to make our profoundest affirmation of faith in the American way of life," he concluded. The applause was dutiful. However, Mr. Stevenson didn't seem disappointed as the thousands of lawyers began to plod out of the ballroom. One of them, a chubby man, rather pale and ill at ease, came over to Mr. Stevenson and, after telling him that he had voted for him in 1952 and again in 1956, said, "I remember 1960 in Los Angeles. That was quite a demonstration they put on for you." "They raise more hell when I'm *not* a candidate than when I am," Mr. Stevenson said, with his laugh.

Later on, in reply to a question, Mr. Stevenson told us that he thought he could speak fairly easily now, although it had taken him many years to reach that point. "I had a terrible time as a young man," he explained. "I was very self-conscious, and I could never speak in public without getting paralyzed with fright." He said that his eldest son, Adlai E. Stevenson III, who is a lawyer and a member of the Illinois House of Representatives, was developing into a good speaker. "He's a very thoughtful student of public life," Mr. Stevenson said. "He has a natural dignity about him, yet he has a wonderful sense of humor. I don't know whether he's got the stomach for the crudities of politics. I don't think he'd ever be any good as a demagogue."

At the Democratic Convention, a week or so afterward, Mr. Stevenson, who was a delegate from Illinois, seemed to enjoy himself. He particularly enjoyed the fact that with him in Atlantic City were his three sons — John Fell and Borden in addition to Adlai III — and John's wife, Natalie, and Adlai III's wife, Nancy, both of whom were delegates, the former from California and the latter from Illinois. Mr. Stevenson joked with the boys about the Convention activities of the two young women, who, he said, had a natural talent for politics. "Natalie is so damn important I want to follow her around and pick up crumbs of wisdom," he said. Later he told us, "I've been going to Conventions since 1948, and this is the first time that I've been able to get to the *Convention*.[3] Heretofore, I've always been locked up in an icebox. When you're being nominated, you can never get out of your hotel room. You eat sandwiches. You walk from microphone to microphone. You put your head out the door and look up and down the hall. Then you settle in to write a speech, and furtive characters peer in at you from time to time. And out of all this comes imperishable American political prose."

In Atlantic City, Mr. Stevenson was again besieged by people who wanted to tell him that they had voted for him. Hotel doormen, ad-

[3] Stevenson actually had attended the 1924 Democratic Convention, at which he was an assistant sergeant at arms. See *The Papers of Adlai E. Stevenson*, Vol. I, pp. 149–150. At the 1948 convention, he made a speech seconding the nomination of Alben L. Barkley for Vice President. See *The Papers of Adlai E. Stevenson*, Vol. II, pp. 518–519.

dressing him as "Adlai," told him that he should be the Presidential nominee, and Mr. Stevenson courteously thanked them. A woman came over to him and said, "You have such a nice warm face," and Mr. Stevenson courteously thanked *her*. A couple of women, both wearing plaid Bermuda shorts, told him that their names were Rhoda and Sally, that they taught second grade somewhere out West, and that he was their "favorite candidate." "We ought to go back to school," Mr. Stevenson said gallantly. "Things have improved."

In the course of some Convention high jinks, Mr. Stevenson said to us, "They used to call me aloof. Actually, I love to be with people. I *enjoy* them. But you can't have things both ways, and when you have to work on a speech, you can't be shut up in your room working and out with people at the same time. However, I've never been able to go for the smash-and-grab kind of person in politics, and, for some reason, that made a certain number of people say I wasn't being practical. It's entirely possible, I think, to be a responsible and completely effective public official without being a smasher-grabber."

One question we'd wondered about for some time was how the legend had arisen about Mr. Stevenson's being "indecisive," and we asked for his explanation of it. "It arose largely from one fact, and that was that when President Truman asked me to be the Presidential candidate in April of 1952, I declined," he told us.[4] "I declined for two reasons. One, I was already an avowed candidate for reelection as Governor of Illinois. I didn't see, in justice to the people of Illinois, how I could be a candidate for two offices at the same time. And, two, I didn't *want* to run for President. I had no such ambition. I wanted to finish the job I'd started in Illinois. For the ensuing six months, I was beset right and left by individuals and delegations from all over the United States putting pressure on me to announce that I was a candidate and to enter the primaries and compete for the nomination. When I refused to do so and never wavered and was very decisive, and then was subsequently nominated at the Convention[5] and accepted, I was told, 'You're indecisive.' Nobody can believe you when you say you're not a candidate. It's a curious thing. The more decisive you are in not seeking an exalted office, the more they say you're indecisive. My very decisiveness was attributed to what they call indecision. Sometimes you look back at it all and it seems almost comic. I don't have any feeling of bitterness. Both times I ran, it was obviously hopeless. To run as a Democrat in 1952 was hopeless, let alone run against the No. 1 War Hero. Even so, if it hadn't been for that going-to-Korea business, I might have beaten him." There was no sound of regret or vanity in Mr. Stevenson's voice; he spoke with as much enthusiasm for the subject, and as much appreciation of its inherent interest, as if he had been discussing some episode in history that he just happened to know something about.

[4] See *The Papers of Adlai E. Stevenson*, Vol. III, pp. 490–491.
[5] See *The Papers of Adlai E. Stevenson*, Vol. IV, pp. 3–6.

The talk turned to Washington, D.C., and we asked Mr. Stevenson whether he liked the place.

"I've lived so much of my life there and know it so well it's difficult not to like it," he said. "Washington was different in the thirties, when I first went there.[6] My feelings are bound up with the way it used to feel during the long evenings — sitting in the gardens of those Georgetown houses in the hot summers, perspiring, with our visions and with our dreams. When I was there during the war,[7] we didn't have much time for fun, but the work itself was fun. In those days, we were interested in ideas. Now it's all so much personality talk, gossip, and rumor — who's up and who's down. The criticism is sort of brittle now, and there's a lot of malice and mischief."

On the first day in Atlantic City, a television interviewer asked Mr. Stevenson, "Governor, how do you feel about the Convention? Are you *sad?*" (He was always addressed as Governor, even though his last title was Ambassador.)

Mr. Stevenson looked far from sad, and he told the television commentator that he wasn't sad. "I'm hoping to see all the many old friends who fought and bled for me in hopeless causes," he said.

In the raucous, emblazoned Convention Hall, he was presented on the stage in the customary man-who fashion ("the man who was twice given the nomination for President by his party"), and the audience received him with a boisterous ovation. It was Mr. Stevenson's mission in Atlantic City to deliver a tribute to Eleanor Roosevelt. Again, he had worked hard, and had come up with a memorable piece of writing to present as a speech. "Thank you, my dear friends, for your welcome — and for all your loyalty and comfort to me in years past when our party's fortunes were not as bright as they are tonight" was his beginning. He continued, "For what I have done and sought to do for our country and our party, I have been repaid a thousandfold by the kindness of my fellow-citizens — and by none more than you, the leaders of the Democratic Party." The audience now seemed politely patient. "It is of another noble American that I am commissioned to speak to you tonight," Mr. Stevenson said, projecting his intimate words into the echoing vastness of the Hall, "She has passed beyond these voices, but our memory and her meaning have not — Eleanor Roosevelt. She was a lady — a lady for all seasons. And, like her husband, she left 'a name to shine on the entablatures of truth — forever.' There is, I believe a legend in the Talmud which tells us that in any period of man's history the heavens themselves are held in place by the virtue, love, and shining integrity of twelve just men. They are completely unaware of this function. They go about their daily work, their humble chores — doctors, teachers, workers, farmers (never, alas, lawyers, so I understand), just ordinary, devoted citizens — and meanwhile the rooftree of creation is supported by them

[6] See *The Papers of Adlai E. Stevenson,* Vol. I, Part Eight.
[7] See *The Papers of Adlai E. Stevenson,* Vol. II, Part One.

alone. There are times when nations or movements or great political parties are similarly sustained in their purposes and being by the pervasive, unconscious influence of a few great men and women. Can we doubt that Eleanor Roosevelt had in some measure the keeping of the Party's conscience in her special care?" It seemed to us, at that moment in Convention Hall, that almost nobody wanted to think about the question he had just asked or the answer to it; now that the nominations were in, the audience's mind was on who else was going to get what. The delegates adjusted their paper campaign hats and shifted in their seats, and many of them looked as though they were now having some difficulty tolerating their former candidate. Nevertheless, he went the course with what he had come to say: "She thought of herself as an ugly duckling, but she walked in beauty in the ghettos of the world, bringing with her the reminder of her beloved St. Francis, 'It is in the giving that we receive.' And wherever she walked beauty was forever there." The delegates gave Mr. Stevenson's speech a nice hand, and the name of Eleanor Roosevelt was not mentioned at the Convention again.

About a month later, on September 22nd, it was Illinois Day at the World's Fair, and who but Adlai Ewing Stevenson, of Illinois, was tapped for the Day. "I've been promising Bob Moses I'd come, and I'm glad I finally made it," Mr. Stevenson said to us as we joined him in one of those Greyhound motorized chairs. He looked expectant, and threw us a Stevenson smile. "Illinois Day gave me the day off from the war in Cyprus," he added, with satisfaction. It was about ten o'clock in the morning, a time that is very popular for ceremonies, and Mr. Stevenson was one of the first of the invited guests to arrive at the Illinois Pavilion for the Day. Among those who turned up later were Benny Goodman, Cab Calloway, Governor Otto Kerner, and Robert Lincoln Beckwith, a great-grandson of Abraham Lincoln and one of the sixteenth President's three surviving direct descendants. A press agent handed out a release stating that none of the descendants have children and that "it is expected the Lincoln blood will discontinue with them." Mr. Stevenson read the release with what seemed to be respectful interest. He looked with pride at the sayings of Lincoln's inscribed on the outside of the Pavilion, among them "WHILE MAN EXISTS IT IS HIS DUTY TO IMPROVE NOT ONLY HIS OWN CONDITION BUT TO ASSIST IN AMELIORATING MANKIND." Then he was ushered into the darkened theatre of the Pavilion, where about three hundred devotees of Illinois were assembled and where the sensational attraction was the six-foot-four-inch mechanical figure of Lincoln, which was to sit, stand, and speak Lincoln's speeches. But first Mr. Stevenson had the privilege of sitting through an hour-and-a-quarter Illinois Day program that included the dedication of a memorial to the late Illinois Secretary of State Charles F. Carpentier; a kind of pageant about the history of the State of Illinois; some folk songs by students at the Old Town School of Folk

Music, in Chicago; a short speech by Mr. Beckwith; a somewhat longer speech by Governor Kerner; and the bestowal of prizes on winners of the Chicagoland Music Festival. Then Mr. Stevenson was introduced. He was brief in his remarks. He said, "Governor Kerner, Mr. Beckwith, Mr. Moses, distinguished guests, sons and daughters of Illinois: We meet here in the midst of the American quadrennial political Olympics, at a time when the air is both figuratively and literally filled with the spoken word. Any man of conscience and sensitivity should exercise particular care in anything he says in public (or, for that matter, anywhere). I am conscious of the remarks of Illinois's greatest son, Mr. Beckwith's great-grandfather, and an intimate friend of my own great-grandfather Jesse W. Fell, of Bloomington. In his message to the Congress in December, 1862, he addressed himself to political leaders of his own and future generations. In the midst of a bitter fratricidal struggle, where tempers and factionalism colored the judgments of many men, Lincoln warned, 'If there ever should be a time for mere catch arguments, that time surely is not now. In times like the present, no man should utter anything for which he would not willingly be responsible through time and in eternity.'" The devotees of Illinois looked blank. The words of Lincoln as Mr. Stevenson spoke them did not appear to make much of an impression. The audience was evidently waiting for the mechanical Lincoln to speak. This Lincoln — a Walt Disney creation, manufactured at a cost, the Illinois press agent told us, of ninety thousand dollars — followed Mr. Stevenson, and its speech was billed as "Great Moments with Mr. Lincoln." Mr. Stevenson listened to it in apparent fascination. The mechanical Lincoln really did sit, stand up, and make a speech — by means of a recording by an actor — in a very deep, melancholy, Lincolnesque voice. We thought the robot was creepy, but Mr. Stevenson admired it. "It's a marvel," he told us. "In one speech, the quotes put together ran all the way from 1838 to 1864."

At the United Nations one afternoon last January, we waited at the entrance to the General Assembly Building for Mr. Stevenson, who was scheduled to deliver a major address before the Plenary Session in General Debate. "The U.N. is finished," the uniformed guard at the entrance where we stood stated to us in a highly certain tone. He was an American, and he knew what he was talking about. "Next year it won't be here," he went on. "Look at the faces of the delegates, especially the Africans. They don't want the U.N. in America. Look at the Ambassador from Hungary. Ice-cold. He doesn't talk to nobody. We're through here. Red China wants to start its own U.N. Who wants this one?"

The session was called to order by the chairman, His Excellency Mr. Alex Quaison-Sackey, of Ghana, at three-thirty. The gallery was packed. With Mr. Quaison-Sackey on the dais sat U Thant. The United States delegation sat with delegates from Upper Volta on its right, delegates from Belgium and Austria behind it, delegates from

Thailand and Syria in front of it, and delegates from the United Republic of Tanzania on its left. Mr. Stevenson — his glasses on, the plastic earphone for translations over one ear, a lumpy briefcase open on the floor at his side — sat putting a few more touches on his speech. Then he seemed to listen intently as the first speaker, the distinguished representative of Mali, talked for quite a while, in French, about being "non-aligned but not for imperialist aggression." There was perfunctory applause. A young man introduced as the Foreign Minister of Morocco made a halting address, also in French, on what we gathered was his interest in peace. There was no applause. Then the Foreign Minister of Pakistan took the floor to discuss, in English, the "crude, absurd, and mischievous" remarks of the distinguished representative of India dealing with what he charged was a fraud that had been perpetrated by India upon the five million people of Kashmir. "They are the ones whose right to self-determination has been denied," he said. "They have the right to be free. Justice must be done!" There was perfunctory applause. The next speaker was the distinguished representative of Afghanistan, who said in a speech in English, which took thirty-five minutes, that Afghanistan was following a policy of friendship with her neighboring African nations; that the United Nations was the only place of hope for saving the world from destruction; that the United Nations' financial crisis, with other crises, was deepening anxiety; but that the Afghanistan delegation was not getting discouraged. There was mild applause. Mr. Stevenson didn't seem to be missing a word. We were sitting on the sidelines, behind some observers who kept calling out friendly remarks in Portuguese to the delegation from Brazil, which was seated nearby. We assumed that the observers were also from Brazil. The noisiest observer was a middle-aged lady who had several rings on her fingers; one ring was set with a pearl the size of a lima bean, which was surrounded by a big cluster of diamonds. She held a mink coat in her lap, and stroked it nervously, without letup. She didn't close her mouth for more than two minutes at a time throughout the address delivered by the distinguished representative of Afghanistan. A number of the delegates looked asleep, or half asleep. Mr. Stevenson glanced occasionally at the text of his speech. Otherwise, he was wholly attentive. At 4:59 P.M., he was called. "The last speaker is the distinguished representative of the United States," the chairman said.

Mr. Stevenson started by saying that it was his first opportunity to extend congratulations to the chairman for the way he had conducted that session of the General Assembly. Then he said, "I have asked to speak at this late date so I can share with all delegations, in a spirit of openness, my government's views on the state of affairs at these United Nations as our annual general debate comes to its conclusion. Certain things which I shall say here today have to do with law, with procedures, with technical and administrative matters. So I want to emphasize in advance that these are but manifestations of much deeper concerns about peace and world order, about the welfare of human society and the prospects of our peoples for rewarding lives."

The group of Brazilians in front of us, including the noisy bejewelled lady, were quiet for the first time. They were paying attention. Everybody in the hall seemed to be awake and listening. What Mr. Stevenson was talking about was the U.N.'s financial crisis, which was mainly the result of more than a hundred and thirty million dollars in overdue assessments owed by Russia, by eight other Communist nations, and by France, Belgium, Paraguay, South Africa, and Yemen. Under Article 19 of the U.N. Charter, any nation that is two years in arrears automatically loses its vote in the General Assembly. It was one of Mr. Stevenson's chores to express the opinion of our government (which happens to carry the largest part of the United Nations expenses) that there should be no voting in the General Assembly until Russia paid at least one-third of its overdue assessments. And so Mr. Stevenson, in his speech, was going to warn the General Assembly against the notion of a "double standard" of assessments for United Nations peacekeeping operations. "We cannot have two rules for paying assessments for the expenses of the organization — one rule for most of the members, and another rule for a few," he said. But before he reached that point in his speech he made some remarks about the United Nations as a whole. "I speak to you as one who participated in the formulation of the Charter of this organization, in both the Preparatory Commission, in London, and the Charter Conference, in San Francisco," he said.[8] "I recall vividly the fears and hopes which filled and inspired us as a second world war ended — fears and hopes which brought us together in an attempt to insure that such a world catastrophe would never again occur. At those conferences we labored long and diligently, we tried to take into account the interest of all states, we attempted to subordinate narrow national interests to the broad common good. This time we would create something better than static conference machinery for keeping the peace and for settling disputes by non-violent means — and endow it with a capacity to act."

The speech had about five thousand words, which he had checked for policy with the State Department, as he always did in his job, but which he had put together himself, in his own remarkable way. It took him about forty-five minutes to deliver. He wound up saying, "I, for one, cannot escape the deep sense that the peoples of the world are looking over our shoulder — waiting to see whether we can overcome our present problem and take up with fresh vigor and renewed resolution the great unfinished business of peace — which President Johnson has called 'the assignment of the century.'" The hall was full of delegates who were supposedly divided, but the applause for Mr. Stevenson was immediate and strong.

8 See *The Papers of Adlai E. Stevenson*, Vol. II, Part Three, Part Four.

For most men, delivering a five-thousand-word speech might constitute a week's, or even a month's, work. For Mr. Stevenson, it was a small and routine part of a twenty-four-hour schedule. The very next morning, he was speaking in the General Assembly again — this time paying tribute to Sir Winston Churchill, who had died three days earlier. Afterward, he conferred with his associates, and then went to a meeting with U Thant, and on to a luncheon for twenty-four people being given by Liu Chieh, the Chinese Ambassador to the U.N. From the luncheon he rushed back to his office to meet with a couple of congressmen from Florida who were en route to Churchill's funeral, and then to confer with Norway's Ambassador to the U.N., who had some ideas about a compromise plan for the countries owing assessments. After that, the new Ambassador from Malta to the U.N. paid a courtesy call on Mr. Stevenson, and for half an hour Mr. Stevenson listened intently to a discussion of the people of Malta (there are three hundred thousand of them), and of the fact that during the sixteenth century, when Malta fell under the rule of the Knights of Malta, no Maltese were members of the Knighthood, and of the possibility of setting up a Malta office in Washington. Having also seen eight other callers, Mr. Stevenson went off to a cocktail reception being given by the American-Arab Association, and after half an hour there he made for a party launching an Indian exhibit at the Union Carbide Building, where he found a mob of celebrated public figures, looking freshly bathed, rested, and barbered, and dressed to the teeth in formal clothes. Mr. Stevenson was wearing the same pin-striped blue suit, by now wrinkled and limp, that he had started the day in at 7 A.M. Vice-President Humphrey was at the party, tall and ruddy-faced and glowing, and was reminiscing about the Inaugural festivities, which had taken place a week earlier. There was a lot of kidding about the big hand Mr. Stevenson had got when he arrived at the Inaugural Ball. Everyone had flocked around *him.* "I never get anywhere, but I get all the applause," Mr. Stevenson said, making Vice-President Humphrey and several other guests laugh. He looked at the exhibit for about an hour, and then made for his apartment at the Waldorf. He had to change to black tie and attend the Diamond Ball for the benefit of the Institute of International Education, in the Grand Ballroom of the Plaza Hotel. His housekeeper, Mrs. Viola Reardy, told him she couldn't find his formal silk shirt and shoes. Mr. Stevenson worried about the possibility of having lost these articles, which were new. "You probably left them at the Inauguration," Mrs. Reardy told him, and Mr. Stevenson put on a regular shirt with his dinner jacket and wore his daytime shoes.

At eight o'clock the next morning, Mr. Stevenson was on a shuttle plane to Washington, where, at the request of the British Ambassador, he was to give the memorial address at the National Cathedral service for Sir Winston Churchill. When he had found time to write the tribute was something we couldn't figure out. It ran to about thirteen hundred words. "Sir Winston Churchill is dead," Mr. Stevenson said at the Cathedral. "The voice that led nations, raised armies, inspired victories, and blew fresh courage into the hearts of men is silenced. We shall hear no longer the remembered eloquence and wit, the old courage and defiance, the robust serenity of indomitable faith. Our world is thus poorer, our political dialogue is diminished, and the sources of public inspiration run more thinly for all of us. There is a lonesome place against the sky. So we are right to mourn." For Sir Winston Churchill the love of freedom was "not an abstract thing but a deep conviction that the uniqueness of man demands a society that gives his capacities full scope," Mr. Stevenson continued. "It was, if you like, an aristocratic sense of the fullness and value of life. But he was a profound democrat, and the cornerstone of his political faith, inherited from a beloved father, was the simple maxim 'Trust the people.' " Near the close of his tribute Mr. Stevenson had a sentence describing Churchill: "The great aristocrat, the beloved leader, the profound historian, the gifted painter, the superb politician, the lord of language, the orator, the wit — yes, and the dedicated bricklayer — behind all of them was the man of simple faith, steadfast in defeat, generous in victory, resigned in age, trusting in a loving providence, and committing his achievements and his triumphs to a higher power."

From the Cathedral, Mr. Stevenson went to the British Embassy for lunch and a reception. Then he went to the State Department for conferences on half a dozen pressing problems of foreign relations. He caught the three-o'clock shuttle plane back to New York, and at four-thirty, in his U.S. Mission office, he started a series of meetings with members of his staff. At six, he attended a cocktail party given for U.N. delegates from the African nations, in the U.S. Mission building, by the Harlem Lawyers Association and Ambassador Franklin F. Williams, the U.S. representative on the U.N. Economic and Social Council. There an editor of the *Amsterdam News* named James Hicks told Mr. Stevenson he'd had trouble getting an advance copy of his speech about Churchill, and added that, come to think of it, during his Presidential campaigns it had always been difficult to get copies of his speeches in advance. "I'm afraid I sit up scribbling until the last minute," Mr. Stevenson told him. "Churchill was always rewriting his speeches until he had to give them." And then he had one of those characteristic funny afterthoughts that constantly bubbled up in him: "But that's where my similarity to Churchill ends."

Mr. Stevenson was due at eight-thirty that evening, in dinner clothes, at a concert of the New York Philharmonic, but when he was about to go home to dress, his secretary sent word to him that a group of educators working for UNESCO were gathered in the Savoy Hilton apartment of his old friend William Benton, the former Senator from Connecticut, who was now the U.S. representative to UNESCO, and that Senator Benton had been stricken suddenly with pneumonia and had to go to the hospital, so there was nobody to speak to the group of people in his apartment. The educators from UNESCO wanted to hear all about the history of the U.N. situation in reference to Article 19, and the problems arising from it. In a manner in which there appeared to us to be no hesitation, no doubt, no resentment, no self-pity, Mr. Stevenson immediately headed for Senator Benton's apartment. Ambassador Marietta Tree, the U.S. representative to the U.N. Trusteeship Council, who was present at the cocktail party, rode up in the car with him; she was on her way to a dinner being given by the Pakistani Ambassador to the U.N., she said.

"I went *last week*," Mr. Stevenson told her playfully. "You'll be offered a hookah. I smoked a hookah last week. Watch your step with that hookah, my girl. Ambassador de Beus, of the Netherlands, smoked the hookah with me last week and then told me, 'My public vice is women. My private vice is the hookah.'"

Mrs. Tree said that she would watch her step.

"And don't eat too much," Mr. Stevenson said. "The food is delicious, but you'll find that nothing is green or ever has been."

"Long time no see!" the Savoy Hilton doorman called out to Mr. Stevenson as he got out of the car.

On the sidewalk, Mr. Stevenson almost collided with a jaunty young man carrying a briefcase. The young man halted and gave Mr. Stevenson an admiring little bow. "My pleasure," the young man said, yielding the right of way to Mr. Stevenson.

"Why, thank you," Mr. Stevenson said, graciously bowing back.

He had less than an hour in which to go home, dress, and keep his date for the Philharmonic, but he walked into Senator Benton's apartment and shook hands, greeting each of a couple of dozen educators as though he had done nothing else that day and had nothing else to do.

A very serious woman there reminded him that they had met some years ago on a houseboat in the Vale of Kashmir. "I believe you said it was the nearest to Heaven you'd ever come," the woman said.[9] "I'm so sorry I wasn't here in this country to cast my vote for you."

"And we couldn't spare it," Mr. Stevenson said.

Mr. Stevenson, rushing no one, held a conversation with everybody in the room. Then the educators sat down, and Mr. Stevenson, taking a chair in a corner of the room, started talking to them. Even here, he began by making his listeners laugh. "I don't often get a captive audience," he said, and everything in his expression signified that he was appreciating the fact that he had one now. They laughed. "It's not often that I get the opportunity to talk to such a literate and cultivated audience," he went on. Again they laughed. He added, "There were times, as a Democratic politician, when I never expected that at

[9] See *The Papers of Adlai E. Stevenson*, Vol. V, pp. 200–202.

all." In the next thirty minutes, speaking quickly, he gave a brilliantly clear, concise, and orderly history, description, and explanation of the events leading up to the current difficulty with the back assessments, of Article 19, of the significance of the deadlock, and of the reluctance of any of the countries — even the Soviet Union — to have an out-and-out confrontation with the United States, because they couldn't be sure they would win. Then Mr. Stevenson allowed time for questions. One man asked him if he thought the Russians wanted to break up the U.N., and Mr. Stevenson said no, he thought they would like only to convert the General Assembly into a static debating forum. As he came to a close, he again, irrepressibly, said something to make his listeners laugh: "I remember my father telling me the story of the preacher delivering an exhortation to his flock, and as he reached the climax of his exhortation, a man in the front row got up and said, 'O Lord, use me. Use me, O Lord — in an advisory capacity!' "

As we were leaving Senator Benton's apartment, we asked Mr. Stevenson how in the world he had the strength and the interest, after the day he had put in — a day that was still far from over — to give that much concentrated attention to this small group of workers for UNESCO. His answer had no note of martyrdom in it but was casual and matter-of-fact. He told us, "You don't like to come in and say, 'What the hell, it's useless to try to explain, it's too complicated.' So you try to tell them the score. They should be informed."

The party given for Mr. Stevenson on his sixty-fifth birthday was held at the River Club, and was attended by a couple of dozen of his close friends, who had started the tradition of giving him such a party fifteen years earlier in the Executive Mansion in Springfield.[10] During the evening, Mr. Stevenson happened to say that he thought "the fifteenth running of this classic should be the last." He also said, "I've heard that a woman's best years are between thirty-nine and forty. My best years have been the past fifteen. For tomorrow is today, and I shall never be any older than I am now." He had been listening for a couple of hours to funny, nostalgic, and loving remarks about himself, including the reading of "A Composite Portrait of Adlai by His Friends on His Sixty-fifth Birthday," in verse, each stanza having been composed by one of his friends. Mr. Stevenson laughed and cried at his party, and scribbled notes of things he wanted to tell his friends at the end. "The best of one's life is one's friends," he said to them. "I've never thought it necessary to be serious about serious things. It takes only a pin to prick the biggest balloon. Horace Walpole said, 'Old age is no uncomfortable thing if one gives up to it with good grace and doesn't drag it about.' I feel there's so much to do, so much to make up, and I do believe that nothing succeeds like excess. My dearest friends, forgive me my excesses, and I'll forgive you your successes. Give me the benefit of your candor and your criticism, but please keep

[10] See *The Papers of Adlai E. Stevenson*, Vol. III, pp. 234–235.

your doubts to yourself, because I have enough of those of my own."

On the winter morning of the first major air strike in Vietnam, we asked Mr. Stevenson some questions about past Presidents of the United States, and in spite of the crisis of the moment, he replied as though our questions were timely and in order. "I think great Presidents are usually the product of their times," he said at one point. "Abraham Lincoln has always been my hero, as he is the hero of most Americans. As President, he contributed to the world the end of slavery, which was an enormous leap forward in history, but then he was assassinated and he didn't have to live through the Reconstruction and the bitterness that followed the war. No one can say what he might have been had he not been assassinated. Bear in mind, however, that I was raised in Lincoln country.[11] My great-grandfather was Lincoln's friend and the first to propose him for the Presidency. It was to him that Lincoln addressed his autobiography. So I was naturally saturated with Lincoln from infancy. The other figure who is very important to me is Woodrow Wilson. He showed us, on the world scene, an extension of what Lincoln preached; namely, that freedom isn't a limited — a parochial — matter but a universal matter. Also, Wilson was the first President I ever met. When I was a boy of twelve, my father took me to visit President Wilson, then Governor of New Jersey, at his summer house in Sea Girt, New Jersey. It was a hot day in August, 1912, and he was running for President. I mounted the stairs of that large frame house alongside my father, and Governor Wilson came out and met us on the porch. He shook hands with me in a formal, courteous way. I was paralyzed with awe. The conversation related mostly to the campaign and how things would go in Illinois. There was a lot of talk about the Democratic Party and the state of mind of people in the Middle West. My father was confident about everything, because of the Bull Moose split. Governor Wilson was extremely courteous to me. He asked me in a friendly, fatherly way if I was interested in politics or in public affairs, and he expressed the hope that I was. You know the way older people often get humble with younger people, and in somewhat that spirit, I think, he made a casual remark about Princeton, and about his having been president of Princeton before becoming Governor of New Jersey. That's what decided me on going to Princeton, right then and there. I came away with the feeling: 'I'm his deathless friend. His supporter. His admirer. That's my man.'" There was affection but no sentimentality in Mr. Stevenson's manner as he talked about Wilson. "And another great President was, of course, Franklin Roosevelt," he went on. "Here, again, there were many contributing factors. The historical ones are obvious. He showed us the way to so many social transformations, bloodlessly. He died in office, from his labors, which always dramatizes and adds an emotional factor to the life of a man." Mr. Stevenson talked for

[11] See *The Papers of Adlai E. Stevenson*, Vol. I, Part One.

some time about President Truman, saying he would be entitled to a high mark in history for the way he dealt with the postwar period. Then he went on to talk about John F. Kennedy's extraordinary mind and spirit and promise. "When President Kennedy was assassinated," he said, "we were all left with a sense of incompleteness."

There was one hot, muggy night last summer, during the political campaign, when we rode back with Mr. Stevenson on a shuttle plane at the end of one of his incredibly full working days in Washington. It was late when we landed at LaGuardia Airport. The city was steaming. Mr. Stevenson was greeted by his driver, who handed him a portfolio of emergency cables and messages to be studied. He did the work in the car as he was riding toward his apartment, and then he remembered that Mayor Wagner had wanted to talk to him about some local aspects of the election campaign, so he asked the driver to stop at Gracie Mansion. It was around ten-thirty when we got there, and we ran into the fading moments of what had been a Young Citizens for Johnson Barbecue, with food prepared by President Johnson's own caterer, imported from Texas. The barbecue seemed to be under the supervision of Lynda Bird Johnson, Robert F. Wagner, Jr., and other very young, very attractive, very recently well-fed Democrats, and they all greeted Mr. Stevenson cordially. It happened that he hadn't had anything to eat since lunch, which he had eaten at the State Department with Dean Rusk. The Gracie Mansion lawn, under festive garden lighting, was strewn with delicious-looking and aromatic-smelling remnants of what had clearly been a great party. Robert Wagner, Jr., said that his father was upstairs, and quickly led Mr. Stevenson up to see the Mayor. Half an hour later, Mr. Stevenson came down. To us, he looked a little hungry but not a bit tired. The party was petering out by then, and the Mayor's guards, who did look tired, were encouraging the young guests to leave. Everybody assumed — wrongly, we thought — that Mr. Stevenson wanted to get away as fast as possible. We thought we saw Mr. Stevenson peering wistfully at the Gracie Mansion lawn. It looked inviting, that hot, humid, misty night, with paper picnic plates dotted about, and with sun-tanned, laughing young men and women standing around in clusters, talking, presumably, about the campaign, and with President Johnson's caterer — fat and jolly, wrapped in a huge white apron, and wearing a chef's tall white hat — still overseeing a long table laden with steaks, sweet corn, and spareribs. But the party was technically over, and a solicitous guard was ushering Mr. Stevenson out to his car. He went. The guard saluted and left him. Mr. Stevenson's driver opened the car door. Just then, a young couple, both tall and skinny and both wearing sandals and blue jeans, the girl with long blond hair falling loosely over the collar of a shirtwaist blouse and the boy with a cultivated fringe of beard, strolled over to Mr. Stevenson, holding hands. They smiled at him and coolly asked him what was going on at Gracie Mansion. A party, he told them. They looked happy and lazy and not impressed, and strolled away, still holding hands. Mr. Stevenson stood there a moment or two, looking down the street after them, and as he got into his car he said, "Summer in New York is pretty wonderful, isn't it?"

On January 26, 1961, President Kennedy met with his cabinet for the first time. When the President called by tradition on the Secretary of State to make the response to his opening statement, Dean Rusk deferred to the new ambassador to the UN. Stevenson said:

As Senior — let me say briefly what I know is in the hearts of all of us as we meet here today for the first time.

We congratulate you — honored to serve with you.

We pledge you our loyalty and our labor to the end that your administration will meet the great demands and solve the staggering problems that confront our country and you as its President.

We wish you health, happiness and success in your great trials and pledge you our ceaseless efforts to insure all three.[12]

Stevenson then spoke from notes — sometimes they were one word such as "Financing," "Cuba," "Tibet," "Hungary," "SW Africa," at other times they were phrases or complete sentences. Excerpts from the notes he spoke from, somewhat rearranged, follow.[13]

Not easy to recapitulate the problems I find in N.Y.

We are on every stage of the world — None larger or more useful than UN

Principal problem — a) How to restore our prestige, influence and confidence in the world thru the great forum of the UN.

b) How to save the UN and strengthen and expand its influence and authority.

Our position has deteriorated. Some of it inevitable — new centers of power and attraction. No longer dependent on us.

Rise of Soviet power and prestige. Sputnik.

Our own mistakes and unpopular positions — military emphasis; intolerance of neutralism; fickle attitude toward UN; colonialism; preoccupation with cold war and anti communist; black-and-white, for or against, when most of uncommitted people are really not much interested in the East-West conflict but are very much interested in modernization and development — Learning how to help others to help themselves — $ and know how not enough — Attitude on China — more diplomatic approaches

---

[12] The text is from a handwritten statement.
[13] Roxane Eberlein transcribed these handwritten notes with skill.

Organize small powers to resist attack on SYG.[14]

Their security is endangered — not ours. Reveals USSR's cynicism about UN.

Cabot Lodge's habit of immediate reaction won more headlines than respect.[15]

Should change emphasis from using UN to *fight* cold war to using it to *end* cold war.

Respect neutrality; not seeking allies but the independance, prosperity, dignity.

Dissociate somehow — colonial.[16] Recapture leadership and confidence of new countries.

K — coming? [17] Should neg[otiate]. in advance. If he comes — propaganda display inevitable.

Should postpone [visit?] to end — act as restraining influence on session. Then call on Pres[ident]. — not summit [meeting]; just get acquainted.

Direct approach to K for cold war truce.

As to UN. — Bankrupt — SYG severe attack — dangerous situation in Congo — have lost our majority. Often irresponsible, immature and cocky. Suspicious of west; impressed by Soviet achievements.

CONGO

[UN] *Trying to keep out all foreign support*

Both superpowers should fade out by tacit agt.[agreement].

Climb down in darkness. Then G A [General Assembly]

Disarmament — nuclear test suspension

African development program

Peaceful uses of Outer Space.

If bored — come up [to the UN] — help figure out. . . .

Harlan Cleveland wrote that a factor in the early adjustment of the relations between Stevenson and Kennedy was "the President's sudden realization that Adlai was making as much news in the New York Times *as he was." The President "was restive," Cleveland added, when he found Stevenson casting a vote in a "highly-publicized forum on a hot*

14 The Secretary-General of the United Nations, Dag Hammarskjöld, was under severe attack, particularly from the Soviet Union, because of the leadership role his office took in the UN operation in the Congo. See Ernest W. Lefever, *Crisis in the Congo: A United Nations Force in Action* (Washington: Brookings Institution, 1965), pp. 25, 49, 50, 55, 56–57, 119, 121.

15 Henry Cabot Lodge, Stevenson's predecessor as ambassador to the United Nations, who had resigned to run for Vice President in 1960. Stevenson refers to Mr. Lodge's abrasive attacks on the Soviet Union.

16 Stevenson hoped that United States policy would not continue to support European colonial powers, including Portugal, in Africa.

17 Soviet Premier Nikita Khrushchev, who at the 1960 UN General Assembly had banged his shoe on the table. He did not attend the resumed session of this General Assembly in 1961.

issue such as Angola, without the President having been aware of 'the U.S. position.'" Cleveland continued: "In fact, most of those 'U.S. positions' didn't require clearance above my desk in Washington, because by the time we took them there usually wasn't any good alternative." Cleveland worked out an arrangement with Arthur Schlesinger, Jr., in the White House to send each day a one-page memorandum telling what positions the U.S. took that day at the UN and "sketching the tactical situation in which the U.S. Representative found himself. That memo went to the President for his bedtime reading folder. Then when he opened the Times *in the morning and saw Adlai's picture on the front page, he was apparently comforted by knowing that he knew about it beforehand."* [18]

Without being allowed access to those papers of Adlai E. Stevenson which were classified after his death, the editor is under serious limitations in trying to present to the reader the arduous nature of Stevenson's life as U.S. ambassador to the United Nations. The daily messages from USUN to the Department of State would help supply such information. They would indicate the number of personal negotiating sessions he had with other representatives, something the unclassified papers do not reveal in detail.

During his nearly four and one half years as ambassador, the UN operation in the Congo and the problem of financing it occupied an immense amount of Stevenson's time. In his first few days as ambassador, for instance, in addition to the many private meetings on the subject, he addressed the Security Council on the Congo on February 13, 15, 16, 17, 20, and 21.

On February 1, 1961, Stevenson attended his first meeting of the Security Council. After an extremely warm welcome by the various delegates, Stevenson spoke.[19]

Mr. President,[20] first let me say that I am very happy to come to this table for the first time in many years under your presidency. Under the rules, I understand that I must succeed you as President the first of next month, and I wish that I did not suspect that you would relinquish that honour with the same enthusiasm with which Mr. Loutfi [21] has relinquished it today.

Listening to such kind expressions and flattery as I have heard here today, I have begun to wonder if you have confused me with Thomas Jefferson, whom Mr. Benitez [22] was good enough to mention, and whose name is always agreeable to a Democrat. I deeply appreciate,

[18] Memorandum to Walter Johnson, April 30, 1973.
[19] The text is from United Nations, *Official Records,* Security Council, February 1, 1961, pp. 7–10.
[20] Sir Patrick Dean, of Great Britain.
[21] Omar Loutfi, permanent representative of the United Arab Republic.
[22] Dr. Leopoldo Benitez Vinueza, permanent representative of Ecuador.

Mr. President, the kind words and good wishes of you and of my colleagues.

I must apologize for my voice; I wish I could say that it was a casualty of the battle for peace instead of a casualty of the New York weather.

I have sometimes said that flattery is all right, Mr. President, if you do not inhale. Well, you have made it very hard for me not to inhale, thanks to the charity and the kindness which have touched me so deeply. In the days, and perhaps the nights, ahead of us I shall always remember with gratitude this hour; and may all of our wishes be as good for all of the peoples of the world as your kind words have been good for me today.

As some of you know, I had a part in the birth of the United Nations in San Francisco in 1945 and in its early walks as an infant in London and then in New York in 1946 and 1947.[23] And now it is fifteen years old and I am pleased to be sharing in the problems of its adolescence. The problems of adolescence are largely those of young love, and I believe that this is true in all countries. Would that all of our problems in this Council were as amiable. Although some of our problems may not be amiable, I hope that we may deal with even the thorniest of them in an atmosphere of tolerance and good will. We are, to use a French phrase, the Nations United. Let us be united, united in a patient and persevering attempt to find the things that we can agree upon and to build upon them a structure of understanding and cooperation against which whatever storms may be ahead shall beat in vain.

To one who has been long absent from these councils, it is striking and heartening that the United Nations has not only survived the turmoil and the conflict of these fifteen years, but has grown to nearly twice its original membership and has become an ever more potent factor in the shaping of world events.

We of the United States wish the United Nations to be still more potent, for the grave dangers of the new nuclear age demand much more unity among the nations. The common concern of all men, expressed in the Charter, is to achieve freedom from war and poverty, disease, ignorance and oppression. That is what binds us all together. Our security and our salvation is the ability of the nations and the Governments to see through the clouds of conflict and discern the truth about our common interests, and then boldly and in concert to act. Only the actions of States, both large and small, can impart vigour to this Organization and can redeem the pledges of the Charter.

We in the United States believe that the times are too dangerous for anything except the truth. The United Nations is a sensitive measure of the tremors which shake the community of nations, tremors which

[23] See *The Papers of Adlai E. Stevenson,* Vol. II, Part Four.

have built up to dangerous levels. But we are not helpless spectators. The tremors are man made, and man can still them. To help the Organization to meet that task, we of the United States will be guided by certain principles, and I hope that I may be indulged for a moment while I mention some of them.

First, we know the great importance which the newer and less developed nations attach to the United Nations. In their search for peace, for mutual tolerance, for economic development, for dignity and self respect, our interest is theirs. We do not seek military allies among them, nor do we wish to impose our system or our philosophy upon them. Indeed, we cannot. Freedom cannot be imposed on anyone. Our concern for these nations is that they should be truly independent members of the peaceful community of nations.

As the oldest anti-colonial Power, the United States is in favour of freedom and of self-determination for all peoples. We rejoice in the rapid and peaceful revolution which has brought into being and into our midst at the United Nations so many new sovereignties. Our great desire is that this transition should proceed peacefully and in good order, with the least possible suffering, bitterness and new conflict. We applaud what has been done to bring about this orderly transition both by the emerging nations and by their former rulers. And we applaud the efforts of this Council to assist the orderly transition in the Congo through the Secretary-General.

Equally important, if not more so, is the work which this Organization can do to further economic development, without which political independence cannot long be sustained. The United States attaches the highest importance to improving the conditions of life and of the peoples in the newly developing countries. In that work the United Nations has already proved its effectiveness as a source of technical assistance, of expert knowledge on potential capital investment, and of administrative personnel, to help those who are determined to help themselves, and without any political condition or any ulterior motive. So we shall support the work of the United Nations in the whole field of economic betterment.

We shall also do all in our power to use the United Nations as a centre for harmonizing the actions of nations.[24] We believe the United Nations is an opportunity for preventive diplomacy which can identify and solve potential disputes before they reach the acute stage sometimes induced by the glare of publicity.

The United States Government is giving its most earnest attention to the impasse over disarmament. We know, as President Kennedy said the other day, that the instruments of war have far outpaced the instruments of peace.[25] We know that progress towards disarmament becomes daily more imperative, and we are ceaselessly aware of the

[24] See the United Nations Charter, I, i. iv.
[25] Inaugural address, January 20, 1961.

vital interest in this problem which is felt by all of the Members of the United Nations.

May I say also that if the United Nations is to continue to function two things are essential. It must be properly financed, and the integrity of the office of the Secretary-General and of the Secretariat must be preserved. We hope all Members, from every region, will join in fulfilling these indispensable minimum conditions.

Finally, with such a fateful agenda it is more than ever important that in these councils we avoid useless recrimination. Free debate is an essential part of the United Nations process, but let us not demean free debate, as you have so eloquently said, Mr. President. In his address to Congress the other day the new President of the United States said that he regards the United Nations as an instrument to end the cold war instead of an arena in which to fight it.[26] We devoutly hope that all of the Governments here represented will share his view, and that our deliberations in this Council may be uniformly directed towards the calm and constructive solution of the problems that confront us. May peace among the United Nations begin with peace among the members of this Council. We are the Security Council, my colleagues, and it should be to us that the peoples of the world look for the security they so desperately long for. They are looking to us, I believe, for leadership — for strong, sober, constructive leadership. If they do not look to this body with confidence it is our fault, so I whole-heartedly pledge myself to the high and challenging task of co-operating with you in our common endeavor to provide the leadership that the world is asking of us. I devoutly hope and pray that we may fulfil this solemn obligation.

Many of Stevenson's old friends helped him celebrate his sixty-first birthday on February 5 at his official residence in the Waldorf Towers.

To Mr. and Mrs. Carl McGowan [27]

February 6, 1961

Dear McGowans:

What a pleasure it gave us that you could get here for the "Old Man's" 61st anniversary party. I hope you'll come back soon and enjoy one of Viola's [28] creations which emerges from under that ancient weapon in modern disguise which you so thoughtfully provided for my kitchen. Who but the McGowans would have thought of this basic utensil! There

---

26 State of the Union message, January 30, 1961.

27 Mr. McGowan was a senior member of the Chicago law firm of Ross, McGowan, Hardies & O'Keefe and from 1950 to 1953 had been Stevenson's legislative aide during his governorship of Illinois. The original is in the possession of Mr. McGowan.

28 Viola Reardy, Stevenson's housekeeper at Libertyville, who had come to New York with him.

were frying pans galore, but only one rolling pin — and ball-bearing at that! [29]

Thanks — and affectionate good wishes to you both.

Yours,
ADLAI

To Louis A. Kohn [30]

February 6, 1961

Dear Lou:

Just a note to say again how pleased I was that you got to the party, which was so thinly represented by the Chicago contingent,[31] and also to thank you again for that handsome and functional gift. I must say it never occurred to me that I would ever own an electric can opener, and in spite of my advanced years my possession of this modern weapon makes me feel young!

Come again soon — and bring Mary Jane.[32]

Affectionate wishes to you both.

Yours,

P.S. And thanks for the clippings! [33]

To Valerian A. Zorin [34]

February 7, 1961

Dear Ambassador Zorin:

You were most kind to send me that magnificent volume of Hermitage reproductions. It afforded some delightful moments to the guests at my birthday party on Saturday evening, and will permit me the pleasure of wandering often through that matchless gallery.

Thank you so much, as well, for the superb wines and vodka. You were good to think of me, and I share your hope for the success of our endeavors in the cause of peace.*

With best wishes,

Sincerely yours,

* And your taste for Russian vodka!

[29] Stevenson had complained that the embassy residence lacked pots and pans. See the *New Yorker*, January 28, 1961, p. 24.

[30] A Chicago lawyer who had been a backer of Stevenson for U.S. senator and who took an active part in his campaign for governor in 1948, serving after Stevenson's inauguration as his appointments secretary. See *The Papers of Adlai E. Stevenson*, Vol. II, p. 455.

[31] A fierce blizzard covered the Midwest and the East, and all planes in Chicago were grounded. Mr. Kohn had come earlier by train.

[32] Mrs. Kohn.

[33] These clippings were not saved.

[34] Permanent representative of the Union of Soviet Socialist Republics to the United Nations.

To Margaret Munn [35]

February 7, 1961

Dear Margaret:

It was good to have a birthday remembrance from Springfield, Illinois — and even better to "hear a voice" from there. Somehow it is difficult for me to think of you sitting at home in the evening, knitting or crocheting — but I shall take your word for it that the potholder is your handiwork!

Many, many thanks — and I shall hope to see you one day when I return to Illinois.

Affec[tionately]

ADLAI

P.S. Margaret Munn was the best thing about the inauguration! [36]

To Mrs. Marshall Field [37]

February 10, 1961

My dear Ruth:

I am writing this letter for your records, to acknowledge the receipt on loan of the following things which you have been good enough to send to my apartment in the Waldorf Towers for my use during the period of my occupancy there and my service at the United Nations.

1) Portrait of General Guye by Francisco Goya — hung in the living room above the fireplace;
2) Coromandel screen in two sections, placed in the dining room;
3) English desk and leather chair, placed in my study; and
4) Two splendid Hazeltine bulls! in the foyer.

You were so good to let me enjoy these lovely things, and I am grateful indeed. I shall see that they are returned at any time at your request.

Cordially yours,

To Mrs. Marshall Field

February 10, 1961

My dear Ruthie:

I am mortified that I didn't call you back before you left. And I am so grateful for both your letter and that exquisite antique "mug." It is so

[35] One of Stevenson's secretaries when he was governor of Illinois. The original is in the possession of Mrs. Munn.

[36] In January, Stevenson had attended the inauguration of Otto Kerner as governor of Illinois.

[37] Vice president and director of the Field Foundation and a close friend and supporter of Stevenson for many years.

lovely, and a precious addition to my meager collection of "important china." But why should you send me a present at all — after bulls, Goya, etc., etc.!

I have been hoping I could come down,[38] but work here plus various public appearances seem to preclude my escape either this week-end or the next, as I find I have to do a formidable broadcast in New York on Sunday the 19th. Perhaps when you get back we can have an evening in the country and a little of that precious fresh air. I am distressed to discover that on the night of the 14th, before the Foundation [39] meeting, I have scheduled a large dinner for the Secretary General — one of the routine courtesies. I am sure, however, that we can meet the next day before the meeting, although lunch is also pre-empted by my duties. Call me when you get back and we will work out something.

Did I tell you that included in the birthday was a splendid, imported French skillet with an angry little mouse sitting in the middle — from Fan [40] and Fiona!

Much love,

To John F. Kennedy

February 11, 1961

Dear Mr. President:

I apologize for taking up again a matter which we have discussed before and which I thought was settled.

There are three Commissions created by the Economic and Social Council of the United Nations on which women have traditionally represented the United States. It has also been the practice in the past for the United States Delegation to the General Assembly to include one woman among the five Delegates, and another among the five Alternate Delegates.

I have suggested, and I understood that you approved, the following appointments:

Commission on the Status of Women: Mrs. Gladys Tillett of North Carolina;

Social Commission: Mrs. Jane W. (Mrs. Edison) Dick of Illinois;

Human Rights Commission: Mrs. Marietta Tree (Mrs. Ronald Tree) of New York.

I proposed Mrs. Tillett for the Commission on the Status of Women because of her experience and interest in that field, and because as a Commission, it is the most active and requires the greatest parliamentary

[38] Mrs. Field was at Chelsea Plantation, her winter home in Ridgeland, South Carolina.

[39] Stevenson served on the board of directors of the Field Foundation.

[40] Fannie Sedgwick, a cousin of Marietta Tree and close friend of Mrs. Field's daughter Fiona.

and political skill. It meets annually for two or three weeks in the spring, usually abroad. Last year it met in Buenos Aires; this year it meets in Geneva.

I proposed Marietta Tree for the Human Rights Commission because of her status in the field of civil rights, and most of all because she has time, talent, acquaintance and facilities in New York which could be most helpful in entertaining and representational work among the Delegates. This Commission has been relatively inactive for the past 8 or 9 years. It meets annually alternating between New York and Geneva for two or three weeks. This year it meets in New York on *February 20*, which makes the appointment particularly urgent.

I suggested Mrs. Dick for the Social Commission because she has had considerable experience in this field, especially in child care and mental health. She served four years on the Board of Welfare Commissioners in Illinois. This Commission has also been relatively inactive and only meets every *two* years for a couple of weeks, also in the spring. I think Mrs. Dick could also be most helpful in representational work and entertaining in New York from time to time in emergencies.

I have promised none of these ladies that they will be appointed to the Delegation for the next General Assembly. My intention, as I told you, is to recommend that Mrs. [Franklin D.] Roosevelt be appointed for the resumed session in March, and also for the regular session commencing in September, as the woman Delegate. I do not exclude the possibility of Mrs. Tillett serving as the Alternate woman Delegate unless you have some other preference. In any event, the appointments need not be made until mid-summer, and there are many able and deserving women.

Mrs. Tree and Mrs. Dick have both accepted and I have been waiting for more than two weeks to hear from Mrs. Tillett. I have spoken to her on the telephone and while she makes no objection to me, I gather from Mr. O'Donnell [41] that Governor [Terry] Sanford of North Carolina has voiced some objection.

While there is no hurry about the appointments of Mrs. Tillett and Mrs. Dick, Mrs. Tree's appointment is urgent if she is to be confirmed and qualify for the meeting of the Human Rights Commission on February 20. She is out of the country at this time, but is returning for briefings on the 17th. Senator Fulbright [42] assures me that her British husband [43] will not be an embarrassment before the Senate Committee.

I am sorry to bother you with this matter, but I felt the foregoing

[41] Kenneth O'Donnell, special assistant to the President.
[42] J. William Fulbright, of Arkansas, chairman of the Senate Committee on Foreign Relations.
[43] Ronald Tree had been Parliamentary Secretary of the British Ministry of Town and Country Planning when Stevenson met him in 1945. Mrs. Tree had retained her American citizenship after their marriage in 1947.

explanation might be helpful, and I am sending it to you by Mr. O'Donnell as a sequel to my telephone conversation with him.

Respectfully yours,

To Mr. and Mrs. Frank Holland [44]

February 11, 1961

Dear Frank and Bea:

I should have written you long before this, but I have been hopelessly
involved in the Congo crisis and getting settled. The work is interesting,
but exacting, and keeps me busy around the clock. My apartment in the
Waldorf Towers hotel is very fine, and sometime you must both come
down and visit me. I also have a car and chauffeur at my disposal, which
eases the difficulty of getting around. I have to get acquainted with all
the chiefs of the other delegations, and there are 98 of them. In consequence, I have had to have a lot of lunches and dinners — at government
expense, thank God!

Mrs. [Ernest L.] Ives was here with me for a few days, and now
Roxane [Eberlein] has come to work in the office, which gives me a little
link with home. But I confess I get homesick and wish I was on the farm
and the ground, instead of the 42nd floor! I hope everything is well with
you and that you will let me hear from you once in a while about conditions at the farm. I suppose you have had a lot of snow and cold weather.
There has been more snow in New York than ever before, and the same
in Washington, where I have to go at least once a week. I hope the
children are well — and also Merlin.[45] Viola [Reardy] is enjoying the
new environment very much and keeping busy, as always, looking after
this large apartment and my many guests.

I had hoped to come home for a weekend this month, but the Congo
crisis makes it unlikely, and the General Assembly will reconvene in
March, which will keep me here for another month, I am afraid.

With best wishes to you all,

Yours,

To Joseph F. Bohrer [46]

February 14, 1961

Dear Joe:

Messages seem to be traveling to New York by dog sled nowadays (did
you hear about our 17-inch snowstorm?), and I have only now learned

---

[44] The couple who took care of Stevenson's farm at Libertyville.

[45] Stevenson's dog.

[46] A childhood friend from Bloomington, Illinois. See his "Boys in Bloomington,"
in *As We Knew Adlai: The Stevenson Story by Twenty-two Friends*, edited and
with preface by Edward P. Doyle, foreword by Adlai E. Stevenson III (New York:
Harper & Row, 1966), pp. 1–14. The original is in the possession of Mr. Bohrer.

that you were in the hospital for surgery. I am distressed — and hope it was nothing very serious, and that you are vertical and completely ambulatory again.

Why don't you and Marjorie [47] come to New York and see the city from my new quarters on top of the Waldorf? It's a magnificent view — but I already long for a glimpse of the Illinois prairie!

Affectionate wishes to you both.

Yours, ADLAI

Belgium granted the Congo independence on June 30, 1960. Five days later Congolese soldiers in Leopoldville and Thysville mutinied against their Belgian officers. On July 11 Moise Tshombe proclaimed the independence of the province of Katanga. On July 12, President Joseph Kasavubu and Prime Minister Patrice Lumumba requested aid from the United Nations. On July 14 the Security Council authorized the Secretary-General to consult with the Congolese government and provide the government with military assistance to facilitate the withdrawal of Belgian forces, maintain order, and protect the country's unity and independence. (The United States and the Soviet Union were the only two permanent members who voted for the action — France, China, and the United Kingdom abstained.) The General Assembly, by an overwhelming majority, decided to finance the operation by assessments on every member. The UN Peacekeeping Force in the Congo between July, 1960, and June, 1964, cost $411 million. In all, some ninety-three thousand men and officers drawn from thirty-four countries served in the Force.

On September 5, 1960, President Kasavubu dismissed Prime Minister Lumumba, who had been receiving some military supplies from the Soviet Union. The Soviet Union continued to view Lumumba as the head of the legal government. A few days later he was arrested by Colonel Joseph Mobutu, chief of staff of the Congolese Army. Lumumba escaped to Stanleyville (in Orientale Province) where he had strong supporters. He was recaptured, however, and imprisoned. In February, 1961, at the request of the Soviet Union, the Security Council discussed Lumumba's arrest. On February 13, 1961, Lumumba was murdered in Katanga. Meanwhile, Lumumba's lieutenant, Antoine Gizenga, had established control in Stanleyville and had secured recognition of his government by a number of Communist nations and the United Arab Republic, Ghana, Guinea, Mali, and Morocco.[48]

"The U.N. Mission to the Congo was by far the largest, most complex, most costly, and most controversial operation ever managed by the sec-

---

[47] Mr. Bohrer's wife, Margaret.
[48] See Lefever, *Crisis in the Congo*, p. 51.

retariat of an international organization," Ernest W. Lefever wrote. "As such, it is rich in irony and paradox. Sent to contain a local crisis, the mission magnified the crisis and compounded the political conflict by internationalizing the Congo. At the same time, the U.N. presence muted the violence of the adversaries. Designed to insulate the Congo from the Cold War, the mission insured that the Cold War would be waged there, but under constraints that furthered the interests of the United States and frustrated the interests of the Soviet Union." [49]

On February 13, 1961, when the Security Council met to discuss Lumumba's death, Soviet Ambassador Zorin attacked Belgium, its allies, and Secretary-General Dag Hammarskjöld. "One can no longer have any confidence in the Secretary-General or his staff," Zorin stated. Many observers at the UN interpreted Zorin's speech as indicating that the Soviet Union intended to intervene unilaterally in the Congo. On February 14, the Soviet Union demanded the resignation of the Secretary-General and the removal of all UN troops within a month. The Soviet Union pledged every possible help and support to Antoine Gizenga in Orientale Province.

Stevenson spoke in the Security Council on February 15.

A TIME FOR ACTION: THE DEVELOPING CRISIS IN THE CONGO [50]

A few days ago a new Administration took office in the United States. This is the first occasion for the United States under the leadership of President Kennedy to speak formally in the Security Council on a question of substance.

But first let me thank you again, all of you both here and abroad who have welcomed my arrival at this table so graciously and so hopefully. While I cannot fulfill your expectations of miracles to come, I can commit my country, my colleagues and myself to a tireless effort to make the United Nations successful, to make this great experiment in international collaboration fulfill the dreams of its founders that one day reason would rule and mankind would be liberated from the everlasting scourge of war.

It seems to be my lot, Mr. President, to address you and my colleagues

[49] *Uncertain Mandate: Politics of the U.N. Congo Operation* (Baltimore: Johns Hopkins Press, 1967), pp. xiii–xiv.

[50] United Nations, *Official Records*, Security Council, February 15, 1961, pp. 5–14. Ambassador Plimpton wrote: "He was a master of words, and words matter at the UN. . . . He came to the UN equipped with moderation and reason. . . . His low, calm, measured voice was all the more effective in contrast to the invective which he so often had to listen and reply to." "They Sent You Our Best," in *As We Knew Adlai*, pp. 256–257.

for the first time in a moment of grave crisis in the brief and tragic history of the Congo and in a moment of equally grave crisis for the United Nations itself. I had hoped that it would be otherwise. Within recent days we have seen successively the withdrawal of two national units of the United Nations Forces, the violent death of the former Prime Minister, Patrice Lumumba, the reported recognition of the Gizenga regime in Stanleyville by the United Arab Republic and a threat by the USSR to provide unilateral assistance outside the United Nations.

What we decide here in the next few days may, we believe, determine or not whether the United Nations will be able in the future to carry on its essential task of preserving the peace and protecting small nations. This is a time for urgent and constructive action. In the midst of passions it is a time when the Security Council must be calm. In the midst of efforts to destroy the United Nations action in the Congo, it is [a] time when we must persevere in the interests not only of the Congo, but also of all of us, large and small. The choice, as always, is a choice of us, the Members of the United Nations. Either we will follow a path toward a constructive and workable solution or we will follow a path of negative recrimination and self-interest.

As a new arrival listening and talking to representatives, I have wondered sometimes in the past ten days if everyone is actually thinking about the Congo, a new Republic struggling to be born, or if the Congo has been obscured by passions and prejudices about the doctors, Kasa-Vubu, Lumumba, Gizenga, Tshombe and so forth. Opinion seems to be polarizing about them, not about the patient. So it is more important than ever to rally strong support to the United Nations in order to save the patient.

For the past fortnight my country has been consulting on a United Nations programme to save the patient, both here and abroad, a programme on which there might be agreement by a large majority of United Nations Members. That effort, in which so many of us have taken part, must not be abandoned. Indeed its urgency is only accentuated by the impact of subsequent events.

As I have said, I had hoped that my first formal remarks to the Security Council on the vexed problems of the Congo could be directed solely to constructive suggestions which would be helpful to the Congolese people in working out their own independence free from outside interference. Instead, I find myself compelled to comment not on constructive suggestions but on a statement [S/4704] [51] and a draft resolution [S/4706] of the Soviet Union which were published in this morning's newspapers, and which is virtually a declaration of war on the United Nations [and] on

[51] This and subsequent references to UN documents or meetings appear in brackets in the original.

the principle of international action on behalf of peace. Permit me to analyse what, stripped of intemperate rhetoric, the statement and the draft resolution propose.

These texts propose the abandonment of the United Nations efforts for peace in the Congo and a surrender of the United Nations to chaos and to civil war. But the statement and the resolution say many things which we are glad to see, things which support positions which my country has always maintained.

As to colonialism, my country fought colonialism in 1776 when, if I may say so, the ancestors of the authors of this statement and this resolution had scarcely stirred beneath their bondage, and we have fought it ever since. My countrymen died to end colonialism in the Philippines and my countrymen have assisted the Philippine people to attain their present high destiny of complete independence. My countrymen have died to end colonialism in Cuba, though some Cubans seem to have forgotten this.

We rejoice, too, to hear the Soviets denounce political assassinations with such vehemence. In this country, it has always been condemned, by whomsoever it is committed, whether by Congolese, by colonialists or by Communists. We condemn any violation of human rights, any death without due process of law, whether of African politicians, Hungarian patriots or Tibetan nationalists. The United States stands clearly for the rights of man, individual men, man himself, as against any tyranny, whether it be the tyranny of colonialism, the tyranny of dictatorship or the tyranny of the majority.

We note that the Soviets demand that Belgian foreign military and paramilitary aid be withdrawn.[52] We of the United States insist that all foreign military aid, from whatever source and to whatever end, be removed from the Congo and that no such aid be permitted to interfere with the free and independent working out by the Congolese people themselves of their own political destiny. We mean this, and we intend to keep on meaning it, and we mean it with particular reference to the threat by the Soviet Government, which we hope we have misinterpreted, that "it is ready to render all possible assistance and support" to a so-called Congolese Government in Stanleyville which has no legal status. The United States intends to use its utmost influence, within the framework of the United Nations, to see to it that there is no outside interference from whatever source with the Congolese people's working out of their own independence. Therefore, we rejoice that the Soviet Union shares the distaste of the United States for colonialism and joins with us in condemning political assassination and in condemning foreign interference in the Congo.

[52] Belgian troops were withdrawn from Katanga in September, 1960, but after that 231 Belgian nationals were assigned to the Katanga regime to direct the gendarmerie and police. *United Nations Review,* Vol. 7, December, 1960, p. 27.

I pass lightly over the Soviet Government's petulant attack on the Secretary-General and that great office. He needs no defence from me, nor does the institution. His record is an open book, a book which all peace-loving peoples recognize as the record of a dedicated international civil servant whose only loyalty is to international justice and to international peace. Let the Soviet Government, if it wishes, pretend that he does not exist. It will find that he is far from being a disembodied ghost and it will find that peace-loving States will continue to support his patient search for the right road to security and peace in the Congo and for all peoples. The United Nations may have made mistakes in the Congo, as who has not, but nothing justifies an intemperate and unjustifiable attack on the integrity of the office itself.

We know that the United Nations has been denounced with equal vehemence by Kasa-Vubu, by Gizenga and by Tshombe. Well, they also attack each other with equal vehemence, but could there be better testimony of impartiality? I would recall, if I may be permitted, that the Christian Scriptures say, "Woe unto you, when all men speak well of you!" Neither the United Nations nor the Secretary-General seem likely to suffer from the affliction of universal approval.

We regret that the Soviet Government does not as yet seem to have seen fit to co-operate with States which truly seek peace in attempting to work out constructive steps for the co-operative solution of the agonizing problems through which the Congolese people are now passing. Instead, the Soviet Government proposes the complete abandonment of the United Nations operation in the Congo in one month. What does this mean? It means not only the abandonment of the Congo to chaos and civil war but, if you please, to the cold war. It means the abandonment of the principle of the United Nations itself. Does anyone doubt that the removal of the United Nations Force would mean chaos? Does this Council, the Security Council, favour abandoning security for insecurity and anarchy? Do we want to withdraw the only elements that stand foursquare against civil and tribal war? Does the Soviet Government really want Africans to kill Africans? The United States does not, and it devotedly hopes that the Soviet Government does not either and that it will join the United States and other peace-loving States in supporting and strengthening the only force that can prevent Congolese civil war, and, indeed, a cold war, the United Nations.

Does the Soviet Government really want to chill what should be warm and temperate in Africa with the icy blasts of power politics? The United States does not; its only interest in the Congo is to support the Congolese people in their struggle for real independence, free from any foreign domination from any source. The United States deplores any war, cold or otherwise. Its only desire is to live in peace and freedom and to let all other peoples live in peace and freedom. It will resist with all its power all assaults on its own peace and freedom, and it proposes to join with all other peace-loving peoples in resisting, in the corporate framework of the United Nations, all assaults on the peace and freedom of other peoples.

In that spirit, we declare that so far as we are concerned Africa shall never be the scene of any war, cold or hot, but we also declare that "Africa for the Africans" means "Africa for the Africans" and not Africa as a hunting ground for alien ambitions. We pledge our full and unstinted support against any attempt by anyone to interfere with the full and free development by Africans of their own independent African future.

We believe that the only way to keep the cold war out of the Congo is to keep the United Nations in the Congo, and we call on the Soviet Union to join us in thus ensuring the free and untrammelled exercise by the Congolese people of their right to independence and to democracy.

But the position apparently taken by the Soviet Government involves more than the unhappy and despicable fate of three Congolese politicians. It involves the future of the 14 million Congolese people. They are the ones with whom we are concerned. We deplore the past, and we condemn those responsible for it, no matter who they may be. But we submit that it is the future that is all-important now and that the best efforts of this Council should be concentrated on the future security of the Congo, and indeed on the future security of all peoples. For it is the security of all peoples which is threatened by the statement and by the proposals of the Soviet Government. Let me make my meaning abundantly and completely clear, if I can.

The United States Government believes, and proudly believes, that the single, best and only hope of the peoples of the world for peace and security lies in the United Nations. It lies in international co-operation in the integrity of an international body rising above international rivalries into the clearer air of international morality and international justice.

The United Nations has not achieved perfection, nor has the United States; and they probably never will. The United Nations, like the United States, is composed of humans. It has made mistakes; it probably always will make mistakes. It has never pleased all people. It cannot please all people. In its desire and wholehearted determination to do justice, it may offend one group of States in 1952; another in 1956, and perhaps still another in 1961. But always the United Nations has tried — and we believe that it will always try — to apply evenhandedly the rules of justice and equity that should govern us all.

Are we callously to cast aside the one and only instrument that men have developed to safeguard their peace and security? Are we to abandon the jungles of the Congo to the jungles of internecine warfare and of international rivalry? This issue even transcends the fate of the suffering

14 million Congolese people. It involves the fate of all of us, of all mankind.

The issue, then, is simply this. Shall the United Nations survive? Shall the attempt to bring about peace by the concerted powers of international understanding be discarded? [53]

May I say that I deeply deplore this outrageous and obviously organized demonstration. To the extent that Americans may be involved, I apologize on behalf of my Government to the members of the Security Council.

I was saying that the issue is simply this. Shall the United Nations survive? Shall the attempt to bring about peace by the concerted power of international understanding be discarded? Shall any pretence of an international order, of international law, be swept aside? Shall conflicts of naked power, awful in their potential, be permitted to rage in Africa or elsewhere, unchecked by international co-operation or authority?

These are questions which call for an answer, not so much by the great Powers as by the smaller ones and the newer ones. My own country, as it happens, is in the fortunate position of being able to look out for itself and for its interests, and look out it will. But it is for the vast majority of States that the United Nations has vital meaning and is of vital necessity. I call on those States to rise in defence of the integrity of the institution which is for them the only assurance for all of us of peace in the years to come. I also call upon the Soviet Union to reconsider its position.

My Government is earnestly determined to co-operate with all Governments in an attempt to improve international relationships and to further friendship among peoples, and it has welcomed evidences of co-operation toward that end by the Soviet Government. Let those evidences be buttressed now by concrete steps, by the Soviet Government's looking toward a constructive solution of the difficult problems that confront us all. Let us join in condemning the past, but let us join in facing the future with calm determination to support steadfastly, and strengthen sturdily, the United Nations — the United Nations, which is the last best hope of us all.

Let me now turn to the Congo and to what can be done to arrest the sad deterioration in that divided country. There are certain fundamental principles concerning the Congo which have had, and will continue to have, the full support of the American people and of the United States Government. It is on the basis of these principles that we have under-

[53] At this point in the speech, demonstrators in the visitors' gallery began shouting: "Vive Lumumba," "Down with the United Nations," "Drive the UN out of the Congo," "Out with Dag Hammarskjöld." Sir Patrick Dean, president of the council, ordered the gallery cleared. It was twenty minutes before Stevenson was able to resume speaking.

taken consultation this past fortnight. We believe that they are shared by others and we are willing to work with any and all who show a willingness to find a solution.

The essential principles of such a solution are, we believe, apparent to all. In the first place, the unity, the territorial integrity and the political independence of the Congo must be preserved. I am sure that Sir Patrick Dean will not object if I repeat that the United States was one of the first anti-colonialists and that, during the 186 years since, we have stood steadfastly for the right of peoples to determine their own destiny. The United States desires nothing for the Congo but its complete freedom from outside domination and nothing for its people but the same indedendent freedom which we wanted for ourselves so long ago and have resolutely defended ever since. Much as the United States was once beset by internal dissensions, so the Congo, since its independence, has been beset by secessionist movements, previously in Katanga and now in Orientale province too. The United States supports the continued territorial integrity of the Congo. So far as we are concerned, its borders are identical with its borders on 1 July 1960. The United States is ready to join with other States which support the Congo's independence and integrity to maintain this principle within the framework of the United Nations.

Secondly, the Congo must not become a battleground, as I have said, for either a cold or a hot war among the big Powers. When the United States was first requested to provide troops for the Congo, we told the Congolese Government to appeal to the United Nations.[54] We then supported United Nations military assistance to the Congo. In contrast to others, the United States has never at any time provided a single tank, a single gun, a single soldier, a single piece of equipment that could be used for military purposes, to anyone in the Congo. We have, on the other hand, responded promptly and vigorously to every request made of us by the United Nations, so that the entire control over our assistance passed from our hands to those of the United Nations. We remain firmly determined, as I have said, to do everything in our power to keep the cold war out of Africa.

Thirdly, we support the United Nations action in the Congo to the fullest measure of our power. The best way to keep the cold war and the hot war out of the Congo, as I have said, is to keep the United Nations in. To those Members which are still contemplating withdrawal, I suggest a long, hard, careful look at what might happen in the Congo if the United Nations Force collapses or if the United Nations mission fails because of lack of support by its Members.

Finally, we believe that the Congolese people must be allowed to

[54] July 12, 1960. See Lefever, *Uncertain Mandate*, p. 10.

develop their own political settlement by peaceful means, free from violence and external interference. The Congo's political problems must, in the last analysis, be worked out by the Congolese themselves. The United Nations can assist in this effort by helping to create peace and stability and by extending its good offices, as it has done in the United Nations Conciliation Commission for the Congo. But only a settlement commanding the support of the Congolese people will long endure.

On these principles — the maintenance of territorial integrity and political independence, the isolation of the Congolese from large-power and small-power interference, continued vigorous United Nations assistance and the settlement of internal political controversies by peaceful means — rests, in our opinion, the only possibility for a solution. We are faced now with the necessity for urgent and effective steps to bring these principles closer to reality. The threat of civil war, of increased unilateral intervention in the Congo on all sides, is increasingly grave. If the United Nations does not take effective action immediately, not only may conflict break forth in full fury in the Congo, but the hopes of African unity may be destroyed for many years to come by the divisions which will be produced among African Nations.

What, then, in those circumstances needs to be done?

First, all foreign intervention outside the framework of the United Nations should cease immediately, and any foreign military or paramilitary personnel in the Congo should be withdrawn. The injunction of the General Assembly resolution [1474 (ES–IV)], adopted with the support of all Members of the United Nations except the Soviet bloc, against any unilateral military aid whatever, whether direct or indirect, should be adhered to fully by all United Nations Members. This applies to those Belgians who are providing military advice and assistance to the Congo. It applies equally to military assistance to the forces in Orientale province. The United States, for its part, does not intend to sit by if others consciously and deliberately seek to exacerbate the present situation. We are prepared to use all of our influence, if other Members of the United Nations do likewise, to prevent such assistance from coming to the Congo, no matter from what quarter it may come.

Equally urgent and immediate steps are needed to avert the extension of civil war in the Congo and to protect the lives of innocent civilians and refugees, should the present passions result in widespread outbreaks of violence. The United Nations political and military authorities on the ground should consult immediately with the Chief of State and with other civilian and military leaders, if necessary, to agree on measures which would best maintain peace and stability and protect the lives of citizens. Such measures must be accompanied also by immediate steps to assure long-range stability and progress.

The Secretary-General proposed to us less than two weeks ago [928th meeting] that measures should be taken to unify, reorganize and retrain the Congolese Army and other armed forces in the Congo with a view to eliminating force as a political element in that afflicted country. The United States supports this proposal. We believe that negotiations to bring this about should be undertaken with the same urgency as the measures I have just mentioned.

On Monday, here in the Security Council [933rd meeting], I deplored the reported death of Mr. Lumumba and his colleagues and supported the Secretary-General's request that his report should be included in the agenda and that the preliminary investigation should be continued. On every occasion when the arrest of Mr. Lumumba has been discussed in the United Nations, the United States has taken the position that he must be treated humanely and with all protection of law and order. We have similarly expressed ourselves through diplomatic channels to the appropriate authorities in the Congo. I believe it has been long known that in our consultations during the past week we advocated the release of all political prisoners and their participation in the political process, once law and order had been restored to the Congo and the possibility of civil war averted. We continue to believe that this must be done for those political prisoners such as Mr. Songolo,[55] about whom the world Press has been less aware. In the case of Mr. Lumumba we support the Secretary-General's investigation, and we believe that it should be continued vigorously until the true facts are known. I earnestly hope that the Katanga forces will co-operate so that the full facts may be brought to light.

The ultimate objective of such steps should be to promote the reconciliation of the political elements in the Congo and a full return to constitutional processes, in a form to be designated by the people themselves. The Government recently appointed by the Chief of State is a step in the right direction. Indeed, any step in the direction of moderation and breadth of base is a step in the right direction. The provision of unfilled Cabinet places for other elements is encouraging. Determined future efforts must be made to broaden the base of the Congolese Government, and Parliament should be convened as soon as conditions of security, law and order permit. Encouragement by the United Nations of such steps is of fundamental importance, we believe.

The measures I have outlined can be carried out with dispatch and effectiveness only through the Secretary-General and the United Nations mission in the Congo. To attempt to discredit and dismiss the Secretary-General at this critical moment would not only wreck the United Nations

[55] Alphonse Songolo and other parliamentarians were being held illegally by supporters of Lumumba in Stanleyville.

mission in the Congo, but dangerously weaken the United Nations itself. This is the measure of the gravity of our crisis. We call upon all members at this table to face these realities soberly and solemnly. We are eager to continue consultations with other nations at this table with a view to producing a draft resolution to carry out measures such as those. We are prepared to meet in the Council by night and by day until we can reach consensus and agreement.

The time for effective action in the Congo is now. We must seize it — and we must seize it quickly.

Senator Wayne Morse of Oregon, who served on the United States delegation to the General Assembly in the fall of 1960, talked on the telephone and then wrote to Stevenson on December 9, 1960, before he accepted the post of permanent representative of the United States to the UN. Morse urged Stevenson to insist that the position be that of Secretary of State for United Nations Affairs. When the Secretary of State and the Secretary of State for United Nations Affairs could not agree on a policy position, Morse proposed that the final decision be made by the President. Morse warned that unless Stevenson insisted on this he would never be able to make a success of his post at the UN. Morse explained that the position papers drafted by lower-echelon officers in the Department of State and sent to the U.S. permanent representative frequently had in the past "pulled" the "rug out from under him" to the great injury of the United States. The permanent representative had to be free from "veto control" at the Department of State, Morse insisted.

Morse added that the Department of Defense had too much influence on State Department officials. As a result, military policies in respect to the North Atlantic Treaty Organization dictated U.S. policy in the UN on colonialism. Asian and African delegations at the UN were aware, Morse wrote, that the United States backed Spain, Portugal, the Union of South Africa, and the United Kingdom on the argument that the U.S. needed military bases or because they were against Communism. Morse pointed out that military minds in the Pentagon lacked sympathy for and understanding of "the great revolution that is taking place in the world on the part of millions of people who want neither Communism nor Western domination."

Morse recommended that Stevenson not accept the post of permanent representative unless President Kennedy agreed to the authority and jurisdiction outlined in his letter. Without this, he stated, "not even an Adlai Stevenson can be effective in this job." Stevenson, however, accepted the ambassadorship without being as specific as Morse had urged.

To Wayne Morse

February 23, 1961

Dear Wayne:

I am going to be in Washington on Sunday, February 26. If it is at all possible for you, I should like very much to have that long deferred talk about your experiences at the UN. I have been literally lost in the jungles of the Congo — not to mention New York! — since I have been here, and my visits to Washington have been infrequent and hurried. This one is, too. But I do not want to postpone any longer a visit with you, if Sunday is at all possible.

The morning would be best for me. I will be staying at 2131 O Street (telephone FE 3-5165) with friends,[56] but I would be glad to come to your apartment.

Yours,

To Mrs. Harry E. Thayer [57]

February 24, 1961

Dearest Joanie:

Thanks so much for my Valentine. It's the loveliest I ever had or ever will have. And to have it delivered in person! You are a glorious girl, and my favorite niece! I love you very much and hope you will come and see me often, with or without Valentine.

Yours,

To Joseph Wyatt [58]

February 28, 1961

Dear Joe:

Thanks so much for reminding me of the CDC's 9th Annual Convention this weekend. I would not want to miss sending my warmest good wishes to Pat Brown,[59] Clair Engle,[60] Libby Smith,[61] and my other California friends — not the least of whom is your retiring President!

I think you know — better than I can tell you — that the California Democratic Council holds a very special place in my heart. I have

[56] Dr. and Mrs. Paul B. Magnuson, with whom Stevenson almost always stayed when in Washington, D.C.
[57] The former Joan Pirie, daughter of Ellen Stevenson's sister, Mrs. Ralph Hines.
[58] President of the California Democratic Council.
[59] Edmund G. Brown, governor of California.
[60] Democratic senator from California.
[61] Elizabeth Rudel Smith, Democratic National Committeewoman from California.

watched it grow from infancy, and have even done my share of baby sitting with this lusty young offspring of California Democracy — one of the most exciting upsurges of political rejuvenation in our time.

My thoughts will be with you this weekend, and always my gratitude for the help and encouragement you have given me in the past.

Cordially yours,

To Grayson Kirk [62]

March 1, 1961

Dear Grayson:

You will note that, as part of our effort to get the very best people in the country into key positions in the State Department, we have been talking to Professor Richard N. Gardner about serving with Assistant Secretary Harlan Cleveland as Deputy Assistant Secretary for International Organization Affairs. His rich background in both international law and foreign economic policy makes him an ideal choice for this spot.

The detailed arrangements have been made between Mr. Cleveland and Dean Warren.[63] However, I understand that the granting of leave to Mr. Gardner will of course require action on the part of yourself and the Trustees. I am therefore writing to draw your urgent attention to the importance which we attach to the earliest possible release of Mr. Gardner for this important service, on a basis which protects his own career as a Professor of Law, and his association with Columbia University.

The high competence and wisdom of the faculty you have assembled at Columbia has caused Columbia to be asked to make more sacrifices in the current recruitment for policy positions in Washington than almost any other University. It is, nevertheless, my earnest hope that the Trustees will be able to make Mr. Gardner's services available to us, in keeping with the high traditions of public service which have been the hallmark of Columbia throughout its distinguished history.

With warm personal regards,

Sincerely,

During the month of March, Stevenson was the president of the Security Council. In addition, the General Assembly resumed its work. Stevenson addressed the Security Council on Angola on March 10 and 15, he spoke to the plenary session of the General Assembly on the Congo on March 21, and he made statements to Committee 1 (Political and Security) of the General Assembly on March 21, 23, and 30.

[62] President of Columbia University.
[63] William Clements Warren, dean of the Law School of Columbia University.

To Robert Benjamin [64]

March 7, 1961

Dear Bob:

As you know, the General Assembly of the United Nations resumes its work this week and Delegations from all over the world will be gathering here in New York City.

I am convinced it is very much in the national interest to welcome the members of these Delegations in a personal way and this is a responsibility I hope you will share with me.

With this in mind I wonder whether you would be willing to help by extending hospitality to some of the visiting delegates during this spring session of the General Assembly.

I have asked Dorothy Hirshon,[65] who has agreed to assist me in this effort, to telephone you and give you the details of what I have in mind.

Sincerely yours,

ADLAI

On March 9, Wallace Irwin, Jr., of the Public Relations Office of USUN, informed Stevenson that the incoming mail of between two hundred and three hundred pieces each day was more than his office had had to handle over an extended period. He wrote: "Most of the letters are expressions of good will, views on public issues, plans and ideas for your consideration, etc. We are hopelessly flooded."

To Harlan Cleveland

March 9, 1961

Dear Harlan:

The flow of mail to this office has increased to the point where the present staff has become hopelessly inundated. Attached is a copy of a press statement which I have been obliged to issue on this subject.

Would you be good enough to arrange, somehow, for the immediate assignment to the Public Affairs Office here, under Mr. Irvin, of a junior officer qualified in this field, plus an experienced clerk-typist, who between them can read and sort incoming mail, match it up with form

---

[64] Director of United Artists Corporation and national chairman of the United States Committee for the United Nations, and an old friend of Stevenson's. The original is in the possession of Mr. Benjamin. Stevenson wrote a number of letters to other friends enlisting their cooperation.

[65] Head of the Hospitality Committee for United Nations Delegates, Inc., in New York City.

replies, and pick out the letters that may need my personal attention? They must be here from now until we get the permanent staff increase which requires Congressional action. I realize this may be difficult and that the Department is also short of people. But every other possible solution has been looked into and found impractical.

This may require an appeal from you to Roger Tubby,[66] to whom I am sending a copy of this.

I am sorry to trouble you with this administrative detail, but it must be solved, and I shall be most grateful to you for your immediate help.

Cordially,

To Maxwell Hahn [67]

March 15, 1961

Dear Max:

I have been meaning to telephone you for the last few weeks to request that payment of any salary to me as President of the Field Foundation be discontinued. I feel we would all be more comfortable if I wasn't accepting any salary in the present circumstances. I have discussed this with Ruth [Field] and she agrees.

Unless you have already terminated, I suggest that you do so as of March 1.

Cordially yours,

Ever since joining the UN in 1955, Portugal had argued that the General Assembly and the Security Council had no right to discuss or recommend action regarding its three African colonies since Portugal maintained they were not colonies but overseas provinces of Portugal itself.[68]

In December, 1960, forty-three Asian and African states submitted a resolution to the General Assembly on "the granting of independence to colonial countries and peoples." The resolution stated that "all peoples have the right of self-determination" and that "immediate steps shall be taken" in all non-self-governing territories "to transfer all power to the peoples of these Territories, without any conditions or reservations, in accordance with their freely expressed will."

Although this resolution had been drafted by the Afro-Asian leaders

---

[66] Assistant Secretary of State for Public Affairs. He had been assistant press secretary to Stevenson in the 1956 presidential campaign.

[67] Executive vice president of the Field Foundation.

[68] See Basil Davidson, *The Liberation of Guiné* (London: Penguin African Library, 1969); James Duffy, *Portuguese Africa* (Cambridge, Mass.: Harvard University Press, 1959); and *A Question of Slavery* (London: Oxford University Press, 1967).

with representatives of USUN, and the Department of State concurred that the United States should vote for it, President Eisenhower ordered the U.S. delegate to abstain after British Prime Minister Harold Macmillan had telephoned him. The resolution passed the General Assembly 89–0, with nine nations abstaining.

Sustained military action by Angolan nationalists led Liberia to place before the Security Council a resolution requesting Portugal to comply with UN policy against colonialism and recommending a UN inquiry into the situation in Angola.

"Stevenson and Kennedy both saw the opportunity to intimate a change in American policy," Arthur M. Schlesinger, Jr., wrote.[69] *Under Secretary of State Chester Bowles, Assistant Secretary of State for African Affairs G. Mennen Williams, Williams's deputy Wayne Fredericks, Harlan Cleveland, and others agreed. The dictator of Portugal, Antonio de Oliveira Salazar, and American's NATO allies were informed in advance that the United States would vote for the Liberian resolution. Although the resolution failed in the Security Council, a month later it passed the General Assembly with U.S. support. "The new administration was now free of automatic identification with colonialism," Schlesinger wrote.*[70]

Before Stevenson spoke in the Security Council on March 15, 1961, Britain, France, Nationalist China, and several other nations had opposed the Liberian resolution, stating that the UN had "no jurisdiction."

Stevenson's speech follows: [71]

The PRESIDENT: [72] Since there are no other speakers, in my capacity as representative of the UNITED STATES, I shall claim the privilege of expressing the views of my Government on the draft resolution [S/4769].[73]

When he first raised the question of Angola in the Security Council, the representative of Liberia, Mr. [George A.] Padmore, recognized that the recent disturbance in Angola was not of itself an immediate threat to the maintenance of international peace and security. At that time he said:

"I believe that there is still time for us to help to build in Angola a future on which neither the Portuguese nor the Africans need be

[69] *A Thousand Days: John F. Kennedy in the White House* (Boston: Houghton Mifflin, 1965), p. 511.

[70] Ibid., p. 512.

[71] United Nations, *Official Records*, Security Council, March 15, 1961, pp. 20–22. *Newsweek*, March 27, 1961, pp. 41–45, in a feature story on Stevenson, reported that when he finished this speech, a "buzz of comment" filled the room. The UN press corps ran for telephones, since "the U.S. had broken with its traditional allies to join sides with the new and neutral nations of Africa and Asia."

[72] On this day Stevenson was the presiding officer of the Security Council.

[73] This and subsequent references to UN documents or meetings appear in brackets in the original.

afraid. But we no longer have centuries, or even decades, in which to accomplish what should be a simple humanitarian task." [934th meeting, para. 7.]

He emphasized several problems with which the United Nations must concern itself: the urgency, in this era of rapid communication, of acting with despatch; the recognition of Angola's problem being a part of the larger African scene; and the desirability of Portugal's availing itself of United Nations cooperation and help in the development of its territories in Africa. It was clear from his remarks that Mr. Padmore was anticipating conditions which, if unchanged, might endanger the peace and security of Africa, if not of the world.

It is in a spirit of seeking the constructive elimination of not just the symptoms, but the sources of friction, that the United States approaches this problem. I regret to find myself in disagreement with the representative of China and other members of this Council who present their position with such logic and force. And while we recognize full well that Angola and the conditions therein do not today endanger international peace and security, we believe that they may, if not alleviated, lead to more disorders, with many unforeseen, unfortunate and dangerous consequences.

We in the United States deplore the violence which occurred in Luanda [74] and the tragic loss of life, involving all elements of the community. Nothing we can do here will restore these people to life. But perhaps we can discourage further violence, which can only make constructive efforts towards the solution of basic problems more difficult.

It is only prudent to view the disorders in Luanda in the context of the dramatic changes which have taken place in so much of Africa in the past few years. Angola is but a part of the over-all picture of evolution on the African continent. The views of the United States have not changed since Jefferson wrote that:

"We hold these truths to be self-evident, that all men are created equal, that they are endowed by their Creator with certain unalienable Rights, that among these are Life, Liberty and the Pursuit of Happiness. That to secure these rights, Governments are instituted among Men, deriving their just powers from the consent of the governed."

[74] For weeks there had been bloody fighting between Angolan nationalists and Portuguese police and soldiers, most notably an attack by several hundred Angolans on a police station in Luanda in early February, with heavy casualties on both sides, and later incidents when police and civilians clashed at the funerals of the attackers.

Those words reflect, we believe, the basic principles which all Governments would do well to observe and to implement with all of the energy at their command.

It is no secret that the General Assembly has been interested for years in conditions within Portugal's African territories. There can be no doubt that the people of Angola are entitled to all of the rights guaranteed them by the Charter, the right of unfettered opportunity to develop their full economic, political and cultural potentialities. I am sure Portugal recognizes that it has a solemn obligation to undertake the systematic and rapid improvement of the conditions of the people of its territories, an evolution which is contemplated by the Charter.

The United States would be remiss in its duties as a friend of Portugal if it failed to express honestly its conviction that step-by-step planning within Portuguese territories and the acceleration thereof is now imperative for the successful political, economic and social advancement of all inhabitants under Portuguese administration — advancement, in brief, towards full self-determination.

The practical difficulties facing Portugal in the immediate future are formidable. If the people of Angola are not given reason to believe that they, too, may hope to participate in determining their own future, the tension which exists today will grow and may well result in disorders which will indeed pose a threat to international peace and security. On the other hand, we all know, and know only too well, the tragic events which have occurred in the Congo, that huge, unhappy State which lies just to the north of Angola. I do not think I would be straining the truth to conclude that much of the Congo's problems result from the fact that the pressure of nationalism rapidly overtook the preparation of the necessary foundation essential to the peaceful and effective exercise of sovereign self-government.

The important thing for us, then, is to ensure that similar conditions do not exist for the Angola of tomorrow. We believe that a beginning should be made promptly within that Territory to foster that educational, social and economic development of which political development is an integral part and to ensure the rapid attainment of political maturity within this area. As we know, political maturity is the crying need everywhere.

On 15 December 1960, by its resolution 1542 (XV), the General Assembly considered that a number of important territories were Non-Self-Governing within the meaning of Chapter XI of the Charter. The Assembly spoke of an obligation which exists on the part of Portugal to transmit information under Chapter XI of the Charter concerning these territories. The Assembly further invited the Government of Portugal to participate in the work of the Committee on Information from Non-Self-

Governing Territories.[75] I mention this because, in the view of my Government, the best course of action for Portugal and the best course of action to promote the interests of the people of the Portuguese territories seems to be through co-operation with the United Nations. In our view, the resolution to which I have just referred was an invitation to Portugal to work with Members of this Organization to ensure the more rapid progress of the peoples in Portuguese territory. I stress the words "work with." The United States does not read any dark dangers into this resolution. This is a gesture of concern, a gesture of goodwill and, beyond that, an effort toward genuine co-operation in the achievement of goals which are shared by all of us and which are recognized in the Charter of this Organization.

Hence, we hope that Portugal will proceed in accordance with the draft resolution now before the Council. In doing so, it would, in the words of Article 73 b of the Charter on the subject of the people of the Non-Self-Governing Territories, work "to develop self-government, to take due account of the political aspirations of the peoples, and to assist them in the progressive development of their free political institutions, according to the particular circumstances of each territory and its peoples and their varying stages of advancement."

I hope that what I have said will be taken in the spirit in which it is intended, to encourage the peaceful evolution of a society in Angola in which men of all races can live together in harmony with mutual respect for the different cultures and ways of life which now exist there.

Eleanor Roosevelt, who was appointed to the United States delegation to the General Assembly, frequently sent Stevenson articles and papers on a variety of issues.

To Mrs. Franklin D. Roosevelt [76]

March 16, 1961

Dear Mrs. R:

Attached, just for your information, are copies of letters I have sent to three people whose papers you were nice enough to forward to me. I wish I could do something useful for them but, as you realize, I have been inundated here.[77]

Cordially,
ADLAI

[75] Portugal refused to participate.
[76] The original is in the Franklin D. Roosevelt Library, Hyde Park, New York.
[77] Stevenson sent one of the papers to the Department of State and recommended to the writers of the other two that they send copies to the Department.

To Alicia Patterson [78]

March 19, 1961

Dear Alicia:

Well, if not April 5th — when? I can catch a tadpole quicker than I can you! . . .

Yours,

A

P.S. Or don't you want to see me!

To Mrs. Franklin D. Roosevelt [79]

March 20, 1961

Dear Mrs. R:

Thanks so much for your letter of the 16th. I am touched and honored that you want me to make the remarks at Hyde Park this Memorial Day, and I accept with great pleasure. I cannot tell at the moment just when I could arrive, but we can be in touch later on about details.

I look forward to being with you on May 30.

Affectionately,

P.S. Will you tell me what to say?

To Andrei A. Gromyko [80]

March 28, 1961

My dear Andrei:

How very thoughtful and generous of you to send me that wonderful caviar, vodka and brandy! They will certainly be savored and enjoyed, and will undoubtedly increase my stature as a host!

With thanks and best wishes,

Cordially yours,

---

[78] Mrs. Harry F. Guggenheim, publisher of *Newsday* and a dear friend of Stevenson's since the 1920's. See *The Papers of Adlai E. Stevenson*, Vol. II, Vol. III. This handwritten letter is in the possession of Adlai E. Stevenson III.

[79] The original is in the Franklin D. Roosevelt Library, Hyde Park, New York. Stevenson added the postscript by hand.

[80] Minister of foreign affairs of the Union of Soviet Socialist Republics. Gromyko and Stevenson had headed their respective delegations at the UN Preparatory Commission meetings in London in 1945. See *The Papers of Adlai E. Stevenson*, Vol. II, pp. 259 ff.

To Mrs. Dennis McEvoy [81]

March 30, 1961

Dearest Nan:

The German Embassy has called today to say that Chancellor [Konrad] Adenauer wants me to dine at the Embassy in Washington on April 13 at 8:00. I note that I have an engagement with you for dinner that evening. Please let me know promptly if it [is] still on, or if you think I can be spared. Do you think I could come in before and after? I don't want to miss *anything!*

If you insist that I forego the Germans, I could do that too — with or without Jackie [Kennedy].

Love,

To Arthur M. Schlesinger, Jr.

March 31, 1961

Dear Arthur:

I find I have to speak on May 30th, Memorial Day, at Hyde Park. Mrs. Roosevelt has suggested that I talk a little about FDR, the genesis of the UN and international organization. I gather that she feels that his thinking about the post-war world and the preservation of peace would be appropriate.

Can you help me? I find that what with commencements in early June and other affairs in late May, I have let the speaking burden get too heavy. Besides, I think this occasion may afford an opportunity to say something thoughtful and useful about the Administration's position. And you know more about that than "the mouthpiece."

Yours,

To John F. Kennedy

April 12, 1961

Dear Mr. President:

They tell me it is from you — and it is indeed a splendid picture of you. But who signed it? [82]

Many thanks for "them kind words."

Faithfully yours,

---

[81] The former Nan Tucker, a member of the family which founded the San Francisco *Chronicle* and a confidante of Mrs. John F. Kennedy. See "They're All Madly for Adlai! He's Still the 'Gov' to a Fiercely Loyal Group," Chicago *American*, May 28, 1961, p. 17.

[82] The President's signature was practically indecipherable.

On April 10, 11, and 14 Stevenson spoke to Committee 1 of the General Assembly on the question of the unification of Korea. Then came the fiasco of the Bay of Pigs.

In November, 1960, President-elect Kennedy was briefed by Allen Dulles, head of the Central Intelligence Agency, about the CIA's training of Cuban exiles in Guatemala for an amphibious assault on Cuba. After Kennedy took office there were many meetings with representatives of the CIA, the Joint Chiefs of Staff, and the Department of State, but conspicuously not Adlai E. Stevenson. When Senator J. W. Fulbright attended one meeting on April 4, 1961, he denounced the entire plan.[83] *Kennedy stated at his press conference on April 12, "There will not be, under any conditions, an intervention in Cuba by the United States Armed Forces."* [84]

On April 14, the Cuban exiles boarded ships in Nicaragua. As part of the CIA plans, planes took off from Nicaragua and at dawn the next morning attacked three Cuban airfields. They were not defectors from Castro's air force and did not take off from Cuba, but they were so described in the CIA cover story.

Meanwhile, at the United Nations, Stevenson was preparing for debates in the General Assembly over Cuba's charge that the United States had aggressive intentions toward it. On January 4–5, 1961, for instance, the Cuban foreign minister had charged at the UN Security Council that the United States had established bases in Guatemala and elsewhere in preparation for an invasion of Cuba.[85]

According to Arthur M. Schlesinger, Jr., Kennedy said he wanted Stevenson to be "fully informed, and that nothing said at the UN should be less than the truth, even if it could not be the full truth." Kennedy

[83] Although Tristram Coffin wrote that Stevenson attended this meeting (*Senator Fulbright: Portrait of a Public Philosopher* [New York: Dutton, 1966], p. 148), he did not, according to Senator Fulbright. Letter to Walter Johnson, July 30, 1975.

[84] New York *Times*, April 13, 1961. See Theodore C. Sorensen, *Kennedy* (New York: Harper & Row, 1965), pp. 297–298, for how Kennedy was assured that the exile brigade could achieve its goals without U.S. intervention.

[85] Ronald Hilton, director of Stanford University's Institute of Hispanic American and Luso-Brazilian studies, stated in the *Hispanic American Report*, November, 1960, p. 583, that it was common knowledge in Guatemala that the CIA was training exiles for an invasion. The *Nation* magazine checked with Hilton and on November 19, 1960, wrote an editorial stating that Castro "may have a sounder basis for his expressed fears of a U.S. financed 'Guatemala-type' invasion than most of us realize." The editorial urged U.S. news media with correspondents in Guatemala to check the story. The *Nation* sent proofs of the editorial and a news release to major news outlets. Only the York, Pennsylvania, *Gazette and Daily* ran an immediate story. On November 28, 1960, the New York *Times* quoted the president of Guatemala as saying the reports were "lies." On April 7, 1961, the *Times* changed a story by Tad Szulc and deleted references to the CIA and the imminence of an invasion. See Victor Bernstein and Jesse Gordon, "The Press and the Bay of Pigs," *Columbia University Forum*, Vol. X, No. 3 (Fall, 1967), for an analysis of the failure of the news media to report the story in advance.

told Schlesinger on April 7, "The integrity and credibility of Adlai Stevenson constitute one of our great national assets. I don't want anything to be done which might jeopardize that." [86]

The next day, April 8, Schlesinger and Tracy Barnes of the CIA talked to Stevenson and Plimpton. Schlesinger wrote: "But our briefing, which was probably unduly vague, left Stevenson with the impression that no action would take place during the UN discussion of the Cuban item.[87] Afterward, when Harlan Cleveland, . . . Clayton Fritchey . . . and I lunched with Stevenson . . . he made clear that he wholly disapproved of the plan, regretted that he had been given no opportunity to comment on it and believed that it would cause infinite trouble. But, if it was national policy, he was prepared to make out the best possible case." [88]

Ambassador Plimpton wrote of the "briefing" that it "guardedly indicated" to Stevenson and others at USUN that "something was likely to happen" on the shores of Cuba. "The financing was to be by Cuban emigres; no U.S. facilities were to be involved (perhaps an abandoned U.S. Army post for preliminary training, which, at USUN urging, would again be abandoned); the impression of one listener, at least, was that there would be a succession of clandestine night landings until a real Oriente force was built up — no hint of any overt frontal assault." [89]

On Saturday, April 15, after the air strike, at the insistence of the Cuban foreign minister, an emergency session of the Political Committee of the UN General Assembly was scheduled for that afternoon. Harlan Cleveland in Washington called the Bureau of Inter-American Affairs to get the facts of the situation. This bureau called the CIA and was told that the strike was by genuine defectors from Castro's air force. Cleveland reported this information to Stevenson. Stevenson thereupon told the UN Political Committee: "These two planes, to the best of our knowledge, were Castro's own air force planes and, according to the pilots, they took off from Castro's own air force fields." Stevenson also showed pictures of the "Cuban warplanes" on the UN screen and pointed out the Cuban markings on them.[90]

Thus not being told the facts (Cleveland did not know them either), Stevenson accepted the CIA cover story as accurate. On Monday, April 17, when the Cuban émigrés landed at the Bay of Pigs, Cuban Foreign

[86] *A Thousand Days,* p. 271.
[87] Plimpton noted: "Certainly there was great lack of candor in that interview." Oral history interview, October 21, 1969, p. 10, in the John F. Kennedy Library.
[88] *A Thousand Days,* p. 271.
[89] "They Sent You Our Best," in *As We Knew Adlai,* p. 263.
[90] Just as Stevenson was completing his statement based on the "information" from Washington, one of his staff brought him a news item off the wire-service ticker reporting what one of the pilots had told the press in Florida when he landed. The story was the same CIA cover story. Harlan Cleveland, memorandum to Walter Johnson, April 30, 1973.

Minister Raul Roa told the UN Security Council that Cuba had been invaded "by a force of mercenaries organized, financed, and armed by the Government of the United States" and that the CIA was the responsible agency. Stevenson replied, wrote one biographer, in "weasel words" [91] that "the United States had committed no aggression against Cuba and no offensive has been launched from Florida or any other part of the United States." Stevenson added that there were "no Americans involved in any action inside Cuba."

A short while after his statement on Monday, Jane Dick met Stevenson at the elevator to the Waldorf Towers. "I was shocked by his appearance," she wrote. "He looked dazedly right through me, apparently not seeing me." Mrs. Dick followed Stevenson to the embassy residence and asked him what was wrong. He replied: "You heard my speech today? Well, I did not tell the whole truth; I did not know the whole truth. I took this job at the President's request on the understanding that I would be consulted and kept fully informed on everything. I spoke in the United Nations in good faith on that understanding. Now, my credibility has been compromised, and therefore my usefulness. Yet how can I resign at this moment and make things worse for the President?" [92]

In addition to being depressed, Stevenson was as angry as he had ever been in his life. "No small part of his suffering at the moment was the seeming confirmation of his darkest suspicions of Kennedy as man and as President," Kenneth S. Davis wrote. "All men make mistakes, of course. But there was in Stevenson's view a kind of mistake that truly honorable and intelligent men never make. Of this kind was the Cuban adventure — or so it seemed at the moment. How could any man of moral sensitivity, with power to control the event, have permitted so criminal a violence to proceed in so soiled and tattered a cloak of lies? How could any man of honor, possessed of normal human sympathies, so ruthlessly use a man of Stevenson's stature, at the expense of Stevenson's honor, merely to lend plausibility to these lies?" [93]

Stevenson's colleagues at the United Nations understood his predicament. Any one of them could find themselves in a similar situation. While they did not lose their respect for him, the entire affair, however, revealed to them the limited influence Stevenson had on vital policymaking in Washington.[94] John Kenneth Galbraith observed on April 25, 1961, "It

[91] Kenneth S. Davis, *The Politics of Honor: A Biography of Adlai E. Stevenson* (New York: Putnam, 1967), p. 458.
[92] "Forty Years of Friendship," in *As We Knew Adlai*, p. 286. Plimpton stated that "Adlai felt absolutely sunk at having misled the United Nations." Oral history interview, John F. Kennedy Library, p. 12.
[93] *The Politics of Honor*, p. 458.
[94] Walter Johnson in 1969 interviewed people in New Zealand, India, and Japan who had served on their countries' UN delegations and staffs while Stevenson was ambassador, and in 1970 he interviewed similar people in Denmark, Sweden, and

wasn't our finest hour." [95] *Richard J. Walton concluded that he should have resigned.* [96]

Many old friends wired or wrote letters to Stevenson pledging their continued support of him in the wake of the Bay of Pigs.

To Mrs. Edward H. Heller [97]

April 21, 1961

Dear Ellie:

Thank you, my dear friend, for "them kind words." They mean much to me — help lighten the pressures — and make it all worthwhile!

My very best to all the Hellers!

Cordially,
ADLAI

To Mary Paul Williamson [98]

April 22, 1961

Dearest MP:

Thank you so much for that telegram. It came just at the height of the Cuban crisis — and I needed it! It has been a bitter week, and a distressing finale for the General Assembly session.

I pray all is well with the Williamsons and Wellings.

Affectionately,

After the close of the UN General Assembly, Harlan Cleveland wrote Stevenson on April 24, 1961: "If the U.S. positions and the objective circumstances have not always been what you (or I) would have wished, your ability to mould and lead a staff and your saving humor and dignity have always been out of the very top drawer of that civilized heritage you personally represent so well. It is, in short, an inspiration to watch you work. And it's fun, even in adversity, to work with you."

Finland. Ralph Bunche observed that such was the respect the UN delegates had for Stevenson that their criticism was directed at Washington, not at Stevenson. Any other U.S. ambassador at the UN would have been destroyed by the situation, Bunche added. See *Adlai: Adlai E. Stevenson in His Own Words and as Remembered by William Attwood et al.,* produced by Arnold Michaelis (CBS Records, 1968).

[95] *Ambassador's Journal: A Personal Account of the Kennedy Years* (Boston: Houghton Mifflin, 1969), p. 88.

[96] *The Remnants of Power: The Tragic Last Years of Adlai Stevenson* (New York: Coward-McCann, 1968), p. 88.

[97] A longtime friend and supporter of Stevenson. He often stayed with her and her husband when he was in California. See *The Papers of Adlai E. Stevenson,* Vol. VI, pp. 385–386.

[98] Daughter of Stevenson's old friends Mr. and Mrs. John Paul Welling. See Harriet Welling, "Friend of the Family," in *As We Knew Adlai,* pp. 42–49.

To Harlan Cleveland

April 27, 1961

Dear Harlan:

I don't believe I have told you properly how grateful I am for your gracious and thoughtful letter. And also for the telegram from the Secretary [of State] which I read during our "post-mortem" staff meeting.

Your own expressions mean a great deal to me as I am sure you realize. But I feel I owe you a vote of thanks more than you owe me one! After all, what we could do here was in large measure thanks to your tireless aid and counsel.

Yours,

To Valerian A. Zorin

April 27, 1961

My dear Mr. Ambassador:

Thank you so much for inviting me to see the Moiseyev Dancers on Saturday, May 6. It is very courteous of you to do so, and I am sorry to have to tell you that I cannot accept. I will be having house guests at that time, and have already made other arrangements to take them all to the performance on that same evening. So — even though I cannot be your guest, I shall not miss seeing those marvelous young people perform once again.

Sincerely yours,

To Cass Canfield [99]

April 28, 1961

Dear Cass:

Thanks so much for your note telling me you are sending James Thurber's new book.[100] I look forward eagerly to receiving it — I could use a little humor these days!

Yours,

To U Nu [101]

May 6, 1961

Dear Mr. Prime Minister:

Ambassador On Sein [102] has sent me a copy of your play, *Wages of Sin*, with your very kind inscription. I am touched by your thoughtfulness and

[99] Chairman of the editorial board of Harper & Brothers, Publishers.

[100] *Lanterns and Lances* (New York: Harper, 1961).

[101] Prime minister of the Union of Burma. Stevenson had first met him in 1953. See *The Papers of Adlai E. Stevenson*, Vol. V, pp. 178–185.

[102] Burmese ambassador to the United States.

impressed indeed by the thought that Burma's first minister is also its foremost playwright. I shall read *Wages of Sin* with great interest.

You were good to think of me, and it is my earnest hope that we shall meet soon again. Meanwhile, may I tell you what a splendid contribution your Ambassador, Mr. U Thant,[103] has made to the United Nations? He has been a great comfort and example to me.

With renewed thanks, and every good wish, I am

Respectfully yours,

To Eugene J. McCarthy [104]

May 6, 1961

Dear Gene:

I have just been obliged to decline an invitation to a party for you on May 21, when I must be in Illinois.

But it reminds me that I have been hoping that you and Abigail [105] would be occupying the guest facilities in this elegant establishment long before this. Please do so — and the sooner the better for the morale of the U.S. Ambassador to the UN.*

Yours ever,

ADLAI

* I find my halo isn't sitting quite as comfortably since they played that Cuba trick on me!

To Ronald Tree

May 8, 1961

Dear Ronnie:

I enclose a copy of my remarks at the Security Council on Angola.[106] They were made, incidentally, before the Soviet delegate spoke. To refresh your recollection, it was our view at the time, that it would be better for the Security Council to adopt a mild resolution than do nothing and let the matter go into the General Assembly where the extremists could gather a whopping Afro-Asian vote.

Of course, the Soviets voted for the resolution too, as they vote for all "anti-colonial" resolutions, but for quite different reasons. There were so many abstentions, however, by our friends (China, Chile, Ecuador, Britain, France, Turkey) that the resolution did not pass. Happily, when it came on in the General Assembly, time was late and the delegates overwhelmed with the Congo, Cuba, Palestine and the financing questions,

[103] Following Dag Hammarskjöld's death in a plane crash in September, 1961, U Thant succeeded him as Secretary-General.
[104] Democratic senator from Minnesota.
[105] Mrs. McCarthy.
[106] March 15, 1961.

with the result that we avoided bitter and violent debate that Angola would normally have provoked.

I am presuming to write you all this in case you are badgered, as you will be, in Portugal.

It was good to see you again. Bon voyage.

Cordially yours,

To John Kenneth Galbraith [107]

May 8, 1961

Dear Ken:

Yesterday I had a call from friends in Chicago advising me that the Indian Government had interrogated the Clow Company about building a pipe factory in India. Accordingly, Kent S. Clow is leaving for India, arriving in New Delhi on next Sunday, May 14 — probably before this letter! I have the impression that he has had little experience in India and has no acquaintance among Indians whose advice might help. Hence, I took the liberty of telling my friends that I would send this note to you suggesting he call at the Embassy in search of friendly counsel about his problems. I would appreciate it if your office will be on the lookout for him and give him such help as they can.

I was sorry not to see you before you left — and you left just in time! While I have survived the Cuban disaster, I had a little trouble convincing the UN of our wisdom and innocence. Latterly I have thought of the story Mrs. [Eleanor] Roosevelt told me a long time ago after she had done a television commercial for oleomargarine. She said her mail was about evenly divided: half were sad that she had damaged her reputation — and half were happy that she had damaged her reputation.

Yours,

To Arthur M. Schlesinger, Jr.[108]

May 11, 1961

Dear Arthur:

May I remind you that in an unguarded moment you agreed to write something for me that would be appropriate at Hyde Park on Memorial Day at the tomb? I had in mind that [Franklin] Roosevelt's contributions to international organization and their relation to the present might be proper, coming from me in the present circumstances.

But whatever you think best will be still *more* proper!

Cordially yours,

[107] United States ambassador to India.
[108] The original is in the Schlesinger papers, John F. Kennedy Library. The postscript was added by hand.

P.S. Thanks for your report on Cuba in Europe.[109] The repercussions of that aberration still ring in my ears.

Mrs. Eugene Meyer [110]

Sunday Evening 6/14 [111]

Dearest Agnes —

I've just come in and find I missed your call. I telephoned back & you were out. Such bad luck!

I *was* tired — and how! — but I'm catching up and please don't worry about me — just let *me* worry about you and your overwork a little!

I'm glad you had such a pleasant visit to Charlottesville [112] & met all those delightful people. After a few months of an almost undiluted diplomatic diet — I miss them — and you!

I will pick you up on the 23rd [of May] at 6:45 at the St. Regis. . . . I'm in agony over that speech and about 10 more I must write — mostly for friends. Or rather I'm *not* in agony — doing nothing, and have no time *to* do anything. Oh for a couple of speech writers — like Agnes Meyer! Have you something I could crib on Ethics in Government for all those intellectual Jews! Help! Help!

The Cuba absurdity made me sick for a week while I had to indignantly defend the U.S. (and got finally a harmless resolution) but I've been surprised how little it seems to have affected my *personal* regard.

Much love to Kay.[113] I pray she is progressing well.

ADLAI

Mrs. John B. Currie wrote Stevenson that watching him at the UN had been an education in how to do things the right way and seeing "all that beautiful work snatched out of your hands and poured into the Caribbean" had made her ill. "Tell me all is not lost!!" she wrote, and added that she had a "mad, mad Passion" for him. Stevenson wrote a note on Mrs. Currie's card and sent it to Marietta Tree. "She writes

[109] Schlesinger discusses his trip to Europe after the Bay of Pigs in A *Thousand Days*, p. 291.

[110] Lecturer and writer on education, widow of the owner of the Washington *Post*, and a longtime confidante of Stevenson. This handwritten letter is in the Agnes Meyer files, Princeton University Library.

[111] Stevenson meant May 14, since he refers in the fourth paragraph to the speech he was to deliver on May 23 at the Jewish Theological Seminary in New York City.

[112] Mrs. Meyer had written Stevenson (no date; early May, 1961) that she had just visited Monticello and the University of Virginia, where he had ardent admirers.

[113] Mrs. Meyer's daughter, Mrs. Philip Graham, whose husband was president of the Washington *Post*.

terrific letters — and has for 10 years.[114] *I don't think I've ever seen her — and want to!"*

To Mrs. John B. Currie [115]

May 22, 1961

My dear friend:

All is *not* lost! And if I felt a little lost your card restored me.

Why don't you come to see me some time when you are in New York and tell me what you would like to do — and all about that mad, mad, mad passion!

Ever,

The Jewish Theological Seminary in New York City created the Adlai E. Stevenson Foundation as part of the Herbert H. Lehman Institute of Ethics. The foundation was to provide scholarships to outstanding students of the institute and the rabbinical school to meet with students in other cultural traditions in search of common values and to make it possible for statesmen and scholars to meet with the students to develop new insights into contemporary problems.

Stevenson spoke at the seminary on May 23, 1961.

AN ETHIC FOR SURVIVAL [116]

I cannot pretend to be an expert in a subject so vast and complex as ethics. But as an ex-politician I can assure you that it is very flattering to be asked to discuss it.

Dr. Finkelstein [117] and his associates at the Jewish Theological Seminary have devoted lives to study and reflection on this subject, and in their presence I feel most humble about expressing any views of my own.

But I *can* express my gratitude to all of you whose contributions have created a foundation in my name for the study of ethics in international relations. In my years in public life I have enjoyed many honors and I have been richly rewarded with the loyalty and confidence of many friends. But nothing has moved or pleased me more. I am grateful that you should consider my name to be a fitting symbol for such a noble undertaking. I hope your generosity has not exceeded your judgment!

But I am sure that the Stevenson Foundation, under the wise and

114 For her first letter to Stevenson, see *The Papers of Adlai E. Stevenson,* Vol. V, p. 216.

115 The original is in the possession of Mrs. Currie.

116 USUN release, May 23, 1961.

117 Louis Finkelstein, chancellor of the Jewish Theological Seminary.

understanding guidance of Dr. Finkelstein and this famous center of theology and thought, will make valuable contributions to the search for those enduring values which transcend the day-to-day frictions which beset the world.

Over the centuries scores of great men have laid down a mosaic of ethical concepts treating with almost every aspect of human life. Yet, strangely enough, in 1961 millions of persons the world over appear to be groping for new ethical guidelines as if they had never before been traced, or as if the old ones were no longer relevant. This seems to me curious, and I wonder if we can trace this uneasiness and search for a new ethic to the nuclear power balance between East and West. Certainly men everywhere are now living under a new shadow of fear as the horrendous and universal implications of nuclear holocaust become more apparent.

We are, it seems, inextricably caught up by a devouring Frankenstein of our own creation — so complex and so volatile that even those directing it appear unable to control it. I suppose that many of us even long for the good old days of limited war with conventional weapons. But with such mistrust in the world, while we dread to go forward we seem to be unable to go back or even to stop this death march.

As the apprehensions caused by this Damoclean power struggle have mounted in the breasts of men everywhere, they have responded with ineffective, piecemeal protests. War is no longer rational, we say, yet the response to our mistrust of one another is more lethal weapons. And then to loudly proclaim that we never plan to use them.

It is no wonder that this is the anxious age and that we want an ethic — an ethic for survival.

Yet the very fact that man is acutely aware that he can no longer resolve his differences by force may well prove to be the key to his salvation. But practical steps are needed — and quickly.

Mere awareness of peril has never been known to eliminate it. The world is still very much a pressure cooker, and new ways must be found to release its tensions through nondestructive channels.

I think a relevant precept to remember in our quest for a world ethic was first stated by Plato when he said: "The creation of a world of civilized order is the victory of persuasion over force." Implicit in Plato's practical thinking is the axiom that men will always be at odds over one thing or another. If such is the case, and so far there is little reason to doubt it, then we must devise means of equal durability for settling our contentions in a nonviolent manner.

It is for the realization of this end that the United Nations was founded. And for an organization so young and still so vulnerable, it has, in good measure, been successful. Its attempts to establish some international ethical standards, of international conduct and human rights, has made it a symbol of hope for millions of people all over the world.

A second and equally important precept is that men have as many similarities as they have differences and, as Prime Minister Nehru said: "We must learn to stress these similarities in order to create a harmonious atmosphere in which we can quietly and amicably work out our disagreements."

These are grand precepts of incontestable validity, but what is to be done about implementing them, and who will do the job? It seems to me that most of the institutions and people needed to further better understanding among men or to arbitrate their differences already exist.

Most countries in the world have religions, laws, educated leaders, scholars, and great institutions of learning. Almost every country has access to the United Nations.

Buttressing all this are millions of other human beings who would like nothing better than to live in peace and friendship with their neighbors, be they down the block or on the other side of the world.

But, whether we care to admit it or not, diplomacy until very recently has been rooted in the Machiavellian principle that: "Where the safety or interests of the homeland are at stake there should be no question of reflecting whether a thing is just or unjust, humane or cruel, praiseworthy or shameful . . . one must take only that course of action which will secure the country's life and liberty."

I suspect that many statesmen still hold to this basic tenet and certainly the Communists acknowledge no greater interest than their own.

But today's statesmen must seek to improve the state of the world as well as the state of the nation. If it was once true that decisions were based solely on the interests of the state, it is now equally true that power politics and war are anachronistic. Today the ideals of individual dignity and liberty, and a human community transcending national boundaries, are the growing notions and the unfolding hope of world community and peace.

In relations among men, it is not enough to help those who are at a disadvantage, but it is necessary also to save, and if possible to increase their self-respect. Perhaps the most significant contribution of the New Deal to our life was not the fact that it brought security and help to many who lacked both before, but that it gave it to them as a right, as citizens of our country, and not as charity, for which one expected gratitude and which was to be accepted with appropriate humility.

The problem of our time hinges to some extent on whether this principle can be applied also among nations. We in America are certainly expending more on the help of less advantageously placed peoples than has ever been expended by any other people. Yet something more is needed — a contribution to the sense of self-respect, of dignity of these ancient societies and civilizations, which are now emerging into effective influence on the world.

How to develop this self-respect among peoples who have never known it as individuals, and having dimly felt it as tribes and nations are losing it in confrontation with the powerful of the earth, is a challenge to our ingenuity, and our wisdom.

Much has already been achieved through the establishment of the United Nations. Once more, we have created an institution, in which the weakest of peoples has a voice, and a vote, which in difficult moments is sought by the powerful.

Yet there remains one aspect of the self-respect of peoples. Like the individuals composing them, so nations and states are more than bodies. They also are minds, and their minds require a sense of dignity, no less than their bodies.

When this sense of dignity is denied them, it is frequently replaced with belligerent and even chauvinistic, unrealistic and unthinking nationalism, which astounds the older and more highly developed peoples. We see this so often among the new countries. But the ferocity and narrowness which are born out of self-depreciation, cannot be exorcised except by appreciation. And this appreciation should itself be offered not as charity, but as a human right. That the small states exercise such decisive influence in the United Nations, for example, is a major contribution to this appreciation, this right, and we can hope that the consciousness of their power in this new forum can and will help to develop self-appreciation, self-confidence and dignity among the new states.

If there were no reason to respect ancient, and what are often called primitive societies and cultures, we could not by sheer will develop that feeling toward them. But fortunately for mankind, there is, in every culture and every society, much that everyone can respect, and from which everyone can learn. There is no group of people so mean and so humble that they have only to be our pupils, and cannot in any respect offer us instruction. That in fact is one of the distinctive qualities of *Homo sapiens*. Wherever he has organized himself as a society (and he has done so wherever he exists), he has created a tradition, a system of sanctions and habits which we might properly call "law," a language, a collective, as well as an individual, conscience.

In each of these traditions, systems of sanctions, and dialects of morals, there is a residue of what might be called wisdom. Much of what is done in the name of this wisdom may seem to us of another world, utter folly, just as no doubt much of what we do must seem bizarre to peoples of other backgrounds.

Certainly, we of the West can scarcely boast of the manner in which we have twice in our time fumbled our way into the most ferocious of all wars, and seem to be preparing for a third even more destructive. No folly perpetrated in any simple and primitive culture can approach the collective folly, as exhibited in the tragedy of the two world wars of the first half of this century, and the menace of a possible third one in the second half.

Yet despite these follies, and those attendant on them, like the world-wide rise in the rate of crime, especially among the youth, Western civilization certainly contains, as no one will deny, much that is wise, and which other peoples could ponder to their benefit. May this not be likewise true of the primitive races? And may it not be that one of the gravest failures of Western thought has been its underestimate of this residue of wisdom in other societies than its own?

Perhaps none of us has ever thought of the Tibetan people, who in our time have been exposed to so much suffering, as one by whom we could be instructed. Their manners and ways certainly seemed strange to most people. What was one to think of a people which considered it wrong to destroy even the most pestiferous insect? And yet is there not something for us to learn from this astonishing respect for life, where it is impossible for a cultured person to kill a fly, as it might be for a similarly situated person among us to walk naked through the streets?

Is it possible that one of the world's urgent needs in our time is really a collective Socrates, who was in his time called by the Oracle of Delphi, the wisest of men, solely, he maintains, because he alone knew his short-comings and tried so hard to learn from all men.

What a remarkable pedagogue he was, who was able to give his young disciples instruction, while at the same time increasing their self-confidence in their own ability to think. And what a glorious place in the annals of history awaits that group of people, and that institution, which seeks above all to make sure that those whom it encounters, realize that they have much to teach.

So I therefore applaud the efforts being made by your Seminary under the guidance and leadership of Dr. Finkelstein to create just such a forum and institution. What has been achieved by your Institute for Religious and Social Studies and by the Conference on Science, Philosophy and Religion, which it sponsors, by the Herbert H. Lehman Institute on Ethics, by your radio and television programs in this area is already impressive. It is perhaps significant that while it cannot be said that the publications of the Conference on Science, Philosophy and Religion are popular reading in this country, I am told some of them have gone through eight editions in Japan.

It is not an accident that an institution, which stands at the apex of your own Jewish tradition, should be so concerned with the problem of mutual respect of men. All great religions and philosophies share the doctrine that men must learn to love and respect one another, and that they have to discover in each other that which demands respect and love. But in your instance, history fortifies this tradition, in a special way. You know as scripture puts it "the spirit of the stranger," for during centuries you have suffered indignity and persecution, probably unparalleled both in extent and continuity in the history of any other people.

And surprisingly in our own civilized century and our highly civilized Western world, your brethren underwent greater torment and suffering than any recorded in your own long history.[118] Yet throughout this period of suffering and indignity, your ancestors knew how to preserve their soul and mind: seeing in their tradition something worth not only dying for but for which they were willing to court contumely and disdain. They had a purpose to fulfill in the human drama, and the cost to themselves as individuals or as a group mattered little, if at all. Not all peoples have such a built-in machinery for the preservation of their own sense of dignity; but intuitively, you, scholars and laymen alike, recognize its importance.

From this, I take it, springs the desire manifested by so many of you here tonight to continue and to expand this aspect of the labors of the great institution in whose name you are gathered here.

Your desire to expand and perpetuate the aspect of your work dealing with ethics and human relations, your aspiration to hold conferences under the aegis of your institute for religious and social studies in other parts of the world, and your ultimate goal of a world academy, which will devote itself solely to the extraction of the wisdom implicit in various intellectual and cultural traditions, seems to me not only praiseworthy, but to hold forth a promise of great good to mankind.

So it is important for religions to explore those common human values which give people everywhere a sense of belonging to a common world community. For if the growing self-consciousness of national cultures increases, the creedal differences in religious systems may be exploited to accentuate tension in the world society.

We would then have, as we have had in the past, the anomaly of universalist religions undermining world brotherhood.

So I see a great opportunity here to further the search for those enduring values which transcend the divisive frictions between nations. While each country supports its national interest through an ethical rationalization, human progress can only be achieved if a way is found to identify the ethical ideas which are the basis for long-range goals helpful to all men.

I am proud and grateful to be identified with such healing scholarship.

[118] See Arthur D. Morse, *While Six Million Died: A Chronicle of American Apathy* (New York: Random House, 1967).

And I would be even more honored and grateful if the foundation just established in my name held an occasional seminar for statesmen. If they could be induced to divorce themselves for even a few days from the griminess of daily politics and plunge into this new Walden Pond, they will, I feel, be much better leaders the rest of the year.

To John F. Kennedy [119]

May 24, 1961

Subject: Meetings with Khrushchev and De Gaulle [120]

I. KHRUSHCHEV

While you will not wish to avoid discussion of such specific questions as disarmament, nuclear tests, Berlin, Laos and Cuba, I suggest that you concentrate if possible on the basic question which governs all of these — the Soviet interpretation of "peaceful coexistence."

From my talks with Khrushchev and others the essential elements of that interpretation appear to be:

1. An absolute taboo on Western intervention inside the Communist Bloc and a free hand for the Soviets to do as they like inside that bloc.

2. Unrestricted Communist aid to "wars of liberation" and Communist or nationalist movements outside the Communist Bloc and a free hand to go as far as they like in this respect, short of provoking general war.

3. The Soviet veto not only on international action *inside* the Communist Bloc (inspection, etc.) and also on international action outside the Communist Bloc (UN Secretariat, Congo).

While Khrushchev will not concede any of the foregoing he might be told that the West could not conceivably accept such a policy or that "peaceful coexistence" could long exist under it. While we recognize that Communists cannot be expected to give up propagating Communist doctrine, are they sufficiently interested in "peaceful coexistence" to accept realistic limitations on means of propagation?

Specifically, can they accept the following limitations: no military action inside either block by the other, or in "neutral" states by either, whether such action on large or small scale. If they wish international disarmament including the suspension of nuclear tests, they must accept inspection without veto.

A fortiori, they cannot veto international action outside their bloc, though they might be offered more opportunity to participate in such action. If the Communists are to be free to engage in political action in the West or in neutral states, they must open up their society to foreign

[119] This document was declassified.
[120] For Kennedy's trip to Europe, see Schlesinger, *A Thousand Days*, pp. 343–378.

political action. If they insist on outlawing the latter, we shall be more and more driven, at no matter what risk or cost, to outlawing the former.

Clearly we could not expect Khrushchev to agree to these points at this time, but I believe it would be advantageous for you to lay bare the fundamentals of the problem as you see it and make it quite clear that we propose to deal in the future much more vigorously with those fundamentals rather than inadequately and tardily with surface symptoms or local crises.

II. DE GAULLE

The Algerian question will doubtless arise. Despite the general sensitivity on this subject and the wisdom of the policy he is now pursuing, it is hoped that you may feel free to emphasize strongly that the present negotiations at Evian must *not* be allowed to break down.[121] If they do, and the war is renewed, as it would be, Communist influence in the whole of North Africa would, I fear, increase rapidly. There would be a very real danger that not only Algeria but Morocco and Tunisia as well would end up under Communist control.

Precisely because of de Gaulle's scornful and unhelpful attitude toward the UN, I suggest you might try to persuade him that, irresponsible and inconvenient as the United Nations may appear to be, it is perhaps the central point at which the great body of uncommitted Afro-Asian States can be influenced and where their ultimate commitment to either European civilization or to Communist political and economic forms is likely to be determined.

I hope you will have occasion to express in some form your disappointment that France has declined to contribute to the Congo expenses, which puts her in the same category as the USSR and gives the latter's disapproval of the UN effort there some color of respectability.

U.S. support and influence on Taiwan for the admission of Outer Mongolia to head off a Russian veto of Mauritania appears to be of great importance to the French Africans (12 votes) and therefore to France.[122] I suggest you record anxiety to help with this if the subject arises.

[121] France began negotiations for peace in Algeria with the Moslem rebel Algerian Provisional Government on May 20, but the talks were suspended on June 13, 1961.

[122] The Nationalist Chinese representative in the Security Council had vetoed the application of Outer Mongolia for admission to the UN in 1955. If Mongolia was vetoed in 1961, the Soviet Union planned to veto the application of Mauritania. In the Security Council, China and the United States abstained in the vote on Mongolia's membership application, which was approved.

To the Right Reverend Joseph E. Schieder [123]

May 25, 1961

Dear Monsignor Schieder:

Thank you for your letter. It is a pleasure to send you good wishes for National Catholic Youth Week.

We are accustomed to hear grown people discuss the problems of youth as if they were quite a separate thing, like a crisis in some distant country. Yet of course the problems and the promise of American youth are our very own affair: the shadow of a future America from which we today are separated by only a few years.

In your theme for this week's observance you have linked youth with the words "Unity" and "Truth." It is well that our young people should accustom themselves to think deeply about the meaning of those words. In a world torn by the clash of cultures and unworthy passions, how are we to be faithful to the moral truths which we perceive? In the presence of a hundred fanaticisms which foster hatred and violence in the name of "truth," how can we hope ever to see mankind — or even our own American people — fully united in a single community of morals? These questions will test our future leaders' qualities: their capacity to learn, their responsibility in a world of difficult ethical choices, their courage and their compassion.

May National Catholic Youth Week help to foster those qualities in the next generation of our nation's leaders.

Cordially yours,

To John Walker [124]

May 26, 1961

Dear Mr. Walker:

I have recently participated in the opening of an exhibition titled "The Traditional Arts of Africa's New Nations" at the Museum of Primitive Art here in New York.

The highly successful opening also served as an occasion to honor United Nations Representatives from the newly-independent African nations. To a man they voiced enthusiastic praise for this highly selective and comprehensive survey of African art.

I am bringing this exhibition to your attention in the hope that a showing can be arranged at the National Gallery of Art. Coming at this time, it will make Americans aware of the depth and strength of the cultural

[123] Director of the Youth Department of the National Catholic Welfare Conference.
[124] Director of the National Gallery of Art.

background of nations which, for other reasons, have been attracting our interest.

At the same time, I feel that it would be an important gesture toward creating better understanding and friendship between our country and the African continent.

Sincerely yours,

To David K. E. Bruce [125]

May 27, 1961

My dear David:

I had hoped to be writing you a letter about this time to be warning you and Evangeline [126] that I was going to add another straw to the camel's back. But my hope for a visit to England en route to the Continent grows less likely. Instead, I seem to be destined for a merciless journey around Latin America — for obvious reasons! I shall be going to Geneva around the 4th of July for the Economic and Social Council meeting, but I am afraid the South American journey precludes London. If I should be going to stay with my sister at her lovely villa in Florence for a brief holiday after the middle of July, what could be more agreeable than a visit from you and Evangeline! And perhaps you will need some kind of escape for a few days after the London season.

But the purpose of this letter was to report that you should be on the lookout for my beloved aunt (by marriage), Lady Mary Spears,[127] and her husband, General Sir Louis Spears. Years ago, as Mary Borden, she was a famous novelist in England. I hope you and Evangeline meet her some day, and I am sure that you will find her most engaging and even useful. He, of course, is a "famous man."

With much love to Evangeline and the children, and, as Mencken said, God save all honest men — if any!

Yours,

To Alicia Patterson [128]

[no date]

. . . OK — You'll be back the 9th.[129] Then how about the 9th for a rendezvous? OK?

And stop being so evasive —

Sincerely
SNUFFY

---

[125] United States ambassador to the United Kingdom.
[126] Mrs. Bruce.
[127] See *The Papers of Adlai E. Stevenson*, Vol. I, p. 225, n. 48.
[128] This handwritten letter is in the possession of Adlai E. Stevenson III. It is postmarked May 29, 1961.
[129] She was at her winter home in Kingsland, Georgia.

After the Bay of Pigs, in order to repair the damage done to the pres-
tige of the United States in Latin America, Kennedy decided that Steven-
son should visit a number of countries. Although Stevenson was reluctant
to make the trip, he ultimately was persuaded to do so.[130]

To Lady Barbara Jackson

May 31, 1961

Dearest Barbara:

I am off on Sunday for Latin America — for ten capitals and three
weeks of remorseless talk and travel. We have things pretty well turned
around now so that the objective is groundwork for the "Alliance for
Progress" conference in Montevideo in July, and economic and social cooperation with the political reprisals against Castro muted. Inevitably,
there will be political talk about parallel action to follow the economic
conference, but the emphasis will be on the future, not the past.

I feel better about the whole project now that we have our philosophical approach on sound ground. Kennedy has come around completely
and now wants no discussion of Cuba whatsoever. But can I convince the
Latins!

I am taking with me a senior Foreign Service Officer, Ambassador Ellis
Briggs,[131] now in Greece, who is an old friend and has a long record in
Latin America. Lincoln Gordon [132] is also coming because of his familiarity with the Alliance for Progress program, as chief of the task force, and
there will also be several people from the Mission and the State Department. I think it is a reasonably good team, and operating without public
appearances, communiques, or ceremonies, we ought to be able to get
a pretty good feeling of the situation throughout the Continent.

I will have a couple of weeks at home when I get back before going on
to Geneva for the Economic and Social Council and some self-education
about our UN activities there and elsewhere in Europe. If the President
goes to the Montevideo Conference at the end of July I suppose I will
accompany him, which makes the travel component of the summer sound
like a political campaign.

Jane [Dick] is full of excitement about her journey with you in
Africa.[133] She acquitted herself extremely well here [134] and is now vacationing in Jamaica with Eddie.[135]

[130] Philip M. Klutznick, letter to Walter Johnson, August 29, 1974.
[131] Stevenson first met Briggs in 1953, when the latter was ambassador to the
Republic of Korea. See *The Papers of Adlai E. Stevenson,* Vol. V, pp. 43–44.
[132] Member of the Council of Economic Advisers and later ambassador to Brazil.
[133] Lady Jackson was in Ghana with her husband, Sir Robert Jackson.
[134] At the UN.
[135] Mr. Dick.

I went yesterday to Hyde Park to make a little speech at Roosevelt's tomb on Memorial Day, and go back to Washington again tomorrow. My incessant activity has not subsided, as you can see. But I pray yours has!

I will try to report progress, but it will be difficult. If you have choices between aquamarine and tourmaline, please advise your lapidary agent c/o American Embassy, Rio, *at once*. I will, of course, execute your every wish, including size, shape, setting, etc.

I haven't begun to tell you all that is in my mind and heart — but in lieu thereof, I send love to all the Jacksons — which is probably more comprehensible than my fragmentary report.

To Arthur M. Schlesinger, Jr.

May 31, 1961

Dear Arthur:

What I was trying to say was that I have the impression that some Latins, at least, resent our lack of interest in their cultural and intellectual ferment. I believe this has been confirmed by some of Jim Perkins' [136] experiences in the Universities. Surely something can be done to begin the process of lessening the anti-Yankee mood of students and faculties.

So long as the United States Administration obviously represented the anti-intellectual, this area was barren. But can't Harvard-on-the-Potomac look on changing University opinion as a most significant revolution — in terms of tomorrow's leaders?

You can't defend or project the "open society" — which we want to make a major theme — so long as the country's chief spokesmen are Chamber of Commerce Marxists — you know "private enterprise is the root of freedom," which has always seemed to me a piece of brassy economic determinism.

America has more sophisticated leadership now, and perhaps a crucial need in Latin America is to begin to change the Yankee image in this respect.*

Sincerely yours,

* Help! Help!

To John L. McClellan [137]

June 3, 1961

Dear Senator: *Re: USUN Budget for Fiscal Year 1962*

Confirming our telephone conversation this morning I am summarizing the facts regarding the above matter as follows:

[136] James A. Perkins, vice president of the Carnegie Corporation and later president of Cornell University.
[137] Democratic senator from Arkansas and chairman of the Committee on Government Operations.

The budget for the United States Mission to the United Nations for Fiscal Year 1962 was reported out in H.R. 7371. The House Subcommittee on Appropriations granted an increase of $110,760 over last year's budget, but cut $90,000 from the requested Mission budget. The Mission has requested 28 additional positions, but because of the $90,000 reduction, we can add only approximately 12 additional persons.

I took the liberty of recommending the restoration of this $90,000 for the following reasons: I really believe these positions are essential if the Mission is to be able to carry out its expanding responsibilities at the United Nations. In spite of the fact that the membership of the U.N. has almost doubled, we are operating now with only about two-thirds of the staff we had 13 years ago. And the recently concluded session of the General Assembly made it clear that all of these requested positions in both the substantive and administrative areas are genuinely needed. I have felt acutely in my few months here the inadequacy of our staff at peak requirements and although I don't question the fact that we can "get along," in the situation here now when our position becomes more difficult all the time, we have to do better than get along. Moreover, some ten additional states will probably be admitted to membership in the near future.

As you know, New York is one of the most expensive cities to live in in the world, and yet the officers assigned to this Embassy which represents us to not one, but to 98 countries, get no extra quarters allowance as they would if they were living anywhere abroad at much less expense. But it is the representational needs of the Mission that are expanding and must be met. Last year's budget (FY 1961) made provision for the expenditure of $17,000, and this amount proved quite inadequate because of the mounting expense of the representational work of entertaining the expanding membership of the United Nations.

We have now moved into the splendid new Mission building, and my experience here re-affirms the need for some additional administrative help, particularly in the telegraphic services, reproduction and general administrative support areas.

I am most grateful for your sympathetic consideration of this rather small matter which is so important to my staff here. I have had, as you know, some experience in several government departments and agencies over many years, and I have never met a more dedicated, loyal and diligent group to whom hours and personal convenience has come to mean little. There has, for example, been no money for overtime since last December, but they continued loyally to work many hours of overtime during the resumed session of the General Assembly. I could list many illustrations of the high morale here, but I will spare you that, confident that our situation will have the careful consideration of your Committee.

With warm personal regards and many thanks for permitting me to impose upon you in this way, I am

Cordially yours,

To Mrs. Henry Cabot Lodge

June 3, 1961

My dear Emily:

I am leaving today for a hurried trip to Latin America, returning about June 22. During my absence the apartment — sua casa — will be vacant save for my elderly housekeeper, Viola Reardy. If you and Cabot can use the place I hope very much that you will. It would please me, and it is where you belong!

Besides, I want you to see what I have done — and don't feel you have to approve the changes!

Cordially yours,

On June 4 Stevenson and his official group flew to South America for a seventeen-day visit to Venezuela, Argentina, Uruguay, Brazil, Paraguay, Chile, Bolivia, Peru, Ecuador, and Colombia. He was accompanied by Ambassador Ellis O. Briggs; Professor Lincoln Gordon; three members of his USUN staff — Charles Cook, Frank Carpenter, and Roxane Eberlein; Harvey Wellman from the Department of State; William Bradford of the International Cooperation Administration (soon to be renamed the Agency for International Development); his son Borden Stevenson; and some eight correspondents.

To Mrs. Ronald Tree [138]

June 15, 1961

Dear M —

. . . I still expect to be in Wash. late on the 22nd, stay there to prepare our report, see [President] Kennedy et al, speak to the National Press Club — and get on to N.Y. Monday night to gather the neglected threads of bureaucracy together; then to Chicago for the week-end, and a visit with the children large & little along a bank where the wild thyme grows. *Then* — on July 3-4 to ECOSOC [139] direct from Chicago by London, Paris or whatnot — where I hope to be reborn.

But will I be alive then? I want to — like I never wanted to before. But — soldiers (and llamas!) surrounded the windswept airport on the

138 This handwritten letter is in the possession of Mrs. Tree. It was written from La Paz, Bolivia.
139 The Economic and Social Council of the United Nations.

Alto Plano at 13500' when we arrived — and almost swooned. Truckloads of same — I mean soldiers! preceded & followed me into the town thru avenues of more soldiers and Indian women in their brown derbies and bright serapes. Now the hotel is surrounded by soldiers shoulder to shoulder & dark rumors of another violent outbreak are interspersed with long pulls on my oxygen tank. So we go to see the Pres[ident] in a house on the outskirts by circuitous routes thru more soldiers and derbied Indians. Then, after an hour of talk of [the] incredible situation in this murderous, treeless, arid land — the word came: They've attacked — 4 dead??? wounded. "But of course, Gov., the police didn't shoot: it was the provocateurs." Better go back to the hotels in disguised cars unattended, one at a time. Whispering in the dark street surrounded by steel helmets & bayonets.

Well here I am — safe if not sound — and sucking oxygen. Poor Ellis Briggs has been in bed "with the Embassy nurse" — since arrival and I don't feel too brisk for the President[']s banquet where I'm supposed to persuade the Veep [140] — large rodent — to support the gov't instead of his armed miners. Well maybe its off — word has just come that they've blocked the approaches and are "throwing rocks."

Lima — 6/16. The dinner went on — I spoke, and firmly — (its so easy to be firm when you've a plane & crew of 10 alerted to fly at any time!) and argued with Lichine [Lechín] — the V.P. — and addressed the press — and fell into bed with my oxygen tank. This morning we were off early with the quaint little Foreign Minister who speaks broken French, so of course we get along famously. Air so clear and crisp and white flashing Andes all about the horizon and squalor and misery all about the foreground. Off — after usual farewells across Lake Titicaca, thru corridors of white volcanoes to Lima, City of the Viceroys for 300 yrs. — and what I wouldn't give for a quiet week-end along the river. . . . Somehow there is never time to *re*live when there isn't enough time to live. "Jelly fish in gilded lobster pot" — indeed! And I thought I'd seen every exotic dish! Did I tell you about my visit with Stressmer? [141] Quadros? [142] No? Perhaps I will — if there's time.

MARCO POLO

On Kennedy's behalf, Stevenson consulted with officials in Latin America on what could be done to improve and accelerate the Alliance for Progress programs for social and economic development.[143]

[140] Vice President Juan Lechín, who was secretary general of the Bolivian Workers Union.

[141] General Alfred Stroessner, president of Paraguay.

[142] Janio da Silva Quadros, president of Brazil.

[143] For the address in which Kennedy proposed the Alliance for Progress, "a vast cooperative effort . . . to satisfy the basic needs of the American people, for

Roxane Eberlein wrote Stevenson's sister, Mrs. Ernest L. Ives, on June 22, 1961: "This has been a tightly packed, exhausting trip for the Governor and the members of his party — though to my mind not nearly as hectic as a campaign swing. It's basically different, of course, because the main work consists of intensive conversations with the officials of one government after the other, and then sending reports to Washington. After a late late South American banquet the Governor looks completely worn out, and yet the next morning he's as energetic as ever." [144] *Ellis O. Briggs wrote: "If there is a worse way to examine a continent than eleven [ten] capitals in seventeen days . . . it has yet to be invented."* [145]

REPORT TO THE PRESIDENT ON SOUTH AMERICAN MISSION, JUNE 4-22, 1961 [146]

By Adlai E. Stevenson

June 27, 1961

I. Introduction

During the period June 4–22, 1961, I visited each of the ten capitals of South America to consult with the Presidents and leading government officials on plans for advancing the "Alliance for Progress" and possibilities of collective action to defend the Western hemisphere against Communist penetration and subversion, including indirect aggression through Cuba. I was accompanied by Ambassador Ellis O. Briggs, Professor Lincoln Gordon, and a supporting staff from the Department of State.

Our mission received everywhere remarkably effective support from our resident Ambassadors and their staffs, as well as excellent briefing and background materials prepared in advance in the Department of State. I should like also to express my gratitude for the way in which our travels were handled by Major Conover and the crew of MATS Constellation 254.

II. Political Appreciation

While every country visited except Paraguay is now under democratic control, the political stability of these democratic regimes is under severe

homes, work and land, health and schools," see the New York *Times*, March 14, 1961.

[144] This letter is in the Elizabeth Stevenson Ives collection, Illinois State Historical Society (E.S.I., I.S.H.L.).

[145] Letter to Walter Johnson, May 12, 1967.

[146] This document was declassified. In the process of declassification, the Department of State deleted two paragraphs. Stevenson spoke to the National Press Club in Washington about the trip on June 26. On the same day, he testified before the House Committee on Foreign Affairs. See U.S. Congress, House, Committee on Foreign Affairs, 87th Congress, 1st Session, H.R. 7372 (Washington: Government Printing Office, 1961), pp. 991–1017. Stevenson kept a diary during the trip, but it was too fragmentary to use.

strain and attack almost everywhere. Communist and other extreme left wing forces have generally gained in strength and aggressiveness in the last year, and the danger of right wing coups d'etat in several countries is still evident.

There follows a brief country-by-country summary in the order of our visits:

Venezuela is still in a state of siege, with continuing fear of a right wing coup, although there are some heartening indications that conservative elements in business and the army now recognize the importance of supporting democratic institutions, and are convinced that President [Rómulo] Betancourt should complete his term. The alternative is further loss of confidence, economic stagnation, and rising radicalism. Left wing violence in the Caracas slums remains acute. Betancourt is trying to push ahead on sound lines, including the restoration of business confidence as well as continued social and economic reform.

In Argentina, President [Arturo] Frondizi's regime is still heavily dependent on army support and on the intricate Florentine political maneuvers of the President. He is making bold efforts to restore fiscal responsibility and to bring about national recovery from the decapitalization of the country under Perón.[147] Eyes are fixed on next year's congressional elections, which will either consolidate the regime or open the way to a possible new attempt at dictatorship.

In Uruguay, social and economic conditions are fortunately not explosive, and the situation is relatively stable, although the system of a collegial executive makes for extreme governmental weakness. The main focus of left wing agitation there is among students and intellectuals.

In Brazil, President [Janio] Quadros is less popular than at the start of his administration, because of his firm austerity measures directed against rampant inflation and financial disorder, and also because of his habits of governing in isolation. Communist agitation in the Brazilian Northeast is increasingly vigorous and dangerous. The President's equivocal attitude on Cuba and diplomatic flirtations with the Soviet bloc arise partly from a desire to demonstrate international "maturity" and independence of the United States, an attitude reinforced by his fear of alienating domestic groups who have an underlying sympathy for the Cuban revolution. . . .[148]

Chile continues to enjoy the broad traditional devotion to democratic institutions. The relative success of President [Jorge] Alessandri in controlling inflation has reduced one serious source of social discontent, but other sources remain in the continuing economic stagnation and the need for positive action on land reform. A dangerous sign was the swing of

147 Former president Juan Perón, who was deposed in 1955.
148 A paragraph was deleted here by the Department of State.

peasant votes this spring to the extreme left for the first time, just when the moderate radical party was gaining support in the towns at the expense of the extreme left. . . .[149]

In Peru political circles are entirely preoccupied with the 1962 Presidential election. While the present regime of President [Manuel] Prado and Prime Minister [Pedro] Beltrán is strong, there is not yet clear certainty that their coalition, made up of moderate Conservatives and the anti-Communist but left wing APRA party, will be able to agree on a candidate. The present antigovernment front runner appears to be Fernando Belaunde, an attractive and vigorous campaigner who is preoccupied with large plans for internal development and studiously avoids committing himself on foreign policy — including Cuba. The underlying Peruvian social structure is probably the most archaic in South America. While the Government is trying to make some social improvements in housing and land settlement, there is no real attack as yet on more fundamental tax and land reform, despite governmental recognition of the need for these measures. Here, too, therefore, the present relative calm — except in the universities — probably conceals explosive under-currents. But we and the ideals of the West have no more firmly declared friends than the present government of Peru.

In Ecuador, a relatively good governmental group is headed by eccentric and unpredictable President [José] Velasco-Ibarra, who combines over-confidence in his ability to deal with left wing forces domestically, with an incomprehensible philosophy concerning the role of Communism in the contemporary world and the security of Latin America from this infection. The general program of his Ministers to improve domestic conditions is good. The student leadership has recently been recaptured from Communist hands, a striking and heartening exception to the general leftward drift of student organizations on the Continent.

The present leadership in *Colombia* is the best on the continent from our viewpoint, but the stability of the regime depends on the finding of a Conservative presidential candidate to carry on in 1962–66, in accordance with the bi-partisan national front arrangement of 1958, which replaced the former dictatorship. Bandit-type violence remains a major problem in several outlying provinces, now aggravated by Communist infiltration. The domestic program of President [Alberto] Lleras [Camargo] is precisely in accord with the Act of Bogota and the thinking underlying the Alliance for Progress.

---

[149] A paragraph was deleted here by the Department of State.

III. *Communist-Castro Influence*

Communist penetration and subversion have clearly increased in vigor and effectiveness since my South American tour in the spring of 1960.[150] This is especially marked among four groups: university students, professors, and school teachers; labor unions; urban slum dwellers, especially where there is severe unemployment; and hitherto unorganized rural areas (outstanding examples are in Northeastern Brazil, Chile, Colombia and Ecuador). A good deal of propaganda material is being imported from Cuba. Several governments commented on activity by Cuban agents, sometimes with the help of the Cuban diplomatic missions. The Cubans appear, however, to be becoming increasingly cautious about gunrunning and blatant abuses of diplomatic missions for subversive purposes.

(Our mission, incidentally, was followed immediately by visits to the same governments by two or three senior Cuban diplomats who were evidently trying to head off any collective action against Cuba instigated by our visit. In response to their standard question about the principles of non-intervention and self-determination, the Colombian Foreign Minister said he had told them that Colombia "adheres to *all* the principles of the American system" and asked: "How many does Cuba believe in?" The Bolivian Foreign Minister told them that Bolivia believes in self-determination which means the continuing right of the people to determine their destiny, and asked if they had that right in Cuba.)

The alignment of Cuba with the Communist movement has greatly added to the appeal of Communism, since it can now take on the guise of an indigenous Latin American revolutionary movement. There is very wide-spread popular sympathy for the proclaimed goals of the Cuban revolution, including land reform, popular education, social equality, removal of foreign business influence, and defiance of the Yankee Colossus. The failure of the April "invasion" attempt gave added impetus to Communist-Castro penetration, since it seemed to imply immunity of left extremism in Latin America from United States retaliation. There is little appreciation among the people of the Sovietization of the Cuban regime, its establishment of a police state apparatus of terror, or other perversions of the original revolutionary objectives of Fidel Castro. But officialdom seems to be largely aware of actual conditions in Cuba.

Much more intensive action is evidently needed to promote the democratic cause in intellectual circles in Latin America. Ministers in several countries commented once again on the absence of cheap paperback translations into Spanish and Portuguese of United States classics (among those named were Jefferson, Lincoln, Emerson, Walt Whitman) and of

150 See *The Papers of Adlai E. Stevenson,* Vol. VII, especially Part Five.

important non-fiction contemporary works, including your own writings and speeches. They point to the contrast with the highly subsidized and widely distributed editions of Marx, Lenin, Mao Tse Tung, and other Communist writers.

A far more affirmative attack on the problems of urban slum conditions and rural insecurity is also evidently needed if these large groups — no longer politically passive — are to see some hope in life under free institutions.

In connection with the misunderstanding of the true character of current developments in Cuba, I believe that excellent use could be made of students and professional intellectuals among the Cuban exiles — especially those who fought with Castro in his early days — to speak and write and circulate among their counterparts throughout the Hemisphere. Their testimony would have a credibility which no North American can achieve under present circumstances.

IV. *Preparations for Economic Conference and Alliance for Progress*

We encountered a unanimous and intense interest in the Alliance for Progress. Your March 13 address [151] was described as having created a profound impression in Latin America — the most favorable since Franklin Roosevelt's announcement of the "Good Neighbor" policy. Without exception, governments emphasized the critical importance of making the Uruguay meeting of the Inter-American Economic and Social Council a "success," and not merely another in the long line of inter-American meetings.

On the other hand, there was no clear or uniform definition of what would constitute "success." There was wide variety in the concept of the meeting's objectives and procedures, and great disparity in the intensity and character of national preparations for the program.

A few governments, notably that of Peru, appeared to believe that the meeting would be the occasion for the cutting of an aid "melon," with little regard to self-help measures or structural reforms in such fields as land tenure and taxation. But all paid at least lip-service to the concept of self-help, and several were in deadly earnest on this front. In terms of technical work on long-term programming for national economic and social development, Colombia, Chile, Brazil, and perhaps Venezuela, seemed to be well in advance of their sister nations. Several others handed us "shopping lists" of public investment projects on which they looked for loans or other aid. Argentina and Chile emphasized the importance for them of economic development as contrasted with social investment. Many governments advanced claims for "special consideration" on political or other grounds.

[151] The address in which Kennedy proposed the Alliance for Progress.

In several cases, less emphasis was placed on outside aid for public investment than on trade and commodity price policies. Argentina, Uruguay, and Chile declared their strong interest in American policy support for their commercial negotiations with the European Common Market. There was the most intense interest in joint action to stabilize primary commodity markets and to raise prices of key export items, notably coffee.

I believe that our mission greatly clarified the thinking of the South American governments on the types of results which we hope might be achieved at the Uruguay conference, especially in the fields of investment programming and the coordination of outside aid. We must clearly expect active discussion of commercial policy and commodity markets, and we should have well-defined positions on these issues. A forthcoming attitude in these fields would do much to overcome the disappointments which are likely with respect to the amounts and conditions of financial aid.

As to aid, it is a fact that the needs are large, the desire for accelerated growth is great, and the capacity for effective use of aid is being rapidly augmented by the systematic programming of public investments, often for the first time. In most cases, the general concepts of needs and priorities are not far out of line with our own thinking. It is evident that large increases in the rate of economic and social public investment and United States aid, as compared with recent years, are expected. Fortunately, most of the governments appear to be thinking mainly in terms of hard loans, which can be financed by the World Bank, Inter-American Development Bank, and Export-Import Bank to the extent that the real creditworthiness permits. (This in turn may be largely dependent on action in the commercial policy and commodity market areas.) If Congress furnishes the authority you have requested for making long-term commitments, there is no question but that the ability of the Latin American governments to carry through sustained development efforts, including the needed structural reforms, will be greatly enhanced.

On the question of the timing of the meeting, Brazil strongly desired a one-month postponement to enable more adequate national and international preparatory work to be completed. Most of the other governments favored a two or three week postponement, although a few emphasized their own readiness to meet on July 15 as scheduled. I understand that the OAS Council is now about to agree on a revised date of August 5 for the meeting of Ministers, to be preceded by an expert-level meeting on August 1. This seems to me a sound conclusion. The publicity concerning the deferred date should of course make it clear that the purpose is solely to permit the completion of more adequate preparations and thus to contribute to a successful outcome.

V. *Collective Political Action Against Indirect Aggres[s]ion and Communist Penetration Based on Cuba*

Our mission demonstrated the vital importance of re-creating confidence in a collective approach to the problem of Communist subversion and indirect aggression, if the inter-American system is to have any hope of survival. The abortive Cuban invasion attempt of mid-April, coupled with subsequent public disclosure and controversy on the extent of our official support of the invasion, has had a bad effect on Latin American public opinion and attitudes toward the United States. Except for Peru and Paraguay, where the main regret is that the invasion failed, governments are unanimous in condemning unilateral United States intervention. On this point, President Quadros of Brazil represented the general official feeling over most of the Continent in describing the April attempt as "disastrous" and any further unilateral intervention as "fatal" to Latin American support for and cooperation with the United States. Outside of Peru and Paraguay, only a few private citizens and one or two political leaders suggested that they would privately welcome unilateral United States military action against Fidel Castro, and even in these cases they would have to condemn such action publicly.

In Brazil, Argentina, Uruguay, and Ecuador, there had been a tendency to regard the Cuban problem as essentially a bilateral quarrel between Cuba and the United States, which might be negotiable if we relaxed our hostility and permitted the larger Latin American states to act as mediators. I believe that I convinced most of the Presidents and Governments concerned that the problem is not a bilateral one, that such issues between us as compensation for expropriated properties are of a secondary order which could be negotiated if other circumstances were favorable, and that the real cause of concern is the establishment of a beachhead for Communist penetration and subversion throughout the hemisphere. It follows that the issue is one of concern to all of the American Republics, affecting Latin America even more than the United States because it is the Latin countries which are vulnerable and actually the object of indirect aggression today. It is they, therefore, who should be primarily concerned with action to deal with this problem. The only country in which the strength of these arguments was not acknowledged at all was Ecuador, where President Velasco seems impervious to rational discussion.

Even where the governments concerned were most sympathetic to our viewpoint, however, as in the cases of Colombia, Venezuela, and Chile, it was strongly felt that no collective action should be officially considered until the economic conference was concluded and had demonstrated its success as a major step toward economic and social better-ment. This conclusion was based partly on the need to obliterate the memory of the April invasion effort, and also on the need to show to dis-sident left-wing elements in their countries that there is real promise of economic and social progress under genuinely democratic regimes work-ing in cooperation with the United States.

As to possible collective action after the Uruguay Conference, the most promising prospect appears to rest in the initiative of President Lleras Camargo (Colombia) for convening a meeting of Foreign Minis-ters acting as an Organ of Consultation under the terms of the Rio Pact.[152] This meeting would occur fairly soon after the economic confer-ence, and would undertake to: (a) reaffirm faith in and adherence to the American system and all of its principles; (b) broaden the definition of aggression in the Rio Pact to include indirect aggression through sub-version among other things; and (c) call upon Cuba to rejoin the Ameri-can community by disassociating itself from the Communist block and renouncing other actions incompatible with the principles of the OAS.[153] Rejection of this challenge would be followed after a suitable interval by a second meeting to consider sanctions designed to isolate Cuba, to reduce the dangers of Communist activity in other countries using Cuba as a base, and to bring economic and psychological pressure on the Cuban regime.[154]

At this time, it is impossible to predict how much support there would be at this second stage for collective sanctions, how extensive such sanc-tions could be, or what their effect would be. Among other unknown factors is the extent to which the USSR would want to support a Cuba isolated from the rest of the Western Hemisphere. The Lleras initiative, nonetheless, appears to be the most hopeful line to pursue at this time, and the only one offering a basis for collective action.

Even at the first stage, however, the action can be meaningful only if

[152] The Inter-American Treaty of Reciprocal Assistance, signed in 1947, which pledged nineteen American nations to mutual defense in case of attack on any one of them.

[153] The foreign ministers met in Uruguay, January 22–31, 1962. They declared "Marxism-Leninism" to be "incompatible with the inter-American system." They urged OAS members to "strengthen their capacity to counteract threats or acts of aggression, subversion, or other dangers to peace and security resulting from the continued intervention in this hemisphere of Sino-Soviet powers." This referred basically to Cuba, which was thereafter "excluded" from "participation in" the OAS. Department of State *Bulletin*, Vol. 48 (1962), p. 278. While all twenty republics — except for Cuba — supported the resolution that "Marxism-Leninism" was "incom-patible," Argentina, Brazil, Chile and Mexico abstained on the vote to exclude Cuba from the OAS.

[154] On February 3, 1962, President Kennedy declared an embargo on almost all trade with Cuba. On March 24, 1962, the United States prohibited the import of goods made in whole or part of Cuban products.

it is supported by two of the three largest Latin American nations — Argentina, Brazil, and Mexico. This point is agreed by all concerned, regardless of whether the legally necessary fourteen votes could be secured without including any, or more than one of these three countries. Mexican concurrence seems very unlikely. The possibilities of Argentine and Brazilian concurrence depend in part at least on first-hand conversations among Presidents Frondizi and Quadros and yourself. Both of these Presidents are lone wolves, giving their Foreign Ministers little responsibility for making foreign policy. Ordinary diplomatic channels will not function with them on a matter of this importance. Their prestige, moreover, is deeply involved in the possibility of meetings with you, either separately or together.

In my view, this is the decisive consideration favoring your attendance at the close of the economic conference at Punta del Este in Uruguay. On other counts, there are balancing advantages and disadvantages. Your presence would have the merit of dramatizing the conference itself, reemphasizing your personal interest in Latin America, strengthening the prospects for effective self-help measures by the Latin governments, and perhaps mustering additional Congressional support here for the provision of resources on a long-term basis to carry out the joint program. On the other hand, there is the possible disadvantage of exciting Latin American hopes and expectations beyond any realistic level of potential accomplishment. There is also the danger of press speculation on the connection between the economic program and our desire for collective political action — a connection which could be exploited by Communist propaganda as the greatest vote-buying bribe in history. If you do attend, special care will be required to minimize these difficulties.

In my judgment, the future of inter-American cooperation is so dependent on the achievement of a community of view among Argentina, Brazil, and ourselves, and the contribution to this achievement of a first-hand meeting at the Presidential level could be so great under present circumstances, that if the decision had to be made now, I think it should be in the affirmative.

In view of the deferral of the economic conference, however, a definite decision can be put off until mid-July without any disadvantage. During the next few weeks the situation may be clarified by a number of diplomatic initiatives, such as the visits of the Colombian and Chilean Foreign Ministers to Argentina, the Chilean Foreign Minister's visit to President Quadros, and the circulation of the Lleras Camargo proposals by Colombian Embassies throughout the continent. I suggest awaiting these developments before making a firm decision.[155]

Respectfully submitted,

[155] Kennedy did not attend the conference.

To Mrs. Eugene Meyer

June 30, 1961

My dear Agnes:

You were sweet to send me that welcome home telegram. It was an exhausting journey but rewarding in many ways, and our mission was accomplished far beyond my hopes.

Now I am off to the Economic and Social Council meeting in Geneva, to be followed by some other business in Europe and then a brief holiday with my sister in Florence. I hope to be back in early August, and that we will then have a weekend and good visit together if you are in these parts.

My thoughts go back to a year ago and the wild preparations for the Convention — and to your gallantry and generosity and remorseless promotion! [156] Bless you, my dear friend.

Affectionately,

To Mrs. Marshall Field

June 30, 1961

My dear Ruth:

I am just back and find your sweet letters. And now I am leaving for the weekend with the children in Libertyville and thence to Geneva next week.

My work there should conclude about the 15th, and I had planned then to go to stay with Buffy and Ernest [Ives] at the Villa Capponi, 3 Via Pian dei Giulari, Arcetri, Florence (phone: 29–2104). The alternative would be to join Bill Benton,[157] as you suggest, but I am afraid he will be way off in Greece by that time. However, I would welcome your views on the alternatives of Florence and the Flying Clipper, at the Hotel des Bergues, Geneva, where I will be staying.

If you come to Florence, I think it will probably be better to go there direct from Paris or from London or wherever you are at that time. Buffy can arrange for a car and all of that after we get there. I may want to have a couple of days in Rome to see the Food and Agriculture Organization people, and also the Prime Minister and some friends. But of all these details we can talk later.

Much love,

[156] For Mrs. Meyer's advocacy of Stevenson for the 1960 Democratic presidential nomination, see *The Papers of Adlai E. Stevenson,* Vol. VII, especially pp. 381, 472–473, 567.

[157] Chairman of the board of directors of the *Encyclopaedia Britannica,* who had invited Stevenson to cruise on his yacht.

To Mrs. Ernest L. Ives [158]

Sunday, July 2, 1961

Dear Buffie:

I am in Illinois for the week-end, before flying tomorrow — Monday — to Geneva — and Carol Evans has come out for the evening. Hence this letter.

My present plan is to stay in Geneva, at the Hotel Des Bergues, until about the 15th of July, attending meetings of the Economic and Social Council and getting acquainted with the UN operations in Geneva.

About that time I hope to come down to stay with you for a week or ten days. I have told Ruth Field that she would be welcome too, if she chooses to come, and I think she will. I would hope that I could get some rest there and do some quiet reading, and perhaps take a motor trip around the countryside to see some of that part of Italy, and perhaps even drive to Rome where I should spend a couple of days before going to Paris toward the end of the month. I suppose we can rent a car in Florence without any trouble, and maybe you and Ernest will want to join us for a few days.

Please let me know at the Hotel Des Bergues if there is any objection to this plan. My recollection is that there is no one staying with you there at that time.

The grandchildren are glorious and this brief visit at home after the brutalities of my trip to South America has been a rebirth.

Love,
ADLAI

To Mrs. John F. Kennedy

July 3, 1961

Dear Jackie:

Included in the list of things that the White House Fine Arts Committee wants to acquire is a Victorian settee and two side chairs which were presented by President and Mrs. Lincoln to Mr. and Mrs. John H. DeWitt.

I have told Mary Lasker [159] that I would be most happy to present these items to the White House, for use in the Lincoln Room — where I have slept! — and I have accordingly sent my check, together with a letter of instructions, to the White House Fine Arts Committee.

The next time I get to the second floor I want you to show them to me.

Affectionately,

158 The original is in E.S.I., I.S.H.L.
159 Mrs. Albert D. Lasker, an old Chicago friend, who with her late husband had founded the Albert and Mary Lasker Foundation to support medical research.

To Mikhail A. Menshikov [160]

July 3, 1961

Dear Mr. Ambassador:

You will recall that one of the reasons for my visit to the Soviet Union in 1958, which you so kindly helped to arrange, was to present to Mr. Khrushchev and the Soviet authorities arguments for the payment of royalties to foreign writers whose works are published in the USSR.[161] You may recall that I prepared a written memorandum on the subject which you were good enough to send to Mr. Mikhailov,[162] Mr. Kabanov,[163] and Mr. Yuri Zhukov,[164] before my arrival in Moscow.

After I arrived I discussed the matter with Mr. Khrushchev and the appropriate authorities. While they were not encouraging, Mr. Leonid Sobelov [Sobolev], President of the Writers Union, was. After my return, you may also recall, I had prolonged correspondence on the matter with the Soviet officials and mentioned it again to Mr. Khrushchev when he was here in 1959.

And now I am happy to see from the enclosed story in the New York Times of June 21, 1961 that the Soviet Union has evidently changed its policy and will pay royalties to foreign authors hereafter. While the newspaper article indicates that the policy was changed at the instance of Captain I. R. Maxwell of England, I am informed that my intervention in Moscow in 1958 and by mail thereafter may have been responsible for this change of Soviet policy.

If you or any of the Soviet officials could give me any information about this matter it would be greatly appreciated.[165]

Sincerely yours,

Rogelio Frigerio, a close adviser of Arturo Frondizi, president of Argentina, wrote Stevenson a long letter on June 24, 1961, that the leaders of the Argentine government had "absolute faith" in him as an interpreter of the "best" American tradition and a worthy follower of Franklin D. Roosevelt's outlook. Frigerio observed that Latin America lacked a specific policy of economic and social development. He warned that if Latin American leaders dedicated themselves to "rhetorical anti-communism" and the people continued to suffer misery, any anti-Communist front would collapse. Moreover, he stated that the United States had to

[160] Ambassador of the Union of Soviet Socialist Republics to the United States.
[161] See *The Papers of Adlai E. Stevenson*, Vol. VII, Part Three.
[162] Nikolai A. Mikhailov, minister of culture.
[163] Unable to identify.
[164] Chairman of the State Committee on Cultural Relations with Foreign Countries.
[165] The editors were unable to locate a reply.

be an associate of the Latin American countries, not a "master." The United States had to accept the juridical equality of states, he wrote, and Latin American nationalism could not be smashed by force. He urged that President Kennedy meet with the presidents of Mexico, Brazil and Argentina to discuss the Alliance for Progress. Kennedy's concept of the alliance to assist in the economic and social development of Latin America, he wrote, had to be implemented in a practical and sincere manner.

To Rogelio Frigerio

July 3, 1961

My dear Senor Frigerio:

I too was disappointed that we did not meet in Buenos Aires, but I was delighted to have your most interesting letter on my return. You may be sure that your views will come to the attention of the Secretary of State and those in our government who are most concerned with the relations of Argentina and the United States and the many and difficult problems facing our hemisphere and, indeed, our Western world.

I do not disagree with anything you say and this hurried journey around South America confirmed my conviction that "the moment is grave and overflowing with danger," as you so aptly put it. But I deeply regret that the meeting of the four Presidents in advance of the Alliance for Progress meeting in Punta del Este, which President Frondizi urged upon me and your letter reiterates, will I fear be impossible for President Kennedy in view of the situation in Congress with this critical session drawing to a close. He hopes, however, to come to Uruguay for the last days of that all-important meeting and I trust that such a meeting can be arranged somehow at that time. I discussed the possibilities with President Frondizi, and if there are any developments in that regard I hope they will be communicated to us through the usual channels as far in advance as possible.

I shall long remember my talks with President Frondizi. I am grateful that I had such a good opportunity to exchange views with him, and I am thankful that your great country has such an accomplished and dedicated man at its helm. Argentina and its President can be most influential in guiding the destiny of our hemisphere. And I am sure that my country wants to help insure that this leadership is in the direction we both believe best. To get this help organized properly and started promptly is why we attach such importance to the Alliance for Progress meeting now set for August 5.

I hope you will honor me with your views on our common problems often.

Cordially yours,

On January 6, 1961, Nikita Khrushchev, in a speech delivered in Moscow, stated: "The positions of the U.S.A., Britain and France have proved to be especially vulnerable in West Berlin. These powers . . . cannot fail to realize that sooner or later the occupation regime in the city must be ended. It is necessary to go ahead with bringing the aggressive-minded imperialists to their senses, and compelling them to reckon with the real situation. And should they balk, then we will take resolute measures, we will sign a peace treaty with the German Democratic Republic."

In March, 1961, President Kennedy asked former Secretary of State Dean Acheson to make special studies of NATO and Germany. When Prime Minister Harold Macmillan visited Washington the following month, Acheson observed at a meeting with Kennedy, Macmillan, and a number of others including Stevenson that should Khrushchev cut West Berlin off from West Germany, the allies had to show immediately that they would meet this challenge. Acheson then suggested a number of military countermeasures including the possibility of sending troops on the highway to West Berlin. The British were dismayed at this concentration on a military showdown and so was Stevenson. He said later: "Maybe Dean is right but his position should be the conclusion of a process of investigation, not the beginning. He starts at a point which he should not reach until we have explored and exhausted all the alternatives." [166]

Tension mounted over the next months. On July 25, Kennedy said over television: "We cannot and will not permit the Communists to drive us out of Berlin, either gradually or by force." He announced that he would ask Congress for an additional $3.25 billion for the defense budget and call up certain reserve and National Guard units. He declared, however, "We do not intend to abandon our duty to mankind to seek a peaceful solution" and added that the United States was determined to search for peace "in formal or informal meetings."

---

[166] Schlesinger, A Thousand Days, p. 381. Schlesinger urged the President to invite Stevenson and Averell Harriman to explain their opposition to Acheson's position, noting that the two men were "deeply dismayed" by Acheson's proposals. Schlesinger added: "Harriman, Stevenson and Acheson are our three elder statesmen in the field of foreign affairs. All have served the republic brilliantly, and all are honorable and towering figures. As a rule of thumb, I would vote with any two of them against the third." Memorandum for the President, April 6, 1961, John F. Kennedy Library.

To John F. Kennedy [167]

. . . *Berlin*

Our efforts to convince Khrushchev of our determination to maintain our Berlin position seem already, judging from the slightly milder tone of his June 28 statement, to be bearing fruit. I am sure they should be continued, but I would hope not in such frantic fashion as to create the impression we expect general war in the fall, or as to distort our treatment of other critical issues we face. (An example is what I understand to be the JCS [Joint Chiefs of Staff] claim we should back up Portugal on Angola because the Azores base will be essential to us if we become involved in a military crisis over Berlin.) I have often had the impression that, whenever the Soviets want to steal a march on us in one or two other places, they heat up the Berlin issue in the confident expectation that we will become so obsessed with it as to neglect or minimize most everything else.

Respectfully,

To William Benton [168]

July 6, 1961

Dear Bill:

I have just sent you a telegram reporting that I can't come aboard as I had hoped at Istanbul for the last week of your cruise. I suspect it will be a disappointment to Ruth [Field], but any complaints will fall upon deaf ears after the adventures she must already have had on the Dalmatian coast.

I am miserably tired after my ordeal in Latin America, and would really like to go home. But Ernest Ives is not well, and I think I owe it to my sister to visit with her for a short while before returning home via Paris the first of August. . . .

I will withhold a report on Latin America until I see you. Your surmise about the success is correct. It went extremely well, but the pace was fearful — 17,000 miles, 10 cities, 18 days — and God knows how many speeches, interviews, appearances, receptions and thousands of words of cables. I think on the whole we are well out of it. I ran into your friends everywhere, and many expressions of regret that you weren't with me,

167 Only the last page of this letter is in the Stevenson files. It bears no date, but may have been written before Stevenson left for Europe.

168 The original is in the possession of the estate of William Benton. Mr. Benton died on March 8, 1973. At the time this volume went to press, his widow and four children had indicated that they wished to deposit his papers at the University of Chicago. This letter was written from Geneva, Switzerland.

together with thanks for the Britannicas that you had strewed so liberally along our path.[169]

I envy you among those Greek Islands more than I can say! And I am beginning to despair of ever getting there.

Yours,

ADLAI

Gerald W. Johnson, a contributing editor of the New Republic *and former editorial writer for the Baltimore* Evening Sun, *wrote that he had broken his hip and suggested that this was one way for Stevenson to slacken his pace.*

To Gerald W. Johnson [170]

July 6, 1961

Dear Gerald:

Your constant advocacy of hip breaking as the absolution of all responsibilities has me a little rattled. But I want you to know that I am not buying any of it. If I could say the same for the bicycles, motor scooters, wee cars, and other beasties and ghoulies that disfigure the shores of this serene Lake, it would be something. I suspect they will break something for me if you don't.

I wish I could tell you about my journey to South America. It was as close to suicide as I have come, and as close to total success, too. I think we pulled some badly scorched chestnuts out of the fire and converted some thinking from negative to positive. But will we follow up? Or was it just a fruitless investment of my good repute in those parts? I want to think that we are on the point of new departures in our relations with Latin America — *really.*

A sensible man would have gone to bed or to grass for a couple of weeks after I got back. Instead, I came to Geneva for more international bickering. Moreover, [John] Calvin's brooding presence seems to have a subtle way of diverting attention from the more agreeable features of life hereabouts and, as you say, "what is to be will be, whether it ever happens or not"! Maybe that's the way I feel about my hip.

I yearn for a visit with you.

Yours,

---

[169] Mr. Benton had accompanied Stevenson on his extensive tour of South America in the spring of 1960. See *The Papers of Adlai E. Stevenson,* Vol. VII, Part Five.
[170] This letter was written from Geneva, Switzerland.

To James Tobin [171]

July 6, 1961

Dear Mr. Tobin:

I have just started to work this morning on the speech I am supposed to deliver to the Economic and Social Council on Monday, and your revised draft is my take-off point. But it is either so good or I am so ignorant that I find it hard to embellish it.

Thank you so much.

Sincerely yours,

To Philip Noel-Baker [172]

July 6, 1961

Dear Philip:

Thanks for yours of June 22 — which I have brought with me among those masses of neglected things, good and bad, which give us all such despair and expectation.

I found the disarmament business going very badly when I returned from South America. The Russians have changed the ground rules since I broke off with Gromyko [173] in April, and refuse to discuss the composition of the forum or the principles to govern its deliberations. Instead, they insist on talking about "general and complete disarmament."

I wish they had told us that when we resumed bilateral negotiations we were to talk substance. Instead, we agreed, as you will recall, in joint statements to Committee 1 of the General Assembly, that bilaterals would be resumed in June on the suspended issues.

It all baffles me a little, although I accept entirely your proposition that what concerns Khrushchev most of all is a re-armed Germany — and I don't blame him. But what a curious way he has of going about disarmament just when we are really ready to do some business.

All I can see now is that the talks in Moscow will get no further and there will be no new forum set up, and we should throw it into the whole Disarmament Commission before they try to make some propaganda about our refusing to discuss disarmament.

The nuclear test negotiations here are a total farce, and the talk is mostly about if and when the farce should be ended.

[171] Member of the Council of Economic Advisers, Executive Office of the President. This letter was written from Geneva, Switzerland.

[172] A member of Parliament and leading advocate of disarmament, with whom Stevenson had worked during the formation of the United Nations. This letter was written from Geneva, Switzerland.

[173] Stevenson and Andrei Gromyko, the Soviet minister of foreign affairs, had held discussions while the UN General Assembly was in session.

In view of their introduction of the Tro[i]ka principle,[174] it is useless to talk about a new forum. I am hoping that the US can seize the initiative on disarmament this fall, and recapture some of the ground we have lost in recent years, perhaps even persuading the Russians to do business on a reasonable basis.

It would be good to talk with you.

Cordially yours,

On July 10, 1961, Stevenson addressed the thirty-second session of the UN Economic and Social Council at Geneva, Switzerland. It was the first time in the history of the United Nations that the chief representative of the United States to the United Nations had made the opening speech on the world economic debate. While in Geneva, Stevenson discussed his recent trip to Latin America with the Latin American representatives to ECOSOC and he also talked with the Polish and Indian representatives.[175]

A BETTER LIFE: ECONOMIC DEVELOPMENT [176]

Economics must always be the servant of society. No amount of steel or cement produced, of oil wells drilled, or acres of wheat harvested is of any consequence except as it fills a human need — unless the steel and cement make decent houses and schools and hospitals, unless the oil warms and transports man and his goods, unless the wheat means bread and strength for those who hunger.

The most efficient factory cannot justify a city's slums. And economic growth is of little avail if it serves only a fraction of the people. It must serve them all.

The greatest challenge of our century is the aspiration of peoples all over the globe to share the abundant fruits of modern science and technology. The example of the industrially developed nations shows that human beings can lead longer, healthier and richer lives than most of the world's population now enjoy, and that each generation can have the satisfaction of bequeathing new opportunities to its children. At the end of the century we will be judged, all of us, by how well we have met these aspirations.

[174] The Soviet proposal to replace the Secretary-General with a three-member committee.

[175] Philip M. Klutznick, letter to Walter Johnson, August 29, 1974.

[176] This speech is reprinted in Adlai E. Stevenson, *Looking Outward: Years of Crisis at the United Nations,* edited with commentary by Robert L. Schiffer and Selma Schiffer, preface by John F. Kennedy (New York: Harper & Row, 1963), pp. 161–170. A summary of the speech appears in United Nations, *Official Records, Economic and Social Council,* July 10, 1961, pp. 37–38.

We must bridge the dangerous chasm between the living standards of the rich and the poor. We must narrow the disparities in the conditions of life between human beings who happen to be born on different parts of the earth.

We seek greater economic equality between nations as well as within nations, not dividing up our present scarcities but sharing in a growing abundance. The world economy must grow in capacity to produce, faster than in the past everywhere. For no one anywhere, any longer, will passively accept the idea that hunger, misery and disease are the immutable destiny of man.

Everyone, everywhere, realizes that in this historic century man has routed the four horsemen of the apocalypse, and that for the first time in human history the ancient evil specters of pestilence and famine have been exorcised. We are crossing a great watershed in history to a time when enough food, shelter and clothing are within the reach of all and new dimensions in human wants and needs are emerging.

It will be no help to the developing countries to slow down the growth of the developed countries. Quite the contrary. For the emerging nations need above all an increased flow of resources from the industrial countries. To be able to provide this aid, and to provide expanding markets for the exports of the less developed economies, the advanced countries will have to progress steadily and rapidly in their capacity to produce.

To meet these and other international responsibilities and to better provide for the wants of our own people, the United States must grow in its own capacity to produce. Therefore, we look to the 1960's as a decade of dynamic and accelerated economic development, demonstrating to all the vigor and vitality of a free economy. And we pledge to do all in our power to make the 1960's a decade of development not only for ourselves, but, we hope, for our fellowmen everywhere.

Our periodic postwar recessions, mild though they have been, have cost us dearly in human disappointment and wasted national opportunities. So the first step in our program for growth is to mobilize the weight of the government's influence to prevent or arrest future interruptions in our economic progress. The idea that the rate of economic growth in a free society does not have to be left to chance, that democratic nations can control their economic destinies, has now become our conviction.

What has happened since 1945 has confounded the pessimists. In no other period of the world's history has there been such a rapid and gratifying recovery from the devastation of war. This recovery has been greatly aided by international cooperation and economic aid. Western Europe and Japan have achieved spectacular results, and we recognize that the record of the Soviet Union, too, is impressive.

In the United States, happily spared the devastation of war and starting from a high level of production and consumption, national production in real terms has increased by more than one-third since the war's end.

If we look further back over the twentieth century, the record of economic and social progress is even more impressive. In the United States per capita income has doubled in the last quarter-century. This growth has been achieved not only through very large investments of new capital but by the growth and improvement of technology, the economies of large-scale production as national and international markets have expanded, and the improvement in the quality of the labor force. It has been achieved while at the same time reducing greatly the hours of work in our factories, mines and farms and providing much more leisure for all of our people.

It has become clear that what happens in research laboratories and in the minds of men can multiply the potentialities of physical factors.

Hours worked, land utilized and capital employed are the elements which, by classical formulas, determine the growth of output. But both the quality and quantity of output have been progressively expanding far beyond what the mere physical combination of these factors would indicate. This we must attribute to intelligence, imagination, inventions, entrepreneurship. Brains have become a real growth industry.

The power of intelligence can manifest itself in every aspect of our lives and in every phase of the development process. We need a concept of social "capital" which goes beyond bricks and mortar and includes investment in education, training and the stock of useful knowledge.

I do not underestimate the need for capital formation. It is true that mere investment without new knowledge and new skills could not have generated the growth in output that we have experienced. But it is equally true that knowledge and skills could not have been productive unless they had been linked to real capital. Indeed, without the prospect of new investment, much of the technological progress would never have occurred at all. If we are serious about accelerated economic growth, we must step up the rate of productive investment. And President Kennedy has made a number of proposals for economic growth based on the need for all three factors: knowledge, brain power, more capital.

Policies designed primarily to stimulate economic growth often turn out to have a desirable incidental effect. Education is a good example. The American tradition values education for its own sake; we led the way in the provision of free public education at all levels of society. But we now feel fairly certain that the resulting improvement in the quality of the labor force has been one of the major factors in our economic growth during the last half-century.

Before I leave the subject of the United States economy, let me say a word about disarmament and arms control. It is no secret that we have been forced to devote a considerable portion of our economy to production for defense. But let me make it perfectly clear that the United States, far from regarding an international armaments agreement as a threat to economic prosperity, would regard such an agreement as an economic opportunity — an opportunity to free our resources from production of instruments of death to the production of the manifold things we need for a better life, for our own citizens and for the citizens of other nations.

This is not to deny that a sudden change in the direction of production tends to be disruptive. This is true for any economy, however organized. But such disruption can be minimized by foresight. The United States is actively studying the economic impact of disarmament and arms control, and is hopefully designing measures to ease the transition. We hope and pray that the day will come when such studies become more than merely an academic exercise, for the United States has no higher priority than genuine disarmament and the building of greater confidence and trust among the great powers who have life and death for the human race in their hands.

The United States is fixing its own economic sights high for the 1960's, but we do not see our goal as a one-nation project. It is a truism that economic development depends primarily on what is done by the country itself. But truisms are also true and we can only help others to help themselves. Our world has become so interdependent, so intertwined, that no country can go forward in isolation. The United States was one of the first to recognize that it is in the interest of all mankind to improve the lot of the less privileged nations, even as we discovered a century ago that to improve the lot of the poor was good for the economy as well as for the soul.

Consequently, when we think of the sixties as a decade of development, we are thinking in terms of a world-wide effort and a general advance, and in working toward this objective, we have sought to refashion our aid program, including increased emphasis to meet the needs of this decade.

Our new program will place primary emphasis on bringing as many countries as possible to the point of *self-sustaining growth* where they no longer need outside assistance. It is not just the goals and the initiatives which will depend primarily on the efforts of the newly developing countries themselves. The greater part of the resources required must also be generated by their own savings and export earnings. On our side, we are prepared to do our utmost to provide that vital margin of help to bridge the gap between their capabilities and their needs.

A study of development during the fifties also makes it clear that private capital has been a most important factor in promoting economic development. Indeed, the country planning economic development without taking into account the great help which foreign private enterprise can provide is like a tennis player who tries to play on one foot.

The resources available from private enterprise, both in terms of capital and know-how, are vastly greater than those available to government. With fairness, good will and good faith on both sides, cooperation between governments and private enterprise, domestic and foreign, can astonish the world with fruitful results for the benefit of people everywhere.

This brings me to another important facet of American economic development policy: Our concern with social justice. We do not have to argue the merits of social justice from the moral standpoint. But the practical economist realizes that it is also essential to any enduring and worthwhile economic development. Neither growth nor political stability can be enduring until all segments of society feel that they have a stake in their country's progress. This is what a distinguished Argentine Minister of Economy [177] had in mind when he used the term "free *social* economy." We have seen it work in the United States; we know it can work elsewhere.

While the United States cannot make decisions for other countries on measures to foster social justice, we plan to offer inducements to make it attractive for any developing country to undertake internal changes in its own best interest. We are determined that the funds provided by the American taxpayers be used, not to enrich the few, but to improve the lot of the many.

Problems of savings, capital formation and external aid are vitally important for the economic growth of the underdeveloped countries. But to dwell on these without reference to the major contribution of international trade would be like casting *Hamlet* without a Prince of Denmark. Trade is the element which binds economies into a closely knitted interdependent world; progress made toward restoring and expanding a healthy multilateral trade has been one of the most encouraging features of the postwar world.

The growth of trade is indispensable to many of the underdeveloped economies which depend so heavily on exports for the materials and equipment so essential for their development. And it is hardly original to say that what happens to commodity prices is a powerful influence for good or bad in raw-material-producing countries, which most of the less developed nations are.

Much effort is currently being directed in the forums of the United

[177] Stevenson possibly refers to Alvaro C. Alsogaray, whom he met during his trip to Latin America in 1960. See *The Papers of Adlai E. Stevenson*, Vol. VII, p. 432.

Nations and elsewhere to exploring means for dealing with the varied and complex commodity problems which affect the welfare of underdeveloped countries. The possible role of commodity agreements and compensatory financing is receiving particularly close consideration. It is clear, however, that arrangements directed solely to the problem of price instability would not suffice to deal with a major aspect of the current commodity situation, for the fact is that oversupply and overcapacity are the most pressing problems now affecting current commodity markets. This is the single most important cause for the persistent downward pressure upon world commodity prices which has prevented these prices from responding fully to improvement in demand.

Obviously what is required above all in tackling commodity stabilization problems is cooperation between producing and consuming countries. And I want to renew the assurance given by President Kennedy that the United States is prepared to give its wholehearted cooperation in such endeavors.

Here, then, are some of our ideas about the tasks we face in the 1960's. They are by no means original, for we have benefited by the ideas and experiences of other nations. We, in turn, hope that our experience in the United States may contribute to the development of societies which have their own traditions, political concepts and economic goals.

The United States has no ambition to determine the future of the rest of the world. With liberation of colonial peoples, dozens of new nations claim a voice in the affairs of the world community through their participation in the United Nations and its various agencies. We welcome their emergence on the world scene. We look forward to working with them to maintain and strengthen a world order which no great power can dominate.

As one crisis after another explodes around the globe, we may at times feel discouraged. Yet tyrannical systems have not succeeded in those areas of the world where workable alternatives exist, however different these alternatives may be from what we in the United States call capitalism or private enterprise.

But the crucial necessity is that aid shall be used effectively by governments willing to make economic and social reforms, so that it will benefit not only a few, but the people as a whole. It is necessary, therefore, that our economic efforts and our efforts in the social field should be united in a single grand design for human progress, for "old moulds have to be broken, and that society which does not translate economic progress is doomed."

I shall go further and say that plans for economic development that do not from the very outset take into account social needs must fail to achieve both their economic and human goals.

What good are impressive production figures if the vast majority of a country's population remains ill-clad, ill-housed, ill-fed, sick and illiterate? In a democratic society — in any good society — the only purpose of economic improvement is to provide a better life for all of the people. If our industrial development creates as many problems as it solves, are we improving the lot of the people? If, because of resistance to land reform, the fruits of improved agricultural methods fall into the pockets of a handful of landowners rather than into the empty baskets of the people themselves, why should the United Nations, the Food and Agricultural Organization and other organizations pour time and money into this so-called improvement?

Many countries have learned the wasteful folly of industrial development without social planning. In those satellite shantytowns which surround and deface so many proud cities, all the social evils which economic progress professes to cure, breed and multiply. With no jobs, inadequate shelter, unsanitary living conditions, scanty food and no schools or recreational opportunities, the standard of living and health goes down instead of up. The restraints of family, tribe and village are broken, giving way to the havoc of juvenile delinquency and crime.

Likewise improved agricultural efficiency without social reform often has similar results. Men and women, pushed off the land by machinery, drift into squalid urban centers and, with no provision to receive these newcomers and help them with their staggering new problems, the same old vicious circle is set in motion.

Then there are the stagnant, *status quo* societies where ambition seems buried under centuries of custom and inertia. Here the problems of the *old* shantytowns may be harder to deal with than those of the *new*. They are so much a part of the landscape that they are forgotten, taken for granted. Who cares about the subhuman dwellers who have lived there since the beginning of time? Is it worth trying to improve their lot if the people themselves don't apparently care?

I say it is not only worth it — it is imperative. A number of years ago, the world trend was described in the world situation as "the revolution of rising expectations." Since then the revolution has accelerated beyond anyone's dreams. Its nature, however, hasn't changed, only intensified.

But it isn't factories and roads and dams, in themselves, that people want. These are vastly important, both as symbols and as means to an end. What they really want are homes, food, jobs, decent clothes, an education for their children, a chance at life in freedom and dignity.

Land reform, urban development, community development, low-cost housing, education, nutrition, sanitation, hygiene, recreation, social welfare — these are the matters that we should be concerned with if we want our economic revolution to succeed.

For if people have a stake in what they are doing, they will work for it. And many social programs underpin or contribute to economic goals as well — some, such as education or housing, in a direct fashion; others, such as nutrition and sanitation, resulting in improved health indirectly. In so far as all of these social programs lift the level of living of the people, they improve the chances for sustained economic progress.

So let us not just give lip service to "balanced economic and social development," as we call it; let us remember that the only point of economic development is social development — or, quite simply, a better life for people.

And remember, too, that it is a better life that people all over the world are demanding today with rising insistence. Each year, in millions and tens of millions, with colossal new-found energy, they are marching onto the stage of history; and that is their demand — a better life! No one can march these great hosts of humanity off the stage again. But it is within our power to help determine their future, whether, in their frustration, they will embrace fanaticism and violence, or whether they will be enabled to move in peace toward that better life which this age has brought within the vision of all.

We know that no final solutions should ever be expected in human affairs. We do not preach a counsel of perfection. There will be no point in history at which we shall be able to say that all crises have come to an end, and that we can live peacefully ever after. But all of us can learn to live calmly and constructively with continuing world crises if we persist in the search, to which this Council is dedicated, for new and more effective means of improving the welfare of human beings.

We have just crossed the threshold of a new decade. Let us so chart our course that this decade may be remembered, not as a period of power struggle, but as a decade of great triumphs in the age-old struggle to provide a better life for men everywhere.

To Seymour M. Finger [178]

July 12, 1961

Dear Max:

I should have written you long ago to thank you for your admirable help in connection with the speech I gave here the other day. It went very well, and there has been considerable comment, all favorable, although the questions indicated they wished I had been a little "more specific." I enclose a copy in more or less final form, although I made additions at the last moment — as usual!

[178] Senior adviser on economic and Soviet affairs at USUN. This letter was written from Geneva, Switzerland.

My stay here has been on the whole restful, and a happy contrast to the ordeal in South America.

Cordially yours,

To Francis T. P. Plimpton [179]

July 13, 1961

Dear Francis:

I will be leaving here presently for a visit with Buffie [Ives] in Italy. On the 24th or 25th I will go to Rome for a couple of days and then to Paris, c/o T. K. Finletter,[180] and plan to return to New York on August 1 — *unless* I am advised to go to London for a day or so. The British here have made "representations" in that direction, but I have thus far discouraged it.

Before talking to the people in Rome and Paris, and possibly London, I would like to have in hand up-to-date information about the status of Chinese Representation [181] and Disarmament, together with whatever other items should be discussed with our allies.

Both the French and British have asked for consultations on CHIREP [Chinese Representation], and there may well be other questions raised.

Perhaps the office in New York can put something together for me and also any information that might be helpful from IO.[182] In the latter connection, any up-to-date information as to the President's plans for attending the meeting in Uruguay would be helpful, together with any available indication as to whether he wants me to go along if he decides to go.

I find you can keep mighty busy at ECOSOC!

Yours,

On July 10, 1961, Agnes Meyer wrote Stevenson that in a recent issue of Encounter *there was an article attacking William Benton, Robert M. Hutchins, and Stevenson for the way they had contributed to weakening the quality of the* Encyclopaedia Britannica.[183] *Mrs. Meyer also criticized the way the* Britannica *used a picture and statement of Stevenson's for promotional purposes. She mentioned that Clayton Fritchey of USUN*

---

[179] This letter was written from Geneva, Switzerland.

[180] Mr. Finletter was now United States ambassador to the North Atlantic Treaty Organization.

[181] The question of seating the People's Republic of China in the UN.

[182] The Bureau of International Organization Affairs of the Department of State.

[183] Harvey Einbinder, "The Britannica," *Encounter*, May, 1961, pp. 16–25. Einbinder, a physicist, published other articles pointing out errors and deficiencies in the encyclopedia and later published *The Myth of the Britannica* (New York: Grove Press, 1964).

and Harold Taylor, former president of Sarah Lawrence College (1945–
1959), were joining her for a cruise to the North Cape of Norway.

To Mrs. Eugene Meyer [184]

July 14, 1961

Dearest Agnes:

Thanks for your glorious letter. Please don't listen to those desparaging
[disparaging] detractors about the Britannica. It is — *by far* — the most
comprehensive and best edited encyclopedia that ever was and probably
ever will be, until it makes a better one. And it *is* making a better one
all the time by continuous revision by some 900 scholars all over the
world, including those from Oxford, Cambridge and the University of
Chicago.

They have spent something like 4 million dollars on editorial revision
alone in the last few years. Moreover, no one makes a profit from the
Britannica except the University of Chicago. Bill Benton has transferred
stock to a charitable foundation.

But I agree with you about the use of my picture in the advertisement
and will do something about that when I return.

I am jealous as I can be of Messrs. Taylor and Fritchey. Why don't you
ever ask me to join you on one of those deluxe cruises!

I shall be back the first of August and can't wait to see you. Please
don't keep me waiting until [after?] you are back. We must have a talk
about many different things, including the Administration, the State
Department and our sons' adventures. Mine, I confess, have been pretty
dull and conventional so far.

Much love,
ADLAI

*After a few days with Mr. and Mrs. Ernest L. Ives in Florence, Italy,
Stevenson visited Rome on July 25 and 26, where he spoke to the
Italian Society for International Organization on July 26.[185]*

*Senator Hubert H. Humphrey wrote Stevenson that he should insist on
talking personally to President Kennedy more than he had done up to
date.*

---

[184] The original is in the Agnes Meyer files, Princeton University Library. This
letter was written from Geneva, Switzerland.
[185] This speech is reprinted in Stevenson, *Looking Outward*, pp. 183–193.

To Hubert H. Humphrey

July 26, 1961

Dear Hubert:

Thank you for your letter and the memorandum. I am astonished —
again — by your reportorial skill.

Perhaps you are right about pressing for more opportunities to talk
with him. Maybe I will do it, but it doesn't come easily. Not that I don't
enjoy it, but I feel that if he wants my point of view he will ask for it.

I shall be back almost by the time you receive this, and will hope to
see you in Washington very soon.

Yours,

*On August 5, 1961, Stevenson, Harlan Cleveland and Arthur M. Schle-
singer, Jr., met with President Kennedy at Hyannis Port to discuss
American strategy at the forthcoming General Assembly of the United
Nations.*

*Stevenson renewed a proposal that he had previously made to the
President that disarmament should be the major theme of the United
States. Kennedy remarked that it did not seem to be a popular issue with
the public or the Congress. He said that he knew how much disarmament
meant to the rest of the world, and it was an issue he could use against
the Soviet Union: "We are ready for inspection; they aren't; and we
should take all the advantage of this we can."*

*Although Stevenson agreed, he told the President: "We can't do this
effectively if we ourselves equivocate. Your first decision, Mr. President,
must be to make sure that you yourself are genuinely for general and
complete disarmament. We must go for that. Everything else in our program derives from it. Only total disarmament will save the world from
the horror of nuclear war as well as from the mounting expense of the
arms race. Your basic decision must be to identify yourself with a new
approach to disarmament. This must be our principal initiative in the
United Nations."* [186]

*According to Schlesinger, Kennedy listened with "interest, but also with
a slight tinge of skepticism." He saw little opportunity for progress on
the issue and, as a result, viewed it as a measure of political warfare.
Kennedy remarked that he understood the "propaganda" importance of
pushing the issue. Schlesinger wrote, "This casual remark stung Stevenson," who insisted that the President had to have faith, not an argument
that was "likely to move Kennedy, and I never felt so keenly the way*

[186] Schlesinger, *A Thousand Days*, p. 478.

these two men, so united in their objectives, could so inadvertently arrive at cross purposes." [187]

At this same meeting, they discussed the question of the seating of the People's Republic of China in the United Nations. As a private citizen Stevenson had favored a solution by which both Chinas would be seated in the General Assembly. USUN and the Department of State prior to this meeting with Kennedy developed a proposal based on the juridical theory that both Peking and Taipei were valid successor states to the "Republic of China" referred to in the Charter of the United Nations. There would be two seats in the General Assembly. The question of the seat in the Security Council would be allowed to "drag, perhaps even winding up in the World Court," Harlan Cleveland wrote. "Our assumption was that Peking would not buy this solution any time soon, but at least the monkey would be off the U.S.'s back." Kennedy "bought the idea" but stated that he had to consult congressional leaders. "After he did that," Cleveland observed, "he concluded that the Congressional reaction would be so troublesome that it would interfere with his legislative program." [188] At the August 5, 1961, meeting Kennedy told the group present that the domestic situation in 1962 would be different. The discussion then revolved around parliamentary ways to stall the admission of the People's Republic. Stevenson objected to one proposed strategy as "too transparent." Kennedy said, "What do you think we ought to do? If you're not for this policy, we shouldn't try it." Stevenson replied, "I'll be for it if you decide it's the policy." [189]

To Mrs. John F. Kennedy

August 7, 1961

My dear Jackie:

It was a glorious visit for me, and I prefer the simplicities of Hyannis to the complexities of the Villa Leopolda, etc!

You and the President have a genius for making people feel relaxed and at home, and I wish I had more opportunity to practice such arts on you here in New York. Please don't forget your promise to come, with suitable disguise, to join your bearded, hairy friend for some nocturnal exploration!

Yours,

[187] Ibid., p. 479.
[188] Memorandum to Walter Johnson, April 30, 1973.
[189] Schlesinger, *A Thousand Days*, p. 480.

To William V. Shannon [190]

August 8, 1961

Dear Bill:

I have just read your column of August 6.[191] That I was your "most enjoyable story" pleases and flatters and honors me beyond measure. And that you thought so well of that campaign and said it so well gives me boundless satisfaction. You almost make me wish we could do it again!

The purpose of this letter, however, was not the foregoing, but to congratulate you on your engagement.[192] I wish I *could* hear your reflections on the institution of marriage, but I can surmise what they are, in view of the contribution that you are making to it! I think I know the young lady, and I wish you would give her my best wishes and affection.

And if you ever escape from that hilltop paradise in Santa Barbara [193] and come back to the East, I insist that you spend a night with me. I know of no acquaintance that I would rather cultivate, and likewise none that has so eluded me.

Bob Hutchins [194] is one of my oldest friends, and I am impressed again with his sagacity. Moreover, I propose to tell him so.

Yours,

To John F. Kennedy

MEMORANDUM FOR THE PRESIDENT [195]

August 8, 1961

SUBJECT: *Nuclear Testing and the United Nations*

1. Last Saturday I sent to the White House and the State Department a proposed Presidential statement in which you would have invited the Soviet Union, first, immediately to discontinue all nuclear testing, and second, to conclude within thirty days a treaty prohibiting all nuclear weapons tests. You would state at the same time that the United States was going to prepare for atmospheric testing, and if your offer was not accepted within one week the US would be obliged to start testing when ready.

2. At a meeting in Washington Tuesday, the Committee of Principals

---

190 Columnist for the New York *Post.*

191 Mr. Shannon had praised Stevenson's 1956 campaign.

192 Mr. Shannon was married to Elizabeth McNelly on August 5, 1961.

193 Mr. Shannon was a fellow in residence at the Center for the Study of Democratic Institutions in Santa Barbara, California.

194 Robert M. Hutchins, president of the Center for the Study of Democratic Institutions.

195 This document was declassified.

decided against using this approach and also against taking any initiative to renew the Kennedy-Macmillan proposal that fall-out testing be banned.[196]

3. On behalf of all the agencies concerned, the Secretary of State has now recommended a new policy under which we would continue to be willing to negotiate a treaty for a controlled test ban, whether for all types of tests or for atmospheric tests only, but in view of the Soviet test series we would not agree to a moratorium on testing during the period of negotiations.

4. I am told that at the meeting of the Committee of Principals it was the consensus that preparations should be made for atmospheric testing, but that such tests could not take place for several months. The proposal that we test in the atmosphere almost at once, for demonstration rather than technical purposes, was rejected — thank God!

5. I think that one more "last chance" challenge to negotiate a treaty within 30 days, with a joint test suspension during that limited period only, would be extremely useful in dealing here with the enthusiasm for the Indian proposal (to ban all tests, with no controls) and with the skepticism about the US-UK resolution (to negotiate a treaty along the lines of our Geneva draft).

6. However, I am not questioning the decision taken in Washington this week. What I do *urgently recommend* is an immediate statement from you or me offering to sign the present draft treaty or to return now to the negotiation table, either in Geneva or perhaps right here in New York. We would make clear that we were making preparations for further tests of our own; express our regret that Soviet actions make them necessary, as a matter of national security; and agree to stop as soon as a treaty is signed.

7. I am not proposing that we should stop our preparations for testing in the atmosphere. I think we should be completely frank in stating that these preparations are going forward. Indeed, the preparations may themselves serve as some incentive toward getting the Soviets back into negotiations. But since we cannot usefully test in the atmosphere for several months, I think we have everything to gain and nothing to lose by using the intervening time to conduct our educational campaign that stresses (a) our willingness to conclude a treaty, (b) Soviet obstruction and duplicity, and (c) the contrast between Soviet unconcern about the dangers of fall-out tests and US reluctance to follow suit.

8. In summary, these are the reasons why I think a new offer to negotiate a treaty would prove useful:

[196] For a discussion of this meeting and the proposal, see Schlesinger, *A Thousand Days*, pp. 454–458, 460–461.

(a) It will be a further boost for the disarmament initiative you took in your great speech here at the UN. And it will show that the United States is supremely desirous of putting an end of nuclear weapons testing, with all its health hazards, its implications in terms of ever more destructive weapons, and its general exacerbating effect on international tensions.

(b) The offer would give us something other than a purely negative line to use as a basis for combating proposals for an uncontrolled, uninspected and unlimited test moratorium. While the present position that test cessation is possible only under a treaty with controls is thoroughly reasonable, it commands indifferent support in the General Assembly. Ninety-six of the 100 members of the UN are innocent bystanders in the nuclear arms race. Fearing that the health and safety of their peoples are jeopardized by continued testing, they are not interested in the rights and wrongs of the situation, or in who tested first. They will make a passionate appeal that the tests must be stopped. If we must test for security reasons, it would help to dramatize the earnestness of our efforts to avoid test resumption before we reached the point of no return.

(c) Our offer should win votes for our resolution and will moderate criticism we will certainly get for not agreeing to an Indian-type resolution. More than that, it will improve our standing with respect to other major political issues about to come up in the General Assembly. I need mention only the Chinese representation problem, the problem of the Secretary-General, and, if it comes into the UN, the problem of Berlin. In dealing with these difficult matters, it is surely best for us to appear as an earnest seeker of ways to diminish tensions.

(d) The renewed offer would focus attention on and dramatize our advocacy of a full nuclear test ban treaty with controls; it would greatly assist the process of public education we had intended in any event to carry out here at the UN.

9. In your press conference yesterday, you did indicate US willingness to negotiate for a test ban treaty, and your conviction that a "moratorium" during negotiations is no longer an acceptable procedure as far as the United States is concerned. But the "news" in your statement was the possibility of atmospheric testing. My suggestion for a formal renewal of our treaty offer is to get the public's attention focussed once again on our desire to negotiate so as to stop tests rather than on the melancholy necessity to continue them.

10. If you prefer to say no more on this subject, I would welcome your authorization to make a statement here, within a very few days, along the lines suggested in this memorandum. One way or the other, a formal US

announcement should be made very soon, before the Soviets complete their present test series.

To Lady Barbara Jackson

August 12, 1961

Dearest Barbara:

. . . I was glad to hear that the [Edison] Dicks had arrived safely, and I am sure this is going to be an enlightening experience for the Commissioner.¹⁹⁷ I have had no word from that distinguished public servant since June, and I'm thoroughly provoked with her for not keeping the boss informed. But forgiveness fills my heart.

As for my head — it's full of disarmament, Germany, Bizerte ¹⁹⁸ and the forthcoming special session of the General Assembly. Meanwhile I have to go to California to make a speech to a formidable international gathering of astronomers! Copy will undoubtedly reach you in due course and you will perceive the sharp descent of my oratorical quality since I left Rome.

Life at the US Mission is a madhouse, as usual. There is more happening than a man can manage — or, at least, than *I* can manage. My frustration about the failure of my negotiations on Bizerte is boundless, and I have discovered another reason why I don't like absolute monarchies, such as France. But the internal situation there may be so delicate that they had to behave in this stubborn way. And now their Ambassador is whispering to me that this incident may lead to their withdrawal from the United Nations. However, that's in confidence and I have heard it before.

. . . Adlai and Nancy [Stevenson] are in Mexico on a long delayed and brief holiday. She is going to bless us all with another baby early next year — although they are shamelessly candid that they don't consider it any blessing at all. Poor girl, I don't know how she manages to do so much with such little evident effort. I hope it isn't to have its sequel years hence.

I am distressed that I can't come to England for the tensions meeting.¹⁹⁹ . . . But I am sure you realize that there is so much to do here after an absence of two months and with the Assembly approaching, that I can't even spare the time — or the money — to go over to Bill Blair's

---

¹⁹⁷ Jane Dick.
¹⁹⁸ In May, 1961, as France began talks with Algerian nationalists which would lead to Algerian independence, Tunisia attempted to drive the French from their military base at Bizerte. The French responded with a bloody attack on Tunisian forces. A special session of the UN General Assembly was called for August 21 to consider an Afro-Asian resolution requiring France to comply with a Security Council order to pull its forces back.
¹⁹⁹ The editors were unable to identify this conference.

wedding,[200] let alone this conference. I had no idea at the time he asked me that you would be there — news that makes it all very painful. . . .

To James M. Gavin [201]

August 14, 1961

Dear General:

Enclosed is a copy of a report which has come to us today, quoting from a newspaper story out of Tunis, alleging statements of mine to Ambassador Slim.[202] You have received a telegram which I sent at the instance of Secretary Rusk, so that you would be prepared to meet any French complaints.

I have said nothing of the kind, and am told that the author of this story is an irresponsible and provocative correspondent for *Afrique Action* here in NY by the name of Simon Malloy. He has a long record of mischief-making, and this seems to be a further example.

Because I attach such value personally, as well as officially, to my long friendship with General de Gaulle, I wanted you to know the facts, and to be adequately prepared to meet any criticism, and to preserve this happy and long-standing relationship if you can. I am told also that it is likely that the French are as familiar with Mr. Malloy's mischief-making as we are!

I wish I could say that the efforts commenced in Paris have borne more fruit. Instead, they have brought on a General Assembly which we view with grave anxiety in view of the almost universal indignation of the Afro-Asians with France.

With my warm regards to Mrs. Gavin, and thanks for your many courtesies in Paris, I am,

Cordially yours,

To Mrs. Ronald Tree [203]

Friday night, August 18, 1961

M —

San Francisco was a success — except that I arrived at 4 AM! The speech was good; humor easy; crowd enormous (5000) and welcome like a campaign.[204] Considering that the local newspapers have had almost

[200] Stevenson's longtime aide William McCormick Blair, Jr., ambassador to Denmark, was to be married to Catherine Gerlach in Copenhagen on September 9, 1961.

[201] United States ambassador to France.

[202] Mongi Slim, Tunisian ambassador to the United States.

[203] This handwritten letter is in the possession of Mrs. Tree. It was written from Washington, D.C.

[204] Stevenson spoke to the International Astronomical Union in Berkeley, California, on August 15, 1961. His speech is reprinted in Stevenson, *Looking Outward*, pp. 151–160.

nothing good to say of me for 10 years, I don't understand why Calif. seems to always embrace me so warmly — but I like it! The astronomers were delightful — including 75 Russians — and no scholars have handled man made barriers like these explorers of a limitless exciting unknown.

Afterward J.F. [205] had a large cocktail party for my friends and his. Pat Brown [206] & wife came and we dined together afterward. His star is down, but rising perhaps a little as Knight [207] and Nixon [208] spar and feint about who will run for Governor. J.F. is *fine* — really — and what a relief it was to see him in such good form. His romance is on "the back of the stove" but she was there looking beautiful, more mature and self confident but still a little weird. Frankie [209] never looked him up and I think he felt really hurt. With his room[m]ate he has bought a sail boat — a lovely cabin sloop with auxiliary engine — and they sail around the bay after work and go on long cruises with friends on week ends — which makes a very good life.

It was hard to leave him; somehow he tugs at my hea[r]t the hardest of all. I had a glorious day with doctor and grandchildren and business at home [210] — including a visit from Alice Albright [211] — who has broken up her affair and seemed much relieved, and gushed away about Frankie etc etc. . . .

Now I am in Washington after a frustrating day with [Dean] Rusk, [George] Ball, Kennan [212] et al re Germany, Bizerte etc. JK sent word to come for breakfast, and then that he was leaving for Hyannis. [Harlan] Cleveland may move to the new aid agency.[213] But [Chester] Bowles now writes me that he can never make do he fears with Rusk and wants it.[214] We've added Arthur Dean [215] to the delegation — and I could go on & on. . . .

As for me I'm beset by people who say I *have* to go to [Bill] Blair's wedding on Wed Sept 6 returning Sunday the 9th. Perhaps I'll do it if my work is in shape and perhaps I'll go to Libertyville for Labor day —

205 John Fell Stevenson.
206 Edmund G. Brown, governor of California.
207 Goodwin Knight, governor of California, 1953–1959.
208 Former Vice President Richard M. Nixon, whom Governor Brown defeated in the 1962 gubernatorial election.
209 Frances FitzGerald, Mrs. Tree's daughter.
210 In Libertyville.
211 Niece of Alicia Patterson.
212 George F. Kennan, ambassador to Yugoslavia.
213 The Agency for International Development, which absorbed the functions of the International Cooperation Administration and the Development Loan Fund.
214 See Chester Bowles, *Promises to Keep: My Years in Public Life, 1941–1969* (New York: Harper & Row, 1971), pp. 619–625, for an earlier letter to Stevenson about his relationship with the Secretary of State.
215 Chairman of the United States delegation to the UN Conference on Law of the Sea in 1958 and 1960 and representative of the United States in negotiations at Panmunjom, Korea, in 1953 and 1954.

with a brief case. The planning for the G[eneral]. A[ssembly]. gets more and more complicated, thanks to China, Berlin, Bizerte, etc. . . .

It was 20 years ago today that my name first appeared on the front page of the N.Y. Times — in connection with the seizure by the Navy of the Kearney Shipyards.[216] What a 20 years it has been — and curiously not half as long as the past week.

Sunday — Foxlease Farm — Upperville — where I came for the night with the Archbolds [217] before going on to N.Y. this afternoon for some pre-assemb[l]y conferring with my "colleagues." With Rusk & Ball we worked on . . . Bourguiba's [218] envoy, for two hours yesterday for a milder resolution on Bizerte — in vain. I fear we will have to abstain — and lose more following among the Afro-Asians — to gain what in Paris?? [219] The expense of DeGaulle's friendship is getting intolerable, and I think the time has come to be very firm with him and Chiang [Kai-shek]. Rusk is coming to that conclusion too, and perhaps JK will too, with consequences for our alliances that are inevitable if not comfortable. . . .

I'm saying nothing — and it is very hard to stop —

Ever —

A

To Chester Bowles

August 20, 1961

Personal and Private

Dear Chet:

I have your letter of August 18 and see great merit in your suggestion of the aid post — especially if you *really want it*.[220] I don't consider it a

216 See *The Papers of Adlai E. Stevenson,* Vol. II, p. 9.

217 Mr. & Mrs. John D. Archbold. Mrs. Archbold, the former Bertrande Benoist, had known Stevenson since his world trip in 1953, when they had been seated at the captain's table of the S.S. *President Wilson.* See *The Papers of Adlai E. Stevenson,* Vol. V, p. 37. This letter was apparently not finished on August 18.

218 Habib Bourguiba, president of Tunisia.

219 Stevenson spoke on the Bizerte question on August 22 and 24, 1961, in the General Assembly. On August 25, the General Assembly adopted, by a vote of 66–0, a resolution calling for French troops to be pulled back to the base at Bizerte and calling their presence on Tunisian soil a violation of Tunisia's sovereignty. The resolution recognized Tunisia's right to demand withdrawal of the troops and called for immediate negotiations between the two countries to achieve a settlement. Although Stevenson wanted the United States to support the resolution, President Kennedy decided, in view of President Charles de Gaulle's shaky position (French generals in Algeria had mutinied in April), that the United States should abstain.

220 Mr. Bowles did not receive the appointment to the Agency for International Development. In November, 1961, he was removed as Under Secretary of State and made a roving ambassador in what was called the "Thanksgiving massacre."

come-down. I consider it a great leap up, in fact, from being just another Under Secretary, as far as that goes.

I have taken the liberty of trying the thing out at the White House and I think you will get some response by the time you get back. We can talk about it at your convenience.

Yours,

To J. W. Fulbright [221]

August 23, 1961

Dear Bill:

Seeing you the other night . . . reminded me that I have a couple of expensive Republican guest rooms in my Embassy, which are available for you and Betty.[222] I hope you will take advantage of them — and the opportunity to educate the Ambassador to the UN!

Besides, he has some troubles that he wants to talk to you about.

Yours,
ADLAI

To Henry Crown [223]

August 23, 1961

Dear Henry:

You have kindly suggested from time to time that I speak to you about my hotel problems in New York. Thus far I have not needed to bother you, and it is with great reluctance that I am bringing to your attention a problem that has arisen in connection with my apartment at the Waldorf Towers. As you know, the government has had this apartment for many years as the Embassy Residence of the U.S. Representative to the U.N. Earlier this year the Manager of the Waldorf asked us to increase the rent from $30,000 a year to $45,000. Due to the impossibility of getting action from Congress on short notice, he agreed to wait until the next budget which is now being prepared.

I am doubtful that the Congress will be willing to support such a large additional expense as this and it might well become necessary for me to look for other quarters. The Manager of the Waldorf has indicated the possibility that it might not be necessary to raise the rent if we gave up two bedrooms. These bedrooms are a great convenience to me for my family and friends and staff, as well as occasional important government

221 The original is in the possession of Mr. Fulbright.
222 Mrs. Fullbright.
223 A prominent Chicago business executive who was a director of the Waldorf Astoria Corporation.

officials passing through the city. I would therefore like to keep them.

However, there is something I could do; this year I will have two full time servants in the apartment [224] and we could dispense with much of the maid service now provided by the hotel.

I would greatly appreciate anything you felt you could do to help me — and the government! But if this would cause you any embarrassment, please don't hesitate to let me know. I am sure you realize that I will wholly understand — and I'll even forgive you *if* you come to see me sometime, preferably with wife. Indeed I would urge you to try those guest rooms sometime!

Sincerely yours,

To Harlan Cleveland [225]

August 24, 1961

It seems not unlikely that the subject of foreign bases will be carried over from the special General Assembly to the regular session. In this connection, I am informed that Cuba may attack the Guantanamo base as directed against Cuba and the struggle of Latin American nations for their independence. We should be prepared for a suitable reply.

I am informed that it is also likely that the Cubans in the General Assembly will refer sarcastically to Puerto Rico as "the so-called free, associated state of Puerto Rico which is neither free, nor associated, nor a state"; that it is a colony which shelters more than ten United States military bases, and that in Puerto Rico and Guantanamo mercenaries are being concentrated to launch attacks against a small, independent country.

We should also be prepared in the General Assembly for sharp and quick responses to any such attacks on our relationship with Puerto Rico.

A

To Mrs. Ernest L. Ives [226]

August 26, 1961

. . . I received some doilies from you, for which I am most grateful. I'm not quite sure what they're for, but there's no hurry about explaining that. Viola [Reardy] is still in Illinois looking after the children. I have been so busy and there is so little use for the apartment that I thought it best to leave her there where she is badly needed.

---

[224] Although Stevenson was considering hiring a second full-time servant, he never did.
[225] This document was declassified.
[226] The original is in E.S.I., I.S.H.L.

The special Assembly on Bizerte is over — thank God! I shall now have to settle down to the preparation for the General Assembly, but I hope to get out to Libertyville for the Labor Day weekend, or to Desbarats with the Smiths.[227] I have only had one day at home, on the way back from California last week, and yearn to see more of the children and grandchildren. Borden [Stevenson] seems in good shape, but he has left his job at Lazard Freres and is currently "unemployed." I hope he has done the right thing but it is hard to keep in communication with him. He has been sharing a house with some friends out in Westhampton during the summer and evidently enjoyed it immensely. I have recurrent and happy dreams of Florence and "the villa."

Love,
ADLAI

Ambassador John Kenneth Galbraith cabled the Department of State and wrote to President Kennedy from New Delhi objecting to the U.S. strategy to prevent the People's Republic of China from being admitted to the UN. The U.S. intended to make the issue an "important question" which would require a two-thirds majority vote for seating Peking. Galbraith termed it "ingenuous and patently bogus." [228]

To John Kenneth Galbraith

August 26, 1961

Dear Ken:

We have all enjoyed your letter about Chinese representation. How I wish you were here for a little conspiratorial reinforcement. I have spoken my piece many times, and I thought the matter was settled last March. Perhaps sometime we will have a chance to talk about this — but too late, I fear.

And after Cuba and now Bizerte, Stevenson is just about out of oratory! Or is the word "credibility"? But who am I to be talking to you about thorny paths, slings and arrows and such?

Well, as we Calvinists say, what is to be will be, whether it happens or not!

Yours,

---

227 Mr. and Mrs. Hermon Dunlap Smith had a summer home in Ontario which Stevenson frequently visited.

228 *Ambassador's Journal*, p. 195.

To Wilson W. Wyatt [229]

August 28, 1961

Dear Wilson:

I have been planning to write you about the Delegation to the General Assembly. After prolonged discussions here and in Washington, we have concluded that we would attempt to alter the practices of the past and convert the Delegation henceforth into a completely professional one, i.e., comprised of officers of the U.S. Mission and the State Department. The Senate has agreed but the House had demurred and insists on its two members for this year. The assumption is that after this year they will have equalized their participation with the Senate, and they too will step aside.

To accomplish this end, we have also had to advise George Meany [230] and Walter Reuther [231] that they cannot serve as Delegates, but would be welcome as consultants. Many others of the type that have served in the past have also been so advised.

This is particularly distressing to me because of your interest, and I hoped that you might be here to sustain me — on the floor, in the cloak-room, and in the bar — during the forthcoming ordeal. Besides, I would like to have some fun! I am sure you will understand the situation, however, and know how disappointed I am — especially on your account, if not on the account of the couple of hundred people who have applied for service on the Delegation this year.

And when are you coming to New York? My guest room is still awaiting your attention. My love to Ann. [232]

Yours,

To William McC. Blair, Jr.

August 29, 1961

Dear Bill:

Up to this minute I have cherished the idea that I could come to Copenhagen for the wedding, but today's additions to the accumulation of problems and provocations have persuaded me that I dare not attempt it.

---

[229] Lieutenant governor of Kentucky, who had been Stevenson's campaign manager in 1952.

[230] President of the American Federation of Labor and Congress of Industrial Organizations.

[231] Vice president of the American Federation of Labor and Congress of Industrial Organizations.

[232] Mrs. Wyatt.

I really am desperate; I try to be casual about it — I suspect more than anyone else. But now that I have lost a week on the Bizerte Assembly, I am desperate for time to get organized for the G[eneral] A[ssembly], which promises to be an acutely uncomfortable three months.

I even had reservations, which I will now relinquish with a groan of anguish.

Agnes Meyer and others have reported on your exemplary conduct and I feel very much isolated from the most important diplomatic development of the season.

I have contented myself with the thought that perhaps I can have a party for you and Deeda [233] when you come to New York. Please bear that in mind and don't commit all your time.

I have talked with Bill Attwood. His condition is bad, but could be far worse.[234] Evidently he was saved from a major catastrophe because he had taken the Salk vaccine shots, or at least some of them. I will try and see him the next time I am in Washington and give you a further report.

My love to Deeda and my deepest regret that I cannot be there to witness this historic event and wish you well.

Yours,

To Walter Mueller [235]

August 30, 1961

Dear Ambassador Mueller:

I have been distressed to learn that some remarks I made about conditions in Chile after my recent visit, in response to questions in the House Foreign Affairs Committee,[236] have embarrassed the Chilean Government. I am confident that you yourself know that I have too much admiration and affection for your country and countrymen to do or say anything intentionally to cause Chile difficulty or offense.

I think you also know that I have spoken and written admiringly about the strength and character and gallant efforts of President [Jorge] Alessandri to restore fiscal responsibility and to advance in an orderly and constructive way the economic interests of his country.

On my return from this last visit, I tried to give the House and Senate Committees and my fellow countrymen a clearer idea of the problems as

---

[233] Catherine Gerlach, Mr. Blair's fiancée.

[234] Ambassador Attwood had contracted polio in Guinea. See William Attwood, *The Reds and the Blacks: A Personal Adventure* (New York: Harper & Row, 1967), pp. 55–57.

[235] Ambassador of Chile to the United States.

[236] Stevenson testified on June 26, 1961. See Hearings before the Committee on Foreign Affairs, House of Representatives, 87th Congress, 1st Session, on H.R. 7372 (Washington: Government Printing Office, 1961).

well as the accomplishments of the people of Latin America, hoping thereby to demonstrate the vital importance of our close cooperation and of our "Alliance for Progress."

During those discussions, I presented my frank and personal views. While there has been a widespread increase of general interest concerning the problems of Latin America, the "Alliance for Progress" will be successful only if there is full and genuine understanding by the informed citizenry of the United States and their counterparts in the other American republics concerning the challenges and opportunities confronting all of us at this critical moment. It is most important, therefore, that the essential public discussion preceding any significant implementation of a new public policy such as the "Alliance" rest upon a clear appreciation of the problems involved.

It was in this spirit that I made my comments regarding economic, social and political conditions prevailing among the South American countries I visited. I had not the slightest intention to detract in any way from the extraordinary accomplishments of the Chilean Government under the leadership of President Alessandri in controlling inflation, stabilizing the Chilean economy, and laying the foundations so necessary for continuing growth and progress. I have spoken and written with admiration of these achievements, publicly and privately, many times following my visits in 1960 and 1961. President Alessandri's program has, of course, been supported by my Government, and it is my sincere hope that the joint efforts of our two countries will bring about still more progress in Chile.

With my warm personal regards to you and Mrs. Mueller, I am

Sincerely yours,

To Lady Barbara Jackson

September 1, 1961

Dearest Barbara:

Instead of writing you, I should be listening to you at this very moment, surrounded by the centuries at Oxford. But the multiplying difficulties here compel me to send word to Bill Blair that I can't even get over there for my old friend's wedding — not that I would be missed among 140 foreign guests!

Your letter of the 22nd was most welcome, and comes just as I am leaving for Libertyville for the Labor Day weekend — my summer holiday! — with the children. And I pray that the weekend won't be spoiled by a summons due to Berlin or nuclear testing or some other horror.[237]

[237] After the Soviet Union resumed nuclear testing in the atmosphere, President Kennedy on September 5, 1961, ordered resumption of U.S. underground tests.

I think you put your finger on or very close to precisely what I was going to ask you to do — a speech directed to the uncommitted. The Soviet have made it clear that they are going to play colonialism for all it's worth again, and such items as Bizerte, Algeria, Angola, South Africa, South-west Africa and the Congo all offer opportunities. Unless we are in a position to support positive action on most of these items, we cannot expect support on some things that interest us, like Berlin. This may mean a break with France on Bizerte and Algeria. It also means that we must be able on other issues to take the initiative in encouraging resolutions which go beyond those of last year; otherwise, we will face sanctions-type resolutions which we cannot vote for and which will therefore make us appear unsympathetic. If we could get ourselves in a position to support some such call for independence in a specified time as the Nigerian ten-year deadline, we could perhaps insist on adding language which at least obliquely made it clear that self-determination applies to Europeans as well as to the rest of the world.

I think what I am trying to say to you is that we confront some horrendous decisions here, on which I have been driving hard since the beginning, as you know. I think a speech which properly mixes support for the ambitions of the uncommitted with a ringing attack on the hypocrisy of the Soviet Union in Eastern Europe will be imperative sometime early in the session. We have made very little of the issue of self-determination in Eastern Europe, and have let the Soviet Union play this theme ad nauseam while they deny East Germany and Eastern Europe any vestige of self-determination — even with tanks, c.f. Hungary. But I fear that so many of these uncommitted peoples don't equate self-determination with white against white, but only white against black, or brown, etc.

So please, please let me have just what you suggested, the kind of speech you think might make sense to the uncommitted and that hits the Russian hypocrisy a shattering blow.

A major initiative of the United States in the Assembly is going to be disarmament — thank Heavens! [238] And I honestly believe that we will come up with a good plan for general and complete disarmament which, properly handled, should vastly enhance our reputation for sincerity and leadership, especially after the resumption of testing by the Soviet Union.

Stevenson at a meeting with Kennedy that day expressed his regret over the decision. See Davis, *The Politics of Honor*, p. 467. Stevenson issued a statement on August 31 on the Soviet announcement of resumption of nuclear testing (USUN press release 3764), and on September 21 he spoke in the General Committee of the UN General Assembly on "The Urgent Need for a Treaty to Ban Nuclear Weapons Tests Under Effective International Control" (USUN press release 3772).

[238] On November 15, Stevenson spoke on disarmament in Committee 1 (Political and Security Committee) of the General Assembly. His speech was published in Stevenson, *Looking Outward*, pp. 40–52.

Neutralists, led as usual by India, will undoubtedly try to water everything down to conciliate the Soviet Union. So I shall need all the eloquence I can summon on this issue, too. If you have some language for
general passages, please let me have that, too.

But perhaps the simplest thing to say is to ask you to send along any
ideas you think should be expressed in the forthcoming Assembly, and
I'll fit them in here and there. I think ideas like the Atlantic Community are useful for general speech material for me, but less so in the
UN.

I have put October 7 on the schedule and will welcome that travel-
worn object with the usual joy. And let me warn you that you shall have
to fight hard to hold your own in the torrential exchange of uncommitted
gossip. . . .

With much love from your harassed Ambassador, — and all the
Stevensons —

p.s. Another subject sure to have a terrific workout is bases around the
world. We had a preview during the Bizerte discussion. Any considered
reflections on this subject would likewise be useful ammunition.

To Alicia Patterson [239]

[No date] [240]

The lady said she was arriving on the 24th for a briefing on the world
situation; the Secretary said she was arriving on the 30th. Well — the
briefing can wait, also the world. But what about the briefer?

BRIEFER

p.s. What about Wed. night Sept. 6 — IF I'm not stuck in Wash. and
if there is no Security Council meeting re Berlin or nuclear testing! And
would the lady be good enough to notify Roxane Eberlein, Yu 6-2424, if
she could keep Wed. night available for confirmation and perhaps stay
at the Embassy which would be a kindness, perhaps a convenience?

*On September 5, Stevenson, Dean Rusk, Harlan Cleveland and several
of the President's White House aides conferred with Kennedy. Rusk
asked whether Stevenson could discreetly inform other delegations that
the United States in the 1962 General Assembly might recommend a
two-China approach, in which Peking and Taiwan would each have its*

---

[239] This handwritten letter is in the possession of Adlai E. Stevenson III. It is
written on Libertyville stationery.
[240] Probably September 2 or 3, 1961.

own seat in the Assembly.[241] *Kennedy authorized Stevenson to do this, adding: "You have the hardest thing in the world to sell. It really doesn't make any sense — the idea that Taiwan represents China. But, if we lost this fight, if Red China comes into the UN during our first year in town, your first year and mine, they'll run us both out. We have to lick them this year. We'll take our chances next year. It will be an election year; but we can delay the admission of Red China till after the election."*[242]

On September 12, Stevenson was again in Washington. He, Arthur Schlesinger and John Kenneth Galbraith, who had returned from India for consultations, had dinner with Mr. and Mrs. Chester Bowles. Galbraith wrote that Bowles, Schlesinger and Stevenson "all talked mournfully" about foreign policy. When Schlesinger mentioned columnist Joseph Alsop's view that world public opinion was unimportant, "Adlai was outraged."[243]

On September 18, Dag Hammarskjöld was killed in a plane crash in Central Africa. Two days later Stevenson spoke to the General Assembly.

HE BELONGS TO ALL MANKIND [244]

. . . It is my privilege to express, on behalf of my delegation and of the people and the government of the United States, our profound sorrow and our deep distress at the tragic death of the Secretary-General, Dag Hammarskjöld. In his passing the community of nations has lost one of the greatest servants it ever had — a brilliant mind and a brave and compassionate spirit.

I doubt if any living man has done more to further the search for a world in which men solve their problems by peaceful means and not by force than this gallant friend of us all. Indeed, he gave his life in a mission of peace — a mission to persuade men to lay down their arms that reason might prevail over force. That his mission was fulfilled this afternoon by a cease-fire in Katanga is a fitting epitaph for this soldier of peace.

Dag Hammarskjöld was the very embodiment of the international civil servant — as the Secretary-General of the United Nations should ideally and always be. He was resolutely impartial, resolutely even-handed and

241 Harlan Cleveland wrote: "But JFK's promise to float a two-China proposal the following year (1962) was sidetracked by China's invasion of Northern India, which caused even Krishna Menon, Adlai's opposite number at the UN, to lose his enthusiasm for seating Peking." Memorandum to Walter Johnson, April 30, 1973.

242 Schlesinger, *A Thousand Days*, p. 483.

243 Galbraith, *Ambassador's Journal*, p. 206.

244 United Nations, *Official Records*, General Assembly, September 20, 1961, p. 14. This speech and Stevenson's address after the funeral service in Sweden are published in Stevenson, *Looking Outward*, pp. 24–29.

resolutely firm in carrying out the mandates with which he was entrusted. He never swerved from what he conceived to be his duty to the United Nations and to the cause of peace. He never wavered under irresponsible invective and unjust criticism.

Mr. Hammarskjöld's skill as a diplomatist was admired in every chancellory of the world, and it was attested to many times when leaders who could not bring themselves to confide in each other were glad to confide in him.

But closer to his heart than the urgent tasks of diplomacy, and more enduring in its value for humanity, is the ideal to whose realization he contributed so greatly in his capacity as head of the Secretariat. That ideal has become an increasing reality; for its sake a great price has already been paid: the ideal of an international civil service whose members are available in fair weather and foul to do the work of the community, and if need be to uphold it with their lives.

Since the founding of the United Nations thirty-four United Nations official and Secretariat members have given their lives in the line of their international duty. Mr. Hammarskjöld and the five Secretariat members who died with him are the latest names on this roll of honor. Every nation has its heroes. But what these people died for, and what thousands of their colleagues still labour for, is something more universal, something which transcends all national and regional interests and all ideologies of power and conquest: the world community of nations.

The future of that community is in great measure in our hands: to build or to destroy; to uphold or to neglect. Today it is only half formed. It is beset with danger and with forbidding problems. But it is the hope of man, it has need of the best energies and the finest talents which we, its members, can put at its service.

Dag Hammarskjöld once said, at a moment of crisis in his life and that of this organization, "The man does not count; the institution does." [245] Yet institutions are made to serve man and it is from the greatest men that they derive their character and their strength.

The memory of this one man — humane, cultured, judicious, possessed of a poetic and philosophic vision, free of passion — other than a passion for the rule of reason and decency — modest and brave, this memory will always be with us as a reminder of the best that the United Nations can be, and of the qualities which it demands of us all.

In closing, let me suggest that the most fitting tribute the United Nations can pay to Dag Hammarskjöld is that he should be buried here by the river at this Headquarters of the Organization to which he gave his life. I suggest this with, of course, final deference to the wishes of his

[245] See United Nations, *Official Records*, General Assembly, Fifteenth Session, Part I, 883rd Meeting, para. 9.

family and of the Government of Sweden whose great son he was, and in the belief, which I know is widely held, that he belongs to all mankind.[246]

I should like to suggest to my fellow delegates that a suitable memorial be provided as a permanent tangible tribute to Mr. Hammarskjöld and to the ideals which he served so nobly, preferably a living memorial to advance the work for peace and international understanding which was his life. I make this suggestion in the knowledge that no memorial, no tribute, can ever be adequate, and that Dag Hammarskjöld's true memorial will be the great new institution in the family of man which it is our duty to build and to nourish.

There is a poem by the great Indian poet Rabindranath Tagore which contains these lyric lines:

> Listen to the rumbling of the clouds, O heart
> of mine.
> Be brave, break through and leave for the
> unknown. . . .

We are indebted to Mr. [James] Reston of the New York *Times* for reminding us this morning of what Mr. Hammarskjöld's response was when these words of Tagore were quoted to him. He said, "I think that these lines express in a very noble way the attitude we must take to this venture called the United Nations. We may listen to the rumbling of the clouds, but we can never afford to lose that kind of confidence in ourselves and in the wisdom of man which makes us brave enough to break through and leave, always leave for the unknown."

Mr. Hammarskjöld has left for the unknown, but bravely and in the cause of us all.

To Leslie N. Jones [247]

September 19, 1961

Dear Les:

I have just noticed that my telephone bill at Libertyville (EM 2-4466) is $36.25 per month for "telephone service," exclusive of all of the other calls.

In view of the fact that I only live there a few days during the year and will be away from there now indefinitely, I wonder if there is some way to discontinue this monthly service charge and bill me only for the calls

---

[246] Mr. Hammarskjöld was buried in Uppsala, Sweden, following services held there.

[247] General counsel of the Illinois Bell Telephone Company and a former associate in Stevenson's old law firm, Cutting, Moore and Sidley in Chicago.

actually made when my son and family are there on occasional weekends.
This is doubtless a too complicated problem for you or your staff, but
I think that occasionally you should have some contact with the cus-
tomers — especially after paying this charge for many years!

Yours,

p.s. If they want to eliminate some extensions, I would be glad to
have them eliminate the one in the library, leaving three.

p.p.s. When are you coming for breakfast and a little enlightenment?

*Theodore Sorensen, Kennedy's White House aide, with the help of
McGeorge Bundy, Kennedy's special assistant for national security, was
drafting the speech the President was to deliver to the General Assembly
of the United Nations on September 25, 1961.*

To Theodore C. Sorensen

September 20, 1961

Dear Ted:

I have been able to spend about eight minutes reading the draft speech,
and have passed my hurried, superficial comments along to McGeorge
Bundy.

I enclose a lot of stuff that I'm afraid comes too late to be of any possible help to you. I would treat it as a quarry and extract a stone here and
there, if you have the time to bother with it — and can find any stones!

Yours,

*Senator Joseph S. Clark of Pennsylvania had an informal group of
congressmen meet with Stevenson to hear him discuss the long-range
prospects for peace and disarmament. Clark wrote that Stevenson's ability
to articulate sound long-range goals was "inspiring."*

To Joseph S. Clark

September 21, 1961

Dear Joe:

You flatter me by asking for my notes, after those dreadful, disorderly,
and depressing remarks. If there were any notes, I prepared them in your
bedroom the night before, and hastily destroyed them after the event.

But I enjoyed the evening more than I can tell you, and a visit with
you becomes ever more precious as the years slip away.

Yours,

President Kennedy spoke to the General Assembly of the United Nations on September 25, 1961. Theodore C. Sorensen wrote: "It was a critical moment in the life of that body, the most critical in its sixteen-year history. The Soviet Union, angered in particular by the UN peace-keeping operation in the Congo, was slowly strangling the organization financially, disrupting its progress and insisting upon three Secretary-Generals." Sorensen added, "But the President believed the UN had to have a future. He hoped he could help to rekindle its hope." [248]

Kennedy told the General Assembly, "We meet in an hour of grief and challenge. Dag Hammarskjöld is dead. But the United Nations lives on. . . . The problem is not the death of one man; the problem is the life of this organization." He urged the General Assembly to reject the Russian proposal for a troika since this would paralyze the United Nations. In the nuclear age the world needed the UN more than ever before, for "a nuclear disaster, spread by wind and water and fear, could well engulf the great and the small. . . . Mankind must put an end to war — or war will put an end to mankind. . . . Let us call a truce to terror." The goal of disarmament, he stated, "is no longer a dream — it is a practical matter of life or death." The President called for negotiations to continue "without interruption until an entire program for general and complete disarmament has not only been agreed but has been actually achieved." The logical place to start, Kennedy declared, was a nuclear test ban treaty.[249] Arthur M. Schlesinger, Jr., wrote: "The momentum of his words, sustained by Stevenson's effective leadership in New York, continued throughout the session." [250] Theodore C. Sorensen wrote of the subsequent session of the General Assembly: "Skillful negotiations, conducted chiefly by Ambassador Stevenson, played a major role. But the President had provided a fresh impetus when it was needed." [251]

During the session the troika proposal was defeated and U Thant of Burma became first the acting Secretary-General, then Secretary-General. (For weeks Stevenson was immersed in the politics of the succession). Steps were taken for new negotiations on disarmament. The General Assembly called for a treaty to ban nuclear tests and authorized a $200 million bond issue to pay for the UN operation in the Congo.

After President Kennedy delivered his speech to the General Assembly, Jane Dick made a sympathetic remark to Stevenson, observing that he might have been addressing the Assembly in that role.

[248] *Kennedy*, pp. 520–521.
[249] New York *Times*, September 26, 1961.
[250] *A Thousand Days*, p. 486.
[251] *Kennedy*, p. 522.

To Mrs. Edison Dick [252]

[no date]

Jane

Bless you! I'm glad someone knows how I occasionally feel!!

I must be in Wash[ington] tomorrow evening for Haile Selassie [253] and will miss . . . reception — and you again!

But it can't be this way forever. . . .

To Theodore C. Sorensen

September 27, 1961

Dear Ted:

I have heard a lot of speeches — good, bad and indifferent. That one was superb!

An old ghost sends his homage to a young one.

Yours,

To Harlan Cleveland

September 27, 1961

Dear Harlan:

I have your letter about the speech drafting problem. My impression is that your writing talents are better than ours and that the first draft for my consideration should be prepared there rather than here.

However, I will proceed on any basis you suggest, but I hate to see Dick Pedersen [254] have to take on anything more, and the limited writing talents hereabouts are sorely pressed as it is.

After prolonged deliberation I have concluded that we propose to the Russians that they ask the Pope to set up a committee of consultation to explain to us how the Holy Trinity works.

Yours,

After attending the funeral of Dag Hammarskjöld in Sweden, Stevenson visited Mr. and Mrs. William McC. Blair in Denmark.

---

[252] This handwritten note is in the possession of Mrs. Dick.
[253] Emperor of Ethiopia.
[254] Richard F. Pedersen, senior adviser for political and security affairs at USUN.

To William McC. Blair, Jr.

October 6, 1961

Dear Bill:

I am mortified that I haven't written you before this — but you know my troubles and my habits! I have reported to Mesdames [Mary] Lasker, [Marietta] Tree, etc., and to sundry gentlemen on my visit with you. My only anxiety is that the picture of charming domestic bliss will bring them all over for a visit. And I wish another visit was in prospect for me, too. I had just enough to whet my appetite, and yearn for more of the Blairs and Denmark.

I miss you!

Yours,

To Andrei A. Gromyko

October 6, 1961

Dear Andrei:

When I saw you the other day,[255] I did not have an opportunity to mention to you the cases of separated families in which, as you know, I have long been interested. I am therefore taking the liberty of sending you now a list of people in the Soviet Union who have applied for permits to join their families in the United States. These are all instances of the separation of very close relatives, and I feel they are deserving of compassionate consideration by the Soviet authorities.

I have been deeply touched by the joy and gratitude of those families that have been reunited in recent years through the favorable action of your Government, and I hope very much that it will be found possible to take similar action in the cases I am now bringing to your attention.

With all good wishes,

Sincerely yours,

To Byron R. White [256]

October 9, 1961

Dear Mr. White:

I have been trying for some time to find a moment to call you about Carl McGowan, whose name is under consideration, I understand, for a district judgeship in Chicago.

[255] Mr. Gromyko was attending the General Assembly meetings in New York.
[256] Deputy Attorney General in the Department of Justice and later an associate justice of the United States Supreme Court.

I have tried to avoid imposing on you and Bobby Kennedy unduly in the matter of judgeships. As you imagine, many people bespeak my intervention. But Carl McGowan is different. He has asked for nothing, and won't. But I don't hesitate to say that he is incomparably qualified. Indeed, I am reminded that when I appointed Judge [Walter] Schaefer to the Illinois Supreme Court,[257] it was over the agonized protests of the Democratic organization. Within two years, they tried to induce him to run for Governor on the ticket, and again four years later!

I am sure you have Carl's dossier. He worked for me for years in the Navy and my law firm and as Governor,[258] and I have never had anyone, several in high places in Washington included, who could match his talent, skill, probity and diligence.

He is a great lawyer. Besides that, he doesn't want to be anything else!

Cordially yours,

To Mrs. Franklin D. Roosevelt [259]

October 11, 1961

Dear Mrs. R —

Among the blessings I count daily, and never more than on your birthday, is the honor of calling such a great lady my colleague and dear friend.

As always, I send you devoted love,

ADLAI [260]

To William Benton [261]

October 14, 1961

Dear Bill:

The lovely cufflinks have arrived. Bless you — again! You have sent me so many gifts, and this is useful and attractive, as usual.

I am obliged to remark at this point that one day this week I misplaced the money clip you gave me, with a large part of my fortune attached! [262] I am still living in hopes that it will turn up somewhere, but the search has been vain so far. I had come to use that handsome golden ornament continuously, and it was a reminder every day of our "collaboration" which means so much to me.

[257] See *The Papers of Adlai E. Stevenson*, Vol. III, p. 333.
[258] See *The Papers of Adlai E. Stevenson*, Vol. II, Vol. III.
[259] The original is in the Franklin D. Roosevelt Library, Hyde Park, New York.
[260] Mrs. Roosevelt replied on October 13, 1961: "I am touched and pleased that you had time to remember me. . . ."
[261] The original is in the possession of the estate of William Benton. See note 168, above.
[262] He lost about two hundred dollars, but it was found about a month later.

I was distressed about the meetings. Actually, it was not Cuba [263] but the negotiations on the Secretary General and a threatened meeting of the Security Council that compelled me to change my plans at the last moment. . . .

What would you think about lunch on next Tuesday, October 17, at my flat? If that's convenient, please telephone my office.

Yours,
ADLAI

To Alicia Patterson [264]

October 15, 1961

Dearest Elisha [265] —

Happy birthday! I love you, even if you are a little more than mature [266] — !

ADLAI

To Mrs. Adlai E. Stevenson, III

October 17, 1961

CHEERS, LOVE AND CONGRATULATIONS FOR THE INCOMPARABLE DAUGHTERINLAW. I HATE THE FATE THAT ALWAYS SEPARATES US ON SUCH ANNIVERSARIES.[267] PRESENT TO FOLLOW, AND ME, TOO, FRIDAY A WEEK.   LOVE

GOV

To Mrs. Ernest L. Ives [268]

October 19, 1961

Dear Buffie:

Life has been so frenetic here that I have had no opportunity to tell you properly that I enjoyed your visit! Everything at the house is going well, except that I have lost my money and gold clip and suffered some other minor misfortunes. The work is at the same absurd pace, but I seem to

---

263 Stevenson spoke in the General Assembly on October 10 on charges by Cuba that the United States was an aggressor.

264 This handwritten letter is in the possession of Adlai E. Stevenson III.

265 In a telegram Miss Patterson once sent to Stevenson, Western Union in transmission changed the signature to "Elisha," to the amusement of both Stevenson and Miss Patterson.

266 She was fifty-five.

267 It was her twenty-seventh birthday. Mrs. Stevenson remarked: "That telegram is a minor example of the qualities that made him the Incomparable Father in Law." Letter to John Woodman, January 23, 1978.

268 The original is in E.S.I., I.S.H.L.

keep going, with a frustrating feeling of inadequate time for proper thought and preparation.

I understand that the alabaster boxes and ash trays are to be forwarded on to you. I have asked Viola [Reardy] to attend to it. I only hope that they come through without breakage. I could have brought them out myself as far as Libertyville. . . .

I understand you are organizing an AAUN [American Association for the United Nations] chapter in Bloomington, and I am pleased, of course. But I hope it isn't too much of an effort. The clipping from Edgar Mowrer [269] was what one has to expect from him. But far more discouraging is the everlasting backbiting and negativism of Dean Acheson.[270]

. . . Please let me know your plans, and how Ernest is doing.

Love,
ADLAI

Early in October, 1961, Stevenson recommended that the President announce that if the Russians would discontinue nuclear testing immediately and conclude a treaty within thirty days, the United States would institute a thirty-day moratorium on testing. If the Soviet Union rejected this, the United States would then have to press on with testing. At a meeting at the White House on October 10, to which Stevenson was not invited, his suggestion was ignored. On October 12 and 17, Stevenson sent memoranda to Kennedy, restating his position. In the latter memorandum Stevenson wrote that he was "disturbed" that the United States was contemplating a new series of tests at Eniwetok. The U.S. held Micronesia under a United Nations trusteeship, he explained, and the Micronesians had bitterly resented earlier tests. "The moral question," he stated, "should really control." However, Stevenson was overruled in Washington, and on October 19, he announced to the Political Committee of the General Assembly a policy that in private he had opposed.[271]

---

[269] Longtime foreign correspondent for the Chicago *Daily News*. The clipping is not identifiable.

[270] Acheson, a "hard-liner" toward the Soviet Union, advocated the use of military force in case the U.S.S.R. blocked access to Berlin. He viewed as "soft" Stevenson, Chester Bowles, and others who criticized European colonialism and advocated assistance to the underdeveloped world. For a discussion of their differences, see Schlesinger, *A Thousand Days*, pp. 299–300.

[271] For a discussion of this, see John Bartlow Martin, *Adlai Stevenson and the World* (Garden City, New York: Doubleday, 1977), pp. 669–672.

NUCLEAR DEATH DANCE: THE NEED FOR A TEST BAN TREATY [272]

An emergency confronts this committee and the world! The Soviet Union is now nearing the conclusion of a massive series of nuclear weapon tests. Unless something is done quickly, the Soviet testing will necessarily result in further testing by my country and perhaps by others.

There is still time to halt this drift toward the further refinement and multiplication of these weapons. Perhaps this will be the last clear chance to reverse this tragic trend. For if testing is stopped, the terrible pace of technological progress will be decisively retarded. A ban on tests is, of course, only the first step; and the control and destruction of nuclear and thermonuclear weapons is the ultimate goal. But it is an indispensable first step.

Accordingly, I must inform the committee that the United States is obliged in self-protection to reserve the right to make preparations to test in the atmosphere, as well as underground.

But the United States stands ready to resume negotiations for a treaty tomorrow. We will devote all our energies to the quickest possible conclusion of these negotiations, either here or in Geneva. If the Soviet Union will do the same and stop its tests, there is no reason why a treaty with effective controls cannot be signed in thirty days and this suicidal business ended before it ends us.

But, I repeat, unless a treaty can be signed, and signed promptly, the United States has no choice but to prepare and take the action necessary to protect its own security and that of the world community.

I trust that this expression of hope for the triumph of reason will convey some measure of the depth of our feeling about the subject and of our desire to do our share to save the human race from a greater menace than the plagues which once ravaged Europe. We believe we have done our share, and more, ever since the United States proposals of 1946.[273] I remind you that if those proposals had been accepted by the Soviet Union, no state would now have nuclear weapons; and we would not now be in such a perilous crisis.

I have claimed the privilege [274] of making this declaration for the

272 This speech is reprinted in Stevenson, *Looking Outward*, pp. 33–39.
273 *International Control of Atomic Energy: Growth of a Policy*, Department of State Publication No. 2702 (Washington: Government Printing Office, n.d.). For an analysis of the "Baruch" plan, see Alice Kimball Smith, *A Peril and a Hope: The Scientists' Movement in America, 1945–47* (Cambridge: M.I.T. Press, 1970), pp. 331–343.
274 Usually deputies to the permanent representatives spoke in the various committees.

United States because few delegates, I dare say, feel more deeply about this matter than I do, in part, perhaps, because I proposed that nuclear tests be stopped almost six years ago — and lost a great many votes in the 1956 Presidential election as a result! [275] Had the nuclear powers agreed even then, think how much safer and healthier the world would be today.

I pray we do not lose still another chance to meet the challenge of our times and stop this dance of death.

I confess a feeling of futility when I consider the immensity of the problems which confront us and the feebleness of our efforts to deal promptly with them. We have lived for sixteen years in the Atomic Age. During these years we have ingeniously and steadily improved man's capacity to blow up the planet. But we have done little to improve man's control over the means of his own destruction. Instead, we have worried and wrangled and talked and trifled while time trickles away, and the hands of the clock creep toward midnight.

I would not imply that the problems of control are easy. Just as the nuclear bomb itself lays open the inner mysteries of science, so the attempt to control the nuclear bomb cuts to the core of our political ideas and mechanisms. As the bomb itself represented a revolution in science, so the control of the bomb may in the end mean a revolution in politics.

But we must not let the very immensity of the problem dwarf our minds and our calculations. We must act — and we must take hold of the problem where we can. One obvious way is to tackle the question of nuclear testing.

No one would argue that the abolition of testing would itself solve all our problems. It would mean only a small beginning in the assault on the evil, ancient institution of war. But, in a world of no beginnings, a small beginning shines forth like the morning sun on the distant horizon. We have talked long enough about the horror which hangs over us. Now is the time for us to get down to business — to fight this horror, not with soft words and wistful hopes, but with the hard weapon of effective international arrangements.

This view shapes our attitude toward the Indian resolution.[276] As I have said, we share the hatred of the sponsors for the whole wretched business of nuclear testing. We are just as determined to stop the spread of such weapons to countries not now possessing them, the contamination of the atmosphere and the bellowing threat of nuclear war. We want to stop these things dead before they stop us — dead!

The world now knows from bitter experience that an uninspected moratorium will not secure the results which the sponsors of the resolu-

[275] See *The Papers of Adlai E. Stevenson*, Vol. VI.
[276] This resolution called for a moratorium on testing, not a treaty.

tion seek. For almost three years, representatives of the Soviet Union, the United Kingdom and the United States met at Geneva to work out a plan to bring nuclear testing to a definitive end. Significant progress was made. The conference adopted a preamble, seventeen articles and two annexes of a draft treaty.

When President Kennedy took office, he ordered an immediate review of United States policy in order to overcome the remaining obstacles to a final agreement. At Geneva, the United States and the United Kingdom submitted comprehensive treaty proposals aimed at ending the fear of nuclear tests and radioactive fallout through a pledge by all signatory nations to cease all tests of nuclear weapons, a pledge backed and secured by effective international inspection.

But the representatives of the Soviet Union reacted very oddly to this generous and determined attempt to reach an agreement. They rejected positions they had already accepted. They renounced agreements they had already made. The whole world familiar with this subject wondered at this Soviet performance. Experts pondered their tea leaves and produced laborious speculation to explain the Soviet change of heart. Alas, we understand today the brutal simplicity of the reasoning behind the Soviet reversal.

We now know that the Soviet representatives at Geneva had long since ceased to negotiate in good faith. We now know that, while Mr. Tsarapkin [277] was delaying action at Geneva, the Soviet scientists and engineers and generals were secretly laying plans for the resumption of nuclear testing — and worse than that, for the resumption of testing in the atmosphere.

Let us make no mistake about it. You cannot decide to resume testing on Monday and actually resume on Tuesday. A sequence of tests of the sort with which the Soviet Union is currently edifying the world requires many, many months of preparation.

In an open society, like ours in the United States, such preparation simply could not be undertaken in secrecy. But in a closed society, like the Soviet Union, almost anything can be done without publicity or disclosure.

And so, while the Soviet representatives condemned nuclear testing at Geneva, the Soviet Government prepared for nuclear tests in Russia. Then they announced their decision to resume testing just two days before the unaligned nations gathered at Belgrade. With no apparent motives except intimidation and terror, Chairman Khrushchev boasted about his 100-megaton bombs.

Today, seven weeks after the Soviet Union began to test nuclear

[277] Semyon Konstantinovich Tsarapkin, head of the Soviet delegation to the Geneva disarmament talks, 1961–1966.

weapons again, and after it had tested more than a score, the Soviet Union has finally told its own people that its nuclear explosions are actually under way. Cushioning the shock, the Soviet leaders announced the *end* of the current series instead of the *beginning*. And Mr. Khrushchev has decided to bring the Soviet program to a crashing conclusion with a 50-megaton bomb.

Are we supposed to be grateful that Chairman Khrushchev has decided not to reach at a single leap his announced goal of the 100-megaton bomb?

As everyone knows, there is no military purpose whatever in such gigantic weapons. For years the United States has been able to build such weapons. But we are not interested in the business of intimidation or bigger blasts.

Now, in a single instant, the Soviet Union intends to poison the atmosphere by creating more radioactivity than that produced by any series since 1945. It may interest the members of this committee to know that from this one test, the 30–60 degree North Latitude band of the world where 80 percent of all of the people of the world live can expect to receive two-thirds as much new fallout as was produced by *all* of the fallout produced by *all* of the tests since 1945. Why must they insist on exploding a 50-megaton bomb? It is not a military necessity.

And no doubt, when the present series of tests reaches its cataclysmic conclusion, the Soviet Union will piously join in the movement for an uninspected moratorium.

Let us be absolutely clear what another such moratorium means. It is clear that it serves neither the cause of peace nor of international collaboration, nor of confidence among nations. We were all in this trap before. We cannot afford to enter it again, and the United States will not.

We do not believe that nuclear testing will ever be abolished by exorcism. It will be abolished only by action. So I plead with the members of this Assembly, which has been called the *conscience* of the world, to demand — not more words, but more deeds.

Standing alone, a treaty banning nuclear weapons would be an immense leap forward toward sanity. It would be a tangible gain for humanity. It would slow down the arms race. It would eliminate all dangers from poisonous materials cast off by nuclear explosions in the atmosphere. It would check the multiplication of new types of nuclear weapons and discourage their spread to additional nations, thereby reducing the hazard of accidental war. Above all, it would mark a great adventure in international collaboration for peace.

Out of our experience with a test ban treaty can come a mutual confidence, the tested procedures and the concerted policies which will enable the world to mount a wider and deeper attack on war itself. If nations can set up a collective system which abolishes nuclear tests, surely they can hope to set up a collective system which abolishes all the diverse and manifest weapons of self-destruction.

The world is asking for bread. Another moratorium resolution would offer it not even a stone. The United States stands ready today, as we have stood ready for many months, to sign a treaty outlawing nuclear tests. As I have said, until such a treaty is signed, we have no choice as a responsible nation but to reserve our freedom of action.

So, at the risk of repetition, let me state again the position of the United States. The current Soviet nuclear test series is approaching its announced conclusion. While thorough analysis of the Soviet tests will require some time, it is already competely clear that they will intensify competition in the development of more and more deadly nuclear weapons. Thus these tests have increased the possibility of ultimate disaster for all of mankind.

There is only one safe and sure way to stop nuclear tests, and to stop them quickly. That is to conclude a treaty prohibiting all nuclear weapons tests under effective controls.

In the last three years the negotiations at Geneva made significant progress toward such a treaty. The United States is still willing and eager to resume these negotiations. If in this fateful moment all three countries involved will really devote their skills and ingenuity to achieve agreement, not evasion, deceit and equivocation, there is, I say, no reason why a nuclear test ban treaty with effective controls cannot be signed within thirty days.

United States negotiators are ready to sit down at the table with Soviet and British representatives for this purpose. But until there is a treaty and tests can be stopped, the United States must prepare to take all steps necessary to protect its own security.

An uninspected moratorium will only lead the world once again into the morass of confusion and deceit. A test ban treaty is the path to peace.

If the Soviet Union really wants to stop nuclear testing, we challenge it to join us now in signing a test ban treaty.

To Robert F. Goheen [278]

October 20, 1961

Dear Bob:

The old, true saying, "Nothing succeeds like success," came to my mind when I heard of the magnificent gift that Princeton has received for a new program of professional education for public service in the Woodrow Wilson School. That our University was chosen for such a

[278] President of Princeton University.

foundation is but one more sign of the fertile soil provided by a strong and vital institution.

It must be obvious to every alumnus that that strength and that vitality cannot be maintained by standing still. If we are to continue as a lodestone for advanced scholarship, we must ceaselessly improve the basic facilities of the University.

That, I take it, is the objective of the $53 million campaign, whose success is so crucial to Princeton's role in national and international affairs. If "nothing succeeds like success," I am sure the news of the new foundation will stimulate Princeton's sons to give generously so that she may live up to the opportunities opening before her.

Cordially yours,

Author John Steinbeck wrote to Stevenson on September 23, 1961, that he had asked Dag Hammarskjöld whether there was anything he could do to help the United Nations while he was on a tour of the world. The Secretary-General said: "Yes — there is. Sit on the ground and talk to people — sit on the ground."

To John Steinbeck [279]

October 20, 1961

My dear John:

Your letter delighted me. Dag's remark about sitting on the ground and talking to people was I thought, in part at least, the echo of a head and heart too long battered by the babble of the great, and after almost a year of consorting with one kind of people here at the UN, I am feeling a little bit the same way.

I hope you *can* sit on the ground and listen during your stroll around the world. I wish I were sitting beside you. Instead, I will be sitting beside [Ambassador V. A.] Zorin and eating too much for lunch. I hope you can find a moment now and then to keep me informed of your progress, together with any observations — which are wise and sometimes humerous [humorous]. Here the pace goes ever faster, and I am incessantly astonished by the conflicts and complications little mortals create for themselves.

With much love to the Fayre Elayne.[280]

Yours,

ADLAI

[279] The original is in the possession of Mrs. John Steinbeck.
[280] Mrs. Steinbeck.

To Walter H. Judd [281]

October 20, 1961

Dear Congressman Judd:

I have just read a statement, purportedly made by you in Minneapolis, in which you said that it was Stevenson's pressure "that caused postponement of the second and crucial phase of the invasion, the knocking out of the T33 planes which would later bomb the invasion craft." [282]

I have said repeatedly that I was uninformed about the plans for an air strike by U.S. forces in Cuba. Evidently you have overlooked my contradiction many months ago of your statement. I hope I need not conclude that you chose to overlook it.

Sincerely,

Sir Julian Huxley, the former director general of the United Nations Educational and Scientific Organization (1946–1948) and world-famous scientist and author, wrote Stevenson about the Conference on the Conservation of Nature which he attended in East Africa and about his own efforts to protect wildlife in Africa.

To Sir Julian Huxley

October 21, 1961

My dear Julian:

I was enchanted with your letter, and the account of all your recent adventures and incredible productivity. It arrived just as I was bemoaning my own fate and the relentless schedule I have been obliged to keep on this job. You make me ashamed of myself and I shall complain no more, but think of you, writing, speaking, traveling, and with such enthusiasm, commitment and enjoyment. Perhaps I need a little of your serum.

Hammarskjold's death was indeed a tragedy for us all, and has resulted in a month of incessant negotiation over a successor, thus far unproductive, but nearing the end, I pray. I went to the funeral in Uppsala, representing our Government, and have never been so moved by such a ceremony. A letter from John Steinbeck from London tells me that he saw Hammarskjold the day before he went to the Congo, and asked him,

---

[281] Republican congressman from Minnesota and a fervent supporter of Chiang Kai-shek.
[282] Retired General James A. Van Fleet made a similar statement, and Stevenson wired him on October 31, 1961, along the lines of this letter.

on the eve of his own departure for a trip around the world, if he had any suggestions for his travel. Hammarskjold said: "Yes, John, sit on the ground and listen — sit on the ground." I have a feeling that you manage to do that, too, and I envy you all the more.

Please give that enchantress [283] my love, and by all means let us see you when you pass this way in the spring.

Cordially,

To Dean Rusk

October 31, 1961

Dear Dean:

Mrs. Katherine Dexter McCormick, the widow of Stanley McCormick of Chicago, and a life-long friend of my family, has owned for many years the Villa Prangins between Geneva and Lausanne. With the new auto-bahn, it will be very accessible to both Lausanne and Geneva. It is a splendid Villa with, as I recall, some 15 or 20 bedrooms, gardens, Lake frontage, etc. It is listed in Switzerland as one of their "Monuments Historiques." While in Geneva last summer I concluded that the arrangements for the Americans who are almost constantly attending meetings there were quite unsatisfactory and that a government-owned Residence would be very useful and also economical.

Accordingly, I have told Katherine McCormick, who is now elderly and has little interest in company any longer, that she should give the Villa to the United States. I have a letter from her today saying that she has decided to give the property to the United States Government if the Swiss Government approves the transfer. I think she is, or plans to be in touch with Mr. James Johnstone [284] in the Department.

Sincerely yours,

To John F. Kennedy

MEMORANDUM TO THE PRESIDENT [285]

November 1, 1961

I am presuming to pass along some "miscellaneous" reflections.

1) Trade and aid next year may take a tremendous beating if some high level public committee doesn't get busy soon. Can't some of the existing talent in this field be remobilized now?

2) For ten years I have been unhappy about the re-arming of Germany

[283] Lady Juliette Huxley.
[284] Deputy Assistant Secretary of State for foreign buildings.
[285] This document was declassified.

and giving them a big "say" in Europe. I suspect it is only by way of disarmament beginning in Central Europe that we can avoid war in the long run. Khrushchev's fear of Germany (which is shared by many of our friends) is the only legitimate part of his tactics, and I am profoundly disturbed when I see Adenauer and Strauss [286] trying to veto discussions and stimulating their U.S. lobby, and now claiming atomic weapons.[287]

3) I wonder sometimes if we can get the deeper insight and the higher truth from the kind of would-be cynical analysis coming out of the Rand Corporation, for example, where, as in so many large bureaucracies with an electronic bias, man has disappeared, and digits and theories and weapons systems take his empty place.

4) I feel a lack of settled principle, which creates an impression of lack of stability and staying power.

A

New Yorker *cartoonist and humorous writer James Thurber died in New York City on November 2, 1961, at the age of sixty-six.*

To Mrs. James Thurber

November 2, 1961

MY DEAREST HELEN, I HAVE JUST HEARD THE SAD NEWS, AND SEND YOU THIS HASTY WORD OF COURAGE AND GRATITUDE FOR ALL YOU DID TO GIVE US SO MUCH OF THE TALENT OF THAT EXTRAORDINARY AND BELOVED MAN. I WILL ALWAYS BE PROUD THAT I COULD COUNT HIM AMONG MY FRIENDS. AFFECTIONATE WISHES.

Stevenson's old friend Helen Kirkpatrick (Mrs. Robbins Milbank), once foreign correspondent for the Chicago Daily News, *invited him to join her husband and her for deer hunting near Saranac Lake, New York.*

[286] Franz Josef Strauss, West German defense minister.
[287] Faced with a loss in his party's strength in the forthcoming West German elections, Chancellor Konrad Adenauer formed a coalition which called for a greater share of NATO command posts for West Germany, a modern nuclear weapons delivery system for all NATO countries, and the abandonment of a number of concessions being proposed to facilitate a settlement of the Berlin problem.

To Mrs. Robbins Milbank

November 5, 1961

Dear Helen:

You tempt me mightily. And not the least of the temptation is to see you in such a new environment. What is a "spike-horn," anyway? If you see any loose furriners up there, let 'em have it! I'm doin' my best to hold the line against the invaders here.

I see no hope of getting there before you leave on the 12th, due to the usual relentless schedule. And I am distressed to have missed you all around. Maybe you'd stop off for an evening with me before you go West. Please do, if you possibly can.

My visit to San Francisco was satisfactory, the crowd enormous and enthusiastic, and the speech adequate.[288] The best of it was a long visit with my beloved John Fell, who is starting up a real estate-investment business of his own, and a day of duck shooting with Roger Kent [289] up in Colusa. If I could add deer shooting with the Milbanks to my 1961 memories, it would be an even more eventful year, but — alas!

Love,

To Frances FitzGerald [290]

November 5, 1961

Dearest Frankie:

You are an angel to invite me to your dance on November 24th. I shall certainly come — unless I am in Illinois for Thanksgiving.

I would rather give thanks with you than just about anything I can think of, with possibly three small exceptions — my grandchildren! And besides, I missed your coming out party.

So let me be a little indefinite, if I may, and full of excited anticipation.

With much love,

P.S. You looked more handsome than I have ever seen you the other night. But you didn't give me much of a look. How about a date with me in Greenwich Village? I'll wear my mustache and side-burns and *we* will collect autographs.

Senator Paul H. Douglas of Illinois wrote Stevenson urging him to be the Democratic candidate against Senator Everett M. Dirksen in 1962.

[288] On October 23, 1961, Stevenson spoke to the San Francisco chapter of the American Association for the United Nations. His speech is reprinted in Stevenson, *Looking Outward*, pp. 132–141.

[289] Leader of the Democratic party in Northern California and a close friend of Stevenson.

[290] Daughter of Mrs. Ronald Tree and a senior at Radcliffe College.

To Paul H. Douglas

November 5, 1961

Dear Paul:

Thanks, dear friend, for suggesting me as Dirksen's opponent. In that role, I am tempted. But I am afraid no one else is tempted to tempt me! And besides, it would be hard for me to leave my present post in the midst of all of our accumulating troubles. But you were gallant and gracious to think of me, and I am flattered.

Yours,

P.s. I wish you and Emily [291] would use my guest room when you are in New York next time.

To Alicia Patterson [292]

[no date]

Dear Madam —

I thought the exploratory discussions opened well. Would it not be well for the principals to meet soon again?

Perhaps you would be good enough to send me a list of available dates for the next two months. I suggest New York, Geneva or Libertyville. Do you insist on Moscow?

Most cordially —
THE U.S. REPRESENTATIVE

P.s. Borden's new address is 44 E 67. . . .

P.s.s. I barely began on my agenda before the elderly doe took flight!

As part of his role as ambassador of the United Nations to the American people, Stevenson appeared every two weeks on a Sunday ABC television program entitled Adlai Stevenson Reports. *The program, which was produced and moderated by Arnold Michaelis, began on October 1, 1961, with Dean Rusk as Stevenson's guest. On October 29 U Thant, Burma's ambassador to the UN, was the guest. On November 12, 1961, Jawaharlal Nehru, Prime Minister of India, appeared on the program.*

MICHAELIS: I know that you have said that anyone who says that he will never compromise is foolish because life is constantly forcing compro-

291 Mrs. Douglas.
292 This handwritten letter is in the possession of Adlai E. Stevenson III. The envelope is postmarked November 9, 1961.

mise on us. Now how do you use compromise in respect of holding to your principles?

NEHRU: Well, you have to draw the line there. That is, compromise about every nonessential and not only what you consider vital and essential. Some line has to be drawn. You çannot draw the sword at every nonessential, that is absurd, childish.

STEVENSON: I think somebody once said that a wise man who stands firm is a statesman and a foolish man who stands firm is a catastrophe, so that maybe we have to find a compromise through wisdom.

MICHAELIS: But even on this very pressing and continually burning question of admittance of Communist China to the United Nations, our government's position, as you know, Mr. Nehru, is opposed to it. Now the conflict, the alleged conflict, between the Soviet Union and China is said to be built on the basis of the Soviets wanting to pursue a course of coexistence and the Chinese being opposed to it. If that is true, and the Chinese in fact are opposed to coexistence, what basis do you see for their admittance to the UN?

NEHRU: Well, my argument for the admittance of China has nothing to do with their views, however bad or whatever they may be, but the fact that you cannot solve any major problem leaving a quarter of the world's population out of it. One has to face that, I would say. Take them in even as a hostile element. Even that is better than keeping them out to go on with their hostility and trying to upset our plans.

MICHAELIS: Do you believe that they really want to join the UN?

NEHRU: It is difficult to say. I imagine they do now, though I must say sometimes I have rather doubted it. And anyhow, I think they have not been so terribly keen as others wanted them to join. I think they like their freedom to do just what they like, to say and do what they like, criticize everybody, and no element of responsibility coming in. Which might to some extent — not very much — take them into the UN.

STEVENSON: Of course they have never renounced the use of force against Formosa, Taiwan, the Republic of China, which makes — hardly makes them qualify for membership in accordance with the literal language of the Charter.

NEHRU: Do other countries — is that so, Governor? Have all the countries renounced their use of force?

STEVENSON: They have by joining the United Nations, except in self-defense, and adhering to the principles of the Charter. The Chinese have asserted repeatedly, I believe, that their claim to Formosa would be enforced if necessary.

NEHRU: One difficulty I have noticed, Governor, is that various countries use the same words in different meanings. Take coexistence. Now the Chinese go on saying that they stand for coexistence, but it seems to me evident the meaning they attach to it is somewhat different than mine.

STEVENSON: Maybe what we should say from now on is not coexistence but we stand against coextinction.

NEHRU: Yes. I will tell you a little story. When Chou En-lai [293] came to India for the first time about six years ago, before the Geneva conference he spent two or three days and at the end of it he asked me to draft a small joint statement to be issued to the press. Well, my Ministry did it. For a long time he looked at it. He said he knows a little English, not too much. He said, "It seems to me all right, but I should like to see the Chinese translation of it." All right. Then when this came he protested, he objected to certain words in it, quite harmless words, no high principle involved. He said in Chinese it sounds funny. Well, I said naturally it may sound funny but you can put any suitable word you like in Chinese but this is the English sense.

You know, for hours we argued about certain words and phrases, quite without any relevance to any principle. Ultimately in the small hours of the morning then [they?] agreed to something.

Now that made me think how difficult [different] is the genius of the Chinese language to that of not only English but all the other languages, including my own, because we are all one family of language, even the Indian languages. Then it struck me these people talk, say they are Marxists. They have read Marx in the Chinese version. What that is I do not know. And other literature. Because the whole background of Chinese is different. I mean the linguistic background, and so they use words with different meanings. It is not that type of language, I would say. Their picture graphs, or whatever they are called, they represent an idea, not a word like in our languages. That is why I think some trouble is caused by different interpretations to words.

STEVENSON: Yes, I am sure. It makes great difficulties in the United Nations, for example, the translation of words, and the meaning of words is not always the same among the languages that we use.

Could you, sir, give me some indication of what — some simple explanation of what you view the policy, of how you describe or define the policy of non-alignment of India and the United Nations?

NEHRU: I could, but of course even what I say would not be a complete thing. Broadly, non-alignment means not tying yourself off with military blocs of nations, nations or a nation. That is, trying to view things

[293] Premier of the People's Republic of China.

as far as possible not from the military point of view, though that has come in sometimes, and trying to view matters independently and trying to maintain friendly relations with all countries.

STEVENSON: That is one thing I have not been able to understand lately. Here we have seen refugees shot in cold blood under the barbed wire in Berlin,[294] we have seen the double-dealing of the Soviet Union in respect to nuclear testing, and now the detonation of an enormous bomb with the consequence, and many others, dire consequences for the human race, and yet I do not see that this stirs up the kind of indignation among the non-aligned people that one would suspect, one would anticipate.

NEHRU: You are right, Governor, to some extent. I think that we will find almost everyone deploring this, but you are right that the degree of indignation may be lesser than elsewhere, than the United States. That depends on how it affects them personally. Now suppose there was a nuclear test in Africa. The African nations would be wild. But the thing is the same whether it is in Africa, Europe, or somewhere else. But it is near to their doors, they personally, see, we are affected by it. And they will shout.

You can only explain that by past conditioning of all these countries. At the Belgrade Conference [295] we had a majority of African countries, newly independent, who are full of their own problems and the rest of the world does not seem to exist for them except vaguely as an imperialist, colonialist world against which they are striving to free themselves. You see, on their background which they have grown into they react accordingly. Of course, if you put to them this they will say, yes, yes, that is very bad. They did say so at Belgrade, it is very bad, and it should not have been done, et cetera. But having said so they reverted to their own problems, you see.

STEVENSON: I think we in the United States share the attitude of India, your attitude about colonialism and about, as you mentioned with such a concern at Belgrade, and also about self-determination. And I believe we share your views that this should be the objective for all peoples everywhere. And not just north and south, but also East and West. And that this great wave of independence that has swept the world and freed a billion people and created 42 new nations, I think, since the war, has not reached some of the other regions of the world.

[294] To prevent refugees from fleeing to the West, the East German government in August, 1961, built a wall between East and West Berlin and strung barbed wire along the entire border with West Germany.

[295] A conference of twenty-five nonaligned nations, including Asian and African states and Yugoslavia, which met at Belgrade September 1–6, 1961. The conference called for immediate talks between Kennedy and Khrushchev to end the arms race and avoid war.

I speak specifically of Eastern Europe where governments have been imposed on the people by force of arms and are maintained in that manner. Isn't, wouldn't it be true that if colonialism and non-colonialism and self-determination applied to Africa that it should also apply to Eastern Europe and give those people an equal opportunity for self-determination?

NEHRU: That would be an ideal thing. But there is a difference in the type. Obviously there is an old style colonial type in Africa and Asia. That is not that type at all. It is not colonialism. It is the domination of a certain group or party, aided by outside elements from another country.

Now, I dislike the second thing also, but it is different. Those elements which went to form the other colonialism really do not apply here. But it may be, of course, and it sometimes is, that the second type is even worse from the human point of view than the other.

MICHAELIS: In other words, you would favor self-determination for all peoples.

NEHRU: Yes, but when you say that, if I agree to that, I don't quite know where it will land me. What I mean is this. Self-determination for a country, for a part of a country, for a district, for what?

MICHAELIS: We are speaking of governments which have had other governments, powers, superimposed on it.

NEHRU: Yes, yes, I think that it would be a good thing if every country as such was given that opportunity. Then that gets tied up with so many other factors. Take this development of the Eastern European countries, partly as a result of the last war and partly conditioned by fear of future wars. See what happened in Hungary — a terrible thing, what happened in Hungary.[296] And yet I think that probably a reason for that was the fear that that was going to lead to a world war. And just at that time the Egyptian invasion by the French and the British was taking place.[297] And it looked almost as though it were going to burst into a world war. If so, the Russians may have thought, "We are going to take no chances in Hungary." You see, the instinct of self-preservation came in.

MICHAELIS: The Soviet's instinct.

[296] In October, 1956, the Soviet Union used military force to suppress a rebellion against Soviet domination of the country.

[297] After President Gamal Abdel Nasser nationalized the Suez Canal, British and French military forces seized control of the canal in October, 1956. Both the United States and the Soviet Union voted in the UN General Assembly to censure them for the invasion. Israel also invaded Egypt at the same time. The UN created the United Nations Emergency Force in the Gaza Strip (UNEF) to facilitate withdrawal of British, French, and Israel troops and to keep peace in the area.

NEHRU: The Soviet's instinct, yes, and they behaved in a brutal manner in Hungary.

MICHAELIS: I am glad to hear you say that today, Mr. Nehru, because, as you know from our press, there are large sections of the American population which feels that you didn't speak out forcefully against the situation in Hungary.

NEHRU: Mr. Michaelis, that shows their lack of touch with what I have been saying. In the first few days, it is perfectly true I said I wanted to know the facts before I said anything. And soon after that I expressed my opinion clearly enough. Always there is a desire not merely to express an opinion — that is easy enough — but to do something in a difficult context to help.

STEVENSON: Non-alignment, Mr. Prime Minister, serves a useful purpose in the United Nations. It spurs negotiations between the aligned countries. It has the effect of sustaining pressure on them in peaceful directions, and it is often a guide to public opinion around the world, and serves very many useful purposes. But when non-alignment leans one way more than the other, it does have the effect of provoking extremism, and it also has the effect of encouraging the Soviet Union to more extreme adventures. And this, in turn, would lead to the same in this country and also to a loss of confidence in the United Nations. I think this problem is something that we have to deal with all the time.

We have felt with respect to your delegation that frequently we don't share common views on political issues in the United Nations. But we do respect your non-alignment. And on other issues in the field of colonialism, in the field of executive action by the United Nations, in the Congo, in the Middle East and so on that you have just mentioned, here we find common ground. And I should like very much to take this occasion, while you are here with me this morning, to express the gratitude of my government for the service that India has rendered in the effort to unify the Congo [298] and in many other cases to establish a United Nations presence, to use this instrumentality more effectively to preserve peace in the world. I think it has been a very useful service, and I am very grateful to you, sir.

MICHAELIS: That gives us the right to enjoy the luxury and privilege of disagreement, since we have agreement in so many areas.

NEHRU: This has nothing to do with non-alignment. Non-alignment is a basic policy, but in its application to particular circumstances or resolutions, that is a matter for judgment. Non-alignment we put aside. That is the background which governs our thinking. But that doesn't arise

[298] India was one of the nations that contributed military personnel to the UN Operation in the Congo (UNOC).

as a resolution. It is not because we are not aligned that we must agree or not agree to something. That requires an independent judgment as to which is likely to lead to the objective aimed at.

We do avoid, generally speaking — we may not succeed always — we try to avoid mere condemnations which often make it difficult to bring differing groups together. But in regard to particular things, we should express our opinion clearly, aiming always at achieving results. It is not a result, in our opinion, merely to damn somebody. That may be necessary sometimes.

STEVENSON: You see, we find it difficult to understand how India can take a position of impartiality between nuclear tests by the United States and the Soviet Union. This form of non-alignment, of trying to find a position of non-identification between right and wrong or good and evil can, I am sure you will appreciate, can cause us some confusion in this country.

NEHRU: There is no difficulty in choosing between right and wrong if the question appears in that sense. It doesn't always appear clearly in that way. But in white and black, there are many shades of grey.

But again, the question is, What you are aiming at. I do not quite know what you have in mind, Governor, about the tests. Obviously the fact that the Soviet Union resumed nuclear tests was a very bad thing from every point of view — in its results, in its breach of a covenant, voluntary covenant, no doubt, still it was bad, bad in itself, bad as an example to be followed by others. And it vitiated the atmosphere of coming together. All that is very bad. There is no question of putting it in the same category as any other, if the United States Government started its underground tests, or whatever it was. But the thing to think is about the future. For us to say, "Well, the Russians have had a go. Therefore it is only right that the Americans should have time to go ahead to equalize," that creates difficulties. The Russians are completely wrong, no doubt. But when we think a thing is evil — that is, a nuclear test — we have to say that at every stage no more. There is no question of equalizing, although Russia may have possibly — I don't know — gained an advantage by some test, I can't help it. That becomes a political, technical and military question, call it what you like, but we are not in a position to judge.

In this particular matter, obviously it was Russia that took the step which we consider very wrong.

STEVENSON: I was very glad to hear you say the other day that you believe that the solution to this matter is in the execution of a treaty providing for control and inspection of nuclear weapons, and the sooner the better.

MICHAELIS: Well, I think that feeling has caught the imagination of all peoples certainly in Britain. I see the other day that Lord Home, the British Foreign Secretary, said that Mr. Khrushchev apparently has extended an olive branch to him. And he said, "If indeed it is an olive branch, I will be happy to climb up on it and sit next to him and coo like a dove with him."

STEVENSON: I hope there is plenty of room on that olive branch. There will be a lot of people trying to get on it.

MICHAELIS: If it happens, then your efforts will have proven successful, Mr. Nehru.

NEHRU: Yes, yes. You see the alternatives are so terrible to contemplate. The reality facing the world today, if there is a nuclear war, is so amazing in its consequences that one tries to avoid it. And I am quite sure nobody wants it in the world. But certain basic, well, urges of an out-of-date mentality govern nations still, all nations. And so they take step by step, til it becomes a matter of national honor not to retire, not to submit to something. And then you have wars.

MICHAELIS: Mr. Nehru had made the statement in part of his writings, that one test of his sobriety and sanity is the fact that he has never suffered a bad headache. Now I wonder if this has been true since the nuclear age came upon us?

NEHRU: Well, it is true, broadly speaking. I don't have headaches and I sleep well even though perhaps not enough sleep. But it is a good sleep.

STEVENSON: I have to say that we have something in common. I have never had headaches either of the technical variety. Of the non-technical variety I am never free of one.

As far as not sleeping is concerned, I find I have no trouble with insomnia during the day. My trouble is only at night.

NEHRU: It is the other way about. I sleep well at night. I sometimes find it difficult to keep awake in the day time.

MICHAELIS: You also made the statement, Mr. Nehru, on a previous occasion that one must journey through life alone. To rely on others invites heartbreak. How heartbroken are you these days?

NEHRU: Well, as one advances in experience and age, one gets a little tougher, used to all kinds of kicks of that type. In one's youth, the heart breaks easily, whether the political heart or any heart. Still, one survives that. Many things happen which are painful, and yet one views them with greater calmness than previously and perhaps with some expectation that things may better themselves.

MICHAELIS: Well, we hope that you suffer less and less heartbreak and that it is the result of the nations of the world coming closer and closer together.

NEHRU: That's so. Ultimately, Mr. Michaelis, heartbreak is always greater in regard to matters affecting one intimately, I would say. I suffer more from something that happens in India which I think is wrong than even a major catastrophe outside for which, well, I don't hold the direct responsibility. I feel a shock about it, but if something happens in front of me, my whole people, myself, that pains me very much more because that seems to mar their future or something.

STEVENSON: Do you feel that the Soviets have intervened in Vietnam and in South Vietnam and in Laos? And if so, why?

NEHRU: My own feeling is that the Soviets are not as much interested in the Southeast Asian States as China. Perhaps they would not like China to throw its weight about there. They came into the picture because they became co-chairman of the Geneva Conference.[299] They have been there. I don't think they care very much. Naturally, they don't want their protegees to be hit on the head. But otherwise, they have no interest or designs there. You know, in Vietnam I suppose everyone is at fault. But the one procedure evolved was that of international commissions. And our point is the international commission of which India is chairman has never had a fair deal, not allowed to function, even [one?] day. It is not allowed to function in South Vietnam because South Vietnam has not acknowledged it.[300] Now, here is something devised to solve questions, to put checks on intrusions. I don't say that it will solve any problem, but it certainly would put a check. It has put a check. It did, but in South Vietnam it is not acknowledged and has not helped at all. I think the first thing is for that link to be re-established and to be made to function. That will not be enough. Other things have to be done too. But I don't think the Soviets have any particular design there, except some people are their friends and they want to pat them on the back and help those, if possible.

MICHAELIS: Governor, November 14th, just two days away, will mark the 72nd anniversary of Mr. Nehru's birth. Won't you join me now in advance in wishing the Prime Minister well at his 72nd and hope that he will continue many, many more years of traveling inside India as well as outside of India?

STEVENSON: I do indeed, sir, we are more honored that you had occasion to come to this country at this time. I am sure we have all profited from

---

[299] The conference in 1954 at which France agreed to withdraw from Indochina. The United Kingdom and the Soviet Union were cochairmen of the conference.

[300] An International Commission for Supervision and Control was created to supervise the agreements. One agreement, blocked by the government of South Vietnam, called for elections in 1956 to unify North and South Vietnam. The Saigon government, like the United States, refused to adhere to the Final Declaration of the conference and was not a signatory to the military accord that "temporarily" partitioned the country.

your wisdom and your philosophical understanding of our times. And I hope you never have a headache.

NEHRU: Thank you, Governor. Thank you, Mr. Michaelis.

MICHAELIS: And we wish you Godspeed on your trip home, Mr. Nehru.

NEHRU: Thank you.

Lawrence Spivak, moderator of the television program Meet the Press, *wrote Stevenson on November 13, 1961, that he had done a superb job on the program with Nehru.*

To Lawrence E. Spivak

[no date]

Dear Larry:

My my, I never thought I would get a fan letter like yours. If you are not careful, I will be inviting you to appear on my program. . . .

Best wishes,

Sincerely,

To John F. Kennedy [301]

November 13, 1961

Dear Mr. President:

In accordance with our understanding I am enclosing a brief memorandum on the "Food for Development" program through the United Nations system, which I mentioned to you the other evening. I hope this will be fruitful and that we can proceed accordingly.

Sincerely yours,

A

MEMORANDUM FOR THE PRESIDENT

November 13, 1961

Subject: Utilization of Food Surplus Through the United Nations System[:] Proposed United States Action in the 16th Session of the General Assembly of the United Nations.

BACKGROUND

In the 15th General Assembly the United States took the initiative in securing the adoption of a resolution (1496) entitled "Provision of Food Surpluses for the Food Deficient Peoples Through the United Nations

---

[301] This document was declassified.

System." This was unanimously approved following an address to the General Assembly by the then President in which utilization of surplus food was among items included.

Following this resolution a report was prepared by the Director General of the Food and Agriculture Organization entitled "Development Through Food — A Strategy for Surplus Utilization," which is one of the most remarkable documents on this subject. The Secretary General in turn submitted a report on the role of the United Nations and its related agencies in the use of food surplus for economic development. The Economic and Social Council, in July 1961, acting on these reports again stressed the use of surplus food in connection with economic and social development programs.

At an April FAO meeting in Rome, Mr. George McGovern [302] proposed on behalf of the United States an initial multilateral program of $100 million in commodities and cash contributions of which the United States committed itself to provide $40 million in commodities, with the possibility of a supplementary cash contribution to be explored in Washington. The President made the first public announcement of this offer on April 22, 1961. This proposal will be acted upon before the end of this month at the FAO Conference in Rome. There is every indication that the proposal will be adopted with special emphasis being placed on the use of food for emergencies, institutional feeding and labor-intensive pilot development projects and programs. The plan provides for cooperation between the FAO and the United Nations in the operation of the program.

These developments, and above all the speech of the President delivered on September 25, raised high hopes in many quarters and in particular among the less developed countries that there might be established as part of the United Nations Development Decade a larger program of food utilization with emphasis on economic and social development.[303] A figure of an additional $400 million for the larger program has frequently been mentioned, although never officially by the United States Government. The issue will arise soon in the General Assembly. Specific proposals are expected of the United States in light of our earlier initiatives. In addition, a speech was made by Ambassador Klutznick in the General Assembly on October 5 detailing the United States concept of a United Nations Development Decade in which he stated, under directions from the State Department, that the United

[302] Director of the Food for Peace program.
[303] For a discussion of Kennedy's views on assistance to foreign countries using excess American agricultural productivity, see Schlesinger, *A Thousand Days*, pp. 168–170, 604–605. Schlesinger called Food for Peace "the great unseen weapon of Kennedy's third world policy." Ibid., p. 605.

States Delegation would have a specific proposal to make later in the present session of the General Assembly.

PROBLEM AND RECOMMENDED ACTION

In view of the impending adoption of an initial program by the FAO and the expectations of further action in the United Nations General Assembly, the problem is to define the position the United States Delegation should take in the General Assembly.

The recommended action is that the United States Delegates be authorized:

1. To strongly endorse and clearly to support the action of the FAO Conference in establishing the initial program.

2. To approve United Nations participation in this program providing for:

(a) the election by the Economic and Social Council, after consultation with the FAO, of a governing committee composed in equal parts of contributing and recipient states, to provide intergovernmental guidance and supervision of the program;

(b) the establishment of a new joint FAO-UN Surplus Utilization Administration to be located in Rome which will operate under the supervision of the Director General of FAO and the Secretary General of the United Nations.

3. To express the hope that the interest of the contributing states and the effectiveness of the initial program will be such as to warrant the expansion both in size and scope of this program, with an increasing emphasis on economic and social development.

4. To state our willingness, subject to Congressional approval, to make substantial contributions to such an expanding program. These contributions would be primarily in commodities, but also in cash. (Pledges of commodity contributions should be made without imposing a specific percentage formula — such as 40 percent of total commodity pledges. In view of the agricultural surplus situation in the world, it would be unrealistic to expect countries other than the United States to contribute more than 20 or 30 percent in commodities of the commodities component of the program.)

To *John F. Kennedy*

November 18, 1961
Personal

Dear Mr. President:

Brooks Hays [304] dropped in to see me the other day and I got the impression that he is not altogether content with what he is doing as congressional liaison for the State Department.

I'm sure you know his talents and interests and special influence among Baptists through the South. It occurred to me that he might be more useful speaking around the country, to combat the extreme rightist movements.

Cordially yours,

William S. Dix, librarian of Princeton University, wrote Stevenson urging him to deposit his papers with the Princeton University Library.

To *William S. Dix*

November 23, 1961

Dear Mr. Dix:

Thank you for your letter, which pleases me — although I have *not* made up my mind just what to do about the papers. That Princeton still wants them is gratifying, however, and perhaps I can reach a decision before long, after I have had an opportunity to talk with all the other interested people. There has been some feeling expressed that the papers relating to my period as Governor of Illinois and prior thereto should go to the University of Illinois or the State Historical Library, and the Presidential campaigns and other papers thereafter could be separated and deposited elsewhere. I suppose Mr. Newman [305] discussed this with you, and I shall look forward to an opportunity to see him when I am in Chicago during the Christmas holidays.

Please give my affectionate regards to Julian. [306]

Cordially yours,

[304] Assistant Secretary of State for Congressional Affairs and former congressman from Arkansas.
[305] Ralph G. Newman, owner of the Abraham Lincoln Book Shop in Chicago.
[306] Julian P. Boyd, editor of *The Papers of Thomas Jefferson*.

To George E. Roosevelt [307]

November 24, 1961

My dear Mr. Roosevelt:

I understand that Andrew Cordier [308] is under consideration for President of New York University. I have known Mr. Cordier since the founding days of the United Nations at San Francisco and London, and in New York. The passing years have increased my respect for him and for his thoughtfulness, competence and industry.

I hesitate to add an unsolicited comment to your files, but feeling strongly as I do about the character and merits of this man, I send you this expression of my regard for him.

Cordially yours,

To Loring C. Merwin [309]

November 24, 1961

Dear Bud:

I've just read your comforting report to the stockholders. But what's this about expenditures for a "fallout shelter?" I hope we haven't fallen for that!

Yours,

Senator Thomas Dodd of Connecticut was a champion of President Moise Tshombe of Katanga and an ardent supporter of the secession of the province from the Congo.[310]

To Thomas J. Dodd

November 24, 1961

Dear Tom:

This is being written in haste, but I want to take a minute to answer your recent letters to me.

It goes without saying that I, too, am distressed over the continuing breach between the Central Government of the Congo in Leopoldville and Mr. Tshombe in Katanga. I not only share your concern, but at this

[307] Chairman of the board of trustees of New York University.
[308] Under-Secretary for General Assembly Affairs of the United Nations.
[309] Stevenson's cousin and publisher of the Bloomington, Illinois, *Daily Pantagraph*. For the Merwin-Stevenson ownership of this newspaper, see *The Papers of Adlai E. Stevenson*, Vol. I, pp. 153–154.
[310] See Lefever, *Crisis in the Congo*, p. 101.

very moment I am engaged in a running fight with Ambassador Zorin in the Security Council over the situation in the Congo.[311]

The Communists have been bending every effort this week to concentrate all attention strictly towards Katanga to the exclusion of all else. As you will see from the attached clippings, I, in turn, have been trying to broaden the scope of any new expression by the United Nations so as to "point up" the situation existing elsewhere including Eastern Province, which I described as "of no less gravity, perhaps in the long run of even greater gravity, than Katanga's secession." My efforts have now brought a threat from Zorin to exercise the veto — and that is where we stand as of this writing. I know that you, too, are pressed for time but hope you will take a minute or two to read the speech I made in the Security Council on November 16, a copy of which I am enclosing. Let's keep in touch.

Meanwhile, best wishes.

Sincerely,

To Irving Dilliard [312]

November 30, 1961

Dear Irving:

It was good to hear from you, and I am distressed that I missed you in New York. Nehru would have been no competition for Dilliard! Another time, please give me advance notice and plan to stay with me.

I, too, am perplexed about the Senate race in Illinois. If you have any further thoughts on the matter, I wish you would pass them along. I have been away from Illinois for so long that I am quite out of touch, although I get constant inquiries.

With affectionate regards to all of the family,

Cordially yours,

To Mrs. Ernest L. Ives [313]

December 1, 1961

Dear Buffie:

Thanks so much for the clipping. Life here has been pretty rugged of late, but there's some light on the horizon. There is even a possibility that the Assembly will finish its work and not have to reconvene after the first of the year. What a blessing that would be! I work almost liter-

---

[311] Stevenson spoke on the Congo in the Security Council on November 13, 21, and 24, 1961.

[312] Editorial page editor of the St. Louis *Post-Dispatch*.

[313] The original is in E.S.I., I.S.H.L.

ally all of the time, and the results are spotty.[314] Tonight I am off to Washington for a session at the State Department and a visit with [President] Kennedy, followed by a dance with the Thorons.[315] My visits have been infrequent lately, due to the pressure of work here, but I hope I can get a better liaison with the Department established somehow in the future.

Adlai and Nancy were here for a visit and seem fine and had a good time. It was a joy to see them after such a long separation.

I hope we can get together during the holidays. Thus far I have no idea when I can be there or how long. I think I should be able to go out [to Libertyville] about the 22nd or 23rd, and plan to take Viola [Reardy] with me and stay at least a week or over New Year's. I am also planning to have a party on Saturday night before New Year's to invite in the old friends I haven't seen for so long. Jane Dick will help me arrange it, and, of course, if you and Ernest would like to come I would be delighted.

This is a shabby letter, but the best I can do in the circumstances.

Love,

ADLAI

On December 4, 1961, Stevenson spoke in Committee 1 of the General Assembly on "International Cooperation in the Peaceful Uses of Outer Space." [316]

The subject before this committee this morning is, as you have indicated, outer space — and what we together decide to do, or not to do, to promote the exploration and use through peaceful cooperation.

This is Year Five in the Age of Space. Already in 4 short years scientific instruments, then animals, then men, have been hurled into space and into orbit around the earth. Within a few more years satellites will bring vast new developments in weather forecasting and in worldwide telephone, radio, and television communications. More than that, rocket booster capacity will become sufficient to launch teams of men on journeys to the

[314] Among other things, Stevenson spoke in the Security Council on November 22 on a complaint by Cuba that the United States was interfering in the Dominican Republic; on November 26 he had as his guest on his television program, *Adlai Stevenson Reports,* Edward R. Murrow, director of the United States Information Agency; he spoke again on November 28 to the Security Council on the Cuban complaint; and on December 1 he spoke in the General Assembly on the question of seating the People's Republic of China in the UN.

[315] Mr. and Mrs. Benjamin W. Thoron. Mr. Thoron was treasurer of the Protestant Episcopal Cathedral Foundation and had known Stevenson since the early 1920's.

[316] The text is from the Department of State *Bulletin,* January 29, 1962, pp. 180–186.

moon and to the nearest planets. And after that, one can only speculate what may come next.

Unhappily this astounding progress in space science has not been matched by comparable progress in international cooperation. In the race of history social invention continues to lag behind scientific invention. We have already lost valuable time that can never be recovered.

Unless we act soon the space age — like the naval age, like the air age and the atomic age — will see waste and danger beyond description as a result of mankind's inability to exploit his technical advances in a rational social framework. In short, unless we act soon, we shall be making the old mistakes all over again.

Despite the urgent need for immediate international action, I fear that we come to this subject ill-prepared to think clearly about it. I suspect that we are handicapped by our heritage of thought about the affairs of this single planet.

We are conditioned to think in terms of nations. Our lives and concepts are predicated upon states whose boundaries are fixed by oceans and rivers and mountain ranges or by the manmade lines drawn sharply across the two-dimensional and finite surface of planet Earth. We are conditioned to think in terms of nations defined by finite areas expressed in finite measurements — nations with more or less known resources and more or less counted populations. And especially we are conditioned to think in terms of national sovereignties.

Such concepts have no meaningful application to the unexplored, unbounded, and possibly unpopulated reaches of outer space, which surround no nation more than any other nation, and which are innocent of the idea of national sovereignty.

We are further handicapped, many of us, by the impression that the exploration of outer space is a matter of concern only to the great powers because they alone have the capacity to penetrate space. That impression gains force from the belief that outer space is unrelated to the day-to-day problems of nations whose energies are absorbed by such earthly daily questions as growing enough food to feed their peoples.

This impression, I submit, is totally and dangerously wrong.

The smallest nation represented here in the United Nations is deeply concerned with this question before us — and so is the poorest of our members. Indeed, they may have far more to gain from the shared benefits of space science — and on just such matters as growing food — than the larger and the richer societies.

Moreover, the small nations have an overriding interest in seeing to it that access to space and the benefits of space science are not preempted by a few nations, that space exploration is not carried forward as a competition between big-power rivals, that the ideological quarrels which so unhappily afflict this planet are not boosted into space to infect other planets yet unsullied by the quarrels of men.

Finally, all nations can play a part in assuring that mankind derives the maximum advantage from space technology in the here and the now and not just in the hereafter. Every nation can cooperate in the allocation of radio frequencies for space communications. Every nation can participate in global systems of weather prediction and communications.

In outer space we start with a clean slate — an area yet unmarred by the accumulated conflicts and prejudices of our earthly past. We propose today that the United Nations write on this slate boldly and in an orderly and a creative way to narrow the gap between scientific progress and social invention, to offer to all nations, irrespective of the stage of their economy or scientific development, an opportunity to participate in one of the greatest adventures of man's existence.

The United States, together with other delegations, today places before this committee a program for cooperation in outer space — a program embodied in the draft resolution [1] now before you. We look forward to constructive discussions of these proposals — and to improvement upon them. They do not represent fixed positions. We are prepared to consider constructive suggestions from any member of the committee so that the widest possible measure of common agreement may be reached. But these proposals do represent our best and most thoughtful effort to put forward in good faith a program of international cooperation for the benefit of all mankind.

Toward a Regime of Law and Order

The first part of this program, embodied in part A of the draft resolution, looks toward a regime of law and order in outer space based on two fundamental principles which should commend themselves to all nations.

The first principle is that international law, including the United Nations Charter, applies to outer space and celestial bodies. Now that man has found means to venture beyond his earthly environment, we should state explicitly that the rules of good international conduct follow him wherever he goes. The *Ad Hoc* Committee on the Peaceful Uses of Outer Space noted in its report of July 14, 1959,[1] that as a matter of principle the United Nations Charter and the statute of the International Court of Justice are not limited in their operations to the confines of the earth.

The second principle is that outer space and celestial bodies are free

[1] U.N. doc. A/C. 1/L.301.
[1] U.N. doc. A/4141.

for exploration and use by all states in conformity with international law and are not subject to national appropriation by claim of sovereignty or otherwise.

The *Ad Hoc* Committee on Peaceful Uses of Outer Space noted in its report that with the practices followed during the International Geophysical Year "there may have been initiated the recognition or establishment of a generally accepted rule to the effect that, in principle, outer space is, on conditions of equality, freely available for exploration and use by all in accordance with existing or future international law or agreements."

This rule has been confirmed by the practice of states in the time since the report was written. It now deserves explicit recognition by this Assembly.

But such a statement on outer space is not enough. In the 2 years since the report was written, mankind has taken giant steps toward reaching celestial bodies. The first manned lunar landing may take place by the end of the present decade. All mankind has an interest and a stake in these monumental achievements. We must not allow celestial bodies to be the objects of competing national claims.

The members of the committee will note that we have not attempted to define where outer space begins. In our judgment it is premature to do this now. The attempt to draw a boundary between air space and outer space must await further experience and a consensus among nations.

Fortunately the value of the principles of freedom of space and celestial bodies does not depend on the drawing of a boundary line. If I may cite the analogy of the high seas, we have been able to confirm the principle of freedom of the seas even in the absence of complete agreement as to where the seas begin.

Freedom of space and celestial bodies, like freedom of the seas, will serve the interest of all nations. Man should be free to venture into space on the same basis that he has ventured on the high seas — free from any restraints save those imposed by the laws of his own nation and by the rules of international law, including those embodied in the United Nations Charter.

Open and Orderly Conduct of Activities

The second part of our program is designed to encourage the open and orderly conduct of outer space activities. The measures proposed in part B of the draft resolution would help all countries participate in space activities and would foster an atmosphere of mutual trust and confidence.

In pursuit of these objectives we proposed that all states launching objects into orbit or beyond should furnish information promptly to the Secretary-General for the purpose of registration of launchings. This information would include orbital and transit characteristics and such other data as launching states might wish to make available. The Secretariat would maintain a record of this information and would communicate it upon request to other members of the United Nations and to specialized agencies.

The establishment of a complete registry or census of space vehicles would mark a modest but an important step toward openness in the conduct of space activities. It would benefit nations the world over, large and small, which are interested in identifying, tracking, and communicating with space vehicles. It could lay the basis for later arrangements for termination of radio transmission and removal of satellites when their lives were ended.

The Secretariat should perform other useful functions beyond these connected with the registry of space vehicles:

It could, in consultation with appropriate specialized agencies, maintain close contact with governmental and nongovernmental organizations concerned with outer space matters.

It could provide for the exchange of information which governments might supply in this field on a voluntary basis — supplementing but not duplicating existing exchanges.

It could assist in the study of measures for the promotion of international cooperation in outer space activities.

Finally, it could make periodic reports on scientific and institutional developments in this field.

It is time to vest the Secretariat with these basic service functions. The report of the *Ad Hoc* Committee on Peaceful Uses of Outer Space suggested that some functions of this kind should be performed by the Secretariat. It noted with approval the conclusion of its Technical Committee that "there is a need for a suitable centre related to the United Nations that can act as a focal point for international co-operation in the peaceful uses of outer space."

We believe that this recommendation should be implemented without further delay, making fullest possible use of existing resources of the Secretariat. We understand that the services specified in this resolution can be performed with the addition of a very small number of personnel. The measures taken to carry out the new functions could be reviewed by the Assembly at its next session.

Weather Research and Prediction

The third part of our proposed program calls for a worldwide effort under the auspices of the United Nations in weather research and weather prediction.

The dawn of the space age is opening vast new possibilities in weather sciences. Satellites and sounding rockets have supplemented other advances in meteorological techniques such as the use of radar and electronic computers. They make it possible for the first time in history for man to keep the entire atmosphere in every region and at every altitude under constant surveillance.

This portends a revolution in meteorology — a peaceful revolution which can benefit all peoples on this earth, particularly in the less developed regions which presently lack adequate weather information. Meteorological satellites hold special promise for the improvement of weather forecasting capabilities in the Tropics and in the Southern Hemisphere, where vast oceans cannot be covered by present techniques.

Increased knowledge of the forces that shape the weather will enable man to forecast typhoons, floods, rainfall, and drought with greater accuracy.

These possibilities will mean the saving of human life and reduction of property damage.

They will make possible the more efficient use of limited water resources and enable the farmer to adjust the timing and the nature of his planting to the rainfall which his fields will receive. Fishing and grazing will also benefit.

Fuels and raw materials can be transported and stored more efficiently with better foreknowledge of the weather.

In short, by making the weather and the events which depend on it the more predictable, we can foster progress in industry, agriculture, and health and contribute to rising living standards around the world.

But the enhancement of our knowledge of the weather is only the beginning. In the more distant future looms the possibility of large-scale weather modification. If this power is to be used to benefit all rather than to gain special advantage for a few, if it is to be used for peaceful, constructive purposes, progress toward weather control should be part of a cooperative international venture.

With these exciting prospects in mind we propose preparatory studies for two coordinated programs in part C of the draft resolution.

The first is an international atmospheric science program to gain greater knowledge of the basic forces affecting the climate. This will yield information essential for improved weather prediction and eventually for possible weather modification.

The second is an international meteorological service program. The aim of this program would be to enable men everywhere to reap the practical benefits of discoveries in basic weather science. Under this program steps could be taken leading to the establishment of a global network of regional weather stations located in less developed as well as developed areas of the world. Weather information obtained from satellites could be transmitted directly to such centers or communicated indirectly after receipt in other areas of the world.

The concept of regional meteorological centers is already accepted and being applied in the Northern Hemisphere, where there are five such centers serving regional needs for weather communications and analysis. The needs of the Tropics and the Southern Hemisphere are now being studied. There is, for example, a plan for establishment of an international meteorological center in Bombay in connection with the 4-year international Indian Ocean expedition.

To put such a world weather network in operation will require cooperative efforts of many nations. The World Meteorological Organization — called WMO — has played an important role in supplying technical assistance in the training of weather technicians, especially in the less developed areas. We believe this activity of WMO should be continued and strengthened in the future. National and international suppliers of investment capital can help finance the establishment of centers in countries which cannot afford them. Nations which have developed weather satellites can make the weather information available freely for use in this system.

So far as the United States is concerned, we stand ready, here and now, to make the weather data received from our satellites available for such a global system. In fact we are already making such data available to other countries. We are developing methods which would permit direct transmission of satellite cloud photography to any part of the world. If this is successful the way will be opened for a marked increase in the timely availability of useful data.

Global System of Communication Satellites

Now the fourth part of the space program looks toward the establishment of a global system of communication satellites.

Space technology has opened enormous possibilities for international communications. Within a few years satellites will make possible a vast increase in the control and quality of international radio, telephone, and telegraph traffic. In addition, something new will be added — the possibility of relaying television broadcasts around the globe.

This fundamental breakthrough in communication could affect the lives of people everywhere.

It could forge new bonds of mutual knowledge and understanding between nations.

It could offer a powerful tool to improve literacy and education in developing areas.

It could support world weather services by speedy transmittal of data.

It could enable leaders of nations to talk face to face on a convenient and reliable basis.

The United States wishes to see this facility made available to all states on a global and nondiscriminatory basis. We conceive of this as an international service. We would like to see United Nations members not only use this service but also participate in its ownership and operation if they so desire.

The United Nations Organization itself stands to benefit directly from the use of satellites both in communicating with its representatives around the world and in disseminating programs of information and education.

As an example of the potentialities of such use, we hope to have before long an experimental satellite which will transmit across the Atlantic, for brief periods, live television excerpts of debates in the General Assembly of the United Nations.

In preparation for these developments the United States proposes that the International Telecommunication Union consider the various aspects of space communication in which international cooperation will be required. This will assure all members of the United Nations a fair opportunity to express their views. It is particularly important that the necessary arrangements be made for the allocation of radio frequencies for space communications.

In order to enable less developed countries to participate in effective use of satellite communications, the Expanded Technical Assistance Program and the United Nations Special Fund should give sympathetic consideration to requests for assistance from less developed countries to improve the state of their domestic communications.

The principles I have mentioned are embodied in part D of the draft resolution now before you. If implemented with dispatch they could help to clear the way for cooperative use of a worldwide system of satellite communications.

Revitalizing the Outer Space Committee

The fifth part of our program seeks to put new life and new responsibilities in the Committee on the Peaceful Uses of Outer Space.

As we all know, this Committee was established 2 years ago for an indefinite period by Resolution 1472 (XIV) [1] with a continuing mandate to study programs on peaceful uses of outer space which might be undertaken under United Nations auspices, to study the legal problems which might arise from the exploration of outer space, and to plan an international conference for the exchange of experience in the exploration of outer space.

We propose that, in addition to the responsibilities laid down in this original mandate, the Committee should review the activities provided

[1] For text, see [Department of State] *Bulletin* of Jan. 11, 1960, p. 68.

for in this resolution and make such reports as it may consider appropriate. In the four previous parts of the resolution we have specifically noted the role the Committee could play in studying the legal problems of outer space, in reviewing the service arrangements undertaken by the Secretary-General, and in examining the proposals for international cooperation in weather and communications.

As my colleagues are aware, Resolution 1472 provided for 24 members of the Outer Space Committee elected for a period of 2 years. We propose to continue the same membership, augmented by the addition of Nigeria and Chad in recognition of the increase in the membership of African states in the United Nations during the past 2 years.

Let the Committee make a fresh beginning. Let the Committee meet early in 1962 to undertake its original tasks and its new responsibilities in connection with these cooperative programs.

We recognize that outer space activities are unique in many respects and that international cooperation is a prerequisite to progress. Although we cannot of course accept the veto in the work of the Committee, we expect that this work can be carried out in a spirit of mutual understanding. We do not anticipate that the nature of the Committee's work would give rise to differences that could not be resolved by discussion. We hope that, proceeding in this spirit, we can finally put life into the Committee created 2 years ago.

I ask the distinguished delegates here to bear in mind that in weather and communications the resolution embodies no commitments to any specific program. It merely calls upon the Secretary-General in cooperation with the specialized agencies, and with other organizations, to submit proposals for action. These proposals will be presented to the Economic and Social Council at its 34th session, to the 17th General Assembly, and to the Outer Space Committee.

In short the resolution in these fields merely clears the way for deliberate consideration of programs by government representatives. Such basic studies ought not be further delayed.

Now we have sought in good faith and so far as is possible to present a program which is above the clash of partisan politics or the cold war. The principles and programs embodied here bestow no special advantage on any state — they are in the interest of all states.

The resolution deals exclusively with the peaceful uses of outer space. The military questions of space are closely entangled with the military questions of earth. We believe that they require urgent study as part of comprehensive negotiations for general and complete disarmament.

This does not mean, however, that the program of peaceful cooperation now before us has no bearing on the issues of peace and war. It does. If put into operation without delay, it can help lay the basis for a relaxation of tensions and facilitate progress elsewhere toward general and complete disarmament.

We Cannot Afford to Delay

Mr. Chairman, I must close with the same theme on which I commenced this presentation: We cannot afford to delay.

The space programs of the great powers are well advanced. Our own nation is proceeding with the development of satellite systems for weather forecasting and communications. In the months ahead important decisions will have to be made. If the opportunity for United Nations action is missed, it will be increasingly difficult to fit national space programs into a rational pattern of United Nations cooperation.

Our first choice is a program making maximum use of the United Nations for at least three reasons:

— because it could bring new vitality to the United Nations and its family of agencies;

— because it would help to assure that all members of the United Nations, developed and less developed, could have a share in the adventure of space cooperation; and

— because a program of such magnitude should be carried out as far as possible through the organizations of the world community.

As I say, this is our first choice. But the march of science is irreversible. The United States has a responsibility to make the fullest possible use of new developments in space technology — in weather forecasting, in communications, and in other areas. These developments are inevitable in the near future. We hope they can take place through cooperative efforts in the United Nations.

I suppose that the great climaxes in the drama of history are seldom evident to those who are on the stage at the time. But there can be little question that man's conquest of outer space is just such a moment, that we — all of us — are on stage, and that how we behave in the immediate will have a profound impact upon the course of human affairs in the decades ahead.

There is a right and a wrong way to get on with the business of space exploration. In our judgment the wrong way is to allow the march of science to become a runaway race into the unknown. The right way is to make it an ordered, peaceful, cooperative, and constructive forward march under the aegis of the United Nations.

I most earnestly recommend your serious attention to the proposals my Government is making to this end.

TEXT OF RESOLUTION [1]

A

The General Assembly,

Recognizing the common interest of mankind in furthering the peaceful uses of outer space and the urgent need to strengthen international co-operation in this important field,

Believing that the exploration and use of outer space should be only for the betterment of mankind and to the benefit of States irrespective of the stage of their economic or scientific development,

1. *Commends* to States for their guidance in the exploration and use of outer space the following principles:

(a) International law, including the Charter of the United Nations, applies to outer space and celestial bodies;

(b) Outer space and celestial bodies are free for exploration and use by all States in conformity with international law and are not subject to national appropriation;

2. *Invites* the Committee on the Peaceful Uses of Outer Space to study and report on the legal problems which may arise from the exploration and use of outer space.

B

The General Assembly,

Believing that the United Nations should provide a focal point for international co-operation in the peaceful exploration and use of outer space,

1. *Calls upon* States launching objects into orbit or beyond to furnish information promptly to the Committee on the Peaceful Uses of Outer Space, through the Secretary-General, for the registration of launchings;

2. *Requests* the Secretary-General to maintain a public registry of the information furnished in accordance with paragraph 1 above;

3. *Requests* the Committee on the Peaceful Uses of Outer Space, in co-operation with the Secretary-General and making full use of the functions and resources of the Secretariat:

(a) To maintain close contact with governmental and non-governmental organizations concerned with outer space matters;

(b) To provide for the exchange of such information relating to outer space activities as Governments may supply on a voluntary basis, supplementing but not duplicating existing technical and scientific exchanges;

(c) To assist in the study of measures for the promotion of international co-operation in outer space activities;

[1] U.N. doc. A/RES/1721 (XVI) (A/C.1/L.301/Rev. 1 and Corr. 1); adopted unanimously in plenary session on Dec. 20 [1961].

4. *Further requests* the Committee on the Peaceful Uses of Outer Space to report to the General Assembly on the arrangements undertaken for the performance of those functions and on such developments relating to the peaceful uses of outer space as it considers significant.

C

The General Assembly,

Noting with gratification the marked progress for meteorological science and technology opened up by the advances in outer space,

Convinced of the world-wide benefits to be derived from international co-operation in weather research and analysis,

1. *Recommends* to all Member States and to the World Meteorological Organization and other appropriate specialized agencies the early and comprehensive study, in the light of developments in outer space, of measures:

(a) To advance the state of atmospheric science and technology so as to provide greater knowledge of basic physical forces affecting climate and the possibility of large-scale weather modification;

(b) To develop existing weather forecasting capabilities and to help Member States make effective use of such capabilities through regional meteorological centres;

2. *Requests* the World Meteorological Organization, consulting as appropriate with the United Nations Educational, Scientific and Cultural Organization and other specialized agencies and governmental and non-governmental organizations, such as the International Council of Scientific Unions, to submit a report to its member Governments and to the Economic and Social Council at its thirty-fourth session regarding appropriate organizational and financial arrangements to achieve those ends, with a view to their further consideration by the General Assembly at its seventeenth session;

3. *Requests* the Committee on the Peaceful Uses of Outer Space, as it deems appropriate, to review that report and submit its comments and recommendations to the Economic and Social Council and to the General Assembly.

D

The General Assembly,

Believing that communication by means of satellites should be available to the nations of the world as soon as practicable on a global and non-discriminatory basis,

Convinced of the need to prepare the way for the establishment of effective operational satellite communication,

1. *Notes with satisfaction* that the International Telecommunication

Union plans to call a special conference in 1963 to make allocations of radio frequency bands for outer space activities;

2. *Recommends* that the International Telecommunication Union consider at that conference those aspects of space communication in which international co-operation will be required;

3. *Notes* the potential importance of communication satellites for use by the United Nations and its principal organs and specialized agencies for both operational and informational requirements;

4. *Invites* the Special Fund and the Expanded Programme of Technical Assistance, in consultation with the International Telecommunication Union, to give sympathetic consideration to requests from Member States for technical and other assistance for the survey of their communication needs and for the development of their domestic communication facilities so that they may make effective use of space communication;

5. *Requests* the International Telecommunication Union, consulting as appropriate with Member States, the United Nations Educational, Scientific and Cultural Organization and other specialized agencies and governmental and non-governmental organizations, such as the Committee on Space Research of the International Council of Scientific Unions, to submit a report on the implementation of those proposals to the Economic and Social Council at its thirty-fourth session and to the General Assembly at its seventeenth session;

6. *Requests* the Committee on the Peaceful Uses of Outer Space, as it deems appropriate, to review that report and submit its comments and recommendations to the Economic and Social Council and to the General Assembly.

E

The General Assembly,

Recalling its resolution 1472 (XIV) of 12 December 1959,

Noting that the terms of office of the members of the Committee on the Peaceful Uses of Outer Space expire at the end of 1961,

Noting the report of the Committee on the Peaceful Uses of Outer Space,[1]

1. *Decides* to continue the membership of the Committee on the Peaceful Uses of Outer Space as set forth in General Assembly resolution 1472 (XIV) and to add Chad, Mongolia, Morocco and Sierra Leone to its membership in recognition of the increased membership of the United Nations since the Committee was established;

2. Requests the Committee to meet not later than 31 March 1962 to carry out its mandate as contained in General Assembly resolution

---

[1] U.N. doc. A/4987.

1472 (XIV), to review the activities provided for in the present resolution and to make such reports as it may consider appropriate.

To Lady Barbara Jackson

December 5, 1961

Dearest Barbara:

Your letter has arrived with the report of your packing boxes and the extraordinary logistical movements in the Jackson household. What does all this mean — or have I missed some letters in between? A simultaneous note from Julian Huxley tells me that he saw you in Ghana and that you were planning to go to Australia for a year. All this is confusing and disturbing. But confusion and disturbance is my daily lot and I suppose I should be used to it.

Anyway, I am not! And I hope your next report will be highly "personalized."

I have to make some speeches in January to outside audiences. If you are full of ideas about what needs saying and perspective, etc., please remember that I never am. Fragments of any kind will be usefully and unusually welcome.

After this Assembly is over I hope to have a week in Illinois catching up with my affairs there. Then I have some distant hope of a holiday in the South, but I am afraid that is not too reliable. I shall be looking for you around the first of February. Do let me have your plans in your usual meticulous detail as soon as you can, because my life isn't as manageable as it used to be.

Devotedly,

Mayor Richard J. Daley of Chicago and Democratic National Committeeman Jacob M. Arvey tried to persuade Stevenson to run for the Senate. President Kennedy told Stevenson "we needed him in the UN." Arthur M. Schlesinger, Jr., wrote: "Kennedy had greatly pleased Stevenson by insisting that he stay." [317]

James Plimsoll, Australian ambassador to the UN, sent the following report to his government on December 4, 1961:

This morning I had a frank talk with Adlai Stevenson about his future. The newspapers reported over the weekend that he had discussed with President Kennedy the possibility of his running for Senator from Illinois.

Stevenson said that the newspapers were more definite than they

[317] *A Thousand Days,* p. 835.

should have been in drawing conclusions. The Democratic Party organization in Illinois had asked him to run and the least he could do was to say that he was 'considering' it as he could not very well turn them down flat. However President Kennedy did not want him to run. Furthermore, he himself had no great inclination to turn back to Illinois politics at this stage of his life. Against this was the fact that he owed something to the Democratic Party machine in Illinois which had backed him as Governor and in his Presidential campaigns. The Democratic Party in Illinois believed that he was probably the only Democrat who could beat Senator Dirksen for re-election. Moreover Stevenson's son, who lived in Illinois was interested in a political career, and Stevenson would be in a position to help him if he were a Senator from his State. In any case for the sake of his son he did not want to get offside with the Democratic Party machine in that state.[318]

To William McC. Blair, Jr.

December 5, 1961

Dear Bill:

I was delighted to have that admirable speech. I have turned it over to Marietta Tree who will doubtless forward to you proper comments!

I have just withstood the blandishments of Dick Daley, Jack Arvey, et al, and decided to stick with this ship which, in spite of my best efforts, is still afloat. I must say I was a little tempted to be my own boss again, but the President was very good about it and may make my life a little easier than it is at present.

Are you coming home for Christmas? If so, please save the night of December 30 for me at Libertyville. I am going to have a party and I need you to do the Smörgåsbord. I need Deeda [319] for other reasons.

Yours,

To John F. Kennedy

December 6, 1961

Dear Mr. President:

I hear you were distressed by reports from Washington about "what I said" following our meeting on Saturday last.

What I said to the press was reported. What I said in response to inquiries from friends was that there were three reasons I would consider returning to Illinois:

(1) that it would be an *easier* job at my age;

[318] Ambassador Plimsoll and the Australian Department of External Affairs released this document to the editor.
[319] Mrs. Blair.

(2) that it would give me more time in Illinois to be with my family; and

(3) that it would give me greater independence.

I want you to know that I also added — I think *in every case* — that the work here was incomparably more important than being another Senator. I made no criticism whatever of my relations with you, Secretary [Dean] Rusk, or anyone else, but I did suggest to one or two of the more informed people that I thought the traditional practice of the State Department in sending minute instructions to the Mission in New York could well be modified in the direction of greater autonomy.

If these remarks have been distorted and caused you any concern, please know that I am distressed. I don't believe I was indiscreet, but if I was I can only ask your forgiveness.

I thought our meetings most satisfactory and concluded to make my statement promptly after notifying [Mayor] Daley that I could not be a candidate. Your expression of gratification was most reassuring.

I am sending you a little memorandum describing our position, as I see it, as a result of the Nuclear Test votes which we discussed and which will point up the need for more long-range planning and, I think, greater autonomy at USUN.[320]

Thanks, too, for that delightful visit at Glen Ora [321] with my beloved Jackie!

Sincerely yours,

To Clara Urquhart [322]

December 7, 1961

Dear Clara:

Thanks for your letter. I enclose a copy of the speech I made in the General Assembly on the representation of China — in accordance with instructions from the State Department! [323] I am sure you will understand that sometimes the Department, the President and his Ambassadors are not in total and exact agreement on policy. However, I am sure you would agree that the admission of Red China on its terms of expulsion of

[320] Stevenson probably refers to his memorandum dated December 8, 1961, below.
[321] The Kennedys' home in Virginia.
[322] A friend of Dr. Albert Schweitzer who had acted as interpreter when Stevenson visited him in 1957 at Lambaréné, French Equatorial Africa.
[323] The speech, delivered on December 1, 1961, is reprinted in Stevenson, *Looking Outward*, pp. 57–67. For the first time, the United States did not attempt to keep the China question off the agenda of the General Assembly. Instead, the United States established by a majority vote that the issue was an important question requiring a two-thirds affirmative vote. The resolution for the seating of the People's Republic of China and the expulsion of the Republic of China (Taiwan) was defeated by a substantial majority.

Nationalist China and the right to use force to conquer that island, is quite incompatible with the Charter of the United Nations and our national interest. Indeed, one wonders if the Russians have not made the case so extreme in order to insure that. I write you all the foregoing in the utmost confidence, of course.

I wish I could promise to do a piece for you. But I really lead a remorseless life, as you can imagine, and keeping up with my speaking [324] and writing commitments here is more than I have been able to manage, without taking on any such formidable task as you suggest. . . .

I had a visit with Fritz and Edith [325] and found them charming and informative as ever. Please remember me to them most affectionately.

Cordially yours,

To Mrs. Franklin D. Roosevelt [326]

December 7, 1961

Dear Mrs. R:

During this time of the year I would like to give a Thousand Dollars to any cause which you designate. This is not a great sacrifice on my part. It is money coming from an article [327] I wrote on the United Nations which I probably should not keep anyway. So please don't hesitate to let me have your recommendation. I think especially of the AAUN [American Association for the United Nations] and wonder if it still has a priority among your concerns.

With much love,

ADLAI

P.S. I should be delighted to come around and talk to you if there is ever a moment in the day.

AES

---

[324] Stevenson spoke in Committee 1 of the General Assembly on December 4 on international cooperation in the peaceful uses of outer space and on December 13 on disarmament, and on December 14 and 15 he spoke in the General Assembly on the seating of the People's Republic of China.

[325] Mr. and Mrs. Fritz Rosenberg. Mr. Rosenberg, Mrs. Urquhart's brother, accompanied Stevenson on a trip through Swaziland in 1955.

[326] The original is in the Franklin D. Roosevelt Library, Hyde Park, New York.

[327] Probably "United Nations: Capital of the Family of Man," *National Geographic,* September, 1961.

To Edward S. Corwin [328]

December 8, 1961

My dear old friend!
You were most kind to send me a copy of your "Higher Law" book.[329]
With its inscription it will be a precious addition to my library. And it
will also be another reminder of you whose friendship and work have
meant so much to me. I am most pleased to have it close by.
I was distressed to miss the recent celebration in your honor in Prince-
ton. That was something I really wanted to do!
As Gerald Johnson says: "Long may you wave!"

Cordially yours,

To John F. Kennedy

MEMORANDUM TO THE PRESIDENT

December 8, 1961

From: Adlai E. Stevenson
Subject: *Nuclear Weapons Questions at 16th General Assembly*
To illustrate the occasional need for long term planning of United
States objectives and positions instead of day-to-day improvisations, I am
taking our recent experience with instructions from the Department on
various nuclear weapons resolutions.
The voting pattern of the United States on this question has already had
a noticeable effect on our general position in the United Nations. Ten or
eleven votes have made us appear to be against nuclear disarmament,
against the cessation of nuclear testing except on our terms, against
free zones, against undertakings by non-nuclear states not to acquire
nuclear weapons and even against an inquiry on the subject, and against
an African effort to keep nuclear weapons out of the African continent.
Looked at from the other point of view, we appear to be fighting for the
use of nuclear weapons, for their proliferation, and for the possibility of
their employment in any continent or area.
Of course, this "image" of the United States is grossly inaccurate.
Nevertheless, it is now rather widely shared by African and Asian delegates, and even some Latin American delegates have voted as if they
gave it at least some credence. The Soviet bloc have been quick to
exploit *our* voting record, and, of course, have voted for most all of these

[328] Professor emeritus of jurisprudence at Princeton University and an authority
on constitutional law and the American presidency, with whom Stevenson had
studied as an undergraduate.
[329] *The "Higher Law" Background of American Constitutional Law* (Ithaca,
New York: Gold Seal Books, 1955).

resolutions. Their voting record on these popular issues does not reveal their shameless hypocrisy, and I suspect the Soviet propaganda machine is making good use of the record.

I think one can safely predict that it won't be long before disarmament and nuclear weapons will arouse the same emotion that the issue of colonialism has aroused in the past.

It seems to me important, therefore, that the United States plot and plan carefully so that we will not emerge on the defensive, but as the foremost apostles of disarmament and ridding the world of the scourge of nuclear weapons. Obviously, to do this will take some planning on more than a day-to-day, resolution-to-resolution basis. Clearly, we can't create the image we want of a peaceful America dedicated to patient, remorseless effort to save the world from nuclear disaster, by continuing in the direction we have been going. Because we have the best disarmament plan, and because our motives are honest and our policy clear (I hope!), we have the essentials of a very successful position on this critical issue. We shall have to take advantage of our opportunity actively and promptly, because the record in this session has gone a long way to exonerate the Russians.

I could add, parenthetically, that all of the NATO delegations at the UN would gladly have abstained on the Swedish resolution for an inquiry on preventing the proliferation of nuclear weapons. Instead, we voted against the resolution, largely, I understand, because of consultations that took place at NATO in Paris.

The process of decision on how we are to vote must be completed at an earlier stage. Otherwise, we cannot exercise our leadership potential with the NATO group or other member states.

If we are not careful, we can lose our sense of proportion. (The Swedish resolution is a case in point. Its implications are minor compared to those of a "ban-the-bomb" resolution, yet we exerted more pressure in accordance with our instructions over the Swedish resolution.)

We shall have to expect new resolutions each year, pressing more and more urgently for disarmament and an end to nuclear weapons. Hence we must prepare on a long range basis to deal with this problem, because we cannot choke off or defeat such resolutions. I think ways may be found to adjust to these emotional issues and to inject some element of responsible thought into their treatment. We did this with considerable success in the colonialism field. We can do it in the field of nuclear disarmament, where our basic impulses are just as much on the side of the angels as in the colonial field.

I conclude that there should be more long range planning on major issues that will come before the United Nations. Too often, in my limited experience, our decisions have been made in Washington at the last moment, and often with little relevance to the political situation at the United Nations. Of course our planning must consider problems from the point of view of domestic as well as international politics, and a course of conduct should be decided on well in advance.

But underlying all of the foregoing is, as I see it, the great advantage in more flexibility of maneuver in the USUN. After all, there is such a thing as being too close to the seat of government, and I suspect there has grown up over the years a tendency to instruct the delegation in too great detail and with too much rigidity.

I believe we have taken at least the first steps toward improvement along the foregoing lines. I will call upon you for help as needed from time to time.

To Mrs. Franklin D. Roosevelt [330]

December 11, 1961

Dear Mrs. R.:

Thanks for your letter. I have sent Mr. Eichelberger [331] a check.

I wish I could come for dinner on the 14th, but I seem to be engaged all the time these days, and that night is no exception. Maybe when the General Assembly is over we can have an evening together. I hope so.

Affectionately,

ADLAI

To John F. Kennedy

December 11, 1961

Dear Mr. President:

I said during our last meeting that I felt we needed changes in the relations between the U.S. Mission to the United Nations and the State Department in two principal respects:

> a) The instructions from the Department should be more generalized and permit greater flexibility and independence of action by the Mission.
>
> b) There should be more advance planning on large and enduring issues that affect U.S. influence and "image."

With respect to a), I have drafted an outline of understanding and discussed it with Harlan Cleveland and Arthur Schlesinger. I understand

---

[330] The original is in the Franklin D. Roosevelt Library, Hyde Park, New York.
[331] Clark Eichelberger, director of the American Association for the United Nations.

they are presenting it to you and Secretary [Dean] Rusk, for what further discussion may be necessary.

With respect to b), I attach a brief memo [332] illustrating the problem by our record on a series of nuclear weapons votes this fall. Assuming the Mission, together with State and other agencies, can make long term plans to improve our influence and "image," we may need your help from time to time to enable the Mission to stick to the agreed line. A good example of how long range planning can improve our position is Portugal. There we have been able to follow through with consistency our planning last spring, thanks to unswerving support from the Department and the White House.

Sincerely yours,

To Mrs. Eugene Meyer [333]

December 16, 1961

Dearest Agnes:

I am delighted to have the information about that charming fellow, Pu-Tai.[334] He has enlivened my household already, and I am confident that there are many miracles to come.

I wish you could come to see him, and I am going to make this my foremost objective in 1962. So look out!

Much love,
ADLAI

To William McC. Blair, Jr.

December 18, 1961

Dear Bill:

I have noted your reservation for February 13–18 in my deluxe pavillion.

What would you think about a party on Wednesday, February 14, or would you prefer some other night?

Let me hear from you as promptly as you can, and also send me any names that you would like included.

The Senate race in Illinois was really no temptation, but I wanted to pay [Mayor] Daley and the people out there the courtesy of serious consideration, and give the President his opportunity if he wanted it.

Things have worked out very well and I think relations with the Department and the White House have been, on the whole, improved.

[332] Probably his memorandum to the President dated December 8, 1961, above.
[333] The original is in the Agnes Meyer files, Princeton University Library.
[334] Mrs. Meyer had sent Stevenson a Chinese Ming porcelain figurine of a god of peace and abundance.

I hope you don't have to work as hard as we do. And I hope your results are better.

Love to Deeda.[335]

Yours

For four hundred years Portugal had three enclaves — Goa, Damao, and Diu — on the Indian subcontinent.

When negotiations for Portugal's withdrawal from these colonies failed, Indian forces massed for action. Washington authorized John Kenneth Galbraith in New Delhi to offer vague American pressure on Portugal in return for a six-month standstill by India.

At midnight December 17, 1961, Indian troops attacked. In the discussions in Washington and at USUN on the American position, there was agreement that the resort to force should be condemned. But, in addition, Stevenson urged that the United States' position should also include a statement that the Portuguese enclaves were anachronistic and there should be a peaceful termination of Portuguese colonialism in India. The Department of State, however, had assured Portugal that the issue of colonialism would not be raised. The references to Portuguese colonialism were cut out from Stevenson's speech over his protests.

At the Security Council on December 18, 1961, "Adlai Stevenson made a very stern and, I think, unfortunately emotional speech," Galbraith wrote.[336] In the speech Stevenson ridiculed Indian Defense Minister Krishna Menon, who in the past had been the Indian ambassador to the United Nations.

Stevenson's first statement to the Security Council on December 18, 1961, follows.[337]

I would like to express the views of the United States at this fateful hour in the life of the United Nations. I will not detain you long, but long enough, I hope, to make clear our anxiety for the future of this Organization as a result of this incident.

When acts of violence take place between nations in this dangerous world, no matter where they occur or for what cause, there is reason for alarm. The news from Goa tells of such acts of violence. It is alarming

---

[335] Mrs. Blair.

[336] *Ambassador's Journal*, p. 286. At a press conference on December 21, 1961, Stevenson said that India had tried to negotiate for fourteen years and then had resorted to force. "Now if you are going to freeze the right of these people to assert their force," he went on, ". . . you have got to open up a channel more fully and firmly on negotiations."

[337] United Nations *Official Records*, Security Council, December 18, 1961, pp. 15–18.

news and, in our judgment, the Security Council has an urgent duty to act in the interests of international peace and security.

We know, as the world knows, and as has been said countless times in the General Assembly and the Security Council, that the winds of change are blowing all over the world. But the winds of change are man-made, and man can and must control them. They must not be allowed to become the bugles of war.

The preamble of the Charter states that the peoples are determined "to save succeeding generations from the scourge of war," and "to practice tolerance and live together with one another as good neighbours." In that connexion, it deserves to be said that all of us at the United Nations owe much to India.

The largest contingent in the United Nations effort to establish peace in the Congo are the troops of India. India has also contributed of its resources in the Middle East. Few nations have done more to uphold the principles of this Organization or to support its peace-making efforts all over the world, and none has espoused non-violence more vehemently and invoked the peaceful symbolism of Gandhi more frequently. That nation is led by a man whom I regard as a friend,[338] who has been a lifelong disciple of one of the world's great saints of peace, whom many have looked up to as an apostle of non-violence and who only this year addressed this Assembly with a moving appeal for a United Nations Year of International Co-operation.

These facts make the step which has been taken today all the harder to understand and condone. The fact is, and the Indian Government has announced it, that Indian armed forces early this morning, on 18 December, marched into the Portuguese territories of Goa, Damao, and Diu. Damao and Diu have been occupied and there is fighting at this moment within the territory of Goa.

So here we are, confronted with the shocking news of this armed attack, and that the Indian Minister of Defence [339] — so well known in these halls for his advice on matters of peace and his tireless enjoinders to everyone else to seek the way of compromise — was on the borders of Goa inspecting his troops at the zero hour of invasion.

Let it be perfectly clear what is at stake here; it is the question of the use of armed force by one State against another and against its will, an act clearly forbidden by the Charter. We have opposed such action in the past by our closest friends as well as by others. We opposed it in Korea in 1950, in Suez and in Hungary in 1956 and in the Congo in 1960. And we do so again in Goa in 1961.

[338] For Stevenson's conversations with Prime Minister Nehru, see *The Papers of Adlai E. Stevenson,* Vol. V, pp. 208–212.

[339] V. K. Krishna Menon. On December 20, Krishna Menon called on Stevenson at USUN. For a description of their "long uncomfortable conversation," see Martin, *Adlai Stevenson and the World,* p. 688.

The facts in this case are, unfortunately, all too clear. These territories have been under Portuguese dominion for over four centuries. They have been invaded by Indian armed forces. The Government of India regards these territories as having the same status as the territories of the United Kingdom and France on the sub-continent from which those countries have voluntarily withdrawn. The Government of India has insisted that Portugal likewise withdraw. Portugal has refused, maintaining that it has a legal and moral right to these territories.

We have repeatedly urged both of the parties to this dispute to seek by peaceful processes the resolution of a problem which has its roots in the colonial past. I do not at this time propose to concern myself with the merits of the dispute. We are not meeting here today to decide on the merits of this case; we are meeting to decide what attitude should be taken in this body when one of the Members of the United Nations casts aside the principles of the Charter and seeks to resolve a dispute by force.

But what is at stake today is not colonialism; it is a bold violation of one of the most basic principles in the United Nations Charter, stated in these words from Article 2, paragraph 4:

"All Members shall refrain in their international relations from the threat or use of force against the territorial integrity or political independence of any State, or in any other manner inconsistent with the Purposes of the United Nations."

We realize fully the depths of the differences between India and Portugal concerning the future of Goa. We realize that India maintains that Goa by right should belong to India. Doubtless India would hold, therefore, that its action is aimed at a just end. But, if our Charter means anything, it means that States are obligated to renounce the use of force, are obligated to seek a solution of their differences by peaceful means, are obligated to utilize the procedures of the United Nations when other peaceful means have failed.

Mr. Nehru, the Prime Minister, has often said himself that no right end can be served by a wrong means. The Indian tradition of non-violence has inspired the whole world, but this act of force with which we are confronted today mocks the good faith of India's frequent declarations of exalted principle. It is a lamentable departure not only from the Charter but from India's own professions of faith. What is the world to do if every State whose territorial claims are unsatisfied should resort with impunity to the rule of armed might to get its way? The Indian sub-continent is not the only place in the world where such disputes exist. The fabric of peace is fragile, and our peace-making machinery has today suffered another blow. If it is to survive, if the United Nations is not to die as ignoble a death as the League of Nations, we cannot condone the use of force in this instance and thus pave the way for forceful solutions of other disputes which exist in Latin America, in Africa, in Asia and in Europe. In a world as interdependent as ours, the possible results of such a trend are too grievous to contemplate.

This action is all the more painful to my country because we have in recent weeks made repeated appeals to the Government of India to refrain from the use of force. These have included not only a series of diplomatic approaches in Washington and in New Delhi, but also a personal message from President Kennedy to Mr. Nehru on 13 December indicating our earnest hope that India would not resort to force to solve the Goa problem. As a culmination of these efforts, the United States Government last Saturday made an appeal to Mr. Nehru, both through the United States Ambassador in New Delhi and through the Indian Ambassador in Washington, to suspend preparations for the use of force, in connexion with a direct offer of United States help in seeking a peaceful solution of the problem.

This resort to armed action is a blow to international institutions, such as the United Nations and the International Court of Justice, which are available to assist in the adjustment of disputes. This is our principal concern. This body cannot apply a double standard with regard to the principle of resort to force. We appeal to India to recognize that its own national interests, as well as those of the entire world community, depend on the restoration of confidence in the processes of law and conciliation in international affairs. Indeed this tragic episode reveals clearly, if nothing else, the need for urgent review of peaceful settlement procedures to deal with the problems of peaceful change. My Government will have more to say about this at an appropriate occasion.

The Council has an urgent duty, in our judgement, to bring this dispute back from the battlefield, so fraught with danger for the world, to the negotiating table. We earnestly urge the Government of India to withdraw its armed forces from the territories they have invaded. We earnestly appeal for a cease-fire and we earnestly urge the Governments of India and of Portugal to enter into negotiations to achieve a solution. In our judgement, we must ask for an immediate cease-fire; we must insist on withdrawal of the invading forces; and we must insist that the two parties negotiate on the basis of the principles of the Charter; for the law of the Charter forbids the use of force in such matters. There is not one law for one part of the world and another law for the rest of the world; there is one law for the whole world, and it is the duty of this Council to uphold it.

Stevenson's second statement to the Security Council on December 18, 1961, follows.[340]

[340] United Nations *Official Records,* Security Council, December 18, 1961, pp. 19–22.

A decision in this case is so urgent that I should like to proceed with the introduction of a draft resolution with only a few further words.

It is clear as crystal on the basis of the facts and the complaint that the issue before the Security Council is not the right or the wrong of Portugal's colonial policy; it is the right or the wrong of one nation seeking to change an existing political and legal situation by the use of armed force. That is expressly forbidden in the Charter. There are no exceptions, except self-defence. And can anyone believe that huge India is acting in self-defence against this almost defenceless territory? The history that lies behind the day's events is well known. We know, as the world knows and has known — it has been said countless times in the General Assembly and in the Security Council, and I said it this afternoon — that the winds of change are blowing all over the world. Surely areas under Portuguese control are not immune to those winds. But I repeat that these winds of change are man-made and man can and must control them in the interests and security of all of us. They must not blow us into war. That is the point at issue here tonight.

Evidently I must remind the representative of India that the United States stand on colonial questions is forthright and we make no apology for it. We whole-heartedly believe in progress, in self-government and in self-determination for colonial peoples. In the past year we have supported many efforts to bring about progress in colonial questions, including two resolutions in this Council [945th and 956th meetings] [341] on Angola and a resolution in the General Assembly [1542 (XV)] on Portuguese Non-Self-Governing Territories. Here in the Security Council last March, when we considered the question of Angola, I said in speaking for the United States that the United States would be remiss if it failed to express honestly its conviction that step-by-step planning within these Portuguese territories and its acceleration is now imperative for the successful political, economic and social advancement of all inhabitants of those territories — advancement, in brief, towards full self-determination. We have not altered that stand.

After listening to some declarations here that the inhabitants of Goa want freedom from Portugal and that it is India's right and duty to use force to liberate them, I am obliged to remind the members of the Council that there are a lot of people in the world — in East Germany and all the way from the Baltic to the Black Sea — who want their freedom too.

Do I detect in this debate an implication that a country such as the United States, for example, is not really anti-colonial unless it approves the abolition of colonies by international armed attack? If so, the United States delegation totally rejects this implication. We are against colonial-

[341] This and subsequent references to UN meetings or documents appear in brackets in the original.

ism and we are against war; we are for the Charter. And the over-whelming testimony of recent history upholds the force and the realism of this position. I have been struck by two contentions made in defence of India's use of force here; first, that Goa is a colony or a Non-Self-Governing Territory and therefore, somehow force is permissible to be employed against it. Secondly, that Portugal has not relinquished control of Goa pursuant to the recommendation contained in General Assembly resolution 1514 (XV) and, therefore, that force is permissible to be used against it and that it is not India but Portugal that is the aggressor.

Let me comment on these contentions in turn. The first fact is that if Goa and its dependencies are a colony or a Non-Self-Governing Territory of Portugal, they are not under the sovereignty of India. In fact, the Assembly last year decided just that, in resolution 1542 (XV). It affirmed that Goa is a Non-Self-Governing Territory of Portugal on which Portugal was required to report, and those who have taken other positions this afternoon supported that resolution at that time. The question is not whether Goa should or should not be under Portuguese authority. As a matter of obvious fact and international law, it is under Portuguese authority. This being the case, India cannot lawfully use force against Goa especially when the peaceful methods in the Charter have not been exhausted. And the claim that Portugal is the aggressor and not India, because it has not followed the recommendation of resolution 1514 (XV), requires an even greater exertion of the imagination. We support that resolution and we hope that it will be intelligently carried out. The Assembly has again acted, with our support, to the same end this year. But resolution 1514 (XV) does not authorize the use of force for its implementation. It does not and it should not and it cannot, under the Charter. If it did, the resolution would lead to international chaos, not to national progress. Resolution 1514 (XV) does not and cannot overrule the Charter injunctions against the use of armed force. It would not have been adopted if it had attempted to do so. It gives no license to violate the Charter's fundamental principles: that all members shall settle their international disputes by peaceful means, that all Members shall refrain from the threat or use of force against any other State.

As I have said, I do not propose at this time to express a judgement on the merits of the territorial dispute between India and Portugal. They seem to me irrelevant. However, even if the United States were supporting entirely the Indian position on the merits, we should nevertheless be firmly opposed to the use of force to settle the question. The Charter, in its categorical prohibition of the use of force in the settlement of international disputes, makes no exceptions, no reservations. The Charter does not say that all Members shall settle their international disputes by peaceful means except in cases of colonial areas. It says again and again throughout its text that the basic principle of the United Nations is the maintenance of peace — not only peace in Europe or peace in America, but peace in Africa, peace in Asia, peace everywhere.

We know that it is the doctrine of the Soviet Union, as the Soviet representative made clear again today, that, while war in general may be reprehensible, what they call wars of liberation and Communist revolutions to overthrow existing governments are quite another breed and are permissible, even desirable.

There have in the past been many wars of liberation or of territorial conquest, depending on your choice of words, but our Charter was drafted in the recognition of the grim fact that in our times war is indivisible, that a war of liberation from colonialism is as likely as any other to lead to a world conflagration, and that the only way to ensure that mankind is spared that catastrophe is strictly, firmly and consistently to oppose the use of force in international disputes, wherever it may occur and however it may be justified.

I therefore submit the following draft resolution [S/5033], in collaboration with the United Kingdom, France and Turkey, and I urge the Council to adopt it promptly:

"The Security Council,

"*Recalling* that in Article 2 of the Charter of the United Nations all Members are obligated to settle their disputes by peaceful means and to refrain from the threat or use of force in a manner inconsistent with the purposes of the United Nations,

"*Deploring* the use of force by India in Goa, Damao and Diu,

"*Recalling* that Article 1, paragraph 2, of the Charter specifies as one of the purposes of the United Nations to develop friendly relations among nations based on respect for the principle of equal rights and self-determination of peoples,

"1. *Calls* for an immediate cessation of hostilities;

"2. *Calls upon* the Government of India to withdraw its forces immediately to positions prevailing before 17 December 1961;

"3. *Urges* the parties to work out a permanent solution of their differences by peaceful means in accordance with the principles embodied in the Charter;

"4. *Requests* the Secretary-General to provide such assistance as may be appropriate."

I hope very much that the Security Council can proceed this evening to vote on this and such other draft resolutions as may be before it.

Stevenson's speech shocked the Indians. Prime Minister Jawaharlal Nehru wrote President Kennedy that he had been "deeply hurt" by Stevenson's "extraordinary and bitter attitude." [342] *B. K. Nehru, Indian ambassador to Washington, stated that Stevenson had such worldwide respect that his speech had damaged the world prestige of Prime Minister Nehru. Indians resented this, he added. It was B. K. Nehru's opinion that Stevenson had delivered such a bitter speech because he felt that India's action lowered respect for international law and the United Nations.* [343] *Rikki Jaipal thought that Stevenson was so critical of India because he "overidealized" India and, therefore, was so disappointed by the military action.* [344]

The resolution urging India to cease hostilities, withdraw its troops, and negotiate with Portugal for a peaceful settlement failed. An Afro-Asian resolution charging Portugal as the aggressor and requesting Portugal to cooperate with India in liquidating its colonial empire also failed.

Stevenson spoke again after the resolutions had been defeated. [345] *Harlan Cleveland called the speech "a hastily written and extremely eloquent statement." He added: "The speech was stronger than his instructions, and was a good (and rare) example of his taking off on the basis of his own moral instincts, and in his own original language."* [346]

I believe that I am the only representative on this table who was present at the birth of the United Nations. Tonight we are witnessing the first act in a drama which could end with the death of the Organization. The League of Nations died, I remind you, when its members no longer resisted the use of aggressive force. So it is with a most heavy heart that I must add a word of epilogue to this fateful discussion, by far the most important in which I have participated since this Organization was founded sixteen years ago.

The failure of the Security Council to call for a cease fire tonight in these simple circumstances is a failure of the United Nations. The veto of the Soviet Union is consistent with its long role of obstruction. But I find the attitude of some other members of the Council profoundly disturbing and ominous because we have witnessed tonight an effort to rewrite the Charter, to sanction the use of force in international relations

[342] Schlesinger, *A Thousand Days*, p. 528.
[343] Conversation with Walter Johnson, April 4, 1969, New Delhi, India.
[344] Conversation with Walter Johnson, April 3, 1969, New Delhi, India. Mr. Jaipal served on the Indian delegation to the United Nations while Stevenson was ambassador. At the time of the interview he was in the Ministry of External Affairs in New Delhi.
[345] United Nations, *Official Records,* Security Council, December 18, 1961, p. 27.
[346] Memorandum to Walter Johnson, April 30, 1973.

when it suits one's own purposes. This approach can only lead to chaos and to the disintegration of the United Nations.

The United States appeals again to the Government of India to abandon its use of force, to withdraw its forces.[347] We appeal to both parties again to negotiate their differences. This is the course prescribed by the Charter. It is the course of wisdom. The inability of the Council to act because of the Soviet veto does not alter this fact.

We will consult overnight with other members of the Council regarding further steps which might be taken by the United Nations and we reserve the right to seek a further meeting at any time.

To Mongi Slim [348]

December 19, 1961

Dear Mr. Ambassador:

Thank you, my dear friend, for that magnificent basket of Tunisian dates which arrived yesterday. You were kind to have thought of me, and I am delighted to have them.

May I take this opportunity to express my gratitude also for the efficient and orderly management of this session of the General Assembly. The task of the President of the General Assembly is an exhausting and endless one, but one at which you have excelled and for which we all owe you our deep appreciation.

Please accept my warmest wishes for the coming Holiday Season.

Sincerely yours,

To Wallace Irwin, Jr.[349]

December 19, 1961

Dear Wally:

I have just called you on the telephone and [was] told that you were at home "sick." I hope it is nothing serious, and merely the normal response to Goa!

I wanted to tell you now [how] grateful I am for that speech, and also for the one on CHIREP.[350] I think these were two of my "finer hours" hereabouts, and far better than I realized during my moments of scattered attention. Perhaps I shouldn't bother to edit your work at all, and they would be still better!

Anyway — many, many thanks, and my admiration for your talent — and patience with me!

Yours,

347 On December 19, the Portuguese in Goa surrendered.
348 President of the 16th Session of the UN General Assembly.
349 Director of Public Services at USUN.
350 The question of seating the People's Republic of China in the UN.

To *John F. Kennedy*

December 23, 1961

Dear Mr. President:

I submit herewith a brief report on the results of the first part of the Sixteenth Session of the United Nations General Assembly.

The three months since the Assembly convened on September 19, 1961, have been critical in the life of the United Nations. The members were faced with several issues of great difficulty, failure on any one of which could have inflicted a grave injury on the United Nations and on the hopes for peace and justice. I mention especially the following:

1. The succession to Dag Hammarskjold.
2. The threat of financial disaster from the Congo operation.
3. Continued danger of secession and chaos in the Congo.
4. The pressure to replace Nationalist China with Communist China.

On each of these issues, whatever the remaining difficulties, the United Nations has achieved better results than we dared to predict in September.

In addition, I am glad to report progress on several topics of major importance, several of which you treated in your address to the General Assembly on September 25. These include the fields of disarmament and the effective prohibition of nuclear testing; your proposal for a United Nations Decade of Development; and your proposal on the peaceful uses of outer space.

1. After prolonged negotiation in which the United States Mission was very active, the General Assembly elected U Thant of Burma to act as Secretary-General until April 1963. The action was unanimous — 103 to 0. Thereby the United Nations overcame a mortal challenge — a challenge to the powers of the office of the Secretary-General and indeed to the very existence of that office; a challenge to the continuance of the United Nations itself as an executive agent of the community of nations and as a friend and protector of small and weak nations.

2. The seat of the *Republic of China* in the United Nations was safeguarded and reinforced, and the claim of Communist China to this seat was rejected, by a decisive vote of 48 to 37. This was the first time this divisive question has been squarely met since it first arose more than a decade ago. Moreover, the Assembly decided by a vote of 61 to 34 that any proposal to make a change in the representation of China would constitute an "important question" requiring a two-thirds majority. Both these votes were great successes for the United States view.

3. The *financial crisis* occasioned by the Congo operation has been

relieved, and may be on the road toward solution. The General Assembly has taken three important steps in this direction. It has voted, first, to ask the International Court of Justice for an advisory opinion as to whether the assessments against member states to support the Congo operation, as well as the United Nations Emergency Force in the Middle East, create binding financial obligations on the member states. If the court says they do, this should stimulate payment by those now in arrears.[351]

Second, the Assembly has further assessed the costs of the Congo operation and of U.N.E.F. through next June 30.

Third, the Assembly authorized an unprecedented $200 million bond issue, to be amortized out of the regular budget of the United Nations. It is hoped that the member nations will now join in purchasing these bonds so as to relieve the immediate financial difficulties of the United Nations and give us a breathing spell in which to devise a long-run solution.

4. The news from the *Congo* today is at last hopeful, after many dark days and weeks. *If* the agreement signed by Prime Minister Adoula and Mr. Tshombe is ratified and carried through, this will indeed be a happy conclusion of a grave crisis for the world and the United Nations.[352] The Central Government can thus turn its attention to consolidating the rest of its vast country.

If secession, disunity and disaster in the Congo, the heart of Africa, is prevented — then the credit must go to the United Nations and to the brave men of many nations who have served it with courage and, in many cases, with their lives.

5. As a result of bilateral negotiations between the United States and the Soviet Union, the Assembly laid the basis for new negotiations on

[351] The General Assembly by overwhelming majorities decided to finance the UN forces in the Gaza Strip and in the Congo by assessments on every member. By the end of 1961, arrears in payments for these operations rose to over $100 million. Most of the $100 million resulted from the defaults of the Soviet Union, countries of Eastern Europe (other than Yugoslavia), and France. But no fewer than seventy members had failed to pay for one or both of these operations. The three-part plan was worked out between the Secretary-General and USUN. It was adopted by the General Assembly by a vote of 58 to 13 with 24 abstentions.

[352] In November and December, 1961, Moise Tshombe's forces in Katanga made repeated attacks on United Nations personnel stationed in Elizabethville. On December 17, United Nations troops started an operation to establish a defense perimeter around Elizabethville. On December 20, Tshombe and Cyrille Adoula, prime minister of the Central Government, met under United Nations auspices. The next day they issued an agreement in which Tshombe recognized the "indissoluble unity" of the Congo and the authority of the Central Government over all parts of the country. Tshombe also promised to return Katanga's representatives to Parliament, to place his gendarmerie under the chief of state, and to respect UN resolutions on the Congo. But within a few days Tshombe began to express reservations and charged that the agreement was imposed on him and would not be valid until it was ratified by the Katanga Assembly. See Lefever, *Crisis in the Congo*, p. 100.

disarmament — thus breaking the deadlock which began when the Soviet bloc walked out of the Geneva disarmament talks in June 1960. Under United Nations auspices the new forum will begin intensive negotiations early next year, reporting on its progress to the UN Disarmament Commission. Among the documents the negotiators will have before them is the United States "Program for General and Complete Disarmament in a Peaceful World," which you presented to the General Assembly on September 25. Thus the stage is set for a new and vigorous attack on this crucial problem.

6. The Assembly also gave great attention to the problems of *nuclear weapons.* It overwhelmingly endorsed the view of the United States and the United Kingdom that there is an urgent need for a treaty to ban nuclear weapons tests under effective international measures of verification and control. This vote was helpful in obtaining the resumption of test ban negotiations in Geneva on November 28.

But the United States was compelled to oppose Assembly recommendations to prevent the testing and use of nuclear weapons, without international controls. In contrast, the Soviet Union cynically voted for those same resolutions — with no provision for controls — while at that very time the Soviet Union was engaged in the most intensive series of nuclear weapons tests in history, and was threatening to use nuclear weapons in case of war. In the long run this hypocrisy will be justly evaluated by the Assembly and by the world.

Moreover, the Soviet Union defied the overwhelming plea of the General Assembly that it refrain from exploding a 50-megaton bomb.

During the Assembly the United States never ceased to expound the fundamental truth that every measure of disarmament and arms control must be accompanied by effective inspection and safeguards. We fully expect that in future sessions of the General Assembly this truth will be accepted by a growing majority of the members.

7. The Assembly unanimously designated the current decade, as you suggested in your address, as the *United Nations Decade of Development.* Under this heading the world organization can now make a comprehensive, long-range attack on the needs for economic and social development which beset more than half of the human race. The contributions which the United Nations can make in this field, by its mobilization of talents and resources without any political strings, are of vital importance to this world objective.

8. Again after long negotiations between the United States and Soviet delegations, the Assembly was able to endorse unanimously a new start for the *Outer Space Committee* with the long-sought participation of the Soviet Union. Further, the Assembly approved the vitally important principle that outer space and the bodies in it are not subject to national

appropriation and are subject to international law — including specifically the United Nations Charter. It further endorsed world-wide collaboration in the use of outer space for the advancement of weather forecasting and even weather control, and for world-wide radio and television communications by satellite — two especially promising technical fields from which all nations, whether advanced or underdeveloped, stand to benefit.

9. On the question of the end of *colonialism,* the Assembly adopted a wise and forthright position reaffirming the goal which virtually all nations now accept, and appointing a committee of 17 nations to concern itself, on behalf of the General Assembly, with this great peaceful transition. In connection with this action, the U.S. Delegation made a major statement of our country's support for the rapid and peaceful evolution of colonial peoples toward self-determination. The United States was happy to find itself in company with the great majority of members, with whom our anti-colonial history and our contemporary interest give us a natural bond of sympathy.

The United States Delegation took this occasion to circulate a detailed memorandum on Soviet colonial practices.[353] That memorandum was informative to delegations from many parts of the world, and will continue to attract attention in the future.

10. The Assembly unanimously approved two resolutions for the *Economic and Educational Development of Africa,* and one to establish an internationally supported World Food Program of $100 million. All three resolutions arose from United States initiatives. All will play an important part in the economic and social development which it is the United States policy to promote among the emerging nations.

But I feel obliged to add a comment in a more sober vein. The recent armed attack on Goa, and the inability of the Security Council to deal with such use of force quickly and decisively, remind us of the dangerous tendency of nations to apply one law in one part of the world or toward one group of states, and a different law to others. If the United Nations should habitually resort to this double standard of judgment, serious consequences for world peace, and for the United Nations itself, are inevitable. Specifically, if the use of force against territory under the control of other states is to be condoned for anti-colonial reasons, it can also be condoned for other reasons — and we will have opened Pandora's box.

This is not a matter of colonialism or anti-colonialism. The United States Delegation has made clear on many occasions the anti-colonial views of the United States. This was a question of the use of force in

[353] See USUN press release 3862, November 28, 1961.

violation of the Charter in the opinion of a large majority of the Security Council.

It is evident that neither the United Nations itself nor some of its members have used as well or as often as they might the procedures for peaceful settlement laid down in the Charter, and the peace-keeping machinery of the United Nations. Nor have we paid enough attention to improving and expanding that machinery.

But we are by no means disheartened. The United Nations in this year has achieved notable and life-giving successes. As for the failures, our only permissible reaction to them is a new dedication to success. If our present methods are inadequate to the task, we must repair and improve them. The task remains what it was: not the facile choice between peace and justice, but peace *with* justice — for only in justice can real peace be attained.

In concluding let me express my appreciation to all the members of the United States Delegation for their devoted and tireless efforts, which contributed so greatly toward the success of our labors. We had a strong delegation and we have worked closely and harmoniously together.

I would also like to express the appreciation of the entire delegation for the effective and vigorous support and guidance which we received in all aspects of our work from you, from Secretary Rusk, from Assistant Secretary Harlan Cleveland and his able staff in the State Department.

Sincerely yours,

Before leaving New York City to spend the Christmas holidays at Libertyville, Stevenson held a press conference on December 21 at which he discussed the record of the 61st General Assembly.[354]

The following letter was dictated before he left New York.

To Erwin R. Steinberg [355]

December 23, 1961

My dear Dean Steinberg:

I am much flattered by your letter of December 23 and invitation to suggest a woman for an honorary degree at Carnegie Tech. Two women occur to me offhand who have contributed conspicuously to our society and had but little recognition.

Mrs. Alicia Patterson Guggenheim, known as Alicia Patterson, is the founder of one of the most successful newspaper enterprises in the country — *Newsday*, published at Garden City, Long Island. She is a Trustee

[354] USUN press release 3906, December 21, 1961.
[355] Dean of Margaret Morrison Carnegie College, Carnegie Institute of Technology.

of Hofstra College and on the Committee at Radcliffe which you are doubtless familiar with. The *Saturday Evening Post* had an elaborate story about her some time ago, and I understand the *New Yorker* is soon to run a profile of this unusual woman. She is about 54 years old and a great-granddaughter of Joseph Medill, the founder of the *Chicago Tribune*. Her father was Colonel Patterson, who founded the *Daily News*. But her views are liberal, rational and advanced!

Mrs. Marietta Endicott Peabody Tree, of New York, is the present U.S. member of the United Nations Commission on Human Rights. She is a daughter of Bishop Malcolm Peabody, retired Episcopal Bishop of Western New York, and a granddaughter of Dr. [Endicott] Peabody, the founder of Groton School. She has been very active in civil rights as a member of the New York Commission, and has also served many civic interests as well as taking an active role in New York and national Democratic politics. Inez Robb did a biographical story about her in the *Saturday Evening Post* a year or so ago.

Doubtless both of these women are known to you and, of course, I could give you much more detailed information if either of them interests you as a possible candidate. The latter, of course, has contributed more to "international understanding," as your letter suggests.

A third suggestion would be Mary Woodard Lasker (widow of Albert D. Lasker), of New York. However, her distinction has been largely in the fields of the arts and medical research. The Lasker Foundation and the Lasker awards in the latter field are doubtless well known to you. I shall not enlarge on her unless you so desire.

And I can think of still others!

Cordially yours,

Stevenson spent the 1961 Christmas holiday season at Libertyville with members of his family.

To Mrs. Ronald Tree [356]

[no date] [357]

. . . "The person who can face both life and love with confidence and courage — and give himself for the sheer joy of giving — is sure to find joy and contentment. For loving *is* living." It sounds well — and is, no doubt, but my trouble seems to be that "life" is so dependent on love.

The holiday in the snowbound house has been glorious with all as-

[356] This handwritten postcard is in the possession of Mrs. Tree.
[357] According to Mrs. Tree, Stevenson dated this postcard, on a later occasion, December, 1961.

sembled in a squalor of toys, disorder and congestion with babes and dogs everywhere. I've only been in town one day with doctor business [358] and lunch with [Mayor Richard J.] Daley. Out here there have been two dances for my age plus my party, which was a triumph of overcrowding and gaiety with dancing in the basement. . . .

[358] He had had a medical examination.

Part Two

1962

S *tevenson returned to the United Nations on January 11, 1962.
By 1962 there were 104 members of the United Nations and the
Afro-Asian nations stepped up their criticism of apartheid in South Africa
and imperialism and racism everywhere.*[1]

*The UN Force in the Congo, Tshombe's refusal to rejoin the Central
Government, and the financial strain on the United Nations of the
Congo operation were omnipresent problems. Flareups along the
Israeli-Syrian border, tension between India and Pakistan over Kashmir,
the Chinese attack on Indian border positions in October, 1962, the resumption of nuclear testing by the United States, the cessation of testing
by the Soviet Union in December, 1962, and the independence of Algeria
were among the complex issues of world politics.*

*In October the world faced a possible holocaust over the introduction
of offensive missiles in Cuba. Stevenson, at President Kennedy's request,
joined in many of the secret meetings of the Executive Committee dealing with the crisis. When the crisis passed, Stevenson was charged in an
article by Stewart Alsop and Charles Bartlett with having proposed
another "Munich" in the Executive Committee deliberations.*

*Amidst the turmoil and unrelenting pressures of the year, Stevenson
found moments of surcease at the marriage of his son John Fell at Big
Sur, California, a brief vacation with his sister and brother-in-law in
Florence, Italy, and a yachting cruise with Agnes Meyer and other
friends, and finally, the Christmas holiday with some of his family at his
home at Libertyville, Illinois.*

[1] See Julian R. Friedman, *Basic Facts on the Republic of South Africa and the
Policy of Apartheid* (United Nations Publication, Office of Public Information #s/72,
1972).

To Mrs. Ronald Tree [2]

[no date] [3]

M —

Excellent! And for one so young and beautiful! Its not fair that you could have so many talents and most so few. I protest — on behalf of the common man! But I bow humbly when I hear how much you have given — and without my help or counsel from me!

But - (1) the word is "administer" — not "administrate."

(2) with larger type could you forgo the glasses? Or are they a "property" to reduce dazzle? . . .

John Steinbeck wrote Stevenson in a jocular spirit asking him to persuade President Kennedy to make Steinbeck ambassador to Oz. Among the reasons he mentioned was the Wicked Witch who melted and ran down over herself. If he could find that secret, he observed, it would be possible to take care of a number of people "who would look better melted down."

To John F. Kennedy

January 3, 1962

Dear Mr. President:

I am loathe to request your personal attention to a question that is manifestly political patronage. Yet I have a feeling you will want to see the attached excerpt from a letter from my long-time friend, John Steinbeck.

You will be particularly attracted by the possibility he suggests that quite a few people we know would look better melted down. After all, we are in search of initiatives in the foreign field and this seems like one of the most promising I have heard of!

Cordially yours,

To Ralph McGill [4]

January 8, 1962

My dear Ralph —

Your reporter handed me your note at the airplane just now. I had heard about your wife's desperate illness, and hence the news of her

---

[2] This handwritten letter is in the possession of Mrs. Tree.

[3] Mrs. Tree dates this letter early January, 1962.

[4] Publisher of the Atlanta *Constitution* and an old friend of Stevenson's. This handwritten letter is in the possession of Mrs. Ralph McGill.

progress was very good indeed. What a time you've had — and my heart goes out to you!

I was glad to see the column — and, of course, flattered. I get provoked to the point of impotent rage by this new breed of Katanga "closed-communion patriots"[5] (wonderful phrase) who obviously have little communion with the facts.

Let us have that deferred breakfast when you come back to New York. I think of no more agreeable way to start the New Year!

Ever yours,
ADLAI

To Edmund G. Brown[6]

January 10, 1962

My dear Pat:

I was in Chicago yesterday and met some of my old friends from the Encyclopaedia Britannica Films Company. You may recall that I brought some of them to the Executive Mansion on my visit to you in Sacramento a few years ago. While I am no longer active in this company, in view of my job in New York, I am still interested in its enterprising exploration of techniques to improve the quality of education. And, therefore, I take the liberty of reporting to you a situation in California which you may not be aware of.

Evidently the revamping of teaching credentials is underway in California and consideration is being given to dropping audio visual as a requirement in your Teacher Training Institutes. Apparently this is part of a move away from the over emphasis on methodology in teacher training to greater emphasis on subject matter. If this is so, it seems strange to me that audio visual would be discontinued.

I certainly applaud the move away from methodology. The over concentration on *how* to teach teachers to teach at the sacrifice of subject matter has long seemed to me ridiculous. But the need for communicating subject matter effectively is the very place where audio visual training comes in. The recent advances in educational communication techniques have been spectacular, as you know, and reflect the rising demand for more effective communication of subject matter to our future citizens.

My EBF friends tell me that there are several committees in California giving consideration to this matter, one of which met this week in Los Angeles. They also tell me that you will be a deciding factor in the ultimate conclusion. Hence this note to bespeak your careful attention to their recommendations.

[5] Stevenson may refer to the American Committee for Aid to Katanga Freedom Fighters.
[6] The original is in the possession of Mr. Brown.

I read with interest and approval, of course, the account of your speech in Washington. I wish I could have seen you. Perhaps I will have that good fortune before long because my youngest son, John Fell, is going to marry Nathaniel Owings' [7] daughter at his place at Big Sur on February 17.

Meanwhile best wishes for total triumph this historic year,[8] and affectionate regards to Bernice.[9]

Cordially yours,

ADLAI

P.S. Encyclopaedia Britannica Films has established a Research Center in Palo Alto which gives me another good excuse for coming to California!

AES

On January 14, 1962, Stevenson received America's Democratic Legacy Award from the Anti-Defamation League of B'nai B'rith. The national chairman of the ADL said in presenting the award: "He is, for Americans, the personification of democratic purpose, and for the world, the embodiment of the spirit of American humanity." Stevenson discussed the Congo on his January 21 television program, spoke in the Security Council on the same question on January 30, and on January 25 and 30 before the General Assembly urged Portugal to grant self-determination to Angola.

To Mrs. Franklin D. Roosevelt [10]

January 15, 1962

Dear Mrs. R.:

Having just returned from a holiday I hasten to put in writing a word of homage and appreciation to you for your faithful and inspiring service as a Special Adviser to our Sixteenth General Assembly Delegation. I know I speak for all my colleagues when I say we were delighted to have you with us and hope to see a great deal more of you in the months to come.

Devotedly yours,

ADLAI

---

[7] A founding partner of the architectural firm of Skidmore, Owings and Merrill.
[8] Mr. Brown was up for reelection as governor of California. He defeated Richard M. Nixon in November.
[9] Mrs. Brown.
[10] The original is in the Franklin D. Roosevelt Library, Hyde Park, New York.

The American-Israel Cultural Foundation was holding a dinner in New York City in honor of former Senator Herbert Lehman. Robert Benjamin, the chairman of the foundation, invited Stevenson to attend. Stevenson sent the following telegram.

To Robert S. Benjamin

January 16, 1962

I REGRET EXCEEDINGLY NOT BEING ABLE TO JOIN YOU IN PERSON AS YOU PAY TRIBUTE TO MY GOOD AND OLD FRIEND HERBERT LEHMAN FOR I CAN THINK OF NO MORE FITTING GUEST OF HONOR FOR THIS EVENING'S FESTIVITIES. HERBERT LEHMAN IS THAT RARE INDIVIDUAL, A NINETEENTH CENTURY GENTLEMAN WITH TWENTIETH CENTURY ENTHUSIASMS, WHOSE BOUNDLESS ENERGY HAS BENEFITED EVERYONE WHO IS PRIVILEGED TO BE HIS CONTEMPORARY. HIS ACCOMPLISHMENTS IN GOVERNMENT, POLITICS, CHARITABLE AND HUMANITARIAN CAUSES, CIVIL RIGHTS AND INTERNATIONAL UNDERSTANDING ARE A CONTINUING INSPIRATION TO ALL WHO WOULD DEVOTE THEIR LIVES TO PUBLIC SERVICE. BUT NO EVENT HONORING THE SENATOR SHOULD FAIL TO TAKE NOTE OF THE GRACIOUS, GENEROUS LADY WHO HAS SHARED HIM WITH US FOR SO MANY WONDERFUL YEARS, AND I SHOULD LIKE TO SAY TO EDITH LEHMAN THAT MY APPRECIATION OF HER HUSBAND EXTENDS TO HER AS WELL.

On January 19, 1962, Stevenson, President Kennedy, and U Thant, acting Secretary-General of the United Nations, lunched at Stevenson's embassy. U Thant wrote Stevenson that he was getting the recipe for the artichoke and shrimp dish from Stevenson's housekeeper.

To U Thant

January 25, 1962

My dear friend:

I am most grateful for your letter. And I suspect my housekeeper will never be the same again.

I hope we can do this again from time to time.

Cordially yours,

To Mrs. Marshall Field

January 31, 1962

Dearest Ruth:

Thank you ever so much for the orchids which ennobled the Kennedy–U Thant–Stevenson encounter, and which ennobled Stevenson for days after! I apologize for not having acknowledged these long since, and am ever so grateful for your eternal thoughtfulness.

Love,

In order to pay for the United Nations force in the Congo, the UN had to issue bonds. Stevenson was to testify on February 7, 1962, before the Senate Foreign Relations Committee urging that the United States purchase its share of the bonds.

To Aage Hessellund-Jensen [11]

January 31, 1962

Dear Aage:

Your message concerning your government's proposal to participate in the United Nations bond issue to the extent of something more than twice your normal assessment rate was most welcome. It comes at an extremely appropriate moment. We are on the eve of Senate hearings in which my government's participation in this issue will be considered. The encouraging news of the attitude of your government and that of the other Scandinavian countries will serve as an inspiration to our people who are intimately concerned with this matter.

I understand that your government and your good self have approached this problem in terms of the vital interests of the world as a whole and of our free nation friendships in particular. Nevertheless, in view of the special situation involved, will you please accept my sincere personal appreciation for your government's as well as your own acts of friendship in this as on so many other occasions.

Sincerely yours,

To Cyril Clemens [12]

February 1, 1962

Dear Mr. Clemens:

Naturally, my favorite is the verse that Mark Twain wrote on the back of a menu at a banquet — in Cleveland, I think — when there was some discussion about the pronunciation of my grandfather's name. From memory and without checking, my recollection is that it went something as follows:

"Lexicographers roar and philologists bray,
And the best they can do is to call him Ad-*lay.*

[11] Permanent representative of Denmark to the United Nations.
[12] Editor of the *Mark Twain Journal.*

> But at longshoremen's picnics
> When accents are high,
> And Fair Harvard's not present,
> They call him Ad-*lie*." [13]

Cordially yours,

To Lady Barbara Jackson

February 2, 1962

Dear Barbara:

I have had the damnedest time trying to get my schedule worked out.

Sunday night, February 4 — your arrival date — I have to have a stag dinner for Adoula.[14] Dinner is at 7. If you arrive in time for me to see you before that, please let me know.

On Monday, February 5, I think we should get together. It is my birthday. Jane Dick will be here and insists on participating. We can arrange something by telephone as soon as you arrive.

On Tuesday, February 6, I am obliged to leave for Washington in order to meet the President by 4 o'clock.

On Wednesday, I have a farewell dinner for Mongi Slim, the President of the General Assembly, at 8 o'clock, formal, at my apartment, where you are expected.

I have had some difficulty trying to get this figured out with Mildred Kenyon,[15] and I hope it is both clear and satisfactory. I yearn to see you.

Love,

Secretary of Labor Arthur J. Goldberg, an old friend from Chicago, sent Stevenson a telegram on his sixty-second birthday.

To Arthur J. Goldberg

February 6, 1962

Dear Arthur:

My heartfelt thanks for that flattering and comforting telegram. I wish it were true. But you will go to heaven for charity, if you don't go some-

---

[13] For different versions of this verse, see *The Papers of Adlai E. Stevenson*, Vol. III, pp. 138, 561.

[14] Cyrille Adoula, prime minister of the Republic of the Congo.

[15] Mrs. W. Houston Kenyon, Jr., with whom Lady Jackson was staying in New York.

where else for other reasons! It is good to have such a loyal and thoughtful friend, and I count myself much richer today after your wire.

Yours,

To Frances FitzGerald

February 8, 1962

Dearest Frankie:

A scarf — a Nassau orange? Such subtlety! And what an improvement in my neck. It's almost worth another birthday — and I have always wanted you around my neck, or vice-versa.

Of course I am expecting you to go to California. John Fell was elated when I reported your imminent arrival. I have a ticket for you (tourist class with me). . . .

On the plane with us will be Buffie Ives, Alicia Patterson, Mrs. Carpenter [16] and Mr. and Mrs. Roger Stevens.[17] If your elusive room mate could disengage long enough, she would be welcome too.

Friday we will stay together at the Del Monte Lodge, and that evening there will be a large Bridal Dinner. The next day comes the wedding at Nathaniel Owings spectacular house, followed by a reception and the conventional festivities. On Sunday we would recapture our health and do some sightseeing.

Don't disappoint me! It's been a long time since we've had a trip.[18]

Stevenson and Miss Jean Wylie, who lived in Ashfield, Massachusetts, corresponded over the years although they never met.

To Jean M. Wylie

February 8, 1962

My dear Jean:

How kind you are to me! Your words and your many gifts convey a sweet presence that I wish I could know better. I love best the beautiful old things you have sent me, full of memories for you that I can almost sense when I look at them.

Thank you so very much for the new supply of china for my office lunches. It is much too good for the purpose, but certainly makes the

---

[16] Mrs. John Alden Carpenter, Ellen Stevenson's mother.

[17] Mr. Stevens, a theatrical producer and real estate broker, had served at Stevenson's request in 1956 as chairman of the Finance Committee of the Democratic party.

[18] In 1957, Miss FitzGerald and her mother, Marietta Tree, had accompanied Stevenson on his trip to Africa. See *The Papers of Adlai E. Stevenson,* Vol. VII, Part One.

sandwiches taste better! And the exquisite bud vase that appeared on my desk with a bouquet of white freesia, on my birthday, enchants me and will remind me daily of a friend who has become very dear.

Affectionately,

To Mrs. Ernest L. Ives [19]

February 9, 1962

Dear Buffie:

I have your letter and will pick you up to go to the airport Friday morning, February 16, at 8:15–8:30. I will have your ticket. Please be downstairs at your apartment so that we will not have to waste any time.

I am getting you a tourist ticket, returning Sunday evening. It saves us about $100. If you wish a first class ticket, be sure to telephone Roxane [Eberlein] promptly.

Love,

ADLAI

P.S. The Florentine donkey is a splendid fellow, ornamenting my desk evermore. Thank you!

Felix Frankfurter, associate justice of the Supreme Court, wrote Stevenson that neither of them needed justification for their gourmet proclivities, but that the late Charles W. Eliot, president of Harvard University, once said: "He who knows not the value of good food is to that extent not civilized." Frankfurter thanked Stevenson for his shrimp and artichoke dish.

To Felix Frankfurter

February 15, 1962

My dear Felix:

If I can now make common cause with Frankfurter *and* Eliot, I feel more comfortable about my shameless admiration for food! Thank you for coming to my rescue — there were whispers that Stevenson didn't know as much about diplomacy as shrimps and artichokes. Of course if they knew no more about the latter than the former, they would be neither diplomats *nor* gourmets.

I hear that I may see you soon here in New York, which makes me very happy. I'll bring neither recipes nor a dispatch case!

Yours,

[19] The original is in the Elizabeth Stevenson Ives collection, Illinois State Historical Library (E.S.I., I.S.H.L.).

Stevenson flew to California on Friday, February 16, attended the wedding of his son John Fell on Saturday, and returned to New York on Monday.

To Mort Sahl [20]

February 21, 1962

Dear Mort:

The retreat from Hungry Eye to previously prepared positions was fast and disorderly, but successful enough to catch the plane for New York. And now that I am back, and Glenn is up and down,[21] I send you this belated word of thanks for your unexpected hospitality — and for the best entertainment I have ever heard you do. I am afraid it was a gross imposition, and hereafter I am going to come without advance notice and pay my own way.

I had hoped so much for a word with you, but the schedule was relentless and so I could do no better than to leave hostages behind.

I hope you will be coming East during the winter and that there will be another opportunity to save the human race — including, of course, the Republicans!

Yours,

To Mr. and Mrs. Nathaniel A. Owings

Feburary 21, 1962

Dear Nat and Margaret:

Well, I'm back, Glenn is down, and the children are up. And how are you! It was a glorious wedding, and obviously you have talents as a producer. Who could have put guests in such beauty and a preacher in such peril? I shall long remember his furtive glances over his shoulder to the Pacific 600 feet below.

I had hoped to call you on Sunday before our departure to thank you for all of your courtesies, but we got to San Francisco barely in time to dine with Mort Sahl and catch the plane back to Chicago. So I must take this means to say again how much we all enjoyed and appreciated your production — and how much we love your daughter!

Yours,

Stevenson had helped influence President Kennedy against resuming nuclear testing in the atmosphere after the Russians had resumed such testing in September, 1961.

[20] Comedian appearing at the Hungry I in San Francisco.
[21] Lieutenant Colonel John H. Glenn, Jr., became the first American astronaut to orbit the earth on February 20, 1962.

To *John F. Kennedy* [22]

MEMORANDUM FOR THE PRESIDENT

February 21, 1962

From: Adlai E. Stevenson

Subject: *Resumption of Atmospheric Tests*

Without more information than I have it is not possible to hazard an opinion as to whether atmospheric testing should be resumed. From what I have heard I assume a decision has been reached, however, to resume tests for legitimate reasons of military security, and not for political and psychological considerations.

The political price of test resumption will be paid most directly in the United Nations and in terms of public opinion around the world. The immediate problem, therefore, is to cushion the shock and moderate the adverse political effects of such testing. There are the following possibilities:

(1) Assuming that it is not realistically possible to delay the announcement on March 1 that the United States will resume atmospheric testing,[23] every effort should be made to channel the controversy out of the United Nations and into the Geneva 18-nation Conference.[24] We should press there for immediate consideration of a test ban treaty together with an agreement to prevent the spread of nuclear weapons as specified in the present U.S. disarmament program, but without prejudice to more general disarmament discussions.

(2) A new test ban agreement, to be most negotiable, should not involve elaborate international controls or inspection arrangements. One possibility would be a comprehensive ban on all testing, with a limited number of inspection challenges by each side to investigate whenever national detection systems indicate that there is clandestine testing. The agreement would be temporary — perhaps of two years duration — so as to allow time to work out a definitive treaty with broader controls, in the context of other disarmament measures. To deal with the problem of clandestine test preparations, we could propose continuous observation of known testing sites and maintain our own standby preparations for resumption of tests. This is not the only type of treaty we might propose,

[22] This document was declassified. The original is in the President's Office Files, Subjects: Nuclear Testing, John F. Kennedy Library.

[23] Kennedy announced in a speech on March 2, 1962, that the United States would resume testing in late April unless the U.S.S.R. agreed to a fully effective nuclear test-ban treaty by that time.

[24] The disarmament conference, which opened on March 14, 1962, was attended by only seventeen nations. It had been created by the UN General Assembly in 1961 as an eighteen-nation meeting, but France, which had wanted a four-power conference, refused to participate.

but it has the virtue of relative simplicity. The important point is to keep pressing for a test ban agreement even as we test.

(3) Other initial steps which we could suggest at the outset of the Geneva meeting to improve our posture include:

(a) a proposal to set aside specified quantities of delivery vehicles (bombers and missiles) for eventual destruction;

(b) immediate cut-off of fissionable materials production, with sequestration of specified quantities of weapons material for ultimate peaceful use;

(c) various measures to reduce the risks of war by surprise attack or miscalculation through systems of fixed or mobile observation groups, aerial observation, and reciprocal inspection in specified zones. (We should prepare the best possible mix of regional security arrangements: area to be covered; limitations to be placed on weapons, manpower and movement; facilities for observation and inspection);

(d) an agreement prohibiting the placing in orbit of weapons of mass destruction;

(e) an updating of the 1925 Convention [25] to prohibit the use of chemical, biological and radiological warfare;

(f) a non-aggression agreement between the Warsaw Pact and NATO countries, perhaps linked with limitations on certain types of forces near East-West demarcation lines;

(g) immediate drafting of the Charter of an International Disarmament Organization and of arrangements for a United Nations Peace Force.

4. I recognize that each of the foregoing measures could involve some disadvantages for the United States, but we must realize that without any of them our disarmament posture is thin and featureless. We should be prepared to offer some specific proposals to offset the Soviet propaganda onslaught calling for immediate and radical disarmament measures without adequate controls.

(5) I assume that the rationale for the decision to resume testing will be set forth fully and persuasively in a statement by the President which will be circulated to all UN Delegations in New York.

(6) I conclude with the suggestion that if testing must be resumed and an announcement is to be made promptly, we should attempt to:

(a) channel the discussion into the 18-nation Conference in Geneva;

(b) urgently propose a new test ban treaty;

(c) propose at the outset an agreement to prevent the spread of nuclear weapons;

---

[25] At the Arms Traffic Convention at Geneva on June 17, 1925, fifty-five states signed a protocol banning poison gas and bacteriological warfare. Although the United States was one of the signers, the Senate did not act on the treaty. B. H. Williams, *The United States and Disarmament* (New York: Whittlesey House, 1971), p. 302.

(d) propose two or three other initial arms control steps of the type suggested above.

Unless we are prepared to come forth with a group of such initial measures, and unless the President indicates in his announcement that he intends to make such proposals, we shall be exposed to widespread protests and growing demands for unrealistic and unacceptable disarmament measures.

The essential point is that test resumption makes it all the more necessary to press for a test ban and other immediate disarmament measures. Otherwise the arms race will ultimately bring us all to grief. Let us *lead*, not *follow*.

Let us *not* insist any longer on unattainable perfection in inspection and control and in this way jeopardize the whole disarmament enterprise.[26]

The following undated memorandum is signed by Stevenson.[27]

The following points may be useful in considering the decision with respect to resumption of nuclear testing:

1. It may be taken for granted that the case for early resumption of tests will be made in its strongest, most concrete terms.

2. It may be assumed that the case for further restraint will *not* be made in very strong or very concrete terms.

3. The difficulty with the second case is that military power can be measured but political and moral power cannot. Indeed we do not seem to have any accepted concept of the value of political and moral factors in the national power equation. (This is despite the fact that if "mutual deterrence" means anything, it means that the military factor in the power equations of the U.S. and USSR cancel each other out; and despite the fact that the real nature of the struggle between the world of consent and the world of coercion is not military but an ideological contest for the loyalty of the non-communist, non-western world.)

4. The semantic problem with the case for restraint on atmospheric testing, therefore, is that the argument tends to be cast in imprecise or sentimental terms. It seems to be a plea for popularity, or for faith in the Russians, or for pacifism — in any case an argument unrelated to real power.

5. The confrontation of opposing arguments in such a semantic context can have only one result: the prompt resumption of testing.

[26] The last two paragraphs are handwritten.
[27] The original is in the President's Office Files, Subjects: Nuclear Testing, John F. Kennedy Library.

6. But to pose the issue in terms of *military* advantage *versus political* advantage can be seriously misleading because it sets up two criteria which, in fact, are almost impossible to separate. Military and political power are both elements of a single criterion which is the only acceptable basis of decision: the *national advantage expressed in terms of total national power and influence.* It is clear that to test is to *gain* something *militarily* and to *lose* something *politically;* while to hold off testing is to lose something militarily and gain something politically. The proper question therefore is: which decision on atmospheric testing is to the *net national advantage?*

7. Presumably the *military* advantage of a given series of atmospheric tests can be forecast with reasonable accuracy.

8. It is also possible to be fairly specific about the disadvantages to the national power equation of immediate test resumption.

For example:

a. Some loss in, or the compromising of, the opportunity for progress on disarmament inherent in a moment of rough equality in nuclear and space technology.

b. Loss of our present advantage over the Soviet Union on the "peace issue." (This is not a sentimental or propaganda point: it is a power fulcrum for drawing the non-western, non-communist world toward closer association with the West, thus adding to total U.S. power in the world arena).

c. Some damage to our growing leadership and influence in the UN, and thus in our capacity to serve U.S. national interests through UN actions.

d. A general loss of world prestige by an act which, rightly or wrongly, would be interpreted as the failure of political leadership to break out of the arms race mentality.

e. Some support for the position of the more reactionary groups within the Soviet leadership, and some support for the Chinese position versus the Russian position on the inevitability of war.

9. If the decision is that the net national advantage lies in further restraint, test preparations could be kept in a state of alert during a limited period of urgent political initiatives. These would be founded on the valid grounds that time is extremely short to prevent another extended round in the nuclear arms race, to prevent the spread of nuclear weapons capability to other nations, and to prevent space exploration from turning into a runaway race into the unknown. The chances for success in such initiatives may be improved by unsettled political conditions within the Soviet Union and by tensions between Russia and China — both of which might encourage Khrushchev to accept agreements which would be extremely popular in all countries, including the Soviet Union.

10. If the decision is that the net national advantage requires immediate resumption of testing it might be advisable to announce with the least possible excitement that the current series of underground tests have shown the need to broaden the experiment by a limited number of atmospheric shots of minimum useful force and limited fallout. It would be most desirable to emphasize simultaneously and repeatedly thereafter that the United States sees no security in a competitive nuclear arms race and is pressing forward to find a mutually acceptable basis for test cessation.[28]

Mr. and Mrs. Albert M. Greenfield, of Philadelphia, old friends and financial supporters of Stevenson's presidential campaigns, spent an evening with him in New York. Stevenson mentioned that it was so expensive for Foreign Service officers to live in New York that he feared that he would lose Ambassador Charles W. Yost as a result. On February 21, 1962, Mr. Greenfield wrote, asking what size donation would help and remarking that they would see Stevenson on September 25, when he was to appear as narrator with the Philadelphia Orchestra.

To Albert M. Greenfield

February 26, 1962

Dear Al:

Thanks for your letter. It was a delightful evening for me, and I wish I could count on another one with you and the charming Elizabeth soon again. September and the Philadelphia Orchestra seems a long way off, both in time and cultural altitude!

The man I spoke to you about is Ambassador Charles W. Yost, a graduate of Princeton and a lifetime Foreign Service officer, whom I enlisted to help me as my No. 3 man here, a year ago. He was then Ambassador to Morocco. He has a Polish wife and two children. The boy is in college and the girl in preparatory school.

Yost is one of those really able, indeed brilliant, Foreign Service officers of whom we have too few. He will soon be made one of the half dozen career ambassadors in our service, I believe. Unfortunately, he is without means except what he earns, and after a long life mostly abroad, finds New York together with the entertaining almost beyond his limited endurance. I am genuinely fearful that after another year he may feel obliged to ask for another Embassy abroad, where he will get the same salary plus a substantial quarters and representation allowance, which

---

[28] This paragraph is crossed out in the document.

together with the lower cost of living virtually everywhere would make his situation much easier.

You have been so good to me so many times, that I am loath to even discuss anything more of this kind. Forgive me for mentioning it, and let me say once more how surprised and impressed I am that you seem to never forget even such casual conversations.

With love to that Unitarian,[29]

Yours,

To Mrs. John F. Kennedy

February 26, 1962

My dear Jackie:

I have known the Brazilian singer and guitarist, Olga Coelho, and the great Andres Segovia, for some time. I am informed indirectly that they would both be most happy to be invited to perform at the White House when the President of Brazil is here. I enclose something about these remarkable people, although I am confident that they are well known to you.

I dread to think of you and Lee going to India [30] —without me!

Affectionately,

To Mrs. Ronald Tree [31]

February 26, 1962

M —

Its absurd. A week has gone by — and there is still no time to report even barest details.

February is the rainy season in Calif, but Sat. dawned bright and blue and cloudless — the first clear day in more than two weeks! So the wedding — luncheon, wedding, reception & evening — were perfect. But the bridal dinner was in a torrent by the sea; and Sunday, the morning after, it rained all day, even up the Carmel valley, where "the sun always shines."

Granny Carpenter, Buffie, the Roger Stevens & I arrived [in San Francisco] Friday noon. Nance & Ad, Borden [Stevenson], the young Ives,[32] Carol Evans,[33] the [Edison] Dicks, Clows [34] etc etc met us [in San

[29] Mrs. Greenfield.

[30] Mrs. Kennedy and her sister, Princess Lee Radziwill, were planning to visit India in March, 1962.

[31] The original is in the possession of Mrs. Tree.

[32] Stevenson's nephew Timothy Ives and his wife.

[33] Stevenson's secretary from 1948 to 1961.

[34] Mr. and Mrs. James B. Clow, Lake Forest friends of Stevenson's.

Francisco] and after TV cameras, press conf., drinks and more than the usual confusion we transferred to a charter plane for Monterrey [Monterey]. There more guests, including the Owings, met us and we scattered — John Fell & me, Buffy, Granny, the Stevens & Dicks to the Del Monte Lodge.

The bridal dinner was as lovely a table as I've ever seen and Ellen [Stevenson] in good humor . . . and very self-conscious. But everything went off alright — and Bob Hutchins, Nat Owings, Adlai & Borden looked after her beautifully. The table was too long, the room too dark and we were seated an hour late with the result that the speaking — aggravated by a bachelor dinner the night before — was not very good. But Adlai, Pat Brown, Bob Hutchins & Nat Owings helped me out admirably. Dear Emily [35] — the bride's mother — was more handsome than ever and utterly inarticulate.

The last moment before John Fell & I started for the Big Sur and the wedding was occupied in trying to find him a collar for his cutaway, collar buttons, the ring and a telephone call from Karim [36] in Switzerland — guess where! The pre ceremony luncheon was divided — 80 people at Jack Morse's [37] and about 10 at the Owings in flashing sunlight, and crashing surf far, far below. I counted more than 100 seals sunning in a cave beneath us — and concluded, all in all that this was incomparably the most spectacular house I've seen in N. America.

The lunch with Ellen & her mother was frightening but went off well — no temper, no violence and Granny was a quiet, refined, gentlewoman thruout. Ellen I'm sure I never met before. Then came the wedding — just family in a tiny grove by a pool and a cross made by that remarkable Natalie in the Mexican fashion — all colors & silver bells — and beyond in all directions the blue, sun lit sea. The bridesmaids were in the colors of the different seasons — yellow, blue, orange, white. I must say I've never seen anything as gay, informal and lovely.

The reception was a few miles away in another spectacular house built originally by Orson Welles for his bride Rita Hayworth. Altho it was more than 100 miles from S.F. masses of people came and it was all very jolly. Ad & Nance & Borden flew back to S.F. with Natalie & J.F. — and said they last saw them heading for his apt & scrambled eggs.

The rest of us stayed at Pebble Beach & caroused and Sunday morning drove out to Helen Russell's [38] famous house & race horse ranch for lunch — in the rain. Thence on to S.F. and evening with Mort Sahl! By

[35] Mrs. John S. Barnes, of Albuquerque, New Mexico.
[36] The Aga Khan, who had been John Fell's roommate at Harvard.
[37] Neighbors of the Owingses at Big Sur.
[38] A San Francisco philanthropist who had been vice chairman of the United Nations Conference Committee of San Francisco in 1945 and later a member of United States delegations to UNESCO conferences.

the time I got back Monday — after 3 hrs sleep & all the nervous strain I was dead — but not dead enough to escape all the maneuvering, conferring & speaking in re the Cuban item in the General Assembly.[39] But by Tues I was in acute pain — and miserable. Dr. Henry Lax [40] pronounced it crystals in the kidney — with stones [41] — and thank God it was soon over and I was back at work doing a TV with Gladwyn Jebb [42] in the afternoon.

Since then I've spent half a day with JFK re nuclear testing & must go back again tomorrow. I'm afraid they are going to count heavily on me to help with the justification, if resumption is necessary — for obvious reasons.

Otherwise life swi[r]ls on in spite of the adjournment of the Assembly Friday night. Tomorrow we have a Security Council session to deal with another Cuban complaint. There is as usual more to report than time to do it in. I made a good speech in Wash[ington] to the Women's Press Club [43] in spite of feeling awful — followed by a reception for all the old friends at Betty Beale's. [44]

I wish I could go on — but it is Monday A.M. & must get off to the office. Perhaps the enclosed assortment will fill in some gaps. I wish I knew when you were coming back etc etc [45] — the schedule is getting out of hand & the pressures rising on all sides. Maybe thats why I liked the enclosed — and hope you do to[o] —

A.

To Lady Barbara Jackson

February 27, 1962

Dear Barbara:

I have been doing a television show every two weeks about the activities of the UN, and American policy generally. The one immediately ahead of us is Paul Hoffman [46] on economic development, on Sunday, March 4, and I wonder if there is any possibility that you could tape

[39] Cuba accused the United States of new plans of aggression and acts of intervention. Stevenson denied the charges in Committee 1 on February 5 and 14 and in the Security Council on March 15, 16, and 23.

[40] Stevenson's physician in New York from January, 1962, until Stevenson's death.

[41] Stevenson had suffered from this condition previously. See *The Papers of Adlai E. Stevenson,* Vol. III, pp. 572–576; Vol. IV, pp. 8, 9, 345–358 *passim.*

[42] A retired British diplomat (since 1960, Baron Gladwyn) who had been acting Secretary-General of the United Nations in 1946 and British ambassador to the United Nations, 1950–1954.

[43] February 22, 1962. USUN press release 3930.

[44] Syndicated columnist with the Washington *Star.*

[45] Mrs. Tree was in Barbados.

[46] Managing director of the United Nations Special Fund and former member of the United States delegation to the United Nations.

one with me on Friday, March 16, in the morning before you go to Washington, or, of course, the 15th if convenient.

The show lasts a half hour and it usually takes us about an hour before the cameras to do the taping. Preparation is minimal. The subject matter would be largely in your discretion. I regret that it would follow so closely after Hoffman, who will be talking with me about economic development and the Special Fund, I presume.

If these dates are not possible, could you keep it in mind for later on during your stay in America? Most any time would do as far as we are concerned, although we don't like to tape more than a couple of days before the Sunday when it appears, in order not to get too disconnected from the news.

Yours,

To Allan B. Ecker [47]

February 27, 1962

Dear Allan:

I am afraid I just don't have time to do whatever it is that is required to fill out the application for the New York Bar. I understand I am supposed to do it all in longhand, and I really can't do it. Perhaps I could do it next summer, somehow. Meanwhile, if there's any way to waive such an absurd requirement, I would appreciate it.

Would you please indicate with a question mark in red ink the questions you want answered on this form? I can dictate them over the telephone or to Miss [Roxane] Eberlein.

It will be inconvenient for me to find in the files in Chicago — where I never go — the copies of all the proceedings in my divorce case in 1949. Likewise, of course, I cannot possibly get letters from employers. After all, I was a partner in Sidley, Austin, Burgess & Smith from 1934 to 1941,[48] and thereafter in the employ of the government, and Governor of Illinois, until I became a partner of Paul, Weiss. Perhaps all this can be spelled out for their satisfaction.

As to degrees, I have an A.B. from Princeton, 1922, a J.D. from Northwestern Law School, 1926, and honorary degrees from some 30 American and foreign universities, including Princeton, Oxford, McGill, Columbia, Northwestern, and so forth, — Doctor of Civil Laws, Doctor of Humane Letters, Doctor of Literature.

I have never been admitted to any courts except the United States

[47] A member of the New York law firm of Paul, Weiss, Rifkind, Wharton and Garrison, which Stevenson had joined in 1957 and with which he planned to resume practice on his retirement from his ambassadorship. See *The Papers of Adlai E. Stevenson,* Vol. VI, pp. 448, 525n.

[48] See *The Papers of Adlai E. Stevenson,* Vol. I, pp. 209–210.

Supreme Court and the Bar of Illinois, so far as I can recall. I suppose I must have been admitted to the Federal courts in Chicago, but I don't have any recollection of when, nor have I done much court work. Just before joining Paul, Weiss, I represented the RCA [Radio Corporation of America] in its case with Zenith Radio Company on a petition for certiorari in the Supreme Court, and while at Paul, Weiss I argued a case in the New York Court of Appeals for the Empire State, Inc. Most of my work was on corporate reorganization and security issues.

If you need letters from judges, I can get them from Felix Frankfurter, Bill Douglas,[49] Earl Warren,[50] and Walter Schaefer and Harry Hershey of the Illinois Supreme Court (both of whom I appointed!).[51]

I am sorry to be so dilatory about this.

Yours,

Philip Noel-Baker wrote Stevenson that he saw encouraging signs for real hope on disarmament. But the general public in both the United States and the United Kingdom, he felt, was characterized by inertia that had to be overcome. He asked whether the Field Foundation would grant funds to educate the public on the issue.

To Philip Noel-Baker

March 2, 1962

Dear Philip:

I was so glad to have your letter of the 15th of February, and find your optimistic tone heartening. While I think that some progress has been made about disarmament, there is a great deal of skepticism, and also the usual vulnerability to pressure of the "prudent." I had hoped that we might have canvassed with Khrushchev by a special emissary the possibilities of progress at Geneva well in advance. But perhaps we can at least come forward with a new "peace offensive" comprised of old elephants.

Moreover, there is obviously more concern with fallout than there is with the weapons themselves, and I am afraid we suffer from the same "vast dead mass of inertia and skepticism" which you do in the UK.

I wish the Field Foundation could be of help, but we have been over the ground so many times that I doubt if it would be useful to raise the question again. It is virtually confined to child care and race relations. However, I am going to take up the suggestion with the Ford Founda-

[49] Associate Justice William O. Douglas, of the United States Supreme Court.
[50] Chief Justice of the United States.
[51] See *The Papers of Adlai E. Stevenson*, Vol. III, p. 275.

tion where they are looking for ways to spend their enormous resources. However, I am afraid they are so fearful of matters affecting
the public interest that little is likely to happen.

I hope I have more of your "outbursts." But I prefer them in person!

Cordially yours,

*On March 6, 1962, Stevenson spoke at Colgate University in his role
as ambassador of the United Nations to the American people. (He also
spoke at North Carolina State College in Raleigh, North Carolina, on
March 7 and on March 13 to the annual conference of the American
Association for the United Nations in Washington, D.C.)*

*The rapid increase in UN membership meant that the United States
no longer was in control of the General Assembly. The nations that had
regularly voted with the United States were now outnumbered. This
led to growing criticism in the United States of the United Nations.*

*Stevenson was introduced by his Princeton classmate Everett Case,
president of the university. Colgate University recorded the question-
and-answer period which followed Stevenson's address.*

THE ROLE OF THE UNITED STATES IN AN
EXPANDING UNITED NATIONS [52]

In all the criticism that has been leveled at the United Nations by
various western critics in recent months, I think I can detect two recurrent themes. The first is that the U.N. has fallen into an unhealthy
and obsessive concern with colonialism, that its Afro-Asian majority can
see no further in international life than the liquidation of the last remnants of the old European empires. As a result of this obsession, they are
said to miss other, more dangerous threats of Communist infiltration and
subversion and end up in a posture which is dangerously one-sided —
treating the western democracies with biased hostility and letting the
Communists get away with the benefit of every doubt.

The second line of criticism — which follows in some measure from
the first — is that the United Nations is neglecting its real function —
which is to keep the peace and uphold collective security. Lured from
the United Nations' true path by their anti-colonialist obsession, the new
nations, so goes the argument, are destroying the UN's fundamental
value as a mediator and conciliator. Disputes are being exacerbated and
blown up by ill-considered meddling — and meddling which always ends
up in bias against the west.

[52] Mr. Case furnished the editor with a transcript of Stevenson's speech and the
questions and answers.

These are serious charges. They have been uttered by responsible people on both sides of the Atlantic, and if they are true, then we have to admit that the value of the United Nations as an instrument of world peace is gravely compromised.

But are they true? They seem to me to be born at best of serious misconceptions about the world which the powers and the United Nations have alike to live in. At worst, they are the product of malice and pique. And whatever the motive behind them, they do not stand up to closer examination.

Let me take first the issue of colonialism. The United Nations, obviously, did not invent it. The issue is there, darkening men's minds with fears and suspicions, whether the U.N. takes any notice of it or not. You may say that it is unfair to the western powers that the obsession with colonialism should still be so strong after 15 years of such wholesale decolonization — the millions of subject peoples freed from western tutelage, the scores of new states brought into being, freely and largely peacefully, in the process.

But before we lump all the "anti-colonialists" together, let us try to be more precise. Loudest of all are the Communists — and least entitled to respect. When Eastern Europe enjoys self-determination, we will listen to them, and not before.

As for the non-communists, it is neither fair nor wise to lash out at a supposed "Afro-Asian Bloc," lumping all the new African and Asian states together as irrational critics of a supposed "Western Bloc." These geographical terms don't define solid blocs at all. They refer to a many-sided array of free nations, each with a wide area of freedom to pursue its own interests and express its own historical experience.

And that experience, of course, varies widely. Among the Asian nations are some whose concern about European colonialism, however deep and active, is somewhat more patient and less fierce than it once was. In fact, the whole subcontinent of Asia — Pakistan, India, Nepal, Ceylon and Burma—has been almost entirely free of Western control for about fifteen years. And these fifteen years of independence have moderated passions and turned many Asian eyes to other issues — especially economic development and security against the menace of atomic destruction.

The shift of interest is far from complete — nor will it be complete as long as colonies remain. There will be dangers for years ahead, both from those who try to stand unmoved against the winds of change and those who are willing in the name of progress to whip the winds of change up to hurricane force. These dangers were all too vividly illustrated in the recent action against Goa.[53]

[53] Stevenson refers to India's invasion and absorption of Goa in December, 1961. See pp. 175–183, above.

Certainly we cannot take Asia's moderation too much for granted. Asia was, after all, dominated for well over a century by Western overlords whose rule, whatever its virtues in many cases, might have been expected to leave deeper scars of resentment than has in fact proved to be the case. Westerners can easily forget their dominion in fifteen short years. What is more remarkable and admirable is the fact that so many Asians appear to be ready to do so as well. If occasionally, some anti-colonialist resolution strikes a chord in their minds, we in the West should not be too surprised. They, after all, were at the receiving end of the colonial experiment. The remarkable fact is how quickly and with what realism and dignity the vast majority are prepared to let the past slip without regret or resentment into history.

But in Africa, we in the West must remind ourselves that colonial control is still a fresh memory or a direct, brutal fact. We do not blame a man for being obsessed with a toothache. We can rise above his discomfort. We don't feel it. But for him it is a dark angry fact. So it still is in many parts of Africa.

The passions unleashed in African minds — particularly young African minds — by bloodshed and exploitation, by discrimination and delay, by the violation of human rights — cannot but color African thinking about general international events. So would such conditions color our thinking if our own neighbors were the sufferers. We demonstrate a comparable feeling when we argue that peace cannot be secure so long as the Hungarian people are tyrannized and oppressed. Why should such a sentiment be acceptable and understandable, and a similar feeling among Africans for their brothers in Angola, say, be called "irresponsible" and obsessed?

We shall make no sense in our international relations if we seek to banish obstinate realities simply by reading new nations lectures on their unadult behavior. For Africans to care profoundly about colonialism in Africa is not "unadult." It is simply and directly human.

Given this background, it would perhaps not have been surprising if the new African states had allowed their votes to be swayed wholly by the colonial issue. Distinguished critics have accused them of such obsessive behavior, but I cannot see how the voting record bears out the accusation. Let us look at the facts. What do we find? Consistent hostility to the West? Consistent support — out of pique and anger — for Soviet resolutions? Utter inability to follow moderate paths on the anti-colonial issue? Complete African — and even Asian — extremism compared with the moderation of Western views? One might expect it, judging by the attacks.

What in fact we find is something wholly different. Take the crucial issue which has confronted the United Nations for a year, and on which Mr. Khrushchev himself staked his personal prestige — an issue, incidentally, made more inflammable by the tragic death of Mr. Hammar-skjold. I refer, of course, to Russia's determination to end all independent executive action by the United Nations and to substitute instead a secretariat hamstrung by the veto from top to bottom. This Communist ploy has been largely defeated, and we have a new and effective Secretary General appointed with no impairment of his powers.

I can testify to the fact that this favorable outcome was not secured by Western pressure and support alone. The West, unaided, could have produced nothing but deadlock. The rescue of an independent, responsible UN Secretariat was accomplished because an overwhelming majority of the United Nations, including virtually all the new Asian and African states, would not go along with an emasculated organization. If this is anti-Western irresponsibility, then we must revise the dictionary.

But even on the specific issue of colonialism, it is, I think, a gross perversion of the facts to accuse the new states of universal irresponsibility. When the resolution calling for a rapid end to colonialism was passed last November 27th, it took the place of a much more violent Soviet resolution which the Soviet delegation had withdrawn — why? Because the Afro-Asian bloc would not support it. In the form in which it was passed, the United States and such members of the British Commonwealth as Canada and Australia voted for it, which surely suggests that it represented a moderate, unobsessed view of the issue.

When sanctions were proposed against South Africa, the resolution, largely under Asian influence, failed to pass. One cannot, therefore, dismiss as "irresponsible extremism" the resolution which *did* pass, condemning South Africa's racial policies and commanding the support of the entire Assembly, save for Portugal. In fact, can anyone doubt that its tone represents what every modern member of world society accepts and supports?

The same moderation appeared on all the leading issues in this most recent resumed session of the General Assembly.

On Angola a moderate resolution, sponsored by 44 countries of Africa and Asia, was adopted by 99 votes to 2 — and a more drastic resolution offered by the Soviet bloc on the same subject was overwhelmingly defeated.

On the ticklish problem of independence for Ruanda-Urundi, Soviet attempts to get all Belgian troops out by July 1, and thus to court another Congolese explosion, were soundly defeated.

On Cuba's charges against the United States,[54] not one African or Asian country — in fact not one country outside the Soviet bloc itself — voted to sustain them or even to take official notice of them.

[54] Charges of continued aggression by the United States against Cuba.

And when the Soviets went to the Security Council in January to demand a new round of shooting in Katanga,[55] they didn't even get the support of the two African states on the Council — Ghana and the United Arab Republic — which are among the most emphatic of the anti-colonialists. There is general evidence here not of obsession but of a careful weighing of words and votes. As for the states singled out for strongest criticism — Portugal and the Union of South Africa — they have flouted the strongly held views not just of the Afro-Asian states, but of nearly the whole of the Community of Nations.

I do not, therefore, find that the criticism of obsessive and biased policies in the United Nations can be substantiated. I would go further and say that in concerning itself with the colonial issue, the United Nations is *not* being diverted from its proper function and purpose of safeguarding the peace and providing the machinery of conciliation. On the contrary, it was inevitable from the beginning that the issue of colonialism, both in the intention of the Charter and in the actual hazards of world politics, would for a time occupy the center of the stage of the United Nations.

When the Charter was elaborated, it stated as a fundamental of international life the equal rights of nations great and small. This democratic principle is, of course, always under attack by those — now on one side, now on the other — who prefer the Orwellian gloss that "some nations are more equal than others." But it stands among the Charter's first principles. Again, the 51 founder members undertook to give due account to the political aspirations of their dependent peoples and to help them to secure "free political institutions." In pressing them to carry through this commitment, the United Nations cannot be said to exceed its terms of reference. The blame should rather be with those nations who have failed and still fail to make any progress towards fulfilling obligations they solemnly undertook.

This is, in some measure, an academic issue. A much more immediate and dramatic justification of the United Nations' concern with colonialism lies in the fact, proven a thousand times in history, that the ending of empires becomes all too easily the beginning of wars. It is a point I hardly need to elaborate. Examples are strewn, like wrecks, on the seabed of the human record. When one system of power collapses — whether from external pressure or internal decay — other systems, aspiring to enjoy its earlier influence and control, move in to fill the vacuum. And in the twilight zones of power, between systems collapsing and others emerging, the dangers of war are at their most acute.

[55] The United Nations Representatives in the Congo were attempting to end the secession of Katanga through negotiations. A temporary cease-fire had been arranged on December 18, 1961.

In fact, seen in this light, one of the most dangerous crises in our world today — the future of Berlin and Central Europe — in Europe — in some measure reflects a post-imperial interregnum. We have still to work out stable alternatives to the old jostling for power between the decaying Turkish and Hapsburg empires and the expanding German and Russian imperialisms. Mr. Khrushchev may not accept the analogy, but communist power in Eastern Europe, far from representing the vanguard of a new and revolutionary world, is the tail end — we hope the tail end — of man's oldest international system — which is imperial control.

Now in this century we are making audacious and heroic efforts to bring the system of imperialism itself to an end. There are three discernible elements in the attempt — all genuinely revolutionary. The first is to apply to nations and peoples the principle we are trying to apply — with comparable ups and downs — to individual citizens: the principle of their equality before the law and of equal weight given to their ultimate political decision. One man, one vote; one nation, one vote.

The effects of this system can be very strange. No one supposes that, in spite of equality of voting rights, the head of the United States Steel has no more influence on American society than an unskilled laborer in one of his plants. There is an element of fiction in the equality.

In the same way Nepal, shall we say, does not pretend to carry the same weight in the world society as, for instance, its neighbor India. Yet its equal vote in the United Nations is a first step towards a covenanted political recognition, by international society, of its right to separate statehood and its right *not* to be handed over to the political control of more powerful neighbors.

The right of small nations to independence in a new post-imperial age is as astonishing as the right of commoners to protection and due process of law in a post-feudal age. And it is an essential part of the struggle to end imperialism — for it substitutes constellations of independent communities, great and small, for the old imperialist penumbra or "spheres of influence" within which most small peoples have hitherto had to live.

The second principle is that great powers recognize this new right of the weak not to be engulfed. Like the coexistence of rich and poor, of influential and weak inside domestic society, laws and constitutions only partially safeguard it. The powerful have, in proportion to their power, a duty to play the game.

I believe that the Western nations on the whole recognize this restraint. Much of the retreat from Western colonialism in the last two decades springs, I believe, from a genuine revulsion against the idea of domination. And it is my hope that the United States, which has "a giant's strength," will always abstain from "using it like a giant" to coerce or overawe the weak.

The third line of attack is most relevant to the peace-making functions of the United Nations. If, in the dissolution of empires, we are left with nothing but the choice between competing systems of power, then it is hard to see how the world can fail to stagger on from one Balkan-type crisis to the next, each time lurching closer to the hideous rim of Armageddon. If every European retreat from direct control threatens to bring in as direct a control by the communists, or to abandon local populations to the outdated paternalism of white settlers—in either of these events we are in for strife.

It is here, as I see it, that the peace-making functions of the United Nations are most vital and most urgently in need of being systematized and expanded. To my mind, the Congo operation, far from representing a usurpation of power by an arrogant Secretariat, is precisely the type of operation which the United Nations should dare to undertake, and in which we must pray to see it succeed.

And the courage of the United Nations and its backers in rescuing the Congo, through all the chaos and all the fog of fanatic propaganda, will stand — let us all hope! — for years to come as a warning against those who would prepare the tinder box for other Congos.

Without the UN, might not Central Africa already offer a total polarization of hostile power? Might we not find Katanga, ranged on one side with white Southern Africans and some Europeans, and on the other side African Nationalism in Leopoldville and Stanleyville, supported by most of Black Africa and all of the Soviet Bloc?

This is precisely the kind of crystallization of conflict every continent must seek to avoid. The long, patient effort of the United Nations to foster unity and stability in the Congo, under leadership which cannot be accused of partisanship with either world bloc, may yet represent the United Nations' most significant triumph and the clearest pointer to where its influence and its spirit can most effectively extend. Here is a lesson in statesmanship and reconciliation which, for the sake of peace and freedom in Africa and the world, should be taken to heart by all who struggle today — both rulers and ruled alike — from Luanda to the Cape.

We cannot undo the world which science is making over for us. With or without an embryonic instrument of international order, the overwhelming need for order remains. It is written into our conquest of space, our instant communication, our common neighborhood of potential atomic death. We can no more live without an attempt at international order than we can run New York's traffic without rules of the road. Critics so often speak and interpret events as though there were some ideal alternative from which we have slipped or which we can attain simply by letting the United Nations fade away. There are no such alternatives. However much like-minded groups of states may concert closer understandings, they must still live in the world with *all* their neighbors, friendly or hostile, aligned or neutral, and struggle for that minimum of order, conciliation and peaceful change which this jostling world ineluctably requires.

If we had no United Nations, it would be necessary to invent one — and it would not differ very greatly from what we have now. This is just about all the law and order our anarchic world will swallow today. If we are to advance to higher standards or greater security, we must work on patiently from the spot we have already reached and not jettison our few working examples of genuine international action in favor of something more ideal — which we shall not get — or more innocuous, which will not meet our needs.

What we have is man's first sketch of the world society he has to create. He can build better than this — so much is obvious. But will he go on building at all if we are forever tearing up the foundations? The experiment of living together as a single human family — and we can aim at no less — is more likely to grow from precedent to precedent, by experience and daily work and setbacks and partial successes, than to spring, utopian and fully formed, from the unimaginable collective agreement of world minds. Let us go on with what we have. Let us improve it whenever we can. Let us give it the imaginative and creative support which will allow its authority to grow and its peace making capacities to be more fully realized.

I think of Colonel [John] Glenn and his comrades — astronauts, citizens, dedicated men — whom I had the honor to escort around the U.N. the other day. In a slack age, we can still be moved by the prospect of discipline and dedication. And in an age in which so many people seem to be condemned to wander lost in their own psychological undergrowth, we can still recognize and acclaim a simplicity of doing and being and giving from which great enterprises spring.

Perhaps there is salvation in the new image of the immense patience and discipline and stripping down of desires and wants that are necessary in the life of those who are fit enough and tough enough to venture out into the new dimension of outer space. Here we can perhaps glimpse some reflection of the kind of discipline and restraint which we all need in some measure if our generation is to achieve great tasks, not only in the upper air but here and now in this bewildered and floundering world.

The sense that something more is required of us than a happy acquiescence in our affluence is, I believe, more widespread than we know. The thousands of young people who volunteer for the rigors and discomforts of the Peace Corps,[56] the uncomplaining reservists, the growing

[56] The Peace Corps, established by executive order on March 1, 1961, to provide skilled manpower to aid underdeveloped countries, had 1,900 members in mid-1962,

body of students with a passionate concern for world peace or for the end of racial discrimination, the unsung citizens all over this continent whose love and service and neighborly good will are the hidden motive forces of our republic — all these people will see reflected in the discipline and dedication of Colonel Glenn and his comrades the proof that great deeds demand great preparation and that no country can hope to master the challenge of our day without a comparable readiness to cut away the trivialities and achieve the freedom which comes from being no longer "passion's slave."

I do not believe that in the last decade our republic has always equaled the brilliant image of youth and energy and regeneration which was once projected to the world when, as a community dedicated to a proposition and an ideal it stirred to life two centuries ago in the United States. Nor do I believe we can fulfill our role in history without a recovery of the original dream.

Therefore I pray that our young astronauts may take us to the stars in mind as well as body, that they may help us recover that sense of our vocation and dedication without which the people, founded and created in a great vision, will not finally endure.

QUESTION AND ANSWER PERIOD

Q: In an expanding United Nations, can we continue to exclude Communist China from membership?

A: I am not sure whether we can or whether we should. But I *am* sure that we will try. This is not a simple question nor is there a simple answer to it. I invite your attention, and I hope you will consider this most carefully — to the fact that it has two aspects. When we talk about the admission of Communist China to the United Nations, it has always been coupled heretofore with the expulsion simultaneously of Nationalist China — the Island of Formosa, Taiwan, Chiang Kai-shek's government. This is something that neither the United States, nor any other member of the United Nations, aside from the Communist Bloc, wants.

So, if they're to be coupled together, if they are part and parcel of the same proposal, then of course, we will have not only the United States, but we will have the aid and support, I suspect, of most of the members of the United Nations, who are willing to be heard on this and who are to be recorded on this question at all. If the question is divided, and it is no longer the question of the expulsion of Nationalist

and Congress had increased its appropriation in expectation of an expansion to nearly 10,000 by September 1, 1963.

China and only the question of the admission of Communist China, then it is complicated by the fact that you still have the question of who will occupy the seat in the Security Council which went to China as one of the original founding members, 1945.

Therefore, what I am trying to do is to indicate to you in a few words that this is a most intricate problem for which there are no simple answers. To say "yes" or "no," to say "yes, this is the way it should be, this is the way it must be, and this is the way it will be," is almost impossible. My own guess is, and I speak to you, obviously with some misgivings about my self-confidence in this matter, is that while we have scored a great victory this last year, there are many people in the United Nations who feel that Red China should be a member; that you can't exclude from a universal organization a quarter of the human race. There are others who feel that it is perfectly obvious not only that China be included but also that the one country that wants China excluded more than anyone else is the Soviet Union. Because, to include Red China would, of course, mean to dilute the control that is now exercised by the Soviet Union over the Communist Bloc. So, it presents many problems. Some people have suggested that the best solution is a two-China policy — that is to say — that both should be members of the United Nations and that this question of the seat in the Security Council should be reserved for further consideration at a later time. They don't cross that bridge. This has been a long way round to your question, sir, and I would have to say to you in conclusion that the judgment, I suspect, of most people, if not all, is that there should be no admission of Red China if it ever contemplates the expulsion of Nationalist China.

Q: What will happen to U Thant after the government that put him into office is no longer there? [57]

A: That is a very good question. My answer to you is that I don't know. But, I suspect, that nothing whatever will happen. He is now an international civil servant who has been selected to serve as secretary general by all the membership; [58] he no longer represents Burma; he is no longer a member of the Burmese delegation; he no longer has any responsibility to the Burmese government. And, therefore, whatever may happen in Burma won't affect him in his position. As to what will happen in Burma, and what effect it might have on him,

---

[57] Burmese Prime Minister U Nu was deposed in a coup on March 2, 1962, and the government was placed in the hands of a revolutionary council, dominated by military leaders, with former defense chief Ne Win at its head.

[58] U Thant had been elected acting Secretary-General on November 11, 1961, following the death of Dag Hammarskjöld, and he became Secretary-General on November 30, 1962.

personally, I mean what he might like to do, on this I can't answer your question. My guess is that what is happening in Burma is a repetition of what has happened heretofore. Whereas U Thant was an appointee of U Nu, the former Prime Minister of Burma was his close friend and ally, and companion in arms in politics, he is also a great Burmese civil servant, and friend I have no doubt of General Ne Win. In fact, I believe he never served in any capacity other than civil service capacity, so to speak. That is to say, as Director of Public Relations, of Public Information in the government of Burma, and in that capacity, I doubt very much if he has had any conflicts with the present government or with General Ne Win. Does that answer your question?

Q: Is there going to be any reconciliation between our policy towards Portugal and our favoring self-determination?

A: No. I am sorry to say there isn't. I feel very sad about this because I have visited Portugal many times, and am devoted to the Portuguese people and to their extraordinarily beautiful and charming hospitable country, but I must say to you that there has been no indication whatsoever by the Salazar government of any concessions to the independence movement in Angola.

Q: Would the United States favor a change in the composition of the present Security Council as a result of the amendment to the charter following the admission of Red China if that comes to pass?

A: My answer to you is that the United States has for a long while expressed emphatically its approval of an enlargement of the Security Council, and also the Trusteeship Council, also the Economic and Social Council in order to accommodate the change that has taken place in membership. These councils were created at San Francisco when the institution was established and there were 51 nations — 51 members — there are now 104 members and there have been no changes whatever in the size or the composition of these councils in the intervening years when the membership was doubled. So it has been the view of our government for a long while that there should be a reconsideration of the membership of these councils and those should be enlarged to accommodate the increase in membership.

Q: Why are some nations in arrears in payment to the United Nations, and what should be done about it?

A: One must bear in mind that there are two aspects of the financial problem of the U.N. There are the regular assessments which each nation pays according to a formula worked out each year by the budgetary committee of the United Nations for the regular budget. In the case of the regular assessments, the payments are almost, with a few exceptions, Nationalist China included, all paid up in full, including the Soviet Union. It is only in the case of the special operations, the Congo, the Near East, the garrisons we have had in the Gaza Strip and the patrolling of the border between Israel and its neighbors, the support of these two special operations in the Middle East and in the Congo. These are the areas in which people have not in all cases paid up. We now have pending — it has just been presented before the World Court — to determine a question that has never been resolved before, and that is whether or not non-payment for a special operation such as the Congo or the Middle East Emergency Committee Force, should result in the loss of the right to vote in the General Assembly which is the penalty provided in the event of non-payment of the regular dues. If the Court determines that is the case, and it is subject to the same penalties as payment of regular assessment, then I think you will find quite a different response. There are a good many members of the United Nations who disagreed on what was going on in the Congo. The Soviet Union was one, France was another, Belgium was another, and therefore, they have not paid their dues. There are others who felt that it was a responsibility of the big powers. There are others who felt it was the responsibility of those powers which were directly involved, and they had no obligation to do so. Until these matters are clarified, and I think they will tend to be within the next year; once they are clarified, then I believe we will have a much better, a more healthy situation. And it is for this reason primarily and for the large accrual of non-paid bills for the Congo operation, for the Middle East emergency force operation, that we are now proposing the $200 million bond issue.

Q: What is your working arrangement between yourself and Mr. Dean Rusk?

A: Well, we both work overtime. I live in New York. Secretary Rusk lives in Washington. I look after the United Nations. He looks after the State Department. We confer weekly and when I spend a day in Washington or he spends a day in New York we discuss matters of common interest and public policy problems generally. I am of the opinion the relationship is very good and very satisfactory.

Q: The Afro-Asian bloc, do they regard the movements and the actions of the Communists — The Soviet bloc, and Red China — do they regard them as colonialism in the same way as they regarded the actions of France and England, Holland and Portugal, as colonialism?

A: I think that is an excellent question. And it is one that has baffled many people. The answer is no — they do not. They don't consider, they aren't as aware, they aren't as conscious, and they don't have the same emotional reaction to Russian imperialism in Eastern Europe as they do to Western colonialism in the African nations. Now why is this? Many people have speculated about it. I think the speculation reduces itself to several comprehensible forms. First of all, they have never known the Russian imperialism or colonialism in Eastern Europe, this is a remote, distant matter. They live in the close familiarity, proximity of experience with Western colonialism in their own countries. Secondly, this one is a colonialism of white and black, the other is the colonialism of white and white. And this likewise invokes a distinction in their minds. I think there are probably other reasons that contribute to this. A long period of passionate nationalism, of the development of their independence revolutions which have generally been directed against the obvious target, the colonial master. And, of course, they don't have this same target in the case of the Soviet Union. All of these, and perhaps even still others I could mention I think contribute to the fact that they don't think of these two things as the same. We do. We, in the West, look at Soviet imperialism, and we detect a form of imperialism which is as vicious, indeed worse than anything that existed heretofore. The independence of all the countries from the Baltic to the Black Sea has been exterminated, extinguished by the Red Army, one by one, always by force, never by option of the people. And in this case we feel that those people are therefore disqualified from complaining about colonialism. But I must assure you this doesn't seem to disqualify them, and they spend the larger part of their almost limitless rhetoric in the United Nations on the subject of colonialism.

Q: What reaction has there been among the neutrals about our decision to resume the testing of nuclear weapons?

A: I can't answer that question because we haven't really gotten any proper appreciation of what the response has been so far. My guess is there is a great disappointment but not very much surprise; that the probability of the resumption of nuclear testing was accepted a long time ago. Not long after the Soviet resumed testing, and after the United States announced it was going to resume underground, it was probably assumed at least by the governments, the leaders who thought in these countries that resumption in the atmosphere would follow in due course. So, while I suspect that there is disappointment, especially among the neutrals, the non-aligned, the non-Communist countries, there is also very little surprise.

Q: Do you see any United Nations intervention in South Vietnam?

A: There has been no indication whatever of any basis on which the

United Nations might intervene in South Vietnam. Therefore, I don't foresee any reason for it at the present.

Q: Do you foresee any easy solution in Cuba?

A: No. I don't see any easy solution in Cuba. I only see one solution to most all questions and that's to elect Democrats. But, even that hasn't saved us in Cuba. This is a very perplexing and difficult problem and I don't purport to be any expert on the subject. I've had to deal with all the Cuban complaints in the United Nations, which have been trying and exhausting. It is interesting to note, however, that while their debates have lasted a long time, they have evoked very little support from the other members of the United Nations, including the neutrals, non-aligned and non-Communist countries. I suspect it will take some time for this course of history to wear out in Cuba, and this is one of those cases, of which there are so many in foreign relations, with which we just have to learn to live.

Harry Golden, editor of the Carolina Israelite, *suggested that Stevenson accompany him on a trip as a syndicated reporter. The two of them needed, he wrote, to continue their discussions on the "Anatomy of Melancholy, Job, Shakespeare, and Damon Runyon." Golden mentioned that at a meeting on civil rights he had been asked what would be the most important development to come out of the struggle for integration. He replied, "The Southern white Protestants are finally being asked to make a choice, either they begin to practice Christianity or — give it up."*

To Harry Golden [59]

March 9, 1962

Dear Harry:

Your letter lifted my spirits — and touched on most everything I want to know just now! But I still want a visit, and I hope you will forget my schedule and worry about yours when you are next in New York.

As far as the trip is concerned, I am afraid there isn't going to be any for the present. I thought to take a journey in the Spring, but dates don't work out, and the difficulties here are multiplying. So I suspect I shall stay home until summer perhaps — and what a pleasant experience it should be! I may have to go abroad for two weeks during the summer for UN business, but I doubt if it would be the sort of journey that would amuse you.

[59] The original is in the possession of Mr. Golden.

Anyway — let's talk it over. Perhaps you can give me a report of how many white Protestants are abandoning Christianity.

Yours,

ADLAI

P.S. Barbara Ward's address is 6 Ash Street, Cambridge 38, Mass. She will be enchanted to hear from you.

To the Reverend Dr. Billy Graham [60]

March 12, 1962

Dear Dr. Graham:

I am writing to you out of a feeling of concern which I am sure you will understand.

Recently I have received several letters attributing to you, on a radio and television broadcast, a statement somewhat as follows: "Members of the United Nations are listed according to their religions, and the United States is officially listed as pagan." All those writing to me have, quite understandably, expressed indignation at the idea of such a characterization of the United States.

On receiving this report, I looked into the matter and have been unable to discover any such listing in the records of the United Nations. I am further advised by the staff of the United States Mission that reports about the alleged existence of such a listing have been received from time to time for several years from citizens who had heard them and were concerned about them; and that investigation has never revealed any basis for these reports.

I would therefore appreciate it greatly if you could help me to find the source of this strange report. If by any chance it does spring from a fact, it must certainly be a fact which has been grossly misinterpreted and distorted.[61]

I need scarcely add that, if any such official assertion were ever issued by the United Nations — which I do not for a moment expect — I would protest it and demand that it be corrected. It would be my duty to do so because the ascription of a "pagan" character to the United States would be grossly false, and deeply offensive to the great majority of Americans.

Meanwhile, my present concern is lest a groundless belief that the United Nations had depicted our country in this false light should arouse among many Americans unwarranted fears and resentments

---

[60] Evangelist, author, and host of the television program *Hour of Decision*.

[61] Dr. Graham replied that he could not find a source for this statement and that he regretted not having checked carefully before using it. He praised Stevenson for the "magnificent" job he was doing at the United Nations.

against the United Nations, whose effective functioning is so important to the freedom and security of our nation.

The purposes of the United Nations — peace and justice among nations, the promotion of economic and social progress and of human dignity and human rights, including the right to worship — all the purposes which the United Nations was founded to advance have their origins to a very great extent in the Judaeo-Christian ethical tradition of which our country is a leading heir. This community of purpose is implicitly recognized by virtually all the major religious groups in this country, including the chief Protestant denominations — the major Baptist conventions, Lutheran, Methodist and Presbyterian, among others — all of whom appoint observers at the United Nations and lend broad public support to our country's participation in it.

I deeply believe that the efforts of the United States as a leading member of the United Nations are not only important to our country's security, but also obedient to the great commandments of love and compassion which we receive from our religious heritage, and which are the deepest source of our country's moral strength. Therefore I am anxious to clear up a public misapprehension which could darken the counsels of the American people concerning these efforts which are so vital to us all.

I would appreciate so much your attention to this matter. Whenever you are in New York I would be happy to talk with you about the United Nations, the problems it confronts, and its value to our country and to Christian ethical ideals.

Cordially yours,

To Stuart Gerry Brown [62]

March 20, 1962

Dear Stuart:

I spoke at Colgate the other night and sorely missed a visit with you in those beautiful snowbound hills.

Gerald Johnson has written a piece after looking rather hurriedly through Ruth [Field]'s files.[63] She wants you to see it before he submits it to a publisher, and I enclose a copy herewith. If you have any comments or subtractions that he should know, please pass them along and I will see that he is informed promptly.

[62] Maxwell Professor of American Civilization at Syracuse University and author of *Conscience in Politics: Adlai E. Stevenson in the 1950's* (Syracuse, New York: Syracuse University Press, 1961).

[63] Mr. Brown had conducted extensive interviews with Democratic leaders on the 1960 nominating campaign. He had been assisted by Mrs. Field and Harold Taylor.

I still hear flattering comments about "Conscience in Politics" — but haven't had the courage to read it yet. Indeed, I haven't read the biography published in 1958.[64] Can you explain this block?

I pray all goes well with you, and look forward to your return.

Cordially,

To Richard N. Goodwin [65]

March 21, 1962

Dear Dick:

I just had a talk with an old friend, Gainza Paz, publisher of *La Prensa*, Buenos Aires. If any change or postponement of the aid program to Argentina is contemplated, I hope you will see that I get a chance to be heard before any action is taken.

Yours,

To Marshall Field IV [66]

March 22, 1962

Dear Marsh:

A week or two ago, Clayton Fritchey showed me the special feature you had on the UN in a recent issue of the Sunday Sun Times — THE HIDDEN ROOTS OF UN STRENGTH by Donald M. Schwartz.[67] Because of the emergency session of the Security Council on Cuba, I did not get around to reading this presentation until last week-end, but once I got into it I was impressed by the quality of this report. No doubt about it — you did get at the root of some of our problems. There are so many misunderstandings about the UN that it is reassuring to see this kind of thoughtful, responsible reporting.

Congratulations on a good job. Also, I hope you will come by for a visit, or a drink, or luncheon, or something when you are next in New York.

Meanwhile, best to you and Kay.[68]

Sincerely,

[64] Kenneth S. Davis, *A Prophet in His Own Country: The Triumphs and Defeats of Adlai E. Stevenson* (New York: Doubleday, 1957). In fact, Stevenson had read both books in typescript. Perhaps he denied having read them so that he would not have to discuss them. See *The Papers of Adlai E. Stevenson*, Vol. VII, for letters to Davis and Brown regarding their books.

[65] Deputy Assistant Secretary of State for Inter-American Affairs.

[66] Publisher of the Chicago *Sun-Times*.

[67] Chicago *Sun-Times*, February 11, 1962.

[68] Mrs. Field.

On March 20, 1962, Senator Henry M. Jackson spoke to the National Press Club.[69] He asserted that while the United Nations was an important avenue of American foreign policy, the alliance with the members of the North Atlantic Treaty Organization was paramount. The United Nations, he felt, played too large a role in shaping American policy. On a television program, Stevenson denied the charge. He pointed out that with the growth of the General Assembly to 104 members, the absolute majority had passed from the West to the Afro-Asian states, and it was inevitable that there would be votes against the United States. When Stevenson was asked whether he thought it was more important to support the NATO allies or the Afro-Asians, he replied: "I do not think these things are alternatives. We support them both." [70]

To Henry M. Jackson

March 22, 1962

Dear Scoop:

After reading your speech, I am all the more persuaded that we should have a talk, and very soon. I will be in Washington on Monday evening to make some sort of tribute to Robert Frost [71] at a dinner Secretary Udall [72] is giving. Perhaps I could see you in the afternoon at your convenience, or preferably the following morning, Tuesday, March 27.

Sincerely yours,

Congressman Sidney R. Yates of Chicago was the Democratic candidate for the Senate against incumbent Everett M. Dirksen. Stevenson had hoped to help organize a fund-raising affair in New York for Yates, but the Democratic National Committee was planning to raise funds for its activities and asked Stevenson to desist.

To Sidney R. Yates

March 23, 1962

Dear Sid:

I enclose a contribution on account. If my recollection is correct — and it's pretty vivid — now is the time when everyone seems to have forgotten your candidacy, and despair is only one step behind insolvency. But I think it's different with you. Everyone seems to know about and

[69] This speech was published in *Vital Speeches of the Day*, April 15, 1962. Stevenson's speech at Colgate University on March 6, 1962, was published in the same issue. Stevenson also answered critics of the UN in a speech in Washington on March 13, 1962, which is published in Adlai E. Stevenson, *Looking Outward: Years of Crisis at the United Nations*, edited with commentary by Robert L. Schiffer and Selma Schiffer, preface by John F. Kennedy (New York: Harper & Row, 1963), pp. 217–226.

[70] *Times of India* (New Delhi), April 10, 1962.

[71] The poet was eighty-eight years old on March 26, 1962.

[72] Secretary of the Interior Stewart Udall.

applaud *your* candidacy — none louder than my son Adlai. I hope he has reported in detail about the preemption of the "New York market" by the National Committee. But if the cut you get from the Congressional Campaign Committee out of the proceeds is unsatisfactory, perhaps we can get a green light, albeit belatedly.

Yours,

Ambassador John Kenneth Galbraith wrote Stevenson describing Jacqueline Kennedy's tour of India and asking when Stevenson was coming for a visit.

To John Kenneth Galbraith

March 24, 1962

Dear Ken:

Thanks for your letter. I have been reading about you and Jackie everyday, and evidently as a tour conductor you have talents that few of us have appreciated.

I wish I could take advantage of them. But the fact is that I am so weary after a year of incessant crises and travails — and now Scoop Jackson! — that I have decided to forego the trip I was hoping to take, and concentrate on my neglected health and family and affairs, if I have any spare time.

I know full well how grateful you are for my consideration, and that it is only a postponement, I warn you!

Yours,

P.S. My love to Kitty.[73] And where was she during the "royal" visit?

To Arthur M. Schlesinger, Jr.

March 24, 1962

Dear Arthur:

Thank you so much for your letter about the International Sociological Association and their invitation to speak on September 6.

I should like nothing more than to try to confuse them a little, but, unhappily, I have all to do to avoid being confused by the international sociological association across the street! [74]

Yours,

[73] Mrs. Galbraith.

[74] USUN was across the street from the UN. Stevenson's discontent with his post at the UN at this time was apparently deeper than this jocular reference would indicate. He had told Agnes Meyer that he was fed up, and she wrote him on March 30, 1962, that the rumor that he was going to resign was all over Washington. She urged him to fight back at his critics and to announce that he would remain at the UN. However, on many occasions, according to Harlan Cleveland, Stevenson himself started rumors that he was about to resign. Memorandum to Walter Johnson, April 30, 1973.

P.S. I will be in Washington Monday and Tuesday and will try to report to you on developments on Capitol Hill re [Senator Henry M.] Jackson.

To Mrs. John Fell Stevenson

March 27, 1962

My dear Natalie:

I am just back from Washington and find your sweet letter. But please let's not use that formal "Mr. Stevenson" any longer. I think "Gov" [75] will satisfy all my ambassadorial dignity — and then some!

I was delighted to hear that you are getting organized, and I can picture the chaos and also the joy.

It now looks as though I was going to come out to Seattle on June 19th to the Seattle Fair. I will hope to stop to see you on the way up or back, and if you would like to go with me, of course you would both be more than welcome.

I apologize for not sending the things you left behind sooner, but I will try to attend to it at once. Things have been thick hereabouts.

With much love, and distinguished sentiments to my last born, I am

Yours,

To Clayton Fritchey and Arnold Michaelis

March 28, 1962

I have talked at length with Hubert Humphrey about the broadcast on Friday.[76] I think we must have the *exact* questions in mind to counter the Jackson speech and not risk the possibility of wandering all over the lot. You know his proclivity — and mine!

Accordingly, please provide me at the earliest opportunity a series of questions which cover most of the basic complaints about the UN that one has heard in recent months — especially in Jackson's speech — and an outline of suggested answers.

This could be *the* most effective answer to Jackson, but it could also be a disorderly discourse without any clear and precise conclusions left in the viewer's mind.

---

[75] After Stevenson's term as governor of Illinois, he continued to enjoy the courtesy title "Governor" and occasionally signed his personal letters "the Gov" or "the Guv."
[76] Senator Humphrey was to be Stevenson's guest on the program of April 1, 1962.

To Adlai E. Stevenson III

March 29, 1962

Dear Adlai:
Don Walsh [77] of the "American" was in to see me this morning. He is a very shrewd politician and said that he would like to talk to you some time. I think you would find him useful, and should call on him.

Love,
DAD

On his April 1, 1962, ABC television program, Adlai Stevenson Reports, *Stevenson opened the discussion by stating:*

The Secretary of State has just returned from Geneva after the first two weeks of the disarmament conference of the seventeen nations that have been meeting there and reported yesterday. I am sure that Senator Humphrey has talked to him personally and has perhaps a better understanding of the current situation than I do.

I think it is well, however, to understand what it was the United States was attempting to do in broadest detail, at least. The plans that were presented by the United States and the Soviet Union are, of course, complicated, but, in general, the United States was attempting to bring about a test ban treaty; that is to say, a treaty banning the testing of nuclear weapons at all levels — underground, the atmosphere, undersea, and so on. We were also attempting to eliminate the delivery of vehicles and reduce all armed forces on a gradual basis, step by step. And, also, to establish an international organization for the verification of steps towards disarmament. And, finally, measures to strengthen the peace-keeping institutions that we have in the world, including a police force of the United Nations.

I think we have made some important beginnings in some of these things, but rather disappointing on the whole with respect to the nuclear test ban treaty because of the intransigent attitude of the Russians about inspection and verification. To them the security of their — the prevention of inspection is a matter of strategic asset, and it has been very difficult for us, of course, to accommodate ourselves to any test ban treaty that doesn't contemplate some kind of protection by verification or inspection.

I think there is some hope, however, that maybe we have some preliminary steps towards arresting the spiraling of the nuclear arms race which,

[77] Business manager of *Chicago's American* and director of public safety during Stevenson's governorship of Illinois.

if it goes on undiminished, will probably double in volume the number of weapons that we now have by 1966.

Later in the program Arnold Michaelis mentioned criticisms like those of Senator Henry Jackson that the Kennedy Administration was turning its responsibility for foreign policy over to the United Nations. Stevenson stated:

Well, under our Constitution, the responsibility for the conduct of our foreign policy is squarely placed with the President. And Presidents have, of course, had varying degrees of interest in the conduct of foreign policy. Our President now, President Kennedy, has a very lively interest. I should suspect that few Presidents have had a greater interest in the conduct of foreign policy.

I am merely his Ambassador at the United Nations. So that I think it would be very — it would be on the face wrong to even hint, to even suggest that the conduct of foreign policy has been transferred from the normal channels to the United Nations here. I think just the contrary is true. And, actually, that the President seeks the advice of his Secretary of State; he seeks my advice; he seeks the advice of his — of the State Department. And, as a result of these consultations, policy emerges which we try to execute here.

When Michaelis mentioned that some critics felt that U.S. security rested in treaties such as NATO rather than in the UN, Stevenson replied:

These are entirely complementary. It would be a great mistake to try to equate — to try to say that the United Nations is an alternative to NATO.

Actually, the conduct of our foreign policy is at several levels. We conduct our foreign policy bilaterally. We conduct our foreign policy at the regional level, such as the Organization of American States or NATO. We conduct it also at the universal level, which is the United Nations that the Senator has been talking about.

And I think we struggle here at the United Nations, at that level, to reach common ground with as many nations as we possibly can on these issues. We have — I think the very fact that we have more friends and fewer enemies here is a contribution to our national security.

It is interesting to recall that over the years in which this institution has existed, the Soviet Union has exercised its veto in the Security Council — that is, opposed decisions of the United Nations — in a hundred different cases. The United States has never had to use its veto. That is to say we have had — in virtually all these cases — we have had the other nations going our way, or we have found it compatible with our interest to go their way.

Now, the idea somehow that this is a disadvantage to us seems to me very odd.

To Clayton Fritchey

April 3, 1962

Last night I had two calls from the White House saying that the President wanted to see me this afternoon and was going to suggest that I make a speech at the first opportunity setting out the whole business of the criticisms of the United Nations advanced by [Henry] Jackson, [Mike] Mansfield, [Arthur] Krock, etc., etc., etc. Harlan Cleveland has proffered his help, here or there, and I suggest that you prepare for me a list of all future speaking engagements for the next several weeks, with the view to selection or creation of an opportunity.

One occurs to me: Chicago on Thursday, April 12, before the Council on Foreign Relations. This would have to be arranged.

To Robert S. Lindsay [78]

April 5, 1962

Dear Mr. Lindsay:

This is in reply to your request for a reference for Mrs. Jean K. Smith, who is negotiating for an apartment through your agency.

As you probably know, Mrs. Smith is the sister of President Kennedy, and it is hard for me to conceive of how you could possibly get a more reliable, attractive, dependable and desirable tenant! [79]

Cordially yours,

On April 2 the Senate resumed discussion of Senate bill 2768, designed to help relieve the financially burdened United Nations by having the United States purchase UN bonds. Senator Mike Mansfield submitted an amendment sympathetic to the bill along with an analysis, which he evidently did not discuss with Stevenson beforehand, of UN fiscal problems. He described the fiscal crisis as a result of UN procedural distortions emanating from the cold war in general and the Russians in

[78] Vice president of Douglas L. Elliman & Co., Inc.
[79] Stevenson sent Mrs. Stephen Smith a copy of this letter with a note: "Dear Jean — Am I honored! ADLAI."

particular. *These procedural distortions were twofold: the inability of the Security Council to function on political problems because of the Soviet veto, which in turn resulted in a shift of these problems to the General Assembly, which was not designed to deal with such matters. In effect, the potential moral force of the General Assembly was being sapped, Senator Mansfield felt, because of the added burden of functioning as a Security Council without sufficient authority to implement its final decisions.*[80]

To Mike Mansfield

April 7, 1962

Dear Mike:

I read your speech about the United Nations. Evidently I failed to answer any questions that you might have about the United Nations when I called at your office the other day. At that time I had not realized that you had such precise criticisms as the speech reveals.

If I can give you any information about the matters that concern you, please let me do so. If you are coming to New York and care to stay the night with me I would be delighted — and please bring your wife! If that is inconvenient, I can, of course, come to see you whenever you wish.

This is as difficult a job as I have ever undertaken, and I had hoped to have my friends behind us.

Cordially yours,

To Henry M. Jackson

April 13, 1962

Dear Scoop:

I am happy to hear that you did not intend to imply any conflict between our interests in NATO — and other regional organizations — and our interests in the United Nations in your speech of March 20.[81] I am afraid this was the impression which the speech widely created. Not only did it suggest a sharp change in the nature and extent of our diplomacy in the United Nations and a withdrawal from our efforts to use United Nations presences and other operational activities in the interests of our own security. But it also made a major case that our participation in the United Nations had, as expressed in a rhetorical question, "at times hampered the wise definition of our national interests" whereas it made a

[80] *Congressional Record*, Senate, April 2, 1962, pp. 5664–5674.

[81] Senator Jackson wrote Stevenson on April 16, 1962, pointing out that he had never said that the United Nations and NATO were in conflict. He closed his letter by saying that a "thoughtful, realistic" review of the United States' role in the United Nations was needed.

second case that "peace depends on the power and unity of the Atlantic Community and on the skill of our *direct* diplomacy." Given its general approach the speech could not fail to be interpreted as implying that our interests in the United Nations and our NATO security interests were more in conflict than they were complementary. It was so understood not only by me but among foreign diplomats.

It would be most helpful if you could sometime in the near future publicly correct this impression by a statement along the lines you have indicated, i.e. that you believe the United Nations is an important avenue of American foreign policy through which we can work constructively to further our vital interests, that our interests in NATO and the United Nations are complementary, and that your previous statement was intended only to raise some danger signals. I think this would help restore the general policy framework and make discussion of specific policy problems more fruitful.

On the question of registration of objects launched into orbit, you are right and I am sorry I misled you in our conversation. We did sponsor a resolution which included this and it was adopted by the Assembly.[82]

As I told you I would welcome the opportunity to give you any further specific information that you might require about United States-United Nations relationships. I can only believe that further understanding would allay your alarms and be reassuring to you.

Sincerely yours,

Israeli forces attacked Syrian positions north of Israel's border. In the debate in the Security Council, Stevenson on March 28, 1962, said that whatever the facts were they did not justify Israeli retaliation; that the peacekeeping machinery must be strengthened and the scale of military actions should not be raised.

To Hubert H. Humphrey

April 16, 1962

Dear Hubert:

I've seen your letter to Secretary [Dean] Rusk of April 2 about the Syria-Israel hostilities — I was about to say "annual hostilities." I hope before you express any views that are comforting to the Zionists you will let us fully explain what was done in the Security Council and why.

I don't need to tell you about my own long and sympathetic record with Israel, but perhaps you don't know how much we did to temper the

---

[82] On March 5, 1962, for instance, Stevenson had sent U Thant a letter describing U.S. space launchings. USUN press release 3933.

action of the Security Council. Someday I hope we will be thanked by the Israelis instead of criticized.

Yours,

To Sir Roy Welensky [83]

April 17, 1962

My dear Sir Roy:

I enclose a wire service clipping purporting to report a statement that you have just made evidently about a speech of mine delivered last week at a seminar on Africa at a Midwest University.[84]

Because I am confident that you could not have read the speech in full, I am taking the liberty of sending you a copy. I think you will find it somewhat less disconcerting than your purported statement suggests, and I doubt if you will find in it any "attack" whatever.

Having had the privilege of visiting your lovely country on two occasions, and meeting you and some of your associates, I feel that I have at least some understanding of the difficult problems you confront. The purpose of this speech was to articulate these difficulties among people who have little familiarity with them.

I think on reading the enclosure you will conclude that I have not been "bitter and unreasoned," but temperate and factual about a situation which we are trying to dampen, not aggravate.

I have happy recollections of my visits with you, and I send you my prayers and best wishes for the success of the difficult and historic work in which you are engaged.

Cordially yours,

To David A. Morse [85]

April 19, 1962

Dear Dave:

Thanks so much for your letter. I am flattered by your invitation to become a member of the committee to nominate Herbert Lehman for the Balzan Peace Prize. Indeed, I can think of no more deserving recipient, nor

[83] Prime minister of the Federation of Rhodesia and Nyasaland.

[84] Stevenson spoke at an African seminar at Lake Forest College, Lake Forest, Illinois. The wire service clipping was not saved. Sir Roy may have objected to Stevenson's statement that the white settler minority in Rhodesia, the Union of South Africa, and the Portuguese territories set the original inhabitants to work in the "new society they, the settlers, direct and control." Stevenson called this the "most explosive" situation in the world. He also warned against "frightening" talk of a white military alliance to stem the "tide of black nationalism." Stevenson, *Looking Outward*, p. 178.

[85] Director-General of the International Labour Office, Geneva, Switzerland.

a more fitting tribute to his dedicated, selfless service to all mankind over many years.

I would consider it an honor and a privilege to be a member of such a committee, and am most grateful for your thought of me.

I was disappointed to miss you when you were in New York recently, but — God willing, and UN crises notwithstanding — I hope to rectify that situation in Geneva this summer!

Yours,

To U Thant

April 19, 1962

Dear Mr. Secretary General:

I was deeply impressed by your speech at the luncheon of the United States Committee for the United Nations — not so much by your kind words about me, though these I greatly appreciate, as by your grave and wise words about the arms race and resulting danger to peace. As you know, this is a constant preoccupation not only with me but with President Kennedy and all those in the United States Government who work on these matters.

May I say that, despite the very heavy burdens you bear, I hope you will find opportunities to speak again soon to an American audience. Not enough Americans realize the tremendous value for the security of this country which comes from the friendship and solidarity achieved between us and other members through the processes of the United Nations, and I can think of no one who can bring this truth home to them so convincingly as you. Needless to say, there is a certain urgency in this situation, and such an address during April or May would be especially timely.

I apologize for intruding this thought into your crowded life, but I can hardly exaggerate its importance.

With renewed admiration and warm regards,

Cordially yours,

To John Steinbeck

April 20, 1962

Dear John:

The last "Stevenson" letter [86] kept me going for a long time, and an appropriate excerpt about your ambition to be Ambassador to Oz also lifted the spirits and hopes of President Kennedy.[87]

[86] Mr. Steinbeck's term for his steady correspondence with Stevenson.
[87] See Stevenson's letter to Kennedy of January 3, 1962, above.

But where are you? When are you coming home? How long am I expected to survive in this desert? And is the Feyre Elaine [88] at your side? I wish she was at mine!

I have little to report except that the world gets no better in spite of your efforts. . . .

To William Proxmire [89]

April 20, 1962

Dear Bill:

Word has just come on the ticker about your speech on the U.N.[90] Thank you so much. I apparently need help in the Congress, in spite of the fact that we have just completed the most successful year in the history of this Mission. I am glad that you realize it, and if you have any suggestions as to how I can keep your colleagues better informed, I would welcome them.

Don't forget that you are planning to stay a night with me in New York.

Yours,

To John F. Kennedy

April 24, 1962

Dear Mr. President:

I will have my thoughts re. Angola on paper for you in a day or so. I also have some ideas about the Congo that might be worth discussing. There are also miscellaneous other matters of less importance. I am planning to be in Washington on Wednesday, May 2, but I could come before if you care to see me.

And I also suggest that you direct the State Department to at least consider acquiring, for the residence of our first U.S. Ambassador to Kenya, Karen House which belonged to Isak Dinesen, the author of "Out of Africa," etc. I am told it is for sale, a beautiful place, and, of course, has historic value and would command a sort of ready-made built-in regard. It presently belongs to Col. and Mrs. D. D. Robson, Karen House, Karen Estates, Ngong, Nairobi, Kenya.

Sincerely yours,

---

[88] Mrs. Steinbeck.
[89] Democratic senator from Wisconsin.
[90] Mr. Proxmire attacked those senators who maintained that the United Nations was useless. See *Congressional Record,* Senate, April 20, 1962.

To Arthur M. Schlesinger, Jr.

April 26, 1962

Dear Arthur:

I have your letter of April 23rd, but Fred Dutton [91] has not appeared in New York, at least to my knowledge.

I have been in touch with his office, however, about briefing and entertainment of the members of the House and Senate Foreign Affairs Committees here in New York.

The Jackson matter continues to cause trouble, and arose today in my talks with the Secretary General. . . . I hope the President will find an opportunity to set the matter straight and also advise Jackson that he does not agree with him, and that the USUN had nothing to do with the presentation of the bond issue case in the Senate,[92] which was managed by the State Department. I was asked to testify and to send Klutznick [93] to Washington because of his special familiarity with the financing problem. In the House I understand it is to be quite different, and that we will have a direct responsibility for the presentation, working with George Ball.[94]

Yours,

To Wayne Morse

April 26, 1962

Dear Wayne:

Bless you for that splendid speech about the UN and our work here.[95] I wish everyone could read it and I am grateful indeed for such an accomplished and effective rescue operation.

I have noted your concern about the resolution in the Syria-Israel incident. I would be happy to give you all of the facts. If you wish them in a word, the resolution this year was milder than any of the previous resolutions adopted by the Security Council condemning Israel for retaliation in force. Our policy on the use of force in violation of the Charter is, of course, of long standing, and we could not risk the consequences of any alteration of it in this case.

The reason Syria was not criticized in the same measure was, of

[91] Assistant Secretary of State for Congressional Relations.
[92] Congress appropriated funds to purchase United Nations bonds.
[93] Philip M. Klutznick, United States representative on the Economic and Social Council.
[94] Under Secretary of State.
[95] Senator Morse spoke in favor of the bill authorizing purchase of UN bonds. See *Congressional Record*, Senate, April 5, 1962, p. 6096.

course, due to the fact that General von Horn and the United Nations Truce Supervisory Organization could not establish who was principally responsible for the provocation. The heavy retaliatory raid was launched by the Israelis from the demilitarized zone. Also, they have consistently obstructed on-the-spot observation by the UNTSO, which makes the establishment of provocation difficult.

But, as I say, more of that if you wish it.

If you want to know what *I* wish — it is that you and Mrs. Morse would pay me that long-promised visit!

Yours,

To Mrs. Ernest L. Ives [96]

April 26, 1962

Dear Buffie:

I want to give away the fee that I received for the speech in North Carolina — after expenses, about $1,180. I think it improper for me to retain moneys earned on government time and in the course of duty.

It occurred to me that there might be philanthropies in North Carolina to which I could give, say, $500. I thought I would return the balance to the [North Carolina State] College, for needy students. Have you any suggestions?

Love,
ADLAI

To Mrs. Eugene Meyer [97]

April 30, 1962

Dear Agnes:

To escape from yesterday's heat in the city, I was touched with brilliance — and promptly drove out to Seven Springs Farm [98] with some friends and had a picnic on your lawn and watched my television show in your caretaker's cottage. All is well, fruit trees in bloom, the grass green and the woods humming with birds. I loved it and dozed happily in the sun. I hope the next time I will find the tennis court in some sort of shape!

I have your note and hope you will put me on TWA 840 from Rome to Athens on the 25th along with your party.[99] Please let me know where you will be staying. And please let me know when you are going to be

[96] The original is in E.S.I., I.S.H.L.

[97] The original is in the Agnes Meyer files, Princeton University Library.

[98] Mrs. Meyer's home at Mount Kisco, New York.

[99] Mrs. Meyer had invited Stevenson to join her party for a yacht cruise among the Greek islands in July.

back in the city and we can have another talk about all these plans —
not to mention the disordered world.

Love,

ADLAI

*In a report to the congregation of K.A.M. Temple in Chicago, Rabbi
Jacob J. Weinstein wrote that the Security Council's rebuke of Israel
for its retaliatory action against Syria made him sadder about the prospects of Gentile understanding of the Jew. He expressed his despair that
Stevenson had joined in the rebuke.*

To Rabbi Jacob J. Weinstein

April 30, 1962

Dear Jake:

Lou[is A.] Kohn has sent me your complaint about the Syria-Israel resolution in the United Nations. I wish you knew all the facts and I doubt if
you could then sustain the same conclusions. This was the mildest of
the four resolutions that have been adopted by the Security Council
about Israel's use of retaliatory force, although the force was the greatest.

The "judge," the Armistice Commission, could not fix who was principally responsible for provocation, in large measure because Israel has
refused access to the Commission in these regions. Hence, there could be
no "equal condemnation" of Syria.

In such circumstances, could the Security Council do anything else?
Indeed, cannot one say that it is surprising that the resolution was as
tempered as it was. Then to be criticized so extensively by the Jewish
community of the United States is a bitter pill, but I am sure that you,
with your taste for justice and concern for facts would not administer the
same.

I hope we can talk about these things someday.

Cordially yours,

*Stevenson's old friend Dorothy Fosdick, a member of the Policy Plan-
ning Staff in the Department of State during the Truman administration,
wrote him that senators like Henry Jackson (on whose staff she was now
working) and Mike Mansfield were seriously concerned about the relation of the United States in the United Nations to the making of national security policies. She added that he had to deal with their concerns
and repair his relations with them.*

To Dorothy Fosdick

May 1, 1962

Dear Dorothy:

I have your letter and confess that I am surprised and grieved by its tone. I had always assumed that we could discuss such concerns as Senator Jackson recited, which have caused me such difficulty, *before* rather than *after*.

But *after* is better than not at all, and I hope we will have an early opportunity to discuss your misgivings and his.

Affectionately,

P.S. I shall refrain from any talk of "brickbats" and "retaliation" which have never had a part in my dialogue with Democrats — let alone you!

Professor Robert Tufts of Oberlin College, who had been a speech-writer in Stevenson's 1952 presidential campaign, wrote that he was mystified that Stevenson was unhappy over the speech by Senator Henry Jackson. Tufts stated that the role of the UN in American foreign policy merited serious discussion.

To Robert Tufts

May 1, 1962

Dear Bob:

I have your letter, and am more perplexed than ever. I also have a sharp note from Dorothy Fosdick that grieves me deeply. I had expected help from my old friends in this trying task, and I had no idea about what gulfs of misunderstanding had opened between us.

I, for one, would be happy to talk with you and Dorothy, and also Senator Jackson, who could find some answers to some of his anxieties by direct inquiry, I am sure.

Cordially yours,

To Philip Noel-Baker

May 3, 1962

Dear Philip:

That I have not answered your letter of March 14th does not mean that it has been neglected, or that the information you have given me about the Institute for Strategic Studies has been overlooked. On the contrary, I have seen that it came to the attention of the American foundation donors, without any revelation of the source of my information. I think what you have to say should be very helpful to them.

The resumption of [nuclear] testing was, as you can understand, a sad day for me, but it was inevitable in view of our analysis of the Russian tests and has evoked much less protest than I foresaw. There is hope here that after the Russians conclude another series, we can get down to the dangerously deferred business of stopping these tests. I hope you share that view.

Cordially yours,

P.S. I may be in London the latter part of June and if I am, I shall, of course, let you know.

To Mrs. Eugene Meyer [100]

May 8, 1962

Dearest Agnes:

On the 15th I must be in Princeton during the day and I will get back barely in time for dinner with the Prime Minister of Norway. On the 16th I am committed to dinner, but can't we get together between 6 and 8 at your convenience? Why don't you stay at my apartment both nights and let my Viola [Reardy] look after you?

I wish I could promise to come over the weekend of the 16th,[101] but I will be in California that weekend enroute to Seattle to speak at the Fair.[102] Surely there will be some other opportunity to get up there during June. Meanwhile, I expect to go out there and sit in the sun on the terrace whenever I get a chance!

I will be in Washington on Friday and part of Saturday of this week and will hope for a glimpse of you somehow — or at least a telephone talk.

Love,

ADLAI

To John F. Kennedy

May 14, 1962

Dear Mr. President:

You were very good to include me in that lovely dinner on Friday, and I am very grateful. I only wish I had been able to stay through the concert and see something more of many friends.

---

[100] The original is in the Agnes Meyer files, Princeton University Library.

[101] Mrs. Meyer had invited him to her farm at Mount Kisco, New York.

[102] The Century 21 Exposition, which had opened on April 20, 1962, the first world's fair to be held in the United States since before World War II.

I assume you or Arthur Schlesinger will let me know when you want to see me again.

Sincerely yours,

To Lady Barbara Jackson

May 16, 1962

Dearest Barbara:

You were "brilliant" on the TV program [103] — and that is not just my assessment, but universal. And I, as I foretold, was self-conscious, hurried and inaudible. Obviously, you have another career coming up. Perhaps I could write a speech for you sometime!

Here, things swirl along at the usual ridiculous intensity and pace. I fight off the smoked salmon and creamed chicken and alcohol, but surrender to too many engagements and too little sleep. I even went to Princeton to celebrate the dedication of a memorial for — Foster Dulles.[104]

I yearn to hear how you found things there,[105] but meanwhile I find you have already sent me a "possible draft" for Boston. I'm sure it's more than possible, and probable. I should think, as for the others, between two and three thousand words would be quite enough.

And that is my two lines for this frantic morning!

Much love,

P.S. . . .

To Richard J. Daley

May 17, 1962

Dear Dick:

Thanks for your letter. I am delighted to hear that the Annual Dinner [106] was such a success. I wish I could have been there.

I share your view that there is nothing for Sid to do but to ignore the gossip about Dirksen and the Administration.[107] I have no doubt that after Congress goes home we will get more positive sounds from this direction.

I shall tell Adlai to drop in on you when you have a spare moment. And I wish the Daleys would drop in on me anytime!

Cordially yours,

[103] Stevenson's television program of May 13. Two weeks earlier, on April 29, Stevenson had discussed disarmament with William C. Foster, director of the United States Arms Control and Disarmament Agency.

[104] The late Secretary of State John Foster Dulles, who had died in 1959. For Stevenson's relations with him, see *The Papers of Adlai E. Stevenson,* Vol. VI, Vol. VII.

[105] She was in Australia.

[106] Of the Cook County Democratic organization, headed by Mayor Daley.

[107] The rumor was that the Kennedy Administration would not be unhappy if Senator Everett M. Dirksen was reelected over his Democratic opponent, Sidney Yates.

To Mrs. Franklin D. Roosevelt

May 18, 1962

Dear Mrs. R.:

I'm sure I needn't tell you of my high regard for Gaylord Nelson,[108] which I know you share.

Jim Doyle[109] has asked me to forward the enclosed letter from Gaylord, who is most anxious to have you as the speaker at his main fundraising affair next fall. And *I* am so anxious to see him win a Senate seat this year that I am unashamedly asking whether you could add this important event to your heavily burdened schedule![110]

Yours ever,

President Kennedy's forty-fifth birthday was the occasion for a fundraising affair at Madison Square Garden. The program was organized by Arthur B. Krim, president of United Artists Corporation, and Anna Rosenberg, a prominent figure in New York and national Democratic politics since the 1930's.

To Mrs. Albert Lasker

May 21, 1962

Dearest Mary:

The fund raising gala for the President worked out well — altogether too well for me. I got home from the Krims' at 3 o'clock in the morning, after several perilous encounters with Marilyn Monroe, dressed in what she calls "skin and beads." I didn't see the beads! My encounters, however, were only after breaking through the strong defenses established by Robert Kennedy, who was dodging around her like a moth around the flame, amid the confusion of artists, artistes, and politicians, and such as me.

In inverse order, the show at the Garden was spotty, the hall was too big for Callas[111] and hardly big enough for some of those screamers from Hollywood, but the [Jerome] Robbins ballet, [Mike] Nichols and [Elaine] May . . . were marvelous.

The dinner beforehand found me with [Paul] Hoffman, Andre Meyer,[112] and the Rosenberg family — ex-Anna,[113] who was as busy as a terrier or-

---

108 Governor of Wisconsin and a candidate for the United States Senate.
109 A Madison, Wisconsin, lawyer and leader of the Democratic party who had helped organize efforts to draft Stevenson for the 1960 presidential nomination.
110 Mrs. Roosevelt agreed to speak.
111 Opera singer Maria Callas.
112 Senior partner of Lazard Frères and Company.
113 Mrs. Rosenberg was to be married to Mr. Hoffman in July.

ganizing everybody and everything. And she and Krim evidently did a hell of a job, although they fell way short of the million dollar mark, Krim tells me. I sat in the box with the President, Vice President [Johnson], about a dozen Kennedys, and — Jim Farley! [114] You can imagine how I enjoyed that proximity.

I spent Sunday at Charlie Noyes's [115] in the sun, the swimming pool, and on the tennis court with Borden and some people from the Mission. It was a healthy contrast to the night before!

I have had no talk with Adlai [III] yet about plans for the Yates party,[116] but I'm sure all will go well, and the universal indebtedness to you — headed by the Stevensons — will mount again.

Summer plans continue a little vague — and I wish Kashmir, Laos, Congo, Ruanda-Urundi and Rhodesia did, too! [117]

De Gaulle's telegram to the President, as read by Nichols and May, said: "Congratulations on your birthday. And if I weren't so busy, I would walk across to see you." I feel the same way! [118]

Love,

To Julian P. Boyd

May 25, 1962

My dear Julian:

I enjoyed the visit to Princeton and the ceremony [119] very much. But I had confidently expected to see much more of you. In that respect I was disappointed.

I am delighted to have the collection of Jefferson portraits, and someday I hope you will come into my Embassy on the 42nd floor of the Waldorf Towers and see the copy of Peale's Jefferson, which is hanging there and which seems to me as good as the original. I am sure it would interest you.

I had a little talk with Mr. [William] Dix about my papers and their disposition in the basement treasure room. This year I am giving the Illinois papers to the State Library in Springfield, and after that transfer,

[114] Former national chairman of the Democratic party.

[115] Charles Phelps Noyes, minister counselor at USUN.

[116] A fund-raising affair for Congressman Sidney Yates.

[117] Stevenson spoke about Rhodesia on June 12 in the General Assembly and about Kashmir on June 15 in the Security Council.

[118] Mrs. Lasker was in Belgium.

[119] The dedicatory ceremonies for the opening of the John Foster Dulles Library. There is a photograph in the *Princeton University Library Chronicle*, Vol. XXIII, No. 4 (Summer, 1962) showing Stevenson, Allen Dulles, Arthur Dean, Dwight D. Eisenhower, Robert Goheen, and Mrs. John Foster Dulles. William Dix remarked that Stevenson was "looking rather uncomfortable at the company he is keeping." Julian Boyd, letter to Walter Johnson, September 12, 1974.

which is very voluminous, I hope to get to the Princeton papers — probably next year. That you will be there and take an interest in them was the decisive consideration.

With all good wishes.

Cordially yours,

To Doris Fleeson [120]

May 28, 1962

Dear Doris:

What's this I read: windshields, cuts and burns.[121] I pray that nothing has happened to that angel face. I am not worried about the spirit or the vocabulary! And how did Kimball get out of it unscathed? Clever fellow that.

If you don't report I will come and see you myself.

Love,

To Nicolas Nabokov [122]

May 31, 1962

Dear Nicolas:

A very very dear young friend of mine, who has just graduated *magna cum laude* from Radcliffe, tells me that she is under consideration for a job on your staff in Paris during the ensuing year. She doesn't seem to have very specific information, and I thought I would take the liberty of writing you, as an old friend, to ask you to let me have the facts — "unvarnished," as they say — so as to help me to help her.

You will remember Marietta Tree. The girl is her beautiful and highly disciplined and intelligent daughter, Frances FitzGerald. As an old newspaper man, I can testify that she has abnormally developed talents as a reporter. She has traveled in my party on several trips in remote places and written extremely mature reports. I think she also has genuine literary taste, and certainly an urgent and consuming curiosity about the world and the people that ornament and enlighten it.

Frankie's "dissertation" at Radcliffe was in the field of Middle Eastern history — which seems a little remote from your interests, but is also a measure of her versatility and catholic interests.

I plan to be in Geneva for a couple of weeks in July this summer, and, after a brief visit with friends in Italy, to have a few days yachting in the

[120] Syndicated newspaper columnist.
[121] She and her husband, Dan Kimball, had been involved in an automobile accident.
[122] Head of the Congrès pour la Liberté de la Culture, Paris, France.

Adriatic. You may be sure that I shall let you know if I get to Paris, and meanwhile I shall be most grateful for any information about this job and whether there is really any suitable place for Frankie.

Cordially yours,

To Arthur M. Schlesinger, Jr.

May 31, 1962

Dear Arthur:

Attached is a speech that I was planning to give at Tufts [University] on next Sunday, June 10. Could you look it over promptly and let me have your reaction.[123] I think it a good idea for me once in a while to talk about domestic affairs, and I haven't done it for a long time. Old soldiers yearn for the battle! Perhaps we could talk about this on Monday or Tuesday when I am in Washington.

Yours,

Stevenson delivered the commencement address at Boston University on June 3, 1962, and five days later he delivered the commencement address at Tufts University. The address at Tufts follows.[124]

We Americans are rightly concerned these days with what the admen call our "image" abroad. We spend millions of dollars explaining ourselves and our policies.

The United Nations brings to our shores people from every state under the sun. They come. They see. They judge. And if there is one thing of which I am sure after my time in the maelstrom, it is this: What we say has little impact compared with what we do.

It is our quality that profoundly determines what others think of us. Visiting delegates may delight in the shining skyscrapers at one end of Park Avenue. But they see the crumbling slums at the other end. They admire our great centers of learning, but they do not overlook the two-shift obsolescent city school where poor children learn the habits of delinquency almost with their letters.

In short, brave pretensions and bold speeches are as nothing in the

---

[123] Schlesinger sent the speech to President Kennedy with a covering memorandum saying, in part: "It is a strong and intelligent speech. Its argument is familiar inside the Administration but may not yet have been put so effectively in public. The only problem raised by the speech is whether it would serve the purposes of general Administration strategy for Stevenson to go out ahead on this issue." Memorandum for the President, June 4, 1962, John F. Kennedy Library.

[124] Both speeches were published in Stevenson, *Looking Outward,* pp. 204–214, 227–234.

balance compared with the solid facts of decency and amenity, of social justice and pioneering reform. And they also note that, with all our pretensions and failures, there is no more socially responsible and successful society on earth. To keep it that way is the job of America's young.

But we know all this, and I refer to it only because the hope of being the nation our dreams and our wealth can make us depends intimately upon their response.

The privilege — and penalty — of their education is that over the coming decades they will be the pacesetters for political and social thought in their communities. They may not accept this responsibility, but that makes no difference. It is inescapable. For if they decide to set no pace, to forward no new ideas, to dream no dreams, they will still be pacesetters. They will simply have decided that there is to be no pace.

They must, therefore, here and now, in their own minds, make the list of their own priorities, the things they would choose to have or do in our great society, if they knew the resources were available. And I will tell them some of the things I would wish to see in America, if our dreams could be realized and our vision of the good society could be planted solidly in our native earth.

I would begin with education: in high schools imaginative enough to check delinquency and give youngsters a sense of the zest and opportunity of life, in college education available to all who can profit by it, in refresher courses and sabbatical years for teachers, in adult education recalling people at every level of attainment to a deepening of their knowledge.

Next, I dream of cities worth living in.

More and more of our people will live in cities and suburbs. I think of the huddled, blighted centers, the commuter chaos, the shapeless sprawls in which the hot dog stand and the used car lot alternate with the filling station and the drive-in diner; the vanishing of parks and spaces, the outward growth of ramshackle subdivisions destined within ten years to be the slums of tomorrow.

We can do better than this.

I have read of Nanking when it was the capital of the Sung dynasty. It was a great city, yet trees and water followed the streets, fountains and waterfalls refreshed the air, gardens divided the city sectors, and in the evening citizens rowed on the lakes, hearing the sound of bells across the water. They had fewer resources than we have. But beauty, it seems, had a compelling priority it lacks in our abundant society. And they loved and cultivated the arts, not as fringe benefits, but as a central purpose in life.

Here, too, I would like to dream of music and theater in every city, of great festivals of the arts springing up in more and more regions and, above all, of citizens themselves learning to use a growing leisure in making their own art.

Another dream is a vast expansion of our national parks and playgrounds, with services expanded and opportunities increased, both for the gregarious and for the solitary lovers of open life — for the latter-day Thoreau looking for his Walden Pond.

Yet I do not, of course, leave out the attack on poverty as a by-product of better living. It is central to our abundance. Most of those who are poor today in America are so because we are slow to bestir ourselves to end the pockets of destitution — in West Virginia, or New England's mill towns, in big city slums, among migrant workers — where the desperately poor are not floated off the bottom of society by any rising tide of general prosperity.

At this point, no doubt, sober heads are being shaken and voices of ancestral wisdom raised to argue that dreams are all very well, but the fundamental need is to get on with the "real business of life," recognize the "limitation of our resources" and "put first things first" — by which, I think, they usually mean more weapons and more consumer goods.

And this is the thesis I want to challenge today. No one denies that education for excellence, beautiful cities, an open-air world and a society without injustice are in themselves good things. They simply argue that we cannot afford them. This I believe to be profoundly untrue.

I do not believe, in our affluent society, that we are, in more than the very shortest run, short of resources. We simply are not mobilizing enough of them.

Secondly, I believe that the kinds of dreams I have described — which become concrete demands for more schools, more teachers, urban renewal, suburban planning and landscaping — are in fact *the* clue to the next stage of growth in the free economy.

Let us begin with the facts about the American economic system today. While other free nations — Japan, West Germany, Italy and even France — have clocked up rates of growth from 5 percent to 10 and 12 percent a year, and while the Communists claim rates as spectacular, we and the British have jogged along at an average of under 3 percent. This is not catastrophic. Indeed, it isn't much below the historical average. But some things about the curve are disconcerting. Clearly, we are operating below our optimum level.

What has gone wrong?

The difficulty is not on the side of supply. I cannot emphasize too much the availability of resources.

We pay a billion dollars a year to stockpile food. We have vast supplies of metals purchased and stored by government. We dump obsolescent weapons, year after year. Petroleum is in surplus, aluminum is in surplus, steel capacity is in surplus, coal has been cut by half to maintain demand, power may well become surplus in another decade of rapid atomic development. And all through the manufacturing industry we are only beginning to see the consequences of automation.

Labor is surplus as it is. What will it become if most major industries can halve or quarter their working force in the next few years?

We have to face the fact that once economies develop beyond a certain level of sophistication, science and technology place at their disposal so vast an array of techniques and inventions that surplus, not shortage, is much more likely to be their habitual state. And surplus left to itself, and seen as a fact, not as an opportunity, depresses markets, makes men redundant, checks investment and leads on to stagnation. Yet surplus is actually a vast opportunity.

The human race has spent all its yesterdays in a state of chronic and crippling shortage. From harvest to harvest, from hand to mouth — so lived the human family until the twentieth century. And so live still perhaps half of the world's population.

If you look at the differences between the rapidly growing economies and ourselves, you will find that the chief factor is the one of demand. Postwar reconstruction started the spurt in Europe and Japan. Now consumer demand is high because these nations are well into the cycle of what the economists call "consumer durables" — cars and dishwashers, television sets and refrigerators.

And these governments also make the maintenance of demand a steady objective of policy, well ahead, incidentally, of surpluses in their budgets. In fact, in France, a technique of stimulating demand has been evolved which countries as various as Britain, Belgium and Spain are thinking of adopting, and Germany and Italy are at least discussing it.

French economists meet with labor and management under the auspices of the planning mechanism established by that innovator of genius, Jean Monnet.[125] There the economists sketch out the consequences — in terms of the need for expansion in steel, power, transport, metallurgy and so forth — of, say, a 5 percent rate of growth. Encouraged by this picture of buoyancy, the managers go back and expand their enterprises accordingly. By doing so, of course, they create the demand that sustains a high rate of growth.

I know no more startling demonstration of the fact that demand is not limited by supply. On the contrary, it is supply that is fashioned, shaped and called into being by organized demand.

For the first time in human history, man, Western man, has the power to build society according to his dreams, not his narrow, primeval necessities. He has received, at the hands of science, a new liberation, a new freedom.

[125] President of the European Coal and Steel Authority, 1952–1955, and chairman of the Action Committee for a United States of Europe.

But what does this fact look like, stripped for a moment of rhetoric and exhilaration? It means that the creation of acceptable demand is our overriding problem.

We face an economy in oversupply, in surplus, in glut. If we are "to get it moving again," we have to make new experiments on the side of demand, creating new needs and objectives, and it is not yet clear how we are to make them.

Let us suppose that as a community we, like our neighbors the French, accepted a 4 to 5 percent rate of growth as the norm. How should we set about the expansion? I admit that there are some technical obstacles of considerable importance — our balance of payments, for instance, or the pressure of rising wages on costs.

But the difficulty I wish to underline is neither of these. I believe they can be handled. The difficulty I see goes deeper. The issue is, quite simply: What, over the next decade, is going to be the *content* of the demand which will set our economy moving again?

And the reason why even the advanced economies of Western Europe cannot help us here is that, very candidly, much of their present lively expansion comes from the fact that they are going through a cycle of demand which we in America completed in the early 1950's.

The "consumer durables" cycle offers immense stimulus to the whole economy. But what happens when a country has not only the proverbial two chickens in every pot, but two television sets in the parlor?

Now I don't for a moment suggest that every household is in this satisfied state. But enough households are sufficiently modernized for this revolution in household equipment to be no longer the prime stimulus to expansion it is in Europe. We have to discover the *next* great surge in demand, and we have to do it not only for ourselves, but for Europe as well.

At present, there are two items of demand upon which we do not mind, apparently, the lavish expenditure of public money. The first is defense. We are approaching a level of $50 billion a year, and the bills go through Congress with hardly a debate. The next is space research. I suspect that we shall spend $40 billion or so, if not more, over the next decade, and space, being limitless, may well offer limitless opportunities for the stimulus of new demand.

Perhaps I should add one other category — roads. No one minds an $80 billion road program, since clearly mobility has an absolute value in our way of life. But after these categories, any sharp increase in public spending — on education, on health, on urban renewal — runs into the stiffest Congressional opposition, and also arouses a lot of local hostility as well.

Yet of the three highly acceptable forms of public demand, two are, after all, limited. Even with completely balanced forces, could we go beyond $60 billion a year? I doubt it. And one day our major road systems will have been built.

We are left with space. And there, I suspect, the limiting factor will remain trained minds and research.

In the private sector, we pin our hopes on new families and on new products. Our population goes on growing, and in our kind of economy this is a great help. As for products, yes, I suppose space research will breed a large field of by-products. We see them already in satellites for better communications. Perhaps top executives' individualized flying machines and the family helicopter are not far off. Color television should make a new revolution of obsolescence. Pocket TV should come soon, to make sure that not even in fifteen seconds' privacy shall we be obliged to think!

Yet I wonder whether the majority of us need to look for a further stockpile of consumer goods, durable or otherwise. Has not the piling up of things and more things reached a point of reasonable satiety?

I suggest that it is possible that the American people need now to think more of their abilities and their capacities, their sources of inner delight, than of a further accumulation of external wants. It was an American poet, Wallace Stevens, who reminded us: "The world without us would be desolate except for the world within us." Does not our soul now need more attention than our body?

We have, therefore, to face the possibility that the present main stimulants to demand upon which our economy depends — arms, space and other public spending, coupled with the vast pouring out of consumer goods of all kinds — will not push us much above our present rates of growth, and these, unchanged, threaten stagnation and deepening unemployment.

Is there any alternative? And here I turn to the beginnings of this address.

Today, what are our choices? We have abundance. We have an economy whose health depends upon the creation of new kinds of demand. Can we then argue that better education, fuller health, a determined onslaught on the last outposts of destitution, beautiful cities, dignified suburbs, great art, great recreation, should not appear on the priority list?

We face the strange and stirring truth that our dreams are turning into our necessities. Now that reality is catching up with our dreaming, are you — above all, you, the young — afraid to dream?

I realize, of course, that at this point our visions will be interrupted by loud, ritual cries against "spending," against "statism" and "big government," and while I do not want to engage in this hoary controversy, I would like to make four brief points.

The revenues, even the higher tax revenues needed for more education and urban renewal, form a smaller load on the community in times of buoyant growth than in times of stagnation.

Next, our public spending on nondefense needs today is, in fact, not only smaller, proportionately, than that of most European governments. It is smaller by one-third than our own prewar level.

Next, the public stimulus is in most fields only a small part of the total expansion achieved. Slum clearance enhances private property values. The rebuilding of city centers often ends with private capital carrying three-quarters of the investment — and the gain.

Or, to give another instance, the TVA [Tennessee Valley Authority] development created a private tourist industry worth $400 million a year for the area. Better park and wilderness services could do the same.

Or again, where would General Motors be without our road system? In fact, if we starve our public services, we nip off a hundred ways in which enterprising private firms can expand their opportunities.

The chief point I would like to stress is, quite simply, that a proper use of public power and policy, far from being hostile to vigorous private expansion, is essential to it. This is the inescapable lesson of the free system's successes since the Second World War.

The Marshall Plan — a public act — salvaged Europe and restored it to heights of prosperity unknown before. The Monnet Plan — a public act — remade the base of France's faltering private economy. Today, in Europe's bounding expansion, the direction of policy everywhere is toward the closest cooperation between public and private authorities, to check excessive wage and price increases, to oversee long-term rates of investment, and to consider, in the open light of public discussion, the great social priorities of the affluent society.

We, in America, may find soon that not only our relative lack of growth but our seeming indifference to national forethought are losing us our place in the vanguard of free men.

This would be treason to our deepest selves. In a world where vision and decision determine resources, and resources no longer limit vision, it is the boldest dreamers who will move to the vanguard of mankind.

The first society to conquer all its remaining poverty, to give all its citizens the chance of full and diverse education, to build for them greater cities, to save and develop their patrimony of natural beauty, and to launch them on a way of life where work and leisure are creatively intertwined — that society will, by its very being, impose its image on the human spirit.

And if any say to me, "How can we dream such dreams? What utopia are you proposing?" I would answer that it is no longer a dream to think of putting a man on the moon. If we can dream that — and our grandfathers would think us madmen — can we not stir up our imagination to encompass what are in fact less impossible dreams?

What is more difficult, to think of an encampment on the moon or of Harlem rebuilt? Both are now within the reach of our resources. Both now depend upon human decision and human will. I pray that the imagination we unlock for defense and arms and outer space may be unlocked as well for grace and beauty in our daily lives. As an economy, we need it. As a society, we shall perish without it.

It will be tragic indeed if, in this hour of our greatest physical opportunity, we cease to seek the American dream.

To Goldie B. Schwarz [126]

June 12, 1962

My dear Miss Schwarz:

Thanks for your letter. I regret that I kept no notes on my tribute to Marietta Tree at that delightful party. I do recall, however, the quotation from Walter Bagehot:

> The water beetle swims upon the water's face
> With ease, celerity and grace.
> If he should stop to think
> How he did it, he would sink.

I believe I went on to say that Marietta's resemblance to the water beetle ended with ease, celerity and grace, which described her manner of doing whatever she did, and that she did a great deal indeed, in politics, diplomacy and for the causes she believes in, including first of all, non-discrimination in housing and equal opportunity for the races.

I am sure I went on and on!

Cordially yours,

To E. Van der Straeten [127]

June 13, 1962

Dear Mr. Van der Straeten:

I was happy to have your letter and the annual report of the Union Minière.[128] The Chairman's declaration was comforting, but I wish I saw brighter prospects for a solution of the difficulties of the Congo. I had hoped that with the assistance of your company and the Belgian Government there would have been far more progress toward reconciliation of Katanga and the Central Government by this time. I have just concluded a long interview with Paul Henri Spaak,[129] who seems particularly

---

[126] Director of special projects of the National Committee against Discrimination in Housing.
[127] Director of the Société Générale de Belgique, Brussels.
[128] The mining company in Katanga, the Congo.
[129] Belgian minister of foreign affairs.

depressed by the deteriorating economic situation in the Central Government. It may be that we can work out some sort of interim credit arrangement on a "package" basis which would yield some results for both Tshombe and Adoula.

Our hope, indeed our prayer, is that we can work out of this situation toward reasonably orderly government before disaster overtakes the Congo and your company as well. Should current negotiations fail, the time would be near at hand when Mr. Adoula may no longer heed, or be free to follow, counsels of restraint. Or if Mr. Tshombe, having made an agreement, fails to live up to it, the chief of the Congo Government will be obliged to assert his authority.

The United States, as you know, has supported the efforts of the United Nations as the best insurance against conflict of great powers in the Congo, and unless the Katanga issue is soon resolved, it seems evident that some other country is bound to raise a question about the non-application of the Security Council's mandate.[130] This would, of course, present a most "awkward situation," to use a diplomatic phrase, and could lead to a United Nations resolution of much more far sweeping character.

Tshombe's government is largely financed by revenues paid by the Union Minière, which has elected to make no payments to the Central Government. I had hoped that this policy would have been reconsidered long, long before this in light of the inescapable obligation which your company has towards the government of Mr. Adoula, the only legal government of the Congo. If, as your people constantly repeat, they fear reprisals from Mr. Tshombe, I believe they should apply to the United Nations for protection.

Obviously, there is some risk involved in any course of action in the Congo, but I believe you will agree that the risks presented by the kind of support we believe should be given to the United Nations are less than the risks of inaction.

I hope you will treat this letter in confidence. I believe a candid exchange of views is the best evidence of friendship, and it is wholly in that spirit that I write you now.

Cordially yours,

Eleanor Roosevelt wrote Stevenson on June 11, 1962, asking him to write Philip Stern and his mother, Mrs. Edgar B. Stern, of New Orleans, to raise money from the Stern Family Fund for the work of the American Association for the United Nations. Stern had served on Stevenson's

---

[130] From March to June, 1962, talks between Prime Minister Adoula and Moise Tshombe were inconclusive. Finally, between December 28, 1962, and January 21, 1963, the United Nations Force ended Katanga's secession.

campaign staff in 1952 and was director of research for the Democratic National Committee from 1953 to 1956.

To Philip M. Stern

June 18, 1962

Dear Phil:

I have long been interested in the program of the American Association for the United Nations and in past years have served as a member of its Board of Directors. Present circumstances prevent me from being actively involved in its affairs, but I am kept closely informed of its activities through its officers.

A number of years ago a grant from the Adele R. Levy Fund made possible the beginning of an AAUN field program to develop regional and local support for the UN through AAUN organization. The grant has been renewed each year and has helped interest other foundations in this project. Many sections of the country are now covered by AAUN field men who work with volunteer leadership in building informed and articulate support for the UN and U.S. policy in the UN. This has been of substantial help in developing the majority opinion of the American people favoring the United Nations.

Today there are still certain areas of the country which present formidable opposition to the UN and U.S. participation in this world body. One such area is comprised of the states of Louisiana, Texas, Oklahoma and Arkansas. Interest and support for the UN exist in these states but are unorganized and reluctant to act. The AAUN feels that substantial progress can be made in developing a UN program in this area if funds can be obtained to initiate a field project. A conditional grant of seven thousand dollars has been pledged by the Western Publishing Foundation if the additional $13,000 needed for the project can be raised.

Knowing of your sympathy and concern for the problems the UN faces in this country as well as on the international scene, may I take the liberty of suggesting this project as one in which both you and the Stern Family Fund might be interested. I will ask Clark Eichelberger, Executive Director of the Association, to call on you in Washington if you would like to hear more about the AAUN.

Sincerely yours,

At the time of the partition of the Indian subcontinent in 1947, the princely state of Kashmir had a Hindu ruler and a predominantly Muslim population. In October, 1947, Northwestern tribal fighters from Pakistan invaded Kashmir. At this point the maharaja decided to join India, and

Indian troops were flown in to stop the tribal fighters, who were now openly supported by the Pakistani army. On January 1, 1948, Prime Minister Nehru agreed to a cease-fire. Pakistan then occupied approximately 40 percent of Kashmir and India the rest. Although Nehru asked the United Nations Security Council to brand Pakistan as an aggressor, the Security Council instead sent a UN team of negotiators to try to reach an agreement. Over the next years a number of proposals were made including a plebiscite, but India refused that suggestion.[131]

In June, 1962, a resolution before the Security Council urged the governments of India and Pakistan to once more enter into negotiations and to refrain from actions that would aggravate the situation. India was opposed to a discussion of the issue by the Security Council. When the resolution came to a vote on June 22, 1962, the Soviet Union exercised its veto. It was the one hundredth veto cast by the Soviet Union. Stevenson, wishing to speak to this issue and not the Kashmir question, asked the president of the Security Council to call upon him as the first speaker after the vote was taken. Before he delivered the speech, and during the times he was interrupted, Stevenson did extensive revisions on the original draft.[132]

Ambassador P. D. Morozov, the Soviet deputy permanent representative to the United Nations, consumed more time interrupting Stevenson's speech than Stevenson used to complete his presentation. The president of the Security Council spoke eight times to clarify points of order, and the permanent representative of Ghana, Ambassador Alex Quaison-Sackey, spoke once. In all, a speech planned for ten minutes took an hour to complete.[133]

I hope the members of the Security Council will not object and will indulge me while I make a few remarks on this historic day in the Security Council. It is a day that should not pass without notice. A permanent member of the Security Council has just cast its 100th veto.

From the beginning of the United Nations one of its special characteristics has been the voting procedure in the Security Council.

We all recall the serious deliberations which took place at San Francisco concerning the nature and the import for the future of the veto right for the permanent members of the Security Council.

[131] For Stevenson's first baptism of fire on the sensitive Kashmir issue, see *The Papers of Adlai E. Stevenson,* Vol. V, pp. 200–204, 225–226. Finally, on February 25, 1975, after agreeing with Prime Minister Indira Gandhi on the accession of Kashmir to India, Sheikh Abdullah returned to power as chief minister.

[132] For a careful study of Stevenson's deletions and additions (some fifty-eight in a speech intended to be ten minutes long), see Michael H. Prosser, ed., *An Ethic for Survival: Adlai Stevenson Speaks on International Affairs, 1936–1965* (New York: William Morrow, 1969), pp. 468–483.

[133] United Nations, *Official Records,* Security Council, June 22, 1962, pp. 21–33. Most of the interruptions are not noted in the official text.

The veto was given to the permanent members primarily because it would be their military and economic power which would have to be used to sustain and enforce Security Council decisions directly affecting vital world interests.

Representatives of small and middle-sized states emphasized their anxiety that the veto might be used to hamstring the Security Council. In order to meet such fears, the four sponsoring members of the conference set forth their conception at that time of unanimity rule, with which the delegation of France also associated itself.

The big powers, including the Soviet Union, specifically stated "It is not to be assumed . . . that the permanent members, any more than the nonpermanent members, would use their veto willfully to obstruct the operation of the Council."

That was the way we started, Mr. President, at San Francisco seventeen years ago, this very week, I believe. What happened since? Before the first year was out the Soviet Union had cast nine vetoes. The Soviet member of the Council has today cast its 100th veto. For fifteen years the U.S.S.R. on occasion after occasion has sought to obstruct the operations of the Council, sometimes where Soviet plans and prestige were directly and clearly involved and at other times when the continuation of friction might contribute to Soviet objectives.

The Soviet Union has used the veto lavishly to prevent states from assuming their rightful place in the United Nations. In fact, fifty-one of these vetos were cast on applications for membership in the United Nations. Ireland, a member of this Council, was denied membership for nine years. So were Jordan and Portugal. Austria, Finland and Italy were kept out for eight years. Ceylon was kept out for seven years. Nepal for six years. Mauritania was vetoed in 1960, and Kuwait in 1961. Korea is still not a member. The veto has been used to tie the admission of clearly qualified states for which there was widespread support to the admission of states and regimes about whose qualifications for membership there were grave doubts. This despite the fact that the tying of the admission of one applicant to that of another has been specifically held by the International Court of Justice to be contrary to the Charter.

The Soviet Delegate used the veto *thirteen* times to assist Soviet bloc activities against the territorial integrity and the political independence of other states. When the Soviet subverted Czechoslovakia in 1948, the Soviet Delegate vetoed Security Council moves to investigate the case. When Communist-supported guerrillas tried to overturn the independence of Greece in 1946 and 1947, the Soviet again vetoed a Security Council resolution. And when Thailand asked the Security Council to act against attempted infiltration from Indochina in 1954, the Soviet again vetoed . . .

[The President of the Security Council, Ambassador Armand Bérard of France, interrupted because the Soviet Ambassador raised a point of order. He said it was an interesting lecture but the history of Soviet vetoes was not on the agenda. Ambassador Bérard said it was the practice of the Council to allow its members to express their opinions or feelings after a vote had been taken. He asked all members to be as brief as they could while remaining within the scope of the item.] [134]

MR. STEVENSON: When interrupted, I was reciting the instances in which Soviet bloc activities of the veto have been used some thirteen times to assist Soviet bloc activities against the territorial integrity and political independence of other states.

After realizing its mistake in boycotting the Council during the North Korean aggression against the Republic of Korea in 1950, I remind the members of the Council that the Soviet Union returned to the Council in August and immediately began to veto Security Council decisions designed to uphold the independence of that country. Fortunately for the Korean people and for this organization, that effort failed because we were able to proceed through the General Assembly. Similarly, in 1956, the United Nations was forced to move in the General Assembly to condemn Soviet intervention in Hungary after the Soviet Union supported its aggression against the Hungarian people by invocation of the veto.

And most recently in 1960 the Soviet vetoed a resolution on the Congo sponsored by Ceylon and Tunisia because the resolution was designed in part to resist Soviet efforts to intervene in the Congo despite the fact that the United Nations peace-keeping operation was already in action; again an emergency session of the General Assembly was required before the United Nations could do what was necessary.

There are still more areas in which the veto has been used to obstruct the operation of the Council.

The veto has been frequently used to prevent the United Nations from investigating . . .

MR. MOROZOV: Point of order.

MR. STEVENSON: The gentleman, I am sure, will have an opportunity to speak after I have concluded what I have to say, which I submit, Mr. President, is entirely consistent with the rules and entirely proper for me to speak.

MR. MOROZOV: I ask for the floor on a point of order.

[Ambassador Bérard called on Ambassador Morozov to state the point of order. Morozov said Stevenson was not staying on the item as the President had asked. Morozov requested that the Council be asked

[134] This and subsequent material in brackets appears thus in the original.

to vote on Bérard's interpretation that it was the practice of the Council to allow its members to express opinions and feelings after a vote had been taken. Bérard was about to put this procedural matter to a vote when Morozov stated that a favorable vote would mean that the majority favored the "waging of the cold war" as the most appropriate activity for the Security Council. When Bérard cited a Soviet statement in the Security Council on July 7, 1948, which supported the president's ruling, Morozov complimented him on "very good stage direction." Finally, Morozov withdrew his request for a vote on Bérard's interpretation.]

MR. STEVENSON: I haven't more to say, Mr. President, but before I proceed I must say that I was not aware, if I understood the representative of the Soviet Union correctly, that my shoe was on the table. I wonder if he could have had me confused with someone else who still has other uses for shoes and tables.[135]

When I was interrupted for the second time, Mr. President, I was saying that the veto has been frequently used to prevent the United Nations from investigating charges brought to the Council by the Soviet Union itself. On at least four occasions, with the use of six vetoes, the Soviet Union refused, after using the Security Council to air its charges, to let its own assertions be examined. I invite your attention to 1950 when the Soviet Union charged the United States Air Force with the bombing of Communist-held areas of China. The Soviet Union vetoed a commission of investigation. In 1952, the Soviet representative climaxed one of the most shameless falsehoods in history — the long crescendo of accusations that the United States and the United Nations troops were employing germ warfare in Korea — by bringing the issue before the Security Council and then promptly vetoing a proposal for an impartial examination.

In 1958, when the Soviet Union purported to be concerned about United States flights over the Arctic Circle, the United States proposed an Arctic Inspection Zone. That too, was vetoed. In 1960, when Soviet fighter planes destroyed a United States RB-47 airplane over international waters, the Soviet Union vetoed two separate proposals for investigations, one of them asking only that the International Red Cross be permitted to assist any surviving member of the plane.

In each of these cases the Security Council tried to exercise its proper peace-keeping function through systematic investigations. In each case, after having brought the charge, the Soviets vetoed the attempt at a remedy.

One of the most disturbing facts also revealed in the history of 100

135 Premier Nikita Khrushchev, during a meeting of the General Assembly in 1960, pounded on the table with his shoe.

vetoes is the consistent effort to prevent the Security Council from developing processes of peaceful settlement. Not only do many of the vetoes I have referred to fall into this category but most of the remaining ones were also cast against efforts to promote peaceful settlements: four times with respect to Spain in 1946; once against a resolution on troop withdrawals from Syria and Lebanon in 1946, not because the resolution was wrong but because it was not extreme enough; twice in connection with problems arising at the time of Indonesian independence; once against the Security Council recommendations for a solution of the Berlin blockade in 1948; once on Goa; twice to prevent extension of the United Nations peace-keeping functions in 1958; and five times since 1960 in the Security Council's consideration of the Congo. The U.S.S.R. also vetoed four resolutions in the field of disarmament.

Distortion of the veto power has been a fact of life in this Council. It is a fact that has led to the Uniting for Peace procedure,[136] adding to the United Nations peace-keeping machinery a flexible means whereby United Nations members can assure that the United Nations' primary function of preserving the peace will be carried out.

The veto does exist, within its proper context, as a recognition of political reality, but it is a privilege to be used not abused, and abused it has been, for the Soviet Union has willfully obstructed the operation of this Council. It has violated that part of the Four Power Declaration at San Francisco — in which the powers agreed not to use their veto willfully to obstruct the operation of this Council.

Now, so much for yesterday and today. What of the future? The Council is a vital and purposeful organization of the United Nations in spite of the veto. It provides vital and purposeful direction and leadership. And in areas of its work where the veto does not apply, we believe the Council might well widen its activities and increasingly provide that direction and that leadership to our affairs. As for the veto itself, we hope that long before the Soviet Union approaches its 200th veto, it will realize that its own interests lie not in national obstruction but in international cooperation, not in willful vetoes for narrow ends but in willing assents for the broad and common good for which the U.N. stands.

Thank you, and my apologies — and I assure you I have had my shoes on all afternoon.

[136] After the Soviet Union returned to the Security Council in August, 1950, Secretary of State Dean Acheson proposed to the General Assembly that it "organize itself to discharge its responsibility [for collective security] promptly and decisively if the Security Council is prevented from acting." Whenever a veto prevented the Security Council from acting, a special emergency session of the General Assembly could be convened by a procedural vote of any seven members. Ruth B. Russell, *The United Nations and United States Security Policy* (Washington, D.C.: Brookings Institution, 1968), pp. 130–131.

To John F. Kennedy [137]

June 28, 1962

Dear Mr. President:

Before my departure for Europe I should like to pass along some of my thoughts on the current situation with respect to disarmament problems, for such use as you may care to make of them.

As I see it the moment is not very propitious even for minimal progress. The general international atmosphere is not good, despite the precarious agreement on Laos.[138] Any one of a half dozen smoldering crises could flare up during the next few months. Internal difficulties in the Soviet bloc are more likely to lead to heightened cold war tensions than the reverse. There are already signs of a tougher tone in Soviet propaganda pronouncements.

In such a period it seems to me to be all the more important for us to go to great lengths to keep disarmament discussions alive. From the tactical point of view such action will be extremely beneficial at the UN and indeed all around the world. More fundamentally, it will do much to keep the channels open and clear away some of the undergrowth. Then, when tensions are again relaxed — as they will be — we could seize the opportunity to move boldly and swiftly for at least a limited measure of agreement.

Even at present we have room for maneuver on one critical issue — the nuclear test ban. On this subject our position is out of date, weakened by our own hints that we would be prepared to water it down, and ripe for beneficial change.

The elaborate 1958 Geneva control system with its cumbersome machinery and intricate tripartite balances, now seems completely unrealistic. Moreover, with the realization that underground testing is of only limited significance, the extensive precautions against clandestine testing contained in the US-UK draft treaty no longer appear necessary. There is good reason to believe that a greatly simplified system, relying principally on national control stations, could function with relative effectiveness and without unacceptable risk. Few nations, even including our Allies, are satisfied with our present position.

With the completion of the current American test series I believe the

137 This document was declassified.

138 For nearly fifteen months, complex negotiations were conducted to bring General Phoumi's conservative forces, Prince Souphanouvong's Pathet Lao, and Prince Souvanna Phouma's neutralists into a government of national unity. On June 11, 1962, Souvanna Phouma announced that an agreement had been reached on a nineteen-member coalition cabinet, headed by himsef as premier. For a discussion of the negotiations and the subsequent breakdown of the agreement, see Roger Hillsman, *To Move a Nation: The Politics of Foreign Policy in the Administration of John F. Kennedy* (New York: Doubleday, 1967), pp. 138–155.

time will have come to seek a new-style test ban agreement based on the proposal made by the eight new members of the Geneva Disarmament Conference. This could provide for a control system including national control stations using standardized equipment, a central technical authority to assess reported data, and the right of international inspection teams to make a small number of on-site inspections annually on the territories of participating countries. A still simpler alternative would be an atmospheric test ban treaty without international controls, as suggested by you and Prime Minister Macmillan last September.

If we could propose such an agreement before or at the next UN General Assembly, our overall political posture would be vastly improved. When the Soviets complete their anticipated tests we might even be able to reach an accord, bearing in mind the Mexican suggestion at Geneva of a cut-off date for nuclear testing around the beginning of next year. If the Soviets objected to such reasonable proposals they would have the greatest difficulty in justifying their position.

Apart from the Test Ban, there are certain other elements in our draft outline of a disarmament treaty on which we should consider making modifications when the Disarmament Conference resumes its meetings in July. In this way we might eliminate some of the more vulnerable aspects of our position before they become rallying points for our adversaries. I have in mind particularly the following:

1. *Proliferation of nuclear weapons.* Our draft treaty outline includes provisions to prevent additional individual states from acquiring nuclear weapons, without preventing their acquisition by organizations or groups of states. As in the case of the test ban, however, there is strong sentiment among a large majority of UN members for reaching a separate and early agreement to halt the spread of nuclear weapons, whether to individual states or regional groups. We are committed to discuss this subject in Geneva, and it will certainly be actively and emotionally debated in the General Assembly.

I think it most important that we adopt a permissive attitude towards decisions by individual states or groups of states to the effect that they will not acquire nuclear weapons or allow them to be stationed on their territories. Since it is inconceivable that we would insist on stationing nuclear weapons in any country without its consent, I do not think we should lose anything substantial by such action.

It will be said that a resolution or agreement in this sense would encourage states to "go non-nuclear." But it seems to me that this tendency already exists; states which allow us to maintain nuclear weapons on their territories today do so for pressing security reasons which will not be lightly disregarded in the absence of a general disarmament treaty. Moreover, I believe we must realistically plan ahead for the day when the bulk of our nuclear strength will be more closely confined to US territory than it is at present. For these reasons I believe we could accept steps that individual states or regional groups might voluntarily take to forswear the possession of nuclear weapons. I think we should avoid opposition to proposals in this sense, either at Geneva or at the next General Assembly. And I would recall that this was the issue on which we were most resoundingly isolated and defeated at the last General Assembly session.

2. *Foreign bases.* The Soviets seem to have made significant headway at Geneva with the charge that by proposing reduction of strategic delivery vehicles but not foreign bases in the first stage of a disarmament treaty, we are seeking to gain unfair advantage. I appreciate the impossibility of agreeing to abolish immediately or even to thin out drastically our strategic bases around the periphery of the Soviet Union. If, however, the development of military technology makes us progressively less dependent on such bases, as I understand is the case, I should think we would want to study carefully the possibility of agreeing to begin the reduction of our overseas bases at an early stage in the disarmament process. We could reasonably ask the Soviets to do the same for their foreign establishments.

In terms of the disarmament treaty this would mean that we might agree to dismantle a certain number or proportion of our bases, or certain specific bases, at given points of time in the disarmament process. If the disarmament treaty were being implemented we would make good on these commitments. If a disarmament agreement were never ratified, we would retain full freedom of action.

From the negotiating standpoint the essential point would be our acknowledgment that foreign bases were a clearly defined element of military power, susceptible of limitation and abolition like other elements. This could not fail to improve the strength of our negotiating posture.

3. *Production allowances.* The US draft treaty outline contains complex provisions under which strategic delivery vehicles may continue to be produced even as we are reducing the strength of our delivery vehicle forces by 30 per cent in the first stage of disarmament. These production allowances exceed simply maintenance needs. While the treaty outline terminology is far from clear, I have the impression that our plan could be manipulated to permit us to maintain and perhaps even increase our overall effective striking power while reducing the size of our strategic delivery force. This anomaly has not escaped either the Soviets or the neutrals, and we should modify our position to eliminate it.

4. *Nuclear weapons.* Our proposals on nuclear weapons themselves have also been severely criticized. We allow such weapons to be retained in national armed forces until the last stage of disarmament. We justify

this on the ground that we do not know how to detect the existence of concealed nuclear weapons. We have suggested a technical study of this problem, though reluctant to begin it as yet, and have laid great stress on the cut-off of military fissionable materials production and the transfer of weapons material to other purposes. This is fairly satisfactory as far as it goes, though hardly negotiable since in the first stage our proposals would hurt the Soviets by requiring them to give up much more, proportionately, than we do.

But our position does not meet the telling argument that no disarmament treaty can be seriously considered if it leaves nuclear weapons in the hands of armed forces until the end of the first disarmament process. Why could we not at least begin, in the very first stage, with a requirement for destruction of a specific quantity of nuclear weapons of a given yield? The destruction process could be verified, and a more general obligation could be accepted to make drastic reductions in stage two, contingent upon the development of methods to control the size of stockpiles of remaining nuclear weapons. Through some such arrangement we could avoid what will otherwise become a serious liability in our position as the disarmament negotiations proceed.

5. *Nuclear weapons for UN Peace Force.* We are accused of insisting that the UN Peace Force which will function when general disarmament is achieved should be permitted to retain nuclear weapons. In fact we have merely attempted to leave the matter open, on the ground that the Peace Force must have the weapons needed to deal with any aggressor and that such an aggressor might possess hidden nuclear weapons.

I would suggest that we agree that the Peace Force should not have nuclear weapons, providing the parties are satisfied at the time that their retention is not necessary. I think we could afford to make such a concession, since we shall certainly not be willing to proceed with the later stages of a disarmament agreement unless we are convinced that it includes satisfactory assurance that nuclear armaments are eliminated.

6. *Time limits.* Under pressure we have agreed to a first disarmament stage of three years and a second of three years more, but we have resisted setting a limit for the third stage or for the disarmament process as a whole. Our hesitancy is used to back up charges that we are insincere. I do not see why, with appropriate qualifications in the event of non-compliance, we could not agree to a time limit of nine years for the entire disarmament process. The least we could do would be to agree that Part I of the disarmament treaty contain a statement that disarmament should be carried out, subject to the treaty provisions, in a period of ———— years (i.e., not filling in the blank at present). Our failure to accept this formulation has not been appreciated by others.

7. *Transition.* We insist on a Security Council veto right in sanctioning

the transition from stage to stage of a disarmament program. This is sharply inconsistent with our general position on the veto. Since the disarmament treaty will presumably contain other escape clauses enabling us to resume freedom of action in the event of non-compliance, we should be willing to abandon the provision for such a veto and to replace it by some other formula under which we could still prevent or delay, for cause, the transition to a subsequent stage. Such action would make it easier for us to attack the Soviet insistence on the veto in UN peace-keeping provisions without seeming to be inconsistent.

There are of course many other details in the United States draft treaty outline which could be usefully modified. I am aware that the Arms Control Agency is carefully studying the possibilities for change. I know, too, that questions of tactics and timing may prevent immediate action on some of the points I have mentioned. But I thought it would be useful for you to have an indication of some of the most important critical comments I have heard regarding the United States position. I sincerely hope that some progress may be made in strengthening that position prior to the General Assembly session in September.

Sincerely yours,

To Mr. and Mrs. Adlai E. Stevenson III

June 30, 1962

Dear Adlai and Nance:

I am off this evening for Geneva, via Florence. I think you have my itinerary, and you can always reach me through Roxane [Eberlein] or Rosemary Spencer if need be. I shall be back on the 8th of August at the latest, and there is always the possibility that I will be called back beforehand. I hope you will write me to Geneva, Hotel des Bergues, and let me know just what your plans are.

Viola [Reardy] is anemic and is having some tests and medical attention. She will then come out there [139] and settle down at the farm, unless you have other directions for her. I think she can do a good deal of work and should keep busy, but not too busy. I have no doubt she is showing the signs both of age and of the exhaustions, nervous and physical, of the past several years, but you will find her much more ready to relax and take things in her stride than in the past.

Roxane is going to take a holiday, possibly, in Evanston, where her sister is living, and I told her to use the farm when you are away. It would be good for Frank [140] to have people there more often and some signs of interest in what he is doing. I detected a little note, when I last

[139] Libertyville.
[140] Frank Holland, Stevenson's farmer at Libertyville.

saw him, of restlessness and, perhaps due to Beatrice's [141] condition, some talk about moving to a house they have built in Clearwater, in Florida. No greater disaster could befall me than to lose Frank, and I would say nothing about even the possibility. I am proceeding on the assumption that, while Beatrice will have to spend the cold weather down there, he will continue here. His plan is to take three weeks in August and build a carport at his house in Clearwater. I think he has had little or no vacation for a couple of years and should be encouraged to stay away as long as he wishes, and I assume that Adlai [IV] and Jimmy [142] can do what's necessary about the place at that time — mow the lawn, gather vegetables and water the sheep. My understanding was that you would be back from Beverly [Massachusetts] by August.

I expect to be back the end of the first week in August, and will hope to get out there, if things are not too pressing here, for a visit. Certainly I want to spend a week, if possible, there over Labor Day when we can all be together.

I *think* John Fell and Natalie are going to meet me in Europe, but I was too late to get them on the yacht,[143] as Agnes Meyer had promised all the places. It may be that someone will cancel and they can come aboard at the last moment. I will motor around Switzerland with them and down to Rome, and then they plan to drive up the coast to Spain and around there a bit before coming back. Of course, John Fell plans to sell his car — and "pay for the trip." And I am no longer one to scoff at his plans!

The news about Borden is unchanged. I find it extremely hard to communicate and there is no job or sustained work in prospect yet. He is getting more and more self-conscious and anxious. If you could have him up to Beverly when you are there and talk about the importance of getting started, in a friendly, understanding way, it might help. . . . I am afraid I have completely failed in the past year, both to be with him enough and to be of any help when I have been. He is extremely elusive and I think uncomfortable with me, but I don't know what to do but to press as gently and helpfully as I can for a change in the situation, which has persisted much too long.

I wish I thought things were going well with your mother and that I could be of some help to you in that trying situation.

Carol Hardin and her mother and father [144] were here the other night. She is having her first baby in August, and has matured and is wise and beautiful, and rapidly becoming the mature member of that extraordinary

---

[141] Wife of Frank Holland, who also worked for Stevenson.

[142] The Hollands' son, who helped his father.

[143] For a cruise in the Greek islands beginning July 26, 1962.

[144] Mr. and Mrs. Adlai S. Hardin. Mr. Hardin's mother was Lewis G. Stevenson's sister. Carol Hardin was Mrs. Geoffrey Kimball.

family. They are going to go back to interior Nigeria for another year and a half. Her brother Adlai is graduating in the top 10% of his class at Columbia, and is staying here [145] in order to study in tranquillity for the New York bar examinations. He is really a first-class boy.

I have told Roxane to get in touch with you if she needs money. . . . I had hoped that John Fell or Borden would pay off all or part of their loans by this time and I would be in good condition. Perhaps they will. But I also have New York income taxes of almost $7,000 to pay on top of everything else — which is a shocking and forgotten burden.

If Nancy wants anything in Europe, linen, etc., etc., please have her let me know. I shall have some time for shopping and Buffie [Ives] can always help. Florence is far cheaper for such things and better than Geneva. I shall also have a day in Athens, in case she has anything in mind there that she would like.

Love,

Stevenson spent four days at Florence, Italy, with his sister and brother-in-law, Mr. and Mrs. Ernest L. Ives. Then he went to rest at the Aga Khan's chalet at Gstaad, Switzerland, before attending meetings of the Economic and Social Council at Geneva, Switzerland.

To the Aga Khan [146]

July 8, 1962

My dear Karim —

After almost three days in this heavenly place we are about to return to Geneva and — work! . . .

I wonder if any weary guest ever left this exquisite chalet more refreshed and with more to be thankful for! I have a long (and I hope good) speech prepared for the conference tomorrow, a fine sunburn, new energy — and a few new pounds, thanks to the fine cuisine. . . .

Your new house is an engineering feat and everything about *this* lovely chalet orderly and beautiful — and quiet. I can imagine what it must be in the winter when all the chalets and ski slopes are occupied! But for what ails me this is perfection and I add another imperishable memory to last year's. Thank you — my dear friend — and with the approval of your kind servants I may come back next week end with a man & his wife from my Mission for some more of this heaven on earth.

I wish I was going to see you on this trip and hear all your news, but after Genoa I'm going yachting with some friends in the Adriatic for a

[145] At Stevenson's Waldorf Towers apartment.
[146] This handwritten letter is in the possession of the Aga Khan.

few days — and then back to New York and work in early August. But John Fell and Natalie may be coming over and if they do I have no doubt Cannes will be on their itinerary. (I hope you are not getting too tired of Stevensons!) I saw him in Seattle a couple of weeks ago [147] and asked them to join me on the yacht. Of course they accepted — and then I discovered the yacht was full! But a motor trip in Italy, a visit with me and home by way of Spain appears to be an adequate substitute. Indeed I think I detected a note of relief when they escaped from the "old people."

And I never felt *younger!* — thanks to you, dear Karim. I pray all is well with you dear Karim, and send you my everlasting thanks — again.

Yours,

To Mrs. Ernest L. Ives [148]

July 10, 1962

Dear Buffy:

We arrived after an effortless and quick flight. . . . and since then I have been absorbed in my chores of the Economic and Social Council meeting. The speech, prepared in part at Villa Capponi, went off fine and I enclose a copy.[149]

I had a cable that John Fell and Natalie will be in Milan on the 18th. I don't know what their plans are or whether they will have an automobile, but it is possible that they may land on your doorstep thereafter. I wish that they could drive me to Rome but it may be too much of an exertion and I will probably do it by air.

A letter from Adlai [III] brings very bad news about Ellen's [150] finances and that Mrs. [John Alden] Carpenter has leased her house at Beverly [Massachusetts] so that they will have to spend their holiday at Libertyville! He asked me to thank you for your contribution to Sid Yates' campaign.

And how can I thank you for taking such good care of my guests and me and arranging that fabulous time at the Palio. I would like to come right back for the second running! . . .

Tomorrow I go . . . for a lunch with Mrs. [Katherine D.] McCormick to discuss her gift of the chateau to the Government. I think it is going to go through and may prove a great blessing to the American Missions in the future. I stopped by the other day but didn't go in the house. The grounds are in perfect order, as you can imagine.

---

[147] Stevenson spoke at the Century 21 Exposition in Seattle on June 15, 1962.
[148] The original is in E.S.I., I.S.H.L.
[149] USUN press release 4022, July 9, 1962.
[150] Stevenson's former wife.

With so many thanks, much love and fondest regards to dear Ernest —
and Happy Birthday! — I wish we were going to spend it together.

ADLAI

*Stevenson was planning to visit Madrid after his trip on the yacht
chartered by Agnes Meyer. He wrote Ambassador Robert Woodward in
Madrid on June 28, 1962, about the visit and explained that Alicia
Patterson would accompany him. Woodward replied that he would
arrange meetings with the foreign minister and other officials.*

To Robert F. Woodward

July 17, 1962

Dear Bob:

Thanks for your letter. You are a good sport to take me in again and I
look forward to it eagerly. For obvious reasons, I had hoped to avoid
publicity and any publicized contact with the Government. However, I
will do precisely what you want, although I hope, if something official
is necessary, it can be confined to a courtesy call on the Foreign Minister
without any entertainment. In view of the fact that he is in San Sebastian,
would that offer me an excuse? If not and you think we should go to San
Sebastian, of course, I will.

As to "dreaming up some other ideas," please relax. All I want to hear
is the gossip about Spain from you and your staff, and do some sightseeing around Madrid. I haven't been there for thirty years, with any time
to spare, and would like to see the conventional sights, even if briefly. In
short, don't worry. I am a tourist in a hurry!

Affectionate regards to you both.

Cordially yours,

P.S. You don't need to worry about Alicia Patterson; she will take what
comes gladly.

Memorandum to: Ambassador Adlai E. Stevenson
From: AEStevenson

Take up with the President and the Secretary [of State] the necessity
for a United Nations man in the major embassies. No one with any substantive knowledge or interest in the embassies in Paris and London. In
the latter, Jones [151] says we sit here watching the balls go over our

[151] George Lewis Jones, Jr., minister at the United States embassy in London.

heads — referring to the communication between Macmillan and the President and bypassing the Embassy.[152]

But more important is the fact that the United Nations has never been part of the Group, and Foreign Service officers with a view to advancement bypass it if they can. This *must* be corrected and promotion granted on the same basis or better in view of the importance of the work and the quality of the workers. . . .

To Mrs. Ronald Tree [153]

August 5, 1962

This morning Alicia [Patterson] and I bid farewell to the fine yacht overcrowded with amusing and v[ery]. agreeable people and are now flying to Rome — where I hope to find my first word of the outside world in more than 10 da[y]s and also certain intelligences which I have not had and sorely need. . . .

It is Sunday, a day of departure from *Mountain* and sea — and this time I'm glad to be departing and impatient to get home and diverted with work. But the Adriatic Odessy was good — Montenegro spectacular and primitive, Dubrovnik and the coast and islands beautiful, sun and sea perfect and my long visit to Tito with George Kennan [154] most interesting and perhaps important. But I've had enough of idleness & thinking, postcard writing and thinking, trying to work and thinking. So it will be good to get home and *have* to work. To do nothing is quite different from having nothing to do; so are serenity and idleness. Yachts are confining and I've been idle without being serene. I hope it is better with you.

And that reminds me to report that I've been ill — high temperature and a big bug with an aching climax at Korcula island on Aug. 2 when I thought I heard a plane southbound high overhead and couldn't get the noise out of my ears or the blinding sun out of my eyes in my darkened aircooled cabin. Odd, but all well now and full of reflections about the appearance I'm afraid we create — in this part of the world at least — of being more concerned with winning wars than preventing them. I'm so glad I have a few years to give to the latter. And I ache to contrive better ways to do it — and to be able to execute them. Perhaps we can talk of this sometime.

[152] He may refer to the letters Prime Minister Harold Macmillan and President Kennedy exchanged over the Soviet resumption of nuclear testing. See Arthur M. Schlesinger, Jr., *A Thousand Days: John F. Kennedy in the White House* (Boston: Houghton Mifflin, 1965), pp. 460–461.

[153] This handwritten letter is in the possession of Mrs. Tree.

[154] United States ambassador to Yugoslavia. He and Stevenson lunched with Marshal Tito on August 3, 1962.

Last night we saw Hamlet way up on the ramparts of Lavechen castle in the ancient walled city — in Serbian. And *never, never* was there a more dramatic and moving performance with the stars overhead. Banquo & Hamlet on the battlements above dimly lit against the night sky and torches flickering along the massive walls of the court where we sat high above the sea. And you know it made little difference that the amazing cast were uttering gibberish! . . .

And now I'm arriving in Rome. It is Sunday and I arrived here just 5 weeks ago at the same moment with heart in throat after weeks in the desert with 17 days of living ahead — and now 17 days later I go back to the desert!

Rome — So good to hear from friends! Embassy here in force. Hope all well in Attica. . . .[155]

To Mr. and Mrs. Robert F. Woodward

August 9, 1962

My dear Woodwards:

My return has been somewhat more spectacular than usual: a) immediate testimony in Congress; [156] b) an infection that is driving me to the hospital; c) an accumulation of work and a deserted office.

But all of these are familiar complaints to you, and I am sustained by happy memories of those two "tranquil" days in Spain. I hope hereafter that you can contrive to find something for your guests to do. Such idleness is befitting an older man!

Alicia [Patterson] and I agreed on the plane that it was "the best part of the trip," and I am *as always,* everlastingly indebted to you both. I pray that it won't be long before I have a glimpse of you here, and that you will bear in mind that there are at least some of the comforts of home at apartment 42 A, Waldorf Towers, ready and waiting eagerly.

I know what an imposition we were, but *you* don't know how happy you made us!

With affectionate regards,

Yours,

To Mrs. Albert Lasker

August 10, 1962

Dear Mary:

I am just back and have improved my return with a professional visit to the Roosevelt Hospital for an acute infection, which has happily sub-

[155] Mrs. Tree was in Greece.

[156] On the need for the United States to purchase United Nations bonds. He had already testified before the Committee on Foreign Affairs of the House of Representatives on June 27, 1962. See Department of State *Bulletin,* July 23, 1962, pp. 149–152.

sided. I can't say I like hospitals, but certainly no one ever had better and more prompt and courteous attention. I find it hard to adjust to work again, but there is so much of it and it is so pressing that I dare say I will have little time to complain or mourn my fate. Congress is still in town, as you know, and raising merry hell about most everything. I think the State Department needs you for a lobbyist, not to mention the Administration, which needs a lot of things!

. . . I hear engaging details of the [Anna] Rosenberg–[Paul] Hoffman nuptials and your galas — including the yachting party around the island. I suspect that Elsa Maxwell will have to look to her laurels if your entertaining genius flowers much more!

I am going out to the [Cass] Canfields' this weekend, and next weekend out with Jim Oates [157] and Rosalind [158] to fish on Long Island! I have hopes for Libertyville for a long visit over Labor Day, and meanwhile Adlai [III] and Nancy are coming to see me next week. The news from their mother is extremely bad. She is destitute and getting more and more neurotic and difficult.

I have visions of that beautiful place in my sleep, and while I am glad to be home, I wish that my journey had included at least a little time in that lovely spot.[159]

With much love,

P.S. I don't know what rumors you heard about me and the merger of the POST. I have talked to Dolly [160] about it, but there is no prospect of a merger with Alicia's paper.[161] I am sure there is nothing of any interest to me in it. I agree with you that two women are harder to work for than [Dean] Rusk and [President] Kennedy. Indeed, I think it's impossible, and so does Alicia. This, of course, for your private information. . . .

To Mrs. Ernest L. Ives [162]

August 10, 1962

Dear Buff:

I got home after a couple of days of frenzied and interesting activity in Spain, only to be laid low by an infection in my jaw! But after a day at the Roosevelt Hospital and a bout with a fine surgeon, I am mending rapidly and almost fit for the battle again.

I have a sweet note from Ruth Field, who evidently had a lovely time

---

[157] Chairman of the board of the Equitable Life Assurance Society of the United States and an old friend of Stevenson's from Chicago.
[158] Mrs. Oates.
[159] Mrs. Lasker's Villa Fiorentina, Saint-Jean-Cap-Ferrat, France.
[160] Dorothy Schiff, publisher of the New York *Post.*
[161] *Newsday,* owned by Alicia Patterson.
[162] The original is in E.S.I., I.S.H.L.

with you, and I am most grateful to you for taking such good care of her.

I found the packages awaiting me in Rome, for which I am most grateful, as well as for your kindness to the children. I have heard nothing from John Fell, and assume that all is well. Are you coming to see me in New York on September 4 on your way home? Actually, I plan to be in Illinois over the Labor Day weekend, but should get back here on the 4th or 5th. So if you want to stop off at that time, it will be entirely convenient for me. Meanwhile, we are putting you down for the opening of the UN on September 18 for a few days.

I have bills from you from Navone for $200, Serraglini for $32, and $5 additional for the boxes for the children — a total of $237. I am enclosing 12,000 lire that I have left over in my pocket, or $19, together with checks for the difference of $220. Ever so many thanks for going to all this trouble for me. I think I am well equipped with Christmas gifts, etc., for years to come!

> Love,
> ADLAI

To Mrs. Edison Dick [163]

August 16, 1962

Jane

I am home a week — thank God!

I've been operated on and recovered from an infection in the jaw — thank God!

I'm exhausted — after my vacation — thanks to me!

I'm swamped — thanks to USUN!

The curtains [164] are up and OK — thanks to you!

So you see I'm full of Thanksgiving. Adlai [III] and Nancy have been here to discuss Ellen [Stevenson] — a sad sadder saddest tale, but leave me today.

That's my news. . . .

To Hubert H. Humphrey

August 16, 1962

Dear Hubert:

I am glad to respond to your request for my views on the implications of the satellite communications bill for our policies and objectives in the United Nations.

---

163 This handwritten letter is in the possession of Mrs. Dick.
164 In the ambassador's residence.

I assure you that if I had any serious concern about this I would somehow have made my views heard long before this.

At the risk of repeating the obvious, let me emphasize that any satellite communications system in which the United States would be interested must be international in scope.

It follows that the corporation envisaged in the bill could not possibly develop a rational communications satellite system without entering into numerous bilateral and multilateral international agreements. Anything else would be a technological and political impossibility. So we start with this fact of life: any system of communication via satellites that makes any sense depends for its existence on international cooperation and agreement. This is the heart of the whole matter.

But for what purpose do we want international cooperation and agreement in developing a workable and useful system of communications via satellites? On this, it seems to me that the language of the bill before the Senate is clear. In the Declaration of Policy and Purpose it is stated:

— that our purpose is to establish a *"global* communications network;"
— that our aim is *"global* coverage at the earliest possible date;"
— that our policy is to do this *"in conjunction and cooperation with other countries;"*
— that our purpose is to "serve the communications needs of the *United States and other countries;"*
— that in doing so "care and attention will be directed toward providing such services to *economically less developed countries and areas;"*
— and that the system herein envisaged should be so designed as to *"contribute to world peace and understanding."*

It therefore seems to me that the bill explicitly recognizes that the system is to be global in scope, including expressly the less developed areas; that it ties this scientific wonder directly to the basic aim of the United States foreign policy which, of course, is to "contribute to world peace and understanding;" and that international cooperation and agreement is the *sine qua non* of the system.

These clear commitments to policy and purpose are given teeth in Section 201, where the President is directed to insure the realization of these policies and FCC [Federal Communications Commission] is directed, among other things, to "insure that all present and future authorized carriers shall have non-discriminatory use of and equitable access to, the communications satellite system . . ."

While I think the bill should have made precise reference to the United

Nations, its language and intent are consistent with the relevant part of resolution 1721 adopted by the General Assembly of the United Nations last December. Included in that long and detailed resolution are these words:

". . . communication by means of satellites should be available to the nations of the world as soon as practicable on a global and non-discriminatory basis."

That the policy set forth in the bill and the policy enunciated by the General Assembly fit each other so neatly is not entirely coincidental. The United States delegation played the leading role in drafting this resolution and supporting its adoption by the assembled nations of the world. Speaking to the General Assembly on December 4, 1961, I stated:

"The United States wishes to see this facility made available to all states on a global and non-discriminatory basis. We conceive of this as an international service. We would like to see UN members not only use this service, but also participate in its ownership and operation if they so desire."

The similarity of purpose — and of language — is again clear.

I understand that some doubts have been expressed as to whether, however clear the language may be, the proposed corporation can be required to give effect to national policy, especially as it bears on foreign participation in an ultimate international system. Once again, it seems to me that the language of Section 201 is adequate when it directs the President to:

". . . insure that timely arrangements are made under which there can be foreign participation in the establishment and use of a communications satellite system."

While, as I say, specific reference to the United Nations has been omitted, Section 201 (a) (4) refers to the authority of the President to supervise relations of the corporation with "foreign governments or entities or with international bodies." The United Nations and its family of agencies are, of course, "international bodies."

The role of one of those international bodies — the International Telecommunications Union — is at least tacitly recognized in the bill itself in Section 201 (a) (7) which directs the President to "so exercise his authority as to help attain coordinated and efficient use of the electromagnetic spectrum" — which is something that can be done only through the ITU. And the hearings have been replete with specific references to the primary role in store for the ITU.

So I am satisfied that the role of the United Nations in a satellite communication system is explicitly intended by the language and legislative history of the bill.

Let me add that in the United Nations General Assembly and its Outer Space Committee, in the International Telecommunications Union, and in bilateral conversations with the Soviet Union and other interested countries, the United States has and will promote the objective which it successfully advocated in the General Assembly — that "communications by means of satellites should be available to the nations of the world as soon as practicable on a global and non-discriminatory basis."

The record seems clear that the United States has been committed — since Year One of the Space Age — to a policy of seeking the maximum amount of cooperation in outer space for which we can obtain international agreement. And that policy guides our actions on space matters before the United Nations and its family of agencies. I believe that the progress that has been made in the UN on this complex and delicate subject is quite hopeful, and I repeat that the United States will continue to press forward in line with our own policy and in the spirit of the UN resolution I have just been describing.

I conclude that the legislation before you provides the President and the executive branch of the government with adequate control and influence to ensure that the instrument proposed here can be fitted or adapted to an international system when we learn enough to design one.

Sincerely yours,

To Francis T. P. Plimpton

August 17, 1962

Dear Francis:

Thanks for your note and the good news about your rapid recovery.[165] We have been in a bit of a flap about the Congo, and [Dean] Rusk has been up here for a couple of days talking with me about all manner of things — mostly that place that you will doubtless remember with such joy! Maybe — repeat maybe — we have a more positive program than heretofore to induce Tshombe to play ball. But the press disclosures have aggravated U Thant's position and, of course, weakened the whole thing.[166]

I go to Washington next week for a day or so to talk about the

---

[165] He was at the Ausable Club at Saint Huberts, Essex County, New York, recuperating from a near-fatal illness he suffered in the Congo.

[166] U Thant promulgated on August 20, 1962, a Plan for National Reconciliation in the Congo. It was based on proposals prepared by the Department of State in cooperation with the British and Belgian governments. Although both Cyrille Adoula and Moise Tshombe endorsed it, they could not come to terms. Finally, the United Nations Force ended Katanga's secession between December 28, 1962, and January 21, 1963. Ernest W. Lefever, *Uncertain Mandate: Politics of the U.N. Congo Operation* (Baltimore: Johns Hopkins Press, 1967), pp. 61, 86, 103, 117, 128, 167.

G[eneral] A[ssembly] with the President and the boys,[167] and over Labor Day, God willing, I hope to go to Illinois for the better part of the week. I think you have nothing to worry about. Things are taking form gradually, and we will only be about a month behind in our preparation — as usual.

Please give my dearest love to that splendid nurse of yours [168] and tell her that I needed her myself for a couple of days when I returned, but all is well now.

Yours,

To Mrs. Ernest L. Ives [169]

August 20, 1962

Dear Buffie:

I have just been looking at the schedule and note that you are down for September 18–20 for the opening. This is entirely O.K. with me, but it occurred to me that the opening of the Lincoln Center for the Performing Arts might be interesting, combined with attendance at some of the UN sessions. The Lincoln Center opens on Sunday, September 23, with a concert by the New York Philharmonic, and on Tuesday, September 25, I have to do a narration of "The Lincoln Portrait" by Aaron Copeland [Copland] with the Philadelphia Symphony and Eugene Ormandy.

I suppose you know that the [Paul] Magnusons are at the Ritz in Paris. I had an infection that threatened my sinus, but by taking out a wisdom tooth they have fixed it up and I am quite all right. I hope you are too. I still dream of those happy days at the Villa, and have a procession of ecstatic letters from Ruthie [Field]. You gave her the time of her life — again.

Timmy [Ives] and Adlai [III] and Nancy have been here to discuss Ellen [Stevenson]'s crisis and other family business affairs. He looked fine and has some new ideas about the business that impressed me very much.[170] Indeed, we are all convinced that by far he is the best business-

---

[167] At the meeting with the President on August 22, Stevenson recommended that in case Kennedy spoke to the General Assembly he should include material on economic and social programs, on disarmament, and a "strong pitch . . . in favor of responsible and moderate action on the part of the General Assembly as a way of increasing public confidence in the United Nations in this country." A memorandum of the discussion is in the John F. Kennedy Library. A "sanitized" version was declassified.

[168] Mrs. Plimpton.

[169] The original is in E.S.I., I.S.H.L.

[170] Mrs. Ives's son, Timothy Ives, was manager of radio station WJVC in Bloomington, Illinois.

man in the family, and you should be extremely proud of the record he is making in Bloomington, both publicly and professionally.

Love,

ADLAI

To Carl McGowan [171]

August 20, 1962

Dear Carl:

They called me from Washington about your appointment [172] just as I was leaving town, and this is the first opportunity I have had to express my satisfaction, gratification, delight, exhilaration — and ecstasy!

Besides what you can do for the law and the bench, think what the proximity of the McGowans can do for Stevenson. The whole thing took much too long, but better late than never and all such banalities, I suppose.

My love to the family and congratulations to you.

Yours,

ADLAI

Ralph McGill, of the Atlanta Constitution; *William Baggs, of the Miami* News; *Harry Ashmore, of the Center for the Study of Democratic Institutions; Harry Golden, of the* Carolina Israelite; *and Stevenson frequently exchanged round-robin letters. McGill wrote Stevenson on August 20, 1962, that Golden, Ashmore, and Baggs were disturbed because he had climbed Mt. Fuji in Japan. "These critics have never been able to do better than lift one foot as high as a barroom rail," he added. The other three were also disturbed, he wrote, that the Japanese Newspaper Publishers and Editors Association had sent a twenty-three-year-old woman staff member along with McGill on the climb of Mt. Fuji.*

To Ralph McGill

August 23, 1962

Dear Ralph:

Thanks so much for your letter. It was a great relief to know the circumstances of that sensational exploit, which has already orbited around the world several times!

And I can't tell you what a relief it was to discover that Harry Golden was misinformed and misinforming.

[171] The original is in the possession of Mr. McGowan.

[172] Mr. McGowan had been appointed a judge of the U.S. Court of Appeals for the District of Columbia Circuit in Washington, D.C.

At all events, I can't overlook the fact that beautiful Japanese maidens either helped you to the top of Mount Fujiyama or helped you to see it at a steam bath. Whatever they did, I wonder if you think that they would do it again. I think I am leaving for Japan presently — and without Dr. Harry Ashmore or Dr. William Baggs! Golden I would accept. I know he couldn't make Fujiyama, with or without such assistance, and I doubt if he likes anything called "Sanno." Possibly I shall join him in Africa as a guide after this conditioning in Japan. I think it's a good thing he's going to Africa although he could do far more good, with less wear and tear and expense, in that glass menagerie on the East River.

I appreciated your report and will hope for more, of the unwritten variety, soon in person.

Yours,

Mr. McGill replied to Stevenson's letter of August 23, 1962, that the charming women who accompanied him and his son to Mt. Fuji did not scrub backs in a bath but translated Japanese haiku poems into French. Stevenson was absolutely right to visit Japan without Baggs and Ashmore, McGill wrote, but he warned that an ambassador should know that Fujiyama meant Fuji Mountain — it was incorrect, therefore, to speak of Mount Fujiyama.

To Ralph McGill

August 27, 1962

Dear Ralph:

That you scaled Mt. Fuji while discussing Japanese haiku poetry with such a charming young lady convinces me that you are the most versatile and vigorous of men. I understand all the better the incontinent jealousy of Mr. Ashmore and Dr. Baggs, whose many pretentions don't, to my knowledge, include either mountain climbing or Japanese haiku poetry. As to the young lady — well, you are winning there too.

In the circumstances, I can only doff my cap — and agree never to say Mount Fujiyama again.

Yours,

To Charles Phelps Noyes [173]

August 27, 1962

. . . 3. I want to send a memo to the President with a copy to [Dean] Rusk and others about the importance and value of USUN as a training

---

[173] The beginning and end of this memorandum are not in the Stevenson papers. It was probably classified.

ground. We have none better, and nothing that offers even approximately the comprehensive experience. Somehow the Foreign Service has never seemed to fully appreciate this great resource, and I want to follow up several talks with the President with some sort of memorandum which might constitute the basis of some remarks at the appropriate time by the President, or an intra-departmental memorandum by the Secretary, etc. . . .

To Alicia Patterson [174]

August 28, 1962

E — What are you doing? Why don't you tell me? Dysentery? Sightseeing? [175] Bridge?

Labor Day week end no good — even if I get there [Libertyville] — thanks to house bulging with babies etc. But how about Tues. night Sept. 4 at Waldorf Towers — or Wed Sept 5?

"A" — DISCOVERER OF
MONTENEGRO

To Felix Frankfurter

August 29, 1962

Dear Felix:

The news of your retirement [176] on the ticker this afternoon brings back many precious memories, tinged with a note of sadness. I wish you were eternal, and I think your mind and spirit and contributions to men and their thoughts will be!

With the gratitude of a citizen, friend, and worshipful admirer,

Yours,

Stevenson asked a number of people to write letters on his behalf so that he could appear before the New York State Supreme Court in case he returned to law practice. The Chief Justice of the United States was one of those who recommended him.

---

[174] This handwritten letter is in the possession of Adlai E. Stevenson III.
[175] Miss Patterson was in Aspen, Colorado.
[176] Justice Frankfurter, who was seventy-nine years old, had been absent from the Supreme Court for five months following a mild stroke, and he cited uncertain health as his reason for resigning.

To Earl Warren

August 30, 1962

Dear Earl:

I have your letter and I am most grateful for your flattering letter to the Committee on Character and Fitness of the Supreme Court of New York. If you don't go to heaven for charity, I hope you won't go anywhere else for anything else!

Our journey together [177] is one of my imperishable memories, and I wish there could be another and more leisurely opportunity to travel with you and that beloved and sainted Nina.[178]

I yearn to see you both.

Cordially yours,

To Philip Jessup [179]

August 30, 1962

Dear Phil:

With the celerity that distinguishes the dispatch of all government business, I have today come across your letter of 12 June, 1962, declining to take jurisdiction of the plea of Harry Wallace, The Prince, Scotland of England.[180] In these unhappy circumstances, I have no choice except to see that justice is done myself. It occurred to me that if that distinguished judicial body was not interested in this case, you might be interested in his offer to sell the right of ascension to the Crown of Scotland for the money he has in the World Bank. But evidently you have no ambition, and are not interested in promotion or ascension. Considering that you have inspired me to such fiendish activity for so many years, to say that I am surprised by your languor and indifference to opportunity and also disappointed, is an understatement to say the least. And the brave Wallace will have to bleed again with nothing by his side but a poor yeoman of the lowland clan of Stevenson.

I look forward to a chance to discuss all these things — with Lois.[181]

Cordially yours,

ADLAI

---

[177] The Warrens had been guests of Agnes Meyer during her yachting trip in late July and early August.

[178] Mrs. Warren.

[179] Judge of the International Court of Justice in The Hague. The original is in the possession of Mr. Jessup.

[180] Mr. Jessup had sent Stevenson a crank letter whose writer claimed the British throne.

[181] Mrs. Jessup.

To Amintore Fanfani [182]

August 31, 1972

My dear Friend:

I am taking the liberty of giving this letter to an American newspaper-man, Marquis Childs, whose name you may identify, and who enjoys an unusual position in American journalism.

Marquis Childs is a columnist situated in Washington for many years, and the senior correspondent of the St. Louis Post-Dispatch, a distinguished American newspaper. Mr. Childs has traveled around the world incessantly for many years, and is presently in Europe. He hopes that he can have a moment with you sometime, and if you can spare the time I think you will enjoy meeting him, and I am sure he will profit immensely from even the briefest exposure to you. I can vouch unequivocally for his discretion, honor, and good judgment.

I think often of our talk last month, and have taken the liberty of passing on to the President some of your views about possibilities of improving our dialogue with the Soviet Union, as well as your remarkable political achievements in Italy.

With warmest good wishes, and renewed thanks for my most agreeable visit this summer, I am

Cordially yours,

Mrs. Franklin D. Roosevelt [183]

[dated 8/ — /62]

Please get out of there quickly! [184] And *please please* let me know if there is anything I can do.

ADLAI

P.S. I'm hoping you can come to dinner with Martha Gellhorn and Tom Matthews [185] on the 12th [of September] —

AES

---

[182] Prime minister of Italy.

[183] This handwritten letter is in the Franklin D. Roosevelt Library, Hyde Park, New York.

[184] Mrs. Roosevelt was in the hospital.

[185] Mr. and Mrs. T. S. Matthews, old friends of Stevenson's. Mr. Matthews, an author, was a former editor of *Time* magazine, and Mrs. Matthews, also an author, had been a war correspondent for *Collier's* magazine.

To Lady Barbara Jackson

September 5, 1962

Dearest Barbara:

. . . That you are leaving on September 13th, bound for England, at least chops a few thousand miles off the space between us.[186] I wish it were still more and that we could have that long deferred conference this very evening. There is so much to ask, to hear, and to discuss — and nothing more important than "Robert Jr." [187] Your description of that fascinating young man renews my eagerness to see him. And perhaps it is especially keen, thanks to the Labor Day weekend in Libertyville with my laughing, bouncing and garrulous grandchildren. I've never had three more enjoyable days, and I think I could have stood some more, although Nancy would dispute that.

After my travels in Europe, I get more and more suspicious that even our best friends are not going to do much fighting for Berlin. And I pray we are not in for a rude awakening one of these days. Surely there are things we can do that would strengthen our own position there and diminish Russia's legitimate fears. But to talk about them publicly has become almost as dangerous as "two Chinas."

We are getting ready for the General Assembly, with many misgivings about some of the issues and with the certainty of a remorseless three months ahead. My difficulties are compounded by mounting demands on my Mission and on me personally. The most recent is substitution for Kennedy at the 100th anniversary of the Emancipation Proclamation at the Lincoln Memorial on September 22. Evidently JFK has to go on a campaign trip — and I'm afraid we need a lot of them! — and, as you will note from Allan Nevins' [188] enclosed letter, the speaking assignment has fallen on my shrinking shoulders.

Nor could it have come at a worse time. All of which is by way of saying the obvious: if you have any thoughts or "purple prose" lying about, please sweep it up and send it on! Whatever it is, it will be better than mine or the contributions I get. Surely this is an opportunity for America to remind the world that there is at least one universally beloved American, and that we have had something to offer in this freedom business, which seems to be the chief interest of innocents and cynics alike.

Also, if I can't persuade President Kennedy to come to the opening of the General Assembly to speak at an early stage of the debate, I shall

[186] Lady Jackson was in Australia.
[187] The Jacksons' son.
[188] Lincoln scholar and research associate at the Huntington Library in San Marino, California.

have to make a speech myself. That will be about the 20th, and I doubt if you have time to put anything together for me before you are afloat.

The other public performances have now reached staggering proportions, and I shan't burden you with a recitation. Meanwhile, the election campaign is gathering momentum, with some disconcerting cracks in the armor already perceptible. That my job forbids me to participate is a welcome escape. But I don't seem to escape the fund raising, and I have been doing a bit of that in Illinois for Sidney Yates, with more to follow for Wilson Wyatt [189] and sundry others.

You have said so many things to which I have not replied, that I feel guilty — and am doubtless afflicted with a creeping stupidity, which alarms me and which I can't attribute to a winter virus in Australia! But a final word as to my summer: The visits in Italy were glorious, the work in Geneva not uncongenial or frustrating, and the cruise on the Adriatic perfect as to weather, and as to relaxed and congenial companions, but not as rewarding for sights — except Montenegro — and "experiences" as I have come to expect. The two days in Spain that followed were fascinating, and provided me with my best summer stories. But they have also provided our Embassy with no little embarrassment, in view of the howling protests of the "opposition" about my visit. That I should ever have been charged with deliberate aid to Franco [190] has been hard to take!

If you find time to write anything for the Lincoln occasion or record any other ideas that need ventilation, I can fit them in somewhere and will be as grateful as ever. If you can't, I shall understand your difficulties and blame myself for putting in my application so late. But somehow there is always an occasion to use what you write, and I hope to go on doing so evermore.

And, finally, I should also like to see you every day — evermore!

With much love,

P.S. Nancy and Adlai asked me especially to send you their affectionate regards, and so would Borden if he were within reach. Actually, he is, but I can't reach him! He has been spending the summer with lighthearted folk at Southampton, but the progress toward industry and profit is meager in the extreme. . . .

A.E.S.

---

[189] Lieutenant governor of Kentucky. President Kennedy told Arthur Schlesinger, Jr., that it would be acceptable for Stevenson to appear at a fund-raising affair for Wyatt, who was running for governor, but that Stevenson should not be co-host. See Schlesinger, Memorandum for the President, August 22, 1962, John F. Kennedy Library.
[190] General Francisco Franco, Spanish chief of state.

To Arthur M. Schlesinger Jr.

September 5, 1962

Dear Arthur:

Note the enclosed letter from Gabriel Reiner,[191] expressing a hope to see the President sometime. I hope he can, too, although I appreciate the difficulties, and I am sure he does, likewise.

But I am prompted to send this along for another reason. You will note that he reflects the view that I have expressed so often: that we should try to make contact with Khrushchev on a political as well as a diplomatic basis, and not sporadically but repeatedly, for the usual long and trying talk fests.

Yours,

To John F. Kennedy

MEMORANDUM FOR THE PRESIDENT

September 14, 1962

Subject: Proposal to Increase IDA Capital

A meeting is being held on September 14 to determine U.S. policy on the proposals of the IBRD [192] to increase the capital of the International Development Association from $1 to $4 billion. I would like to urge support of this proposal for the following reasons:

1. The IBRD estimates that IDA will commit approximately $500 million of its resources during the current fiscal year. These commitments, coupled with commitments already made, will exhaust IDA's stock of "hard money" available for the development loans. Action during this fiscal year to augment the capital of IDA is therefore necessary to enable the institution to make further commitments in Fiscal 1964 and later years.

2. Based on experience IDA already has and its estimates for the coming year, Eugene Black [193] forecasts $600 million a year as a reasonable level of IDA activity in Fiscal 1964 and thereafter. Following the formula used in the initial capitalization of IDA, in which countries made their contributions to capital in five annual installments, he concludes that an additional $3 billion of capital is necessary to support the desirable rate of lending operations in the period FY 1964–FY 1968. We see no reason to question the soundness of these figures.

3. Development lending through IBRD–IDA has proved itself as an

---

[191] The travel agent who had arranged Stevenson's trip to the Soviet Union in 1958.
[192] International Bank for Reconstruction and Development (the World Bank).
[193] Chairman of the World Bank.

effective instrument of U.S. foreign policy. Indeed, it is perhaps the optimum kind of multilateral cooperation in economic development for both economic and political reasons. The institutions are agencies of the United Nations and act in the name of the U.N. system. At the same time, the United States and its principal allies retain control both through the device of weighted voting and in the day to day management of the institution. The Soviet bloc does not participate. The less developed countries do, and most of them find distinct advantages in receiving advice and assistance from these international institutions in which they participate — in spite of the fact that these institutions are largely managed and controlled by the Atlantic nations and nationals. Finally, the experience of the IBRD–IDA in development, the high quality of their officials, the prestige they command in all continents — all of these factors make them prime institutions through which to exercise American power and influence in the development field.

4. A major increase in IDA capital provides a unique opportunity to draw in additional resources from the countries of Western Europe and Japan. This is precisely the opportunity we are looking for to get these countries not only to commit more resources for economic development but to finance development on easier credit terms. No other device readily comes to mind by which we can get these countries to finance economic development through no-interest fifty year credits with ten year grace periods in repayment. In increasing IDA's capital we should insist on a renegotiation of country quotas so that the European Six [194] contribute at least as much as the United States. But we shall have leverage to do this only if we take the leadership before the world in seeking a major increase in IDA resources along the lines of Eugene Black's proposal.

5. Recent experience in the Congress suggests that we will have continued difficulty in obtaining Congressional support for increased U.S. capital aid on a bilateral basis. Increasing IDA's resources from $1 to $4 billion offers a politically attractive way of increasing the flow of U.S. aid to less developed countries. It is politically attractive because the Congress would see in this proposal an effective way to assure that our allies assume their fair share of the aid burden. The U.S. would have to put up no more than $1 billion of the $3 billion — and less if the European percentage can be increased above the present figure. This would be paid over in five installments of $200 million a year. Following the procedure used for the first $1 billion, only one Congressional authorization would be needed, although there would be annual appropriations of the five installments.

[194] The members of the European Economic Community: France, West Germany, Italy, Belgium, the Netherlands, and Luxembourg.

6. The increase of IDA from $1 to $4 billion would be the most important single thing we could do to give vitality to the United Nations Development Decade. It would strengthen our posture very greatly in the United Nations General Assembly, in the Economic and Social Council, and in the forthcoming United Nations Conference on Trade and Development. It would enable us to eliminate for the foreseeable future serious pressures for a SUNFED, a United Nations capital development fund. It would greatly strengthen the free world's contribution to United Nations actions in economic development and offer another dramatic contrast of the comparative contributions and approaches to development of the Free World and the Soviet bloc.

7. The proposal to divert the approximately $70 million of IBRD annual earnings not earmarked for reserves to IDA should *not* be pursued at this time. It is too likely to be used as an excuse by some countries to avoid substantial commitments to increase their contributions to IDA capital. Moreover, we are currently considering proposals to apply these Bank earnings to other uses under U.N. auspices — peaceful settlement activities, "presences," and technical assistance and preinvestment efforts of the U.N. Without getting into the merits of these latter proposals, I would hope that the State Department will not take any position inconsistent with them now until we have had a chance to consider them thoroughly.

8. The negotiation of an increase in IDA capital from $1 to $4 billion with an increase in the quota of Western Europe and Japan will require a difficult political effort. The present moment offers a uniquely favorable opportunity to make this effort. Eugene Black is engaging his great personal prestige in this proposal. It is to be part of his valedictory to the organization. The Treasury Department supports the proposal.

9. I understand there is opposition to this proposal, but I think it would clearly be in the national interest of the United States not to lose this opportunity to further strengthen multilateral cooperation for economic development, under U.N. auspices but under Western control.

The General Assembly opened on September 18, 1962. In the days just before this, Stevenson was involved in briefings for the American delegation, in both Washington, D.C., and New York. On September 20 and 21 he addressed the General Assembly. On September 22, 1962, he delivered an address at the Lincoln Memorial to commemorate the one hundredth anniversary of the Emancipation Proclamation.[195]

[195] The text is from Stevenson's reading copy, which he deposited in the Library of Congress. Words underlined by Stevenson for emphasis are printed in italics. The speech was published in Stevenson, *Looking Outward*, pp. 244–248.

This day just a hundred years ago, America reached a *turning* point.

It was five days after Antietam. In the South Mountain defiles and on the fields around Sharpsburg ghastly clumps of dead soldiers lay unburied. The foul weeds of *civil* war — *hatred, fury, cruelty* — grew ranker as the lists of slain and wounded filled the bulletin boards, and the hospital trains crept *North* and *South* between lines of harrowed watchers. In *Europe,* leaders pondered intervention; some ready to take harsh advantage of the New World's *agony;* some, like Gladstone, racked with anxiety to stop the slaughter.

And then came the *flash,* the lightning stroke that enables men to see the changes wrought by the storm. A haggard President told his cabinet and his *Maker* that if the foe was driven from Union soil, he would declare the slaves "forever free." Within *hours* headlines all over this land clamored with the word "Emancipation!" Within *days* every slave had heard the news. Within *weeks* people all over the world were hailing the redemption of young America's promise.

Like *all title deeds* of human progress, the Proclamation of Emancipation meant *more* than it *said.* Morally it meant that American civilization and human bondage were *irrevocably* incompatible. And a panoply of *larger* freedoms was bound up in that first small step. For the Proclamation touched not the fate of *Americans* alone; it gave courage to the oppressed from the Thames to the Ganges; it inaugurated a *new* age of world-wide reforms. It was an application of the basic tenets of the nation, tenets which gave promise, said Lincoln, that "in due time the weight would be lifted from the shoulders of all men."

Since we admit so readily our *gratitude* and our *debt* to *other* nations for their enrichment of our national fabric, I hope it will not seem immodest to others that Americans take such pride in the momentous milestone we commemorate today, nor in the globe-circling spread of our spirit of *national* independence and *individual* freedom. During the past two centuries the two have walked *hand* in *hand.* Beside *national* independence in 1776 stood the goal of individual *freedom;* beside the preservation of the Union in 1862 stood the same great idea — planted there by the most *beloved* of American leaders.

And *today* — just a century later — freedom is *again* at stake. This time the whole world-wide society of men is perilously divided on the issue. *National* independence has swept the earth like wildfire, but *individual* freedom is *still* the great *unfinished* business of the world. Once more we doubt whether the human experiment can survive half *slave* and half *free.* Once more we *feel,* as men did in Lincoln's day, that the future of mankind itself depends upon the outcome of the struggle in which we are engaged.

In this *context,* with this *urgency,* with these *fears,* it would be easy enough to slip into the path of cloudy rhetoric. I could paint you a picture of this world struggle in which our *adversaries* would be *pitch black* and we — "the land of the free and the home of the brave" — would be *lily white*.

But since today we celebrate not only the *act* of Emancipation, but also the *Great Emancipator* (who sits brooding behind me,) it is well to point out that Lincoln, throughout all the *agonies* and *defeats*, and the breathtaking *triumphs* of the Civil War, *never* made such a speech. Never did he define his cause — this overwhelming cause of freedom — in terms of *white* and *black*, *good* and *bad*, *excellence* and *evil*. Abraham Lincoln of Ill. never stooped to cheap rhetoric. Instead, he continued, *obstinately* and *greatly*, to see human *affairs* and human *emotions* in all their *complexity* and *ambiguity*, and to *refuse* the snap judgments into which *self-righteousness* can so easily lead us all. If ever a leader *lived* by the Biblical injunction — "Judge not, lest ye be judged" — it was Lincoln. For him, *truth* was the groundwork of freedom, and you could no more build victory upon *delusion* than you could sustain society in *slavery*. And *this* is reason enough for his *saintly* rank among world statesmen.

So if today we wish to honor both the *act* of emancipation and the *man* who framed it, we have to follow in the *same* dedication to *truth,* and the *same* abhorrence for pretension and self-deceit. We *know* that we uphold the cause of *freedom*. Equally we *know* that we risk *betraying* it if we have any illusions about our *failures* and *insufficiencies*.

If the issue between North and South sometimes seemed ambiguous to Lincoln; if, as in the Second Inaugural, he recognized the equal complicity of *Northerners* organizing the slave trade and *Southerners* profiting by the results, so, too, today we must approach the theme of freedom in the *world* context with some of Lincoln's *modesty* and *accuracy.*

Are we the pure-souled defenders of freedom when Negro citizens are anywhere denied the right to *vote,* or to equal education, or to equal opportunity, to equal dignity? Can we be surprised if, abroad, *friends* with *sadness* and *enemies* with delight, observe the *inequalities* and *injustices* which still mar our American image?

In his day, Lincoln was bitterly attacked for this unwillingness to take the straight partisan line, to claim all *virtue* for the North, all *evil* for the South, to *praise himself* and his *cause,* to *damn* all his adversaries. His sense that issues might be relative and ambiguous roused men of rougher certitude to furies of denunciation, and Lincoln was accused of weakness, even of *treachery,* because he could not go along with the single-minded jingoism of much of the propaganda of his day.

So *today,* there is a danger that those who do not see things in the *stark* contrasts of black and white will be denounced as *feeble* and even *treacherous.* It is therefore worthwhile recalling that Lincoln's sense of the complexity of all great historical issues did not hold him back for one hour from "doing the right" as God gave him to see the right, or deter him from emancipating the slaves and fighting a great war to its finish to ensure that the Union would be preserved and the Emancipation honored.

So today — that we make no claim to *final righteousness* will help us to keep open all the paths to *negotiation* and fruitful compromise. It does not — any more than it did for Lincoln — make us compromise with *violence, aggression* or *fraud.* We shall stand all the *firmer* for not standing in a *false* light. Our defense of freedom will be all the *stronger* for being based, not on *illusions* but upon the *truth* about *ourselves* and our *world.*

Freedom must be rooted in *reality* or it will *crumble* as *errors* are revealed and *faith* is shaken. Only the truth can make us free.

The *immortal* document that the Great Emancipator read to his advisers just one hundred years ago *closed* one era of American history and *opened* another. It freed the *Negro* from his age-old bondage; it freed the *white* people of the South from an outworn and crippling institution; it freed the *Republic* from the darkest stain upon its record. It gave freedom a *mighty* impulse throughout the globe. And it will surround the rugged features of President Lincoln with an *unfading* halo.

But it marked a *beginning,* not an end; it was a call to a *new battle* — a battle which rages around us now in every part of the world in this *new* time of testing.

Truth was never the enemy of liberty, and it is no coincidence that the greatest statesman of liberty, the greatest champion freedom has ever known, was also the man who claimed *least* infallibility for himself and for his cause. And *we* can be humble as he was humble, knowing that the *cause* of *freedom* is greater than its *defenders,* and can *triumph* in spite of all their shortcomings.

In this *spirit,* we dare declare that the *concern* and *dedication* of our Union is the freedom of *all* mankind. With this *candor,* we can claim to be Lincoln's heirs in the unfinished work of emancipation.

To Mrs. Franklin D. Roosevelt [196]

September 30, 1962

Dearest Eleanor —

I have been getting regular bulletins from Maureen [197] and PRAY it won't be long before I can come to see you — and what a long deferred visit it will be! How I wish that preparation for the General Assembly

[196] This handwritten letter is in the Franklin D. Roosevelt Library, Hyde Park, New York.

[197] Maureen Corr, a member of Mrs. Roosevelt's staff since 1948. See Joseph P. Lash, *Eleanor: The Years Alone* (New York: W. W. Norton, 1972), p. 175.

and all those trips to Washington had not interfered with the visit to Hyde Park we had planned before I went abroad! My situation reminds me a little of the lad who wrote his girl: "I'll cross the coldest mountains, the darkest forest, the burning desert, the endless prairies, to be with you." And then a P.S. "I'll see you Saturday night if it doesn't rain!" Well somehow the rains and trouble have been incessant since I got back from Europe.

The General Assembly is off to a better start than usual — at least for the punctual dispatch of business — thanks to our stern President — Zafrullah Khan. [198] But the agenda is overcrowded and with all the new states [199] the job of our mission is becoming more and more exacting — and we need *you* more and more, both your advice and your influence! Every *day* people ask tenderly about you — and every *night* I PRAY that your recovery will be swift.

I love you dearly — and so does the whole world! But they can't *all* come to see you and perhaps I can when David gives me permission.[200]

Devotedly,

ADLAI

Stevenson's friend and loyal supporter, actress Vanessa Brown, wrote him on October 1 that she and others were organizing a "write-in" campaign to make him governor of California in November. (Governor Edmund G. Brown and Richard M. Nixon were the candidates of their respective parties.) She wrote Stevenson that if he did not wish them to continue he must say "no" immediately.

To Vanessa Brown [201]

October 3, 1962

Dear Vanessa:

I have your letter of October 1 about the write-in campaign for me for Governor of California, in which you are evidently deeply involved. I am afraid I have not fully understood what was going on out there

[198] Permanent representative of Pakistan to the United Nations and president of the Seventeenth General Assembly.

[199] In a statement on September 12, 1962, in the Security Council, Stevenson welcomed Jamaica and Trinidad and Tobago as new members. Also during September, 1962, Ruanda and Burundi were admitted to UN membership.

[200] It is not clear whether Stevenson knew that Mrs. Roosevelt was suffering from aplastic anemia. He had visited the hospital, but since Mrs. Roosevelt did not wish to be seen in her invalid condition, her doctor, David Gurewitch, turned him away. For Mrs. Roosevelt's illness, see Lash, *Eleanor: The Years Alone*, pp. 324–332.

[201] The original is in the possession of Miss Brown (in private life Mrs. Mark Sandrich, Jr.).

before this, and I hasten to send you at once my emphatic expression of hope that this activity will be discontinued. I am sure you realize that I am neither ungrateful nor insensible of the honor that you and your friends are doing me. On the other hand, my support for the Democratic ticket in California is clear and not qualified by any personal ambitions whatsoever.

I wish there was some way I could thank you and all those who are involved in this project, and also apologize for my uncooperative attitude. I feel ungrateful, especially in view of the time and effort and money that you and other friends seem to have expended. I wish I had understood it all sooner.

So, with my gratitude and my apologies, I urge you to discontinue this campaign.

Cordially yours,

On October 10, 1962, Roxane Eberlein wrote Mrs. Ernest L. Ives that Stevenson was making one speech after another at the UN,[202] *attending professional lunches and dinners, "and even going to two or three receptions a day—a chore he generally skipped last year, but is faithfully performing this year." The embassy residence was frequently occupied by visiting friends. The daughter of Mr. and Mrs. Hermon Dunlap Smith wrote him from Radcliffe College to ask if she and her roommate could stay with him before attending a football game at Princeton University.*

To Adele Smith

October 11, 1962

Dearest Adele:

Yes, by all means come, and bring your roommate if you wish. So far as I can tell *now*, the apartment will be empty on November 8 and 9. Moreover, I was planning to go to Princeton myself on the 10th for the game. Let me know if you want a ride. Unhappily, I have a dinner on Wednesday, November 8, at 8, but I would love to see you beforehand if you get here in time. I think there will be another diplomatic do, at the apartment, on Friday evening, but surely we can find a little time if you can't come until then. Indeed, I would be happy to include you in the dinner, although I'm not sure how entertaining it would be.

The opportunity to present you a diploma at Radcliffe in the spring

---

[202] He spoke in the Security Council on October 4, twice in the General Assembly on October 8, and in Committee 1 of the General Assembly on October 10.

is dangerously tempting. And let us by all means talk about it. I yearn
to see you!

Much love,

*On July 26, 1962, quantities of Soviet arms, including missiles and
technicians, had begun arriving in Cuba. On September 2, a joint
Soviet-Cuban communique stated that at the request of Cuba, the Soviet
Union had agreed to furnish arms and send specialists to train Cuban
military personnel. Two days later President Kennedy warned that
while the United States had no evidence of "significant offensive capability either in Cuban hands or under Soviet direction," if it turned out
otherwise, "the gravest issues would arise."* [203]

*On September 11, the Soviet Union announced that the military
equipment sent to Cuba was designed "exclusively for defensive purposes." Then Soviet authorities charged that the United States was "preparing for aggression against Cuba" and "if the aggressors unleash war
our armed forces must be ready to strike a crushing retaliatory blow at
the aggressor." At a press conference two days later, President Kennedy
stated that the Soviet shipments did not constitute a serious threat, but
if Cuba were to "become an offensive military base of significant
capacity for the Soviet Union, then this country will do whatever must
be done to protect its own security and that of its allies."* [204]

*Meanwhile, U-2 overflights of Cuba were increased and Congress
gave the President standby authority to call up military reserves. On
October 3, the foreign ministers of the American republics (Cuba had
been excluded from the Organization of American States on January 31,
1962) expressed concern over Cuba becoming an armed base for hemispheric penetration and subversion.* [205]

*On October 8, at the 17th Session of the UN General Assembly,
President Osvaldo Dorticos of Cuba attacked the United States' economic blockade of Cuba and charged the United States with aggressive
intentions toward Cuba. Dorticos quoted a statement made a few days
before by the Cuban Council of Ministers: "Were the United States
able to give Cuba effective guarantees and satisfactory proof concerning the integrity of Cuban territory, and were it to cease its subversive
and counterrevolutionary activity against our people, then Cuba would
not have to strengthen its defenses. Cuba would not even need an army,*

---

[203] New York *Times*, September 5, 1962.
[204] New York *Times*, September 12, 1962.
[205] For a useful survey of the events leading up to the confrontation of the two
superpowers, see *Events in United States–Cuban Relations: A Chronology, 1957–1963*,
prepared by the Department of State for the Committee on Foreign Relations, United
States Senate (88th Congress, 1st Session, committee print, January 29, 1963).

and all the resources that were used for this could be gratefully and happily invested in the economic and cultural development of the country. Were the United States able to give us proof, by word and deed, that it would not carry out aggression against our country, then, we declare solemnly before you here and now, our weapons would be unnecessary and our army redundant. We believe ourselves able to create peace." [206]

Stevenson replied: "*The President of Cuba professes that Cuba has always been willing to hold discussions with the United States to improve relations and to reduce tensions. But what he really wishes us to do is to place the seal of approval on the existence of a communist regime in the Western Hemisphere. The maintenance of communism in the Americas is not negotiable. . . .*" [207]

On October 14, a U-2 flight returned from overflying Cuba and taking photographs which, when they were developed, revealed a launching pad, buildings for ballistic missiles and one missile on the ground. When President Kennedy received the evidence on October 16, he called a meeting of a group known as the Executive Committee, later called the ExComm by the press. The committee carried on its work with utmost secrecy. Among those who participated in the succession of meetings (although not all of them attended every meeting) were the President; Vice President Lyndon B. Johnson; Secretary of State Dean Rusk; Secretary of Defense Robert McNamara; Attorney General Robert Kennedy; General Maxwell Taylor, personal adviser to the President on military affairs; CIA director John McCone; Secretary of the Treasury Douglas Dillon; McGeorge Bundy, special assistant to the President for national security affairs; Theodore C. Sorensen, special counsel to the President; Under Secretary of State George W. Ball; Deputy Secretary of Defense Roswell Gilpatric; Llewellyn Thompson, ambassador to the Soviet Union; Under Secretary of State Alexis Johnson; Assistant Secretary of State for Inter-American Affairs Edwin Martin; and Adlai Stevenson. Among others brought in at times were former Secretary of State Dean Acheson and former Secretary of Defense Robert Lovett.

---

[206] Richard J. Walton wrote: "In short, if the United States guarantees Cuba's territorial integrity, Cuba will get rid of its nuclear weapons. Since that was precisely the agreement between Kennedy and Khrushchev that ended the fearful confrontation, it is inescapable that Kennedy did not have to go to the brink to have the missiles removed. A diplomatic avenue was expressly offered by the Cubans." *Cold War and Counterrevolution: The Foreign Policy of John F. Kennedy* (Baltimore: Penguin Books, 1973), p. 115.

[207] USUN press release, October 8, 1962.

After lunch on Tuesday, October 16, Kennedy described the photographic evidence to Stevenson. The President said: "We'll have to do something quickly. I suppose the alternatives are to go in by air and wipe them out, or to take other steps to render the weapons inoperable." Stevenson replied: "Let's not go to an air strike until we have explored the possibilities of a peaceful solution." Four months before his death, Stevenson recalled: "I was a little alarmed that Kennedy's first consideration should have been the air strike. I told him that sooner or later we would have to go to the U.N. and it was vitally important we go there with a reasonable case." [208]

Kennedy asked Stevenson to remain in Washington and join in the discussions.

"In the Executive Committee consideration was free, intent and continuous," Arthur M. Schlesinger, Jr. wrote. ". . . Every alternative was laid on the table for examination, from living with the missiles to taking them out by surprise attack." [209] On Wednesday, October 17, Robert McNamara suggested a naval blockade to stop further entry of offensive weapons and possibly force the removal of missiles already in Cuba.

Theodore C. Sorensen wrote that the President was "annoyed by a somewhat ambivalent handwritten note" from Stevenson.[210]

To John F. Kennedy [211]

[October 17, 1962]

Dear Mr. President —

I have reviewed the planning thus far and have the following comments for you:

As I have said I think your *personal* emissaries should deliver your messages to C[astro] and K[hrushchev]. There is no disagreement as to C. As to K an emissary could better supplement the gravity of the situation you have communicated to Gromyko. And *talking* with K would afford a chance of uncovering his motives and objectives far better than correspondence thru the "usual channels."

As to your announcement, assuming it becomes imperative to say something soon, I think it would be a mistake at this time to disclose that an attack was imminent and that merely reciting the facts, empha-

---

[208] Quoted in Elie Abel, *The Missile Crisis* (Philadelphia: Lippincott, 1966), p. 49.
[209] *A Thousand Days*, p. 802.
[210] *Kennedy* (New York: Harper & Row, 1965), p. 695. Sorensen did not mention Stevenson's name in his text, but later confirmed that it was Stevenson. Letter to Walter Johnson, August 17, 1972.
[211] This letter was declassified. Cuba 1962, Countries Series, President's Office Files, John F. Kennedy Library.

sizing the gravity of the situation and that further steps were in process would be enough for the *first* announcement.

Because an attack would very likely result in Soviet reprisals some-where — Turkey, Berlin, etc. — it is most important that we have as much of the world with us as possible. To start or risk starting a nuclear war is bound to be divisive at best and the judgments of history seldom coincide with the tempers of the moment.

If war comes, in the long run our case must rest on stopping while there was still time the Soviet drive to world domination, our obliga-tions under the Inter-American system, etc. We must be prepared for the widespread reaction that if we have a missile base in Turkey and other places around the Soviet Union surely they have a right to one in Cuba. If we attack Cuba, an ally of the USSR, isn't an attack on NATO bases equally justified. One could go on and on. While the explanation of our action may be clear to us it won't be clear to many others. Moreover, if war is the consequence, the Latin-American re-publics may well divide and some say that the U.S. is not acting with their approval and consent. Likewise unless the issue is very clear there may be sharp differences with our Western allies who have lived so long under the same threat of Soviet attack from bases in the satellite coun-tries by the same IRBMs.

But all these considerations and obstacles to clear and universal under-standing that we are neither rash, impetuous or indifferent to the fate of others are, I realize only too familiar to you.

I know your dilemma is to strike before the Cuban sites are opera-tional or to risk waiting until a proper groundwork of justification can be prepared. The national security must come first. *But the means adopted have such incalculable consequences that I feel you should have made it clear that the existence of nuclear missile bases anywhere is* NEGOTIABLE before we start anything.

Our position, then, is that we can't negotiate with a gun at our head, a gun that imperils the innocent, helpless Cuban people as much as it does the US, and that if they won't remove the missiles and restore the status quo ante we will have to do it ourselves — and then we will be ready to discuss bases in the context of a disarmament treaty or any-thing else with them. In short, it is they, not the US, that have upset the balance and created this situation of such peril to the whole world.

I confess I have many misgivings about the proposed course of action, but to discuss them further would add little to what you already have in mind. So I will only repeat that it should be clear as a pikestaff that the US was, is and will be ready to negotiate the elimination of bases and anything else; that it is they who have upset the precarious balance in the world in arrogant disregard of your warnings — by threats against Berlin and now from Cuba — and that we have no choice except to restore that balance, i.e. blackmail and intimidation *never,* negotiation and sanity *always.*

Yours —

ADLAI E. STEVENSON

Wednesday morning Oct 17.

P.S. I'm returning to New York and can return, of course, at your convenience.

Over the next two days the proponents of air strike and the proponents of the blockade (since a blockade is technically an act of war, it was decided to refer to it as a quarantine) argued their respective merits. In order that Soviet officials would not be alerted that highly secret meetings were taking place in Washington, President Kennedy departed on a campaign swing to support Democratic candidates for Congress. Stevenson returned to New York to attend an important meeting at the United Nations.

On Friday, October 19, Robert Kennedy argued persuasively for the quarantine. Someone at that meeting remarked that the United States would have to pay a price to get the missiles out of Cuba and mentioned that we might have to agree to withdraw our obsolescent Jupiter missiles from bases in Italy and Turkey.[212]

On October 20, 1962, Stevenson prepared the following memorandum for President Kennedy. It was probably prepared in New York before Stevenson joined the ExComm meeting later that morning.

To John F. Kennedy [213]

October 20, 1962

POLITICAL PROGRAM TO BE ANNOUNCED BY THE PRESIDENT

1. Recent developments with respect to offensive capability in Cuba constitute the gravest threat to the peace and security of the Caribbean area as well as to the world. Thus they can and should be discussed by

[212] Robert F. Kennedy, *Thirteen Days: A Memoir of the Cuban Crisis* (New York: W. W. Norton, 1969), published posthumously, is important for these tense days. The Joint Congressional Committee on Atomic Energy and the Secretary of Defense had recommended removal of these missiles in 1961. President Kennedy months before the missile crisis had directed the Department of State to arrange for the withdrawal of the Jupiter missiles from Turkey.

[213] This document was declassified. Theodore C. Sorensen papers, John F. Kennedy Library.

the Security Council and measures should be taken to avert any immediate danger and to find, through negotiation, [a] permanent solution to the problem.

2. Ambassador Stevenson will propose to the Security Council tomorrow (?) a resolution whereby the UN would dispatch immediately observation teams to all strategic nuclear missile sites maintained on the territory of any country other than the three major nuclear powers. These observation teams, which would be placed in Cuba, Italy, and Turkey, would insure that no surprise attack could be mounted in any of these countries pending a permanent solution to the problem of foreign missile bases.

3. If the Soviet Union justifies these missile bases in Cuba as necessary to guarantee that country against foreign invasion, I reply that there is, in fact, no such threat to Cuba. But the United States would agree, along with the other American states, to guarantee the territorial integrity of Cuba, and we propose the immediate dispatch of a UN force to Cuba, modeled on the United Nations Emergency Force, to effectuate this guarantee. But to insure the security of the hemisphere we must insist on the prompt dismantling of these missile sites in Cuba and the withdrawal of all Soviet military personnel. Concurrently the United States will evacuate our base[s] at Guantanamo, Turkey, Italy and withdraw all forces and weapons therefrom.

Because of the danger of escalation the Soviet Union's clandestine action in Cuba has endangered the whole world and demands that we all hasten the conclusion of nuclear and general disarmament before it is too late. We can draw no better lesson from this experience. And the United States stands ready to consider with the Soviet Union the elimination of the NATO strategic bases situated in Italy and Turkey and all other bases on the soil of countries other than the nuclear powers in the context of the disarmament treaties now under consideration.

On Saturday, October 20, Stevenson returned to Washington and joined an ExComm meeting that had been going on for several hours. Stevenson spoke in favor of a quarantine as against an air strike. He recommended that simultaneously with a speech the President planned to make to the nation on Monday, October 22, the United States should call for an emergency session of the UN Security Council. The President agreed with Stevenson's assertion that the United States should introduce a resolution before the Soviet Union did so. Stevenson, also, while approving the quarantine, insisted that approval of it by the Organization of American States was vital.

On Saturday afternoon President Kennedy presided over a National

Security Council meeting with a larger group of people than ExComm. Stevenson strongly advocated that the United States make it clear to the Soviet Union that if it withdrew its missiles from Cuba, the United States would guarantee the integrity of Cuba and withdraw from the naval base at Guantanamo, and he repeated what someone else had said at earlier meetings that we might want to consider giving up the missile bases in Turkey and Italy. Stevenson's suggestions were sharply attacked by Dillon, Lovett, and McCone.[214] President Kennedy said that while he had had reservations about the Turkish and Italian bases for some time, now was not the time to suggest removal, nor could the United States withdraw from Guantanamo under threat from the Soviet Union. The President issued orders to prepare for the quarantine.

Robert F. Kennedy wrote: "Stevenson has since been criticized publicly for the position he took at this meeting. I think it should be emphasized that he was presenting a point of view from a different perspective than the others, one which was therefore important for the President to consider. Although I disagreed strongly with his recommendations, I thought he was courageous to make them, and I might add they made as much sense as some others considered during that period of time." [215]

According to Elie Abel, "The bitter after taste of that Saturday afternoon stayed with him until his death." [216] The exchange with Dillon, Lovett and McCone later led to published charges that Stevenson had "wanted a Munich." [217]

On Sunday, October 21, Stevenson wrote down his thoughts about strategy at the United Nations. There was no hope of achieving enough votes in the UN to authorize action against Cuba in advance. The Organization of American States, however, offered the possibility of multilateral support. At the UN the United States had to seize the initiative. To prevent resolutions against the quarantine, the United States had to propose a political path out of the military crisis. His proposals for negotiating required the removal of missiles, installations, and Soviet personnel under UN supervision. In evidence of American good faith, he would offer guarantees of no invasion of Cuba and of withdrawal from Guantanamo. The bases in Turkey and Italy, he now wrote, should

---

214 But Sorensen stated that even the "synopsis" prepared by the "air-strike hard-liners" earlier in the week had included not only a call for a summit meeting but also a pledge that the United States was prepared to withdraw promptly all nuclear forces based in Turkey, including aircraft as well as missiles. *Kennedy*, p. 696.

215 *Thirteen Days*, p. 50.

216 Abel, *The Missile Crisis*, p. 80.

217 For a discussion of this article and its repercussions, see pp. 348–352, below.

not be included. This might be considered later in the context of general disarmament.

Stevenson's memorandum follows.

1. WHY THE POLITICAL PROGRAM SHOULD BE IN THE SPEECH

Military action by us with respect to Cuba will raise worldwide fears of a nuclear war. It will also raise questions about our full objectives. The world will be watching us closely to see whether we combine our military might and determination with political acumen. Inclusion of a political program in the initial speech will drive home the essential point: that the United States wants a political settlement, not an escalated military involvement. In the absence of such an offer at the very outset we risk being in the world position the UK was in at the time of Suez. [Should further military action be necessary after the speech we would be credited with having tried to avoid the necessity.] [218] The offer would not sound "soft" if properly worded; it would sound "wise." An offer in a subsequent speech (such as in the SC [Security Council]) would not create the necessary initial impact on world opinion. It might even give the appearance of a retreat, from our initial position.

2. WHAT "NEUTRALIZATION" WOULD MEAN

The political program needs a catch word which will strike imaginations as portraying a fair offer. "Neutralization" is the best that comes to mind, "demilitarization" a second best. By "neutralization" we would mean a result along the Austrian type.[219] The main content of the program would in fact be "demilitarization." i.e. removal of Soviet military installations, equipment, and personnel under UN observation. Such neutralization and demilitarization would immediately and drastically reduce the troublemaking capability of the Cuban regime, and would probably result in its early overthrow. In the initial proposal a tightrope needs to be walked between making Khrushchev *directly* agree to replace the present Cuban Government with a non-communist one (which would make it almost impossible for him to talk), and any implication that we would settle for the present government. The crux of the problem is getting the USSR out militarily and putting as much "neutral," e.g. UN influence, in as possible in order to bring about consequential political change.

[218] This sentence appears in brackets in the original.
[219] A treaty signed by Great Britain, France, the United States, the Soviet Union, and Austria on May 15, 1955, restored full sovereignty to Austria. The Treaty prohibited Austrian possession of major offensive weapons, and Austria proclaimed its permanent neutrality.

3. *WHY GUANTANAMO IN AND ITALY AND TURKEY OUT*

Within the scope of vigorous US military action to defend our security, an offer to exchange Guantanamo for removal of Soviet installations in Cuba would be regarded both worldwide and domestically as a gesture showing our wisdom and good faith. It is the element of concession (of little real importance) which would give a proposal for "neutralization" of Cuba (i.e. withdrawal of Soviet military support) "balance." The entire political context in which the offer would be made, in other words, would be different than the one now prevailing. An offer in effect to exchange Guantanamo for the Soviet sites *in the absence of US military response to the Soviet moves* would be weak. In conjunction with such steps it would be regarded as a far-reaching step by us to grasp peace out of the brink of war.

Turkey and Italy should not be included in the initial offer. Their inclusion would divert attention from the Cuban threat to the general problem of foreign bases. Furthermore, Turkey and Italy should be consulted in advance. The inclusion of bases in these countries in an inspection arrangement in response to the USSR's broadening of the issue *would* at a later stage be a powerful move.

TACTICS IN UN SECURITY COUNCIL

There are two and sharply different tactics we can use:

1. Propose a broad political program for the demilitarization of Cuba: The components would be (a) stop all foreign military build up, (b) dismantle and evacuate all foreign military installations, (c) guarantee integrity of Cuba, (d) UN observer force, and (e) end the blockade.

2. Propose simply a military standstill in Cuba, supervised by UN.

The first has the disadvantage of pledging our withdrawal from Guantanamo, if and when Soviet military are withdrawn and Soviet missiles and aircraft dismantled or neutralized. It has, however, the following important advantages:

1. The single act of the week which will have most impact on world opinion and arouse most fears of immediate war, despite our efforts to concentrate attention on the Soviet missile sites, will be our naval blockade. In order to obtain the broad political support which we need in this crisis, we should have a broad political program which will cover our military action by demonstrating our

genuine willingness to remove *all* foreign military presence from Cuba.

2. In fact, if this proposal should be accepted and carried out, the Soviets would have lost an important military asset in Cuba, while we would have lost a base which is of little use to us. This would be a major victory, not a defeat.

3. If we demand merely that the Soviets get out of Cuba, it will be widely alleged we are seeking uncompensated military and political advantage at serious risk to world peace, and we will obtain little support. In the UN we risk failure to hold the seven votes we need in the SC, not to mention the two-thirds we may need in the GA [General Assembly].

(A possible alternative to the offer to withdraw from Cuba would be an offer to evacuate our missiles from Turkey and Italy. This would be less desirable because (a) our missiles in these countries could be a very important bargaining counter at the Summit meeting and should not be thrown away in advance, (b) the effect in Turkey, particularly if there is not careful advance preparation, might be very serious.)

The second tactic for the SC, proposal of a military "standstill," is the best approach if it is judged inexpedient even implicitly to offer the evacuation of Guantanamo at this time. This tactic, however, will fail to divert world attention from a military action, will obtain far less political support, will probably be no more acceptable to the Soviets than the broader approach since it also would establish a UN presence at their missile sites, and would run the further risk of being twisted in the Council to apply an immediate "standstill" to our blockade. This tactic would, in effect, delay any political program until the Summit meeting.

The first alternative, therefore, seems very much to be preferred.

Kennedy, however, regarded any political program as premature. He wanted to concentrate on the introduction of the missiles and their removal. He rejected, therefore, Stevenson's recommendation.[220]

Meanwhile, Schlesinger, Harlan Cleveland, Thomas W. Wilson and others in the Department of State worked on a speech for Stevenson to deliver at the United Nations. On Monday, October 22, Kennedy instructed Schlesinger to go to New York to assist Stevenson. Before he left, Schlesinger went over a draft of the speech with the President, Dean Rusk, Robert Kennedy and others. The Attorney General said to Schlesinger: "We're counting on you to watch things in New York. . . .

[220] Schlesinger, A *Thousand Days*, p. 810.

We will have to make a deal at the end, but we must stand absolutely firm now. Concessions must come at the end of negotiation, not at the beginning." [221] Meanwhile John J. McCloy was assigned to assist Stevenson at the United Nations. "As a Republican," Robert F. Kennedy wrote, "he made our efforts there bipartisan, and as a counter balance to Stevenson's point of view, he had initially favored a military attack and an invasion of Cuba." [222]

On Monday, October 22, at 7 P.M., President Kennedy spoke to the nation — and for the next few days people trembled at the prospect of a nuclear holocaust. He described the Soviet missiles in Cuba and termed the Soviet action "a deliberately provocative and unjustified change in the status quo which cannot be accepted by this country." He emphasized that his initial steps were a quarantine on all offensive military equipment under shipment to Cuba, an intensified surveillance of Cuba, an immediate convening of the Organization of American States to deal with this threat to the security of the hemisphere, a request for an emergency meeting of the UN Security Council, an appeal to Khrushchev "to abandon this course of world domination, and to join in an historic effort to end the perilous arms race and to transform the history of man." He declared that any missile launched from Cuba against any nation in the Western Hemisphere would be regarded as an attack by the Soviet Union on the United States requiring full retaliatory response against the Soviet Union.

Stevenson managed to find time to reply to a letter from Frances FitzGerald, who was in Paris, France, working for the Congress for Cultural Freedom. She had asked Stevenson if John Steinbeck would give an interview for the Paris Review. She also asked Stevenson for copies of his recent speeches and described her Paris apartment to him. She mentioned that a speech of his was reprinted in the Senegalese magazine Afrique Nouvelle and asked if he would like an audience in Busenbuhu to read his speeches.

[221] Ibid., p. 811.
[222] *Thirteen Days*, p. 48. Mr. McCloy wrote: "In some respects this was a rather awkward relationship because I am sure that President Kennedy's motive in asking me to come to New York was to counteract what he thought might be a too soft attitude on the part of Adlai. When I got to New York, I did not find that he had any such attitude. . . . I even found him tougher than I was prepared to be and I always sympathized greatly with him over the position he found himself in at the United Nations at the time of the missile crisis. I thought the way he presented the case of the United States once it was disclosed that the missiles were there was most effective." Letter to Walter Johnson, July 24, 1967.

To Frances FitzGerald

October 22, 1962

Darling Frankie:

I have your letter, and I'm mortified that I'm compelled by circumstances, with which you are not unfamiliar, to reply in this hurried and unsatisfactory way. I am sending you a batch of recent Stevenson utterances. And let this be a lesson to you! Don't read them, don't even say you read them — unless you want to read the Emancipation Proclamation piece.

To get down to business, as you so gracefully call your literary charms. I am writing John [Steinbeck] to ask if he would undertake the interview, and if he would make a suggestion. He is, as you know, something of a recluse, although not really, but at least he lives in Sag Harbor! However, I see him from time to time when he comes to town, and he seems in good and gay fettle (I wish I was!).

I can't say I saw the reprint in *Afrique Nouvelle*. My reading seems to be limited to the assaults of the Russians and similar aggravating items. I even have some doubts as to whether I care to have an audience in Busenbuhu! All of which reminds me of happy days, and has even suggested from time to time that you should go back to the Congo, to save it for the Western world — and take *me* along to save *you!*

Your mother [223] has told me about your new apartment, and your description leaves me swooning with curiosity, and a restless yearning for Paris and its new and special charm.

I hope the work is going well, and I am shattered by the thought that Frankie is now an editor, along with everything else. I had meant to send her a birthday greeting yesterday, but instead I was closeted with *Il Presidente* and the others concerned with matters which you now know all about. Forgive me, and let me add that the most engaging child of my acquaintance is now the most engaging young lady — which, as the Russians say, all the world knows!

With so much love,

p.s. You were an angel to have even noticed my Lincoln recitation with the Philadelphia Orchestra. [224] Confidentially, I'm preparing for a new career. Why not?—I've tried everything else!

Stevenson at the United Nations had requested a meeting of the Security Council for the next day. Much of his time until he spoke on

[223] Marietta Tree.
[224] He narrated "A Lincoln Portrait" at Lincoln Center in New York City on September 25.

Tuesday, October 23, was devoted to talking to delegates from other nations.

At 4 P.M. on October 23, 1962, Stevenson spoke to the Security Council.[225]

I have asked for an emergency meeting of the Security Council to bring to your attention a grave threat to the Western Hemisphere and to the peace of the world.

Last night, the President of the United States reported the recent alarming military developments in Cuba. Permit me to remind you of the President's sobering words:

"Within the past week, unmistakable evidence has established the fact that a series of offensive missile sites is now in preparation on that imprisoned island. The purpose of these bases can be none other than to provide a nuclear strike capability against the Western Hemisphere. Upon receiving the first preliminary hard information of this nature last Tuesday morning at 9 A.M., I directed that our surveillance be stepped up. And having now confirmed and completed our evaluation of the evidence and our decision on a course of action, this Government feels obliged to report this new crisis to you in full detail.

"The characteristics of these new missile sites indicate two distinct types of installations. Several of them include medium-range ballistic missiles, capable of carrying a nuclear warhead for a distance of more than 1,000 nautical miles. Each of these missiles, in short, is capable of striking Washington, D.C., the Panama Canal, Cape Canaveral, Mexico City, or any other city in the southeastern part of the United States, in Central America or in the Caribbean area.

"Additional sites not yet completed appear to be designed for intermediate-range ballistic missiles — capable of travelling more than twice as far — and thus capable of striking most of the major cities in the Western Hemisphere, ranging as far north as Hudson's Bay, Canada, and as far south as Lima, Peru. In addition, jet bombers, capable of carrying nuclear weapons, are now being uncrated and assembled in Cuba, while the necessary air bases are being prepared."

In view of this transformation of Cuba into a base for offensive weapons of sudden mass destruction, the President announced the initiation of a strict quarantine on all offensive military weapons under shipment to Cuba. He did so because, in the view of my Government, the recent developments in Cuba — the importation of the cold war into the heart of the Americas — constitute a threat to the peace of this hemisphere, and, indeed, to the peace of the world.

Seventeen years ago, the representatives of fifty-one nations gathered in San Francisco to adopt the Charter of the United Nations. These na-

225 United Nations, *Official Records,* Security Council, October 23, 1962, pp. 2–17.

tions stated with clarity and eloquence the high purpose which brought them together. They announced their common determination: "to save succeeding generations from the scourge of war . . . to reaffirm faith in fundamental human rights . . . to establish conditions under which justice and respect for the obligations arising from treaties and other sources of international law can be maintained, and to promote social progress and better standards of life in larger freedom." And in one sentence, Article 2, paragraph 4, they defined the necessary condition of a community of independent sovereign States, in these words:

"All Members shall refrain in their international relations from the threat or use of force against the territorial integrity or political independence of any State, or in any other manner inconsistent with the Purposes of the United Nations."

In this spirit, these fifty-one nations solemnly resolved to band together in a great co-operative quest for world peace and world progress. The adventure of the United Nations held out to humanity the bright hope of a new world, a world securely founded on international peace, on national independence, on personal freedom, on respect for law, for social justice and betterment, and, in the words of the Charter, for "equal rights and self-determination of peoples."

The vision of San Francisco — and I was there — was the vision of a world community of independent nations, each freely developing according to its own traditions and its own genius, bound together by a common respect for the rights of other nations and by a common loyalty to the larger international order. This vision assumes that this earth is quite large enough to shelter a great variety of economic systems, political creeds, philosophical beliefs and religious convictions. The faith of the Charter is in a pluralistic world, a world of free choice, respecting the infinite diversity of mankind and dedicated to nations living together as good neighbours, in peace.

Like many peoples, we welcomed the world of the Charter, for our society is based on principles of choice and consent. We believe the principles of an open society in the world order will survive and flourish in the competitions of peace. We believe that freedom and diversity are the best climate for human creativity and social progress. We reject all fatalistic philosophies of history and all theories of political and social predestination. We doubt whether any nation has so absolute a grip on absolute truth that it is entitled to impose its idea of what is right on others. And we know that a world community of independent order offers the best safeguard for the safety of our shores and for the security of our people. The commitment to the world of the Charter expresses both our deepest philosophical traditions and the most realistic interpretation of our national interest.

Had we had any other vision of the world, had we sought the path of empire, our opportunities for self-aggrandizement immediately after the war would have been almost unparalleled. In 1945, we were incomparably the greatest military Power in the world. Our troops and planes were dispersed at strategic points around the globe. We had exclusive possession of the terror and the promise of atomic energy. Our economic strength was unmatched. If the American purpose had been world dominion, there could have been no more propitious moment to set out on such a course.

Instead, our commitment, then as now, was to the world of the Charter — the creation of a community of freely co-operating independent States bound together by the United Nations. In the service of this commitment, and without waiting for the peace treaties, we dismantled the mightiest military force we had ever assembled. Armies were disbanded wholesale. Vast supplies of war equipment were liquidated or junked. Within two years after the end of the war, our defence spending had fallen by nearly $70 billion a year. Our armed forces were slashed from more than 12 million to one and a half million. We did not retain a single division in a state of combat readiness. We did not have a single military alliance anywhere in the world. History has not seen, I believe, a more complete and more comprehensive demonstration of a great nation's hope for peace and for amity.

Instead of using our monopoly of atomic energy to extend our national power, we offered in 1946 to transfer the control of atomic energy to the United Nations. Instead of using our overwhelming economic strength to extend our national power, we contributed more than $2.5 billion to the United Nations Relief and Rehabilitation Administration, much of which went to the relief of suffering in the communist countries. And after 1948, we contributed many more billions to the economic restoration of Europe — and invited the communist countries to participate as recipients in this programme. Instead of using our substance and strength to extend our national power, we supported the movement for independence which began to sweep through Asia and Africa — the movement which has added fifty-nine new members to the United Nations in the years since 1945. Since the war, we have contributed $97 billion of economic and military assistance to other nations — and, of this sum, $53 billion has gone to the nations of Asia, Africa, and Latin America.

I have often wondered what the world would be like today if the situation at the end of the war had been reversed — if the United States had been ravaged and shattered by war, and if the Soviet Union had emerged intact in exclusive possession of the atomic bomb and overwhelming military and economic might. Would it have followed the same path and devoted itself to realizing the world of the Charter?

To ask this question suggests the central paradox of the United Nations. For among the States which pledged fidelity to the idea of a pluralistic world in San Francisco were some who had an incompatible vision of the future world order.

Has the Soviet Union ever really joined the United Nations? Or does its philosophy of history and its conception of the future run counter to the pluralistic concept of this Charter?

Against the idea of diversity, communism asserts the idea of uniformity: against freedom, inevitability; against choice, compulsion; against democracy, dogma; against independence, ideology; against tolerance, conformity. Its faith is that the iron laws of history will require every nation to traverse the same predestined path to the same predestined conclusion. Given this faith in a monolithic world, the very existence of diversity is a threat to the community future.

I do not assert that communism must always remain a Messianic faith. Like other fanaticisms of the past, it may in time lose its sense of infallibility and accept the diversity of human destiny. Already in some countries we see communism subsiding into a local and limited ideology. There are those who have discerned the same evolution in the Soviet Union itself; and we may all earnestly hope that Chairman Khrushchev and his associates will renounce the dream of making the world over in the image of the Soviet Union. It must be the purpose of other nations to do what they can to hasten that day.

But that day has not yet arrived. The conflict between absolutist and pluralistic conceptions of the destiny of mankind remains the basic source of discord within the United Nations. It has given rise to what is known as the cold war. Were it not for this conflict, this Organization would have made steady progress toward the world of choice and justice envisaged at San Francisco.

But because of the Soviet rejection of an open world, the hope for progress and for peace has been systematically frustrated. And in these halls we spend much of our time and our energy either engaged in or in avoiding this incessant conflict. It began even before the nations gathered at San Francisco. As soon as the defeat of the Nazis appeared certain, I remind you that the Soviet Union began to abandon the policy of wartime co-operation to which it had turned for self-protection. In early 1945, Moscow instructed the communist parties of the West to purge themselves of the sin of co-operation, and to return to their pre-war view that democratic governments were by definition imperialistic and wicked. Within a few weeks after the meeting at Yalta, the Soviet Union took swift action in Romania and Poland in brutal violation of the

Yalta pledges of political freedom for those countries.[226] At the same time, it began a political offensive against the United States, charging that the United States Government — the Government of Franklin Roosevelt — was engaged in secret peace negotiations with Hitler. Roosevelt replied to Stalin that he deeply resented these "vile misrepresentations." At the end of March 1945, Roosevelt cabled Winston Churchill that he was "watching with anxiety and concern the development of the Soviet attitude" and that he was "acutely aware of the dangers inherent in the present course of events, not only for the immediate issue but also for the San Francisco Conference and future world co-operation."

It is important to recall these facts, because the Soviet Union has tried in the years since to pretend that its policy of aggression was a defensive response to the change of administration in the United States, or to Churchill's 1946 speech at Fulton, Missouri,[227] or to some other event after the death of Roosevelt. But the historical record is clear. And as soon as the Soviet Government saw no further military need for the wartime coalition, it set out on its expansionist adventures.

The ink was hardly dry on the Charter before Moscow began its war against the world of the United Nations. The very first meeting of the Security Council — and I was there — was called to hear a complaint by Iran that Soviet troops had failed to withdraw from the northern part of that country on the date on which they had agreed to leave. Not only had they declined to go: they had installed a regime of their own on Iranian soil and had blocked Iranian troops from re-entering part of Iran's own territory. The Soviet Union, in short, was violating the territorial integrity and denying the political independence of Iran — and doing so by armed force. Eventually the United Nations forced a reluctant agreement from the Soviet Union to live up to its pledge.

This was only the beginning. At the time of the German surrender, the Red Army was in occupation of Romania, Bulgaria, Hungary, Poland, Eastern Germany and most of Czechoslovakia. And there it stayed. It stayed in violation of the agreement reached at Yalta by the heads of the Allied Powers — the agreement which pledged the independence of and promised free elections to these nations. By 1948, five nations and half of a sixth, with a combined population of more than 90 million, had been absorbed into the communist empire. To this day the peoples of Eastern Europe have never been permitted to exercise the Charter right of self-determination.

[226] See Edward R. Stettinius, Jr., *Roosevelt and the Russians: The Yalta Conference,* edited by Walter Johnson (New York: Doubleday, 1949).

[227] In this speech Churchill used the phrase "iron curtain" to describe the division between Western and Eastern Europe. For this and other events described by Stevenson in this speech, see Walter Johnson, *1600 Pennsylvania Avenue: Presidents and the People, 1929–1959* (Boston: Little, Brown, 1960).

Before the suppression of Eastern Europe was complete, the Soviet Union was fomenting guerrilla warfare and sabotaging economic recovery, assailing neighbouring regimes through all the instrumentalities of propaganda and subversion. Nor were such activities confined to Europe. In Malaya, in the Philippines, in Burma, in Indo-China, the Communists encouraged and supported guerrilla uprisings against constituted governments.[228] In one event after another, on one stage after another — the rejection in the United Nations of the United States plan for the internationalization of atomic energy, the rejection of the Marshall Plan, the blockade of Berlin, and, finally, the invasion of South Korea — the Soviet Union assailed political independence, resisted the world of the Charter and tried to impose its design on a communist future.

Let me recall to this Council the record with regard to international agreements. The Soviet Government has signed treaties of non-aggression, as it did with the Baltic States and Finland — and then systematically invaded the countries whose integrity it had solemnly promised to respect. At Yalta and in a succession of peace treaties it pledged to the liberated countries of Eastern Europe "the right of all peoples to choose the form of government under which they will live, the restoration of sovereign rights and self-government to those peoples who have been forcibly deprived of them by the war" — and then it systematically denied those rights and consolidated that deprivation. In 1945 it signed a thirty-year pact of mutual assistance and non-aggression with China, pledging that its military aid and economic support would be "given entirely to the National Government as the Central Government of China" — and violated that treaty almost before the Chinese negotiators had left Moscow. At Potsdam it promised that "all democratic political parties with rights of assembly and of public discussion shall be allowed and encouraged throughout Germany" — and within its own zone promptly repudiated that promise. At Geneva in 1954 it agreed not to introduce arms into Viet-Nam — and sent guns and ammunition to the Viet Minh. It denounced nuclear testing — and then violated the moratorium which for three years had spared the world the danger of nuclear tests. Within this Council it has thwarted the majority will one hundred times by the use of the veto.

The record is clear: treaties, agreements, pledges and the morals of international relations were never an obstacle to the Soviet Union under Stalin. And no one has said so more eloquently than Chairman Khrushchev.

With the death of Stalin in 1953, the world had a resurgence of hope. No one can question that Chairman Khrushchev has altered many things in the Soviet Union. He has introduced welcome measures of normalization in many sectors of Soviet life. He has abandoned the classic com-

---

[228] For Stevenson's own observations in 1953, see *The Papers of Adlai E. Stevenson*, Vol. V.

munist concept of the inevitability of war. He has recognized the appalling dangers of nuclear weapons.

But there is one thing he has not altered — and that is the basic drive to abolish the world of the Charter, to destroy the hope of a pluralistic world society. He has not altered the basic drive to fulfill the prophecies of Marx and Lenin and make the whole world communist. And he has demonstrated his singleness of purpose in a succession of aggressive acts — in the suppression of the East German uprising in 1953 and the Hungarian revolution in 1956; in the series of manufactured crises and truculent demands that the Allies get out of West Berlin; in the resumption of nuclear testing; in the explosion — defying a resolution of the General Assembly — of a fifty-megaton bomb; in the continued stimulation of guerrilla and subversive warfare all over the globe; in the compulsive intervention in the internal affairs of other nations, whether by diplomatic assault, by economic pressure, by mobs and riots, by propaganda, or by espionage.

The world welcomed the process known as "de-Stalinization" and the movement toward a more normal life within the Soviet Union. But the world has not yet seen comparable changes in Soviet foreign policy. It is this which has shadowed the world since the end of the Second World War, which has dimmed our hopes of peace and progress, which has forced those nations determined to defend their freedom to take measures in their own self-defense. In this effort, the leadership has inevitably fallen in large degree on the United States. We do not believe that every action that we have taken in the effort to strengthen the independence of nations has necessarily been correct. We do not subscribe to the thesis of national infallibility for any nation. But we do take great pride in the role we have performed.

Our response to the remorseless expansionism of the Soviet Union has taken many forms. We have sought loyally to support the United Nations, to be faithful to the world of the Charter, and to build an operating system that acts, and does not just talk, for peace. We have never refused to negotiate. We have sat at conference after conference, seeking peaceful solutions to menacing conflicts. We have worked for general and complete disarmament under international supervision. We have tried earnestly — and we will [not] stop trying — to reach an agreement to end all nuclear testing.

We have declined to be provoked into actions which might lead to war — in the face of such challenges as the Berlin blockade, such affronts to humanity as the repression of the Hungarian revolt, such atrocities as the erection of that shameful wall to fence in the East Germans who had fled to the West in such vast multitudes.

We have assisted nations, both allied and unaligned, who have shown a will to maintain their national independence. To shield them and ourselves, we have rebuilt our armed forces, established defensive alliances, and, year after year, reluctantly devoted a large share of our resources to national defence.

Together with our allies, we have installed certain bases overseas as a prudent precaution in response to the clear and persistent Soviet threats. In 1959, eighteen months after the boasts of Chairman Khrushchev had called the world's attention to the threat of Soviet long-range missiles, the North Atlantic Treaty Organization, without concealment or deceit — as a consequence of agreements freely negotiated and publicly declared — placed intermediate-range ballistic missiles in the NATO area. The warheads of these missiles remain in the custody of the United States, and the decision for their use rests in the hands of the President of the United States, in association with the Governments involved.

I regret that people here at the United Nations seem to believe that the cold war is a private struggle between two great super-Powers. It is not a private struggle; it is a world civil war — a contest between the pluralistic world and the monolithic world — a contest between the world of the Charter and the world of communist conformity. Every nation that is now independent and wants to remain independent is involved, in this grim, costly, distasteful division in the world, no matter how remote, no matter how uninterested.

We all recognized this in 1950, when the Communists decided to test how far they could go by direct military action and unleashed the invasion of South Korea. The response of the United Nations taught them that overt aggression would produce not appeasement, but resistance. This remains the essential lesson. The United Nations stood firm in Korea because we knew the consequences of appeasement.

The policy of appeasement is always intended to strengthen the moderates in the country appeased, but its effect is always to strengthen the extremists. We are prepared to meet and reconcile every legitimate Soviet concern, but we have only contempt for blackmail. We know that every retreat before intimidation strengthens those who say that the threat of force can always achieve communist objectives — and undermines those in the Soviet Union who are urging caution and restraint, even co-operation. Reluctantly and repeatedly, we have to face the sad fact that the only way to reinforce those on the other side who are for moderation and peaceful competition is to make it absolutely clear that aggression will be met with resistance, and force with force.

The time has come for this Council to decide whether to make a serious attempt to bring peace to the world — or to let the United Nations stand idly by while the vast plan of piecemeal aggression unfolds, conducted in the hope that no single issue will seem consequential enough to mobilize the resistance of the free peoples. For my own Government, this question is not in doubt. We remain committed to the principles of the United Nations, and we intend to defend them.

We are engaged today in a crucial test of those principles. Nearly four years ago a revolution took place on the island of Cuba. This revolution overthrew a hated dictatorship in the name of democratic freedom and social progress. Mr. [Fidel] Castro made explicit promises to the people of Cuba. He promised them the restoration of the 1940 Constitution abandoned by the [General Fulgencio] Batista dictatorship; a "provisional government of entirely civilian character that will return the country to normality and hold general elections within a period of no more than one year"; "truly honest" elections along with "full and untrammelled" freedom of information and political activity.

That is what Mr. Castro offered the people of Cuba. That is what the people of Cuba accepted. Many in my country and throughout the Americas sympathized with Mr. Castro's stated objectives. The United States Government offered immediate diplomatic recognition and stood ready to provide the revolutionary regime with economic assistance.

But a grim struggle was taking place within the revolutionary regime, between its democratic and its predominant communist wings — between those who overthrew Batista to bring freedom to Cuba, and those who overthrew Batista to bring Cuba to communism. In a few months the struggle was over. Brave men who had fought with Castro in the Sierra Maestra and who had organized the underground against Batista in the cities were assailed, arrested, and driven from office into prison or exile, all for the single offence of anti-communism, all for the single offence of believing in the principles of the revolution they had fought for. By the end of 1959, the Communist Party was the only party in Cuba permitted freedom of political action. By early 1960, the Castro regime was entering into intimate economic and political relations with the Soviet Union.

It is well to remember that all these events took place months before the United States stopped buying Cuban sugar in the summer of 1960 — and many more months before exactions upon our Embassy in Havana forced the suspension of diplomatic relations in December 1960.

As the communization of Cuba proceeded, more and more democratic Cubans, men who had fought for freedom in the front ranks, were forced into exile. They were eager to return to their homeland and to save their revolution from betrayal. In the spring of 1961, they tried to liberate their country, under the political leadership of Mr. Castro's first Prime Minister and of a Revolutionary Council composed without exception of men who had opposed Batista and backed the Revolution.[229] The people and Government of the United States sympathized with these

---

[229] For a somewhat different interpretation, see Tad Szulc and Karl E. Meyer, *The Cuban Invasion: The Chronicle of a Disaster* (New York: Praeger, 1962). In fact, former Batista supporters led the Bay of Pigs invasion.

men — as throughout our history Americans have always sympathized with those who sought to liberate their native lands from despotism. I have no apologies to make for that sympathy, or for the assistance which these brave Cuban refugees received from our hands. But I would point out, too, that my Government, still forbearing, refrained from direct intervention. It sent no American troops to Cuba.

In the year and a half since, Mr. Castro has continued the communization of his unfortunate country. The 1940 Constitution was never restored. Elections were never held and their promise withdrawn — though Mr. Castro's twelve months have stretched to forty-two. The Castro regime fastened on Cuba an iron system of repression. It eradicated human and civil rights. It openly transformed Cuba into a communist satellite and a police state. Whatever benefit this regime might have brought to Cuba has long since been cancelled out by the firing squads, the drumhead executions, the hunger and misery, the suppression of civil and political and cultural freedom.

Yet even these violations of human rights, repellent as they are — even this dictatorship, cruel as it may be — would not, if kept within the confines of one country, constitute a direct threat to the peace and independence of other States. The threat lies rather in the submission of the Castro regime to the will of an aggressive foreign Power. It lies in its readiness to break up the relations of confidence and co-operation among the good neighbours of this hemisphere, at a time when the Alliance for Progress — that vast effort to raise living standards for all peoples of the Americas — has given new hope to the inter-American system.

Let me make it absolutely clear what the issue of Cuba is. It is not an issue of revolution. This hemisphere has seen many revolutions, including the one which gave my own nation its independence.

It is not an issue of reform. My nation has lived happily with other countries which have had thoroughgoing and fundamental social transformations, like Mexico and Bolivia. The whole point of the Alliance for Progress is to bring about an economic and social revolution in the Americas.

It is not an issue of socialism. As Secretary of State Rusk said in February [1962], "our hemisphere has room for a diversity of economic systems."

It is not an issue of dictatorship. The American Republics have lived with dictators before. If this were his only fault, they could live with Mr. Castro.

The foremost objection of the States of the Americas to the Castro regime is not because it is revolutionary, not because it is socialistic, not because it is dictatorial, not even because Mr. Castro perverted a noble revolution in the interests of a squalid totalitarianism. It is because he has aided and abetted an invasion of this hemisphere — an invasion just at the time when the hemisphere is making a new and unprecedented effort for economic progress and social reform.

The crucial fact is that Cuba has given the Soviet Union a bridgehead and staging area in this hemisphere; that it has invited an extra-continental, anti-democratic and expansionist Power into the bosom of the American family; that it has made itself an accomplice in the communist enterprise of world dominion.

There are those who seek to equate the presence of Soviet bases in Cuba with the presence of NATO bases in parts of the world near the Soviet Union. Let us subject this facile argument to critical consideration.

It is not only that the Soviet action in Cuba has created a new and dangerous situation by sudden and drastic steps which imperil the security of all mankind. It is necessary further to examine the purposes for which these missiles are introduced and these bases established.

Missiles which help a country to defend its independence, which leave the political institutions of the recipient countries intact, which are not designed to subvert the territorial integrity or political independence of other States, which are installed without concealment or deceit — assistance in this form and with these purposes is consistent with the principles of the United Nations. But missiles which introduce a nuclear threat into an area now free of it, which are installed by clandestine means, which result in the most formidable nuclear base in the world outside existing treaty systems — assistance in this form and with these purposes is radically different.

Let me state this point very clearly. The missile sites in NATO countries were established in response to missile sites in the Soviet Union directed at the NATO countries. The NATO States had every right and necessity to respond to the installation of these Soviet missiles by installing missiles of their own. These missiles were designed to deter a process of expansion already in progress. Fortunately, they have helped to do so.

The United States and its Allies established their missile sites after free negotiation, without concealment and without false statements to other Governments. There is, in short, a vast difference between the long-range missile sites established years ago in Europe and the long-range missile sites established by the Soviet Union in Cuba during the last three months.

There is a final significant difference. For a hundred and fifty years the nations of the Americas have laboured painfully to construct a hemisphere of independent and co-operating countries, free from foreign threats. An international system far older than the United Nations — the inter-American system — has been erected on this principle. The principle of the territorial integrity of the Western hemisphere has been woven into the history, the life and the thought of all the people of the Americas. In striking at that principle, the Soviet Union is striking at the strongest and most enduring strain in the policy of this hemisphere. It is disrupting the convictions and aspirations of a century and a half. It is intruding on the firm policies of twenty nations. To allow this challenge to go unanswered would be to undermine a basic and historic pillar of the security of this hemisphere.

Twenty years ago the nations of the Americas were understandably disturbed by the threat of nazism, so today they look with equal concern on the conquest of Cuba by a foreign Power and an alien ideology. They do not intend to applaud and assist while Mr. Castro and his new friends try to halt the march of free and progressive democracy in Latin America.

Yet, despite the ominous movement of affairs in Cuba, the reaction of the hemisphere and of my own Government continued to be marked by forbearance. Despite Mr. Castro's verbal assaults on other nations in the hemisphere, despite his campaign of subversion against their Governments, despite the insurrectionary expeditions launched from Cuba, the nations of the Americas retained their hope that the Cuban revolution would free itself. But Mr. Castro's persistence in his campaigns against the Governments of this hemisphere, his decision to become the junior partner of Moscow, finally destroyed that hope.

If Cuba has withdrawn from the American family of nations, it has been Mr. Castro's own act. If Cuba is today isolated from its brethren of the Americas, it is self-inflicted isolation. If the present Cuban government has turned its back on its own history, tradition, religion and culture, if it has chosen to cast its lot with the Communist empire, it must accept the consequences of its decision. The hemisphere has no alternative but to accept the tragic choice which Mr. Castro has imposed on his people — that is, to accept Cuba's self-exclusion from the hemisphere.

One after another, the Governments of this hemisphere have withdrawn their diplomatic representatives from Cuba. Today only three still have their ambassadors in Havana. Last February [1962] the American states unanimously declared that the Castro regime was incompatible with the principles on which the Organization of American States had been founded, and, by a two-thirds vote, excluded that regime from participation in the inter-American system.

All this, I remind the Council, took place before Soviet arms and technicians began to move into Cuba in a massive, continuous stream. But, even then, the Governments of the hemisphere were willing to withhold final judgment so long as the Soviet weapons were defensive. And my Government — the United States Government — and the United Nations were solemnly assured by the representatives of both Soviet Russia and Cuba that the Soviet arms pouring into the island, were, in fact, purely defensive weapons.

On 11 September, just over a month ago, the Soviet Government said in an official statement: "The armaments and military equipment sent to

Cuba are designed exclusively for defensive purposes." The Soviet Government added that Soviet rockets were so powerful that "there is no need to search for sites for them beyond the boundaries of the Soviet Union." And last week, on 18 October, Mr. Gromyko, the Foreign Minister of the Soviet Union, told the President of the United States at the White House that Soviet assistance to Cuba "pursued solely the purpose of contributing to the defence capabilities of Cuba," that "training by Soviet specialists of Cuban nationals in handling defensive armaments was by no means offensive," and that "if it were otherwise, the Soviet Government would never have become involved in rendering such assistance." [230] This once peaceable island is being transformed into a formidable missile and strategic air base armed with the deadliest, far-reaching modern nuclear weapons.

The statement issued by the Soviet Government this morning [S/5186] [231] does not deny these facts — which is in refreshing contrast to the categoric assurances on this subject which it had previously given. However, that same statement repeats the extraordinary claim that Soviet arms in Cuba are of a "defensive character." I should like to know what the Soviet Union considers "offensive" weapons. In the Soviet lexicon, evidently, all weapons are purely defensive, even weapons that can strike from 1,000 to 2,000 miles away. Words can be stretched only so far without losing their meaning altogether. Yet semantic disputes are fruitless, and the fact remains that the Soviet Union has upset the precarious balance and created a new and dangerous situation in a new area.

This is precisely the sort of action which the Soviet Government is so fond of denouncing as "a policy of positions of strength." Consequently, I invite the attention of the Council to another remark in the Soviet Government's statement of this morning: "Only madmen can now take their stand on 'positions of strength' and expect that policy to bring them any success, to allow them to force their own dispositions on other States."

I need only mention one other curious remark in the Soviet Government's statement of today, and I quote once more: ". . . who has authorized the United States to assume the role of arbiter of the destinies of other countries and peoples . . . Cuba belongs to the Cuban people, and only they can be masters of their fate." [232] This latter sentence is, of course, a succinct statement of United States policy towards Cuba. It is, however, very far from being Soviet policy towards Cuba.

When the Soviet Union sends thousands of military technicians to its

---

[230] See Schlesinger, *A Thousand Days*, p. 805, for a discussion of this. For a different version of the entire crisis, see Anatoly A. Gromyko, "The Caribbean Crisis," *Voprosy Istorii*, August, 1971, an article by the son of the Soviet minister of foreign affairs in 1962.

[231] This and subsequent references to UN documents appear in brackets in the original.

[232] United Nations, *Official Records*, Security Council, October 23, 1962.

puppet in the Western Hemisphere, when it sends jet bombers capable of delivering nuclear weapons, when it installs in Cuba missiles capable of carrying atomic warheads and of obliterating distant points, when it prepared sites for additional missiles with a range of 2,200 miles, when it does these things under the cloak of secrecy and to the accompaniment of premeditated deception, when its actions are in flagrant violation of the policies of the Organization of American States and of the Charter of the United Nations, this clearly is a threat to this hemisphere. And when it thus upsets the precarious balance in the world, it is a threat to the whole world.

We now know that the Soviet Union, not content with Mr. Castro's oath of fealty, not content with the destruction of Cuban independence, not content with the extension of Soviet power into the Western Hemisphere, not content with a challenge to the inter-American system and the United Nations Charter, has decided to transform Cuba into a base for communist aggression, into a base for putting all of the Americas under the nuclear gun, and thereby to intensify the Soviet diplomacy of blackmail in every part of the world.

In our passion for peace we have forborne greatly. There must, however, be limits to forbearance if forbearance is not to become the diagram for the destruction of this Organization. Mr. Castro transformed Cuba into a totalitarian dictatorship with impunity; he extinguished the rights of political freedom with impunity; he accepted defensive weapons from the Soviet Union with impunity; he welcomed thousands of Communists into Cuba with impunity: But when, with cold deliberation, he turns his country over to the Soviet Union for a long-range missile launching base, and thus carries the Soviet programme for aggression into the heart of the Americas, the day of forbearance is past.

If the United States and the other nations of the Western Hemisphere should accept this new phase of aggression we would be delinquent in our obligations to world peace. If the United States and the other nations of the Western Hemisphere should accept this basic disturbance of the world's structure of power we would invite a new surge of aggression at every point along the frontier. If we do not stand firm here our adversaries may think that we will stand firm nowhere — and we guarantee a heightening of the world civil war to new levels of intensity and peril.

We hope that Chairman Khrushchev has not made a miscalculation, that he has not mistaken forbearance for weakness. We cannot believe that he has deluded himself into supposing that, though we have power, we lack nerve; that, though we have weapons, we are without the will to use them.

We still hope, we still pray, that the worst may be avoided — that the

Soviet leadership will call an end to this ominous adventure. Accordingly, the President has initiated steps to quarantine Cuba against further imports of offensive military equipment. Because the entire inter-American system is challenged, the President last night called for an immediate meeting of the organ of consultation of the Organization of American States to consider this threat to hemispheric security and to invoke articles 6 and 8 of the Rio Treaty [1] in support of all necessary action. They are meeting now. The results of their deliberations will soon be available to the Security Council.

I am submitting today to the Security Council a draft resolution [S/5182] designed to find a way out of this calamitous situation. It reads as follows:

"The Security Council,

"Having considered the serious threat to the security of the Western Hemisphere and the peace of the world caused by the continuance and acceleration of foreign intervention in the Caribbean,

"Noting with concern that nuclear missiles and other offensive weapons have been secretly introduced into Cuba,

"Noting also that as a consequence a quarantine is being imposed around the country,

"Gravely concerned that further continuance of the Cuban situation may lead to direct conflict,

"1. Calls as a provisional measure under Article 40 for the immediate dismantling and withdrawal from Cuba of all missiles and other offensive weapons;

"2. Authorizes and requests the Secretary-General to dispatch to Cuba a United Nations observer corps to assure and report on compliance with this resolution;

"3. Calls for termination of the measures of quarantine directed against military shipments to Cuba upon United Nations certification of compliance with paragraph 1 above;

"4. Urgently recommends that the United States of America and the Union of Soviet Socialist Republics confer promptly on measures to remove the existing threat to the security of the Western Hemisphere and the peace of the world, and report thereon to the Security Council."

I have just been informed [233] that the Organization of American States

[1] Inter-American Treaty of Reciprocal Assistance, signed at Rio de Janeiro on 2 September 1947. See United Nations, *Treaty Series*, vol. 21 (1948), I, No. 324*a*.

[233] The Organization of American States had been meeting since 9 A.M. Harlan Cleveland in Washington was watching Stevenson deliver this speech on television when he received a telephone call informing him that the OAS had acted. Cleveland telephoned New York and dictated an insert for Stevenson's speech, which was taken to Stevenson's table by an aide. Then a phone rang in Cleveland's office. President

this afternoon adopted a resolution [1] by 19 affirmative votes containing the following operative paragraphs:

"The Council of the Organization of Inter-American States, meeting as the provisional organ of consultation,

"*Resolves:*

" . . .

"1. To call for the immediate dismantling and withdrawal from Cuba of all missiles and other weapons with any offensive capability;

"2. To recommend that the member States, in accordance with articles 6 and 8 of the Inter-American Treaty of Reciprocal Assistance, take all measures, individually and collectively, including the use of armed force, which they may deem necessary to ensure that the Government of Cuba cannot continue to receive from the Sino-Soviet Power military material and related supplies which may threaten the peace and the security of the Continent, and to prevent the missiles in Cuba with offensive capability from ever becoming an active threat to the peace and the security of the Continent.

"3. To inform the Security Council of the United Nations of this resolution in accordance with Article 54 of the Charter of the United Nations, and to express the hope that the Security Council will, in accordance with the resolution introduced by the United States, despatch United Nations observers to Cuba at the earliest moment."

The issue which confronts the Security Council is grave. Were it not, I should not have detained you so long. Since the end of the Second World War, there has been no threat to the vision of peace so profound — no challenge to the world of the Charter so fateful. The hopes of mankind are concentrated in this room. The action we take may determine the future of civilization. I know that this Council will approach the issue with a full sense of our responsibility and a solemn understanding of the import of our deliberations.

There is a road to peace. The beginning of that road is marked out in the draft resolution I have submitted for your consideration. If we act promptly, we will have another chance to take up again the dreadful questions of nuclear arms and military bases and the means and causes of aggression and of war — to take them up and do something about them.

[1] Subsequently circulated as document S/5193.

Kennedy asked if there was some way of getting word to Stevenson of the action by the OAS. Cleveland replied that he had sent a message, but Stevenson apparently had not seen it. Just then, Stevenson picked up the note and added it to his speech. Kennedy, watching him on television, said, "Oh, I see it. He's picking it up and reading it now." Harlan Cleveland, *The Future Executive* (New York: Harper & Row, 1972), p. 7.

This is, I believe, a solemn and significant day for the life of the United Nations and the hope of the world community. Let it be remembered not as the day when the world came to the edge of nuclear war, but as the day when men resolved to let nothing thereafter stop them in their quest for peace.[234]

On Wednesday, October 24, 1962, U Thant made an important intervention. He proposed to Khrushchev and Kennedy the voluntary suspension of all arms shipments to Cuba and of the quarantine for a two- to three-week period to enable the two nations to get together and solve the crisis peacefully. He offered his own services to the two countries. Stevenson and McCloy in New York phoned the President and urged him to keep the diplomatic option alive.[235] The next day both Kennedy and Khrushchev welcomed U Thant's action, but Kennedy warned that the missiles had to be removed. That same day, Thursday, October 25, 1962, as the world stood at the abyss, Stevenson again spoke to the Security Council after Ambassador Zorin had stated that there were no offensive weapons in Cuba.[236]

Today we must address our attention to the realities of the situation posed by the build-up of nuclear striking power in Cuba. In this connexion I want to say at the outset that the course adopted by the Soviet Union yesterday to avoid direct confrontations in the zone of quarantine is welcome to my Government. We welcome also the assurance by Chairman Khrushchev in his letter to Earl Russell that the Soviet Union will take no reckless decisions with regard to this crisis.[237] And we welcome most of all the report that Mr. Khrushchev has agreed to the proposals advanced by the Secretary-General. Perhaps that report will be confirmed here today.

---

[234] Kennedy immediately dictated a telegram: "Dear Adlai: I watched your speech this afternoon with great satisfaction. It has given our cause a great start. . . . The United States is fortunate to have your advocacy. You have my warm and personal thanks." Schlesinger, *A Thousand Days*, p. 814.

[235] Stevenson told the Senate Foreign Relations Committee: "At a critical moment — when the nuclear powers seemed set on a collision course — the Secretary-General's intervention led to the diversion of the Soviet ships headed for Cuba and interception by our Navy. This was an indispensable first step in the peaceful resolution of the Cuban crisis." Hearings before the Subcommittee on International Organization Affairs, Senate Foreign Relations Committee, 88th Congress, 1st Session, March 13, 1963, p. 7.

[236] United Nations, *Official Records*, Security Council, October 25, 1962, pp. 1–6.

[237] Bertrand Russell sent messages to both Khrushchev and Kennedy urging them to alleviate the crisis. Bertrand Russell, *Unarmed Victory* (New York: Simon & Schuster, 1963), pp. 42–45.

My Government is most anxious to effect a peaceful resolution of this affair. We continue to hope that the Soviet Union will work with us to diminish not only the new danger which had suddenly shadowed the peace but all of the conflicts that divide the world.

I shall not detain the Council with any detailed discussion of the Soviet and the Cuban responses to our complaint. The speeches of the communist representatives were entirely predictable. I shall make brief comment on some points suggested by those speeches and some other points which may have arisen in the minds of Members of the United Nations.

Both Chairman Khrushchev, in his letter to Earl Russell, and Ambassador Zorin, in his remarks to this Council, argued that this threat to the peace has been caused not by the Soviet Union and Cuba but by the United States.

We are here today, and have been this week, for one single reason: because the Soviet Union secretly introduced this menacing offensive military build-up into the island of Cuba while assuring the world that nothing was further from its thoughts.

The argument of the Soviet Union, in essence, is that it was not the Soviet Union which created this threat to peace by secretly installing these weapons in Cuba, but that it was the United States which created this crisis by discovering and reporting these installations. This is the first time, I confess, that I have ever heard it said that the crime is not the burglary but the discovery of the burglary, and that the threat is not the clandestine missiles in Cuba but their discovery and the limited measures taken to quarantine further infection. The peril arises not because the nations of the Western Hemisphere have joined together to take necessary action in their self-defence but because the Soviet Union has extended its nuclear threat into the Western Hemisphere.

I note that there are still some representatives in the Council — very few, I suspect — who say that they do not know whether the Soviet Union has in fact built in Cuba installations capable of firing nuclear missiles over ranges from 1,000 to 2,000 miles. As I say, Chairman Khrushchev did not deny these facts in his letter to Earl Russell, nor did Ambassador Zorin on Tuesday evening, [1022nd meeting] [238] and, if further doubt remains on this score, we shall gladly exhibit photographic evidence to the doubtful.

One other point I should like to make is to invite attention to the casual remark of the Soviet representative claiming that we have thirty-five bases in foreign countries. The fact is that there are missiles comparable to those being placed in Cuba with the forces of only three of our allies. They were established there only by a decision of the Heads

[238] This and subsequent references to UN meetings appear in brackets in the original.

of Government meeting in December 1957, which was compelled to authorize such arrangements by virtue of a prior Soviet decision to introduce
its own missiles capable of destroying the countries of Western Europe.

In the next place, there are some troublesome questions in the minds of
Members that are entitled to serious answers. There are those who say
that, conceding the fact that the Soviet Union has installed these offensive missiles in Cuba, conceding the fact that this constitutes a grave
threat to the peace of the world, why was it necessary for the nations of
the Western Hemisphere to act with such speed? Why could not the
quarantine against the shipment of offensive weapons have been delayed
until the Security Council and the General Assembly had a full opportunity to consider the situation and make recommendations?

Let me remind the Members that the United States was not looking
for some pretext to raise the issue of the transformation of Cuba into a
military base. On the contrary, the United States made no objection whatever to the shipment of defensive arms by the Soviet Union to Cuba,
even though such shipments offended the traditions of this hemisphere.
Even after the first hard intelligence reached Washington concerning the
change in the character of Soviet military assistance to Cuba, the President of the United States responded by directing an intensification of surveillance, and only after the facts and the magnitude of the build-up had
been established beyond all doubt did we begin to take this limited action of barring only those nuclear weapons, equipment and aircraft.

To understand the reasons for this prompt action, it is necessary to
understand the nature and the purposes of this operation. It has been
marked, above all, by two characteristics: speed and stealth. As the
photographic evidence makes clear, the installation of these missiles, the
erection of these missile sites, has taken place with extraordinary speed.
One entire complex was put up in twenty-four hours. This speed not only
demonstrates the methodical organization and the careful planning involved, but it also demonstrates a premeditated attempt to confront this
hemisphere with a fait accompli. By quickly completing the whole
process of nuclearization of Cuba, the Soviet Union would be in a position to demand that the *status quo* be maintained and left undisturbed —
and, if we were to have delayed our counteraction, the nuclearization of
Cuba would have been quickly completed.

This is not a risk which this hemisphere is prepared to take. When we
first detected the secret and offensive installations, could we reasonably
be expected to have notified the Soviet Union in advance, through the
process of calling a meeting of the Security Council, that we had discovered its perfidy, and then to have done nothing but wait while we
debated, and then have waited further while the Soviet representative in
the Security Council vetoed a resolution, as he has already announced he

will do? In different circumstances, we would have done so, but today we are dealing with dread realities and not with wishes.

One of the sites, as I have said, was constructed in twenty-four hours One of these missiles can be armed with its nuclear warhead in the middle of the night, pointed at New York, and landed above this room five minutes after it was fired. No debate in this room could affect in the slightest the urgency of these terrible facts or the immediacy of the threat to peace.

There was only one way to deal with the emergency and with the immediacy, and that was to act, and to act at once, but with the utmost restraint consistent with the urgency of the threat to the peace. We came to the Security Council, I would remind you, immediately and concurrently with the Organization of the American States. We did not even wait for the OAS to meet and to act. We came here at the same time.

We immediately put into process the political machinery that we pray will achieve a solution of this grave crisis, and we did not act until the American Republics had acted to make the quarantine effective. We did not shirk our duties to ourselves, to the hemisphere, to the United Nations or to the rest of the world.

We are now in the Security Council on the initiative of the United States, precisely because having taken the hemispheric action which has been taken, we wish the political machinery, the machinery of the United Nations, to take over to reduce these tensions and to interpose itself to eliminate this aggressive threat to peace and to ensure the removal from this hemisphere of offensive nuclear weapons and the corresponding lifting of the quarantine.

There are those who say that the quarantine is an inappropriate and extreme remedy; that the punishment does not fit the crime. But I would ask those who take this position to put themselves in the position of the Organization of American States and to consider what they would have done in the face of the nuclearization of Cuba. Were we to do nothing until the knife was sharpened? Were we to stand idly by until it was at our throats? What were the alternatives available? On the one hand, the Organization of American States might have sponsored an invasion or destroyed the bases by an air strike, or imposed a total blockade of all imports into Cuba, including medicine and food. On the other hand, the Organization of American States and the United States might have done nothing. Such a course would have confirmed the greatest threat to the peace of the Americas known to history and would have encouraged the Soviet Union in similar adventures in other parts of the world. It would have discredited our will and our determination to live in freedom and to reduce, not increase, the perils of this nuclear age. The course we have chosen seems to me to be perfectly graduated to meet the character of the threat. To have done less would have been to fail in our obligation to peace.

To those who say that a limited quarantine was too much, in spite of the provocation and the danger, let me tell them a story, attributed, like so many stories of America, to Abraham Lincoln. It is a story about a passerby in my part of the country who was charged by a farmer's ferocious boar. He picked up a pitchfork and met the boar head on and it died. The irate farmer denounced him and asked him why he did not use the blunt end of the pitchfork. The man replied by asking, "why did the boar not attack me with his blunt end."

Some here have attempted to question the legal basis of the defensive measures taken by the American Republics to protect the Western Hemisphere against Soviet long-range nuclear missiles, and I would gladly expand on our position on this, but in view of the proposal now before us, presented last night by the Acting Secretary-General, [1024th meeting] perhaps this is a matter for discussion which, in view of its complexity and length, could be more fruitfully delayed to a later time.

Finally, let me say that no twisting of logic, no distortion of words can disguise the plain, obvious and compelling commonsense conclusion that the installation of nuclear weapons by stealth, the installation of weapons of mass destruction in Cuba poses a dangerous threat to peace, a threat which contravenes paragraph 4 of Article 2 of the Charter, and a threat which the American Republics are entitled to meet, as they have done, by appropriate regional defensive methods.

Nothing has been said here by the representatives of the communist States which alters the basic situation. There is one fundamental question to which I solicit your attention. The question is this: what action served to strengthen the world's hope of peace? Can anyone claim that the introduction of long-range nuclear missiles into Cuba strengthens the peace? Can anyone claim that the speed and the stealth of this operation strengthens the peace? Can anyone suppose that this whole undertaking is anything more than an audacious effort to increase the nuclear striking power of the Soviet Union against the United States and thereby magnify its frequently reiterated threats against Berlin? When we are about to debate how to stop the dissemination of nuclear weapons, does their introduction into this hemisphere by an outside State advance sanity and peace? Does anyone suppose that if this Soviet adventure went unchecked, the Soviet Union would refrain from similar adventures in other parts of the world?

The one action in the last few days which has strengthened the peace is the determination to stop this further spread of weapons in this hemisphere. In view of the situation that now confronts us, and the proposals made here yesterday by the Acting Secretary-General, I am not going to further extend my remarks this afternoon. I wish only to conclude by reading to the members of the Council the letter from the President of the United States which was delivered to the Acting Secretary-General just a few minutes ago in reply to his appeal of last night. He said to U Thant:

"I deeply appreciate the spirit which prompted your message of yesterday. As we made clear in the Security Council, the existing threat was created by the secret introduction of offensive weapons into Cuba, and the answer lies in the removal of such weapons. In your message and in your statement to the Security Council last night, you have made certain suggestions and have invited preliminary talks to determine whether satisfactory arrangements can be assured. Ambassador Stevenson is ready to discuss promptly these arrangements with you. I can assure you of our desire to reach a satisfactory and a peaceful solution of this matter."

That letter is signed "John F. Kennedy." I have nothing further to say at this time.

When Stevenson finished speaking, the ambassador from Cuba stated that the weapons were "exclusively of a defensive nature." Then the Soviet ambassador, who also was the presiding officer of the Security Council that month, spoke and denied there was any "evidence" of the introduction of offensive weapons into Cuba. He added that all the evidence the United States possessed was "fake evidence" produced by its "intelligence service." Then Ambassador Zorin asserted to Stevenson: "Even now, you cannot advance any grounds except, I repeat, the fake evidence supplied by your Intelligence Service."
A few minutes later Stevenson spoke again to the Security Council, as the public watched the proceedings on television.[239]

I want to say to you, Mr. Zorin, that I do not have your talent for obfuscation, for distortion, for confusing language and for double-talk — and I must confess to you that I am glad I do not. But, if I understood what you said, you said that my position had changed: that today I was defensive because we do not have the evidence to prove our assertions that your Government had installed long-range missiles in Cuba. Well, let me say something to you, Mr. Ambassador: We do have the evidence. We

[239] United Nations, *Official Records*, Security Council, October 25, 1962, pp. 10–14.

have it, and it is clear and incontrovertible. And let me say something else: Those weapons must be taken out of Cuba.

Next, let me say to you that, if I understood you, you said — with a trespass on credulity that excels your best — that our position had changed since I spoke here the other day because of the pressures of world opinion and a majority of the United Nations. Well, let me say to you, sir: You are wrong again. We have had no pressure from anyone whatsoever. We came here today to indicate our willingness to discuss U Thant's proposals — and that is the only change that has taken place.

But let me also say to you, sir, that there has been a change. You, the Soviet Union, have sent these weapons to Cuba. You, the Soviet Union, have upset the balance of power in the world. You, the Soviet Union, have created this new danger — not the United States.

You asked, with a fine show of indignation, why the President did not tell Mr. Gromyko last Thursday about our evidence, at the very time that Mr. Gromyko was blandly denying to the President that the USSR was placing such weapons on sites in the New World. Well, I will tell you why: because we were assembling the evidence — and perhaps it would be instructive to the world to see how far a Soviet official would go in perfidy. Perhaps we wanted to know whether this country faced another example of nuclear deceit like the one a year ago, when in stealth the Soviet Union broke the nuclear test moratorium. And, while we are asking questions, let me ask you why your Government, your Foreign Minister, deliberately, cynically deceived us about the nuclear build-up in Cuba.

Finally, Mr. Zorin, I remind you that the other day you did not deny the existence of these weapons. Instead, we heard that they had suddenly become defensive weapons. But today — again, if I heard you correctly — you say that they do not exist, or that we have not proved they exist — and you say this with another fine flood of rhetorical scorn. All right, sir, let me ask you one simple question: Do you, Ambassador Zorin, deny that the USSR has placed and is placing medium and intermediate-range missiles and sites in Cuba? Yes or no? Do not wait for the interpretation. Yes or no? [240]

THE PRESIDENT (translated from Russian): I am not in an American court of law, and therefore do not wish to answer a question put to me in the manner of a prosecuting counsel. You will receive the answer in due course in my capacity as representative of the Soviet Union.

MR. STEVENSON (United States of America): You are in the courtroom of world opinion right now, and you can answer "Yes" or "No." You have

---

[240] In addition to the pictures of the installations in Cuba, senior United States officials had been informed that Khrushchev had told a visiting American businessman that there were nuclear warheads in Cuba. Harlan Cleveland, memorandum to Walter Johnson, April 30, 1973.

denied that they exist — and I want to know whether I have understood you correctly.

THE PRESIDENT (translated from Russian): Please continue your statement, Mr. Stevenson. You will receive answer in due course.

MR. STEVENSON (United States of America): I am prepared to wait for
my answer until Hell freezes over, if that is your decision. I am also
prepared to present the evidence in this room.

THE PRESIDENT (translated from Russian): I call on the representative of
Chile.

MR. [DANIEL] SCHWEITZER (Chile) (translated from Spanish): Mr. President, I had not expected the incident which has just occurred, and I
should prefer to speak after you have replied, if you should deem it
necessary, to the comments or questions addressed to you by the United
States representative. I should be glad to yield the floor to you for that
purpose.

MR. STEVENSON (United States of America): I had not finished my statement. I asked you a question, Mr. President, and I have had no reply
to that question. I will now proceed, if I may, to finish my statement.

THE PRESIDENT (translated from Russian): By all means, you may proceed.

MR. STEVENSON (United States of America): I doubt whether anyone in
this room, except possibly the representative of the Soviet Union, has
any doubt about the facts, but in view of his statements and the statements of the Soviet Government up until last Thursday, when Mr.
Gromyko denied the existence of or any intention of installing such
weapons in Cuba, I am going to make a portion of the evidence available right now. If you will indulge me for a moment, we will set up an
easel here in the back of the room where I hope it will be visible to
everyone.

The first of these exhibits shows an area north of the village of
Candelaria, near San Cristóbal in the island of Cuba, south-west of
Havana. The map, together with a small photograph shows precisely
where the area is in Cuba. The first photograph shows the area in late
August 1962. It was then, if you can see from where you are sitting,
only a peaceful countryside. The second photograph shows the same
area one day last week. A few tents and vehicles had come into the
area, new spur roads had appeared, and the main road had been improved.

The third photograph, taken only twenty-four hours later, shows
facilities for a medium-range missile battalion installation. There are
tents for four or five hundred men. At the end of the new spur road

there are seven 1,000-mile missile trailers. There are four launcher-erector mechanisms for placing these trailers in erect firing position. This missile is a mobile weapon which can be moved rapidly from one place to another. It is identical with the 1,000-mile missiles which have been displayed in Moscow parades. All of this, I remind you, took place in twenty-four hours.

The second exhibit, which you can all examine at your leisure, shows three successive photographic enlargements of another missile base of the same type in the area of San Cristóbal. These enlarged photographs clearly show six of these missiles on trailers and three erectors. That is only one example of the first type of ballistic missile installation in Cuba.

A second type of installation is designed for a missile of intermediate range, a range of about 2,200 miles. Each site of this type has four launching pads. The exhibit on this type of missile shows a launching area being constructed near Guanajay, south-west of the city of Havana. As in the first exhibit, a map and small photograph show this area as it appeared in late August 1962, when no military activities were apparent. A second large photograph shows the same area about six weeks later. Here you will see a very heavy construction effort to push the launching area to rapid completion. The pictures show two large concrete bunkers or control centres in process of construction, one between each pair of launching pads. They show heavy concrete retaining walls being erected to shelter vehicles and equipment from rocket blast-off. They show cable scars leading from the launching pad to the bunkers. They show large, reinforced-concrete buildings under construction. A building with a heavy arch may well be intended as the storage area for the nuclear warheads. The installation is not yet complete and no warheads are yet visible.

The next photograph shows a closer view of the same intermediate-range launching site. Here you can clearly see one of the pairs of large, concrete launching pads with the concrete building from which launching operations for three pads are controlled. Other details are visible, such as fuel-tanks. That is only one example, one illustration of the work going forward in Cuba on intermediate-range missile bases.

Now, in addition to missiles, the Soviet Union is installing other offensive weapons in Cuba. The next photograph is of an airfield at San Julián in western Cuba. On this field you will see twenty-two crates designed to transport the fuselages of Soviet Ilyushin-28 bombers. Four of the aircraft are uncrated and one is partially assembled. These bombers, sometimes known as Beagles, have an operating radius of about 750 miles and are capable of carrying nuclear weapons. At the same field you can see one of the surface-to-air antiaircraft guided-missile bases, with six missiles per base, which now ring the entire coastline of Cuba.

Another set of two photographs covers still another area of deployment of medium-range missiles in Cuba. These photographs are on a larger scale than the others and reveal many details of an improved field-type launching site. One photograph provides an over-all view of most of the site. You can see clearly three of the four launching pads. The second photograph displays details of two of these pads. Even an eye untrained in photographic interpretation can clearly see the buildings in which the missiles are checked out and maintained ready to fire. A missile trailer, trucks to move missiles out to the launching pad, erectors to raise the missiles to launching position, tank-trucks to provide fuel, vans from which the missile firing is controlled — in short, all of the requirements to maintain, load and fire these terrible weapons.

These weapons, these launching pads, these planes — of which we have illustrated only a fragment — are part of a much larger weapon complex, of what is called a weapon system. To support this build-up, to operate these advanced weapon systems, the Soviet Union has sent a large number of military personnel to Cuba, a force now amounting to several thousand men.

These photographs, as I say, are available to members for detailed examination in the Trusteeship Council room, following this meeting. There I shall have one of my aides who will gladly explain them to you in such detail as you may require. I have nothing further to say at this time.

When Stevenson finished speaking, the ambassador of the United Arab Republic praised both the United States and the Soviet Union for stating that they were willing to discuss the "arrangements proposed" by U Thant.

Ambassador Zorin then spoke and denied again that there were "offensive weapons" in Cuba. As to the "evidence" introduced by Stevenson, Zorin reminded the Security Council that on April 15, 1961, Stevenson introduced photographs of a "Cuban aircraft" with the "markings of the Castro Air Force" as evidence that Cuban defectors had strafed Havana. Since those photographs were faked by the Central Intelligence Agency, Zorin asked, what was the value of the present photographs? "He who lies once is not believed a second time." [241]

Stevenson replied: [242]

[241] Ambassador Plimpton stated that Stevenson was reluctant to show the photographs of the missile sites, since he was still angry over having been misled at the time of the Bay of Pigs. Oral history interview, October 21, 1969, p. 12, John F. Kennedy Library.

[242] United Nations, *Official Records*, Security Council, October 25, 1962, pp. 16–17.

I shall detain the Council only a moment.

I have not had a direct answer to my question. The representative of the Soviet Union said that the official answer of the Soviet Union was the Tass statement that the USSR does not need to locate missiles in Cuba. I agree: the USSR does not need to do that. But the question is not whether the USSR needs missiles in Cuba. The question is: has the USSR missiles in Cuba? And that question remains unanswered. I knew it would remain unanswered.

As to the authenticity of the photographs, about which Mr. Zorin has spoken with such scorn, I wonder if the Soviet Union would ask their Cuban colleagues to permit a United Nations team to go to these sites. If so, Mr. Zorin, I can assure you that we can direct them to the proper places very quickly.

And now I hope that we can get down to business, that we can stop this sparring. We know the facts, Mr. Zorin, and so do you, and we are ready to talk about them. Our job here is not to score debating points: our job, Mr. Zorin, is to save the peace. If you are ready to try, we are.

"The Stevenson speech dealt a final blow to the Soviet case before world opinion," Schlesinger wrote.[243] During the next three days Khrushchev and Kennedy exchanged messages and the crisis eased. U Thant visited Cuba on October 31 and Deputy Premier Anastas Mikoyan arrived in Cuba on November 2. Meanwhile, at the UN, Stevenson and McCloy were engaged in intricate negotiations with the Russians for the removal of the offensive weapons. Khrushchev replaced Zorin with First Deputy Foreign Minister V. V. Kuznetsov. Stevenson took this as a helpful sign, since he and Kuznetsov had had lengthy discussions in the Soviet Union in 1958.[244] On November 20, Kennedy announced that all known offensive missile sites had been dismantled and removed from Cuba and that the United States now would end the quarantine. Although the military crisis was past, Stevenson and McCloy were busy negotiating with Soviet representatives over Cuba until January, 1963.[245]

[243] *A Thousand Days*, p. 824.

[244] See *The Papers of Adlai E. Stevenson*, Vol. VII, pp. 253, 257. In a memorandum to President Kennedy dated October 31, 1962, Schlesinger wrote that Stevenson had just had a cordial lunch with Kuznetsov. "Stevenson came away with the distinct impression that Kuznetsov is seeking discussion on a much wider basis than Cuba alone; that he has come up not only to wind up the Cuban affair but to engage in a general exploration of outstanding issues; Kuznetsov obviously has no negotiating authority, but seems to be feeling out the prospects of laying the groundwork for a broad talk on a high level." Schlesinger papers, John F. Kennedy Library.

[245] See the letter to U Thant signed by Kuznetsov and Stevenson and dated January 7, 1963, p. 370, below.

To Mrs. Ernest L. Ives [246]

October 30, 1962

Dear Buffie:

I have received some more doilies, napkins, etc., in packages with the enclosed label. Did you send me these, or have I someone to thank? They are lovely, and I can use them either for myself or for wedding presents.

It has been a trying period and we're not out of the woods by far. However, I am fine and the dramatic denouement of the Cuban matter has lifted all our spirits, and none more than mine. Some day soon I hope to be able to tell you all about it.

Love,
ADLAI

John Steinbeck received the Nobel Prize for literature on October 25, 1962.

To John Steinbeck

November 1, 1962

Dear John:

Cheers! The news from Oslo is the best news from any foreign capital in a long time — not excepting Moscow or Havana.

I had promised before that news came to pass on to you a request from Miss Frances FitzGerald, the delightful young daughter of our friend, Marietta Tree, who is now working in Paris. She was approached recently by the editor of the *Paris Review,* who asked her to find out whether you would be willing to be interviewed for that magazine. I wrote to Frankie on October 22nd, promising to sound you out, but something happened that day which has prevented my keeping my promise until now — and, meanwhile, something has happened to *you,* which has doubtless brought on you an avalanche of similar requests.

If, nevertheless, there is any possibility that you would want to be interviewed for the *Paris Review,* and if you have any particular friend among the critics — preferably an American — by whom you would like to be interviewed, I will pass the good news on to Frankie promptly.

Do let me know when you and the Fayre Elaine [247] come to town. I hope we can foregather soon and talk of many things.

Yours ever,

[246] The original is in E.S.I., I.S.H.L.
[247] Mrs. Steinbeck.

Harry Golden wrote praising Stevenson's speech of October 25, 1962, and saying that he had used some phrases that were "pure gold."

To Harry Golden [248]

November 2, 1962

Dear Harry:

Thanks for your "pure gold." As far as my recent language is concerned, I can't tell the difference between gold — brass — or crass! I hope *you're* right.

Yours,
ADLAI

To Anastas I. Mikoyan [249]

November 2, 1962

Dear Mr. Minister:

One thing that Mr. McCloy and I neglected to discuss with you last night was the list of items that the United States considers in the category of offensive weapons within the meaning of the exchange between President Kennedy and Chairman Khrushchev. Such a list is appended to this letter. We trust that the weapons you plan to remove include all those on this list.

With the thanks of Mr. McCloy and myself for our dinner with you last night and the opportunity to talk with you, I am

Yours respectfully,

List of Weapons deemed offensive by the United States in accordance with the exchange of letters between President Kennedy and Chairman Khrushchev

1. Surface-to-surface missiles including those designed for use at sea and including propellents and chemical compounds capable of being used to power missiles.
2. Bomber aircraft.
3. Bombs, air-to-surface rockets and guided missiles.
4. Warheads for any of the above weapons.
5. Mechanical or electronic equipment to support or operate the above items such as communications, supply and missile launching equipment including Komar class motor torpedo boats.

[248] The original is in the possession of Mr. Golden.
[249] A copy is in the papers of Arthur Schlesinger, Jr., John F. Kennedy Library.

To V. V. Kuznetsov [250]

November 3, 1962

Dear Mr. Kuznetsov:

In view of the inability thus far to implement the ground inspection by an international agency in Cuba to verify the dismantling and removal of offensive weapons from Cuba in accordance with agreements reached by Chairman Khrushchev and the President, I thought it might be helpful to give you a brief resume from time to time of our aerial reconnaissance of Cuba. You may be able to supplement our information about the removal, at least pending such time as an international inspection on the ground can take place.

Accordingly, I am enclosing a brief memorandum of the results of our survey of yesterday. I call particular attention to the disturbing evidence of the continued assembly of the IL–28 bombers, in contrast with the affirmative evidence that we have in respect of the dismantling of the missile sites.

In view of the difficulty of finding any adequate alternative to verification on the ground in accordance with Chairman Khrushchev's letter, we take the liberty of suggesting that you communicate to Mr. Mikoyan the urgent importance of Dr. Castro's agreement to permit thorough international verification on the ground that the removal has been completed in a manner consistent with Chairman Khrushchev's agreement.

Sincerely,

To Anastas I. Mikoyan [251]

November 6, 1962

Dear Mr. Minister:

I was distressed to hear the sad news about your wife.[252] And I take this means of sending you my personal and profound condolence. That it should come at such a time adds, I know, to your anguish. You and your sons have my utmost sympathy.

Sincerely yours,

On November 9, 1962, the General Assembly put aside other business as delegate after delegate expressed grief over the death of Eleanor Roosevelt, which had occurred two days earlier. It was the first time that

---

[250] A copy is in the papers of Arthur Schlesinger, Jr., John F. Kennedy Library.
[251] This letter was addressed to the embassy of the U.S.S.R., Havana, Cuba.
[252] Mrs. Mikoyan had just died.

any private citizen had been so honored. Stevenson said that this eu-logy [253] *and another he delivered in New York on November 17, 1962, were the most difficult, and certainly the saddest, of any tasks he had ever been called upon to perform.*[254]

I stand here for the second time in little more than a year sad in heart and in spirit.[255] The United States, the United Nations — the world — has lost one of its great citizens. Mrs. Eleanor Roosevelt is dead; a cherished friend of all mankind is gone.

Yesterday I said I had lost more than a friend. I had lost an inspiration. For she would rather light candles than curse the darkness, and her glow had warmed the world.

My country mourns her, and I know that all in this Assembly mourn with us. But even as we do, the sadness we share is enlivened by the faith in her fellow man and his future which filled the heart of this strong and gentle woman.

She imparted this faith, not only to those who shared the privilege of knowing her and of working by her side, but to countless men, women and children in every part of the world who loved her even as she loved them. For she embodied the vision and the will to achieve a world in which all men can walk in peace and dignity. And to this goal of a better life she dedicated her tireless energy, the strange strength of her extraordinary personality.

I do not think it amiss to suggest that the United Nations is, in no small way, a memorial to her and to her aspirations. To it she gave the last fifteen years of her restless life. She breathed life into this Organization. The United Nations has meaning and hope for millions, thanks to her labours, her love, no less than to her ideals — ideals that made her, only weeks after Franklin Roosevelt's death, put aside all thoughts of peace and quiet after the tumult of their lives, to serve as one of this nation's delegates to the first regular session of the General Assembly. Her duty then — as always — was to the living, to the world, to peace.

Some of you in this hall were present at that first historic session of the Assembly in London seventeen years ago. More of you were witnesses to her work in subsequent sessions in the years that followed. The members of the Third Committee — the Committee on social, humanitarian and cultural questions — and the Commission on Human Rights, which

[253] The text of the November 9 eulogy appears in United Nations, *Official Records, General Assembly Plenary Meeting*, pp. 725–726, and is reprinted in Stevenson, *Looking Outward*, pp. 113–115.
[254] Stevenson, *Looking Outward*, p. 113.
[255] He refers to his eulogy to Dag Hammarskjöld.

she served so long as Chairman — you, in particular, will remember the warmth, the intelligence and infectious buoyancy which she brought to her tasks. You know better than any of us the unceasing crusade that helped to give the world, after years of painstaking, patient travail, one of the most noble documents of mankind: the Universal Declaration of Human Rights.

This is not the time to recount the infinite services of this glorious and gracious lady; the list is as inexhaustible as her energies. But devotion to the world of the Charter, to the principles of the United Nations, to a world without war, to the brotherhood of man, underscored them all. And happily for us, she could communicate her devotion, her enthusiasm, to others. She saw clearly; she spoke simply. The power of her words came from the depth of her conviction.

"We must be willing," she said, "to learn the lesson that co-operation may imply compromise; but if it brings a world advance it is a gain for each individual nation. There will be those who doubt their ability to rise to these new heights, but the alternative," she said, "is not possible to contemplate. We must build faith in the hearts of those who doubt, we must rekindle faith in ourselves when it grows dim, and find some kind of divine courage within us to keep on till on earth we have peace and good will among men."

Albert Schweitzer wrote:

"No ray of sunlight is ever lost, but the green which it wakes . . . needs time to sprout, and it is not always granted to the sower to live to see the harvest. All work that is worth anything is done in faith."

While she lived, Mrs. Roosevelt rekindled that faith in ourselves. Now that she is gone, the legacy of her lifetime will do no less.

Mr. President, I trust you and the Members of the Assembly will forgive me for having taken your time with these very personal thoughts. The issues we debate in this hall are many and grave. But I do not think that we are divided in our grief at the passing of this great and gallant human being who was called the First Lady of the World.

John Steinbeck wrote Stevenson that he would be happy to be interviewed for Paris Review *and suggested author George Plimpton, the son of Francis T. P. Plimpton, as a possible interviewer.*

To Frances FitzGerald

November 9, 1962

Frankie darling:

Here's a typical letter from Steinbeck. Whom shall we get? Would George Plimpton like to try to handle him? I would love it — but I'm crushed with work and worry just now. And how I yearn for you!

Love always,
YOUR OLD FIANCE

P.S. A proper letter will follow — God and the clock willing!

To Barry Goldwater [256]

November 13, 1962

Dear Senator Goldwater:

I have just seen the press reports of your speech in New York last night, in which you refer to a statement by me to the General Assembly of the UN on September 20th of this year.[257]

I would be obliged if you would not again distort my utterances by quoting them out of context. In the press today you are reported as saying:

"I am more concerned over a civilian like *Adlai Stevenson telling the United Nations that we are prepared to take 'risks' to lessen the chance of an* intensified arms race with Russia than I am about military men who regard the Soviets as an implacable foe which will never deal in honor."

You have carefully neglected to quote the rest of the paragraph. The entire paragraph, as you must know, reads as follows:

"We have demonstrated again and again during long negotiations that we are prepared to take certain risks to lessen the chance of an intensified arms race. *But we are not prepared to risk our survival.* If other nations permit — as we have agreed to do — the degree of international inspection technically required for mutual security, we can end the arms race. *But we cannot stake our national existence on blind trust — especially on blind trust in a great and powerful nation which repeatedly declares its fundamental hostility to the basic values of free society.*"

256 Republican senator from Arizona.
257 See USUN press release 4043, September 20, 1962.

I hope that as a United States Senator you feel some obligation to be accurate and responsible in your public statements. And I trust you will keep that in mind if you have occasion to refer to any speech of mine again.

Sincerely yours,

Alicia Patterson gave Stevenson a check to help one of the USUN staff pay his expenses.

To Alicia Patterson [258]

November 15, 1962

Bless you — my love, love. He is elated and oh! so grateful! And so is

ADPAI

P.S. And thanks for "the perfect rose"! I like these permanent reminders of ———

On November 17, 1962, Stevenson delivered a eulogy at the Memorial Service for Eleanor Roosevelt at the Cathedral of St. John the Divine in New York City.[259]

One week ago this afternoon, in the Rose Garden at Hyde Park, Eleanor Roosevelt came home for the last time. Her journeys are over. The remembrance now begins.

In gathering here to honor her, we engage in a self-serving act. It is we who are trying, by this ceremony of tribute, to deny the fact that we have lost her, and, at least, to prolong the farewell. And — possibly — to say some of the things we dared not say in her presence, because she would have turned aside such testimonial with impatience and gently asked us to get on with some of the more serious business of the meeting.

A grief perhaps not equaled since the death of her husband seventeen years ago is the world's best tribute to one of the great figures of our age, a woman whose lucid and luminous faith testified always for sanity in an insane time and for hope in a time of obscure hope, a woman who spoke for the good toward which man aspires in a world which has seen too much of the evil of which man is capable.

She lived seventy-eight years, most of the time in tireless activity as if she knew that only a frail fragment of the things that cry out to be done

---

[258] This handwritten note is in the possession of Adlai E. Stevenson III.
[259] The text is from Stevenson, *Looking Outward*, pp. 290–295.

could be done in the lifetime of even the most fortunate. One has the melancholy sense that when she knew death was at hand, she was contemplating not what she achieved, but what she had not quite managed to do. And I know she wanted to go when there was no more strength to do.

Yet how much she had done — how much still unchronicled! We dare not try to tabulate the lives she salvaged, the battles, known and unrecorded, she fought, the afflicted she comforted, the hovels she brightened, the faces and places, near and far, that were given some new radiance, some sound of music, by her endeavors. What other single human being has touched and transformed the existence of so many others? What better measure is there of the impact of anyone's life?

There was no sick soul too wounded to engage her mercy. There was no signal of human distress which she did not view as a personal summons. There was no affront to human dignity from which she fled because the timid cried "danger." And the number of occasions on which her intervention turned despair into victory we may never know.

Her life was crowded, restless, fearless. Perhaps she pitied most not those whom she aided in the struggle, but the more fortunate who were preoccupied with themselves and cursed with the self-deceptions of private success. She walked in the slums and ghettos of the world, not on a tour of inspection, nor as a condescending patron, but as one who could not feel complacent while others were hungry, and who could not find contentment while others were in distress. This was not sacrifice; this, for Mrs. Roosevelt, was the only meaningful way of life.

These were not conventional missions of mercy. What rendered this unforgettable woman so extraordinary was not merely her response to suffering; it was her comprehension of the complexity of the human condition.

Not long before she died, she wrote that "Within all of us there are two sides. One reaches for the stars, the other descends to the level of beasts." It was, I think, this discernment that made her so unfailingly tolerant of friends who faltered, and led her so often to remind the smug and the complacent that "There but for the grace of God . . ."

But we dare not regard her as just a benign incarnation of good works. For she was not only a great woman and a great humanitarian, but a great democrat. I use the word with a small "d" — though it was, of course, equally true that she was a great Democrat with a capital "D." When I say that she was a great small-d democrat, I mean that she had a lively and astute understanding of the nature of the democratic process. She was a master political strategist with a fine sense of humor. And, as she said, she loved a good fight.

She was a realist. Her compassion did not become sentimentality. She understood that progress was a long labor of compromise. She mistrusted absolutism in all its forms — the absolutism of the world [word] and even more the absolutism of the deed. She never supposed that all of the problems of life could be cured in a day or a lifetime. Her pungent and salty understanding of human behavior kept her always in intimate contact with reality. I think this was a primary source of her strength, because she never thought that the loss of a battle meant the loss of a war, nor did she suppose that a compromise which produced only part of the objective sought was an act of corruption or of treachery. She knew that no formula of words, no combination of deeds, could abolish the troubles of life overnight and usher in the millennium.

The miracle, I have tried to suggest, is how much tangible good she really did; how much realism and reason were mingled with her instinctive compassion; how her contempt for the perquisites of power ultimately won her the esteem of so many of the powerful; and how, at her death, there was a universality of grief that transcended all the harsh boundaries of political, racial and religious strife and, for a moment at least, united men in a vision of what their world might be.

We do not claim the right to enshrine another mortal, and this least of all would Mrs. Roosevelt have desired. She would have wanted it said, I believe, that she well knew the pressures of pride and vanity, the sting of bitterness and defeat, the gray days of national peril and personal anguish. But she clung to the confident expectation that men could fashion their own tomorrows if they could only learn that yesterday can be neither relived nor revised.

Many who have spoken of her in these last few days have used a word to which we all assent, because it speaks a part of what we feel. They have called her "a lady," a "great lady," "the first lady of the world." But the word "lady," though it says much about Eleanor Roosevelt, does not say all. To be incapable of self-concern is not a negative virtue; it is the other side of a coin that has a positive face — the most positive, I think, of all the faces. And to enhance the humanity of others is not a kind of humility; it is a kind of pride — the noblest of all the forms of pride. No man or woman can respect other men and women who does not respect life. And to respect life is to love it. Eleanor Roosevelt loved life — and that, perhaps, is the most meaningful thing that can be said about her, for it says so much beside.

It takes courage to love life. Loving it demands imagination and perception and the kind of patience women are more apt to have than men — the bravest and most understanding women. And loving it takes something more beside — it takes a gift for life, a gift for love.

Eleanor Roosevelt's childhood was unhappy — miserably unhappy, she sometimes said.[260] But it was Eleanor Roosevelt who also said that "One

[260] See Joseph P. Lash, *Eleanor and Franklin* (New York: W. W. Norton, 1971).

must never, for whatever reason, turn his back on life." She did not mean that duty should compel us. She meant that life should. "Life," she said, "was meant to be lived." A simple statement. An obvious statement. But a statement that by its obviousness and its simplicity challenges the most intricate of all the philosophies of despair.

Many of the admonitions she bequeathed us are neither new thoughts nor novel concepts. Her ideas were, in many respects, old-fashioned — as old as the Sermon on the Mount, as the reminder that it is more blessed to give than to receive. In the words of St. Francis that she loved so well: "For it is in the giving that we receive."

She imparted to the familiar language — nay, what too many have come to treat as the cliches — of Christianity a new poignancy and vibrance. She did so not by reciting them, but by proving that it is possible to live them. It is this above all that rendered her unique in her century. It was said of her contemptuously at times that she was a do-gooder, a charge leveled with similar derision against another public figure 1,962 years ago.

We who are assembled here are of various religious and political faiths, and perhaps different conceptions of man's destiny in the universe. It is not an irreverence, I trust, to say thàt the immortality Mrs. Roosevelt would have valued most would be found in the deeds and visions her life inspired in others, and in the proof that they would be faithful to the spirit of any tribute conducted in her name.

And now one can almost hear Mrs. Roosevelt saying that the speaker has already talked too long. So we must say farewell. We are always saying farewell in this world, always standing at the edge of loss attempting to retrieve some memory, some human meaning, from the silence, something which was precious and is gone.

Often, although we know the absence well enough, we cannot name it or describe it even. What left the world when Lincoln died? Speaker after speaker in those aching days tried to tell his family or his neighbors or his congregation. But no one found the words, not even Whitman. "When Lilacs Last in the Dooryard Bloomed" can break the heart, but not with Lincoln's greatness, only with his loss. What the words could never capture was the man himself. His deeds were known; every schoolchild knew them. But it was not his deeds the country mourned; it was the man — the mastery of life which made the greatness of the man.

It is always so. On that April day when Franklin Roosevelt died, it was not a President we wept for. It was a man. In Archibald MacLeish's words:

> Fagged out, worn down, sick
> With the weight of his own bones,
> the task finished,

The war won, the victory assured.
The glory left behind him for the others,
(And the wheels roll up through the night
in the sweet land
In the cool air in the spring
between the lanterns).

It is so now. What we have lost in Eleanor Roosevelt is not her life. She lived that out to the full. What we have lost, what we wish to recall for ourselves, to remember, is what she was herself. And who can name it? But she left "a name to shine on the entablatures of truth, forever."

We pray that she has found peace, and a glimpse of sunset. But today we weep for ourselves. We are lonelier; someone has gone from one's own life who was like the certainty of refuge; and someone has gone from the world who was like a certainty of honor.

C. K. McClatchy, associate editor of the Sacramento Bee, *sent Stevenson an editorial critical of Senator Goldwater and described Richard M. Nixon's outburst against reporters after he had been defeated in his race for governor of California. McClatchy observed that all the candidates for public office endorsed by the* Bee *won except the candidate for superintendent of public instruction. He also mentioned that his father-in-law, George F. Kennan, was thinking of resigning as ambassador to Yugoslavia since Congress paid no attention to his policy recommendations on Yugoslavia.*

To C. K. McClatchy

November 21, 1962

Dear "C.K." —

I was delighted to have your letter and most grateful for your excellent editorial about Goldwater. They have been coming in from various places including a delightful reflection by one gentleman who said he did not know so much lard could be poured into one suit!

I hardly need tell you what a relief it is to have Mr. Nixon out of Washington and out of Sacramento — and out! I think you can congratulate yourselves on another triumph of editorial sanity — in spite of that superintendent of public instruction you described so vividly.

Carol Evans has been trying to find a suitable job and you know her talents and her capacity for thoughtful effective work. I am delighted that you are helping her for she needs to stay in California with her family if she can.

I share your anxiety about George Kennan. I saw him in Yugoslavia this summer and we spent a couple of days together visiting Tito. He seemed a little depressed and discontented with his relationships there. To lose him would be a major misfortune and I hope if anything develops along these lines you will let me know well in advance.

My love to Grace [261] — and when I come out to see my fifth grandchild in San Francisco, I will come to see your third in Sacramento.

Yours,

To Ralph McGill

November 21, 1962

Dear Ralph:

I've been saving your kind telegram of October 25th to answer myself — and hence I've saved it for almost a month! You were good to go to that trouble, and it pleased me immensely, coming from you.

I think we'll work out of this crisis well, but I have no doubt there will be others to follow. The quick decision of Khrushchev to withdraw the missiles was, I am sure, due to three factors: the threat of military action by the United States, the solidarity of the hemisphere, and the sudden realization that, after the Security Council confrontation and the exposure of the plot, they risked losing the confidence and good will so painstakingly developed over many years among the nonaligned Afro-Asians. And perhaps the latter was the most important of all. I think this factor is well to bear in mind, because it is only through the UN that the exposure could be dramatized and made indeed visible to all of the Afro-Asians, whom the Soviet Union had spent so much money and time neutralizing.

I hope on another visit you will not be too considerate of my time!

Yours,

On November 29, 1962, Anastas Mikoyan visited the White House. Stevenson wrote the following note before the visit.

To John F. Kennedy [262]

[no date]

Mr. Pres.

If and when you see Mikoyan I think it would be profitable to talk to him a) about Russia's future intentions in Cuba — to leave him with

[261] Mrs. McClatchy.
[262] This handwritten note is in the Sorensen papers, John F. Kennedy Library.

the feeling that as long as Cuba threatens the political stability of Latin America he can't expect us to restore normal relations & trade with Cuba — indeed the mistrust and hostility of the Hemisphere vs. Cuba can only increase. He should have no illusions when he returns to Moscow about the danger of further subversive activity from Cuba.

I think also it might be helpful if you could express your hope for a more extensive detente now that we have made a start in Cuba — with some emphasis on nuclear testing, Berlin etc.

A E STEVENSON

John Steinbeck sent Stevenson a draft of his speech of acceptance of the Nobel Prize for literature.

To John Steinbeck [263]

December 2, 1962

Dear John —

I was never more flattered — Stevenson criticizing Steinbeck! Well, I've tried and tried — and I can't move around a word or an idea — or even a comma. I suppose I'm a hell of a critic — but I think you've "said something" — briefly, honestly and powerfully. And I think I know when to keep my silly hands off. And this piece is a Hands Off!

How I wish I could hear you —

Let me know when you get back — and thanks again & again for coming to that party. They made $10,000 — on you!

Kisses to Elaine — and Bravo! for you —

ADLAI

P.S. I'm keeping the copy — *No,* I'm returning it — hoping you'll autograph & return to me.

AES

On December 8, 1962, Stewart Alsop and Charles Bartlett published an article, "The White House in the Cuban Crisis," in the Saturday Evening Post. *It contained a photograph of an agonized Stevenson and a caption stating: "An opponent charges 'Adlai wanted a Munich. He wanted to trade U.S. bases for Cuban bases.' " The authors quoted one member of the Executive Committee: "At first we divided into hawks and doves, but by the end a rolling consensus had developed, and except for Adlai, we had all ended up as dawks or hoves." The authors stated further that*

---

[263] This handwritten letter is in the possession of Mrs. John Steinbeck.

*only Stevenson dissented from the ExComm consensus — "He wanted
to trade the Turkish, Italian and British missile bases for the Cuban
bases."*

*In fact, Stevenson supported the consensus. He had talked about the
Turkish and Italian bases, but others had as well.*

*On December 1, 1962, President Kennedy had told Arthur M. Schle-
singer, Jr., that Alsop and Bartlett were writing an article and asked him
to warn Stevenson that he was being accused of advocating a Munich.
"Everyone will suppose that it came out of the White House because
of Charlie," the President said.[264] "Will you tell Adlai that I never talked
to Charlie or any other reporter about the Cuban crisis, and that this
piece does not represent my views."*

*Pierre Salinger, the President's press secretary, at a press conference on
Monday, December 3, 1962, was asked to comment on the Alsop-Bartlett
article. The transcript reads:*

> MR. SALINGER: Let me read you a short statement on that.
> QUESTION: By the President?
> MR. SALINGER: My statement.
> "The proceedings of the National Security Council have been secret
> since its founding in 1947 and will continue to be. The various posi-
> tions of members of the National Security Council taken during de-
> liberations must also remain secret in order to permit access by the
> President to the frank expression of views.
> "I can state flatly, however, that Ambassador Stevenson strongly
> supported the decision taken by the President on the quarantine and
> brilliantly developed the United States position at the United Nations
> during the days which followed. He also played the key role in the
> negotiations at the United Nations on the Cuba matter."

*After the Salinger press conference, one or two of Stevenson's friends
in the press told Stevenson that Bartlett would not have dared write the
article the way he did unless he was sure he was saying what Kennedy
wanted. When Schlesinger talked to Stevenson that afternoon, Stevenson
"said grimly that, if the President wanted him to go, he did not have to
go about it in this circuitous fashion." [265]*

*Schlesinger then told the President that people all over Washington
interpreted the article as a signal that he wanted to get rid of Stevenson.
The President insisted that he did not want Stevenson to resign. "In the
first place," he stated, "where could I possibly find anyone who could do*

---

[264] Bartlett had introduced Kennedy to Jacqueline Bouvier. See Schlesinger, *A Thousand Days*, p. 835.

[265] Ibid., p. 837. The National Security Council refused to declassify two memoranda that Arthur Schlesinger sent to President Kennedy on December 2 and 3, 1962,
on the Alsop-Bartlett article.

half as good a job at the UN? Look at the alternatives — Adlai would do a far better job than any of the others. In the second place, from a realistic political viewpoint, it is better for me to have Adlai in the government than out. In the third place, if I were trying to get him out, Charlie Bartlett is a good friend, but he's the last medium I would use." [266]

When Schlesinger reported to him what Kennedy had said, Stevenson answered: "That's fine, but will he say it publicly?"

The next morning the New York Daily News headlined: "Adlai on Skids over Pacifist Stand in Cuba." [267] Clayton Fritchey phoned the White House and told Schlesinger: "Something must be done. Adlai is very close to throwing in the towel." Schlesinger urged Kennedy to write a letter to Stevenson "making clear your continued confidence in him," adding that Charles Bartlett had assured Fritchey that the President had had "absolutely nothing" to do with the article.[268]

On December 5, Kennedy's letter to Stevenson was released to the press.

Dear Adlai:

This is just a note to tell you again how deeply I regret the unfortunate stir which has arisen over the statements contained in the Saturday Evening Post article. I think you know how greatly we have all admired your performance at the United Nations in general and during the Security Council discussions and private negotiations connected with the Cuban crisis in particular. I have, of course, valued your advice very highly. That we have eliminated the nuclear menace from Cuba is the best evidence of the prudence of our policy and its execution, in which you played such an active part.

Our Government has many important challenges in the days ahead; and your continued work at the United Nations will be of inestimable value. Meanwhile, it goes without saying that you have my fullest confidence and best wishes.

Sincerely yours,

That same day in a television program Stevenson called the Alsop-Bartlett article "wrong in literally every detail." [269] He pointed out that

---

[266] Ibid.

[267] It was of course worldwide news. The Melbourne, Australia, *Herald*, for instance, carried stories on December 5 and 6, 1962. After describing the rumors that Stevenson was to lose his UN post, the December 6 article commented: "As a politician he is astute but perhaps hampered by his innate magnanimity, his humility, and the quality that Cassandra of the *London Daily Mirror* once called 'a kind of gentle greatness that is so rare as to be almost non-existent in politics.'"

[268] Memorandum for the President, December 4, 1962. Schlesinger papers, John F. Kennedy Library.

[269] See Stevenson's memorandum to Arthur Schlesinger, Jr., analyzing his position with regard to Cuba during the crucial days of this crisis, pp. 385–388, below.

*he had supported the quarantine days before the decision was made.
"What the article doesn't say is that I opposed . . . an invasion of Cuba
at the risk of nuclear war until the peace keeping machinery of the UN
had been used." On the question of bases, he added: "I said that, if the
United States started a negotiation about the elimination of the bases
with Mr. Khrushchev, we would have to develop well in advance the content, the political content, of whatever our position would be. Among
these would inevitably be the subject of bases which Mr. Khrushchev
would raise." [270]*

*Stevenson told a friend that if worse came to worst and the United
States had had to give up bases to get the Soviet bases out of Cuba, this
was not an unthinkable compromise if the alternative was nuclear war.
He added that Kennedy should not have let the article happen and that,
moreover, Kennedy had not publicly said a word of condemnation of the
participants in the affair.[271]*

*Stewart Alsop wrote that Kennedy had not inspired the article nor was
he the "nonadmirer" who said that "Adlai wanted a Munich." "But it is
true," Alsop added, "that Kennedy read the piece for accuracy, and proposed a couple of minor changes." [272] Alsop wrote in 1973: "The President
proposed a few changes in the piece. One of the changes was in the
section dealing with Adlai Stevenson and Cuba. It was his clear intention
to give this section a tone less critical of Mr. Stevenson. The actual result
was precisely the opposite since the President cut out two or three sentences which reflected Clayton [Fritchey]'s explication and justification
for Stevenson's position on the bases. Stevenson's position was thus made
to seem less rational than in fact it was. One moral seems to be that over-
worked Presidents are lousy editors. Another moral that I have since
abided by is not to submit any article to anybody in advance, including
Presidents." [273]*

Don A. Schanche, then executive editor of the Saturday Evening Post,
*and Clay Blair, the managing editor, "seriously questioned the use of
such an explosive remark ["Adlai wanted a Munich"] without attribu-*

[270] New York *Times*, December 6, 1962. See Stewart Alsop, "Footnote for the Historians," *Saturday Evening Post*, January 26, 1963, for his view of the criticisms of
the Alsop-Bartlett article. See also Stevenson's letter to Stuart Gerry Brown dated
March 11, 1963, pp. 398–399, below.

[271] Bethia Currie, "Notes of Conversations with Adlai Stevenson," p. 25. Ambassador Plimpton stated that Stevenson "was hurt more than anything else. I'm sure he
must have thought of resigning, but he isn't [sic] the resigning type." Oral history interview, John F. Kennedy Library, p. 16.

[272] *The Center: People and Power in Political Washington* (New York: Harper &
Row, 1968), p. 191. Otto Friedrich quoted a *Saturday Evening Post* editor as saying
that Kennedy read the article twice before it was published and that the President
wanted the words "Adlai wanted a Munich" published. *Decline and Fall* (New York:
Harper & Row, 1969), p. 39.

[273] Letter to Walter Johnson, July 9, 1973.

tion. Stew Alsop then told us in confidence that the quotation was the President's own and that he had read it and approved it. Blair asked Alsop and Bartlett to ask JFK to read it a second time. Alsop reported back that the President had read it again and said, 'I want it in.' " [274]

Chester Bowles wrote: "*As I think back over this period I am impressed and disturbed by the fact that Kennedy at no point, in regard to either Stevenson or myself, said that the leaked charges against us were false. In each case he simply expressed his regret that a leak had occurred.*" [275]

To Lady Barbara Jackson

December 8, 1962

Dearest Barbara:

Your letter of November 8 is still sitting here neglected and contributing to my remorse and chagrin. But I really have been busy — and how! What with the incessant negotiations with the Russians and all of the UN work, plus incessant commuting to Washington, I have now had to face — once again — the assaults of malicious — with overtones of White House — conspiracy that have excited the press and agitated my friends. The latter have quickly converted a hatchet into a boomerang — and the President has been forthright and noble in his responses.

But the incident leaves some bad scars — the suspicion among the working press of favoritism and news management, the insecurity of the President's most secret discussions — and finally — which worries me most — the impression I fear that there are many people in the higher councils of the Government who really wanted an invasion of Cuba, and maybe still do, with all of the risks of reprisal and escalation.

How I missed you in these weeks of worry and work, of depression and satisfaction. Actually, as you know, the policy adopted by the President in the last analysis coincided with my recommendations, and has worked out so well that I sometimes can scarcely believe it. How often has the Soviet Union backed down — and out — without risking war, without cost to the United States, and by using the peacekeeping machinery we have so laboriously constructed? Or perhaps that sentence should have read — when, if ever, has the Soviet Union withdrawn from a position of strength before?

The factors that contributed to it — the threat of force, the solidarity of the Western Hemisphere, were almost overshadowed in my opinion by the sudden realization in Moscow that they risked the loss of all the confidence and good will they had built up so expensively and patiently

---

[274] Don A. Schanche, letter to Walter Johnson, October 17, 1974.
[275] Letter to Walter Johnson, December 5, 1972.

among the non-aligned countries by the exposure in the Security Council of Soviet duplicity and dangerous daring.

I have been, therefore, delighted with the policy and its execution and proud to have had an active part in both. But I confess that I wish there were not quite so many and vocal bloody-minded gentlemen in our Capitol. As for me personally, I am not going to belabor you with masses of clippings, but I think there is little left for me to worry about as far as my position in the United Nations is concerned or at the White House for that matter.

I have not heard from you for so long it worries me. Nor have I seen Robert [Jackson], although Paul Hoffman tells me he will be here after the first of the year and I may have a chance to visit with him then. I wish he would come and stay with me, and I wish most of all that I knew what you were doing and where — and all the details — of your current activities — health and spirits — and also I wish I knew what your Spring schedule was for the United States. It is difficult to make mine, without synchronization possible.

If your pen is still full of ink, and your head and heart full of wisdom and fire, I have, as usual, two more major chores ahead of me. One is a speech in New York on January 22 on the challenges to democracy in the next decade in the world context. Then I have to make a speech at Notre Dame on February 18 on a topic that hasn't been chosen yet! Any suggestions for either would be lifelines to the drowning. But — please — please don't overburden yourself as I seem to have been doing since the last campaign — sustained I suspect by repetition rather than production.

I have a little something to send you for Christmas but I am not sure where to send it. Indeed, I'm not sure I should send it — given its modest character.

The boys are well. Borden has a job at last — John Fell's wife is having a baby in January, and Adlai and Nancy and their children are flourishing in spite of Sidney Yates' defeat for the Senate.[276]

There is so much to report and so much to hear that I am as always, bewildered and paralyzed!

Much love,

Stevenson's old friend Ben W. Heineman, chairman of the board of the Chicago and Northwestern Railroad, wrote that the Alsop-Bartlett episode was outrageous. If people around the President were to give advice at the peril of having it taken out of context and with inaccurate and partial revelations, he warned, the country was in trouble.

[276] Senator Everett M. Dirksen had been reelected.

To Ben W. Heineman

December 8, 1962

Dear Ben:

Thanks for your letter. It heartens me. And, as you know, I agree with you emphatically about the implications of this incident which go far beyond the malice toward me. I have the one great comfort, and it is my conviction, that the President knew nothing about it. Indeed, he seems to be, if anything, more upset and agitated than I am.

I hope to be home over the holidays and will look forward to a visit with you.

Cordially,

To Pierre E. G. Salinger

December 10, 1962

Dear Pierre:

I have just read the TIME piece which worried the President,[277] and have written John Steele the attached letter trying to correct those of his misinterpretations and misstatements about which I have any personal knowledge.

Let me also say that the remark in the LIFE magazine story by [John] Steele [278] implying that I was dissatisfied with the first statement that you and the President released, on Monday of last week, and felt it "cavalier" is quite wrong. I believe I told you and the President that I was satisfied with the statement, and I have so stated publicly repeatedly. I believe that the feeling that it was cavalier and insufficient emerged from the newspapermen and their interpretation, which evidently Steele shared.

Cordially yours,

To James J. Kilpatrick [279]

December 10, 1962

Dear Mr. Kilpatrick:

Thank you for the kind remarks in your letter of October 17 concerning my part in the State Department briefing for out of town newspapermen. I hope you will forgive the delay in replying to your letter, which arrived just as the Cuban crisis began to occupy practically all of our time at the Mission.

[277] "The Nation: The Administration: Stranger on the Squad," December 14, 1962, pp. 15–18.

[278] "The Adlai Stevenson Affair," *Life,* December 14, 1962, pp. 44–46. The story carried the headline "Hard facts support the Ambassador against irresponsible charges."

[279] Editor of the Richmond, Virginia, *News Leader.*

I have read your editorial of October 17 with interest and am glad to answer the question you posed in it. The United Nations is not intervening in the internal affairs of the Congo, since it was invited by the legitimate government of the Congo to come to its assistance for the purpose of maintaining order in that strife-ridden country. It remains there at the invitation of the Central Government. You are right that our basic policy favors the self-determination of peoples. However, the people of Katanga have no more right to self-determination outside the framework of the nation than do the people of any state of our union. Katanga is a province of the Congo. I think it is well worth noting that no government in the world has to this date ever recognized Katanga as an independent country. Moreover, Provisional President Tshombe is presently insisting publicly that Katanga is not in a state of secession from the Congo but on the contrary is anxiously desirous of taking actions which will assure its full return to its role as an integral part of the Congo nation. He has repeatedly stated publicly that he supports Secretary General U Thant's plan of national reconciliation, which has as its principal purpose the full integration of Katanga into the political and economic life of the Congo.

Lastly, you state that our policy "calls for the overthrow of a stout and friendly anti-Communist." You imply that the Central Government leans toward the Communists. While Tshombe has proclaimed himself anti-Communist, his policy has threatened the very kind of chaos and division which, without the presence of the United Nations in the Congo, would invite the cold war into the unfortunate country and permit the Communist bloc to find a secessionist government of another sort which it could support. On the other hand, the Central Government is headed by a Prime Minister who has clearly shown his dedication to the independence of his country, particularly as it might be threatened by Communist subversion.

It is our judgment that the future of the Congo, and its ability to avoid the chaos which would result from its abandonment by the United Nations, will be most enhanced by the degree to which Prime Minister Adoula is able to unify his country, politically and economically.

With cordial best wishes,

Sincerely yours,

To the Reverend Theodore M. Hesburgh [280]

December 11, 1962

Dear Father Hesburgh:

I realize that Mr. [Clayton] Fritchey has already telephoned you to convey my pleasure at receiving your most gracious letter of November

[280] President of the University of Notre Dame.

7th, and my acceptance of the great honor which the Senior Class and the Administration have seen fit to pay me. But I could not rest without writing myself to tell you how complimented I am by your thought of me. Indeed, I would have written long since were it not for the continuing — on occasion, I must admit they have appeared to be continual — series of meetings, both here and in Washington, necessitated by the Cuba crisis. During that period, there was no chance to read my correspondence. I find that situation doubly regrettable now that I have read your good letter; it would have furnished a welcome respite!

But even now, when our transactions with the Soviet Union are moving toward a conclusion, word of my selection by students of your great University as recipient of your annual Patriotism Award is heartwarming and gratifying news. I look forward to meeting you, the members of your faculty and staff, and the student body on February 18th, at which time I hope to be able to express my appreciation more fully.

In the meantime, please accept my thanks and my best wishes for the Christmas season.

Cordially yours,

Agnes Meyer wrote Stevenson that he had come out of the Alsop-Bartlett affair with a triumph, but she expressed concern over the way the White House did things.

To Mrs. Eugene Meyer [281]

December 15, 1962

Dearest Agnes:

You were sweet to write me, and I am flattered and grateful that you have shared some of my recent troubles — although they haven't troubled me as much as they seem to have troubled some of my friends.

I had hoped to have some lovely long evenings with you during this autumn, but life has been a little unkind to both of us, it seems to me.

Perhaps the New Year will bring something better — but it can't bring more love and gratitude and good wishes to you and all your glorious breed!

Devotedly,

ADLAI

P.S. I'm leaving for Libertyville on the 22nd, hoping to stay over New Year's.

[281] The original is in the Agnes Meyer files, Princeton University Library.

To Francis Brown [282]

December 19, 1962

Dear Mr. Brown:

Since I am certain you have long ago discovered that both politicians and diplomats tend toward the verbose, I trust it will come as no surprise that my review of DAG HAMMARSKJOLD/SERVANT OF PEACE [283] runs somewhat longer than requested.

It was your suggestion about placing Mr. Hammarskjold and his speeches "in the setting of their time" which inspired me to such evangelical fervor. I do, however, understand your space problems and apologize if I have added to them.

With every good wish,

Cordially yours,

To Dr. Albert Schweitzer

December 20, 1962

Dear Doctor:

I have just learned from Mr. Lisle Ramsey [284] of a special invitation to visit the United States that has been extended to you by a group of Americans who are, like myself, among your great admirers. The news is pleasant, of course. But I, as well as my fellow citizens, would be even more pleased to learn that you feel it possible to accept the invitation.

It would be an act of pure selfishness on my part to urge you to do so, for I know and sympathize with your understandable reluctance to leave Lambarene for long periods. What I can do in good conscience, however, is to tell you that your visit would be welcomed with cheers by my fellow countrymen!

Whatever your decision, you have, as always, my heartfelt good wishes — and never more than on January 14th.[285] Would I might be there to express them in person!

I have been meaning to write you for many months, not only to convey my affectionate good wishes, but also to report on the prospects for some of the things to which we both attach such importance.

With the completion of the nuclear testing series by both countries, I

---

282 Editor of the *New York Times Book Review*.

283 *Dag Hammarskjold: Servant of Peace. A Selection of His Speeches and Statements*, edited by Wilder Foot (New York: Harper & Row, 1962). The review appeared in the *New York Times Book Review*, April 14, 1963.

284 Mr. Ramsey, of St. Louis, was organizing a citizens' committee to sponsor the visit of Dr. Schweitzer.

285 Dr. Schweitzer's eighty-eighth birthday.

have been persuaded that the Russians are now prepared to reach a tolerable agreement to terminate testing forever. Indeed, during the Cuban crisis, some of Khrushchev's correspondence gave me new heart in this regard.[286] Indeed, I am still hopeful, but, as is so often the case, the words don't seem to be followed by appropriate action at the negotiating table in Geneva. I have, as you know, pressed long and earnestly for a liberal approach by the United States and I think our position is now entirely sensible and reasonable. The Soviet apprehensions, at least professed, about espionage, seem to me quite fictitious and I suspect what underlies it all is divided opinion in the Kremlin about taking any steps toward opening their closed society until they see clearly the consequences. Moreover, the Chinese and other rightist elements in the communist world are not making it any easier for the reasonable ones to lead effectively and confidently.

With God's help and some rational thinking we managed to resolve the Cuban crisis without the disaster that might well have followed. Here again, the Russians gave evidence, verbally at least, of a desire for broader detente. About that we will have to wait and see and, I pray, be ever-ready to meet and negotiate. In spite of much of what you read and hear about tough and hard line sentiment in the United States, I want to assure you that this view is neither dominant nor serious in the Administration in Washington.

I think often of my visits with you [287] and of our correspondence which I wish were more frequent. But I have a strong feeling that you know far better than I about what is going on in the world, and of the hopes and fears that seem to be in everlasting contest for the mind's mastery.

I occasionally see visitors to Lambarene who bring me happy and comforting reports about you and the hospital. An old and beloved friend, Mrs. Elizabeth Paepcke,[288] counts her visit with you last summer among her most cherished memories. And I can understand why!

With affectionate and respectful regards, and all that Christmas wishes mean, I am

Cordially yours,

Robert F. Kennedy recommended to Cuban exiles that they send New York lawyer James B. Donovan to Havana to negotiate the release of prisoners from the Bay of Pigs invasion. Kennedy and others led the drive

---

[286] On December 19, 1962, for example, Khrushchev wrote Kennedy that the "time has come now to put an end once and for all to nuclear tests."

[287] For Stevenson's visit to Dr. Schweitzer at Lambaréné, see *The Papers of Adlai E. Stevenson*, Vol. VII, pp. 32–34.

[288] Widow of Stevenson's friend Walter Paepcke, of Chicago, who had been chairman of the board and chief executive officer of the Container Corporation of America.

to get food and drugs for ransom. On December 23, 1962, the first prisoners reached Florida.

To Robert F. Kennedy

December 22, 1962

Dear Bob:

To complete the record, let me report that one of my men, Jack Cates,[289] who knows Ambassador Lechuga,[290] talked to him following our conversation yesterday, and made our position clear. Lechuga was very cordial and reported our position to Havana exactly as presented.

And now I read in the morning papers that all is well. For this happy outcome to such long and agonizing negotiations, I think you are entitled to our gratitude as much as anyone else. Certainly you have mine, and with it my admiration for your assistance in what I am afraid I would have long since written off as hopeless.

Yours,

Stevenson spent the holidays with members of his family at Libertyville.

To Mrs. Ronald Tree [291]

December 28, 1962

M —

Do you know her? Have you ever seen her? [292] I think not. . . .

Yes, I'm struggling out of the sea of tissue paper, broken toys, mounds of damp diapers — and, with waves of fatigue, have escaped from the old homestead, the grasping little hands and shattering noise. And you?

Yates gets the job [293]—and Rowan [294] an Embassy abroad. All is well — I think! But the Congo is burning again, and Cuba beckoning. So it looks like N.Y. tomorrow instead of Georgia next week. Nancy [Stevenson] and the babes are grounded with influenza in L'ville [Louisville], and I am bereft — and healthy.

Talking with . . . brought forth this New Year's confection.

[289] Alternate United States representative on the council of the Organization of American States.

[290] Carlos Lechuga, permanent representative of Cuba to the United Nations.

[291] This handwritten letter is in the possession of Mrs. Tree.

[292] Stevenson enclosed a picture of a painting.

[293] Sidney Yates, after his defeat by Senator Everett M. Dirksen, was appointed United States representative on the Trusteeship Council, with the rank of ambassador.

[294] Carl Rowan, Deputy Assistant Secretary of State for Public Affairs, was appointed ambassador to Finland.

Beauty crowds me till I die,
Beauty, mercy have on me!
But if I expire today
Let it be in sight of thee.

And I hope its sun, sea and beauty for you.[295]

P.Q. H.

To Lady Barbara Jackson

December 31, 1962

Dearest Barbara:

Perhaps you are already familiar with the conspiracy to elect you to the Board of the Rockefeller Foundation. I subscribe to Barry Bingham's [296] expectation that the effect of your charms would exceed our persuasion, but has anyone consulted you about all this?

My skies are still cloudy — what with a more mountainous accumulation of work than ever before, changes in the Mission — Cuba, the Congo, and the Alsops! But I think I see a distant light as the chilly, frigid winter moves on. But I wish I had your exact schedule more clearly in mind. I hope you will send it along as soon as you can. Meanwhile, I will look forward to Robert [Jackson]'s arrival and an opportunity for a first-hand report.

I got back to Illinois for a few days over Christmas but was called back — as always — to Washington, so it was not, on the whole, a very rewarding visit to the prairies. However I am hoping to have a few days in Georgia, shooting quail at Alicia [Patterson]'s place before the grind begins in earnest again, and Congress convenes.

Having ahead of me a speech on the prospects for democracy in the next decade disturbs me, and I hope your thoughts on that subject are as interesting and illuminating as usual. But whatever they are, I hope I get them before I have to put something together for a most formidable audience on the 22nd of January.[297]

I sent you a little gift, but unfortunately it went to Picketts instead of Jersey, and I suppose it has vanished in the Customs House, as they usually do. I pray you are well, and send you dearest love,

P.S. Art Buchwald [298] says what Washington needs is an aquarium because fish don't talk!

---

[295] Mrs. Tree was in Barbados.

[296] Publisher of the Louisville *Courier-Journal.*

[297] The tenth anniversary convocation of the Center for the Study of Democratic Institutions, held in New York City.

[298] Syndicated columnist based in Washington.

John B. Oakes, an editor of the New York Times, wrote Stevenson that when his grandfather, Vice President Adlai E. Stevenson, visited Chattanooga, Tennessee, seventy years ago, he was met by Mr. Oakes's father, who was mayor of the city.

To John B. Oakes

December 31, 1962

Dear John:

I was delighted with your letter of December 20 and the thought that our family acquaintance goes back 70 years. I hope it will go on for 70 more!

If I could see the text of Grandpa's address on that occasion, I would be pleased. Although, I confess, I can anticipate his old-fashioned oratorical style, he was a marvelous story teller and there just might be a useful and humorous nugget embodied in the rhetoric.

When do we have another breakfast? And when do we have another newspaper? [299]

Happy New Year!

Yours,

The card Stevenson sent out to those who sent him Christmas greetings follows.

I am so grateful for your thought of me at Christmas. And — with warmest wishes for all the years ahead — I send you a favorite and familiar prayer — by a man I wish was a relative!

ADLAI E. STEVENSON

New York — 1962

"Give us grace and strength to persevere. Give us courage and gaiety and the quiet mind. Spare to us our friends and soften to us our enemies. Give us the strength to encounter that which is to come, that we may be brave in peril, constant in tribulation, temperate in wrath and in all changes of fortune, and down to the gates of death loyal and loving to one another."

ROBERT LOUIS STEVENSON

[299] The *Times* was shut down by a strike that lasted from December 8, 1962, until April 1, 1963.

Part Three

1963

*I*t was a year of accomplishment — and a year of tragedy.
    What Adlai E. Stevenson had been advocating since 1956 — the suspension of nuclear testing in the atmosphere — was achieved.

But before the year was out, the assassination of the young President left a pall over the country.

By 1963 there were 111 members of the United Nations. The secession of Katanga was ended by the United Nations Force, but the question of paying for the entire operation remained a vexing problem. The General Assembly in December, 1961, had adopted a three-part plan to finance the Congo operation and the UN Emergency Force in the Middle East.[1] It asked the International Court of Justice for an advisory opinion as to whether the assessments against member states to support both operations created binding financial obligations on the member states. The General Assembly further assessed the costs of both operations through June 30, 1962. And, third, the General Assembly authorized a $200 million bond issue to be amortized out of the regular budget of the United Nations.

Under this three-part plan, while assessments were levied on every member, the less developed countries were given reductions of up to eighty per cent of their normal assessment. In order to accomplish this, the United States agreed to make voluntary contributions above its normal thirty-two per cent share. The Kennedy Administration had difficulty persuading Congress to do this. Moreover, a number of congressmen objected to the U.S. purchasing one half the bond issue, asserting that this was a device to have the U.S. pay what the Soviet Union and other countries owed. President Kennedy, Secretary of State Dean Rusk, Stevenson and other high officials assured Congress that the defaulting countries would be required to meet their obligations, since Article 19 of the UN Charter provided that a member in arrears by more than two

[1] See Stevenson's letter to President Kennedy of December 23, 1961, pp. 184–188, above.

years in its contributions "shall have no vote in the General Assembly." In July, 1962, the World Court affirmed the binding character of the assessments. That December the General Assembly accepted the court's decision by 76 to 17 with 8 abstentions. In May, 1963, a special session of the General Assembly requested that the delinquent countries pay their arrears. Over thirty countries did so, but the Soviet Union and the East European countries (other than Yugoslavia) continued to refuse to pay anything for either operation. France continued to refuse to pay anything for the Congo operation. Unless they changed their policies, the Soviet Union and the defaulting East European countries would face Article 19 in 1964 and France would face it in 1965.

Portugal, with its medieval mentality, came under increasing attack for its unwillingness to grant even self-government to its African colonies, and apartheid in South Africa was bitterly assailed at the United Nations.

Stevenson, with "chronic stamina," presented the American position at the Security Council and in the General Assembly, at committees, at receptions, and in the corridors of the UN building. He continued his biweekly television program Adlai Stevenson Reports [2] and he spoke and spoke to the American people about the importance of the United Nations.[3] And he was harassed by anti-UN pickets in Dallas one month before President Kennedy was shot on the streets of that city.

After the death of John F. Kennedy, President Lyndon B. Johnson insisted that Stevenson must remain as ambassador to the United Nations. At the beginning of the new administration, Stevenson was treated with respect — and deference.

In January, 1963, Arthur Hoppe, columnist for the San Francisco Chronicle, rode with Stevenson from La Guardia Airport to the UN building. Hoppe wrote that "there was a gentleness about him. Almost a sadness." As Stevenson talked, Hoppe recalled President Kennedy delivering his State of the Union speech — "so cool, so self-possessed, so decisive, so brilliant. And I thought of what the hard New Frontiersmen in Washington say privately about Mr. Stevenson — 'egghead,' 'indecisive,' 'no guts.'" Hoppe added: "And I think I understood clearly for the first time the root of the differences, whatever they may be, between Mr. Kennedy and Mr. Stevenson. It is not, I think, that Mr. Stevenson is indecisive. It is rather that he is not sure he is right. Not absolutely sure.

[2] The American Broadcasting Company discontinued the program after May 26, 1963. New York *Times*, May 7, 1963.

[3] The Gallup Poll, January 7, 1963, reported that of those interviewed about Stevenson as ambassador to the UN, 64 per cent approved, 11 per cent disapproved, 25 per cent had no opinion. Arthur Schlesinger, Jr., sent this poll to President Kennedy on January 10, 1963. Schlesinger papers, John F. Kennedy Library.

That is to me a warmly human quality — a quality I much admire." [4]
The first of Stevenson's papers to start the year 1963 is an undated handwritten note to Marietta Tree.

To Mrs. Ronald Tree [5]

"Only — but it is rare —
When a beloved hand is laid in ours,
When, jaded with the rush & glare
Of the interminable hours,
Our eyes can in another's eyes read clear;
When our world-deafened ear
Is by the tones of a loved voice caressed,
A bolt is shot back somewhere in our breast
And a lost pulse of feeling stirs again:
The eye sinks inward and the heart lies plain,
And what we mean, we say, and what we would,
we know."

S F and Matthew Arnold

Most of one's life it is impossible to say what is really true! And then —
but it is rare — the pulse of feeling stirs again — the heart lies plain —
and what we mean we say, and what we would we know!

To Valerian A. Zorin

January 2, 1963

Dear Ambassador Zorin:

The news of your impending departure reached me in Chicago, and I deeply regret that I have not had an opportunity to call upon you and Madame Zorin to bid you farewell.

Our service here together for the past two years has given me a warm respect for your powers of advocacy and presentation, and great admiration for your tireless representation of your country both in the United Nations and in all of the related activities.

I trust that your health will be good and that the new work which your Government doubtless has in mind for you will be satisfying. That you will do it with the same diligence and skill, I have no doubt.

[4] San Francisco *Chronicle*, January 17, 1963. Harlan Cleveland wrote: "In my observation, AES was decisive about matters of national and international policy; and indecisive only in matters touching his own person, and his own personal future." Memorandum to Walter Johnson, April 30, 1973.
[5] This handwritten letter is in the possession of Mrs. Tree.

With kindest regards to you and Madame Zorin, and my distress that my few hours in New York did not afford me an opportunity to call upon you, I am

Cordially yours,

To Dr. C. W. Mayo [6]

January 2, 1963

Dear Chuck:

Your letter was most kind and most welcome, and I am very grateful. The Saturday Evening Post article irritated me, not so much because of another attack based on falsehoods from a familiar quarter — the Alsops — but because of the impression it created, especially abroad, that for some mysterious reason risking nuclear war was noble and American, and peaceful settlement, through means we had created, un-American and ignoble.

I am grateful to you and Alice [7] for the additional names for the Foundation [8] and am sending them along to Mr. Bookbinder [9] to bring up when additions are considered again.

It is a joy to me to find us after all these years joined in a common interest. But I wish I could see how I can manage it with all there is on my plate these days.

All the best —

To Mr. and Mrs. Walter Lippmann [10]

January 2, 1963

Dear Walter and Helen:

I returned from Illinois to find my refrigerator loaded with splendid cheeses! Thank you, my dear friends, for satisfying so generously an irresistible appetite — if not the doctor's orders!

I am afraid I will miss you on this trip to New York since I am going out of town again today and returning to Washington Monday next. I will try to reach you by phone there, and call on you Monday afternoon if you are free.

With so many thanks — affectionate regards — and best wishes for the New Year!

Yours,

[6] Of the Mayo Clinic, Rochester, Minnesota.

[7] Mrs. Mayo.

[8] Stevenson was chairman of the Eleanor Roosevelt Memorial Foundation, which was in the process of being organized.

[9] Hyman H. Bookbinder, who became director of the Eleanor Roosevelt Memorial Foundation.

[10] Mr. Lippmann, columnist and author of numerous books on political subjects, and his wife had been friends of Stevenson's for years.

On January 6, 1963, Carl Sandburg's publishers, Harcourt, Brace and World, celebrated the poet's eighty-fifth birthday with a dinner party at the Waldorf-Astoria Hotel. John Steinbeck and William O. Douglas, Associate Justice of the Supreme Court, were among the speakers. Stevenson, unable to be present at his old friend's celebration, sent the following statement.

CARL SANDBURG, YES [11]

Traditionally, Americans count their blessings on Thanksgiving day. But I have the temerity to suggest to this distinguished gathering that January 6th is not only an occasion for celebrating our dear friend's birthday, but an appropriate date on which to celebrate the many blessings that are Carl Sandburg.

How do we love him? Let me attempt to count the ways.

— As the poet who has heard the heartland of America singing — and made the rest of us listen, and recognize the magnificent melody all but drowned out by the raucous din of our continual "building, breaking, re-building."

— As the spinner of the delightful "Rootabaga Stories," which for forty years have enchanted our youngsters, and those fortunate parents who have managed to retain a sense of humor in spite of the toll taken by growing up.

— As the generous custodian of American folksongs, whose guitar and songbag have given us rich cause for pride in our heritage (I suppose, since it's Carl's birthday, we mustn't blame the Greenwich Village variants on *him*.)

— As the matchless scholar and historian whose biography of Lincoln towers, like the man himself, over all the rest.

— As seer, sage, philosopher, whose wisdom — and wit — have inspired and sustained us all at many a difficult moment. Is there a better motto for Americans than Carl's reminder that "Nothing happens unless first a dream?"

— As raconteur extraordinary, convivial companion, ageless and beloved friend.

Since I have unblushingly borrowed phrases from Carl Sandburg since my entry into public speaking (Aside to any worried publisher present: with due credit, of course.), I have no compunction about ending *this* message with words of his which, as with so many other topics, seem to me a far better description of the subject under discussion than I could write myself:

[11] The text is from a carbon copy.

"Under his wrist is the pulse, and under his ribs the heart of the people."

To Carl I send my warmest birthday greetings. It is to the other celebrants that I send my congratulations, for it is *our* good fortune to have been given the opportunity of sharing in tonight's festivities. And if, at some time during the evening, the guest of honor should let you in on the secret of his enviable shock of hair, I would be grateful if one of you would take pity and forward the magic word to this reluctantly absent guest.

To U Thant

January 7, 1963

Dear Mr. Secretary General:

On behalf of the Governments of the United States of America and the Soviet Union we desire to express to you our appreciation for your efforts in assisting our Governments to avert the serious threat to the peace which recently arose in the Caribbean area.

While it has not been possible for our Governments to resolve all the problems that have arisen in connection with this affair, they believe that, in view of the degree of understanding reached between them on the settlement of the crisis and the extent of progress in the implementation of this understanding, it is not necessary for this item to occupy further the attention of the Security Council at this time.

The Governments of the United States of America and of the Soviet Union express the hope that the actions taken to avert the threat of war in connection with this crisis will lead toward the adjustment of other differences between them and the general easing of tensions that could cause a further threat of war.

Sincerely yours,[12]

To Lady Barbara Jackson

January 12, 1963

Dearest Barbara:

Your note of January 7 has just come. I also have a recent, long, delicious letter from you which I have read once or twice and will consume again and again.

The Belafonte[13] record came in due season and was played in Libertyville during my brief stay there at Christmas. I am mortified that I have not thanked you sooner. Indeed, I am mortified about a myriad of things and people due to my hopeless incapacity to deal with Christmas this

---

[12] This letter was signed by both Stevenson and Kuznetsov.
[13] Harry Belafonte, popular singer and actor.

year. The presents have not been acknowledged, the Christmas cards are far behind — and the New Year is advancing! I thought I had mentioned the record in another letter, but evidently I did not and I hereby apologize with gratitude to you for this wonderful addition to my musical library and education. And, by the way, does it impress you to know that I have been to two Rubenstein [Rubinstein] and two Symphony concerts this winter — and I'm going to another next week! Moreover, that's about all I have done after dark, save for the everlasting parties — some good and some dreary. Can it be that the stimulating change of scene that the UN brought me is diminishing?

As for the speech at Notre Dame [University] on February 18, I am enclosing a letter from Father [Theodore] Hesburgh which is literally all I know about it. I am also enclosing a speech on "Patriotism" which I made at the American Legion Convention in 1952,[14] as of remote if any interest.

I really don't know what I should do. Do you think to anatomize patriotism in contemporary terms would be misunderstood and only provoke the usual suspicions, or is there something to say about the relationship of education to real patriotism? . . . Can there be real patriotism without criticism and the preservation of the right to criticize without misconstruction and abuse in a free society, etc., etc.? I wish I could give you some better guidelines but I haven't really thought about the thing at all or what would be useful and expedient in terms of my present posture which, by the way, seems to have been little damaged by the efforts of Messrs. Alsop and Bartlett; the latter, by the way, I suspect, for your information only, got most of their untruths from jingoists at CIA who, as you can imagine, were for immediate and all-out military action to erase, among other things, the memory of the Bay of Pigs.

I shall find time, God willing, to write further soon. I was distressed that I had only a brief telephone conversation with Robert [Jackson] enroute to an airplane, but he has promised to stay with me when he returns and I shall bear in mind your anxieties about overwork and too much travel. He sounded keen about his work and in good spirits, but seeing him would have been more revealing.

There is so much to report, and to inquire about, that, again — I give up in hopeless despair!

Love,

Stevenson was beginning to donate some of his papers to various institutions, and he hired Ralph Newman, of the Abraham Lincoln Book Shop in Chicago, to appraise them for purposes of income tax deductions.

14 See *Major Campaign Speeches of Adlai E. Stevenson, 1952,* with an introduction by the author (New York: Random House, 1953), pp. 17–22.

To Ralph G. Newman

January 15, 1963

Dear Ralph:

I made a speech to North Carolina State College sometime last year and presented the original typescript with my notations to the North Carolina State College Library.[15] A copy of the speech is enclosed.

Last spring I made a speech about Robert Frost at a dinner for him in Washington, and the Library of Congress and Dartmouth College both asked me to present the original to them. I haven't checked the files, but I believe I sent it to you and asked for your advice and also for an evaluation. Miss Eberlein tells me that we have not heard from you about this yet. I enclose a copy to refresh your recollection.

You will recall the speech last fall on the Emancipation Proclamation, which I subsequently presented to the Library of Congress at its request.

In anticipation of the appalling difficulties I seem to have each year with my income tax return, I would like to have as promptly as possible your evaluation — if any! — on these gifts and also some information for my file as to what disposition you have made of the document about Robert Frost.

Also, would you let me know for my file when I can expect the evaluation of the material sent to Springfield, for my 1961 and 1962 income tax records?[16] It is probable that I will leave the country long before the April 15 income tax filing date and will, therefore, have to get my return in around the first of March, which means that I will have to get started pulling the threads together long before. And this is one of the more important threads!

After consultation with several people, I have begun to wonder if I would not be making a mistake in giving my post-Governor papers to Princeton [University] instead of keeping them all together at the State Historical Library in Springfield.[17] I appreciate that there will be a substantial tax benefit loss by giving them to Springfield, but perhaps it is offset by accessibility to any future researchers, and also to myself if I would ever want to do any work among them in my old age in — I hope — Illinois.

So I must ask you if you have any thoughts on this subject, although that decision can wait until later in the year.

Sorry to burden you, but I am most anxious to get my affairs in shape.

Cordially yours,

[15] Stevenson was not always so considerate of the future editor of his papers. He sometimes gave away the reading copies of his speeches, containing his last-minute corrections, and left no record of their whereabouts.
[16] Stevenson deposited his papers from the period of his governorship of Illinois in the Illinois State Historical Library.
[17] He gave these papers to Princeton University.

To Lady Barbara Jackson

January 17, 1963

Dearest Barbara:

I have just reread your letter of January 3rd. And "Why not the unity of mankind?" I think it is a fine idea for a Notre Dame effort and, as you say, perhaps something trenchant can be said about one of the day's cliches.

The Congo is finally — thank God! — reaching the conclusion of the secession phase,[18] and now the hard, trying business of real nation-building must commence. I hope the UN can disengage somewhat and not have to suffer the abuse of the past two years from all the faint hearts and doomsdayers.

The work here continues to mount with or without a General Assembly and I sometimes despair of ever getting on top of it all and finding a moment for rest and reflection. Also it now seems not unlikely that I will finally have to do some chores in Europe toward the end of March and early April, but I shall make a gallant effort to be back in time for the Easter reunion, if not before. But more of this as my plans jell.

I am distressed that I have not been able to give you more information on Robert [Jackson] and his state of mind and health but I hope to have a talk with Paul Hoffman about him soon. If I hear anything of interest you may be sure that I will pass it on promptly.

Much love,

P.S. Did you receive a modest Christmas offering?

To Mr. and Mrs. Hermon D. Smith [19]

January 17, 1963

Dear Dutch and Ellen:

On Friday evening, February 8th, I propose to have a birthday party — cocktails-buffet — from 6 pm on — and on.

I am asking only the old hawks, the veteran hard line celebrants of this annual occasion from Illinois, and a few local doves. Please come! And please let Roxane Eberlein know at your convenience at YU 6–2424.

Oh, to be 60 again!

Ever,
ADLAI

---

[18] Between December 28, 1962, and January 21, 1963, the UN Force in the Congo ended the secession of Katanga. On June 14, 1963, Moise Tshombe left the country for self-imposed exile.
[19] The original is in the possession of Mr. Smith.

To Mrs. Eugene Meyer [20]

January 18, 1963

Dear Agnes:

I think Mr. [Hyman] Bookbinder has notified you that we have decided to defer the next formal meeting of the Board of Trustees of the Eleanor Roosevelt Foundation until the bill has passed Congress and we can have a signing ceremony, followed by a meeting in Washington.

I may have some difficulty in getting to Washington on Saturday, February 9, for your party for Dobrynin.[21] I wish it could be the next week. However, I will make every effort. I have no clue as to whether you should or should not invite McGeorge Bundy. Certainly, I have no personal objection to it.

I think Dobrynin's top-level contacts in Washington have been largely with Llewelyn Thompson [22] and Chester Bowles and, as you know, I have seen him somewhat, and have promised to lunch with him when I am in Washington next.

I'm afraid August is a little late for me for the yacht. But again I might be able to come for a week before I have to get back. My work in Geneva [Switzerland] usually concludes around the 15th to 20th of July. If I can come, even for a short while, could I bring along my son Adlai and his wife, Nancy? Or is the ship already full?

I wish I saw you more often!

Much love,
ADLAI

To Mrs. Hugh Gaitskell

January 18, 1963

My dear Dora:

The news has come only this very minute,[23] and I send you this hasty note of heartfelt sympathy. I have known few men whose friendship I valued more highly and whose companionship I enjoyed as much. Unhappily, it was all too infrequent, and now there can be no more.

I know how brave you are and how good and gallant those dear girls will be. All the same, I wish I could be there to pay you and them a visit

[20] The original is in the Agnes Meyer files, Princeton University Library.

[21] Anatoly F. Dobrynin, Soviet ambassador to the United States.

[22] Llewellyn Thompson, Foreign Service officer and former ambassador to the Soviet Union (1957–1962).

[23] Her husband, the leader of the Labour Party in Great Britain, had just died. For Stevenson's public statement, see USUN press release 4142.

and, if I could, give you some inkling of the respect in which Hugh was
held by so many in this country, and by none more than

Your sorrowing and devoted friend,

*Stevenson gave an address at the tenth anniversary convocation of the
Center for the Study of Democratic Institutions, held in New York City
on January 22, 1963.*[24]

When Bob Hutchins lured me here to speak at this meeting, he said,
with customary modesty, that it would surpass in importance the Constitutional Convention. I thought he might be exaggerating a bit, but,
looking around this room, I'm not so sure.

I understand all these famous and wise men, foreign and domestic,
have been dissecting democracy morning, afternoon and evening for two
days. I wonder if the time hasn't come to leave the poor thing alone to
recuperate!

And my discomfort isn't relieved by the subject Dr. Hutchins has
assigned to me: "The prospects for Democracy around the world"!

Have you no little questions, Dr. Hutchins? For I am neither prophet
nor philosopher, but an ex-politician and a practicing diplomat, although
many would doubtless dissent from both of these claims.

But if my qualifications for speaking to this exalted company are
dubious, let me say that when it comes to faith in democracy, I refuse to
take a back seat even for my distinguished predecessors on this platform.
Because I believe in democracy and freedom, and I believe in their
ultimate triumph with the fundamentalist fervor of a survivor of Valley
Forge or a Presidential campaign — not to mention two! As Macauley
[Macaulay] said of Lord Brougham, or vice versa, "I wish I was as sure
of anything as he is of everything." Well the one thing I'm sure of is that
constitutional democracy is that form of government, as Bob Hutchins
says, which best fulfills the nature of man. Moreover, my faith, I remind you, has survived some rather disillusioning experiences.

And that's why I'm glad to be here among people of like convictions
who are trying so hard to make freedom and democracy working realities.
And that's why I toil in the tangled vineyards of the United Nations,
where the leaders of the whole world are trying to practice parliamentary
democracy on a global scale.

Bernard Shaw said that democracy was a device that insures we shall

24 USUN press release 4145. This speech is reprinted in Adlai E. Stevenson,
Looking Outward: Years of Crisis at the United Nations, edited with commentary
by Robert L. Schiffer and Selma Schiffer, preface by John F. Kennedy (New York:
Harper & Row, 1963), pp. 249–259.

be governed no better than we deserve. The Center for the Study of Democratic Institutions, as I understand it, can be thought of, then, as a kind of national insurance plan — a way of making certain that we will deserve better and better.

For years Robert Hutchins talked about the need for a democratic version of the Platonic Academy, to deal with new questions of freedom and justice as they emerged on the changing horizon of our times. Finally, with the establishment of the Center, his dream came true.

Now, I gather from a few delicate hints that the time has come to think about an endowment policy for this insurance plan—and I am pleased to lend my endorsement to what the Center has already done and promises to do in the years ahead. For busy, battered bureaucrat though I be, I am a staunch believer in the leisure of the theory class.

Ten years ago last July, as Governor of Illinois, I welcomed the Democratic National Convention to Chicago. And I hope you will forgive me for resurrecting some of my words, because I think, Mr. Hutchins, they have some relevance to the work of your Center.

"This is not the time for superficial solutions and everlasting elocution," I said in 1952, "nor for frantic boast and foolish word . . . Self-criticism is the secret weapon of democracy . . . We dare not just look back on great yesterdays. We must look forward to great tomorrows. What counts now is not just what we are *against,* but what we are *for. Who* leads us is less important than *what* leads us — what convictions, what courage, what faith." [25]

I should like to think that these words apply to the Center for the Study of Democratic Institutions and the work that goes on there. For we have all learned that modern technology can strengthen the despot's hand and the dictator's grasp — and for that reason, if no other, we know that democracy is more necessary now than it ever was.

Of course, democracy is not self-executing. We have to make it work, and to make it work we have to understand it. Sober thought and fearless criticism are impossible without critical thinkers and thinking critics. Such persons must be given the opportunity to come together, to see new facts in the light of old principles, to evaluate old principles in the light of new facts, and by deliberation, debate and dialogue to hammer out the consensus that makes democracy possible. And this, as we all know well, though some of us forget from time to time, requires intellectual independence, impenitent speculation, and freedom from political pressure. In a word, it requires centers of the kind found on Eucalyptus Hill in Santa Barbara [California]. And centers need money.

I hope you will provide the money to make it possible for this Center

---

[25] See *The Papers of Adlai E. Stevenson,* Vol. IV, p. 13.

to go on. And I hope the day may come when such centers are multiplied the world over. For democracy's need for wisdom will remain as perennial as its need for liberty. Not only external vigilance but unending self-examination must be the perennial price of liberty, because the work of self-government never ceases. The work of an institution like this Center in Santa Barbara is similar to the work of the church in this regard — it will be required as long as final salvation eludes us, which will be until the end of time.

The study of democratic institutions — how to create them, how to sustain them — how to preserve them — will be necessary as long as men continue to seek faith in themselves, continue to harbor hope in their own capacity to progress, and cherish the charity that unites them in a common cause.

And with a world undergoing such rapid change in geography, politics and economics, the need to adapt our old and venerated institutions to the changes is urgent.

Ten years ago, Robert Oppenheimer [26] said: "In an important sense, this world of ours is a new world, in which the unity of knowledge, the nature of human communities, the order of society, the order of ideas, the very notions of society and culture have changed, and will not return to what they have been in the past. . . . The world alters as we walk in it, so that the years of man's life measure not some small growth or re-arrangement or moderation of what he learned in childhood, but a great upheaval."

I suppose whether democracy can prevail in the great upheaval of our time is a valid question. Certainly, after 150 years of uninterrupted expansion of the idea of government by consent of the governed, it has recently met with mounting and formidable challenges all over the world from Fascist, Nazi, Communist authoritarians, and a variety of dictatorships. And we have good reason to know how clumsy, slow, inefficient and costly it is compared to the celerity, certainty, and secrecy of absolutism.

But the important thing is that it *has* survived. The important thing is that even the absolutists masquerade as democrats; even the military and quasi-military dictatorships strive in the name of democracy to manage the public business. And all of them say that authoritarianism is only a necessary transition to democracy.

Why? Because it is the most popular form of government yet devised; because it is, as it always has been, not only the prize of the steadfast and the courageous, but the privilege of those who are better off; because, in

[26] Atomic physicist and former chairman of the general advisory committee of the Atomic Energy Commission. See Philip Stern, *The Oppenheimer Case: Security on Trial* (New York: Harper & Row, 1970).

short, as Jefferson said, it is "the only form of government which is not eternally at open or secret war with the rights of the people."

I have, therefore, no doubt that, distant as it may be for many people, it will ultimately prevail, that it will rewin lost ground, that it will expand its dominion — that it can withstand the wild winds that are blowing through the world — if, and I repeat if, we who are its custodians continually re-examine and adapt its principles to the changing needs of our changing times.

Years ago, Reinhold Niebuhr [27] observed that "man's capacity for justice makes democracy possible; but man's inclination to injustice makes democracy necessary."

And I suppose that most of us, if we were asked to name the most profound issues at stake in the world today, would say the issues of freedom and democracy. We would say that the Western world, for all its errors and shortcomings, has for centuries tried to evolve a society in which the individual has enough legal, social and political elbow room to be not the puppet of the community, but his own autonomous self.

And we would say that the enemies of freedom, whatever the magnificent ends they propose — the brotherhood of man, the kingdom of saints, "from each according to his ability, to each according to his needs" — miss just this essential point: that man is greater than the social purposes to which he can be put. He must not be kicked about even with the most high-minded objectives. He is not a means or an instrument. He is an end in himself.

This, I take it, is the essence of what we mean by democracy — not so much voting systems or parliamentary systems or economic or legal systems (though they all enter in), as an irrevocable and final dedication to the dignity of man.

In this sense, democracy is perhaps mankind's most audacious experiment. This dignity and equality of the human person could hardly be further removed from the existential facts of human existence. There is precious little dignity or equality in our natural state.

Most human beings have to spend their lives in utter vulnerability. All are murderable and torturable, and survive only through the restraint shown by more powerful neighbors. All are born unequal, in terms of capacity or strength. All are born to the inherent frailty of the human condition, naked and helpless, vulnerable all through life to the will of others, limited by ignorance, limited by physical weakness, limited by fear, limited by the phobias that fear engenders. It is not surprising that, given this basic defencelessness, the natural condition of man has not been far removed from Hobbes's definition of it as "nasty, brutish and short."

[27] Professor of applied Christianity at Union Theological Seminary.

For nearly 3,000 years now, the political and social genius of what we can permissibly call "Western man" has struggled with these brute facts of our unsatisfactory existence. Ever since the Hebrews discovered personal moral responsibility and the Greeks discovered the autonomy of the citizen, the effort has been made — with setbacks and defeats, with dark ages and interregnums and any number of irrelevant adventures on the side — to create a social order in which weak, fallible, obstinate, silly, magnificent man can maintain his dignity and exercise his free and responsible choice.

The task has never been easy. Each step has been a groping in the dark — the dark of violence and brute power and overweening arrogance. Yet we have learned some of the preconditions and expedients of freedom. And we have incorporated them in societies and institutions. What we seek to defend today against new critics and new adversaries is essentially a great body of *experience* — not theories or untried ideals, but a solid mass of lived-through facts. First in time came the great medieval discovery that the king must be subject to the law.

Equality before the law has been expanded and safeguarded by consultation and representation — in other words, the vote. This is not simply a device for peacefully changing government — although it is that, too. It is not only a means of allowing the wearer to say where the shoe pinches. It is, in addition, a means of offsetting the natural inequalities which grow up in any society, however organized, as a result of the unequal endowment of people.

The head of, say, General Electric, has more means of influencing society than a small town electrician. Against the advantages of brains and money, the vote is the only advantage the small man has. His voice, or vote, added to millions of other voices, offsets the accumulated power of society's entrenched positions.

But equality before the law and at the ballot box are only strands in the seamless robe in which all our liberties are woven together. Carelessly unravel one — and the robe itself may come apart.

Another is enough social and economic opportunity for each man — even the poorest — to hold his dignity intact. The widest access to education and training, equal opportunity for talent to find its niche, security of income and work, the chance of health — all these belong to a social order of responsible and respected citizens. We no longer define democracy solely in political terms. The great effort of this century has been to work out its economic and social implications.

If we take these three main strands of democracy — equality before the law, constitutional, representative government, and social and economic opportunity — it is clear that they face — as evolving free society has always faced — new challenges in our own day. It is profoundly concerned with the extension of the concept of democracy — extension in depth, for we now believe that no human being, however lowly his occupation or poor his resources, can be excluded from the dignity of man — extension in space, for the whole world is now a community and we have to find ways in which the idea of a truly human society can be realized on a planetary scale. The two processes, going forward simultaneously in every part of the globe, make up the vast revolutionary ferment of our day.

What we have to attempt today is the building of intercontinental forms of free community — certainly the most testing experiment of all those made so far by free men. Yet our past achievements give us the right to hope for future success.

One form of association already exists between virtually all the nations of this globe and, whatever work we may accomplish on a regional basis, progress at the United Nations in the direction of a free society of equals must be part of our effort to extend the principle of liberty as the essential working principle of mankind.

How are we to set about this task? There is one method which, I most profoundly hope, we shall avoid — and that is the method of self-righteous exhortation. We have, I fear, sometimes displayed an unattractive tendency to lecture new governments on their constitutional shortcomings and to point, sometimes openly, sometimes implicitly, to the superior performance of the West.

We can admit that free government *is* a Western invention — by all odds, its finest political achievement. But there are several things we must remember as well. We must remember that it took about eight centuries to develop these patterns of life in our own culture. We must remember that our form of democracy is the most subtle and sophisticated form of government in the world; other more primitive, still developing peoples cannot be expected to master it overnight. But move towards it they will; and such institutions as the United Nations help to train their leadership in our ways. Moreover, new states always face appalling problems of readjustment and we must be smart enough to recognize when and how these alien leaderships move our way.

If now we see in Africa single party rule dominated by one leader, with changing policies and political choice severely restricted, we should not hold up our hands in horror but remember that this is not far from our politics of two centuries ago. We might even have the modesty to admit that in Northern Ireland and the American South, for example, we, too, practice single party government.

Where we have every right to express our alarm is in the breakdown of constitutional protection by the law. The danger lies not so much in parliamentary failure as in judicial failure. Yet even here our alarm should be expressed in modest terms. In 18th century England, a man could be hanged for stealing a sheep, and horrible ships took convicts to Australia for no more than petty larceny. Nor was Europe's recent Fascism precisely a law-abiding mode of government.

No — the way ahead does not lie through sermonizing carried on by people whose own eyes are too full of beams to judge clearly the others' motes. It lies rather in a sustained effort to work out, within the United Nations and in partnerships with other nations, the chief lines of advance towards a more coherent and viable world community, with freedom as its working principle and constitutionalism as its political habit. No one is likely to underestimate the appalling complexities of the task. But the outlook must have seemed as daunting to the lawyers struggling against Stuart despotism or the Founding Fathers attempting to turn federalism into a workable system.

The task is indeed "piled high with difficulty." We should attempt it, therefore, with all the more vigor and clarity and I would suggest that the three criteria I stressed in domestic democracy are relevant, too, to the global democracy we painfully must try to build.

Today, the first of all tasks is to restrain the nation-state from taking law into its own hands — in other words, from using force to assert its will — or, in the final word, from making war.

From domestic society, we know the only way to banish lawless violence and fratricidal strife is by accepting rules of peaceful change and adjustment, and building an impartial police force to enforce the peaceful solutions that are agreed. This I take to be a task of the United Nations. However, no world body can yet take on the tasks of global peace. Some of our vast modern states are still, like the medieval barons, too powerful to be controlled in their feudal fastnesses.

But perhaps we have reached a first stage of restraint on arbitrary power. Troubled areas — Palestine, the Congo, Laos — are policed not by rivals whose rivalry would lead to war, but by an external and impartial third force.

Could we not extend the principle? Could we not aim at the policing by the United Nations of more and more areas in which the rival interests of powerful states threaten to clash? Global systems of restraint may still evade us. But history suggests we can start from the particular instance and then extend the principle — and every area withdrawn from the naked arbitrament of force is an area saved for the constitutional working of a sane human society.

Does the second principle I have picked out — the procedure of equal voting — apply to the building of a free world society? The critics say the new states, holding the balance of power by means of their combined vote, drive the United Nations on towards ferocious extremes of anti-colonialism and attempt to impose other imprudent policies on the Great Powers which must disrupt the whole organization. Meanwhile, the great foot the bill.

There is much to be said on this score. For the moment, let me only say that in world society, the small nation — like the small man in domestic society — is most likely to be vulnerable. His equal voice, his capacity to unite it with other small voices, is a measure of protection against his inequality. We see the need for this countervailing power inside our states. So let us not be too quick to denounce it in the world at large.

There is a further reason for being cautious and patient about the workings inside the United Nations of the potential ex-colonial majority. If we turn to the third principle of democracy — equality of esteem, equal dignity, equal access to the social and economic possibilities of society — we find that the disproportions which distort true community inside our states are present in world society, too. This Afro-Asian bloc — a misnomer, for, save on the colonial issue, there is no bloc — represents most of the world's most truly underprivileged peoples. If they cling to their U.N. status, it is because, as citizens of our planet, they have not yet much else to cling to. Pushed to the first outskirts of modernity by Western investment and trade, emancipated before they had received either the training or the powers of wealth creation needed for a modern society, they are caught between two worlds — the powerful, affluent, expanding world of the developed "North," and the traditional, pre-technological, largely poor world of the underdeveloped "South."

This division in world society is a great obstacle to the expansion of the confidence and community the world needs for a truly human society. And it threatens to become worse if such experiments as the European Common Market or the Atlantic community prove to be, vis-a-vis the less fortunate parts of the world, a rich man's club, exclusive in its commerce, its investments, its arrangements and its interests. The gap exists. We must not make it worse.

What can we do? I would like to suggest that we, the wealthiest, most fortunate of all the developed states of the "North," have two lines to follow, both of them essential if we in this generation are to make our full contribution to the advance of world democracy.

I know there is much dissatisfaction about aid, much feeling that it is wasted and never achieves a "breakthrough," and dribbles away down thousands of unspecified drains and ratholes. Yet just so did the Victorians talk about tax money devoted to lifting the standards of the very poor in early industrial society. There were the "good poor" who said "please" and "thank you" and touched their forelocks. Then there were the "bad poor" who kept coal in the bath tub. But over a couple of generations, it was the raising of all this unfortunate mass of humanity that turned Western society into the first social order in history in which everyone could expect something of an equal chance.

After ten years, we are only at the beginning of the experiment of international aid. We are learning greatly. We see the relevance of some policies, the supreme obstacles offered by others. We discriminate more. We are learning to be better givers.

Our second task is harder. It is harder for us than for any other member of the world's wealthy elite. It is to see that the last vestiges of discrimination inside our own society are speedily abolished. It is no use talking of ourselves as the vanguard of freedom and democracy while any of our fellow Americans can be treated like a James Meredith at the University of Mississippi.[28]

Must we not, as lovers of freedom and as—too often—self-styled prophets of the free way of life, sometimes lapse into a shamed silence when we even have to talk about social injustice, let alone deal with it — 100 years after the Emancipation Proclamation?

I must end as I began. The essence of democracy is the dignity of man. We shall create a free world order on no other basis. If we attack Communism — as we must — for its contempt for political dignity, we must attack as unrelentingly lapses in social dignity.

It sometimes seems to me today as though running through all the great issues of the day — the anti-colonial revulsion, the political contest with Communism, the unification of Europe, the clamor of poorer lands for advance — there runs the underlying desire for some lasting realization of the dignity of man — man with a measure of political autonomy, man with

---

[28] James Meredith by order of the federal courts was admitted to the University of Mississippi. Governor Ross Barnett denounced the order and declared that he would impose state sovereignty in the matter. On September 20, 1962, Governor Barnett flew to Oxford, Mississippi, to block Meredith's enrollment. Meredith, flanked by federal marshals, walked past jeering people to try to register. Barnett refused to accept his credentials. The Justice Department went back to court again. On September 24, the federal circuit court ordered all employees of the university to enroll Meredith and enjoined the governor from interfering. Nevertheless, on September 25, Barnett personally blocked Meredith again by refusing to let him in the door. The circuit court ordered Barnett to appear on September 28 to show cause why he should not be held in civil contempt. At midnight September 29, the White House ordered the Mississippi National Guard into federal service, sent federal troops to Memphis, and ordered all people to cease and desist. President Kennedy appealed on television for compliance, but when Meredith arrived on campus September 30 the marshals had to defend themselves with tear gas against the rioting crowds. Federal troops were called in only after fifteen hours of tumult, with two dead and hundreds injured. Meredith remained at the university under the protection of federal marshals until he graduated the next year. See Richard Bardolph, ed., *The Civil Rights Record: Black Americans and the Law, 1849–1970* (New York: Thomas Y. Crowell, 1970), pp. 478–485.

the economic elbow room to live above the torturing doubts of food and work, man with the dignity to look his neighbor in the face and see a friend.

Isolate the problems, measure their magnitude, measure our progress in dealing with them — and you have my answer to Dr. Hutchins' little question — "The prospects for democracy around the world."

And this, I take it, is what the Center for the Study of Democratic Institutions is all about — the steady effort to discover the common good in democratic fashion, by assembling together persons from varied backgrounds, with diverse specialities and competences for discussion and debate.

The Center may be a pioneering effort, but its roots are sunk deep in the Academy of ancient Greece, the medieval university, the New England Town Meetings, and a long list of later devices to make democracy work. Getting good men to think together, though not to think alike; bringing the cumulative wisdom of such persons to bear on present and emerging problems; and, through publications, broadcasts, and meetings like the one just finished, widening the circles of discussion and debate.

I think this unique institution merits your generous support. And let me repeat that I hope this is only the first of the chain of centers for the study of democratic institutions that will some day girdle the globe. For freedom rings every time opinions anywhere are allowed to clash — and we shall not be content until freedom rings all over the world.

In these remarks I have quoted some moderns. I should like to close with a few words from an ancient. Plutarch wrote: "Only those persons who live in obedience to reason are worthy to be accounted free. Only they live as they will who have learned what they ought to will."

If you have no engraving over your door in Santa Barbara, Mr. Hutchins, that quotation might not be half bad.

To Robert Benjamin [29]

January 30, 1963

Dear Bob:

You will recall that at our meeting on January 25th, it was suggested that I write to all trustees about their own contributions to the Eleanor Roosevelt Foundation.

Very shortly, perhaps at a bill-signing ceremony at the White House, the official campaign for funds will be launched. It would be most helpful if we could announce that the trustees have already pledged an initial sum of large proportions. The figure of a million dollars was suggested as a minimum for such announcement — not including labor gifts.

[29] The original is in the possession of Mr. Benjamin.

Could I ask you to try to determine as quickly as possible what your own contribution will be and advise me? Although we are engaged in a "one-shot" drive, your contribution can be phased out over a number of years, perhaps up to five. Please let me also know whether there are any restrictions on disclosing the amount of your contribution.

With much appreciation for your dedication to this effort, I am

Sincerely yours,

Secretary-General U Thant was asked at his press conference on January 29, 1963, to comment on Stevenson, about whose imminent resignation there were strong rumors. U Thant said: "In my experience of public men, I have very rarely come across a statesman of Ambassador Stevenson's stature, with mellow wisdom, perceptive thinking and balanced judgment. . . ."

To U Thant

January 31, 1963

My dear Friend:

How can I thank you for your charitable and flattering words at your press conference yesterday!

This, at best, can only be an inadequate expression of my gratitude for your confidence and good will.

Cordially,

On January 31, 1963, Arthur M. Schlesinger, Jr., requested that the following analysis by Stevenson of his position with regard to Cuba during the missile crisis be filed with the minutes of the Executive Committee.

To Arthur M. Schlesinger, Jr.[30]

[no date]

I have at long last reviewed the entire file on the Cuban crisis in view of Alsop's most recent article.[31]

[30] This document was declassified. ExComm Meetings subseries, National Security Council series, National Security Files, Papers of President Kennedy, John F. Kennedy Library.

[31] Stewart Alsop and Charles Bartlett, "The White House in the Cuban Crisis," *Saturday Evening Post*, December 8, 1962. For a discussion of this article and its repercussions, see pp. 348–352, above.

I can summarize the import of my oral comments and written memoranda as follows:

1. We should not launch an air strike or invasion until we had used the peacekeeping machinery of the OAS and the Security Council.
2. We should institute a blockade limited to weapons only, and not including POL [petroleum, oil, and lubricants]. The latter should be added if escalation of the blockade became desirable to increase the pressure. The blockade should not be made effective until after the OAS acted, with substantial support for our resolution from the Latin Americans.
3. We had an obligation under Article 51 of the Charter to take the issue to the United Nations Security Council, and we would also gain a political advantage by doing so ourselves before the USSR or some other country did so. But we should not proceed in the Security Council before announcing our blockade, because of the danger of political moves by someone else (USSR?) to prevent us from acting militarily. So we should do it concurrently with the President's announcement of the blockade.
4. In the President's speech and in the Security Council we should, in addition to the blockade and threat of attack to wipe out the missiles, suggest a political program which would (a) counter objections to our military action, (b) offer a realistic possibility of achieving our objectives without the risk of military escalation, and (c) exploit the tension prevailing to bring about a drastic favorable change in the Cuban political situation. (My hypothesis was that, as a result of the United States military steps and the Security Council hearings and the possible resolutions it might adopt, the USSR might relieve the immediate danger to peace by rendering the weapons inoperable, but not immediately remove them, let alone withdraw Soviet military personnel from Cuba. Moreover, if US–USSR negotiations followed, which seemed likely, whatever happened in the Security Council, we would have to be ready with a political program anyway.)
5. I suggested that the various components of a political negotiation might include:

a) "Neutralization," both military and political, of Cuba (into an entity like Austria) or at least "demilitarization," i.e., removal of *all* Soviet military forces and aid and possibly limitation on Cuban arms. Either of these objectives was seen as a way of ending in a reasonable period of time Communist domination of the Cuban Government.

b) United Nations observer teams in Cuba *at once* to insure against surprise attack against anyone and to serve as a long-range guarantee to us of Cuba's "neutralization" or "demilitarization."

c) Guaranty of territorial integrity and "political independence" of Cuba by American states.

d) A United States demand for total Soviet evacuation of Cuba would inevitably produce counter demands, and the achievement of such a major political change in Cuba would justify similar "demilitarization" by us of Guantanamo, the military utility of which was limited anyway.

e) Reaffirmation of our willingness to consider, after the immediate offensive weapons threat had been removed, elimination of all foreign missile bases in the context of the pending disarmament treaties. But we should reject the idea of bargaining on the withdrawal of missiles from Turkey and Italy in connection with Soviet missiles in Cuba because it would divert world attention from the danger to world peace of the Soviet move in Cuba, and would cause political repercussions in Turkey and Italy.

The above political objective was, of course, more far-reaching than merely dismantling and withdrawal of the missiles, as it included at a minimum total withdrawal of Soviet forces. Contrary to the Alsop-Bartlett assertions, we did not and never would have suggested trading Guantanamo for the limited objective of merely rendering the missiles inoperative.

When the President decided not to include *initially* any political program other than an offer of a US-Soviet meeting, I proposed that in the United Nations I call for both the dismantling and "withdrawal" of the missiles and offensive weapons *under United Nations supervision* (not just rendering them inoperable), and without making any political offer of our own to bring this about.

Note that Alsop's essential accusation is that I proposed to trade Guantanamo for "neutralization of the missiles" instead of "neutralization of Cuba." This is a totally different proposition from what I proposed.

At the meeting on Saturday, October 21,[32] when the President, as I recall, asked everyone's final position, I opposed air strike and invasion until the peacekeeping machinery of the OAS and UN had been used and proposed a political program along the above lines. When you came to New York on Monday, after the basic lines of policy had been decided, we also made some oral suggestions to you about the last draft of the speech which the President was to give that night, because we felt

32 The meeting took place on Saturday, October 20, 1962.

that it was not entirely clear that the missiles themselves were actually present in Cuba and that we were demanding their "withdrawal" and withdrawal of other offensive weapons, as well as the dismantling of the sites. Our letters to the President of the Security Council and the Secretary General demanding an immediate meeting of the Security Council, together with our draft resolution to submit to the Council, had already been prepared and provided for *"withdrawal"* of offensive weapons as well as dismantling of the sites.

To Mrs. Ronald Tree [33]

February 4, 1963

M —

Saturday afternoon to Greenwich [Connecticut] swooning with fatigue, trying to read the papers, the brief case and neither reading, retaining or falling asleep. . . .

[Sunday] Evening I dined with Ruth [Field] alone — and then at 9 to . . . fund raising for the Democratic Study Group [34] at the Savoy Hilton — (that lobby, elevator, hall, entrance — everything — does something to me) — hosted by Stephen Currier [35] and very badly attended. Hope [Home] by 11 to work — and of course promptly fell asleep.

Monday — Up, fresh, bright, brisk & well this morning to greet two gentlemen from Seville — our host or something at the Bull fight on our departure day (a thousand years ago) bringing me a painting of bull done in the blood of the bull killed that day & by the American bullfighter who killed him — Also album of photos taken in that muddy bull ring etc. The painting is good: I may give it too [to] you — something to remember me by & convenient — only 4 feet by 3.

Lunch with Kenneth Royall, big N[ew] Y[ork] lawyer, Truman's Sec[retary] Defense — Stevenson fan, determined I *must* be V[ice] P[resident] — no one else even remotely possible. Am slowly developing a new line — suggested by Ruth [Field] and good, I think. If I get a minute to put it on paper I'll submit it for Mrs [Jane] Dick's approval before using.

This afternoon very effective Pak[istan]. speech vs. India — 2½ hours — in S[ecurity]. C[ouncil]. Far better than Zafrulla's [36] last year. Then adjourned until Wed.

Queen Fredericka [Frederika] called Sunday afternoon to report she

---

[33] This handwritten letter is in the possession of Mrs. Tree. She was in Barbados when it was written.
[34] Of the House of Representatives.
[35] The philanthropist.
[36] Sir Muhammad Zafrullah Khan, foreign minister of Pakistan.

was called back to Greece, leaving at once. So my cocktail party cancelled. Dined with Mary Lasker, Chester [illegible] — . . . they to opera, me to 42A to see [Mr. and Mrs. Ernest L.] Ives — who are out. Now to sleep again — to dream — to lie awake — to wonder, wander, wonder —

A

Did I thank you properly for the birthday? Can I? But it will endure forever where precious things are kept.

To William McC. Blair, Jr.

February 8, 1963

Dear Bill:

I have your letter and will be here for the first part of your visit. If you want to stay with me in the apartment — of course I would be delighted. And so would Viola [Reardy]! But if you prefer those familiar quarters in the Savoy-Hilton, I will understand.

I have promised to speak at the NATO War College in Paris on March 25, which means I will have to leave here around the 23rd. After a few days there, I do have some travelling to do in Britain, Brussels, and possibly Holland and Germany. After that I had hoped to take a brief holiday before returning around Easter time.

From this schedule it looks as though I won't have much chance to see you and Deeda,[37] which is very distressing. But any reunion would be better than none. And you will have a very warm welcome in your native land which rings with applause for your performance.

Meanwhile, I am doing my best to see that you get a new post which will really be a challenge to your talents.[38] Yemen is a possibility. What do you think? There is also talk of Outer Mongolia. Rest assured that I am always looking after your interests.

With much love to Big Blair, Little Blair, and Beautiful Blair!

Yours,

To Bessie McReynolds Moore [39]

February 13, 1963

My dear Bessie:

If I were you I would have me stay after school and write on the blackboard 100 times (at least!): "I must learn to acknowledge gifts promptly." — and perhaps even a good pasting with a ruler might do me some good.

[37] Mrs. Blair.
[38] Mr. Blair was completing his assignment as ambassador to Denmark. He was appointed ambassador to the Philippines.
[39] One of Stevenson's teachers in Bloomington, Illinois.

Yes, my dear, I received your wonderful, wonderful "flower garden" which I treasure even more because each leaf and bud were put there with your own loving hands. How can I ever thank you? I only hope you will forgive me for taking so long to tell you all this.

I am having your gift sent to Illinois — because all my treasures are there — and when the day comes for me to return to them — a part of you will be there too.

Much love,

To Irving Kupcinet [40]

February 13, 1963

Dear Irv:

I was delighted to have your birthday greetings. With the 60's well advanced, I'm reminded of the story about Theodore F. Green's [41] 90th birthday and the lady who asked him how it felt to be 90. With a sour expression he said it felt fine — considering the alternative!

Yours,

ADLAI

To Mrs. Eugene Meyer [42]

February 20, 1963

Dearest Agnes:

This belated note is written on an airplane — where I seem to spend most of my time!

First, the dinner for Ambassador and Mrs. Dobrynin was a great success, and you and Kay [43] and darling Lally [44] were gallant as always. Your guests really had a good time and I thought Mme Dobrynin's performance was disarming and delightful.[45] It was a memorable evening for me and I pray not too painful for you.

Second, this will serve to introduce an old and esteemed friend of mine from New York who is now the Official Liaison Officer of the State Department's protocol office. She is a grand girl, enterprising and humorous. I suspect she wants to talk to you about THIS — the Hospitality and Information Service for Diplomatic Residents and Families in Washington. This is a huge problem for us in New York, and I wish I was sure

---

[40] Columnist for the Chicago *Sun-Times*. The original is in the possession of Mr. Kupcinet.

[41] Democratic senator from Rhode Island, 1937–1961.

[42] The original is in the Agnes Meyer files, Princeton University Library.

[43] Mrs. Meyer's daughter, Mrs. Philip Graham.

[44] Mrs. Meyer's granddaughter, Elizabeth Graham.

[45] Stevenson had asked Mrs. Dobrynin to sing and play the piano.

that we are doing it as well as they are in Washington. I suppose Elly Israel will call you some day and if you can see her, even briefly, I will appreciate it.

Third, in the last week Princeton [University], at a formidable ceremony, presented me the Woodrow Wilson Award (including 1,000 very welcome dollars!); Notre Dame [University] gave me its patriotism award and 4000 people had to listen to my oratory; [46] and on its 40th anniversary the Chicago Council on Foreign Relations had its largest meeting in history and again the innocent multitude had to listen to me in exchange, or is it *retaliation,* for the honor they did me.[47]

My office has sent you these speeches. The only one I recommend is Notre Dame, and sometime I would like to know what you think of that theme.

I have heard nothing about family developments for days, and pray that things are going better.[48] If not and if I can help in any way, I know you or Lally will let me know.

Much love,
ADLAI

P.S. John Fell's wife presented me for my birthday a) one of her most enchanting paintings, and b) a 10½ pound grandson!

To John Fell Stevenson [49]

February 22, 1963

Dear John Fell:

In the excitement I forgot your usual birthday present — plus one to grow on! [50]

No father ever had a more satisfactory son — or daughter-in-law. Bless you both and also Mao! [51]

Love,
DAD

P.S. I am having a silver mug engraved for JF II — but I think it's a mint julep cup!

---

[46] The Notre Dame speech is published in Stevenson, *Looking Outward,* pp. 260–269.

[47] USUN press release 4151, February 19, 1963.

[48] Philip Graham's health was deteriorating. He died on August 3, 1963. See John Bartlow Martin, *Adlai Stevenson and the World* (Garden City, New York: Doubleday, 1977), p. 753.

[49] The original is in the possession of John Fell Stevenson.

[50] Stevenson gave his sons a dollar for each year of their respective ages, "plus one to grow on."

[51] The nickname of their son, John Fell Stevenson, Jr.

To Lady Barbara Jackson

February 23, 1963

Dearest Barbara:

In a few minutes, I am leaving for Antigua [British West Indies] to stay with the [Archibald] MacLeishes for a few days — and thaw out! It has been an appalling winter of work and travel and long days and late nights. The patriotism piece was superb, and saved me again.[52] I sometimes wonder what would happen if you weren't always at hand to rescue me and sustain my ill-deserved reputation! I enclose a copy of what came out.

The evening was extraordinary — 4,000 students, faculty and townsfolk, and the best undergraduate preliminary speaking I have ever heard. The speech was "enthusiastically received," to coin a phrase. And what's more, the thoughtful Fathers were really intrigued and we talked late into the night.

I was distressed to hear about your flu, and pray that you aren't overdoing. Perhaps I should have sent you a warmer bed jacket!

I have shared your bitter feelings about de Gaulle's performance.[53] But isn't the only sensible thing for us to do to resume the dialogue with France as soon as we can and face the realities of a rapidly changing alliance? Indeed, I have had some gestures from the French here — support for the Congo and suggestions from Paris about talking with de Gaulle and Couve[54] while I am there. Kennedy has behaved well, I think, and with considerable restraint in spite of his indignation. I think the way de Gaulle did it was almost worse than what he did. But we shall have to re-examine the fingers on the nuclear trigger and subordinate our resentment to the realities of the new Europe. And, as you say, de Gaulle does give way before the facts. And the mutual involvement of America and Europe is a *fact,* I suppose, as long as the Russians are in the background — or is it the foreground? We haven't handled things well from this end, I concede. And I think the young men in Washington know it, too.

[52] The speech Stevenson delivered at the University of Notre Dame.

[53] On January 14, 1963, President Charles de Gaulle had stated that if Great Britain was admitted to the Common Market, the European community would be transformed and "it would appear as a colossal Atlantic community under American domination." As to the concept of a coordinated Western nuclear policy, "France intends to have her own national defense. . . . It is entirely understandable that this French enterprise should not seem very satisfactory to certain American quarters. In politics and strategy, as in economics, monopoly naturally appeals to him who enjoys it as the best possible system." He also asserted: "No one in the world . . . can say whether, where, when, how, or to what extent American nuclear arms would be used to defend Europe." New York *Times,* January 15, 1963.

[54] Maurice Couve de Murville, French foreign minister.

And now for the plans and schedules, which are a mess. I am leaving here for Paris about March 21st and hope to get back in time for Easter in Libertyville with you. Thereafter, I will be in New York continuously until after you have left. And I can fit in with anything that you can contrive. I have canceled a trip to the West Coast in early May and I think all will be well. The General Assembly will probably reconvene, to discuss the long term financing of the peace keeping operations of the UN, around the first of May. By all means, plan to stay with me whenever you get a chance, and definitely the last weekend in April. I am putting you down on the schedule for Friday-Sunday, April 26–28. If "Beyond the Fringe" [55] is here, we'll do it or anything else that you suggest.

And speaking of British actors, that enchanting Dorothy Tutin, whom we met in Stratford in 1958,[56] has been here with "The Hollow Crown," and captured the sophisticates *en masse*. She brought back many memories of that glorious journey through the English countryside.

And this brings me to England again. The British have been cooking up all kinds of projects for my few days there, March 27–April 1, including a speech or speeches at Coventry, Birmingham, Manchester. I don't think I can begin to do all they have in mind, if I'm going to do any useful conferring. But I shall certainly have to make at least one or two major efforts designed to relieve pain, heal wounds, bridge gaps, warm hearts, etc., etc. As the foremost practitioner of all these arts I am at your feet again! If you have any ideas as to what sort of talk would be suitable in the critical mood in Britain, please record them if you have time and send them along. I shall have to be working hard on my NATO lecture for March 25, and I'm really at a loss as to what sort of public talk is both realistic and useful in the UK, with all that's going on, and going right and wrong. I am sure our British friends are right that I could be of some use, not only in the talks in London but before the public in the provinces. But I feel helpless and bewildered. So again, help! help! — but only if you can without too much exertion.

I wish I knew more about Robert [Jackson], Robin [57] and you. As for me, I have weathered the winter without illness, lost 10 to 15 pounds in the past year, with more to go — and John Fell's Natalie has just presented me a 10½ pound grandson. Because of a certain resemblance, he has been nicknamed "Mao." We have been having acute Ellen [Stevenson] trouble, but Adlai III has measured up with more than competence. There are at least a thousand other things to talk about, but I'll spare you more for the present.

With ever more love,

55 A British satirical revue appearing on Broadway.
56 For Stevenson's visit to England en route to the Soviet Union, see *The Papers of Adlai E. Stevenson*, Vol. VII, pp. 225–226.
57 The Jacksons' son.

P.S. Thanks for your birthday cable. We had a riotous party of the old friends, and there was much talk of you. Indeed, there's much talk of you everwhere I go, and even after a year's absence and an interminable newspaper strike, nothing changes.

To Mrs. Eugene Meyer [58]

March 4, 1963

Dear Agnes:

I came back Saturday from Antigua after a week in the sun — with a stiff back, an infected foot, a bad cold, conjunctivitis, and a sunburn. But I had a good time!

I find your note and am delighted that you're getting off to Florida for a little rest. You must need it dreadfully. Don't worry about the Foundation.[59] We can talk of that later.

Please, please let me know if there's anything I can do in the troubles.

Yours,

ADLAI

To Thomas K. Finletter [60]

March 4, 1963

Dear Tom:

I have your letter and dinner on the 25th [of March] suits me perfectly.

Couve de Murville has asked me to lunch on Saturday, March 23rd, and I have accepted. I will probably go on to London on March 26th or 27th, depending on that schedule which is still in disorder. I think there are some other things I want to do in Paris, and now plan to arrive on Pan American Flight 114, at 8:25 A.M. on Friday, March 22. I think I shall be busy that evening but I hope to have a chance to see you during the day and also Chip Bohlen,[61] et al. Perhaps I will conclude to come a day earlier after I have had a further talk with the French here and in Washington.

Marietta [Tree] returned yesterday from Barbados and suggested that she might come up from Geneva for the weekend to see you all and Frankie [FitzGerald]. Perhaps if you are not already engaged, we might do something together on Saturday night or Sunday.

You are most kind to invite me to stay with you, but I think in view of my disorderly behavior, I had best stay at the Ritz where I have

---

[58] The original is in the Agnes Meyer files, Princeton University Library.

[59] A meeting of the trustees of the Eleanor Roosevelt Memorial Foundation.

[60] Ambassador to the North Atlantic Treaty Organization.

[61] Charles Bohlen, ambassador to France.

already made a reservation. But I suspect I shall be at your house most of the time!

Love to Gay! [62]

Yours,

p.s. Could you have a car meet my plane? And if you have any suggestions for my lecture on Russian objectives and tactics in the UN, and the peacekeeping prospects for the UN after Katanga and Cuba which would be of special interest to the officers, they would be most welcome. I can perhaps work them into whatever I am able to prepare, after I get there.

To Mr. and Mrs. Archibald MacLeish

March 5, 1963

Dear Ada and Archie:

I know I have been to Antigua — but it must have been a long time ago. In this turmoil, all perspectives change — the troubles come close, the joys recede. Yes, I can remember everything that happened and that I saw and felt on Antigua. I only wish I could remember everything I *heard.*

But, most of all, I remember my hosts — their thoughtfulness, their charming house, their good health and gaiety, their rum punch and myriad talents — from croquet to massage!

Bless them for merciful kindness and a holiday that I would like to repeat — next week!

Thanks — and don't forget 42A Waldorf Towers.

Love always,

To Lady Barbara Jackson

March 7, 1963

Dearest Barbara:

I am mortified that I have been so unconscionably remiss. I have swallowed all of your scripts, and thank God for them! That you had to write while you were ill and have had such perfunctory response makes me ashamed, but my gratitude is boundless — so — "Mss. received; bless you!" And to those "two lines," let me add a few more.

I am going to Paris on March 20, and plan to stay at the Ritz to keep out of the Finletters' hair until the 27th when I go to the Bruce's [63] in London. I will be there until about April 1st when I must go on to Brussels for a day or so and then to Bonn and Berlin. Thereafter — if

---

[62] Mrs. Finletter.
[63] Ambassador and Mrs. David K. E. Bruce.

circumstances here permit — I may go down to Madrid for a few days with my friends the Woodwards.[64] Due to all the uncertainties, I cannot be sure just when I will be back. But I think it probably unlikely that I can get back in time to get to Illinois for Easter. Surely, however, I will be here not later than the 1st of the following week. Thereafter I hope we can have more time together than your schedule indicates. Please conserve whatever you can for me. And please take over the apartment while I am away. Viola [Reardy] will be there to look after you and Roxane [Eberlein] will be on hand to help.

My week in Antigua yielded a strained back, conjunctivitis, an infected foot, insomnia induced by the wind, a lot of croquet, sun, swimming — and I fasted for a week and gained two pounds! The Mac-Leishes were helpful as always and I can report that they are in the soundest health of mind and body of any of my friends of any age! I think some day we must visit them together, but first I would like to persuade them to move to the non-windy side of the Island. Ada has stopped singing as you know, which is a pity.

I am not sure whether I will see de Gaulle in Paris, but I will see plenty of Couve [de Murville] and will not overlook the points you make — especially about stirring up the isolationist sentiment in this country. Actually I have seen little sign of it yet. Indeed, about all we see or hear is the irritability of Congress about Cuba, foreign aid — including the UN! — and I suspect it is all a reflection of the frustrations that come with the realization that our position in the world is changing and that if de Gaulle can't dominate it, neither can we!

Pat Dean [65] is coming in this afternoon to talk to me about my England schedule, and if there are any further developments, I will add them as a postscript to this letter. I hardly know what to talk about except the old themes to new music and some hard realism.

With much love,

P.S. I am touched and delighted by the thought that Mao [66] will enter life from a Jackson launching pad! I haven't seen the young man yet and am planning now to go out there the end of May, before my round of commencements starts.

P.P.S. Our troubles here are multiplying in all directions. The future financing of peacekeeping operations is the worst, with Congress digging its heels in and the Administration a little short on courage.[67]

[64] Ambassador and Mrs. Robert Woodward.

[65] Sir Patrick Dean, permanent representative of the United Kingdom to the United Nations.

[66] His grandson John Fell Stevenson, Jr.

[67] Stevenson testified before the Subcommittee on International Organization Affairs of the Senate Committee on Foreign Relations on March 13, 1963. His testimony is reprinted in Stevenson, *Looking Outward,* pp. 119–131, under the title "What's in It for Us."

To Mrs. Ronald Tree [68]

March 10, 1963

M —

. . . Without taking breath he [69] took off for Wash[ington] and attended an extravagantly beautiful dinner dance at the White House — sitting between Jackie [Kennedy] & Phyllis Dillon [70] at small round tables in the oval room with some 50 other guests. Around the walls at uneven distances were 12 violins playing gently & wildly Viennese & Hungarian music during the dinner. The company was a mixed bag of lovely ladies — C[layton]. Fritch[e]y for example arrived with Joan Fontaine [71] who danced for long hours of romantic madness with H[ubert]. Humphr[e]y. But I'm ahead of myself. As dinner — elaborate & good — approached the end the Pres[ident]. who was in a light hearted mood made some graceful & flattering remarks about Mr Black,[72] the guest of honor. . . .

The company repaired to the adjoining red & green room where large fires enlive[n]ed the softly lit rooms and, added to the oppressive heat. When the tables were removed from the oval room . . . the lights were shut off and the gayety, enhanced by a large number of younger people who arrived after dinner proceeded far into the morning lit by only a few candles around the walls.

. . . Sat. was work with a little head trouble, lunch with [Dean] Rusk . . . then the interminable evening at the Gridiron [Club] dinner of [spurious?] good fellowship, poor skits and splendid speeches — Romney [73] was good; Hubert [Humphrey] terrific and [President] Kennedy very relaxed, witty and for the first time master of the scene. If I can get a copy of HH's I'll send it. He promised it to me and I gather everyone in Wash contributed to it.

Pleasant talk with the B[arry]. Binghams — pere et fils — about, guess who? and extremely warm reception for AES from all sides from Ev[erett]. Dirksen to Jimmy Byrnes.[74] Felt very much like a respected, indeed beloved, and amiable elder statesman. Horrors!

[68] This handwritten letter is in the possession of Mrs. Tree. It was written aboard the Sunday night 11 P.M. air shuttle between Washington, D.C., and New York City.
[69] Stevenson refers to himself.
[70] Wife of Secretary of the Treasury C. Douglas Dillon.
[71] Motion picture and stage actress.
[72] Eugene Black, former president of the World Bank.
[73] George Romney, governor of Michigan.
[74] James F. Byrnes, former Secretary of State and former governor of South Carolina. It was Byrnes who first recommended Stevenson to Jacob M. Arvey, chairman of the Cook County Democratic Central Committee. See Arvey, "A Gold Nugget in Your Backyard," in *As We Knew Adlai: The Stevenson Story by Twenty-two Friends*, edited and with preface by Edward P. Doyle, foreword by Adlai E. Stevenson III (New York: Harper & Row, 1966), pp. 50–65.

. . . Sunday was a pleasant walk across Georgetown in warm bright early spring . . . read another enchanting long letter from F[rances] F[itzGerald] — who I almost dread to see. I can feel my heart misbehaving already. . . . saw many old, old friends, and was thence transported by Nan McEvoy to the Sulgrave [Club] for large, dull lunch by Pete Brandt [75] and Mark Childs [76] for Post Dispatch moguls. From there to Bill Beale's, Pres[ident]. of Gridiron [Club], Betty's [77] brother, and to the huge Gridiron reception at Statler [Hotel]; then an hour in line billing, cooing and fainting from fatigue at the AAUN [American Association for the United Nations] rout at the Mayflower [Hotel]. The evening concluded with the *best of all* — Mary McGrory's.[78] It was like an underground meeting of the IRA [Irish Republican Army], and I laughed to the danger point. It all started when she told me she had gone to a German hairdresser and asked for some blond streaks in a blond head! So when I arrived en route to airport with bag and baggage — the dizzy blonde shouted put 'im in the bedroom and lock the door, and the evening was off! And so was I at 9:30 to get the 10 shuttle. Toni and Chubb [79] were there — but I had almost no talk with them — except Toni's affectionate farewell and promise to tell me all about how it felt to win!

This must stop now — it's Mon. AM and I haven't even told you about the extraordinary young woman who rode in with me from the airport. . . .

To Stuart Gerry Brown [80]

March 11, 1963

Dear Stuart:

On second thought I feel that I should not send you the Cuba paper [81] I mentioned, for all the obvious reasons. However, I can summarize my views very briefly, as follows:

1. I felt and said emphatically that we should not take military action by air strike or invasion at least until we had used the Organization of

[75] Raymond P. Brandt, contributing editor and former Washington bureau chief of the St. Louis *Post-Dispatch*.

[76] Marquis W. Childs, chief Washington correspondent of the St. Louis *Post-Dispatch*.

[77] Betty Beale, syndicated columnist with the Washington *Star*.

[78] Feature writer for the Washington *Star*.

[79] Governor and Mrs. Endicott Peabody of Massachusetts. Mr. Peabody was Mrs. Tree's brother.

[80] The original is in the Stuart Gerry Brown papers, Syracuse University Library. See Stuart Gerry Brown, *Adlai E. Stevenson, A Short Biography: The Conscience of the Country* (Woodbury, New York: Barron's Woodbury Press, 1965), p. 188.

[81] The memorandum requested by Arthur Schlesinger, Jr., which Schlesinger filed with the minutes of ExComm on January 31, 1963. See pp. 385–388, above.

American States and the Security Council of the United Nations to bring about the peaceful removal of the threat from the nuclear missiles. This is what was done.

2. I favored the quarantine against additional arms shipments to Cuba, but opposed including petrol, oil and lubricants in the first instance. This is what was done.

3. I proposed that in the event that the missiles were rendered inoperable as a result of the OAS-UN proceedings, but had not been withdrawn from the island, that the US should be prepared to negotiate for their withdrawal and for the demilitarization of Cuba by the withdrawal of all Russian forces. And for any such comprehensive result, we should be prepared to pay the price in the context of mutual evacuation of bases. I think the confusion arose because somebody interpreted my position as offering to trade a base in exchange for rendering the missiles inoperable, i.e., removing the gun from our head, rather than the larger package of removing the Russians from Cuba. But obviously the US has long pursued a policy of refusing to negotiate under threat and I had no such idea at the time.

Perhaps on another visit we can amplify this in greater detail, as well as many other proposals that emerged during that week, if you wish.

It was good to see you. . . .

Cordially,
ADLAI

To Mrs. John F. Kennedy

March 13, 1963

Dear Jackie:

Just in case your husband didn't tell you, he has agreed to serve as Honorary Trustee and approves of your serving as such also! [82] The only other trustees will be: President and Mrs. [Harry] Truman, President and Mrs. [Dwight] Eisenhower, and President [Herbert] Hoover.

With all good wishes,

Cordially yours,

P.S. I've been trying to think if I ever a) had a better time, b) saw a lovelier party, and c) ever had a better seat at dinner.

While I'm loath to make such boyish confessions, the answer in each case is NO! — and especially item c) — a shock from which I hope *never* to recover. Thanks, blessings — and love ever — ADLAI

P.S. On Sunday, Oct. 18 a remarkable young pianist [83] is coming to play

---

[82] Of the Eleanor Roosevelt Memorial Foundation.
[83] Eugene Indjic, a protégé of Mrs. John Alden Carpenter.

at the apartment. It will be a small group — Could you come? No hurry — just keep it on your schedule.

AES

To Robert Woodward

March 20, 1963

Dear Bob:

I have your note of March 16. My schedule now — and it changes from day to day — is to arrive in Madrid on Air France Flight #515 from Paris at 7:10 P.M. on Friday, April 5. I expect to have with me Mrs. Marietta Tree, the U.S. Member of the Commission on Human Rights, and possibly her daughter, Frances FitzGerald, who is living in Paris. I am not sure about the latter and will let you know. If it would be more convenient to put them and me up in a hotel — please do so.

I have no plans in mind for that weekend except not to cause you and Virginia any inconvenience. I could get a car and go off with the girls for an excursion somewhere, if you are occupied. If not, perhaps we could go together and see some sights. Anything will do!

On Monday, April 8, I must fly to Rabat [Morocco], leaving Madrid around 3 P.M. and arrive in Rabat about 5 P.M. I hope Marietta can go too. That night I will see the Foreign Minister, and the following morning, the King, and then go on in a Moroccan Government plane to Marrakesh for the night and the following day.

On the afternoon of the following day, April 10, I plan to fly to Fez and stay the night there. I believe the Air Force has arranged to put on a plane to fly us from Fez to Seville on Thursday evening, April 11. Perhaps it would be inconvenient to go until the next morning. I had thought to stay in Seville to see the Easter festivities on Friday and Saturday and go to Madrid somehow on Sunday in time to catch TWA Flight 901 leaving Madrid at 5:25 P.M.

The Moroccan trip is of special interest to President Kennedy and I wish very much that you and Virginia could go with me. The work would be negligible, and we have not "shown the flag" there for quite a while. Meanwhile Morocco has become a member of the Security Council, and the Ambassador here is extremely eager for me to make this visit. Please come along if you possibly can. He has arranged for accommodations, planes and so on. Our problem would be simply to get to Rabat. Perhaps it might even be well to make two reservations on the plane on Monday afternoon, April 8, and reservations for yourselves if you can manage it.

. . . This would be an experience I have long looked forward to, and I pray I won't be called back.

Yours,

While in Paris, Stevenson visited, among others, former Premier Pierre Mendès-France. Stevenson departed from France the day he wrote this letter.

To Pierre Mendès-France

March 26, 1963

My dear Friend:

I am dictating this hastily as I am leaving for the airport, where I am to resume my journey.

I am distressed that I didn't have an opportunity to see you again and to tell you about my experiences here in Paris. Actually, little transpired with which you are not already familiar. There were a few encouraging developments of special interest to me, especially evidences of increasing French interest in participation in the United Nations and a cordial atmosphere that implied, at least, some anxiety to establish less formal and more intimate relations with the United States. Likewise, I had the impression that apprehension about economic exclusion of the United States from Europe is not in French contemplation.

On British admission to the Common Market, the attitude can be phrased generally as — welcome, when Britain decides to be European. On the multilateral nuclear force idea, disapproval was clear and emphatic. They seemed to encourage U.S. exploration of the idea with other members of NATO however.

I repeat that I am disappointed not to have seen you again and regret that my schedule got quite out of hand and left me with no time to do some of the things I wanted to do.

With all good wishes and my warmest hope for another opportunity to see you again, I am

Cordially yours,

To Lady Barbara Jackson

March 26, 1963

Dearest Barbara:

A sheaf of records were awaiting me and have been extremely useful. How I wish I could say things the way you can write them. Actually, one isn't saying very much around here just now and I rather regret the inhibitions. I have had talks with our people and also Couve de Murville, Pompidou [84] and a couple of other Ministers. I made no effort to see deGaulle and perhaps it is just as well at this stage. There are some encouraging signs, but few on the major points, and I doubt much

[84] Georges Pompidou, prime minister of France.

can be done until a few months time has had its effect. I have gotten in repeated good hard licks on America's liability [reliability] [85] and constancy as an ally to combat the current propaganda. I think it has been effective and it has even provoked some firm, friendly response from the French.

The schedule has been appalling and the speeches and "appearances" incessant, and I shall be glad to move on to London tomorrow — where things will be no better!

I don't know what you will find when you get back to New York — but I know what I will find! My plan is to go direct from Idlewild Easter night to Washington, to speak the following morning at the Pan American Day celebration, returning to New York Monday evening or Tuesday morning. That night we have a Latin American reception at the Embassy and I have to go to a Greek dinner. I expect to go back to Washington on Thursday, April 18, to make my reports, and I see from my schedule that you will be there on the 19th. I have to be back in Washington [New York] and talk that night to present an award of some kind at a public ceremony of some kind to Lloyd Garrison,[86] but perhaps I can see you during the day.

I asked Roxane [Eberlein] to get tickets for the Royal Ballet on May 3. I think perhaps it may be imperative to go to Illinois — with you — on Thursday, April 26. As I wrote you, Frank Holland wants to leave not later than the 1st of June,[87] and I simply must get a replacement started. This looks like the only weekend I can get out and I would not have to be back in New York before Monday or Tuesday, April 30. Please see if you could arrange to do this with me, because the time is going to be too short at best.

Stevenson changed planes in New York City and flew to Washington to speak before the Organization of American States on the occasion of Pan American Day, April 15, 1963.[88]

On March 16, 1963, he had received word that his television program Adlai Stevenson Reports *had been selected for the 1962 George Foster Peabody Award for "Television Contribution to International Understanding."* [89]

[85] The secretary at the U.S. embassy in Paris to whom this was dictated transcribed the word incorrectly.
[86] Stevenson's old friend and former law partner.
[87] Stevensons' farmer in Libertyville was retiring to Florida.
[88] The speech is published in Stevenson, *Looking Outward,* pp. 194–203.
[89] Among those who had recently appeared on the program were Ralph J. Bunche, January 20; Harlan Cleveland, March 3; George W. Ball, March 17; and Thomas K. Finletter, March 31.

To *Clayton Fritchey*

April 26, 1963

Can you weave something appropriate from the Notre Dame speech for use at De Paul [University] and let me have the draft as far in advance as possible.

Also, for future TV shows, please bear in mind that I am not able to read the type on memoranda originating from your office. I wonder if these can be put on larger type so that I can follow them without putting my glasses on and taking them off constantly.

To *John Fell Stevenson*

May 1, 1963

Dear John Fell:

I enclose a copy of a letter I have just written to Emily.[90] I hope it has the desired effect. I also enclose her letter for your information.

My plan now is to come out there on Friday afternoon, May 24. I'll let you know the time later. I had thought on Saturday to try to arrange for the christening of C.K. McClatchy's child,[91] preferably in San Francisco. If that is inconvenient, I suppose we could drive to Sacramento and stay the night there with them or with [Governor] Pat Brown. Also, the Rotary Club of Berkeley, California, has dedicated a tree, in a grove of Redwoods in Tilden Regional Park, to me in recognition of my contribution to the cause of peace during the last year, and I gather that they want to have some kind of ceremony. I am telling them that I will be in San Francisco that weekend if it is a suitable time for them.

If everything goes well, we should be able to go up to Vancouver on Sunday, May 26, and have Monday, Tuesday and Wednesday there before I have to appear before the University of British Columbia on Thursday, May 30. The trouble is that I find the Kelloggs[92] are in Japan and I don't know now whether we can go to Salt Spring Island as I had hoped. If not, do you know of any place around the Vancouver area where we could go for a few days holiday in the woods? If not, we could always stop at the Corbetts[93] in Portland and go up to their ranch on the Metolius River where you have been before. I shall have to leave Vancouver to come back East on Thursday night, May 30, or Friday, I suspect.

[90] Mrs. John S. Barnes, of Albuquerque, New Mexico, Natalie Stevenson's mother.
[91] Stevenson was the child's godfather.
[92] Mr. and Mrs. John Kellogg, old friends from Chicago, who had a summer home in Canada.
[93] Mr. and Mrs. Alfred Corbett, who had been avid supporters of Stevenson in his campaigns.

If you have any suggestions about how to use the time from my arrival until May 30, let me know. It may be that we should give up the whole idea of going to British Columbia, or the Corbetts, and stay in San Francisco, or perhaps ask the Milbanks [94] for refuge at their place at Delmonte. Perhaps we could even visit the [Nathaniel] Owings for a couple of days which might be a good thing to do for several reasons. Anyway, assuming that Emily is not going to join us, you might talk all this over with Natalie and telephone me collect at your convenience so that I can plan accordingly.

Another possibility is to motor part way to Vancouver — say to Medford or Portland — to see something of that part of the country. I have only seen it from the air. . . .

Love,

To Arnold Michaelis and Clayton Fritchey

May 2, 1963

I note that we are going to tape the next TV show at 12 on Monday, May 6. My only chance to review what we are going to talk about will be Friday or Saturday morning, which leaves little time to talk to Pat Dean.[95]

I wonder if this wouldn't be a good time to review some of the really difficult questions and try to get more content into the program than we had last time. What about Outer Space, Nuclear Testing, Southern Rhodesia, Apartheid, Yemen, Congo re-training, the Malaysian Federation, and of course financing — and — the British position, our position, Congressional attitudes, the Russian position, delinquencies under Article 19 when the [General Assembly] Special Session opens.

And what about trying to elicit some statement on the British present position on the Common Market, the Community of Europe, the Atlantic partnership, and NATO national nuclear forces and multilateral forces. We also have to say something about the UAR [United Arab Republic]-Israel and Jordan.

If we can't cover all of these things, perhaps we can pick out some which we could talk about with some enlightenment to the viewer, as well as illustrating the broad area of agreement, and also at least hint at any disagreements with the UK.

As I dictate this memorandum, I am reminded again that I really wonder if we can possibly continue to put on a tolerable program with-

[94] Mr. and Mrs. Robbins Milbank. Mrs. Milbank, the former Helen Kirkpatrick, was a foreign correspondent for the Chicago *Daily News* before her marriage.

[95] Sir Patrick Dean, permanent representative of the United Kingdom to the United Nations.

out more preliminary thought about material selection and more research in depth. I am afraid this will take more talking with our guests as well as with our Mission staff.

To Frank Carpenter [96]

May 2, 1963

Regarding . . . [the] question on the announcement by the Presidents of Bolivia, Brazil, Chile, Ecuador, and Mexico that they were ready to sign an agreement not to manufacture, receive, store or test nuclear weapons or launching devices, and expressing the hope that other Latin American Governments would adhere in order that Latin America be recognized as a denuclearized area as soon as possible, my answer would be as follows:

"The announcement indicates the deep concern of many people in Latin America about the spread of nuclear weapons and the imperative need for arms control. The United States, of course, feels the same way, and has been struggling for years to reach an acceptable agreement with the Soviet Union to stop testing and start to reverse the trend.

"We will be interested in hearing what our other Latin American neighbors have to say. Some will doubtless point out that Cuba would have to be included, or that some safeguards by inspection would be necessary, that the transportation of such weapons across Latin American territory may be necessary for the deterrent defense of the hemisphere, and that the whole question of a denuclearized Latin America should be discussed in the Organization of American States."

To Rómulo Betancourt [97]

May 2, 1963

My dear Mr. President:

You were so kind to write me and I apologize for not acknowledging your letter long before this.

As you well know, your visit to the United States was an extraordinary personal triumph, and a great service to your country and to our relations. I am distressed that I had so little opportunity to be with you and Mrs. Betancourt and my beloved Virginia.[98] I hope you will give them all my affectionate regards.

I am enclosing a copy of the speech I made on the morning of my return from Europe at the Pan American Day ceremonies in Washington.

[96] Director of news services at USUN.
[97] President of Venezuela.
[98] The Betancourts' daughter.

Speaking of Europe, I think that "disarray" is an exaggeration, but while I expect that the economic community, the Common Market, will evolve steadily, I fear the progress toward a political community will be retarded. The immediate problem, of course, is how to accommodate Europe's reasonable anxiety to have more control over its nuclear destiny. The proposal for a multilateral nuclear force has attracted much attention and debate, as you know. The difficulties cannot be minimized but few alternatives have been advanced. Meanwhile we cannot but view with misgiving the development of separate nuclear capabilities. I wish so much that I can accept your invitation for a talk and a weekend in Caracas, to talk about these and other matters, soon.

The unanimous support of the Latin Republics for the election of Ambassador [Carlos] Sosa-Rodriguez as President of the General Assembly this Fall is, of course, a source of great satisfaction to me personally and to my government. I am sure he will discharge this formidable responsibility with skill, dignity, and with credit to Venezuela.

With warmest regards and great respect, I am

Cordially yours,

To Thomas H. Kuchel [99]

May 2, 1963

Dear Tom:

Wire service reports of your speech [100] in the Senate today, fragmentary though they may be, impel me to write immediately to express my appreciation, especially of those sections of your remarks which dealt with some of the curious canards which have been levelled at the United Nations, and at the United States for participating in the Organization.

My staff and I are constantly called upon to reply to similar allegations. I can assure you that we are much heartened by the forthright manner in which you have laid many unfounded charges to rest. I am further heartened by the report of the bi-partisan approval evoked by your remarks, for the principles of the United Nations Charter stem, as you know, from our own traditional beliefs in the equality of all men before God and the law, and in the dignity and freedom of the individual — beliefs that are the proud heritage of *all* Americans.

I would be pleased to have your office send me a copy of the full text of your speech, and look forward to acquainting myself with it first hand.

With every good wish,

Cordially yours,

[99] Republican senator from California.

[100] In a Senate speech on May 2, 1963, Mr. Kuchel denounced the John Birch Society and said that right-wing extremists did the "devil's work far better than Communists do."

To Lady Barbara Jackson

May 14, 1963

Dearest Barbara:

I've just had a summons from the White House for Monday evening, June 3rd. Together with other Washington appointments, it seems certain that I shall have to be in Washington that night, accordingly, I must break our date in New York. However, I wonder if you couldn't come up to Washington from Williamsburg [Virginia] and I could ask either Laura Magnuson or Florence Mahoney [101] to put us up.

The speech in Chicago [102] was a great success. Yesterday, we had a visit here from Cardinal Suenens of Belgium, personally dispatched by the Vatican to amplify the encyclicals in a speech at the UN, followed by a luncheon at which I was given an award.[103] You can be sure that the portions about the Pope and the encyclicals did double duty!

I pray you found all well in Jersey [104] on your return and have even succeeded in erasing all memories of Virginia Woolf! [105]

The General Assembly opens today. . . . I think our financing plan is taking form and, properly handled, can generate a considerable degree of support. I wish I had any confidence that the Congress won't cause difficulties mid-stream.

Summer plans are still vague, and after another weekend in Libertyville with the children, trying to do some work on this wretched book,[106] I feel more and more anxious to stay there for a quiet holiday in July instead of traveling the familiar trail in Europe. We shall see!

Much love,

To James Wechsler [107]

May 15, 1963

Dear Jim:

I have just read the program of the ADA [Americans for Democratic Action] Annual Convention and the touching piece about Adlai Steven-

---

[101] A Washington socialite active in Democratic party affairs and an associate of Mary Lasker in the Lasker Foundation.

[102] He spoke at the annual scholarship dinner of De Paul University on May 9, 1963. The speech is published in Michael Prosser, *An Ethic for Survival: Adlai E. Stevenson Speaks on Foreign Affairs, 1936–1965*, pp. 335–365.

[103] The United States Committee for the United Nations gave him an award "for his dedication to public education." USUN press release, May 13, 1963.

[104] She was at her home on the Channel Island of Jersey.

[105] Stevenson had taken her to see the Broadway production of *Who's Afraid of Virginia Woolf?* by Edward Albee. They left in the middle of the performance. Roxane Eberlein, memorandum to Walter Johnson, March 17, 1973.

[106] He was writing the introduction to his book of speeches, *Looking Outward: Years of Crisis at the United Nations.*

[107] Editor of the New York *Post.*

son.[108] I would welcome an opportunity to meet that remarkable man, if you can arrange it sometime. And perhaps it's just as well that *you* don't know him any better — although it is something that he has looked forward to for many years and is determined to do something about!

With gratitude, and everlasting affection,

Yours,

To Mrs. Felix Irwin [109]

May 17, 1963

Dear Mrs. Irwin:

I appreciate your thoughtfulness in sending me a copy of the resolutions adopted by the Seventy-second Continental Congress of the National Society of the Daughters of the American Revolution. The views expressed by your organization are always of interest.

In accordance with your request, I have studied those texts marked in blue, and have taken regretful note that the resolution dealing with the subject with which I am most closely concerned is apparently based on allegations which, although they have been given wide currency, have no foundation in fact. I share with your membership an abiding interest in history, and my respect for historical accuracy leads me to take the liberty of calling your attention to the following:

In re: Paragraph One — It would be foolish for me to quarrel with the statement that "an anti-western majority can be organized. . . ." In theory, such an occurrence is possible. In practice, however, such has never proven to be the case; nor is it likely to occur in the future. The fact is that the story of the last General Assembly — when the U.S. position was the majority position better than four times out of five — is the standard story of succeeding Assemblies over the past 17 years. The fact is that in 17 years the Soviet Union has never once succeeded in building a majority for any proposition of substance against the opposition of the United States. And the fact is that in 17 years, the United States has never felt obliged to exercise its veto in the Security Council to protect its interest, while the Soviet Union has used the veto 100 times. Hence, perhaps it is small wonder that the Soviet Union has talked for years about the anti-communist bloc — a majority! in the United Nations.

The United Nations is a parliamentary body based on western traditions of democratic procedure and majority rule. If the United States were to withdraw because it feared the consequences of the democratic method, it would be denying on the international level the principles,

---

[108] Mr. Wechsler was the author of the article.
[109] Recording secretary of the Daughters of the American Revolution.

methods and techniques which we swear by on the national and local levels — practices that are among our proudest heritages.

In re: Paragraph Two: — The United Nations has neither attacked nor subjugated the Congo province of Katanga. By its very nature, when the United Nations enters a situation, it can have no enemies. Its goal in the Congo was not to attack or subjugate anyone. Its help was requested by the Congo Government to restore order and protect the integrity of the country, so that the Congolese people could work out their own future peacefully. The United Nations' actions in the Congo were entirely consistent with Resolutions adopted by the Security Council and the General Assembly which recognized — as does your organization — the inherent right of every government to maintain its political independence and its territorial integrity against insurrection from within as well as aggression from without.

In re: Paragraph Three — Article 52 of the Charter notes that Members are not precluded from making regional arrangements, and urges Members to make every effort to achieve pacific settlement of local disputes through such arrangements before referring them to the Security Council. It does not set up any regional organizations, nor, with the exception of four regional economic commissions, does the United Nations have any regional organizations.

NATO is an independent alliance of fifteen nations and has no connection whatsoever with the United Nations. It is not a regional organization of the United Nations. NATO affairs, military or otherwise, are the concern of its fifteen members and are not subject to review or interference of any kind by the United Nations.

No "military affairs concerning the United Nations" pass through the hands of the Under Secretary for Political and Security Council Affairs (incorrectly called the Assistant Secretary of the Political and Security Council in your resolution.) His office provides staff services and documentation for the Security Council; it has never been involved with actual peace-keeping operations and plays no part in the decision-making process. You may be interested, in this connection, in the enclosed list of the principal UN commanders of the past 17 years.

In re: Paragraph Four — The United States Government has never endorsed the "world government" concept. In the State Department's view, as long as the Soviet Union remains militarily powerful, and aggressive, there is no likelihood in the foreseeable future of agreement among governments on the substantial relinquishment of national sovereignty involved in this concept.

That I do not agree with the last paragraph of your resolution is, I think, abundantly clear. My disagreement is based on long acquaintanceship with the United Nations and its record — its faults and its drawbacks as well as its accomplishments. I hesitate to impose further upon your time by continuing this already lengthy letter. I trust you will permit me instead to enclose a statement which I recently had the privilege of making before the Senate Subcommittee on International Organization Affairs of the Committee on Foreign Relations. It is concerned with the value of the United Nations to the United States, and I am grateful for the opportunity of sharing these thoughts with you.

Sincerely yours,

To Mrs. Ernest L. Ives [110]

[no date] [111]

Dear Buffy —

Having glorious time with the children and the [Nathaniel] Owings. Christening [112] — in Unitarian church! — went beautifully, followed by sp[l]endid lunch by Owings. I spoke at dedication of redwood tree in Berkeley & flew down here to Big Sur for night in Owings' remarkable house. . . . Back to S F this — Mon — PM; dinner party at John Fells ancient house, redeemed by Natalie, & thence to Vancouver for Commencement of Univ of B[ritish]. C[olumbia]. Back to N.Y. by Friday or Saturday.

Love
AES

P.S. Alicia [Patterson] came out to be Godmother!

To John W. McCormack [113]

May 29, 1963

Dear John:

With regard to House Bill H.R. 6283, you were good enough to suggest that I send you a memorandum about the Bill which was introduced by Congressman Fascell [114] on May 14, 1963, and in which I am very much interested.

The Bill includes three essential elements. The first is designed to permit the U.S. Representative to the United Nations greater latitude in the assignment of his deputies and associates in whatever manner best serves the interest of the United States. The second section of the pro-

---

[110] This handwritten letter is in the Elizabeth Stevenson Ives collection, Illinois State Historical Library (E.S.I., I.S.H.L.).

[111] Probably written May 27, 1963, from California.

[112] Of John Fell Stevenson, Jr.

[113] Speaker of the House of Representatives.

[114] Dante B. Fascell, Democratic representative from Florida.

posed amendment would provide statutory authority for the appointment to the European Office of the United Nations in Geneva of a U.S. Representative. The third would authorize a special quarters allowance to certain officers of our Mission here in New York with heavy representational responsibilities so that they may be able, within their means, to lease quarters in Manhattan suitable for this purpose.

My principal interest is in rectifying the unfortunate anomaly that exists because the United Nations happens to be located in the United States instead of a foreign country. The officers assigned to New York, the most expensive post in the world, get no housing allowances. However, such allowances are paid to all Foreign Service personnel serving abroad, even though living costs may be less. The lack of a housing allowance for our Mission officers creates obvious difficulties and it seems to me to be inherently unfair. Further, it inhibits the recruitment of our best diplomatic talent for service at the Mission.

It is our intent to limit this quarters allowance to those officers who have important representational responsibilities and on the basis of our present staff not more than 20 would be eligible. It is difficult to estimate with precision the annual cost of these allowances. However, I believe that after the first two or three years the cost would level off to about $60,000.

The group of Mission officers who have representational duties would be required to reside in Manhattan in such accomodations that would be suitable for entertaining diplomatic officers of other governments and of the United Nations. The allowance would cover only the difference between the normal rental cost to Federal employees of this rank and what it would cost to reside in Manhattan as a diplomatic representative of our government. The officer would be required to accept the first $3,000 in rental costs as a personal expense and he would be reimbursed only for the actual rental costs, which may exceed this figure. The quarters allowance thus granted to my group of diplomatic specialists could not become a precedent for simliar requests from other Federal agencies.

I am sorry to bother you with this, but it has become quite urgent in view of the extreme financial burden that must be borne by our dedicated officers in serving their country at the U.S. Mission.

Whatever you can do to help us out of this financial dilemma would be most welcome. It was good to have a visit with you, and I wish they were more frequent!

Cordially,

To John Fell Stevenson

June 4, 1963

Dear John Fell:

You and Natalie should please execute the attached leases where indicated, have your signatures notarized beneath Phyllis Gustafson's [115] certificate, and then forward to Tim Ives at 209 East Washington, Bloomington, for execution by the Peoples Bank and Aunt Buffie and Uncle Ernest [Ives].

Last night I saw the [Nathaniel] Owings at the White House dinner for the President of India and we had a jolly reunion afterward with Lady Jackson, who is here to make a speech.

Be sure to let me know all the expenses in connection with my visit out there, and I really would like to reimburse you for the dinner for *my* friends.

. . . I have thought that if you are going to look after my oil investments henceforth, I should pay you $1000 a year, at least for the present, for "oil and miscellaneous investment advice." I presume such an expense would be proper and deductible if someone else was doing it, and I will clear it with the auditor. Meanwhile you should remember to send me a bill for my tax file at the end of the year for $500, and thereafter on a semi-annual basis for a like amount.

The visit was a huge success and I can hardly wait to come back again! Here things are popping right and left and I'm afraid I'm in for more troubles over financing the UN, Portuguese territories in Africa, apartheid in South Africa, etc., etc. I am more and more inclined to stay in America this summer if I can work it and try to have some time on the farm to catch my breath before the General Assembly. It may be, however, that I will conclude to go abroad for some meetings in Paris and the regular session in Geneva around the first of July, returning before the end of the month after a visit with Aunt Buffie.

I have sent Aunt Buffie and Alverta [116] pictures of the baby at the christening. I enclose some more prints in case you want them.

I enclose some photo strips and have indicated a couple that might be nice to have. Perhaps you would want to send one of each to the [C. K.] McClatchys. . . .

Love to Natalie and Mao,

---

[115] Private secretary to Adlai E. Stevenson III.

[116] Alverta Duff, housekeeper in Stevenson's Bloomington home during his youth and an employee of the family since that time.

To John F. Shelley [117]

June 5, 1963

Dear Jack:

I am so grateful to you for inserting in the Congressional Record the article about the United States Mission to the United Nations and my-self, which appears in the current issue of *Holiday Magazine*.[118] I wish it had been a little more about the Mission and its work and a little less about AES! But such pieces certainly help to advance public under-standing of this unique operation and its difficulties. So, I am happy that you inserted it, and flattered by your gracious words about me.

I was in San Francisco the end of May for a few days to see my son, John Fell, who is living there, and his wife and new baby. I concluded not to bother you although I hope some time for an opportunity to discuss with you the exchange of correspondence and the conferences we have had with Mayor [George] Christopher regarding the United Na-tions Commemorative Ceremonies in 1965, on the 20th anniversary of the San Francisco Conference. By that time, you will be Mayor, and I think it would be wise if you could follow and approve the plans in some in-formal way.

I could tell you all about it in a few minutes in Washington sometime at your convenience. There's no hurry.

With renewed thanks and warmest wishes,

Cordially yours,

To Harlan Cleveland

June 7, 1963

Dear Harlan:

In accordance with plans I discussed with Ambassador [Sidney] Yates when he was appointed, we have worked out a schedule for an orienta-tion trip for him to Africa, primarily its trouble spots, this August. Mrs. Yates will go with him and Dick Pedersen will also accompany him. The schedule of visits is attached. It is virtually immutable because of the difficulties of scheduling air transportation in Africa.

I especially want Ambassador Yates to get into the areas which are likely to give us most difficulty in the United Nations — Angola, South Africa, Mozambique and Southern Rhodesia. We would expect the Portuguese to be the most touchy. To make acceptance most likely we

[117] Democratic representative from California.
[118] June, 1963. Mr. Shelley inserted it in the *Congressional Record*, May 23, 1963, pp. 9268–9272.

thought his visits to non-independent areas and South Africa might be described as informational in nature, (i.e. not for the purpose of presenting United States policy proposals) the aim being to see some of the country, to talk with United States Representatives in the area, and to talk with such governmental officials as might be useful. If asked about "nationalist" leaders the reply might be that it is not his purpose or plan to see them; any incidental contacts that might occur would only be arranged in consultation through the United States Missions and in accordance with normal local practice.

In the major independent African capitals (Lagos, Leopoldville, and Cairo) talks in the Foreign Offices on their views toward African colonial problems would help provide perspective. A visit to Lisbon is scheduled at the end so that Ambassador Yates will have a first-hand impression of the territories before he talks to the Foreign Office. Although no visits are scheduled to Spanish territories, which are not currently politically touchy in the United Nations, a visit is scheduled for Madrid in light of Spain's active role in the Non-Self-Governing Territories Committee and for purposes of comparisons with Portuguese views.

I would appreciate your advice on how Portugal and South Africa can best be approached in order to maximize the likelihood of a favorable reply, e.g. should it be done informally here or by the Department either in Washington or through capitals. I presume the best way to approach Nigeria, Congo, the UAR [United Arab Republic] and Spain would initially be informally here, with arrangements in all places subsequently being made by the Embassies and Consulates concerned. . . .

Sometime later in June I presume a circular should go out from the Department to the various posts concerned. We will prepare a draft for this. It probably should be delayed until after the Portuguese and South Africans are firmed up, however, particularly as refusals in Angola or Mozambique would force a revision of the schedule.

Sincerely yours,

On June 12, 1963, Stevenson delivered the commencement address at Radcliffe College.

FIFTY PERCENT OF OUR BRAINS [119]

Nietzsche said that women were God's second mistake. And Radcliffe is my third mistake.

I made a commencement address at Vassar College one time and wisely concluded that I would never make that mistake again. But I did. The

[119] The text is from Stevenson, *Looking Outward*, pp. 281–289.

next time it was Smith [120] and once more I resolved never to face all those disconcerting, lovely young faces again. And here I am, as uncomfortable as I look, making the same mistake for a third time — and of all places at Radcliffe, which to a Princetonian is such a luminous and pretty part of Harvard.

I've been wondering *why* I make this foolhardy mistake again and again. Perhaps, like the ancient Greeks, I am so desperate for learning that I even turn to lecturing to acquire it. Or is it, as Dr. Johnson wrote, that one of the last things we men are willing to give up, even in advanced age, is the supposition that we have something to say of interest to the opposite sex? But, of course, it's neither. I'm just an old man who can't say no — to President [Mary I.] Bunting and certain charming young ladies of my acquaintance.

In previous appearances at women's colleges, my solemn remarks were addressed to women specifically — about the place of educated women in our society; about bringing up children in a neurotic world; about the conflict between the office desk and the kitchen sink. After listening to my highly instructive addresses I came to the enlightened conclusion that women would not be truly emancipated until commencement speakers ignored the fact that they were women and directed their remarks to graduating students who happened to be women and not to women who happened to be graduating.

So, like most of my decisions, I shall of course ignore it and talk to you as women.

I proceed at once, then, to the central question. The question is whether the wonderfully diverse and gifted assemblage of humans on this earth really know how to operate a civilization. Survival is still an open question — not because of environmental hazards, but because of the workings of the human mind. And day by day the problem grows more complex.

However, there is something even more difficult — something even more essential — than comprehending the great complexities. And that is comprehending the great simplicities.

Let me mention only a few. The first is that human ingenuity has shot far ahead of human responsibility. The destructive intelligence has far out stripped the moral imagination.

Another simplicity is that this world exists for people before it exists for anything else — whether we are talking about ideologies or politics or economics. It exists for people ahead of nations, notions, machines, schemes or systems.

[120] See *The Papers of Adlai E. Stevenson,* Vol. IV, pp. 495–502. For a comment on this speech, see William E. Leuchtenburg, *A Troubled Feast: American Society since 1945* (Boston: Little, Brown, 1973), p. 74.

Therefore, this world must be made safe for people. And it must be made fit for people.

And a third simplicity is that each of us is born with a capacity for growth — not just physical growth but growth of the ability to think, to create works of beauty, to live freely and wondrously, and to add to the lives of others.

And that is where you come in. For nowadays trained intelligence is the nation's best weapon in the battle for a world fit for people and safe for people. We can no longer be content — in the old Ivy League-Oxbridge tradition — to educate a few supremely well. We have to educate every citizen capable of intellectual development. We have to cherish and expand every "erg" of brain power.

Our gravest social evils now spring from the neglect of training and opportunity. One thinks of the immature adolescents in our big cities, often from colored families, who are flung skill-less on a labor market which is hungry only for skills. Our greatest social opportunities — in every field of research and discovery — spring from the scale of the investment we are prepared to make in minds. Some economists are ready to argue that perhaps 60 percent of our gains in output and productivity over the last fifty years can be traced back not to physical capital — in plant and tools — but to mental investment, to quick brains and visionary imagination.

But I believe the need for trained minds extends far beyond the limits of economic life. The forces of science and technology have made the world one, abolished space, given us instant communication, brought the world's leaders into our homes and showed us all the cultures of our shrinking globe co-existing with our own in a familiarity we might not have felt for even the next county a hundred years back.

In such a transformed environment, we cannot rely on tradition or habit or what has been called the "conventional wisdom." We can rely on only the rational response of trained minds — minds that can discern facts and judge outcomes, minds sufficiently informed of the lessons of the past to know when, say, an analogy from Thucydides makes sense in the modern context and when it does not, minds disinterested enough to distinguish between a prejudice and a principle, minds steady enough to weigh risks and imaginative enough to take them. Genius consists in anticipating events and knowing how to accelerate or prevent them.

At any time of great social upheaval — and no age has undergone such changes as our own — profound emotions, above all the emotion of fear, are unleashed. There always seems to be so much to lose when changes are proposed — even though more will be lost if the changes are not accomplished.

In the summer before the French Revolution, all of France was gripped by a deep malaise, an underlying panic to which contemporaries gave the name of *la grande Peur* — the great Fear. In our country, where vast social transformations, especially in the relations between the races, have to be achieved, you will find, too, a fringe of hate and fear — an appeal to panic, ignorance and suspicion.

Again, I ask, with what can we combat these panic reactions except with steady intelligence in command of the facts, with the moderation that comes from knowledge, with the freedom that springs from objectivity? Today, as always, it is the truth that makes us free. But how in this confused and confusing world, can we recognize the truth and adhere to it unless we have the tools for truthseeking — a critical faculty, a certain humility in face of the facts, the coolness and disinterest which comes from habits of study, concentration, and judgment? A mind clear of cant, a mind that "is not passion's slave," is *not* the natural state of our grasping egos; it is something we have to achieve, and it is something which is the proudest aim of education to produce.

So, I repeat, for all who love the human city and wish to see its commerce proceed in dignity and peace, commencement day is or should be a day of rejoicing. And indeed, as I look about, I do rejoice. For Radcliffe is about to launch another task force of intelligent and disciplined good will. And we can take comfort from the fact that one of the truly revolutionary consequences of modern science is that the great majority of you here today will be alive and effective some fifty years hence — yielding a steady return in terms of good sense, good work and calm and rational influence.

When, on commencement day, a man looks forward to his unfolding future, he is unlikely to see, as it were built into it, any marked discontinuity. He will change jobs and places, no doubt, but probably remain broadly within his chosen calling, advancing in it with what skill and industry he has, establishing his family and his reputation, and hopefully ending as chairman of the board. Of course, there are exceptions. I, for one, can guarantee that there are few discontinuities as marked as those of politics and public affairs. Starting from scratch over and over is the lot of most of us.

But for most women there is a large and obvious "discontinuity" to be faced — by most of you, I suspect, fairly soon — and that is to be married and raise a family. Then — in our servantless society — will follow some years in which the life of the mind will co-exist, with some difficulty, with the life of the diaper and the kitchen sink. From the kind of work pursued in the Greek ideal of the academy, you proceed to the work which in the Greek definition is the work of the slave. For the Greeks, the servile quality of domestic work lay precisely in its recurrent rhythm — meal after meal, bed-making after bed-making, washing day after washing day.

Is this, then, the parabola of your future — from scholar to slave? The contrast is too savage, no doubt, but the dilemma is one on which we must reflect.

Let us put into the balance first of all the obvious, unquestionable joys and rewards of family life — love, companionship, the excitement of unfolding young minds, the satisfactions of dreary work well done. And in our democratic society where politics are in large measure a "do-it-yourself" job, much community action depends upon voluntary work and many housewives will be able to make their contribution as educated citizens, too.

So, I don't suggest in our free, open society that woman's home is her prison. On the contrary, it will be for many of you the proud center of a rich and satisfying life.

And yet my doubts persist. It is partly a social concern. Fifty percent of our brains are locked up on the female side. (Perhaps your estimate is even higher!) Can we afford to waste a large percentage of this intellectual power? Can we afford not to use it in the sciences, in the professions?

It is also an individual problem. Many women *are* content with the domestic role. But some are not. And since with women as with men, brain power comes not as an evenly distributed mental quota but often in large patchy concentrations, it is frequently where the talents are highest that the frustration is greatest, too. Social and individual waste reach a peak when the young woman who has it in her to be, say, a brilliant atomic physicist, or a pioneering sociologist, or an historian of formidable insight finds herself in front of the dishes and the diapers. The case may be exceptional. But surely in a free society we must never let the tyranny of the normal trample down the supreme contribution of the unique.

Another problem, as I have said, is that today a woman of forty is still young. She has thirty years or more of active life ahead of her. Is there not here again a factor of waste if, after ten or twenty years of housework, reentry into active professional, civic or academic life is not available?

In a world still very largely run by men, you will not find many ready-made answers to these questions — even though they are urgent for you and should be urgent for all of us. Men, clearly, have had some difficulty in making up their minds about women and their role: Freud remarked that after thirty years of research into the feminine soul, he still could not answer the great question: What do women want? Some philosophers dismiss you as a "second sex," inferior, says Schopenhauer, in every respect to the first. Lord Chesterfield was not alone in thinking women "only children of a larger growth." And we all know the restricted sphere of influence Bismarck allotted you in children, kitchen and church. But I like best Maeterlinck's observation — that woman is mysterious — like everyone else!

You have, of course, had noble defenders too — Plato, John Stuart Mill, Erasmus, Darwin, Shelley. One of the most unequivocal recent statements in favor of removing all irrational restraints upon your capacities came from that remarkable man, Pope John XXIII.

Certainly our Western tradition has never denied you souls — as did the ancient world — or made your total segregation an essential foundation of the social order. But contemporary reactions to the role of women in our society remain ambiguous, and, as a result, women often lack a clear, confident picture of their status and even their identity, and for some this uncertainty reaches a tragic pitch of frustration.

Nor do some of the impersonal forces in our society help to clarify the issue. When were women so bombarded with the suggestion that their success depends upon the right mascara on the eyelash and the right beguiling whiff of irresistible perfume? The aspect of glamour, of allure, of conquest screams at you from a million color ads and television screens. Influenced by these hosts of persuaders, you could come to believe that your rating as a woman, as a wife, as a mother depended on the sheen of your hair, the softness of your hands, your ability to do fifty hot, vexing, repetitive jobs, and emerge looking like Jackie Kennedy or Princess Grace [of Monaco].

I remember one of those masterly [James] Thurber drawings portraying his furiously funny view of the war between the sexes. A shapeless Thurber male leans aggressively over the back of a sofa at a startled and equally shapeless Thurber female. "Where," he hisses at her, "where did you get those great brown eyes and that tiny mind?" Can you have such perpetual insistence upon those aspects of women which are determined by her sex, and not diminish in some degree her other attributes — intellectual power, executive ability, common sense, mature wisdom?

Her image can be molded in other ways, too. "A woman preaching," said the great Johnson, "is like a dog on its hind legs. It is not that she does well. The remarkable thing is that she does it at all." It is frustrating, it is humiliating, it can be destructive of ease and confidence if women have to feel like dogs on their hind legs whenever they leave the domestic haven to which so much of the folk thought of our society assigns them.

None of all this should, however, discourage you. Many great social transformations have occurred *against* the grain of accepted thought and practice, and if society is slow to realize how much it loses by this potential stifling and inhibiting of half its brain power, there is a good deal that can be done to speed up the recognition. Radcliffe is the sponsor of one such approach in your Institute for Independent Study, at which women receive fellowships to enable them to carry on their scholastic and professional interests part-time to prepare themselves for greater participation in the post-domestic years.

I would hope to see every university in America provided with similar institutes.

In devising institutes for retraining, in fashioning tax patterns which encourage both continuous and post-domestic professional life, in reconsidering problems of responsibility and promotion, we have to use genuine social inventiveness, and with institutes such as yours — and with others of similar intent — an initiative of first class importance has been taken.

Society could help more than it does to give its women citizens the fullest sense of participation. Yet I believe that for men and women alike the fundamental liberations, the genuine experiences of equality, depend not only upon the opportunities — or disabilities — society offers, but also on the reactions and beliefs of the human beings involved. Confusion of roles, problems of identity have their origins in divided and uncertain minds, and there are ways, I think, in which all of us, as members of this strange, varied, immensely talented yet sometimes delinquent human family, can confront the future with some hope of making better sense of the years ahead.

In what I have to say now — (do not be perturbed, this *is* the peroration) — I confess that I have been profoundly influenced by a great and noble woman whose friendship was one of the exhilarating rewards of a public career in which the rewards were not, shall we say, the most notable feature. Since Eleanor Roosevelt's death last year, I have reflected often on what made up the peculiar quality of her greatness. And I can only conclude that it was her absolute disinterestedness. She did everything because it was worth doing. She did nothing because it would help to enhance her own role. Of that she seemed to be unconscious. Work was there. Work had to be done. And it would require all her energy and concentration. But the fact that Eleanor Roosevelt was doing it interested her not at all.

I have never known her equal for objectivity, for unbiased judgment, for a sort of divine fairness and simplicity which sprang from the fact that she never felt her own interests or status or reputation to be involved in her activities.

I recall the beguiling statement of an eighteenth-century lady, who wrote that she did not find the garden of the Doge of Venice so remarkable as the fact that she was sitting in it. For Eleanor Roosevelt, what she did, what her role might be, how people thought of her, her image, her repute — all this meant nothing. The work to be done meant all.

So this is the thought that I would leave with you as you start to play all the various parts which life will bring you — do them all if you can for the sake of the work, do them as little as possible for the sake of yourself. Resist those obsessive commercial voices. Be indifferent — if possible

— to any limited view of your part in society. See your life as a whole, with times, no doubt, of concentrated domesticity, with times beyond when you will have leisure and energy and experience for work.

All these forms of work and dedication will be fruitful, will support your self-respect and give you tranquility, if they are done with self-forgetfulness because they are good in themselves. None of them, on the contrary, will release you if you are imprisoned in a narrow, inward-looking self and see them as means of self expression, self fulfillment, and heaven knows what other confusions of purpose and integrity.

That this mood of detachment is more difficult for women than for men in our society I do not doubt. If people constantly exclaim that you as a woman are doing this or that, your role, not the work in hand, can appear the main objective. But never doubt one thing. The more the work is done for its own sake, the more it imposes its own respect. The more objective and disinterested your efforts, the more rapidly shall we all — men and women alike — reach that condition for which a famous English woman pleaded so eloquently when she wrote: "Let us consider women in the grand light of human creatures, who in common with men are placed on earth to unfold their faculties."

May every one of you stand beside us males, not as the classical help-meet one step behind, but shoulder to shoulder, "in the grand light of human creatures."

To John F. Baldwin [121]

June 17, 1963

Dear Congressman Baldwin:

In response to your letter of May 31 I am happy to supply the following information to use in replying to questions from your constituent, Mr. Fred C. MacDougall. For the sake of clarity I will repeat the questions and then provide the answers:

Question 1: *"The United States [sic] Political and Security Council has always been under the authority of a Communist officer. Why? He is the Assistant Secretary General for Political and Security Council Affairs, Eugeny D. Kiselev. Are we as a Nation nuts? Any military action where the UN is consulted goes direct to Communist Russia.*

Answer to Question 1. In speaking of the "United States Political and Security Council" I believe Mr. MacDougall is referring to the post of Under Secretary for Political and Security Council Affairs of the United Nations.

The Under Secretary for Political and Security Council Affairs has always been a Soviet national, except for a period of three years when

[121] Republican representative from California.

the position was held by a Yugoslav national. The occupant of this post is in charge of a section of the Secretariat which provides administrative services for meetings of the Security Council and for the two Political Committees of the General Assembly. Military operations, however, such as those in the Congo or Middle East, as well as other responsibilities assigned the Secretary-General by the Security Council, are administered from the Office of the Secretary-General itself. The Under Secretary for Political and Security Council Affairs is not necessarily consulted, or even informed, on all political and security matters. The ability of the United Nations successfully to carry our [out?] peace and security operations in Korea, in the Congo, and in the Middle East, over the objections of the USSR and at a time when a Communist filled this post, suggests that our interests have not been adversely affected by the situation to which you refer.

Question 2: *"Who is the Commander and Chief of our troops that are assigned UN duty? What has been the percentage increase of U.S. troops being assigned UN duty in the last two years: What has been the percent decrease of U.S. troops under our President's command? (Remember, U.S. troops assigned UN duty are not under the President's command as Commander in Chief)."*

Answer to Question 2. The Commander in Chief of U.S. troops assigned to the UN command in Korea is General Guy B. Meloy. He is simultaneously Commander of United States Forces in Korea, Commander of the Eighth Army in Korea, and Chief of the UN Command. The United States serves as the command of UN forces in Korea at the request of the Security Council. The assignment of U.S. forces to Korea as part of the UN Command has not decreased the number of troops under the President's control. U.S. forces remain under the direct command of General Meloy and, thus, under the President as Commander in Chief. There has been no increase in the number of U.S. troops assigned to UN duty in the last two years. The number of U.S. soldiers serving there has been approximately 50,000 for the last three years.

With every good wish,

Cordially yours,

To Mrs. Ronald Tree [122]

June 19, 1963

. . . Friday night I went out to Crowfields [123] . . . Usual gay luncheon but a bad rainy day. Persuaded Quaison-Sackey [124] to postpone Angola-

---

[122] This handwritten letter is in the possession of Mrs. Tree.

[123] The country home of Mr. and Mrs. Cass Canfield in Bedford, New York.

[124] Alex Quaison-Sackey, permanent representative of Ghana to the United Nations.

Stevenson and Eleanor Roosevelt on their way to the United
Nations General Assembly hall, March 7, 1961

Listening to the debate in the General Assembly on the question
of seating the People's Republic of China, October 22, 1962

At graveside services for Eleanor Roosevelt at Hyde Park, New York,
November 10, 1962. To Stevenson's left is Ralph Bunche; to his
right are Dwight D. Eisenhower, Mr. and Mrs. Harry S. Truman,
Vice President Lyndon B. Johnson, President and Mrs. John F.
Kennedy, Mrs. Lyndon B. Johnson, and members of the
Roosevelt family

Soviet Permanent Representative Nikolai T. Fedorenko talking with
Stevenson before a meeting of the Security Council, July 24, 1963

President Kennedy shaking hands with Secretary-General U Thant outside
the UN after the President's official visit and speech to the General
Assembly, September 20, 1963

Hyman H. Bookbinder (left) and Philip M. Klutznick discussing the
charter of the Eleanor Roosevelt Memorial Foundation with
Stevenson at the White House, October 11, 1963

With President Johnson two days after the
assassination of President Kennedy

Christmas, Libertyville, 1963. Stevenson surrounded
by Katie, Lucy, and John Fell II

Stevenson and Attorney General Robert F. Kennedy at a press conference at the UN on January 28, 1964, following Kennedy's visit to the Far East

A birthday surprise: Stevenson with President and Mrs. Lyndon B. Johnson at the White House, February 4, 1965

(PHOTO BY Y. R. OKAMOTO — COURTESY OF THE LYNDON BAINES JOHNSON LIB

Stevenson, Vice President Hubert H. Humphrey, and Secretary of Defense
Robert S. McNamara at a cabinet meeting, February 11, 1965

Stevenson and conductor Howard Mitchell following Stevenson's narration
of Aaron Copland's *Lincoln Portrait* in performance with the National
Symphony Orchestra in Washington, D.C., May 30, 1965

Stevenson and R. Keith Kane, Fellow of Harvard College, outside
University Hall on Commencement Day, June 17, 1965, when
Stevenson received an honorary degree from Harvard
University

apartheid S[ecurity] C[Council] to July 22 — and what a terrible two to three weeks that will be, with US in defensive position and losing some more of our African influence — unless big meeting I had yesterday in Department [of State] produces some more positive position. . . .

Sunday — Amherst [125] — a pretty setting and uneventful except for long, tiring motor journey. [Francis T. P.] Plimpton now sick with throat infection, [Charles] Yost on vacation in Mexico, and me doing their work — including winding up interminable negotiations on financing.

Monday — Hugh Foot [126] and [C. K.] McClatchys for breakfast — he [Foot] more Cassandra about Southern Rhodesia than ever. . . . To Saks to get my brass button beauty altered. An interminable evening at [Arthur] Krims' with Field Foundation. Ruth [Field] brought me home. Seems better. Worried . . . with editing Marshall's biography.[127] Now I have to rewrite section on the Daily News in 1944.[128]

Tuesday. Dr. Lax. OK — down 2! pounds! Lunch with Rosenbergs [129] from South Africa and Lisa Howard,[130] who makes *superb* report on her 8 hours with Castro. In secret she reports that he asked about me, what I thought of him and possibility of arranging a clandestine meeting. Horrors! Then to Washington for evening on the yacht with 12 Senators ostensibly to tell them about the financing resolution and my troubles [131] — but mostly listening to them. [Glenard P.] Lipscomb of California, by the way, moved the House yesterday to cut $19,000,000 from US appropriation to UN and we were saved by gallantry of — Rooney! [132] — with only 6 Republicans voting with us.

Tues. — today — Cabinet meeting. Review of world by [Dean] Rusk and presentation of civil rights message and bills by Bobby [Kennedy].[133]

---

[125] Stevenson received an honorary degree from Amherst College on June 16, 1963.

[126] British consultant to the United Nations Special Fund.

[127] Presumably Stephen Becker, *Marshall Field Third* (New York: Simon & Schuster, 1964).

[128] Stevenson had tried to buy the Chicago *Daily News* in 1944. See *The Papers of Adlai E. Stevenson*, Vol. II, pp. 209–211.

[129] Mr. and Mrs. Fritz Rosenberg, of Johannesburg, whom Stevenson had met in 1955 through Clara Urquhart, Mr. Rosenberg's sister and Dr. Albert Schweitzer's interpreter.

[130] A roving reporter for the American Broadcasting Company who had recently interviewed Fidel Castro.

[131] On June 21, 1963, Stevenson spoke in Committee V of the General Assembly on UN financing of peace-keeping operations. See USUN press release 4224.

[132] Democratic Representative John J. Rooney, of New York, chairman of the subcommittee of the House Appropriations Committee dealing with the Department of State. The reason for the exclamation point is that Mr. Rooney was ordinarily tightfisted with appropriations.

[133] On June 19, 1963, President Kennedy requested Congress to enact a civil rights bill which, among other things, called for equal accommodations in public facilities and gave authority to the Attorney General to initiate school desegregation suits.

Message excellent but rough seas ahead for the bills — and how will we look if they fail! Mood of Washington subdued and anxious as race riots spread and ever more extreme leadership pushes out the Wilkinses! [134] Liberal Senators come to Laura [Magnuson]'s after yacht trip and stay to 1 AM — mostly urging me to forget the administration point and speak on my own. . . . And now — after Cabinet lunch at Lyndon [Johnson]'s — I'm on the shuttle back to New York in dreadful heat. Tomorrow must speak in C[ommi]ttee 5 to conclude the debate on financing and hope to have it in the plenary by Tuesday — and then adjourn this absurdly long session and go to Ill[inois]. for a few days of business and Ellen [Stevenson] trouble before leaving for Europe July 1.

. . . Fearful may not get there until morning 5th. . . .

Have neglected corres[pondence]. with Bill B[lair] shamefully. Please explain my constant predicament. . . .

To Thomas K. Finletter

June 19, 1963

Dear Tom:

I am arriving in Paris on Sunday evening, June 30, on TWA Flight 802, arriving at 9:55 P.M., and plan to stay at the Ritz until July 4th or 5th, en route to Geneva.

I hope while I am there it may be possible to arrange some informal talks with some of the NATO Ambassadors about the developing situation in Africa, particularly with reference to the Portuguese Territories. The Africans here are going to call a meeting of the Security Council on July 22, and four Foreign Ministers, including Mongi Slim of Tunisia, have been designated by the Conference at Addis Ababa [135] to present the case in the Security Council.

As you know, the situation in Africa is getting daily more acute and I think President Kennedy may write to [Premier] Salazar directly urging Portugal to take some steps in their own interest, and indicating the probability that we will not be able to help much longer.

It has seemed to me for more than a year now that we should be urging the other principal NATO partners to bring similar pressure to bear on Portugal to make some gesture in the direction of self-determination for the territories. It is for this reason that I think some talks in Paris with the Ambassadors might have some effect in that direction.

[134] Roy Wilkins, executive secretary of the National Association for the Advancement of Colored People.

[135] A number of African nations met in Ethiopia in May, 1963, and denounced Portugal's refusal to grant independence to its African colonies and condemned apartheid in South Africa. The United States was warned that mere verbal condemnation of South Africa would not satisfy the African countries.

I yearn to see you and Gay! [136] Please don't plan anything for me. We'll plan something — ad hoc!

Yours,

Archibald MacLeish wrote Stevenson on May 31, 1963, that an easy path for the Eleanor Roosevelt Memorial Foundation to follow would be to give money to various charities. But rather than taking the easy way, he urged that it was more important to support activities which were vital to Mrs. Roosevelt, which would make some people angry just as she had done in her lifetime.

To Archibald MacLeish [137]

June 21, 1963

Dear Archie:

Your piece about Mrs. Roosevelt and the purposes of the Foundation was splendid.

We have been having a devilish time trying to get some agreement and, unfortunately, I was obliged to be absent at the last meeting. At all events, they have made sort of a tentative decision to place the Foundation's major emphasis on human rights and race relations — which suits me perfectly.

I feel, however, that it should be in some enduring form if the money is sufficient — perhaps an Institute connected with some major University where some really useful work could be done in the fields of human rights and race conflict the world over. As you have said so eloquently, these were her interests — not cancer and such things.

I wish to God I saw you occasionally!

Love to Ada.[138]

Yours,

To John F. Kennedy [139]

June 26, 1963

Dear Mr. President:

When the African states bring *Apartheid and Portuguese Territories* before the Security Council starting about July 22, the United States will

[136] Mrs. Finletter.

[137] The original is in the MacLeish papers, Library of Congress.

[138] Mrs. MacLeish.

[139] The original is in the papers of Arthur Schlesinger, Jr., John F. Kennedy Library. This document was declassified. Schlesinger wrote on the document that Kennedy showed it to the British ambassador, the British foreign secretary, and the British minister of defense.

be under direct fire for the first time. This is apparent from the provision in the Addis Ababa resolution calling on us to choose between Africa and European colonial powers, the fact the Conference adopted a paragraph on United States racial policies, and the increasing African demand for the application of sanctions (especially, of course, by us) and for expulsion (on which Permanent Members of the Security Council have a veto power). The attendance of four African foreign ministers also shows that the Council session will be a major drive and not just another UN discussion of the issues.

Accordingly, it seems clear that we are approaching a decisive situation from which the Africans will draw conclusions about the long-run nature of our policies.

The issue will be posed in the Security Council — first on Portuguese Territories and then on Apartheid. It will be essentially the same on both: The Africans will present resolutions calling for far-reaching sanctions against Portugal and South Africa; we will not favor UN sanctions because we do not believe these provisions of Chapter VII of the Charter apply to such situations; the United States and the United Kingdom will take the blame for the defeat of sanctions, even if others share our viewpoint, because we are the ones whose approval would make their adoption possible and application meaningful; the ire of the Africans may consequently continue to shift from Portugal and South Africa to us.

What do we do in such a situation? The tactics are fairly easy, the substance more difficult. The tactics are to be for an alternative resolution which not only puts us morally on the right side but which calls for measures of implementation that we can support and which are sufficiently responsive to give the Africans reasonable satisfaction.

The problem of substance is to decide what measures are adequate for this purpose. This becomes increasingly difficult as African patience wears thinner in the face of the adamant Portuguese and South African policies.

The minimum answer I can see is for us to support, in the Council, resolutions which would contain (a) "condemnation" of their policies, (b) "recommendations" against arms supplies that could be used to enforce those policies, and (c) provisions for a "meaningful" United Nations function. The nature of a "meaningful" UN function is not yet altogether clear to me. But some version of a rapporteur to visit the Portuguese Territories with terms of reference which include self-determination and some kind of a Special Representative to consult governments on measures against Apartheid — as suggested by the Norwegian Representative — might be sufficient. I also believe we should call on Portugal to talk to its own *nationalist* leaders on the application of self-determination in its territories. This is the way the issue ultimately will be solved — as it was in Algeria — and advocacy of this now should be well received in Africa.

Other states — Norway, Venezuela, China, and the Philippines in particular — have a comparable problem, and I believe that only some such approach as the above will enable them even to refuse to approve sanctions.

Beyond the specifics of the Council session, we will be watched closely by other states in terms of our fundamental policy. In *oversimplified* terms, they want to know whether, if it comes to that, we will stand for self-determination and human rights and, therefore, for the mind of Africa, or whether we will give our Azores base and the tracking stations in South Africa priority. Obviously, we want to avoid such a showdown and will do our best toward this end. But the Africans have the capability, and I believe the intention, of posing the problem in such a way that important risks will have to be assumed, one way or another.

It seems to me that when such risks must be faced — and I fear they will have to be faced this summer — your decisions should favor our future relations with the people of Africa.[140] The satisfactory position of the United States which has now been established in Africa through the stands we have taken since 1961 (on such issues as Angola and the Congo) could easily be reversed by our posture on these extremely emotional questions, compounded as they are by our own problems.

The Defense Department and perhaps some of our allies may have conflicting views. And I suspect this will be a difficult decision for you from both the international and domestic point of view. To lose the Azores base, for example, may appear to some in Congress and the country like a hard bargain for the uncertain advantage of good will in Africa.

So, I hope you can give this problem careful consideration. I am planning to return from Europe on July 25. If there are other things to do there I can stay longer. If the Security Council meetings start sooner, I can, of course, return sooner to discuss our position with you and Dean Rusk.

Sincerely yours,

To Mrs. Ronald Tree [141]

June 27, 1963

M

Nietz[s]che: There is always folly in love. But there is always reason in the folly. It is necessary to have in one chaos — to give birth to a star that dances.

---

[140] For a discussion of how Dean Rusk differed with Stevenson on this question, see Martin, *Adlai Stevenson and the World,* p. 763.
[141] This handwritten letter is in the possession of Mrs. Tree.

Have you never said Yes to joy? Then, my friends, you have said Yes to all suffering. All things are enchained, entangled, united by love.

> AES: Hunger perhaps may cure your love,
>   Or time your passion greatly alter;
>   If both should unsuccessful prove
>   I strongly recommend a halter.

You are in Berlin — amid all the excitement. I am in L'ville [Libertyville] — sun and silence — and I wouldn't *trade,* but I would *join.*

It's hard to work — I can't set paper to pencil, or vice versa, — or subdue the desire to read — unless it be to write bits to you. Is the price of rich revery poor production? . . .   a.

To Mrs. Marshall Field

June 29, 1963

Dearest Ruth:

I returned to New York Saturday night too late to telephone you farewell. Your angelic letter of sympathy arrived and I am more grateful than I can tell you.[142] It *does* help.

Until Geneva!

Love,

As so many times before, Stevenson started a diary of his trip. And as in the past, he did not continue it. In fact, this time he wrote only one page.

June 29 — 1963

Left Libertyville for N.Y. in evening after 3 days of business troubles with Adlai; joy with those enchanting grandchildren; attending Pablo Casals oratorio . . . at the opening of Ravinia & visiting this dear old friend during the intermission; acting as Godfather to Letitia Last, Marnie Dick's[143] eldest, and writing an introduction — very poor I fear — for my next book, "Looking Outward," to be published by Harpers in October. The introduction is a month overdue and I must send it in for better or for worse. As for the selections from the last 2½ years that comprise the book — I haven't even read them over, let alone selected them!

Roxane [Eberlein] met me at Idlewild to catch up on mail and dictation. Packed — to bed late after packing.

[142] Alicia Patterson was dying.
[143] Daughter of Mr. and Mrs. Edison Dick.

June 30 —

Up early — to catch 9:30 Pan Am to Paris — but due to strike at Orly [airport] we must land in Brussels — damn it — with appointment commencing at 9 AM tomorrow in Paris.

Stevenson spoke at the 36th session of the Economic and Social Council in Geneva, Switzerland, on July 10, 1963, when the following letter was written.

To Mrs. Eugene Meyer [144]

July 10, 1963

My dear Agnes:

You were sweet to write me about Alicia.[145] As you know, she was one of my closest and dearest friends and it was a bitter blow — compounded by inability to get back for the funeral.

I wish I were joining you on the yacht. Instead, I shall be joining my colleagues in the Security Council for a forthcoming oratorical orgy over the Portuguese territories in Africa and apartheid in South Africa.[146] Please think of *me* when you are languishing on the sunny after-deck!!

I pray that all goes well with the family and my beloved Lally [Graham].

Devotedly,
ADLAI

To Mrs. Edison Dick [147]

July 11, 1963

My dear Jane:

I have read and re-read your letter about the funeral.[148] Somehow, in a few words, you have brought the whole thing to life. It sounds like a suitable conclusion but why was a conclusion necessary! It seems unthinkable that she is gone and I, for one, will have a hard time reconciling myself to life without the comforting assurance that she would always be there when needed.

[144] The original is in the Agnes Meyer files, Princeton University Library.

[145] Alica Patterson had died on July 2. Mrs. Ives wrote: "Alicia meant so much to Adlai, and the death was such a severe blow to him. . . ." Letter to Walter Johnson, August 25, 1975.

[146] Stevenson spoke in the Security Council on the Portuguese colonies on July 26 and 31, on South Africa on August 2, and on Southern Rhodesia on September 11.

[147] The original is in the possession of Mrs. Dick.

[148] Stevenson was in Europe at the time of Alicia Patterson's funeral.

I hope when I get back we can talk about her and what she meant to us all — gaily!

Love always,

To Mrs. Daniel Caulkins [149]

July 13, 1963

Dearest Babs —

Bless you for that cable about Alicia. It was a cruel blow from which I shan't quite recover — ever. Her delicious, irreverant voice, her grumpy growls, her realism and loving long loyalty were a part of my life for almost 40 years. I had a curious premonition — or rather an uneasy feeling — the first experience of that kind I've ever had. I'll tell you about it.

Your letter filled me with gratitude, visions of the "glistening" morning in that cool, lovely garden you have made so like yourself — and also anxiety. It sounded a little triste and I was reminded that you so often do — on paper — yet *you* never are. You must explain your two selves to me someday. Some things don't end, and works of memory, sadness and finality are often, I suppose, the symbols not of endings but of continuity — a paradox of the heart.

After a few wild days of work in Paris, I came to Geneva where I've just made a memorable, if I do say so, speech. From here I go on to Italy on Monday July 15 — thence to N.Y. for the Angola-apartheid ordeal in the Security Council on July 25. If you are the[re]abouts perhaps there will be a telephone call & I can have a vocal cocktail to wake me up compounded of 1 part sadness & 10 parts lilting laughter.

I'm here at Karim Khans lovely chalet for a couple of days of "rest" — i.e. tennis, hiking, eating & drinking. Bless & embrace you —

L'AMBASSADEUR DES ETATS UNIS!

To Mrs. Ernest L. Ives [150]

July 17, 1963

Dear Buffy —

I'm sitting in Orly airport wa[i]ting for my plane to take off to N.Y. — and on to Washington this evening.[151] It was a bitter blow to have to forego another vacation — after 24 hours — at Villa Balbianello.[152] Please tell Ruth [Field] how disappointed I am and how much I had looked

---

149 Sister of Mrs. Cass Canfield. This handwritten letter is in the possession of Mrs. Caulkins.

150 This handwritten letter is in E.S.I., I.S.H.L.

151 President Kennedy had summoned him back to the United States.

152 Francis T. P. Plimpton's villa on Lake Como.

forward to our holiday with you, and fun in the sun. I've written a note to Betty Beale who has been such a good and loyal press friend for so long. I'm sure you'll have fun together — she is so bright and gay and sharp.

In the airport in Zurich on Monday I met an old French friend — a former minister of finance and a very distinguished friend of the U.S. — M. Edgar Faure and his wife, who has just published a book. They told me their married daughter — Sylvie Lisfranc — was staying at a little hotel in Florence — the Belvedere or something like that. If you could invite her for tea or something it would be nice — but if inconvenient forget it and I'll explain when next I see him that I never got to Florence — damn it!

They've called my plane & I must go. Love to Trees, Ruth [Field], Betty [Beale] — and you & Ernest!

ADLAI

P.S. I had hoped to pick up some art books for Natalie [Stevenson] & some clothes for her & Nancy [Stevenson] — also some of the usual embroideries etc. for wedding presents and trinkets for Christmas presents. If you run across anything suitable please get them for me — but I feel so broke this year I don't want to spend much — say $200 max[imum]. And please don't go to much trouble. I know how much you have to do.

Alicia [Patterson]'s death was a dreadful blow — I've never had a more loving, loyal, fascinating friend. And she was counting on this visit so much!

AES

And please write me what you think about Ruth [Field] — Is she well etc.

To Freda Kirchwey [153]

July 23, 1963

Dear Mrs. Kirchwey:

Thank you for your letter of July 17th which I find on my return from abroad.

I note with interest your views about the utility of the [military] bases in Spain. I am sure you appreciate that this is a matter which concerns the State Department and the Defense Department and not the United States Mission to the United Nations.

I must say I was surprised by the flyer which says that "democratic

---

[153] Head of the Committee for a Democratic Spain.

Americans were shocked by my praise of Franco Spain." There has been no such praise.

Sincerely yours,

Atomic scientist Leo Szilard suggested to Stevenson the need for discussions of the long-term objectives the United States should pursue in the field of limiting weaponry.

To Leo Szilard

July 23, 1963

Dear Leo:

Your letter of July 12 reached me just as I left Geneva for Italy, and I am distressed that I did not have an opportunity to see you while I was there.

While I think we will conclude a Test Ban Treaty which may be a major opening in the disarmament field, I think your idea of private discussion of long-term objectives in the government is excellent. Actually I have been disappointed the past few years by the lack of long-term plotting and planning— at least as far as I am concerned. Perhaps it goes on somewhere in Washington, but most of what I see are the immediates, with heavy overtones of political considerations.

Let me discuss the idea further with some people on the government side, and perhaps we can have a talk about where and how to implement it when you return.

Cordially yours,

To Harlan Cleveland

July 23, 1963

Dear Harlan:

If you could find time to look through the attached,[154] [and] let me have your reactions, I would appreciate it.

I suppose there is a lot of long-term thinking going on in Washington, but I seldom come across it, which is such a contrast to the old days in [Franklin D.] Roosevelt's administration.

Possibly Leo Szilard has an idea here that is worth exploring a little further. In all events, I should like to have your reactions. Perhaps Arthur Schlesinger would have some reactions too.

Yours,

[154] Szilard's proposal.

To Roger W. Tubby [155]

July 29, 1963

Confidential

Dear Roger:

I have been meaning to write to you ever since I returned, but the ensuing chaos left no opportunity.

I am most grateful to you for your everlasting courtesies while I was in Geneva. But I was disappointed that we didn't have more time together, and I shall hope for better luck another time — if there is another time.

I have read with utmost interest your letter to Secretary Rusk of July 16. As you can imagine, I agree with it heartily, and I am fearful that our present action in the Security Council on Portuguese Territories may leave us with our goodwill in Africa impaired and our ill-will in Portugal increased.[156] It has been a difficult case to handle, but of course if Portugal really did anything in the direction of self-determination, this trying interval would be quickly obliterated, and we could emerge with increased authority and influence among the Africans.

In a few days we will move into Apartheid. Meanwhile I hope to take up in Washington, and perhaps here, your suggestion of an approach to Verwoerd.[157]

Love to Anne.[158]

Cordially,

To Lady Barbara Jackson

July 29, 1963

Dearest Barbara:

I meant to send you immediately on my return the enclosed announcement of the action of the Board of the Eleanor Roosevelt Foundation regarding future programs. I also enclose a subsequent proposal for action within this broad field, specifically with regard to race relations problems in the United States. I also enclose, for your information, some material

---

[155] United States representative to the European office of the United Nations in Geneva, Switzerland.

[156] At a meeting at the White House on July 18, 1963, President Kennedy decided that the United States would not press Portugal on its African colonies. The military bases in the Azores were essential, he said, particularly in view of the forthcoming treaty with the Soviet Union and Britain that would ban nuclear testing in the atmosphere. Arthur M. Schlesinger, Jr., *A Thousand Days: John F. Kennedy in the White House* (Boston: Houghton Mifflin, 1965), p. 582.

[157] Hendrik F. Verwoerd, prime minister of South Africa.

[158] Mrs. Tubby.

on Harold Taylor's [159] "Friends World College" — an experimental project which started this summer and has attracted at least the vigorous interest of Ruth Field. I think she feels that it might be a suitable activity for the Foundation to support. I have reservations, and a preference for the more specific human rights' program we discussed in Europe.

It becomes more apparent with time that some sharpening of the objectives of the Foundation is necessary if we are going to interest the money in the amounts that we have talked about. My broad vision of an Institute or Center for Race Relations throughout the world certainly should be discarded or sharpened soon. I am afraid in my absence we have not made much progress in this direction, but I have no doubt that you will shed some light on the possibilities when you have time.

The days since I returned have been busy with the Portuguese territories in Africa case in the Security Council. I hope that we don't end up with our goodwill on both sides impaired. But it is not unlikely! However, if the Portuguese should actually *do* something in the direction of self-determination as a result of our more moderate approach, it would restore African confidence in our leadership. I pray they will, but you know how stubborn they are. We hope to finish this case today and perhaps Apartheid by the end of next week.

Things with Ellen [Stevenson] have deteriorated and the situation becomes more acute and difficult for all concerned. Perhaps we are approaching a climax which may lead to court proceedings.[160] John Fell, Adlai and their families are well, but Borden may have to have an operation, and John Fell's oil enthusiasm has got us all into some trouble and possible loss.

Robert [Jackson] arrived yesterday but I was in the country. Am hoping to see him at the apartment this evening.

I pray your journey to Brussels was rewarding, and that you are finding some time for rest and recuperation from your exertions in the Greek Islands!

Love,

At 9 P.M. on July 31, 1963, Stevenson sent the following "priority" telegram to the Secretary of State.

[159] Adviser to the Field Foundation and former president of Sarah Lawrence College.

[160] In 1964, her mother and three sons filed a petition in the Circuit Court of Cook County for the appointment of a conservator for her estate. She was declared incompetent, and the Continental Bank was appointed conservator. See Martin, *Adlai Stevenson and the World*, pp. 773–74.

To Dean Rusk [161]

Following SC [Security Council] meeting on Portuguese territories in Africa, on Wednesday, Stevenson confronted [Alberto F.] Nogueira (Foreign Minister — Portugal) with Elbrick's [162] report on Fragoso's [163] statement that US was behind African resolution and that we would be held responsible by Portugal. Stevenson expressed shock and surprise at such statement in view of very moderate US draft resolution which had been shown to Nogueira and extreme exertion of US delegation to moderate African resolution in Portugal's interest, together with final abstention by US [164] because of further objections which Africans had refused to satisfy.

Nogueira repl[i]ed by asking Stevenson whether US wanted friendly relations with Portugal to which Stevenson replied of course it did and he assumed Portugal wanted friendly relations with US also. Nogueira then said Portugal did not like way US always calculated [conciliated?] Africans at expense of its friends. Stevenson asked what conciliation there had been in this case and pointed out that expulsion, sanctions, Chapter VII, and other objectional features had been dropped at US insistence. Nogueira then changed course and said he was speaking of US policy in Africa generally, and that US was always pressing Portugal to give a little — and then a little more — and a little more. He said he did not object to US position on self-determination but that independence was not only kind of self-determination. Stevenson emphatically agreed and pointed out that US had vigorously argued this position with Africans for a long time, repeating his surprise that Fragoso should abuse US in spite of extreme exertion over past ten days to confine resolution to tolerable bounds. Nogueira protested use of word "abuse" as too strong, and Stevenson said call it "criticize."

There followed discussion of self-determination and repeated insistence that GOP [government of Portugal] would not act in response to pressure from UN. Conversation concluded with some slight evidence of conciliation on Nogueira's part but no direct retraction of Fragoso statement. Nogueira asked Stevenson to ascertain if President or Secretary wished to see him before his departure for Portugal.

In afternoon, Nogueira sought out Stevenson to say that there was nothing personal intended in morning conversation; that Portugal had not

161 This document was declassified.

162 Charles Burke Elbrick, United States ambassador to Portugal.

163 José Manuel Fragoso, director general of political affairs and international administration and secretary of foreign affairs of Portugal.

164 President Kennedy instructed Stevenson to abstain. The vote was 8–0, with the United Kingdom, France, and the United States abstaining. According to John Bartlow Martin, "Stevenson was disgusted." *Adlai Stevenson and the World*, p. 768.

abused US and that there might have been some misunderstanding of what Fragoso had meant. He then asked Stevenson for his views as to what Portugal might do, and Stevenson replied that indispensable ingredient was some unequivocal recognition of principle of self-determination followed by conferences with view to implementation. Nogueira said Roberto,[165] for example, represented nobody and they would not talk with him, and repeated familiar theme that in past there was no indigenous independence movement in Portuguese territories. Parted in courteous and apparently good-humored mood.

On August 2, 1963, Stevenson spoke in the Security Council on the South African question.[166]

All of us sitting here today know the melancholy truth about the racial policies of the Government of South Africa. Our task now is to consider what further steps we can take to induce that Government to remove the evil business of apartheid, not only from our agenda but from the continent of Africa. The policy of apartheid denies the worth and the dignity of the human person, and for this very reason we must try to express our feelings with as much restraint as we can muster. Self-righteousness is no substitute for practical results.

It is all too true that there is scarcely a society in the world that is not touched by some form of discrimination. Who among us can cast the first stone or boast that we are free of any semblance of discrimination by colour or religion or in some other form? I take the liberty of quoting to you a few lines from a speech I made in Geneva a couple of weeks ago. I said:

"In my country too many of our negro citizens still do not enjoy their full civil rights because ancient attitudes stubbornly resist change, in spite of the vigorous official policy of the Government. But such indignities are an anachronism that no progressive society can tolerate and the last vestiges must be abolished with all possible speed. Actually, in the last few years we have made more progress in achieving full equality of rights and opportunities for all of our citizens than during any comparable period since Abraham Lincoln's Proclamation of Emancipation freed our Republic and our national conscience from a heavy burden. The very struggles which now call world-wide attention to our shame are themselves signs of a progress

---

165 Holden Roberto, leader of an independence movement in Angola.
166 United Nations, *Official Records*, Security Council, August 2, 1963, pp. 12–17.

that will be increasingly visible in the months ahead. The sound and the fury about racial equality that fills our Press and airwaves are the signs of the great thaw. The long [log] jam of the past is breaking up."

I wanted to repeat what I said in Geneva so as to leave no doubt that the United States position is not one of self-righteousness or self-satisfaction. The question before us, however, is how and when the log-jam of racial discrimination will be loosened and brought into the mainstream of the United Nations Charter.

We all suffer from the disease of discrimination in various forms, but at least most of us recognize the disease for what it is: a disfiguring blight. The whole point is that, in many countries, governmental policies are dedicated to rooting out this dread syndrome of prejudice and discrimination, while in South Africa we see the anachronistic spectacle of the Government of a great people which persists in seeing the disease as the remedy, prescribing for the malady of racism the bitter toxic [toxin] of apartheid.

Just as my country is determined to wipe out discrimination in our society, it will support efforts to bring about a change in South Africa. It is in the United States' interest to do this; it is in the interest of South Africa; it is in the interest of a world which has suffered enough from bigotry, prejudice and hatred.

The past two decades have seen an explosion of nationhood unequalled in history. Certainly, the pace of decolonization in Africa has been nothing less than phenomenal, and it offers a record of progress far beyond what the most optimistic among us could have expected in 1945. The new States of Africa are gaining strength, resolutely fighting to build prosperous, dynamic societies, and to do this in co-operation with other African States.

But, as this meeting of the Security Council so graphically emphasizes, the full potential of this new era cannot be realized because of South Africa's self-chosen isolation. Worse yet, progress in Africa is overshadowed by the racial bitterness and resentment caused by the policies of the South African Government; and it is the duty of this Council to do what it can to ensure that this situation does not deteriorate further, and that the injustice of apartheid comes to an end, not in blood and bondage, but in peace and freedom.

What we see and hear, however, offers us at present little hope. Indeed, the situation is worse than it was three years ago, when the Council first met on the question of apartheid. Speakers before me have reviewed the record of previous discussions of apartheid by this Council and the General Assembly. As they have pointed out, we have called repeatedly upon the Government of South Africa to consider world opinion, to co-operate with the United Nations, and to set in motion some meaningful steps toward ending discrimination and the policies and practices that would offend the whole world, wherever they were pursued.

Outside this Organization, many Members — not the least of which is my own Government — have attempted repeatedly to persuade the South African Government to begin moving along the lines of these resolutions. I myself have had something emphatic to say on this score, on two occasions, in the Republic of South Africa — things that it grieved me to say after enjoying so much courtesy and hospitality from the friendly and gracious people of the [that?] lovely land. But it is only stating a fact of life to say that the visible result of all these discussions and resolutions here in the United Nations, and all the diplomatic activities so far, is zero. It is only stating the obvious to say that, up until this time, our efforts have yielded no tangible results. It is only calling things by their right name to say that we are confronted for the moment with a deadlock between the overwhelming majority of mankind and the Republic of South Africa. There has been no forward motion; indeed, there has been retrogression — calculated retrogression.

Need I read the bill of particulars? For the past fifteen years, the Government of South Africa has built a barrier between the races, piling new restrictions upon old: all South Africans must carry identity cards indicating racial ancestry; segregation in religion, education and public accommodation is virtually total; freedom of employment is limited; wages rates for the same work and the same responsibility are different, according to the colour of one's skin; freedom of movement is inhibited; strikes by Africans in South Africa are illegal; Africans in South Africa are prohibited from residing, from doing business, or acquiring real property, in most cities and in large areas of the countryside; voters are registered on separate rolls according to race. This is not the whole story; but the point is that these and other measures of discrimination, aimed at the total separation of races into privileged and under-privileged segments of society, do not represent inherited social defects for which remedies are being sought: but injustices, deliberately and systematically imposed, in the recent past.

We are all agreed, and we have proclaimed again and again, in this body and in the General Assembly, and in many other forums of the United Nations, certain basic views about the issue before us. However, we must restate them again and again so that we can sum up where we stand, and deliberate with clarity and with candour on how to move forward.

First, we have affirmed and reaffirmed that apartheid is abhorrent. Our belief in the self-evident truths about human equality is enshrined in the Charter. Apartheid and racism, despite all of the tortured rationalizations that we have heard from the apologists, are incompatible with the moral, social, and constitutional foundations of our societies.

A second basic principle on which we are agreed is that all Members of the Organization have pledged themselves to take action, in cooperation with the Organization, to promote observance of human rights, without distinction as to race.

Thirdly, we continue to believe that this matter is of proper and legitimate concern to the United Nations. We have often stated, in the General Assembly, our belief that the Assembly can properly consider questions of racial discrimination and other violations of human rights where they are a Member's official policy and are inconsistent with the obligations of that Member under Articles 55 and 56 of the Charter, to promote observance of human rights, without distinction as to race.

Moreover, the apartheid policy of South Africa has clearly led to a situation the continuance of which is likely to endanger international peace and security. We also believe that all Members, in the words of the resolution passed almost unanimously by the sixteenth General Assembly, should take such separate and collective action as is open to them in conformity with the Charter to bring about an abandonment of those policies. The United States supported that resolution and has complied with it.

I should like to take this occasion to bring up to date the record of the measures the United States has taken to carry out this purpose. First, we have continued and indeed have accelerated our official representations to the Government of South Africa on all aspects of apartheid in that country. We have done this through public words and private diplomacy, expressing our earnest hope that the South African Government would take steps to reconsider and revise its racial policies and to extend the full range of civic rights and opportunities to non-whites in the life of their country. And we have observed to the South African Government that in the absence of an indication of change, the United States would not co-operate in matters that would lend support to South Africa's present racial policies.

We have utilized our diplomatic and our consular establishments in South Africa to demonstrate by words and by deeds our official disapproval of apartheid and, as the United States representatives informed the Special Political Committee of the General Assembly on 19 October last,[5] the United States has adopted and is enforcing the policy of forbidding the sale to the South African Government of arms and military

---

[5] *Official Records of the General Assembly, Seventeenth Session, Special Political Committee*, 334th meeting, para. 30.[167]

[167] Footnotes 1–4 appear in speeches by others prior to Stevenson's.

equipment whether from Government or commercial sources, which could be used by that Government to enforce apartheid either in South Africa or in the Administration of South West Africa. We have carefully screened both government and commercial shipments of military equipment to make sure that this policy is rigorously enforced.

But I am now authorized to inform the Security Council of still another important step which my Government is prepared to take. We expect to bring to an end the sale of all military equipment to the Government of South Africa by the end of this calendar year, in order further to contribute to a peaceful solution and to avoid any steps which might at this point directly contribute to international friction in the area. There are existing contracts which provide for limited quantities of strategic equipment for defence against external threats, such as air-to-air missiles and torpedoes for submarines. We must honour these contracts. The Council should be aware that in announcing this policy the United States, as a nation with many responsibilities in many parts of the world, naturally reserves the right in the future to interpret this policy in the light of requirements for assuring the maintenance of international peace and security.

If the interests of the world community require the provision of equipment for use in the common defence effort, we would naturally feel able to do so without violating the spirit and the intent of this resolution. We are taking this further step to indicate the deep concern which the Government of the United States feels at the failure of the Republic of South Africa to abandon its policy of apartheid. In pursuing this policy the Republic of South Africa, as we have so often said, is failing to discharge its obligations under Articles 55 and 56 of the Charter whereby Members pledge themselves to take joint and separate action in co-operation with our Organization for the achievement, among other things, of "universal respect for, and observance of, human rights and fundamental freedoms for all without distinction as to race, sex, language, or religion."

Stopping the sale of arms to South Africa emphasizes our hope that the Republic will now reassess its attitude towards apartheid in the light of the constantly growing international concern at its failure to heed the numerous appeals made to it by various organs of the United Nations, as well as appeals of Member States such as my Government.

As to the action of the Council in this proceeding, we are prepared to consult with other members and with the African Foreign Ministers present at the table and we will have some suggestions to make. It is clear to my delegation that the application of sanctions under Chapter VII in the situation now before us would be both bad law and bad policy. It would be bad law because the extreme measures provided in Chapter VII were never intended and cannot reasonably be interpreted to apply to situations of this kind. The founders of the United Nations were very careful to reserve the right of the Organization to employ mandatory coercive measures in situations where there was an actuality of international violence or such a clear and present threat to the peace as to leave no reasonable alternative but resort to coercion.

We do not have that kind of a situation here. Fortunately for all of us, there is still some time to work out a solution through measures of pacific settlement, and any solution adopted by this Council must be reasonably calculated to promote such settlement. It is bad policy because the application of sanctions in this situation is not likely to bring about the practical result that we seek, that is, the abandonment of apartheid. Far from encouraging the beginning of a dialogue between the Government of South Africa and its African population, punitive measures would only provoke intransigence and harden the existing situation. Furthermore, the result of the adoption of such measures, particularly if compliance is not widespread and sincere, would create doubts about the validity of, and diminish respect, for the authority of the United Nations and the efficacy of the sanction process envisioned in the Charter.

Also, views on this matter differ so widely that we cannot hope to agree on the necessary consensus to make such action effective even if it were legitimate and appropriate. And as for suggestions of diplomatic isolation, persuasion cannot be exercised in a vacuum. Conflicting views cannot be reconciled *in absentia*. Instead, we believe that still further attempts should be made to build a bridge of communication, of discussion and of persuasion. If the human race is going to survive on this earth wisdom, reason and right must prevail. Let us not forget that there are many wise and influential people in that great country who share our views. It is regrettable that the accomplishments in so many fields of human endeavour in South Africa are being obscured by a racial policy repugnant to Africa and to the world. Certainly, one ultimate goal for all of us is to assist South Africa to rejoin the African continent and to assist in the development of all the peoples of Africa. And that is why my Government has looked with such favour on the idea of appointing special representatives of the Security Council who can work energetically and persistently and be free to exercise their own ingenuity and to pursue every prospect and every hint of a useful opening.

We cannot accept the proposition that the only alternative to apartheid is bloodshed. We cannot accept the conclusion that there is no way out, no direction in which to go except the present collision course towards ultimate disaster in South Africa. Certainly there are alternatives and they must be identified and they must be explored before it is too late.

It is a matter of considerable regret to my delegation that the Government of South Africa has chosen to absent itself from these proceedings. But aside from regrets, it is exceedingly difficult in this shrunken interdependent world to live in self-ostracism from international society. In this world of instant communication, it is progressively more hazardous to fly in the face of world opinion. And certainly the obligation to talk about dangerous disputes is too solemn to be ignored by even the most stubborn of leaders today.

There is nothing inherently immutable in any impasse in human affairs. Many a seemingly hopeless cause has prevailed in the course of history. I had occasion just last week to recall here that negotiations over the testing of nuclear weapons [168] looked hopeless for five long, dreary, frustrating years, until the impasse was broken suddenly, to the vast relief of an anxious world. And, as I said, the stalemate was broken because men refused to give up hope, because men declined to give in to despair, because men worked consistently and doggedly to break the deadlock. Manifestly this treaty does not solve all of the problems in connexion with nuclear armaments. But every long journey begins with a single step, and this is a beginning.

So I should like to suggest very emphatically that we approach the problem of apartheid in South Africa as a similar challenge to ingenuity, to the instinct for survival for humankind. As President Kennedy said with reference to the atomic treaty, "We must not be afraid to test our hopes." It is in the spirit of testing our hopes that this sad episode will end in reason and not in flame that I, on behalf of my Government, solemnly and earnestly appeal to the Government of South Africa to change course and to embark on a policy of national reconciliation and emancipation.

In January and February, 1963, the Soviet Union, the United Kingdom, and the United States conducted negotiations for an agreement to ban nuclear testing in the air, in outer space, and underwater. On May 27, thirty-four senators introduced a resolution supporting the ban. On June 10, President Kennedy spoke at American University on world peace. He pointed out that the Russians and the Americans had a mutual interest in halting the arms race and in outlawing nuclear tests. In mid-July Ambassador at Large Averell Harriman, who had been ambassador to the Soviet Union during World War II, headed a delegation that met with the British and the Russians in Moscow to reach an agreement.

At the beginning of August, Stevenson accompanied Dean Rusk to Moscow to sign the test ban treaty — a step Stevenson had first urged in

[168] Stevenson spoke in the Security Council on July 26, 1963, on the signing of the test ban treaty. USUN press release 4231.

1956.[169] *President Kennedy had not planned to include Stevenson in the delegation that went to Moscow. Arthur Schlesinger, Jr., wrote Kennedy on July 29, 1963: "When we talked on Friday, I underestimated Adlai Stevenson's strength of feeling about going to Moscow. . . . He feels that this was an issue on which he was prematurely right, that he has been vindicated, and that no one could be a more appropriate participant in the final ceremony." Schlesinger added that Clayton Fritchey "says that Adlai feels more strongly about this than about anything else for a long time and urges that you call him. . . . Personally I [Schlesinger] doubt whether his presence in Moscow would cause any political damage. I don't think most people, even senators, notice this kind of thing particularly."* [170]

To Mrs. Ernest L. Ives

August 8, 1963

Dear Buffie:

Thanks for your letters, and for buying me all those things. I have added up the enclosed accounts, and they seem to total $226.30. My check is enclosed. While the things have not come yet, I presume they will in time, and I hope you will also return these sales slips so that I will know what the gifts are worth when I give them away.

The trip to Moscow was memorable, and also brought back a lot of memories to me about the campaign of 1956, and all the abusive things that were said about my test ban proposal. I guess 7 years is too far to be in front of history.

I saw Ruth [Field] before I went away and heard her ecstatic account of her visit with you. Letters from Marietta [Tree] and Betty [Beale] say the same thing, with more colorful adjectives about the efforts you made to make their visit in Florence happy, especially Marietta.

I understand full well what you say about Betty Beale's manner, but she is a bright and interesting girl, and in her business she has to be pretty aggressive to get a story. Speaking of stories, I enclose one of hers which you may have already seen.

I hope to go up to Maine for a visit with Ruth [Field] and Brooke Astor,[171] and thence to Illinois to see the children over Labor Day. It's been a long, hard grind, with few interludes, and I look forward to a holiday eagerly.

Things are reaching a crisis with Ellen [Stevenson], and it has been

[169] See *The Papers of Adlai E. Stevenson*, Vol. VI, especially pp. 118, 277, 283–284, 439–446.
[170] Memorandum for the President, July 29, 1963, in the Schlesinger papers, John F. Kennedy Library.
[171] Mrs. Vincent Astor, of New York City, an old friend of Stevenson's.

extremely difficult for Adlai [III] to handle it all in addition to his job and large family. I wish I could be of more help. Borden's situation is unchanged but he seems well in spite of the fact that he has too little to do.

All the girls reported how well Ernest [Ives] seems, and I hope they were not misled. Your last letter raises some doubts, but if things get no worse, I should think you could count on the Venice and Athens visit. I hope you can make it, and I shall be eager to hear all about it when you return.

Love,

On August 10, 1963, Senator Estes Kefauver died. Stevenson made the following statement.[172]

Estes Kefauver was a modest gentleman, a colorful political figure, a tireless public servant and an implacable foe of privilege and monopoly. The people have lost an old friend and companion in arms. In 1956 when a nuclear test ban was a major political issue and not as popular as it is today he never wavered. Already grieved by the death of the Kennedy baby [173] this is a very sad day.

To Mr. and Mrs. Hermon Dunlap Smith [174]

August 15, 1963

My dear Smiths:

First, let me tell you how eternally grateful I am for your helpful counsel to Adlai about our distressing and everlasting problem. I rather feel that there is no "right" thing to do; that the present situation is taking a severe toll of Adlai and the other boys, emotions as well as money. Certainly any aggravation of her "persecution" complex is to be avoided. But I fear that legal proceedings and probable bankruptcy will not only result in publicity to enable her to charge that she has been abandoned, and perhaps even further aggravate the persecution complex more than the appointment of a conservator. The latter at least is a sincere effort to help her. I hope to get out there for the week following Labor Day, or perhaps before, and then we can reach some decision. I

[172] The text is from a handwritten draft.
[173] On August 7, Jacqueline Kennedy gave birth prematurely to a boy, who was named Patrick Bouvier Kennedy. Despite intensive medical efforts, the baby died on August 9.
[174] The original is in the possession of Mr. Smith.

rather feel that the most important thing for me now is to try to help make life tolerable for the boys.

Adele [175] was with me for a fortnight but unhappily I had to be away most of the time. She is fit as a fiddle and seems really interested in her work at the United Nations. Unhappily, with some other lodgers scheduled, I have had to evict her for a while.

The visit to Desbarats [176] over Labor Day is tempting, and I hope to get my schedule worked out soon. I have not been there for years, and dream of those cool woods and waters. Perhaps we can even disconnect the telephone! I will send you further word about this as my plans evolve.

Love,
ADLAI

To John Steinbeck [177]

August 15, 1963

My dear John:

Your memory of the bitter attacks when I proposed a nuclear test ban in 1956, touches me deeply. As you surmise, my heart and head have been full of poignant and persistent recollections for the past several weeks, and I am comforted that someone hasn't forgotten, now that the bandwagon is so crowded! I guess seven years *is* too far to be ahead of history!

I had hoped so much to come out to Sag Harbor to see you and Elaine [178] but my prospects are dim. I hope to get away on August 22nd for a holiday in Maine and Illinois, returning the 8th of September, in time to get ready for the forthcoming African assault in the General Assembly which opens on September 17th. Perhaps you and Elaine would like to come to one of the early sessions and see the assortment of characters we will have hereabouts. But most of all, I hope that we can have a proper visit before you go to Russia. . . .

With love to you both,

Yours,
ADLAI

To Mrs. Edison Dick

August 15, 1963

Dear Jane:

I shall have to plead guilty again! I am a lousy correspondent. Moreover, my schedule has been even worse than I am! Somehow I had labored

---

[175] The Smiths' daughter.
[176] The Smiths' summer home in Ontario.
[177] The original is in the possession of Mrs. John Steinbeck.
[178] Mrs. Steinbeck.

under the absurd illusion that this was going to be a quiet period! Instead, we have had apartheid, Portuguese territories, Moscow, Kefauver's
funeral, State Department conferences, Appropriation Hearings — and
more to come!

Yesterday in the [State] Department, we reviewed the staffing for the
General Assembly in a preliminary way and I think you will be well
taken care of, especially if Jack Bingham [179] can assume primary responsibility for the discrimination item. Dick Gardner [180] told me about all
your kindness, and I suspect you have another scalp hanging from your
belt — a hairy one at that!

I had a session with the Chairman of the House Foreign Affairs Committee [181] yesterday about the delegation appointments. There is even a
possibility that we won't have any Congressional members this year due
to the fact that Congress will be in session until Christmas. In that
event, I shall probably add to the delegation, Ambassador Charles Stelle,
the disarmament expert from Geneva, and Bill Attwood, who is here
between posts while his wife has a baby. He should be a big help with
the Africans and to me personally — for "editorial" work.[182] All in all,
I think the delegation is shaping up well although Francis [Plimpton] is
still away and we have not worked out the item assignments by any
means. As usual, the biggest problem will be Committee 5 [183] — which no
one wants — and for good reason!

We expect a bloody session, dominated by the Africans, and probably
attended, at least at the outset, by a lot of Chiefs of State. So — go to
sleep — rest up — and lie in the sun. That prescription will give you
better preparation than reading all that documentation!

Much love,

To Lady Barbara Jackson

August 15, 1963

Dearest "White Elephant": [184]

After Geneva came Angola. After 10 days of that — and a disappointing final decision from on high [185] — came apartheid. There we did

[179] Jonathan B. Bingham, United States representative on the UN Economic and
Social Council.

[180] Richard N. Gardner, Deputy Assistant Secretary of State for International Organization Affairs.

[181] Thomas E. Morgan, Democrat of Pennsylvania.

[182] William Attwood had just completed two years' service as ambassador to
Guinea. He had traveled around the world with Stevenson in 1953, when he was
foreign editor of *Look* magazine, and had assisted Stevenson in speechwriting in
1960.

[183] The committee dealing with administrative and budgetary questions.

[184] The editor is unable to explain this salutation.

[185] The White House.

better. Then came Moscow — a memorable experience which brought back poignant memories of the bitter attacks of seven years ago. To see all the faces on the bandwagon, and to hear their enthusiastic endorsements, was a little ironic. A few newspaper writers and commentators have evoked the past, but precious few. My dear friend, John Steinbeck, has reminded me of the dangers of getting seven years ahead of history. And there have been a few letters from friends around the country who remember.

But I was delighted to be there, and to witness the signing and to participate in the discussion of next steps with the British and the Russians.

I found Robert [Jackson] in fine fettle and he left a most splendid plant behind him. Please thank him for me, and also tell him that guest presents from the Jacksons are strictly forbidden; that I will forgive him this time. I am expecting him back again on August 27, although I again will be away all the time he is here — on my belated vacation in Maine and Illinois.

Don't think for a moment that you are ever going to escape the recitation of my troubles! But I hope you will at least demand equal time!

I am glad you see some possibilities in the idea of an Eleanor Roosevelt Institute of Race Relations, but I hope you won't spend too much time on it at the expense of anything else. I have hinted discreetly that you might be preparing something — to the great elation of my hearers, but I have said nothing about further possibilities in that direction. However, I have mentioned to Bill Benton, who is as usual looking for an editor for the Encyclopaedia Britannica, that it might be worth talking to you sometime. He seized the idea aggressively but I suspect by this time he has communicated with some of his other advisers. I am not sure that it would interest you at all, even if it were available, but it is a formidable job with a huge salary, and I could see no harm in exploring it a bit. I hope you don't mind.

[Estes] Kefauver's funeral brought back memories of campaigning in the hills of southern Illinois, 15 years ago this summer — a small sunbaked town, filled with hearty, pure bred, early American stock, in their Sunday best, awkward, shy, hospitable, and a little excited. It warmed my heart and I came away with a feeling that I know more about Estes now than I had ever known during his lifetime.

I hope to get away the end of next week after further preparations for the General Assembly, for a visit with Ruth Field and Brooke Astor in Maine and thence to Illinois for a week with the children. Adlai has been having acute troubles regarding his mother lately, as you know, and I feel frustrated and anxious to help if I possibly can.

I expect to be back here by the 8th of September.

Much love,

To Mrs. Estes Kefauver [186]

August 16, 1963

My dear Nancy:

This is just to tell you that you are beautiful and brave, and everybody loves you!

And to remind you that the guest rooms at the United States Embassy on the 42nd floor of the Waldorf Towers, are available for all Kefauvers — on short notice.

Your buoyant spirit turned a funeral into a bright memory for all of us. I think Estes would have liked it just that way.

Affectionately,
ADLAI

To Mrs. Philip Graham [187]

August 26, 1963

Dearest Kay —

Everyone has written you everything that can be said.[188] I wish I had something new and comforting to add besides expressions of admiration for your unwavering and gallant goodness, faith and loyalty.

God's ways we cannot understand, but as Fra Giovanni said and I have come to know, there *is* joy and glory in the darkness, could we but see. And YOU *can* see. I like to think you have *already* seen — and the day breaks and the shadows flee away.

Let me come to see you when you get back. I know that if I can be of help, any how, any where, any time, — you will quickly summon your

Devoted
ADLAI

To Mrs. Eugene Meyer [189]

August 29, 1963

Agnes dear —

How I wish I could have joined you and Kay and Lally on the boat [190]

[186] The original is in the Estes Kefauver papers, University of Tennessee Library.

[187] This handwritten letter is in the possession of Mrs. Graham.

[188] Her husband had committed suicide on August 3, 1963. See the New York *Times*, August 4, 1963.

[189] This handwritten letter is in the Agnes Meyer files, Princeton University Library.

[190] Mrs. Meyer, her daughter, Mrs. Katherine Graham, and Mrs. Graham's daughter, Elizabeth (Lally) were on a yacht cruise and cabled Stevenson on August 7 inviting him to join them.

and your telegram to Moscow touched and tempted me. Unhappily I had to hurry back to N.Y. and the Security council — and to travel all the way to Istanbul and back for a couple of days was beyond my pocket book, if not my heart — which has been with you all — all the way!

I was so relieved to read in your "circular" report [191] that Kay entered in with such fortitude and interest. Surely it was the best thing that could have happened to her during those trying days — family, distance, old friends and new scenes. You couldn't have arranged things better and I couldn't have arranged my summer worse! (But I pray her sudden departure didn't leave the boys forlorn and confused.)

I have written Kay a note — wholly inadequate and another lost conflict between my reserve and my emotions. But I deny the indictment of Mesdames Meyer and Pierson [192] — and I don't FEEL that all women are serpents with long hair!! I just ACT that way. And with this subtle encouragement I think I'll change my style. So! — all Meyer-Graham women — Beware the wolf!

I've had an extraordinary letter from darling Lally — that, thank God, she recovered the full depth of her love for her father in time; that life and death hold no fears for her any more; that her equilibrium and exuberance are unimpaired; that she is not too modern to acknowledge and respect the power and comfort of religion and faith — all come thru clear and strong, and fill me with joy. I am so proud to have the love and confidence of this remarkable woman — who yesterday was a girl. And besides she loved and appreciated Alicia [Patterson] with a warmth and perception I never suspected, (You know what that means to me!) and wrote her father an amazing letter just after her death.

Your adventures on the Black Sea excited and amused me. I visited Samson and Trebizoni in 1926 on the way to Batum and the USSR.[193] I yearn to hear more and will hope to see you soon after your return. At the moment I'm visiting friends in this forest of Arden [194] for the Labor Day week-end (my vacation!). After a couple of days in Illinois for family business, grandchildren and E[leanor] Roosevelt Foundation speeches I plan to come to Washington for a conference with Pres. Kennedy.[195] From Friday evening, Sept. 6, to Sunday afternoon when I

---

[191] A letter sent to many friends while she was on the cruise.
[192] Mrs. Drew Pearson.
[193] See *The Papers of Adlai E. Stevenson*, Vol. I, p. 168.
[194] He was visiting Mr. and Mrs. Hermon Dunlap Smith in Desbarats, Ontario.
[195] Stevenson discussed with the President, Dean Rusk, George Ball, Harlan Cleveland, and others at a White House meeting on September 9, 1963, increasing the membership of the Security Council and the Economic and Social Council; continuation of the UN force in the Congo; and the question of the admission of the People's Republic of China. At this point, the President said, "We should do what is necessary to keep Red China out and to maintain our position." When the question of supplying South Africa with three submarines was raised, Stevenson

must return to N.Y. I could be free if there is any prospect of seeing any or all of you. . . . In any event I will call you or Kay Friday afternoon — unless I find a message with my secretary — Roxane [Eberlein] in N.Y. — or Norma Bandoni [196] at the State Department.

Hooray for American plumbing — I wish there was more of it right here — and dearest love to you all —

ADLAI

When Stevenson received the message that the United States Senate had ratified the nuclear test ban treaty by a vote of 80 to 19, he issued the following statement to the press.[197]

I have been working for an agreement to stop nuclear testing since the 1956 Presidential campaign. So this is a happy day for me. And I think this first step on the long, rocky road to safety and sanity is an historic day for the world.

To Women Strike for Peace [198]

September 25, 1963

Dear Ladies:

Your flowers on the day of the ratification of the Test Ban Treaty pleased me immensely. It is comforting to know that some people remember the history of this issue. I shall always be proud of my connection with it — and your flattering recollection.

Sincerely yours,

On October 2, 1963, Roxane Eberlein wrote Mrs. Ernest L. Ives: "The Governor is Foreign Ministering like mad. [He] Returned from Washington after the White House dinner for [Emperor] Haile Selassie, then lunch for the South Africans, a big [Dean] Rusk reception at 42 A, followed by a dinner at [Andrei] Gromyko's. Tomorrow he's going out to

---

said that "from the point of view of our position in the United Nations, it would be better not to provide the submarines, but he realized there were other considerations that must be weighed in making a decision on this matter." Memorandum of Conversation, September 9, 1963, John F. Kennedy Library. This document was declassified.

[196] Stevenson's secretary when he was at the Department of State.

[197] USUN press release, September 24, 1963.

[198] An organization which, along with the National Committee for a Sane Nuclear Policy (SANE) and the American Friends Service Committee, publicized the effects of radioactive fallout and the dangers of nuclear weapons.

the airport with [Mayor Robert] Wagner for Haile Selassie's arrival here."

Robert F. Woodward, United States ambassador to Spain, wrote Stevenson that his daughter Mary was a student at Sarah Lawrence College. He asked Stevenson whether there had been any reactions to the treaty with Spain granting military bases to the United States.

To Robert F. Woodward

October 7, 1963

Dear Bob:

I pray there will be an opportunity soon to get in touch with Mary. What with daily and nightly bi-laterals and tri-laterals with [Andrei] Gromyko, Home [199] et al, 70 foreign ministers and the general debate in the Assembly, all I've been able to add is a few hours of sleep — now and then. But it won't always be this way. It can't!

The base agreement renewal was evidently largely discounted here and caused little comment. The Russians have never mentioned it. But Spain's forward steps in Africa have invited much favorable comment. We are working on Castiella's [200] advice that "a moment of silence" would be the best way to advance the Portugese and he seems to think Spain can be of some help in Lisbon. I think we may be able to get the Portugese-Angola case in the Security Council, now set for early November, postponed until after the General Assembly. The Apartheid case [201] may be more difficult to defer.

. . . Marietta [Tree] adds her affectionate regards to you both to mine.

Yours,

On October 15, 1963, Stevenson spoke at the annual banquet of the Planned Parenthood Federation of America in New York City.[202]

As the grandfather of five children under six, I am beginning to wonder if I'm not coming to the Planned Parenthood Federation a little late.

---

[199] Lord Home, the British foreign secretary.

[200] Fernando Maria Castiella, the Spanish foreign minister.

[201] A number of African countries demanded economic and political sanctions against South Africa for its policy of apartheid against Africans and Asians living in South Africa. The General Assembly adopted a resolution leaving to individual nations the action each might take. Stevenson spoke in Committee III of the General Assembly on the Draft Declaration on the Elimination of All Forms of Racial Discrimination on October 1 (USUN press release 4249), in the General Assembly on the same subject on November 20 (USUN press release 4312), and in the Security Council on apartheid in South Africa on December 4 (USUN press release 4328).

[202] The text is from USUN press release 4262.

Moreover, I planned and planned to have a daughter — and ended as the father of three sons! But some of my other plans have gone astray too — take 1952, for instance, or 1956!

So I have reason to be in favor of better planning. And I'm not faint hearted about it, like the condemned man who was about to be hanged. As he started to ascend the rickety scaffold, he shrank back and said: "Is this thing safe?"

We are always hearing predictions about future increases in population, only to discover a little later that the predictions were on the conservative side.

It's like the distressed householder who called the police to come rescue him during a flood: "I'm standing in two inches of water," he yelled over the phone. The harassed officer replied: "Sorry, but that's not an emergency." "But," said the householder, "I'm on the second floor."

And that's where we seem to be these days with the flood tide of population — on the second floor, if you please.

It is something to which we cannot be indifferent. I share with Rousseau the conviction that as soon as any man says of the affairs of state "what does it matter to me?" the state may be given up for lost.

And so the presence of so many of you crowded into this room tonight is very reassuring. Because you do care.

I know there are some who don't believe it is possible to find a formula for family planning that is both effective and universally acceptable. But, I recall Browning's line: "Do the things you cannot do so your soul shall grow."

That's what you have to do, and are doing. And we try as best we can to practice that at the United Nations. The results are not always spectacular, but we are learning not to be easily discouraged. We try not to neglect any work of peace that is within our reach, however small. We have constantly to carry on, or re-begin, the work of building the institutions and practices of a non-violent world, keeping always in mind, beyond the setbacks and disappointments, our own vision of a peaceful future for men.

And it is a vision, I would say, that the opening of the present session of the United Nations General Assembly has projected more hopefully than in preceding years.

I don't mean to imply that we are suddenly threatened with total harmony, or that the light of sweet reason is about to shine forth, or that peace is about to break out. Any such dangers are remote. But I would say, too, that more and more nations are less and less flouting the general consensus of most nations.

Some do it grudgingly, some with poor grace; some are even reluctant to admit they are doing it at all, and some are just letting it happen. A few, of course are still unmoved. But we are inching forward. That in itself is a miracle, a small miracle, but a miracle nonetheless — and a very timely one.

For within the very recent past, discovery of some of the secrets of the atom has put such destructive force into the hands of the great powers that the whole purpose of armed struggle is becoming meaningless. The conventional wisdom about national security which has instructed the leaders of all states in all times past, has suddenly become obsolete. And so it is that the unconventional wisdom of a national security based on developing means and procedures for the peaceful settlement, or at least, the containment of vital differences among states has suddenly become even more urgent — if that is possible — than ever before.

And this, not at all strangely, is linked directly with the reason we meet here tonight. For within the very recent past, too, scientific discoveries have so extended the average span of life that population growth threatens to frustrate all our costly efforts to achieve significant improvements in living standards. So it is not only in the attainment of peace that conventional wisdoms must give way to the unconventional wisdoms.

To say the obvious, ours is a world of multiple revolutions, of vast ferment, of pervasive change, of political turmoil. Oliver Wendell Holmes once said: "We need education in the obvious more than in investigation of the obscure." This observation seems to me particularly apt with regard to the work that brings you together here tonight.

Last year, Richard Gardner, Deputy Assistant Secretary of State, told the General Assembly on behalf of the United States Government that world population growth was "a matter of transcendent importance for the United Nations." "Transcendent" is a word to use most sparingly, but since Mr. Gardner's statement ten months ago, the population of the world has gone up even more swiftly so that there are now 45 million more people than when he spoke. In the next decade, man's numbers will swell by a full half billion and probably 100 million more.

So I would like to endorse the word "transcendent." Whether or not any one nation at the moment can be said to have a "population problem," mankind's runaway growth in the Twentieth Century must concern every nation. And within the family of nations we must do our utmost to help each other understand and deal with it. As Professor George Zeegers, the eminent Catholic sociologist of Geneva said recently, "the expected growth of world population . . . puts before humanity great problems, the like of which it has never known before."

A more informal way of stating it would be to say, "this thing is bigger than all of us." But it need not be if we become concerned with the quantity of life as well as with the quality of life. This depends to some extent on the quality of people; for I think our own estimate of ourselves, the human species, is somehow amiss these troubled days, in a way that bears obliquely but deeply on our approach to population.

Sometime ago I came across a comment that the major problems confronting the world today could be summarized as bombs, babies and bulldozers: Nuclear bombs and missiles which might destroy civilization overnight; an excess of babies which could frustrate efforts at economic development; and bulldozers which are well on their way to leveling the world's countryside to make way for a chaotic urban sprawl.

In short, the more we learn about our expanding universe, the more we must be impressed with the minuteness of our planet, and of our species, in the infinity of space. We are learning to master the physical universe faster than we learn to control ourselves. Surely man's view of himself has been rudely shaken and diminished since those quaint pre-Copernican days, brief centuries ago, when he looked upon himself and his world as the hub around which all else turned. And yet, for all our new knowledge and for all our peering even farther into space, we have yet to discover anything like man — indeed, any inklings of sentient life — or any other place than this earth where he could live.

Our reason tells us that the galactic vastness of space may contain other creatures, some other organic intelligence. But our most advanced instruments have yet to find it: The satellite Mariner II confirmed, in the first space probes of another planet, that the temperature of Venus is 800°; reports about the moon, meanwhile, indicate an equally unlivable temperature at the other extreme — around zero minus 500. So our own mother earth, and our own species, should again begin to seem uniquely precious.

For practical purposes in our time, therefore — and perhaps absolutely and forever — man is alone. Will he recognize, in God's wisdom, that his needs for his fellow men far outweigh his arguments with them? Can he grasp and act wisely on the simple truth that we are living on a small jewel of a star which is our only habitat and hope, and that its God-given resources must therefore be nurtured and cherished for the benefit of all mankind, rather than plundered and fought over? There may be a special irony that the so-called population crisis — calling attention to a potential excess of humanity in relation to resources — may finally drive home this fact. Perhaps the necessity of confronting the population dilemma will finally usher in the brotherhood of man.

In addressing this audience, I need not dwell further on the importance of population problems, nor on the spreading awareness of the implications of population trends evident throughout the world and our own country. Nor do I need to read to you the lengthening roster of diplomats and statesmen of many countries who have spoken out on this subject —

including Senator [Ernest] Gruening of Alaska. But I do want to say a few words about the role of leadership in this field, and the special contributions of the United Nations.

If we look behind the words of diplomats and statesmen, we find that their leadership often lies in discerning and articulating the existing balance of forces which moves beneath the surface of popular opinion. There are not many areas in which governments and international organizations move creatively to lead public opinion in new directions. Yet I believe that population problems provide one of the rare opportunities.

For in this field, marked by deep differences of conviction, by slogans, by emotion, it may be possible for statesmen to discern underlying principles not fully apparent to the intense partisan. In this field we need not fear differences of conviction. In this field, so intimately intertwined with the most basic facts of human life and existence, we *must* fear ignorance, inattention, easy solutions.

We know, only too well, that there is no one, simple solution to this many-faceted population problem. And even with respect to the most important aspect, responsible parenthood, the obstacle is not the intransigence of one group or another.

The obstacle is not political timidity; it is not lack of consensus. The true obstacle is the long neglect of population problems, only now beginning to be remedied by scientists, by theologians, by administrators, by social scientists, and by statesmen. The simple, shocking, fact is that we know very little about human behavior in this vital area.

Our ignorance would be even greater if it were not for the work of the United Nations. With remarkable foresight the pioneers of the UN provided for a special organ on population problems — the Population Commission of the Economic and Social Council. They also provided a corresponding population section in the Secretariat which over the past seventeen years has patiently and tirelessly, assembled the basic data which have enabled us now to begin to chart the dimensions of world population problems.

And now their work is beginning to bear fruit:

Last December, for the first time in its history, the General Assembly debated the question of "Population Growth and Economic Development." As a consequence of that debate, the Secretary-General is conducting an inquiry among all the members of the United Nations and the Specialized Agencies which will, for the first time, assemble the views of all member governments.

This December there will convene in New Delhi under United Nations auspices an Asian Population Conference, the first formal conference of governments ever held in this field.

In April the Economic and Social Council adopted a comprehensive resolution on the intensification of the demographic work of the United Nations.

I venture to predict that these first steps presage a lasting interest in population problems by the most important organs of the United Nations system.

Are there principles which should guide the United Nations and associated agencies as it moves to grapple with so complex a problem? I believe that there are.

The greatest contribution which the United Nations can make is the encouragement of attention, of sound knowledge, and of careful analysis of problems deeply involving the most basic human values. Population problems are not an area in which drama contributes nearly so much as thought.

Last December the General Assembly found itself divided on the question of technical assistance for dealing with population problems. Yet a careful reader of the records of that debate will find little concrete specification of precisely what would be involved in a program of United Nations technical assistance. I believe that interest in technical assistance will be more nearly universal when we clarify what it is we are talking about.

The United Nations already possesses authority to lend technical assistance in all aspects of population problems. Quite apart from legal authority, however, there is no reason for the United Nations to supply particular birth control devices which are repugnant to many of its members. The limited resources of the United Nations are insufficient for this purpose. What is more important, such materials are already available from certain governments and through private channels. The less developed countries are perfectly capable of securing these materials without special provision for technical assistance or external financing.

With respect to population there are, however, several vital tasks which the United Nations should be equipped to perform in its technical assistance programs and related activities:

First, the United Nations should be able to help member countries to learn more about their own population trends, particularly in relation to the implications for economic and social development. The inquiry currently being undertaken by the Secretary-General may provide some information on the need for this kind of technical assistance.

Second, the United Nations should be prepared to extend technical assistance to member countries which desire to undertake surveys of the attitudes of their people toward marriage, child-rearing and family size. Surprisingly little is known about this important subject, even in the case of our own country.

Third, the United Nations, along with such agencies as UNESCO and the World Health Organization, can advise countries upon request on how to transmit information on family planning consistent with the cultural and religious values of their people — so that individual parents will have free access to the growing fund of knowledge in this field.

Fourth, our knowledge of the basic life processes involved in human reproduction needs to be enlarged, so that parents can have the knowledge they need to overcome both involuntary parenthood and involuntary childlessness. As President Kennedy said last April, we need to "know more about the whole reproductive cycle," and this knowledge should then "be made more available to the world." The World Health Organization has been enabled to make a small start in this direction by the pledge of the United States last May of $500,000 to initiate research on human reproduction.

Fifth, the United Nations can help less developed countries build effective institutions for health and social services. These are not only desirable for their own sake — they are essential to the success of family planning policies at the village level.

The common element in all these activities is the development and dissemination of knowledge. It should be made unequivocally clear that in this field, as in others, the United Nations and its related agencies will not engage in propaganda, and will not seek to influence the policies of member countries. But the United Nations system can and must provide international mechanisms for making knowledge available to all countries who desire it for the purpose of finding solutions to their population problems, and for expanding and deepening that knowledge. To this effort the United States has pledged its wholehearted support.

But the United Nations system, with its many instrumentalities and its rich fund of experience, still is but one of the resources available to the international community. What about our own government, with its resources for foreign assistance, its vast research laboratories, and its familiarity with the immense reservoir of experience gained by foundations and private firms?

We ourselves will help other countries, upon request, to find sources of information and assistance in dealing with problems of population growth.

Within limits of scientific feasibility — and the more prosaic and abrasive limits of the availability of trained personnel — the Government is well launched toward this objective. The National Institutes of Health have committed more than $3.4 million a year to reproductive studies — a figure that is destined to grow. Within the National Institutes of Health, the new Institute of Child Health and Human Development embraces research in human reproduction as one of its specific and important functions.

As this new institute becomes more firmly established, expansion of federally-supported research in this field may be expected — assuming that scientific institutions are ready and able to merit federal support.

For its part, the Agency for International Development, which as you know is responsible for United States foreign assistance programs, is currently surveying the needs of developing countries for U.S. assistance in collecting and analyzing basic data on population trends needed for national development planning. This is an outgrowth of the long-standing AID program under which the United States had made skilled demographers and statisticians available to countries for census-taking and vital statistics.

AID is also in a position to refer requests for medical assistance in the population field to appropriate agencies of the U.S. Government, such as the Public Health Service, to private organizations, to universities, and to foundations. And AID is prepared to support scientifically meritorious research on the economic and social determinants and consequences of population trends.

Finally, let me say a few words about one of the most distinctive of American resources: the rich diversity of private organizations which American citizens so generously support through their own efforts, organizational and financial.

I do not need to tell you who are assembled here at the Annual Dinner of the Planned Parenthood Federation of America how much imagination, dedication, and practical idealism has gone into the programs of voluntary organizations such as this.

Your immense contribution is drawing attention to a problem which, as I have already said, is of transcendent importance not only to the United States but increasingly to the world.

I salute you particularly for your work during the many years during which few, even among the best informed, recognized the true importance of the looming population problem.

And I urge you now to continue your contributions to understanding on a problem which, together with the problem of building a peaceful world, will determine the success of all our efforts in this century to secure the future of the human race.

The work and vision of people like you all over this shrunken globe will, I am confident, hasten the day when men will no longer live as strangers, or war against each other as hostile neighbors, but learn to live together in the world, to respect each other's differences, to heal each other's wounds, to promote each other's progress, and to benefit from each other's knowledge.

Trygve Lie, the first Secretary-General of the United Nations, was in a hospital in Oslo, Norway.

To Trygve Lie

October 22, 1963

My dear Trygve:

I have just heard the news of your illness and send this hurried message of urgent prayers for your speedy recovery.

I have seen you in trouble so many times that I have no doubt that you will survive another and emerge stronger than ever.

But I can imagine how difficult it must be for you to submit to the tyranny of a hospital! This time you must capitulate!

Your countless admirers are thinking of you, and none more than your old and respectful friend — the undersigned!

Cordially,

To Nikolai T. Fedorenko [203]

October 23, 1963

Dear Nikolai:

Some five years ago, I discussed at length with officials in Moscow, Soviet adherence to the Universal Copyrights Convention, with a view to the protection of works of American authors published in the Soviet Union, and works of Soviet authors published in this country.[204]

At that time I filed an elaborate brief on the subject and, if you wish, I could doubtless find a copy. However, I now have a letter from the Authors League of America suggesting that reconsideration of the Soviet position may now be possible.

I enclose an excerpt from this letter and perhaps sometime we could discuss this further possibility of improving relations between our governments and peoples.

Cordially yours,

To Omar N. Bradley [205]

October 23, 1963

My dear General:

I have your letter of October 8th with regard to a contribution by the Field Foundation to the George C. Marshall Research Foundation. I, per-

[203] Permanent representative of the Union of Soviet Socialist Republics to the United Nations and a scholar in Chinese philology.
[204] See *The Papers of Adlai E. Stevenson*, Vol. VII, Part Three.
[205] Retired General of the Army and chairman of the board of the Bulova Watch Company.

sonally, have been most enthusiastic about this effort to gather and preserve all of the material relating to General Marshall. Indeed, I recall several fascinating evenings with him years ago, and my futile efforts at that time to persuade him to commence the recording of his memories. Everytime he talked, more and more emerged, and I count it as one of my most enduring experiences. To the historical value of the record of his life, I can add my own inordinate admiration.

All this background makes it the more difficult to say to you that the project is so remote from the purposes of the Field Foundation that I can confidently predict their negative reaction. As you may know, the Field Foundation, since it was established by Marshall Field, has been devoted to child care and race relations, with a few exceptions — and those mostly relating to special situations in Chicago. The Board of the Field Foundation has clung religiously to these fields, within broad limits. Repeatedly efforts have been made from outside and even from within to accommodate urgent and worthy but unrelated cases, but always in vain.

Because of you, because of General Marshall, and because of the importance of what you are doing, I write this letter with the utmost difficulty.

With my everlasting admiration and warmest personal regards, I am

Cordially yours,

On October 24, 1963, Stevenson spoke about the United Nations at Dallas, Texas. The previous day the National Indignation Convention held a "United States Day" with retired General Edwin A. Walker as speaker. He denounced the United Nations. The next day handbills with pictures of President Kennedy were distributed in Dallas: "Wanted for Treason. This Man is wanted for treasonous activities against the United States."

As Stevenson spoke that evening there was hooting and heckling; placards and flags were waved. When the police removed a protestor, Stevenson paused in his speech and said: "For my part, I believe in the forgiveness of sin and the redemption of ignorance." When he finished speaking he walked to his car through a crowd of jostling pickets. A woman screamed at him and he stopped to quiet her. Another woman hit him on the head with a picket sign. A man spat at him. As the police broke through to him, Stevenson, wiping his face with a handkerchief, said, "Are these human beings or are these animals?" [206]

[206] When asked if he thought they should be put in jail, Stevenson replied: "I don't want to send them to jail. I want to send them to school." Roxane Eberlein, memorandum to Walter Johnson, March 18, 1973. And to the woman who hit him with the picket sign Stevenson said: "It's all right to have your own views, but don't hit anyone." The woman responded, "All right," and left the scene. New York *Times*, October 25, 1963.

After President Kennedy read about the incident, he was impressed with Stevenson's presence of mind and his coolness. The President asked Arthur M. Schlesinger, Jr., to call Stevenson and tell him "we thought he was great." When Schlesinger reached him, Stevenson joked a bit about the night before and then said, "But, you know, there was something ugly and frightening about the atmosphere. Later I talked with some of the leading people there. They wondered whether the President should go to Dallas, and so do I."

Schlesinger wrote that he was reluctant to pass Stevenson's message to the President "lest it convict him of undue apprehensiveness in the President's eyes." Several days later Stevenson called Schlesinger and expressed relief that Schlesinger had not given the message to President Kennedy. Stevenson mentioned that he had received a reassuring letter from a leading Dallas businessman stating that the incident had had "serious effects on the entire community. . . . You can feel that your visit has had permanent and important results on the City of Dallas." [207]

Stevenson spoke in Los Angeles on October 23 at a luncheon sponsored by the Los Angeles World Affairs Council, the Los Angeles Bar Association, and the Southern California Council of the American Association for the United Nations [208] and then had several days' vacation with his son John Fell before returning to New York City.

To Edwin W. Pauley [209]

October 30, 1963

Dear Ed:

After Dallas and Los Angeles, what I needed was precisely your prescription — duck hunting! I am more grateful than I can tell you for giving John Fell and me all that luxurious transportation and that memorable afternoon at Island Farms. If you spoiled duck hunting in the East for me, it is a small price!

I had intended to talk with you about the Eleanor Roosevelt Memorial Foundation, created after her death by an Act of Congress, with a view to avoiding a multiplicity of fund-raising projects in her name.

Aside from the miscellaneous things that the Foundation proposes to do — including building wings to the Franklin D. Roosevelt Library at Hyde Park, to house *her* materials — the ultimate and major focus will

---

[207] Schlesinger, *A Thousand Days*, pp. 1020, 1021. Harlan Cleveland thinks that Stevenson drafted a letter to Kennedy urging him not to go to Dallas but decided not to send it since the President had more security information available than he had. Interview with Walter Johnson, June 12, 1972.

[208] USUN press release 4275.

[209] President and chairman of the board of Pauley Petroleum, past treasurer of the Democratic National Committee, and Democratic National Committeeman from California, 1944–1948.

be in the field of human rights. At the end of the road I can envisage something like an Eleanor Roosevelt Institute of Human Rights attached to some major university, and doing both research and training and adult education in this particular field. The goal is $25,000,000 — and it looks very distant indeed to me! However, we have "Founder" contributions of $25,000 and up from 40 or more thus far, and several contributions of over $100,000 to $250,000. Labor Unions feel confident that they can produce around 8 or 10 million dollars over a period of time — so I am not downhearted — but on top of everything else it has been a frightful chore for me.

All this is by way of saying that if you feel disposed to help with this project to keep that noble woman's memory alive, I would of course be delighted.

And perhaps you will let me know when you are in New York and we can talk about ducks and oil and things!

Cordially,

P.S. I have just discovered that you evidently paid for my hunting license — and enclose my check for $28, with apologies for the oversight and renewed thanks for that lovely day!

A.E.S.

To Earl Cabell [210]

October 30, 1963

Dear Mr. Mayor:

When I returned from the West Coast this week I was shown a clipping of the letter that you wrote to the *Dallas Morning News*, about the incident that occurred in your city. It is most heartening to see the leader of a great community speak up in such a forthright manner. In talking with the press, I have done my best to put this incident in perspective and to underline the fact that with the exception of a few zealots, I was treated with the utmost courtesy during my visit in Dallas. I thought my visit to your city was most worthwhile and I am glad I came.

Best wishes,

Sincerely,

[210] Mayor of Dallas, Texas.

To Stanley Marcus [211]

October 30, 1963

Dear Stan:

I seem to have become, albeit unintentional, something of a hero. And I rather think that President Kennedy is convinced that you and I rigged it all! At all events, everyone from U Thant down is convinced that it is the best publicity that the United Nations has had in those regions for a long time.

All of which only attests to my gratitude to you and that gallant Jack Goren for your many courtesies and infinite hospitality.[212] I really enjoyed the visit more than I can say — and especially the opportunity to meet Mrs. Marcus and that charming daughter of yours.

I hope I shall have the opportunity to see you and Jack here in New York soon — to thank you both again. And, I hope not contrary to your advice, I have urged President Kennedy not to delete Dallas from his forthcoming itinerary.

Cordially yours,

To Mrs. Eugene Meyer [213]

November 1, 1963

My dear Agnes:

Thanks for your note about the episode in Dallas. Actually, I never had a warmer or more enthusiastic reception anywhere, and the idiot fringe was small if vocal and violent. The deluge of messages, editorials, etc., that followed made it all the more worthwhile. Indeed, U Thant assures me that the United Nations has never had better advertising, especially in that opaque area where little light penetrates. And I even had a telegram from an unknown lady expressing her regrets and saying that she admired my "magnitude!"

I am distressed that there have been so few opportunities to see you during the autumn. But I have had some fragments of visits with Kay [Graham] here in New York and find her strong and calm, and I think even happy with her work, in spite of all the unfolding problems.

I hope that it won't be long before we have a reunion — here or in Washington!

Dearest love,

ADLAI

211 President of Neiman-Marcus, Dallas, Texas.
212 Mr. Marcus introduced Stevenson at the Dallas meeting, which Mr. Goren had helped to plan. See Sanley Marcus, *Minding the Store* (Boston: Little, Brown, 1974), for a description of the incident.
213 The original is in the Agnes Meyer files, Princeton University Library.

P.S. I want so much to talk to you about the Eleanor Roosevelt Foundation. On top of everything else it has been a heavy burden, but things are beginning to take shape, including the program, and I am more hopeful that we may have something important in hand. The money is coming slowly, but coming nonetheless!

To Peter B. Mohn [214]

November 1, 1963

Dear Mr. Mohn:

I'm sorry it has taken me so long to reply to your letter, for I fully sympathize and to some extent share the dilemma of the liberal today who wonders how to answer the shrill cries of arch-conservatism, which seem so loud though they come from a distance so far to our right.

On the other hand, my recent brush with a group of reactionaries has reinforced my conviction that their noisiness is in inverse proportion to their numbers. The inside story of Dallas was a resounding ovation by thousands of people, though the outside story of the rude and fearful few got most of the attention. But even more encouraging has been the outpouring of letters and telegrams, most of which were not limited to protesting the behavior of the demonstrators but also indicated a growing respect for and faith in the United Nations. Although I am aware that support of the UN is not the only measure of America's political maturity, I do think it is an important one, because those who continually attack the UN are the same individuals who have attacked almost every other intelligent and outward-looking effort since World War II.

Despite these obstructive activities, however, the country as a whole supported the Marshall Plan, NATO, Point Four, Alliance for Progress, Decade of Development, the World Bank, International Monetary Fund, Special Fund, etc.

It is also a fact that the noisy, bad mannered, disruptive opposition we are talking about has also opposed the new test ban treaty, opposed the Korean War, and tried to force the UN out of the Congo, but again they did not succeed.

All of this, it seems to me, is quite a demonstration of intelligence, far-sightedness and world mindedness on the part of a great majority of Americans.

I was very glad to hear from you, and to read the thoughtful editorials you enclosed, which I think is another indication that good sense is being published and read all over the country. I would say too that those of us who support enlightened national and international politics must

[214] City editor of the New Ulm, Minnesota, *Daily Journal.*

not be silent, lest those who do speak up mistake themselves for voices in the wilderness.

Cordially yours,

To John Connally [215]

November 1, 1963

Dear Governor:

I want you to know how grateful I am for the statement which you issued following the unfortunate little incident in Dallas the other day. Actually, as you know, my speech had as warm and enthusiastic a reception in Dallas as I have ever had anywhere, and the demonstrators were but a minute handful. In my statements to the press, I repeatedly invited attention to the warm reception I had in Dallas and the unimportance of the demonstrators as a reflection of public opinion.

After this incident, I feel all the more confident that the President's visit to Texas will be gratifying — to you as well as to him!

With renewed thanks for your prompt and gratifying reaction, I am

Cordially yours,

To James P. Warburg [216]

November 4, 1963

Dear Jim:

Over the weekend I read the excerpt from your biography [217] with delight. Now I can hardly wait for the book! I have no comments except a reservation about what you say on Page 25, about being disappointed "by his last minute attempt in 1960, to secure the Democratic nomination for a third time."

Actually, I think had you been closer to that episode, you would have fully appreciated my infinite difficulties, and might delete this clause. You may recall that immediately after the election in 1956, I announced that I would not seek the Democratic nomination again. For the ensuing four years, I had a tough time, and spent a good deal of it out of the country, including much of the Spring before the Convention of 1960.[218] As the Convention approached, I refused repeatedly requests from Mrs. [Eleanor] Roosevelt, Senator [Herbert] Lehman, Senator [Mike] Monroney, Senator [Eugene] McCarthy, Senator [Hubert] Humphrey,

[215] Governor of Texas.
[216] Banker, philanthropist, and author of many books.
[217] *The Long Road Home* (Garden City, New York: Doubleday, 1964), his autobiography.
[218] See *The Papers of Adlai E. Stevenson*, Vol. VII.

et al, that I announce my candidacy. Indeed, I never did, but that did not seem to deter them.

Meanwhile, I refused vigorous overtures to assist in a "stop Kennedy" movement with Lyndon Johnson, [219] and tried to preserve a position of strict neutrality to the end. Although a member of the Illinois Delegation, I even declined to appear again on the floor after the first episode, but, as I say, a group of determined supporters kept at it excessively, and with a view to establishing in the delegates' minds my availability if a deadlock should develop.

Sometime, perhaps I could tell you more about this long ordeal to make me a "candidate" after I had said I would not be one, and for four years even avoided questions about whether I could be drafted. In a word — I did not make a "last minute attempt to secure the Democratic nomination."

It was good to have even a glimpse of you and Joan [220] the other day, and I hope there will be more.

Yours,

To Kenneth O'Donnell [221]

November 4, 1963

Dear Kenny:

I have had a deluge of correspondence since my incident in Dallas. The enclosed letter [222] is thoughtful and of possible interest in anticipation of your visit there, and the President's understanding of the local situation.

But I do doubt his gloomy conclusion that the idiot fringe is in fact "winning their fight in Dallas." On the contrary, my guess is that the President will have an enthusiastic and sincere reception.

Cordially,

On November 7, 1963, Stevenson spoke and presented the award of the American Jewish Committee to Robert S. Benjamin.[223]

. . . Speaking at dinners of the American Jewish Committee I have a feeling is becoming a habit with me — perhaps it is one of my better

[219] See *The Papers of Adlai E. Stevenson,* Vol. VII, pp. 499–500, 501, 505, 529, 530.

[220] Mrs. Warburg.

[221] Special assistant to the President. Mr. O'Donnell arranged Kennedy's visit to Dallas.

[222] A letter from Bob Walker, news director of WFAA Television in Dallas.

[223] This speech was transcribed from a tape recording in the possession of Arnold Picker, of United Artists Corporation, New York City.

habits — and I shall long remember, Mr. Rosenwald,[224] the dinner that night when you honored me with your American Liberties Medallion. I recall I sat and listened mostly, of course, while my friend Jacob Blaustein [225] described my virtues with such eloquence and imagination that I had an uneasy feeling as he went along that there had been some mistake and that Benjamin Franklin was about to receive the award. (Laughter) Thinking back, though, it did seem to me that he went to rather great lengths to explain just why I was entitled to the award. After all, we were among friends at that time and not in Dallas. (Laughter and applause) Since I've been here no one has asked me about anything except Dallas. Perhaps I should break the suspense. I have come here tonight not to hit Bob Benjamin on the head, not to bury him, but to praise him. But I shall take a moment or two to say a few words about a matter that I think deeply concerns Bob Benjamin as it does me, and that is the present public attitude in some areas of the country and among some people toward the United Nations. Down in Dallas, for instance, General [Edwin] Walker, who is known to some of you, is so distressed over the United Nations and the United States Ambassador to the United Nations, that he is flying the American flag upside down. The other day someone asked me if anything should be done about it, and off the record, of course, I said I thought that the General himself was upside down and maybe it wasn't much to worry about. But my reception in Dallas, I want you to know, for a speech about foreign affairs and about the eighteenth anniversary of the United Nations was just about the warmest I have ever received anywhere, in or out of politics, yet with five thousand inside the hall cheering and fifty outside the hall jeering, the latter, as is usually the case, got the attention in the headlines. However, as it turned out, the incident, I think, had a salutary effect, and for this I am grateful. The indignation demonstrated, I believe, that the extremists are a very small minority and that their views and their manners are repugnant to the great bulk of our citizens. As it was in the time of Senator Joe McCarthy, I am sure it is still a mistake, to use Thomas Jefferson's expression, to underestimate the good sense of the American people, although there is still an occasional politician among us who seems to doubt it. After all, we live in a day when modern weapons are ten million times more powerful than the world has ever seen and are only minutes away from [us at] any time, we live in a day when two thirds of all mankind are struggling to overcome degrading conditions of poverty, illiteracy and disease, and we live in a day when nearly all nations of the world are engaged in a joint effort to keep the peace and to improve the lot of mankind. The focus of this effort is in that remarkable experiment, the United Nations. While I am

[224] William Rosenwald, a philanthropist active especially in the United Jewish Appeal and the American Jewish Committee.
[225] A Baltimore business executive and philanthropist.

not worried about the lunatic fringe, I am, like Bob Benjamin, aware that the endeavors of this organization must be understood and must be supported by the masses of the people in our free society whose beliefs are reflected in government decisions.

Let me, then, say no more about my Texas reminiscences except to comment that someone who wired me that I was too magnanimous in my reaction to those pickets down there, yet this telegram that I picked up was from a lady in Boston who ended her generous and charitable remarks in these words: "I also love your magnitude." (Laughter) And here I thought I had been reducing for the last six months. But I must say I am getting used to telegrams about my appearance. You know it turned out that my tilt with the Dallas pickets occurred on the very anniversary of another tilt I had just one year before to the day with Ambassador Zorin in the Security Council over the placing of the Russian missiles in Cuba. I should like to say parenthetically that between Mr. Zorin and the pickets, Mr. Zorin was much more polite (Laughter), and he didn't carry any signs and didn't even have much to say. In any event, during that debate I received a telegram from a retired Los Angeles schoolteacher which said, "Dear Ambassador Stevenson, I really admire you so much. Your posture, however, is negative. Why don't you sit up straight so that you'll make a good impression on the underdeveloped countries?" (Much laughter) Now all these remarks about my magnitude and posture are really calculated to bring me at last to the business at hand, which is my very good friend, Bob Benjamin.

There has never been any question about his posture, a posture of a tireless and inspiring public service, whether it has to do with the United Nations, the American Jewish Committee, with human relations, indeed, with the whole spectrum of our affairs. In these respects, Bob, we all love your magnitude. There is really not much, I am sure, that I can tell any of you that you don't already know about him as well as I. After all, you selected him for this award, so you must think about him much as I do. I had, however, one story that does come to mind and it happened during that same Cuban affair that I was talking about a moment ago. I was supposed to appear on a television program somewhere just as the crisis in the Security Council was reaching a climax, and casting around for somebody to fill in for me at the last moment I naturally thought of Bob Benjamin, and then, when we reached him about two hours before the show was to commence, he was on a tennis court in Long Island. All he said was, "Give me time to change into a suit and I will come right in." As I understood later, it wasn't until he was seated in the studio and the cameras were focused on him he suddenly discovered that he was still wearing tennis shoes. But when it comes to friends in need, I think Bob Benjamin always wears his running shoes, and for this I believe we are all fortunate. As the National Chairman of the United States Committee for the United Nations, he has brought new life to the cause of world peace in this country. I can tell you that Bob Benjamin is a major reason for so many Americans knowing and understanding what that world organization is doing, and that it is mankind's best hope for peace and security in these troubled times. If he did nothing else, he deserves my thanks and yours, and I believe the entire country's, and of course he does much besides. He is one of the leaders of your Committee, and in countless unsung and unheralded ways he has advanced the cause of human relations in equal rights and better government. Today we in the United States are committed as never before in our history to solving our problems of racial discrimination by giving every man his rights as a human being, and as a son of God, and as an American citizen to whom equality is a birthright and not a privilege. And when we solve these problems, as we shall, it will be because of the dedication and the leadership of men like Bob Benjamin, like Morris Abram,[226] like so many of you who are here tonight. The finest tribute I could pay to Bob Benjamin is to say that he reminds me of Eleanor Roosevelt. Since her death last year I have often reflected on what made up her special quality of greatness, and the most important, I think, was the absolute quality of her disinterestedness. She did everything because it was worth doing — work was there, work had to be done. That was the reason she did it. Not because it would enhance her personal role or her personal position, or her personal prestige. Of that she seemed oblivious. And so it is with Bob Benjamin. Whether it is the United States Committee for the United Nations, whether it is the American Jewish Committee, the Citizens Committee for International Development, the Eleanor Roosevelt Foundation, it is not the projection of his own role that's important, it's the work, the job that must be done. And to it he gives his heart, he gives his imagination and the entire quality of his tireless energy. Yes, I think Bob Benjamin deserves your award tonight, and I count myself profoundly flattered that you have asked me to present it to him, for the inscription on this splendid bowl says, "An exceptional leadership in mankind's struggle to achieve human dignity and equality." To this inscription, though, I should like to add a philosopher's words: "All work that is worth anything is done in faith." And Bob Benjamin's work is meaningful because his is the faith of decency, and of humility, of equality, and of social responsibility. We are all better because of it and because of him. Thank you. (Much applause)

---

[226] A partner in Paul, Weiss, Rifkind, Wharton & Garrison and president of the American Jewish Committee.

To Lady Barbara Jackson

November 13, 1963

Dearest Barbara:

. . . The session is grinding on and will undoubtedly establish a mark for the dullest on record. But the relative tranquillity across the street has brought no relief to the U.S. Mission, and the thundering herd still mills around these offices day and night, leaving me little time for trips to Washington, which I miss, and trips to Illinois, which I miss still more.

Things are reaching a climax with respect to Ellen [Stevenson], but when that happens it will be a relief from a deteriorating situation that has taken such a heavy toll on the boys and caused such embarrassment to so many friends. John Fell and Natalie are staying with me for a few days on business, and next week Adlai and Nancy are arriving. On Thanksgiving, they are going to join me and the [Ernest] Ives at Ruth Field's in South Carolina for a long weekend of hunting, resting — and sunning, I hope!

Mary Spears has just left after a fortnight with me, looking very frail but full of spirit. . . . She has left me a memorandum from Louis [227] about the situation in Ghana, which seems to contain more concern about U.S. criticism of the U[nited]. K[ingdom]. than anxiety about [Kwame] Nkrumah. I don't understand it after the way we have supported the U.K. on most everything.

Talks between [Alberto Franco] Nogueira and the African leaders about Angola have ended without much progress, and the Africans are whipping each other up to new emotional heights in the Fourth Committee. Yesterday Tanganyika (which has become one of our most hostile "friends") even charged us with conducting underground nuclear tests with South Africa. I went into the committee this morning and let 'em have it, which I've decided is the only way to treat this sort of extremism which is increasing right and left. It is clear now that the African target is no longer Portugal, South Africa and Southern Rhodesia, but the US and the UK. Meanwhile France sits mute and musing.

And I haven't begun to report! At home, I think [Richard M.] Nixon is emerging as a probable compromise candidate after [Governor Nelson] Rockefeller destroys [Senator Barry] Goldwater, which I am sure he is determined to do at any cost. Political prophecy this early is hazardous, but a replay of Kennedy vs. Nixon seems to me likely, with the probable result that Kennedy will win by something better than an eyelash this time. The disaffection of the South and the rising irritation among the whites, however, may be assuming formidable proportions. I don't in-

---

[227] General Sir Louis Spears, husband of Mary Borden Spears, who was Ellen Stevenson's aunt.

clude the right wing lunatic fringe (that spit on the Ambassador to the UN), because I can't believe they are numerous enough to be significant.

I wish I could go on, but the time has come to do the cocktail parties and change clothes for the evening appearance. I worry about your exhausting travels, and even two lines would be comforting. I have not bothered you with speech writing, in view of your own burdens, but I must add that on top of everything else the Eleanor Roosevelt Foundation is a formidable load. Your piece at Lincoln Center was a godsend! [228]

Love always,

To Benoit Bindzi [229]

November 13, 1963

Dear Mr. Ambassador:

The other night you told me that you were awaiting my reply to your *note verbale* about the article in THE [New York *Daily*] NEWS of October 21–22.

I had not understood that you were awaiting a further word from me. However, I am happy to tell you again that I deeply regret the unfortunate charges of traffic obstruction and the offensive comments of the reporter who wrote these articles.

As you know, I spoke personally to Mr. Richard Clarke, Editor of THE NEWS, and requested that he publish your letter of protest. As published, the letter is somewhat abbreviated to accommodate the newspaper's space problem. I regret the deletions.

Finally, let me say again that under our Constitution the American press is entirely free; in peacetime, for all practical purposes, it is immune to government authority, and hence is free to publish or not to publish material as it sees fit.

With renewed expressions of my regard and respect for you, for President [Ahmadou] Ahidjo and the Government and people of the Cameroons, I am

Sincerely yours,

To Mrs. Harold Hochschild [230]

November 19, 1963

My dear Mary:

Thank you so much for the loveliest, long, quiet, comfortable night I have had for months! And thank you, also, for a delightful luncheon and

---

[228] Stevenson spoke at the International Tribute to Eleanor Roosevelt at Lincoln Center in New York on October 21, 1963. USUN press release 4271.

[229] Permanent representative of the Federal Republic of Cameroon to the United Nations.

[230] The former Mary Marquand, a friend of Stevenson's since his undergraduate days at Princeton.

an opportunity to see some old friends.

All in all, I count that weekend in Princeton the most civilized I have ever had. Moreover, it even improved my bronchitis!

. . . Perhaps . . . you will all come and have dinner with me in New York some night. Meanwhile, my utmost thanks for your kindness, and

Much love,

P.S. Your letter has just come. Hooray! A new career — cook for the HKHs!! [231] Give me a try-out in the Adironda[c]ks.

A

On Friday, November 22, 1963, four weeks after Stevenson's visit to Dallas, President Kennedy was assassinated on a Dallas street.

Stevenson was at the UN having lunch with members of the Chilean delegation when Francis W. Carpenter, director of news services for USUN, brought him the news that the President had been shot. As they walked to the U.S. Mission building, Stevenson said: "That's in Dallas. Maybe I should have insisted that he not go to Dallas." They watched television in Stevenson's office. Carpenter wrote: "When the death was announced, there was immediate silence. Stevenson was quite poker-faced. In moments of stress he just works away. His first thought was that he had to get some word of consolation to Jackie and the family. He dictated telegrams, then wrote out a statement of two or three paragraphs in longhand." [232]

To Mrs. John F. Kennedy

November 22, 1963

I PRAY FOR YOU AND ALL OF US. DEVOTEDLY,

ADLAI

To Mr. and Mrs. Robert F. Kennedy

November 22, 1963

DEAR ETHEL AND BOB, A FEW MINUTES AGO IN THE GENERAL ASSEMBLY WE STOOD IN SILENT PRAYER. THERE WERE TEARS IN THE EYES OF ALL OF US, AND THAT'S THE WAY THE WHOLE WORLD IS TODAY. MY OWN SORROW IS IMMEASURABLE, SO I CAN IMAGINE YOURS.

---

[231] Mrs. Hochschild wrote that because Stevenson had shaken their cook's hand, she might refuse to cook any more, in which case he would have to cook for them.
[232] Quoted in the New York *Post*, November 22, 1964.

To Mr. and Mrs. Edward M. Kennedy

November 22, 1963

THE SHOCK AND GRIEF AT THE UNITED NATIONS TODAY IS TESTIMONY TO THE WORLD'S DEEP SENSE OF LOSS. MY PERSONAL SORROW IS IMMEASURABLE. MY DEEPEST SYMPATHY AND PRAYERS GO TO YOU AND YOUR FAMILY.

To Mr. and Mrs. Stephen E. Smith

November 22, 1963

DEAR JEAN AND STEPHEN, THE WORLD HAS LOST ITS CHAMPION. ALL IN THE UNITED NATIONS ARE BEREFT. MY DEEPEST PERSONAL SORROW GOES TO YOU AND ALL YOUR FAMILY.

To Mrs. Peter Lawford

November 22, 1963

DEAREST PAT, THE WORLD IS GRIEVING WITH YOU AND YOUR FAMILY. MY PERSONAL SORROW IS ACUTE AND I SEND YOU DEEPEST SYMPATHY.

To Lyndon B. Johnson

November 22, 1963

YOU HAVE MY PRAYERS AND WHATEVER STRENGTH I HAVE IS AT YOUR COMMAND ALWAYS.

Stevenson issued the following statement to the press on November 22.

The tragedy of this day is beyond instant comprehension. All of us who knew him will bear the grief of his death to the day of ours. And all men everywhere who love peace and justice and freedom will bow their heads.

At such a moment we can only turn to prayer — prayer to comfort our grief, to sustain Mrs. Kennedy and his family, to strengthen President Johnson, and to guide us in time to come. May God help us.

To Mrs. Edison Dick [233]

[no date]

Jane

Sometime I hope to be able to express — perhaps in silence — my thanks for your letter after Kennedy's death.

Yes — you were always there in every crisis. Pray God you always will be!

Sometime after President Kennedy's death, Stevenson told Harlan Cleveland that his relations with President Lyndon B. Johnson would be better than those with Kennedy since Johnson was a man of Stevenson's generation. Although Johnson paid greater deference to Stevenson than Kennedy had done, after a few weeks of Johnson's presidency their relationship deteriorated.[234]

At 2:30 P.M. on Saturday, November 23, 1963, Johnson held his first cabinet meeting. Stevenson made the following statement.[235]

Mr. President,

When President Kennedy's Cabinet met for the first time following his inauguration, I presumed to speak on behalf of my colleagues, in view of my background and seniority in the Party and its leadership. I said to him that while of course we were all subject to the frailties of mortal men, he could count on us to discharge our assignments to the best of our abilities, and execute his orders with absolute fidelity to him.

Except for three changes, the same group of men surrounds you, Mr. President, on this sad and dismal afternoon. All of us suffer with you the same grief at the cruel and untimely death of the leader we, like you, respected, obeyed, and loved. All of us served him loyally.

While we cannot obscure our loss, we are, I know, mindful, too, that

[233] This handwritten letter is in the possession of Mrs. Dick.

[234] Harlan Cleveland, interview with Walter Johnson, June 12, 1972. Stevenson told Arthur Schlesinger, Jr., after talking with President Johnson following Kennedy's funeral, that he believed he would play a much larger role in foreign policy than under Kennedy. Schlesinger said later, "It turned out that he was in worse shape with Johnson than he had been with Kennedy because Rusk quickly got more power." See Martin, *Adlai Stevenson and the World*, pp. 781–782.

[235] The text is from the ribbon copy with Stevenson's handwritten corrections and interlineations. Alfred Steinberg wrote that Stevenson's "wretched reading" of this statement "bore none of his own low regard for the new chief executive." *Sam Johnson's Boy: A Close-up of the President from Texas* (New York: Macmillan, 1968), p. 618. For Stevenson's earlier relations with Johnson, see *The Papers of Adlai E. Stevenson*, Vol. VI, Vol. VII.

this is only a moment's pause in the nation's business and that the brutal burden of leadership has suddenly fallen on your shoulders.

To share as best we can that crushing burden is our task now, Mr. President. And I can say with the confidence of experience with your Cabinet that your will is our command, and that we will serve you with the same fidelity we served your predecessor.

Finally, Mr. President, let me echo what Dean Rusk has said. Your unique qualities of character, wisdom and experience are a blessing to our country in this critical hour, and our confidence in your leadership is total. Seasoned by three years of the stark reality of responsibility, we trust we have deserved the confidence you have so graciously expressed — and I speak with certainty, Mr. President, when I promise you we will all do our damnedest to merit it in the future.

Stevenson spoke at the UN memorial service for John F. Kennedy on November 26 [236] and then went to spend the Thanksgiving holidays at Ruth Field's Chelsea Plantation in Ridgeland, South Carolina.

To Arthur M. Schlesinger, Jr. [237]

November 28, 1963

Dear Arthur —

I didn't have a chance to see you in the turmoil. I will be back in New York Sunday evening Dec. 1, and I hope you will consult me before you *do* anything.[238] Not that my views will be worth much but they — and I — are always at the command of the beloved Schlesingers.

Would you please see that Jackie gets the enclosed *personally* [239] — Thanks.

Ever —

ADLAI

To John Fell Stevenson [240]

December 4, 1963

Dear John Fell:

We had a lovely Thanksgiving all together with Ruth [Field] . . . at Chelsea — and talked much of you and Natalie.

[236] USUN press release 4318.
[237] This handwritten letter is in the Schlesinger papers, John F. Kennedy Library.
[238] Schlesinger remained on the White House staff for four months.
[239] Mrs. Kennedy on December 4, 1963, thanked him for his letter and sent him a silver shoe from his 1956 campaign which her husband had kept in his stud box.
[240] The original is in the possession of John Fell Stevenson.

By unanimous agreement, I was also instructed to invite you and Natalie and Mao to Libertyville for the Christmas week — all expenses included. Please let me know as promptly as you can. I pray it will be possible. You can never tell how many reunions we shall have. Granny Carpenter [241] will be there for Christmas Day, too.

Love,
DAD

On December 9, 1963, Stevenson addressed the General Assembly of the United Nations in its commemoration of the fifteenth anniversary of the Universal Declaration of Human Rights.[242] With the world still shocked over the assassination of President Kennedy and President Johnson largely unknown to the world Stevenson emphasized the continuity of America's dedication to universal human rights.

As a common standard of achievement for all, the Declaration of Human Rights was a milestone in history. It was a great stride along the road to justice and to peace. For the first time the international community accepted the proposition that a precondition of peace was human rights — the rights that tyranny, oppression and bigotry had too long denied to man. We meet here today to commemorate this act. In the words of an immortal champion of those rights, it is altogether fitting and proper that we should do this.

For the United States, in particular, this ceremony has added significance. In addition to marking the fifteenth anniversary of the Universal Declaration of Human Rights, we in the United States also celebrate this week the 172nd anniversary of our own Bill of Rights.

It is a matter of pride for us that the two have so much in common — that from our distant past we can take increased hope in the world's future, a future in which dignity and equality shall be the inalienable right of all men everywhere.

As a bridge to the future the Universal Declaration has a profound significance. However, unless we cross the bridge, unless we use it as an instrument to right the wrongs that still oppress so much of the human family, the Declaration will sometime wither on the shelves with all the other pious affirmations of good intentions.

Today, gratified though we may be that the Declaration has gathered

[241] Mrs. John Alden Carpenter.
[242] United Nations, *Official Records,* General Assembly, December 9, 1963, pp. 9–10. On December 10, 1963, Stevenson delivered a speech in the same vein at the Human Rights Day ceremony held at the National Archives building in Washington, D.C.

reverence and respect for fifteen years, human rights still remain the great unfinished business of all men, as all speakers here this morning have testified. So this is not an occasion, it seems to me for lighthearted celebration. It is a moment for sober reflection. The war that the Declaration declared is not yet won. Only when every man in every land can truly say that he has attained every right that is his due, only then will we have the right truly to celebrate. And perhaps none of us will be here when that great day comes.

In marking this anniversary I would like to call your attention to some words recently uttered by the new President of this country, Lyndon Johnson:

"Justice" — he said — "is not a practical thing which can be measured in terms of percentages. Any degree of injustice is complete injustice. And until we achieve complete justice we can regard progress only as a series of steps towards the goal. Each step should hearten us; but should not lull us into self-satisfaction that the job has been done." [243]

And so it is that the Universal Declaration of Human Rights must not be regarded as an end. Noble it is, but it is only one step towards the establishment of a universal standard of justice. It should hearten us, yes; "but should not lull us into self-satisfaction that the job has been done."

President Kennedy, in the last address that he was to make at this rostrum,[244] told us truthfully and bluntly what that job was, and he was equally candid whether referring to the United States or to others. And if I may digress for a moment, I should like to suggest that all world leaders who come to this rostrum discuss with equal candour the stubborn ills that plague their own societies. Would that we did not have such ills in America. But until they are cured, and I can assure you that we shall never be secret or furtive about them, we shall continue to battle them and discuss them openly where all may see and hear. For this, too, is a human right — the right of men to know what is being done to combat the evils among them. President Kennedy said:

"But man does not live by bread alone — and the Members of this Organization are committed by the Charter to promote and respect human rights. Those rights are not respected when a Buddhist priest is driven from his pagoda, when a synagogue is shut down, when a

[243] Speech to the Capital Press Club in Washington, D.C., May 18, 1963.
[244] Kennedy spoke to the General Assembly on September 20, 1963.

Protestant church cannot open a mission, when a Cardinal is forced into hiding, or when a crowded church service is bombed.

"The United States of America is opposed to discrimination and persecution on grounds of race and religion anywhere in the world, including our own nation. . . .

". . . We are unalterably opposed to apartheid and all forms of human oppression. We do not advocate the rights of black Africans in order to drive out white Africans. Our concern is the right of all men to equal protection under the law — and since human rights are indivisible, this body cannot stand aside when those rights are abused and neglected by any Member State.

"New efforts are needed if this Assembly's Declaration of Human Rights, now fifteen years old, is to have full meaning. And new means should be found for promoting the free expression and trade of ideas, through travel and communication and through increased exchanges of people, books and broadcasts. For as the world renounces the competition of weapons, competition in ideas must flourish — and that competition must be as full and as fair as possible." [1]

I have taken the liberty of quoting rather extensively not what I have said, but what two Presidents of this country have said recently, because this could have been said anywhere in the world by any leaders concerned with prejudice, oppression, social irresponsibility and discrimination. To press forward the frontiers of the human intellect and spirit is the task of all leaders everywhere, and the United Nations by this historic declaration has charted the way to lift from the conscience and shoulders of mankind the ancient burdens of man's inhumanity to man. It is for us to follow the chart, to get on with the great unfinished business of human rights which are at the core, the very heart of our effort to bring about a peaceful change in the affairs of the human family.

The history of tyranny and of injustice is much older than the history of freedom and justice. Yet now we know full well that no society, national or international, can prosper or long endure if it does not grant the people full human, political and economic rights. When the battle for the rights of man will be won is not predictable, but this must not lessen our determination that, in the end, it will be won and that it will be won peacefully.

Eleanor Roosevelt, who gave so much of her heart and tireless energy to the Declaration, was once asked: "Where, after all, do universal rights begin?" And she answered: "In small places close to home, so close and

[1] United Nations, *Official Records*, General Assembly, 1209 meeting, pp. 4–7.

so small that they cannot be seen on any map of the world . . . they are the world of the individual person."

So let each of us go forth from here to places close to home, and there let each of us strive to finish the work that we, in this Assembly, have solemnly proclaimed "the highest aspiration of the common people."

At Stevenson's urging, President Johnson spoke to the General Assembly of the United Nations on December 17, 1963.

To Lyndon B. Johnson

December 18, 1963

Dear Mr. President:

I'm sure you know by now what a great success your visit to the United Nations has been. The press reaction, as you probably have been told, is overwhelmingly favorable. And just a few minutes ago we sent a telegram to the Department reporting in detail the enthusiastic comments of many individual delegates here at the United Nations. It was a worthwhile day all around.

It goes without saying that I personally appreciated your making this effort, for I am sure we will be reaping substantial benefits from it in the months ahead.[245]

With best wishes,

Sincerely,

On the adjournment of the General Assembly, Stevenson spoke to a press conference at the United Nations on December 18, 1963.[246]

This is the third year in a row that I have had the pleasure of meeting with you ladies and gentlemen of the United Nations Press Corps to discuss the work of the General Assembly.

There is no need to tell you again how much store we set by the United Nations. President Johnson made that clear yesterday both in what he said and equally in what he did — the fact that he thought it important to come here and meet personally with the delegates to the General Assembly. I think we should underline here the President's declaration:

[245] Johnson replied that the United States was fortunate to have Stevenson in the United Nations and thanked him for his unstinting support.

[246] This speech and the questions and answers were transcribed by USUN and issued as press release 4349.

"The United States wants to see the cold war end, and wants to see it end once and for all."

We have seen very clearly in this Assembly how much can be accomplished when there is even a small rise in the political temperature. The declaration against placing nuclear weapons in orbit; [247] the declaration of the legal principles in the use of outer space; the sharp reduction in cold war polemics — all these are welcome progress, welcome steps on that long road called general and complete disarmament which can only be traversed one step at a time.

In this respect, the 18th Session is well described as a transitional session — part of a world-wide shift from arguing about peace in the abstract to building the machinery of peace in a very practical organization called the United Nations.

If we are in a time of transition, let us hope it is transition to a world of diversity in which no nation or bloc thinks of itself as presently or potentially in charge of the world. Certainly the tightest bloc, which we have called the monolithic communist world, is full of cracks, and diversity is no longer a monopoly of any region or grouping. A world more safe *for* diversity is not yet a world more safe *with* diversity.

There are dangers, of course, when any big iceberg begins to crack. The fissures in the Communist world have caused the aggressive, lone-wolf foreign policy of Communist China to stand out as both more obvious and more threatening to the rest of the world.

All in all, this Assembly has both reflected and contributed to the easing of cold war dangers which started with President Kennedy's speech at American University last June and the coming into force of the limited Nuclear Test Ban Treaty this autumn.

Now, as the disarmament negotiators go back to their tasks in Geneva next month, cooperation comes in for a new test. They will talk of technical problems like static observation posts and nuclear production controls — but the big question is wholly non-technical: it is whether each military power is willing enough and bold enough and imaginative enough to find agreed ways of slowing the arms race to a halt, and building simultaneously the international peacekeeping machinery which will permit the first steps toward practical arms control and reduction.

The Assembly's record on colonial and racial questions is a paradoxical mixture of strong sometimes unfair and provocative words and, for the most part, sober actions. We hope that the Republic of South Africa takes careful note of the unanimity and force of world opinion. Policies of

[247] The Soviet Union and the United States issued a joint statement of intent not to orbit weapons of mass destruction in outer space. This was combined in a General Assembly resolution on October 17, 1963, with a request for continued abstention in the future.

government-sponsored racial discrimination are contrary to the Charter and the universal elementary principles of freedom.

There is still a sincere desire in the United Nations membership to make the inevitable change peaceful — but the other side of the coin is that the maintenance of peace requires willingness to change.

On the Portuguese territories, a resolution of the Security Council has asked the Secretary General to continue efforts to get the Portuguese and interested African states to work through negotiations toward self-determination for the Portuguese territories in Africa.

The United Nations' biggest contribution on any really difficult issue is to start a process of quiet diplomacy looking toward a solution, and not merely to raise the dust of mutual recrimination.

It is certainly not too late to talk, as some would contend, about the growing political conflict in the southern third of Africa. It is also not too early for positive action to move toward equality of rights and equality of treatment, in Africa and elsewhere.

The Africans who feel strongly about their grievances, have not followed hot words with irresponsible action. The intemperate scenes and walk-outs which characterized some United Nations conferences last summer have not been repeated in this Assembly.

The good sense, restraint and orderly procedure which they have evidenced here is a favorable augury for the future handling of these difficult colonial and racial issues, which will continue to occupy an important place on the United Nations action agenda.

Support for United Nations peacekeeping activities was reaffirmed when the Assembly overwhelmingly endorsed a six months extension of the United Nations Operations in the Congo and a year's financing on an equitable basis of the United Nations Emergency Force in the Middle East.

The United Nations is helping maintain the peace in Yemen, in Kashmir, in Korea and throughout the Middle East under continuing Security Council and General Assembly mandates. Thus in a practical way experience is being gained and procedures are being developed that can be used in restoring and maintaining peace in future security crises in other parts of the world.

But the steady development of the United Nations peacekeeping capacities requires a solution to familiar problems — the payments past due from some members, and arrangements for financing future peace and security operations.

The United Nations' peacekeeping capacities — indeed its future as an action agency — is threatened by the refusal of the Soviet Union and some other countries to pay their assessed share of legally constituted operations.

The law on this subject is clear. The International Court of Justice has ruled and the General Assembly has accepted the ruling,[248] that members have Charter obligations to pay their assessments for peace-keeping as well as for the regular budget. The proper solution is for the Soviet Union and other debtors to pay up. This is what we would like to see happen. If it does not, if the delinquent countries insist on challenging the Charter, it would be a grievous blow to this Organization — because it would erode the support of some large and loyal contributors to its growth. We believe that if the other members want to preserve the Organization they must preserve its Charter.

So I want to say once more on behalf of the United States that we regard financial support of the United Nations peacekeeping operations as an essential obligation of the Member States. And I think I have already made it plain that I feel just as strongly about the United States of America's own financial contributions to the United Nations.

Coming up over the horizon is a series of issues in the field of trade and development. As the President said yesterday, one of our urgent tasks is "the steady improvement of collective machinery for helping the less developed nations build modern societies." This means the streamlining of Technical Assistance and pre-investment work at United Nations Head-quarters and the strengthening of the resident representatives of the United Nations in many countries, to enable the United Nations family of nation building agencies to act more like a family.

Strengthening the United Nations in the development field is urgent because of the danger of rising tensions between poor countries and rich countries — and the possibility that these tensions could merge with racial tensions that sometimes divide the world along similar lines. The rich and the poor could work more effectively together, and as the United Nations itself is effectively organized for this purpose, it can be enormously helpful to both by providing a political framework for mutual assistance.

We are glad that the 18th General Assembly began to get down to cases on the enlargement of the Security Council and the Economic and Social Council, to achieve better representation for Member States that did not exist when the original agreements were made on the distribution of seats.

The United States abstained on the final vote because, for a permanent member of the Security Council, this is an especially serious business that requires full consultation through our own constitutional processes between the executive and legislative branches of our government.

[248] On July 20, 1962, the International Court of Justice ruled that under articles 11, 14, and 17 of the Charter of the United Nations, the General Assembly was empowered to finance peacekeeping operations. The General Assembly in December, 1962, accepted the decision by a vote of 76 to 17, with 8 abstentions.

But we would like to see something worked out on this, and regret the rigidity which still characterizes the voting of our Soviet friends in this matter. If you ask me whether they are using the Chinese Communists to conceal their own attitude, I cannot answer.

Now before anyone accuses me of radiating only sweetness and light — to which no UN Ambassador should plead guilty — I want to point out that the spirit of detente I noted earlier was not present in every area of the Assembly's work — particularly in the Third and Sixth Committees. There the cold war did not thaw as much as elsewhere.

I need hardly say that this 18th Session of the General Assembly was not an unqualified success in other ways too.

It did not, for example, see the end of the Russian veto — indeed it saw one more added to make a total of 101 in the Security Council; it still saw some abuse of the principles of free and open debate; it still saw a tendency, although less than in previous sessions, to introduce unrealistic resolutions that have little chance of implementation; and it still saw needless inscription of items on an already overburdened agenda.

But, let me emphasize, these are not failures of the organization as such. They are failures of the membership.

Certainly, the Secretary General and his staff deserve our thanks and admiration for the splendid manner in which they have carried on their work. And here, too, let me say a word about the splendid performance of the President of the Assembly, Dr. Carlos Sosa-Rodriguez.

This was an orderly, well run session, and it marked a still further improvement in the general status and accomplishment of the Assembly, which can only enhance respect for the Organization. It was, I think, one of the least contentious sessions in recent United Nations history. Much of this is due to Dr. Sosa-Rodriguez, and he deserves and has our congratulations and thanks.

Perhaps, the 18th session will not go down as one in which miracles were worked; but I believe it may well be remembered as the session that proved that great and small powers do have the ability to look in the same direction and to labor together for the benefit of all.

We must remember that the history of the United Nations consists largely of problems, pitfalls and progress. As we have had occasion to say, the UN was built for trouble and thrives on it.

This fact, plus the improved disposition of our Communist friends to cooperate and to use the UN machinery instead of abusing it, encourage our hope that the prophets of doom and gloom will again be proven wrong, together with the derisive critics of the UN who usually see it as either dangerously effective or innocuously ineffective.

And now before we part I would like to express my warmest compliments to all of you here today for your conscientious and distinguished efforts to keep the world informed about what is happening behind the draperies of this house of glass.

Let me assure you I do not compliment you with any hopes that you will make your cross-examination any easier.

But I want to emphasize my high regard and appreciation of the day-in-day-out excellence of your coverage.

Yesterday someone wished me a Merry Christmas and for a Happy New Year. Let me wish all of you a Merry Christmas and a Happy New Year. May you have safe journeys back to your homes wherever they may be. While our world is not yet one; it is surely unique, and precious to us all alike.

- - - - -

AMB. STEVENSON: I have concluded my formal statement and will be happy to attempt to answer any questions that you choose to ask me.

QUESTION: Governor, when you were in Dallas just before the tragic occurrence and then when you returned here in New York I think you addressed the AFL-CIO, you were at that time very greatly preoccupied with this anti-UN movement which you expressed here, I think, in your speeches in the form of such expressions as rightism and extremism. Well, now, much blood has flown under the bridge since then and President Johnson is now in the White House. I hear nothing said about the extremist movement or the rightist movement. I wonder whether you think in this evaluation of events whether President Johnson will have to face the same skeptical movements which you had described as being afraid of the UN either as being innocuous or perhaps too effective — whether you are preoccupied with those fears to the same extent as you were preoccupied with them in that period preceding Kennedy's tragic death?

ANSWER: It is impossible for me to predict what the state of mind will be at the extremities of thought in this country in the future.

I have had a feeling that the effect of this tragedy that has befallen this country and the world has been to sober somewhat the extremist view and that perhaps we can look forward, if not with confidence at least with hope, to a decrease, a diminution in the extent of the attacks of the lunatic fringe.

I think it is the better part of caution, however, to anticipate that we shall never be wholly without extremist views in this country, where we prize the freedom of speech so highly, and where we are all pledged to preserve it, and that doubtless there will be recurrences of criticism of the UN from both the extremist right and perhaps the extreme left as we have known in the past.

In a word, I am tempted to think, at least, and pray that there has been some decrease in the heat, in the emotion that we have witnessed in recent years.

QUESTION: Mr. Ambassador, I have three topics in mind. I would be very grateful if you would allow me to elaborate these topics and ask you questions related to them. These are the questions of the People's Republic of China, Cuba and, thirdly, Malaysia.

As regards the People's Republic of China, may I remind you of the statement made by Mr. Roger Hilsman, the Assistant Secretary of State for Far Eastern Affairs, in San Francisco on December 13, in which he outlined the United States policy toward Peking and in which he left the door open to talks with China.[249] A few days ago there was a news analysis in the New York *Times* insinuating that the United States does not ignore the stability of the Peking government and that eventual recognition of the People's Republic of China might follow. Membership of the People's Republic of China, as you know, was also a most significant topic during the Eighteenth Session of the United Nations General Assembly, especially in the Special Political Committee on the question of equitable representation in the Security Council and the Economic and Social Council. Further, President Kennedy in one of his speeches, according to the New York *Times,* has said: "In a year or two it will no longer be possible to negotiate a disarmament treaty without the participation of Communist China." Further, there have been negotiations going on recently between the United States and the Ambassador of the People's Republic of China in Warsaw.

My question on this matter referring to these elaborations is: Is there any possible recognition of the People's Republic of China by the United States Government in the near future? And would you mind to give your comment?

ANSWER: I think the problem of China rests in Peking, not in Washington. If there are to be any changes in its relations with other powers, including the United States, those changes must originate in Peking. As long as the Communist Chinese persist in their present aggressive and lone wolf policies, there is not likely to be any improvement in their relations with the United States or, I believe, with the United Nations.

By their aggressive, lone wolf policies, I refer to the fact that the war still goes on in Korea, that they have encouraged and are encouraging the Vietcong, that they are stirring up the Pathet Lao, and that this continuous aggressive behavior is of Peking manufacture — not of Washington.[250]

[249] See Roger Hilsman, *To Move a Nation: The Politics of Foreign Policy in the Administration of John Kennedy* (New York: Doubleday, 1967), Part VII.
[250] For aggressive actions of the United States in Vietnam at this time, see *The Pentagon Papers: The Defense Department History of United States Decisionmaking on Vietnam,* Senator Gravel edition (Boston: Beacon Press, 1971), Vol. II, *passim.*

QUESTION: Would you mind continuing with the other topics on Cuba and Malaysia?

ANSWER: Perhaps we'd better move around. I will come back to you. I think it is only fair to the others.

QUESTION: Thank you very much, sir.

QUESTION: Ambassador Stevenson, as you noted, President Johnson said yesterday that the United States wants an end to the cold war once and for all. What steps would you suggest could now be taken to try to end that cold war, and would exploitation of the split between the Soviet Union and Red China be one of them?

ANSWER: Well, do you mean steps by the United States or by the United Nations or by the allies?

QUESTION: Both parties to the cold war.

ANSWER: Well, I would hope very much that we could make, as I said a moment ago, some progress in the field of disarmament, in the mutual reduction of arms. I think this would all contribute to a relaxation of anxiety and fear. I would hope very much that we could find enlarged areas of agreement between the East and the West, both in the political field and also in the economic field. I think it is in all of these areas — the continuity and the proper financing of this organization is one illustration.

I think the cold war has laid its frozen fingers on our relations in every area and, therefore, any relaxation that can take place in any area is a contribution.

As far as the exploitation of the division between the communist world — between Communist China and the Soviet Union, I do not think that it is a matter of exploitation, at least for the West. I think this is an internal problem within the communist family. But it has given rise, as I indicated in my prepared statement, to cracks in the monolithic concept of the world, to encouragement for those who believe in diversity and that the world shall not have any single boss. I think these all contribute to an improved climate.

QUESTION: Governor, what do you regard as the chief element or elements exacerbating cold war tensions?

ANSWER: Mistrust of one another I think would be the principal one, this of course, depending on which side you are on. In our judgment, it results largely from the concept of the closed society. The fact that there is, perhaps, very sincere mistrust about the objectives, the peaceful objectives of this country and the Western Allies within the Soviet Union. Certainly the fear of Germany is open and notorious. All of these things I think contribute on their side.

On our side, we can only look back over the history of these postwar years at the repeated examples of aggressive purpose and the disturbing declarations of philosophical intention.[251]

All of these things I think are what have created the climate of the cold war, without going into minute detail.

QUESTION: Ambassador Stevenson, the essential work of the Eighteenth Session here has not only been summarized as the three D's for decolonization, disarmament and development, but from what you said in your statement this morning could we add a fourth D — if not a big D perhaps a little d — for detente?

ANSWER: Yes, I think we could; yes, a very agreeable addition.

QUESTION: Sir, going back to this statement of your Assistant Secretary of State for Far Eastern Affairs, Mr. Roger Hilsman, the interpretation put on that by your own Americans is it has changed Washington's posture and you are trying to get the people to accept the facts of life as regards Red China. You answered this question to a certain extent, but still I think this question is important enough for you to elaborate a bit and tell us whether the United States attitude towards the Peking regime would undergo some changes in the United Nations? I think this is an important question for you to elaborate a little about it.

ANSWER: Well, I don't know what more I can say, sir. I don't know what you mean by elaborate about it. I made it clear, I thought, that in our view the problem of the relations with Peking depend on Peking, and as long as it persists in its present aggressive policies, there is little likelihood of any improvement in our relations. And that decision can't be made here. It can only be made there. It is just that simple.

The speech that Mr. Hilsman made the other day represented no change in the American position. We have been ready, open, waiting, willing to extend the hand of friendship and of cordiality and of co-operation to all peace-loving nations. Until that time comes, I am afraid there can't be any change in our position.

QUESTION: What I would ask is whether you, being a member of the Cabinet anyway, whether under Mr. Kennedy and Mr. Johnson some efforts will be made to contact Red China and its emissaries to see whether they would listen to reason. I think they are also making certain moves in that direction, sir, if I am not too wrong.

ANSWER: I am sorry I can't answer that because I just don't know whether any such moves are contemplated. I am very happy to hear what you say, however, that the Chinese have such moves in mind. If you don't mind, I will report that to my government!

251 For Stevenson's earliest negotiations with the Russians, see *The Papers of Adlai E. Stevenson,* Vol. II, Part Four.

QUESTION: Governor, you said, if I understood your prepared statement correctly, that the two disarmament questions in the foreground are static observation posts and nuclear production control. Now, yesterday the President mentioned non-proliferation. Do you think there is any priority of any of these three topics in the disarmament negotiations? And what is your evaluation of that?

ANSWER: Well, sir, I think it is apparent to all that the greatest likelihood of progress rests in the field of static observation posts and measures against surprise attack. This, like all the other possibilities, presents difficulties. However, the difficulties would seem perhaps to be less than those in the case, say, of non-dissemination of nuclear weapons, the East-West non-aggression pact and the others. So I would think that the priority would be, first, attention to measures against surprise attack.

QUESTION: Governor, I wanted to ask if the United States is determined to deny the right to vote in the Assembly to the Soviet Union and any other nations that remain in arrears in this next year?

ANSWER: Well, I would hope very much that this situation would never arise, as I tried to make clear. It is a matter, we think, of primary importance to the survival of this organization as well as to its effectiveness. And that means of remedying this delinquency should — and I hope will be — found, so that the question will not arise. But, certainly, if it does, likewise, we believe that rigid adherence to the law, to the Charter is essential to the Charter's preservation. Once you begin to contaminate or erode or interpret the Charter too flexibly, you very soon will have no sustaining body of legal structure to support the United Nations. This is one reason why we have been so meticulously careful to try to avoid the imposition of sanctions under Article VII in cases which do not clearly represent threats to international peace and security. We feel that it is the responsibility of all those who believe and are determined to see this organization survive to put the utmost emphasis on the Charter and on its compliance. And the same is true with respect to Article 19.

QUESTION: Sir, looking at the pattern of voting in this Assembly, do you find any tendency of the new small Asian and African countries to attempt to take over political power from the big powers through the pressure of numbers? I am thinking of the vote on expanding the councils and various other votes that have taken place.

ANSWER: Well, I should not care to put it that way — taking over control. I think that the power rests with the Afro-Asians by force of numbers and that they are conscious of their responsibility in exercising that voting power responsibly and intelligently and with restraint. While I am perfectly conscious that they know this power lies within their hands, I cannot point with any confidence to anything that has happened here in the Assembly to show that they intend to use it to their self-interest, excluding the interests of others. I do not believe that has been the case. As I attempted to say, that what often seemed intemperate and hot and provocative words have usually been followed by sober action.

QUESTION: Mr. Ambassador, both the United States and France seem to have given the same explanation in the Assembly and in the Special Political Committee why support to the expansion of the councils could not be given, yet France voted No and the United States together with the United Kingdom abstained. Now, does this abstention mean, sir, that the Administration is going to recommend to Congresss to ratify the change in the Charter?

ANSWER: I cannot predict with certainty what will ultimately happen with respect to the resolutions that were adopted yesterday. I did try to point out in what I have said that we have a problem — perhaps other countries have it likewise — which is the relationship between the legislative and the executive branches of our government, that for a matter like this which would require an amendment to the Charter of the United Nations there would have to be Senatorial ratification, ratification by the United States Senate. And that, therefore, there would have to be advance consultation between the executive branch and the Senate. For us here to commit the United States to a position — even if we made reservations — without that prior consultation would be both unwise tactically and also might create repercussions which would embarrass us later. So we felt, therefore, that we had to abstain consistent with our constitutional processes.

QUESTION: Governor, on the basis of what happened in the House Appropriations Committee last week, would you interpret this to mean that maybe there is not as strong support of the United Nations in the Congress as the President's word indicated yesterday?

ANSWER: Well, I think you also saw what happened yesterday in the Senate in which a substantial portion of the cuts were restored. I think it would be premature to try to draw any conclusions about the United Nations from what has happened in the House until the aid bill is passed through both houses. I do not believe there is any diminution. My own impression is that, if anything, this session of the General Assembly and the improved climate in the world has enhanced respect for the United Nations in the United States Congress. And that what you have witnessed here is the growing misgiving that we have seen not only in this country but elsewhere in the world about the extent to which it can support foreign aid at a time when we have an imbalance in our balance of payments and also when the tax burden is very heavy and when there is increasing feeling somehow that we have done our share and that maybe we should cut back.

QUESTION: Governor, this leads, I think, into the question I had in mind. Are there any specifics or are there likely to be in the President's suggestions yesterday that the global application of the American New Deal experience might be indicated?

ANSWER: Well, I think what he was saying was that he had had intimate personal experience with the evolution of the domestic New Deal in the 1930's and what he was envisioning now was an extension of these principles of concern for the welfare of peoples to the world scene.

QUESTION: What are the specifics?

ANSWER: Well, I think the emphasis in this brief speech — the principal emphasis was on economic development — the poor nations.

QUESTION: Yes, but does this envisage a new program of some kind, a new approach?

ANSWER: No, I don't think it envisions any new approach except to indicate his concern for this field and for his anxiety to see something effective done about it, both within the United Nations through the multilateral method as well as the old bilateral method. I think, if anything, this indicated, if any conclusions could be drawn from what he said, it would be the attention he paid to the multilateral method through international organizations, including the United Nations as well as the other international lending agencies.

QUESTION: You said that you hoped that Article 19 would not — the question would not arise. Since the Soviet Union has repeated at this Assembly anyway its opposition concerning the Congo financing, do you have any indication or can you see the possibility that the Soviet Union might give some money under some other chapter? And would that be acceptable?

ANSWER: Well, I can't imagine giving money under any other chapter, but I can conceive the Soviet Union changing its mind. I remind you that it was only October of a year ago when they flatly rejected in this very committee room my proposal for a suspension of nuclear testing in the atmosphere, under water and in outer space. Within six or seven months, they had accepted this proposal.

QUESTION: Governor, one subject that has not been touched on — or hardly touched on — even by yourself, sir, is the matter of human rights in this past Assembly. In the Third Committee, the United States Delegation seemed to indicate a change in policy from the old policy of insisting only on persuasion and education in the field of human rights to an interest on behalf of the United States in implementation of the Covenants on Human Rights which have been discussed here now for nine years and is still on the table. I wonder, sir, whether the United States Delegation will be prepared in the next Assembly to use its influence and prestige toward final adoption of the two draft Covenants on Human Rights? I wonder also, sir, whether the United States Delegation would use its influence and prestige behind an agenda item lost in the shuffle this year calling for a new declaration on elimination of all forms of religious discrimination?

ANSWER: I know of no change in the United States policy with respect to human rights.

I think our votes in Committee Three on the covenants to which you referred indicated what our position was and also the arguments we made about any infringement of the United States constitution on freedom of assembly and speech and so on.

Now, as to the covenants that are going to be discussed and the declaration that's going to be drawn up by the Commission on Human Rights, I understand that's going to take place in the next meeting of the Human Rights Commission.

We are very much in favor of human rights; we are very much in favor of expression of human rights by the United Nations; and we hope to demonstrate that in ratification by our Congress.

QUESTION: May I ask explicitly, sir, is the United States Delegation in favor of final Assembly determination on the two draft covenants regarding human rights that have been pending here since 1954?

MRS. [MARIETTA] TREE: Sir, the implementation clauses, as you know, have not been drawn up yet. I would imagine that would take several years of action by the Third Committee. And so the final position is not known on the two covenants.

QUESTION: Mr. Ambassador, may I go back to your remarks on the Chinese question? You have said that the improvement of relations between Peking and the United States as well as the United Nations will depend upon Peking's change of policies, and you mentioned several points like Pathet Lao and the Vietcong, but you did not say anything about Taiwan. In view of Roger Hilsman's remarks that the United States now accepts the stability of the Peking regime and the refusal of both Taiwan and Peking to accept the two China theory, does it mean that you are giving up your two China theory?

ANSWER: I didn't know we ever had one! Our position is very clear that the Chinese Communists still claim Taiwan. They still are bombarding the islands. They are still encouraging the Vietcong. They are still at war in Korea. They are still stirring up the Pathet Lao. These are all policies that originate in Peking. Until this attitude changes, until the present aggressive position of the Chinese People's Republic is altered, there can be no change in our policy toward them.

As far as recognition of the stability and the continuity of the mainland government, I think there is nothing new about that. This is a fact of life which we have all realized for many years.

I am afraid I can't amplify my previous remarks beyond that.

QUESTION: Are you concerned about the continuing split between Peking and Delhi?

ANSWER: I am concerned about any area of the world in which there is a major threat of war or of the increase in tension which could ultimately alter the present balance both of power and of peace. So that the split between Delhi and Peking insofar as it constitutes a threat to international peace and security to the territorial integrity of India is of concern, naturally.

QUESTION: Mr. Ambassador, may I ask you, do you consider the recent cut in the Soviet military budget as a valuable contribution to the relaxation of tensions?

ANSWER: Yes — while I have never seen any analysis of it, I do not know how to interpret it, I do not know yet what it means — but I think these are all steps in the right direction.

QUESTION: Do you expect to take — to devote all your time to the next General Assembly, or do you expect to be devoting a large part of your time to the election campaign?

ANSWER: Well, under our system, as you know, people who are engaged in the conduct of foreign policy are not supposed to participate in partisan political activities. So that if I am in this position during the campaign next fall, I shall be obliged not to participate. I shall be obliged to devote myself to this work and, therefore, not participate in the campaign.

QUESTION: Well, do you expect to be here?

ANSWER: Yes, I do.

QUESTION: I suppose that raises the obvious question: Would you accept the nomination for the Vice Presidency?

ANSWER: It seems to me this is where I came in ten years ago! [252]

[252] He refers to his refusal to be a candidate for the Democratic nomination for President in 1952. See *The Papers of Adlai E. Stevenson,* Vol. IV, pp. 3–10. On

I think my job is to stay here and mind the shop across the street for the President and do the best job I can for President Johnson and for my country.

QUESTION: Governor, under the present Charter of the Security Council, seven affirmative votes are required to carry a decision. Assuming that the present proposals for enlargement get through with your Senate, with the Soviet Union and also France, what is the United States position on what should be the new affirmative votes required?

ANSWER: Well, if I understand your question, I think it is answered by the resolution itself, which calls for nine as a majority of the Security Council comprising fifteen members, and that is what we would be called upon to approve. That is incorporated in the resolution.

QUESTION: Thank you very much, Mr. Ambassador.

ANSWER: Before you go, may I say that yesterday someone said to me that he wished me a Merry Christmas and/or a Happy New Year. I would like to wish you all a Merry Christmas *and* a Happy New Year!

Mrs. Agda Rössel, the permanent representative of Sweden to the United Nations, had just been appointed ambassador to Yugoslavia.

To Agda Rössel

December 23, 1963

Dearest Agda:

I tried to reach you on the phone before I left for Illinois, to say Good-bye — and found that you had already said Goodbye! Somehow the autumn has been a failure in one major respect for me — I have seen so little of you, and that long hoped for evening together is still ahead of us.

It has been a joy to be with you here in New York these past few years, and I think I regret your departure more than any of your devoted admirers.

But I am confident this isn't the last of our association. Meanwhile, until we meet again, I send you confident hopes for the future, and

Dearest love,

Stevenson spent the holiday season at Libertyville.

Meet the Press on Sunday, December 22, 1963, Stevenson said that he would accept the vice presidential nomination if President Johnson asked him but that he would not seek the nomination. He added that the chance of Johnson's asking him were "very remote." New York *Times*, December 23, 1963.

To Mrs. Ronald Tree [253]

December 28, 1963
8 A.M.

M —

Peace, and be at peace with your
    thoughts and visions.
These things had to come to you and
    you to accept them.
This is your share of the eternal burden,
The perpetual glory. This is one moment,
But know that another
Shall pierce you with a sudden painful joy
When the figure of God's purpose is made
    complete.
You shall forget these things, toiling
    in the household,
You shall remember them, drawing by
    the fire,[254]
When age and forgetfulness sweeten
    memory.
Only like a dream that has often been
    told
And often been changed in the telling,
    They will seem unreal.
Human kind cannot bear very much reality.

(Have I sent you that before?)

A frenzied day preparing for Christmas, a glorious, exhausting Christmas, with all the young and younger. A day & night in Bloomington [Illinois] with [Mr. and Mrs. Ernest] Ives, [Mr. and Mrs. Loring] Merwins et al, mostly business, much telephoning to N.Y. re Cyprus–Greece,[255] and after a midnight S[ecurity] C[ouncil] meeting a reprieve until Monday at least.

[253] The original is in the possession of Mrs. Tree.
[254] Stevenson has slightly altered this line from T. S. Eliot's *Murder in the Cathedral,* which originally read, ". . . droning by the fire."
[255] Peace between the Greek Cypriot and Turkish Cypriot communities on Cyprus had broken down. Both Greece and Turkey were threatening intervention. A United Nations peacekeeping force was sent to restore order. For Stevenson's first experience with the situation in Cyprus, see *The Papers of Adlai E. Stevenson,* Vol. V, pp. 318–320.

This morning we go hunting at —2° — but the sun is bright and the snow and *moon* so white. The ghost, and the creak at the top of the stair, — is always there.

A

P.S. Return to N.Y. 1/5; to Jamaica 1/9; return to N.Y. 1/18. . . .

Part Four

1964

The year 1964 was a sad one for Adlai E. Stevenson. He knew that he was getting old — his letters reveal it. He also knew that his influence in Washington was slight. Yet the pace he set for himself was as astonishing as ever. "He does more than 40 men," Marietta Tree observed.[1] The New Yorker marveled at "his fantastic energy."[2]

The civil conflict in Cyprus, the problem of financing the United Nations operation in the Congo, the tension between Israel and the Arab states, the shaky neutrality of Cambodia and Laos, the covert war the United States was conducting against North Vietnam and the Tonkin Gulf incident and Senator Barry Goldwater's attacks on the United Nations were some of the developments which added to the difficulties and challenges of Stevenson's post as permanent representative of the United States to the United Nations.

To Mr. and Mrs. Glenn Anderson [3]

January 2, 1964

Dear Glenn and Lee:

I am deeply distressed! A year later, I find in Libertyville a list of presents received for Christmas 1962, including a lovely lounging jacket. You have never been thanked. But you are thanked now — double!

I hope you don't conclude that this oversight is an illustration of my administrative incompetence. Perhaps it is, but with 24 hours at home and four grandchildren on my shoulders, it's a wonder I got out of the house last Christmas alive, with or without my papers!

Bless you, my dear friends, and the happiest, happiest New Year yet.

Yours always,

[1] Quoted in a United Press International feature story on Stevenson's social activities. See the *Wisconsin State Journal*, December 27, 1964.

[2] "The Talk of the Town," *New Yorker*, July 24, 1965, described in detail Stevenson's working days and nights at the United Nations. See pp. 4–20, above.

[3] Mr. Anderson was lieutenant governor of California.

To Carl Sandburg [4]

January 6, 1964

THE ONLY THING THAT RECONCILES ME TO GROWING OLDER IS SEEING WHAT AGE HAS DONE FOR YOU AND WHAT YOU HAVE DONE FOR AGE. TIME SEEMS TO MARCH ON FOR EVERYONE BUT YOU: THIS IS TRUE POETIC LICENSE!

MY BEST WISHES FOR A HAPPY BIRTHDAY AND A HAPPY NEW YEAR.

Daniel Schweitzer, who had been the permanent representative from Chile to the United Nations, wrote Stevenson on December 30, 1963, from Chile expressing anguish over the death of President Kennedy and hope that President Johnson would work toward the "noble" objectives that had motivated Kennedy. He then expressed the hope that Stevenson would become President.

To Daniel Schweitzer

January 7, 1964

Dear Daniel:

I was touched by your letter and your characteristic thoughtfulness and perception.

Actually, the transition has been effected without disorder and, I believe, with little public anxiety. If anything, my relations with the new President, a very old friend, will be more intimate and informal than before. But let us not speak of another political campaign! I have had enough of the extreme exertion of our political life.

I thought often of you in recent days and wished that you might have been here. I pray that all goes well with you, and am delighted that you find Ambassador Cole [5] . . . so sympathetic. . . .

Most affectionately,

To Clayton Fritchey

January 8, 1964

I am trying to put together a complete file of my speeches, statements and articles, and find there are serious gaps in our files, especially as regards magazine articles. I would like to suggest that you have your

[4] A telegram.
[5] Charles W. Cole, United States ambassador to Chile.

staff send up *two* carbon copies of every typescript at the time it is sent to the publisher.

Added by hand: The files here are in a mess. Pls. have someone make it their business to send up 2 copies of everything that goes out over my name — articles, press releases, statements, etc. I *think* we have complete files on speeches.

AES

To Lady Barbara Jackson

January 10, 1964

Dearest Barbara:

I said goodbye to Robert [Jackson] and headed for the airport en route to Jamaica for my long-planned week in the sun with the [Edison] Dicks. At the airport, the inevitable happened and I returned to the Mission, this time because of the crisis in Panama.[6] But so it has always been — and doubtless always will be.

The only consolation is that at last I have a moment to write you a note of thanks for your recent and informative letters. First let me say that Robert seems to be his old self again — full of bounce, interest and enthusiasm. I don't think it is simulated and that he really seems happy and content with his lot, at least as an interim solution. Certainly he never looked better as you will see before you get this.

So much has happened hereabouts that I hardly know where to begin. Indeed I probably will only begin before the telephone rings again and I have to resume negotiations and drafting for a Security Council meeting tonight, over this miserable business in Panama [7] which might have been instigated by the government to incite nationalistic feelings and divert attention from the growing popularity of the opposition in the forthcoming elections. In any case, it has been a grave misfortune and will doubtless set back the evolution of our new relations with Panama and the Canal.

Having known Lyndon Johnson for more than 30 years, I feel that the relationship will be even better than with Kennedy. Certainly Johnson

[6] Rioting broke out in the Canal Zone on January 9, 1964, when a group of students defied the order that the United States and Panamanian flags were to be flown together. On January 10, Panama severed diplomatic relations with the United States and demanded a revision of the Panama Canal treaties. Panama protested to both the United Nations and the Organization of American States, and the UN Security Council and the council of the OAS were called into emergency session. On January 10, however, Panama deferred its request for UN action and agreed with the United States to submit the dispute for mediation to the Inter-American Peace Committee of the OAS.

[7] Stevenson spoke on this issue in the Security Council on January 10, 1964. USUN press release 4353.

has gone to pains to make that clear, and has responded affirmatively to all of my suggestions in the days of the transition. Actually I think in the election he may have an easier time than Kennedy would have had, although it is difficult to predict this so early. Certainly he has taken the job upon his shoulders with speed to show good business confidence, southern reassurance, a better Congressional attitude and rapidly emerging foreign confidence in the continuity. Of course this won't last but he will probably get the tax bill,[8] and at least a modified civil rights bill,[9] and maybe Medicare [10] or some other important legislation through this session which should put him in very good shape for the election. Meanwhile, the Republicans are in the worst predicament I have ever seen! But all this you know!

Speaking of Johnson, by the way, he has made it perfectly clear that he considers B[arbara] W[ard] his favorite contemporary writer!

I see little prospect of getting to Kuala Lumpur,[11] what with the problems piling up in all directions and especially the problem of future financing of the UN peacekeeping operations. On this we have aired some new ideas to create some inducements to the Russians and French to pay up and to avoid a major confrontation in the next General Assembly. If the atmosphere appears favorable among the major allies, I will commence negotiations with the Russians which may well lead to Moscow. All this, of course, in the utmost confidence.

I had hoped so much to make my long delayed journey to Australia, New Zealand, Southeast Asia and Japan, including Kuala Lumpur, but for the third year I suspect it will have to be postponed.

Meanwhile I am confronted with the usual burden of speech making which, after discarding 90% of the requests, seems to be as remorseless as ever. Two in particular concern me. The first is on February 12th, a huge affair in Springfield [Illinois], primarily to launch a campaign to restore the old State House to its condition in Lincoln's time. I have not been sure what I should talk about and had hoped to think it over in Jamaica. It occurs to me that a possibility might be to pick up the theme

8 A bill was passed on February 26, 1964, providing for significant reductions in federal individual and corporate taxes over the calendar years 1964 and 1965.

9 The Civil Rights Act of 1964, guaranteeing the right to vote, prohibiting discrimination in public accommodations and empowering the district courts to enforce this prohibition, and authorizing the Attorney General to institute suits to protect civil rights, among other provisions, was passed after long and heated debate and was signed on July 2, 1964.

10 A bill providing for medical care for persons over sixty-five to be financed by Social Security, which failed to pass in 1964. Medicare legislation was eventually passed on July 30, 1965.

11 Stevenson may refer to the conference of foreign ministers of the Philippines, Indonesia, and Malaya, held at Bangkok, Thailand, February 5–10, 1964, at which it was agreed that Thailand would supervise a cease-fire between Indonesia and Malaya that had been negotiated by Robert F. Kennedy.

in Lincoln's speech to the Young Men's Lyceum in Springfield in 1838 (I think), in which he talked about violence, disorder and prejudice, using that as a takeoff to Kennedy's assassination and similar evidence of extremist views in our country now as periodically in the past. Perhaps one could build on that uncertain foundation an essay on the difficulty of conducting a democratic government with a large component of irrational talk and opinion. Lincoln was similarly afflicted throughout the Civil War.

Perhaps you will have a better idea of something to talk about, germane to the present with Lincoln connections. At all events, the self-righteous, complacent way we criticize others and foul our own nest seems to me to have continuing relevance and timely pertinence now, especially with the prospect of some real break-through in East-West relations — and I haven't said one word about Goldwater! [12]

If you have a spare moment — which you don't! — and could send me anything appropriate to Lincoln's Birthday that occurs to you — I would greet it with cheers and sighs of relief!

I am not going to bother to send you any of my recent speeches because there hasn't been a good one for months!

My next concern is a Dag Hammarskjold Lecture at Princeton in early March. Thinking back to the Godkin Lectures at Harvard ten years ago [13] at the same time (I wonder why I hark back to that distant time so often!) it has occurred to me that I might do something on a little larger screen than UN shop talk, and develop some of the elements of a movement toward the international community. How do we handle our domestic extremists? How do we maintain an alert, resilient and flexible attitude, given our own compunction for improving ourselves — with our own propaganda and the popular attitudes to which our so-called leaders feel they have to make complaisance? Are we ready to pay the price of disarmament? Do we know what it is? How can we enlarge the room for maneuver when so many of us seem to be afraid to depart from the safe paths of public approval? In this connection, I was profoundly provoked by the suspicious and cynical response of our Kremlinologists to Khrushchev's New Year's message which contained something really new and hopeful.[14] I think that my allies and I are getting on top of

[12] Senator Barry Goldwater had published *Why Not Victory? A Fresh Look at American Foreign Policy* (New York: McGraw-Hill, 1962), a book hostile to Stevenson's point of view, and was a strong contender for the Republican nomination in 1964.

[13] See *The Papers of Adlai E. Stevenson*, Vol. V, pp. 433–489.

[14] Khrushchev sent a personal message on January 2, 1964, to all governments with which the U.S.S.R. had diplomatic relations, calling for an international agreement renouncing the use of force for settling territorial or frontier disputes. The proposal was widely viewed as a Soviet propaganda gesture, and observers pointed out that while such an agreement would prohibit United States troops in Taiwan, Korea, or

that, however, and that in the published response we will have some balance. You know as well as I the conditioned reflexes in our East-West dialogue, and there are other debilitating elements — like the growing Congressional temptation to make foreign policy by legislation (the Hickenlooper amendment for no aid to Argentina because it repudiated our oil contracts; tariff punishment to Yugoslavia and Poland,[15] and now there is a group in the Department seriously advocating using foreign aid for short term purposes only, an attitude highly sympathetic to many Congressmen.)

But I have gone on with this too long, and my purpose is simple and obvious: to enlist your help, but not at the expense of one hour of lost sleep — please!

The holiday at home with all three sons and dependents was a great success, in spite of countless family problems and a sub-zero temperature the whole time. And if only I could get a few days in the sun to reflect and plot and plan about my perplexing future — there would be no complaints from

> Your devoted —

P.S. How I hate to send these dictated, typewritten letters, but my opportunities for something better seem to never improve!

PPS. And — I have not thanked you for the War Requiem. I found it was a stereo record which does not work on my machine so I have traded it with Adlai and you will be greeted by its beauties in Libertyville. Also, if you could get me another Faure Requiem, it would be a welcome birthday-cum-next Christmas present. My own is all but worn out and also has a way of disappearing into other peoples' houses!

Stevenson spent a week in Jamaica with the Edison Dicks.

To Mrs. Edison Dick

January 22, 1964

Dearest Jane:

I have not written you, and I am mortified. As perhaps you suspect, I stepped out of that fairyland into the usual turmoil here and have barely caught my breath yet. But you will be pleased to hear, weather notwithstanding, the comment on my appearance, color and demeanor is

---

Vietnam, it would leave the Communist countries free to conduct "just wars of liberation." The State Department responded on January 3 that the proposal was "not objective" and was "disappointing," but promised to give it careful study.

[15] Congress refused to extend "most favored nation" status to these two countries.

all good. Evidently I flourished in spite of wind and wave — which I attribute more to the Dicks than to Jamaica!

It was a glorious holiday, and I am as grateful as I can be.

I will expect you and Eddie for the night of Friday, January 31st, at 42 A. Adlai and Nancy have had to decline the birthday party and I am asking Roxane [Eberlein] to arrange for a luncheon with Leona Baumgartner [16] on the 31st.

Love,

To Lady Barbara Jackson

January 23, 1964

Dearest Barbara:

I am having to dictate this very hurriedly — what with Panama, Indonesia, Cyprus, Tanganyika, Zanzibar, de Gaulle, Red China, and a thousand other new and old headaches! [17]

I enclose an excerpt from the speech of January 27, 1838, to the Young Men's Lyceum of Springfield. It is a long, ponderous speech mostly calling for strict compliance with the laws, and I am not sure that my idea of comparing our troubles with the violence of those troubled times is a very good one.

The Lincoln speech is, of course, on February 12, and I hope to get at it myself about a week beforehand. If you have any ideas as to what would be appropriate at this time, please pass them along.

The Dag Hammarskjold lecture is on March 23rd.

I am troubled about our Godkin anniversary because I am tentatively committed to join Agnes Meyer on a boat in the West Indies on the 10th of March for one week. I have had little success with her regarding money I had hoped to get for the Eleanor Roosevelt Foundation, and promised her a long time ago that I would try to find time to join her cruise for a few days. That, however, must remain indefinite until I can see how the work here evolves.

I think Easter in Libertyville should work well. Immediately thereafter I may have to go abroad for my NATO lectures and some other chores. My schedule is not firm but I shall probably be gone from about the 1st of April until the 20th. The World's Fair opens on April 22, and the Anniversary of the Eleanor Roosevelt Memorial Foundation Charter is on April 23. There are doings in which I am involved, of course, in New York in connection with both. And, by the way, I can hardly tell

[16] Commissioner of health of New York City and adviser on public health to many governments.

[17] "Each was important in UN politics," Harlan Cleveland observed, "and he was usually the man in the middle." Memorandum to Walter Johnson, April 30, 1973.

you the headache the Foundation has become. I shall have to see it through for a few more months. The Kennedys are now going out for 10 million dollars for their library [18] which of course cuts across my bows and causes me no end of trouble. What with the Library, the Cultural Center, and all the other memorials, I think there is increasing restlessness in this country — especially since there has never been a memorial to Franklin Roosevelt yet.

Forgive this hasty note, and bless you!

Love,

To Mrs. Lyndon B. Johnson

January 25, 1964

Dear Lady Bird:

Jean Kintner [19] seems to be deeply distressed that you are unable to come to the luncheon she is arranging on April 9th on behalf of the Eleanor Roosevelt Memorial Foundation. I am presuming to write you to urge you to reconsider and come, if you possibly can, because:

1) The Kennedy Library drive will seriously interrupt our campaign.
2) It was gallant of Jean Kintner to undertake the thankless job of Co-Chairman.
3) I can think of no more effective way for you to evidence your devotion to Mrs. Roosevelt and her work, especially here in New York where she is all but deified.

I don't want to be a pleader, and I shall not impose on you again — unless it is to go with me to the theater! And next time I hope it will be *before* the fall!

Yours,

To Emanuel Celler [20]

January 25, 1964

Dear Manny:

I am distressed by a report from Bill Benton regarding your disappointment at not being named a Trustee of the Eleanor Roosevelt Memorial Foundation. I had not heard of this before — let alone that you felt that a commitment had not been honored. I was aware of your interest in the Foundation, and deeply grateful. As to the promise, I am bewildered.

[18] The John F. Kennedy Memorial Library.
[19] Wife of Robert Kintner, president of the National Broadcasting Company.
[20] Democratic representative from New York City.

The original Trustees were named in consultation with the President, and subsequent Trustees have been suggested by the Nominating Committee and submitted to the President for appointment in accordance with the Act. During the months that you were so vigorously seeking the necessary legislation, I understand that you were dealing primarily with James Roosevelt [21] and Hyman Bookbinder. Both of them reported to me frequently on how much you were doing for us. I am sending them a copy of this letter and will seek a fuller explanation of what might have been said at that time.

After the designation of the first Trustees in the Bill itself, I recall a meeting in which it was decided that no Members of the House or Senate should be submitted to the President because of the difficulty of discrimination among your many friends. While Hubert Humphrey took the leadership in the Senate, there are, as you know, scores of other Congressmen who had many years of close association with the Roosevelts, and might expect like treatment. Moreover, there were 35 sponsors of the Bill in the Senate. It was pointed out also, at some point, that having Members of Congress on the Board might make it difficult to seek grants from Federal Agencies for programs of the Foundation because of limitations written into some recent welfare bills.

While I doubt if the Foundation will ever ask for Federal appropriations, we have not ruled out the possibility of seeking funds from such agencies as HEW [22] and Labor and Area Redevelopment.

As you probably know, neither Jimmy Roosevelt nor any members of the family are Trustees. While they have all been designated as Ex-Officio members, they have no vote.

I hope to have a chance to talk with you about this myself, in view of our long and happy relationship, and I am sending you this preliminary letter only because I don't want you to think for a moment longer that I have defaulted on any promise. Moreover, I shall take the whole matter of Congressional representation on the Board of Trustees up again at the next meeting, and should they conclude that the present policy is unsound, your willingness to serve will certainly have sympathetic and prompt consideration.

With assurances of my appreciation and all best regards, I am

Cordially yours,

[21] Eldest son of Mr. and Mrs. Franklin D. Roosevelt.
[22] The Department of Health, Education, and Welfare.

To Walter Jenkins [23]

January 31, 1964

Dear Walter:

In addition to my telephone request to you about the President's appearance in New York in April in behalf of the Eleanor Roosevelt Memorial Foundation, may I also ask if he could spare two minutes to record a message for a "TV spectacular" about Mrs. Roosevelt?

We could prepare a draft script, and the cameras will, of course, be brought to wherever the President wishes. It should be done sometime before March 1.

I would appreciate it so much if you could enlist his cooperation for these two chores.

Cordially yours,

To Mrs. John B. Currie [24]

February 5, 1972

Dearest Bethia:

You are marvelous!

You make it "pay" [25] to get older, and since I have no choice in the matter anyway — you make it a joy!

Thank you, my dear, for your wonderful and perfect birthday gift. I am all the more touched and encouraged because of my perpetual distress at not being able to give the Foundation the time I should.

Bless you!

Yours,
ADLAI

To Robert M. Hutchins

February 6, 1964

Dear Bob:

I have agreed to speak at the Honors Day Convocation at the University of Illinois on May 1st.

Dr. David Henry [26] has given me the following guidelines:

"1. Honors Day is the time when we give institutional emphasis to the central purpose of university life — the personal and institutional dedica-

---

[23] Special assistant to President Johnson.
[24] The original is in the possession of Mrs. Currie.
[25] Mr. and Mrs. Currie sent a check to the Eleanor Roosevelt Memorial Foundation as Stevenson's birthday present.
[26] President of the University of Illinois.

tion to learning and the advancement of learning. Any views that you have on the place of higher education in the national life and for the encouragement of young people to live by high standards of intellectual achievement would, of course, relate to the theme of the occasion.

"2. A large number of parents will be present as their young people are honored. Here we have 'grass-roots' America expressing pride in scholarly attainment, and supporting university work and all that it stands for in all aspects of life.

"3. Our students today are sophisticated in public affairs and tremendously interested in international relations, as you know. Any encouragement of this interest in a broad view of their future, from your present vantage point, would be a tremendous inspiration.

"I know that you will not feel bound by these comments — they are suggested only to help you build a bridge to the local audience. Obviously anything that you have to say will be warmly received."

Feeling that you probably have very little to do — and are impatient for assignments — I thought you might be good enough to devote four minutes to picking out some suitable examples of your reflections on these subjects — which I will then weave together. If it works well — you'll get no credit. If it doesn't — I will murmur something about my ghosts!

In short — what the hell do I say about "excellence," in my condition.

Yours,

P.S. I am not asking you to write anything — just to give me something to read.

On February 12, 1964, Stevenson returned to Springfield, Illinois, to speak at the Lincoln Day Dinner of the Abraham Lincoln Association.[27]

Springfield is filled with many fond memories for me. I count the four years I lived here as your Governor the most rewarding of my public life. And the warmth of your welcome, the presence of so many old friends, make tonight a remembrance to be included with those I treasure most.

Nor am I unmindful of the great honor you have done a Democrat by inviting me to speak at this historic Lincoln Day Dinner. I was a little uneasy when I was asked to come back to Springfield tonight to lend a hand to the campaign to restore the old capitol. While I accepted with alacrity, I also thought of Lincoln's story about the judge who was getting

---

[27] The text is from USUN press release 4361.

ready to pass sentence on a man he knew well. Moved by the old ties of friendship, the judge leaned down from the bench and sadly asked: "My friend, when would you like to be hung?"

And I am not sure whether I have diplomatic immunity in Springfield!

I turn to the reason for our gathering, incidentally, with more than a little of the farmer's feeling about spring plowing: the job is important, but the terrain is familiar and there is little chance for originality — particularly here in the town where Lincoln walked with his friends and where his memory is enshrined in every heart and mind.

No flash of lightning illumined the Kentucky countryside, no clap of thunder rolled from the hills 155 years ago today. But well they might, for what came into the world then was not merely "the grandest figure in the drama of the Nineteenth Century" — but one that stands tall and commanding on the crowded canvas of all the centuries.

Carl Sandburg has said:

"Not often in the story of mankind does a man arrive on earth who is both steel and velvet, who is hard as rock and soft as drifting fog, who holds in his heart and mind the paradox of terrible storm and peace unspeakable and perfect . . . The people of many other countries take Lincoln now for their own . . . millions there are who take him as a personal treasure. He had something they would like to see spread everywhere over the world."

Coming to you as I do from the United Nations, I can attest to the verity of those poetic words. The people of many countries do take Lincoln for their own, for to them he left a legacy — that freedom and equality are the essential ingredients of a life of dignity.

Today, even as in his time, freedom and equality are the burning issues of a world in ferment. There is no quarter of the earth which has not been touched by this wave of human aspiration; it is even more the mark of our century than the fury of the atom. The legacy that Lincoln left to all humanity is now the heartbeat of our time.

Lincoln was a man of all ages, of all civilizations. His words were those of love and understanding for the whole human family. They transcend national boundaries and are as timeless and pertinent today as when he uttered them.

In the year that has passed since we last met to celebrate the memory of Abraham Lincoln, another great President has been shot down by a mad assassin, another great American leader has been cut off before his work was finished. And the tragedy of President Kennedy's death was compounded by an atmosphere of violence and lawlessness — a disorder so stark that the world could watch while yet another assassin shot down the first, even while he was in the custody and under the protection of the police. Never mind that any leader is at the mercy of the insane.

Added to the racial conflicts of recent months, the double killing — of the famous and of the infamous — projected both to ourselves and to the world at large a picture of malice, passion and violence in America.

The picture is dark enough in its immediate consequences. No great country can seem quite so confident of its greatness and civilization when its elected leader is murdered in the street. But the evil goes deeper. President Kennedy's death was more than a tragedy for the country and the world. It was a torch, a flare, lighting up a sullen, menacing landscape. Lawlessness, violence, even the verbal violence that "seeks to wound but fears to strike," destroy more than the image of America. They undermine its political foundations as well.

Significantly enough, the menace of violence to America's free institutions was one of the very first issues discussed by Abraham Lincoln in public. A few weeks after the mob murder of Elijah Lovejoy in Alton in 1838, Lincoln spoke to the Young Men's Lyceum here in Springfield. In those days speeches counted because people listened and talked about what was said. He was not yet 29, but his words already contained the basic idea of the Gettysburg address 25 years later.

He asked the members a pointed question: What, he inquired, is the greatest danger threatening the republic and its political institutions? It was not foreign invasion, he replied; all the armies of the Old World, commanded by a Napoleon, could not take a drink from the Ohio or leave a footprint on the Blue Ridge. No, the peril was internal; if it appeared, it must spring from within. "As a nation of freemen, we must live through all time, or die by suicide."

The danger, Lincoln believed in those far off days of [President Martin] Van Buren and the great depression which followed the panic of 1837, might already be visible, for evil tendencies and forces of dark omen walked among the American people. And the worst was the increasing disregard for law. Mad impulse, wild passion, hate and violence — what Lincoln called a "mobocratic spirit" — were taking the place of sober judgment throughout the land and weakening the fabric of law and justice.

In this eloquent speech, Lincoln was indicting a spirit of violence which was especially characteristic of the rough frontier where he had lived. In the decades after 1838, and especially after the Mexican War, the slavery struggle made its almost overwhelming contribution to the spirit of hatred, passion and brute force in America. Lincoln, who entered national politics at the very time the country plunged into the Mexican conflict, was soon immersed in all the inflamed feeling of the day. But as he opposed the war, so he opposed the excited partisanship and sectional animosities. From his early years, he had counted himself an intellectual and spiritual follower of Thomas Jefferson and Henry Clay. It was

Jefferson who, shrinking from the fevers and rancors of the Presidential election of 1800, bade Americans in his first inaugural address to cultivate brotherhood, for they were all Federalists and all Republicans. Jefferson heard with anguish the angry quarrel over the admission of Missouri, "a firebell in the night," and bent all his influence to compose the sectional dispute.

As the slavery struggle grew in intensity, Lincoln maintained his stand beside Henry Clay and Daniel Webster, those champions of reason, moderation, and obedience to law. His devotion to the spirit of reason and moderation, and above all to the rule of law, never wavered. On any moral issue, such as the expansion of slavery, he was adamant; in any contest between right and wrong, justice and injustice, progress and reaction, he took a rigid stand. But he always defended his position by appeals to reason — by clear, logical argument; and like Webster, he believed that temperance, candor and magnanimity should be supplemented by a fraternal regard and sympathy. Like President Johnson he may have often used the Prophet Isaiah's words "come now and let us reason together"!

But now the slavery issue, like the rough frontier, is far behind us; the days of its feverish excitements are all but forgotten; it no longer has any power to move men to passion. We are far advanced in a new century of enlightenment and progress, when the public is more intelligently informed than ever before, and when our national affluence has all but banished class divisions.

Why is it, then, that senseless rancors still excite men; why is it that half truths, slander, suspicion, malevolence mislead and excite so many citizens in this thrice-blessed land?

Theodore Roosevelt liked to quote a proverb which he ascribed to the Arabs: "A man is half the son of his father, and half the son of his time." And it is certain that in such a time, in such an atmosphere there is a mighty mischief, with incalculable consequences, like the grievous loss our time has suffered in President Kennedy's death.

If we are to find a remedy for these ugly ingredients in our life, we must go deeper than merely to say that ignorance is invincible, and that distorted minds are uncontrollable. Ignorance is *not* invincible, and malice *can* be exorcised. While we cannot wholly guard against the diseased mind, we will do well to recall that Great Britain has had no noteworthy political assassination since a maniac killed Prime Minister Spencer Percival [Perceval] in 1812.

Perhaps one of the explanations for the persistence of prejudice and passion lies in the fact that an era of expanding government controls, of rapid and universal change, of social amelioration, and enlarged civil rights, inevitably produces conflicting reactions. A reform which appears to some as a step forward will seem to others a step backward. The law which curbs a monopoly business, imposes standards on a broadcasting industry, or opens all hotels to minority elements, will seem to the consumer, the viewer of television, or the Negro, just and necessary equality and protection. But to the beneficiaries of such controls, it will seem a gross infringement upon their liberties. The protesting group will tell us, in all honesty, that we should turn back to the Jeffersonian principle of non-interference with the individual. It pains them in principle as well as pocket to give up what they had. It especially pains some of them to be told to do so in the name of a higher morality.

From this pain and this clash of opinion, misunderstanding and ill-feeling inevitably spring. Among the men who cling to the principles of respect for vested rights and individualism free from governmental restraint, extremists are certain to arise, just as extremists arose among the defenders of slavery. For that matter, extremists arise on the reform side too in the familiar fanatics and demagogues.

Our era from the inauguration of Franklin Roosevelt to the death of John Kennedy, has been one of rapid, continuous and far-reaching change in the social and economic spheres, and of an impressive enlargement in the powers of the government. The openings for misunderstanding, friction, and antagonism on the socio-economic level have therefore been growing larger. Pockets of resentment are visible all over the map, and politicians and publicists and citizens have been quick to exploit them for their several reasons. To the domestic anxieties, international living in a shrinking world full of foreigners and unfamiliar conflicts and mortal dangers had added larger and more obscure fears, frustrations and resentments.

Would Lincoln have a remedy? The answer lies plain in his written words and his career. Patriotism is not enough; or rather, our old definitions of patriotism have been narrowly inadequate. It is not enough to affirm our loyalty to existing laws and institutions, for they must be changed for the better. We must be patriotic in the sense of being disinterested when healthy change imposes penalties upon us; magnanimous in recognizing that large national groups have suffered from injustice and have a right to expect reform; and public-spirited in supporting new ideas and policies. True patriotism is no superficial matter. It will be proved by disinterest, and magnanimity, and public spirit, in facing the overdue shifts and readjustments, painful as they may be.

Lincoln always emphasized obedience to law. But he went far beyond in enjoining his countrymen not merely to respect the law, but to show a patriotism devoid of fanaticism, and infused with the spirit of magnanimity. The words of his second inaugural will always echo down the generations: "With malice toward none, with charity for all, let us strive to do the work we are in." [28]

Thus there are two sides to the preservation of our free institutions — respect, certainly, for law and due process, but equally a constantly renewed effort to see that our laws are such as free men can respect.

It is the tension between these two needs that gives our free society its dynamic equilibrium. Press for change by too much violence, and the fabric itself will give. Let the need to change become too glaring and too frustrated, then violence is inescapable.

Free society has no easy options, no escape either into rigidity or into anarchy. It must survive the endless clash, which is what makes it both the most precarious and the most adaptable social order ever worked out by men.

Today we feel the clash with especial force because times of great social upheaval are always times when violence of speech and action follow from the fears stirred up by the need for change. In 1838, America was beginning the quickening slide into conflict over slavery, a conflict which came because the social evils and inequalities could not be changed in time. Today, much of the aggression and unreason in our politics springs from the same deep roots of fear and resentment and our overwhelming need is to see to it that we act in time.

The needed reforms are not easy reforms. They require multiple and radical changes. It is not simply the disabilities under which 20 million Negroes have labored so long that we face, but the stark fact that perhaps twenty per cent of our people — including 11 million children — live below the poverty line; that urban decay, linked with this poverty and exacerbated by racial tension, is eating out the heart of our great cities; that automation is demanding higher skills just as a new flood of postwar children, all too often unskilled, begin their search for work.

We shall not exorcise these problems by the politics of verbal violence. We shall not exorcise the violence by turning our backs on the problems themselves. We have to brace ourselves for a social effort as great, perhaps, as the waging of war itself if the promise of a free society is to be made good within the framework of unbelievable affluence and unforgivable squalor that make up America today.

The ebullitions of fanatic intolerance which so frequently recur in the United States are always distressing and sometimes alarming. But one

[28] This condensation and alteration of Lincoln's statement is surprising in that Stevenson was well versed in Lincolniana. The original statement reads: "With malice toward none, with charity for all, with firmness in the right as God gives us to see the right, let us strive on to finish the work we are in, to bind up the nation's wounds. . . ." Second Inaugural Address, March 4, 1865.

fact is more alarming still; the apathy, the silent indifference, of so many enlightened men and women. In their hearts they condemn fanaticism, but they neither speak out to rebuke it nor take action to repress it.

When a large organization [29] arises to demand the impeachment of our Chief Justice; when influential groups call for the abolition of the income tax; when a candidate for President [30] declares for getting out of the United Nations and forsaking the only hope for collective security and world law, we need not apprehend any imminent peril. Chief Justice Warren will not be impeached; the income tax will not be repealed; we will not get out of the United Nations. These steps would be condemned by the elementary common sense of our people. But the advocacy of such excited, ill-considered and foolish acts can nevertheless do untold harm, for it begets a frame of mind among the ignorant and thoughtless in which extreme courses seem natural.

It is sad to see these eruptions of folly; yet it is sadder still to see so many good people passively inert in dealing with them. They are the tares in the seed wheat, and they should be torn out before they can do any more harm. An aroused public sentiment, a militant commitment to truth and justice in our national life, can destroy their power for evil and save the basic principles upon which the republic in Washington's day was founded, and in Lincoln's day was preserved.

Perhaps there is no greater service that the ordinary citizen and voter can do, each in his own locality, than to raise his voice against any evidence of slander, prejudice, muckraking and race baiting, from whatever side it may appear.

An alert, informed, courageous citizenry, eschewing violence, open to reason, respecting adversaries, ready to conduct its public debates in the spirit of Voltaire: "I abhor your views and I would fight to the death for your right to express them" — that is part of the eternal vigilance that is the price of free institutions.

Now, as in 1838, the main enemy is not without. It is within — in the violence thrown out by social upheaval, in the slowness of our reactions to the human tragedies underlying the upheaval. Now, as in 1838, we have not created our framework of liberty. We are inheritors charged with preserving a priceless legacy. And whatever its scale, whatever the test to our nerves and courage, we must accept the charge.

In Lincoln's words: "This task, gratitude to our fathers, justice to ourselves, duty to posterity and love for our species in general, all imperatively require us faithfully to perform."

[29] The John Birch Society.
[30] Senator Barry Goldwater.

To Mr. and Mrs. Otto Kerner [31]

February 15, 1964

My dear Helena and Otto:

After a few hours in New York — or is it Kashmir and Cyprus! [32] — my happy day in Springfield seems far away. It *was* a happy interlude and a treat I shall long remember. To revisit that mansion and see all those old friends was a joy that has been too long deferred.

Thank you for all your courtesy, and all best wishes,

Yours,

To Allan Nevins

February 15, 1964

My dear Allan:

Enclosed is a copy of the speech I made in Springfield to a very large audience on Wednesday night. I am everlastingly grateful to you for your help. It went off well — thanks, I am sure, in large measure to your contributions.

I shall not impose on you soon again — I hope — but your everlasting readiness to come to my rescue is a constant temptation!

I was much interested in what you had to say about the homicidal contributions of the Chandler family [33] to the demise of the West Coast [edition of the] *New York Times.* From what the family tell me, the latter became an intolerable burden and they had no choice but to give up the experiment. Why it did not have more support in California I find hard to understand. But then that is not the only thing I find hard to understand about my beloved native state!

I hope you will be coming East soon and will let me know in advance. Meanwhile, thanks and thanks again!

Yours,

To Mrs. Lyndon B. Johnson

February 17, 1964

Dear Lady Bird:

To say the least — I am ecstatically delighted to have your letter of February 10, and I know Jean Kintner will be overjoyed.

[31] Mr. Kerner was governor of Illinois.

[32] Stevenson spoke in the Security Council on Kashmir on February 14 (USUN press release 4362) and on Cyprus on February 19 (USUN press release 4364) and March 4 (USUN press release 4367).

[33] Owners of the Los Angeles *Times.*

I also know of the overwhelming demands on your time, and I am everlastingly grateful to you for responding so favorably — so promptly — and so wonderfully — to my plea for help.

The formidable task of getting the Eleanor Roosevelt Foundation firmly started and on its way will need all the help I can get — and your presence at the luncheon on April 9th will do more good than you can possibly know!

Bless you!

Yours,

On February 19, 1964, Stevenson spoke in the Security Council on the troubled situation in Cyprus.[34]

During the nineteen fifties, the political problems of Cyprus were the subject of bitter dispute in the General Assembly of the United Nations year after year. Finally, however, a carefully balanced settlement was reached, with the agreement of all of the parties: Greece, Turkey, the two communities in Cyprus itself and the United Kingdom. I think we all breathed a sigh of relief at that time and allowed ourselves to hope that, with the conclusion of the Zurich Agreements and the establishment of the Republic of Cyprus, the peace which was so longed for and so needed by the people of that historic island had finally been achieved.

We were therefore deeply distressed when new fighting broke out last December which resulted in hundreds of deaths and has now threatened to rupture the whole fabric of peace in the eastern Mediterranean.

All members of the Council are familiar with the melancholy events of the past several weeks to which Sir Patrick Dean has referred. Tension between the two communities reached a flashpoint on 21 December, and violence and bloodshed erupted on a serious scale. When it became clear that additional help was needed, President Makarios, on behalf of the Greek community, and Vice-President Kücük, on behalf of the Turkish community, invited the United Kingdom, in co-operation with the Governments of Greece and Turkey, to undertake to restore stability and preserve peace.

Since 26 December a British force has sought to keep the peace on the island. Today, the United Kingdom has despatched further troops to troubled Cyprus. I believe that all of us here, and most particularly the representatives of Cyprus, owe a debt of gratitude to the United Kingdom for undertaking this unenviable task.

Political efforts to resolve the problems were also promptly started. A

[34] United Nations, *Official Records,* Security Council, February 19, 1964, pp. 11–15.

conference of the parties was, as we know, convened in London in an effort to work out a solution of the political issues which divided the two communities on the island. But that conference, alas, was unable to produce an agreement. Despite the determined efforts of British forces on Cyprus, violent incidents multiplied and bloodshed continued. With the Government of Cyprus and the leaders of the Cypriot communities unable or unwilling to control the passions which had been unleashed, it became clear that the restoration of public order, so imperative before the long-range political problems could be attacked anew, would require a considerably larger number of troops.

The United Kingdom told the Government of Cyprus that it could not continue to shoulder alone the responsibility for peace on the island. The conclusion was obvious that a larger and more broadly based peace-keeping force was required to augment the British forces if order were to be re-established and maintained throughout the island. The Government of the United Kingdom then proceeded to consult with the Governments of Greece and Turkey, which are also parties to the international agreements that led to the establishment of the Republic of Cyprus in 1960. It also consulted with my Government. A plan for the establishment of such a force, including provision for an impartial mediator to help settle the dispute, was agreed to by Greece and Turkey, and by the Cypriot Vice-President, Dr. Kücük. Archbishop Makarios, however, raised a number of objections.

The other parties made a new effort to meet these objections, and a revised plan within the framework of the United Nations and agreed to by Greece, Turkey and the United Kingdom and by my Government, was put before Archbishop Makarios on 12 February. On the following day, he informed representatives of the United Kingdom and of my Government that this revised proposal was also unacceptable, although he agreed in principle to the need for an international peace-keeping force. We are frank to say that we deeply regret that the President of Cyprus was not able to agree to the latter proposal — a proposal which represented a solid recommendation of the Governments of all the guarantor Powers — the United Kingdom, Greece and Turkey — and also of the United States.

A tragic loss of life and property occurs daily in Cyprus; international complications increase; and a solution daily becomes more difficult. The recommendations of the guarantors would, we believe, have helped to avoid all of this.

I think we all know that the Treaty of Guarantee forms an integral part of the organic arrangements that created the Republic of Cyprus. In fact, it is a so-called basic article of the Constitution of Cyprus. That Treaty assures the independence, territorial integrity and security of the

Republic, as well as respect for its Constitution. It assigns to the Guarantor Powers certain responsibilities regarding the maintenance of the Constitution and of the Treaty itself, including the carefully negotiated balance and protection of the two Cypriot communities. It was signed after literally years of soul-searching negotiation and approved by all of the parties. This Treaty or any international treaty cannot be abrogated, cannot be nullified, cannot be modified either in fact or in effect by the Security Council of the United Nations. The Treaty can be abrogated or altered only by agreement of all of the signatories themselves or in accordance with its terms.

No one is threatening to take the territory of Cyprus, no one is threatening its independence — Turkey or Greece or anyone else. What is possible is — and I quote the language of the Treaty: "action" expressly authorized by article IV of the Treaty "with the sole aim of re-establishing the state of affairs created by the present Treaty."

Time is wasting. While we talk people are dying, and any moment violence and bloodshed may erupt again on a large scale, with predictable and grave consequences. The important, the imperative, the urgent thing to do is to restore order and communal tranquillity and do it quickly before new violence breaks out, before the atmosphere is further poisoned, before the positions of the parties on the political issues that divide them become more inflexible and, indeed, before peace in the Eastern Mediterranean is endangered.

I repeat that the urgent business before the Council and the responsibility of the Government of Cyprus is to restore communal peace and order and to stop the bloodshed. The sooner that we in the Security Council turn our attention to this, the better it will be for all. I respectfully urge that the Security Council not be deflected from this purpose. Once we have met this problem and communal peace is restored, no question of any action under the Treaty of Guarantee would arise.

The United States has no position as to the form or the shape of a final settlement of the Cyprus problem. The leaders of the two communities must work out their differences together. But in the present climate this is patently impossible. The two communities are holding each other at gun point. To serve any helpful purpose in this inflammable case, the Security Council must make an effective contribution to the re-establishment of conditions in which a long-term political solution can be sought with due regard to the interests, the rights and the responsibilities of all parties concerned. We have made it clear at all times that the United States is prepared to participate in a peace-keeping force but only on the request of all the parties. We have made this unequivocally clear to Archbishop Makarios, and I can assure the representatives of the Soviet Union that the United States, while prepared to help, will be delighted if it does not have to be involved in keeping the peace between Greeks and Turks in Cyprus. And it must be equally clear that neither the United States nor any of the Western Powers are seeking to impose their will on the Government of Cyprus.

I shall not dwell at this time upon the assertions of the representative of the Soviet Union whereby the anxiety that most of us have that peace must be restored to Cyprus is some sort of a NATO plot. No one is even proposing that the international force be comprised just of NATO military units. The parties will have to agree upon the participants in any such force.

I have outlined why the United States supported the proposals developed for a peace-keeping force in Cyprus. I have said that the United States is deeply concerned with this grave situation and the imperative need to keep the peace in the Mediterranean area. Peace on that island today is as precarious as it is precious, and we do not know what new violence tomorrow may bring. The need for such a peace-keeping force is, I repeat, critically urgent. Clandestine arms shipments have recently increased the dangers. The world cannot stand by as an idle and silent witness to the fire that is consuming Cyprus and which could spread so rapidly.

We must ask ourselves what the Council can and should do in these circumstances. That is clear. We should go straight to the point at which we can really be most helpful. I suggest that we must bring about a prompt agreement on an international peace-keeping force for Cyprus, the need for which has been recognized by all, including President Makarios. This may require that we introduce into these consultations an expert in the peace-keeping field of recognized impartiality and stature. No one better fills such a requirement than the Secretary-General of the United Nations. We therefore recommend that the Council appeal to the parties concerned, in consultation with the Secretary-General, to move ahead quickly in working out such arrangements. Other States can make a contribution toward the establishment of a peace-keeping force. Those that can do so should co-operate freely and generously in this endeavour.

Strenuous efforts will also be required to bring about agreement between the two parties on a political settlement which will permit them to live in peace with each other. Therefore, we would also strongly urge that the Government of Cyprus and the Guarantor Powers, in consultation with the Secretary-General, be asked to designate an impartial mediator to assist in achieving a settlement. Let us address ourselves to these two priorities and let us, I beg leave to say, do so quickly.

In conclusion, let me say how much the United States values the spirit of co-operation which Greece and Turkey have shown in these dangerous weeks. They have demonstrated great restraint at a difficult moment in history. Both Governments, I believe, are to be commended for approaching Cyprus' problem which has such sensitive implications for both of them, with a sense of responsibility not only to the respective communities in Cyprus but also, more importantly, to the entire world community. We should be grateful to both of them.

To Katharine Schlesinger [35]

February 21, 1964

Dearest Kathy:
You're a fickle girl! A long time ago you told me you were coming to New York to talk about a job. Instead of that, I think you came and saw someone else — perhaps younger? Perhaps more handsome?
But I can forgive even that — if you will try again!

Love always,

To Mrs. Ronald Tree [36]

February 23, 1964

Sticks and stones are hard on bones,
Aimed with angry art;
Words can sting like anything.
But *silence* breaks the heart.

To Clayton Fritchey

February 25, 1964

I would hope that in the Eleanor Roosevelt speeches language could be included, provided by Harold Taylor, which would suggest in some exciting and inspirational way the magnitude of the human rights problems, the needs, the opportunities and the devices by which the Foundation might be of help.

It is no longer sufficient to talk about her and the importance of a memorial to preserve her memory. Something of this kind indicating the significance and importance of the Foundation's program should be included. Perhaps Harold Taylor has already written suitable materials or could do so if requested.

It is apparent that I am going to be tied up solidly for the week. Today I must go to Washington. This weekend I hope to make a long

---

[35] Daughter of Mr. and Mrs. Arthur Schlesinger, Jr.
[36] This handwritten note is in the possession of Mrs. Tree.

postponed visit to Libertyville for a variety of reasons, and before I know it these ERF speeches [37] will be on top of me.

To Adlai E. Stevenson III

February 25, 1964

Dear Adlai:

Of course, I was distressed not to get to Chelsea.[38] We have been having a hell of a time with Cyprus [39] — and still are.

Roxane [Eberlein] has put together the attached list of gifts for '63, which is the best we have been able to do from her records. So far as I know, this covers everything except possibly some small cash expenditures, which I believe we can disregard.

Perhaps I can talk to you on the phone during the week about how things are going. Dutch [Hermon Dunlap] Smith has been here, but was not very enlightening. I had hopes of getting out there to Libertyville for the coming weekend to do some work on my files in the basement, to ready them for an examination by the Librarian at the State Library in Springfield. I can't be sure if I can come, however, in view of the situation here.

Love,

H. Steven Lord and a companion, Miss Reed, were on a street corner waiting for a cab when Stevenson approached. They shook his hand and he conversed with them. Mr. Lord wrote Stevenson to thank him for talking to them.

To H. Steven Lord

March 3, 1964

My dear cab-whistling friend:

But I should thank *you!* And I do — for recognizing me; for being so courteous and so flattering.

With warm regards to Miss Reed — and my hope that we shall all meet again,

Cordially yours,

[37] He gave four speeches for the Eleanor Roosevelt Memorial Foundation in Florida during March and spoke at the foundation's luncheon in honor of Mrs. Lyndon B. Johnson in New York City on April 9 (USUN press release 4380).

[38] Chelsea Plantation, the winter home of Ruth Field in South Carolina.

[39] In addition to having spoken on Cyprus in the Security Council on February 19, 1964, Stevenson was also active in private negotiations on the dispute. He issued statements to the press on Cyprus on February 17 (USUN press release 4363) and March 4, 1964 (USUN press release 4367).

On March 7, Stevenson and his son Borden flew to Florida, and after fund-raising for the Eleanor Roosevelt Memorial Foundation they joined Agnes Meyer, who had rented a yacht to sail in the Caribbean. Stevenson wrote the following description of his trip.

In early March went with Borden to Palm Beach — spent luxurious night . . . spoke next day at lunch to small group of rich people for Eleanor Roosevelt Foundation. . . . Large dinner that night at Biltmore Hotel for ER Foundation and another speech[.]

After lunch moved to home of Stuyvesant Peabody [40] — old friend from Chicago. — After dinner visited with Leon Mandel [41] and Carola [42] on their yacht. Night at Peabodys.

Next morning flew to Miami in private plane with Elliott Roosevelt. . . .[43]

At Miami spoke at large business men's lunch at Du Pont Hotel — for ER Foundation. Sat with Jack Knight.[44] Press conference. Stayed at Elliott Roosevelt's house. Good visit with Bill Baggs of Miami News. Wrote fine, flattering column about me. Large cocktail party for political donors to ERF — followed by large dinner at Fontainbleu Hotel. Phil Klutznick and I spoke.

Sat up too late talking with Elliott and current wife — Pat Peabody of Seattle, mostly about Mrs. Roosevelt.

Monday morning Mar 12 Borden & I flew to Antigua via San Juan expecting to meet Mrs. Meyers yacht — the Panda. At Antigua in the late afternoon there was a message that the boat was in St. Vincent! We spent an expensive night at Mill Reef Club, arose at 5:30 and drove back to the airport to catch the Island hopping plane to St. Vincent — but found the yacht at St. Lucia.

"Panda" was a beautiful refitted 3 mast schooner formerly belonging to Emperor Bao Dai of Viet Nam — shades of my visit to him in the jungle in 1953 and dining on Gaur meat! [45] Mrs. Meyer, feeble and insecure after her eye operation and illness, Luvie Pierson [46] — Drew [Pearson] was at Caracas for inauguration of new Pres[ident]. . . . (why didn't U.S. send me, everyone asked, when I knew retiring Pres. [Rómulo] Betancourt & Venez. so well)[.] Dr[.] David Paton — eye doc. from Johns Hopkins and pretty wife — Joan. Delightful, gay young couple & good companions for Borden.

[40] Former president of the Peabody Coal Company.
[41] Chairman of the board of the Mandel Brothers department store in Chicago.
[42] Mrs. Mandel.
[43] Second son of Mr. and Mrs. Franklin D. Roosevelt.
[44] John S. Knight, publisher of the Miami *Herald* and other newspapers.
[45] See *The Papers of Adlai E. Stevenson*, Vol. V, p. 101.
[46] Wife of syndicated columnist Drew Pearson.

After look around St. Lucia we sailed over to Martinique — anchored in pretty bay for swim and night. Next day sailed around so. coast — under canvas — Fort de France.

Capt. . . . young very attractive ex R[oyal] N[avy] officer told me Panda belonged to Sterling Morton Hamill of Chicago — my old girl Suzie's [47] son. Crew all negro — 5 agile sailors, chef and 2 stewards.

Wandered around Fort de France, sailed across big bay to cove and fine beach. Met some local friends; inspected nearby real estate project; swam and spent night on deck under the stars.

Next day sailed up West coast of Martinique. Reading Bitter Lemons, Durrell's fine book about Cyprus [48] — my current headache — Charlie Yost's book [49] and The Spy who Came in Out of the Cold [50] — great thriller!

Anchored in cove in Les Saintes — where great sea battle of Rodney & De Grasse [51] was fought in 1784. Great story!

Mistake! The Saints was later. That night we anchored at La Soufrer (?) [Soufrière] on South end of Dominica because Roseau harbor too unprotected.

Went ashore to see negro village & plant of Rose's Limejuice. Negroes still speak French after 150 years of British colonial rule. Fascinating talk with village priest — French — recognized me at once. Recalled my last visit to Dominica with Marietta & Ronald Tree in 1957.[52] Ten years there ministering to the natives. Couldn't join us on board for dinner because of regular evening service at his 100 yr old church.

Why are all W. Indian towns so squalid! Slums of Empire.

That evening Drew Pierson [Pearson] suddenly appeared — escorted to Souffriere [Soufrière] by auto of John Archbold. Bertie [Archbold] had recognized him on plane flying up from Caracas via Barbados, where the Archbolds had boarded the plane.

I went back with the chauffeur & spent the night with Bertie — beloved girl! — and John at Springfield — their charming plantation in the lush, tropical mountains above Roseau. Stopped there with [Ronald] Trees — just 7 years before.

---

[47] Suzette Morton Zurcher, daughter of Preston and Sterling Morton, of Chicago. For her relationship with Stevenson, see John Bartlow Martin, *Adlai Stevenson and the World* (Garden City, New York: Doubleday, 1977), pp. 446–447.

[48] Lawrence Durrell, *Bitter Lemons* (New York: Dutton, 1957).

[49] *The Age of Triumph and Frustration: Modern Dialogues* (New York: Speller, 1964).

[50] John Le Carré, *The Spy Who Came in from the Cold* (New York: Coward-McCann, 1964).

[51] After Admiral de Grasse's French fleet had helped General George Washington defeat the British at Yorktown, de Grasse sailed to the West Indies to capture British possessions. He was stopped by Admiral George Rodney's fleet in April, 1782.

[52] See *The Papers of Adlai E. Stevenson*, Vol. VI, pp. 489–490.

Next morning others joined us for glorious picnic at Chelsea (Chatham?)
Plantation of Archbold down near the sea. Talked to Wash[ington]. by
phone! Bathed in mountain stream — memories of 1957! Joined boat in
mid afternoon and sailed up coast — anchoring near Portsmouth where
we had lunch . . . in 1957.

Next morning fine sail in brilliant sun over the Rodney-De Grasse battle
area to the Saintes. After swim in the lovely cove — anchored off the old
town and went ashore for walk around just at Angelus time. Pretty Creole
women and children going to church for evening service.

Next morning — early — sailed up to large town on W. side of Guade-
loupe. Borden & I went ashore and took taxi over to Pointe a Pitre — 1½
hours across beautiful, tropical, highly developed island. Big commotion
at airport — many police. Gen[eral] De Gaulle's plane about to arrive
en route to Mexico.

Flew Air France to St. Martin's island where Borden & group have
bought land. . . . Stayed at Passengrau guest house at Phillipsburg on
Dutch side. . . . took long motor ride around island to see real estate
development possibilities. Passed house with "Welcome Adlai" sign &
went in for visit with Mr. & Mrs. —————— McDonald — old Stevenson fans
from Conn[ecticut]. Jolly dinner at Passengrau with Borden's friends,
including . . . attractive people from Poughkeepsie who have come
there to live. Talked constantly of investment prospects. Island dry, good
climate, fine beaches, windy, near St[.] Croix & St. Juan. Next mor[n]ing
inspected possible site for new hotel project. . . .

Interesting Swedish colony at Simpson Bay — still blond after 300 years
on island. Too much intermarriage.

Flew back to N.Y. arriving evening of Mar[ch] 19th — I think.

To Mrs. Ronald Tree [53]

March 21, 1964

M —

Late Sat. afternoon. . . .

Things as usual . . . mad frenzy to get Dag Hammarskjold lecture finished for tomorrow at Princeton [University]; wriggled thru Kashmir for
present; [54] Cambodia next; [55] big hand at Dem[ocratic]. dinner in DC;

---

[53] This handwritten letter is in the possession of Mrs. Tree.

[54] The debate on the dispute between India and Pakistan over the border province
of Kashmir resumed on March 17, 1964, but was recessed for six weeks on March 20.

[55] Border negotiations between South Vietnam and Cambodia were broken off on
March 20, 1964, following an attack on a Cambodian village for which Prince Norodom Sihanouk, the Cambodian chief of state, blamed both the United States and
South Vietnam. The two countries apologized on March 21, and Cambodia demanded
reparations from the United States.

session with LBJ & urgent invitation to stay all night — after agreeable talk on USUN & disagreeable battle on Panama [56] — which is sure to end up in S[ecurity] C[ouncil], at present rate.

Much gossip re Salinger's departure,[57] rumored resig[nation]. of [Dean] Rusk etc etc. *But to the important: LBJ quickly approved Yates for Bingham & Tree for Yates.*[58] But who for Human Rts — ? Jane [Dick] whom he doesn't know . . . ?

. . . May cable you before you get this; [59] so suggest you prepare press release *as you would like it.* LBJ wants lots of publicity about his female appointments — and this would be his most important. Also any suggestions for shuffling the commission welcome!

. . . Sunday AM — . . . This morning clear, fresh snow — soon will go for a walk & lunch with [Cass] Canfields . . . tea at Mary L[asker]'s & an evening for my myriad speeches & problems. Tomorrow a hideous two weeks begins — speeches, travels, income tax etc. . . .[60]

B[arbara]. Ward has to return to England 2 weeks earlier than planned. Saw her briefly in Wash[ington] where she has been wowing her audiences, as usual. She will join me in Ill[inois]. for Easter — for the 6th time, I think. Because our visits can be few I told her I would save Sat Ap[ril] 11 for her but *Sunday Ap 12* I was mighty busy! The [Daniel] Caulkins and [Cass] Canfields are both going to be away that weekend.

Do you think I should have a birthday party for *you* on Ap 12? How about my big dance? If so please send list promptly. I want to do it — and you are such a good cause.

I pray all is well. . . .

S F

---

[56] A settlement of the dispute between the United States and Panama had been worked out by a committee of the Organization of American States, and the two countries agreed to accept it on March 12, 1964, but immediately disagreed as to its meaning. President Johnson stated on March 16 that he did not believe there was "a genuine meeting of the minds" between himself and Panamanian President Roberto F. Chiari over the accord.

[57] Pierre Salinger had resigned as President Johnson's press secretary.

[58] Jonathan B. Bingham resigned from USUN to run for Congress. Sidney Yates replaced him as representative on the Trusteeship Council, and Mrs. Tree took Yates's old position as special representative.

[59] Mrs. Tree was in Barbados.

[60] Stevenson spoke at Princeton University on March 23, at the University of California at Berkeley on April 2, and at the Commonwealth Club in San Francisco on April 3.

To Roxane Eberlein [61]

March 23, 1964

Roxane

I don't have Barbara Jackson's number at home. Please confirm that she is arriving Thurs afternoon Mar 26 and we are going to dinner at the [Paul] Hoffmans (what time is it? — put on sch[edule]).

Friday Mar 27 we go to Ill[inois] leaving at 4 PM. I have reservations for her going & returning (please get them — tourist) — she wants to return to Boston (?) on Tuesday Mar 31 at what time? (I plan to stay in Chicago leaving for Calif on Wed — have you that reservation?) I think for that part of the trip & returning I will go 1st class.

My trip to Chicago — S[an] F[rancisco] — N[ew] Y[ork] should be charged to the office. Barbara's going & returning I should pay.

Confirm that she is retur[n]ing on Sat Ap 11 & tell her Babs Caulkins has invited us for Sat night & any other couple she would like in the country — to let me know whether she would like to go or stay in town & go to Becket [62] so I can let them know.*

Also confirm that I am expecting her Friday night April 24 — Would she prefer Hamlet with [Richard] Burton (if it has opened? Can you get tickets now?) or the opening of the Lincoln Center Ballet which takes place that night. Is she staying at 42A Sunday night Ap 12? She knows I have to be out that night. . . .

Is anyone drafting anything for the Univ of Calif for me? When can I see it?

On the night I get back — Ap 5 — I have to present an award to Eva La Gallienne [63] at the opening of the Nat'l Repertory Theatre. Who asked me to do this? I must find out from someone something about La Gallienne, what sort of remarks would be appropriate about her, the theatre & the occasion. Perhaps you could make preliminary inquiries which I could follow up on Wed[nesday].

* Or would she like me to have a big bang up dinner party for her that night? Up to 20. I think it would be fine & she might like to see her NY friends. Or would she like just a few people early — and take them all to Becket? Who?

Stevenson gave the Dag Hammarskjöld Memorial Lecture at Princeton University on March 23, 1964.[64]

[61] This handwritten memorandum is in the possession of Miss Eberlein.
[62] A film based on a play by Jean Anouilh and starring Richard Burton and Peter O'Toole.
[63] Eva Le Gallienne, actress and author.
[64] The text is based on USUN press release 4374.

The United Nations and therefore the world has been fortunate to have three strong Secretaries General — Trygve Lie of Norway, Dag Hammarskjold of Sweden and U Thant of Burma. While serving on the American Delegation in London in the first days of the United Nations and latterly in New York, I had something to do with the selection of Trygve Lie [65] and U Thant. And it was my good fortune to know Dag Hammarskjold well, and my sad lot to attend his funeral in the lovely old cathedral at Up[p]sala. Like the others who came from all over the world, I walked behind him to the cemetery through the streets of the ancient town, lined with thousands of silent, reverent people. Upsala was the world that day when he was laid to rest in the northern autumn twilight, for he was a hero of the community of man.

Norman Counsins [66] tells a story that says a lot about Dag Hammarskjold as a peace-maker.

He had scheduled an interview with a magazine writer one evening. The writer suggested that they have dinner at a restaurant, which the Secretary-General accepted. He further suggested that they take his car, which the Secretary-General also accepted.

Upon leaving the building, the writer recalled to his embarrassment that he had driven into town in a battered old jeep. The Secretary-General was delighted. "Sometimes I think I was born in one," he said.

But the writer's embarrassment had only begun. Four blocks away, a taxi cab darted in front of the jeep and there was a harmless collision.

I don't have to suggest the reaction of the cab driver or the quality of his prose. But the writer was not without a temper himself, or the prose to match the cab driver. It looked as though the disagreement was about to escalate into active hostilities. At this point, Hammarskjold climbed out of the jeep and stepped around to the cab driver.

"You know," he said, "I don't think anyone quite realizes how tough it is to drive a cab in New York City. I don't know how you fellows do it — ten, twelve, fourteen hours a day, day after day, with all the things you've got to contend with, people weaving in and out of traffic and that sort of thing. Believe me, I really have to take my hat off to you fellows."

The cab driver defused immediately. "Mister," he said, "you really said a mouthful." And that was the end of the incident.

But it wasn't the end of the story. A few blocks later the unfortunate writer ran out of gas. And who should drive by? The same cab driver pulled up and said, "What's the matter chum, any trouble?"

"Out of gas," said the disgruntled writer.

[65] See *The Papers of Adlai E. Stevenson,* Vol. II, pp. 304–305.
[66] Norman Cousins, editor of the *Saturday Review.*

Well, you can guess the end of the story: The cabbie offered to get some gas, invited the driver's "nice friend" to come along with him, and drove off with the Secretary General of the United Nations in the front seat — leaving the writer to ponder the role of the peace-maker in today's tense society.

No one ever doubted Dag Hammarskjold's selfless dedication to peaceful settlement of any and all disputes among men and nations. None questioned his deep personal commitment to the principles of the Charter of the United Nations, whose first business is the peaceful settlement of disputes.

But this can be said of other men: Hammarskjold was unsurpassed, but he was not alone in his devotion to peace. What distinguished his service to the United Nations is that he came to see it for what it is: a specific piece of international machinery whose implicit capabilities can only be realized by the action of the members and the Secretariat working within its constitutional framework.

There was no doubt in Dag Hammarskjold — nor is there in many others — that the United Nations is the most remarkable and significant international institution ever conceived. But Hammarskjold also understood that the machinery not only needs lofty goals and high principles but it has to work in practice — that it has limited, not unlimited functions; that it has finite, not infinite capabilities under given circumstances at a given time.

He saw that the effectiveness of the organization is measured by the best consensus that can be reached by the relevant majority of the relevant organ — and that reaching that consensus is a highly pragmatic exercise.

Understanding all this, Dag Hammarskjold — himself a key part of the machinery — helped make the machinery more workable, more adaptable, more relevant to the immediate political needs. By doing so, he helped expand the capacity of the machinery to act effectively. This, I think, was his greatest contribution to the United Nations, and thus to world peace.

His was dedicated service — backed by diplomatic skill, by administrative talent, and by a sharp sense of political reality.

The overwhelming political reality of Hammarskjold's day was the division of the world into opposing and rigid military alliances, led by two incomparable centers of power and influence — with the two halves of this bi-polar world engaged in a cold war paced by an uncontrolled and seemingly uncontrollable nuclear arms race — while everyone else held his breath lest the "balance of terror" get too far out of balance.

Many came to accept this as a continuing — almost natural — state of affairs which would continue until one side collapsed or the two sides collided in World War III. We now know that it was a transitory and unhealthy condition of the world body politic.

The cold war has not sunk out of sight, but the field of contest may be shifting radically — and for the better.

The nuclear arms race has not passed into history, but at least it has, for the first time, been brought within a first stage of control.

For these and a large variety of other reasons, the world is a very different world from that which existed when Dag Hammarskjold went down to his death in that cruel crash in Africa two and half years ago. We therefore will be wise to tailor our thinking about the role of the United Nations he served so well not to his world of 1961 but to our world of 1964 — which is to say:

— a world which is no longer bi-polar but in which multiple centers of power and influence have come into being;

— a world which at long last is approaching the end of the historic struggle for military superiority — by acquiring absolute military power;

— a world in which the myth of monolithic blocs is giving way to a bewildering diversity among nations;

— a world in which realities are eroding the once rigid political dogmas;

— a world in which not only imperialism but paternalism is dying;

— a world in which old trading systems, monetary systems, market systems, and other elements of conventional wisdom are being challenged and changed;

— a world which at once makes breath-taking new discoveries and is crippled by ancient feuds — which is both fabulously rich and desperately poor — which is making more progress than ever before and seeing much of it wiped out by an explosive population growth;

— and finally, a world in which fundamental issues of human rights — which have been hidden in closets down the long corridor of history — are out in the open and high on the agenda of human affairs.

For the first time in history the world is being changed radically within the span of an average lifetime: we enter one world and leave quite a different one. As E. B. White once said of New York, "the miracle is that it works at all."

Not even the sloganeers have caught the full essence of these times; we do not yet know what to call this particular passage of history. Since the end of the Second World War we have spoken of the "atomic age" and the "jet age" — of the era of "rising expectations" and the "epoch of the common man" — of the "first age of space" and the "first age of mass politics." Each of these labels identifies at least one of the swirling phenomena of our times, but none of them will do as an over-all title.

We should try to come to grips with the central theme of our times —

with that aspect of current affairs which gives them their characteristic stamp and flavor — with that label which may not tell all but puts its finger on the most important thing that is going on.

You will recall that back in 1947 a certain "Mr. X" — who turned out to be my friend George Kennan — wrote an article for *Foreign Affairs* [67] in which he introduced the famous label, the "Policy of Containment." He invented the phrase but he did not invent the doctrine; the United States already was busily, heavily, expensively, and dangerously involved in containing the ruthless, heavyhanded outer thrust of Stalin's Russia — wherever he might strike or lean.

This was the main pattern of world events for a number of years and "Containment" was a meaningful description of the main purpose of United States policy. It was therefore a great public service, for in the free world effective foreign policy is difficult without the understanding and appreciation of the public. How can one rally support for a policy if one can't even describe it? In the absence of a suitable description, each individual action of government is dangerously exposed to attack and suspicion, but if it is known to be part of a larger and well-understood design, it becomes less difficult to act quickly and coherently. However, this is not a lecture on the glorious virtues and crippling vices of sovereign public opinion in a genuine democracy.

When we look back with pride on the great decisions that President Truman made, we see now that he had the inestimable advantage of public understanding. He could react to Korea quickly because he didn't have to stop to explain, to pull public opinion up alongside. It was quite clear to all that this was but another phase of Containment, just like the Berlin airlift and the guerila war in Greece, and NATO.

Up until the post-war years, Americans had been brought up on the idea of fighting every conflict to a decisive finish — to total victory, to unconditional surrender. But when the nuclear age revealed the hazards of this course, it was neither easy nor popular to introduce the concept of limited action, primarily to preserve the status quo. This nuclear necessity went against the American grain; it was (and to some still is) both confusing and frustrating. It took patient explaining, and all of us can be grateful that Mr. X gave identification and illumination to a policy that was already being practiced. He showed us why the Greeks thought it so important to have "a word for it."

We can, as I say, be proud of our performance under the Containment policy. Above all we can be proud that the tendency once noted by Lord Acton did not operate in our case: the possession of great power — unprecedented and overwhelming power — did not corrupt the American government or the American people.

[67] July, 1947, pp. 566–582.

But as unquestioned leader of an alliance constantly threatened by external military pressure, we had to stand up and be counted for more; we had to stand firm; we had to confront force with force until the tanks faced each other gun barrel to gun barrel, along Friedrichstrasse in Berlin — until the Korean invaders had been thrown back across the 38th Parallel — until the Navy drew an armored noose around Soviet missile sites in Cuba — and until, at long last, Soviet leaders became convinced that free men will answer steel with steel.

During this whole period the positions and actions taken by the United States Government to contain aggression had broad public understanding and support. In a sense the policy of containment was too easy to understand. It tended to reinforce a simplistic view of a black-and-white world peopled by Good Guys and Bad Guys; it tended to induce a fixation on military borders to the exclusion of other things; and it tended to hide deep trends and radical changes which even then were restructuring the world.

And, of course, the policy of containment — being a reaction to Soviet communist aggressiveness — necessarily had a negative and static ring to it. This had the unfortunate effect of partially obscuring the positive and progressive purposes of U.S. policies in support of the United Nations, in support of regional unity in Europe and elsewhere and in support of economic and social growth throughout most of the world where poverty was a centuries-old way of life.

Nevertheless, the doctrine of containment was relevant to the power realities of the times — to the struggle to protect the independent world from Stalinism — and to the defense of peace — which is quite a lot!

Indeed, the doctrine may not yet have outlived its usefulness. If the present Soviet leaders have come to see that expansion by armed force is an irrational policy, it is by no means clear that the Chinese Communists — pretending to read out of the same book — have yet come to the same conclusion.

No doubt we shall have to stand firm again — and face danger again — and run risks again in the defense of freedom.

We cannot and will not resign from whatever degree of leadership is forced upon us by the level of threat used against us, our allies, and our friends.

But as anyone willing to see clearly already knows, the current course of world affairs calls for something more than a "policy of containment."

What, then, *is* the dominant theme that marks the character of contemporary world affairs?

I would suggest that we have begun to move beyond the policy of containment; that the central trend of our times is the emergence of what, for lack of a better label, might be called a Policy of Cease-Fire, and Peaceful Change. I would suggest, further, that we may be approaching something close to a world consensus on such a policy.

No analogy is ever perfect, but if the Policy of Containment stands for "limited war," then the Policy of Cease-Fire perhaps stands for "limited peace." I believe this mutation is occurring simply because the H-bomb has made even "limited" war too dangerous.

Cease-Fire and Peaceful Change may strike some as a curious way to describe a period so jammed by violence, by disorder, by quarrels among the nations — an era so lacking in law and order. But I do not speak wistfully; I speak from the record.

It is precisely the fact that so much violence and so many quarrels *have not led to war* that puts a special mark on our times.

Only a few decades ago, if a street mob organized by a government sacked and burned the embassy of another government — if rioters tore down another nation's flag and spit upon it — if hoodlums hanged or burned in effigy the head of another state — if ships or planes on lawful missions were attacked — you would expect a war to break out forthwith. Lesser excuses than these have started more than one war before.

And only a few decades ago, once hostilities broke out between the armed forces of two nations, it was assumed with good reason that since the war was started, the war would proceed until one nation or one side had "won" and the other had "lost" — however foolish or futile the whole thing might be.

It also was assumed that the only way fighting could be stopped was by surrender — unconditional or negotiated — confirmed by signatures on a document and ritualized by the presentation of swords by the vanquished to the victors. That was in the nature of the institution called war. This is how it was.

But this is *not* the way it has been for well over a decade now and I think we should begin to notice that fact. Scores and scores of what used to be called "incidents" — far too many of them — have occurred around the world without leading to hostilities or even ultimatums. The fact is that in the last decade, nearly every war, partial war, incipient war, and threat of war, has either been halted or averted by a cease-fire.

It is still a very foolish and dangerous thing to insult another nation or desecrate its property or take pot shots at its citizens or equipment. But there are other forms of penalty than mass slaughter and, happily, the world is beginning to avail itself of them. Firing has started and then stopped — organized hostilities have been turned on and then called off — without victory or defeat, without surrender or peace treaty, without signatures or swords.

This is what seems to be happening. If so, it is perhaps the most important and certainly the most hopeful news for many a moon. As Al Smith kept saying, let's look at the record.

Just after the last war, the Soviet Union sent two armored divisions through northern Iran toward the Turkish and Iraqi frontiers while Bulgaria massed troops on its southern frontier to form the other prong of a huge pincers movement against Turkey. Then the Security Council of the United Nations met in London for the first time, and presently the Soviet troops went back into the Soviet Union. Not a shot had been fired.

Since that time there have been some twenty occasions on which the armed forces of two or more nations engaged in more or less organized, formal hostilities, which in another day would have been accompanied by declarations of war — wars to be fought until "victory" was atttained by one side or the other. Eight of these could be classified as outright invasions, in which the armed forces of one nation marched or parachuted into the territory of another; only one of them — the mis-matched affair between India and Goa [68] — was settled in the traditional way in which wars have been settled in the past.

On at least another twenty occasions there has been minor fighting on disputed frontiers, or armed revolts which usually involved the national interests of an outside state. Any of them would have qualified as a *causus belli* in another day.

At this very moment the agenda of the Security Council of the United Nations lists fifty-seven international disputes. Some of them have been settled, some are quiescent, and others could flare again at any moment. The point here is that more than half a hundred international quarrels have been considered by somebody to be enough of a threat to the peace to take the case to the court of last resort.

This is not exactly peace — at least not the kind of peace that people have dreamed and hoped and prayed for. But the record suggests that if fighting breaks out somewhere tomorrow, the chances are good that the next step will not be the sound of trumpets but the call to cease-fire.

And the chances are good that the step after that will not be an exchange of swords but an exchange of words at a conference table. This is no guarantee that a way will be found to remove the root of the trouble: in the Middle East, Southeast Asia, and the Far East there are temporary armistice lines that have been temporary now for more than a decade. But in these affairs there are no victors and no vanquished — and in this sense we are all winners.

This record of violence-without-war suggests, then, that we may have slipped almost imperceptibly into an era of peaceful settlement of dis-

[68] This statement led to another attack on Stevenson by the Indian press. See the *Hindustan Times* (New Delhi), March 25, 1964.

putes — or at least an era of cease-fires while disputes are pursued by other than military means.

Without making light of life-and-death matters, one can conclude that it has become distinctly unfashionable to march armies into somebody else's territory. I can think of no better evidence than the fact that the Organization of African Unity — an institution hardly out of its swaddling clothes — quickly arranged cease fires when fighting broke out on the borders between Morocco and Algeria and again between Somalia and Ethiopia.

How has all this come about? I shall not attempt anything like a definite answer. I would only suggest in passing that *perhaps* Korea was the end of the road for classical armed aggression against one's next-door neighbor; that *perhaps* Suez was the end of the road for colonial-type military solutions; and that *perhaps* Cuba was the end of the road for nuclear confrontation.

Perhaps man is adjusting once again to his environment — this time the atomic environment. *Perhaps* the leaders of nations around the world — small as well as large nations — have absorbed the notion that little wars will lead to big wars and big wars to annihilation. *Perhaps* we are edging toward a consensus on the proposition that nobody can afford an uncontrolled skirmish any more — that the only safe antidote to escalation is cease-fire.

I emphasize *"perhaps"* — for we must work and pray for that historical judgment on these times.

Yet skirmishes will occur — and will have to be controlled. Countless borders are still in dispute. Nationalism and rivalry are rampant. Ethnic and tribal and religious animosities abound. Passions and hatreds — ignorance and ambition — bigotry and discrimination — are all still with us.

The question is what can be done to make sure that this is in fact an era of peaceful settlement of disputes among nations.

For one thing, we can pursue this consensus on recourse to non-violent solutions. Most of the world is in agreement right now — though there are a few who would make a small exception for his own dispute with his neighbor. Yet there is reason to hope that the aggressors are extending their doctrine of no-nuclear-war to a broader doctrine of no-conventional-war — on the grounds that you cannot be sure there will be no nuclear war unless you are sure there will be no conventional war either.

For another thing, we can get on with the urgent business of expanding and improving the peacekeeping machinery of the United Nations. Most of the cease-fires I have been speaking about have been arranged by the United Nations and the regional organizations. Most of the truces and negotiations and solutions that have come about have come about with the help of the United Nations. Even if the will had existed, the way would not have been found without the machinery of the United Nations.

Violence — which there will be — without war — which there must not be — is unthinkable without an effective and reliable system of peacekeeping.

How should we and how can we improve the peacekeeping machinery of the United Nations?

Cyprus has vividly exposed the frailties of the existing machinery: The Security Council, by an impressive unanimous vote, first saved the situation with a cease-fire resolution providing for a UN peacekeeping force, but shortly afterward war nearly broke out again before the UN could put the resolution into effect.

There were no troops immediately available, and the Secretary General could not marshal the UN force with the speed so urgently required. Then there was no assurance of adequate funds to pay for the operation. While these handicaps were overcome, the Secretary General has not yet found a Mediator of the conflict. While I am confident that he will soon be designated, it took over two weeks (instead of two days or two hours) to get the peacekeeping operation going, and then only because armed intervention appeared imminent.[69]

In short, when time is of the essence, there is a dangerous vacuum during the interval while military forces are being assembled on a hit-or-miss basis.

And we further risk an erosion in the political and moral authority of the UN if troops trained only for national forces are thrust without special training into situations unique to the purpose and methods of the United Nations. For a UN soldier in his blue beret is like no other soldier in the world — he has no mission but peace and no enemy but war.

Time and again, we of the United States have urged the creation of a United Nations International Police Force, trained specifically for the keeping of the peace.

Perhaps it is too early to contemplate a fixed UN international force which would be permanently maintained for use for any and all purposes — for the world's emergencies differ one from another, and there can hardly be one treatment for all of them. But surely it would make sense for member countries of the United Nations to indicate what forces, equipment, and logistic support they would be willing to train for peacekeeping service, and to supply on a moment's notice. And surely it would make sense for the UN itself to add to its military and planning staff

[69] Neither Greece nor Turkey invaded Cyprus at this time. On March 4, 1964, the Security Council adopted a resolution establishing a peacekeeping force for Cyprus, and on March 25, U Thant named Sakari S. Tuomioja, the Finnish ambassador to Sweden, as mediator.

so that peacekeeping operations can be set in motion with the utmost speed and effectiveness.

There are some encouraging signs of progress. Recently it was announced that Scandinavia would create a permanent force for use on UN peacekeeping Missions. This would include Denmark, Sweden, Norway and Finland, although it is not yet clear if Finland would join in an integrated command or form an independent unit. Other nations, such as Canada and the Netherlands, have also shown interest in creating a United Nations stand-by force. So things are moving.

There is also movement on the fiscal front. Last year it seemed hopeless that the United Nations General Assembly would be able to agree on a financing formula which would permit its vital Congo operations to continue. But it did, and in the process paved the way for further developments in this all-important area.

This next month a United Nations working group will be meeting in an endeavor to formulate agreed methods of financing future peacekeeping operations, so that there will be less need for controversy each time such an operation is to be financed.

It is true that every United Nations peacekeeping effort is and probably always will be different from any other, and that no simple financing formula can fit them all, but agreement on certain principles and improvements in mechanisms should be possible and useful for the future. The United States will join wholeheartedly in the search for such agreements.

There will, however, be a shadow over that working group — the shadow of unpaid assessments for past United Nations peacekeeping operations. No less than $92 million of such arrears are owed by the Soviet bloc and a few other countries that have refused to pay their share of the cost of such operations — principally those in the Middle East and in the Congo.

But the Soviet claim that the assessments for these operations were not legally imposed and are not legally binding was rejected by the advisory opinion of the International Court of Justice in 1962, and that opinion was accepted by a decisive vote of the General Assembly that fall. Yet the Soviets are still refusing to pay.

What can be done about it?

Article 19 of the United Nations Charter provides that a member whose arrears amount to as much as its last two years' assessments "shall have no vote" in the General Assembly. This Article has caught up with the Soviet Union and certain other countries, which means that if at the time the next General Assembly meets the Soviet Union has not paid at least some $9 million of its arrears, it will have no vote in the Assembly.

The United States, and I believe all the members, want to avoid such a situation — in the only way it can be avoided, namely by a Soviet payment — in whatever form.

We think the best way to avoid the penalty and preserve the UN's financial integrity is for the members to make it abundantly clear that they support peacekeeping operations, that they want all members to pay their fair share of the cost, and that the Charter must be applied in accordance with its terms, and without fear or favor.

It is our earnest hope that the overwhelming sentiment of the members will prevail, and that the Soviet Union and others will find the means, in one way or another, to provide funds that will make unnecessary any Article 19 confrontation.

At the same time, the United States and others are exploring the possibility of adjustments to avoid the recurrence of this unhappy situation. Not many members would agree with the Soviet Union's contention that the General Assembly has no right to recommend a peacekeeping operation and that the Security Council should have the exclusive right to initiate such operations. Nor would many agree to abolish the General Assembly's exclusive right, under the Charter, to apportion and assess expenses.

But it should be possible to give new emphasis to the position of the Security Council by providing that all proposals for initiating a peacekeeping operation should first be presented to the Council, and that the General Assembly should not have the right to initiate such an operation unless the Council had shown that it was unable to act.

Also when it comes to the apportionment of the costs among the members by the General Assembly, we are exploring possible arrangements whereby the viewpoints of the major powers and contributors to the cost could be assured of more adequate consideration, and also the possibility of more flexible methods of distributing the cost.

I mention the fact that these possibilities are being discussed to make clear that the United States is using every effort to reach agreement as to future peacekeeping arrangements, in the hope that agreement as to the future will facilitate solution as to the past and provide a more firm foundation for a peacekeeping structure that has already proved itself so valuable.

Let me make it quite clear that it is the Charter that imposes the penalty of loss of voting privileges for non-payment of assessments. The United States has never presumed to think it could negotiate this requirement of the Charter with the Soviet Union and it has not entered into these exploratory talks for this purpose. But we are eager to discuss a sound system for financing future peacekeeping operations, a system which involves no change in the terms of Article 19 of the Charter and, indeed, presupposes settlement of the arrears problem.

We hope and believe that these efforts to preserve the peacekeeping function will have the support of all members, and certainly of all members who believe in the efficacy, indeed the indispensability, of the United Nations as a force for peace in the world.

Finally, if we are going to get the nuclear genii back in the bottle and keep it there, we shall have to improve our techniques for arriving at basic solutions to problems which remain even when a cease-fire has gone into effect.

I referred earlier to the point that the doctrine of containment was essentially a negative and static concept — as it had to be for its purpose. But a simple cease-fire is static, too; it is a return to the *status quo ante*. And that is not good enough for a world in which the only question is whether change will be violent or peaceful.

The world has known periods of relative peace and order before. Always the order was assured by a system designed to preserve the *status quo*. And this is precisely why the system of order broke down — because the *status quo* is indefensible in the long run.

What the world needs is a *dynamic* system of order — a system capable of bringing about not just a precarious halt to hostilities, but a curative resolution of the roots of hostility. This is to say that a dynamic system of order must be one which helps parties to a dispute to break out of rigid stalemates — to adapt to new times — to manage and absorb needed change.

It is easier to write this prescription than to fill it. But if conflicts are to be resolved and not just frozen, it is manifest that only through the United Nations, the community of nations, can the workable system of peaceful change evolve. The United Nations is a shared enterprise; it speaks for no nation, but for the common interest of the world community. And most important, the United Nations has no interest in the *status quo*.

To conclude: I believe there is evidence of new beginnings, of evolution from containment to cease-fire, and from cease-fire to peaceful change. We have witnessed the first concerted and successful effort to avoid the confrontation of naked force. The Cuban crisis has been followed by the nuclear test ban treaty and a pause in the arms race. We see growing up in the interstices of the old power systems a new readiness to replace national violence with international peacekeeping. The sheer arbitrament of force is no longer possible and less lethal methods of policing, controlling and resolving disputes are emerging. Do we perceive, perhaps dimly, the world groping for, reaching out to the fuller vision of a society based upon human brotherhood, to an order in which men's burdens are lifted, to a peace which is secure in justice and ruled by law?

As I have said, I believe that now, as in the days of the Founding Fathers, even the faintest possibility of achieving such an order depends upon our steadfast faith. In their day, too, democracy in an age of monarchs and freedom in an age of empire seemed the most remote of pipedreams. Today, too, the dream of a world which repeats at the international level the solid achievements — of law and welfare — of our domestic society must seem audacious to the point of insanity, save for the grim fact that survival itself is inconceivable on any other terms.

And once again we in America are challenged to hold fast to our audacious dream. If we revert to crude nationalism and separatism, every present organ of international collaboration will collapse. If we turn in upon ourselves, allow our self-styled patriots to entice us into the supposed security of an impossible isolation, we shall be back in the jungle of rampant nationalisms and baleful ambitions and irreconcilable conflicts which — one cannot repeat it too often — have already twice in this century sent millions to their death, and next time would send everybody.

I believe, therefore, that at this time the only sane policy for America — in its own interests and in the wider interests of humanity — lies in the patient, unspectacular, and if need be lonely search for the interests which unite the nations, for the policies which draw them together, for institutions which transcend rival national interests, for the international instruments of law and security, for the strengthening of what we have already built inside and outside the United Nations, for the elaboration of further needs and institutions of a changing world for a stable, working society.

If we in the United States do not carry these burdens, no one else will. If we withdraw, retreat, hesitate, the hope of today, I believe without rhetoric or exaggeration, will be lost tomorrow.

We have called this land the "last best hope" of man — but "last" now has overtones of disaster which we would do well to heed. With Churchill, I can say that "I do not believe that God has despaired of His children." But I would say also, in the words of the Scriptures: "Let us work while it is yet day."

Simon H. Rifkind and Lloyd K. Garrison discussed with Stevenson plans for his rejoining the law firm of Paul, Weiss, Rifkind, Wharton & Garrison. On March 5 Mr. Rifkind wrote Stevenson that all the partners were eager that he rejoin the firm and the suggested date was January 1, 1965, or an earlier date.

To Simon H. Rifkind

March 27, 1964

Dear Si:

❈ ❈ ❈ ❈ ❈ ❈ 70

I appreciate so much your letter of March 5 reviewing our understanding, and find it wholly satisfactory.

I confess I am a little uncertain about some current developments. In the first place, it seems likely that the General Assembly will be postponed until after the elections, which means that it will run well into 1965. Meanwhile with all the political and bureaucratic uncertainties, I have been urged to give no hint of possible retirement from this position, at least for the present. However, I believe any uncertainties will be resolved by the date you suggest — January 1, 1965.[71]

Meanwhile, I will keep you informed of any developments which could affect the plan.

❈ ❈ ❈ ❈ ❈

Yours,

To John J. Rooney

March 25, 1964

Dear Mr. Chairman:

This is to renew my invitation to you, and any of the Members of your Committee [72] that you can enlist, to visit us in New York.

Each time I go to Capitol Hill on a call, I remember, hopefully, that you indicated at our last meeting that you might find it convenient to come up to see us some time.

Moreover, so far as I know, you have not inspected "your building," [73] and besides, we have a lot to talk to you about in connection with our future financing problems, especially in the peacekeeping field.

Forgive me for being persistent, but it is the only way I ever do anything, and perhaps you suffer from the same occupational resilience!

Cordially yours,

---

70 Lloyd K. Garrison wrote that Mr. Rifkind could not remember why these asterisks appeared in this letter. Letter to Walter Johnson, April 3, 1973.

71 Lloyd Garrison wrote: "Judge Rifkind does remember that Adlai kept postponing his departure from the U.N. from that which was mentioned in the agreement. This happened every month or so. The last the Judge remembers was that Adlai said he felt confident that he would be returning to us before Labor Day [1965]." Ibid.

72 The Subcommittee on Appropriations of the House of Representatives.

73 Stevenson refers to the new USUN building.

On his return from speaking in California on April 2 and 3, Stevenson delivered the address at the Eleanor Roosevelt Memorial Foundation luncheon in honor of Mrs. Lyndon B. Johnson on April 9.

To Mr. and Mrs. Albert Greenfield

April 10, 1964

My dear Albert and Elizabeth:

While the memory of my meeting with you is still so vivid, I must thank you again for all your help with the Eleanor Roosevelt Foundation and for that fine dinner. I feel as though I had become a permanent nuisance to my friends, and I shall try not to burden you again — or at least until something else comes along!

Yesterday we had a huge luncheon — 2800 women — with Lady Bird Johnson as the attraction, and it went off extremely well. I don't know yet what the box office was, but I'm told I will be "delighted."

And I am also delighted to have had another visit with *you*. I shall always be proud to be able to call Albert and Elizabeth Greenfield my friends — and what friends!

Affectionately,

To Richard C. Beake [74]

April 13, 1964

Dear Richard:

Commencing May 1st, I am increasing your salary to $275 per month, payable as before.

I would hope it will now be convenient for you to assume your separate telephone bill.

I hope Nancy [Stevenson] has attended to the tree spraying and trimming. I shall remind her about it.

With affectionate regards to your family,

Yours,

P.S. Walking along the river, I noticed that there are still a lot of uncut roots from the wild grapevines that are smothering some of the crabapple trees. If you have time, this is a good season to clip them at the ground level.

---

[74] The new caretaker at Stevenson's Libertyville farm, replacing Frank Holland.

To Mrs. Edison Dick [75]

April 17, 1964

Jane dear —

. . . I'm on the way back from Wash[ington] to N. Y. — still no final action on the changes in USUN — and will be going abroad May 3 or 4 for 2 or 3 weeks. Why don't you and Eddie come down to Univ[ersity] of Ill[inois] with me for the Convocation on Friday, May (?). I hope Adlai and Nancy will come too. I might go over to Bloomington for the night and back to L'ville [Libertyville] on Sat; East on Sunday. I would rather do Bloomington later when there was more time. So perhaps we could fly down to Urbana and back together. I think the Univ. will supply a plane.

I don't expect to go to Geneva this summer and hope to have some time in Ill. in June or July. . . .

Love from my people to your people—

ADLAI

P.S. Things have been swirling at the usual pace. With E[leanor] R[oosevelt] Foundation added I've had a hell of a year — 3 years! And now there's this damn Senate business again.[76] This time from N.Y. But it is nice to know that your political demise has been exaggerated.

To Mrs. Eugene Meyer [77]

April 29, 1964

Dearest Agnes:

I have been worrying about you. Yesterday I had a call from Drew Pearson with a comforting report on your "condition." I am leaving for Europe for three weeks in a day or so, and will be hoping that the last vestige of your illness will be gone when I get back, and that we can have an evening with the pictures of the cruise.

I hope you won't forget to send along the money for the Eleanor Roosevelt Foundation. The office prods me from time to time. And if you can also pledge anything for future years it would improve our plans more than I can say. Things have been gathering momentum lately since Orin Lehman took over as Director, and I am more hopeful. But it is exhausting — I have to speak repeatedly and see people — a distasteful chore

---

[75] This handwritten letter is in the possession of Mrs. Dick.
[76] There was talk that Stevenson should run for the United States Senate from New York.
[77] The original is in the Agnes Meyer files, Princeton University Library.

on top of the normally brutal schedule. It has complicated my life almost beyond endurance!

Dearest love,
ADLAI

Stevenson released the following statement to the press April 30, 1964 [78]

I don't wish to be considered for the Democratic nomination in New York for the United States Senate.[79] And I feel that I should say so, decisively and promptly, to avoid any embarrassment or difficulty for my Party, for the candidates and for my friends and supporters.

While I will always want to help my Party as best I can, my present responsibilities in President Johnson's administration, in connection with the conduct of foreign affairs at this critical and hopeful time, must take precedence.

I am most grateful to all of those in New York who have urged me of late to be a candidate for the Senate. I greatly appreciate their interest. I faced the same problem in 1952 [1962] when political leaders in Illinois urged me to run for the Senate.

Mrs. Edison Dick sent Stevenson the draft of an article she had written about him. The following letter was dictated in New York City before Stevenson flew to Italy.

To Mrs. Edison Dick

May 4, 1964

Dear Jane:

I think it's marvellous! I really do. I have read it hurriedly and made some even more hurried suggestions. If I have any criticism it is, as you surmise, about the portion towards the end, which seems to overlook entirely that much of my problem in New York is official dinners, lunches, etc., which I *have* to go to. But you must write what you think.

[78] The text is based on a typewritten draft with handwritten corrections and interlineations by Stevenson.

[79] Robert F. Kennedy received the nomination. According to Theodore C. Sorensen, he was told by Lyndon Johnson that Stevenson had asked him to get the support of party leaders for Stevenson's candidacy. "When I told him I was for Bobby," Johnson said, "he never said another kind word about me." *The Kennedy Legacy* (New York: Macmillan, 1969), p. 46. See also Lyndon B. Johnson, *The Vantage Point: Perspectives of the Presidency, 1963–1969* (New York: Holt, Rinehart & Winston, 1971), p. 100.

I would like to get in the thought somewhere that my interest has been in foreign policy *per se* more than its execution or annunciation. I have had, as you must know, many frustrations and controversies with the Department [of State], but have tried to stick scrupulously to the State Department line even though it does not always coincide with my own views. Hence I think it would be a mistake to give the impression that I am wholly content with the present position.

I wonder if you could also use as illustrative of something the fact that I have been asked to run for the Senate — by the party leaders — from two of our major states in two years, Illinois and New York. As I said, "even though I am out of politics, it is comforting to discover that my political demise has been voluntary rather than involuntary." I most earnestly hope that something can be done with this. While I think it is a little over-written in places, I am sure that a redraft would sharpen and shorten it, and none could do that better than you.

Perhaps Clayton Fritchey would have as good an idea as anyone as to where to turn for a publisher. MacCall's, which specializes in women's work might be a good possibility. Moreover, it pays well! Parade or one of the Sunday magazine sections of the newspapers might be a possibility. They have enormous circulations, as you know.

I am more than a little grateful for your charity and forgiveness of my countless sins. I think its best virtue is its candor, simplicity and the grace of the writing more than the subject. But, my dear, you do get in an occasional extra word.

Libertyville was so beautiful, to leave it was inhuman cruelty. I hope you can get out to see the jonquils and the magnolia while they're still in glorious bloom.

Love, and thanks again,
ADLAI

Stevenson kept a diary for a few days in the spring of 1964.

Thursday, April 30, 1964
Caught 6 PM plane to Chicago. Night with Adlai III, Nancy and babies at L'ville [Libertyville]. Wet and overcaste [overcast].

Friday 10:30 AM
Loring Merwin met me at O'Hare & we flew in Univ[ersity]. of Ill[inois]. plane to Urbana for my Honors Day Convocation speech.

Lunch at Student Union with Pres[ident]. & Mrs. David Henry, sundry Deans & Trustees. . . .

Convocation in new Assembly Hall (seats 16 000!) great white mushroom on the green prairie. . . . Splendid!

Large crowd — maybe 5–6000. Made excellent speech on education for liesure [leisure] in automated age etc.

Hon[orary]. degree of Dr. of Humane Letters. Reception for honor students and families.

Flew back to Chi. with Mr. and Mrs. Clement . . .[80] in time for Dutch [Hermon Dunlap] Smith's birthday party at Lake Forest. . . .

Sat. May 2

Beautiful day — jonquils out, emerald grass, carpets of spring beauties beneath the maples in tiny leaf.

Children glorious. Played tennis with Adele & Dutch & Ellen [Smith].

At 3:15 bid reluctant farewell and caught 4 PM plane to N.Y. Roxane [Eberlein] met me. Repacked suit case for Europe and boarded 8:30 Pan Am. plane to find Marietta [Tree] already aboard.

Uneventful flight. Arrived Rome at 11 AM — Sunday, May 3.

Transferred to Alitalia plane to Naples. Met by consulate people; Commander & wife from Navy HQ. and Ricardo and Betty Sicre.[81] Drove direct to their beautiful new 96′ yac[h]t — Rampager — tied up to restaurant on quai of Marina Piccola. First time in Naples since June 1953 when we paused on world trip for few days at Positano — Bill Blair, Bill & Sim Attwood, Walter Johnson & I.[82]

Naples booming — what a contrast to those cold, dark days during the war — November, December 1943 — and all the horrible destruction in the port and industries and that cold, damp villa near the barracks where we slept in misery.[83]

Up anchor — and out of the little port in brisk wind & bright sunshine — dead tired after journey. Sailed past great U S supply ship over to Capri. Giovanni Agnelli's beautiful sloop moored nearby. Sailed around island — great cliffs — Augustus threw his enemies off? — past the huge rocks — the tunnel, the blue grotto — memories of 1953.

Took taxi up to town for walk around with Ricardo & M[arietta]. Walked back to ship — and there was Ava Gardner — arrived by helicopter from Naples! altho I had asked the Sicre's not to have her.

Late dinner.

---

[80] Mr. and Mrs. James W. Clement, of Chicago. Mr. Clement, a member of the board of trustees of the university, had served in the state administration when Stevenson was governor of Illinois.

[81] Old friends now living in Spain.

[82] See *The Papers of Adlai E. Stevenson*, Vol. V, p. 357.

[83] For Stevenson's mission to Italy in December, 1943, see *The Papers of Adlai E. Stevenson*, Vol. II, pp. 173–176.

Monday May 4

Awoke refreshed after long sleep. Ship under way for Positano. Climbed up past villa I had in 1953 — with Ricardo & M[arietta]. Explored town — vastly grown and readyied [readied] for summer influx. Bright & warm. Swam off boat. Huge Lo[b]sters for lunch on deck. Very gay. Up anchor and away to Amalfi. Sun bath on top deck. Paused briefly; didn't go ashore. Sailed on to Agraphali [Agropoli]. By taxis to Paestum — 12 kilometers — to see the splendid ruins of temples to Hera, Ceres and Neptune on the flat rich plain — just at sundown. New tombs nearby uncovered by farmer — very neat & rectangular. Bones etc all removed to museum at Paestum which, of course, was closed. Who were they — pre Greek?

Stopped in Agropoli to buy vegetables — fenuchi with salad dressing with cocktails!

Dinner was a splendid pasta with sausages & meat balls & glorious sauce — very piquante — cooked by Ava [Gardner], who then went to bed afraid to face it & anxious about our reaction! Strange, lovely, lush girl. (last night she climbed alone up to Capri in the middle of the night[.])

Tuesday, May 5

Up anchor at 6:30 for the Aeolian islands. Anchored off Stromboli — smoking volcano — near desolate village — on the NW point opposite the great rock surmounted with a white lighthouse. Pop. now 650 or less — deserted houses. Delicious swim off the yacht. After another glorious lunch pulled up 150' of anchor and cruised past Panarea to Lipari. Anchored in harbor and went ashore at sunset to explore the castle — Greek and neolithic excavations and ancient tombs in exquisite citadel overlooking stage set square. M[arietta] and I want to rent one of little bldgs surrounded with ancient churches and gardens in Castle grounds high above the sea and charming unspoiled town.

Ava cooked magnificent pasta for dinner — and then went to bed refusing to eat it!

Wednesday, May 6

Back to see the town, mail letters and climb to the castle again by daylight. Lovely museum — archeological, Greek and Roman. Fine cathedral. Melange of churches, gardens, tombs.

Lunch, water skiing, swim and siesta in hot sun. At 3 up anchor for Milazzo, past Vulcano island, on Sicily. Arrived at 5:30 & tied up at quai to take water & spend night.

Betty, M[arietta] & I took ancient fiacre for castle on cliff above the big town. Dismounted and walked rest of way to desterted [deserted] abandoned castle built on earlier citadel in 13th century. Watchmen asked if we were Germans. They can enter only with pass. "Americans!" Opened the great iron gates and led us thru ruined, dark passages to the highest part — what used to be a prison. Walked back to boat thru busy town — little poverty in Italy any longer.

Lipari — Ava water skied perfectly — after she finally got up!

Joined the evening paseo — another beautiful soft evening — blue sky, pale & high stars.

American woman and her small daughter came aboard — "to see the first Americans in many months.["] Lives in ancient tower & castle above bay where we stopped to swim before entering harbor. Lived in India 5 yrs; writing novel; came from Boston; evidently very lonesome. Told us much about Sicily & Milazzo. Likes Vulcano better than Lipari — no tourists — and I thought they hadn't found Lipari! Never got her name.

Dinner on board — and to bed tired again!

Thurs. May 7

Sailed out of Milazzo in another day of bright sunshine for the straits of Messina — following along the rugged green coast of Sicily — past S[c]ylla — the great rock off the Calabria coast & Charybdis, the whirlpool and terror of the ancient mariners. Shipping and strange fishing boats with tall steel masts & lookouts and long catwalk bow sprits — probably tuna or bonita.

Much building along the coast of Sicily as we approached the harbor of Messina. Tour of port — saw the exact place where I boarded the LST for Reggio Calabria in Nov. [December] 1943 — also the Municipia where the meeting with the A.M.G. [Allied Military Government] officers took place that cold rainy night when the British officer proposed the Xmas party for the children — hungry wretched urchins — and concluded his moving plea that we "do something" for them "because the little bastards will steal it all anyway."

85 000 killed in eruption of Etna & earthquake in 1909 — 5000 in 1943 bombing.

Now the quai is no longer rubble; everything is rebuilt and the city is busy & prosperous.

Another glorious lunch on board & we headed down the coast for Taormina arriving as the sun was sinking low.

Took a cab along the coast road and up and up thru crowded streets around horseshoe turns, past countless hotels and old villas to the Greek theatre — certainly as beautiful, spectacular setting as there is in the world — sitting on a ridge between two rocky hills surmounted by a castle & overlooking the sea.

Walked down thru past the Timeo hotel . . . thru blocks of tourist shops. Another soft luminous night sitting, strolling, dreaming in the plazas. Met Ricardo & Ava at Hotel San Dominico for drink in quiet old Victorian room & wandered thru the lively streets some more — As we were leaving to return to the yacht she announced she was flying back to Naples in the morning at 7! — to send her enormous luggage!

Quiet dreamless night in port of Taormina.

Fri. May 8

Set off for Catania early — along coast of Sicily. Arrived Catania at noon. Nice doctor picked us up on quai & took us to Alitalia. Usual interminable business of getting tickets for Monday AM at 7! to Rome.

Walked around busy, businesslike Milan of Sicily — cathedral & church closed — back to ship for another delicious paella. Then off to Syracuse — reading history of Sicily in newly acquired guide books.

Tied up at quai in Syracuse — again in soft evening light & walked thru lovely old town — lovely churches — St. Agatha who was martyred here — built on Greek temple using great Doric columns. Vespers in all churches. Beautiful ancient palaces — now banks, public bldgs, stores. Balconies in narrow winding streets. Joined the "paseo" again in the plazas. Saw ruins of Greek temple of Apollo amid noise of Vespas & little Fiats hurrying in every direction.

Back to ship for — octopus with wonderful stuffing — and more wonderful sleep!

Sat. May 9

We saw more of this incredible museum of antiquities — Syracuse — where Archimedes was accidentally killed during the sack of the town by Marcellus (2nd B C) while quietly pursuing his studies. The Greek theatre — 475 B C — one of largest known — the street of tombs with deep ruts in the rock made by chariot wheels for hundreds of years — the mouth of the acquaduct [aqueduct] and rushing torrent carrying water under the theatre from 13 miles away. (Greek dramas were performed in early morning when view was best!) The alter [altar] of Hieron II hewn out of rock — 650' long 75' wide — destroyed by the Spaniards. In the Latormia [Latomia] del Paradiso in whose sheltered depths paths wind among luxuriant fruit trees — almonds, orange, lemon, naspoli — we entered the Ear of Dionysius — huge S shaped cavern 75' high like a vaulted Gothic cathedral. The floor was a pool of water — the echoes eyrie [eerie].

Adjoining is the Gratta dei Cadari where rope makers have plied their trade for centuries. An old man making hemp threads sold me a sample of his card. Hewn out of the rocks, the high pink walls are huge pillars — and countless million hours of labor to chisel the vast cavern — make it a wonder and a beauty.

Then to the Roman amphitheatre of 2 c "only a little inferior to

Verona.["] (Where, how did they get so many "beasts" for the gladi[a]-torial spectacles of all the Roman theatres!)

Then out on the Catania road past the "tomb of Archimedes" & a path leading to the Latomia del Filosofo where the legend says Philoxenus and Cythero were confined for expressing too candid an opinion of the verses of Dionysius!! Climbing higher along the great spur of rock we reach the enormous Castle of Euryalus — the most complete & important Greek military work extant built in 402–397 on the plateau of Epipolae W[est]. of Syr[acuse]. — to defend the city from the Phoenicians. In those days the sea came up to the S. walls — now there are several KM's [kilometers] of fertile plain. I don't recall seeing previous Greek fortresses. It was full of laughing young girls — school classes — buzzing with talk. In a deep recess — or moat — an animated & delightful lady was teaching an out door class of attentive teenagers.

We passed countless sights and came back from the staggering Castello to the ship — thence by motor boat across the harbor for a swim — champagne, bread & cheese. I explored a promentory [promontory] — opposite entrance to harbor — and an abandoned farm house complete with ruined chapel & glorious view of city, sea, harbor and country. I'm afraid Ricardo isn't interested in buying & restoring it!

Back to beautiful Rampager (cost $350 000) for another incredible lunch — rice lubana[?] (rice, fried bananas & sauce of tomatoes, onions oil & peppers) followed by fried fish — shrimps, octopus, tiny sole, small red fish & a delicious soft white larger fish — popped into the pan from the sea. Then sliced blood oranges and fraises du bois!!

X — Loup de mer.

Siesta!

M[arietta] & I took long walk — lovely little acquarium [aquarium] of small rare fish in settings like submarine pictures. Pool of Arethusa — nymph who was pursued by river god and fled from Pelepon[nesus]. & became a pool in Ortygia — the island of ancient Syracuse. Walked around sea side of old town — back thru busy streets to ship.

Sunday May 10

Got to work on my papers early. Visited archeological museum with M[arietta] — materials going back to pre-Greek 2000 BC. Didn't see famous collection of coins — plaster copies — exquisite! Revisited cathedral built around Greek temple. What a splendid sight it must have been.

"Set sail" for Broccoli (!) little town on far side of Catania bay — explored old castle, swam — lunch — siesta in sun & tied up at Catania at sunset.

And there awaiting us was . . . a charming vivacious English speaking retired Navy officer with two telegrams for me. Son works in Am[erican]. consulate in Naples & poor man had motored all the way from Syracuse to deliver them.

40 yrs in Italian Navy; escaped from Shanghai with family — 3½ mos. journey to Italy — 9 yrs. commander Port of Naples. Now has own almond factory — and can't find "a peasant" — everyone working for the big Gulf refinery & new industries in Augusta — now Syracuse where his pretty, fat, intelligent daughter is a secretary. A few years ago — 3 or 4 — Syracuse was a poor quiet tourist town. Now there is no unemployment & terrible traffic jam. Told us Mafia active only in Palermo area. Never has been tolerated in Catania or Syracuse.

Walked around town before dinner with Ricardo & Betty [Sicre] & ended up in Red light district — crowded with young men on Sunday night — where helpful Madam said "Nau[g]hty street — not for you" and we retreated. Found our way back to boat thru dark deserted streets — for dinner & good talk with dear Sicres. What a relaxed, luxurious, restful cruise it has been!

Monday, May 11

Couldn't sleep — up at 5:30! Comdr. of Port sent car & sailors to take M[arietta] and me to airport. Farewell to crew. . . . Sicres up too [to] see us off. Leave later themselves to fly back to Spain.

Left Catania at 7:15 by air for Rome. Drove in Pan Am car to Astra Antigua — closed! Then along Lido beach (— 250 000 Sunday visitors) and thru lovely forest of Roman pines. A little walk, a little talk. Roman road to Anzio.

. . . Goodbye to M[arietta] — for Teheran and Kabul for Human Rts. [Rights] conference, Returning by Beirut, Cairo & Algiers.

Haircut — cost $2.00! Used to be 50c.

. . . Then met Sarragat [84] . . . Foreign Minister who [is] going to the Hague for Atlantic Council meeting. Photographs & talk. Economy of Italy OK but communism very bad and govt. "feeble" — can't do anything about it. "Movies, TV, Radio — all communist!"

Ambassador Frederick Reinhart [85] called me at airport for greetings — coming to U.S. in July with P[rime] M[inister]. . . .

Off at 1:35 by Alitalia for Hague.

Stevenson met with various ministers attached to the North Atlantic Treaty Organization at The Hague. He spent one day in Paris and then flew to Sweden to speak at Uppsala University. He arrived in London on May 18, 1964, to stay with Ambassador and Mrs. David K. E. Bruce.

[84] Giuseppe Saragat, Italian minister of foreign affairs, 1963–1964.
[85] United States ambassador to Italy.

To Mrs. Ronald Tree [86]

May 19, 1964

. . . Your letter from Persia has come. . . . Now I feel a little better —
I've had lunch . . . done my annual horrendous press conference and 3
TV performances and at least that much is behind me. I arrived yester-
day — Mon. afternoon — from Stockholm after a lively experience at
Uppsala 9 AM to 2:30 AM and a day in the country with the P[rime]
M[inister]. The Bruces had a dinner party laid on — hardly my dish. . . .
A[rthur]. Schlesinger is staying here, leaving for home in a day or so
after a month in Europe. The Mods and the Rockers are at it; Nicky
[Bruce] is incomparably the brightest most engaging child I've ever
seen!

This morning — Tues. — I went to the Embassy — worked on the
phone on my schedule, talked to all the droppers in — and now — later —
I'm a little sick again. . . .

Then to Gladwyn Jebb's for more talk, talk; then back here for supper
with the Bruces. . . .

Talked with NY on the phone today — no reason to hurry back but I
want to go home, London doesn't interest me any more and I wish
[President Charles] De Gaulle had been in Paris and I could have had
those talks.

So glad and not surprised the carpets are red; the people good and
the work satisfying. Pray no tourista. Extreme restraint about everything. . . .

a.

*On Stevenson's return to the UN, the question of aggression in Vietnam
was on the agenda of the Security Council. On May 21, 1964, Stevenson
spoke to the Security Council.* [87]

The facts about the incidents at issue are relatively simple and clear.
The Government of the Republic of Viet-Nam did in fact mistakenly
cross the ill-marked frontier between their country and Cambodia in
pursuit of armed terrorists on 7 and 8 May 1964, and on earlier occasions.
This has been repeated and acknowledged here again by the representative of the Republic of Viet-Nam.

[86] This handwritten letter is in the possession of Mrs. Tree.
[87] United Nations, *Official Records,* Security Council, May 21, 1964, pp. 5–14. For
a discussion of the situation in May, 1964, see *The Pentagon Papers: The Defense
Department History of United States Decisionmaking on Vietnam,* Senator Gravel
edition (Boston: Beacon Press, 1971), Vol. II, Vol. III.

The Government of the Republic of Viet-Nam has expressed its regrets that these incidents occurred with some tragic consequences. It has endeavoured to initiate bilateral discussions with the Cambodian Government in order to remove the causes of these incidents. But these efforts have not yet produced any useful result.

These incidents can only be assessed intelligently in the light of the surrounding facts, namely the armed conspiracy which seeks to destroy the Government and the very society of the Republic of Viet-Nam itself.

It is the people of the Republic of Viet-Nam who are the major victims of armed aggression. It is they who are fighting for their independence against violence directed from outside their borders.[88] It is they who suffer day and night from the terror of the so-called Viet-Cong.

The prime targets of the Viet-Cong for kidnapping, for torture and for murder have been local officials, school teachers, medical workers, priests, agricultural specialists and any others whose position, profession or other talents qualify them for service to the people of Viet-Nam, plus, of course, the relatives and children of citizens loyal to their Government.

The chosen military objectives of the Viet-Cong — for gunfire or arson or pillage — have been hospitals, school houses, agricultural stations and the various improvement projects by which the Government of Viet-Nam for many years has been raising the living standards of the people. The Government and the people of the Republic of Viet-Nam have been struggling for survival, struggling for years in a war which has been as wicked, as wanton and as dirty as any waged against an innocent and peaceful people in the whole cruel history of warfare. It seems to me that there is something both grotesque and ironic in the fact that the victims of this incessant terror are the accused before this Council and are defending themselves in daylight while terrorists perform their dark and dirty work by night throughout their land.

I cannot ignore the fact that at the last meeting of this Council, the representative of the Soviet Union digressed at great length from the subject before the Council to accuse the United States Government of organizing direct military action against the people of the Indo-Chinese peninsula. For years, too many years, we have heard these bold and unsupported accusations in the halls of the United Nations. I had hoped that such malicious fairy tales would be heard no more, but since another fanciful accusation against my country has been made by the Soviet representative I am sure that the members of the Council will permit me

---

[88] The United States government's official position that the war was imposed on South Vietnam by aggression from Hanoi is "not wholly compelling" in light of the Pentagon Papers. "Most of those who took up arms were South Vietnamese and the causes for which they fought were by no means contrived in North Vietnam." Neil Sheehan et al., *The Pentagon Papers as Published by the New York Times* (New York: Quadrangle Books, 1971), p. 71.

to set him straight on my Government's policy with respect to South-East Asia.

First, the United States has no, and I repeat "no," national military objective anywhere in South-East Asia. The United States policy for South-East Asia is very simple. It is the restoration of peace so that the peoples of that area can go about their own independent business in whatever associations they may freely choose for themselves without interference from the outside. I trust that my words have been clear enough on this point.

Secondly, the United States Government is currently involved in the affairs of the Republic of Viet-Nam for one reason, and for one reason only, because the Republic of Viet-Nam requested the help of the United States and other Governments to defend itself against armed attack fomented, equipped and directed from outside.[89]

This is not the first time that the United States has come to the aid of peoples prepared to fight for their freedom and their independence against armed aggression sponsored from outside their borders nor will it be the last time, unless the aggressors learn once and for all that armed aggression does not pay, that it no longer works, and that it can no longer be tolerated in the nuclear age.

The record of the past two decades makes it clear that the nation with the will for self-preservation can outlast and defeat overt or clandestine aggression, even when that internal aggression is heavily supported from the outside and even after significant early successes by the aggressors. I would remind the members of the Council that in 1947, after the aggressors had gained control of most of the country, many people felt that the cause of independent Greece was hopelessly lost. But as long as the people of Greece were prepared to fight for the life of their own country, the United States was not prepared to stand by while Greece was overrun.

This principle does not change with the geographical setting. Aggression is aggression, organized violence is organized violence. Only the scale and the scenery change. The point is the same in Viet-Nam today as it was in Greece in 1947 and in Korea in 1950. The Indo-Chinese Communist Party, the parent of the present Communist Party in North Viet-Nam, made it abundantly clear as early as 1951 that the aim of the Viet-Namese communist leadership is to take control of all of Indo-China. This goal has not changed. It is still clearly the objective of the Viet-Namese communist leadership in Hanoi.

[89] In the spring of 1961, President Ngo Dinh Diem of South Vietnam was reluctant to accept a proposal by President Kennedy to increase American forces in the country. However, by the fall of 1961, when his government became shaky, he appealed to the United States to become a cobelligerent. Ibid., p. 98. On May 13, 1961, Kennedy ordered covert warfare against North Vietnam. Ibid., p. 96.

Hanoi seeks to accomplish this purpose in South Viet-Nam through subversive guerrilla warfare, directed, controlled and supplied by North Viet-Nam. The communist leadership in Hanoi has sought to pretend that the insurgency in South Viet-Nam is a civil war, but Hanoi's hand shows very clearly. Public statements by the Communist Party in North Viet-Nam and its leaders have repeatedly demonstrated Hanoi's direction of the struggle in South Viet-Nam. For example, Le Duan, First Secretary of the Party, stated on 5 September 1960: "At present, our Party is facing a momentous task . . . to strive to complete the revolution throughout the country." He also stated: "The North is the common revolutionary base of the whole country." Three months after the Communist Party Congress in Hanoi in September 1960, the so-called National Front for the Liberation of South Viet-Nam was set up pursuant to plans outlined publicly at that Congress.

The International Control Commission in Viet-Nam, established by the Geneva Agreements of 1954, stated in a special report which it issued on 2 June 1962, that there is sufficient evidence to show that North Viet-Nam has violated various articles of the Geneva Agreements by its introduction of armed personnel, arms, munitions and other supplies from North Viet-Nam into South Viet-Nam with the object of supporting, organizing and carrying out hostile activities against the Government and armed forces of the Republic of Viet-Nam.

Infiltration of military personnel and supplies from North Viet-Nam to South Viet-Nam has been carried out steadily over the past several years. The total number of military cadres sent into South Viet-Nam via infiltration routes runs into the thousands. Such infiltration is well documented on the basis of numerous defectors and prisoners taken by the armed forces of the Republic of Viet-Nam.

Introduction of communist weapons into South Viet-Nam has also grown steadily. An increasing amount of weapons and ammunition captured from the Viet-Cong has been proven to be of Chinese communist manufacture or origin. For example, in December 1963, a large cache of Viet-Cong equipment captured in one of the Mekong Delta Provinces in South Viet-Nam included recoilless rifles, rocket-launchers, carbines and ammunition of Chinese communist manufacture.

The United States cannot stand by while South-East Asia is overrun by armed aggressors. As long as the peoples of that area are determined to preserve their own independence and ask for our help in preserving it, we will extend it. This, of course, is the meaning of President Johnson's request a few days ago for additional funds for more economic as well as military assistance for Viet-Nam. And if anyone has the illusion that my Government will abandon the people of Viet-Nam — or that we shall weary of the burden of support that we are rendering these people — it will be only due to ignorance of the strength and the conviction of the American people. We all know that South-East Asia has been the victim of almost incessant violence for more than a decade and a half.

Despite this fact, it has been suggested that we should give up helping the people of Viet-Nam to defend themselves and seek only a political solution. But a political solution is just what we have already had, and it is in defence and in support of that political solution that Viet-Nam is fighting today. The United States has never been against political solutions. Indeed, we have failthfully supported the political solutions that were agreed upon at Geneva in 1954 and again in 1962. The threat to peace in the area stems from the fact that others have not done likewise.

The Geneva Agreements of 1954 and 1962 were, precisely, political agreements to stop the fighting, to restore the peace, to secure the independence of Viet-Nam and Laos and Cambodia, to guarantee the integrity of their frontiers and to permit these much-abused peoples to go about their own business in their own ways.[90] The United States, though not a signatory to the 1954 Agreements, has sought to honour these agreements in the hope that they would permit these people to live in peace and independence from outside interference from any quarter and for all time.

To this day there is only one major trouble with the political agreements reached at Geneva with respect to Viet-Nam, Cambodia and Laos in 1954 and again with respect to Laos in 1962. It is this: the ink was hardly dry on the Geneva Agreements in 1954 before North Viet-Nam began to violate them systematically with comradely assistance from the regime in Peking. Nearly a million people, as you will recall, living in North Viet-Nam in 1954 exercised the right given to them under the Geneva Agreement to move south to the Republic of Viet-Nam. Even while this was going on, units of the Viet-Minh were hiding their arms and settling down within the frontiers of the Republic to form the nucleus of today's so-called Viet-Cong — to await the signal from outside in order to rise and strike.[91] Meanwhile, they have been trained and sup-

[90] The 1954 Geneva Agreements called for an election in 1956 to unify the country. President Diem, with the encouragement of the United States, blocked any election because he knew he would lose. Ibid., pp. 52, 53.

[91] The Pentagon study states: "From 1954 to 1958 North Vietnam concentrated on its internal development, apparently hoping to achieve reunification either through the elections provided for in the Geneva settlement or through the natural collapse of the weak Diem regime. The Communists left behind a skeletal apparatus in the South when they regrouped to North Vietnam in 1954 . . . but the cadre members were ordered to engage only in 'political struggle.' In the years before 1959 the Diem regime was nearly successful in wiping out the agents, who felt constrained by their orders not to fight back. Their fear and anger at being caught in this predicament, however, apparently led them to begin the insurgency against Mr. Diem, despite their orders, sometime during 1956–57." Ibid., p. 72.

plied in considerable measure from North Viet-Nam — in violation of the Geneva Agreement, the political settlement. They have been reinforced by guerrilla forces moved into the Republic of Viet-Nam through Laos — in violation of the Geneva Agreement, the political settlement.

This is the reason — and the only reason — why there is fighting in Viet-Nam today. There is fighting only because the political settlement for Viet-Nam reached at Geneva in 1954 has been deliberately and flagrantly and systematically violated.

As I say, this is the reason why my Government — and to a lesser extent other Governments — have come to the aid of the Government of the Republic of Viet-Nam as it fights for its life against armed aggression directed from outside its frontiers in contemptuous violation of binding agreements. If the Government of the Republic of Viet-Nam is fighting today, it is fighting to defend the Geneva Agreement which has proven undefendable by any other means. If arms are being used in Viet-Nam today, it is only because a political solution has been violated cynically for years.

The same disregard for the political settlement reached at Geneva has been demonstrated — by the same parties — in Laos. Violation has been followed by a period of quiet and then another limited aggression. Throughout the period since July 1962, when the Laotian settlement was concluded, the Prime Minister of Laos, Prince Souvanna Phouma, has with great patience and fortitude sought to maintain the neutrality and independence of his country. He has made every effort to bring about Pathet Lao co-operation in the Government of National Union.

Now, in the past few days, we have seen a massive, deliberate, armed attack against the forces of the coalition Government of Prime Minister Souvanna Phouma. The attack was mounted by a member of that coalition Government, with the military assistance of one of the signatories of the Geneva Agreements.[92] These violations are obviously aimed at increasing the amount of Lao territory under communist control.

The military offensive of recent days must be seen as an outright attempt to destroy by violence what the whole structure of the Geneva Agreements was intended to preserve. Hanoi has persistently refused to withdraw the Viet-Namese communist forces from Laos despite repeated demands by the Lao Prime Minister. Hanoi has also consistently continued the use of Laos as a corridor for infiltration of men and supplies from North Viet-Nam into South Viet-Nam.

It is quite clear that the communists regard the Geneva Agreements of 1962 as an instrument which in no way restrains the communists from pursuing their objective of taking of Laos as well as South Viet-Nam. The recent attempt to overthrow the constitutional Government headed

[92] Ibid., pp. 92–95, contains a discussion of the situation in Laos at this time.

by Prime Minister Souvanna Phouma was in large part attributable to the failure of the machinery set up by the Geneva Agreements to function in response to urgent requests by the Government of Laos. This machinery has been persistently sabotaged by the communist member of the International Control Commission, who has succeeded, by misuse of the so-called veto power, in paralysing the machinery designed to protect the peace in that area, and thereby undermining support for the Souvanna Phouma Government. Today, however, that Government which was created under the Geneva Agreements, remains in full exercise of its authority as the legitimate Government of a neutralized Laos. The other Geneva signatories must live up to their solemn commitments and support Prime Minister Souvanna Phouma in his efforts to preserve the independence and the neutrality which the world thought had been won at Geneva. These solemn obligations, we submit, must not be betrayed.

My Government takes a very grave view of these events. Those who are responsible have set foot upon an exceedingly dangerous path.

As we look at world affairs in recent years, we have reason to hope that his lesson has at last been learned by all but those fanatics who cling to the doctrine that they can further their ambitions by armed force.

Chairman Khrushchev said it well and clearly in his New Year's Day message to other Heads of Government around the world. In that letter he asked for:

". . . recognition of the fact that the territory of States should not, even temporarily, be the object of any invasion, attack, military occupation or other measure of force directly or indirectly undertaken by other States for political, economic, strategic, frontier or other reasons of whatsoever kind."

There is not a member of this Council or a Member of this Organization which does not share a common interest in a final and total renunciation — except in self-defence — of the use of force as a means of pursuing national aims. The doctrine of militant violence has been rendered null and void by the technology of modern weapons and the vulnerability of a world in which the peace cannot be ruptured anywhere without endangering the peace everywhere.

Finally, with respect to South-East Asia in general, let me say this. There is a very easy way to restore order in South-East Asia. There is a very simple, safe way to bring about the end of United States military aid to the Republic of Viet-Nam. Let all foreign troops withdraw from Laos. Let all States in that area make and abide by the simple decision to leave their neighbours alone. Stop the secret subversion of other people's independence. Stop the clandestine and illegal transit of national frontiers. Stop the export of revolution and the doctrine of violence. Stop the violations of political agreements reached at Geneva for the future of South-East Asia.

The people of Laos want to be left alone. The people of Viet-Nam want to be left alone. The people of Cambodia want to be left alone. When their neighbours decide to leave them alone — as they must — there will be no fighting in South-East Asia and no need for American advisers to leave their homes to help these people resist aggression. Any time that decision can be put in enforceable terms, my Government will be only too happy to put down the burden that we have been sharing with those determined to preserve their independence. Until such assurances are forthcoming, we shall stand for the independence of free peoples in South-East Asia as we have elsewhere.

Now, if we can return to the more limited issue before this Council: the security of the frontier between Cambodia and the Republic of Viet-Nam.

My Government — if there is any misunderstanding about this, let me put it straight — is in complete sympathy with the concern of the Government of Cambodia for the sanctity of its borders and the security of its people. Indeed, we have been guided for nearly a decade in this respect by the words of the Final Declaration of the Geneva Conference of 21 July 1954, which said:

> "In their relations with Cambodia, Laos and Viet-Nam, each member of the Geneva Conference undertakes to respect the sovereignty, the independence, the unity and the territorial integrity of the above-mentioned states, and to refrain from any interference in their internal affairs."

With respect to the allegations now made against my country, I shall do no more than reiterate what Mr. [Charles] Yost, the United States representative, said to this Council at the last meeting: the United States has expressed regret officially for the tragic results of the border incidents in which an American adviser was present; our careful investigations have failed to produce evidence that any Americans were present in the crossing of the Cambodian frontier on 7 and 8 May; and there is, of course, no question whatever of either aggression or aggressive intent against Cambodia on the part of my country.

Let me emphasize that my Government has the greatest regard for Cambodia and its people and its Chief of State, Prince Norodom Sihanouk, whom I have the privilege of knowing. We believe he has done a great deal for his people and for the independence of his country, and we have demonstrated our regard for his effort on behalf of his people in very practical ways over the past decade. We have no doubt that he wants to assure conditions in which his people can live in peace and security. My Government associates itself explicitly with this aim. If the people of Cambodia wish to live in peace and security and independence — and free from external alignment if they so choose — then we want for them precisely what they want for themselves. We have no quarrel whatsoever with the desire of Cambodia to go its own way in peace and security.

The difficulty has been that Cambodia has not been in a position to carry out, with its own unaided strength, its own desires to live in peace and tranquillity. Others in the area have not been prepared to leave the people of Cambodia free to pursue their own ends independently and peacefully. The recent difficulties along the frontier which we have been discussing here in the Council are only superficially and accidentally related to the Republic of Viet-Nam. They are deeply and directly related to the fact that the leaders and armed forces of North Viet-Nam, supported by Communist China, have abused the right of Cambodia to live in peace, by using Cambodian territory as a passageway, a source of supply, and a sanctuary from counter-attack by the forces of South Viet-Nam, which is also trying to maintain its right to live in peace and go its way. Obviously, Cambodia cannot be secure — its territorial integrity cannot be assured, its independence cannot be certain — as long as outsiders direct massive violence within the frontiers of its neighbouring States. This is the real reason for troubles on the Cambodian border, and this is the real reason why we are here today.

Now it is suggested that the way to restore security on the Cambodian–Viet-Namese border is to reconvene the Geneva Conference which ten years ago reached the solemn agreement which I have just read to the Council. While I hesitate and dislike to disagree with my friend from Cambodia, I submit that we can surely do better than that, and that there is no need for another such conference. A Geneva conference on Cambodia could not be expected to produce an agreement any more effective than the agreements we already have. This Council is seized of a specific issue. The Cambodians have brought a specific complaint to this table. Let us, then, deal with it. There is no need to look elsewhere.

We can make, here and now, a constructive decision to help meet the problem that has been laid before us by the Government of Cambodia — to help keep order on its frontier with Viet-Nam, and thus to help eliminate at least one of the sources of tension and violence which afflict the area as a whole.

Let me say that my Government endorses the statement made by the representative of Cambodia to the Council at the last meeting when he pointed out that States which are not Members of the United Nations are not thereby relieved of the responsibility for conducting their affairs in line with the principles of the Charter of this Organization. We could not agree more fully. Yet the regimes of Peking and Hanoi, which are not Members of this Organization, are employing or supporting the use of force against their neighbors. That is why the borders of Cambodia have seen violence. That is why we are here today. And that is why the United Nations has a duty to do what it can to maintain order along the frontier between Cambodia and Viet-Nam — to help uphold the principles of the Charter in South-East Asia.

As for the exact action which this Council might take, my Government is prepared to consider several possibilities. We are prepared to discuss any practical and constructive steps to meet the problem before us.

One cannot blame the Viet-Namese for concluding that the International Control Commission cannot do an effective job of maintaining frontier security. The "troika" composition of the International Control Commission, which under the Geneva Agreements on Viet-Nam and Cambodia requires that decisions dealing with violations which might lead to a resumption of hostilities can be taken only by unanimous agreement, has contributed to the frustration of the International Control Commission.

The fact that the situation in South Viet-Nam has reached the crisis stage is itself dramatic testimony of the frustration to which the International Control Commission has been reduced. With the exception of the special report on 2 June 1962, to which I have referred, condemning communist violations of the Geneva Agreements, the Commission has taken no action with respect to the communist campaign of aggression and guerrilla warfare against South Viet-Nam.

The representative of Cambodia has suggested that a commission of inquiry investigate whether the Viet-Cong has used Cambodian territory. We have no fundamental objection to a committee of inquiry, but we do not believe it addresses itself to the basic problem that exists along the Viet-Namese–Cambodian border. More is needed in order to assure that problems do not continue to arise.

Several practical steps for restoring stability to the frontier have been suggested and I shall make brief and preliminary general remarks about them. I wish to reiterate that, as Mr. Yost said, we have never rejected any proposal for inspection of Cambodian territory. One suggestion is that the Council should request the two parties directly concerned to establish a substantial military force on a bilateral basis to observe and patrol the frontier and to report to the Secretary-General.

Another suggestion is that such a bilateral force should be augmented by the addition of United Nations observers and possibly be placed under United Nations command in order to provide an impartial third-party element representative of the world community. We also could see much merit in this idea.

If I am correctly informed, a third suggestion is to make it an all-United Nations force. This might also be effective. It would involve somewhat larger United Nations expenditures than the other alternatives, but if this method should prove desirable to the members of the Council the United States would be prepared to contribute.

We would suggest that, whether one of these or some other practical solution is agreed upon, it would be useful to ask the Secretary-General to offer assistance to Cambodia and to the Republic of Viet-Nam in clearly marking the frontiers between the two countries. One of the difficulties is that there are places where one does not know whether he stands on one side of the frontier or the other. Certainly it would help to reduce the possibility of further incidents if this uncertainty could be removed.

In conclusion, and with my apologies for detaining the members of the Council so long, let me repeat that I am prepared to discuss the policy and the performance of my Government throughout South-East Asia, but that the issue before us is the security of Cambodia and the Cambodian–Viet-Namese border. I have expressed my Government's views on that subject. I hope other members of the Council also will express their views on that subject, and that the Council, which is the primary world agency for peace and security, can quickly take effective steps to remedy a situation which could threaten peace and security.

To William Benton [93]

May 25, 1964

Dear Bill:

At the airport leaving Paris, I tried to pay the young man from the Embassy for my room at the [Hotel] Crillon. He told me that you had already taken care of it. I seem to be always thanking you for something and now I do so once again!

I wish our breakfast had afforded a little more time. There is always so much to talk about, and now I will look forward to an account of your adventures in the Soviet Union when we meet — I hope — in Chicago at the E[ncyclopaedia] B[ritannica] meetings after your return.

My journey was exhausting and amusing — a profitable weekend in Sweden followed by a couple of days in London and then my orders to return to New York at once in view of the Security Council meeting on Southeast Asia. I made a formidable speech the day after my arrival

[93] The original is in the possession of the estate of William Benton. See note 168 to Part One, above.

here, but I am afraid we have a lot of trouble ahead in that unhappy area. . . .[94]

Yours,

ADLAI

Senator Wayne Morse sent Stevenson copies of speeches he had made on the floor of the Senate on May 6 and 13, 1964, opposing United States military action in Vietnam as unjustifiable under international law and incompatible with the Charter of the United Nations. On June 11, 1964, Morse criticized Stevenson on the floor of the Senate for failing to fulfill his responsibilities to the United Nations.

To Wayne Morse

May 27, 1964

Dear Wayne:

I was in Europe when your letter of May 14th arrived, and when I returned a few days ago I had to plunge at once into the Security Council action over Viet-Nam and Cambodia. Hence the delay in acknowledging your note to me.

It goes without saying that the questions you have raised are serious and thoughtful, and deserve a thoughtful answer. I shall get around to this as soon as the situation lets up a little here at the United Nations. Right now we are working incessantly on the whole Indo-China problem.

In connection with this situation, I will probably soon have to be in Washington, in which case I hope I can talk with you candidly and fully.[95]

Meanwhile, please forgive this interim response.

Sincerely,

Stevenson made the following statement on the death of Prime Minister Jawaharlal Nehru.[96]

May 27, 1964

India has lost its father and the whole world grieves. Within Prime Minister Nehru's frail body burned the fires of freedom, justice and hope. At a critical time for his country and the world, we have lost a towering leader whose wisdom is sorely needed. My sympathy goes out to his country, his daughter and his family.

[94] Stevenson spoke in the Security Council on Cambodia on May 26 and June 4, 1964.

[95] There is no record in the Stevenson papers that this talk occurred. A letter from Walter Johnson to Senator Morse was unanswered at his death.

[96] The text is based on USUN press release 4400.

To Lyndon B. Johnson[97]

MEMORANDUM

May 28, 1964

From: Adlai E. Stevenson
Subject: *Indo-China*

The following suggestions (pursuant to our telephone conversation) are without benefit of full information about the situation on the ground or our contingency military planning.

We must demonstrate to the world that all peaceful remedies through the United Nations have been exhausted before resorting to escalation of United States military action. In fact, we have an obligation to report to the Security Council before taking such action.

I.

Cambodia

As of today, there is no possibility of a large and effective UN force to *protect* the border. A commission to inquire into the situation and make recommendations seems likely. This would be very meagre but it would at least get a UN foot into the door.

The resolution will call on all States, especially the Geneva powers, to respect the neutrality of Cambodia. Though there will be no reference in the Security Council resolution to a Geneva Conference, Prince [Norodom] Sihanouk will continue to call for one to guarantee Cambodia's neutrality. While the United States has opposed a Geneva Conference on Cambodia at this time because such a conference would become involved in Laos and Viet-Nam as well, we should recognize in our own mind that there will eventually be another Geneva Conference on some part of the Indo-China problem and be prepared at that time to deal with a neutrality guarantee for Cambodia. Sihanouk wants to get Hanoi and China on the line and, of course, that would be to our advantage too.

II.

Laos

These suggestions are on two assumptions: A. *with* French support in the Security Council, and B. *without* French support.

A. *With French Support for United Nations Move*

    1. Souvanna[98] appeals to the Security Council for aid, and states

[97] This document was declassified.
[98] Prince Souvanna Phouma, the Laotian premier.

he will be forced to appeal for help in defending presently held territory unless the Security Council acts at once.

2. US endorses appeal for UN aid and indicates in its absence we prepared to take other steps.

3. Proposed Security Council resolution would provide for:

a. Cease-fire and standstill,
b. UN observers to check on cease-fire and standstill and to report violations,
c. Geneva Conference to restore coalition government or, failing that, to partition Laos. I would not insist on Pathet Lao withdrawal from the Plaine des Jarres which they will not agree to.

4. If Security Council is unable to act (by Soviet veto), move US forces into Mekong Valley, *but not beyond,* and use US Air Force against Communist advances and Communist bases in Laos.

5. We could also *consider* possibility (if Soviet vetoes) of going to a Special Session of the General Assembly *before* taking step 4, deferring Article 19 problem to Regular Session of the General Assembly in November.

B. *Without French Support for United Nations Move*

1. Take United States military steps under Paragraph 4, above, based on request from Souvanna Phouma.

2. Announce publicly our objectives (especially their limited nature) at *same* time and call for establishment UN observer arrangements, indicating United States prepared to *withdraw* when the UN observers are in position to police the cease-fire and standstill.

3. Call Security Council session to explain US moves simultaneously with taking them.

C. *Prospects for French Support*

1. Our intentions should be discussed with French and UK in advance.

2. Our objective should be to get the UN into Laos — if possible without prior US involvement, if necessary, after it.

3. If French understood alternative to a UN operation in Laos would be direct US intervention, they might support us. But [t]his alternative would have to be clear to them.

4. Once French were in line the issue would have to be discussed fully with U Thant to overcome his vigorous opposition to UN involvement in Laos.

D. *Reason for moving militarily first if French
do not support UN track*

If we went to the UN *before* moving militarily in the absence of French support for a UN role, we would get 6 votes in the Security Council at the most. The French and others would also use the UN to make it more difficult for us to move militarily.

E. *Objective*

In either approach our main aim should be to introduce the United Nations into Laos with sufficient physical presence and political will that it would make any further Pathet Lao military action politically costly and build the basis for a political settlement.

III.

Vietnam

Regardless of how serious the situation in Vietnam seems to us, world opinion is simply not sufficiently prepared for either US military action in North Vietnam or a US appeal to the United Nations. The first would be widely considered an irresponsible escalation of the war likely to bring in Communist China. The second would not produce a useful Security Council resolution because most members of the Council still believe the war is essentially a civil war and Hanoi assistance only of secondary importance. So at present, before or after military action on our part, we would be more likely to get a UN resolution against us than one for us.

There is grave question in my mind whether US armed intervention in North Vietnam, consisting of more than sabotage and harassment, makes military sense. However, if the situation in South Vietnam is so grave that military reaction against North Vietnam is the only way out, much more political preparation is necessary. This could best be done either by bringing the *Laos* situation promptly to the UN, as suggested above, or by going to a Geneva Conference on Laos in conjunction with the threat or fact of US military action there. In either case South Vietnam could join in the complaint against Hanoi concerning use of Lao territory for attack on Vietnam.

If over a period of time at the UN or in Geneva we can demonstrate clearly that it is Hanoi which keeps the Vietnam War going, we can perhaps build up the necessary support for UN action or justification for US action.

Stevenson spoke at the twentieth anniversary dinner of the Citizens Committee for Children of New York on June 1. The next day he addressed the Women's National Democratic Club in Washington, D.C. On

June 4 he spoke in the Security Council on Cambodia. On June 7, 1964, he delivered the Commencement Address at Colby College, Waterville, Maine.[99]

I wish to thank the trustees and faculty who have elected to confer upon me a Doctorate of Letters. Coming as it does from a college that has sustained the finest traditions of higher education for so long, I value this degree and your recognition immensely. Even more, I was going to add, than the excuse to come to Maine on this lovely June day.

The truth is I cannot resist a student audience. Moreover I think we older people ignore students at our peril these days. While sometimes their emotion exceeds their judgement, student demonstrators have even been toppling governments all over the world in the last few years. It is getting so that old-fashioned dictators can't enjoy a safe night's sleep any more.

Happily for us, students have not tried to overthrow the Government of the United States, but they certainly are making their views felt in public affairs. I think especially of the participation of American students in the great struggle to advance civil and human rights in America.[100] Indeed, even a jail sentence is no longer a dishonor but a proud achievement. Perhaps we are destined to see in this law-loving land people running for office not on their stainless records but on their prison records.

But I would not want to leave the impression that I think our students are very radical these days. They aren't! There are a few on the extreme left and a few on the extreme right, but the great majority seem to occupy the center. Maybe the *extreme* center. Also, they have other things on their minds — especially in the Spring. Looking around at all this youth and beauty, I think it may be contagious.

In considering my role here today, I have in mind Goethe's remark that there are many echoes in the world, but only a few voices. All truisms, unfortunately, tend to be echoes, and therefore a little boring. So if I bore you today it is because I want to bore you to *distinction*. If a commencement speech has any virtue at all, it ought to help the listeners attain that "peculiar grace" that Browning wrote about — that of learning how to live before living.

To me that means learning, in some degree at least, how to carry on a little of the Lord's work, no matter what kind of a career you finally turn to.

So, if you will forgive me for taking a day off from my business of for-

---

[99] The text is based on USUN press release 4409.

[100] Among other things, he may have been thinking of the work of the Student Nonviolent Coordinating Committee in the South and the Free Speech Movement at the University of California at Berkeley.

eign affairs and war and peace, I want to express on this commencement day some layman's views about education in the context of human rights, employment, technology and automation — subjects that are very much in my heart and mind these days because they are certain to affect us as citizens of the republic and the world more and more.

I turn to Goethe again for the thought:

"What you have inherited from your fathers, earn over again for yourselves, or it will not be yours."

You have inherited freedom, but as you leave this campus you will still have to *earn* it for yourselves.

I could suggest no harder task in a day when the sweeping changes of science and technology have confronted us with a society in which the whole human experiment has been thrown into an alarming turmoil. Space has been annihilated. Electric communications carry ideas and words around the world as round a village.

Astronauts watch dawns and dusks chase themselves across the face of this little planet. We are united in a single neighborhood — which a few bombs can wipe out forever.

Within this village world, human beings learn about other human beings and conditions by direct information and confrontation. No longer will the ill-housed, ill-educated, ill-fed suffer their indignity meekly and in silence. The mood within our society and all around our narrow world is the revolution of rising expectations — to recoin a phrase I have already coined.[101]

How right was Santayana when he said:

"Men who will not learn from history are destined to repeat it."

To survive this revolution, education, not wealth and weapons, is our best hope — that largeness of vision and generosity of spirit which spring from contact with the best minds and treasures of our civilization.

Here at Colby, with its fine tradition of teaching free men to be wise, you need not search far for inspiration. I think, of course, of Elijah Lovejoy of the Class of 1826, a hero of our young republic.[102]

Here was a man who lived the audacious heritage of our founding fathers; a restless thinker who was unafraid to stand up and rock the boat, who passionately believed the American Revolution was meant not

[101] Stevenson always believed that he had coined this phrase, which he had actually heard while in Asia in 1953. It appears to have originated with Harlan Cleveland, who in 1949 gave a speech at Colgate University entitled "Reflections on the Revolution of Rising Expectations." Stevenson did give the phrase wide currency, however, beginning with his Godkin lectures in 1954. See *The Papers of Adlai E. Stevenson*, Vol. V, p. 456.

[102] See Paul Simon, *Lovejoy: Martyr to Freedom* (St. Louis: Concordia Publishing House, 1964).

only for some men but for all men, who embraced the radical idea of his day that the enslavement of black by white was wrong and should be ended.

Slavery has ended: but some of the evils of indignity and inequality it fostered still live on in our society. That is the dilemma of our day. Until we cope with it, we shall not cope with our new and irrevocable environment — an environment we ignore at our own peril.

I say this because the world is now too small for anything but the truth; it is also, as one of America's great preachers observed, too small for anything but brotherhood.

Both these facts were the concern of Lovejoy. As I had occasion to say a dozen years ago at the dedication of a monument in Alton, Illinois — for it was there that he became a martyr to his principles — he served a cause which will be remembered long after the struggle over the actual abolition of slavery is forgotten.

That greater cause is the right and duty of the individual to speak out for the truth. Knowing the danger he faced, he said:

"I am impelled to the course I have taken because I fear God. As I shall answer to my God in the great day, I dare not abandon my sentiments, or cease in all proper ways to propagate them. If the civil authorities refuse to protect me I must look to God; and if I die, I have determined to make my grave in Alton."

Today, even as when first I had occasion to recall these sobering words, I know of no more moving statement of the right to speak freely.

But it is much more than that, too.

It reminds us we have not only the right, but the duty to speak on the burning issues of our time. Lovejoy knew the distinction and so spoke up in terms of what he felt obligated to say — not merely what he was entitled to say.

The distinction is an important one; and only those who observe the one as well as claim the other fully serve the cause of truth.

Much of the talk these past months about our struggle for equal rights has centered around the Civil Rights Bill, which hopefully will be passed by the Senate before June is out.[103]

But legislation is not an end — it is only a beginning: and this is particularly true of legislation that — vital as it is — no more than spells out rights and liberties already guaranteed to *all* our citizens by our inviolate constitution. As such, it merely sets the framework within which the real struggle will be fought out.

---

[103] A filibuster against the bill had been carried on in the Senate since March 30, 1964. Cloture was finally voted on June 10, and the Senate passed the bill on June 19.

And in this struggle let us not forget the true enemies are the appalling inter-locking vicious circles of abject poverty, ill health leading to school drop-outs, school drop-outs leading to lack of skills, lack of skills to poor jobs or no jobs, no jobs leading back to the lowest income and then back to the sicknesses which the people cannot afford to cure.

The slums and tenements, the poor schools, the joblessness — this is the great unfinished business which the Civil Rights Bill does *not* remedy.

What it boils down to is that human rights and poverty are simply two sides of the same coin. So while the Civil Rights Bill is a new beginning, a new chance, most of the work still remains to be done.

The lesson for all of us, therefore, is: fight against injustice and for its victims, yes; but cure the miseries through homes and cities and schools and work places good enough for all the citizens of this great land. And do not, above all, do not wait too long, for time is about the only commodity in America of which we do not have enough.

How to use the time we do have is a question. But our answer up to now has been disappointing. There has been more rhetoric than action; and I say this more in sorrow than in anger, because *all* of us share in the blame.

Providence distributes brains and capacity pretty evenly and makes no distinction between skin colors. Yet we waste untold numbers of our most precious resources because they cannot play a full part in our civic and professional life. And they cannot because they have not been trained.

A law that all men can respect is essential; no less so is breaking the bottleneck that now chokes off equal opportunity for the Negro in education and employment. For without employment, without the equal opportunity to earn a living, without the education that modern science now demands for better jobs in our society, human rights for the Negro will be a mockery.

The growth of automation compounds the problem. All of us are affected by it, but the Negro more than the white. For limited as he is today by lack of educational opportunity, he will fall behind even more tomorrow when even the simpler jobs will require some form of training.

The implications for all of us and our economic security are profound. No nation can enjoy a general prosperity where a large segment of its population is forced to remain backwards and hence poor.

In March of 1962, for example, when total unemployment in this country was at 6 per cent, it was at 10.4 per cent among those with four years of schooling or less, and 8.5 per cent among those with five to seven years of schooling. Forty per cent of those without work had eight years of schooling or less, although this group accounted for only thirty per cent of the labor force.

The man who is unemployable because of lack of education has become one of the problems of the highly technical modern society.

To which let me add the postscript that unemployment today is roughly three times as high among non-whites as it is among whites.

It seems to me, therefore, it is in the enlightened self-interest of all of us to stop mere talk about the problem, to stop being polite about it, and to attack inequality of opportunity wherever it exists, no matter how close to home.

We need the Negro in every human endeavor not because they are Negro; we need them because they are citizens of America. We need them for that same reason in all phases of our public life, in every level of government; every strata of elective office, in all the arts, all the sciences, all the technologies.

Of course, to give a man a job or elect him to office solely because of his race or religion would be but another form of discrimination. But clearly where the discrimination now exists, it must be erased. And it is right here in our educational complex that the process must begin. It is here in the universal city of the mind that the great social problem of our age must find its solution. Otherwise education will fail us in our crisis.

Five years ago, I had occasion to point out in a lecture — I'm full of remembrances today of things past — that I doubted if any society had ever faced so great a moral challenge as ours, or needed more desperately to draw upon its deepest source of courage and responsibility.

Well, I would say this is still true today, and it is not alone because of the challenge we face in putting our house in order. For even as we do, we must no less prepare ourselves for the complexities of our new technological society. The future welfare of all of us — white and black — rests upon the quality of our response. And again, education provides the key.

It is no longer a question of whether automation will come, or whether it is good or bad. It is here and obviously it is a matter that affects all of you very directly.

Automation has been making its presence felt for many years now; but yours is the generation that will feel its full impact. It will shape your lives as little else. And to speak of problems and careers and aspirations without considering the automated shock waves already rippling and spreading with ever increasing force is to offer you crusty concepts of irrelevant ideas.

Certainly, at no time in history have we had greater need of shared knowledge to help humanity meet a new challenge and raise itself above the old level of brute life. Without it we have no answer to Hamlet's question:

"What is a man
If his chief good and market of his time
Be but to sleep and feed?"

My point in all this is that the attainment of your hopes and aspirations depends, I feel, primarily on your recognition of the fact that never has the world had more need of dedication to learning or more reason to explore its implications further.

Our accelerating scientific knowledge and our exploding technology so steadily remap the regions of the mind that we can no longer dare to think of education as a static, one-shot thing which ends at a certain point in youth and is then lived on as capital ever after.

Automation and the new technological society now flowering throughout the world demand both a better array of skills at the outset and a wholly new concept of renewed education throughout life.

But even this will not suffice, for we must also devise new policies and institutions fully to meet the new challenge envisioned more than 2000 year ago when Aristotle, in a flash of prescience, predicted that when looms would weave by themselves man's slavery would end.

Now, at long last, looms *are* weaving by themselves, and we are fast approaching the time when machines will perform pretty much every other form of drudgery.

Now let me emphasize, I speak not alone of what you will *do*. Equally important, I feel, is what you *will not do*, for one of the fruits of the new technology with its still uncharted possibilities of automated work will be the growth of leisure. And make no mistake, this is a problem that may well threaten the future well being of our society as we know it.

History, of course, is replete with examples of how leisure time contributed to the greatness of society. In the Golden Age of Athens, where drudgery was done by slaves, culture flowered.

But just as the slaves did the work and enabled Athenians to follow other pursuits, so will the machines — the slaves of our automated age — free us to follow interests other than work.

Social and individual waste, however, reach a peak when people who have highly developed skills don't know how to enjoy the rich satisfactions of life. And as a society concerned with individual happiness we must never permit the tyranny of nothingness to trample down the contribution of the unique.

Clearly, this throws us back on education in the broadest sense. Maybe, as one learned professor recently put it, we must no longer think of "earning a living" so much as "learning a living," seeing our lives as chances not only to gain our daily bread and secure our physical survival, but as "values of soul making," in Keat[s]'s splendid phrase.

In the more leisured society we are about to face, training in all forms of excellence — in the arts, in literature, in history, in physical culture — could be the balance to any over-specialization on the technical or scientific side. Once again, we have to see this as a process in which men and women throughout their lives can use their new leisure for deepening knowledge and insight, and hence enjoyment.

Perhaps you will have a better idea of what the problem is if I tell you that not so many decades ago, the work week in the steel industry in America was almost twice what it is today. I can't foretell what the American work week of the future will be, but some respected economists forecast that Americans will have (I started to say enjoy) 660 billion more hours of leisure in the year 2000 than in 1950.

I also noticed a recent estimate that in 25 years or less 2 per cent of America's population in factory and on farm, will be able to produce all the goods and food the other 98 per cent can consume. Even if these forecasts are exaggerated they foreshadow something of what's ahead.

And that's why the President of the American Academy of Political and Social Science says leisure is "growing much faster than our capacity to use it wisely." He is right, and perhaps the time is not far off when we will see departments of leisure in our state governments, along with the teaching of leisure skills in schools and colleges. Certainly, devising even the means of teaching leisure skills will be a mighty contribution to social inventiveness.

It has been said a civilizing education cannot aim or wish to produce a nation composed exclusively of saints, philosophers, and artists, but it ought to aim at producing one in which every educated man can to some extent participate in the experience of the saint, the philosopher and the artist.

And to this thought I would add some words of Andre Malraux: ". . . culture is the free world's most powerful guardian against the demon of its dreams, its most powerful ally in leading humanity to a dream worthy of man."

Now you may well ask why the United States Ambassador to the United Nations has concerned himself in his remarks to you with such matters as civil rights, education and technology. My answer is twofold:

First, we will get through the vast social revolution of our day on one condition only — that we face it with information and reason and not ignorance and fear.

And second, in our interdependent world there is no longer any line of demarcation between social problems and political problems. The past has shown that the solution of one depends upon how well we understand the other. And the extent to which we succeed in doing both will be the test of our success in maintaining an open society, which essentially is a society of opportunity for all.

As the leaders of that society in our world, I would have us set an example of how a free people elevates the quality of its domestic life. For in so doing we add immeasurably to the prestige and influence of our voice around the globe. And we set the pace for others to follow as we both search for the wider interests which unite all the nations and strengthen the international instruments we have helped to build inside and outside the United Nations.

In the long run, this is how we shall achieve the abstract ideals into which we have put our faith, and reach out to the fuller vision of our greatest traditions — to the rights of all men, to human brotherhood, and to a world-wide peace secure in justice and ruled by law.

Last month I spoke about the social-technological revolution at the ancient University of Uppsala in Sweden. I concluded with some words written in a simpler time by the 18th century Swedish botanist, Linneaus [Linnaeus], who, like Elijah Lovejoy, was a citizen of the world!

"Thou sawest my happiness when I was still lying in darkness. Thou settest my clock, Thou cuttest my bread, So why, Almighty Hero, shouldst Thou forget me now? My house I have built by the grace of God. Therefore I sleep unafraid."

By the grace of God, we shall build safe the house that is our nation and our world. And when we do, we, too, shall sleep unafraid.

Every age needs men who will redeem the time by living with a vision of things that are to be.

This is my prayer today for you, and for all young people everywhere.

To Charles P. Noyes

June 18, 1964

Dear Charles:

Your resignation will be a great loss not only to the U.S. Mission, but to me personally. You were the first person I asked to join me when I became Permanent Representative of the United States to the United Nations almost four years ago, thus resuming an association in the work of the United Nations that began at the San Francisco Conference more than nineteen years ago.[104]

Having you at my side as Counsellor of the Mission during these critical years has given me great comfort and confidence and relieved me of countless anxieties. In the trying months ahead all of us in the U.S. Mission will miss your counsel, wisdom and unequalled experience, and none more than I.

---

[104] See *The Papers of Adlai E. Stevenson,* Vol. II, Part Four.

But I understand the important personal reasons that have dictated your resignation, and I respect your decision, and accept your resignation effective August 1, 1964.

I have always felt that one of the finest things that can be said about any man is that he has served his country well. And you have — indeed! And more than once.

With my gratitude and best personal wishes,

Cordially yours,

To Lady Barbara Jackson

June 18, 1964

Dearest Barbara:

As usual, I have been planning a fine long, thoughtful letter for weeks and weeks, and nothing has happened. Thank God we have Cambodia versus Vietnam, the world versus South Africa, about 15 speeches and endless travels out of the way — so now we can start on Cyprus! [105]

Robert [Jackson] writes me that you will be coming on the 23rd. I hope part of it will be reserved for me, and not just June 30th. I am not sure how much I approve of Johnson's bold assault on my domain, but I seem to be defenseless. [106]

Cyprus and Vietnam are his worst problems, of course, and I seem to be up to my ears in both of them with the usual minimal opportunities for consultation. They did, however, unanimously agree on my scenario for Vietnam, including reversing the instant rejection of the Polish proposal. [107] I shall have lots to talk to you about, and lots to hear after you have done my homework for me at the White House!

I can't say that I have any confidence that the President will press for a larger proportion of aid through international agencies against the formidable opposition of George Ball. However, in the long run, I think things will move more and more in that direction.

Adlai [III] has been asked to run for the legislature in Illinois and has accepted. The Republicans have Eisenhower's brother at the head of their ticket, so the contest is to be renewed — and this time we will win!! [108]

[105] Stevenson spoke in the Security Council on Cyprus on August 9, September 11, and September 17; on South Africa on June 16 and 18; and on Cambodia on June 4.

[106] The President had told reporters that he was a disciple of hers and that he particularly admired her book *The Rich Nations and the Poor Nations* (New York: Norton, 1962).

[107] Stevenson probably refers to the proposal that the International Control Commission, created by the 1954 Geneva Accords, patrol the border between South Vietnam and Cambodia.

[108] As a result of Illinois's failure to redistrict, all candidates for the legislature had to run at large. Both Adlai III and Earl Eisenhower led their respective tickets in November, and Adlai III served one term as a state representative.

Aside from Eleanor Roosevelt Foundation troubles, my most formidable speaking obligations are: a short bit on patriotism at a large stadium affair in San Francisco on July 25, a speech before the American Bar Association on August 13th, and a testimonial to Mrs. Roosevelt at the Democratic Convention.

I am mortified that I have not followed up on the contribution to the World Rehabilitation Fund. I will send $1,000 to you or directly to the Fund, as you designate. This is so far off the reservation for the Field Foundation that I am loath to tackle the Board, but I am going to take it up with Ruth [Field] at once and see what I can do through her personally. Perhaps she will even join me in recommending it to the Foundation.

Dearest love,

To Clayton Fritchey

June 18, 1964

I have had letters and comments from several people about how deathly sick and tired I always look on television — including "Face the Nation" on Sunday.

I wonder if there is some way we could experiment with make-up to improve this gargoyle?

As a result of repercussions from Stevenson's commencement speech at Colby College, Clayton Fritchey, on June 20, 1964, sent the following letter to U.S. News & World Report:

Ambassador Stevenson has read your reference to his commencement speech at Colby College, which apparently was based on a press report implying that he endorsed anarchy as a means of advancing equal rights.[109]

This is not his view at all. He has repeatedly condemned illegality and violence over many years. Indeed, that is why he is working in the United Nations.

In a speech at the New York World's Fair (April 20th, 1964), when the opening of the Fair was endangered by a threatened auto "stall-in," Governor Stevenson denounced this proposal and said:

"Civil wrongs do not make civil rights, so there should be respect for law and order."

And earlier this year, on Lincoln's Birthday, in Springfield, Illinois, he said among other things:

[109] The story appeared in the June 22, 1964, issue.

"Lincoln always emphasized adherence to law. But he went far
beyond in enjoining his countrymen not merely to respect the
law, but to show a patriotism devoid of fanaticism and infused
with the spirit of magnanimity.

'Thus there are two sides to the preservation of our free institutions — respect, certainly for law and due process, but also
a constantly renewed effort to see that our laws are such as free
men can respect."

I am enclosing the Colby speech, so that you may see the context
in which these remarks were made. The audience did not misunder-
stand his irony.

But in any case, students and others who have been *illegally* arrested, *illegally* fined, and *illegally* jailed for exercising their constitutional rights in the course of trying to advance the cause of civil
rights have nothing to be ashamed of. I think you will agree with
Ambassador Stevenson that the right of protest, within the limits prescribed by the Constitution, is one of our country's most cherished
privileges.

As a lawyer, however, Ambassador Stevenson feels strongly about
reckless or provocative abuse of this privilege, not only because of
illegality but also because such activity may set back progress in civil
rights.

Ambassador Stevenson would appreciate your publishing this letter
in your columns.

*The letter was not published. Stevenson sent the following memoran-
dum to Fritchey about this letter:*

To Clayton Fritchey

June 24, 1964

The word "humorous" should be inserted before "irony" in the letter.
Also exclamation marks after "prison records!"

———

This speech reminds me again how important it is to edit *before* release
to the press. This release should have omitted the 3 so called humorous
paragraphs.

To Clayton Fritchey [110]

[no date]

Mr. Fritchey —
Yesterday at [the] White House Wayne Hayes [111] said he had two demands from constituents for my immediate resig[nation].[112] Another Congressman — whom I didn't recognize — said something similar —

AES

Senator Edward M. Kennedy was severely injured in an airplane crash at Southampton, Massachusetts, on June 19, 1964.

To Mrs. Edward M. Kennedy

June 20, 1964

DEAR JOAN, MY SYMPATHY AND PRAYERS. THANK GOD THE CALL WAS NO CLOSER. HE HAS A LONG GOOD AND USEFUL LIFE AHEAD.

To Sir John Masterman [113]

June 23, 1964

My dear Sir John:
Thanks for your welcome letter. With pride an Honorary Fellow sends congratulations on the 250th anniversary of the second founding of Worcester College in Oxford. What a joy it would be to participate in the celebration, and only the everlasting fevers of this manic world keep me in New York.

I cherish the thought of joining you, Sir John, and Oliver Franks [114] in that enchanted place and I keep thinking of Yeats' words about Oxford, which you know so well:

"I wonder anyone does anything here but dream and remember; the place is so beautiful one expects the people to sing instead of speaking."

However, I know that the scholars *do* speak and sing, learn and prepare for service to the world in the splendid traditions of Worcester.

[110] This memorandum is handwritten.
[111] Wayne Hays, Democratic representative from Ohio.
[112] These demands apparently arose from the speech at Colby College.
[113] Former provost of Worcester College, Oxford.
[114] Provost of Worcester College, Oxford, and former British ambassador to the United States.

Only another crisis kept me away from you while I was in London in May. Another time even that won't deprive me of this long delayed reunion.

Meanwhile, my warmest wishes to you and please remember me to Sir Oliver.

Cordially yours,

To C. K. McClatchy

June 27, 1964

Dear "C.K.":

It was good to have your letter and I am flattered, as always, by the editorial note on my comments about Fulbright's speech.[115]

Our eyes have been on California of late and once more I thank the deity for the "Bee" papers. I think you did the right thing all around, as usual. And, as you say, maybe there is consolation for everyone in the final eclipse of Nixon. Or is it final?[116]

My love to Grace,[117] and let me know when you come this way.

Yours,

To Archibald MacLeish[118]

June 27, 1964

Dear Archie:

Although I am an ex-politician, I am always prepared to make a deal. Yes, you are excused from attending any meetings unless I urge you specially to be present, if possible. But the foregoing consideration is on condition that you help me with a tribute to Mrs. Roosevelt that I may have to make at the Democratic National Convention. What with this and that — and there are a lot of both these days — I am afraid I will be in my usual predicament as the dread day approaches, i.e., August 25 or 26.

So, could you, would you let your pen soar and help me lift the sweating delegates' hearts?

I wish, I wish, I wish you and Ada[119] were coming to New York and

---

[115] The Sacramento *Bee* on June 17, 1964, praised Senator J. W. Fulbright's statement that the nation had to be courageous enough to shape its foreign policy to the times and not be a captive of the rigid past. The editorial also praised Stevenson's words of support: "I think he is right in that we have always to search for new perspectives. We have to be willing to face ugly facts and not be diverted by agreeable myths."

[116] Stevenson sensed that Nixon's inability to secure delegates for the 1964 Republican presidential nomination was not the end of his political career.

[117] Mrs. McClatchy.

[118] The original is in the MacLeish papers, Library of Congress.

[119] Mrs. MacLeish.

could settle in my Embassy for a few days this summer. I will promise not to bore you with the [Eleanor Roosevelt] Foundation, Vietnam, Laos, Cyprus, the Congo, Apartheid or any of these tiresome things that seem to be chewing up my life!

Yours,

ADLAI

Stevenson's Aunt Julia Hardin was celebrating her ninetieth birthday. Stevenson sent her the following telegram.

To Mrs. Martin D. Hardin

June 30, 1964

REJOICE WITH ALL THE CLAN ON THIS ANNIVERSARY DAY OF A GREAT LADY AND MY BELOVED AUNT. DEAREST LOVE AND HEARTFELT REGRETS THAT I MUST BE BETWEEN TURKEY AND GREECE [120] INSTEAD OF JULIA AND LETITIA [121] ON SUCH A MEMORABLE BIRTHDAY.

To Mrs. Eugene Meyer [122]

[no date]

Dearest Agnes —

Sunday afternoon I spent two solid hours with the Greek Prime Minister [123] — but it was worth it and cleared up a lot of things. It also cleaned up my week end!

Thank you, thank you for that delicious moment of sunlight, gaiety and beauty! But I'm distressed that we had no time together.[124] Please give me another chance when you get back.

Good fishing! And dearest love —

ADLAI

P.S. The Republicans remind me of an old story — about the passer by who stopped to ask an old fisherman on the bank of a muddy lake — if "they were biting"? "Well, ['] he replied, ["] if they are they must be biting each other."

While you are away if I want to come out to the farm for a swim and tennis some Sunday or Saturday I hope it will be alright —

AES

[120] In addition to speaking in the Security Council on June 19 on the role of the UN peacekeeping mission in Cyprus, Stevenson took an active part in private negotiations with representatives of Greece and Turkey.

[121] His Aunt Letitia Stevenson, Mrs. Hardin's sister.

[122] This handwritten letter is in the Agnes Meyer files, Princeton University Library.

[123] Over the Cyprus dispute.

[124] He spent a day at her home in Mount Kisco, New York.

To Daniel D. Mich [125]

July 8, 1964

Dear Dan:

I noted — with gratitude! — several kindly references to me in the July 14 issue.[126]

And I also noted (page 28) an old lithograph of "a rousing reception for Grover Cleveland in 1892." A copy of this rare item of Americana is my proud possession. It is *not* a reception for Cleveland. It is entitled "The Lost Bet" and is an interesting picture of a German (Republican) pulling a buggy surmounted by an Irishman (Democrat, of course) brandishing a whip and followed by a brass band, at the corner of Clinton and 12th Street (now Roosevelt Road) in Chicago. The people in the background make up a wonderful cross-section of Chicago at that time. The banner overhead is "Cleveland and Stevenson." Evidently the photograph was sent to Paris and there colored, enlarged and lithographed and sent back to this country for sale as a memento of the 1892 campaign. It bears the name of the lithographers and the words "Paris 1893."

Some day I hope to show it to you — in Chicago. It would make an interesting bit for an article on campaign advertising and commercial exploitation, if you ever try to put one together.

Cordially yours,

To Dean Rusk

July 11, 1964

Dear Dean:

For your information I am enclosing a copy of a letter I have just sent to Harlan [Cleveland]. The handling of news relating to United Nations matters in Washington rather than New York, has caused repeated difficulties. I had hoped that as time went on we would be able to guide it more from this end and avoid some of the conflicts, leaks and embarrassments to both USUN and State.[127]

Sincerely yours,

---

[125] Editor of *Look* magazine.

[126] An article in *Look* by David Brinkley, "Elections Are No Fun Anymore," mentioned how gracefully Stevenson acknowledged his defeat in 1952. And a photo-essay by Richard Harrity, "Again, They Are Readying the Convention Halls," ended the article with a statement by Stevenson: "More important than winning the election is governing the nation."

[127] Rusk replied on July 28, 1964, agreeing that there was need for better coordination.

To Harlan Cleveland

July 11, 1964

Dear Harlan:

We have talked from time to time about the problem of dealing with the press on matters that relate to the United Nations. A further instance occurred in connection with the Russian peace-keeping proposals as you know. I think we should agree upon something like the following and try to adhere to it in the future:

1. When a new situation comes up, immediate consultation between the US Mission and the Department (usually IO) [128] to decide these points:
    a) Should there be an official reaction? If so, should comment be *on* or *off* the record?
    b) Should it come from the US Mission or from the State Department?
    c) If it is to be on the record, should it be attributed to Ambassador Stevenson or to an official of the Department?
2. If this protocol were adopted, it would mean that both USUN and the Department would reach a decision before either talked with the press.
3. It seems to me that we should do everything possible to agree on the most effective response — to present a united front to the press and to preserve the dignity of both the Mission and the Department.

I feel that the Mission's views should be carefully considered in coping with the press aspects. Perhaps we could find an occasion to talk more about this in the near future.

Sincerely yours,

To Lady Barbara Jackson

July 11, 1964

Dearest Barbara:

Thanks so much for these scripts. Thus far I have only seen the one for ECOSOC and I am confident that it will put some attractive flesh on the bare bones. I don't know yet whether I'll be able to go to ECOSOC but whoever does will share my gratitude! [129]

---

[128] The Bureau of International Organization Affairs.
[129] The tense situation over Cyprus, among other problems, kept him in New York City. On June 4, 1964, President Johnson had warned Turkey not to invade Cyprus.

As to the American Bar Association annual banquet on August 13, I have been thinking of something as follows: I regret that it is so opaque and ill-considered. But the time problem is ever with me.

State the simple goals of US foreign policy. For Americans our *goals* are not an issue. The *means* are a subject for political debate whether one likes it or not.

A little on the great problems and dangers confronting the world: Cyprus, Viet-nam, Laos, Malaysia, NATO versus De Gaulle, China versus Russia, North versus South etc. In this context it is not hard to criticize but maturity and restraint are tough. Develop the responsibility of a privileged, educated portion of the public, especially lawyers, to exercise and instruct in maturity and restraint.

From there I had thought to pass from the context of the forthcoming presidential campaign into a section on the measure of a nation, i.e. is it looking forward or backward? And then a soaring section on looking ahead — the golden age theme — the "great society" and the US potential. The magnitude of the resources that we have has been obscured and hidden by a $50 billion defense budget. Knock off 10% and we could erase slums, raise every school system, etc.

Have we really begun to think about what to do with an economy of abundance? — a familiar line for you!

The ultimate and greatest challenge to the human mind is to see and adapt to an accelerating rate of change. Change has always been resisted. Can we keep pace with it? Here perhaps I could pick up some of your previous thoughts about the problems created by automation and develop the good side of it.

For a conclusion I had thought of saying something, as we discussed, about the difficulty, costliness, confusion, conflicting opinion etc. — including the political conformity. Why, for example, has it become *daring* to say that [Fidel] Castro is no threat to the United States, as Senator Fulbright did? But perhaps this section would be more appropriately included at the outset with maturity and restraint, which are really difficult disciplines in an open free speech society. Perhaps it would be better to end on the golden age theme and hopefulness in the midst of danger and disorder.

I am afraid this is pretty thin preliminary thinking. Perhaps you will have some different ideas. Anything would be welcome. It seems a pity for me, in my sort of special position, to miss an opportunity to take advantage of this largest and most influential "trade" association group for some thoughtful counsel and I hope I can take full advantage of it. With things as they are, however, I doubt if I'll be able to get at it much before early August and by that time we must have Cyprus back in the Security Council and God knows what else.

I had only the briefest time with Robert [Jackson]. He seems in the best possible spirits and shared with me some confidences about his present job and the probability of another important offer, emerging from the Commonwealth Conference. I felt very proud to be on the inside!

Political alternatives are as opaque as ever. Yesterday, I spent two or three hours with Hubert Humphrey. He thinks, for your information, the President will want him to stay in the Senate. If the Republicans put a Catholic on the ticket with [Barry] Goldwater, he feels that the President may be tempted to do likewise — but not Bobby [Kennedy]. Meanwhile, the New York politicians tell me that if LBJ does not have a Catholic on the ticket, they think he will put extreme pressure on Wagner,[130] a Catholic, to run for the Senate in New York. If Johnson does have a Catholic Vice Presidential candidate, they warn me to look out; that the pressure will be on me from New York.

I wish there was time for more!

Love,

P.S. After a preliminary look at the Rep[ublican]. Platform I am tempted to use the ABA to answer the frightening foreign policy parts. We are back to concepts once found only in the lunatic fringe! Perhaps ridicule and "once over lightly" would be the best treatment. Or perhaps, for this organization of rich Republican lawyers, to ignore it as such would be more effective.

I feel we should have open hearings of the Democratic Platform Committee the preceding week and tear this apart. And, of course, I'll have to be the principal witness. God: I wish you were going to be here!

XX
AES

And now I'm off to Poughkeepsie for another ERF [Eleanor Roosevelt Foundation] speech.[131]

To Thomas Hamilton [132]

July 13, 1964

Dear Tom:

Sunday I was dozing on a raft at Piping Rock Beach Club when a handsome lady and bevy of young men emerged from the sea. I saw them vaguely through one half shut eye. And when they had gone, Pauline Plimpton [133] said: "I thought you knew Tom Hamilton's wife."

---

[130] Robert F. Wagner, mayor of New York City.
[131] The postscript and this sentence were added by hand.
[132] Chief of the UN bureau of the New York *Times*.
[133] Mrs. Francis T. P. Plimpton.

I almost dove in after her! Please ask her to forgive my rude indifference; I can't recognize anyone upside down and asleep. Curious isn't it!

Yours,

To Mrs. Marshall Field

July 13, 1964

Dearest Ruthie:

Yesterday I had lunch . . . with the [Francis T.P.] Plimptons and we stopped for a plunge in your delicious pool on the way back. I wandered around the old house for a few minutes — largely to check the success of our vandalism! [134] It has not succeeded. The beautiful pots are still standing on their pedestals smothered in vines. Another at the near end of the balustrade has toppled off and broken in the weeds. Don't you think you'd better instruct your salvage crew to get busy?

Moreover, I looked long and longingly at the bronze eagle over the front door. This, too, must be retrieved before it is too late.

And if you have no place for it, I am sure there is a place in Libertyville!

Lest you think my larcenous designs are limited, let me add that the great square lead boxes are also too beautiful to abandon to the ravages. But of these things we can talk when you get back. I would — seriously — try to salvage the vases, because one can't tell what will happen during the summer.

Things have been swirling as wildly as usual around here, and in a moment I am off to Poughkeepsie to make a speech for the Eleanor Roosevelt Foundation. Its situation is as desperate as ever, and evidently getting more so. I am going to have a session tomorrow afternoon with [Philip] Klutznick, [Robert] Benjamin, Anna [135] and perhaps one or two others, to be sure we are on the right track. I am afraid [Harold] Taylor's program of miscellaneous bits and pieces to students here and there is attracting more ridicule than approval. I am tempted, myself, to forget it all and go back to the original concept of an institute supported by what funds we end up with at New York University.

On Field Foundation developments, I have nothing new to report. No news about Marshall [Field IV] has reached me, but I suspect there will be some developments by the time you get back.[136] And that can't be too soon for

Your devoted

---

[134] Mrs. Field gave her Long Island estate to the State of New York. She and Stevenson had previously visited the estate to see what should be removed.

[135] Mrs. Paul G. Hoffman.

[136] Mrs. Field was in Italy.

To Lady Barbara Jackson

July 20, 1964

Dearest Barbara:

This Lippmann piece[137] suggests a theme I had in mind for the American Bar Association speech — rationality vs the popular appeal of irrationality.

Also doesn't "extremism" and "moderation" offer an opportunity to say something sensible about law observance and law enforcement — as keystones of self-government. Change by laws vs change by violence must be practised *at home* by minority and majority alike if we hope to persuade nations to do the same.

San Francisco was the week that was![138]

Dearest love,

P.S. I'm extricating myself from the Senate race in N.Y. — somehow! Hope you are in Cornwall [England] — resting! & I wish I were too.[139]

To Ernest L. Ives[140]

July 21, 1964

My dear Ernest:

The *Goldwasser* has arrived and provoked a deluge of mirth among my visitors. But reflections on the Republican Convention no longer elicit much mirth! Something was unleashed there that has a disturbing echo of Nuremberg.[141] Few thoughtful people any longer discount the danger or make any light hearted assumptions about the election. In short, the mood is getting more serious, and rapidly.

Buffie's report of her hives and troubles to Roxane [Eberlein] was distressing, but I pray that she has recovered. I have successfully resisted the pressure to come to Geneva as usual for a speech this week. There is too much going on here, and I am trying to find a respite over weekends when possible. I have had no word from Ruth [Field], but I

---

137 Walter Lippmann's column in the New York *Herald Tribune,* July 16, 1964.

138 The Republican National Convention, held in San Francisco July 13–16, 1964, nominated Senator Barry Goldwater for President on the first ballot and Representative William E. Miller for Vice President. The ticket was seen as a victory for the conservative wing of the party.

139 The postscript was added by hand.

140 The original is in the Elizabeth Stevenson Ives collection, Illinois State Historical Library (E.S.I., I.S.H.L.).

141 The scene of gigantic Nazi rallies in the 1930's.

assume that she is enjoying that lovely place, which *I* enjoy — in my dreams! [142]

Love to you all,

ADLAI

To Mrs. Ronald Tree [143]

July 21, 1964

. . . It's early morning — after one of those tense taut nights — and I'm writing this now so Harlan [Cleveland] can deliver it to you to-morrow. . . . And there is much to do here — I can't figure out what happens to my days — there's seldom time to go out to lunch; I'm home weary every night; the mail and papers pile up hopelessly. Francis [Plimpton] left yesterday for Europe — after our last run with the Russians. [Ambassador] Federenko goes to Moscow today — (he suggested *he* go to Illinois and *I* go to Moscow!)

Charlie Yost gets back today — thank God — and takes over the Cyprus and Congo load. I go to Washington for several days this afternoon or tomorrow. On Thursday I'll see [President] Johnson and urge him to do a TV fireside on the racial trouble. He has Harlem and Chicago [144] as well as Miss[issippi]. and Georgia now. I'll also reconfirm MT for Yates [145] and tell him about my plans — if he wants to know. After 4 hours last night of talk I think the NY promoters are beginning to understand that I'm not going to run for the Senate. I must also talk to LBJ about my role in the campaign, if any. Some say he might ask me to resign after the Convention and campaign full time. . . .

I hope — so does Dr. Lax — to go to Maine on July 30 returning Aug. 5 — my holiday. Perhaps I'll change it to Ill[inois]. Sorry — no time for all the gossip. . . .

To Julian P. Boyd

July 23, 1964

Dear Julian:

I am not sure that the American Historical Association knows what it has done, but it has conspicuously inflated my ego. But I am a sensible and prudent old man — and I shall decline your invitation to speak at the annual meeting of the Association on December 30.[146] The reasons are twofold — first incompetence and second this is the brief

---

142 Mr. and Mrs. Ives were in Florence, Italy, where Mrs. Field was visiting.
143 This handwritten letter is in the possession of Mrs. Tree.
144 There were riots in both cities.
145 Mrs. Tree was about to replace Ambassador Sidney Yates at USUN.
146 Mr. Boyd was president of the association.

interval in the year when I can visit my sons and grandchildren in Chicago or San Francisco.

I have never been more flattered and I think I'll set your letter aside so that historians will take note of the fact that historians invited me to speak!

Cordially yours,

To Mrs. John B. Currie [147]

July 24, 1964

My dear Bethia:

The inelegantly wrapped ambrosia was — elegant! [148] It has brightened the summer, and a glimpse of you would brighten it more.

Perhaps you and John would consider coming to a festivity at the United States Mission on the evening of August 5. We will have Miss Joan Baez playing her guitar and singing those delicious songs with which you rural folk in Connecticut are doubtless familiar.[149]

Gratefully and affectionately,

ADLAI

Harry Golden wrote Stevenson on July 20, 1964, that the Goldwater movement should not have come as a great surprise since the time comes when the "newly-arrived" takes over from the "aristocracy."

To Harry Golden

July 28, 1964

Dear Harry:

I don't know whether it's a fascist movement or not, but certainly the newly arrived took over, as you say. I pray they will let go in November.

I think you have hit it about right. Somehow, this curious character has raised the standard to which all of the fearful, frustrated, suspicious and hateful can repair for mutual support. That there are so many of them depresses me deeply. And ditto that they should come from the most recent beneficiaries of liberal democracy.

But I don't despair. "Prosperity" may not be enough, but peace lies close to the heart of every man — and especially every woman. Goldwater's path is straight to war.

Moreover, if we can stir around in the ashes of our old affirmations of

---

[147] The original is in the possession of Mrs. Currie.
[148] Mrs. Currie had sent Stevenson some wild berry jellies.
[149] Miss Baez also spoke out against the war in Vietnam.

national purpose, I think we will find some fire to warm the torpid spirits.

I have had enough experience to know better about the "people" by this time, but I am still convinced that there is more sense in the goodness than in the fear and ignorance around us.

Come soon; I will get John Steinbeck out of his molehole, and we'll attack the wagon ring — shooting from both hips!

Bury Goldwater!

Yours,

To John Steinbeck

July 28, 1964

Dear John:

I lost you and Elaine [150] in the confusion last night — just as I was about to waltz away with her.

I have written our friend Harry Golden today and enclose a copy. I am sure that you are right: that we must take this miserable thing very seriously.[151] Just how to rob it of success is, of course, the problem. I have felt that the President may be putting too much emphasis on the health of the economy and not enough on peace. I think he has in mind that that will come later, and a draft speech that I have just worked on a bit goes in that direction.

I wish I could promise to come out to see you but my schedule is so rugged and unpredictable that I can't. I am leaving tomorrow for Maine until August 5th — my summer holiday!! Perhaps thereafter we can consult.

Meanwhile, any suggestions you have as to what to say will get into the blood stream pretty quick. Just send them to me here. Meanwhile I will hope to go to South Hampton [Long Island] the weekend of August 8th — but I fear that the hope is forlorn!

Yours,

To Lyndon B. Johnson

July 28, 1964

Dear Mr. President:

At the State Department today, I was asked for any suggestions for Presidential appointments to the Board of Directors of the Satellite Corporation, and I gave them the following names:

150 Mrs. Steinbeck.
151 The presidential candidacy of Barry Goldwater.

1. Newton Minow — former Chairman of the FCC [Federal Communications Commission].
2. Joseph McConnell — Executive Vice President of Reynolds Metals, and Chief of U.S. Delegation to the ITU [International Telecommunications Union].
3. James F. Oates, Jr. — Chairman and Chief Executive Officer of Equitable Life Assurance Company, former Chairman of People's Gas Company of Chicago.
4. William E. Stevenson — former Ambassador to the Philippines, President of Oberlin College, Director of the Red Cross in Europe and Africa during the war, and a former Wall Street lawyer.
5. Paul Porter.[152]

I think all of these gentlemen will bring with them the variety of experience, talent and good judgment needed for the position. I shall be happy to give you more information about any of them upon request.

I enjoyed the dinner at the White House immensely. But explaining the "surrey with the fringe on top" in broken French to the President of Madagascar was an assignment beyond my competence!

Cordially yours,

In February, 1964, the United States started clandestine military operations against North Vietnam. In May, 1964, President Johnson was presented with a thirty-day plan for graduated military pressure that would culminate in full-scale bombing attacks. Included with the plan was a proposed congressional resolution "authorizing whatever is necessary with respect to Vietnam." In June a Canadian diplomat warned the premier of North Vietnam of the great "devastation" that would result from any escalation by North Vietnam.

On July 30, South Vietnamese naval commandos under General William C. Westmoreland's command raided islands in the Gulf of Tonkin. On August 2, the United States destroyer Maddox, on an intelligence-gathering patrol in the Gulf of Tonkin, was attacked by North Vietnamese PT boats. On August 3, the destroyer C. Turner Joy joined the Maddox. On August 3, South Vietnamese commandos raided the coast of North Vietnam. On August 4, North Vietnamese PT boats allegedly attacked the two destroyers.

In Washington, President Johnson ordered air strikes against North Vietnam and the Administration drafted a resolution, which was sent to Congress, that authorized the President to "take all necessary measures"

[152] A member of the Washington law firm of Arnold, Fortas & Porter and former chairman of the Federal Communications Commission.

against aggression in Southeast Asia. The Pentagon Papers *give no indication that Johnson told the leaders of Congress about the United States command's responsibility for the covert raids on July 30 and August 3.*[153]

Secretary of Defense Robert McNamara, in secret sessions of the Senate Foreign Relations Committee, denied knowledge of any attacks by the South Vietnamese on July 30 and August 3. The Tonkin Gulf resolution passed the Senate on August 7 by a vote of 88 to 2, and passed the House of Representatives by 416 to 0.

Although Stevenson was not consulted on the policy adopted, he had to defend it in the Security Council. According to John Bartlow Martin, "At the onset of the crisis, talking to someone in the [State] Department, probably Cleveland, Stevenson said with heavy emphasis, 'But are our hands clean? What the hell were our ships doing there in the first place?' "[154]

Stevenson spoke in the Security Council on August 5, 1964.[155]

Having asked for this urgent meeting [S/5849],[156] I take the liberty of replying to the request of the representative of the Soviet Union for a postponement. I asked for an urgent meeting in the light of armed attacks on the high seas. There have been two such armed attacks in the past two days. Despite these aggressive actions, my Government has sought to dampen the explosive potentialities, the implications of which we must all be aware, and to reduce the likelihood of expanding the conflict.

We have already agreed, at the request of the Soviet Union, to delay until this afternoon. Any further delay would seem to me improper because the Council should be fully and promptly informed about the circumstances. I am sure all of the members know that the Council has acted and can act with great rapidity when the need arises. Indeed, there have been several recent examples of the speed with which this body can respond. One such example was on the evening of 27 December of last year, when at 5 o'clock the representative of Cyprus requested the representative of the United States, in his capacity as President of the Security Council, to convene an urgent meeting. I recall that the Soviet representative, shortly thereafter, was found willing, even anxious,

153 See Joseph C. Goulden, *Truth Is the First Casualty: The Gulf of Tonkin Affair, Illusion and Reality* (Chicago: Rand McNally, 1969), pp. 82–162, for an account of what the Administration did not tell Congress and the American people.

154 *Adlai Stevenson and the World*, pp. 808–809.

155 United Nations, *Official Records*, Security Council, August 5, 1964, pp. 2–15.

156 This reference appears in brackets in the original. See United Nations, *Official Records*, Security Council, Supplement for July, August, and September, 1964.

for a speedy response. The Council in that event convened six hours later, at 11.15 in the evening.

More recently, during the afternoon of 13 March, the representative of Cyprus again sought an urgent meeting of the Council and, without undue delay, the Council convened at 6 o'clock that evening.

Members will note that in both instances the Council was convened at the request of a Member State which feared that hostile action against it was imminent. In the present instance a series of deliberate hostile actions have already taken place. But even more important—and I had not thought it necessary to remind any member of the Security Council — the Charter of the United Nations provides not for deliberate consideration, but explicitly calls for immediate reporting to the Council, of measures taken by Members in the exercise of their right of self-defence.

Under these circumstances, while I should like very much to accommodate the representative of the Soviet Union, I am unable to agree with the idea that we should now delay the deliberations of the Council. If the Council wishes to adjourn after hearing our statement, we would certainly have no objection, in order to give time to other delegations as well to receive their instructions. But that we should proceed now, consistent with the language of the Charter requiring of all Members, imposing as a duty upon them, the immediate reporting of such circumstances, I feel is self-evident.

At this point the representative of Czechoslovakia stated that his delegation did not wish to participate in the Security Council debate since they possessed "only one version of the events which have taken place. . . . What urgency is there for the Security Council to hear only the American version of the events? . . ."

A few minutes later Stevenson spoke again.

I have asked for this prompt meeting to bring to the attention of the Security Council acts of deliberate aggression by the Hanoi regime against naval units of the United States.

Naval vessels of my Government on routine operations in international waters in the Gulf of Tonkin have been subjected to deliberate and repeated armed attacks. We therefore have found it necessary to take defensive measures.

The major facts about these incidents were announced last night by the President of the United States and communicated to other Governments. At the same time I was instructed to request this meeting. I shall recount these facts for the members in chronological order.

At 8 A.M. GMT on 2 August of this year, the United States destroyer

Maddox was on routine patrol in international waters in the Gulf of Tonkin, proceeding in a south-easterly direction away from the coast about thirty miles at sea from the mainland of North Viet-Nam.

The *Maddox* was approached by three high-speed North Viet-Namese torpedo-boats in attack formation. When it was evident that these torpedo-boats intended to take offensive action, the *Maddox,* in accordance with naval practice, fired three warning shots across the bows of the approaching vessels. At approximately the same time, the aircraft carrier *Ticonderoga,* which was also in international waters and had been alerted to the impending attack, sent out four aircraft to provide air cover for the *Maddox.* The pilots were under orders not to fire unless they or the *Maddox* were fired upon first.

Two of the attacking craft fired torpedoes which the *Maddox* evaded by changing course. All three attacking vessels directed machine-gun-fire at the *Maddox.* One of the attacking vessels approached for close attack and was struck by fire from the *Maddox.* After the attack was broken off the *Maddox* continued on a southerly course in international waters.

Now, clearly this was a deliberate armed attack against a naval unit of the United States Government on patrol on the high seas, almost thirty miles off the mainland.

Nevertheless, my Government did its utmost to minimize the explosive potential of this flagrant attack in the hopes that this might be an isolated or uncalculated action. There was local defensive fire. The United States was not drawn into hasty response.

Then, on 3 August, the United States took steps to convey to the Hanoi regime a note calling attention to this aggression, stating that United States ships would continue to operate freely on the high seas in accordance with the rights guaranteed by international law, and warning the authorities in Hanoi of the "grave consequences which would inevitably result from any further unprovoked offensive military action against United States forces." This notification was in accordance with the provisions of the Agreements adopted at the 1954 Geneva Conference.[1]

Our hopes that this was an isolated incident did not last long. At 2.35 P.M. GMT on 4 August, when it was night-time in the Gulf of Tonkin, the destroyers *Maddox* and *C. Turner Joy* were again subjected to an armed attack by an undetermined number of motor torpedo-boats of the North Viet-Namese navy. This time the American vessels were sixty-five miles from shore, twice as far out on the high seas as on the occasion of the previous attack. This time numerous torpedoes were fired. The attack lasted for over two hours.

[1] Geneva Conference on the problem of restoring peace in Indo-China, held from 8 May to 21 July 1954.

There no longer could be any shadow of doubt that this was a planned deliberate military aggression against vessels lawfully present in international waters. One could only conclude that this was the work of authorities dedicated to the use of force to achieve their objectives regardless of the consequences.

My Government therefore determined to take positive but limited and relevant measures to secure its naval units against further aggression. Last night aerial strikes were thus carried out against North Viet-Namese torpedo-boats and their support facilities. This action was limited in scale — its only targets being the weapons and facilities against which we had been forced to defend ourselves. Our fervent hope is that the point has now been made that acts of armed aggression are not to be tolerated in the Gulf of Tonkin any more than they are to be tolerated anywhere else.

I want to emphasize that the action we have taken is a limited and measured response fitted precisely to the attack that produced it, and that the deployments of additional United States forces to South-East Asia are designed solely to deter further aggression. This is a single action designed to make unmistakably clear that the United States cannot be diverted by military attack from its obligations to help its friends establish and protect their independence. Our naval units are continuing their routine patrolling on the high seas with orders to protect themselves with all appropriate means against any further aggression. As President Johnson said last night, "We still seek no wider war."

Let me repeat that the United States vessels were in international waters when they were attacked. Let me repeat that freedom of the seas is guaranteed under long-accepted international law applying to all nations alike. Let me repeat that these vessels took no belligerent actions of any kind until they were subjected to armed attack. And let me say once more that the action they took in self-defence is the right of all nations and is fully within the provisions of the Charter of the United Nations.

The acts of aggression by the North Viet-Namese in the Gulf of Tonkin make no sense whatsoever standing alone. They defy rational explanation except as part of a larger pattern with a larger purpose. As isolated events, the kidnapping of village officials in the Republic of South Viet-Nam makes no sense either; neither does the burning of a schoolhouse or the sabotage of an irrigation project or the random bomb thrown into a crowd of innocent people sitting in a cafe.

All these wanton acts of violence and of destruction fit into the larger pattern of what has been going on in South-East Asia for the past decade and a half. So does the army of terrorist gangs in South Viet-Nam by the regimes of Hanoi and Peking. So does the infiltration of armed personnel to make war against the legitimate Government of that nation. So does the fighting in Laos, and all of the acts of subversion, and all of the propaganda, and the sabotage of the international machinery established to keep the peace by the Geneva Agreements, and the deliberate and systematic and flagrant violations of those Agreements by two regimes which signed them and which, by all tenets of decency, law and civilized practice, are bound by their provisions.

The attempt to sink United States destroyers in international waters is much more spectacular than the attempt to murder the mayor of a village in his bed at night; but they are both part of the pattern, and the pattern is designed to subjugate the people of South-East Asia to an empire ruled by means of force, of rule by terror, of expansion by violence. It is only in this larger view that we can discuss intelligently the matter that we have brought to this Council.

In his statement last night President Johnson concluded by emphasizing that the mission of the United States is peace. Under the explicit directions of President Johnson, I want to repeat that assurance in the Security Council this afternoon: our mission in South-East Asia is peace.

We hoped that the peace settlement of 1954 would lead to peace in Viet-Nam. We hoped that that settlement and the 1962 supplementary Agreements signed at the Geneva Conference [1] would lead to peace in Laos. Communist governments have tried aggression before and have failed. Each time the lesson has had to be learned anew. We are dealing here with a regime that has not yet learned the lesson that aggression does not pay, cannot be sustained, and will be thrown back by people who believe, as we do, that people want freedom and they want independence, and not subjugation and the role of satellites in a modern empire.

In South-East Asia we want nothing more, and nothing less, than the assured and guaranteed independence of the peoples of that area. We are in South-East Asia to help our friends preserve their own opportunity to be free of imported terror, of alien assassination, managed by the North Viet-Nam Communists based in Hanoi and backed by the Chinese Communists from Peking.

Two months ago when we were discussing in this Council the problems created on the Cambodia–South Viet-Nam frontier by the Viet-Cong, I defined our peace aims in South-East Asia, and I should like to take the liberty of repeating them because of their pertinence here today. I said then:

[1] International Conference on the Settlement of the Laotian Question, held in Geneva from 12 May to 23 July 1962.

". . . There is a very easy way to restore order in South-East Asia. There is a very simple, safe way to bring about the end of United States military aid to the Republic of Viet-Nam. Let all foreign troops withdraw from Laos. Let all States in that area make and abide by the simple decisions to leave their neighbours alone. Stop the secret subversion of other people's independence. Stop the clandestine and illegal transit of national frontiers. Stop the 'export of revolution' that has taken place in that area. Stop the violations of political agreements reached at Geneva for the future of South-East Asia.

"The people of Laos want to be left alone. The people of Viet-Nam want to be left alone. The people of Cambodia want to be left alone. When their neighbours decide to leave them alone . . . there will be no fighting in South-East Asia and no need for American advisers to leave their homes to help these people resist aggression. Any time that decision can be put in enforceable terms, my Government will be only too happy to put down the burden that we have been sharing with those determined to preserve their independence. Until such assurances are forth coming, we shall stand for the independence of free peoples in South-East Asia as we have elsewhere." [157]

That is what I said to the Council in May; that is what I repeat to this Council in August.

When the political settlements freely negotiated at the conference tables in Geneva are enforced, the independence of South Viet-Nam and of South-East Asia will be guaranteed. When the peace agreements reached long ago are made effective, peace will return to South-East Asia and military power can be withdrawn.

At this point the representative of the Soviet Union spoke. He stated that the Security Council only had "one-sided information about the alleged attacks by torpedo-boats of the Democratic Republic of Viet-Nam against United States destroyers." He introduced a resolution inviting representatives of the Democratic Republic of Vietnam to participate in the discussions of the Security Council.

The representative of France agreed that a representative of the Democratic Republic of Vietnam should be invited, "as a matter of urgency, to participate in our debate without a vote."

After this, Stevenson spoke again.

[157] United Nations, *Official Records*, Security Council, May 21, 1964, paragraphs 61–62.

I have little comment on Mr. Morozov's extensive remarks, except to observe that, for a representative who, at 3.30 P.M., protested that he could not possibly get instructions until tomorrow, he had quite a bit to say at 4.30 P.M., submitting even a draft resolution.

His suggestion that the Council should condemn the United States for defending itself and its ships against unprovoked attack in international waters is certainly a novel concept — that the North Vietnamese can attack United States ships outside of their territorial waters, but that the United States ships may not defend themselves.

I repeat again that the objective of the United States is peace, and not war; we want no wider war in Viet-Nam or anywhere else. But if others attack us, let there be no doubt that we will defend ourselves, as I trust the incidents in Viet-Nam in the past few days have made clear.

I must comment for a moment on the draft resolution that has been presented. The United States, let me say at once, has no objection to authorities of Viet-Nam being heard by the Council — indeed, to answer for their grave use of military force; and thus we have no objection to their being notified, in prompt terms, that the Council would be glad to have their views. We also believe, however, that, if the North Vietnamese are invited, the Republic of Viet-Nam should also be invited to appear.

The attack on our destroyers was an extension of Hanoi's aggression against the Republic of Viet-Nam, and the representative of the Soviet Union has also made accusations in his remarks against the Republic of Viet-Nam. Perhaps the best way, then, to handle this matter might be to provide an opportunity for informal consultations among Council members so that appropriate invitations could go forward.[158]

To Bill Moyers [159]

August 7, 1964

I don't know who is doing what about the foreign affairs plank for the platform. I prepared the enclosed hastily with a view to getting some of the points on paper for elaboration — or contraction!

[158] Stevenson also spoke twice in the Security Council on August 7, 1964, about the situation in Vietnam.

[159] Special assistant to President Johnson.

ADLAI E. STEVENSON — FIRST DRAFT OF FOREIGN AFFAIRS PLANK FOR DEMOCRATIC PLATFORM

August 5, 1964

FOREIGN AFFAIRS 1965–69

Peace and Defense

1. No greater threat confronts mankind than nuclear war, which could destroy or impoverish all of us — friend and foe alike. Therefore the overriding national purpose is world peace. Exercises in brinkmanship, which could easily escape control and hurl the world over the edge into nuclear catastrophe, must not and will not be initiated by the United States. If such follies are commenced by an adversary, however, as in the Cuban crisis of 1962, they will be met with unyielding firmness.

2. Weakness is a temptation, and until there is effective disarmament, we must maintain nuclear and conventional forces so strong that aggression against us or our allies would be fatal to the aggressor — and he knows it. We have and shall maintain such forces and weapons. The awesome responsibility for the control of these forces, and particularly of the nuclear deterrent in all its forms, must rest with the President representing the whole people of the United States.

3. We shall at the same time work patiently and tirelessly for general and complete disarmament by international agreements which provide for rapid, progressive, balanced reduction of armaments under adequate international inspection. We shall hope to find acceptable partial measures as negotiations proceed. But genuine security will not be achieved until comprehensive disarmament has finally been agreed upon and carried out.

4. In the meantime we favor rigid control of nuclear weapons to prevent disaster through miscalculation or accident. We believe that their production should be limited to states now producing them and their control to states now controlling them separately or jointly. We also favor the exclusion of such weapons from those regions of the world the nations of which agree they should be excluded.

5. We shall faithfully and effectively maintain NATO and our alliances. We shall continue to assist by all necessary means those nations which are under armed Communist attack as long as they desire our assistance and are willing to fight for themselves. This assurance applies particularly at the present time to the Republic of Viet-Nam and the Kingdom of Laos, where armed insurgency is fomented, armed, supplied, directed, and to a large extent, manned by their Communist neighbors.

6. At the same time we are ready and eager to negotiate on any subject with any state which makes clear by its deeds that it desires to live in peace with its neighbors and not to interfere in their internal affairs by force or subversion.

7. We maintain our solemn commitment to the United Nations and its family of sister agencies, as the most effective instrument for avoidance or settlement of international disputes and for nation building through economic, technical, and cultural development. The United Nations represents a vital national interest of the United States because we consider it the best hope of the world for the creation of durable international institutions in which peace in the future must primarily depend.

Political Relations

1. We are committed to the steady strengthening of the bonds which unite the Atlantic Community. We are prepared to proceed as far along this road of equal partnership as our allies are. We perceive no incompatibility between an Atlantic Community and a United Europe, and will continue to work for both. It is up to our allies and friends to determine how far, how fast, and in what ways they wish to move toward unity, but we applaud their goal and will support and assist progress toward it.

2. We favor the peaceful reunification with the Federal Republic of Germany of the Eastern Zone now under Soviet occupation. We favor the reduction of tensions in Central and Eastern Europe and friendly and profitable relations among the nations of that region, including the Soviet Union. At the same time we shall oppose with our full strength any attempt to alter the status quo in West Berlin by the use of force.

3. We earnestly wish to improve relations with the Soviet Union and its European allies. We will welcome and respond to demonstration of their sincere and practical desire to do so. We cannot expect that the grave differences between us, which have largely arisen from their attempt to export Communism by force or subversion, can be overcome quickly. But we hope that gradually, by tested stages, the traditional common interests between Americans and Western and Eastern Europeans, will demolish the artificial barriers which have been erected during the last fifty years.

4. Our relations with Latin America are of first importance. It shall be our constant concern to strengthen these relations, multilaterally through the OAS [Organization of American States] and bilaterally with each country. What is most vital to ourselves as well as our Latin American neighbors is rapid economic and social progress and reform throughout the Hemisphere, so that all its peoples may enjoy the fruits of the modern technological revolution. If their governments with our help

cannot rapidly begin to satisfy the legitimate demand for modernization, the people of Latin America may well turn in desperation to extremism.

The economic and social plight of Latin America aggravated by the population explosion, is the real threat to the Hemisphere; Communist subversion, whether from Havana, Peking, or Moscow, is dangerous only because of this underdevelopment. Nevertheless, the Castro regime in Cuba is an alien disease in our midst from which infection may spread. We are, with our allies in the OAS, taking all necessary precautions to assure that Cuba is quarantined and the disease isolated, until the Cuban people regain control of their own affairs and restore democratic government.

5. We reaffirm our commitments to our allies in the Far East. We view with the utmost gravity the expansionist actions and designs of the Communist Chinese regime and its Asian allies, which are a serious threat to the independence and security of all of East and South Asia and to the peace of the world. As stated above, we shall assist and help to defend all peoples who defend themselves and ask for our assistance from aggression by these regimes. At the same time we shall always be prepared to negotiate peaceful settlements, on the basis of the United Nations Charter and pertinent international agreements, with those who demonstrate the will to carry out such settlements.

6. We have a profound concern for the continent of Africa, its old and new nations, and the welfare and development of its peoples. We welcome the growing role which Africa is playing in world affairs, the efforts of African nations for greater unity in their vast continent and the struggle for political stability and economic development. We shall continue to support racial equality and mutual understanding throughout the continent, and political self-determination for those African peoples who have not yet obtained it.

Economic Relations

1. A rising standard of living is the birthright of every citizen of the modern world. It is also the central plank in the platform of every political party and the indispensable ingredient of political stability on all continents. Where economic development is neglected, obsolete and unnecessary human suffering will continue; where it is stalled, the false Communist promise and the real Communist threat will take root and flourish.

The United States therefore will continue, both bilaterally and through international organizations, to assist generously in the development of emerging nations which are willing and able to use such assistance for the benefit of their peoples. We will have in mind that no claim of interest in the welfare of others can be genuine, or no opposition to the spread of Communism realistic, which does not consistently support and carry out foreign aid programs of the magnitude and scope which modern times require.

After President Johnson announced that no member of his cabinet was eligible for the vice presidential nomination, Nan Tucker McEvoy wrote Stevenson expressing displeasure with the decision.

To Mrs. Dennis McEvoy [160]

August 10, 1964

Dearest Nan —

I'm suffering no pain — but that you thought I deserved some extra consideration pleases me. Better to have never been mentioned at all than to be thus dismissed.

Bless you my beloved Nan —

ADLAI

To Mrs. Ronald Tree [161]

August 10, 1964

I've just come home from USUN — after receiving the Turks' acceptance of the cease-fire! [162] I had thought to have a little quiet celebration of yesterday's hard-won triumph alone and then settle down to my Am[erican]. Bar [Association] speech. . . .

Things are bad in the UN: trouble everywhere. U Thant is wobbling about Art[icle]. 19 [163] and if we ever get out of the S[ecurity] C[ouncil] I'll have to start in earnest on the financing. Meanwhile [Francis T. P.] Plimpton is away and I foolishly told him he could stay another 10 days and go to Israel. [Clayton] Fritchey of course is in Maine with Ruth [Field] when things have been worse than any time since Cuba. Thank God for [Charles] Yost — and now [Richard F.] Pedersen is back. But there will be time to talk of all that — perhaps.

Archie and Ada [MacLeish] are here. Last night I staggered back for

---

160 The text is from a handwritten draft.

161 This handwritten letter is in the possession of Mrs. Tree.

162 Turkish planes attacked Greek Cypriot positions on August 7–9, and there were fears of a full-scale war between Greece and Turkey as a result. Stevenson in the Security Council on August 9 proposed a resolution calling for an immediate cease-fire, which was adopted by a vote of 9–0, with the Soviet Union and Czechoslovakia abstaining. Turkey and Cyprus agreed to the cease-fire on August 10.

163 The article of the UN charter providing that a nation could be deprived of its seat in the General Assembly if it was two years in arrears on payments.

dinner with them and Burton [164] and Taylor [165] — no one else — and it was about the most amusing night of my life in 42A. Even Liz took my fancy — and Archie and Ada enjoyed it even more. . . .

Yes, Senate is hot again. Bobby [Kennedy] is mad to run now and Steve Smith [166] is making unctuous calls daily about getting together. "He doesn't want to do anything if I'm interested" etc. [Mayor] Bob Wagner is holding out but the K's have unleashed the mafia. I stalled him just not to give them any easy satisfaction. . . . But *starting* a new career now is senseless; instead I'm going to *end* me.

Today NYU [New York University] — which has $25 million from Ford [Foundation] — asked me to become the "distinguished professor" — a new chair, occasional lectures, serious and limitless aid on my "book," [167] plus 3 mos. holiday — *and* a house in the Mews! I said I was doubtful about the Chair but interested in the house. Do you remember? . . . Can't you come on the 20th? *Please* try — things may thicken. And of course you can do the TV on "PEACE" even if you don't know anything about it, nor I, therefore. . . .

P.S. Cyprus has been the closest crisis yet, since Cuba. I'll tell you about the stalling tactics of Morosov [Morozov], Rossides [168] et al! 'Twas a glorious victory.'

On August 13, 1964, Stevenson spoke to the annual meeting of the American Bar Association in New York City.[169]

I had thought to talk to you about the relation of the work of the United Nations and that porridge of "principles" and declarations called "international law." As the common law grew out of the blood and bone of men's lives — their quarrels, their frustrations, their defeats and desires — so a new international law is growing out of the United Nations Charter — crisis by crisis, case by case.

But now that the quadrennial political fit is upon us once more it seems to me the proper season to recall that we are not just lawyers, or diplomats, or politicians or plumbers — but citizens, voters and Americans. A good diplomat, according to Talleyrand, improvises what he says, and carefully prepares what he doesn't say. So, as a good — and ex-

[164] Actor Richard Burton, who was playing *Hamlet* on Broadway.
[165] Actress Elizabeth Taylor, who was married to Mr. Burton.
[166] Kennedy's brother-in-law.
[167] Stevenson had not definitely decided on a topic for the book he planned to write after leaving the United Nations.
[168] Zenon Rossides, permanent representative of Cyprus to the United Nations.
[169] The text is based on USUN press release 4434.

hausted — diplomat I propose to improvise a little about the upcoming campaign.

I have heard that the object of the exercise — from one side at least — is to offer the voter a "clear choice" of leadership. Although the trumpet gave forth a less certain sound from Hershey [170] yesterday, if I correctly interpret the words that came to us from San Francisco, there will, indeed, be a conspicuous choice available.

But, it seems to me the dominant philosophies of the two major parties in recent years have been quite distinguishable; indeed I have been at considerable pains during much of my adult life to insist on just that point.

And yet I have thought that the strength of the American political system lay precisely in its lack of extreme contrasts — in its rejection of dogma — in the fact that rigid ideology really has no relevance to our great political parties. And this system has remained intact for more than a century — the most stable, durable, and adaptable system the world has ever seen.

But now, as society and the world become more complex, some people want to repeal the whole thing. They seem to yearn for the old simplicity — for the shorthand analysis — for the black-and-white choice — for the cheap-and-easy answer — for the child's guide to good and evil. The very color and diversity of our pluralistic society seems to confuse them; they want it plain and unitary.

But you know as lawyers — and most Americans know by instinct — that goals worth believing in are always just out of reach — liberty is never quite secure, and problems yield to solution only to reveal new problems. Of course we have problems — unprecedented problems: what to do with more food than we can eat; how to find productive work for all, now that men no longer have to work as pack animals or drones; how to use leisure time, now that man does not have to struggle from dawn to dusk to live; how to raise the level of education, now that literacy is not enough; how to provide medical care, now that so many of us have a chance to live to a ripe age.

These are problems of a society that has come so far that its concerns are with the distribution, not the production, of wealth — with care for the aged, not infant mortality — with higher education, not the fight for survival — with the use of leisure, not the abuse of labor.

But if we have problems and blemishes, we also have the means to do

[170] Senator Barry Goldwater and Representative William Miller met with Republican leaders, including former President Eisenhower, at a party unity conference in Hershey, Pennsylvania, on August 12, 1964. Goldwater softened his conservative image considerably, promising to repudiate extreme right-wing groups and to support the Social Security program, the United Nations, and the Civil Rights act.

something about them. The *increase* in our gross national product over the past three years was more than the *total* annual product of 85 members of the United Nations. The *increase* in the value of goods and services produced this year compared to last year probably would be more than enough to finance the replacement of every urban slum dwelling in the land.

Even a minor downward adjustment of marginal military expenditure permits us simultaneously to maintain a mighty defense establishment, reduce the deficit, lower taxes, and mount a war on poverty. A 10% cut in defense spending for one year would pay for the present level of federal support to vocational training for the next 250 years, or the federal contribution to the fight against juvenile delinquency for centuries hence.

Have we begun to understand the significance of these magnitudes — to comprehend the meaning of an economy of abundance — to grasp the implications of the ongoing agricultural revolution, the march of automation, the potentials of computer technology, nuclear energy, satellites communication, and the whole thundering impact of science upon society?

And perhaps it is well that we should not take the momentous change in the human condition quite so much as a matter of course as do our grandchildren. For we have stolen a new Promethean fire. Perhaps the gods are jealous. We need to reflect deeply on these overwhelming new powers.

For these are the new servants — or the new masters — of mankind. It was Aristotle who said that when the looms work themselves, there will be an end to slavery. Now the looms do virtually work themselves. One machine in a couple of hours already produces the output of a year's handicraft. What this unimaginable increase in energy and capacity and supply can do for human society is already a little prefigured in the American economy — the first economy to break the sound barrier of general affluence.

And if — as under providence we hope — arms spending can now be stabilized while the economy continues to grow, we can look forward to an almost unimaginable expansion in all the instruments and services of the good life.

Such extraordinary freedom of resources and choices adds a wholly new dimension to the concept of liberty. Certainly it gives "the pursuit of happiness" a range which would have astounded our founding fathers. I find these prospects of abundance, not simply for a small elite but for all Americans, an exhilarating prospect, in keeping with the promise of our great republic.

Yet, like all human prospects, this vista of growing prosperity is shadowed.

First, we are not yet agreed, as a nation, upon the policies and mechanisms needed to secure steady growth.

Second, we are still unable to share it fairly and widely enough.

And third, over us all still hangs the appalling dilemma — that while we can harness the energy of the atom, replace human drudgery with mechanical power, make the deserts bloom and unlock the riches of the oceans, we can also, in one final holocaust, annihilate the human experiment.

The means of life are, in a full apocalyptic sense, the means of death as well. Never has the human condition appeared so splendid and so precarious. Never has man seemed so magnificent and so forlorn.

Let us look at these three shadows. The first — the means of securing a higher and steadier rate of growth in our economy — is, of course, at the core of politics throughout western democracy.

Is equilibrium between labor costs and prices possible without an unacceptable degree of central interference? The dilemmas of federalism and states rights in an economy of 190 million people and continental in size in which so many vast businesses and unions are highly centralized are real dilemmas and deserve serious discussion.

I would like to think that in our forthcoming political dialogue, these profound differences would be seriously debated — not in terms of slogans and epithets, not in terms of "creeping socialism" or "fascist reaction," but in terms of the real dilemmas when certain needs of the economy point towards more centralized decision making and others point in the opposite direction.

This debate is all the more urgent in that the proper management of our economy includes the vital issue of how we can lessen some of the dangerous disparities of income and of opportunity between different groups and different regions. And our problem is intensified by the fact that the race line and the poverty line tend to coincide, and that the highest proportion of unskilled unemployed workers — especially young workers — are Negro.

So the urgent problem of countering poverty in the midst of affluence brings us to the heart of our profoundest domestic challenge — the achievement of civil rights and equal opportunities.

As all responsible Negro leaders realize, looting and rioting and hooliganism are no remedy and only set back their cause. Violence, whether it is the silent terror of murder in the deep south or the screaming violence of urban mobs in the north, must be rooted out. But the causes remain. Leave men unskilled, frustrated, hopeless, and violence will recur.

The war on poverty and the struggle for civil rights then are two sectors in the same battle. Carry forward the first and we have some hope of triumphing in the second. Do nothing and we face a state of semi-siege and recurrent violence.

Here again it is surely the patent duty of both parties to project the true shape of our possibilities and our decisions.

The third and darkest shadow is that we now have the means to annihilate the human race. Suddenly the pursuit of peace — the pioneering work of peacekeeping and peacemaking — the control of armaments — the construction of world order and community — has become the most important business of the human race.

The world has talked of peace for so long that we may overlook the fact that we *are* doing something about it.

In the last decade nearly every war, partial war, incipient war, and threat of war has either been halted or averted by a cease-fire. Firing has started and then stopped — organized hostilities have been turned on and then called off — without victory or defeat, without surrender or peace treaty, without signatures or swords.

And this nation has spent the better part of two decades, untold billions, and thousands of lives to prove that aggression does not pay, that the first commandment of the nuclear age is to leave your neighbors alone, and to build the international institutions of collective peacekeeping. That policy has paid important dividends.

The first brake has been placed on the nuclear arms race.

The accumulation of weapons has been slowed down.

Steps have been taken to minimize the possibilities of war by accident.

Weapons of mass destruction have been banned from outer space.

Serious study and negotiations for arms control and disarmament are under way.

The peace machinery of the United Nations has gained in experience, capacity, and usefulness.

A community of international agencies has come into being to fight world poverty — seed-bed of world disorder.

A more hopeful dialogue has been opened between the nuclear powers; tensions have slowly relaxed; and projects for cooperation on great scientific enterprises have started.

And at last a tacit agreement has been reached on a mutual interest in survival.

All this has taken hard, patient, purposeful work — and, I might add, steady hands and cool heads. At Check Point Charlie, in the air corridor to Berlin, in the Formosa Straits, in the Caribbean, and now in South East Asia — from crisis to crisis our armed men, administrators, diplomats and presidents have proved that victory for peace takes restraint along with firmness, wisdom along with weapons. We have learned that bluff is dangerous, bluster cheap, that recklessness can be fatal; and we have also learned that the organized, audible opinion of the world expressed through the United Nations is a powerful and persuasive influence for peace.

Now, however, this tacit understanding between the two great nuclear powers is under violent attack. In the first place, the critics claim, it is miserable appeasement to accept a world partly under hostile ideological control. The enemy must be made to disgorge people groaning under the heel of exploitation and despotism. He must be threatened right up to the brink of war with the menace of nuclear punishment and it will be found, then, that his nerves are not up to the strain and he will give way. All this negotiating, all this talk, all these "hot lines" from White House to Kremlin are simply capitulation to the sworn opponent. Such weakness, such slackness must be rigorously suppressed. The people must rise against such betrayals and in their place put the stern, pure, audacious strength of worldwide — Marxist-Leninist — class war.

I have, of course, been referring to the Chinese Communists' deadly attack upon Mr. Khrushchev's policies. These jingoists base their attack on the ground that Moscow is now appeasing the "paper tiger" of the United States and betraying the worldwide responsibility to lead humanity into the unified communist world of tomorrow.

If these strident calls sometimes have strange undertones and overtones of language that we hear nearer at home, do not be deceived — or even surprised. The two ends of the political spectrum, like the two ends of the tuning-fork, often vibrate in harmony. Both extremes in international politics are lethal and for the same reason — they ignore the fragility of man's survival; they play deadly games on the brink of disaster; they misread the facts of power and the restraints of responsibility; they gamble with the very pre-condition of our survival in the nuclear age.

Yet, it is painfully clear that not everyone has yet learned that aggression and brinksmanship do not pay — be it in Vietnam or Cyprus. It is all too evident that military power is still relevant to world affairs. When there is no doubt about aggression — when all restraints have failed — then there can be only one course of action: to put power in the service of peace by using power to restrain further aggression.

As President Johnson put it at Syracuse last week, "aggression unchallenged is aggression unleashed . . . there can be no peace by aggression and no immunity from reply."

And let me tell you, Gentlemen, that the decision as to whether United States power must be used — and when — and where — and at what level — is the heaviest responsibility of government in this day. For the consequences of one false step are incalculable — one hasty response — one impulsive or ignorant reaction — one failure to communicate clearly the purpose of a national action.

So we live with a dual reality. On the one hand, there is the increasingly effective international machinery for peacekeeping. On the other there is the persistence of aggression which can be influenced only by the existence of the power to stop it.

We have no alternative but to keep the balance between an appeasement which would betray us by weakness and a brinksmanship which would destroy us by miscalculation. On this tightrope above the abyss, we cannot indulge in adolescent showmanship or Chinese acrobatics. We have, sanely, calmly to preserve both our strength and our caution, our full defensive might and our ever-readiness to negotiate, our dedication to the cause of allied freedom and our search for reasonable accommodation.

This path is not exciting. It sets no trumpets braying or drums beating. It revolts the ideologists — in Peking and anywhere else. But this adventure has in it the most precious of all possibilities — that our children and our grandchildren may survive to build a saner, better, more law-abiding world.

Perhaps this is, in fact, the theme that runs through all today's possibilities and dilemmas. We have created for ourselves almost unimaginable means of power — power to create, power to destroy. Our moral load is, therefore, heavier than ever before. This vast abundance, this soaring technology, these space-conquering instruments are all at our disposal — for good or ill.

But it is, I believe, the common experience of history that vast power is of infinite danger unless it is kept under the firm restraints of reason, of generosity, of realism and of good sense. We do not take our best decisions when we are lashed with pride or lathered with resentment. We do not act most sanely when slogans and catch words fill our ears and smother our reason.

The greatest issues of our day — civic order, civil rights, peacekeeping, conciliation and law — these above all command the response and the responsibility of wise and temperate — I almost said moderate! — men.

And I firmly believe that you gentlemen — the servants of law and reason — are called upon to play a part and give a lead to our fellow citizens.

Our freedom depends upon our wisdom and our restraint. Let them be the watchwords in this election year. And let the word once more go out round the world that in the very citadel of freedom, the processes of open debate, open conviction, and open choice are more maturely honored and respected in this time of crisis than in any previous campaign.

The greatness of the issues calls out for greatness in ourselves — to vindicate democracy, to speak for freedom, and to make our profoundest affirmation of faith in the American way of life.

To Lady Barbara Jackson

August 14, 1964

Dearest Barbara:

Your letter of August 13th has just come, and tranquility, clotted cream and pilchards and sunny Cornwall [England] make my head swim. Here, we have battered our way through Viet-Nam and Cyprus, and now politics is smothering us.

Bobby [Kennedy] has reconsidered his Sherman statement [171] and has moved back into New York with all his troops to seize the Senatorship with little opposition in view of my reluctance to leave my present post at this time.

The Bar Association speech was a triumph. You will note that I took considerable liberties with your manuscript. And, of course, there were the usual sallies and wisecracks here and there. The press has been fine but I suspect [Barry] Goldwater will have me in his sights pretty quick — because the subtlety was not very subtle!

I was delighted to hear about your return in the autumn and would like to stake out a prior claim for any extra time before someone else moves in — and you know who! [172] Moreover, the opportunity is so obvious that I call hurriedly and prayerfully for something for Cornell on October 9. I enclose a copy of Jim Perkins' [173] letter which tells me as much as I know about what is expected of me — which is nothing. He writes, by the way, that he would like me to come on the previous night in order to be there for all of the 9th, but if you are coming on the night of the 8th, I shall plan to stay here and will get to Cornell sometime on the morning of the 9th, in time for the Convocation. I may be in Chicago for some EB [Encyclopaedia Britannica] meetings on the 6th and 7th. Bill Benton will be in New York only on the 9th before he has to return to Paris, and suggests breakfast that morning with you and me. It makes the schedule pretty tight and I am not sure we can manage it, but we will wait and see.

[President] Johnson has asked me to stick to my post during the campaign. I had offered to resign. I suspect my role will be to make thinly-veiled speeches to non-political gatherings which has at least the saving grace of reducing the wear and tear, although I can see the restlessness of a retired race horse when the trumpets blow in the adjoining field.

As to my future "plans" — frankly, now that Johnson has thrown out

---

[171] William Tecumseh Sherman's famous statement to the 1884 Republican National Convention: "I will not accept if nominated and will not serve if elected."
[172] Stevenson apparently refers to a possibility that President Johnson might ask her to draft speeches for his campaign.
[173] James A. Perkins, president of Cornell University.

the baby and all the Cabinet with the bath water,[174] I don't see any —
unless [Dean] Rusk resigns. For that I have only rumors and no evidence,
nor any assurance that Johnson would want me in any event.

I wish I could assure you that Hubert [Humphrey] had the Vice Presidency settled but I doubt if he does. A friend had lunch with him yesterday and tells me by telephone that he is still in doubt as far as anything
the President has said. But his position in the Party is gaining strength
continuously and I rather think he gets more obvious with the passage of
time — *if* Johnson feels that he can spare him from the Senate. I agree
that we need a little zest and generosity all along the line in politics, and
certainly he is the incomparable contributor of both.

Adlai [III] is running for the legislature in Illinois, as you know, and
is coming on for the Convention with Nancy. And Natalie [Stevenson] is
an Alternate Delegate from California!

Please get an option on that Greek Island. I am ready! But from the
way things have been going in the Cyprus case, I am not sure but that
I am a public enemy in Greece this time.

Love always

p.s. Ada and Archie MacLeish have been with me for a few days,
and we spent an hilarious evening with who but Richard Burton and
Liz Taylor! It brought back memories of that over-crowded gala!

To Mrs. Albert Lasker

August 14, 1964

Dearest Mary:

I have examined your amusing brief on smoking and am deeply impressed — and am still smoking! [175] — but the volume is going down. I
wish I could say the same for the work. Instead, we have had Viet-Nam
and Cyprus in rapid order and I have been called back from two "vaca-
tions." Now, we have New York politics and the rising protest against
the [Robert] Kennedy invasion from the Liberal Party, the Roosevelt-
Lehman Reform groups, Labor, et al. But you can't stop somebody with

---

[174] Stevenson had been interested in the vice presidential nomination and asked his
close friend J. Edward Day, a former Postmaster General, to start an approach to the
President to secure the nomination for him. Day, interview with Walter Johnson,
May 26, 1966. In order to forestall speculation and to end pressure from Robert F.
Kennedy, Johnson announced that no member of his Cabinet would be considered
for the vice presidential nomination. According to Harlan Cleveland, Stevenson "was
really disappointed" when Johnson made this decision. Memorandum to Walter
Johnson, April 30, 1973. For other examples of Stevenson's interest in the vice presi-
dency, see Martin, *Adlai Stevenson and the World*, pp. 806–807.

[175] Stevenson had given up smoking after an operation in 1954 but had resumed
the habit since coming to the United Nations.

nobody, and I have refused to alter my position. So, of course, he can get the nomination, but winning is another matter what with the widespread disaffection. . . .

I hope you keep out of it and that rumors I hear are not verified. Meanwhile, I promised to have a talk with him [Kennedy], and perhaps I can be helpful in improving the "image," and getting some of the dissidents to go along with some consideration on his part.

I spoke at the American Bar Association Banquet last night, and the reception was gratifying. And now I must go to work on the foreign relations plank of the Platform and testify before the Platform Committee on Monday of next week.

All of the foregoing exertion makes my midnight reveries of life in Fiorentina [176] more painful. Some hot sun, blue sea and ripe figs — and the blue haze on the mountains above the Bay — cause me to wonder if I have lived two different lives.

I have been to Washington occasionally for some dinners, conferences, et al, and the President was here the other day. He seems fine and is as sure-footed as ever — especially now that he has thrown out the baby and the whole Cabinet with the bath water — and Lady Bird is gracious, busy, and travelling around the country.

Archie and Ada MacLeish have been staying with me and we had a riotous evening in spite of Cyprus and weariness, with who but Richard Burton and Liz Taylor.

And now, after sundry interruptions, another is upon me, and I shall have to conclude this letter — if by your grace it can be called a letter — with much love and wistful memories,

Yours,

To Stuart Gerry Brown [177]

August 14, 1964

Dear Stuart:

I am sending you a collection of miscellaneous speeches in accordance with your request.[178]

As to your second request, I can't say that the relationship with [President] Johnson has been much different. The consultation and contact at first was much more intimate and personal due to his difficulties and my long acquaintance with him.

As you know, in the spring of 1960, when I reaffirmed my decision

---

[176] Mrs. Lasker's villa at St.-Jean-Cap-Ferrat, France.
[177] The original is in the Stuart Gerry Brown papers, Syracuse University Library.
[178] Mr. Brown was writing *Adlai E. Stevenson, A Short Biography: The Conscience of the Country* (Woodbury, New York: Barron's Woodbury Press, 1965).

to seek no delegates to the Convention and make no effort to get the nomination, I told him that while I would do nothing to stop Kennedy, I would also not endorse him or, for that matter, either of them. I stuck to that in spite of importunities — and with consequences with which you are familiar. I rather suspect that President Johnson well remembers those days, and I have enjoyed a comfortable personal relationship with him and Lady Bird, and that includes a bed at the White House on request, and many opportunities to talk to him.

But the fact of the matter is that my life here is so exacting and since visits to Washington are usually for expressed purposes, casual, relaxed conversation is just about as difficult to contrive now as it was in [President] Kennedy's time. Moreover, with the pressures mounting on him, and on me here, the contacts save for formal meetings have, if anything, diminished as time has gone on. As you know, the social occasions at the White House are manifold but they allow little time for "close personal relations." I am usually included with all of the preferences of rank and seniority and a very warm personal relationship. But I confess I would like to have more opportunities for the quiet, "low down" talks which are so hard to arrange at this pace of life and especially if you are living in different cities.

I am afraid the foregoing doesn't help very much.

I can understand that the prospect of returning to winter in America is distasteful.[179] I feel sometimes after a series of interminable Security Council ordeals that I am going to escape — never to return!

I hope you are getting on with your work, and send you both my affectionate regards.

Yours,

Stevenson made the following statement to the press on August 23, 1964.[180]

I think Robert Kennedy is the strongest available Democratic candidate for the Senate. I have conferred with many people with a view to assuring him the support of all elements in the Democratic Party. I think he will have widespread support.

I have known Mr. Kennedy for many years and, if elected, I believe he will be an effective Senator and will further the efforts of Mayor [Robert]

---

[179] Mr. Brown was at the East-West Center of the University of Hawaii. Although Hawaii had become a state in 1959, it was still frequently referred to as though it were not part of the United States.

[180] The text is based on a typewritten copy.

Wagner and so many others to improve and strengthen the Democratic Party in New York.

May I take this opportunity to express again my gratitude to all the citizens of New York who have proposed me for the Senate. I announced last April and have frequently repeated that, in these perilous times, I felt my work in our foreign relations should take priority over any further personal political ambitions. But my appreciation for these expressions of confidence is boundless. I hope my friends will join me in supporting Mr. Kennedy.

Stevenson delivered a tribute to Eleanor Roosevelt at the Democratic National Convention on August 27, 1964.[181]

Thank you, my dear friends, for your welcome — and for all your loyalty and comfort to me in years past when our party's fortunes were not as bright as they are tonight.

For what I have done and sought to do for our country and our party, I have been repaid a thousand fold by the kindness of my fellow citizens — and by none more than you, the leaders of the Democratic Party.

I have been proud to march with you in seven Presidential campaigns, and to lead two of them. But I have never been prouder than I am tonight — to follow two such brilliant and bold leaders, and old and dear friends, as Lyndon Johnson and Hubert Humphrey. They will, I predict, leave the future of our country and our world in their debt.

But it is of another noble American that I am commissioned to speak to you tonight. She has passed beyond these voices — but our memory and her meaning have not — Eleanor Roosevelt.

She was a lady — a lady for all seasons. And, like her husband, she left "a name to shine on the entablatures of truth — forever."

There is, I believe, a legend in the Talmud which tells us that in any period of man's history the heavens themselves are held in place by the virtue, love and shining integrity of twelve just men. They are completely unaware of this function. They go about their daily work, their humble chores — doctors, teachers, ordinary devoted citizens — and meanwhile the rooftree of creation is supported by them alone.

There are times when nations or movements or great political parties are similarly sustained in their purposes and being by the pervasive, unconscious influence of a few great men and women. Can we doubt that Eleanor Roosevelt had in some measure the keeping of the Party's conscience in her special care? That her standards and integrity steadied our

[181] The text is based on a mimeograph copy.

own? That her judgment persuaded the doubters and "too-soon despairers"? That her will stiffened the waverers and encouraged the strong?

I do not suggest some unworldly saint dwelling in remote regions of unsullied idealism. On the contrary, as we all know Eleanor Roosevelt was a bonny fighter, at her best down in the arena, face to face with opponents and ideas she disapproved. Like that other grand old veteran of so many Democratic wars — Herbert Lehman — in ripe old age she took on tasks that might have daunted people half her age. Whether it was Communist bosses in the United Nations or shoddy politicians, whether it was exploiters of the poor or traducers of the faith of freedom — she sailed in, tall, courteous, good tempered, implacable, and thwacked them with the dispassionate energy of a good mother chastising a bad boy.

She did not carry our conscience by remote control. It was precisely her involvement that gave her such tremendous influence. Long before the civil rights issue moved to the forefront of the nation's consciousness, she was there, quietly reminding us of the inequalities practiced in our land.

Throughout the depression, her patient journeys brought to the President and dramatized for the nation the misery and neglect of millions.

During the gray days of national peril she heartened the wounded and the weary.

And during the affluent fifties, when misery ran for cover before the national complacency, she never ceased to remind us of the slums, disease and deprivation which still make up the dark face of this shining American planet.

And again when we emerged from the war, blinking and surprised, to the role of world leadership, there she was at the center of the effort, reminding her countrymen of their duties as citizens in the greater society of man.

She thought of herself as an "ugly duckling," but she walked in beauty in the ghettos of the world bringing with her the reminder of her beloved St. Francis, ". . . it is in the giving that we receive." And wherever she walked beauty was forever there.

There are always in any society, as there are in ours at this moment, plenty of men and women who would like — despite Abraham Lincoln's warning — to "escape history," to evade "the fiery trial," to turn back the clock. Eleanor Roosevelt never would and never did. She trained herself from the beginning of her life to face the realities, however unwelcome they might be, and face them she did, not only in the world around her but in her own family, in her own life. Few human beings are called upon to make decisions as difficult as some of hers. Fewer still — fewer women in any case — have ever been subjected to personal abuse as malicious and persistent. But never did she hide, run, wince or lower her head. Falsity withered in her presence. Hypocrisy left the room.

And never did she fail to act. If anything equalled the courage of her confrontation with the facts it was the candor and warmth of her response. She saw the state of our world as well as the most cynical, the most despairing, but she never despaired, she was never cynical, she never gave up. She believed in the human heart because she knew her own, and she proved by love what all the despair of a despairing time will never disprove — that hope is more powerful than fear.

She has left us — our counselor, our friend, our conscience. But there can be no doubt where she would be directing our great party today.

She would bid us add to the equality we guarantee, the extra dimension of opportunity without which even rights can seem so much emptiness.

She would tell us to look at our great cities and ask whether, in the midst of overwhelming affluence, we can afford such misery, such squalor, such hopelessness.

She would tell us to labor on in the vineyards of the world, to succor the needy, to underpin the rule of law, to check aggression, and, with remorseless purpose, to seek peace among the nations.

She would ask us to engage ourselves profoundly in the war on poverty at home and abroad.

She would urge us to build the great society not only for America, but for all God's children.

And she would bid us do all this not from party spirit or partisan prejudice or anger or bitterness or fear or contempt. She would ask only for the positive emotions — love of one's unfortunate neighbor since "there but for the grace of God go I" — love of our party as a mighty engine of social betterment, love for a world community threatened by the same annihilation — and, above all, love for America, which our Founding Fathers first dedicated to the great propositions of freedom, equality and happiness, and which can never fulfill itself until these magnificent promises can be turned into even more magnificent facts.

This is the spirit in which she would have us go out to join the everlasting battle for something better.

This is her lasting legacy to humankind — and to the Party she loved and worked for all her life.[182]

---

[182] Alfred Friendly, covering the Democratic National Convention for the Washington *Post*, recommended that the Sunday *Post* carry the full text of the eulogy, adding: "We are not likely to get anything better than this until they resurrect Lincoln." Eric Sevareid said on the Columbia Broadcasting System: "Now I know why Mr. Stevenson wasn't elected President. We Americans never elect poets to be President."

To Mrs. Walter Kerr [183]

August 29, 1964

Dear Jean:

Your telegram arrived — just in time! Enclosed is a copy of my utterance about Mrs. R., and "A Lady for All Seasons" evoked applause.

But the appearance of AES, and the ghost of Eleanor Roosevelt, which used to raise such a tumult, was muted this time, thanks to the immediately preceding film about President Kennedy and the orgy of emotion. I don't know whether they placed me there deliberately, but I didn't mind, and the words of the multitudes afterward were comforting.

I have missed you — but I always do!

Dearest love,

P.S. I am hoping, praying to get away for some long deferred rest and relaxation with my grandchildren, and some reflections on Atlantic City and that ghost-filled hall.

I shall be returning after Labor Day for a formidable autumn which should exorcise all the ghosts in my political past!

Stevenson vacationed with the Hermon Dunlap Smiths at their summer home in Canada and then went to Libertyville.

To Mr. and Mrs. Hermon Dunlap Smith [184]

September 7, 1964

My dear, dear Smiths —

The summons has come & I'm off to N.Y. — Malaysia and Cypress [185] — in a few minutes, without even time to write you a proper letter of thanks for perhaps the best R & R I've ever had! And, thinking of 35 years of Desbarats, that's saying a lot. Maybe it came just when I needed it most; but I suspect the largest component was the Smith family — three generations — and their mysterious gift for hospitality and quiet repose in that lovely, tranquil environment. And this time even the journey down

---

[183] Author and playwright and wife of the drama critic of the New York *Herald Tribune.*

[184] This handwritten letter is in the possession of Mr. Smith.

[185] Stevenson spoke about the situation in Malaysia in the Security Council on September 10 and on September 17. He spoke on Cyprus on September 11 and again on September 17. On September 3 Malaysia had asked for an urgent meeting of the Security Council, charging that Indonesian aircraft had dropped thirty paratroopers in South Malaya on September 2.

was painless and on time! But what a pity to waste any part of a blue and white northern summer day in an airplane.

I send you blessings and thanks from the heart, head & sinews — *

* double thanks for letting Marietta [Tree] come too — she needed it as much as I! Love always — ADLAI

To Lady Barbara Jackson

September 10, 1964

Dearest Barbara:

I am dictating this hurriedly so that Robert [Jackson] can take it with him. He has been with me for a few days, but, as usual, I have seen all too little of him. He seems blithe and gay and animated and very positively interested in his job — with endless travels already booked. I don't see how he does it. All I want to do is unpack for keeps.

But instead the campaign is upon us and I shall have to be going around the country quite a bit speaking before "non-partisan audiences" — conventions, world affairs councils, etc. On top of that we now have the guns of Malaysia, Indonesia, Greece, Turkey and the USSR trained on the US Mission. But it was always thus!

I wish I could answer all of your inquiries wisely and quickly. I can't. But of one thing I am as sure as you are — that Hubert [Humphrey] has had his just deserts at last, and as time goes on will reassure more and more people. I only hope that very zest, generosity and gaiety which we admire doesn't get too exuberant and embarrass him.

I am embarrassed that I haven't sent you the Eleanor Roosevelt speech long before this, and a copy is enclosed. It was a great success, and in some quarters I am now labeled "Old Eloquence." I concede at least the "old"!

The balance of your material I can use in the endless speeches I have to make about her during the fall, when our campaign for funds [186] will peak. My hope is that after November I can extricate myself from that job, which has been almost too much and not well handled, I fear. Perhaps then we will know how much money we have left over after the fixed commitments and can reach some rational conclusion as to its use and the future role of the Foundation in the field of human rights.

Your surmise about [Robert] Kennedy's motivation is, of course, correct. It's a long story in which I was deeply involved, and I hope I can reconstruct it for you when that moment of leisure arrives. A wistful hope! I suspect he will win, although there is much opposition even within the Democratic party and a great deal of sympathy for Keating,[187] who has

[186] For the Eleanor Roosevelt Memorial Foundation.
[187] Senator Kenneth Keating, who was defeated for reelection by Kennedy.

earned liberal support on both sides by his stand against [Barry] Goldwater.

I enclose a preliminary schedule of my speaking engagements. You will note that I have to be in Saint Louis on Tuesday, October 6, and at Northwestern University to dedicate the new campus the following day. I will probably fly back to New York on Thursday, October 8, in time to meet you and we can go up to Cornell together on Friday, October 9 in a private plane, which the University will provide, in the morning as you suggest.

I am sure this schedule will not hold: they never do. Other things will be slipped in, and what with USUN, Roosevelt Foundation and the campaign I have a wicked, weary fall ahead of me. Hence your proffer of help is even more welcome than usual. What more can I say! I think you have as much background as I have about the Cornell Centennial. If I didn't have to worry about that one, it would be a great relief. And I won't! However, if you get anything ready that you can send me in advance, it will be helpful for the editing and advance copies which they are sure to demand for release to the press. Perhaps I could even use some of it for the Northwestern University speech at the dedication of their huge new campus.

I stop my suggestions for your contributions here only because I don't want to impose on you further. So the suggestion that any thoughts on the international scene which occur to you and sly digs at Goldwater would be useful is only parenthetical. I thought Bill Fulbright made a good point the other day when he said that "there is a kind of romantic mysticism in the Goldwater view of the world, not unlike that of the Communists themselves. Both groups seem to believe that there is something unnatural and immoral" about survival of more than one set of beliefs about man and human societies. Elsewhere he said that the Goldwater Republicans "propose to change the basis of American foreign policy from a commitment to defend the free world to a commitment to liberate the Communist world." [188]

Are we witnessing in the Goldwater talk a new summons to the religious wars and a rejection of the democratic idea of human diversity?

After the Convention and a couple of days in New York with John Fell and Natalie, I took refuge at the [Hermon D.] Smiths' camp in Canada, followed by Labor Day weekend with the children at Libertyville. It may not have been as good as the sun, sea and cream of Cornwall, but it was mighty good for what ails a weary old politician quietly receding into the shadows. But of the future there will be much to talk about when you arrive. And the prospect of your two months in America makes everything brighter!

Love always,

[188] See the *Congressional Record*, Senate, September 8, 1964, p. 21676.

John H. Sengstacke, editor and publisher of the Chicago Daily Defender, *sent Stevenson a memorandum by Chuck Stone of his editorial staff, criticizing Stevenson's attitudes toward Negroes.*

To John H. Sengstacke

September 14, 1964

Dear John:

I've been so swamped by all the recent crises at the UN, plus Atlantic City, that I'm only now getting around to personal correspondence that has been piling up. So please forgive this delay in answering your letter and the memorandum from Mr. Stone.

In this letter I intend to deal point-by-point with Mr. Stone's bill of particulars, all of which add up to the charge that I am indifferent or hostile to the interests of Negroes. This, at a time when Goldwater and Miller are attacking me almost daily for being too "extreme" in support of Civil Rights. As you must have noticed, the Republican candidates are now attacking me harder than any other Democrat for my speeches in behalf of racial equality and the right of protest. I don't mind their attacks; I expect them; but it is a poor reward indeed when someone like Mr. Stone ignores all I have done over the years, and tries in the most unfair way to depict me as unfriendly to my Negro fellowman.

I must say in all candor, John, that Stone's attack seems to me full of downright malice, for there is not a single charge of his that will bear examination.

He begins his indictment by asserting that Adam Powell [189] switched to Eisenhower in 1956 because "he was so appalled by my refusal to campaign on a strong Civil Rights platform."

You *know* that this is untrue. I fought hard for a very strong Civil Rights plank in 1956, and got one, that, of course, is a matter of record.[190] You will also recall that Eisenhower, in sharp contrast, refused to say a word in behalf of the 1954 Supreme Court desegregation decision, which was then very controversial. Despite Eisenhower's position, Adam Powell saw fit to endorse him, but, so far as I recall, he was one of the few prominent Negro Civil Rights spokesmen to do so.

I am happy to say that in both of my campaigns in 1952 and 1956 I had the overwhelming support of the Negro community. I think you will agree that the American Negro never had a better friend than Mrs. Roosevelt. Mr. Stone seems to have overlooked that in 1956 she had this to say about me:

"As Governor of Illinois he desegregated the National Guard; he fought for a State Fair Employment Practices Commission; he issued

[189] Adam Clayton Powell, a black Democratic representative from New York City.
[190] See *The Papers of Adlai E. Stevenson*, Vol. VI, especially pp. 177–180.

and enforced orders for the first time in any state denying the facilities of the state employment services to any employer practicing discrimination, and deleted all references to race in employment service records; he reorganized and strengthened the State Commission on Human Relations; he encouraged and supported desegregation of public schools in southern Illinois; he appointed many qualified Negroes to state office. . . ."

I might add that my actions as Governor merely carried on similar activity undertaken when I was Assistant Secretary of the Navy from 1941 to 1944, and when the first steps were taken toward removing racial barriers in that Service.[191]

Mr. Stone's second point is that, at my first press conference after coming to the UN, I "angrily snapped" and "made a nasty retort" when I was asked if I intended to appoint Negroes to the UN staff. I don't think I have ever made a nasty retort during a press conference in my life, and I certainly did not on this occasion. I have just refreshed my recollection of this conference by reading a transcript of it and I can find nothing that would suggest that I did not intend to appoint Negroes.

On the contrary, I had every intention of increasing the role of Negroes in the U.S. Mission. And this intention I have certainly made good on since coming here.

When I came to the Mission it included only one Negro officer, Mrs. Carmel Marr, who acted as one of our legal advisers. That had been the entire extent of Negro officer representation at the U.S. Mission for a number of years before I arrived.

I am proud to report that this situation has been greatly improved. There are now a number of Negroes serving in high capacity. This list includes Frank Williams, our Representative to the Economic and Social Council, with the rank of Ambassador; Frank Montero, who I personally recruited as my Special Assistant; John Means, a principal economic adviser; Ernest C. Griggs III, one of our top advisers on political and security affairs; and Mrs. Marr, who has been given larger responsibilities. In addition to this, I obtained the services not only of Carl Rowan, but John Morrow, former Ambassador to Guinea; Ambassador Mercer Cook; and Ambassador Clifton Wharton.

We have also enlarged the number of Negroes serving in administrative jobs at the Mission. The "light-skinned colored girls" charge is both odious and provably untrue.

The press widely circulated Representative Powell's false charge that our Mission had only one Negro on a staff of 500. The fact is we have

191 See *The Papers of Adlai E. Stevenson*, Vol. II, p. 134.

16 Negroes (and two more are being added next month) out of a total roster of 120.

As you can see from the above, Negro representation is a matter that has been constantly on my mind since coming to the Mission, and so I find Mr. Stone's distortions a poor reward for all I have tried to do.

The only documentation Mr. Stone offers for his various rumors and allegations is reference to vague, anonymous "sources" and "certain quarters" at the State Department, Democratic National Committee, and the White House. I can only say that I would be very surprised if any responsible official in any of these quarters would accuse me of "being antagonistic to adding Negroes to the UN staff." Surely Mr. Stone should at least be able to tell you personally who these alleged informants are.

This letter is not sent to you for publication, but for the information of you and your associates. I value your friendship and good opinion, and therefore have gone to some length to set the record straight.

Best wishes,

Sincerely,

To Simon Michael Bessie [192]

September 16, 1964

Dear Mr. Bessie:

It was a great pleasure to receive Newton N. Minow's new book, "Equal Time," recording the author's chairmanship of the Federal Communications Committee [Commission].

As his former law partner, I was probably less astonished than most when this little known young man greeted the television giants, the lords of fifty million living rooms, with the words:

"Gentlemen, your trust accounting with your beneficiaries is overdue. . . . Never have so few owed so much to so many."

This book records his patient, incisive, consistent remarks to the broadcasting industry and its huge audience. He envisioned the enormous promise of a communications revolution to make a "vast wasteland" more productive. Now the publication of "Equal Time" reveals the careful design and simple logic of the plans for beauty and significance in broadcasting, which Mr. Minow framed for America and the world.

The public needs more such advocates. Educational television appears solidly established. Some of the promise of public affairs programming has been fulfilled. All-channel receiver legislation, effective this year, can light up seventy new channels in the Ultra High Frequency band.

[192] President of Atheneum Publishers.

In response to Mr. Minow's urging, more and more broadcasters are meeting their obligation to air responsible opinion on matters of public controversy.

Unfortunately some of the vital parts of Mr. Minow's program for enrichment are yet unrealized. I hope the book finds wide readership and stirs more public discussion.

With my best wishes,

Cordially yours,

To DeWitt Wallace [193]

September 16, 1964

Dear Mr. Wallace:

I have just read Dr. Mario Lazo's article on the Bay of Pigs invasion in the September issue of the Reader's Digest.[194]

Dr. Lazo writes that the invasion failed because a proposed air strike, supposedly planned for Monday morning, April 17, 1961 was canceled by President Kennedy. Dr. Lazo then suggests that Mr. Kennedy canceled the air strike at the insistence of Secretary [Dean] Rusk and myself.

Dr. Lazo has apparently not read or has ignored the public statements I issued long ago denying that I intervened or even knew about the proposed air strike. I was in New York the entire time, and the old story that Dr. Lazo has repeated about my participation in the Washington decisions is wholly incorrect.

Sincerely yours,

MEMORANDUM FOR THE FILES

September 26, 1964

Yesterday, Dean Andrew Cordier [195] visited with me and on behalf of the President of Columbia, asked me to consider a distinguished professorship at the (graduate) School of International Relations at Columbia if and when I left the Government. The volume of the lecturing load and the subject matter would be up to me. He wants me to have a blank check as to what I would do with the students, and, as in the case of NYU,[196] assured me all the research assistance necessary for any writing.

---

[193] Founder and president of the *Reader's Digest*.
[194] "Decision for Disaster: At Last — The Real Truth about the Bay of Pigs."
[195] Dean of the Columbia University Graduate School of International Affairs and former undersecretary for General Assembly affairs of the United Nations.
[196] New York University had offered Stevenson a similar professorship.

To James A. Wechsler [197]

September 29, 1964

Dear Jimmy:

I have agreed to speak about 5 minutes at the Liberal Party rally for President Johnson on October 15 — thus violating the latter's admonition to keep out of partisan political meetings this fall!

Perhaps I can do something light-hearted as a non-partisan diplomat — with a paragraph or so of meat re foreign policy.

Excerpts from a speech in Philadelphia last week are enclosed — in case my favorite speech-writer might feel inspired to suggest something to a weary old admirer — who is about to set sail for two weeks of refined campaigning, etc.

Yours,

On October 2, Stevenson spoke in Cleveland. Four days later he spoke in St. Louis. On October 7 he spoke at Northwestern University. Two days later he spoke at Cornell University. On October 11 and 12 he spoke at dinners honoring Eleanor Roosevelt.

He wrote the following letter to his eldest son, who celebrated his thirty-fourth birthday on October 10, 1964.

To Adlai E. Stevenson III

October 12, 1964

Dear Bear:

At 34 I was working in the FACA [198] in Washington, as Assistant General Counsel; my father was dead, my mother was an invalid, my father-in-law was in deep and perpetual financial trouble; I had two children, no home in Chicago, a meagre income, an insecure base as a lawyer and a compelling interest in public affairs on the liberal, democratic side, and we were in the depths of depression with the first rays of hope barely visible.

I can't readily assess the differences in our positions. But I am sure you are way ahead on most counts. And certainly in self-confidence and purpose. Bless you!

Love,

[197] Editorial page editor and columnist of the New York *Post*.
[198] For Stevenson's work with the Federal Alcohol Control Administration, see *The Papers of Adlai E. Stevenson*, Vol. I, pp. 274–276.

To Mrs. Walter P. Paepcke

October 14, 1964

Dearest Pussy:

Your postcard lifted my heart and even eased my wounded finger!

It arrived while I was in the hospital for an operation on a finger broken in the line of duty, i.e., peace-keeping! But the combatants were Merlin, a dalmation of ancient lineage,[199] like your naughty Baron, and two monsters residents of my neighbors. . . .

The victim was, as usual, the peace-keeper, and I have had a wretched time traveling about the country making speeches and nursing a badly broken paw. But by October 21st I will be ready. I can't tell at the moment what my situation will be that evening for dinner due to a long standing engagement for the opening of a play, but please plan to stay the night here. Unhappily, the next day I have to leave to speak in Nashville,[200] etc., returning in time for a formidable speech on Sunday evening, October 25th,[201] at which you will be most welcome.

I hope you can stay longer this time and give me a chance to catch up on your intercontinental misconduct. Your neglect has been shameful!

Love,

To Penelope Tree [202]

[no date]

Penelope dear —

Do you like my penmanship? If not, try writing with your thumb and forefinger with a 2 pound bandage on the rest of your hand.

I broke my finger — in pieces — trying to keep peace between some dogs and am just back from 3 hours on the operating table. So *weep* — don't *laugh!* And reflect on the perils of peacekeeping!!!

Your mother tells me you have broken the school rules and are in acute trouble and spiritual agony.[203] Well — at some time or other we all break the rules, get in trouble, & suffer acutely. I'm sorry you did it at all — but that is behind you now and I'm *glad* you did it when you were so young, have suffered the remorse, — *and won't do it again!*

---

[199] His dog in Libertyville.

[200] On October 22, he spoke at the United Nations Day ceremonies in Nashville, Tennessee. Two days later he spoke at Louisville, Kentucky.

[201] He addressed the American Jewish Congress in New York City and received the Stephen Wise award.

[202] This handwritten letter is in the possession of Mrs. Ronald Tree, Miss Tree's mother. It is postmarked October 15, 1964.

[203] Miss Tree was attending Concord Academy in Concord, Massachusetts.

It is only by experience — not copy book maxims — that we can help *others* — which is the greatest joy of all. And every glimpse, every bit of news about you, good or bad, helps your devoted and loving old

Yo Yo [204]

To DeWitt Wallace

October 15, 1964

Dear Mr. Wallace:

Thank you for your letter of September 28.

I do not know what more I can say.

I have stated as unequivocally as I know how, that I was not consulted or informed about any of the air strikes in connection with the Cuban invasion of April, 1961. The gist of Mr. Monahan's [205] memorandum to you seems to be that he and Dr. [Mario] Lazo know better.

He says their information comes from unidentified "reliable sources"; unnamed "highly respectable individuals"; and from unspecified "sources we respected."

Evidently my word is no match for "reliable sources." I guess there is nothing more I can say.

Whatever the intent or motive, the effect of the article has been to leave, uncontradicted, the impression that I was instrumental in calling off the air strike. I wasn't!

Sincerely yours,

To Bill Moyers

October 19, 1964

Dear Bill:

I have your letter advising me that the President would be pleased to have me do "everything possible for Bob Kennedy consistent with my current duties and responsibilities."

During the campaign I have proceeded on the assumption that I should not speak at partisan rallies and have confined myself to foreign policy speeches before non-partisan gatherings. Accordingly, I have declined speaking invitations from Democratic candidates in virtually every State. I have spoken before non-partisan meetings in Pennsylvania, New York, Illinois, Missouri and Ohio, and am presently going to Tennessee, Kentucky and California.

I have, however, accompanied Bobby Kennedy and introduced him at

[204] Miss Tree had given Stevenson this nickname because he said that in practicing diplomacy he found the word "yo," meaning "yes and no," of great usefulness.

[205] James Monahan, a senior editor of the *Reader's Digest*.

a political rally in the Bronx, and also spoke at the Liberal Party Rally for President Johnson, including an emphatic endorsement of Kennedy. I have, of course, spoken to many influential individuals and small private groups both before and since his nomination. And my written endorsement of his candidacy on August 23rd attracted considerable press attention — and also some sharp criticism from the anti-Kennedy sources!

If the President now wishes me to alter this procedure and campaign actively in and about New York, I shall try to do so although my schedule leaves little time for the office and New York before election. But the President should bear in mind that such appearances attract conspicuous notice in the papers and make it extremely difficult to discriminate as to other candidacies around the country.

Please call me on the telephone if you wish to discuss this further.

Sincerely yours,

P.S. I should add that I have agreed to speak at a dinner for Salinger [206] in Los Angeles on October 29th, which is another departure from the original plan.

To Samuel N. Friedel [207]

October 22, 1964

Dear Congressman Friedel:

Please assure the members of the Maryland Chapter of the American Jewish Congress that the United States Government continues to be vitally concerned with the arms race in the Near East. We have repeatedly stated our opposition to the introduction of sophisticated offensive weapons into the area and our strong hope for an abatement of the arms race and the tensions engendered thereby.

Israel's security has been a long-standing concern to this Government. We are, therefore, pleased that in the considered judgment of American military experts, Israel's security is well assured at present and for the foreseeable future. Israeli leaders, despite concern over specific developments, have confirmed the accuracy of this assessment and have consistently stressed the competence of the Israel Defense Force to meet possible contingencies. Despite our conviction that the present situation in the Near East gives no cause for immediate worry, the United States Government is aware of possible threats to the future security of the area and is constantly seeking ways to keep these under control.

You undoubtedly recall that one of the first acts of the administration after President Johnson took office was to make clear that the essentials of

[206] Pierre Salinger was campaigning for the U.S. Senate in California.
[207] Democratic representative from Maryland.

our foreign policies remained unchanged. The continuity of our policy in the Middle-East was emphasized. In looking back on the record, I feel the late President Kennedy best expressed our commitment to the security of Israel and her neighbors when he stated at his press conference on May 8, 1963, "We support the security of both Israel and her neighbors. In the event of aggression or preparation for aggression, whether direct or indirect, we would support with appropriate measures in the United Nations, adopt other courses of action of our own to prevent or to put a stop to such aggression which, of course, has been the policy which the United States has followed for some time." This statement stands valid today.

While I do not profess to be an expert on the nuclear capability of the United Arab Republic, I am attaching a summary of our findings on this controversial issue as expressed by the Assistant Secretary for Congressional Relations [208] in reply to a recent inquiry. I hope this will answer some of the questions raised by your constituents.

It is always good to hear from you.

With all best wishes,

Sincerely yours,

To Edwin C. Austin [209]

October 27, 1964

Dear Ed:

I am reliably informed . . . that on November 11th the firm is celebrating your 50th Anniversary at a dinner. To say that I wish I could be there is hardly necessary.

Of those 50 years, I can claim to recall bits and pieces of all of them, save the first 13. Perhaps they were the hardest — for you. The next 13 were the hardest for me! But I will long remember your patient efforts to instruct me in some of the rudiments of law practice — including the use of the library for research, and not sleeping — and the men's room — well, not for reading the newspapers.

But I remember too with what charity you often asked us "younger men" for our opinion, and the solemn panic with which I occasionally uttered something. Nor did I overlook the fact that you were generous enough to disregard the fact that it was usually either irrelevant or inconsequential.

---

[208] Frederick G. Dutton. The two-page statement is not included here since it did not emanate from Stevenson or USUN.

[209] A senior partner in the Chicago law firm of Sidley, Austin, Burgess and Smith (now Sidley and Austin). For Stevenson's earlier relationship with this firm, see *The Papers of Adlai E. Stevenson,* Vol. I.

I would like to add that you were never in a hurry, never impatient, never irritable, and always considerate and thoughtful. I wish anyone could now say as much for me!

Memories of "the office" are crowding in from all directions as I dictate this hurried note, and, so far as you are concerned, they are all so respectful and admiring and tender that I can even forgive you for once asking me to help write a brief on the unconstitutionality of the Holding Company Act. Indeed, I am becoming so maudlin that I am even forgiving you for being such a good Republican.

And, by the way, thanks for letting me be such a good New Deal Democrat!

I know you will be there for many years to come. I wish I could spend a few of them with you, especially since I have some things on my conscience — those ERPI bills in Bemidji, Minnesota that I never collected.[210]

Press on, young man!

Affectionately,

To Arthur Ochs Sulzberger [211]

October 27, 1964

Personal

Dear Punch:

I have been hearing reports that, in pursuance of your policy of rotation, there is some possibility of changing your Bureau Chief at the UN,[212] and also eliminating the UN Column on Sunday.

I hope you won't think that I am butting into your business, or interfering with the conduct of the paper, but, as an old friend, I hope you will keep in mind that we have some trying months ahead for the UN. I refer to the confrontation with Russia over financing of peacekeeping efforts, a new struggle over seating of Communist China in the UN, and several other issues that will arise. These matters are not only of international importance, but they are of great concern to the American public.

Thus, it seems to me most likely that there will be a lively interest in the coming session of the G[eneral] A[ssembly], and now, more than ever, the public will depend on experienced and sophisticated reporting of UN developments.

Most of us at the UN, and I think this is true of foreign delegations as

---

[210] One of Stevenson's duties with the firm during the Depression was to try to collect money owed to clients.

[211] President and publisher of the New York *Times*.

[212] Bureau chief William Hamilton, who asked Stevenson to write this letter. The transfer did take place.

well as ours, have come to rely on the Times coverage of the UN as almost quasi-official. This not only goes for the daily coverage, but also for the "perspective" column on Sunday. Finally, there is also the influence of the Times coverage on other American papers. There is no doubt in my mind that the significant attention the Times has always given the UN has had a lot to do with the growing coverage by other papers both here and abroad — for which we are grateful indeed!

Forgive me for this intrusion, but I wanted to pass my thoughts on to you in a personal way for whatever they may be worth.

With best wishes,

Sincerely,

On October 29, Stevenson flew to Los Angeles to speak at a dinner for Senate candidate Pierre Salinger. On October 30 Stevenson addressed a World Affairs Council luncheon, and at a press conference the same day he issued the following statement.[213]

I have come here to make a non-partisan speech in behalf of a bi-partisan foreign policy — one that has been supported for twenty years by the leaders of both major parties. Strong support of the United Nations has been very much a part of that bi-partisan policy, but now, I am sorry to say, we have a Presidential nominee who for years has been constantly hostile to the UN.

During the present campaign, however, Senator Goldwater has discovered how devoted the American people are to the United Nations, so now he says, and I quote:

"I've never said let's get out of the UN. I don't know how that rumor got started."

Well, I'll tell you how it got started:

As far back as December 21, 1961, the Associated Press reported him saying — quote —

"The U.S. no longer has a place in the U.N." End quote.

And as recently as February 7, 1964, he said, quote —

"I have come to the reluctant conclusion that the United States no longer has a place in the United Nations" — end quote. That is from the Nashville Tennessean.

On January 16, 1962, at Miami University, he said — quote:

"The anti-peace countries have more of a say in the UN than we do; let's forget the whole thing and join up with our allies." End quote.

[213] The text is based on a mimeograph copy.

Speaking for myself, I thought we had already "joined up with our allies."

This reminds me of what Thoreau said when he was asked if he had made his peace with God. He said: "I didn't know we had quarreled."

Now what did the Senator say in 1963. Well, on June 5, 1963, for instance, he was interviewed on WOR–TV and was asked whether he would, as President, favor getting out of the UN. His answer was, and I quote:

"I would, at this bet, having seen what the United Nations cannot do, I would have to suggest it." End quote.

Even as late as the New Hampshire campaign this year, Senator Goldwater was making his old charge that the UN was going to be dominated by the enemies of the U.S., and therefore — quote —

"I see no advantages of staying in it." New York Times, February 2, 1964.

And at a press conference at Keene, New Hampshire, on January 22, 1964, the Senator even went so far as to say — quote —

"Unless we revise the UN Charter, I can see no reason for *any* Western power (not just the U.S. but any Western power) to stay in the United Nations." End quote.

Perhaps that will give the Senator some idea of how the rumor got started that he was critical of the United Nations.

I might add that I have in my briefcase a number of other Goldwater attacks on the United Nations, all of them unfair and distorted, but I think these quotes will do.

From California, Stevenson flew to Santiago, Chile, to represent the United States at the inauguration of President Eduardo Frei. As a result he missed the election victory celebrations of Adlai III and Robert F. Kennedy.

To Robert F. Kennedy

November 6, 1964

Dear Bobby:

Down in Santiago, Chile, I wasn't surprised when the good news came in from New York. But I was mighty relieved, all the same! And the jubilation among the Chileans would have warmed your weary heart.

I wish I could have been in New York for the celebration — old politicians die so slowly.

Best wishes for your limitless future and love to Ethel [Kennedy].

Yours,

To Pierre Salinger

November 6, 1964

Dear Pierre:

Damn it! And just when I thought it was in the bag.[214] Why does California have to always be so eccentric? But it was a gallant battle, and I am proud that Natalie [Stevenson] had even a tiny part in it. I wish I had had more.

Yours,

To Lyndon B. Johnson

MEMORANDUM FOR THE PRESIDENT [215]

November 18, 1964

From: Adlai E. Stevenson

A Reassessment of United States Foreign Policy 1965–70
The United States met with courage, intelligence and imagination the unprecedented responsibilities which were thrust upon it as the leading World Power during the first decade after the war. During the second decade the aspect of the world scene changed substantially. During the third decade it will change even more. Consequently, some of the United States policies which were triumphs in 1950 have become barely adequate by the mid-6o's and are likely to be obsolete and in some cases counterproductive before 1970. Pragmatic adaptation to the evolving climate and environment is essential if our security and leadership are to be maintained.

Elements of Change in the World Scene
The principal elements of change in the environment which confront us are the following:

1. *Polycentrism or splintering in the Communist bloc and movement.*
Even though some papering over of Sino-Soviet differences will occur, the monolithic bloc has already disintegrated beyond repair, basic reconciliation between Russia and China is extremely unlikely, and the vast consequences of this rift in Eastern Europe, Asia and Africa have only begun to appear.

---

[214] Salinger had been defeated in his campaign for the Senate.
[215] This document was declassified. A copy was sent to Secretary of State Dean Rusk on November 20, 1964.

2. Expansion of the power and influence of Communist China

The more aggressive of the Communist Great Powers will henceforth be more and more able to influence events, particularly in the Far East and Africa, often without or even against the Soviet Union.

3. Shift of emphasis in the Soviet Union.

The ouster of Khrushchev [216] completes the transfer of power to the post-revolutionary generation of party bureaucrats and technocrats who, without diminishing fidelity to Communist dogma or Russian Great Power interests, will probably prefer to concentrate primary attention on internal reorganization and productivity.

4. Polycentrism and splintering in the Western Alliance.

The United States has long promoted a stronger, more independent and more united Europe in close alliance with us. Unfortunately, present trends seem to be toward stronger, more independent but less united European states in looser alliance with us.

5. Limitations on strategic military stability.

While United States strategic military predominance seems relatively secure, there are serious encroachments on the stability of the current "balance of terror":

(a) Proliferation of nuclear weapons.

(b) Communist "wars of liberation" through tactics which cannot be overcome solely by military force exercised from outside.

(c) Impatience with the growing economic burden of armaments.

(d) Impatience with the failure to reduce armaments and mitigate the continuing danger of nuclear war.

(e) Obstacles to effective United Nations peacekeeping.

6. Instability and radicalism in the underdeveloped world.

As the "founding fathers" in new countries die off or are ousted by younger leaders, there is a clear tendency toward increasing instability and radicalism in those countries, with consequent exacerbation of their differences with the West and among each other; regional organizations are still too weak to deal effectively with these conflicts, so that polycentrism is also prevalent among the non-aligned. Moreover, the prospects for reasonably rapid economic development, which is necessary to political stability, are diminished by the unchecked population

[216] Nikita Khrushchev was replaced on October 14 and 15, 1964, by Leonid Brezhnev as first secretary of the Communist Party and by Aleksei Kosygin as premier of the Soviet Union.

explosion and by the increasing reluctance of developed nations to provide needed capital and favorable terms of trade.

7. Revival of global polycentrism.

The increasing reascertion of national independence in the Communist,
Western and non-aligned worlds, while tending somewhat to relieve the
cold war between blocs, also tends to recreate an international anarchy
which no single Great Power, such as the United States, can dominate,
and no regional or international organization, such as the United Nations,
is yet strong enough to control.

Therefore, in face of increasing military, and in the underdeveloped
world political and economic, instability neither the United States alone,
the West as a whole, nor existing international institutions are under
present conditions able to exercise the authority necessary to prevent
those instabilities from provoking over the next decade a series of
calamities.

Inadequacy of Old Prescriptions

These vast changes and challenges cannot be successfully met simply
by more of the same old prescriptions: more United States and Western
armament, more NATO unity, more alliances with small states in the
Far East, more bilateral military and economic aid to underdeveloped
states in Asia and Africa. Most of these measures continue to be desirable, but they are increasingly inadequate and unreliable.

It is very doubtful that further substantial increase in United States
armament is necessary or usable, or that further substantial increase in
Allied armament would be feasible, or, to the extent feasible, centrally
controllable. With the three principal Western European powers and the
erstwhile East European satellites in an increasingly ambivalent political
situation, there is little prospect, or indeed advantage, of further developing NATO on a primarily military basis; it has about reached the limits
of internal tolerance in this respect and, in the absence of sharply renewed Soviet aggressiveness, its future progress will probably be more
in the political and economic than in the military field. In the two former
domains its potentialities as the instrument of a maturing Atlantic Community can hardly be exaggerated.

Geographical Shift in the Communist Threat

The principal threat to the United States since 1945 has been the
Soviet Union. It remains potentially almost as great a threat as ever.
The current effort to minimize the Sino-Soviet rift may even momentarily
bring about a deterioration in US-Soviet relations. However, in longer
perspective and progressive disintegration of the Communist bloc de-

prives the Soviet Union of some of the capabilities, the increasing concern of its population and leadership with a rising standard of living and more relaxed disciplines deprives it of some of the incentives, for an aggressive foreign policy. There is a real possibility that over the next few years the Soviet Union and its European allies (no longer satellites) may, if given the opportunity, become more European and more tractable. This will not, of course, occur immediately, rapidly, totally or without appropriate Western response. It will not occur at all if favorable opportunities are not periodically offered by the West.

The principal threat to world peace and Western security in the foreseeable future will almost certainly be Communist China. It is arrogant, aggressive, resourceful and resolute. It is already stronger militarily than any other state in Asia except the Soviet Union and its military strength, including its ability to make and deliver nuclear weapons, is likely to grow much faster than has been forecast. Politically its prestige among colored peoples as the most powerful and successful colored nation will prosper, and it will use that prestige and a disproportionate share of its resources to extend its influence and create maximum disorder in Asia and Africa.

Containment in the Far East

If the thesis is accepted that henceforth by far the greater actual threat to us and the West comes from China than from Russia, two consequences follow: (1) that we should mobilize far stronger forces in East Asia for the containment of China than the unsatisfactory coalition of the United States plus half a dozen small states (SEATO has never really amounted to more) on which we have so far relied, and (2) that we should actively explore and exploit in Europe possible new opportunities for partial military disengagement and partial political relaxation in order to facilitate a greater concentration of attention and, it may be hoped, of defensive force on the Far East *by both sides in Europe.*

Under this strategy we would attempt to encourage India and Japan to play more of a role as military and political counterweights to Communist China, while realizing that Indian economic backwardness and Japanese reluctance to re-enter the military arena in a substantial way would place limitations on their role. We would continue to encourage further British, Australian and New Zealand concentration on this threat. We would also, by making another very serious effort to lower tensions and relieve fears on both sides in Central Europe, make it more feasible and more rewarding for the Soviet Union to demonstrate increasing political and military concern with the potential threat to its Asian frontiers. This would be supplemented by further attempts to improve bilateral

US-Soviet relations, most importantly in the field of trade where mutual advantages, both economic and political, seem clearly to exist. Until steps along these lines have been successfully taken, it is unlikely that the unfavorable situation in which we find ourselves throughout most of Southeast Asia can be corrected and the Communist momentum there brought to a halt.

We will probably not, however, be able thus to re-enforce the ring around Communist China if we do not at the same time demonstrate to potential allies and neutrals that the ring is directed against Chinese aggressiveness, not against the Chinese people or even Chinese domestic Communism, and that we are quite ready to negotiate modus vivendi or even real settlements, on a quid pro quo basis, whenever Peiping is ready to accommodate itself to a peaceful world. Such a posture would involve more vigorous efforts to develop a meaningful continuous dialogue with the Peiping regime, analogous to that we maintained with the Soviets even in the worst days of the Cold War. The point of contact might be either in Warsaw or in some new locus which, it may be hoped, would emphasize the increased significance both parties attach to the dialogue. Such a new posture would also involve progressive relaxation of our opposition to China's participation in international conferences, particularly in disarmament, and in the United Nations. A quid pro quo for this latter concession would clearly have to be self-determination for Taiwan. However, the fact is that we shall not much longer in any case be able to prevent Chinese Communist admission into the United Nations and international negotiations relevant to its power situation and that the Chinese leaders, well aware of this fact, will not be prepared to pay a high price for such admission.

Consequences in Europe

Would this shift of emphasis and concentration from West to East undermine our European Alliance? The answer is: not if it is adroitly handled. There is already an increasing desire among West Europeans to improve relations with Russia and the other East Europeans. De Gaulle and the British Labor Government are likely to press further forward in this direction, in any case. There is also a growing feeling that it is no longer necessary to spend such large sums or immobilize such large forces for European defense. Defense requirements, which originally constituted the main factor of unity inside NATO, are fast becoming a main factor of disunity and disarray.

The exception, of course, is Germany, which very naturally continues to be preoccupied with the threat from the East and with its own artificial division. Any settlement which would relieve tensions in Central Europe and permit greater concentration by both the West and the

Soviets on the containment of China would have to involve solid assurances and advantages for the Federal Republic. On the other hand, the Germans should not be permitted through their excessive nervousness to veto any forward movement in their area to the detriment of the worldwide security of the West. After all, the Soviet Union would also have to receive solid assurances and advantages before it would agree to relax in Central Europe and shift a significant part of its military attention and resources to the Far East. The major reorientation of Soviet foreign policy which is here postulated, while constituting a return to historical norms and a natural reaction to Chinese aggressiveness inside the Communist camp, would nevertheless be a highly debatable and difficult step for the Kremlin to take and would call for great discretion and sophistication by the West if we are to facilitate the . . .[217] not obstruct it.

Control and Reduction of Armaments

Another necessary area of adaptation is that of disarmament. The importance of checking further nuclear proliferation is obvious, though there would seem to be little hope of persuading either the Chinese or the French to renounce the option, even though lacking the capacity, of nuclear equality with the US and the USSR. This factor of creeping proliferation must be considered in conjunction with three other negative factors in the armaments field — the enormous diversion of resources from more constructive tasks, the fact that despite all our safeguards the possibility of nuclear disaster through accident, miscalculation or escalation still hangs over us, and the growing frustration and anger of nonnuclear states that they are subjected to this lethal hazard without having themselves the slightest control over it. When these factors are coupled with the notable advantages to both the US and USSR of controlling and drastically reducing nuclear armaments before the Chinese Communists develop their own to a significant degree, both the necessity and the feasibility of much more rapid progress at Geneva would seem to be clear.

"Small" Wars and "Wars of Liberation"

This conclusion also seems to be supported by the fact that the immediate threat to international security is not directly in either the nuclear nor the large-scale conventional field. The actual and explicit, as distinguished from the potential and implicit, threat arises from two quite different types of wars, in which, however, the same relatively modest sorts of weapons are used. The first is a war between middle or small powers (Israel-Arab, India-Pakistan, Malaysia-Indonesia, Ethiopia-

[217] A word or words are missing from the declassified document sent to the editor.

Somalia, Greece-Turkey) which, if it broke out, could easily spread and involve Great Powers. The second type is the "war of liberation," which in its turn may be of two varieties, the genuine war of independence from a colonial master or a dominant minority, and the Communist "war of liberation," which may start as the first variety but is transformed into a war *to impose* a dominant minority, either the Communist or an allied extremist party.

Both these types of wars are very difficult for a single Western Power or even a coalition of Western Powers to deal with successfully, particularly if new or underdeveloped states are involved, because charges of "neocolonialism" are likely to create serious confusion and hostility not only in the country concerned but often throughout the whole adjacent region. Also, the nature of guerilla warfare, which is that generally employed in the Communist variety of "wars of liberation," is not one which Westerners, no matter how excellent their training and equipment, are well fitted to fight among and against colored populations. Sometimes, as in Vietnam or Borneo, there appears no feasible alternative but it is generally so precarious and disadvantageous a venture that Western Powers should exhaust all other possibilities of checking this type of war before becoming directly involved themselves.

Peacekeeping by Regional Organizations

Regional organizations have in this respect very obvious assets and should where possible be encouraged. The OAS coupled with the Alliance for Progress is the most highly developed instrument of this kind and could become even more useful if the radicalization of political regimes, which is presently so characteristic of underdeveloped countries, should spread more widely in Latin America. Even this regional organization, however, has serious limitations, as shown by its inability to deal effectively with the Cuban situation, which demonstrates once more that in checking radicalization an ounce of prevention is worth a pound of cure.

The Organization of African Unity is of course much more recent, more primitive and more ineffective. Despite some successes, as in the Moroccan-Algerian affairs, it has not yet proved to be a reliable peacekeeping instrument nor does it seem likely to become so in the near future. Nevertheless, it already has substantial value as a means of mobilizing African opinion and applying it politically if not militarily. Its future depends, first, on its avoiding domination by a few radical members and hence remaining truly nonaligned and, second, on its gradually developing more effective peacekeeping procedures and instruments. A danger, of course, is that it could become almost wholly obsessed with "liberating" Southern Africa. We and our allies should learn to take OAU more into account, to encourage its alertness to Communist subversion in Africa, and to help to strengthen it without trying to dominate it.

In Asia, of course, there is no broad and effective regional organization. Whether one can be created which will assume more of the burden of holding the line in Southeast Asia and elsewhere, depends on the degree to which India, Japan, Australia and New Zealand can be drawn into common defense arrangements as the Chinese threat expands, and how the hostile or unaligned elements *inside* the area to be defended, Indonesia, Cambodia, Burma, even Pakistan, are to be won over or truly neutralized.

With regional organizations and their individual members in Latin America, Asia and Africa, a further dilemma arises in that we need to arm them against external enemies but not against each other or against their own people. In fact, those remote from large-scale Communist threat should, in the interests of regional peacekeeping, be induced to disarm rather than arm. But how to do this when the Communists are usually ready to offer them arms when we do not? Eventually this problem will have to be brought into the complex of general disarmament negotiations, but for the present it can probably best be handled on the regional level.

United Nations Peacekeeping

This analysis of the serious inadequacies of other peacekeeping procedures, whether unilateral, Western or regional, emphasizes the vital importance of rapidly developing United Nations peacekeeping capabilities. The difficulties of doing so — Soviet, French and other opposition, the financing tangle, inherent administrative and logistic shortcomings — hardly need explanation. The point is that the general need for effective United Nations peacekeeping is so great that all of these obstacles must be overcome realistically and promptly. Practicable though far from ideal ways around Soviet and French opposition have already been found and repeatedly used; improvements in provision and supply of forces, of which the recent Ottawa Conference is an indication, are gradually being made. The principal remaining stumbling block is financial and it is absolutely essential in the United States national interest that, whether we "win" or "lose" on Article 19, practical and widely acceptable means of financing United Nations peacekeeping, to which the United States would contribute substantially, must be found. We clearly must not let the Communists exercise an indirect veto on United Nations peacekeeping by in any way tying our financial support to such operations, which is required to make them work, to Communist financial support of such operations, which is not required to make them work. What the Communists are trying to block now is not primarily the levying of General

Assembly assessments or the application of Article 19 to themselves, but the whole process of United Nations peacekeeping, particularly as applied to Communist-inspired or supported "wars of liberation." The primary United States objective in this area should be, not to make the Soviets pay up for the past or contribute in the future (desirable as these would be), but to ensure to the best of our ability that United Nations peacekeeping is revived and re-enforced despite Communist opposition, whatever twist or turn that opposition may take.

The North-South "Gap"

Another calamitous element in the evolving environment is one on which countless volumes have been written and speeches made but which still has failed to obtain the public recognition necessary to deal with it effectively. This is the enlarging gap between developed and underdeveloped countries. Means must be promptly found to convince public opinion in the former, despite its growing cynicism and weariness, that the world which will result from the aggravation of this development gap will be an extremely dangerous one for their children to live in. A failure of development to proceed with sufficient speed in underdeveloped countries — and what is "sufficient" will differ in each one — will inevitably result, despite whatever force can be exerted from outside, in the seizure of power by more and more extreme regimes in more and more countries. Even where these regimes are not Communist and in alliance with the Chinese, as some of them probably will be, they will be increasingly ready to attack white "bastions" in Asia and Africa. Eventually, if the disease is not checked, a general North-South confrontation, more uncontrollable and bloody than the East-West confrontation, may eventually emerge. In concrete, practical terms this means that the governments, legislatures and peoples of developed countries *must* be persuaded, despite their impatience with their alleged role of "Santa Claus," that larger bi-lateral and multilateral economic aid and technical assistance programs, as well as arrangements for trade and investment favorable to the underdeveloped countries, are in hard cold fact as much in the interest of North as of South, and that the alternative is disaster.

The Population Explosion

Finally, and closely related, is the problem of exploding populations, particularly in underdeveloped countries where aid and savings must be increasingly diverted from economic development merely to keep ever more numerous bodies and souls together, but also in some developed countries where the coincidence of geometrically progressing automation with rapid population growth can seriously upset even the modern guided economy. Both a forthright campaign of public education and a general program of governmental aid, such as have been successful in Japan, are required, first, merely to permit standards of living to rise but also, more fundamentally, to check the crazy automaticity of death control without birth control which, if unchecked, would before many more decades escalate all the problems of the world into intractability, intolerability, war and catastrophe.

Conclusion

In summary and conclusion, what is proposed in this memorandum is that the United States, reassessing realistically the trends of the times at this moment of danger and opportunity, should take account and advantage of those trends: (1) by beginning to shift the center of containment from Europe to the Far East and broadening the participation in containment in the latter area; (2) by encouraging, in consonance with the changing moods and basic needs of our allies, a gradual rapproch[e]ment as it occurs; (3) by pushing forward more boldly with the control and reduction of armament, particularly nuclear; (4) by developing rapidly, in face of reviving radicalism and international anarchy in Asia and Africa, improved methods of regional and United Nations peacekeeping; and (5) for the same general purpose, by expanding substantially international instruments and resources for accelerating economic development, international trade and investment, and balanced, progressive and complementary economic growth throughout the world.

On November 18, 1964, Stevenson spoke at the United World Federalist dinner, where Norman Cousins, editor of the Saturday Review, *received the Publius Award.*[218]

Publius was three men; [219] as you know from your scholarship — or at least from your program. The same is true of Norman Cousins. How can one man fill so many roles — distinguished editor, brilliant writer, indefatigable traveler, and constant toiler for peace — except on the chess table or the tennis court. And constant Counsellor and conscience of a former candidate for President — and I don't mean Nixon.

But there's an old English saying that three are too many to keep a secret, which proved to be true in the case of the original Publius. (And,

[218] A copy of this speech containing Stevenson's handwritten corrections is in the possession of Mr. Cousins.

[219] To help overcome formidable opposition to the ratification of the United States Constitution, Alexander Hamilton decided to publish a series of essays in New York newspapers. He enlisted the aid of James Madison and John Jay, and they published the essays under the name of Publius. The essays were later collected as *The Federalist*.

I could add, is demonstrated every day in the United Nations.) So we must assume the Publius we honor tonight is indeed one man, who sees as clearly as Hamilton, Jay and Madison that united we stand, divided we fall — and applies this principle to the world.

The parallel between the American Federalists of 1789 and the World Federalists is clear and often noted. One historian of the Nineteenth Century described the states, before the union as "The hope of their enemies and the fear of their friends."

The same is true of our disunited nations. If we cannot create a community of states, abiding by basic laws to safeguard the world, the un-United Nations will indeed be the hope of its enemies. One more nation now has the bomb — an aggressive, expansionist, dangerous nation.[220] But the proliferation of nuclear power even among allies or neutrals will indeed make each of them the fear of their friends.

It goes without saying that the more push buttons exist, the more likely it is that one of them will get pushed. No nation can guarantee to be forever free from madmen, one of whom could exterminate civilization with a flick of a finger. We know we have an awesome weapon — that we could kill more people than may be our enemies. And we in turn could be "over-killed," though I suppose that's no worse than getting plain killed, from a personal point of view. There is evidence that the other major nuclear power, the Soviet Union, knows this too.

But what of Red China, whose spokesmen have proclaimed that war is a means of spreading communism, that if half the world died the other half would remain, while imperialism would be razed to the ground?

There are a lot of people on mainland China, and the nation could certainly survive with fewer, but they themselves undoubtedly do not feel expendable. Sooner or later they may even be able to express this preference for existence over obliteration to their government.

As Norman Cousins said: "Even the most insulated and arbitrary government or system has to be concerned today about the turnings of the popular mind. Some systems may be less attuned than others but at some point all must pay attention."

The half of the world that Mao optimistically predicted as surviving would surely distrust any government — including their own — which had triggered such a catastrophe.

You may recall that it took nine ratifications from the thirteen founding states to make the Constitution binding. After the nine had agreed, the other four saw that it was not to their advantage to be left out.

---

220 The People's Republic of China announced on October 16, 1964, that it had exploded an atomic bomb, and it demanded a summit meeting to outlaw nuclear weapons and effect the destruction of all existing stockpiles of such weapons.

It does not seem now that Communist China minds being left out of the [nonproliferation] treaty which she called a "fraud" and a "trap." This in spite of the fact that her bomb is small.

It is not likely that it will be used in the near future. She has simply joined what might be called the power-elite of the planet.

I do not by any means depreciate this threat, and the pressure it applies upon other nations to join the power-elite. But most of the world believes that there is too much kill and over-kill already.

Prime Minister Shastri of India said the other day: "We have to arouse the conscience of the world against nuclear weapons. The UN is the proper forum where this should be taken up, and a united voice should be raised in the UN that would not allow the countries of the world to go against the Moscow test-ban treaty. Its sphere has to be further extended."

Such views have been expressed over and over by individuals, by resolutions of the UN and countless organizations — even by the non-aligned conference in Cairo a couple of weeks before the Chinese explosion — But no one in the whole world has raised his voice more often more eloquently than Norman Cousins — and his devoted admirer Albert Schweitzer. Indeed, Norman was so convincing that I followed my conscience and urged a test ban treaty in the campaign of 1956. Of course it was ridiculed by the opposition and I'm told it didn't cost me more than 3 or 4 million votes.

Such views have been expressed over and over and we must keep everlastingly at the task of peace and security. There is, of course, the little question of "how" — with which I am occupied all the time, and by that I mean seven days a week. But if those nations which want peace and disarmament will reconcile their differences and stand together, those which stand on the other side will be lonely indeed.

As in the case of the test ban treaty, we do not need absolute unanimity, any more than the original states did, to proceed toward a community of states under law. And some day, for practical reasons as well as moral ones, the disadvantages of standing alone, brandishing a bomb, will be apparent to all mankind.

Norman Cousins has long been a prophet of that day, and he has hastened us toward it.

I would like to quote him again, as I present this award:

"There is a primitive, colossal energy in the simply stated but insistent call by enough people for a situation of reasonable safety on earth, for an end to anarchy in the dealings among states, and for easier access by members of the human family to one another."

He has sounded that call, as Publius did in his time, and it gives me great pleasure to express the pride in his leadership of the United World

Federalists — and the gratitude of countless others besides — myself included!

To U Thant

November 24, 1964

Dear Mr. Secretary-General:

In my letter of October 26th I promised to inform you of any significant developments with respect to the observance of 1965 as International Cooperation Year.

I am now writing to alert you to what I consider a highly significant television series to be presented in late 1964 and, at various intervals throughout the coming year, which will attempt to dramatize the work of the United Nations. The idea for this series originated with a group of prominent Americans who felt, in particular, the need to acquaint the people of this country more intimately and fully with the important social and economic work of the organization. This series is being produced by the Telsun Foundation, a nonprofit organization created especially for the purpose. The $4,000,000 cost of the series will be underwritten by Xerox Corporation. No commercial advertising will accompany the presentations.

The television series will deal with a number of important themes and cover in depth such diverse topics as international narcotics control, the problem of stateless refugees, and peacekeeping operations. A distinguished group of international actors, playwrights, producers and composers have agreed to accept only Guild minimums for their part in the series, which means, in effect, they are voluntarily contributing their talent for this effort.

I will continue to inform you of other activities commemorating International Cooperation Year as they are brought to my attention.

Sincerely yours,

To Hubert H. Humphrey

November 26, 1964

Dear Hubert:

This is to remind you:

1. To read the memo I gave you, which is "confidential." [221]
2. To speak to the President about opening the convocation on *Pacem*

---

[221] The memorandum to the President of November 18, 1964, which Stevenson had just given Senator Humphrey at lunch.

in Terris [222] on February 18 in New York — which Bob Hutchins informs me you have agreed to close on the 20th. This would afford an excellent opportunity to the President to say something to a distinguished group of scholars from around the world about Pope John and the ecumenical movement, poverty, peace, etc.

3. If the subject should arise, to tell the President that you doubt if I am prepared to stay on this assignment indefinitely — and will talk with me again sometime at your leisure.

4. Send Muriel [Humphrey] back to New York and Stevenson whenever life becomes intolerable for her with H.H.!

Yours,

The controversy over Article 19 of the charter of the United Nations consumed an immense amount of Stevenson's time during 1964. [223] *When the General Assembly was to open in the fall, Article 19 would have caught up with the Soviet Union and the Eastern European nations except for Yugoslavia. In 1965 it would have caught up with France.*

According to Richard Gardner, the Johnson Administration wanted to avoid, if possible, the application of the article. [224] *But it was committed to the article in order to secure appropriations from Congress, to uphold the principle of collective financing, and to keep open the possibility of UN peacekeeping efforts in the future. The Administration did not want to have to apply the sanction and deprive the delinquent nations of their votes in the General Assembly since participation in the UN by the big powers was important to a viable world organization. Since President Kennedy, Rusk, Stevenson and other officials had stated to Congress that Article 19 would be strictly enforced against the defaulters, the Administration by negotiations hoped to persuade the delinquent nations to pay as much as possible.*

On March 1, 1964, Stevenson proposed to Soviet Ambassador Fedorenko that arrears be settled in a manner not detrimental to positions of principle. Stevenson observed that in making a "voluntary" payment adequate to avoid Article 19 no country was abandoning its position as to

---

[222] An encyclical issued on April 10, 1963, by Pope John XXIII which called for the formation of a supranational government, perhaps based on the United Nations, to insure peace. The encyclical also advocated a nuclear test ban and disarmament.

[223] For the development of this problem, see pp. 184–185, 223–224, 481–482, 488, above.

[224] "The Article 19 Crisis: A White Paper," an unpublished essay containing a detailed account of the controversy over Article 19 and a skillful analysis of American policy-making. A memorandum from Francis T. P. Plimpton to Walter Johnson, March 19, 1973, has been helpful as well.

the legality of the UN operations in the Congo and the Middle East.
Moreover, in the future the delinquents would not be asked to pay for
UN peacekeeping operations they objected to. On March 21 the Soviet
Union rejected the proposal and warned that certain actions could lead
to the breakup of the UN.

In August, 1964, after a visit to the Soviet Union, U Thant gave Washington officials the impression that he did not intend to press the Soviet
Union for payment and he made it clear that it would be unwise to apply
Article 19. But both houses of Congress, in a joint resolution adopted
without a dissenting vote, called on Stevenson to try to persuade the
defaulting countries to pay their debts. If they did not do so, Article 19
must be applied. Congressman Gerald Ford of Michigan reflected the
mood of Congress when he said: "I would like to state categorically that
I fully support what I believe to be the intent of this concurrent resolution, but in my support of it I want it clearly understood that the President and our representatives at the United Nations shall be very hard
and tough. There is no room for compromise. Our U.N. delegates should
demand that these other nations make their payments as they are
required to do under the Charter and the World Court decision. This is
not a negotiable issue in the U.N. Payment is to be made, or else." [225]

During the autumn, after lengthy discussions among Stevenson,
Francis T. P. Plimpton, Charles Yost and high officials in the Department
of State, it was decided to make credible the threat of applying Article 19.
It was hoped that the Russians and other defaulters, realizing that a
majority in the General Assembly would vote to apply Article 19, would
before the vote make "voluntary" contributions. On October 8, 1964,
USUN sent a memorandum to all UN members warning of the serious
consequences for the UN if Article 19 of its own charter was not enforced. Early in November the Department of State dispatched a circular telegram to American embassies — except to those in the Soviet
Union, Eastern Europe, and France — instructing the ambassadors to
emphasize at the highest governmental level why Article 19 had to be
supported. Failure to support Article 19, the ambassadors were instructed to say, could have serious consequences on U.S. support for the
UN.

While these steps were being taken to demonstrate the viability of
the sanction, Stevenson and others at USUN were explaining that the
U.S. was not insisting on a "victory" for its position but a resolution of
the question whereby both sides would maintain their legal positions. It
was emphasized that only a fraction of what was owed by the defaulters
needed to be paid, and these payments would not be earmarked for the
Congo and Middle East operations. In order to continue negotiations on

[225] Congressional Record, House, August 17, 1964, pp. 19884–19886.

this "voluntary" payment concept, the U.S. agreed to postpone the open-ing of the General Assembly from November 10 to December 1.

On November 20 Stevenson and Soviet Ambassador Fedorenko dis-cussed ways of avoiding a confrontation. Stevenson explained that while money must be forthcoming from the Soviet Union, it should be done in such a way that the legal position of both was preserved and no defeat for either side was involved. Fedorenko again rejected, however, the "voluntary" fund proposal, but he asked what would happen if all mem-bers of the UN wanted a postponement of the Article 19 issue. "Steven-son then took a historic step," Richard N. Gardner wrote. "Possibly, he replied, the issue could be postponed until March by dispensing with voting; perhaps the whole Assembly could be postponed." [226] In other words, the issue would be postponed through the Assembly's avoiding a vote and acting only by "consensus," without objection.[227]

According to Arnold Beichman, Stevenson's telegraphed report of this meeting caused consternation in the Department of State. He had changed United States policy without authorization.[228]

The next day Stevenson persuaded Dean Rusk to go along with the no-voting proposal. Beichman stated: "Stevenson's resolution of the dead-lock, even though it flouted State Department policy, had to be accepted because, confronted by a determined USUN Chief, the Department lacks a damage control mechanism." [229]

The no-voting plan was presented to the public as representing no change in policy but merely as a tactic to allow time for negotiations. But the State Department officials "who had been working on the Article 19 issue for more than three years knew it was more than that," Richard N. Gardner wrote. "In effect, the careful policy of firmness plus flexibility was being altered at the very moment it was beginning to bring results." [230]

[226] "The Article 19 Crisis: A White Paper."

[227] Letters that Stevenson wrote to Frank Altschul on March 8, 1965, and to Hamilton Fish Armstrong on March 15, 1965, suggest that Stevenson was trying to resist American insistence on the letter of the law, and that he placed the blame for the near-confrontation on United States domestic politics. Charles Yost stated that Stevenson had qualms about the legalistic approach and that Ambassador Plimpton's views did not always accord with Stevenson's. Interview with Walter Johnson, April 9, 1973.

[228] *The "Other" State Department: The United States Mission to the United Na-tions — Its Role in the Making of Foreign Policy* (New York: Basic Books, 1967), p. 155.

[229] Ibid., p. 157. Ambassador Plimpton recalled: "Adlai and I genuinely thought that there was a real chance that the Russians would make a voluntary contribution if they were given time through the no-vote device. . . . Unfortunately, as I've in-dicated, we were wrong." Oral history interview, October 21, 1969, p. 63, John F. Kennedy Library. He added that USUN should not have agreed to a "no-vote Gen-eral Assembly." Instead, USUN should have pressed for a showdown vote. Ibid., p. 60.

[230] "The Article 19 Crisis: A White Paper." Gardner also wrote: "On Friday, No-vember 20, 1964, two events occurred that will long be debated by historians exam-

Ambassador Plimpton wrote: "The General Assembly then proceeded to meet and act by 'consensuses' announced by the President, the 'consensus' as to an election being reached by informal ballots in his office. The Russians hinted they would make a voluntary contribution if they were allowed to vote, but would never disclose (even to U Thant) whether the contribution would be sufficient to make Article 19 inapplicable. Afro-Asian support, never certain, wavered with the urge to pass resolutions, and the charade finally ended, as the Assembly was about to adjourn, with a 'procedural' vote joined in by the defaulters." [231]

To Carlos Lacerda [232]

December 1, 1964

Dear Carlos:

I'm so disappointed that I missed you in New York on your last visit. I'm afraid I was in Washington when you were here — and vice versa.

We have today survived the opening of the General Assembly without major disaster after long weeks of negotiation with our Russian friends. There is just a chance indeed that we may be able to negotiate a settlement of the financial-peacekeeping impasse and have something more orderly to exhibit to you when you return.[233]

Cordially yours,

To John Fell Stevenson

December 4, 1964

Dear John Fell:

Please let me know — also Adlai — as promptly as possible if and when you are coming back for Christmas. There are many arrangements that Nancy will have to make. Also let me know about Emily Barnes [234] and her plans.

Things have been more hectic than usual here and I have had little time for family planning. I hope to be able to get out to Libertyville a day or so before Christmas and stay until after New Year's. But everything continues in doubt. I will try to keep you informed.

---

ining the Article 19 crisis. The first event took place in Ghana. Jacob Malik, a high official of the Soviet Foreign Ministry, hinted to Ghanaian officials that the Soviet Union was prepared to accept the 'rescue fund' plan. Malik expressed grave anxiety about the effects of a confrontation over Article 19 and urged the Ghanaian government to take up the 'rescue fund' compromise in an attempt to achieve a settlement of the question. This information was immediately reported to the U.S. Embassy in Accra and relayed to the Mission and the State Department."

[231] Memorandum to Walter Johnson, March 19, 1973.

[232] Governor of the state of Guanabara, Brazil.

[233] On December 1, 1964, Stevenson issued a press release on the no-voting formula. Department of State *Bulletin*, December 21, 1964, p. 891.

[234] Natalie Stevenson's mother.

I hope your ski companion from Austria is not going to become a visa problem after he comes to this country. Sometimes these cases become embarrassing if they overstay the period of their visa. . . .

And how are you, Natalie and John Fell!

Love,

To Lyndon B. Johnson

December 7, 1964

Dear Mr. President:

Some time ago you asked me about possible replacements for Angie Duke [235] and I suggested Ambassador William McCormick Blair.[236]

I have thought about the following possibilities, all of whom I believe have the conventional and additional qualifications you mentioned:

Ambassador W. Walton Butterworth [237]

Ambassador Randolph Kidder [238]

Joseph J. Jova, presently DCM [Deputy Chief of Mission] in Chile

Ambassador Robert McClintock

Ambassador Anthony Akers [239]

Of the foregoing, I think McClintock and Akers are the most readily available. You know Tony Akers, and while I regard him highly, I suspect Bob McClintock, most recently our Ambassador in Argentina, has more experience and enterprise. Moreover, he is an accomplished linguist and has a beautiful and animated Chilean wife.

Ralph Kidder's experience is extensive and certainly his wife, a granddaughter of Theodore Roosevelt, has all the qualities of energy, taste and enterprise you and Lady Bird have in mind.

But, probably because I know him so well, I still think Bill Blair could do the job perfectly, and I am sure his wife would catch on rapidly. However, I wonder if you should bring him back from the Philippines so soon.

Please let me know if you want my reaction to anyone else — or *anything* else!

Sincerely yours,

Congolese rebels in Stanleyville seized a number of whites as hostages. United States military transport planes flew Belgian soldiers to rescue them. Some hostages, however, were killed before the Belgian troops

[235] Angier Biddle Duke, chief of protocol in the Department of State.
[236] United States ambassador to the Philippines.
[237] United States ambassador to Canada.
[238] United States ambassador to Cambodia.
[239] United States ambassador to New Zealand, 1961–1963.

could occupy the city. On November 25, 1964, the Soviet Union denounced the landing of Belgian troops as a "flagrant act of armed intervention." For days the debates in the Security Council were bitter and acrimonious. When Stevenson was attacked in racist terms by one African representative, he responded angrily: "I have served in the United Nations from the day of its inception off and on for seventeen years. But never before have I heard such irrational, irresponsible, insulting and repugnant language in these chambers — and language used, if you please, contemptuously to impugn and slander a gallant and successful effort to save human lives of many nationalities and colors." [240]

To Sir Robert Jackson

December 11, 1964

Dear Robert:

It is a lovely cat — and is going home at Christmas to join my dogs.

You have made me *really* proud of that veto message so long ago! [241] But the Africans are rapidly sapping the remnants of my humor. We have suffered such abusive language in the last two days as never before in the history of the United Nations, and my patience is all but exhausted.

Happy Christmas and love to Barbara.[242]

Yours,

To Mrs. John F. Kennedy

December 17, 1964

My dear Jackie:

Would you like to go on a little junket with me to Washington on Sunday — fly down in a special plane in the afternoon and fly back fairly early in the evening. Here is the background:

Some time ago, Paul Hoffman and I got the Xerox Corporation to put up four million dollars to make a series of television "spectaculars" dramatizing some of the lesser known activities of the UN. They will be shown on prime television time over NBC and ABC during 1965. Many of the most famous movie producers, directors, writers, actors and actresses have contributed their services.

The first picture, Carol for Another Christmas, has just been completed

---

[240] United Nations, *Official Records,* Security Council, December 9, 1964.

[241] As governor of Illinois, Stevenson in humorous language vetoed a bill requiring cats to be restrained by means of a leash, and his veto message became widely known. See *The Papers of Adlai E. Stevenson,* Vol. III, pp. 72–74.

[242] Lady Jackson.

under the direction of Joe Manckeweicz. It will be shown for the first time at a private preview at the State Department Auditorium, under the auspices of the Secretary and Mrs. Rusk, on this Sunday at 5 P.M. There will be a buffet-reception at the John Quincy Adams room of the Department afterward. A special plane will fly a group of the movie people down to Washington leaving around 3 P.M. Sunday afternoon and returning to New York after the buffet.

It occurred to me that this might interest you and possibly Lee [243] as well. And think how nice it would be for your —

Devoted

P.S. If you want to come, just call me at YUkon 6–2424.

To Robert E. Kintner [244]

December 19, 1964

Dear Bob:

Good Lord, is it true that I have really been on MEET THE PRESS seven times? Once more and I ought to be entitled to permanent possession of the program. Anyhow, Bob, these appearances always offer opportunities of greatly increasing the popular understanding of many difficult situations and so I have been glad to take the witness chair from time to time when I have thought there was something useful to be said. It was nice of you to write to me.

Hope to see you during the holidays. Meanwhile, all the best to you and Jean.[245]

Sincerely,

P.S. The recordings [246] have just arrived, and I am so grateful!

Clayton Fritchey wrote in an undated memorandum that Stevenson was receiving a good press in the Chicago Tribune, *the New York* Daily News *and the Dallas* News. *These newspapers, traditionally hostile to Stevenson, praised his statements on the Congo rescue mission.*

Stevenson wrote on the memorandum:

Horrors! What are you doing to me?!!

AES

---

[243] Mrs. Kennedy's sister, Princess Lee Radziwill.
[244] President of the National Broadcasting Company.
[245] Mrs. Kintner.
[246] Of Stevenson's appearance on the program on November 13, 1964.

To Fernando Ortiz Sanz [247]

December 23, 1964

My dear Fernando:

Now that your term as President of the Security Council of the United Nations is coming to an end, I want to tell you how much I admire the skillful and judicious manner in which you have presided over the almost continuous meetings of the Council during the past month.

Among other items, you have had to deal with the conflicts in Cyprus, between Israel and Syria, and in the Congo. After long experience in the Security Council, I think I can say with confidence that the debates have never been conducted with more impartiality, efficiency and despatch.

I am proud to be able to call you my friend. And I wish it was my prerogative to thank you when you relinquish the Presidency on January 1, although it would be hard to thank you as gracefully as you thanked me a few weeks ago!

May I add to my professional admiration, my personal sentiments and best wishes for Christmas and the New Year.

Cordially yours,

The debate in the Security Council on the Belgian–United States rescue operation at Stanleyville occupied much of Stevenson's time all through December. The United States came under bitter attack. On December 10 the representative of Guinea, L. Beovogui, stated that Belgian, South Africa, Rhodesian, and Cuban mercenaries, "recruited and financed in the United States," massacred "hundreds upon hundreds of defenceless Congolese citizens." He continued: "The so-called civilized Government and countries which today denounce what they call rebel atrocities did not then express any indignation. . . . Is it because the thousands of Congolese citizens who have been murdered by the South Africans, Rhodesians, Belgians and Cuban refugee adventurers had dark skins like the coloured United States citizens who were murdered in Mississippi?" [248]

Mr. O. Ba of Mali charged: "Under the guise of a humanitarian action, the United States and Belgian Governments launched against the innocent population of Stanleyville and the surrounding area one of the most murderous operations which the Congo has witnessed. . . . In fact, it was a premeditated, cold-blooded act. The timing of the events shows

[247] Permanent representative of Bolivia to the United Nations.
[248] United Nations, *Official Records*, Security Council, December 10, 1964, p. 6.

that the freeing of the hostages was only a pretext for a criminal undertaking planned long before. The objective of the imperialist aggressors in that part of Africa was none other than the fall of Stanleyville, the stronghold of popular resistance to foreign domination and aggression." [249]

Near the close of his lengthy statement, Mr. Ba declared: *"We also wish to tell the United States of America that we refuse to let it play the role of international policeman, to set itself up as a judge of other nations. The sovereign equality of States is one of the great basic principles of the Charter to which we are deeply attached. This principle must be scrupulously respected by all, if we are not to become the jungle of nations. We want to help the United States not to export the 'ugly American' to Africa as it did to Asia."* [250]

Stevenson addressed the Security Council on December 14 and 24. His statement on the day before Christmas follows: [251]

Mr. President, just about everyone has spoken twice, so I will take the liberty of doing so, too. I shall not detain the Council long, however, as about everything that can be said, and should be said about this case has been said, including quite a bit that should not have been said.

When I spoke here a week ago [1174th meeting] [252] about the role of the United States in the Congo and in the mission to rescue the civilian hostages of many nations, held by the rebels in Stanleyville, I had high hopes that this role would be correctly understood, if not indeed applauded by the nations which had signed the complaint against my country. I had high hopes because the rescue mission was inspired by principles which I thought unassailable and by motives which I fancied were shared by all men of goodwill and of humane instincts everywhere.

In the intervening days of this debate I have been torn between disbelief at the incessant parrotlike repetition of absurd charges and sorrow that several African nations are disdainful, even resentful, of my country's long and consistent efforts to help achieve the unity, integrity and peaceful development of the Congo by assistance in many forms, first by the United Nations and subsequently by the central Government.

Yet these same countries proclaim again and again that an independent stable Congo is what they want. I believed them at first, and now I wonder what their real objectives are.

I heard no such complaints about United States aid during the years of the struggle to end secession in Katanga and preserve the unity of the

[249] Ibid., pp. 9–10.
[250] Ibid., p. 17.
[251] United Nations, *Official Records*, Security Council, December 24, 1964, pp. 6–10.
[252] This and subsequent references to UN meetings appear in brackets in the original.

Congo, when the troops of many Members of the United Nations were transported to the Congo in United States vessels and aircraft, used American equipment and were supported by American voluntary contributions and matching bond purchases when other means of financing failed. We did our part, as did many other nations, and in view of the accusations by a small group of African States, I am proud to recall in the Council today the part that we played at that time.

But for the most part, I have heard only a repetition of charges that my Government was insincere in its efforts to extricate the hostages, and that together with Belgium we planned aggression in the Congo, using the rescue mission as a pretext, and that we alone are responsible for frustrating peace and order in this troubled country.

Perhaps the most outrageous, the most despicable charge that we have heard in the Council during these proceedings was the one made yesterday that the United States and Belgium intentionally kept their nationals in the regions occupied by the Congolese rebels in order to have a pretext for intervention by military means. In effect, the Foreign Minister of the Congo (Brazzaville) accused my country [1184th meeting] of deliberately baiting a trap with unsuspecting human beings, of deceitfully leaving them to the tender mercies of outlaws and terrorists in order to have a pretext for intervening subsequently against those outlaws.

I shall say no more about this repulsive charge. I am sure, however, that, like the racialism that has emerged in this discussion, it will have been noted well by all responsible men.

The facts are that my Government sought to persuade all Americans, except the staff of our Consulate in Stanleyville, to leave the region prior to the occupation of Stanleyville by the rebels on 5 August. Our consular officials remained because it was their duty to stay until all others were out. These consular officials were, however, imprisoned and held as hostages until released by the rescue mission. Some Americans left, but others, particularly missionaries, refused to leave their posts at the side of the Congolese people to whom they had devoted their lives. Some in the bush could not be notified in time. Some who sought to leave failed to reach the airport before it was seized by the rebels. Some who had left the region returned, against our advice, in order to tend their flocks.

I have heard also some strange doctrines asserted here, provoked, I hope, more by emotion than by mature reflection. For example, that African States can intervene against a neighbouring African State while denying the right of other States to answer that State's call for help. I have heard a rebellion equated with a legitimate government — which must indeed be the first attempt to use the United Nations to validate an armed attack against a Member State.

And I have heard that the United States Government is indifferent to the death of Negroes in Mississippi and of Africans in the Congo, and that my country habitually seeks to overthrow unsympathetic Governments. I heard too, from a non-African source, the charge that my country sought to establish in the Congo a beachhead for colonialism in Central Africa for the purpose of monopolistic exploitation of the Congo's natural wealth. But thus has that source misdescribed for years of United States public or private efforts to assist underdeveloped nations, efforts which it cannot otherwise assail. The technique is old and familiar; what is new is the small chorus of African voices that now echo the same refrain.

The representative of Czechoslovakia claimed [1181st meeting] that NATO, which exists for the defence of Western Europe, had intervened in the Congo. He was quite mistaken. Two members of the North Atlantic Treaty Organization have taken certain steps at the request of the Government of the Congo. These steps have been fully explained and justified at this table. On the other hand, the communist States have never attempted to deny that they have intervened, often through military assistance, in what they call "wars of liberation." On some occasions they have assisted genuine nationalist movements fighting for the liberation and the independence of their countries. In many cases, however, they intervene in countries already independent and Members of the United Nations, on behalf of subversive movements or open rebellions against indigenous national Governments.

This is the sort of intervention by the established government of one independent country against the established government of another independent country which, if continued, will tear apart the fabric of international co-operation and world peace. This is precisely the sort of intervention in which the communist countries normally, regularly and as a matter of doctrine engage. We hardly think that this qualifies them to denounce others who furnish aid to recognized, sovereign Governments resisting armed rebellion inspired from abroad.

The bulk of the charges against my country appear to fall in the category of motivation rather than of facts, although, in some cases, the latter also are disputed. Allegations have been made which call into question the good faith of my Government and of the statements which I made here last week. This I can only regret, since motives — and other men's speculations concerning them — are, unfortunately, not provable. I have, as I said, explained my country's motives and purposes at length in my earlier remarks. I can only hope, in the light of what is known of my country's long record of assistance to other nations in their efforts to improve the lot of their peoples, that the leaders of the Governments represented here among the complainants will examine, in the privacy of their consciences, what I have said to this Council. If they do, I believe they will find that they do not themselves really believe their intemperate remarks. And if we question motives, I too could question theirs.

Socrates said in the *Dialogues* of Plato: "The partisan, when he is engaged in a dispute, cares nothing about the rights of the question but is anxious only to convince his hearers of his assertions."

And I recall, too, a Danish proverb, which has its equivalent in all countries, I dare say, that "Empty waggons make the most noise."

It is said that no foreign civilian was killed by the rebels before the Belgian paratroopers landed in Stanleyville. This too is demonstrably false. I reported earlier that thirty-five foreign civilians were murdered by the rebels in the several months immediately preceding the 24 November rescue mission. I have here a partial list of foreign civilians killed by the rebels this year prior to 24 November. The figure now amounts to sixty-four persons — and the end of this grisly story is not yet. I will spare you, gentlemen, the names, the places and the manner of their deaths. The list, however, is available for anyone who chooses to examine it.

History will record the long efforts of the Congolese Government to obtain help in the training, the disciplining and the equipping of its army in order to preserve law and order within its boundaries against the day when the United Nations forces would have to leave and that the United States and Belgium were among those who answered that call. It will record the fact that the rebellion was against the Government of Prime Minister Adoula in the beginning — a fact which the complaining nations seem to overlook. It will record Mr. Adoula's appeals to African nations to help him fill the void created by the final departure of the United Nations forces. It will recall their failure to respond, and it will also now record their denunciation of those who did. And it will also record the unashamed — indeed exultant — admissions by the Chiefs of State of Algeria and the United Arab Republic, President Ben Bella and President Nasser, that they are sending arms to the rebels to help overthrow the Government of the Congo and that they will continue to do so.

It seems to me I have been challenged here again and again to prove the complaint of the Government of the Democratic Republic of the Congo that members of the Organization of African Unity were assisting the rebels.

A few days ago we heard speakers say in this Chamber that the complaint of the Government of the Congo should be dismissed because "it has no substance," to quote the words literally — dismissed without substance when the charge is admitted, when we have an alarming preview of the kind of legality and of international conduct that they intend to practise regardless of what they preach about African brotherhood and unity.

Contrary to the bold assertions of the Foreign Minister of Kenya that the United States is frustrating peace in the Congo, I remind you that the promise of the United States to co-operate with the Organization of African Unity has already been reaffirmed in this Council and I repeat again that the United States, in spite of everything — the disappointments, the accusations, the contradictions in the reasoning — stands ready to co-operate with the OAU, with the Security Council and with the Government of the Congo in finding a solution, a *bona fide* solution, to the problems, political and economic, which beset this great country. And I now wish to appeal once more for an end to this ugly, abusive and dangerous polemic which has demeaned this hall of justice, peace and international fraternity. A calm and constructive approach to the perpetual problems posed by the Congo's long, hard struggle to preserve its independence, its territorial integrity and its unity may get results. But bitterness, hatred and falsehood will get results too, results that no one in his right mind cares to contemplate at any time, let alone on the eve of Christmas, the birthday of the Prince of Peace.

I say to the complainants that the hand is extended. If others will grasp it we may still be able to act before it is too late.

To Mr. and Mrs. Francis Carpenter

December 24, 1964

My dear Dorothy and Frank:

I have a confession to make. And it only increases my thanks! As I rushed out of the apartment for the plane to Illinois, I found a gift from [Ambassador] Fedorenko. And what did I do? I extracted that delicious fruit cake from my suitcase and sent it to Fedorenko! He doesn't deserve it, and my children do. But this is diplomacy, and you saved me in the nick of time.

As for the marmalade — no one could get that!

Love and everlasting thanks for all your kindness and loyalty,

Stevenson's Christmas card for 1964 follows.[253]

My dear friend — your Christmas message pleased me very much and I am most grateful.

I send you some words that seem appropriate to the season of hope —

---

[253] The message on the outside of the card was a reproduction of Stevenson's handwriting.

because they have often helped me in the clamor and conflict of my daily work among all the nations.

New York — 1964   ADLAI E. STEVENSON

"Grant us a common faith that man shall know bread and peace — that he shall know justice and righteousness, freedom and security, an equal opportunity and an equal chance to do his best, not only in our own lands, but throughout the world. And in that faith let us march toward the clean world our hands can make."

— An excerpt from a prayer by
Stephen Vincent Benét

Part Five

1965

*T*he increasing escalation of the war in Vietnam, American intervention in the Dominican Republic, the unpaid assessments to the
United Nations, and his declining influence in Washington were among
the most difficult situations Stevenson faced until he died on a London
street on July 14.

John Steele, the Time-Life *bureau chief* in Washington, wrote: *"President Johnson's taste runs to swift analysis of a situation, often brief
debate, and then crisp decision making. Stevenson worried a problem,
pondered it, qualified it, then came up with a recommendation. As the
President's decision-making group grew ever smaller, Stevenson was
moved ever further away from its epicenter."* [1]

On August 6, 1964, U Thant talked with Dean Rusk, Adlai E. Stevenson, Charles Yost, Averell Harriman, and William Bundy at the State Department and suggested that leaders from Hanoi and Washington should
talk face to face to end the fighting in Vietnam. Through the highest-
ranking Soviet citizen in the UN Secretariat, U Thant asked the Soviet
government to sound out the North Vietnamese about the idea. On
September 23, U Thant told Stevenson he had received a favorable response from Hanoi. Stevenson reported this to Washington. On October 15, Stevenson told U Thant that Johnson was too preoccupied with
the election and Stevenson advised U Thant to shelve the initiative for
the time being.[2]

[1] *Life*, July 23, 1965, p. 3.
[2] At the time of the publication of *The Pentagon Papers* in 1971, four volumes in
the study were not published. They have since been declassified. They are identified as Vol. VI, C. 1; Vol. VI, C. 2; Vol. VI, C. 3; Vol. VI, C. 4. Only Vol. VI, C. 1,
entitled *Settlement of the Conflict: History of Contacts—Negotiations, 1965–1966*
is pertinent to the period when Stevenson was UN ambassador. This volume does not
include mention of the U Thant–Stevenson peace initiative. Washington used Blair
Seaborn, chief Canadian representative on the International Control Commission,
who did not have access to Ho Chi Minh or other top officials, to transmit messages
to Hanoi. Other approaches to Hanoi are also discussed in this volume, including
the Soviet refusal in March, 1965, to be an intermediary. See pp. 117–120. I have

Stevenson later told Eric Sevareid that "someone in Washington insisted" that the attempt be postponed.[3]

After the November elections, Stevenson told U Thant that Washington, checking through its own channels, had received the impression that Hanoi did not want a conference.[4] U Thant on December 1, 1964, discussed the North Vietnamese offer with Ambassador Fedorenko and with Foreign Minister Gromyko.[5]

Early in January, U Thant pressed Stevenson for an answer from Washington. Stevenson, on his own initiative, asked the Secretary-General where the meeting might take place.[6] U Thant replied that Burma would be ideal. Stevenson asked U Thant to find out whether Burmese officials would provide facilities for the secret talks. On January 18, 1965, the Burmese agreed to provide the facilities.

U Thant told members of the Senate Foreign Relations Committee: "Ambassador Stevenson was informed and said he would convey this information to Washington. On January 30, Ambassador Stevenson told the Secretary-General that word had come from Washington that the United States could not hold these conversations because it would be difficult to keep them quiet and if there were any publicity, the Government of Prime Minister Quat in South Vietnam might fall." [7]

On February 16, 1965, Stevenson met with U Thant to find out whether there had been any reaction from Hanoi to the January 30 statement that the United States would not send a representative to the proposed meeting in Rangoon. The Secretary-General had received no reaction up to that date.[8] Then the Secretary-General suggested that the way to proceed would be to issue a statement which would be short of a cease-fire proposal but which would contain "some form of words regarding a more congenial climate for negotiations." U Thant suggested that if

relied for factual data on an unpublished manuscript written by U Thant. Richard J. Walton, 24 Cornelia Street, New York, New York, kindly sent excerpts from this manuscript.

[3] *Look,* November 30, 1965, p. 84.

[4] David Kraslow and Stuart H. Loory, *The Secret Search for Peace in Vietnam* (New York: Random House, 1968), p. 99. See also Mario Rossi, "U Thant and Vietnam: The Untold Story," *New York Review of Books,* November 17, 1966.

[5] Francis T. P. Plimpton, letter to Walter Johnson, November 15, 1968, after an interview with U Thant.

[6] Unpublished manuscript by U Thant. See also "A Conversation with U Thant, Secretary-General of the United Nations," by members of the Committee on Foreign Relations of the United States Senate. The conversation, which took place on March 22, 1967, was published for the committee by the United States Government Printing Office, March 16, 1972.

[7] Ibid.

[8] U Thant, letter to Walter Johnson, November 13, 1972. According to U Thant's notes, Stevenson "appeared distressed" at the United States' massive bombing of North Vietnam on February 7, while Premier Kosygin was in Hanoi as a guest of the North Vietnamese government.

bilateral talks were not possible, a seven-nation meeting might be held (perhaps in Rangoon), consisting of the two Vietnams, the People's Republic of China, the Soviet Union, France, the United Kingdom, and the United States.

Stevenson discussed this with Dean Rusk, who made it clear that the bilateral meeting had never been seriously considered because the United States could not possibly meet secretly behind the back of our ally. Stevenson argued that the United States should say it was ready to negotiate and propose a meeting of the seven nations. If an agreement was reached, Stevenson recommended that the United Nations be involved in implementing it.⁹

Stevenson left for Jamaica on February 19. On February 24, U Thant held a press conference and charged that the United States government was withholding the truth about the possibility of peace talks from the American people. In response to a question, the Secretary-General said: "I am sure that the great American people, if only they knew the true facts and the background to the developments in South Vietnam, will agree with me that further bloodshed is unnecessary. The political and diplomatic method of discussions and negotiations alone can create conditions which will enable the United States to withdraw gracefully from that part of the world. As you know, in times of war and of hostilities, the first casualty is truth."

Harlan Cleveland phoned Stevenson in Jamaica to be sure he understood what he considered to be the background of U Thant's charge. Stevenson described the background to Cleveland, starting with U Thant's proposal in August, 1964. Stevenson explained that Dean Rusk had dismissed the proposal on the ground that the United States could not talk with Hanoi behind Saigon's back.

After U Thant's press conference, reporters asked the White House about U Thant's "proposal." The White House, without checking with the Department of State, announced that U Thant had never made any proposal. Press Secretary George Reedy stated, "I know nothing about any proposals he has offered. The White House is not engaged in any negotiations." To a further question, Reedy replied that "there is no authorized negotiations going on, period." When a reporter reiterated that U Thant had said there were, Reedy stated: "Gentlemen, I am not going to get into a semantic confusion here. Obviously there are at various times diplomatic contacts going on at various levels of government throughout the world but from the standpoint of authorized negotiations going on, meaningful negotiations, no." Later Reedy was asked: "George, would the White House necessarily be the first channel of communication if a

⁹ On February 16, Stevenson sent a memorandum to President Johnson describing his conversation with U Thant.

proposal is made through Ambassador Stevenson at the United Nations or would any such proposals go automatically first to the State Department?" Reedy answered: "I am not going to go into the question of channels . . . but I think an honest answer to your question would be that there are no meaningful proposals for a negotiation that are before our government." [10]

When the White House statement was published, Harlan Cleveland phoned the White House and explained that although the Department of State considered U Thant's suggestion to be a "procedure," not a proposal, U Thant considered it to be a proposal.

At about 10 P.M. on February 24, Dean Rusk phoned U Thant. A memorandum of their conversation follows:

Memorandum of telephone conversation between Secretary Rusk and U Thant

1. At about 10:00 P.M. this evening, Secretary Rusk called Secretary-General U Thant regarding the Secretary-General's press conference of today.

2. The Secretary started by saying that there had been quite a reaction in Washington to the Secretary-General's implication that the truth was being withheld from the American people. Compared to other nations involved in the Vietnamese affair, the Secretary said, Americans are certainly much more fully informed.

3. U Thant inquired whether the Secretary was informed of his talks with Governor Stevenson over a period of the last year and a half. The Secretary said he was informed, but didn't see what bearing that had on this question of withholding truth from the American people.

4. U Thant said he had made "proposals" about Vietnam.

5. The Secretary said he was aware of that but that the proposals were just procedural, and did not deal with substantive questions or give any indication that talks would lead to agreement.

6. U Thant said he had sounded out Hanoi and that Hanoi had agreed right away to the idea of direct talks with the United States. However, he said that in answer to a similar approach he had heard nothing from the United States on this subject in six months.

7. The Secretary said that bilateral talks were out of the question, particularly since there were no indications they would be fruitful. The Secretary expressed his concern at U Thant's public statements that Burma was not getting any outside assistance. As the Secretary-General would know, Burma was receiving disguised military assistance from the U.S. Government in considerable volume; it was chargeable to our military aid appropriations on this end but treated on the other end as a purchase in local currency at a special rate.

[10] White House press release 618, February 24, 1965, 4:23 P.M. Eastern Standard Time, pp. 2–3.

8. U Thant said that when he was in Rangoon he discussed the whole Southeast Asia problem there, and formed the impression that Burma was not getting any military aid from anybody.

9. Reverting to the Vietnam issue, the Secretary asked whether the Secretary-General had any real indication from Hanoi of their willingness to stop the aggression.

10. U Thant said his approaches had dealt only with procedure. The Secretary said it was dangerous to consider only procedure without knowing whether anything could be accomplished through a procedure.

11. U Thant said again that he had had no response from Governor Stevenson on his "proposal." He had the impression that Ambassadors Plimpton and Yost were not informed of his discussions with Governor Stevenson. The Secretary said he was asking Ambassador Yost to see U Thant in the morning, and U Thant said he would reveal to Ambassador Yost the state of his efforts in this matter.

12. The Secretary asked whether U Thant thought he could do something to correct the impression left by his press conference, that he was aiming his comments at the American people over the heads of their own Government. The Secretary-General demurred at this interpretation of his remarks, and said the New York newspapers had not read them that way. But frankly, he went on, most Americans don't know the true facts about the war in Vietnam.

13. The Secretary repeated his earlier comment that the U.S. Government had informed its people very fully; especially was this so when compared to the Governments of the other countries involved.

14. The Secretary said he would ask Ambassador Yost to discuss further with U Thant the next morning the U.S. Government's reactions to his press conference comments on Vietnam.[11]

Harlan Cleveland stated: "The basic problem (I think) was that Stevenson did not like the answer he got from Secretary Rusk, hoped it would be moderated in time, and therefore did not pass it along to U Thant in a timely manner. This produced a growing resentment in U Thant, which finally boiled over in his February 24 press conference." [12]

After President Johnson spoke at ceremonies in San Francisco on June 26, 1965, to commemorate the twentieth anniversary of the founding of the United Nations, he left the podium and had a private talk with U Thant. Johnson told U Thant that the United States could not accept the proposed meeting with the North Vietnamese in Rangoon because

[11] This document was declassified. National Security Files, Agency File, USUN Re: SYG Statement Vietnam, Lyndon B. Johnson Library.

[12] Interviews with Carol Evans, May 24, October 11, 1972. The dictation was submitted to Cleveland and he approved it as an accurate record of his remarks. During late September, 1972, he consulted classified files in the Department of State to refresh his memory.

that would have undermined the Saigon government and led to its collapse.[13] *When Johnson and Rusk visited the United Nations in September, 1965, the two of them met with U Thant and Ralph Bunche. Johnson told U Thant that "he had never heard of the peace initiative."* [14] *Then Rusk said to the Secretary-General: "Stevenson was not authorized to reject the approach and he should have kept the channels open."* [15]

Eric Sevareid wrote: "Rusk has made that same argument to me privately, that he never told Adlai not to pursue the U Thant probes. This struck me as silly. Adlai never did have any authorization to pursue them or any encouragement to do so. What was he to do, continue on his own, entirely unsupported by his superiors and colleagues in Washington? How could he have done so when all of his soundings in Washington received negative reactions or, apparently, in the case of Rusk himself, no reaction at all?" [16]

According to a State Department document:

> Stevenson later told Cleveland that the answer from Washington was always: "There may be a time . . . but not now." (Stevenson–Cleveland Telcon, Feb. 13/65). Secretary Rusk's recollection was that it was one of those things he talked over with Stevenson along with others and because (at the time they were getting messages from various intermediaries) it did not have the mark of seriousness, he was very much afraid it was a move to embarrass us with Saigon and there was doubt of anything substantive. We did not reject it — we simply did not indicate that we wanted to go ahead at that time but put it on shelf for consideration for future. (Rusk-Ball Telcon, Nov. 17/65) [17]

[13] U Thant, interview with Walter Johnson, April 10, 1973.

[14] Ibid. President Johnson's statement is not believable. On February 16, 1965, Stevenson sent him a memorandum of his conversation of February 16 with U Thant through Johnson's aide Horace Busby. Furthermore, Bill Moyers, who was on the President's staff, wrote Adlai E. Stevenson III on August 17, 1972: "I did play some role because your father sent his original memo to the President through me, feeling, he later told me, that it would be assured of getting to Mr. Johnson. It did go immediately to the President and he called Secretary Rusk. . . . My wife and I subsequently had lunch with your father in New York and he lamented the murky ending to which the initiative and his memo came. He never understood why no one at any high level gave U Thant the benefit of any doubt." Moreover, Johnson had discussed the proposal with U Thant in San Francisco on June 26.

[15] "A Conversation with U Thant . . ." by members of the Committee on Foreign Relations of the United States Senate, p. 3. See Richard Barnet, *Roots of War: The Men and Institutions Behind U.S. Foreign Policy* (Baltimore: Penguin Books, 1973), pp. 90–91, 109, 111, for an analysis of why U Thant's proposal was ignored.

[16] Letter to Walter Johnson, August 16, 1968. Charles W. Yost wrote: "I do not believe that U Thant's proposal was 'turned down.' It was simply left in suspense without a reply for many months so that in effect it lapsed." Letter to Walter Johnson, September 18, 1968.

[17] "Chronology of U Thant Suggestion that DRV and U.S. Representatives Meet in Rangoon to Discuss Restoration of Peace in Viet-Nam." The "sanitized" declassified

Although some classified documents dealing with Vietnam were declassified for this volume, some requests were refused. The editor therefore presents the following selections with considerable trepidation. The
material that was declassified is so identified in footnotes. The remainder
of the material came from the unclassified Stevenson papers or from
interviews.

NOTES OF A ONE-HOUR AND TEN-MINUTE TALK WITH
PRESIDENT JOHNSON, JANUARY 5, 1965 [18]

Me [He?] — Could never replace you — brilliant job. Hate to think
what might have happened to UN. Want to make statement of appreciation, admiration, gratitude, and hope that you will continue throughout
my administration. I know how loyal and helpful you have been.

I said I appreciated his confidence but felt after 4 years might want to
go after G[eneral] A[ssembly]. I said he could understand how might want
to do something else and would talk again — hoped it wouldn't be for
long time. Suggested didn't have much policy consultation. Told him
others could handle domestic program and he should concentrate on
foreign. Said he agreed — 80%. But was going to try to drive his huge
program through before he got in trouble with Congress. They suffered
from inferiority complex. Properly. He knew! Would always pick at the
Executive to assert themselves — old idea that Executive derisive of corn-
fed tobacco-chewing Congressmen.

Proposed "bicker session" — AES[,] [Robert] McNamara[,] [Dean]
Rusk[,] [McGeorge] Bundy. Wanted ideas about China. Constant
references to V[iet] N[am]; all military proposed was bomb bomb bomb.
Would be Senate debate. Bad thing. Could collapse any time. Talked
about communication with Ho Chi Minh. What did I suggest? Please
talk with Wayne Morse and report to him. Remind he put him on the
F[oreign] A[ffairs] C[ommi]ttee day he joined Dem[ocratic] party.[19] I
said he had said such nasty things about me doubted any influence.
He — has said nasty things about everyone — except his wife.

Story of Wilson's visit [20] — State shove MLF [21] down his throat, or

---

version of this document sent to the editor had no date on it. The material covers
the period from November, 1963, to October 7, 1966. National Security Files,
Agency File, United Nations, Vol. 1, Lyndon B. Johnson Library.

[18] The original is in the possession of Adlai E. Stevenson III.

[19] Mr. Morse had been Republican senator from Oregon from 1945 until 1956,
when he ran successfully for the seat as a Democrat. Mr. Johnson was then majority
leader of the Senate.

[20] On December 7, 1964, Prime Minister Harold Wilson talked with Johnson, who
asked for limited or token British troops to be sent to Vietnam. Wilson refused.
Manchester *Guardian*, August 7, 1971.

[21] The United States proposal for a multilateral force of surface vessels manned

else! Close election — like LBJs — 4 seat maj[ority].; run on pound. Felt sorry for him — wouldn't hold him up and shake everything out of him. Told State to soft pedal MLF — and gave Wilson something to take home. — Made a friend.

Talked about past year — 85 heads of state for [President Kennedy's] funeral — 33 more since — Kennedys called him a buffoon — couldn't run without legislative program — had to drive it thru last year before election. Wanted to make as few changes in Cabinet and top [people?]. . . . Valued McN[amara] and Wirtz [22] highest — does job, concise, efficient, don't whine, Wirtz settles strikes, pulled State of Union speech together. Lady Bird and family love him. Everybody congratulating LBJ. Agnes Meyer — Mary Lasker. . . .

. . . Going to make H[ubert] H[umphrey] his closest in Public eyes — pile things on him. Resent[ment] of way JFK treated him very clear.

Sent for reporters and photogs for pictures of us — said just another of our periodical talks over 5 continents — especially Art. 19, Africa, VN etc and UN.

Skeptical if an advisory consultant position would be agreeable to me. Always running into Sec State here and Ambs. abroad. Thought [Dean] Rusk[,] [George] Ball et al conscientious and able. But never a new idea.

Gave me 2 lighters & tie clasp!

Looked brown and well — large paunch. Drank 2 orange drinks.

Couldn't talk about VN in speech — nothing to say.

With Congress — like a country dog. If stand still screwed to death; if run chew you out.

To Richard N. Goodwin [23]

January 5, 1965

Dear Dick:

My "holiday" was ruined by the Congo, Article 19, Security Council "considerations," etc. and two about-trips to Illinois to see the children, clear up the wreckage, do the diapers, put out the dogs and cats, etc., etc.

Hence inaugural production possibilities were nonexistent. But some tired old cliches fell from my palsied lips. Here they are — unedited! [24]

Perhaps you could salvage a word here or there. Please don't try to do

---

by crews made up of personnel from all NATO navies and armed with Polaris missiles. Only West Germany had responded favorably to the proposal.

[22] Willard Wirtz, Secretary of Labor and a former law partner of Stevenson.

[23] Special assistant to President Johnson.

[24] Stevenson submitted a draft for the President's inaugural speech at Johnson's request.

a rhetorical "jewel." It would sound too contrived and, *I think,* diminish him.

Hastily,

NOTES ON TELEPHONE CALL FROM MCGEORGE BUNDY ON BEHALF OF PRESIDENT JOHNSON, JANUARY 8, 1965

Bundy: How much LBJ hopes I can stay on here. Twenty people called after my statement on TV. Country has never had this kind of representation. Could I say "I have no present intention of quitting?"

Said Yes. He will generate a statement by [George] Reedy that LBJ has asked me to stay on and I have no present intention of leaving.

To Lady Barbara Jackson

January 8, 1965

Dearest Barbara:

And still we have no settlement with the Russians. Article 19 has almost caught up with the Congo for total time expenditure and frustration. Every time we get anywhere near a settlement with suitable face-saving scenery for the Russians, they back away and try to get a little more, in the usual fashion. With all the new Afro-Asians who are both casual about the constitutional integrity of the Charter and intimidated by the Russian threats of withdrawal, etc., plus the effective work of the Communist sympathizers, it gets harder and harder to negotiate anything. On top of it all, U Thant has been laid up with an ulcer and enfeebled. I can't predict what will happen, but if we have to have a confrontation I think our prospects of winning are slowly improving as the implications of exclusively volunteer financing of all UN operations begin to filter through.

And now we have Indonesia! [25] Well, there is, in short, no change in my circumstances and the "holidays" consisted of the Christmas weekend, then back to New York and back to Illinois for the New Year's weekend. But even that interrupted interval was a joy, with all the children and the bundles in good health and appetite. We spoke of you often and "Lady J's" absence was deplored by all, commencing with Katie.[26]

I had a long session with the President this week and he bathed me with gratitude, appreciation, and sincere insistence that I continue indefinitely. But I reserved my final decision until after the Assembly. So we should

[25] President Achmed Sukarno withdrew Indonesia from the United Nations in January, 1965, and threatened to establish a new organization made up of the "new emerging forces."
[26] Katherine Randolph Stevenson, daughter of Adlai E. Stevenson III.

have ample time to talk about it all when you return. I hope you will let me know your plans as precisely as possible. Can I assume that you will be here for my birthday party on February 5th? I have it on the schedule, and this year the party is given by the [James F.] Oates and [Edison] Dicks at the River Club.

Had it not been for you, I would have had nothing to contribute to the inaugural grab bag. I changed it about a bit, and what they don't use I can salvage for my General Debate speech in the General Assembly, I think. So your precious words are never wasted.

And while speaking of precious words, I am taking you literally and enclose a copy of the speaking engagements, with miscellaneous minors omitted. I have indicated the ones that will trouble me most, especially if the General Assembly gets going with a bang, not a whimper!

There is much much more to report, but it will have to wait — as usual! I pray all is well in Jersey [27] and that the holiday has given you a little peace and quiet after that horrendous schedule here and in Africa. Everyone that comments is bewildered by your strength and resilience and everlasting good humor.

Tell Robert he has first lien on 42A for '65.

Dearest love,

P.S. John Dewey got back onto the schedule, thanks to a brutal assault by the labor leaders in New York.[28]

P.P.S. And I'm not yet off of the Eleanor Roosevelt Foundation job, in spite of all my dexterous efforts!

To Mrs. Eugene Meyer [29]

January 8, 1965

Dearest Agnes:

A letter from Bill Dix, the Librarian at Princeton explains what you refer to in your letter of December 29th.[30]

I am flattered and grateful of course. But how in the devil am I ever going to find the time to sit evening after evening to record my "history?" But "oral history" is the fashion, now that no one has time to write, and I suppose I will get around to it some time — thanks to you.

I was even more interested in your invitation to Barbados but I fear

---

[27] The Jacksons' home in the Channel Islands.

[28] He was to receive the John Dewey Award from the United Federation of Teachers on March 13, 1965.

[29] The original is in the Agnes Meyer files, Princeton University Library.

[30] Mrs. Meyer had sent Mr. Dix funds to tape interviews with Stevenson on his life. The interviews were never conducted.

I shall be in the trenches all of February except for a few days speaking at the University of the West Indies in Jamaica. If I can't resist, however, don't be surprised if I turn up!

Love,
ADLAI

To Lady Barbara Jackson

January 13, 1965

Dearest Barbara:

I am back this very minute from the inauguration of Governor [Otto] Kerner in Springfield and a day at the Encyclopaedia Britannica Films meeting in Chicago.

Last night, following our usual dinner, they exhibited your picture on Britain. It was splendid and for the first time in more than 10 years I heard there was not a criticism! Moreover, they expect to work at once on plans for a premiere showing in New York, hopefully when you can be here.

As a capsule of the problems of Britain's economy it was splendid, and I'm afraid you may have still another career ahead.

Beware of Hollywood!

Love,

P.S. And this afternoon we may come to a showdown on Article 19, I fear!

To Otto Kerner

January 13, 1965

Dear Otto:

While the memory is still fresh, let me thank you and Helena [31] again for your many courtesies to me on that memorable day in Springfield. Every visit to that old house is full of reminders of the past, and it gives me a special satisfaction to have you living there for another four years. Besides, I'll be back!

Adlai [III] looks forward to his service in the legislature with an eagerness I had little expected in that much beset young man who has already had such a surfeit of politics and public life. I hope he will have some opportunity to be of service to you. I am sure he wants to, but he inherits a diffidence and shyness which may inhibit him a bit at first!

I have looked at the schedule on my return and I am afraid I must decline your invitation to speak at the affair on February 11th at the

[31] Mrs. Kerner.

Chicago Historical Society. From all indications, that will be a critical time for us, and moreover I seem already to have a conflicting engagement here.

You were good to think of me, and I am flattered and grateful.

Please let me know if there is anything I can ever do here or in Washington to ease your burdens, and give my affectionate regards and thanks to Helena. I do not overlook my honorable situation at her right on Monday evening!

Cordially yours,

To Philip M. Kaiser [32]

January 18, 1965

Dear Phil:

Some day I must try to recapture and tell you the incident in 1956 when I got word that [General Douglas] MacArthur was going to announce for me and was dissuaded with difficulty.[33]

I hope things go better for you in London than they do for me in New York these days.

Best wishes, my dear friend,

To Jack J. Valenti [34]

January 18, 1965

Dear Jack:

Jack Shelley, the Mayor of San Francisco, is pressing me for confirmation that the President will attend the closing ceremonies of the Twentieth Anniversary Commemorative Session of the United Nations in San Francisco on the morning of June 26, 1965. I hope you will see that this gets properly emblazoned on the appointment book, and as the situation develops we can talk about it again before he need make any final commitment.

As you know, the United Nations is at a critical period and his appearance at the Commemorative Session would be a significant gesture of support. If he could indicate his hope to attend, it would generate responses elsewhere in the world and strengthen the morale of many UN members and private organizations supporting its work.

As you will recall, the International Cooperation Year and the Com-

[32] Minister at the United States embassy in London.

[33] There is nothing in the Stevenson papers substantiating this statement. Neither William McC. Blair, Jr., nor Barry Bingham knows of the incident. Letters to Walter Johnson, October 17, 1974.

[34] Special assistant to the President.

memorative Session received emphatic encouragement at the meeting with the President in Washington. I should like to be able to send Jack Shelley and the Chairman of the Citizens Committee for International Year, Mr. Mortimer Fleishhacker, Jr., some encouragement now — if you can give it to me!

Cordially yours,

To Eduardo Frei Montalva [35]

January 18, 1965

My dear Mr. President:

This will introduce my old and dear friends, Mr. and Mrs. John Gunther. You are doubtless familiar with Mr. Gunther's books and his distinguished place in the literature of this country.

Mr. and Mrs. Gunther are travelling through Latin America preparatory to another book on the area of maximum interest to my country, and I am bold enough to ask you to give him a few minutes of your time, although I know full well your formidable schedule.

All the news I hear about the progress of your program is reassuring. And my heart and head are full of happy memories of your Inauguration. I am proud that I can say I was there on that historic occasion.

With warm regards and great respect,

Cordially yours,

During January the possibility of achieving voluntary contributions from the delinquent nations became increasingly remote. It was, however, decided by Stevenson and officials of the Department of State to make one more attempt to rally support for Article 19. On January 26, 1965, Stevenson spoke in the General Assembly.[36]

Like all here present, we have heard the news of the death by violence of the Prime Minister, Hassan Ali Mansour, of Iran with shock and with grief. On behalf of my delegation and my Government, I extend our heartfelt sympathy to the people of Iran, His Majesty the Shah and the Government of Iran, and the delegation of Iran to the United Nations, and most especially to our beloved and respected colleague, Mr. [Mehdi] Vakil, who has today lost a brother-in-law as well as a distinguished leader of his people.

Mr. President, this is my first opportunity to express publicly, on

[35] President of the Republic of Chile.
[36] United Nations, *Official Records,* General Assembly, January 26, 1965, pp. 11–16.

behalf of the delegation of the United States, our congratulations to you on your election as President of the General Assembly, and our admiration — I shall now add — for the manner in which you have conducted that office in most difficult circumstances.

I have asked to speak at this date so that I can share with all delegations, in a spirit of openness, with candour and with simplicity, my Government's views on the state of affairs at the United Nations as our annual general debate comes to its conclusion. Certain things which I shall say here today have to do with law, with procedures, with technical and administrative matters. So I want to emphasize in advance that these are but manifestations of much deeper concerns about peace and world order, about the welfare of human society and the prospects of our peoples for rewarding lives.

There can be little doubt that we have reached one of those watersheds in human affairs. It is not the first, of course, and surely not the last. But this is clearly a critical point in the long, wearisome, erratic, quarrelsome but relentless journey towards that lighter and brighter community which is the central thread of the human story.

Twenty years ago we took a giant stride on that historic journey. We negotiated and signed and ratified the Charter of the United Nations. The first purpose of the United Nations was to create a new system of world order. Those who drafted the Charter were acutely conscious of earlier efforts to find collective security against war and were determined to do better this time.

I speak to you as one who participated in the formulation of the Charter of this Organization, both in the Preparatory Commission in London and in the Charter Conference in San Francisco, under circumstances so eloquently recalled by Dr. [Alberto] Lleras Camargo in his memorable address on the International Cooperation Year in this hall last evening.[37] I too recall vividly the fears and hopes of those days as the World War ended in the twilight of an old era and the fresh dawn of a new one — fears and hopes which brought us together determined to ensure that such a world catastrophe would never again occur. At those conferences we laboured long and diligently; we tried to take into account the interests of all States; we attempted to subordinate narrow national interests to the broad common good.

This time we would create something better than static conference machinery, something solid enough to withstand the winds of controversy blowing outside and inside its halls. This time we would create workable machinery for keeping the peace and for settling disputes by non-violent means, and we would endow it with a capacity to act. This time we would create working organizations to stimulate economic

[37] See *The Papers of Adlai E. Stevenson*, Vol. II, Part Four.

growth and social welfare and human rights — and put resources back of them. And this time we would create a constitutional framework flexible enough to adapt to an inevitably changing environment and to allow for vigorous growth through invention, experiment and improvisation within that framework.

Twenty years ago nobody could see, of course, what the post-war years would bring. But there was a widespread feeling, in those bright, cool days on the rim of the Pacific, that the United Nations was our last chance for a peaceful and secure system of world order, that we could not afford another failure. For the character of war had evolved from a clash of armies for strategic ground to the possibility of the destruction of populations and the indiscriminate destruction of wealth and culture; the weapons of war had evolved from field artillery to block-busting bombs, and then to a single warhead that could wipe out a city; and recourse to war had evolved from what was cruel to what could be suicidal insanity.

Twenty years ago there was a widespread feeling, too, that it already was late in the day to begin loosening the strait jackets of unbridled sovereignty and unyielding secrecy, to begin systematically to build the institutions of a peaceful, prosperous international community in the vulnerable, fragile, interdependent neighbourhood of our planet. For science and technology were making the nations interdependent willynilly, and interconnected whether they liked it or not. Science and technology were making international co-operation and organization a modern imperative in spite of ideology and politics, and were paving the way for a practical assault on world poverty, if the world was up to the challenge.

It may well be that twenty years ago people expected too much too soon from this Organization. In the workaday world we quickly discover that social and scientific and institutional inventions — even important and dramatic ones — do not swing wide the doors to Utopia, but only add new tools to work with in the solution of man's problems and the abatement of man's ills. In the workaday world we also discover, over and over again, that man himself is a stubborn animal, and in no way more stubborn than in his reluctance to abandon the iron luggage of the past that encumbers his journey towards human community. In the workaday world we discover, too, that to be effective an international organization must be relevant to contemporary world realities, and that there may be conflicting views as to just what those realities are.

So we have learned how real are the limitations upon a single enterprise so bold and so comprehensive in its goals as the United Nations. We have learned how heavy are the chains of inherited tradition that inhibit man's journey towards wider community. We have learned that the United Nations will be no less — and can be no better — than its membership makes it in the context of its times.

And yet, we have seen that the Charter of this Organization has made it possible to maintain a hopeful rate of dynamic growth; to adapt to changing realities in world affairs; to begin to create workable international peace-keeping machinery; to begin to grapple with the complex problems of disarmament; to stimulate effective international cooperation; and so to move, however erratically, down the road towards that international community which is both the goal of the Charter and the lesson of history. I am proud to say that not only has the United States given of its heart and mind to this endeavour, but that over the years we have contributed more than $2,000 million to the support of the United Nations and its activities.

The progress which this institution has fostered has been accomplished despite the unprecedented character of the Organization, despite the intractable nature of many of the problems with which we have dealt, despite the so-called cold war which intruded too often in our deliberations, and despite a series of debilitating external and internal crises, from which the Organization has, in fact, emerged each time more mature and better able to face the next one.

In the short space of two decades, the United Nations has responded time after time to breaches of the peace and to threats to the peace. A dozen times, it has repaired or helped repair the rent fabric of peace. And who can say that this has not made the difference between a living earth and an uninhabitable wasteland on this planet?

During that time, the United Nations has sponsored or endorsed all the efforts to halt the armaments race and to press on toward general and complete disarmament in a peaceful world. Its efforts were not fruitless. Agreement was reached on a direct communications link between Washington and Moscow — a step lessening the risk of war through accident or miscalculation. A Treaty was signed — long urged by the General Assembly — the Treaty banning nuclear weapons tests in the atmosphere, in outer space and under water.[38] The two States presently capable of stationing nuclear weapons in outer space expressed in the United Nations their intent to refrain from doing so, and we adopted a resolution [1884 IXVIII)] [39] here calling upon all other States to do likewise. In short, the efforts of the last twenty years have at last begun to arrest the vicious spiral of uncontrolled nuclear armament.

In the short span of twenty years, the United Nations also has created

---

[38] Signed in Moscow on August 5, 1963.
[39] This and subsequent references to UN documents or meetings appear in brackets in the original.

a versatile range of international agencies which are surveying resources, distributing food, improving agriculture, purifying water, caring for children, controlling disease, training technicians — carrying on research, planning, programming, investing, teaching, administering thousands of projects in hundreds of places, so that, to quote the Charter, "we the peoples of the United Nations" may enjoy "social progress and better standards of life in larger freedom." These activities are now being financed at the impressive level of some $350 million a year.

In its brief life the United Nations has also taken major strides toward creating an open community of science — for the peaceful use of atomic energy, for the application of technology to industry, agriculture, transport and communications and health, for a world-wide weather reporting system, for shared research in many fields, and for co-operative regulation of the growing list of tasks — life frequency allocation and aerial navigation — which cannot even be discussed except on the assumption of international co-operation and organization.

We have proved in practice that these things can be done within the framework of the Charter of the United Nations whenever enough of the Members want them done and are willing to provide the means to get them done. In the process we have left well behind us the out-dated question of whether there should be a community of international institutions to serve our common interests. The question now is how extensive and effective these organizations should become — how versatile, how dynamic, how efficient — and based on what assumptions about the sharing of support and responsibility.

And yet, in spite of this history, we have reached a fork in the road ahead of this Organization, and thus in our search for world order and our journey toward a wider community.

Is this to over-draw the picture, to over-dramatize the situation in which we find ourselves? Not, I think, if we recollect the historic character of warfare. I assume that we are all convinced that the revolutionary advance in destructive capability — and the danger that little wars anywhere can lead to bigger wars everywhere — has made war an obsolete means for the settlement of disputes among nations. Yet World War II, I remind you, occurred after it already was clear to intelligent men that war had become an irrational instrument of national policy, that another way must be found to settle international accounts and to effect needed change.

The reason is not hard to find: the level of destruction does not obliterate the inherently double character of warfare. In our minds we tend to associate war — and correctly so — with the ancient lust for conquest and dominion; we tend, rightly, to identify war as the instrument of conquerors and tyrants.

Yet in every war there is a defender who, however reluctantly, takes up arms in self-defence and calls upon others for aid. And this is the other face of war: war has been the instrument by which lawlessness and rebellion have been suppressed, by which nations have preserved their independence, by which freedom has been defended. War is an instrument of aggression — and also the means by which the aggressors have been turned back and the would-be masters have been struck down.

As long ago as 490 B.C., Miltiades and his heroic spearmen saved Greek civilization on the Plain of Marathon. Nearly 2,500 years later, the gallant flyers of the Royal Air Force fought in the skies over Britain until the invading air armadas were turned back, while the indomitable legions of the Soviet Army fought on and on at Stalingrad until at last they broke the back of the Nazi threat to the Russian homeland.

All through the years we have been taught again and again that most men value some things more than life itself. And no one has reminded us more eloquently and resolutely that it is better to die on your feet than live on your knees than the noble spirit that left us the other day in London — Sir Winston Churchill.[40]

As long as there are patriots, aggression will be met with resistance — whatever the cost. And the cost rises ever higher with the revolution in weaponry. At Marathon 200 Athenians lost their lives. At Stalingrad 300,000 invaders lost their lives.

There, precisely, is the difficulty we are in. Now, in our day, the end result of aggression and defence is Armageddon — for man has stolen the Promethean fire. Yet resistance to aggression is no less inevitable in the second half of the twentieth century than it was 2,500 years ago.

The powers of the atom unleashed by science are too startling, too intoxicating, and at the same time too useful as human tools for any of us to wish to abandon the astonishing new technology. But if we will not abandon it, we must master it. Unless the United Nations or some other organization develops reliable machinery for dealing with conflicts and violence by peaceful means, Armageddon will continue to haunt the human race; for the nations will — as they must — rely on national armaments until they can confidently rely on international institutions to keep the peace.

This, it seems to me, makes the present juncture in our affairs historic and critical. This, it seems to me, is why the Assembly should be able to perform its proper functions in the event of an emergency, and why the issue before us must be resolved.

What then is the issue before us? It is, in essence, whether or not we

40 Churchill had died at the age of ninety on January 24 after having suffered a cerebral thrombosis ten days earlier.

intend to preserve the effective capacity of this Organization to keep the peace. It is whether to continue the difficult but practical and hopeful process of realizing in action the potential of the Charter for growth through collective responsibility, or to turn toward a weaker concept and a different system.

This choice has not burst upon us without warning. Some three and a half years ago, the late Secretary-General Dag Hammarskjold, in what turned out to be his last report to the General Assembly, foreshadowed this choice quite clearly. There were, he said:

". . . different concepts of the United Nations, the character of the Organization, its authority and its structure.

"On the one side, it has in various ways become clear that certain Members conceive of the Organization as a static conference machinery for resolving conflicts of interests and ideologies with a view to peaceful coexistence, within the Charter, to be served by a Secretariat which is to be regarded not as fully internationalized but as representing within its ranks those very interests and ideologies.

"Other Members have made it clear that they conceive of the Organization primarily as a dynamic instrument of Governments through which they, jointly and for the same purpose, should seek such reconciliation but through which they should also try to develop forms of executive action, undertaken on behalf of all Members, and aiming at forestalling conflicts and resolving them, once they have arisen, by appropriate diplomatic or political means, in a spirit of objectivity and in implementation of the principles and purposes of the Charter." [1]

If that language of Mr. Hammarskjold's seems mild and diplomatic, the warning was nevertheless clear. If it was relevant then, it is no less relevant now. If we needed an Organization with capacity for executive action then, how much more do we need it now.

There have been many challenges to the ability of the United Nations to act, from the abuse of the right of the veto to the effort to impose a "troika" to replace the Secretary-General. Now we are faced with a challenge to the Assembly's right even to engage in peace-keeping functions or to determine how they are to be financed and to adopt assessments to support them.

The decision to invest the General Assembly with the power over the

[1] *Official Records of the General Assembly, Sixteenth Session, Supplement No. 1A* (A/4800/Add.1), sect. I.

United Nations finances, its power of assessment, was made in 1945 when the Charter was adopted. Ever since then, an overwhelming proportion of the Members have been paying their assessments on the assumption and understanding that this was, in fact, the law — and that the law would be applied impartially to one and all.

Almost from the outset these assessments have included peace-keeping activities. Starting in 1947 the United Nations Truce Supervision Organization in Palestine, the United Nations military observer in Kashmir, the United Nations Observation Group in Lebanon and other similar missions, were financed by mandatory assessments under Article 17. For ten years no Member of the United Nations thought to refuse — as some are now doing — to pay these assessments, or to condemn them as illegal — as they now do.

When the assessments for the United Nations Emergency Force in the Middle East and the Congo operation were passed year after year by large majorities in the General Assembly, the Members clearly understood them also as mandatory obligations.

This was the understanding of States when they made voluntary contributions above and beyond their regular scale of assessments to reduce the burden on Members less able to pay.

This was the understanding on which the Members approved the United Nations bond issue, and it was the understanding on which the Secretary-General sold — and over sixty Member States bought — some $170 million of these bonds.

As the Secretary-General so aptly put it last Monday, the question is whether the United Nations will, in the days ahead, be in a position "to keep faith with those who have kept faith with it" [1315th meeting, para. 14].

When the argument was presented — in spite of unfailing United Nations practice — that peace-keeping assessments were not mandatory because peace-keeping costs could not be expenses of the Organization within the meaning of Article 17, that question was taken to the International Court of Justice for an opinion.[1] We all know that the Court confirmed the principle which the Assembly had always followed: peace-keeping costs when assessed by the Assembly — and specifically those for the Congo and the United Nations Emergency Force — are expenses of the Organization within the meaning of Article 17. We also know that the General Assembly, by a resolution adopted at the seventeenth session [resolution 1854 (XVII)], accepted that opinion by an overwhelming vote — thus confirming that the law was also the policy of this Assembly as well.

[1] *Certain expenses of the United Nations (Article 17, paragraph 2, of the Charter), Advisory Opinion of 20 July 1962: I.C.J. Reports 1962*, p. 151.

The Assembly's most important prerogative may well be its power of assessment. It is the heart of collective financial responsibility, and as the Secretary-General also said last week:

". . . a policy of improvisation, of *ad hoc* solutions, of reliance on the generosity of a few rather than the collective responsibility of all . . . cannot much longer endure if the United Nations itself is to endure as a dynamic and effective instrument of international action." [1315th meeting, para. 15.]

It is your power of assessment which is being challenged. It is the power of each Member of the General Assembly — and particularly those smaller nations whose primary reliance for peace and security and welfare must be the United Nations. And, make no mistake about it, it is your power to keep or to abandon.

We can live with certain dilemmas and paradoxes; we can paper over certain ambiguities and anomalies; we can ignore certain contradictions of policy and principle in the interests of pursuing the common interest of majorities in this Assembly. And we can, of course, change our procedures and devise new procedures, within the framework of the basic law, for handling our affairs in the future. Or we can indeed change the law. But we cannot have a double standard for applying the present law, under which we have been operating in good faith for the past two decades.

We cannot have two rules for paying assessments for the expenses of the Organization: one rule for most of the Members and another rule for a few. If this Assembly should ignore the Charter with respect to some of its Members, it would be in no position to enforce the Charter impartially as to others, with all the consequences which will follow with respect to the mandatory or voluntary character of assessments.[41]

This is not to say the procedures under which the Assembly exercises its authority should not conform to changed conditions and to political realities. Indeed, it is all-important that they do.

That is why my Government has suggested that a special finance committee, perhaps with a membership similar to the Committee of

41 Richard Gardner wrote: "It is one of the ironies of history that Ambassador Stevenson was prepared to deliver this statement . . . when the battle over Article 19 had nearly been lost—and that he was unwilling to make a statement of this kind earlier when it might have changed the course of events." When Stevenson met with delegations to get their support to invoke Article 19, he presented the course of action implied in these two paragraphs as only one of several courses to follow. Gardner concluded that "the inference drawn from his presentation was that he wanted no action taken to bring the matter to a head." "The Article 19 Crisis: A White Paper" (unpublished essay), pp. 29–30.

Twenty-One,[42] be established by the Assembly to recommend to the General Assembly in the future the ways and means under which it should finance any major peace-keeping operation — and that this committee should consider a number of alternative and flexible financing schemes whenever it is called upon for such recommendations.

We are not dogmatic about this proposal and we are prepared to examine patiently variations and alternatives with other Members — we have been for months and months. Certainly it should not be beyond the ingenuity of such a committee, on a case-by-case basis, to devise ways of assuring financing arrangements for the future which are generally acceptable, particularly to the permanent members of the Security Council.

But in favouring procedural changes we do not challenge the basic law of the Charter: we seek improved working procedures. We do not seek to undo the past, but to smooth the future.

We support the primacy of the Security Council in the maintenance of peace and security and would support an increase in its role; but we seek to maintain the residual right of this Assembly to deal with such questions in the event the Security Council fails to do so.

We support the right, under the Charter, of the General Assembly to assess the membership for the expenses of this Organization, so long as it enforces this power equitably and impartially; we will also support steps to assure that the views of all are taken fully into account.

We believe, as I have said, that the Assembly should continue, within the scope of its powers, to be able to deal, free of a veto, with problems of peace and security should the need arise. We are prepared to seek ways of accommodating the principle of sovereign equality and the fact of an unequal distribution of responsibility.

The question here is whether the United Nations will demonstrate again, as it has in the past, a capacity for flexibility and adaptation, which has permitted it to grow under the Charter as it has been accepted by most of us, interpreted by the Court, and endorsed by this Assembly.

My Government is quite clear about its own choice, lest that be a secret to any of you. We want to continue to do our full share in designing and supporting — morally, politically and materially — any sound expansion of the peace-keeping machinery of this Organization. We feel that there are possibilities for a more diversified family of weapons of peace in the United Nations arsenal — from conciliation procedures, to small teams available for investigation of complaints and for border inspection, to logistical plans for peace-keeping missions.

My Government also intends to continue the search for meaningful

[42] The Working Group on the Examination of the Administrative and Budgetary Procedures of the United Nations.

and verifiable steps to limit and, hopefully — hopefully, I repeat — to halt the arms race. For a peaceful world delivered of the burden of armaments, we will pursue with the urgency it merits the objective of stopping the spread of lethal weapons and of halting the multiplication of nuclear arms. This most urgent objective is in the common interest of all mankind. For if we fail to achieve it soon, all the progress attained thus far would be brought to naught and the goal of general and complete disarmament would become more distant than ever.

My Government is prepared to support a further enlargement of the capacity of the international agencies to wage the war against poverty. We would, for example, like to see the combined Special Fund and Technical Assistance Programme raise its budgetary goal well beyond the present $150 million once the two programmes have been merged satisfactorily. We would like to see a further expansion of capital for the International Development Association. We would like to see a further expansion in the use of food for development. We would like to see some major experiments in bringing to focus the whole family of United Nations agencies.

We would like to see, among other things, the Centre for Industrial Development intensify its work and become an effective laboratory for spreading the technology of the industrial revolution to the far corners of the planet. We feel that there are good opportunities for building up the institutions and programmes dealing with the transfer and adaptation of science and technology, and for developing the wise use of the world's most precious resources.

And, too, we wish to see the final chapter written in the drama of decolonization, and written peacefully. We, too, wish to explore the desirability of creating some new United Nations machinery in that most neglected area of the Charter called human rights. We, too, want to press on in such fields as weather forecasting, nuclear energy, resource conservation, and the conversion of sea water.

My Government is as anxious as any delegation represented in this Assembly to get on with these priority tasks, to press ahead towards the peaceful solution of disputes, towards co-operative development, towards building the law and institutions of a world community in which man can some day turn his full talents to the quality of society and the dignity of the individual.

This is what we have believed in and worked for at the United Nations for two decades now. This is what most of the Members have believed in and worked for as long as they have been Members.

What, then, is the alternative? What if the Assembly should falter in the exercise of its own authority? What if the Assembly should repudiate its own history, reject the opinion of the International Court, reverse its own decision with respect to that opinion, and shut its eyes to the plain meaning of the Charter, and thereby the treaty which gives it being?

I have no prophetic vision to bring to the answer to this question — for this would be a step in the dark, down an unfamiliar path. I can only say with certainty that the United Nations would be a different institution than most of the Members joined and a lesser institution than it would otherwise be.

I do not have to draw a picture of the uncertainties, the delays, the frustrations and no doubt the failures that would ensue were Members able to decide with impunity which activities they, unilaterally, considered to be legal or illegal and which, unilaterally, they chose to support or not to support from year to year. And so our world would become not a safer but a more dangerous place for us all, and the hopes for a strengthened and expanded and more useful United Nations would have been dimmed.

I must say in all earnestness that my delegation would be dismayed if at this stage in history the Members of the Assembly should elect to diminish the authority of this Organization and thereby subtract from the prospects for world order and world peace. If the General Assembly should now detour on the long journey towards an enforceable world order, I fear we will set back the growth of collective responsibility for the maintenance of peace.

Wise men drew a lesson from World War I and established the League of Nations. President Woodrow Wilson took the lead in that great experiment, and my countrymen, in hindsight, deeply regret that the United States did not take up its share of the burden in that historic enterprise. But the lesson of World War II was not wasted on this country, as our active leadership in establishing the United Nations and its Charter attests.

Who can say whether we shall have another chance to draw a lesson from another global conflict and start again? But this we know full well: we, the human race, are fellow travellers on a tiny space ship spinning through infinite space. We can wreck our ship. We can blow the human experiment into nothingness. And by every analogy of practical life, a quarrelsome ship's company and many hands on the steering gear is a good recipe for disaster.

In such a world there can be only one overriding aim — the creation of a decent human order on which we can build a reasonable peace — not simply the precarious peace of balances and alliances, not simply the horrifying peace of mutual terror, but the peace that springs from agreed forms of authority, from accepted systems of justice and arbitration, from an impartial police force.

That is why our commitment to an effective working, tenacious United

Nations is so deep, and why, in the most literal sense, the United Nations carries with it so much of the hope and future of mankind.

This is our position not because we, among the Members, are uniquely dependent upon the United Nations for the security and safety of our citizens.

This is our position not because we, among the Members, especially look to the United Nations for guidance and help for our economic development.

This is our position not because we found it advantageous to our narrow national interests to treat assessments as mandatory; we found it a price worth paying in recognition that others also shared the principle that all Members bear some measure of responsibility for maintaining the peace.

This is our position, rather, because we believe that in the nuclear age the only true national security for all Members lies in a reliable and workable system of dealing with international disputes by non-violent means — because we believe that we shall continue to face crises and problems which, by definition, can only be dealt with internationally — because we believe that workable, effective international institutions are a plain necessity of our day and age — because we believe that in every secure community shared privileges demand shared responsibility — and because we believe it unwise and unsafe and unnecessary to take a side road at this stage of the journey on which we set out together two decades ago.

Beneath all the complexities of the issue that now threatens the future capacity of this Organization, there are some very simple, very basic, very plain points to remember.

My nation, most nations represented here, have paid their assessments and have kept their accounts in good standing.

My Government, most Governments represented here, want to resolve this crisis without violence to the Charter and to get on with our international business.

That is why we have all stood available to discuss this issue at all times.

What we have sought is not defeat for any Member of this Organization. What we have sought is the success of the United Nations as a living, growing, effective international organization.

But the Assembly is now nearing a fork of the road, and I have attempted to put the issue frankly because the Assembly may soon again have to decide which branch of the road it will take.

And the very least that we can do is to be absolutely clear just what we are doing when we exercise that option.

Finally, I, for one, cannot escape the deep sense that the peoples of the world are looking over our shoulder — waiting to see whether we can overcome our present problem and take up with fresh vigour and with renewed resolution the great unfinished business of peace, which President Johnson has called "the assignment of the century."

The day Stevenson delivered a eulogy to Winston Churchill, he was accompanied by a staff writer for the New Yorker. *Stevenson flew to Washington, D.C. at 8 A.M. He delivered the eulogy at the National Cathedral, lunched at the British embassy, went to the Department of State for a conference, flew back to New York City at 3 P.M., held a staff meeting in his office at 4:30 P.M., and attended a cocktail party in the USUN Mission building. As he was about to leave, he received a phone call saying that William Benton had suddenly been taken to the hospital and there was a group of educators in Benton's apartment. Would he come and talk to them about the United Nations? After greeting each individual, he talked to the group for thirty minutes. The* New Yorker *wrote: ". . . he gave a brilliantly clear, concise, and orderly history."* [43] *At 8:30 P.M. he attended a concert of the New York Philharmonic.*

EULOGY TO WINSTON CHURCHILL [44]

January 28, 1965

Today we meet in sadness to mourn one of the world's greatest citizens. Sir Winston Churchill is dead. The voice that led nations, raised armies, inspired victories and blew fresh courage into the hearts of men is silenced. We shall hear no longer the remembered eloquence and wit, the old courage and defiance, the robust serenity of indomitable faith. Our world is thus poorer, our political dialogue is diminished and the sources of public inspiration run more thinly for all of us. There is a lonesome place against the sky.

So we are right to mourn. Yet, in contemplating the life and spirit of Winston Churchill, regrets for the past seem singularly insufficient. One rather feels a sense of thankfulness and encouragement that throughout so long a life, such a full measure of power, virtuosity, mastery and zest played over our human scene.

Contemplating this completed career, we feel a sense of enlargement and exhilaration. Like the grandeur and power of the masterpieces of art and music, Churchill's life uplifts our hearts and fills us with fresh revelation of the scale and reach of human achievement. We may be

[43] July 24, 1965.
[44] The text is based on USUN press release 4495.

sad; but we rejoice as well, as all must rejoice when they "now praise famous men" and see in their lives the full splendor of our human estate.

And regrets for the past are insufficient for another reason. Churchill, the historian, felt the continuity of past and present, the contribution which mighty men and great events make to the future experience of mankind; history's "flickering lamp" lights up the past and sends its gleams into the future. So to the truth of Santayana's dictum, "Those who will not learn from the past are destined to repeat it," Churchill's whole life was witness. It was his lonely voice that in the Thirties warned Britain and Europe of the follies of playing all over again the tragedy of disbelief and of unpreparedness. And in the time of Britain's greatest trial he mobilized the English language to inspire his people to historic valor to save their beleaguered Island. It was his voice again that helped assemble the great coalition that has kept peace steady through the last decades.

He once said: "We cannot say the past is past without surrendering the future." So today the "past" of his life and his achievement are a guide and light to the future. And we can only properly mourn and celebrate this mighty man by heeding him as a living influence in the unfolding dramas of our days ahead.

He used to say that he was half American and all English. But we put that right when the Congress made him an honorary citizen of his mother's native land and we shall always claim a part of him. I remember once years ago during a long visit at his country house he talked proudly of his American Revolutionary ancestors and happily of his boyhood visits to the United States. As I took my leave I said I was going back to London to speak to the English Speaking Union and asked if he had any message for them. "Yes," he said, "tell them that you bring greetings from an English Speaking Union." [45] And I think that perhaps it was to the relations of the United Kingdom and the United States that he made his finest contribution.

In the last analysis, all the zest and life and confidence of this incomparable man sprang, I believe, not only from the rich endowment of his nature, but also from a profound and simple faith in God. In the prime of his powers, confronted with the apocalyptic risks of annihilation, he said serenely: "I do not believe that God has despaired of his children." In old age, as the honors and excitement faded, his resignation had a touching simplicity: "Only faith in a life after death in a brighter world where dear ones will meet again — only that and the measured tramp of time can give consolation."

The great aristocrat, the beloved leader, the profound historian, the

[45] See *The Papers of Adlai E. Stevenson*, Vol. V, p. 388.

gifted painter, the superb politician, the lord of language, the orator, the wit, — yes, and the dedicated bricklayer — behind all of them was the man of simple faith, steadfast in defeat, generous in victory, resigned in age, trusting in a loving providence and committing his achievements and his triumphs to a higher power.

Like the patriarchs of old, he waited on God's judgment and it could be said of him — as of the immortals that went before him — that God "magnified him in the fear of his enemies and with his words he made prodigies to cease. He glorified him in the sight of kings and gave him commandments in the sight of his people. He showed him his Glory and sanctified him in his faith . . ."

Stevenson's caretaker in Libertyville wrote him, describing a severe ice storm that had damaged many trees on the farm.

To Richard Beake

February 1, 1965

Dear Richard:

I am heartsick about the news that Viola [Reardy] brought and your letter confirms. By all means hire someone to help you clean up the mess, and I hope you can get Hall [46] out there to trim and paint the worst wounds before the sap rises.

I don't know when I can get out there to look things over, but you can confer with Adlai or Nancy whenever necessary. I suppose the pipe froze under the kitchen sink — as usual — but if the house is not being used, perhaps that will take care of itself in time. Thank heavens you had enough water for the sheep, and I am delighted that the new lambs survived the storm.

I guess there is nothing we can do about repairing the backstop on the tennis court until the spring.

I was relieved to hear that you could make do without the electricity. Perhaps it's a good thing for your children to know how their great grandparents had to live on the Illinois prairie!

Thanks for your letter, and best wishes,

P.S. Archibald Enoch Price has sent me a proposal to spray the elms against Dutch elm disease during the dominant [dormant?] period. In view of the damage, I think Hall should send me a new proposal after the clean-up work and repairs have been completed.

[46] A tree surgeon with the firm of Archibald Enoch Price, of Winnetka, Illinois.

To Elizabeth Carpenter [47]

February 1, 1965

Dear Liz:

Respecting you as a master critic — I am delighted that you approve of my speech about Churchill at the Cathedral. How I wish that the President had sent me to London for the funeral of my old friend!

Frank Carpenter reports that the Carpenters, [Jack] Valentis, and Abels [48] will be invading this community on February 19, 20 and 21. I don't charge that you contrived these dates knowing that I was going to be out of town, but I am distressed all the same.

However, the U.S. Embassy in the Waldorf Towers is at your disposal and I hope that you will use it. I can provide two double rooms, one double bed and one single, and my housekeeper, Mrs. Viola Reardy.

I am obliged to go to Kingston, Jamaica, to speak at the University of the West Indies, together with the Queen Mother, on February 20th, and I suspect I may have to leave here on the 19th — God and Article 19 willing!

I hope very much that you will find an opportunity to send for Mrs. Emily Otis Barnes for that interview we discussed.[49] Her address is: 25 West 54th, telephone CO 5-2757.

Hastily and affectionately,

To Nikolai T. Fedorenko

February 2, 1965

Dear Nikolai:

You were most kind to invite me to hear Milashkina in PIQUE DAME at Lincoln Center on February 15.

I wish very much that I could hear this remarkable soprano. But I must go that night to the opening of "The Greatest Story Ever Told." The Eleanor Roosevelt Memorial Foundation is one of the beneficiaries of the proceeds and I am the Chairman of the Foundation. So, I must see a motion picture instead of listening to that great singer. It will have to be a very good picture to compensate me!

Sincerely yours,

On February 5, 1965, Stevenson celebrated his sixty-fifth birthday.

[47] Press secretary to Mrs. Lyndon B. Johnson.
[48] Elie Abel, a news broadcaster for the National Broadcasting Company, and his wife.
[49] Stevenson had recommended Natalie Stevenson's mother for a job.

To my dear friends on the second floor [50]

February 6, 1965

Nothing pleased me more on my birthday than your marvelous chorus. Little did I know that we had such a distinguished musical group in the Mission. And as for the librettist — what is she doing wasting her time down there with you singers!

I hope our choral society can meet more frequently. And if you need a good tenor (90% proof), there is a frustrated singer on the 11th floor.

Blessings — and may you all have many happy returns of the day!

To Hubert H. Humphrey

February 8, 1965

Dear Hubert:

Thanks from the heart for your note about the Churchill tribute. I won't tell Rembrandt or Picasso! [51] And I won't ask; I'll just wonder how you have time for such thoughtfulness.

I *pray* you and my beloved Muriel can find an evening sometime for refuge — rest — recreation with me in New York.

And perhaps there will be an opportunity to *talk* sometime, too. How much you mean to so many these days! — and to none more than me.

Yours,

P.S. And now I find your birthday telegram. "Wonder" becomes "marvel"! As for the candle — I lit both ends, of course. It cast a lovely light!

To Roxane Eberlein [52]

February 9, 1965

Tell Jerry [53] when he comes back to pick up some sandwiches Viola [Reardy] is making for lunch.*

Did we *rent* a car just to bring me from Waldorf this AM — It seems *so* unnecessary — with cabs all about and Doctors orders to walk more?

* Also there is a draft of speech for H[ubert] H[umphrey] for the Pacem in Terris convocation on desk in my study — *I think* — which Viola may be able to find and I wish Jerry would bring it back.

50 The Public Affairs Section of USUN.

51 The Vice President had written that Stevenson could do with words what Rembrandt and Picasso did with a brush.

52 This handwritten note is in the possession of Miss Eberlein.

53 Jerome Aprile, Stevenson's regular chauffeur. That morning, he drove the ambassador's car to the airport and another car drove Stevenson to his office.

To Loring C. Merwin

February 9, 1965

Dear Bud:

I am so grateful for your telegram, Marjorie's [54] lovely letter, and the editorial! [55]

I was distressed to hear about Marjorie's operation and I hope all has gone well. The party was riotous, as usual — if not more so — enriched with wit, humor, verse, song, food and drink! Somehow the familiar faces from far and near looked no older.

But I announced that this was the 15th running of the classic — and the last!

Yours,

To Anatoly F. Dobrynin

February 9, 1965

Dear Anatoly:

Your birthday letter pleased me a great deal. I am flattered, and grateful for your thought of me and send you and Mrs. Dobrynin my warm thanks and best wishes.

I wish I saw more of you both!

Cordially yours,

To Mary McGrory

February 9, 1965

My dear Mary:

Thank you for that kind letter about the Churchill rhetoric. If you approve, my cup is full.

I agree that both HHH [Hubert H. Humphrey] and AES should have been in London, but nobody ever asks me about these things either! [56]

I despair of ever seeing you here or of ever finding time there!

Love always,

[54] Mrs. Merwin.

[55] On February 6, 1965, the *Pantagraph* published an editorial entitled "Adlai Stevenson at 65." Among other things, the editorial stated: "Mr. Stevenson, at an age when many men retire, sets a pace that keeps his aides exhausted and the public marveling. If he can be spared for future service, he can become the Churchill of America. At 65 he puts the thoughts and dreams of people into electrifying words."

[56] At the funeral of Winston Churchill in St. Paul's Cathedral on January 30, 1965, Chief Justice Earl Warren represented President Johnson, who could not attend because of illness.

Stevenson delivered the following speech to the American Bankers Association in New York City on February 10, 1965.[57]

Our government has and can have only one overriding aim — to keep the world from war. There could also be no more ambitious aim, since war appears to be the one constant of human history.

However, mankind has not spent its entire time in fratricidal slaughter. Over large areas and for long periods men have lived at peace. These times and places coincide with the existence of steady institutions to mitigate clashes of interest and settle disputes. Peaceful times are also times of reasonable prosperity, when the temptation to grab your neighbor's hunting grounds is not acute.

In this century, we have known too little of either condition. While science and technology have made the weapons of destruction more and more terrible, the first half of this century saw two world-wide wars and one devastating depression also on a world-wide scale. We cannot, therefore, say that peace is a self-regulating principle in the 20th century, and I think it would be wise if we looked again at our recurrent disasters to see whether we are on the way to repeating them again.

In solving the problems that confront us, I suggest we have to look all the time beyond the narrow national interest to the wider community of man within which all national interests must coexist peacefully and cooperatively if we are not to wreck the human city. And if this is true of our economic existence, how much more true is it of our agonized political search for peace.

Once again our civil society is our model and our terrible recent wars our warning — for in 1914 and 1939, there were no institutions available to buy time and compel second thoughts. And that brings me to my own front yard. For the United Nations is the greatest post-war institution created to keep the peace this time and to create the preconditions of peace.

So much has been said by and about the United Nations recently, and so little has been done that I don't see how the most conscientious citizen can fully understand the merry-go-round on the East River.

First of all, we have had what we call the annual "general debate" with which the General Assembly opens. With 115 nations expressing their views about the state of the world the oratory has reached Niagara proportions.

Yet some of the greatest speeches I have ever heard have been made in the General Assembly, often by the representatives of small nations.

"If you were to make little fishes talk," said Oliver Goldsmith to Samuel Johnson, "they would talk like whales."

[57] The text is based on USUN press release 4499.

At the United Nations we have tried to substitute words for bullets, and so words are all important. If a delegate really has something significant to say, he will be listened to no matter how small his country may be.

La Rochefoucauld, the French seventeenth century writer, once said: "A man is like a rabbit: you can catch him by the ears."

That's the whole point of our general debate — to catch the world by the ears. . . .

On balance, as I have indicated, these statements by the member nations are full of rumblegumption, which is an old Scottish word for common sense; but in all candor, I must admit there are days when the debate is debased by demagoguery and shameless propaganda. (But who are we in this free speaking democracy to complain too much about that!)

We had such a moment only a few weeks ago when a number of nations indulged in unprecedented verbal violence against the United States for our actions in the Congo, particularly the rescue of innocent hostages from death and torture by the Congolese rebels.[58]

Great powers must practice restraint in the face of criticism. As a Spanish writer said long ago: "There is always time to speak a word and never time to unspeak it." We must always keep in mind that our very wealth and power tend to generate hostility. And there are many people at large in the world who are doing their best to discredit America and its motives and methods.

We cannot expect other nations always to see things as we do, or expect the very young nations to act like mature ones, or, rather, like mature ones *should* act. So we must keep our composure and try to be a little more philosophical about our changing position in the world and in the United Nations.

It has been hard for some of our people to realize that the United Nations is not a United States organization; that we and our western friends are not even a majority any longer. And perhaps it is even harder to get adjusted to the new realities — that there are other great centers of power and influence in the world; that we are not universally beloved or acknowledged as the conscience and policeman of the world; that as we have inherited much of the British burden of the 19th century so have we inherited much of the blame, not only for our own mistakes but as the scapegoat for the mistakes, failures and frustrations of others; that, in short, we now have to work for everything we get.

The General Assembly this session has been deadlocked by the dispute over the payment of peacekeeping costs. Those who refuse to pay assessments for peacekeeping costs in the Congo or the Gaza Strip, and those like the United States and the United Kingdom who say they

58 See pp. 651–656, above.

should pay like all the rest or lose their vote in the Assembly in accordance with the Charter have been on a collision course for a long time and collided head on in this session. The neutrality of many smaller states has surprised me. And I think of a story Brooks Hays [59] told me about the country boy in Arkansas who wanted a job on the railroad. The rural station master gave him a test.

"Two trains are on collision course. One," he said, "is approaching from the west at sixty miles an hour, another from the east at sixty miles an hour. What would you do?"

"I'd run and get my brother. He's never seen a big train wreck."

That phrase "collision course" is too familiar to me for comfort. Most of us at the United Nations have already seen all the wrecks we ever want to, and that's why we have all wanted to avoid a head-on collision over Article 19 of the UN Charter, which provides that members shall lose their vote in the General Assembly if they fall over two years in arrears in paying their UN assessments.

This has posed not only a legal but a grave political problem, and has finally, over several years, produced one of the most acute crises in the history of the United Nations but by no means the first.

From time to time, you probably have seen headlines proclaiming the UN on the verge of bankruptcy. That is not the case. Insofar as the regular, administrative budget of the UN is concerned, there is no problem. In fact, the record of financial responsibility, since the UN was founded twenty years ago, has been surprisingly good. Russia and the Soviet Bloc have always met their assessments for the normal activities of the United Nations. Even the original debt of sixty million dollars, borrowed from the United States to launch the organization, has been steadily amortized.

So, the financial plight of the UN stems almost exclusively from emergency expenses for special peacekeeping operations, notably in the Congo, and the Middle East in the wake of Suez. The United States and a large majority of other nations believe the Charter is clear and that the General Assembly has the power to assess members for these operations as well as normal ones. A minority, notably Russia and France, contend the Charter does not so endow the Assembly. They say that as peacekeeping is the responsibility of the Security Council, financing peacekeeping must also be the exclusive responsibility of the Security Council, where the USSR and France have a veto.

The dispute was taken to the Court of International Justice, which rendered a 9 to 5 opinion upholding the majority position. After that the General Assembly voted overwhelmingly to affirm the Court's ruling.

Despite this, Russia has declined to pay its share of the Congo and Middle East operations.

[59] Former representative from Arkansas.

As was long ago foreseen, this put Russia on a collision course not just with the U.S. but with the UN itself. There was bound to come a day when the Soviet Union's arrearage finally exceeded the limit permitted by the Charter, raising the question of Article 19 — the loss of its right to vote in the General Assembly.

This day came in December when the session of the General Assembly finally convened, but the actual showdown was put off by an agreement not to vote, to take action only on a non-objection basis. This has been possible because nobody — including the United States and Russia — has wanted to force a showdown in which many members would refuse to take sides and which might have grave consequences and permanently impair the usefulness of the United Nations.

The United States has not been inflexible. While we believe the constitutional integrity of the Charter must be preserved, and with it the principle of the General Assembly's power to tax and its residual authority to recommend peacekeeping operations where the Security Council is paralyzed by a veto, we have not insisted that the delinquents adopt our legal interpretation. We have not insisted that they pay up; we have long since agreed to a "voluntary contribution" sufficient to satisfy Article 19, without prejudice to anyone's legal position. We have indeed suggested that we too would make a voluntary contribution to help the organization restore its financial stability. The trouble is that the Soviets have insisted that they would not make even a voluntary contribution of undetermined amount unless we permitted voting to resume in the Assembly in violation of the Charter. We are not trying to score a victory over the Soviet Union and France; we are simply trying to score a success for the United Nations. We have been trying for long, weary, frustrating months to preserve the principle of the taxing power and peacekeeping influence of the General Assembly — which is the only recourse of the smaller countries.

Moreover, we have been urging the Russians since last March to discuss with us new procedures for peacekeeping operations and their financing for the future which might be more acceptable, but to no avail.

That is where matters stand now. The prospect is for another and longer adjournment while we try to negotiate a solution of the impasse. This Assembly has been stalemated, but not the UN. The modern world, the nuclear age, without collective security, without the UN, is unthinkable. Our job is not only to preserve it but to make it even more effective. We believe in it; most every other country does too, including the smaller countries. The issue is not just payment of arrears or sanctions. That is the smallest part of it. The real question is one of principle — of an effective peacekeeping instrument. And in the last analysis I believe as firmly as ever that the majority of the membership will not deny their parliament, the General Assembly, the right to deal effectively with peacekeeping; that they will insist on some role for the Assembly in preserving the peace of the world.

It is not we — the United States — who have used the right of veto to frustrate the majority will. On the contrary we have supported the United Nations in every way from the start; we have paid the lion's share of the cost of peacekeeping operations, and we have still to use the veto for the first time. It is they who evidently want only such peacekeeping operations as they can control in their political interest or none at all.

So I urge you not to believe the Cassandras who gloomily predict that the United Nations is going to collapse; that as the League of Nations failed because the US and the Soviet Union were *not* in it at the end, the United Nations will fail because they *are* in it. It is in a great crisis, but, as all institutions must change with changing conditions, this one will change somewhat too, but it will emerge from this crisis as it has from others because it has long since demonstrated its indispensability to the human race and withstood all manner of criticism and cynicisms, and dealt with all the most stubborn problems of the post-war world in spite of all its imperfections and frustrations.

When I listen to people complain about the UN and contemplate the state of affairs if we had no organized machinery to keep people talking instead of fighting, I think of the poor Roman who felt sorry for himself because he didn't have a shoe, until he saw a man who didn't have a foot.

There are those who criticize the United Nations for doing too little, for being merely a debating society. And then there are those who complain that it is doing, or trying to do, too much; that it is gradually becoming an action, as well as debating, society — that it is developing the capacity — for instance — to intervene effectively in situations that threaten the peace and stability of the world.

I think it is fair to say that the United States has encouraged this latter trend; that we have welcomed this evolution. I think it is equally fair to say that, on balance, Russia has not welcomed it.

The Soviet position has been that the Security Council, where it has a veto, has *exclusive* jurisdiction over all peacekeeping efforts. The United States believes that the Security Council has *primary*, but *not* exclusive jurisdiction. We have always felt the General Assembly has residual powers in this respect, and that it has the right to step in when the Security Council, through veto or otherwise, finds itself helpless to act in a situation that threatens the peace and security of the world.

But peacekeeping, be it in Korea, or Cyprus, or the Congo, or the Middle East, costs money, so there would be little point to the General Assembly intervening if its operations could not be adequately financed.

There are those who, like Russia and France, feel that, irrespective of the Charter, it is not realistic or practical to try to force a major power to pay for peacekeeping operations to which it is opposed. Frankly we are prepared to concede that, in developing a financing formula for the future, this view cannot be ignored. Our thinking, however, is that it can be given greater weight without depriving the General Assembly of all power and influence in the great decisions.

In any case, as we go into the new negotiations, our objective will be to preserve and, if possible, improve the peacekeeping capacity of the UN, which in recent years has done so much to halt or avert nearly every war, partial war, incipient war, or threat of war.

At this moment the Agenda of the Security Council of the United Nations lists fifty-seven international disputes. Some of them have been settled, some are quiescent, and others could flare again at any moment. The point here is that more than half a hundred international quarrels have been considered by somebody to be enough of a threat to the peace to take the case to the court of last resort — the United Nations.

This is not exactly peace — at least not the kind of peace that people have dreamed and hoped and prayed for. But the record suggests that if fighting breaks out somewhere tomorrow, the chances are good that the next step will not be the sound of trumpets but the call to cease-fire.

This is no guarantee that a way will be found to remove the root of the trouble: in the Middle East, Southeast Asia, and the Far East there are temporary armistice lines that have been temporary now for more than a decade. But in these affairs there are no victors and no vanquished — and in this sense we are all winners.

This record of violence — without war — suggests, then, that we may have slipped almost imperceptibly into an era of peaceful settlement of disputes — or at least an era of cease-fires while disputes are pursued by other than military means.

Man is adjusting once again to his environment — this time the atomic environment. The leaders of nations around the world — small as well as large nations — have, I believe, slowly absorbed the notion that little wars will lead to big wars and big wars to annihilation. *Perhaps* we are edging toward a consensus on the proposition that nobody can afford an uncontrolled skirmish anymore — that the only safe antidote to escalation is cease-fire.

I emphasize *"perhaps"* — for we must work and pray for that historical judgment on these times.

Yet skirmishes will occur — and will have to be controlled. Countless borders are still in dispute. Nationalism and rivalry are rampant. Ethnic and tribal and religious animosities abound. Passions and hatreds — ignorance and ambition — bigotry and discrimination — are all still with us.

If we did not have this organization in our troubled, revolutionary times, to preserve some semblance of reason and order in the nuclear shadows of our times; if we had no hope of evolving institutions for living in the international community as we have in our local communities, I can safely assert that we would have to start all over again to create such institutions. And it would be more difficult now than it was in the twilight of the last war and the dawn of a new and more hopeful day at San Francisco twenty years ago.

Most public interest in the United Nations centers on its peacekeeping activity, on the polemics of the cold war, on conflict, not cooperation. Yet, in fact, only 2,500 of the 23,000 members of the staff of the United Nations and its specialized agencies are working on peacekeeping operations: the other 20,000 are working on peace-building operations.

The enormous contribution the United Nations is making toward economic progress — helping countries to leap into the 20th Century — is scarcely comprehended, even by the well-informed. A newspaperman explained the lack of publicity this way:

"If you build a fifty-seven story building in the heart of Manhattan, you'll get a mention in the real estate section. But if you blow up a two-story building anywhere, you'll make the front page."

Reading so much about disagreements, some people get the idea that they are total. They may assume that if two countries oppose each other on topic "A," they also necessarily oppose each other on "B" through "Z."

We are engaged in nothing less than a massive unique effort to transfer and adapt science and technology from the limited areas in which they have flourished to the international community as a whole.

If more people can begin to grasp the fact of this great development — if they can begin to sense its significance — if they can share some of the hope that it justifies, they will appreciate better the pioneering work of the United Nations in its adolescent years.

This has been a political effort in the world community as it was in our own community. Electricity had been harnessed fifty years in the United States before it was put to work on the farm. It was political will that put it there.

It was political initiative which built TVA, the Grand Coulee Dam, the super highways, years after we knew how.

It was a political trigger which started the huge programs of research in science in universities and private industry.

And it is also political will which has inspired the members of the United Nations to establish programs of technical assistance. For we know that peace can never be secure when half the world envies the other half.

Winston Churchill said, "It is quite certain that mankind would not agree to starve equally, and there might be some very sharp disagreements about how the last crust of bread was to be shared."

Since the depression we have gradually got over the Robin Hood notion that to give to the poor we must rob the rich. We discovered nationally that everyone is better off in an affluent society. And although we have not yet won our own war on poverty, we have long abandoned the concept that it must be shared to be reduced.

The United Nations rejects that concept, too. In water resources, there are 91 projects underway. One is the Mekong Delta in Southeast Asia, where the river basin could be used for irrigation, flood control, and electric power — if it wasn't used for war!

Others include desalinization, which could have been available by the early 1950's if we had spent one-tenth of what the Manhattan project cost us to develop the atomic bomb.

In fisheries there are 22 projects to increase the harvest from the seas.

In locust control, projects in 38 countries may soon bring this ancient scourge under control.

And not long ago, agreement was reached to eradicate the rhinoceros beetle which causes severe damage to the coconut palm in the South Pacific.

One hundred countries are cooperating in a world weather watch. In two years our satellites have discovered 20 hurricanes, typhoons and other tropical storms and observed the behavior of 62 others.

Nothing, of course, is more global than the weather and the world is even getting together to do something about it at last — Mark Twain to the contrary notwithstanding.

An elderly lady in Seattle had an idea along these lines. "Why couldn't the delegates," she wrote me, "take a break every twenty minutes or so, and go out into the corridors and sing songs? Surely this would show the delegates that they could be in harmony at some point."

While I welcome all suggestions for reducing friction among nations, I felt obliged to point out the practical difficulties to her proposal. I'm afraid group singing would only increase the discords!

The role of government is to create a favorable climate and a steady stimulus for every force which can benefit mankind.

America has been operating on this principle. And as our federal government has provided the central impetus to reduce the differences in standards of living among our states, so indeed can the United Nations assume much the same role in the world.

And let us not underestimate the *political* importance of *economic* factors abroad any more than we do at home. Finally, let me repeat that, in spite of all the harsh words, most of the world knows full well that the economic growth, stability and magnanimity of the United

States, together with the simple fact that we have no ambitions in the world save peace, freedom and justice for all mankind, breaks through the clouds and confusion, the doubts and fears, and has been the greatest single contribution to the post-war survival of the human race.

To Horace Busby [60]

February 16, 1965

Dear Horace:

Thanks for your note.

The "memorandum" the President requested at the close of the Cabinet meeting regarding the political settlement in Viet-Nam was enlarged into a whole scenario of possible action in the Security Council and discussed with the President on Saturday by George Ball, I understand.

I have had a very significant talk today with U Thant and take the liberty of enclosing a copy of my report.[61] The President may wish to see it as a reflection of his views and concern.

Sincerely,

MEMORANDUM OF CONVERSATION [62]

February 16, 1965

Participants: Governor Stevenson
              Secretary General U Thant

Subject: Vietnam

(For more than a year U Thant has been urging bilateral talks between the United States and North Viet-Nam, with a view to exploring the possibility of a negotiated settlement of the war. After all of these proposals were reported to the State Department but not deemed feasible, U Thant himself renewed the proposal at length in the State Department at lunch in August 1964. Without reviewing the intervening events, he informed me that in December, through the Soviet Union he had made a sounding in Hanoi and that Hanoi was ready and willing to discuss Viet-Nam with the United States. He also informed me that Ne Win had changed his position, evidently at U Thant's urging, and would offer

---

[60] Special assistant to the President.

[61] It may have been this memorandum that Stevenson read in February to Henry Brandon of the *Sunday Times* of London. Brandon wrote that Stevenson pleaded "eloquently for the need to offer negotiations." When Stevenson finished reading, he remarked to Brandon: "I doubt whether they will pay any attention to this in Washington." *Sunday Times,* July 18, 1965.

[62] This document was declassified. National Security Files, Agency File, Representative of the United States to the United Nations, Lyndon B. Johnson Library. Harlan Cleveland sent a copy of this memorandum to Dean Rusk and George Ball.

Rangoon as a venue for discreet conversations. He also proposed Pakistan as perhaps the best available intermediary with Hanoi if we would consider his suggestion of bilateral talks.)

During U Thant's conversation with Ambassador Yost on Friday, February 12th, he said that he was still waiting to hear from Governor Stevenson about his suggestion, having received a "positive" response from Hanoi.

On February 16th, I called on U Thant and his views were substantially as follows:

"I do not think a Security Council meeting on Viet-Nam very realistic at this time although there is rising sentiment for such a meeting in view of the fact that fighting is going on and the United States has an obligation under the Charter to seek a peaceful solution. I doubt if a Security Council meeting could be successful because the other side would deny the competence of the United Nations, assert that the ICC [International Control Commission] was still in existence; the Soviet Union would say that it was a war of liberation, an indigenous civil war against colonialist puppets, and doubtless veto any resolution calling for a cessation of infiltration and a cease fire to be followed by negotiations.

"But I feel very strongly that further attempts at a negotiated solution should be made because there is a definite discernable trend toward closer rapprochement between Peking and Moscow and I am apprehensive about the resumption of the 1958 Peking-Moscow axis. Indeed, I consider it most dangerous and in sight. Hence I have been for a negotiated settlement for the past two years. Moreover, many of the Afro-Asians are very critical of the retaliatory bombing attacks. Already, Shastri, the Pope, de Gaulle, Ne Win and others have made statements. General Ayub is going to Peking in March and a statement is probable then or after Ne Win's visit to Ayub in Pakistan calling for a negotiated settlement.

"All of these developments weaken the United States position and it will be further affected by renewed bombing if it should take place.

"While I have strong misgivings about a Security Council meeting, I think the United States could state its position in a Security Council paper for circulation to the membership, and add such documentary and photographic support as it wishes. The other side could then reply if they cared to. The United States could express its readiness to negotiate and doubtless make a very strong case for its military action in the protection of South Viet-Nam's independence and territorial integrity. I am apprehensive about a Security Council meeting because it could also further damage US–USSR relations which had been improving until the unfortunate dispute over Article 19.

"If the United States is fearful of any sign of weakness, or if the

Congress would cause difficulty, or South Viet-Nam, and therefore the United States is reluctant to propose negotiations itself, I would be prepared to do so. I like the idea of a meeting with the two Viet-Nams, Communist China, the Soviet Union, France, the United Kingdom and the United States. I am not sure whether Ne Win would still wish to be host in Rangoon, and for a meeting of 7, Geneva might be better. The quick response I received from the Soviet inquiry in Hanoi that they were prepared to meet the United States anytime is further evidence, I think, that Hanoi is still anxious to keep flexible and not become a vassal of China. I would not wish to include in any proposal for such negotiations reference to infiltration or cease fire, but I could contrive some formulation of words regarding a more congenial climate for the negotiations.

"If any agreement was reached, I could see, as I have repeatedly said, the possibility of a useful United Nations involvement."

To Lyndon B. Johnson [63]

February 17, 1965

Dear Mr. President:

I am writing to you in elaboration of views I expressed on the Vietnam situation at the Cabinet meeting on February 11.

I have admired greatly your prudent and careful approach to this critical situation and to choices that are very difficult. But at least our purpose in Vietnam is clear and firm: to end the aggression and secure the genuine independence of the Republic of Vietnam — by peaceful means if possible, by military means if necessary.

I do not believe that we should pursue a harder military line with all the risks it involves without at the same time making it emphatically clear that we prefer a peaceful solution and that we are ready to negotiate. Moreover, I believe that escalation of the war would diminish our maneuverability and that we should move quickly.

In this connection, you will be interested to know of my conversation on Tuesday, February 16, with Secretary-General U Thant. He has offered to propose, if we agree, that the United States, United Kingdom, France, the USSR, Communist China, and North and South Vietnam open talks to explore the possibilities for peaceful settlement. He has serious reservations about going to the Security Council, believing Peking and Hanoi would deny the competence of the United Nations, USSR–US relations would suffer further damage from the debate and that any resolution calling for an end to infiltration and cease-fire would surely be

[63] This document was declassified. National Security Files, Agency File, Representative of the United States to the United Nations, Lyndon B. Johnson Library.

vetoed. He believes events are moving rapidly towards rapprochement between Moscow-Peking, accelerated by the air attacks in Vietnam; and that a proposal calling for negotiations would provide the USSR with a handle to bring Hanoi and Peking around rather than vice versa.

Bearing in mind the foregoing and based on the informal discussions I have had with Dean Rusk, George Ball and a few other officials in the Department of State, I have outlined a course of action below for your consideration.

Specifically, I suggest the following two steps:

First, an early statement by you which would (a) express our firm intention to continue all necessary military measures to stop the aggression; (b) succinctly set forth our peace (war) aims; and (c) indicate our readiness to explore the willingness of the Communists to accept a peaceful solution.

Such a statement would be circulated to the Security Council for the information of its members, possibly with also a full documented story of Communist aggression and infiltrations. A suggested statement is attached. (Tab A)

Second, by prior arrangement the Secretary-General would follow up our readiness for exploratory talks a few days later with an appeal to the United States, United Kingdom, France, Communist China, USSR and North and South Vietnam to open discussions to determine whether there exists an acceptable basis for a peaceful settlement safeguarding the security and freedom of the Republic of Vietnam.

It should be clearly understood that such an appeal by the Secretary-General does not include preconditions to talks re stopping infiltration and cease-fire. He can not include such preconditions because the other side denies that they are doing the firing and still insists that it is an indigenous civil war against "puppets of the imperialists."

I believe that our statement and the Secretary-General's proposal should be made within a very few days since military preparations or actions by the other side could make it more difficult for us to move onto the negotiations track. Our intentions should, of course, be discussed fully beforehand with the Government in Saigon.

Such a course of action would have broad support at home and abroad. It would provide the Soviets with ammunition in Peking and Hanoi. Such a proposal by the Secretary General would be more difficult for the Communists to reject than if made by us. It would move towards internationalizing the problem. It avoids the appearance of the United States suing for peace. It would set us on a diplomatic-military track which can not be attacked as either unlimited expansion of the war or appeasement. This course can be presented persuasively to the Government in Saigon and other key Asian allies as the political adjunct of our military step-up

and not as a sign of weakened resolve. I realize fully that Peking or
Hanoi may not bite. If they do, we can begin to talk. If they don't, they
would bear the onus. This would help justify politically necessary military action on our part.

If the above course is pursued, we should defer, pending the Communist reaction, any decision to convene the Security Council. I realize
there would be advantages to such a meeting. We could propose or encourage submission of a resolution calling for Seven-Power preliminary
talks of the kind we have in mind. We could present Communist infiltrations dramatically and graphically. If such a proposal was vetoed, or
Peking and Hanoi deny the Council's competence once again and refuse
to appear, the onus again would be on the other side.

However, I share the Secretary-General's reservations regarding early
recourse to the Council, and I think it would be better to pursue the
above diplomatic track and allow the Communists time to react. As the
Secretary-General says, an early public debate in the Security Council
will force Soviets to side with Hanoi and Peking and bring Moscow and
Peking closer together rather than farther apart.

One final point: the worst possible course would be for us to go into
the Security Council without a specific program for negotiations. A move
into the Council following another air strike designed to justify such a
strike without an accompanying proposal for peaceful settlement will, I
fear, put us on the defensive and build up pressure for negotiations on
terms and conditions perhaps less favorable. We would certainly be faced
with proposals seeking to tie our hands militarily.

I am sending copies of this letter to Dean Rusk.

Respectfully,

Enclosure: Tab A —
    "Suggested Statement by
    the President."

Tab A

Suggested Statement by the President

The regime in Hanoi is conducting a war of aggression against its
neighbor, the Republic of Vietnam. The conduct of this aggression depends increasingly both on arms and North Vietnamese armed units infiltrating across a line established by international agreement. The level
of troop infiltration has increased substantially in recent months and is
composed almost entirely of members of the regular armed forces of the
regime in Hanoi.

The Republic of Vietnam and the United States have responded to this aggression, in self-defense, and have in recent days undertaken operations against major staging areas and supply depots where infiltrating forces assemble for clandestine entry into the Republic of Vietnam. The United States in concert with the Republic of Vietnam will continue to take all necessary military measures to stop the Communist aggression against the Republic of Vietnam. The aggression must stop or be stopped.

Our sole aim is to secure and maintain the political independence and territorial integrity of the Republic of Vietnam which will permit it to develop its institutions and live in peace with its neighbors free from outside interference.

The United States is ready to withdraw its military forces from South Vietnam if — but not until — Hanoi decides to leave its neighbors alone and effective international machinery is established to guarantee the political independence and territorial integrity of the Republic of Vietnam.

We believe these objectives are attainable if there is a will to peace on the other side. We are willing to explore by any means which are honorable and constructive whether such a will to peace exists.

I am requesting Ambassador Stevenson to circulate this statement to the Security Council for the information of its members.[64]

To Mrs. Lyndon B. Johnson

February 18, 1965

My dear Lady Bird:

You were an angel to come up here for the opening of the "Greatest Story Ever Told." [65] It was certainly the longest story ever told. But, as one of my diplomatic colleagues said, anyway it had a happy ending!

I know how much inconvenience and energy even such a brief visit exacts. And I hope it's some comfort to you to realize what pleasure it gave so many — and none more than

Your devoted

Albania almost upset the no-voting agreement in the General Assembly (see pp. 644–647, above). The Assembly on February 16, 1965, was about to accept by consensus a resolution establishing a special committee on peacekeeping operations. Albania, however, demanded that the Assembly return to its normal procedures. The Albanian delegate re-

[64] On February 27, 1965, Stevenson submitted the document, entitled "Aggression from the North: The Record of North Viet-Nam's Campaign to Conquer South Viet-Nam," to members of the Security Council.

[65] The movie was shown to benefit the Eleanor Roosevelt Memorial Foundation on February 16, 1965.

fused to withdraw his proposal, which would have required a vote. Thereupon, the President postponed the Assembly for two days. Then, over the protests of Albania, the Assembly voted to rule voting out of order.[66]

Stevenson made the following statement to the General Assembly on February 18, 1965.[67]

Since 1 December, this Assembly has agreed, without objection, to act on the basis of a procedure the purpose of which has been to avoid a confrontation on a matter of basic principle so that, with adequate time, an agreed solution consonant with the provisions of the Charter shall be reached. Agreement has also been reached that the Assembly should proceed by recessing, after disposing of certain important items, to permit a new effort to be made to seek that solution.

One Member of the Assembly [68] has now challenged these procedures, previously agreed to by all Members in the best interests of the Organization. We are therefore faced with a situation where a procedural vote is regarded by many Members as necessary to confirm the clear desire and wishes of the overwhelming majority of the General Assembly.

Inasmuch as the procedural vote for which the President has called in connexion with his ruling deals only with the issue of whether the Assembly should or should not continue to proceed on a non-voting basis, and not with the substantive business of the Assembly, the United States considers that such a vote would not involve or prejudice the question of the applicability of Article 19 and that the question can in no way be affected by it. Accordingly, so that the overwhelming majority may not be frustrated by one Member and so that the Assembly may complete the substantive business currently before it on a consensus basis, the United States will raise no objection to the procedural vote on the challenge to the President's ruling.

He made a further statement to the General Assembly on February 18.[69]

I regret that I have felt it necessary to ask for another moment on this platform to exercise my right of reply to some remarks uttered here a moment ago by the representative of the Soviet Union, who charged me

[66] Ruth B. Russell, *The United Nations and United States Security Policy* (Washington, D.C.: Brookings Institution, 1968), pp. 202–203.
[67] United Nations, *Official Records,* General Assembly, February 18, 1965, p. 7.
[68] Albania.
[69] United Nations, *Official Records,* General Assembly, February 18, 1965, pp. 24–25.

with presuming to act as judge of the procedures of the General Assembly and with intolerable behaviour, and so forth, if I understood him aright. I should like to take leave to point out that the procedures were not determined by the United States; they were determined and decided by everybody in the General Assembly and reaffirmed this afternoon by an overwhelming vote — and I thought that that included the Soviet Union.

The Soviet representative criticized me for even mentioning the United States position on Article 19 when I rose here to consent to a vote in order to enable the Assembly to proceed with its business. But he did not hesitate to make a speech in justification of the Soviet position and of its refusal to pay its assessments under Article 19 in continued defiance of the opinion of the International Court of Justice and of the vote of the overwhelming majority of the General Assembly expressed in a formal resolution.

I had thought that the Soviet Union wanted to avoid a debate on Article 19 and a confrontation at this time, and it was because, as I said when I came here earlier, almost all of the Members also wanted to avoid a showdown at this time, that I did not insist on a prior decision by the Chair as to who was eligible to vote on the Albanian challenge to the President's ruling, but announced that on such a procedural matter I would not object to a vote to enable the General Assembly to finish its work.

If I have disappointed the representative of the Soviet Union in trying to accommodate the President and the Members, I regret that he did not express his objection to my agreement to a procedural vote at an earlier hour. From those who wanted to avoid confrontation, I had expected something better than this surly utterance from the representative of the Soviet Union. I deeply regret that the representative of the Soviet Union has ended the Assembly on such an unhappy note, with not only an attack on the United States, but a rigid, uncompromising reaffirmation of its rejection of the powers of the General Assembly in the field of peace-keeping.

I can only hope that the attitude presented by the Soviet Union today will not prevail in the consultations to which they have agreed.

On behalf of my Government, let me say, in conclusion, that we intend to enter the consultations in good faith, and we can only hope that the Soviet Union will do likewise.

Stevenson flew to Jamaica on February 19, 1965, and spoke at the University of the West Indies the next day.[70]

[70] The text is based on a USUN press release.

This University is fortunate to have such a gracious and eminent personage for its Chancellor. And I only wish the words were mine to say how deeply my introduction by Her Royal Highness [71] has placed me in her debt.

I am honored to be invited to speak here on this memorable day in the history of the University of the West Indies — a history that the world community of scholars expects to be long and distinguished.

My gratitude for your flattering invitation is multiplied by the privilege of meeting again Her Majesty, the Queen Mother, and witnessing the fitting award to her of your first honorary degree. This is not the first time I have seen her so honored. For Her Majesty and I were awarded honorary degrees at the bi-centennial convocation at Columbia University just 11 years ago.[72] How I happened to be included in the distinguished group of honorary doctors that day I never understood. Nor have I thought it discreet to inquire! But I have always treasured that meeting, as I will this one. In my own country and here on this lovely island in the sun, we owe much — much more than we can ever say or repay — to the courage and determination of the England of King George, Queen Elizabeth, Winston Churchill. So it is honor indeed for me to be here today with this gallant lady.

This is not my first visit to Jamaica or to this University. Indeed I have travelled joyfully around this lovely island from Port Antonio to Negril. I have even been to Accapong! And at the "Jamaica 300" celebration some years ago, before your independence, I made a speech here in Kingston — which surely must have been the first time an American politician ever joined in celebrating 300 years of British rule in North America! At the next Presidential election I was defeated, by the way; but I don't hold that against you, because I was defeated at the previous one, too! Indeed you have always been so friendly to me here, I have sometimes wondered if I didn't run for President in the wrong country!

So I am very much honored that you asked me again through my dear friend and colleague, Ambassador Egerton Richardson.[73] I came with alacrity and will leave with reluctance. And I'll be back to Jamaica and the West Indies as often as providence permits, because these islands and their stirring history have fascinated me since boyhood.

In her gracious welcome, Her Royal Highness, the Chancellor was good enough to refer to the combination of British tradition and American ideas as a happy one. I agree. And while I doubt if I can bring you any new ideas, if a visitor may be permitted a comment about your domestic affairs, I think the West Indies have been singularly blessed

---

[71] Princess Alice of the United Kingdom.
[72] See *The Papers of Adlai E. Stevenson*, Vol. IV, pp. 369–376.
[73] Permanent representative of Jamaica to the United Nations.

by wise leadership in the British tradition. Progress and political stability cannot be assured by leadership alone, but they can hardly be secured without it. And here, from the ashes of barbarity, piracy and slavery, have grown industry, agriculture and commerce on an expanding scale and with them civil order, education and a rising standard of living, not for just a few but for all — and now, beckoning vistas of an even brighter future in these small lands. But, as Thomas Huxley said: "Size is not grandeur, and territory does not make a nation."

You have lessons to teach all of us, not the least of which has been your peaceful transition from British colony to independent nation blessed with the heritage of British justice and public responsibility.

To these blessings we must surely add this flourishing university, first established in close partnership with London University and now launched on its proud career of independence. The fact that you now have a registration of 2,500 students when in 1948 you had just 33 points up the remarkable demand for your services. Another fact, however, that more than 10,000 West Indians still must seek higher education in the United States, Britain or Canada, underscores how great is the scope for further efforts.

In this you share the world's destiny.

I came across some startling figures about all this not too long ago. In 1950, it appears, there were upwards of 6 million college and university students throughout the world. When the decade of the 60's began, the figure had doubled. By the beginning of 1970, it will be higher still.

However, if you would really grasp the problem, you must look below the college level where 70 million children now attend schools in 200 countries around the world. This figure is greater than the world has ever known, but it palls into insignificance when we realize that there are at least 250 million more children for whom no education exists.

But I did not come here today to hurl statistics at you. I did come to talk about the central role the expanding university has to play in our shrinking world. In our day of sweeping scientific and technological change, when all of society has been thrust into an alarming turmoil, there can be no enduring peace unless *all* men everywhere learn to cope with their new and irrevocable environment. That is the real meaning of the educational statistics, the real scale of the educational challenge.

My concern about all this prompts me to take a day off from my usual business of foreign affairs and express to you on this commencement day a layman's thoughts about learning — thoughts close to my heart and which I would share with you.

It is, of course, par for the course that a graduating class be told it carries special responsibilities for the future. Do any of you remember Mark Twain's classic remark — which I always think of at commencements: "To do good is noble. But to tell *others* to do good is also noble, and much less trouble." I would not wish to deny you this imperishable bit of truth even as you leave this valley and the hills of Mona, and set about on the work of your life.

A wise man has said that a university's great task is not only to reflect yesterday, but to illuminate tomorrow. To do so, however, it first must help you to understand today.

For to me it is a certainty that we shall not attain tomorrow unless we control the forces that today have been unleashed in the small world in which we now live — a world in which, as I have said, the whole environment of the human species have been revolutionized.

All of us today — in whatever hemisphere, in states large and small, in nations ancient and nations new, in every culture — we have all been thrown into the violent slip stream of world history. The vast turbulence of scientific and technological change engulfs us all, washes away the ancient landmarks and leaves mankind to struggle for mastery on a world scene of headlong development and transition.

To an audience such as you I need hardly list the characteristics of this revolution — instant communication, the abolition of space, the interdependence of economic trends, the awful risk of annihilation. You know all this as well as I do. I mention them only because, as Chesterton once remarked, "Truisms are also true" and we must not let familiarity with the world's vast transformations slip into contempt for its equally stupendous risks.

As planet earth swings us through the heavens, none of us can escape the propinquities and risks of this strange, mortal journey. All of us are new to it. You may perhaps feel that you are more unfamiliar than older states with the rigors of our new world community. But in America — independent for nearly two hundred years, long since out of the colonial hatchery, astride two oceans, in resources and arms the most powerful state on earth — we, too, find strange this new inescapable world community. We believed until the day before yesterday that those same two oceans — with the British Navy as unobtrusive governess — could keep the bogeys away. Even after the first world war, we tried to retreat to isolationism. Even today, voices are raised suggesting we might do worse than try it again.

The truth is that our planet, our little space ship, is in many ways a drafty, uncomfortable and even dangerous place. And if our space ship had an escape hatch, I suspect, even now, there would be some people shouting — "Stop the world, we want to get off." But we can't. There is nowhere else to go and all of us, big nations, small nations, white men, black men, Christians, Moslems, Buddhists, Communists, Capitalists — we have to find out how to run the machine or face extinction.

There is no more awesome fact. And the fact is no easier to confront after two hundred years of supposed maturity than on the very morrow of independence. It confronts every nation, old or new, with a completely new set of challenges. None of us can subtract ourselves from the tides and currents of world opinion, emotion and ideology. By radio, by word of mouth, by visits and conferences, by propagandists and agitators — the various versions of world history, all trying to make sense of the unruly facts — or impose sense on them — compete for our attention and loyalty. We cannot switch them off unless we are ready to abolish hearing itself.

None of us can now pursue our own economic interests in our own way — large States can't because of the havoc they can create abroad; small ones can't because they have to adjust their policies to inescapable outside pressures. And no nation can pursue a political objective in blind disregard of others' needs and policies. The smallest local dispute has within it the seeds of escalation. Relatively speaking, large States may escape some of these economic and ideological and political pressures. But it is only a matter of degree. Sometimes a mouse can disentangle the net more skillfully than the lion. What is certain is that we are all in the net.

How can these facts of interdependence best be absorbed into the world's political dialogue? It is, I think, when we ask this question that the crucial role of the university comes into perspective. We have to have educated men and women in society with enough grasp of history and world development to face objectively and coolly the chaos of ideas, theories, doctrines, ideologies, anathemas and damnations. All these claim to interpret the facts — but if some truce among them is to be found, we must know the facts.

What forces have propelled the world wide thrust of western colonialism — and all but obliterated it overnight? What meaning can be precisely attached to the word "neo-colonialism"? What exactly is the effect of foreign investment on local economies? In Asia? In Africa? In the new world or Australia? Does the critique contained in Lenin's "Imperialism: The Last Stage of Capitalism" bear any genuine relation to the facts? If so, which facts?

I cite these questions because they seem to me to be the kind of questions with which citizens in new States and developing countries are likely to be confronted, and which must be judged factually if thought is not to be washed away in tides of prejudice and emotion. But the facts must be found. The habit of judgment must be learned. Evidence must be respected. And where else can all this come about save in school and university?

I would judge that in virtually every university in the modern world a strong, lively school of international studies could make an essential contribution to genuine national independence — the independence enjoyed by cool minds, clear of cant, who survey their world through eyes of informed judgment.

But I see the university's task here as more than one of instruction. Our new life on the global space ship requires far more research into the concrete problems of how we are to live creatively in our cramped quarters. Our scientific knowledge so far gives us little more than brute physical proximity. It does not tell us how to cope with it. There is, then, a large and, I would think, exciting field here of basic and applied research — to examine and expand the kind of institutions which, in the light of man's history — and, I would add, his psychology — are needed to give us a civilized world-wide human order in the age of atom and rocket — and potential annihilation.

By what reasonable steps can we extend and strengthen the idea of a worldwide rule of law? Should not every law school have a research section devoted to the rapid evaluation of the new reach of international law? Should not the law schools of various countries establish contact with one another to elaborate joint programs of research, to exchange findings, explore possibilities and create wherever feasible a common academic approach?

In the political field, Europe, Africa, Latin America and indeed your neighbors in the Caribbean are all, at this moment, experimenting with forms of supra-national association. The United States federal form of government may or may not be a suitable model.

But how much active work is going on in the political departments of universities to bring this into clearer focus, how many universities are reaching out to see what ideas and possibilities the others may have to share?

Or, if we approach supra-national institutions from a rather different perspective, how much inter-university research has been stimulated on the issue of strengthening the authority of the United Nations and modifying claims of total national sovereignty? Joint projects by universities in countries of differing political viewpoints might yield interesting results.

As any politician will tell you — and I do not shun the label — the world of active politics is always long on pressures, compulsions, ambitions, compromise and balancing acts. It is always short on new creative policies and ideas.

And here I say to you what I recently told an American University — the more universities can, as it were, nourish the political process, the more promising will become our search for a more stable world. It is virtually impossible for governments to create the research teams needed for this. But universities can do so, and provide invaluable assistance to public action — as well as invaluable contributions to their own research.

For surely it is the special task of the academic mind, dedicated as it is to the loftiest of human tasks, the dispassionate, objective search for knowledge to reinforce the unities and common sanctities of the family of man.

When we turn to the facts of economic interdependence, the university's function is no less crucial. It has here a double role of enlightenment and training. All the nations have to learn the hard lessons of economic survival. You may think that new nations have more difficulty in coming to terms with an international existence in which major economic issues are still defined and determined by forces far beyond the reach of sovereignty. But in more or less degree this peculiar combination of sovereignty and powerlessness confronts us all. The most powerful economic community in the world — my own — is reminded by such persistent troubles as our unfavorable balance of payments that we cannot live in this world without being profoundly affected by its reactions.

None of us, great or small, can survive without policies and institutions which reconcile local interests with the sweep of economic interest and change all round the world. Indeed, I believe the most hopeful feature of the world after 1945 — compared with the world after 1919 — is that statesmen were wise enough after the second world war to create new functioning international agencies through which nations could reconcile their interests and avoid for all time the disasters of 1929 when each state's efforts to secure only its own survival ended in the shipwreck of all. The International Monetary Fund, the World Bank and the International Development Association, the General Agreement on Trade and Tariffs, regional groupings and development banks, such United Nations conferences as those on technology or on trade and development — these are the new instruments through which we can all mediate our differences and work for a more smoothly functioning world economy.

And one of the essential tasks of a university is to explain the functioning of this international economic system to which we all belong whether we like it or not, and to train men and women to work in this new field of world-wide economic diplomacy.

I hardly think I need to say much about this essential task of training. We are beginning to get the processes of education into proper perspective in our studies of the needs of economic development. Some experts reckon that in the last 70 or 80 years perhaps two-thirds of the increase in our powers to produce wealth came not from more and better machines but from better trained and more sophisticated minds. When you see large, old-established powers such as Britain and America making educational reform and advance a central feature of government policy, you will understand to what degree the upgrading of skills, the enlargement of capacity, the production of skilled people at every level are the precondition of successful adaptation and growth.

Thus your university stands at the very center of the modern state's central preoccupation.

Moreover, it seems to me, universities such as yours which are young enough and flexible enough to experiment with new educational possibilities can take advantage of the variety of university models round the world and look boldly for the types and programs which best suit their own needs. Returning to our two English-speaking models — in America and in Britain — I find it significant that just as America is beginning to put more emphasis on quality and on the building of an intellectual elite, the British show growing concern at the relatively small proportion of young people receiving higher education, and are considering heroic measures to expand their colleges.

There is, we thus discover, no virtue in either extreme. Modern society needs its intellectual standard bearers, a love of excellence, an unrestrained respect and admiration for the best minds and the best gifts. But it must make sure that intermediate skills are not neglected, that the applied sciences receive proper respect, that all with the talent for higher education have access to it. Every society must work out its own balance between these needs. It is not an issue that can be solved by outside advice and interventions. These are the most intimate matters of national vocation and style.

Yet there is one area in which I believe external assistance can be effective and acceptable. In all developing nations there is an early bottleneck when the new flood of students threatens to engulf the available teachers and thus lower standards just when they ought to rise. A judicious policy designed to supplement the teaching force from outside can at this point greatly accelerate educational growth.

In any nation, great or small, at any time of man's long unfolding history, there has always been a most desperate need for a citizen body of trained and expert minds, free of prejudice, open to reason, respectful of others, able to live in peace and dignity with their fellow citizens. Too much of history is the record of rabid violence and passionate unreason, of societies and civilizations swept away because restraint and justice gave place to anarchy and war. But the need was never so urgent as it is today.

On the risks of atomic annihilation I will not dwell. As I said before, the only danger is that we should allow our imagination to become stalled into accepting the appalling risk of annihilation. But there is a further reason for the urgency — and on this I would like to insist. In this age of greatest danger we are trying to get away from the oldest method of world management known to man — the rule of the weak by the strong. Until the day before yesterday, international society knew nothing but a system of rival imperialisms. The rise and fall of their dominion made up the whole troubled external history of man.

Now, with an audacity which ought to leave us breathless, we are trying to assert the democratic principle in the world at large. All states great or small — like all men powerful or weak — have a right not to be ruled by powerful neighbors. More, each has a responsibility to world society, a voice, a right and a vote. As that old Cromwellian John Lilburne put it: "The poorest he . . . has a life to live as the richest he," and we are trying to make this the foundation of a new kind of international order.

The United Nations rests on this fundamental assumption of equal representation and equal responsibility. And you who in one way or another over the coming years will take up the task of building your nation, take up at the same time the task of building the world.

Your voice in the United Nations may be only one. But it is heard. Your vote may be a single vote but combined with others, it can create a majority. The initiative now open to small powers, their field of operation and responsibility, create a wholly new dimension in world politics, one which, if properly developed, could open up new possibilities for peace.

In a world under the dominion of rival imperialisms, nothing can be interposed between the confrontations of brute power. World history is strewn with the lamentable consequences of this iron rule of force. Today we have set up in the United Nations an alternative to the old violence. Of all its functions, the peace-making and peace-keeping function, though the most disputed, is the most essential for the alternative — the practice of brinks and confrontations — is the sure way to ultimate war.

I know the news from the United Nations these past few months has not been the best. But do not be discouraged; I am not.

The financial dilemma that now threatens the future of the United Nations is serious. I would not say otherwise. But I can assure you that the United States approaches the discussions and negotiations that will be held during this recess of the General Assembly with a constructive spirit and with a desire to achieve a harmony of views.

For we believe in the United Nations; we believe in its capacity to keep the peace and promote a better life for all in larger freedom. And it is this belief that shall guide us in the weeks and months ahead.

So do not heed the Cassandras who gloomily predict that the United Nations is going to collapse; that as the League of Nations failed because the United States and the Soviet Union were *not* in it at the end, so the United Nations will fail because they *are* in it.

It is in a serious crisis, but, as all institutions must change with changing conditions, this one will change somewhat, too, but it will overcome
this crisis as it has others, because it has long since demonstrated its indispensability to the human race, and dealt with all the most stubborn
problems of the post-war world in spite of its imperfections.

We know there are governments in the world that want to destroy
the UN; others that aim to sharply limit its peace-keeping capacity.

The great powers alone cannot make this new system work. Indeed, on
occasion, they do not even wish to make it work. The lions entangle
themselves and each other in the lethal net. But now there are new possibilities of creative intervention. From one end of the world to the other
the smaller powers whose survival depends upon peace in the lion's den,
can concert their policies and use their new found freedom of action to
continue and expand the experiments in peace-keeping already successfully begun — postponing confrontations, dispatching fact-finding missions, supporting the strengthening of an independent international
policing system, urging on the great powers in season and out of season
the habits of peaceful settlement, the reactions of decent restraint.

But they will carry the burden of this new responsibility only if they
themselves accept the task, approach it with cool and objective minds,
and do not allow their majority position to be subverted to limited interests or to self-regarding ends. The democracy of the worlds — like the
democracy of nations — depends upon the restraint and decency of the
majority. It is an enormous, an awesome responsibility. Yet it is one
which nations, new to independence, seeking a distinctive role, establishing a particular identity, can embrace with pride. Nothing like it has
been seen in the world before. It is the only genuinely new factor in the
world's long frustrated search for peace. I doubt if any nation, any people can ask for a greater vocation than to play a vital, a decisive part in
the survival of the human experiment.

And may I end by telling you my conviction born of many visits to
these brilliant islands and of many journeys into the great parent Continent of Africa that peoples touched with the African heritage have an
especial gift and therefore an especial responsibility for the forces of life,
of joy, of spontaneous zest — the life-giving, life-enhancing forces which
must be made to triumph over the forces of negation and death.

In the words of your own poet, Claude McKay — who is not just a
citizen of Jamaica, but of the world —

> ". . . in the socket-chiseled teeth of strife,
> That gleems in serried files in all the lands,
> We may join hungry, understanding hands,
> And drink our share of ardent love and life."

That is my parting wish for you today — and for young people everywhere — that you get — and give — your share of ardent love and life.
Bless you all.

*Stevenson stayed in Jamaica three days at the winter home of Edison
and Jane Dick. It was here that Harlan Cleveland phoned Stevenson and
learned in detail about U Thant's peace initiative on Vietnam. While in
Jamaica, Stevenson visited with Katherine W. Caulkins. She sent him a
poem by Stephen Spender.*

To Mrs. Daniel Caulkins [74]

February 24, 1965
. . . Today I have read it for the 10th time — the quote from the
Chinese and the quote from Bell — and, best of all, what you say.

With a written word, uncontrived and natural; with a spoken word
musical and vibrant, you can make me happy, relaxed, *content.* A curious
magic given to few; enriches and enslaves —

*The following document was sent to President Johnson on February 27,
1965, immediately after the conversation it describes took place in New
York City.*[75]
From Ambassador Stevenson in New York — February 27 [1965]

Following summarizes two-hour Stevenson-Thant conversation this morning attended by [Ralph] Bunche and [Charles] Yost.

Stevenson made three preliminary points. *First* was that he and Washington had assumed *conversations* on Vietnam which he had had with
Secretary General over period of months and suggestions which latter had
made were *strictly confidential* between them and would not be revealed
to anyone. There was therefore consternation in Washington, which he
fully shared, when these matters were disclosed in detail in the Secretary
General's press conference. This development had created *very serious
doubts as to whether it was any longer possible to have confidential exchanges with Secretariat about international affairs of vital concern to
United States.*

Second, Stevenson described in some detail United States Military *aid to
Burma* over considerable period of years, emphasizing payment received

[74] This handwritten letter is in the possession of Mrs. Caulkins.
[75] This document was declassified. National Security Files, Agency File, Representative of the United States to the United Nations, Lyndon B. Johnson Library.

was only 10 to 20 percent of value and that in convertible currency. He also pointed out that members of Congress were aware of these arrangements and may publicly challenge Secretary General which would of course be intensely embarrassing to Burmese Government.

Third, Stevenson noted *inaccuracy of Secretary General's claim* that International Court had not decided whether Security Council or General Assembly should be considered as competent to assess membership for peacekeeping operations and indicated lengthy passages in International Court decision where this point had been covered.

Stevenson then went over at length and in detail points set forth in Department's telegram. He emphasized repeatedly the fact that, despite existence of several channels of contact, there has been no indication whatsoever that Hanoi is prepared to talk about calling off its effort to take over Viet by force. He also emphasized the fact that all previous successful negotiations with Communists since the war have been preceded by private indications that Communists were willing to talk about a mutually acceptable settlement. Stevenson added that in this case, as recently as 10 days ago, Hanoi authorities had told third party whose identity he was not free to disclose [76] that they would not talk with United States on any basis as long as a single American remains in Vietnam, that they are not disturbed by United States attacks, and that South Vietnam is crumbling and victory is in sight.

Stevenson noted that situation has been aggravated in recent weeks by rapid increase in flow of men and arms to South Vietnam. Total number of men is in tens of thousands and equipment now arriving is virtually all Chinese and Russian.

Stevenson reported that President Johnson was particularly distressed at the public revelation of procedural proposals discussed between United States and that this revelation makes it more difficult to discuss such matters with Secretary General in the future. The President had further been deeply disturbed by Secretary General's reference to "facts" and "truth," which had conveyed implication that truth being withheld from American people, though this was presembly [sic] not what Secretary General meant to convey. The President has repeatedly said that he would do anything for peace and this continues to be his policy. However, there has been no indication whatsoever from other side, except Hanoi's response to Secretary-General's suggestion of bilateral talks, that they in any way reciprocate this policy. United States present intention is to continue measured response to Viet Cong attacks but not to escalate hos-

[76] Probably J. Blair Seaborn, Canadian commissioner on the International Commission for Supervision and Control in Vietnam.

tilities substantially. However, if these measures have no effect in checking Hanoi aggression, United States will have to examine other and more dangerous steps.

Stevenson concluded by asking again whether Secretary General had any information on North Vietnam intentions and by repeating that we would be most interested if at any time he were able to obtain indications that they are willing to stop infiltration and negotiate settlement guaranteeing South Viet independence.

Secretary General expressed appreciation for Stevenson's statement and replied by saying that his approach to problem had for some time been governed principally by three considerations.

First and most important was that *United States should not create conditions which would bring about rapproachement between Peking and Moscow.* If this occurred it would be most dangerous event of 1965 and perhaps of many years to come. Secretary General referred to his conversations with Khrushchev in Moscow last July in which latter had said he wished to wash his hands of Vietnam since it was too far away and too close to Peking. Thant said he had reason to believe Kosygin and Brezhnev had been following same policy until last January. Secretary General stressed his belief that detente between United States and Soviets is most essential element in maintaining peace of world and that he himself has been working to this end through every means available to him. Thant mentioned Couve de Murville's belief that Moscow is still most reluctant to realign with Peking, that Soviet arms being delivered to Hanoi by sea rather than through China, and that Moscow will realign with Peking only if United States pushes too hard in Vietnam.

Secretary General's *second* major consideration was his belief that *Hanoi does not wish to be close to Peking and that it is still not too late to draw it farther away from Peking.*

Secretary General's *third* consideration was *mood and attitude of Asian countries* toward Vietnam. He referred to statements of Ayub, Shastri and Ne Win calling for negotiations, to widespread demand in this same sense in much of Asian press, and to Ayub's forthcoming visit to Peking. He suggested that more and more Asian public opinion is being alienated from United States because it is beginning to see racial aspect in United States military intervention. He believes all countries in area except Thailand feel that *the more the situation in Viet is aggravated the more likely it is that Communists will take over.* He predicted that if United States air action is stepped up, even Asians who are anti-Communist will feel obliged to react negatively to such action.

These are the reasons, Secretary General repeated, why he has sought to find ways of improving the situation, beginning with his suggestion for broadening the South Viet Government and continuing through his proposal of bilateral negotiations to recent suggestion of "5-plus-2" conference. (US, UK, USSR, Communist China, France plus South Vietnam and North Vietnam)

He then sought to explain his treatment of subject in press conference by saying Bill Frye's story in Chicago Sun Times of February 19 had revealed almost all of details of Thant-Stevenson conversations. Secretary General had confided these conversations only in Bunche and Narasimhan [77] and he was certain no one in Secretariat had leaked to Frye. However, following Frye's story, United Nations Public Information Office and Burmese Permanent Representative [James] Barrington had been deluged with queries and news agencies had transmitted story all over world, it having appeared even in Burmese papers. In press conferende [sic] he therefore had alternative in replying to questions either to lie or to deal with subject as generally as possible, which he had tried to do. However, he had been asked whether United States was included among "parties primarily concerned" to whom he had made suggestions and he had been obliged to answer yes. Thant mentioned he had informed Lord Caradon [78] of his approach to Hanoi before appearance of Sun Times story and it was possible leak might have come from UK [United Kingdom] Mission. He had, however, told Caradon of 5-plus-2 idea only after Sun Times story, had told Couve of both bilaterals and 5-plus-2 only last Monday (February 22), and [Ambassador] Fedorenko [of the USSR] of 5-plus-2 only last Tuesday. He had never conveyed any of these suggestions to Peking.

Thant then said that he very much regretted that some of his statements had put United States Government and Stevenson in embarrassing situation. He said he had highest admiration for President Johnson and has been telling Soviet for past two years that he is wise, sober and statesmanlike leader.

However, he continues to feel that *three factors he had just outlined require that negotiations take place.* While he had not felt that private bilateral contacts required any terms of reference, he realizes that conference of any kind, such as 5-plus-2, does require such terms. He felt initiative for proposing terms of reference for negotiations should come from one of parties concerned, though he would be glad to transmit them.

[77] C. V. Narasimhan, United Nations chef de cabinet and Under-Secretary for General Assembly Affairs.

[78] The former Hugh Foot, at this time consultant to the Special Fund of the United Nations.

He mentioned incidentally, that when South Viet Observer Duc had called on him February 25 and insisted on knowing what proposals he had made, he had mentioned idea of 5-plus-2 conference in Geneva and had suggested that either United States of [sic] South Viet Vietnam might propose terms of reference.

Turning to United States military assistance to Burma he mentioned that Ne Win had told him last summer that Burma is not accepting any foreign military assistance and that he, Thant, had not known of arrangements with United States. Yesterday he had asked Barrington whether latter knew of such arrangements and Barrington had replied that, while he was not aware of recent developments, he had known of these arrangements when in Burmese Foreign Office in 1959.

Secretary General also mentioned that Suslov[79] had expressed to him yesterday Soviet Government's unhappiness that Secretary General in his press conference had explicitly not advocated withdrawal of United States troops from Vietnam. Secretary General had replied that he had no thought of pleasing everyone and that Suslov should tell his Government that precondition of United States withdrawal is unrealistic, will not happen, and will only prolong war.

Secretary General concluded by once more expressing regret for embarrassment caused by his press conference and asked Stevenson to inform President that his principal preoccupation is to prevent Moscow and Peking from coming together again.

Stevenson replied that this is also one of our major preoccupations, but how is it to be done? We had hoped Kosygin would restrain Hanoi when he visited there but North Vietnam had set up trap for him by planned and coordinated attacks in the South and as result, instead of restraining them he had promised more aid.

As to terms of reference for negotiations, Stevenson said that our terms would obviously be that negotiation should deal with stopping North Vietnam infiltration and guaranteeing independence of South Vietnam, but that we would be very glad to hear of any indication Secretary General might hear of any modification of Hanoi intentions.

In conclusion, Stevenson declared frankly that United Nations position in Washington is at all-time low and that it will be difficult in future to discuss international affairs candidly with Secretariat. We very much regretted Secretary General had not seen fit simply to deny Frye's story or at least to let us know in advance that he planned to respond to press

[79] Vladimir P. Suslov, United Nations Under-Secretary for Political and Security Council Affairs.

conference questions on this subject. However, Stevenson said, he wishes to keep channel to Secretary General open. United States of course wants negotiations if there is any sign they would lead to acceptable results, but other side seems to have rejected any such basis. It is clear to United States that their objective there is conquest of all Indochina. If United States should give any sign of entering negotiations merely as prelude to pulling out and permitting Communist takeover, all small countries of the area would be convinced they would be next in line of attack and would be unprotected. United States policy is that Hanoi either slows down or we step up.

Secretary General [brought] conversation to close by saying he had been considering for last few days whether it would be worthwhile to sound out North Vietnam through Soviets as to their intentions, but his tentative conclusion is that their response would probably not be helpful. It did not appear, however, that he had entirely ruled out such an approach.

The instructions from the Department of State which Stevenson presented to U Thant were a clear rejection of Stevenson's letter of February 17 to President Johnson, when he had written: "It should be clearly understood that such an appeal by the Secretary-General does not include preconditions to talks re stopping infiltration and ceasefire. . . ."

NEGOTIATIONS ON VIETNAM [80]

March 1, 1965

In the considerations on Vietnam which we presented to the Secretary General February 27 there were some general points about negotiations with the Communists which were based primarily on analogy and could easily prove inapplicable in the present case.

Our instructions [81] said: "None of the important political negotiations of modern times would have been successful if there had not already been advance indications that both sides wanted to 'talk turkey' and work out some reasonable accommodation." The instructions then cited in support of this thesis the Berlin blockade, the Korean armistice, the Cuba missile crisis, and the Nuclear Test Ban Treaty.

It is true there were encouraging indications from the Communists in advance of formal and public negotiations in each of these cases, but why were these indications forthcoming? They were forthcoming in the

[80] This document was declassified. National Security Files, Agency File, Representative of the United States to the United Nations, Lyndon B. Johnson Library. The photocopy of the document does not indicate whether the original went to President Johnson or to the Secretary of State.

[81] Instructions from the Department of State, February 26, 1965. This document was declassified. National Security Files, Agency File, Representative of the United States to the United Nations, Lyndon B. Johnson Library.

Berlin case because the blockade had failed and our airlift had made it look ridiculous, in the Korean case because during two years we had fought to a stalemate which the Communists saw they could not break, in the Cuban missile crisis because the alternative seemed to be general nuclear war, which the Soviets did not want, and in the limited test ban because both sides had decided such a treaty would be in their interests.

The situation in Vietnam is analogous to none of these. The Communists have for some time been winning in South Vietnam, and it is an attempt to reestablish a military and political equilibrium that we have undertaken our air strikes north of the 17th parallel. It is quite apparent to the Communists, however, as to ourselves, that we may not be able to establish this equilibrium in Vietnam without resort to much wider war, which for good reasons we may not be willing to bring about. Until we demonstrate that we have usable and effective military and political means of restoring an equilibrium in Vietnam, we would be foolish to expect any favorable "advance indications" concerning negotiations.

Do we have these usable and effective means? That remains to be seen. We can and presumably will continue and increase our air strikes between the 17th and 19th parallels. It is possible that over a period of time these will convince the Communists that either the damage suffered or the danger of escalation is too great to tolerate and they will show a willingness to negotiate. It seems unlikely, however, that we can inflict enough real damage in this area to give them pause or even that they themselves will refrain from escalating if confronted by a series of air strikes which would call into question the solidity of Peking and Moscow's assurances to Hanoi. It is at least questionable, therefore, whether this course of action on our part will produce indications of a willingness to negotiate.

We could certainly proceed to strike centers of population or industrial targets farther north, and this would presumably inflict great damage. It might also produce a willingness to negotiate, but unfortunately it would be more likely to produce one or more of the following: (1) a greatly increased invasion of South Vietnam via Laos by DRV [Democratic Republic of Vietnam] forces, sufficient to make the situation in the south much worse than it already is; (2) appearance of substantial Chicom [Chinese Communists] forces as "volunteers" in North Vietnam; (3) a much more explicit Soviet commitment to Hanoi and the probable appearance there of Soviet military "technicians." It is quite possible that an escalation of this magnitude would produce Communist willingness to negotiate, but it is also possible that Peking and Hanoi, for different reasons, would persist in the escalation and Moscow would be unable to control them.

Such substantial escalation on our part as bombing centers of population would also have very damaging consequences for us, whether or not the immediate results of the escalation were militarily helpful. (1) Even presently friendly Asian opinion would be shocked and alienated by our bombing Asian noncombatants on a large scale. (2) Even our friends in Asia, whatever their present attitudes, would subsequently hold it against us if we took action which either (a) brought North Vietnamese troops openly and on a large scale into South Vietnam and Laos, and/or (b) brought Chinese Communist troops into Indochina. (3) Most important of all, close Moscow-Peking cooperation would be reestablished for some time to come and our position in all parts of the world would thereby be rendered much more difficult.

It therefore seems clear that our situation in Vietnam is nowhere nearly so favorable as it was in Berlin, Korea, Cuba and on the test ban at the time positive "advance indications" were received from the Communists, and that there is therefore little reason to expect such indications at this time. There is also serious doubt whether repeated air strikes between the 17th and 19th parallels will be sufficiently effective to bring about a change of mood among the Communists; air strikes on centers of population probably would, but the worldwide political consequences of such action would very probably outweigh any military advantages it might produce.

The tentative conclusion of this analysis is that: (1) our only usable military option is the *limited* air strikes mentioned above (with possible extension to *isolated* military targets farther north); (2) this may be effective in changing the Communist attitude toward "realistic" negotiations but probably will not; (3) within a few weeks at best, therefore, we shall have either to escalate military action in a way certain to produce very damaging consequences to our worldwide position, or to risk the politico-military situation in Vietnam sliding further downhill, or to enter negotiations *without* the favorable advance indications we had in Berlin, etc.

Under these circumstances it would seem wise not to be inhibited by those precedents which were far from being analogous and to enter into some sort of negotiations soon if they can be arranged without unacceptable pre-conditions. The essential point, as history shows, is that negotiations, after the agony of getting them under way is over, are themselves a *stabilizing factor* in the overall politico-military picture, even if they drag on for many months, as was the case in Korea, without a satisfactory conclusion. Once under way, we should not plan to break them off prematurely, any more than we plan to break off our military action prematurely.

To Harry F. Guggenheim [82]

March 3, 1965

Dear Harry:

I apologize for neglecting your letter of February 2nd suggesting a column for the Newsday syndicate.

You tempt me sorely! But it is obvious that I can't even consider this as long as I am in government and I sometimes wonder if I'll even be alive when I'm out of it!

All in all, Harry, I suspect I had better not flirt with any future plans, at least for the present.

I wish I saw you more often, and do give my affectionate regards to the Ethridges.[83]

Cordially yours,

To Hamish Hamilton [84]

March 3, 1965

My dear Jamie:

The accumulation of messages regarding my literary efforts — past and future — plus another birthday, remind me:

(a) that I am now eligible for social security and therefore shall have no more birthdays, and
(b) that I have no more thoughtful friends than the Hamiltons of Hamilton Terrace!

Bless you and Yvonne [85] for your approval of the Churchill effort and the hint that there might be a book rattling around in my empty head. If there is — or was — I am afraid it has been strangled by Vietnam, Article 19 and assorted frustrations. But, believe me, I am flattered that Hamish Hamilton, Doubleday, Harpers, et al, view with any interest the possibility of a book.

At the moment I view the possibility of a visit with the Hamiltons with far more interest! Is there a possibility? If you don't come here, I shall have to come there!

Affectionately,

ADLAI

[82] Publisher of *Newsday*.
[83] Mr. and Mrs. Mark Ethridge. Mr. Ethridge was vice president and editor of *Newsday*.
[84] Founder and managing director of Hamish Hamilton, Ltd., of London, publishers of British editions of a number of Stevenson's books. The original is in the possession of Mr. Hamilton.
[85] Mrs. Hamilton.

To Mrs. John F. Kennedy

March 3, 1965

Dearest Jackie:

Would you like to be "the crowning jewel of an otherwise fantastic Feria?" [86] If so, your jewel box is at hand, although presently imprisoned by South East Asia, the Middle East, Article 19, and sundry alarms.

But, after all, how can you see the world save in the tender care of a safe, old chaperon like me!

Love always,

On March 4, 1965, Stevenson narrated Dore Schary's reenactment of Abraham Lincoln's Second Inaugural Address on the steps of the Capitol. He left immediately afterwards for Vienna to attend the funeral of President Adolf Schärf of Austria.

To Mr. and Mrs. James Riddleberger [87]

March 8, 1965

My dear friends:

We landed in Paris in bright sunshine before I had even opened my briefcase. But reflections on my brief and delightful adventures in Vienna were more profitable than those endless papers! This was only my second state funeral abroad and I had not realized how agreeable funerals could be! I have you to thank for that — you and those relaxed and sensible Austrians.

You were so good to me, so painlessly efficient and considerate of my state of exhaustion. Indeed, I came away refreshed and felt it had been a holiday weekend!

Paris was the same. Tom Finletter and Chip Bohlen were waiting lunch for me and there was as much gaiety as worry. Perhaps we should all live abroad for a bit now and then and change pace and perspective.

If there are any letters to write — Chancellor [Josef] Klaus, the Chief of Protocol etc., I hope you will let me know, or better still, write them yourself and sign my name. I wholly neglected to mention it — thanks no doubt to enough sleep for a change, or that postcard snow.

I'll try not to send any more travellers to you — but you don't make it

---

[86] Mrs. Kennedy had sent Stevenson a clipping from an unidentified French newspaper containing a photograph showing them arm in arm and describing rumors that they were to be married. As a result of this, she wrote, she could not now attend a "Feria" with him.

[87] United States ambassador to Austria and his wife.

any easier not to! Please let me know when you are in New York, and many, many thanks for so much hospitality. I had hoped I was a statesman but I think I'll tell LBJ that I'm best at ceremonial visiting — and hope for another one in Austria.

Cordially yours,

To Paul W. Gates [88]

March 8, 1965

Dear Professor Gates:

I have been meaning to write you for a long time to thank you for your letter of December 15, and the enclosures.[89] The latter are most interesting to me. They bring back many memories of my boyhood, and my Aunt Julia Scott — at least we always called her "Aunt Julia," although she was our Great Aunt.[90]

I accompanied my father as a boy many times on his trips to the farms, and I have imperishable recollections of being stuck in the mud by day and eaten up by mosquitoes at night in half the counties of central Illinois. I wonder if this generation will ever have any idea of what travel was like before the "hard roads."

Someday I am going to come to Cornell and spend a day in the library scratching around among my family's documentary bones!

Cordially yours,

To Eugene Ormandy [91]

March 8, 1965

My dear Mr. Ormandy:

I am so grateful for your reassuring words about the Lincoln Portrait recording.[92] I thought the music exquisite and stirring. But, as for the narration, it seemed to me too muted and bloodless. Somehow, doing it in the studio separated from the orchestra diminished my sense of participation.

But if you were really pleased, I am delighted!

With my utmost admiration, I am

Cordially yours,

[88] Professor of American history at Cornell University and an authority on American land policies.

[89] Mr. Gates had sent Stevenson copies of material that Lewis Stevenson collected while managing Mrs. M. T. Scott's land.

[90] Mrs. M. T. Scott, sister of Mrs. Adlai E. Stevenson. Mrs. Scott was the mother of Julia Scott, who married Carl Vrooman of Bloomington, Illinois.

[91] Conductor and music director of the Philadelphia Orchestra.

[92] On March 4, a film was made in Washington, D.C., on Lincoln's Second Inaugural Address, with Stevenson as narrator.

To Frank Altschul [93]

March 8, 1965

Dear Frank:

I have not overlooked your thoughtful and very penetrating letter of January 28, about the Article 19 issue in the late and unlamented General Assembly.

I had hoped to see you long before this and to talk about it a bit and to explain why things were done and not done, and I shall hope for such an opportunity soon. Meanwhile, please bear in mind that this issue got involved in our domestic politics at an early stage. Happily, the Congressional "get tough" attitude has subsided with time and with better understanding of the issue.

Perhaps we may be approaching a time when we can deal with this more rationally. I marvel at how we can conduct a foreign policy at all, with one eye on domestic politics — and sometimes two eyes!

Yours always,

To Jean M. Wylie

March 13, 1965

My dear Jean:

I am just back from three days (and three speeches!) in Washington and must leave very shortly to attend a luncheon of the United Federation of Teachers, receive their John Dewey Award — and make another speech! After such a week, I am more than ever longing for the Caribbean holiday I have been promising myself. If all goes well, I shall be off on a cruise the last week or ten days of this month.

But it has been on my mind that I have not yet thanked you for your birthday thought. I am still carrying *your* briefcase on all my major travels and could not let you add another to the collection. In just the last month, yours has been with me to Jamaica, where I spoke at the commencement exercises of the University of the West Indies, and to Vienna, where I attended the funeral of the Austrian President. The latter trip took place last weekend on less than 24 hours notice and was rather agreeable on the whole, for it included a gay overnight reunion in Paris with my friends the [Thomas K.] Finletters. I was informed late on Wednesday that I would have to go to Vienna. Early Thursday I left for Washington to fulfill an engagement, narrating the background to a re-enactment of Lincoln's Second Inaugural on the steps of the Capitol. At five in the

[93] Member of the board of directors of the General American Investors Company and secretary of the Council on Foreign Relations.

afternoon I left for Vienna, where I arrived at nine the next morning in a dense fog and had to circle the airport for two and a half hours. A wild ride into town with motorcycle escort got me to my destination on the stroke of noon, just as the ceremony was starting. Paris the next day, and home on Sunday.

And so, you see, my life continues to be anything but quiet, and I still lament the fact that I can't keep in closer touch with my friends. If I didn't talk so much in public, I might be able to talk more in private — and to let you know more often that I think of you and bless you for your constant kindness to me.

Affectionately always,

To Hamilton Fish Armstrong [94]

March 15, 1965

Dear Ham:

I have neglected your letter of March 2nd, pending some estimate of developments in the United Nations. My notes indicate that you expect a script by May 5th.[95]

In view of the deliberation with which negotiations are being organized,[96] let alone conducted, relating to the future of peacekeeping, I have little hope that we can have this written by May 5 — even if Charlie Yost could find the time to write it!

It seems quite unlikely from present indications that we will be able to foretell the future with any confidence before mid-summer. The Vietnam trouble is, of course, slowing up negotiations, and the probability of any settlement. And the Soviets and French show an inertia which now seems like a wise tactic for us too.

All in all, I think it probably hazardous for you to count on the kind of piece we discussed for the June issue. Of course if things change, we can reconsider and perhaps put something together reasonably quickly. I hope this is not too disappointing, and I am sure it is not wholly unexpected.

Love to Christa.[97]

Yours

José Rolz-Bennett, of Guatemala, the deputy chef de cabinet of the United Nations, sent Stevenson a rubber ball that golfers used to

[94] Editor of *Foreign Affairs.*
[95] Mr. Armstrong had asked Stevenson to write an article on key matters pending before the UN.
[96] Over Article 19 and the payments for the peacekeeping forces.
[97] Mrs. Armstrong.

strengthen their hands and fingers during the idle months of winter. He wrote that it might help restore full mobility to Stevenson's fingers injured in his "peacekeeping" between the dogs at Libertyville.

To José Rolz-Bennett

March 18, 1965

Dear Jose:

Thanks so much.

I have started squeezing. Indeed, I like it more than dictating or discussing! Do you think the Secretary-General would object if I brought it into the Security Council? It would be such an agreeable diversion in the Cyprus debate! [98]

Yours,

To David Lawrence [99]

March 19, 1965

Dear David:

I have your letter of March 15th suggesting an interview on various aspects of the United Nations.

It may be that something of this kind would be helpful and in principle I gladly accept. However, for the present, there are so many uncertainties, and the East-West situation is so rigid as a result of Vietnam that I hesitate to make a firm commitment — as you will understand.

Perhaps we could talk about this again around the 1st of May. Efforts concerning the future of peacekeeping may have made some progress by then, and the future prospects for the Organization will be clearer.

I appreciate your suggestions.

Cordially yours,

To Mrs. Albert Lasker

March 19, 1965

Mary dear:

We have all been writing the General Services Administration urging them to be patient.[100] I think that there is enough money in sight to at least warrant a loan to enable us to get on with the Wings, which be-

[98] Stevenson spoke in the Security Council on the situation in Cyprus on March 19.
[99] Newspaper columnist and chairman of the board and editor of *U.S. News & World Report.*
[100] The Eleanor Roosevelt Memorial Foundation had pledged funds to construct additions to the Franklin D. Roosevelt Library at Hyde Park, New York, which was administered by the General Services Administration.

come more expensive every day, and my present thought is to try to interest the AFL-CIO — our largest debtor — to either loan us the money itself or endorse the Foundation's note to the bank.

All of this illustrates the hellish predicament I am in, and I wish we could get somebody to replace me quickly to attend to this sort of thing and to keep after the collection of pledges.

I have made a further plea to Phil Klutznick to assume the Chairmanship and he has dodged me successfully so far. I wish the Executive Committee and the Nominating Committee could meet without me, and reach some decision. After all, I have done what I could for more than two years, and I should not be asked to continue.

We finished Cyprus today and I am happy to get off tomorrow morning to Antigua for a week, God willing, on Brooke's [101] boat, but you may be sure that I shall carry with me a heavy brief case!

I trust you had a lovely "dolce" time . . . I wish I had been there!

Love,

To Clayton Fritchey

March 19, 1965

I am afraid I must do this [102] — much as I regret it. Within this context, I hope to talk in more or less outline form about the position of the United States and the West, and our transition from domination in the immediate post-war period to first, a bi-polar society, and then a society of multiple centers of gravity. Perhaps we could dig up some thoughtful writing about the parallel between the fragmentation of the free society and closed society. Both monoliths have collapsed, but the struggle will go on in the new situation.

At this point I suggest we could talk about the advantages of a united Europe and an Atlantic Community as a position of strength in the contest. I suppose I should comment on the rapidity with which the sacrifice of individual freedom follows national independence in the liquidation of Empire. In short the distinction between the free society and freedom.

I could go on, and I shall try to do some thinking about this while I am away. It would seem to me that the same speech could be effective and informative both for the Prudential Center in Boston [103] and for the Publishers in New York.[104] I am sure there must have been a lot of recent

101 Mrs. Vincent Astor, of New York.
102 There is no evidence in the Stevenson papers that would make it possible to identify which speaking engagement Stevenson refers to.
103 On April 20 he spoke at the dedication of the center and on the same day addressed a joint session of the Massachusetts legislature.
104 He spoke at the annual dinner of the Bureau of Advertising of the American Newspaper Publishers Association on April 22.

writing on "the State of the West" — and perhaps I should read some of it.

With a speech of this kind, I think it might be better to first do an outline of the sound, thoughtful and significant points and then wrap the words about later.

On March 20, 1965, Stevenson flew to St. Kitts in the British West Indies to join Mrs. Vincent Astor and several other people for a cruise. While aboard the yacht, he read a number of books, including Richard J. Whalen's The Founding Father: The Story of Joseph P. Kennedy (*New York: New American Library, 1964*). *Stevenson wrote in his diary: "Read from the Founding Father — the story of Joe Kennedy and his remorseless, ruthless ambition for money — any way to get it — and status. Power? . . ." Stevenson returned to New York City on Sunday, March 28.*

To Dean Rusk [105]

March 31, 1965

Following my talk with U Thant on Monday regarding rumors of a possible trip to Hanoi and Saigon and his role in the Viet Nam situation, [Ralph] Bunche asked me to see him following my luncheon with the Secretary General today. Bunche told me that U Thant had discussed with him and with [José] Rolz Bennett, another Under Secretary, an idea which had now taken the form of the following proposed message to the United States, North Viet Nam, and South Viet Nam. He was careful to explain that the Secretary General had no intention of making any move on Viet Nam unless ground work made it look worth while. Hence he was submitting this preliminary suggestion to Stevenson first. If the United States reaction was negative, he would drop it. If United States reaction was positive, he would consider any suggestions in the text which we might care to make and thereafter follow up any suggestions we might care to make in the text and for timing of its release. The message is as follows:

"My serious concern over the dangerous situation in Viet Nam has only deepened since the statement I made on this subject on February 12, 1965. If anything, since that date, the situation there has worsened and the threat of a wider war is even graver. Nor, unhappily, do I see any immediate sign of hope for an improvement if present trends continue.

Naturally, I continue to be conscious of my responsibilities under

[105] This document was declassified. National Security Files, Agency File, Representative of the United States to the United Nations, Lyndon B. Johnson Library.

Article 99 of the Charter as well as of my broad duty as Secretary General of the UN, to do whatever I reasonably and legitimately can in pursuit of peace.

In the light of existing circumstances, therefore, I feel obliged to make a new effort in the form of a most urgent appeal to the three governments directly involved militarily in the conflict in Viet Nam. Consequently, I am addressing this identical appeal to your government and to the governments of [North Viet Nam and the United States].[106]

I am convinced that no one of the governments involved in the Viet Nam war would wish to see the war escalate beyond control. I am equally convinced that these three governments are themselves aware of the incalculable dangers to the peace of the world that would result from such an escalation. Obviously, a first and essential objective with regard to that conflict is to bring about an immediate cessation of hostilities. I am sure also, that you will agree with my often stated view that the solution of the problems of Viet Nam must, and indeed, can only be sought around the conference table rather than on the field of battle. In order to create that climate of quiet, which alone would be congenial to a search for a peaceful solution, it is imperative to bring a quick end to the fighting. Therefore, I now appeal most earnestly and urgently to your government to agree, along with the other two governments directly concerned, to a temporary cessation of all hostile military activity, whether overt or covert, across the 17th parallel in Viet Nam, for a duration of three months, as from the date of the acceptance of this appeal by the three parties to which it is addressed.

I trust, that your government will accord to this appeal the most serious attention and will find it possible, in the interest of peace and for the good of humanity, to respond favorably to it.

In the event of a favorable response from the three governments, I would be fully available for such assistance and service as the parties might feel that I could usefully afford in the imperative quest for a peaceful solution.

I intend to make this message public as soon as it has reached the three addresses."

In response to my question, Bunche informed me that the Secretary General would consider any appropriate language extending the 17th parallel to include the infiltration through Laos. He also will welcome any suggestions, if we wish to make them, with respect to policing re-

---

[106] A blank was left at the end of this sentence; the appropriate governments were inserted here in each letter.

quirements during the cease fire period. Further, he would consider suggestions for any changes in the language, including further steps such as a personal visit by the Secretary General to Viet Nam preparatory to negotiations.

Harlan Cleveland is in New York today, and I am discussing this and some of our ideas with him. He will be back in Washington tomorrow, Thursday morning.

Stevenson received the third annual Eleanor Roosevelt Political and Public Service award at a dinner held on April 12, 1965. Mrs. Danny Kaye produced a show patterned on the television program This Is Your Life. *The characters ranged from a Bloomington, Illinois, childhood sweetheart to his former law partner Willard Wirtz. The skit was written by Edward D. McDougal, Jr. Parts of it appear in Volume I of* The Papers of Adlai E. Stevenson: Beginnings of Education, 1900–1941, *pp. 240–241, 562–563.*

To Harry S. Truman

April 14, 1965

Dear Mr. President:

Your telegram to the Eleanor Roosevelt Memorial Award Dinner touched me deeply and I am so grateful for your thoughtfulness and for your charitable words about me. To be linked in any way with Eleanor Roosevelt is an honor; and that *you* did the linking gave me my finest hour!

I was distressed that Southeast Asia and Washington kept me away from the Freedom House dinner [107] in your honor. It would have been a joy to see you again! Perhaps, with Margaret's [108] help, I'll have an opportunity to see you on another visit to New York.

With affectionate regards to Mrs. Truman and heartfelt thanks to you,

Cordially yours,

To Art Buchwald

April 15, 1965

Dear Art:

Time is passing, hence this letter of thanks for your incomparable contribution to the Eleanor Roosevelt Award dinner.[109] For me, the memory will last forever — and be refreshed every time I read my favorite contemporary philosopher, commentator — and friend.

[107] April 13, 1965.
[108] Mr. Truman's daughter, Mrs. Clifton Daniel, who lived in New York City.
[109] The columnist had played one of the parts in the skit.

Be sure to let me know if the Secret Service surrounds you — not that I could help, of course!

> Yours always

To Dean Rusk [110]

> April 15, 1965

Wednesday evening, Stevenson called on [Ralph] Bunche again regarding U Thant's intention to call for a cessation of hostilities in Vietnam by all parties in a speech to the UN Correspondents Association at noon today, Thursday.

Bunche informed Stevenson that he had presented Stevenson's objections to such a call at this time to Secretary General and latter had, evidently a little reluctantly, agreed not to make his appeal at this time. Draft of what SYG had intended to say is attached.

> He added

that if asked questions at the lunch he would have to say that he was giving thought to what he could do to stop the fighting in Vietnam.

SYG instructed Bunche to tell Stevenson that his cease-fire proposal had already been once deferred on Stevenson's suggestion, that having now deferred it again, he wants it understood that he will feel obliged to make an appeal some time because it is his primary responsibility to do what he can to stop the fighting even if only temporarily in order to create better conditions for talks, and that his thinking was in contemplation of the Monsoons beginning the end of April and increased guerilla activity which would challenge US to vigorous response with ever more serious consequences. SYG wants US reactions and consultations with Stevenson as to how and when to use it with best results. Stevenson promised US reactions and consultations and reminded Bunche that when original cease-fire proposal was made to Stevenson on March 31st, SYG had invited US suggestions for timing and language changes. Hence Stevenson was surprised that SYG had contemplated immediate declaration without time for such consultation. S. also urged SYG to ask Yugoslavia and countries of the 17 non-aligned to insist on an answer to their appeal from Hanoi.[111]

---

[110] This was dictated over the classified phone by Stevenson. The document was declassified, but it was "sanitized" by the Review Board. It is printed here as it was received by the editor, including the gaps. National Security Files, Agency File, Representative of the United States to the United Nations, Lyndon B. Johnson Library.

[111] On April 1, 1965, the seventeen heads of government of the nonaligned countries called for the start of negotiations on Vietnam without any preconditions.

Stevenson then reviewed all of reasons why timing was unwise and his gratification that SYG had agreed to defer any immediate appeal. Stevenson also suggested that any favorable reference to Pearson's speech by U Thant in answer to questions from the press at today's lunch would be unwise unless it included mutual obligation to stop infiltration, etc.[112]

Yesterday

On April 20, 1965, Stevenson spoke at the dedication of the Prudential Center in Boston and, on the same day, he addressed a joint session of the Massachusetts legislature. Stevenson spoke at the annual dinner of the Bureau of Advertising of the American Newspaper Publishers Association in New York City on April 22, 1965.[113]

I commend to you something the distinguished able and overburdened Secretary General of the United Nations, U Thant, said yesterday at the ANPA luncheon:

"It is a truism that 'news' is what sells newspapers, and I do not question the need for an element of drama and excitement in the popular press . . . but this is an attitude which, if carried too far, can produce a gloomy or sensational picture of events which cannot fail to have important repercussions on the opinions and reactions of peoples and governments. An undue concentration on violence and conflict inevitably creates a heated atmosphere which is unfavorable to reason and conciliation."

In that connection I want to say that to cover 114 nations and a huge secretariat, all dealing with a vast variety of problems, is not an easy task. On the whole, I have found the correspondents who cover the United Nations informed, temperate, and responsible. It is well that they are, because I sometimes suspect that many delegates from abroad form their judgments of our country more from what they read in our papers than from what the likes of me tell them.

It is well that your foreign affairs reporters are competent because the reporting and interpretation of foreign affairs, is becoming, perhaps, the greatest single responsibility of the press — that is, if you consider the preservation of peace as our paramount problem.

Once upon a time, I too was a newspaper man on the Daily Pantagraph of Bloomington, Illinois, and have fancied myself just a frustrated jour-

---

[112] Canadian Prime Minister Lester B. Pearson said in a speech at Temple University on April 2, 1965, that suspension of air strikes against North Vietnam "at the right time" might be helpful in getting a dialogue on Vietnam started among the principal parties.

[113] The text is based on USUN press release 4530.

nalist ever since. But after a good many years of alternately admiring and damning foreign correspondents I'm not sure that I yearn for the task of cramming into ten or fifteen columns a day the complex happenings of our turbulent world, let alone reducing to 200 words on the editorial page the blinding light of undiscovered insight and the simple answer to complex questions.

But I am reconciled to your difficulties by contemplation of my own. And you may be reconciled to your difficulties by recalling Nikita Khrushchev's comment at a Moscow reception last summer. Western correspondents had complained that it was hard to get news about the Soviet-Chinese ideological negotiations then going on in Moscow.

Khrushchev retorted: "Any fool could be a journalist — if the job were not so difficult."

Your editors and reporters will once again be on their mettle next week, when the members of the United Nations Disarmament Commission — all 114 of them — gather to take up again the formidable task of stopping the arms race and pushing ahead toward that distant yet urgent goal called general and complete disarmament. There will be plenty of noise to report, and those interested only in reporting noise will be content with the show. But for those who want to report what the noise portends, the assignment will be no job for fools.

Those of us who feel that arms control is near the heart of foreign policy are bound to feel at times that we do not have much these days to sustain our hopes. But we have to have the irresponsible gumption of the lady who was stopped by a policeman for going the wrong way on a one-way street, and decided that the best defense was counter-attack. "Officer," she said indignantly, "have you ever considered that the arrow may be pointing the wrong way?"

In the Disarmament Commission next week, can we escape the tedious litany of familiar reiteration? Can we break the circle of fear and suspicion? We have a global arms race and a number of regional arms races. They are directly the product of fear and suspicion and of the absence of political settlements of international conflicts.

Since the second world war, we ourselves have spent about $800 billion on our military establishment — an amount that exceeds the production of all the nations of Asia, Africa and Latin America this year. Literally hundreds of billions of dollars were spent by the Europeans and ourselves, mainly to convince aggressors that aggression does not pay and has no future — whether in Central Europe or in Korea or anywhere else — including Viet-Nam.

In each major region of the world, aggressions and threats and uncertainties about the intentions of neighbors are driving up the cost of nationhood and driving down the standard of living.

Communist China is depriving the people of that great and ancient land of the chance for rapid development — because it wants to finance nuclear threats and conventional adventures.

The militancy of Asian communists in turn causes the South Koreans to keep more than a half million men under arms, forces Taiwan to maintain 600,000 armed men and South Viet-Nam a quarter of a million men; keeps Thailand armed and alert; galvanizes India into an unprecedented defense effort; and even keeps the Soviet Union patrolling the world's longest border to deal, so the Soviets say, with hundreds of Chinese incursions into Soviet Asia.

Throughout the world, there is competitive buying and competitive selling of arms — and competitive begging and granting of arms as well. For too many political leaders, in too many countries, the first answer to every difficult question is the threat or the use of force. Some of them suffer from the same confusion that overcame the young American who was applying for a government job, and answered the standard question: "Do you favor the overthrow of the government by force, subversion or violence?" with a single word "violence."

There is, after all, something grotesque, unreal, and nightmarish about a world with 20 million men under arms and a military budget of $120 billion dollars when we can't seem to find 20 thousand men and $120 million dollars for international peacekeeping by the United Nations.

Even Ogden Nash, whose verse is seldom bitter, had an edge as he wrote these lines:

> "When geniuses of every nation [114]
> Hasten us toward obliteration,
> Perhaps it will take the dolts and
>   geese
> To drag us backward into peace."

The goal of general and complete disarmament is, of course, to achieve a better and safer world through the application of the principles of the Charter of the United Nations, and the steady development of international law and effective peacekeeping arrangements.

If we are ever to begin the process of general disarmament, we must start by halting the present arms race, and particularly the nuclear race, and we must begin with those areas of arms control where agreement seems possible — and we must begin now.

This is precisely the aim of the program of action which the United States has placed before the eighteen nation disarmament conference in Geneva and which we are prepared to discuss next week in New York.

[114] Stevenson has misquoted this line, which reads: "When geniuses all in every nation."

At Geneva we have set out, at the direction of President Johnson, a series of versatile and far-reaching proposals: an offer to explore an agreement to stop any increase in the numbers of strategic nuclear weapons, stopping production of fissionable materials for weapons, and beginning the process of actual destruction of bombers. We are anxious to see the test ban treaty extended to ban underground tests, and we are prepared to discuss practical measures to guard against surprise attack.

These proposals are concrete and practical. Unlike the slogans and generalities which characterize many of the Soviet proposals, ours are accompanied by technical and scientific detail. We know they would not be accepted when first offered. They deal with complex matters of military balance, and scientific technology and verification, and we accept the need for a full exchange of views before others could be expected to agree on them. Thus, we are not wholly discouraged by the lack of progress at Geneva last year. There is no short road to arms control or disarmament.

But there is one area in which time is pressing and action urgent. This is the dangerous spread of nuclear weapons capabilities. Many countries will soon have peaceful power reactors turning out plutonium as a by product. And with plutonium you can manufacture nuclear weapons. It is essential that international safeguards keep pace with the threat. The United States strongly supports such safeguards.

Similarly we strongly favor a non-proliferation agreement to prevent the transfer of nuclear weapons to states which do not possess them and to prevent the latter from producing or seeking such weapons or seeking such control. This agreement has been delayed too long by Soviet arguments relating to the discussions of a multilateral or allied nuclear force.

Why should we not conclude a non-proliferation agreement now and, by so doing, provide reassurance that any further allied nuclear arrangements would be consistent with the principle of non-dissemination? Why should we not conclude a comprehensive test ban agreement which would be an important complement to any non-proliferation agreement? Why should past differences remain forever unresolved?

Red China has poured its scarce resources into building a nuclear weapon capability which underscores the need for action. Now Peiping's neighbors are confronted with a new threat to their security. The political pressure to follow suit is rising dangerously. If they do, others will follow. But such a chain reaction would only lessen everyone's security. That is why we applaud the announced policy of India to confine its scientific talents to the peaceful uses of atomic energy.

But we are mindful of the concern for their security felt by Peiping's neighbors who have refrained from nuclear weapons production. President Johnson said on October 18, 1964: "The nations that do not seek national nuclear weapons can be sure that if they need our strong support against some threat of nuclear blackmail, then they will have it."

In short, we recognize the legitimate security concerns of others, whether allied to us or not, and this problem continues to engage our earnest attention.

Before I leave the subject of disarmament, let me note a tendency on the part of some of the smaller nations to complain about the lack of progress in dampening down the major arms race while they themselves are negotiating for the acquisition of advanced jet aircraft, or other advanced lethal weapons. Sometimes this is done out of exaggerated assessments of their security needs or for prestige considerations. In either case, the result is to add fuel to regional arms races. Regional initiatives for arms agreements might also enhance regional security. And, equally important, it would release badly needed funds for economic and social development. As the world's leading provider of assistance for such development, the United States would certainly welcome local initiatives in this area.

But disarmament is not the only thing I want you publishers to think about. I want you to think about the United States. I hope you don't think I'm frivolous, because to know ourselves, let alone to see ourselves as others see us, is a formidable assignment few of us ever finish.

Every nation has difficulty in thinking objectively about itself. There is so much that is understood and taken for granted, so much that is accepted as uncritically as climate or geography. But I believe the American people have some special difficulties in thinking about themselves. In the first place, we are the only great power in history who jumped to overwhelming great powerhood with virtually no outside contacts on the way up. The isolation of the first century of our republic is unique by any standards.

There was little reason for us to think about ourselves, about our place in an evolving world context, about the views of others, about the impact of our policies. If I may use the phrase without irreverence, I think America, of all the powers in the world, came nearest to an immaculate conception.

Now I come to the second difficulty confronting our view of ourselves. We were the first community to come into being with a declared and positive political, even messianic aim. We sprang from the womb of history "dedicated to a proposition" — a new society destined to prove that man could be governed yet free, a new policy which would be "the last best hope of man."

Now this is pretty heady stuff. I believe that it has profoundly influenced our development. We are today that paradox, a profoundly conservative nation with a vast liberal ideal to conserve. Our stirring dreams

are all of liberation and greater equality, of legal rights and social en-
franchisement. We cannot change our dreams, for we wrote them into
our Constitution. We are, if you like, birthright radicals, since we have
to conserve the most soaring political aspiration ever conceived by man.

Yet this vast ambition, this sense of legislating for all mankind which
gives the Declaration of Independence its luminous glory, have also had
profound and less desirable effect upon our intermittent efforts at intro-
spection. It is much more agreeable to think on one's community as the
"last best hope of man" than as a settler society which secured a whole
continent in "fee simple" by exterminating the original inhabitants. It is
much easier to hold up the banner of freedom against godless tyranny
than to remember the plight of the American Negro a hundred years
after emancipation. These darker pictures are not the whole truth about
America — but they are a part of the truth and the side of it which
in our rhetoric, our diplomatic posture and our own imagination we tend
to leave out.

We entered history suddenly and inescapably. And once again our
manner of doing it gave a further twist to our self-imaginings. For in 1945
we entered a world virtually stripped of all power save our own. Is it
possible to picture any circumstance more traumatic than this? Here was
the United States, largely unconscious of the scale of its wealth and
power, which had had no previous world policies, strategies or even
views — save that of continuing invulnerability via isolation or the Monroe Doctrine — pitchforked into a vast vacuum where only its power, its
policy, its strategy seemed likely to have any effect.

Once again, I doubt if any nation ever had unsought leadership thrust
so suddenly upon it. To go to bed a separate American people and wake
up to find a large part of the world at the bedside clamoring for solutions — this is perhaps a suitable description of the American plight between 1944 and 1947.

Yet this untried community, this inexperienced leadership produced,
at virtually no notice, astoundingly successful policies. One looks back
with a kind of awe at the audacity and vision of those first post-war
years — on the one hand the rallying of the free world to the policy of
containment in Greece and Turkey, in the North Atlantic Treaty Alliance,
in Berlin, and, with United Nations support, in Korea; on the other, the
bold use of American resources in the Marshall Plan to restore the war-
devastated European economy in four short years, and to do so on a
cooperative basis which foreshadowed Europe's later experiments in
unification.

These were stunning achievements. America, emerging as a world
leader for the first time, put up a performance that the wisest veteran
could hardly have matched. Yet I believe that our very success has had

consequences for our present posture in world affairs that, some fifteen years later, are not altogether happy. We have in a sense been a little hypnotized by our achievement. The sense of unique and successful leadership in a grateful and reasonably compliant coalition has come to be the posture we understand best. Anything else makes us uneasy and at times resentful.

In the Atlantic arena, the policies have proved so efficient that the evils they were designed to meet have, if not vanished, at least so sharply changed their character that we confront a new situation, demanding new initiatives. Success has changed the circumstances with which we have to deal. As H. L. Mencken said, "By the time everyone accepts a truism, it is no longer true."

What we have to ask ourselves today is not whether our policies have been good in the past. That is no longer the question. In this mutable world of breakneck change, we have constantly to re-examine both our assessments and our strategies. Past success, the sense of our "manifest destiny," knowledge of our material resources and superiority — all these are not good guides if they confuse us about our present problems and possibilities.

As becomes more and more obvious, West European recovery and East European relaxation create wholly new conditions for Atlantic co-operation. The fear is less. The sense of recovered power is greater. I do not myself believe that the underlying unity is lost. If attacked, the alliance would stand. To this extent, containment continues to be the successful base of our policy.

But Russian aggression is no longer the major issue. The major issues now are the divided state of Europe and particularly of Germany, and the degree to which Western Europe, including West Germany, needs or does not need its own independent nuclear defense, now that its reconstruction and economic expansion give it the preconditions for making great power claims. Concerning these issues the Europeans are sharply divided among themselves.

In this situation, no amount of American "leadership" or pressure can quickly change the underlying deadlock. So this is probably not a time for bold initiatives and audacious breakthrough in Europe. It is rather a time when America with modesty and good will should explore the less sensational channels of growth and consolidation, listening attentively to the views of others on the chances of reunification by agreement, discussing the same issue in low key with the Russians, linking European security with the wider context of disarmament, encouraging the British to accept their European role, encouraging the increase of trade between East and West, making every effort to keep all possible channels of agreement open.

The phase is new. The diplomacy must match it. And if, in this phase, America is as often a listener as a talker, this too reflects the changes in power and responsibility that are taking place in the Atlantic world.

The grand design of a lasting partnership between equals still stands. But the old leader has to learn the new habits of genuinely equal partnership. It is not easy — but now is the time.

In the world beyond the Atlantic, we are beginning to see that neither straightforward containment nor over-simple formulas of economic assistance provides the whole answer to the vast and multiplying dilemmas of the "third world."

In principle, it is true that the readiness of America to use its great strength to underpin the security of smaller powers threatened by outside, often communist, intervention holds good in this shrunken world.

There can be no doubt, for instance, that prompt British and American arms support for India under Chinese attack in 1962 helped to stabilize the situation. Likewise there can be no doubt that our two-pronged war and peace policy in Vietnam is equally directed toward stabilization there. Our measured but unequivocal military response is our contribution to the containment of those who today in Asia, as yesterday in Europe, will not leave their neighbors in independence and freedom. Our offer to discuss unconditionally, on the other hand, emphasizes our desire for a peaceful settlement and our willingness to discuss it with our adversaries as well as our friends.

This parallel track might provide the basis, if the governments and peoples of the area would participate, for a long-term policy of political stabilization and economic development in Asia which could be as successful as that jointly pursued in the West by the Europeans and ourselves.

Let me turn your attention to another irritating difficulty. Throughout the developing world, the overriding memory is of colonial domination by Western force of arms. The white faces, the troops, the weapons — however different their intentions — revive old fears and feuds. After aiding most everyone's independence, America finds itself suspected of neo-imperialism. Many of its non-European allies, some of them still unstable and prone to internal revolution, are in no position to screen the United States from such charges. There are even cases where a direct American presence, by reviving the colonial bogey, weakens the position it is intended to reinforce. We have to face the risk and paradox of strength increasing insecurity.

Again, in the field of economic assistance, America's expectations have been frustrated. Far from quick accomplishment, the programs stretch on and out, and the goal of growth without special assistance seems further off than ever. And in the short run, so many recipients seem to take an almost malign pleasure in biting the hand that aids them, that the burning library [115] is almost becoming, in many Americans' minds, the symbol of its relations with states it has been trying to help.

In short, for the Americans, the troubled mid-sixties seem to offer few of the rewards of the successful late forties and early fifties. The exhilarations of single-handed world leadership are fading. A long, ungrateful grind in a chaotic and ungrateful world would perhaps be nearer to peoples' estimate today. It is this greyness, this bitterness, that underlie many of the current American pleas to "be through with it all," to get out and pull back to the old safe manageable limits of American sovereignty, and let the rest of the troubled world look after itself.

Now I am not going to argue to an audience like this about the impossibility of American withdrawal, of American neo-isolationism. We killed isolation at Oak Ridge and Los Alamos for ourselves and for anyone else. Our planetary society is now one, even if only in the unity of potential annihilation. We cannot get off and float about outside this particular spaceship. We and the human race are going to survive — or not — together.

What I do suggest is that the new epoch calls for a rather different kind of involvement, a subtle shift in our attitudes, both to ourselves and to our diplomacy.

Our brief U.S. experience is compounded of two extremes — long isolation and brief supremacy. Now we have to learn the middle term — of patience, of cooperation, of genuine sharing in the formulation and execution of policies, of readiness to compromise, even, I would say, of humor and self-depreciation and readiness to admit that on occasion the mistakes have been ours.

The essence of the new approach is more genuine consultation, a more conscious search for the consensus, a greater readiness, in President Johnson's phrase, to "reason together." Where we can avoid the direct confrontations of American power by substituting an international policing apparatus, we should hasten to do so. The Gaza Strip, the Congo, Cyprus have all involved us in less expense, misunderstanding and abuse than the more direct confrontations of Southeast Asia. Our power and our will to use it remain the underpinning of worldwide freedom. But we should seek to mediate its application through the international institutions which seek to express the general judgments of mankind.

Similarly greater reliance on international action would, I think, give added effectiveness to our programs of economic support. The admirable activities of the lending agencies and of the United Nations agencies, the western consortia for aid to India and Pakistan, President Johnson's pro-

[115] He refers to the burning of United States Information Service libraries in a number of places.

posal for cooperative development in Southeast Asia are precedents and models.

The more our aid expresses recognition of the commitment of wealthy nations to the advancement of poorer neighbors, the less it comes in the guise of America's national self-interest, the more effective it will be — both for promoting worldwide growth and stability and frustrating communist propaganda.

In conclusion, may I express my conviction that, even in the perplexing, less black and white, world of the Sixties, we still have cause for confidence. Our allies in Europe are now strong enough to support themselves, to help others, and to argue with us. That gives them satisfaction and us tangible benefits. Our friends in the less developed world, while individually still greatly in need of aid and understanding, are collectively more assertive and more ready to play a part in the world. Sometimes that is irritating, but, since self-reliance and independence are our way of thinking, it is even more irritating to the communists.

By the nature of things we can adjust to a plural and polycentric world much more easily than they can. That is precisely what President Kennedy and President Johnson have been doing in foreign affairs during the past five years. We have made a good beginning. But much remains to be done.

In our new more fluid world, with its more diffuse power, its "polycentrism," its shifting balances and alliances, America is not called on to do everything, to lead everything, to bring everything to its own kind of conclusion. But it is called upon to use its wisdom for the concerting of common policies, its skill for the immediate negotiation of workable compromises, its patience and fortitude for the times when compromises and workable policies fail to emerge, and its ultimate vision and faith for a world society in which men and nations can be free.

As the astronomer Fred Hoyle has said: "The most important factor in our environment is the state of our own minds." The more rapidly and exactly we can adjust the state of our minds to the changes in the state of the world in the last twenty years, the more informed, the more sophisticated and the more successful our foreign policy will be.

There, too, I am sure you will agree, you share the responsibility with your Government. In the Forties the American newspaper played a great role in explaining to the American people the nature of the challenge, and what was required of them to meet it. I am confident you will be equally alert, as we move with the times into another era, to explain in what respects the same challenge persists and in what respects it or the instruments for dealing with it have been transformed.

That great lady, Eleanor Roosevelt, once said of herself: "What one has to do, usually can be done." That has usually been true of the American people. I believe they will recognize that, where leadership is more difficult because less unilateral, it is bound to be different but no less necessary.

To James Hester [116]

April 26, 1965

Dear Jim:

My secretary tells me that you called this morning while I was across the street at the Disarmament Commission meeting. I think I earned all of my Honorary Degrees today! — listening for hours to the Soviets' numerous and irrelevant attacks — and replying, also for hours! [117]

I wish I could accept your invitation to speak at NYU's Commencement on June 9. But, while I won't be in Europe that morning, I shall have to be in Chicago — if I survive that long!

Thanks so much for your flattering thought of me — and I suppose you are entitled to insist that that cherished Degree be earned twice!

With warmest regards,

Cordially yours,

To Lyndon B. Johnson

MEMORANDUM FOR THE PRESIDENT [118]

April 28, 1965

From: Adlai E. Stevenson

Subject: *Secretary-General's Proposal for Temporary Cessation of Hostilities in Vietnam*

Although the Secretary-General has so far deferred to our wishes by delaying his appeal for a cease-fire in Vietnam, I cannot be sure that he will defer some action indefinitely following his return from Europe on

[116] President of New York University.

[117] The Soviet spokesman stated: "The United States of America is opposed to the destruction of nuclear delivery vehicles at the beginning of the process of disarmament, and does not wish to hear about the elimination of foreign military bases." He added later: "Fantastic sums are being spent in the United States on the development of still newer and more modern means of destruction." He continued: "The most barbaric means of destruction are being used to the full by the United States militarists on battlefields many thousands of miles from the United States territory." Stevenson made a lengthy reply in the afternoon session. Among other things, he said: "Every step to increase our military capability since our unilateral disarmament — which was not reciprocated by the USSR — at the end of the Second World War has been taken in response to the expansionist policies of the communist world, first of the Soviet Union and now Communist China." See United Nations, *Official Records, Disarmament Commission*, April 26, 1965, pp. 1, 3, 5.

[118] This document was declassified. National Security Files, Agency File, Representative of the United States to the United Nations, Lyndon B. Johnson Library.

Friday, May 7. He is acutely conscious of his responsibilities as Secretary-General, troubled by criticism that he as Secretary-General and the UN as an institution have not been able to contribute to a solution in Vietnam, and strongly convinced that the continued use of force holds no promise for a settlement but only the ever-increasing danger of wider warfare, as well as a reorientation of Soviet foreign policy from limited detente with the West to close cooperation with Communist China.

Given this estimate of the Secretary-General's mood, we have set down below some of the advantages and disadvantages of acquiescing in an appeal by the Secretary-General for a cessation of hostilities in Vietnam.

Advantages

1. If we are receptive to the idea of the Secretary-General's appeal, we will obviously be in the best position to influence its contents and timing.

While we do not exclude an appeal to cease *all* hostilities, the Secretary-General may not think it wise to make an appeal broad enough to cover the fighting *within* South Vietnam because North Vietnam could more easily reject his appeal on the ground that it does not control the Viet Cong. Moreover, we doubt if it would be in our interests to accept an appeal which would prevent us and the South Vietnamese from continuing the war against the Viet Cong.

We believe the Secretary-General would be willing to make an appeal whose principal paragraph would be along the following lines:

"Therefore, I now appeal most earnestly and urgently to your Government to agree, along with the other two Governments directly concerned, (SVN and DRV) to: (a) a cessation for a period of ——— of all military activity in Vietnam, both overt and covert, across the boundaries, land, sea or air, of either of the Zones established in the Agreement on the Cessation of Hostilities in Vietnam of July 20, 1954, such cessation to take place as of the date of the acceptance of this appeal by the three parties to which it is addressed; (b) immediate discussions, in whatever manner the parties prefer, designed to strengthen and maintain the cessation of military activity and to seek the bases for a more permanent settlement." The Secretary-General proposed a three-month cessation but would take a shorter period if we prefer.

2. A favorable US response to the Secretary-General's appeal (conditional on a favorable response from North Vietnam) would greatly reinforce and add to the improved US image which stemmed from the President's April 7 speech.[119]

[119] In a broadcast speech at Johns Hopkins University, President Johnson said that the United States was willing to engage in "unconditional discussions" to end the war in Vietnam and proposed a large-scale program of economic development for Southeast Asia, perhaps including North Vietnam. His proposals were almost immediately rejected by North Vietnam, as well as Communist China and the Soviet Union.

3. Rejection of the Secretary-General's appeal by North Vietnam would do serious damage to the Communists' international posture and, at the same time, provide us with further justification in the eyes of the world community for continuing our air strikes against the North.

4. An appeal from the Secretary-General would place him on record as implicitly admitting that North Vietnam is engaged in the use of force against South Vietnam.

5. The Secretary-General, by making such an appeal, would become the center of the effort to terminate hostilities in Vietnam, a fact which would facilitate a later move on our part — should we so desire — to involve the United Nations in the role of supervising or policing a negotiated settlement.

Disadvantages

1. International pressure on the United States to cease its air strikes against the North will probably increase rather than decrease, and a favorable US response to the Secretary-General's appeal might be interpreted by some as a sign of weakness. This would not, however, be the case and could be counteracted by vigorous prosecution of the war against the Viet Cong.

2. Another possible disadvantage, one we are unable to assess, is the adverse effect the temporary cessation of air strikes against the North might have on the morale of the South Vietnamese.

3. If air strikes against the North were stopped in response to the Secretary-General's appeal, I suppose we would be subjected to pressure not to resume them even if we subsequently found that the North was continuing its infiltration of the South.

4. In this connection, our judgment (and the Secretary-General's) is that unilateral surveillance by the US and SVN is the only practicable means available for the immediate future to police a cessation of hostilities. An effective international police force could not be agreed [to] and established fast enough to deal with this situation.

We are also frankly dubious that surveillance by some international body — whether the UN or some other *ad hoc* body — would serve our interests at this stage. While it could easily check whether air strikes against the North had been halted, it would find it very hard, if not impossible, to check whether infiltration from the North had stopped. We might find ourselves in the position of claiming that the North had not lived up to the cease-fire bargain without confirmation from the international body. However, an international force to police an agreed settlement would be quite a different thing.

There is one fundamental strategic and political factor which underlies the whole problem.

The broader objectives of US policy are, in general, to demonstrate that Communist conquests, labeled as "wars of liberation," cannot be carried out successfully and, in particular, to "contain" Communist Chinese ambitions to dominate Southeast Asia and North Vietnamese ambitions to absorb South Vietnam.

The United States has the force to carry out these tasks, *if* the American people have the steadfastness to pursue them over many years. Experience in Europe shows that the job can be done, but also shows that it can be done much more successfully as a cooperative venture by many threatened states than by the US alone.

The same applies in large degree in Asia. One vital tactical factor must be so to carry out our operations there as to contribute to rather than to inhibit the eventual creation of a great defensive coalition. Essential members of an effective coalition in Asia would have to be, among others, Japan and India, the absence of which has made SEATO [Southeast Asia Treaty Organization] of limited value.

Our tactics in Vietnam so far, necessary as they are from other points of view, have not generated widespread Asian support, except among the small, weak states directly under the gun. This may not seem to matter at the moment, but how long will the American people be willing to carry almost the whole burden of containment in Asia.

On the other hand, our bold, determined action in Vietnam in the past three months has probably already persuaded the major Communist Powers that they can no longer pursue "wars of national liberation" in Asia, even in a relatively covert form, without very grave risks to themselves; the risk for the Soviets of a total breakdown of their policy of "peaceful coexistence" with the West, the risk for the Chinese of an unequal direct conflict with the United States. This realization is too recent to have yet produced a visible effect, but it is probably there and will give some pause to further Chinese expansionist plans.

It may be, therefore, that the lesson has already, or will soon, be driven home sufficiently so that we might begin to tailor our tactics more specifically to the longer-run objective, that is, to creating an Asian consensus and eventually an Asian coalition for the containment of China, a coalition in which the United States would of course participate heavily but which it would not have to carry almost entirely on its own back.

Another paramount political consideration is, of course, to reverse as quickly as we can, without other major drawbacks, a situation which tends willy-nilly to drive the Soviets into following a common policy with the Chinese, rather than Khrushchev's policy of open hostility to the Chinese. This of course works against our interests everywhere and, inter alia, inhibits the Soviet Union itself from participating in the containment of China, as it might otherwise wish to do to some degree.

In 1961, the dictator of the Dominican Republic, General Rafael Leonidas Trujillo, was assassinated. A year later Juan Bosch was elected president. But in September, 1963, a military junta overthrew him. On April 24, 1965, a popular rebellion broke out and toppled the ruling military junta. On April 28, President Johnson ordered the Marines to intervene in the civil war, and 23,000 United States troops were landed over the next few days. Johnson explained to the nation that he had ordered the intervention to protect the lives of Americans and other foreigners in the country. The American ambassador, W. Tapley Bennett, however, had recommended armed intervention not just to protect foreigners but to "prevent another Cuba" from arising out of the turmoil. On May 2, Johnson announced: "We know that many who are now in revolt do not seek a Communist tyranny. We think it's tragic indeed that their high motives have been misused by a small band of conspirators who receive their directions from abroad. . . ." [120]

Before speaking to the nation on April 28, President Johnson had congressional leaders and high officials, including Stevenson, to a meeting at the White House where Johnson explained what action he had authorized and read the speech he intended to deliver that evening. The speech went further than the mission to rescue foreigners. One line stated that the United States would always stand ready to help the Dominican Republic preserve its freedom. Stevenson asked the President to reread the sentence. When he did so, Stevenson asked the group: "What does that mean?" Eventually Johnson crossed out the line. [121]

On April 29, 1965, the council of the Organization of American States met in Washington, D.C., for bitter debate. A number of the ambassadors would not support the intervention without thorough consultation with their governments. They did agree, however, to ask the dean of the diplomatic corps in the Dominican Republic to try to arrange a cease-fire. On April 30 this was achieved. Brazil, Honduras, Paraguay, Nicaragua, and Costa Rica sent troops to join the United States forces.

A special committee of the Organization of American States went to the Dominican Republic. On June 18 the committee proposed free elections in 1966, a general amnesty, and the establishment of a provisional government.

The intervention ordered by Johnson prevented the insurgents from

[120] Stevenson watched the speech on television. He was surprised by this statement. Jerome Slater, *Intervention and Negotiation: The United States and the Dominican Revolution* (New York: Harper & Row, 1971), furnishes little or no support to the official rationale that there was a danger of a Communist takeover. See also Theodore Draper, "The Dominican Crisis," *Commentary*, December, 1965, and "The Dominican Intervention Reconsidered," *Political Science Quarterly*, March, 1971.

[121] Eric Sevareid, "The Final Troubled Hours of Adlai Stevenson," *Look*, November 30, 1965, p. 84.

gaining control of the government, but it triggered both in the United States and abroad widespread criticism of American motives and actions.[122]

The Soviet Union brought the Dominican case before the Security Council, condemned the "armed intervention" as a violation of the UN Charter, and demanded immediate withdrawal of United States forces. The Soviet resolution was defeated, but the United States, lacking strong Latin American support, agreed to a resolution that described the Security Council as "deeply concerned at the grave events in the Dominican Republic," called for a cease-fire, and invited the Secretary-General to send a representative to report to the Security Council on the "present situation." [123]

On May 3, 1965, Stevenson spoke to the Security Council.[124]

I think it is interesting to note that Cuba has asked for permission to speak to the Council in regard to this item on the agenda relating to the Dominican Republic, and we should be glad to hear the Cuban representative explain his country's role in this matter.

This, I would remind the Council, is the same Cuba which conspired with the Soviet Union to introduce into this hemisphere long-range ballistic missiles which were trained on the cities of the North and South American continents. This is the Cuba which stands charged with aggression by the Organization of American States and which because of that aggression was excluded from participation in the OAS and later cut off from diplomatic relations with the other members of that organization.[125]

This is the Cuban Government which stands condemned by the OAS for training and dispatching saboteurs and terrorists to other countries of Latin America, with the publicly expressed intent to overthrow the democratic Governments there established — Venezuela, Colombia and others.

Too long, perhaps, have we pretended that these things cannot be, that modern nations would not wish to interfere in the domestic concerns of others. But round the world we see this aggressive communist intervention carried on under the anomalous title of "freedom fighters."

I should like to remind the Council that this matter is being discussed at the request of the Soviet Union, and now the communist Government of Cuba has requested to participate in the discussion. My delegation finds this combination extremely interesting, and it emphasizes again the close relationship between the communist movement and what is going

[122] See, for instance, the speech by Senator J. W. Fulbright in the Senate, October 22, 1965.
[123] United Nations, *Official Records,* Security Council Resolution 203, May 14, 1965.
[124] United Nations, *Official Records,* Security Council, May 3, 1965, pp. 1–2.
[125] Mexico did not sever diplomatic relations with Cuba.

on in the Dominican Republic today. If the Castro Government feels it is so closely associated with the problem, it might be very useful to have it explain its part in this unhappy situation. We have no objection to seating the Cuban Government at this table for the discussion this afternoon.

After the Soviet ambassador called upon the Security Council to condemn "the armed interference by the United States in the domestic affairs of the Dominican Republic as a breach of international peace and as an action incompatible with the obligations assumed by the United States under the United Nations Charter," Stevenson spoke to the Security Council.[126]

We have heard from the representative of the Soviet Union about the Congo, about Viet-Nam, about Panama and about Cuba; we have even had some comments about Alabama and American business. I must say that after the recent experience we have had in United Nations bodies with Soviet polemics, reminiscent of the days of Stalin and Vyshinsky, I am not surprised that the Soviet Union has again used a United Nations body — this time the Security Council — to digress into a whole catalogue of complaints about United States resistance to communist expansion or assistance to those resisting aggression.

I used to marvel at the audacity of the Soviet Union in pointing an accusing finger at others — the Soviet Union, which signed a pact with Hitler, which forcibly added 264,000 square miles and over 24 million people to its own territory and population in the aftermath of the Second World War, which subjugated all of Eastern Europe, which crushed the uprisings in East Germany [1953] and Hungary [1956] and which has persistently sought to enlarge its domination elsewhere beyond its borders.

When one hears, as we did this morning, the Soviet Union, which has politically enslaved more people than any nation in this century, attack the good faith, the sincerity and the honesty of the Government of the United Kingdom, which has politically liberated more people than any nation in this century, one gets the measure of the Soviet cynical disdain for fact or fairness in the pursuit of its goals. Thus, when there are difficulties in the Western Hemisphere in which the United States is in any way involved, we know from experience that the Soviet Union will issue a loud and self-righteous blast accusing the United States of aggression or intervention, or both. Of course, it did not do so when the Soviet Union itself installed long-range missiles in Cuba; nor does it hesitate to denounce the United States while itself aiding and abetting the Castro

[126] United Nations, *Official Records,* Security Council, May 3, 1965, pp. 11–19.

regime to foment the forceful overthrow of established Governments throughout the Caribbean area. But whenever any defensive action is taken against subversion and disorder, the Soviet Union is the first to cry aggression.

Of course, the Soviet Union knows perfectly well that the Western Hemisphere has an active and effective regional organization, the OAS, to which the Republics of the Western Hemisphere are deeply attached and which they prefer to be the vehicle for resolving the problems of this Hemisphere. The Soviet Government also knows that the OAS has for several days been dealing with the situation in the Dominican Republic and has made substantial progress.

However, since the Soviet Union cannot use the Organization of American States for its customary attacks, it always hastens to bring such matters to the Security Council, where it can. Most of the Members of the United Nations are quite familiar with these tactics and with the traditional charges that they always involve. You will remember similar charges last year to the effect that the United States was committing aggression against Panama. I believe it is now apparent to all that Panama continues to enjoy its full sovereignty and independence. The same will be true of the Dominican Republic, if the agents of foreign Powers do not succeed in first exploiting and then taking over a democratic revolution as they did in Cuba and as they have tried and are trying to do in Venezuela and in other countries of the region. That this is the objective in the Dominican Republic is apparent from the very eagerness of the Soviet Union and of Cuba to exploit the present ambiguous situation in the Security Council before the full facts about this desperate strike for a Communist take-over in the Dominican Republic becomes more obvious.

I do not propose here to review in great detail the history of the Dominican Republic over the past five years or to speculate at any length on the origins or the political motivations of the mixed forces which have led to a state of anarchy in that unfortunate country. However, I do believe that it is relevant to our discussion to recall that the people of the Dominican Republic have suffered from constant turmoil and political conflict following in the wake of the long and tyrannical reign of the former dictator, Trujillo.

It is also relevant to recall that the final overthrow of that regime was brought about in part by the action of the OAS in adopting diplomatic sanctions against the Trujillo dictatorship. At that time, and in the period both preceding and following the election of Juan Bosch as President of the Dominican Republic, the Government of the United States supported every effort of the Dominican people to establish a representative democracy.

After the last remnants of the Trujillo regime had departed and the

Council of State was established, my Government, in conjunction with the Organization of American States, assisted in the preparation of an electoral code, made available information and procedures on the mechanics of elections and, finally, again in conjunction with the OAS, observed the actual elections, the first free elections held in the Dominican Republic in over thirty years. Both prior to and following those elections my Government has pursued extensive efforts to build a stable and free society capable of economic, social and political development. Let there be no doubt in anybody's mind of my Government's devotion to the cause of representative government in the American republics.

The members of this Council know well the instability which often follows the end of authoritarian regimes and the difficulties of a people unfamiliar with the practices of democracy in establishing effective government. The Soviet Union itself has had some experience with the difficulties of transferring power without public participation and approval.

About a week ago the instability which has plagued the Dominican Republic since the fall of the Trujillo regime erupted and the officials who had governed there for a year and a half were violently forced out. Rival groups strove to capture power; fighting broke out between them and among them; and the Dominican Republic was left without effective government for some days. As the situation deteriorated, certain of the contending forces indiscriminately distributed weapons to civilians; armed bands began to roam the streets of Santo Domingo, looting, burning and sniping; law and order completely broke down. The Embassies of Mexico, Guatemala, Peru, Ecuador and the United States were violated and the Embassy of El Salvador burned.

The great majority of those who joined in this insurgent cause in the Dominican Republic are not Communists. In particular, my Government has never believed that the PRD — the Dominican Revolutionary Party, led by President Bosch — is an extremist party. United States co-operation with President Bosch and his Government during his tenure following the ouster of President Trujillo speaks for itself. But, while the PRD planned and during its first hours led the revolutionary movement against the Government of Reid Cabral, a small group of well-known Communists, consistent with their usual tactics, quickly attempted to seize control of the revolution and of the armed bands in the streets. Quite clearly this group was acting in conformity with directives issued by a Communist conference that met in Havana in late 1964 and printed in Pravda on 18 January 1965. These directives called for assistance and continuing campaigns in support of the so-called "freedom fighters" to be organized "on a permanent basis so that this work will not dwindle to sporadic manifestations or disunited statements." They went on to say: "Active aid should be given to those who are subject at present to cruel repressions — for instance, the freedom fighters in Venezuela, Colombia, Guatemala, Honduras, Paraguay and Haiti."

This deliberate effort to promote subversion and overthrow Governments in flagrant violation of all norms of international conduct is responsible for much of the unrest in the Caribbean area.

In the face of uncontrollable violence, the Government which had replaced the Reid Cabral Government also quickly crumbled in a few days. Many of its leaders, and also others from the initial leadership of the revolt against the Reid Cabral Government also sought asylum.

In the absence of any governmental authority Dominican law enforcement and military officials informed our Embassy that the situation was completely out of control, that the police and the Government could no longer give any guarantee concerning the safety of Americans or of any foreign nationals and that only an immediate landing of United States forces could safeguard and protect the lives of thousands of Americans and thousands of citizens of some thirty other countries. At that moment, the United States Embassy was under fire; the death toll in the city, according to Red Cross estimates, had reached 400; hospitals were unable to care for the wounded; medical supplies were running out; the power supply had broken down; and a food shortage threatened.

Faced with that emergency, the threat to the lives of its citizens, and a request for assistance from those Dominican authorities still struggling to maintain order, the United States on 28 April dispatched the first of the security forces that we have sent to the island. Since their arrival, nearly 3,000 foreign nationals from thirty countries have been evacuated without loss, although a number of the United States military personnel have been killed or wounded. We have made a full report to the Organization of American States; we have successfully evacuated some 2,000 Americans and about 1,000 persons of other nationalities; we have established the secure zone of refuge called for by the OAS; we have supported the dispatch by the OAS of the Committee which is at present in Santo Domingo; we have proposed that other American States make military forces available to assist in carrying out the mission of that Committee and the OAS is considering such a resolution this afternoon.

To refresh your recollection of last week's events, let me remind the Council of the sequence.

On Tuesday, 27 April, this situation was considered by the Inter-American Peace Committee. On Wednesday, 28 April, the OAS was formally notified by the representative of the Dominican Republic about the situation in his country, and my Government called for an urgent meeting of the Council of the Organization of American States to consider ways to bring an end to the bloodshed by a cease-fire and to restore order so that the people of the Dominican Republic could settle their own political affairs without further recourse to arms.

At the same time my Government notified the President of the Security Council [127] of the action that it had taken to evacuate citizens of foreign nationality and to set in motion the machinery of the Organization of American States.

The Council of the OAS met on Thursday, 29 April, and as a first step called for an immediate cease-fire on all sides, and then addressed an appeal to the Papal Nuncio in Santo Domingo, requesting him to use his good offices to help effect a cease-fire and a return to peace.

The Council of the OAS continued in session and, in the early hours of 30 April, took a second action urgently calling upon all parties "to pursue immediately all possible means by which a cease-fire may be established and all hostilities and military operations suspended in order to prevent any further tragic loss of life." By the same resolution, the OAS Council decided:

> "To make an urgent appeal to the same authorities, political groupings and forces on all sides to permit the immediate establishment of an international neutral zone of refuge, encompassing the geographic area of the city of Santo Domingo immediately surrounding the embassies of foreign governments, the inviolability of which will be respected by all opposing forces within which nationals of all countries will be given safe haven."

At the same time, on the initiative of the representative of Venezuela, an urgent meeting of the Foreign Ministers of the Organization of American States was called for 1 May to consider what further measures should be taken to restore peace to the Dominican Republic.

The Security Council was immediately informed by the OAS of all these actions, in accordance with Article 54 of the Charter of the United Nations. In accordance with the OAS resolution of 30 April, United States forces in the Dominican Republic have now established, as I said, a safety zone. As I have said, 3,000 persons have now been evacuated, representing some thirty countries, including fourteen countries of this hemisphere; more than 5,000 persons, 1,500 of whom are American, and others of foreign nationalities are still awaiting evacuation.

These evacuations continue and efforts are being made to secure the safety of some 5,000 people who are awaiting evacuation, including 1,000 American citizens and 500 citizens of other countries who remain in peril throughout the Republic. In addition, my Government has distributed

[127] This letter is USUN press release 4536.

more than 6,000 tons of food and medical supplies to all elements in Santo Domingo, to relieve the suffering of the population.

The Council of the OAS, on the afternoon of 30 April, took another step. It dispatched the Secretary General of that organization, Dr. Jose Mora, to the Dominican Republic. He departed on Saturday and is now working with the Papal Nuncio and others to restore order.

On Saturday the OAS again convened as a meeting of consultation the Ministers of Foreign Affairs. This time it dispatched a five-member committee composed of Argentina, Brazil, Colombia, Guatemala and Panama "to go immediately to the city of Santo Domingo, to do everything possible to obtain re-establishment of peace and normal conditions." The Committee was directed to give priority to two tasks: in the first place "to offer its good offices to the Dominican armed groups and political groups and to the diplomatic representatives for the purpose of obtaining urgently: (i) a cease-fire; and (ii) the orderly evacuation of persons who have taken asylum in diplomatic missions and of all foreign citizens who desire to leave the Dominican Republic"; and secondly, "to investigate all aspects of the current situation in the Dominican Republic that led to the convocation of this Meeting." This Committee, the members of the Council may be interested to know, is now actively at work in the Dominican Republic.

The members are no doubt aware that as a result of these repeated appeals a cease-fire was first agreed to — on the initiative of the Papal Nuncio — late in the afternoon of 30 April by the military leaders and by some of the leaders of the opposition forces, and on 1 May it was also signed by Colonel [Francisco] Ca[a]mano, their most authoritative leader. Although the leaders of the opposition forces declare that they no longer control many elements which are still shooting in and around Santo Domingo, this agreement began to take effect among the organized forces Saturday and Sunday, and the situation in the city was much improved by yesterday afternoon.

However, lawlessness and disorder have by no means been eliminated. It has become clear that communist leaders, many trained in Cuba, have taken increasing control of what was initially a democratic movement, and many of the original leaders of the rebellion, the followers of President Bosch, have taken refuge in foreign embassies.

The American nations will not permit the establishment of another communist government in the Western hemisphere. This was the unanimous view of all the American nations when in January 1962 they declared, "The principles of communism are incompatible with the principles of the inter-American system." This is, and this will be, the common action and the common purpose of the democratic forces of the hemisphere, as President Lyndon B. Johnson has said. For the danger is also a common danger, and the principles are common principles. So we have acted to summon the resources of this entire hemisphere to this task.

At the same time, we have increased our own forces in the light of the urgency of the situation. The OAS Committee now in the Dominican Republic has called for the urgent shipment of more food and medical supplies to be made available to the Secretary General of the OAS, and the organization adopted a resolution to that effect just this morning. The United States will respond promptly.

The OAS has before it today, I repeat, a resolution which would request Governments of the American States that are capable of doing so to make available to the OAS contingents of their military, naval or air forces, to assist in carrying out the Committee's mission. The same resolution would also provide for the Meeting of Consultation to continue in session in order to take the necessary steps to facilitate the prompt restoration of constitutional government in the Dominican Republic and the withdrawal of foreign forces.

In this connexion, I should like to reaffirm the statement made by Ambassador Ellsworth Bunker, representing the United States, in the OAS meeting on Saturday. He said:

"My Government regrets that there was no inter-American force available to respond to the request of the authorities and the needs of the people of the Dominican Republic, and for the protection of the lives and the safety of other nationals. And my Government would welcome the constitution of such a force as soon as possible."

The efforts of the Organization of American States to deal with this tragic crisis in the Dominican Republic have been carefully considered, prudent and reasonable actions. Heroic efforts to end the bloodshed by cease-fire have been made by the Papal Nuncio. The Secretary General of the OAS is in the island contributing his prestige and abilities to this effort. The Inter-American Commission on Human Rights is also in Santo Domingo and functioning actively.

In the face of these energetic and productive steps, the Soviet effort to exploit the anarchy in the Dominican Republic for its own ends is regrettable, if familiar.

My delegation welcomes the discussion in the Security Council of this situation in the Dominican Republic. Members of the Council are well aware, however, that Article 33 of the United Nations Charter states that efforts should be made to find solutions to disputes first of all by peaceful means, including "resort to regional agencies or arrangements." This, of course, does not derogate from the authority of this Council. It merely prescribes the procedures and priorities envisaged by the authors of the two charters, the Charter of the United Nations and that of the OAS, for dealing with disputes of a local nature, procedures and priorities that have been followed consistently in analogous situations in the past.

In the light of the actions already taken, it would be prudent, it would be constructive and in keeping with the precedents established by this Council to permit the regional organization to continue to deal with this regional problem. The United Nations Charter, in Article 52, specifically recognizes the authority of regional organizations in dealing with regional problems. The Council recognizes the desirability of encouraging regional efforts, and I may add, the confidence of this Council in the abilities of regional organizations to deal with their own problems has been justified by the historical record.

In closing I should like to make two things quite clear. First, the United States Government has no intention of seeking to dictate the political future of the Dominican Republic. We believe that the Dominican people, under the established principle of self-determination, should select their own government through free elections. It is not our intention to impose a military junta or any other government. Our interest lies in the reestablishment of constitutional government and, to that end, to assist in maintaining the stability essential to the expression of the free choice of the Dominican people. This intent is in full accord with the basic democratic tenets of the Organization of American States and the inter-American system, the charter of which calls for the maintenance of systems of political organization "on the basis of the effective exercise of representative democracy."

The United States intends to continue to work with the OAS in assisting the Dominican people to return as soon as possible to constitutional government. With the good will and the sincere support of all parties concerned, we are confident that the Dominican people will ultimately be able to have the democratic and progressive government which they seek, and we feel that the members of this body should encourage such a peaceful and orderly evolution in this small republic which has suffered so long from tyranny and civil strife.

Secondly, as President Johnson has emphasized, the United States will never depart from its commitment to the preservation of the right of all of the free people of this hemipshere to choose their own course without falling prey to international conspiracy from any quarter. Our goal in the Dominican Republic is the goal which has been expressed again and again in the treaties and agreements which make up the fabric of the inter-American system. It is that the people of that country must be permitted freely to choose the path of political democracy, social justice and economic progress. Neither the United States nor any nation can want or permit a return to that brutal and offensive despotism which earned the condemnation and punishment of this hemisphere and of all civilized humanity. We intend to carry on the struggle against tyranny, no matter in what ideology it cloaks itself. This is our mutual responsibility under the agreements that we have signed and the common values which bind us together.

Thirdly, we believe that change comes, and we are glad that it does, and it should come through peaceful process. But revolution in any country is a matter for that country to deal with. It becomes a matter calling for hemispheric action only — and I repeat, only — when the object is the establishment of a communistic dictatorship.

Let me also make clear that we support no single man or single group of men in the Dominican Republic. Our goal is a simple one: we are there to save the lives of our people and to save the lives of all people. Our goal, in keeping with the principles of the American system, is to help prevent another communist State in this hemisphere, and we should like to do this without bloodshed or without large-scale fighting.

The form and the nature of a free Dominican Government, I assure you, is solely a matter for the Dominican people. But we do know what kind of government we hope to see in the Dominican Government, for that is carefully spelled out in the treaties and agreements which make up the fabric of the entire inter-American system. It is expressed time and again in the words of our statesmen and the values and hopes which bind us all together. We hope to see a government freely chosen by the will of all the people. We hope to see a government working every hour of every day feeding the hungry, educating the ignorant, healing the sick, a government whose only concern is the progress, the elevation and the welfare of all the people of that country.

After the Soviet ambassador in strong language criticized United States foreign policy since the end of World War II, and the Ambassador of Cuba denounced United States intervention as "one of the most criminal and shameful acts of this century," Stevenson spoke again to the Security Council.[128]

I do not intend to detain the Council for long at this stage, but I must reserve the right to speak again at somewhat greater length as the discussion proceeds, in view of some of the statements that have been made here this afternoon by the representatives of the Soviet Union and Cuba.

I have been interested by the fact that of late the Soviet Union representative seems always to bring two documents with him: one is his

[128] United Nations, *Official Records*, Security Council, May 3, 1965, pp. 45–47.

speech, and the other is his right of reply, prepared in advance. I wonder if we had not better re-label the right of reply the right to reply by unlimited extension of one's speech.

I should like to enquire: Did I cast any shadows on the gallant struggle of the Soviet armies in the last war? No, not one. Indeed, the Soviet Union representative could have found, had he wished to do so, some words of mine to quote in praise of that struggle.

But I do not think that any diversionary rhetoric can change the facts of history, can change the fact that since the war the world has been afflicted by some aggressive Powers, but the United States has not been one of them.

The Soviet Union representative has mentioned some moths in the lion's skin as examples of United States sins: Viet-Nam, the Congo, Korea. I would point out to the Security Council that all have been cases of attempts to protect the integrity and independence of States from outside interference.

I am not surprised that the Soviet Union representative is touchy about some of the record of the past twenty years, including its acquisition of great amounts of territory and its alliance with Nazi Germany. But I am surprised at exactly how touchy he has turned out to be. The Soviet Army did indeed, as I have said, fight most gallantly in the Second World War. We are all profoundly indebted to it for that, although I would hardly ascribe the entire credit to it, as the Soviet Union representative seemed to do. We were indeed prepared to continue in the post-war world the co-operation with the Soviet Union that had prevailed during the war. The blame for the great gulf which followed that war lies squarely and solely on the policies of the Soviet Union during that time.

I regret that in recent weeks the Soviet Union representative has revived — first in the Special Committee on Peace-keeping Operations, then in the Committee on the definition of aggression, then in the Disarmament Commission, and now in the Security Council — the language and techniques of the Stalin era. I hope that this is only a passing phase and that the frustrations of the Soviet Union's troubles with its former ally [China] will not continue to plague us here.

I shall not speak any further about the history of the Soviet Union, as he has seen fit to speak about the history of my country. Russia did expand from the Duchy of Moscow to the Arctic, to Central Asia, and all the way to the Pacific. Facts which, I think, are familiar to all of us hardly need repetition here.

I should like to turn, for only a moment, to the extensive remarks of the representative of Cuba.

While it is not easy, I shall disregard the extreme offensiveness of many of the Cuban representative's remarks, such as his references to pirates in Washington and liars in the White House committing criminal acts. If he had spent as much time learning facts as he has spent learning epithets and insults, I think that he would have had some trouble getting quite so emotional about the imperialistic objectives of the United States in the Dominican Republic.

History will, I think, speak on the full significance of the present situation in the Dominican Republic, just as it will speak on the rescue mission in the Congo. And when it has spoken, it will be clear that the role of United States forces in the Dominican Republic has been constructive, and not destructive, of the freedom of the Dominican Republic.

I remind the representative of Cuba too that it has been necessary, as I have said, to send United States troops to several countries since the Second World War: to Korea, to Lebanon, to the Congo to evacuate foreigners, and to Viet-Nam. In no case have those troops derogated from the sovereignty and independence of the country in which they have been employed. Indeed, one of the main reasons for their dispatch has been to help preserve that independence, whether threatened by direct aggression or by the modern forces of subversion and totalitarian techniques.

The representative of Cuba has used freely some extreme language to express his conclusions about the sins of the United States and our malevolent purposes in the Dominican Republic, but few facts to support his conclusions and a good many false statements. Let me assure the representative of Cuba that he is misinformed and that I can categorically deny that the United States has done any bombing in the Dominican Republic. Nor have we been fighting against constitutionalists — to use his word. We have been fighting against fighting, trying to stop bloodshed and to restore order. I can assure him — to pick up an argument of his — that, unless there are nations and international organizations that will denounce aggression and will protect against aggression whether by armies or by agents, there surely will be no free States left. This is the danger in the future — not conquest of anybody by the United States. We have not invaded the Dominican Republic; we have acted to protect foreigners in a revolution, in concert with our fellow representatives in this hemisphere, and to protect the Dominican people from a communist seizure of the country while the Dominicans themselves determine their future.

However, the extensive attacks we have heard may be pertinent in a way to the subject before us, for they serve to remind us how easily and how quickly a revolution offered to and accepted by a people in the name of democratic freedom and social progress can be betrayed. It reminds us of the grim struggle which took place within the Cuban revolutionary regime which overthrew Batista, the struggle between those who overthrew Batista to bring freedom to Cuba and those who overthrew Batista to bring Cuba to communism. It reminds us of the tragic outcome of that struggle: brave men who had fought for the revolution with Castro were turned upon, suddenly assailed, arrested and driven from office into prison or exile, all for the single offense of believing in the principles of the revolution they had fought for. This stark reminder of revolution betrayed will remain for ever in the minds and hearts of all the citizens of the Western Hemisphere and it cannot but influence actions which are taken to bring order out of chaos in the Dominican Republic.

I had not thought of referring to the contemptuous epithets he has used with reference to sister Republics of this hemisphere — "lackeys," "lickspittles" and so on. However, it was curious that he first quoted with approval what they said when they expressed concern and doubt about our urgent response to the call for help and he then denounced them in these repulsive epithets when they discovered the facts and joined to help in stopping the bloodshed and to restore order to the Dominican Republic and give the people of that beleagu[e]red land a chance to restore constitutional democracy to their country.

In the Security Council's continuing discussion of U.S. intervention in the Dominican Republic, Stevenson spoke on May 4, 5, 6, 7, 11, 13, 14, 19, 20, 21, 22, and 24 and on June 9 and 18.

To Lady Barbara Jackson

May 11, 1965

Dearest Barbara:

Things have been beyond description lately and "two lines" have been as elusive as peace. About speeches, I enclose something that has interested me a great deal and may be worth some reflection in anticipation of Toronto or even Harvard.[129] I have been so submerged in Southern Rhodesia, Dominican Republic, Vietnam et al. that I haven't had the opportunity to reflect on futures. But there is much to talk about. I wonder if you might find it convenient on your arrival to stay with me on Thursday, May 20th. Perhaps I shall have to ask you to go to an American Jewish Committee dinner in honor of Herbert Lehman. The speakers will be Hubert Humphrey and Martin Luther King. I am sure you will be most welcome, and afterwards we can have a talk.

---

[129] He was to speak at both universities.

Between now and then, I hope to get my mind on Toronto et seq. and perhaps you will be proliferating ideas meanwhile — as usual!

Goodbye — I am leaving for the Dominican Republic across the street!

Love always,

To Harry S. Truman

May 11, 1965

Dear Mr. President;

Only revolution in the Dominican Republic, war in Viet Nam, crisis in Southern Rhodesia and perpetual conflict in the United Nations could have obscured your birthday.

Though belatedly, I send you congratulations and renewed thanks for all you have done for our country and for me personally.

With affectionate regards to Mrs. Truman and prayers for health and happiness for all the Trumans,

Cordially yours,

P.S. Enclosed is a "token" for the [Truman Memorial] Library — which I am determined to see again and soon I hope.

To Mrs. Eugene Meyer [130]

May 11, 1965

Dearest Agnes:

Alas! I must be in S[an] F[rancisco] for the 20th anniv[ersary] ceremonies of the UN on the June 26 week end.[131] But please give me another chance. I yearn to see you and had hoped to be at the garden party this afternoon. Instead I was in the S[ecurity] C[ouncil] wrangling about the Dom Rep. and there is no relief in sight.

Love always

To James Wechsler

May 12, 1965

Dear Jimmy:

I am deeply grateful that you did not consult me![132] As you well sensed, everything has not been to my liking of late.

[130] This handwritten letter is in the Agnes Meyer files, Princeton University Library.
[131] Mrs. Meyer had invited Stevenson for a tennis weekend.
[132] Mr. Wechsler wrote a column for the New York *Post* attacking the intervention in the Dominican Republic. He telephoned Clayton Fritchey and asked that Stevenson be told that he had deliberately refrained from asking for an interview. See James Wechsler, "The Stevenson I knew," *Progressive,* September, 1965, p. 30.

I still hope we can have a proper talk one of these days.

And I am always flattered and touched by your references to me — even if I don't say so!

Yours,

Arthur M. Schlesinger, Jr., sent Stevenson a copy of a letter he had written to two White House aides on May 10 expressing his concern that instead of being neutral in the civil war in the Dominican Republic, we were supporting another right-wing government. Schlesinger warned that the Administration would be charged with prejudging the nature of the revolution, for unnecessarily ignoring the Organization of American States, and for sending far too many troops. On May 30, 1965, Stevenson talked to Schlesinger in Washington, D.C. and Stevenson said to him that "if we did so badly in the Dominican Republic, I now wonder about our policy in Vietnam." [133]

To Arthur M. Schlesinger, Jr.

May 14, 1965

Dear Arthur:

I am so glad you sent me your splendid letter about the Dominican Republic. Nothing has caused me as much trouble since the Bay of Pigs and it goes on and on.

It reminds me that I wish I could see you more often.

Indeed I must see you! I have a commencement speaking engagement at your Alma Mater (top secret!) and I need some advice as to what to talk about. I have been a good boy for years and haven't imposed on you but the moment is fast approaching. Perhaps you will be here one day and could let me know in advance. If not, I will try to chisel a moment out of those dreadful days in Washington.

Yours,

To Howard F. Gillette [134]

May 27, 1965

Dear Howard:

I have emerged from the streets of Santo Domingo and the jungles of Vietnam long enough to catch my breath and re-examine the schedule.

I am grateful for your letter of May 12, [135] and have accepted the

---

[133] Schlesinger, interview with Walter Johnson, April 8, 1973.

[134] General secretary of the alumni of Harvard University.

[135] Mr. Gillette had sent Stevenson a program for the commencement at which he was to receive an honorary degree.

Chief Marshal's spread for June 17th. While I have not yet tried to master the whole schedule, I must do something about the "guests" promptly. But first may I ask if, having no wife, it would be possible for me to bring Lady Jackson (Barbara Ward) to the Pusey [136] dinner on the 17th. If you have any reservations whatsoever, I am sure she will understand and, of course, I will. She knows the Puseys very well and I thought it a nice courtesy as long as she is going to be in Cambridge at that time. She is also, as you know, a former commencement speaker. [137]

As for my guests at the commencement exercises, I would like to bring my son, Borden Stevenson, 44 East 67th Street, New York, who is a Harvard graduate. I would also like to invite my son and his wife, Mr. and Mrs. Adlai E. Stevenson, 1519 North Dearborn Parkway, Chicago, Illinois. He is also a Harvard alumni, and I am not at all sure they will be able to come.

If additional guests are permitted for the commencement exercises, I would like to include the Honorable Marietta P. Tree, 123 East 79th Street, New York, and Mrs. John Alden Carpenter, Sunset Hill, Beverly, Massachusetts. The former is an Ambassador of the United States on my staff and a sister of Chuck Peabody; [138] the latter is my former mother-in-law. My children will be staying with her.

It will be good to see you and Mary. [139]

Cordially yours,

On May 28, 1965, Stevenson spoke at a convocation at the University of Toronto. Two days later in Washington, D.C., at a Memorial Day concert he narrated the Lincoln Portrait *by composer Aaron Copland. "With rugged simplicity, he spoke the words of Lincoln so eloquently that even fidgeting school boys sensed a moment to remember," Dorothy McCardle wrote.* [140]

On June 1, Stevenson delivered an address at the fifty-sixth annual convention of Rotary International at Atlantic City. Three days later he spoke at the sixty-seventh annual meeting of the Arkansas Bar Association at Hot Springs National Park.

[136] Nathan M. Pusey, president of Harvard University.
[137] She had delivered the commencement address in 1957.
[138] Endicott Peabody, former governor of Massachusetts.
[139] Mrs. Gillette.
[140] Washington *Post,* May 31, 1965.

To Mrs. Ronald Tree [141]

May 30, 1965

M —

It is Sunday — a whole week — and, thank God, it has been *another* such week! It is always better, easier that way — no time for reflection, reverie — just little flashes here and there, by day and by night — of Lusaka,[142] *where* you were sleeping, *what* you were thinking, how harried and angry, frustrated and fierce, you felt; yes, and how nice, statistically and otherwise, it would have been to add another country. Then there was the news of the eggs — and where were *you!*

I'm in a beautiful Canadian Air plane — the PMs [Prime Minister's] flying from Ottawa to Wash[ington] after my visit to Toronto & Ottawa. I may be able to slip in a clipping or so to give you at least a superficial idea of all that transpired on this eventful journey from which I emerge unscathed and content that neither the US or AES lost any ground. I have *never* had more fulsome, extravagant introductions at all the public appearances — doubtless inflated to compensate for the hostile pickets [143] — which were not very hostile to an old veteran of Dallas hawks — and the demonstrations which may have been noisy for Canada but were muted for us.

I shall not attempt to rehearse the week, let alone the stuffed schedule in Canada. This time is *really* your turn to deliver the *details*. As for me it is sufficient to say that the speech — prepared under difficult circumstances — went off gloriously and I had what they said was the only standing ovation in the experience of their convocations. The luncheon by the PM & the afternoon with Mike [Lester B.] Pearson at his country retreat were all easy, relaxed, agreeable & useful. The dinner with 2000 alumni in the great hall — given by the Massey Fdn [Foundation] — was done with great style & dignity and the utterances about me very moving. Last night the U S Ambass[ador's] dinner in Ottawa was heavier but tolerable in spite of exhaustion.

And now its 2 PM — Wash is below — I'll try to get a tennis game; rehearse my Lincoln Portrait perform[ance] outdoors with the Nat[ional] Symphony, go to the reception and then catch up on sleep at Laura [Magnuson]'s.

Monday — All went well in Wash — clips enclosed — and now I'm back in the office on Decoration Day and the loveliest day I've *ever* seen in N.Y! . . .

---

141 This handwritten letter is in the possession of Mrs. Tree.

142 She was in Africa with the UN Committee of 24.

143 When Stevenson spoke at the University of Toronto, pickets carried signs denouncing United States foreign policy.

Tues night — 1:00 AM — Decoration Day went like all the rest — no, gloriously! — as I struggled to get thru the day's office work and then a speech for this morning in Atlantic City to the Rotary International. I flew off in a small plane with Luther Hodges [144] & Borden [Stevenson] & re entered that great hall full of shades & horrors of last summer's convention and the indescribable disorder — even ours — to find 12 000! — literally — people waiting for me. The speech worked — why I don't know — and I flew back to N.Y., again content — right over the Traymore — but with that uncomfortable questioning — what am I doing all this for — for me? . . . for who?

Tonight it was two receptions and then a dinner for Erhard [145] & a reply to his speech. Now — at 1 AM — George McGhee [146] has left and I'm alone — at last — with nothing except these blank pages and a speech to do for Arkansas day after tomorrow — and no time tomorrow.

But this whimper of self pity is unworthy. . . . Your exhaustion is greater than mine. And I can picture those sweaty nights trying to get ready to retaliate tomorrow in a strange room in a strange land surrounded by strange people — and diverted even by occasional thoughts less strange. . . .

I *pray* you are well — fit — and fighting.

. . . I want so much to telephone Penelope [147] . . . Frankie [148] — yes — I'll try to see her.

To Mr. and Mrs. Hugh Patterson [149]

June 8, 1965

My dear friends:

My happy weekend on the farm was interrupted — as usual! — by more Dominican trouble and instead of rolling in the lush green grass of Illinois, I'm duelling with our adversaries in New York.

But while the memory of Arkansas is still fresh, let me thank you again for making it such a happy and profitable one. And please remember your promise to let me know when you come this way.

Cordially yours,

---

[144] Secretary of Commerce, 1961–1965, and former governor of North Carolina.
[145] Ludwig Erhard, chancellor of West Germany.
[146] United States ambassador to West Germany.
[147] Penelope Tree, Mrs. Tree's daughter.
[148] Frances FitzGerald, Mrs. Tree's daughter.
[149] Mr. Patterson was the publisher of the *Arkansas Gazette*.

To Charles Hanly [150]

June 11, 1965

Dear Mr. Hanly:

I apologize for neglecting your letter of May 28th. I am afraid it got lost among my papers when I returned from Toronto.

I appreciate the candor of your comments on United States policy in Vietnam and in the Dominican Republic, but I am afraid it would serve no purpose to re-argue the case by letter. I hope the speech I made at Toronto served at least in part to explain my Government's position.

I am sure you know that President Johnson is as eager as anyone to find a peaceful solution in both cases. The United States has made more than 13 efforts, directly or indirectly, to induce Hanoi to negotiate a peaceful solution in Vietnam. I assumed it was apparent to everyone by this time that Peking and Hanoi are not interested in a peaceful solution as long as there is a prospect of winning by a military decision.

In the Dominican Republic, military intervention has prevented a continuation of the blood-bath and at least an opportunity to enable the people to choose their own government by free elections.

Sincerely yours,

To Lyndon B. Johnson

June 11, 1965

Dear Mr. President:

I was alarmed by your remark at the National Security Council meeting this morning that you might not go to San Francisco. After the widely publicized reports that you were definitely going to speak at the concluding session, any rumor, let alone any decision that you were not going at all, would cause consternation and, I fear, grave damage in the UN, not to mention bitter disappointment in San Francisco.

Internationally, I suspect there would be several interpretations, none advantageous to us. In the UN, I have no doubt feelings would be offended. In San Francisco, where they had expected chiefs of state and a large meeting as at the time of the 10th Anniversary, you are, of course, the only major "attraction."

I could multiply reasons why I hope you do not reconsider. I hope I shall have an opportunity to do so before you conclude not to go. We need help these days, and this occasion affords a fine opportunity which I am sure you can exploit most effectively.[151]

Sincerely yours,

---

[150] Of the University of Toronto.
[151] The President replied on June 14 that he doubted that he should go to San Francisco. However, he eventually decided to attend the United Nations twentieth anniversary ceremonies, and he spoke there on June 25.

On June 13, 1965, Stevenson received an honorary degree from Williams College, where he delivered the commencement address.[152]

I am grateful for the honor you have conferred on me. Coming as it does from this illustrious college which has for so long commanded respect far beyond our borders, it has great personal significance for me.

Every June I decide that I will never make another commencement address. There is nothing more perishable than commencement speeches. But then come another June, and I find I'm commencing commencements all over again. I'm sure it is vanity. All politicians, even old ex-politicians, like to be mistaken for scholars. And after five years at the United Nations I can't resist an invitation to speak — where there is no right of reply.

I assure you I will long remember the reception you have given me. The beauty of this tranquil place brings back memories of another commencement here at Williams during the last war, 22 or 23 years ago. I came here on such a lovely June day as this with the Secretary of the Navy, Frank Knox, who was my boss. Everyone said he made a fine speech — which pleased him, and pleased me even more — because I wrote it. I wish someone else had written my speech, for now it is my turn — and it is your unhappy assignment to have to listen.

I wish I could have brought you a neat package of instant truths about our world that would in one blinding flash of insight set things right. Goethe said that there are many echoes in the world, but only a few voices. All truisms, unfortunately, tend to be echoes, and a little boring. So I would like to bore you today not to extinction but to distinction. I would like to help you graduates attain that "peculiar grace" that Browning wrote about — of learning how to live before living. But I can't.

So I have concluded to follow Mark Twain's recommendation:

"To do so is noble: to tell others to do good is also noble, and much less trouble."

I have no trouble telling you to be noble and do good. And I suppose if these days of ferment, demonstration and protest on the campus mean anything, they mean a lot of young people are genuinely concerned about the great issues and are trying to be noble and good. I seem to be less concerned about it all than some of my contemporaries — probably because I have been picketed, applauded and abused everywhere from Texas to Toronto, by the far right and the far left — and the far center, perhaps.

[152] The text is based on USUN press release 4585.

A friend of mine, Adam Yarmolinsky,[153] said not long ago that if it is the proper function of prophetic tradition to comfort the afflicted and to afflict the comfortable, it would seem that these young prophets on the right are busy comforting the comfortable, while those on the left are only afflicting the afflicted!

But a decade ago they were neither afflicting nor comforting. They were withdrawing from politics and the conflicts of real life. They were more concerned with their own future, their families and private lives. But we don't hear so much now about the young graduates whose first question to a prospective employer was about pension plans and early retirement options.

This violent swing of the pendulum from small private concerns to large public concern — be it civil rights in the United States, war in Vietnam or intervention in the Dominican Republic — cannot, I think, be too alarming, in spite of all the accompanying immaturity and emotion.

But if I could offer one word of advice about the nobility of doing good I would say that movements that focus on moral goals, no matter how noble, without consideration of the means to achieve those goals, reflect neither a meaningful commitment to morality nor a practical hope of improving the human condition. Any movement, whether conservative or radical, cannot responsibly tell us where it wants to go without telling us how it proposes to get there.

And with that sage advice let me talk a bit about the state of this world you can help to manage better.

Nobody needs reminding these days that our first concern must be for the survival of the human experiment. We repeat it so often that we have all but rubbed the meaning off the words. This is the danger of a world of total communication — we communicate the daylights out of everything — and I should know, being, alas!, a notable practitioner myself.

But we must try to keep sense in the words we use — especially in the words of crisis — and I would like not only to repeat the all-too-often repeated cliches about survival, but to try to make you feel that, if anything, the risks and dangers are understated. If you accuse me of trying "to make your flesh creep" — well, remember this was the celebrated role of Charles Dickens' "fat boy" — and let the role fit where it must!

We know that space and time are annihilated inside this small small spaceship we call "planet earth." We can blow it up. We can annihilate the thin envelope of soil on which our nourishment depends, and contaminate the thin envelope of air we breathe. This apocalyptic risk exists

---

153 Economist and author and Deputy Assistant Secretary of Defense for international security affairs.

simply because our modern means of science have made neighbors of us all.

But this absolute propinquity comes at a time when the chances of conflict are uniquely high. We live in a twilight of power systems with few settled frontiers of world power. We live in a time of growing misery for the many and hence of a possible international class war. We live in a time of acute ideological conflict. Each has caused crises in the past. Together, they threaten catastrophe.

What can we do about our triple crisis? Can we do anything about it? I will confess to you from the start that I am an optimist — not, I trust, of the Pollyanna type, but as one who draws confidence from facts as well as from hopes. For the fact is that while our crises are in some measure old — as old as human living and striving — some of our means of dealing with them are new — as new as our new environment of political freedom and scientific advance.

For political freedom is new. It is only in the last two centuries that we have tried to practice it even on a continental scale. Now we have at least made a start in applying some of its principles on a global scale. For make no mistake about it. For all its frustrations, muddles and inconsistencies, international organization is an attempt to apply democratic principles to our planetary society.

Hitherto in the whole history of man, it has been the role of small nations both to put up and to shut up — to put up with alien domination and to shut up about resentment and discontent. Only since the American and French revolutions have peoples — even small peoples — felt they had a right to run their own affairs. Only since President Wilson has that right been formalized as part of a world philosophy of freedom. Only in the United Nations has it been realized over the face of the globe on such a flood tide of freedom that scores of new nations have been precipitated into sovereignty in one short decade.

The whole basis of the United Nations is their right, great or small, to have weight, to have a vote, to be attended to. The age of the colony, the dependency, the sphere of influence, the white man's burden, the civilizing mission — all in theory have given way before the new right of peoples to be themselves.

This is a vast gain. But it is precarious. It depends upon its universal acceptance. Small powers do not automatically preserve their rights and independence by seeing them subscribed [inscribed?] in the United Nations Charter. They still have to cope with the problem of powerful neighbors who may or may not respect their autonomy and whom they have not the power to withstand alone.

I myself believe that overt aggression against smaller neighbors is now unlikely. The world suffered too recently and directly from Hitler's aggressions to accept any longer armies crossing the frontiers in the full panoply of war. Two such open aggressions across frontiers — in Korea and at Suez — were checked by the near unanimous opposition and action of the world community. But we face today the more devious problem of covert aggression and subversion, by "wars of national liberation," as the Communists call them, which have nothing to do with either nation or liberation.

This is a far more delicate business. Since Cuba, we know how irrevocable such a takeover can be, and how little it is thereafter subject to popular control. Yet we know, too, how easy it is to mistake genuine local revolt for Communist subversion.

For this opaque, uncertain type of crisis we need new international machinery to ensure that if local disorder leads to civil war the frontiers can be sealed against external intervention, order can be restored and free elections held. We have been trying to move in that direction in the Dominican crisis. It could be the basis of a negotiated settlement in Vietnam. Such a policy was effective to a large extent in the Congo; and it is keeping order in Cyprus.

I do not underestimate the difficulties of setting up such a policing system. But I believe it is the direction in which we must try to move in the next decade. It could give greater security to the small powers living in the interstices between the great systems. It could restore order in the disorderly regions where power is disputed. It could point the way to the impartial police which one day must take the place of individual arms and the precarious "balance of terror." We must start where we can; and today, of all the avenues towards security and disarmament, I would place the experiments in international peacekeeping at the very head.

But we shall not keep peace in a world mined by misery, hunger and despair. Here, too, let us try to keep meaning in the cliches — the rich nations, the poor nations, the developed north, the underdeveloped south, the industrialized state, the emergent states. How many words we have used up to describe and finally obscure the horrendous gap between wealth and poverty in our contemporary world.

But truisms are true! Cliches mean what they say. America can add $30 billion to an annual gross national product of some $630 billion in one year. And that, my friends, equals the entire gross national product of Latin America. These are the contrasts. One continent's almost casual surplus is as great as the whole apparatus of living among its neighbors.

The gap grows worse. Since 1960 — when the United Nations decade of development was launched — the wealth of the wealthy has been growing at two and three times the speed of the national income of the poorest group. Let us be quite specific about this. On the latest estimates issued by the United Nations, the nations whose gross national product on a per capita basis is above $700 — America's incidentally, is the highest in the world at $2500 — have been increasing their wealth by about 3 to 3½ per cent a year. In the next group — with per capita figures of $250 to $700 — a number of lively nations, including Greece and Israel and Taiwan, have been growing by about 5% a year. They are the next recruits to the ranks of full development, and incidentally most of them have received massive economic assistance in the last 15 years and thus offer a convincing answer to the skeptics who doubt the effectiveness of foreign aid.

But below, among the nations whose gross national product per capita is below $200, the rate of growth has been from zero to a mere 2% — and more often zero. Yet this group covers half mankind and over 100 countries.

These figures are inescapable. The poor are caught fast in the ancient trap of poverty, and across the whole globe stretches the darkening shadow of injustice and despair.

What do we do about it? Pass by on the other side? Lecture the needy on the virtues of thrift? Scold them for their birth rates? Point with pride to our own achievements and — in almost the same breath — regret that we cannot afford to do anything? There was almost a consensus in the middle of the 19th century that nothing much could be done about poverty. But such was not the case. Over the last century, the poorer classes inside our developed western world have secured a larger share of the economy's steadily expanding production. And the richer members of society, by means of a progressive tax system, have shared more of their wealth with their less fortunate neighbors. And since tax money went into better schooling and housing and health and skills, this in turn increased the capacities and abilities of the mass of the people, increased their productiveness, and so created yet more wealth to share.

If such changes can be brought about inside domestic society, we can repeat the success in the larger economy of the world. The proletarian nations of today are no more feckless, thoughtless, idle and child-ridden — to quote a few of our current pessimisms — than were the proletarian classes of the day before yesterday. And the same strategies are available.

Confronted with so many economists — and also with my watch, I won't spell it out. But I will ask you to remember something you learned here at Williams: that it is not the active, reforming, liberal societies that have been swept into the discard of history. It is, on the contrary, those which were too proud, too rigid, too blind and too complacent to change in time.

And what chance have we of transcending the world's ideological struggle if we are not prepared to tackle it at its roots . . . its roots in injustice and resentment, in the contrasts of wealth and misery, in the memories of colonial control, in the profound resentment of the white man, in the growing readiness to make him the scapegoat of every form of human ill?

Let us make no mistake about this. Marxism as an ideology is a failure. The East Europeans are deserting it. The Russians are crossing it with the profit motive. The Chinese are re-writing the Gospel according to Mao. It is a faulty, inadequate, inconsistent interpretation of the majesty and destiny of man.

But Marxism as the last great outburst of the spirit of prophecy is something else again. Only in western civilization does this note sound out — of outrage at injustice, of compassion for misery. This note, like the voice of Jeremiah or Isaiah or of Christ himself cannot be stilled. It echoes round the world. It cries out, as of old, as the laborers in the coffee plantations and tea gardens and cocoa forests are, by the chance workings of the market, deprived of the fruits of their labor. It stirs the passions of multitudes as they stream, homeless, shelterless, into the world's great slums and read of the swimming pools, the multiple houses and automobiles of the privileged few.

We have no alibis today with which to face those ancient judgments. As we add in one year the entire national income of Africa to our own wealth, as we pour out our $50 billion on arms, as we shoot another $5 billion of equipment towards the empty moon — here on earth the "sentence of the watchers" goes forth upon our society.

"I was hungry and ye fed me not."

"I was naked and you did not clothe me."

"I was homeless and you gave me no shelter."

These judgments do not change. Rather, they acquire a new dimension because of the very dimensions of our good fortune. If we use this first great liberation of our resources only to be more comfortable, we can be sure that God is not mocked, and as we have sown indifference, so we shall reap destruction.

This fate is not determined. We have the means. We have the choice. We can "remake the face of the earth." But the decision has to be made soon. For all the while, the margins of the world's patience ebb away.

Why do I talk to you about this one aspect of our world? Because this is the battleground. You have the weapons, and you will soon be the warriors.

Good luck!

To Bill Moyers

June 14, 1965

Dear Bill:

I am presuming to send you a copy of a telegram [154] I sent to Ellsworth Bunker on the Dominican Republic,[155] as of possible interest to you or Mac [McGeorge] Bundy. I have an impression that my views seldom come to the President's attention.

Cordially yours,

To Mrs. Ernest L. Ives [156]

June 16, 1965

Dear Buffie:

I have just read your lovely letter about the villa in Italy. I am so relieved that you are feeling well and enjoy it as much, indeed more than ever. I wonder if you saw Florence Eldridge [157] and her husband, Frederic March.[158]

Do you remember Marc Connolly [Connelly], author of "Green Pastures" and Lloyd Lewis's [159] best friend? He is delightful, witty and fat and a little feeble. He tells me that he is arriving at the Hassler [Hotel] in Rome on June 28th, and I think would love an invitation for a day or so at the villa if it is convenient for you. He will be in Rome about a week.

I have had a hideous month, but the end is in sight, with the Harvard [University] commencement and speech tomorrow, followed by the San Francisco celebration of the 20th anniversary of the UN. Thereafter I am most indefinite. I had hoped to stay at Libertyville for a while and get a good rest and tend to my papers in the basement. There is talk now, however, of the necessity of a major speech at the Economic and Social Council meeting in Geneva. If I have to do it, I would leave here July 4th or 5th and be in Geneva for perhaps a week. Thereafter, if I am not called back, I might come to see you for a few days or go to London, where I have some things to attend to. I suspect I will have to

---

[154] This telegram is not in the Stevenson papers.

[155] Ambassador Bunker was in the Dominican Republic with two other ambassadors from the Organization of American States.

[156] The original is in the Elizabeth Stevenson Ives collection, Illinois State Historical Library (E.S.I., I.S.H.L.).

[157] Stage and film actress.

[158] Stage and film actor.

[159] Author and newspaperman and a close friend and neighbor of Stevenson until his death in 1949. For Stevenson's remarks at his funeral, see *The Papers of Adlai E. Stevenson*, Vol. III, pp. 71–72.

leave it indefinite. But you might let me know what the situation is in the house after the 12th.

John Fell and Natalie have been with me for several days and it has been a joy, of course. But they have had to go back to California, on account of his business, before the Harvard commencement, and I am disappointed. Adlai and Nancy are also anchored in Illinois, due to the legislature. But I hope to have Borden in attendance.

I regret that I have not been able to figure out the Kentucky dates. I hope to be able to catch my breath, though, soon and clean up a mess of neglected things, including that one. If, as Roxane [Eberlein] says, you would prefer August 9th or thereabouts, why don't we leave it at that and I will try to adjust my schedule accordingly.

As for shirts, if you can get one yellow one — more yellow than cream — and a blue one identical with the last one, please do so. But no more ceramics! I haven't begun to unload my present inventory.

Love to you both,

ADLAI

On June 17, 1965, Stevenson addressed the annual Commencement meeting of the Harvard Alumni Association.[160] Arthur M. Schlesinger, Jr., recalled that Stevenson expressed the anxieties he had about American policy to him in Washington a few days before he made this speech.[161]

Goethe said there are many echoes in the world, but only a few voices. These days everyone is voicing or echoing their views about Viet-Nam, the Dominican Republic and student demonstrations and picketing. I claim without shame that I am really a battle scarred, if not scared, veteran of the demonstrators and picketers. I've been picketed, applauded and abused from right and left and center everywhere from Texas to Toronto for more years than I like to remember. Indeed my honorary degree should have a P.D. — a Doctor of Pickets.

I don't share the concern of some of my contemporaries about student demonstrations. I like their involvement in great issues. But if I could offer them one word of advice I would say that to state goals is easy; to tell us how to get there is not so easy. A moral commitment is hardly meaningful without a practical hope of improving the human condition.

But now I must speak a bit, and you must listen. I hope we both

---

[160] The text is based on USUN press release 4588.

[161] "Adlai Stevenson," essay accompanying the record album *Adlai,* produced by Arnold Michaelis, Columbia Records D2S–793, no date.

finish our work at about the same time. I will suggest how we might, I say "might" advisedly, get to some of our goals in the world.

Twenty years have passed since we made the last peace — exactly the same span of time from Versailles to Hitler's war. This is the sobering fact which today overshadows our troubled world. Last time, not all our good intentions, not all our last-minute efforts and improvisations, could stave off catastrophe. Can we be sure that on this grim anniversary we may not be failing once again? This question dwarfs all others, for in the nuclear age we have peace — or we have nothing.

We know all about our errors in 1919. They were, simply, to repeat the policies of the last century — high moral tone and non-involvement. President Wilson attempted through the League of Nations to bring our idealism down to earth in the first sketch of a functioning world society based on law, on self-determination, on the organized institutions of peace. But this dive into reality was too much for us. We retreated to an old isolation and continued to mistake exhortation for power.

Could we have repeated this error in 1945? Perhaps, but in fact, we were presented with the opposite temptation. What a heyday of conquest we could have had — alone with the atom bomb, alone with a healthy economy in a shattered world, alone with our energy unleashed and unbroken by the ordeal of war.

But we are not conquerors. We are perhaps the most unwilling great power in history. And certainly no great power has been plunged so suddenly from the temptations of lofty non-involvement to the opposite temptations of almost total power. Yet we did not lose our idealism. We set up the United Nations on the basis of equality and self-determination, and have helped mightily to make it work ever since. We have pressed for de-colonization. We offered to internationalize atomic energy. We gave Europe the Marshall Plan — first proposed from this platform. We preached the ideal of unity and federation to Europe. All this was very far from a selfish exercise of our power.

But of course it *was* power. The United States was dominant. The Western alliance was guided by us. The United Nations majorities voted with us. The economic assistance was all from us. The Communists were largely contained by us.

It is a great record of magnanimous and responsible leadership. But I suspect we became used to the idea that although all nations are equal, we were somehow a little more equal than anyone else. And of course for any nation this sense of leadership is very heady stuff! I have myself said of flattery that "it is fine provided you don't inhale." The same is true of leadership. It's fine — and we did inhale.

Today, however, we face entirely new conditions. Preponderant power is a thing of the past. Western Europe has recovered its economic strength and military potential. Russia commands a vast war machine with a full nuclear arsenal. China adds incipient nuclear power to massive armies. And both exploit the new techniques of covert aggression — the so-called "wars of national liberation" — which have nothing to do with nation or liberation — and can be stretched to cover any use of outside interference to remove any government, whatever its policies, that is anti-Communist or even non-Communist.

Our idealism is frustrated, too. The "third world" of post-colonial states seems to have much less stability and staying power than we expected. Just as Western colonialism ends, some of them seem ready to fight it all over again under the guise of "neo-colonialism." Meanwhile, the new tactics of subversion, infiltration, deception and confusion seem to be little understood, to say the least. Even in Europe the partnership we looked for from a unified continent has been challenged and circumscribed by reassertions of national power.

So we face a new situation — less manageable and less appealing. What do we do about it? There are those who would bid us accept the inevitable. If Europe is strong enough to defend itself, let it do so. If China is recovering its ancient influence in Asia, so what! We can't stop it. If weak, developing nations want to try communism, let them learn the hard way. We've done the best we could with aid and advice.

In these arguments we can detect some of the old isolationist overtones and assumptions. But in a world much less closely knit than this, isolation has not saved us from two global wars. It launched us on a worldwide depression. It saw the Far East all but devoured by a single military clique.

Would we now keep the peace by leaving the levers of power largely in the hands of vast imperial systems whose ideological aim is still to dominate the world? And at what point should we cry "halt" — and probably confront a nuclear holocaust?

The old isolationism was always too naive about power and about the pretensions of power. We must not make that mistake again.

But equally we must not make the opposite mistake and put too much faith in power. We have among us advocates of much stronger action. For them it is the idealism of America that is at fault. Get the allies back into line. Confront Russia over Berlin and East Germany. Bomb China's nuclear capacity before it increases. Back any anti-Communist Government anywhere. Teach everyone they can't push us around.

But this won't work either. What power have we to coerce our friends in Europe? What assurance have we that direct action against either communist giant will not unleash the nuclear war from which we would suffer as much as they? How can we be sure that unlimited support of any authoritarian anti-Communist Government may not merely hasten the day when their citizens become communists as the only means to change?

If total isolationism is no answer, total intervention is no answer, either. In fact the clear, quick, definable, measurable answers are all ruled out. In this new twilight of power there is no quick path to a convenient light switch.

What then can we do? What are the options? I want to suggest that the extremes are not exhaustive. In between — less exciting perhaps, less nationally satisfying, but safer and more humane — are other routes and methods which recognize the limits of our power, allow for our traditional idealism, take account of the world's ideological struggle, and include no fantasies of either total withdrawal or total control. But they are all paths which demand a high degree of genuine partnership, of genuine cooperation. As such they will often seem more arduous and more tedious than the old pursuits — for it is easier to command than to persuade.

How do we apply a new sense of partnership and cooperation to the dilemmas of our time? In Europe we have to help defend against renewed Soviet pressure westward. Equally we have to remove the grievance of a divided Germany which obstructs genuine peace in Central Europe. And, to compound the problem, to defend the West we must take a hard line with Russia. But our only hope of reunifying Germany peacefully is with Russian good will. I do not believe a divided, splintered, nationalist Europe cut off from America can accomplish this complicated balance. Either its divisions will enfeeble it militarily, or a resurgence of German nationalism will postpone possible reconciliation with the East.

Our best policy is, I think, on the one hand to keep our defense commitment to Europe unequivocal and to explore all reasonable ways of transferring greater responsibility to them — by joint planning, by joint purchasing, by joint burden sharing, by our readiness to consider any pattern of cooperation the Europeans care to suggest. And if, at some future time, they move towards political union, then, clearly, the question of nuclear responsibility will have to be reconsidered.

But at the same time let us seek all possible ways, together with our European allies, to increase peaceful and profitable contacts with Eastern Europe and the Soviet Union. There were small signs not long ago of a modest thaw in the dead winter of the old cold war. We should be ready for all such signs — in trade, in scientific research, in cultural exchanges, in tourism, in anything, in short, that opens the two systems to each other and substitutes knowledge and reality for myths and fears. Just the other day President Johnson said directly to the Soviet people:

"There is no American interest in conflict with the Soviet people anywhere."

Had I been talking with you even a year ago, I would have been
more optimistic about these possibilities. Today, the drama in South-
east Asia and the dilemmas faced by Russia in its relations with its stubborn, dogmatic Chinese associate have shrouded our hopes of yesterday.
But the aim is not at fault — to prove that we at least want to end this
tragic breach in human society, want to overcome the barriers that un-
naturally divide an ancient continent and culture, want to explore with
our fellow citizens of a threatened world the dilemmas and the possibilities of a stable peace.

In Asia, too, I do not believe our aims are false. The right we seek to
defend is the right of people, be it in Korea or South Viet-Nam, not to
have their future decided by violence. I do not believe this right can be
secured by retreat. Retreat leads to retreat just as aggression leads to
aggression in this still primitive international community. Already an
active apparatus of subversion has begun its work in Thailand. And it is
only a few years since Malaya beat down a long and murderous attempt
to impose communism by force. The Tibetans were not so fortunate. And
the Indians have found the neighborhood of 800 million Chinese hardly
a guarantee of peace and security.

So the aim of reenforcing the right of peoples, large and small, to
determine their own destiny does not seem one that we dare allow to
go by default. The old, old principle that powerful neighbors, for reasons
of power alone, must prevail never gave the world peace in the past. I
question whether it will do so even in the nuclear age.

But if you ask me whether the task of defending and upholding this
right should be the responsibility of any one power, particularly of a
large white western power whose past behavior in its own hemisphere
has not, shall we say, been wholly without "imperialist" overtones, then
I say emphatically "No."

Let us be quite clear about this. The United States has no desire to
dominate. We have no delusion of omnipotence or omniscience. We do
not cheat ourselves with the purple rhetoric of "manifest destiny." We
do not see ourselves as self-appointed gendarmes of this very troubled
world. And we do not rely on muscle instead of diplomacy.

But although we are not even a direct party to most of the world's
disputes, we have had to take a disproportionate share of the burden,
because the international community is not prepared or ready to do so,
or to do so fast and far enough in a given crisis.

In South Viet-Nam the task of upholding the principle of self-
determination and popular sovereignty is ours in part by the chances of

history, but in part by default. We should use every persuasion, every instrument available to put responsibility where it belongs — in the international community, with international guarantees and policing, and in a long term settlement resting not only on our arms but on the will and authority of the United Nations.

This is what we seek. That the Communists have rejected every overture from every quarter — more than 13 — for negotiations without preconditions does not alter our aim — to stop the fighting, to create the international machinery to safeguard the people's right to peaceful choice and to underpin the whole post-colonial settlement. Only the right of self-determination brought it into being. Only that right, properly reinforced, can defend it now.

So I am suggesting that our role is not absolute responsibility. Rather it is to seek patiently, yes, and modestly, to persuade our fellow nations to take on the indispensable tasks of peace and law. And if we want the new nations to recognize the reality of the threat to self-determination in Southeast Asia, for example, we must be ready to recognize the reality to them, for example, of the threat of continued colonialism in Southern Africa. We can hardly proclaim the duty to safeguard the right of free choice in the Caribbean and deny its validity on the other side of the Atlantic. The credibility of our posture rests on its consistency.

Safeguards for the right of choice, like safeguards for peace itself, must depend ultimately on multilateral foundations and the concept of collective security enshrined in the United Nations Charter. At a time when peace is so precarious, it is shameful that the great peacekeeping institution must beg for the means of keeping the peace. But I believe its financial troubles may soon be over. It has been on a sick bed long enough. But it is not a death bed. It is suffering not from death pangs but from growing pains. The simple truth is that as long as the world is in crisis, the United Nations will be in crisis. That's what it is there for. As long as there is global tension, there will be tension at the global headquarters. When it ceases to reflect the troubles of the world, then you can start worrying about its demise.

But external pressures is not the only threat to self-determination. Of the UN's 114 members, perhaps two-thirds are vulnerable and unstable not because of great power ambitions and rivalries. The instability springs from the growing gap between their aspirations and the hard economic reality of making their way in the post-colonial world. The fact that sugar prices fell by half last winter is not unconnected with the crisis in the Dominican Republic. Nor has the stability in Latin America been reinforced by a ten-year decline in primary prices that wiped out the effect of all incoming capital, public or private.

These are roots of disorders exploited by external subversion. To suppose that our world can continue half affluent and half desperate is to assume a patience on the part of the needy for which — to put it mildly — history gives us no warrant at all.

But, like peacekeeping, this vast global task is not a task for one nation or for nations acting singly. The developed states together must redress the imbalance. While America can give and has given a generous lead, we have to accept once again the patient, modest, unsensational tasks of consulting and persuading.

The developing nations have started to act together in the framework of the United Nations trade and development conference. The developed nations' policies should also be internationalized more and more by working in and through the United Nations group.

If only one government is giving a country aid, it easily comes to play too pervasive a part on the local scene. Suspicions of neo-colonialism arise. Issues of prestige, of paternalism, of dependence begin to obtrude.

The answers to these dilemmas is once again the way of consultation and joint action to bring a sizeable part of the needed flow of capital under international bodies in which donors and recipients can work out their problems together.

No doubt much of this seems more difficult than the role of direct benefaction. But our readiness to act not as benefactor but as partner could lead to increasing respect, closer understanding, the sense of community, and perhaps, at last, enough confidence to dissipate the myths of "neo-colonialism" and erase the memories of earlier servitudes and humiliations.

In short, what I believe we should seek in this new age of more limited power but still unlimited challenge is not so much new policies, but a new emphasis, a new tone. We should be readier to listen than to instruct — with that curiosity which is the beginning of wisdom. It will take a greater effort of imagination for us to see the world through others' eyes, to judge our policies as they impinge on others' interests.

For what we attempt today is to extend to the whole society of man the techniques, the methods, the habits — if you will, the courtesies — upon which our own sense of citizenship is based. In our free society we ask that citizens participate as equals. We accept their views and interests as significant. We struggle for unforced consensus. We tolerate conflict and accept dissent. But we believe that because each citizen knows he is valued and has his chance for comment and influence, his final loyalty to the social order will be more deeply rooted and secure.

As heirs to the tradition of free government, what else can we do? Our founders had the audacity to proclaim their ideals "self evident" for all mankind. We can hardly be less bold when "all mankind" is no longer an abstraction but a political fact in the United Nations, a physical fact for the circling astronaut.

Nor should we despair. The art of open government has grown from its seeds in the tiny city states of Greece to become the political mode of half the world. So let us dream of a world in which all states, great and small, work together for the peaceful flowering of the republic of man.

Linus Pauling, the distinguished scientist and winner of the Nobel prize in chemistry and the Nobel Peace prize, wrote on May 17 that Stevenson had made a false statement when he referred to the Soviet missiles in Cuba as nuclear weapons. On June 9, Pauling wrote that if Stevenson did not reply to his letter it would be clear that he had lied.

To Linus Pauling

June 19, 1965

Dear Dr. Pauling:

I have been obliged to neglect much of my mail of late. Hence this tardy acknowledgment of your letter of May 17. You may be assured, however, that it was from no hesitation to clarify the matter on which you wrote. If you knew anything about the circumstances of my life at the United Nations during the past month and my speaking schedule in Canada, Arkansas, New Jersey, and at Williams and Harvard you might be disposed to reconsider the language in your letter of June 9.

You are correct that the Soviet missile installations in Cuba were not for ICBMs but for MRBMs and IRBMs and perhaps the phrase I used in my extempore remarks — to which you object so vigorously — was technically imprecise. But the missiles would have had a range extending over most of the United States and many populous targets in Latin America. They were long range enough to constitute a military and political threat to our security as well as to our populace and to that of much of Latin America. "Long range" is a comparative term. I am informed that the Soviets term the IRBM, which has a range of 2200 nautical miles, a "long range missile." The Soviets term the ICBM "a super long range" missile.

I am not aware of the significance of your comments on the propellants used in these missiles. But I am perplexed by your statement that they were not nuclear missiles but "rockets of the ordinary sort." Of course these missiles were intended to carry nuclear warheads and so far as I can recall the Russians never denied it. They were thus nuclear missiles and any description of them as such is neither a "false statement" nor will it "mislead the American people." [Nikita] Khrushchev certainly had no doubt about the effectiveness of these weapons when he stated before the Supreme Soviet in December 1962, for the benefit of the Germans, that "our rockets have come back from Cuba. We have added them to the defense equipment which covers our western borders." Nor had Fidel Castro any doubts as to their purposes or power when, on March 31, 1965, in an Havana radio and TV program referring to the missile crisis and reported in the American press, he said, "The Cuban people did not hesitate to face the dangers of thermo-nuclear war . . . We agreed to the installation of strategic thermo-nuclear rockets on our territory and, in addition, not only were we in agreement that they could be brought here, but we disagreed that they should be taken away."

Sincerely yours,

To Theodore H. White

June 19, 1965

Dear Teddy:

You were so good to send me a copy of your new book.[162] I have already heard about the Graham Memorandum from the press — and from Kay![163] I wish I could drop everything — especially the Dominican Republic — and start reading right this minute. Instead, I have to start writing again on the last utterances — thank God! — of one of the worst months of my life.

But I know it won't be long before I can watch the past unfold — as only you can unfold it.

So many thanks, and love to Nancy.[164]

Yours,

To Ricardo Sicre

June 19, 1965

Dear Ricardo:

Thanks for your letter. It made me jealous![165] It has been a hideous couple of months here what with the Dominican Republic, incessant Security Council meetings, endless travels and speeches. But after the San Francisco doings things may quiet down a bit. I suspect I may go

162 *The Making of the President, 1964* (New York: Atheneum, 1965).
163 Mrs. Philip Graham. Mr. White had included in his book a memorandum that Philip Graham had drafted regarding Kennedy's selection of Lyndon Johnson to be the vice presidential candidate in 1960.
164 Mrs. White.
165 Mr. Sicre was in Madrid, Spain.

to Geneva for a week to the Economic and Social Council meeting about the fifth or sixth of July, but I'm afraid there is little prospect of getting off for a visit with you and Betty [166] on the boat — although a long rest, far away, is precisely what I need and want.

I am so glad to hear that your financing company worked out. . . . My son, Borden, tells me that he has been in touch with you about a remarkable match project. I think what our family fortunes need is a little of that Sicre know-how.

I'm sure Emil [167] will enjoy Georgetown [University] — although he belongs at Princeton! You will note that my loyalty persists in spite of the fact that I have just become an Honorary Doctor of Laws at Harvard.

Love to Betty and if she is going to be in Geneva between the fifth and 15th of July, tell her to be sure to let me know.

Yours,

On June 23, 1965, Stevenson spoke at a dinner celebrating the dedication of the Equitable Life Assurance Building in Chicago. It was the last speech he delivered in Chicago. It is not published here, since it covered much of the same material as his speech at Williams College. From Chicago, Stevenson flew to San Francisco to participate in ceremonies to commemorate the twentieth anniversary of the founding of the United Nations. President Johnson, as a result of Stevenson's urging, attended and spoke. Harlan Cleveland, Thomas Wilson in Cleveland's office, and Stevenson drafted a speech which contained a solution to the UN's financial crisis and Johnson was to state that while the U.S. considered its position on Article 19 to be sound, it would no longer insist on its being invoked if the membership of the UN did not wish to do so. Instead, the U.S. would reserve the same option to withhold payments for UN expenses on which it had strong political objections. The speech, however, was leaked to James Reston of the New York Times and Johnson refused to deliver it.[168]

The speech Johnson delivered was pedestrian and lacked the strong words of financial support for the United Nations which were in the

---

[166] Mrs. Sicre.

[167] Mr. Sicre's son Emile.

[168] Stevenson's successor, Ambassador Arthur Goldberg, made the statement at the UN on August 16, 1965, thus disengaging from Article 19. Johnson thought that Cleveland had leaked the speech. But Cleveland was away from Washington when Reston was writing the story. When he returned, there was a message to call Reston. Cleveland called him about eleven P.M., and Reston read him the story, which had already gone to press. Cleveland recalled: "I told him that probably meant the President wouldn't use it, but it was too late to stop it, to comment on it, let alone to participate in the 'leak.'" Memorandum to Walter Johnson, April 30, 1973.

unused speech.[169] *In a United Nations broadcast over the American Broadcasting Company on July 15, 1965, Edward P. Morgan mentioned how worried Stevenson had been at San Francisco over what the President was going to say in his speech.*[170]

Among the papers in Stevenson's briefcase after he died in London on July 14 was an undated handwritten document entitled "My argument to LBJ." It read:

Easier to kill Art. 19 *now* — in its last gasp. The alternative of enforcing it is not available to us now.

Either indicate clearly now or wait until last moment. Better now — get some real credit. At end just accepting the inevitable.

Not doing it now looks as tho we are reviving the issue — and it will be harder to yield later.

Step aside *before* we are run over. Better take some initiative now when we can get something out of it.

On June 26, Stevenson addressed the United Nations commemorative meeting.[171]

This is the end of a commemorative occasion. Some of us here today who were midwives at the birth of the United Nations can never forget those days here in San Francisco in the twilight of the war, when an old world was dying and a new world was coming to birth.

We shared an audacious dream — and launched a brave enterprise.

It seemed so easy then — when all was hope and expectation. I remember my own sense of pride, of history, of exultation — and the special responsibility that fell upon the host country to that historic conference.

Inescapably I remember, too, both the triumphs and the failures. For over these churning, fearful, and expectant years, we have been up and we have been down.

But up or down, my government and my people have never lost faith in the United Nations.

The hope, the expectation, was mirrored by the vote — 89 to 2 — by which the United States Senate approved the ratification of the Charter

[169] James Reston, *The Artillery of the Press: Its Influence on American Foreign Policy* (New York: Harper & Row, 1967), p. 55. These strong words were deleted from the speech on Johnson's orders. Cleveland, memorandum to Walter Johnson, April 30, 1973.

[170] A transcript of this broadcast is in the Morgan papers, Wisconsin State Historical Society.

[171] The text is based on USUN press release 4597.

of the United Nations in 1945 — a few weeks after the Charter was signed here in San Francisco in this very hall.

And our Congress only this week — in a rare mood of unanimity — reaffirmed that support and dedicated this country, once again, to the principles of this Organization.

This Concurrent Resolution referred specifically to this twentieth anniversary event, to International Cooperation Year, to the "important and, at times, crucial role" which the United Nations has played in defense of the peace — and to its other "valuable service" to human rights and the fight against hunger, poverty, disease, and ignorance.

The Resolution then stated: "Now therefore, be it

"Resolved . . .

"That it is the sense of the Congress that the United States of America rededicates itself to the principles of the United Nations and to the furtherance of international cooperation within the framework of law and order . . ."

Thus in this week of memory and anticipation did the representatives of our democratic diversity declare again our unity and our commitment in matters that touch the peace of the world.

We welcome the counsel of all our brethren, large and small, on this long, rough voyage to world community.

We make no claim to omniscience or omnipotence; we, too, believe that to the humble many things are revealed that are obscure to the mighty.

Out of twenty years of humbling experience, we all know that we need the United Nations more today than we needed it twenty years ago — that we shall need it more twenty years from now than we do today — that the United Nations is a simple necessity of our times.

We know that the issue therefore is not one of survival but of how rapidly or how slowly, how surely or how hesitantly, how skillfully or how clumsily, we shall get on with the work we took up here so short a time ago.

And the record of the United Nations is full of evidence of skillful action by men and women of many nations.

There is time, even in a short address, to salute the Secretary General and the international civil servants of the UN family of agencies who pioneer day in and day out in our emerging world community.

We have time to extend our congratulations to those delegates from the younger nations who have joined our ranks since the Charter first was signed — who have added diversity to our company — who have given us all an intimate sense of wider community — who have contributed their minds and talents, their vision and wisdom to the conduct of our affairs.

We have time, too, to pay our respects to those hundreds of men of the United Nations who have given their lives in the cause of peace — to those tens of thousands from fifty-four countries who have helped the United Nations keep the peace — and to those other thousands of Blue Berets who at this moment stand guard for peace in Gaza, Cyprus, and Kashmir, even as we meet here, peacefully, in San Francisco.

We have time here to offer thanks to those unsung heroes of the United Nations who are responsible for curing 37 million children of the yaws, and 11 million more of trachoma, and another million of leprosy — and to those who have protected 162 million people against tuberculosis, and lowered the incidence of malaria by over a hundred million people a year — and to those nameless men and women of the United Nations who have helped find new homes and new lives for more than a million refugees.

These are a few — and only a few — of the things that we the people of the United Nations have done together in the time-speck of two tearing decades.

In the bright glow of 1945 too many looked to the United Nations for the full and final answer to world peace. And in retrospect that day may seem to have opened with the hint of a false dawn.

Certainly we have learned the hard way how elusive is peace — how durable is man's destructive drive — how various are the forms of his aggression.

We have learned, too, how distant is the dream of those better standards of life in larger freedom — how qualified our capacity to practice tolerance — how conditional our claims to the dignity and worth of the human person — how reserved our respect for the obligations of law.

Our world is still as brave, though not so new, as it seemed in this place two decades past. But the world's leaders, and their peoples, are deeply troubled — and with cause:

There is war in Viet-Nam — and in other places, too.

There has been revolution and bloody violence in the Dominican Republic — and in other places, too.

There are still border troubles in Kashmir, communal bitterness in Cyprus, violence in the Congo.

There is shattering ideological conflict; there is subversion and aggression — overt and clandestine; there is tension and mistrust and fear.

The nuclear threat is spreading and the means of self-destruction are still uncontrolled.

Meanwhile the economic gap between the developed and developing nations grows wider. Human rights and political rights and self-determination are cynically denied. Hunger, disease and ignorance still afflict the majority of God's children.

I agree with Ambassador [Benoit] Bindzi of the Cameroon that these are symptoms of an unstable, dangerous world — too dangerous and too unstable, for the General Assembly to remain in its present deadlock.

We all know that the deadlock must be broken before we sit down again in the General Assembly nine weeks hence.

If there be disputes which keep us apart — there is much, much more to be done which draws us together.

Change, guaranteed by the inventions of science and the innovations of technology, accelerates, threatens and promises.

Already science has destroyed any rational excuse for war between states.

Already science induces statesmen to reach for national prestige not in the conquest of someone's territory, but in the conquest of everyone's environment.

Already science and technology are integrating our world into an open workshop where each new invention defines a new task, and reveals a shared interest, and invites yet another common venture.

In our sprawling workshop of the world community, nations are joined in cooperative endeavor: improving soils . . . purifying water . . . harnessing rivers . . . eradicating disease . . . feeding children . . . diffusing knowledge . . . spreading technology . . . surveying resources . . . lending capital . . . probing the seas . . . forecasting the weather . . . setting standards . . . developing law . . . and working away at a near infinitude of down-to-earth tasks — tasks for which science has given us the knowledge, and technology has given us the tools, and common sense has given us the wit to perceive that common interest impels us to common enterprise.

Common enterprise is the pulse of world community — the heartbeat of a working peace — the way to the great society.

Yet we are all impatient. We are all concerned that the scope of our work is still too narrow — that the pace of our work is still too slow — that our best efforts to date risk being overwhelmed by the enormity of the tasks and challenges that press upon us from all sides.

We need time to perfect our peacekeeping machinery to the point where no nation need use its own armed forces save in the service of the international community.

We need time to adjust to the thundering impact of science and technology upon human society and human tradition.

We need time to get on with international cooperation toward disarmament, toward a decent world diet, toward peaceful exploration of outer space, toward international development.

And we the members of the United Nations need time at home to struggle with all those great domestic tasks of welfare and justice and human rights which cry out for the priority attention of all national leaders, regardless of the size or the wealth of or the social system of any particular country.

Is there no way to quicken the pulsebeat of our common enterprise? Is there no short-cut to a better world society? Is there no way to make time our ally — and use it better to serve us all?

Of course there is. For the enemy is not change but violence. To induce needed change without needless murder what we require above all is a truce to terror. We need a moratorium — a breathing spell free from acts of international violence.

We need — all of us — a respite from the malignant claims which violence levies upon our energy and our attention and our resources.

There is not a single dispute in this world — however sharply the issues may be drawn — which would not look different two decades from now, after time and change have done their erosive work on the sharpest corners of conflict.

If we could somehow bring about a Truce to Terror we would soon discover that world order will come not through the purity of the human heart nor the purge of the human soul, but will be wrought from a thousand common ventures that are at once possible and imperative.

Mr. President, on behalf of myself, on behalf of my government, on behalf of the vast bulk of my countrymen, let me say this:

We believe in the United Nations; we support the United Nations; and we shall work in the future — as we have worked in the past — to add strength, and influence, and permanence to all that the Organization stands for in this, our tempestuous, tormented, talented world of diversity in which all men are brothers and all brothers are somehow, wondrously, different — save in their need for peace.

For all our desperate dangers, I do not believe, in the words of Winston Churchill, "that God has despaired of His children."

For man in his civil society has learned how to live under the law with the institutions of justice, and with a controlled strength that can protect rich and poor alike. This has been done, I say, within domestic society. And in this century, for the first time in human history, we are attempting similar safeguards, a similar framework of justice, a similar sense of law and impartial protection in the whole wide society of man.

This is the profound, the fundamental, the audacious meaning of the United Nations. It is our shield against international folly in an age of ultimate weapons. Either we shall make it grow and flourish, arbitrator of our disputes, mediator of our conflicts, impartial protector against arbitrary violence, or I do not know what power or institution can enable us to save ourselves.

We have the United Nations. We have set it bravely up. And we will carry it bravely forward.

On June 27, 1965, Stevenson appeared on the National Broadcasting Company's program Meet the Press.[172]

MR. BROOKS: [173] MEET THE PRESS comes to you today from San Francisco, where the United Nations is celebrating its 20th Anniversary.

Our guest is Ambassador Adlai Stevenson, who played a leading role in the formation of the United Nations and is now this country's U.N. Representative. Ambassador Stevenson heads the U.S. Delegation to the anniversary celebration.

Now, we will have the first question from Lawrence E. Spivak, Permanent Member of the MEET THE PRESS Panel.

MR. SPIVAK: Ambassador Stevenson, after 20 years the United Nations is believed by many both here and abroad to be in serious crisis and on the verge of complete collapse.

What shape do you really think the U.N. is in today?

AMBASSADOR STEVENSON: I think it is in much better shape than your question would indicate. Actually, the United Nations is a reflection of the situation that exists in the world. If the world is tense, there will be tension in the United Nations. I think that if the United Nations ever ceases to reflect the situation that prevails in the world, then is the time when one had better begin to worry about its demise.

MR. SPIVAK: But, Mr. Ambassador, isn't one of the purposes of the United Nations to relieve the tensions of the world, not merely to reflect the tensions or to add to the tensions?

AMBASSADOR STEVENSON: Yes, most certainly it is; it is to dissolve the disputes that create the tensions, but that it hasn't always succeeded in doing this is small wonder, given the divided world, given the existence of national rivalries, uncontrolled, unbridled, given all the circumstances with which we have had to deal in these past twenty years.

MR. SPIVAK: I would like to take up one or two particular things. The General Assembly has been paralyzed for many months now because of Article 19 and the refusal of the Soviet Union and France to pay the peacekeeping assessments.

Will the General Assembly remain paralyzed much longer, or do you see a solution to that problem?

AMBASSADOR STEVENSON: I certainly hope not. I think it is imperative that the Assembly, when it reconvenes, conduct its business in the

---

[172] A transcript was published by Merkle Press, Inc., Washington, D.C.
[173] Ned Brooks, announcer for the program.

normal way and that the deadlock that has paralyzed it during this past session must be broken. I believe it will.

MR. SPIVAK: How will it be broken?

AMBASSADOR STEVENSON: I think it will be broken by an action taken by the General Assembly itself to determine what it wishes to do with respect to the application of Article 19 or with respect to the assessments for peace-keeping operations.

It has been the view of the United States, and I think of the vast majority of the membership, that they should be financially responsible. That is to say, that if they authorize a peace-keeping operation, the members should pay for it, especially peacekeeping operations of which they themselves approve.

MR. SPIVAK: Do you think that the financial problems are going to be solved through the enforcement of Article 19 or just by forgetting it?

AMBASSADOR STEVENSON: I don't think anybody wants a confrontation over Article 19 any more now than we did when the last Assembly convened the first of last December. How it will be done, I don't yet know. A subcommittee of the United Nations, called the Committee of 33, representing 33 states has been considering this matter for some time. I suspect it will have to consider it somewhat further.

MR. SPIVAK: Great Britain, Mr. Ambassador, and Canada, and some of the Scandinavian countries, have made voluntary contributions in order to break the paralysis. Is the United States prepared to make voluntary contributions in the same way?

AMBASSADOR STEVENSON: I can't answer that question, obviously, because that would depend at least to some extent upon the Congress, what the attitude of the Congress is, and the matter has not been presented to the Congress. They would have to provide the money.

MR. SPIVAK: On Article 19, I believe you led the fight to apply Article 19. Now are you going to abandon that fight?

AMBASSADOR STEVENSON: This is a decision that if we had made it, I wouldn't be at liberty to tell you, but I don't think that this decision has been reached by any means.

MR. LISAGOR: [174] There seems to have been considerable disappointment among the United Nations delegates here that President Johnson didn't come to forgive the delinquents their back dues or make some other dramatic proposal.

Were you led to believe that he might in fact say something about Article 19 which would change the U.S. position on it?

174 Peter Lisagor, of the Washington bureau of the Chicago *Daily News*.

AMBASSADOR STEVENSON: I thought the President had made it clear even before he came that he didn't expect to make any dramatic announcement here, that he looked upon the meeting in San Francisco as a birthday, as a ceremony, a commemorative ceremony on the 20th Anniversary of the founding of the United Nations and not an occasion for negotiation or for dispute.

MR. LISAGOR: Why, then, did almost all the delegates seem to expect him to make some kind of spectacular proposal?

AMBASSADOR STEVENSON: Sometimes the wish is father to the thought.

MR. LISAGOR: To follow up Mr. Spivak's earlier questioning, isn't it a fact that the United States will have to abandon its position on the back assessments if the U.N. General Assembly is going to be viable? [175]

AMBASSADOR STEVENSON: It has always seemed curious to me that they ask the United States, which has met every one of its commitments to the United Nations, which has by far been its most generous contributor, its consistent, unqualified supporter from its inception to this date — that we should always be called upon to make concessions, especially if we are trying to establish in the United Nations a constitutional institution which has respect for both its Charter and its terms and for the organs that it has created, including the World Court which has handed down [an] advisory opinion that these assessments for peacekeeping operations are costs of the organization and therefore payable by all of the members. Somebody has to stand fast for this concept of constitutionalism.

I can't answer your question as to what we are going to do finally, but I am surprised that they always ask us to do something. And it is not only us; it is virtually all the West Europeans, all the Latin Americans and so on, that share these views.

MR. LISAGOR: But what the Russian delegate said here, which was that the United States had created — artificially, he suggested — a financial crisis in the U.N. Doesn't it then follow that the United States will have to change its position?

AMBASSADOR STEVENSON: I don't know that it follows, becauses we haven't created an artificial crisis. The crisis was created by the non-payment of the assessments levied on the Soviet Union, France and the other Communist states, and it is interesting to note, if I may add this, that the Soviet Union itself voted for the Congo operation that it now refuses to pay for.

MR. FRYE: [176] Mr. Ambassador, may I ask you to turn for a minute to

[175] See pp. 673–686, above.
[176] William Frye, United Nations correspondent for the *Christian Science Monitor*.

the problem of Vietnam. President Johnson appealed to the UN individually and collectively to put pressure on Red China and North Vietnam for peace talks.[177] Does the United States really want the UN collectively, as he put it, to intervene in Vietnam, and if so, why don't we make some move to bring the subject before the UN?

AMBASSADOR STEVENSON: You have a couple of questions. I think in the first place one must bear in mind that neither Communist China nor North or South Vietnam are members of the United Nations, that last year at the time of the Tonkin Gulf incident when I did bring it to the United Nations, to the Security Council, it invited North Vietnam to come. Ever since then it has sarcastically rejected any — even the propriety of any concern by the United Nations in the conflict in Vietnam.

The Chinese, of course, have done likewise. Indeed they are doing their very best to destroy the institution of the United Nations.

In addition to that, it is problematical as to what — if it were possible to bring them all before the United Nations even though they are nonmembers and have indicated that they will not come — the United Nations could do in the present circumstances. But I shouldn't leave you with the idea that the United Nations is not interested in it. Actually it sent a commission there at the time of the trouble between the government and the Buddhists, if you will remember, a Human Rights commission. And last year, at the instance of Cambodia it sent a commission to Cambodia and to South Vietnam, the United Nations did, to see if it could resolve the border dispute between those two countries. I have no doubt that if a peaceful settlement is arrived at in due course to stop the fighting in Vietnam — and pray to God that it is — the United Nations will have an important role to play in the future in policing compliance with any agreement that is reached with respect to Vietnam.

MR. FRYE: You have mentioned the absence of Red China as a handicap to UN activity in the Vietnam business. Do you mean to imply that you feel Red China should be invited and seated as a full member?

AMBASSADOR STEVENSON: I didn't say that — I don't believe I said that or hinted at it, did I?

MR. FRYE: A number of delegates did in the past few days.

AMBASSADOR STEVENSON: Yes, I know many do. The trouble with that, of course, is that the Chinese have made it very apparent that the only terms and conditions on which they would come into the United Nations would be through the expulsion of Taiwan, and they have

[177]For Johnson's rejection of U Thant's peace initiative, see pp. 665–666, above.

refused to renounce the use of force with respect to Taiwan and made conditions virtually impossible.

MISS FREDERICK: [178] Why has the United States not been willing up to this time to have Secretary General Thant issue a cease-fire appeal to all parties in the Vietnam war?

AMBASSADOR STEVENSON: I am sure if he felt it was the time to do it or that that was the best thing to do that he would do it. I think perhaps there have been other tracks that have been pursued during this interval. Having offered to go to Hanoi, having been told to stay home, that they didn't care to see him; having offered to go to Peking, having been told that he would not be welcome; I think he has concluded that perhaps these other tracks — and there have been some 13 or 14 of them that have been attempted in the past year, some of them through other channels, not just the United States by any means — had to be exhausted. Whether or not such an appeal by the United Nations would elicit any more affirmative response than the other tracks have failed to elicit, I very much doubt.

MISS FREDERICK: Would the United States be willing to accept a cease fire if the other side does, if U Thant made such an appeal?

AMBASSADOR STEVENSON: Oh, I wouldn't have any doubt that — the President has already suspended the bombing on one occasion. He has offered to negotiate without pre-conditions; he has pursued every conceivable avenue to open negotiations. Were it possible to bring the fighting to a stop pending some, at least, discussion of the possibility of negotiations — you would find the United States very responsive if the other side complied. One problem, of course, would be, how would you determine compliance?

MISS FREDERICK: Governor, with all due respect to your knowledge, I believe that in the President's speech at Johns Hopkins University he offered unconditional discussions, not negotiations, and Ambassador [Henry Cabot] Lodge has pointed out a difference. Would you say there was a difference?

AMBASSADOR STEVENSON: This quarrel about — this semantic argument about discussions and negotiations, frankly, has never — perplexes me.

MISS FREDERICK: Would the United States be willing to negotiate with the National Liberation Front, the political arm of the Viet Cong?

AMBASSADOR STEVENSON: I don't think the question is properly addressed to the United States. After all, this is a problem for South Vietnam, for Saigon, for that government.

[178] Pauline Frederick, United Nations correspondent for the American Broadcasting Company.

MISS FREDERICK: Isn't the United States a party to this conflict?

AMBASSADOR STEVENSON: Oh, very much so. Do you mean as to what the United States' position would be?

I think it would depend, as I tried to indicate, very much on what the position of South Vietnam would be, whether it would choose as a sovereign government to deal with rebels in its own lands.

MISS FREDERICK: According to information that has come to Secretary General Thant, as I understand it, the Chinese Communists have said that the Viet Cong are the proper interlocutor for such negotiations. So, consequently, wouldn't this seem to indicate that if the United States were willing to talk to the Viet Cong, there might be more chance to open discussions than there have been up to the present time?

AMBASSADOR STEVENSON: It might be, and I think we have indicated — I am not too sure about this, but I think we have indicated that it is for Hanoi to determine whom it wants to sit at its table. If it wants to include a representative of the Viet Cong among their delegation to any conference, that would be for them to determine. We would have no objection.

MR. SPIVAK: Governor, I don't like to labor the financial problem, but I would like to ask one more question on it.

AMBASSADOR STEVENSON: It has been labored pretty thoroughly.

MR. SPIVAK: On June 17th at Harvard, referring to the U.N., you said, and I quote: "I believe its financial trouble may soon be over."

You must have had something specific in mind because I know you don't generalize upon occasions like that. What did you have in mind?

AMBASSADOR STEVENSON: It has to be resolved in the course of this summer before the Assembly reconvenes. The financial solvency of the organization has to be re-established. It seems to me pitiful that an organization which was created by the responsible leaders of virtually all of the countries of the world to keep the peace must be begging for the means of keeping the peace. This is a paradox that seems to me intolerable, and a solution must be found.

MR. SPIVAK: To come back to it again then, a majority of the Senate Republicans called upon the President either to seek the enforcement of Article 19, which you fought for, or publicly acknowledge that Article 19 is a dead letter.

Is the financial situation going to be resolved by either one of these?

AMBASSADOR STEVENSON: I can't answer that, because I don't think that decision has been made.

It might be resolved that way; it might be resolved by perhaps the debtors paying up.

MR. SPIVAK: A decision made by whom, by the United States, do you mean?

AMBASSADOR STEVENSON: By the United States.

MR. SPIVAK: By the President then?

AMBASSADOR STEVENSON: I think he would have to do it in cooperation with the Congress and with the Executive Branch. I am sure he would want to consult.

MR. LISAGOR: Governor Stevenson, to get back to President Johnson's call on U.N. members individually and collectively to help out to bring the Communists to the conference table, do you see any realistic diplomatic intervention by any member of the United Nations which would produce the result the President called for?

AMBASSADOR STEVENSON: Yes, I can't — even in such a lawless world as we live in, I can't but believe that virtually any state — perhaps I should express it as a hope — would respond to the collective opinion of the world, were it made emphatic, were it made clear and were it made with virtually unanimity — that this would be a mighty influence on the Viet Cong and on Hanoi.

MR. LISAGOR: Can I ask you a rather blunt question about the United Nations and the Vietnamese situation?

If a vote were taken today ——

AMBASSADOR STEVENSON: I know you would ask a blunt question whether I gave you permission or not, so go ahead.

MR. LISAGOR: If a vote were taken in the U.N. today on American action in Vietnam, would the United States be condemned?

AMBASSADOR STEVENSON: I don't think they would be condemned for trying to defend South Vietnam from aggression from its northern neighbor. I think there would be a good deal of feeling in the United Nations that the bombing was a mistake.

MR. LISAGOR: Many of your liberal friends, as you know, appear to feel that you oppose American policy in Vietnam and in fact have called upon you, a few have, to resign your position and to speak out.

I would like to ask you first whether you do oppose American policy in South Vietnam?

AMBASSADOR STEVENSON: No, I think we have to hold the line somewhere. After the war it was largely the United States, happily with the cooperation of many other countries, that established and made the containment policy effective. We are now confronted with a similar situation in Southeast Asia and the United States, having the power and having the will, has seen fit to try to hold the line against Communist expansion, or domination by China in that area, and I think that this is probably something in the long run which will be in the interests of peace in the world and security for all of us.

The problem of how to do it and the problem of dealing with the type of intransigence we have encountered there is, of course, exceedingly difficult and complicated. I don't want to leave the impression, if I have, that I am opposed to this policy. I suppose every one of us would disagree on details about anything, virtually anything, and I don't hesitate to say that as to every detail of the conduct of our policy, I am not always in agreement, nor, I suspect, are any of our responsible officials, and that is what you have a President for. He is the one who has to make the final decisions, however uncomfortable and distasteful they may be.

MR. FRYE: The Russian delegate has been giving you personally rather a hard time of late, especially in the Security Council. He called you a "reptile," I believe, at one point. You appeared to attribute this at one stage to a revival of Stalinism. At another point, to Red Chinese pressure.

To what extent do you feel there has been a revival of Stalinism in Moscow, and how deep has been the impact of Chinese pressure on their policy?

AMBASSADOR STEVENSON: This is purely speculation, of course, but it is very obvious that the Chinese are now challenging the Russians for the leadership of the Communist parties throughout the world and that naturally enough the Russians are going to contest any challenge to their leadership very vigorously, so that what you have is the United States often emerging as the scapegoat between these two contending forces.

In other words, it is competitive whipping of the United States for the attention of the Communist parties, and I think there has been a good deal of that.

MR. FRYE: President Johnson also asked for individual pressure on Hanoi and Peiping, which pressure obviously could only come from Moscow. Is Moscow privately being helpful to any extent in bringing about a Vietnam peace negotiation?

AMBASSADOR STEVENSON: I can't talk with confidence about that because I don't know. I am very sure that the Soviet Union is anxious to avoid any dangerous escalation of this war and that it doesn't want to see it pass on into higher and higher levels of threat to all of humanity any more than we do.

MISS FREDERICK: Both the Soviet Union and the United States have now invoked regional alliances in entering, respectively, Hungary and the Dominican Republic. Do these precedents set by the two big powers give the green light to any regional group to take enforcement action although the Security Council is supposed, under the Charter, to approve such enforcement action?

AMBASSADOR STEVENSON: I don't consider that this was enforcement at all.

MISS FREDERICK: Do you mean the OAS force is not down there keeping the peace?

AMBASSADOR STEVENSON: It is not enforcing anything.

MISS FREDERICK: Isn't that a peacekeeping ——

AMBASSADOR STEVENSON: Enforcement — we have always interpreted the Charter and I think virtually all the membership, Miss Frederick, interprets that language, that word, as enforcing a decision.

We are down there to keep the peace, to prevent one party from enforcing its will on the other.

MISS FREDERICK: The United States is keeping ——

AMBASSADOR STEVENSON: The OAS, the Inter-American Peace Force.

MISS FREDERICK: But if shooting breaks out, the OAS Force led by the United States is supposed to try to stop it, isn't it? Doesn't that make it enforcement?

AMBASSADOR STEVENSON: No, that is not our interpretation of what was intended by that language of the Charter at all.

MISS FREDERICK: In other words, the OAS has the primary role in the Dominican Republic, whether you call it enforcement action or what. How does this affect other possible regional organization actions, such as the Arab League, or the Organization of African Unity, stepping into areas in their regions?

AMBASSADOR STEVENSON: Yes, I think you raise a very good point there, and I think it is a serious one that causes us a good deal — at least me — a good deal of anxiety.

Those organizations, the OAU and the Arab League, of course, are not as developed by any means, nor do they have the historical experience that the OAS does, that the Organization of American States does, but when the Organization of American States undertook to prevent, to stop the bloodshed and prevent these people from getting at each other's throats indefinitely in the Dominican Republic, it did undertake an action which I suppose is nonexclusive, and that means that others could do likewise.

MR. SPIVAK: Ambassador Stevenson, the Soviet Union has exercised its veto power 104 times, and we haven't exercised it at all. Would you be in favor of abolishing the veto?

AMBASSADOR STEVENSON: No, I think not at this stage because I am afraid — if I would say it, it would be meaningless. The Soviet Union would never assent to it. I am not even sure our own Senate would assent to it. I am happy to say we have been able to persuade the majority in the United Nations from the beginning to go along with us and therefore have not needed to use the veto.

MR. BROOKS: I am sorry to have to interrupt, but I see that our time is up. Thank you very much, Ambassador Stevenson, for being with us.

To Roxane Eberlein [179]

June 28, 1965

I borrowed $35,000 from Brown Brothers Harriman — to make another investment with Mr. Swig.[180] I might as well reduce the loan with any available balance. Hence, please send a check payable to Brown Brothers Harriman to Charles Woodford for $5,000 which I should be able to spare — with a letter somewhat as follows:

Dear Charles: I enclose my check for $5,000 which I wish you would credit against the loan of $35,000. I hope to be able to pay off the balance in installments from time to time. Sincerely yours.

Tell both Mrs. [Ruth] Field and Senator [William] Benton that I expect to stay in Libertyville for a few days and will not be back in New York for dinner on July 1st — unless I get a summons. You might tell Mrs. Field that I will take the liberty of calling her in case I get back sooner and can still join them for dinner. In any event, I will be in touch with her promptly on my return.

I will have to defer a decision about Dr. Lax until I find out whether I am going to Geneva on the 5th.

Please ask Bill Benton if the visit to [Prime Minister] Harold Wilson is off or on, and let me know in Libertyville together with the dates. You might tell him that I am still uncertain as to whether I am going to Geneva or not. If I do, I will hope to be in London July 9th or 10th and would be delighted to join him at Chequers.

Make me a reservation on TW[A] 821 — Lv JFK 9:15 P.M. — on July 5th. If there is a flight that leaves earlier in the evening, I'd just as soon take that.

[179] This memorandum was written from San Francisco.
[180] Benjamin Swig, owner of the Fairmont Hotel in San Francisco, who advised Stevenson on investments.

To Joan Baez

July 2, 1965

My dear Joan:

I am distressed that my remorseless schedule prevented me from even crossing the street to see you. You were sweet to write me that nice note and it would have been a joy to have a visit with you.

Instead, I sat in the sun in the Greek Theatre for a spectacular Convocation that lasted for hours!

With affectionate regards,

Yours,

To J. Edward Day [181]

July 4, 1965

Dear Ed —

I've read a few pages and laughed & laughed.[182] Thanks! And, Lord, how I miss you and that effervescent humor. Most of the time I feel parched and dry these days.

And another book to come! I thought you were practicing law. I go to Europe next week [183] for a brief ordeal & when I get back we will meet in Wash[ington] — pray Lord.

Love to Mary Louise [184] & all the children.

ADLAI

To Roxane Eberlein [185]

July 6, 1965

R.E.

Ask John Nagel [186] how much deduction I can use for 1965 assuming income and other deductions about the same for 1965 as 1964. I have 17,500 of deductions for damage to trees — appraised by Archibald

---

[181] This postcard was written from Libertyville. The original is in the possession of Mr. Day.

[182] Mr. Day had just sent Stevenson a copy of his book *My Appointed Round* (New York: Holt, Rinehart and Winston, 1965) and wrote that he was dedicating his next book, *Humor in Public Speaking* (West New York, New York: Parker Publishing Company, 1965), to Stevenson.

[183] Stevenson was to speak at a meeting of the Economic and Social Council of the United Nations in Geneva, Switzerland.

[184] Mrs. Day.

[185] This handwritten note is in the possession of Miss Eberlein. It was written from Libertyville.

[186] Stevenson's tax consultant.

Enoch Price of Winnetka [Illinois] — and will want to make a further gift of papers to Princeton [University] this year to use up the allowable deductions.

See letter from [Benjamin] Swig re 35 000 investment for 5% interest in S[an]. F[rancisco]. building. Put original of letter in bank file.

I have issued check for $1000 to Viola Reardy dated July 5, 1965 unnumbered — "account number 275840" — this is an interest free loan to enable her to fix her house up for rental in Boyne City [Michigan]. She is going up there from Libertyville July 7 and will let you know how to reach her. I've said I would not need her before July 20 & will let her know when to come back.

James Wechsler in the New York Post, *June 28, 1965, described Stevenson's performance on* Meet the Press *and the letters he was receiving asking that he resign, and wrote: "What Stevenson seemed to be saying . . . was that a man does not lightly walk out on a major government mission unless convinced that conflicts over strategy have become irreconcilable issues of principle. The obscure twilight zone lies between 'detail' and doctrine." Wechsler added that too often Stevenson was reduced to the role of debater rather than a creator of policy.*

To James Wechsler

July 6, 1965

Dear Jim:

It has taken me too long to catch up with your column "Stevenson's Role" of June 28th. Belated thanks, which are no less emphatic and warm!

You always seem to understand with such clarity what is obscure to others. But that you can express publicly with greater clarity than I can privately, is, Sir, humiliating! Yet it is not as awkward for me as the constant role of "debater" instead of "creator." There you touch the nerve with precision!

I pray we can have that leisurely talk soon.

Yours — again!

To Borden Stevenson

July 6, 1965

Dear Borden:

Tomorrow is your birthday, and I had hoped to spend the day, or some of it, with you. Instead, I must leave tonight for Geneva, as you know.

Hence I must enclose the customary check — and it seems a very impersonal recognition of this important day in your life.

I have wanted so much to hear more about your journey but it seems so hard for us to get together. I will dictate some introductions which the office will send you or which you can pick up before your departure. I hope they will be of some help.

I will be back in New York between the 15th and 18th of July, I think. Please let me hear from you, and the date of your return as promptly as possible.

Love,

On June 9, 1965, Dwight Macdonald wrote Stevenson and asked for an appointment for a number of writers and social critics to discuss American policy in Vietnam and the Dominican Republic. Enclosed with the letter was a "Declaration to Ambassador Adlai Stevenson" expressing the signers' "dismay" at the escalation of the war in Vietnam.

The printed declaration, initiated by Artists and Writers Dissent, 224 West 4th Street, New York, New York, was distributed widely. Stevenson had a copy of the declaration in his briefcase when he died. On the reverse side of the page Martha Gellhorn wrote Stevenson, July 4, 1965, supporting the declaration and adding that since he would not resign and Eleanor Roosevelt was dead there was no leader of great strength and conscience to speak out.

Another printed letter (undated) headed "Volunteers For Stevenson — 1965 — An organization dedicated to the ideals spelled out by Governor Stevenson in his Presidential campaigns of 1952 and 1956; and in his reluctant bid for the nomination in 1960" was also being circulated. It stated, among other things:

We, the volunteers of brighter yesterdays, wait in ever increasing despair for some sign of the Stevenson who so inspired us. . . . We, the Volunteers for Stevenson of the past, the crusaders of happier yesterdays still hold fast to your vision of the today that should have been — and yet can be. It was you, Governor Stevenson, who inspired in us not only an extra measure of pride in our country but a sacred responsibility in our citizenship. You gave us much — and we, in turn invested much in you. . . . The nation and the world desperately need a strong and eloquent voice to oppose the policy which is leading mankind towards the final confrontation. We implore you to be that voice. With full knowledge of the sacrifice we ask, we who have loved you plead with you now to resign. Outside of the United Nations, free of the bonds of the present administration, you may yet save America from the predictable disaster towards which we are drifting."

Stevenson also had a copy of this letter in his briefcase when he died. The declaration read:

We speak to you as fellow citizens. We have watched in dismay as our government — by its actions in Vietnam and the Dominican Republic — has clearly violated the United Nations Charter, international law, and those fundamental principles of human decency which alone can prevent a terrifying, world-wide escalation of suffering and death.

We urgently ask you, as our government's representative in the United Nations and as a man who has in the past stood for the best hopes of realizing American ideals, to consider your complicity in what this government is doing. We mean not only the persistent escalation of the war in Vietnam but also the willingness of this government to resort to unilateral military interventions, thus dangerously weakening the United Nations.

We urgently ask you to consider your complicity in the persistent misstatements of facts by this government and by you as its representative. We refer you to numerous discrepancies between official government statements and on-the-scene reporting by responsible newsmen on such papers as The New York Times and the New York Herald Tribune.

In the past you have expressed your commitment to a world of law and to an honest, compassionate search for peaceful solutions to conflict. Therefore, we believe this must be a time of deep inner conflict for you, and we urge you to resolve that conflict in the interest of restoring sanity to this government's foreign policy.

We urge you to resign as United States Ambassador to the United Nations, and having done that, to become spokesman again for that which is humane in the traditions and in the people of America. By this act, you can contribute immeasurably to the prospects of world peace. By remaining in your post — without speaking truth to power — you will have diminished yourself and all men everywhere.

On June 21, Stevenson talked to eight of the signers of this declaration: Kay Boyle, Paul Goodman, Nat Hentoff, Dwight Macdonald, former Congressman William S. Mayer, A. J. Muste, David McReynolds, and Harvey Swados. Clayton Fritchey attended the meeting for a few minutes but left in order that Stevenson would not be embarrassed by having a staff member present. Fritchey stated: "Stevenson had a decent respect for the opinions of the intellectual community. When they talked to him, he did not know about President Johnson's plans for putting troops into Vietnam. Johnson did not tell him or consult him, but we at USUN had heard rumors about it. Stevenson, at the time of the meeting, was much more disturbed over the invasion of the Dominican Republic. Stevenson felt that he could not resign. It was better to stay and try to persuade Johnson to change. Stevenson did not like prima donnas who resigned with big publicity. He was not a prima donna. But, at the same time, he was thinking that if you cannot do something from the inside and it is a great issue, shouldn't you resign? At the time of the meeting, Stevenson had reached this point in his thinking." [187]

Hentoff wrote of the meeting:

He received us — the delegation who had come in June to ask him to resign — with grace. That rare, unforced, unfeigned grace that friends tell me Joseph Welch [188] had, that Duke Ellington [189] has — the more so when he is serious and not public. There was much more of a dialogue than I had anticipated. We were there for an hour and a quarter. At first, he tried — loyally, some would say — to present again and to defend again the Administration's line. But the more forceful among us — Dwight Macdonald, Harvey Swados, David McReynolds, Paul Goodman — would not let him demean himself. And finally — though only intermittently — there were echoes of the Stevenson of the 1952 campaign.

I am not saying he was explicitly in opposition to LBJ with us. We were strangers. But his concern with what he had compelled himself to do broke through at times. Clearly he was not secure in himself with what had happened in the Dominican Republic. At another point, when one of us referred to the transmogrification of the USIA [United States Information Agency], he snapped — and not at us — "I would not have permitted that!" Viet Nam was more complex than Santo Domingo. But after a remarkably lucid, I thought, analysis by David McReynolds of how this country was compounding error, let alone immorality, Stevenson said, anguished, "But what the hell CAN we do?" Alternatives were suggested, but the implication from his side of the room was that they could not be "sold." To LBJ. To the public. It wasn't clear. He wasn't clear.

At the end, he said — and I did not feel it to be rhetoric — "You honor me by coming. I do not have the chance often these days to have this kind of dialogue." Leaving, I was depressed. I had the sense of his impotence — and the sense of his knowing and caring deeply, hopelessly about the impotence. He could not resign. That was not the way he played the game. And because he could not — would not — change the rules, he had been trapped by them. . . .[190]

[187] Clayton Fritchey, interview with Walter Johnson, April 6, 1973.
[188] The Boston lawyer who represented the Army in the Army-McCarthy hearings in 1954.
[189] Composer, pianist and orchestra leader.
[190] *Village Voice,* July 22, 1965.

Macdonald wrote a description of the meeting from notes he made at the time.

Asked about Dominican intervention at first said he regretted it, but when we pressed him as to why, he seemed to retreat to official line. Me: "Do you really think there were those 52 Communist leaders in Bosch regime?" S[tevenson]: "I don't know about Communists in the D.R." "But you *must* — who else?" S: "It's all very speculative . . . It wasn't *wholly* because of the threatened Communist take-over. Bloodshed was threatening, so we *had* to intervene to stop it — also to guarantee free elections." After much argument from us — S: "I think you've made one misstatement: the situation was that the Bosch people were in a bad situation militarily and welcomed US troops. It's like Eisenhower sending the marines to Lebanon." (Can imagine the uproar this caused. . . .) Then: "Perhaps it did represent stretching the Monroe Doctrine a little."

At one point, forget context: "I think you could be extremely useful as an articulate group with strong ideas on foreign policy."

He smiled when we asked him if he had considered resigning: "No, I will not resign. I would never take advantage of my political position to resign for political reasons.[191] That's not the way we play the game." Goodman (I think): "But don't you feel you have a greater obligation to the people of the US, and of the world, than to the Administration."

"I think I meet that by representing my country at the UN — no, I wouldn't think of resigning."

Us: Why don't we negotiate with the Vietcong for peace in Vietnam? S: "Can you imagine us going over the heads of the South Vietnamese government to negotiate with the Vietcong?" US: "Then why doesn't Administration bring pressure on SV govt. to negotiate? S: "Because we cannot ask that govt. to negotiate with a force that is trying to overthrow it." Us: "But can't call SVN govt. a govt. — reasons — much clamor — (session often rather spirited — S. always polite, listened to all arguments attentively, gave impression of answering, or trying to, in same spirit). Can't recall his words to that but tune was same — it is a govt, etc.

Us: Why not take the Vietnam war to the UN? S: Because North Vietnam not a member — also "The UN has in fact been very active, though not officially. . . ." Some point S. said we must keep on present course at UN and outside UN "until we can substitute international organization for national power." Also, at another point: "On principle what do you suggest we do in the UN. Because I do agree it might be desirable." We told him, no sale.

[191] Roxane Eberlein wrote that Stevenson knew what a commotion his resignation would cause. Memorandum to Walter Johnson, March 12, 1973.

Someone brought up a recent scandal — Johnson's easing out head of Voice of America for some political reason, or maybe putting him in position had to resign (Rowan think it was).[192] S: "Well, I can't defend that." [193]

Goodman recalled that at one point Stevenson told them: "It is appalling to deal with government people who don't know history, the history of diplomacy, and who are like children." [194]

Several days after the meeting, Paul Goodman wrote Stevenson that he must not condone lies. "When you are put in the position of repeating them, we are deeply ashamed," he wrote. "Please, go down and nail them and get yourself fired."

Several days before he died in London on July 14, 1965, Stevenson gave a copy of his intended reply to Goodman to Philip Kaiser, minister at the American embassy, for comment. It was typewritten but had numerous corrections by hand. Whether it is the final draft is not clear. It is quite possible that in this draft Stevenson was probing, looking for a formula that would allow him to stay in his post but one that the intellectual community could accept.[195] Mr. Kaiser sent the letter to Adlai E. Stevenson III after he had shown it to Walter Johnson in London in November, 1965. Adlai III sent a copy to Mr. Goodman and released the letter to the press.

To Clayton Fritchey

July 6, 1965

I attach a copy of a letter I have drafted in reply to a letter from Mr. Paul Goodman. I left copies with Joe Sisco [196] in the Department [of State] for review before sending it to Mr. Goodman. He will return it with any comments and changes.

Perhaps you could then look it over and see that it is mailed to Mr. Goodman, and also consider whether it should be published in view of the extensive publication of the appeal to me to resign.[197] The latter I have also left with Mr. Sisco which he will doubtless return.

---

[192] The New York *Times*, July 14, 1965, reported that the feeling was that Carl Rowan had been forced out because he was neglecting his administrative tasks.

[193] Letter to Walter Johnson, August 14, 1967. See also Macdonald's column in *Esquire*, June, 1967, p. 189. Richard J. Walton describes the meeting in *The Remnants of Power: The Tragic Last Years of Adlai Stevenson* (New York: Coward-McCann, 1968), pp. 174–180.

[194] Interview with Walter Johnson, October 14, 1968.

[195] Clayton Fritchey, interview with Walter Johnson, April 6, 1973. Fritchey added that had Stevenson been sure about the letter, he could have mailed it himself without leaving copies for him, Joseph Sisco, and Philip Kaiser.

[196] Assistant Secretary of State, replacing Harlan Cleveland.

[197] Fritchey did not send the letter to Goodman or release it to the press. He felt

Perhaps you will want to consider sending copies to the other people who comprised the delegation that called upon me if you think it suitable. Perhaps a copy should also go with a letter of transmittal, explaining that I am abroad, to Ralph Ginzburg.[198] His letter to me is attached.[199]

To Paul Goodman [200]

[no date]

Dear Mr. Goodman:

Thank you for your letter. Its arguments, I think, rest on a simple presupposition: that I share your belief in the disastrous trend of American foreign policy and that I must therefore resign to underline my disagreement, rally public opinion against it and nail the "lies" into which it is being presented to the people.

But it is precisely this pre-supposition that I do not share with you, and I would like to send you my reasons for believing that, whatever criticisms may be made over the detail and emphasis of American foreign policy, its purpose and direction are sound.

---

that the letter—drafted, he believed, by Barbara Ward—took too hard a line and that the reasoning in the letter did not represent Stevenson's thinking. (Sisco agreed with Fritchey.) Fritchey decided to hold the letter and discuss it with Stevenson on his return to USUN. Fritchey wrote out comments for the discussion. The first dealt with the statement in the letter that the United States had drawn a line in Europe and now must do it in Asia. Fritchey planned to point out that the United States had accepted the Soviet Union's absorption of the Baltic states and control over Eastern Europe and therefore the reasoning in the letter implied that China should have control over Thailand and other nations along its border. Interviews with Walter Johnson, January 25, 1967, April 6, 1973. Barbara Ward wrote that Stevenson did not discuss the letter with her. Letter to Walter Johnson, August 12, 1972. Adlai E. Stevenson III and his wife Nancy were at Libertyville over the Fourth of July, 1965, when Barbara Ward was there. He recalls "vaguely some discussion of the Paul Goodman letter. Dad was annoyed and troubled, particularly at the suggestion that his advocacy of administration policy was immoral." Letter to Walter Johnson, September 13, 1972. Marietta Tree, who was walking with Stevenson near the U.S. embassy in London when he had his fatal heart attack on July 14, 1965, wrote: "Adlai did talk to me about this letter he was drafting to go to Paul Goodman. I wouldn't rely 100% on my memory, but I think I remember that he told me it was drafted originally by Barbara Ward and that he was very concerned about the letter as well as perplexed. Goodman and Company, after all, represented his own constituency and he did not want to let them down. At the same time, he could not depart from the President's policy. In any case, he stewed a good deal about it to me on various occasions." Letter to Walter Johnson, May 1, 1973. Harlan Cleveland talked with Stevenson in Geneva just before Stevenson left for London. Stevenson did not mention the letter from Goodman nor his response to it to Cleveland. Letter to Walter Johnson, November 30, 1974.

[198] Publisher of *Eros* magazine.

[199] This letter is not in the Stevenson papers.

[200] This letter was released to the press on December 14, 1965, by Adlai E. Stevenson III. The New York *Times* published it on December 15, 1965.

Our overriding purpose must be to avoid war. Yet we still live in a state of international anarchy in which each nation claims absolute sovereignty and great powers believe they can enforce the aims and interests which they consider paramount.

I believe that the ultimate disaster of atomic conflict can be avoided in this situation only by the pursuit of two clear lines of policy.

The first is to establish a tacitly agreed frontier between Communist and non-Communist areas of influence on the understanding that neither power system will use force to change the status quo. On the other side of it there may [be] change, of course, but not outside intervention, of [over] that line.

The second is to move from this position of precarious stability toward agreed international procedures for settling differences, towards the building of an international juridical and policing system and toward a whole variety of policies designed to turn our small vulnerable planet into a genuine economic and social community.

If you like, the first policy is static and defensive, the second creative and constructive. Both have to be pursued together.

The period from 1947 to 1962 was largely occupied in fixing the postwar line with the Soviet line. It is not a very satisfactory one since it divides Germany and Berlin. But the Russians respect it in Europe. So do we.

The Russians are perhaps not wholly committed to it since their doctrine included the right to encourage "wars of national liberation." These, we know, can lead to the imposition of governments which are not later answerable to any form of popular approbation or control. However, the missile crisis of 1962 may have convinced the Russian leaders that interventions of this sort beyond the tacit frontier of the two worlds are in fact too costly and dangerous.

We have no such line with the Chinese. Since they are in an earlier, more radical stage in their revolution, it may be more difficult to establish one. Should we try? And is the line we stand on in [201] half way across Vietnam a reasonable line? Should we hold it?

Let me take the second point first. I have no doubt that if France had handled the forces of decolonization in the prompt and orderly fashion of the British, the situation in South East Asia might be much more stable today. It can even be argued that in 1954 we should not have taken any action to guarantee a non-Communist regime to South Vietnam. Yet we did so in South Korea and it was reasonable to argue that the refugees streaming south from Hanoi had as much desire to avoid Communism as the people of South Korea. In any case, the line inherited by the Democratic Administration is the 17th Parallel. History

[201] The word "in" was inserted in Stevenson's handwriting.

does not always give us the most convenient choice. What sane statesman would choose West Berlin, for instance. Yet can one doubt its pivotal significance?

Since this *is* the line, should we hold it? The answer depends on the assumptions made about Chinese power. In the past, some Chinese dynasties have been aggressive, claiming sovereignty over wide areas of Asia, including all South East Asia and even some of India. So far, the new Communist "dynasty" has been very aggressive. Tibet was swallowed, India attacked, the Malays had to fight 12 years to resist a "national liberation" they could receive from the British by a more peaceful route. Today, the apparatus of infiltration and aggression is already at work in North Thailand. Chinese maps show to the world's chagrin the further limits of the old empire marked as Chinese. I do not think the idea of Chinese expansionism is so fanciful that the effort to check it is irrational.

And if one argues that it should not be checked, I believe you set us off on the old, old route whereby expansive powers push at more and more doors, believing they will open until, at the ultimate door, resistance is unavoidable and major war breaks out.

As President Johnson pointed out the other day, my country has suffered 160,000 casualties since the last war, but aggression didn't succeed — with our help — in Greece or Turkey, Iran or Formosa, Korea or Lebanon. And I think timely resistance has vastly enhanced the hope for peace and the prospects for the evolution of the principle of peaceful settlement of disputes enshrined in the U.N. Charter.

While I hesitate to draw historical comparisons with the Chinese, I remind you that the French Revolution led to prolonged war before the limits of France's power to control its neighbors were established.

My hope in Vietnam is that relatively small scale resistance now may establish the fact that changes in Asia are not to be precipitated by outside force. This was the point of the Korean War. This is the point of the conflict in Vietnam. I believe Asia will be more stable if the outcome is the same in both — a negotiated line and a negotiated peace — a just and honorable peace which leaves the future of the people of South Vietnam to be decided by them and not by force from North Vietnam.

This brings me to my second point — the hope of transcending the static policy of "containment" and moving to the more creative tasks of building a world security based on law and peaceful settlement.

I believe that we must seek a negotiated peace in Vietnam based upon the internationalization of the whole area's security, on a big effort to develop, under the U.N., the resources of the Mekong River and guarantees that Vietnam, North and South, can choose, again under international supervision, the kind of governments, the form of association and, if so decree the type of reunification of the two states they genuinely want to establish.

If we can achieve this, we begin to offer the small nations of the world an alternative to being within the spheres of influence. We are more decisively beyond the age of empires. We would begin to establish procedures by which local revolutionary movements, such as the rising in the Dominican Republic, and for that matter Zanzibar, are not automatically a prey to outside intervention.

I believe, for instance, that the U.N. effort in the Congo did prevent Central Africa from becoming a South East Asia, and I would make the strengthening of these U.N. procedures and activities a cardinal principle in a policy aimed at substituting "due process" for violence as the basis of international life. Meanwhile, I do not believe the opposite policy of retreat in Asia or anywhere else would make any contribution whatsoever to the ideal that violence shall not be the formal arbitrator in world affairs.

It is my conviction that American policy is groping its way toward this difficult but essential ideal, and this is the reason both for my support of the policy and for my continuance in a position which gives me some hope of assisting its advance in that direction.

Now it is possible for honest men to differ on every aspect of this interpretation. You may believe that Communist powers are not expansive. Or you may believe that the changes they seek to support by violence are beneficent changes which can be achieved by no other route. Again, you may believe that a return to some form of non-involvement in world affairs is the best posture for America. Or you may genuinely believe that America is in Vietnam "for sheer capitalist greed." These are all possible attitudes and I do not impugn the good faith of those who hold different views.

I would only ask them, in the name of the courtesies and decencies of a free society, that they should equally refrain from impugning mine.

Yours sincerely,

Soon after arriving in Geneva, Stevenson renewed his talks with U Thant about the possibility of peace in Vietnam. Following this conversation, Stevenson phoned Dean Rusk in Washington, D.C. After describing the Secretary-General's ideas, Stevenson's handwritten notes of Rusk's response read:

No chance of 2 & 2 — ask Couve [de Murville] for his suggestions. Any participation by VC would collapse whole position in VN — Can do much better than that on the ground. See him in N.Y.[202]

[202] Stevenson's rough notes of his talk with U Thant and Rusk's response were in

Stevenson sent the following cable to the Department of State on July 7, 1965, describing his talk with U Thant.[203]

I met with U Thant for long talk Wednesday morning in Geneva. He meets [Maurice] Couve de Murville in Paris at four on Thursday and [Harold] Wilson at lunch in London on Friday.

His views on current situation re Vietnam are summarized as follows: Soviets will take no further active role and he thought [Nikolai T.] Fedorenko has been instructed not to discuss Vietnam with him. Soviet either has no present influence or will exert none at risk of clash with Peking.

Still convinced that Hanoi is more and more under influence of Peking and doubts if Hanoi has complete control of Viet Cong. Doubts if there will be any change in Hanoi-Peking attitude for next 2–3 months because they expect to capture all principal towns except Saigon before end of monsoon. Recalled that he had proposed an appeal for cessation of all hostilities in April before the monsoon and also that Soviet had risked further trouble with Peking when they opened channel for US-Hanoi private talks in Rangoon at his request last autumn which US did not choose to pursue.

With regard to an appeal for talks with a cease fire as the first order of business, U Thant said the question of representation of the Viet Cong will immediately arise. If US could consider negotiations with Saigon, Hanoi and Viet Cong seated at the table, he thought it well worth while to transmit the suggestion to Hanoi from U Thant through Couve during meeting in Paris tomorrow. He repeated several times that it was only realistic that the discussions of a cease fire would have to include those who are doing the fighting. While not essential, he would recommend that "an honest broker" sit with the four to use his good offices to keep the talks going, and asked for reactions to Nyere [204] if Ayub would not act personally. In response to inquiry if I had any suggestion for a mediator, I replied that I had none for the present because I suspected that no meeting including representatives of the Viet Cong was possible.

U Thant still thinks his original suggestion best; i.e. his appeal for a cessation of all overt and covert hostilities for 1–3 months while peace talks proceed because this course would be more of an inducement to Hanoi. He offered to sound out Couve on this suggestion also if we are interested.

---

his luggage when he died. Roxane Eberlein transcribed the fragmentary notes for this volume. Only those on Rusk's response are included here, since the others are covered in Stevenson's cable of July 7, 1965, to the Department of State.

[203] This document was declassified. National Security Files, Agency File, Representative of the United States to the United Nations, Lyndon B. Johnson Library.

[204] Julius K. Nyerere, president of Tanzania.

Pursuant to telephone conversation with Secretary [of State], I am informing him that in present circumstances any meeting including Viet Cong cannot be considered and therefore he should only elicit suggestions from Couve and Wilson and report them to me in New York next week.

With regard to suggestion of a Security Council meeting to call for resumption of the Geneva Conference, U Thant was skeptical. He thinks Peking and Hanoi will object and therefore the Russians, and perhaps the French. However, he offered to sound out the Russians on the understanding that US and USSR would avoid verbal violence and agree in advance not to veto a call for resumption of the Conference. However, he anticipates that representation of Viet Cong in a Geneva context would also arise in any consultation with the Soviet.

He could shed no light on the meaning of Dobrynin's remark to the Secretary, "Stop the bombing and see what else happens."

On July 9, 1965, Stevenson spoke at a meeting of the Economic and Social Council in Geneva.

STRENGTHENING THE INTERNATIONAL DEVELOPMENT INSTITUTIONS [205]

Mr. President,

We meet here in Geneva at the midpoint of the year of international cooperation and the midpoint of the decade of development [as Amb. Pachachi [206] has reminded us]. Let us be neither *cynical* nor *despondent* about the gap between these brave titles and the fact that at the moment, our world community is chiefly notable for *minimal cooperation* and very *lopsided development*. Our *aspirations* are there to spur us on, to incite us to better efforts. They are emphatically *not* there as a *blind* or a *cover* or as *rhetoric* to suggest that we are really doing very well.

I take as the understood *premise* of everything I say that as a world community we are *not* developing as we should and that our record of cooperation is *inadequate*, to say the least. But I *believe*, I *hope*, we can

[205] The text is from the typewritten copy that Stevenson used in delivering the speech. Words and phrases that he underlined for emphasis are italicized. His handwritten additions are enclosed in brackets. Other changes, corrections, and deletions are indicated in the footnotes. On a separate sheet of paper he jotted down the following notes for his informal opening to the speech: "After admirable speeches etc. I suspect you will detect some echoes in what I have to say — I am reminded of the young daughter of a clergyman etc." An excerpt from the speech was reproduced in *I Can Hear It Now/The Sixties*, written and edited by Fred W. Friendly/Walter Cronkite (Columbia Records, Inc., 1970). The speech was published in Department of State *Bulletin*, July 26, 1965.

[206] Ambassador Adnan Pachachi, permanent representative of Iraq to the United Nations, 1959–1966.

do *better* and that the nations meeting in *1970* will say: "Ah, yes, 1965 was a kind of *turning point*. That was the moment at which we began to realize how much *better* our performance has to be."

How *much* better can best be registered by a glance at *where* we are now.

We launched the Decade of Development because we realized, as a world community, that while our wealth was *growing* its *distribution* had become increasingly *unbalanced*. I need hardly repeat the figures — the developed market economies and the developed centrally planned economies make up about [one] [207] quarter of the world's population and account for *three* quarters of the world's *trade, production,* and *investment*.

By the chances of *history* and *geography,* these developed nations are largely to be found to the *north* of the Tropic of Cancer. Ideology makes no difference here. Soviet Russia belongs by *income* and *growth* to the *developed "north,"* Ghana to the *developing "south"* in our new economic geography.

These facts we knew in *1960*. In the last 5 years the contrasts have grown more vivid. The developed nations with per capita incomes of above $700 a year have *grown* — the index I use is gross national product per head of population — by not less than 3 percent a year.

Below them a smaller group of nations, which are in the range of $200 to $700 per capita, have grown even more rapidly — by 4 to 8 percent a year.

But at the *bottom* of the scale at a figure of $200 per head and less, comprising over a hundred nations making up over two-thirds of humanity, the rate of per capita growth has in many instances been less than the average of 2.3 percent of the developing countries as a whole. *Population* growth has swallowed up their margins, and *per capita* growth hovers around *zero*.

I

This is the statistical picture which emerges from the present data about world development. But how *bare* and uninformative such numbers really are. They tell us nothing about the rates of child mortality — *ten* times higher among *poor* than *rich*. They give us no picture of the homeless *migrant* living without *water* or *shelter* on the fringe of Asian or Latin American cities. We get no *feel* from them of the ache of hunger or the debility that comes from diets without enough protein and vitamins.

These are the *hidden* miseries about which we talk with our figures of per capita gross national product, our statistical comparisons, our imper-

[207] "One" has been substituted for "a" here.

sonal percentages. We are talking about *pain* and *grief* and *hunger* and *despair* and we are talking about the lot of half the human race.

II

But we are *also* talking about another phenomenon — the extraordinary *increase* in resources available to human society taken as a whole. These 3- or 4-percent increases in the national growth of *developed* societies mean an *unparalleled* expansion of *new* resources.

Under steady and responsible economic management, we cannot *see* — and we certainly do not *want* [208] — any *end* to this process of expansion. Out of the *research* that is connected with *weaponry*, with *space*, and with the whole wide range of needs of our civilian economy, we are constantly making *new* breakthroughs — new *methods*, new *products*, new sources of *food* or *energy* or *medical* relief that increase our capacity to reproduce wealth still *further*. We have harnessed energy to take us into outer space and to convert saline waters into drink for the thirsty. The isotopes which grow from *nuclear* experiments can revolutionize *medical* and *agricultural* research. And we know not what *new*,[209] still undiscovered sources of abundance lie *ahead*.

We have to begin to *grasp* and *digest* this new, astonishing *liberation* of our terrestrial resources, for only after such an understanding can we hope to act on the *scale* and with the *audacity* that our profound problems of *poverty* and *hopelessness* and *obstruction* demand. We shall conquer, no doubt, the *dark* face of the moon. But I would hope we can with equal confidence conquer the *dark* face of *poverty* and give men and women *new life, new hope, new space* on this planet.

III

Let's face it: We are nowhere *near* conquering world poverty. *None* of us — neither the *weak* nor the *strong*, the *poor* nor the *rich*, the *new* nations nor the *old* — have yet taken seriously enough the contrast between the *abundance* of our *opportunities* and the *scarcity* of our *actions* to grasp them. It is *good* that the *rich* are getting *richer* — that is what economic development is *for*. But it is *bad* that, despite our considerable efforts in the first half of this decade, the *poor* are still *poor* — and progressing more slowly than present day society can tolerate.

What shall we do to improve the trend during the next 5 years? There is *something* for *everybody* to do. There are tasks for *all* of us, and it won't *help* the poorer [210] countries for us to sit around this table blaming the state of the world on each other. There are clear and present tasks for

---

[208] Dashes have been substituted for commas around this phrase.
[209] The comma has been added by hand.
[210] "Poor" has been changed to "poorer."

the *developing* countries in doing what they know is *necessary* to their own economic growth and social progress. There are tasks, equally *clear* and equally *present,* for the industrialized countries. And there are tasks — a growing number of much *larger* tasks — for UN organizations themselves.

I think each of us should come to this table vowing to bring proposals that his nation *can* — and *intends* to — *do* something *about.* In that spirit I will not rehearse here my views on how the *developing* nations can better help *themselves* but will suggest what the *wealthier* countries can do to help and how the UN itself can do *more* about development, and do it *better.*

[*PAUSE*]   IV

Let me suggest *first* the sense of a convergent *strategy* for the industrialized nations. Its aim should be to see to it that more of the *wealth* and *purchasing* power of our expanding world economy will be used to stimulate economic growth in the developing nations.

We can accomplish this aim only by the *coordinated* use of a *variety* of *means:* by the direct transfer of resources from developed nations to developing nations through effective *aid* programs; next, by assuring the developing countries greater access to the expanding *markets* of the world; next, by working to reduce fluctuations in the *export* earnings of the developing countries; next by *working* harder, doing more specific research, on what the more developed countries can do to help the less developed create *more* wealth *faster;* next, by helping to slow down the vertiginous growth in the number of *people* which the still fragile developing economies have to support. A steady, overall four per cent rate of growth in national income is in itself a difficult achievement. Its effects are tragically nullified if the rate of population growth is 3% or even more.

These five strands of a convergent strategy contain no *mysteries.* We have discussed them over and over again. What has been lacking has been an adequate *urgency* of *purpose* and *decision* and a real determination to face the full costs.

There is no doubt that we can *afford* whatever direct transfer of resources can really be put to effective use. There are so many man-made obstacles in the development process that there is a kind of natural *limit* to the transfer of resources from the richer countries to the poorer countries.

In my judgment, we are in no danger at all of *harming* our *own* healthy economies by *maximizing* our efforts to promote international development. Our problem, rather, is to step up the *training* of people, the *surveying* of resources, and the *investigation* of opportunities — in a word, the *pre-investment* work — which still sets the ceiling on *direct* investment, public and private, in the economic growth of most developing countries.

With my next point — improved *trading* opportunities [211] — I come to all the issues at stake in the continuing work of the new UN Trade and Development Board and its committees, and of the GATT.[212] These are some of the problems we must face *together. Primary* prices are *unstable,* and many have tended downwards in the last decade. The tariff structures in the industrial countries hit harder at the processed and manufactured goods than at raw materials.[213] Internal taxes discourage the consumption of tropical products. And finally, there is need for greater effort to improve *production* and *efficiency* in the *export* industries of the developing countries.

The enormous *uncertainties* of trade, the unstable, fluctuating export earnings, interrupt the development process, too much and too often.[214] The world has already put into effect some means of providing *compensatory* finance and balance of payments support to help the developing countries deal with such difficulties. Perhaps we will never find an ideal solution, but I think we have by no means reached the end of the road in dealing with these problems. We must [215] continue to do everything practicable to provide to developing countries resources that are effectively related to the fluctuations in their export trade.

When I say we need a concerted attack on these obstacles, I do not mean a great *debate* in which the attack is concerted *against* the governments of the wealthier countries. Complaints about *other* countries' policies have their place in international politics.[216] They seldom change what the other nations actually do, but they help make the complainant a hero to his own countrymen — and that has its place in politics too. But when it comes to *trade* between the world's "north" and the world's "south," we need not a general *debate* about general *principles* but *concrete proposals, direct negotiations, specific* nose-to-nose *confrontations* about particular *ways* the developing countries can *increase* their *exports* and how the rest of us can *really* help, commodity by commodity.

---

[211] "For the developing countries" has been deleted here.

[212] The General Agreement on Tariffs and Trade, adopted by sixty signatories in 1947, which provided for the phased elimination of tariffs, quotas, and preferences in order to achieve freer trade.

[213] This sentence has been bracketed in pencil, with a question mark in the margin.

[214] This sentence originally read: "Many of the developing countries suffer enormous uncertainties and interruptions of trade, with their unstable, fluctuating export earnings." Several words have been added by hand but crossed out.

[215] This word has been corrected from "much."

[216] A period has been substituted for a dash and the next word capitalized.

V

Another vital contribution the industrialized nations can make to development is to expand their own *research* into the *causes* [217] and *cures* of poverty. Partly this is a matter of putting extra *emphasis* on those fields of science that are especially relevant to the needs and possibilities of the developing countries. We stand here in the presence of exciting breakthroughs in *nutrition,* in *farming,* in *water use,* in *meteorology,* in *energy.* All these are *vital,* and it is particularly gratifying that the United Nations advisory group of scientists have put the development of *water* resources and the evolution of new *high*-protein diets at the top of their list of points needing special attack.

Mr. President, while I am on this subject, I should like to say a special word about the work of the Advisory Committee on the Application of Science and Technology to Development. My Government will make known in due course its detailed views with respect to the specific proposals made by this group in the report which is before us.[218] As to the report itself, I would only say at this time that it is *clear, precise,* and *professional* — high testimony to the quality of work that *can* be done in our international community. On behalf of my delegation, I should like to congratulate all members of the Advisory Committee, the many experts of the Specialized Agencies who contributed to it, and the members of the United Nations Secretariat under whose supervision the work went forward.

But I have *more* in mind than the *merits* of the recommendations put forward and the *quality* of the report as a whole. I have in mind the *background* of this report and the process by which these proposals have taken shape for our consideration.

The background of the report, as we all know, is the Conference on the Application of Science and Technology to problems of the developing areas, held here in Geneva in early 1963.[219] That conference was *criticized* by superficial observers. They said that the whole thing was much too *big* — too many *people,* too many *subjects,* too many *papers,* too much *talk* to do any good. They said that the whole thing was much too *vague* — too *general,* too *unfocused,* too *disparate.* And perhaps there was something in some of this criticism.

But it was a *start.* And the big thing is that we did not let it die. We maintained the momentum generated at that conference. We went on to the *next* step. Within a few months after the close of that conference, this

[217] "Cause" has been changed to "causes."
[218] UN document E/4026.
[219] For this background, see the Department of State *Bulletin,* February 4, 1963, p. 188, and February 25, 1963, p. 302.

Council recommended the establishment of an expert committee of advisers to *carry on* — to *pick up* where the conference *left off* — to *sort* the *important* from what is merely *useful.*

I have no doubt, Mr. President, that what followed was a difficult and tedious exercise for the Committee of Advisers. But they went about it systematically. They consulted and took evidence. They worked steadily and quietly. And out of *thousands* of things that might be good to do, they have derived a few *dozen* of things which it is *urgent* and *necessary* to do — which, in fact, it would be *outrageous not* to do. They have *resisted* dreams of *tomorrow's science*,[220] and thought hard about *today's technology.* They have refrained from proposing yet another agency and come to grips instead with *existing* agencies — what more *they* might do, what we know they *can* do *better*, with *foreseeable* resources.

So what began as a seemingly unmanageable project has been *tamed, mastered*, and *transmitted* into a sensible list of specific proposals of priority value and manageable proportion. This is no small accomplishment in so short a time. And we can all take heart from this exercise. It bodes well for the work of the Council, and of the U.N. system at large.

VI

The Advisory Committee focused of course on *science* and *technology* — that is what it was asked to do. But we need *research* and *inquiry* fully as *much* in great areas of *social confusion* and *uncertainty.*

I must be content [today] with one vital *example.* All through the developing world we face an increasing crisis of accelerated and uncontrolled *urbanization.* Men and women and children are streaming into the great cities, generally the *capital* cities, from the *monotony* and all too often the *misery* of *rural* life, and they are *moving*, bag and baggage, long before *farming* can afford to *lose* their labor or the *city* is *ready* to put them to work and accommodate them properly.

This *rootless, hopeless, workless* urban poverty is the greatest single cause of misery in the world. Can we *lessen* or *redirect* this flow? Can we *prepare* the urban world better to *receive* it? Or improve the *rural* world enough to *diminish* the flood? We don't know, because we have not sought seriously to *find out.* We lack *adequate* policies, because we have so few *facts* and so few people *trained* to develop and implement programs. For too long we have proceeded on the false assumption that people would *really* rather live in *villages* than anywhere,[221] and that it is *better* for society if they *did.* The trouble is they *don't* — even when the village is *modernized* and *sanitized* and *electrified*, people move into *larger* towns and cities.

---

220 The comma has been added by hand.
221 The comma has been added by hand.

Some countries have in fact recognized that the problem is not *less* urbanization but *more* urban areas — not just one or two in each country. Some are experimenting with *regional* development programs — and here I mean regions *within* countries — in an effort to create *new* urban centers which will not only *deflect* migration headed for already over-crowded capital cities but will have an *impact* on the surrounding *countryside* and *improve rural* living in a wide area around the new cities. But the process of *decentralization* is *difficult* and *complex* and failures — temporary or permanent — are as common as *successes*.

This is the *background* against which we helped *launch,* and heartily *welcome,* the unanimous decision of the Social Commission to recommend a research training program in *regional* development — using as a laboratory the current efforts being made in a variety of different *lands,* political *systems* and *cultures* to deal with the problems of urban *in-migration.*

With some *systematic* research perhaps some *useable* conclusions can be drawn about how *best* to encourage an *appropriate* pattern of urban development which will avoid the *blight* and *misery* so visible in so many cities throughout the world. This is precisely the *kind* of research we need if the full weight of modern discovery and modern resources is to be brought to bear on the *social* as well as the *technical* problems of the developing world.

VII

In this *same* context — of science applied to an *explosive human* and *social* problem — we have to make a wholly new attack upon what President Johnson has called "The *multiplying problems* of our *multiplying peoples.*" It is perhaps only in the last five years that we have come fully to realize on what scale they are proliferating. Since 1960, under United Nations auspices, censuses have been held in scores of countries,[222] in *nine* of them for the first time. They have all underlined the *same* fact — that population is increasing more rapidly than had previously been imagined and that this accelerating growth, in all developing lands, is eating into the pitiful margins needed to give *bread* and *hope* to those already born. [¶] We have to find the *ways* of *social, moral,* and *physical* control adequate to stem the *rising, drowning flood* of people. We need more *knowledge,* we need more *cooperative* effort. In fact, *much* that we do *elsewhere* will be *undone* unless we can act in this vital field. [PAUSE]

Aid, trade, research, population control — in *all* these fields we can mount a *convergent* attack upon the great *gap* between *rich* and *poor.* But we must *also* mount it *together.* And that brings me to some quite

[222] The comma has been corrected from a period.

concrete suggestions about international organizations, in the development field — in what *direction* they should be *going*, and how *fast* they should be *growing*.

VIII

The organizations of the UN family perform a rich *variety* of useful labors. At a moment when one of the central political organs in the UN is temporarily hung up on a constitutional hook,[223] it is worth reflecting on the *success* and *growth* of the Specialized Agencies, and of the central *funds* which provide a growing fraction — more than *half* in some cases — of the resources they appy to the business of development. These agencies are an illustration — and a good one — of the proposition that international politics is not a *game* in which an inch *gained* by one [224] player must mean an inch *lost* by another.

The *reality* is that international agreements *can* be *reached* — and international organizations *can* be *formed* — and international *common law* can be *elaborated* — on subjects which draw nations *together* even as they continue to *quarrel* about the *frontiers* and *friends* and ideological *frenzies* which keep them *apart*.

So let's look for a moment at the *political* merits of *functional* organizations — the kind that work at *peace* through *health,* or *food,* or *education,* or *labor,* or *communications,* or *meteorology,* or *culture,* or *postal* service, or *children,* or *money,* or *economic* growth — or the exploration of *outer space* — organizations, that is, for the pursuit of some *specific* and *definable* task beyond the frontiers of *one* nation, a task for which *technology* is already *conceived* or *conceivable,* for which a common *interest* is mutually *recognized,* for which institutions *can* — and therefore *must* — be *designed*.

Organizations like these *begin* by taking the world as it *is*. No fundamental *political* reforms are *needed; no value systems* have to be *altered; no ideologies* have to be seriously *compromised*.

These organizations start from where we *are*,[225] and then take the *next* step. And that, as the ancient Chinese guessed long ago, is the *only* way to get from *here* to *there*.

These organizations tackle jobs that can be managed through *imperfect* institutions by *fallible* men and women. *Omniscience* is not a prerequisite; the peace of the world does not *stand* or *fall* on the success of any one organization; *mistakes* need not be *fatal*.

These limited-purpose organizations *bypass* the obstacle of *sovereignty*. National independence is not *infringed* when a nation voluntarily accepts

---

[223] Stevenson refers to the question of application of Article 19.
[224] "Our" has been changed to "one."
[225] The comma has been corrected from a period.

in its own interest the *restraints* imposed by cooperation with *others*. *Nobody* has to play who doesn't *want* to play, but for those who *do* play, there are door prizes for all.

All these special characteristics of the *functional* agencies are important to their *survival value* and *growth potential*. The best example is also momentarily the most dramatic. In the midst of the military, political and diplomatic *turmoil* of Southeast Asia, the governments which are working together to promote the regional development of the lower Mekong Basin have continued to work there in surprising and encouraging harmony.

IX

But a certain *shadow* hangs over the affairs of the technical agencies — a shadow which threatens to *compromise* the very virtues we have just been discussing. That shadow is *political* controversy — and it has *no place* on the agenda of the technical agencies.

I shall not attempt to draw sharp lines along the sometimes murky borders between the *politico-ideological* and the *functional* fields — between just what is *doctrinal* and just what is *technical*. The *important* distinctions are *clear* enough. The difference between appropriate content for the general debate in the *General Assembly* and appropriate content for debates on international *labor* or world *literacy* or world *health* does not need much elaboration. We can all recognize that the remaining problems of *colonialism* have practically *nothing* to do with the problems of *health* — and vice-versa. We have organizational arrangements for dealing with *both*. We have *times* and *places* set aside — we have *agenda* prepared and *representatives assigned* — for dealing in *separate* and *orderly* ways with these and other subjects.

Yet we cannot overlook a disturbing tendency to *dilute* the proceedings of the technical agencies with ideological *dispute* — and to steal *time, energy* and *resources* needed to help the developing countries,[226] and *divert* it instead to *extraneous* issues calculated to stir *everybody's* emotions without raising *anybody's* per capita *income*.

This *limits* the *value,* inhibits the *growth,* hurts the *prestige,* and crimps the *resources* of the technical agencies. It is a *wasteful* exercise.[227] It is only to be hoped that these *diversionary* tactics will *fade* from our forums so we may get along more *promptly* with the *practical, useful, technical* tasks which lie before us in such profusion.

The great *spurt* in useful activity by the UN *specialized* and *affiliated* agencies has come about through the good *sense* of the members, expressed in a series of actions by the Economic and Social Council and in

[226] The comma has been corrected from a period.
[227] "And moreover a futile exercise" has been deleted and "exercise" inserted.

the General Assembly, and designed to provide new resources to break down the main obstacles to development.

Through the Expanded Program of Technical Assistance and the [228] Special Fund, the members have already provided close to one billion dollars to help the developing countries *organize* the *use* of knowledge and to get ready to make effective use of large *capital* investments. Now these two programs, on the recommendation of the Council,[229] are to be merged in the 20th General Assembly to become the *UN Development Program.*

We are reaching this year, for the *first* time, the target of $150 million a year for that program. My Government believes that this has been a *useful* and *efficient* way to provide technical assistance and pre-investment capital. The target should now be raised. For our part, we would be glad to see the target set substantially higher. [Personally?]

We also think that the use for development of *non-commercial* exports of *food* from some of the *surplus* producing countries, has been promising. At a meeting in Rome last week, we have already indicated that we would be glad to see the World Food Program continued, with a target for the next three-year period, almost *triple* that of the three year experimental period now coming to an end. We hope that *other* nations which foresee non-commercial *surpluses* in their agricultural horoscope, will *join* in expanding the World Food Program as another way to transfer needed resources for the benefit of the developing countries.

We are also pleased with the progress of *industrial* development. The establishment of the Center for Industrial Development in the UN Secretariat has clearly proved itself a sound and progressive move. We think the time has come to move *further* along this line, and find much promise in the suggestions made by the distinguished representatives [230] of the United Kingdom [,Lord Caradon and Miss Castle,] [231] on this subject. We emphatically [232] agree that it will be necessary to secure *additional* resources for the promotion of industrialization. We believe, however,[233] that rather than to establish yet another special voluntary fund, such resources could *best* be made available by special arrangements within the framework of the new UN Development Program.

X

Beyond *raising* the *target* for the Development Program and *expanding* the World Food Program, and giving a special *push* to the work on

[228] "UN" has been deleted here.
[229] The comma has been corrected from a period.
[230] "Representative" has been changed to "representatives."
[231] Barbara Castle, British minister of overseas development.
[232] "Strongly" has been changed to "emphatically."
[233] The comma has been corrected from a period.

industrialization, I would foresee *another* kind of development activity to which I believe every government should accord a very high priority indeed. This is the field which might be called *truly international* development.[234]

So far, we have tended to define the word "development" to encompass only the elements of an *individual* country's economic growth and social progress. Some regional projects have gained favor as well. But clearly visible now on the horizon are programs and projects in which the operating agency will not be a *national* government or a *private* company or even a small *group* of governments in a *region* — but rather one of the UN's *own* family of world wide organizations.

The best example — one that is *already* requiring our attention — is the world weather watch now being planned by the WMO.[235] In the preliminary design work already underway, it is proposed, for example, to:

— Probe into atmosphere from satellites in orbit;

— Establish group stations to read-out what the satellites have to say and to process and communicate weather information throughout continental regions;

— Establish floating weather stations to give more coverage to vast oceanic areas, particularly in the Southern Hemisphere;

— Possibly even launch balloons from international sites which will travel around the world at a constant level making weather observations as they go.

The *major* components of the World Weather Watch must continue to be the *national* facilities, operated primarily for *national* purposes, and also contributing to the needs of the world. But we are speaking here of *additional* facilities, some of which may need to be *internationally operated* and perhaps *internationally owned* and which may be very *costly* even at the start. Money would have to be raised on a *voluntary* basis and placed in the hands of an *international* agency — the WMO, perhaps or some *new* operating facility.

Here, then is a *new* kind of problem for us to think about before it *overtakes* us. Here is a great *big* development project, involving activity inherently *international* which will have to be *financed internationally*. We would propose that the UN Development Program start experimenting with *this* kind of development activity, *modifying* as necessary the *rules* and *procedures* that were drafted with *national* development projects in mind.

Maybe such large projects will have to be financed in some *special* way. But for a *start*, we would like to see the new UN Development program, with its rich experience in financing various kinds of development, work

234 "Program" has been deleted here.
235 The World Meteorological Organization.

on this subject and present to its own Board, and to this Council, an *analysis* of the problem of meeting the costs of global international operations.

XI [PAUSE]

If all these suggestions for *raising* our *sights* — yes, and our *contributions* — give the impression that the United States believes in the *strengthening* of international development institutions, you may be sure that that impression is *correct.* [¶] Most of these institutions *need* to be strengthened to meet, within their respective areas, the challenge of the requirements and aspirations of the developing countries. Equally, and perhaps even *more* important, their policies and actions need to be *harmonized* for there is no room left in this world for narrow *parochialism.* The various aspects and problems of economic and social development — *modernization* of *agriculture* and *industrial growth, health* and *production, education* and *social welfare, trade* and *transportation, human rights* and *individual freedom* — have become so closely *inter-related* as to call for inter-locking *measures* and *programs.*

These *basic* conditions in the contemporary world give *meaning* and *urgency* to the Review and Reappraisal of the Economic and Social Council's role and functions which U Thant proposed in this Chamber a year ago. The position of my Government is set forth in our submission to the Secretary General reproduced in Document E/4052/Add.2 and needs no further explanation.

But there are just a few points I want to stress:

With the UN system as *envisaged* in and *established* by the Charter, the General Assembly and ECOSOC are the two *principal* intergovernmental organs with overall responsibilities for UN policies and activities in the economic and social field, their *orderly* development and *effective* implementation.

Whatever the *record* of the Council in the *past* — and we believe that it is a *good* record — it has become evident that the Council faces ever increasing difficulties in the discharge of its functions due to the ever widening *scope* of the United Nations and the *multiplication* of machinery.

To make the Council *fully* representative of the [236] enlarged membership of the UN, its *size* will soon be increased by the necessary ratifications of the Charter Amendment.

We believe that the *role* of the Council as a *preparatory* body for the General Assembly, and acting under its authority needs to be *clarified* and *strengthened.* It should make a significant contribution to the work

[236] "Total" has been deleted here.

of the General Assembly by drawing its attention to *major* issues confronting the world economy, by formulating *proposals* for [237] action; by providing supporting *documentation;* and in *preparing* and *reviewing* programs with a sense of *financial responsibility,* and thus assisting the preparation of budget estimates by the Secretary General for appropriate action by the Committees of the General Assembly.

In stressing the *coordination* function of ECOSOC every care needs to be taken to *encourage* rather than to *hinder* the work of *functional* and *regional* economic and social bodies and the activities of the Specialized Agencies and other related organizations. [We believe] The role of these functional organizations in achieving coordination within their areas of competence needs to be more fully *recognized.*

The Review and Reappraisal proposed by the Secretary General is a difficult task and adequate time must be allowed for it. Many of the constructive suggestions he made yesterday regarding *research, documentation,* and sound *budgeting* are directly related to the work of the Council and deserve most careful thought. It is our hope that the Council at the *present* session will make the necessary arrangements to *facilitate* and assure such study in depth and full consideration.

We assume the Review will go through several *stages,* including consideration by both the Council and the General Assembly. The Council will have to undertake thorough preparatory work in order to enable the General Assembly and its Committees 2, 3 and 5 to reach informed conclusions and to take the necessary actions.

Last but not *least,* and this I cannot stress strongly enough — the Review will require the closest possible cooperation between all members of the Council representing developed and developing countries. The Council will wither away, whatever conclusions are reached by the Review, unless there is a *will* among *all* of us to *make* it succeed. And succeed it *must* as an *indispensable* organ of the United Nations for the achievement, beyond anything we have experienced to date, of constructive [238] cooperation in the economic and social fields and as a powerful aid to [239] development. [Insert] [240]

In this connection I listened with interest *and* to Am. Pachachis thoughtful observations on the role of the Council. We appreciate the weight and importance of his statements. They open the way to a frank and constructive discussion. The spirit in which they were offered give us hope and encouragement.

[237] "Relevant" has been deleted here.
[238] "International" has been deleted here.
[239] "The promotion of economic" has been deleted here.
[240] The paragraph which follows is handwritten on a separate sheet.

XII

Finally, let me repeat [241] that the need for *joint* action in the wide field of development is *obvious.* Whether we are talking about *aid,* or *trade* or *research,* or urban redevelopment,[242] or industrialization — whether we are talking about *scientific discovery* or about *institution building* — we hold that there are no *monopolies* of *trained minds* and *disciplined imaginations* in *any* of our countries.

Joint action is, after all, the *final* significance of *all* we do in our international policies today. But we are *still* held back by our old parochial *nationalism.* We are still *beset* with dark *prejudices.* We are still *divided* by *angry,* conflicting *ideologies.* Yet all around us our *science,* our *instruments,* our *technologies,* our *interests* and indeed our deepest *aspirations* draw us more and more *closely* into a *single neighborhood.*

This must be the *context* of our *thinking* — the *context* of *human interdependence* in the face of the vast new dimensions of our science and our discovery. Just as Europe could never again be the old *closed-in* community after the voyages of Columbus *we* can never again be a squabbling band of nations before the awful majesty of outer space.

We travel *together,* passengers on a little space ship,[243] *dependent* on its *vulnerable* reserve of *air* and soil; *all* committed for our *safety* to its *security* and *peace;* preserved from annihilation only by the *care,* the *work,* and I will say, the *love* we give our *fragil* craft. We cannot maintain it *half fortunate, half miserable, half confident, half despairing, half slave* — to the ancient enemies of man — half *free* in the liberation of resources *undreamed* of until this day. No *craft,* no *crew* can travel safely with such vast *contradictions.* On their *resolution* depends the *survival* of us *all.*

Stevenson left no notes of any conversation with Maurice Couve de Murville in Paris, but on July 10 he kept brief notes of his talk with Prime Minister Harold Wilson at Chequers. Stevenson described his conversation with U Thant in Geneva. Wilson explained that a British Commonwealth mission was in Hanoi sounding out the possibility of a "just and honorable peace." But the mission had been unable to see

---

241 "Say" has been changed to "repeat."
242 "Development" has been changed to "redevelopment."
243 This phrase of Stevenson's has had wide use since 1965. See, for instance, R. F. Dasmann, *Planet in Peril?: Man and the Biosphere Today* (Harmondsworth, Middlesex, England: Penguin Books, 1972), preface, and Friends of the Earth, *The Stockholm Conference: Only One Earth: An Introduction to the Politics of Survival* (London: Earth Island, Ltd., 1972).

North Vietnamese Premier Ho Chi Minh. Moreover, the British were being criticized by Hanoi for not having "denounced US bombing." Wilson explained that he had little hope for the peace mission. Stevenson noted that Wilson felt "at end of day will have to talk with VC."

While in England, Stevenson talked to a number of officials and visited with old friends. On July 12, he appeared on the British Broadcasting Corporation's television program Panorama. *A short time before he died on July 14, Thomas Barman, diplomatic correspondent for the BBC, interviewed him.*[244] *That evening the BBC, after considerable discussion over the propriety of using the discussion, broadcast it in a somewhat edited form.*[245]

The discussion on Panorama, *July 12, 1965, follows.*[246]

ROBIN DAY: Ambassador, or as I believe you prefer to be called from your earlier days Governor, what brings you to England?

ADLAI STEVENSON: Well, I came to England on my way back to the United States after a visit to Geneva to attend the portion of the Economic and Social Council meeting of the United Nations there and to make a speech and I stopped off here on my way home to see some of your officials and also to see some old friends.

DAY: And in the course of seeing some of our officials and old friends, have you taken the opportunity of discussing the Vietnam matter at all?

STEVENSON: Yes, I have a little bit, not very much yet, I expect to perhaps in the next few days discuss it even a little more.

DAY: What reaction have you found in Europe and in Britain as to the wisdom or otherwise of America's current foreign policy, particularly in Vietnam?

STEVENSON: Yes, well, I think there's a good deal of confusion about it, one finds not only in Europe but even in my own country some misapprehension about the direction of American policy in South-East Asia, and that's reflected elsewhere too. For the most part, however, I haven't found, talking to officialdom, anything like the degree of confusion or apprehension about it or misunderstanding of it that one encounters in the public.

DAY: Does the replacement of General [Maxwell] Taylor by Mr. Cabot Lodge as America's Ambassador in Saigon signify a change of policy?

[244] Thomas Barman, *Diplomatic Correspondent* (London: Hamish Hamilton, 1969), pp. 201–202.
[245] W. S. Bonarjee, letter to Walter Johnson, March 18, 1968.
[246] The text is from a mimeograph copy released by the British Broadcasting Corporation.

STEVENSON: Not so far as I know, I've been away now for a week, but my impression is that it doesn't represent any change at all; I remember very well at the time that Max. Taylor undertook this task that he would, he agreed to serve for only a year and that year is now about up and I think consistent with that understanding the President has concluded to let him off and make a replacement and he has chosen Ambassador Lodge who has served there previously and who has other qualifications for that task.

DAY: Well, would you agree with what Senator Fulbright is reported as saying, namely, that this change could, and I quote, "possibly mean greater emphasis on the political aspects of the problem?"

STEVENSON: Possibly, although I don't know. Certainly the political aspect of the problem has always been uppermost, I think, in people's minds who are at all familiar with the situation in Vietnam and that this isn't a war that can be resolved by military means, nor can we find a solution there except by political means.

DAY: May I ask you, Governor, about reports and suggestions that you yourself are not altogether happy with President Johnson's policy in Vietnam?

STEVENSON: Well, I've heard these reports, indeed I had many letters and petitions and representations and delegations and even pickets and so on, but I think it's unfortunate because actually I don't share this — any misgiving about the direction of our policy, especially with respect to Vietnam. Here I think the ultimate disaster of atomic conflict is probably going to be averted in this situation or in any other situation by the pursuit of lines of policy which have become, in the course of time, very clear, that, as we did in Europe, we shall have to draw a line between the Communist and the non-Communist world areas, so that neither power system can force a change by force.

DAY: What answer have you given to the many people, many of whom are your admirers, political admirers, that you should resign from your job in protest against the policy there?

STEVENSON: Well, I've told those that have called upon me in person that I have no such intention and I've explained to them why, but I have not published anything or written anything or said anything publicly about this. I suspect maybe when I get home, if the volume of this sort of protest is large enough, I shall have to do so.

DAY: In a recent television interview in America, Governor, you said this, you said that you were not always in agreement on every detail of the administration's conduct over the Vietnam policy. Well, what exactly did you mean there?

STEVENSON: Well, I said I am not always in agreement on every detail of any policy. I didn't confine it to Vietnam.

DAY: But it was in the context of ——

STEVENSON: Yes, and I daresay that nobody who participates in the conduct of foreign policy is in agreement on every detail anyway. The problem of, the job of the President is to reach a conclusion between competing ideas, conflicting ideas. But for the most part, and in the larger aspect of the policy, I think on the whole this is a practical illustration of the importance of stopping aggression where we can and this is what we, this was the point of the Korean war. The United States has suffered some hundred and sixty thousand casualties, as you know, since the last War. But aggression has not succeeded in either Greece or Turkey, it's not succeeded in Iran, it hasn't succeeded in the Lebanon, it hasn't succeeded in Korea, it hasn't succeeded in other places as well, with the help of the United Kingdom and other countries as well. Sooner or later, one has to face the fact that the world is still in the state of anarchy and there are some countries that believe they can impose their will by force.

DAY: May I put to you one of the things that Mr. Walter Lippmann has said recently, he described America's choice in Vietnam as "between the devil of unlimited war and the deep blue sea of defeat." Is there any other course?

STEVENSON: I think so. It's bold of me to disagree with my old and dear friend, Walter Lippmann, but I don't believe it need be stated in such extreme terms as that. I had rather hoped that, and still believe that the limited form of resistance which we pursued for five years while the North Vietnam was attacking South Vietnam before the United States ever struck in the North at all,[247] would prevail. It didn't prevail. But now the time has come when we have to take such measures to meet force with force as are necessary to ensure that it does and that reason will prevail and that they will come to the conference table, they will find their way along with us and with the others that are very involved and I hope that with the benefit of the advice and counsel of other countries who are more concerned with peace than they are with conquest, that we will find a solution of this matter as we have elsewhere in the world which will enable us to pursue a peaceful, not only a peaceful solution but the development of all of South-East Asia. It's not only Vietnam, it's all these other countries that are involved. Aggression begets aggression, retreat begets retreat and we either stand, as we discovered in Europe, and hold the line at appro-

247 Whether Stevenson was aware of American covert action against North Vietnam is not clear.

priate places or we don't, and if we don't then aggression succeeds and they knock on door after door and find that they open, they ultimately come to the ultimate door where resistance becomes imperative and then you have a holocaust, you have major war. This is what we're trying desperately to avoid in South Vietnam.

DAY: Well, can I ask you about that, how can America continue the fight against Communist forces in Vietnam by meeting force with force without escalating or stepping up the conflict further and further?

STEVENSON: Well, I don't know, I could answer that question better after the present monsoon season is over, after this present Vietcong offensive. I must say one can't but deeply deplore this war. I saw something of it there with the French forces in the north in the Red River delta more than ten years ago,[248] and I know how desperate, how wicked, how evil it is and how very difficult it is for Westerners and I deeply deplore the fact that American forces have to fight in Asia anywhere but this is the lot and what country should know more about that than the United Kingdom, which preserved the peace for a century? You have to meet these problems, as I say, where they arise and not to do so, I think may lead on to even greater evils.

DAY: President Johnson, Governor, in his speech at San Francisco, you will remember, appealed to members of the United Nations to do what they could to help get Communist China and North Vietnam to the conference table. Now what, in fact, can the U.N. or its members do in this Vietnam situation?

STEVENSON: Well, I think the cumulative effect of the moral authority of the world is a very powerful weapon, perhaps more powerful than guns and bombs, and that want [?] [249] the world authority to make its view very clear and very emphatic in Hanoi and in Peking, that it wanted a solution of this matter and it wanted a peaceful solution, one that preserved the right of self-determination of a small people, that they would get it. This would have an enormous effect and I think this is what President Johnson was calling for in his speech at San Francisco.

DAY: Do you think that the U.N. would be a more useful vehicle for negotiations, particularly in the Vietnam matter, if Communist China were admitted?

STEVENSON: Well, as things stand now, you see, it's a rather moot question. Communist China is doing its very best to destroy the United Nations. It has never agreed to become a member of the United Na-

---

[248] See *The Papers of Adlai E. Stevenson,* Vol. V, Chap. Seven.
[249] The text is not clear at this point.

tions, except on condition that Taiwan, that Formosa was expelled. And very few members want to see that happen. It's always imposed impossible conditions just as it's imposing impossible conditions now. It says, with respect to Vietnam, that it certainly will talk "with you on our conditions," namely that the United States' forces get out and that the National Liberation Front, that is to say the Vietcong, shall dominate the scene and impose its own will on South Vietnam.

DAY: What is your ——

STEVENSON: We have offered to talk, on the other hand, as you know, unconditionally.

DAY: Well, what is your opinion, Governor, of the visit to Hanoi of Mr. Harold Davies who, as you know, is a junior Minister in the British Government?

STEVENSON: Well, it's my understanding that the Davies mission to Hanoi was an effort to explain to the authorities in North Vietnam what the purpose and objectives of the Commonwealth mission were. And we've generally supported, as you know, the purpose of the Commonwealth mission which is entirely consistent with the some thirteen or more initiatives that the United States has taken and many of them by and with the cooperation of the United Kingdom to bring this matter to the conference table. I don't think we can afford to leave any stone unturned if you believe in peace, and certainly we do. And certainly you do, and certainly, I think, most of the civilised world does, and that it doesn't want to see this war escalate. As President Johnson has so repeatedly said, we don't want any larger war,[250] we want to see this thing resolved as quickly as possible and as a fair and honourable peace, a just and honourable peace that will enable these people to determine for themselves their own future.

DAY: Governor Stevenson, thank you.

After the Panorama *interview Stevenson had supper with a number of reporters, and "he talked off the record of many of the doubts and frustrations he felt about American policy in South East Asia and more particularly over the Dominican Republic."* [251]

[250] In March, 1965, President Johnson authorized air strikes against North Vietnam and sent two Marine battalions to Vietnam. The following month, Johnson approved an 18,000–20,000-man increase in "support forces." In June, U.S. troops were made "available for combat support." In July, Johnson approved the deployment of about 100,000 men. By the end of 1965, U.S. forces in Vietnam totaled 184,314. Neil Sheehan et al., *The Pentagon Papers as Published by the New York Times* (New York: Quadrangle Books, 1971), Chap. 7.

[251] David J. Webster (deputy editor of *Panorama*), letter to Walter Johnson, March 31, 1967.

After supper Stevenson asked his old and trusted friend Eric Sevareid to come with him to the embassy residence and talk. After Stevenson's death Sevareid reported over the Columbia Broadcasting System some of what Stevenson had talked about.[252] *Sevareid then published in* Look *a lengthier report of the conversation.*[253] *The* Look *article is authentic Stevenson, talking to someone who understood him and was perceptive about him. He said what was in his soul to one of the few people with whom he had real rapport.*[254]

[252] See the Chicago *Sun-Times,* July 18, 1965.
[253] November 30, 1965.
[254] Fred W. Friendly described the article as the most distinguished piece of journalism done outside of Vietnam in 1965 by a broadcast journalist. "Vietnam: What Lesson?" *Columbia Journalism Review* (Winter, 1970–1971), p. 15.

THE FINAL TROUBLED HOURS OF ADLAI STEVENSON

I loved Adlai Stevenson, unreservedly, and for me there was a brutality about that week in mid-July when he died.

On Monday, the twelfth, I had sat up with him until well past midnight, and he bared his heart in a rush of talk. What he said that night revealed a profound frustration, a certain resentment that stopped just short of bitterness. We had not talked so intimately for several years, and I went away with my feelings of sadness for him overlaid with a kind of selfish feeling of elation that our old affection had been revived and confirmed.

Two days later, in the late afternoon, I was sitting in a warm bath in my room at London's cavernously old-fashioned Hyde Park Hotel, looking through the notes I had scribbled on the hotel stationery after the Monday conversation. In an hour or so, I would dress and go to the American Embassy residence in Regent Park to dine with Adlai, Ambassador David Bruce and his wife, Evangeline, and their current houseguests. The phone rang. It was Patricia Bernie, the London office manager for CBS News, telling me in halting sentences that Governor Stevenson had just died on the street near the Embassy in Grosvenor Square.

With all sensation somehow suspended, I dressed in a hurry and caught a cab to the Embassy. There at the curb, standing beside her car, was Mrs. Katharine Graham, president of The Washington Post Company, one of the Bruces' houseguests and an old friend.

I am no good in moments like this. We stood there, distraught, unable to say much of anything to one another. Mrs. Graham kept glancing about. Then she exclaimed, "There she is, there is Marietta."

Mrs. Marietta Tree, the statuesque and beautiful delegate to the United Nations Human Rights Commission, got out of a car with Phil Kaiser, Minister of Embassy, another old friend. It was Mrs. Tree who had been strolling with Adlai when he said he felt faint and then fell down; it was she who had tried to blow her own breath into his mouth and lungs, kneeling on the cement. They were returning from St. George's Hospital, where Adlai now lay.

Mrs. Graham hurried to join them, and I followed, up the steps to the Embassy's glass doors, then into the elevator to the second floor, where the Bruces were waiting in the Ambassador's office. Every one of us in that small elevator had known and loved Stevenson for years; he had been the centerpiece of many mutual gatherings. He was still the centerpiece, but we were like strangers. I glanced once at Mrs. Tree. Her eyes dilated as she caught my glance, and her face seemed to stiffen. They went into Bruce's office, and I rode back to my office in Hallam Street to begin a long night of writing and recording for radio and television, culminating in a live discussion about Governor Stevenson on a BBC program when I very nearly broke down completely and publicly.

A flurry of controversy and some angry feelings in high places resulted from what I broadcast to America that evening and from what others said. I did not report all he had told me, but I said that he was planning to resign from the UN post. From Paris, David Schoenbrun of Metromedia Stations reported a conversation of the previous week and stated that Stevenson had referred to President Lyndon B. Johnson's intervention in the Dominican Republic as a "massive blunder." The President, through Bill Moyers, his press secretary, responded with anger, saying it was a disservice to Stevenson's memory to quote him when he was dead and could not answer.

Later, the White House told me its reaction was directed solely at the Schoenbrun story, not at mine, but for a time I suffered painful worries that I may indeed have harmed the memory of a dear friend. I do not think so now; I think what I reported had to be reported, if the historic record is to be truthful and complete, though perhaps I should have waited until after his funeral. I am not quite sure. In any case, Adlai's state of mind at his death should be known, and I think it is entirely proper for me to relate it in detail now. I do so without attempting to evaluate his various remarks about high policy, but with a sense of certainty that I report him accurately.

On Saturday, July 10, Stevenson flew to England, and a paragraph in the London papers said he had spent that day with Prime Minister Harold Wilson at Chequers, the official country residence of British premiers, a house that will forever bear the imprint of Winston Churchill's presence. On Monday, the Embassy told American news offices in London that Mr. Stevenson would be interviewed on the BBC that night by Mr. Robin Day, a tough cross-examiner. In fact, the Embassy had arranged the interview, with America's "image" overseas in mind. Most Englishmen thought highly of Stevenson. They did not associate him with their developing picture of the United States Government as aggressive, military-minded and reckless. If Stevenson were to talk to the British people in explanation and defense of Vietnam and the Dominican intervention, he could dilute the efforts of the British "teach-inners" and their far-left-wing associates. The interview could help make up for Henry Cabot Lodge's disastrous performance in an Oxford debate a month earlier.

I went to the slightly shabby BBC studios at Lime Grove in the west end of London. Adlai arrived with Evangeline Bruce, shook hands with a dozen British and American reporters, expressed surprise at finding me in London, then sat down before the cameras and fielded Day's questions with his customary sincerity. Even Robin Day seemed subdued under the Stevenson spell and pressed but lightly. Deftly, Stevenson reminded the British people that the United States had suffered 160,000 casualties among its young fighting men *since* World War II. His way of saying that America had had precious little help in these postwar struggles to contain Communist imperialism was to suggest that the British people, above all others, knew what it means to "stand alone"—a reference to the London blitz, when all Britishers felt they were the world's heroes, and, in a way, were.

After the broadcast, Adlai sat at a long table in a reception room, before a plate of cold beef and potato salad, and, between swallows, answered the reporters' questions, "for background only." He won them by his modesty, by his willingness to acknowledge that his country, too, was capable of mistakes, by granting that sometimes American rhetoric obscured American wisdom. Once, he referred to President Johnson with a smile as " my lord and master," and the reporters chuckled. It was obvious that however much he admired the President, the two men were hardly *simpatico.*

When the meeting broke up, Adlai pushed toward the door and, putting a hand on my arm, said, "You come along with me." He gave a sigh as we settled in the back seat of the Embassy limousine. We drove a few blocks and he said, "Oh, Lord, Pamela Berry is giving a party in Westminster, and I guess I'm supposed to be there." He hesitated a moment with the slight expression of pain I had seen a hundred times over the years, when he thought he might be offending some friend. "Let it go," he said finally, "let's go on to the house."

The American Embassy residence is Winfield House, once the home of Barbara Hutton, and surely the most munificent residence in all London. No ambassadorial couple has used it with more grace than the handsome Bruces and their handsome children. The great house was almost totally dark when Adlai and I found our way through the entrance hall and switched on a light. We took a small elevator to an upper floor and found more light switches in a warmly elegant library and sitting room. Adlai mixed a drink for each of us at a little table by the door. Then we relaxed, I in an easy chair, he at one end of the adjoining sofa, for what proved to be his last long talk with any of his many friends in my profession of journalism.

I quickly understood that he had not brought me back to the house merely for my company, merely as a gesture of friendship. He wanted to tell me certain things he had on his mind and, in a curiously pathetic way, to seek advice from someone he could trust.

He began almost abruptly. He simply had to get out of the UN job. He was tired. He was 65 years old. He had stuck with the task that President John Kennedy gave him (Stevenson had really wanted, very much, to be Secretary of State) for four and a half years — longer than UN ambassadorships usually ran for any government. And he was not at all happy in his official relationship with Washington.

He twisted his body — now grown very stout in the middle, I noticed — in my direction and sharply asked, "What do you think?"

I was taken aback. Here was a world statesman, an original public figure, a moral authority in his own right asking me how to make the final big decision of his life. I hesitated and said, "As a citizen, I hope you will stay in the job, but as a friend, I must say I have thought for a long time that you should resign." I said I thought he had been extremely patient in an impossible situation where he could not really speak as the Adlai Stevenson the world admired but only as public defense counsel for policies he did not always privately approve.

"I guess I've been too patient," he said. Then, with the wry, deprecating smile, "I guess that's a character weakness of mine."

He said he had to decide that very week. What this meant, as I understood it, was that unless he resigned right away, there would scarcely be time for Washington to make new arrangements before the General Assembly opened its session in September.

Big decisions of a personal nature are made in the viscera; the mind just ratifies them later. Adlai Stevenson had already resigned in his guts, and his mind was groping for the ways and means.

It would be very hard just then, partly because all manner of his intellectual and academic followers who violently objected to our Vietnam and Dominican Republic actions were trying to get him to repudiate his Government and his President. These efforts deeply exasperated him. These simple, if high-minded, followers did not grasp the delicacy of his official relationship with Washington. They underestimated his sense of duty to his office and vastly oversimplified the American problem in foreign affairs. It seemed clear to me that Adlai could not resign without specifically and forcefully repudiating these well-meaning followers, though we did not get to that tactical problem in our talk.

What was equally clear was that he hated, in advance, the moment when he would have to walk into President Johnson's office and hand him his resignation. I am sure he feared a blast of counter pressure from Johnson to persuade him to stay on, and, he complained, "He will then ask me who should replace me at the UN, and I have simply been unable to think of the proper person."

But at no time did he fundamentally criticize the Vietnam or the Dominican policies. If he had strong negative views about the latter, he may have restrained them with me because he may have known I was on record in support of the Caribbean intervention, hateful as that necessitous procedure was.

"Couldn't the President have waited, say three days, so we could round up more Latin-American support?" he asked me.

I said that personally I didn't think so, that events in Santo Domingo had been moving fast and that I could not imagine very many Latin governments volunteering official support in advance for an American intervention in Latin America. Their domestic politics simply would not allow them to, whatever their private desires.

"But did we have to send in so many troops," Adlai said, "20,000 of them?" I said the Pentagon had initially asked permission to land 30,000, and Stevenson was surprised to hear this. I also said the line the men had to cover from the Dominican airport to and through the city and around the international safety sector was 16 to 19 miles. That required a great many men, for thorough security.

Adlai said, "You may be right. You may be right." He took my glass, walked back to the little bar and replenished our drinks. Suddenly, he seemed extremely tired, and I suggested I let him go to bed. No, he wanted to talk a bit more. He drifted into a description of his Saturday at Chequers and of Prime Minister Wilson, whom he admired. "You know," he said, "Wilson wouldn't stop. He must have shown me every john in that house."

(A week later, at 10 Downing Street, Mr. Wilson recalled that tour of Chequers and said, "Adlai seemed to want to see every room in the house." Wilson also told me he had shown Stevenson the Rubens painting that Churchill had decided needed improvement. Churchill painted a mouse into the picture. "Imagine," said Wilson to me, "the self-confidence of a man who would alter a Rubens!")

The talk wandered back and forth — the UN, Washington, Vietnam, the Dominican Republic, and Stevenson's view of a future life for himself. He recalled the day in President Johnson's office when the President gave the order to send a small detachment of Marines to rescue the imperiled foreigners in Santo Domingo. Among those in the office, besides Adlai and Mr. Johnson, were Secretary of State Dean Rusk, Special Presidential Assistant McGeorge Bundy and Vice-President Hubert Humphrey. The President read aloud the statement he intended to make over television and radio. It went further than the simple mission of rescuing foreigners. It included a line that stated the United States would always stand ready to help the Dominican Republic preserve its freedom. This was the first hint that anybody in high office was thinking about the danger of a Communist coup. This sentence had far-reaching political implications.

Mr. Stevenson said he asked the President if he would mind rereading that particular passage. Mr. Johnson did so. "What does that mean?" Stevenson asked the group in general. There was, as I understood it, no specific reply, but Mr. Johnson began to frown and to ponder the point.

"I leaned over toward Humphrey — Hubert's my buddy! — and whispered, 'Say something!'" Stevenson said.

Hubert put his finger to his lips and shook his head.

"I walked over to Mac Bundy, who was looking out a window, and said, 'What do you think?'

"Bundy said, 'I'm in two minds.'" Stevenson seemed scornful of this response as he told me the story.

At length, the President picked up the phone and called Thomas C. Mann, Under Secretary of State for Economic Affairs. Mann, known as the hard-boiled realist on Latin affairs, told the President he couldn't see anything wrong with the sentence. But eventually, so Adlai said, the President looked over at him, said, "I think you're right," and with a pencil crossed out the questionable line.

And that, so Adlai believed at the time, was it — a very limited operation with a very limited aim. He told me that when the President went on television the following Sunday, saying that Communists were in control of the Dominican rebellion and, in effect, that we would not permit another Cuba — that this was a startling surprise to him, the man who then, of course, had to defend the heavy intervention at the United Nations.

This was only one of the last of what he obviously felt were personal humiliations, even though they were not so intended. In the same period, last spring, the President was planning his big speech for San Francisco at the twentieth anniversary of the founding of the United Nations. Stevenson was asked to write the first draft of the speech. He did so, including several concrete policy proposals. Then an article appeared in the New York *Times* by James Reston, shrewdly anticipating the Presidential proposals. Probably for this reason, the President had the speech almost entirely rewritten.

When Stevenson, who was, after all, America's chief delegate to the United Nations, called down to the White House to have the final draft read to him, Presidential Assistant Richard Goodwin, a Stevenson friend, was unable to comply. He told Stevenson that President Johnson had given him a flat order to show the speech to no one, specifically including

Stevenson and Secretary Rusk. "The literature that remained in the speech," Stevenson told me, "was mine. All the meat was taken out."

I had the impression this incident deeply offended him. Yet, in all the long discussion that night, he did not utter a word of specific criticism of Mr. Johnson. I had the feeling that he had great respect for the President's capacities, but no warm regard for him as a person.

At one point, Adlai chuckled.

"Come to think of it," he said, "I was the one who got young Congressman Johnson his commission when I was assistant to Secretary of the Navy [Frank] Knox during the war."

I asked him about Dean Rusk, who had the post that Stevenson had wanted. There was a faint shrug of the shoulders, and he replied, "Oh. . . . I just can't seem to make him out. He's so sort of wooden."

When President Kennedy died, Stevenson did not know whether the new President would want him to stay on at the UN or whether he wanted to stay on himself. When he next saw Mr. Johnson, the President urged him to call in the reporters and announce that he had "enlisted for the duration."

Adlai demurred at this, he told me, and limited himself to a statement that he would not desert the ship in a crisis.

Stevenson had to be the agent of American foreign policy at the UN, but, of course, he saw himself as something more than that. Too many crowds, in too many foreign countries, had adored and cheered him as a kind of universal symbol of peace, high thought and the goodness in man. He wanted, personally and directly, as Adlai Stevenson the man, to help bring the world to safety. The Vietnam war deeply worried him.

He settled further in the sofa and told me stories of negotiation efforts that were not then known to the public — or to me. I do not know that people have premonitions of their death. Yet, as he talked, the thought flickered through my mind that he was telling me these things out of a sense of urgency that they be known.

In the early autumn of 1964, he went on, U Thant, the UN Secretary-General, had privately obtained agreement from authorities in North Vietnam that they would send an emissary to talk with an American emissary, in Rangoon, Burma. Someone in Washington insisted that this attempt be postponed until after the Presidential election. When the election was over, U Thant again pursued the matter; Hanoi was still willing to send its man. But Defense Secretary Robert McNamara, Adlai went on, flatly opposed the attempt. He said the South Vietnamese government would have to be informed and that this would have a demoralizing effect on them; that government was shaky enough, as it was.

Stevenson told me that U Thant was furious over this failure of his patient efforts, but said nothing publicly.

Time was passing, the war expanding. The pressures on U Thant, supposedly the Number One peacemaker of the globe, were mounting from all sides within the UN. So he proposed an outright cease-fire, with a truce line to be drawn across not only Vietnam but neighboring Laos. U Thant then made a remarkable suggestion: United States officials could write the terms of the cease-fire offer, exactly as they saw fit, and he, U Thant, would announce it in exactly those words. Again, so Stevenson said to me, McNamara turned this down, and from Secretary Rusk there was no response, to Stevenson's knowledge.

At the time of this incident, it was official American policy that the fighting would go on until North Vietnam "left its neighbors alone," to use the phrase the State Department was then using. In other words, the Communists would have to quit first. It was not until April, in his Baltimore speech, that President Johnson changed all this and anounced that the United States was willing to negotiate for peace without preconditions.

(Some days after Stevenson's death, I broadcast on CBS Radio the essentials of this story, without attribution to its source — "the rule of compulsory plagiarism," the Washington press corps calls this often necessary practice. I was aware of no reaction, but about two weeks after that, when I was vacationing in France, the same account — without mention of U Thant — was published in the New York *Herald Tribune* and on many front pages in France and other countries. Washington officials brushed it off with the statement that there had never been any serious peace opportunities in the fall and winter. We will never know; history, after all, does not disclose its alternatives. But there can be no doubt that Adlai Stevenson, who was working closely with U Thant in these attempts, was convinced that these opportunities should have been seized, whatever their ultimate result.)

Clearly, he was not telling me about those opportunities, or possibilities or whatever one should call them, entirely because of a concern that we might have gotten peace in Vietnam. He was relating them as prime examples of the frustrations of his job at the UN. He was accustomed to making policy, not to being told what the policy was to be and how he was to defend and explain it before the world. In particular, he could not bear having certain White House and State Department people whom he regarded as mere youngsters telling him what to do. He felt these men simply did not understand his difficulties at the UN, and he doubted their wisdom about this dangerous world. At times, when he was in the middle of a UN debate with a Communist adversary — on TV and before the listening world — he would receive phone calls from Washington, or notes would be slipped to him, instructing him on how he should complete his arguments. The tactic, apparently, had driven him wild.

The summer night wore on; it was well after midnight now. I told

Stevenson that whatever he did after leaving the UN, it was important that he write his personal memoirs.

"I know, I know," he said. "Cass Canfield [chairman of the executive committee of Harper & Row, Publishers] has been after me a long time. But, hell, I haven't kept notes or diaries the way you fellows do. I find writing very hard work. How fellows like Art Schlesinger can pour it out the way he does, I just don't understand."

I reminded him of what Dean Acheson had done when he left office as Secretary of State. He had not tried full-scale, documented memoirs for print — partly because he did not want to involve men who were still living — but had, instead, written a series of rather light but fascinating descriptions of various famous figures he had dealt with, including Churchill. Stevenson perked up at this suggestion, and seemed to mull it over for a time in silence.

He said he felt he had served his time as a government servant, about 30 years of it, and when he left the UN, he did not intend to take another public office. He would practice law, living in New York but often working out of his Chicago law office, which would enable him to see his grandchildren often. He had a large place in his heart for these children. Adlai, after all, had lived without a wife or a settled home for more than 15 years. I had known for a long time that he was essentially a lonely man, and he knew I knew it, but he always stopped just short of saying so. "Ah, well," he said finally, "for a while, I'd really just like to sit in the shade with a glass of wine in my hand and watch the people dance."

He was fighting to keep awake. I stood up, and he acquiesced. As we neared the door to the hall, a little blond man with spectacles appeared in the lighted doorway. We had not heard his approach. Adlai introduced us. This was Truman Capote, the novelist, another house guest of the Bruces, returning from an evening engagement. He said something, and Stevenson and I found the elevator. On the way down, he said, "That young fellow has written a new book that will earn him $2,000,000. Imagine!"

He went all the way to the front entrance with me, finding those light switches again. Then he asked the waiting driver to take me to my hotel and to come around for him in the morning at nine-thirty. Adlai had an appointment at the British Foreign Office. We shook hands. He cuffed me lightly on the shoulder as I turned to go out.

Governor Stevenson died of exhaustion; he just wore himself out. I don't know how else to put it. Of course, the gathering frustration was part of this, but he did not die of a broken heart. If others regarded him as a "tragic" figure, I don't think he thought of himself that way. Let others call his life a failure; I think it was a wonderful success. When he was 50 years old, almost nobody but his private friends knew his rare quality;

when he died 15 years later, a million people cried. And he had this effect on the world of civilized people without using any of the instruments of power. He did it with words alone, and with that wry grin in his battered, lopsided face.

It will not be for me to try to analyze his character, to recall his wit and common sense; others are very busy at that task — the books and record albums are already piling up. All I know as a political reporter is that Adlai Stevenson injected humor and happiness and sophistication into American political life, and you have to have spent half your life listening to the normal run of American politicians to really understand what a fantastic accomplishment that was.

I find I don't think much about his public moments, but about the private times together: when he scolded me, early in 1952, for doing a broadcast about him as Presidential timber; when I telephoned him after the Illinois delegation, on the eve of the '52 convention, had refused to agree not to nominate him, and there was desperation in his voice; when, two days after that nomination, he confessed under my prodding that he had gone across Springfield at midnight and sat in "Mr. Lincoln's house" to try to gather strength for the ordeal; when we drove up to Granada in Spain, and he debated with himself out loud as to what he should do or not do about the 1960 nomination; when he called me over from London to Paris in the summer of 1961, and we sat in the Notre Dame gardens early in the morning while he remonstrated with me over a column I had written about Latin America; when he grabbed me in a crowd during the '56 campaign and said, "Hey, Eric, I'm one up on you — this morning a lady outside the church in Virginia said, 'Danny Kaye's the funniest and Eric Sevareid's the best-looking, but *you're* the one we love!' "

Adlai was a wonderful public figure, but he was essentially a private person. He was intensely *aware* of his friends. That was, I think, the real reason his friends loved him so much.

In a way, I suppose, that's a rather self-serving reason. (Years ago, a fellow officer asked Gen. Walter Bedell Smith to explain why he loved Eisenhower in spite of all Eisenhower's failings. Smith said, "When I am really honest with myself, I have to admit I love that guy because he makes *me* feel powerful.")

Adlai didn't make me feel powerful, but he made me feel importantly alive, and he made me feel trusted. There was something else, of no meaning to anybody but me; I am cursed with a somewhat forbidding Scandinavian manner, with a restraint that spells stuffiness to a lot of people. But Adlai saw through all that unfortunate facade. He knew that inside I am mush, full of a lot of almost bathetic sentimentality about this country, the Midwest, Abraham Lincoln, and the English language. He knew that while I can't easily give affection, I cannot easily withdraw it.

He was what the French call "a friend of the heart" because he saw through to your heart.

So, like a good many other people, I will never forget this man. But I will never fall in love with a politician again. I haven't the right to, in my kind of work, and there is too much pain in it.

END

Acknowledgements

The editor is most grateful to Stevenson's sister, Mrs. Ernest L. Ives, for her infinite patience and her considerate help at all stages in the preparation of this Volume. U Thant, Professor Stuart Gerry Brown, Roxane Eberlein, Harlan Cleveland, Francis T. P. Plimpton, Marietta Tree, Arthur Schlesinger, Jr., Charles Yost, and Clayton Fritchey read the first draft of the manuscript. Their suggestions have been most valuable. The editor is also deeply grateful to Adlai E. Stevenson III and his brothers, John Fell Stevenson and Borden Stevenson, for their help and cooperation.

Little, Brown and Company, Mrs. Eugene Meyer, Mrs. Marshall Field III and the Field Foundation, Mrs. John French, Mr. and Mrs. Harold Hochschild, Arnold M. Picker, Robert Benjamin, Newton N. Minow, James F. Oates, Jr., Francis T. P. Plimpton, Benjamin Swig, Philip M. Klutznick, Mrs. John Paul Welling, William McCormick Blair, R. Keith Kane, Simon H. Rifkind, Wilson W. Wyatt, William Benton, Daggett Harvey, Mr. and Mrs. Edison Dick, William McC. Blair, Jr., Lloyd K. Garrison, J. M. Kaplan, Jerrold Loebl, Hermon D. Smith, Edward D. McDougal, Jr., Glen A. Lloyd, Mr. and Mrs. Gilbert Harrison, Irving B. Harris, Edwin C. Austin, Archibald Alexander, Jacob M. Arvey, Paul Ziffren, Frank Karelsen, George W. Ball, C. K. McClatchy, Maurice Tempelsman, Barnet Hodes, Scott Hodes, Mrs. Ernest L. Ives, Timothy Ives, and the J. M. Kaplan Fund, Inc., provided funds to defray the editorial expense of these volumes. The University of Hawaii kindly assisted in defraying the cost of typing the manuscript.

The editor is grateful to Roger Shugg, of the University of New Mexico Press; Larned Bradford, of Little, Brown and Company; and Ivan von Auw, of Harold Ober Associates, for their encouragement and support.

The late William S. Dix, Alexander P. Clark, and Mrs. Nancy Bressler, of the Princeton University Library; Emmett Dedmon, of the Chicago *Sun-Times;* and Judy Fresco have been most cooperative. Phyllis Gustafson in Senator Adlai E. Stevenson's Washington office helped in many ways. Adele Sugawara checked the manuscript with great patience and typed the final draft with skill. John Woodman has been an exceptional copy editor for all the volumes in this series. Jean Whitnack, former manager of the Copyediting Department of Little, Brown and Company, and her successors, Sara Hill and Mike Mattil, have contributed much to these volumes. The indexes for the volumes were prepared by Bernice Colt and Ruth Cross. Proofreading was done by Zelda Fischer and Cecil Waters.

Special thanks goes to Roxane Eberlein for the painstaking care with which she read the manuscript and helped in many ways to search for additional material, including furnishing a list of classified documents which enabled the editor to request that they be declassified.

The archivists at the John F. Kennedy Library have been most helpful, particularly John F. Stewart, Sylvie Turner, William W. Moss, and Megan Desnoyers. Daniel Brown and D. F. Barrett, of the Freedom of Information Staff, Bureau of Public Affairs, Department of State, expedited requests for declassification review of some classified documents.

WALTER JOHNSON

Index

Index

foreign policy, U.S. (*continued*)
toward People's Republic of China, 485, 487, 491–492, 634–635, 799, 809n, 810; "by legislation," 504; "containment," 531–533, 634–635, 741, 743, 749, 798–799, 811; "goals" of, 583; for Democratic platform, AES and, 597–601, 611; AES makes "nonpartisan speech" for "bipartisan policy," 629–630; AES memo to Johnson on reassessment of, 631–640, 643; AES on isolationism, 744, 779–780; denounced, (by Soviet ambassador) 760, (by Canadian pickets) 767n, (by intellectual community) 804–805; AES draft of letter on, 809–812; AES on "confusion" about, 829–833. *See also* colonialism; State, U.S. Department of
Foreign Relations Committee. *See* Senate, U.S.
Formosa. *See* Taiwan
Fosdick, Dorothy, 243, 244; letter to, 244
Foster, William C., 246n
Fragoso, José Manuel, 435–436
France, 224; and Algeria and Tunisia (Bizerte), 67, 107, 108, 109, 110, 117; and Berlin, 88; and Suez, 143; in UN (mentioned), 181, 261, 392, 401, 470, 489, 493, 596, (and financial aid to UN) 13, 67, 185, 224, 366, 502, 638, 644, 645, 694–696, 792, 794, (abstains from voting) 31, 57, 435n, (opposes Liberian resolution) 46, (and Chinese representation) 100, (threatens withdrawal) 107, (refuses participation in disarmament conference) 203n, (and Indochina) 564–566; economic growth of, 252, 253, 254, 256; and Common Market, 290n, 392n, 401; signs Austrian Treaty, 304n; and nuclear weapons, 636; and Vietnam peace talks, 663, 702, 703, 720, 729; in Indochina, 832, (withdrawal from) 147n, 177, 810. *See also* Paris
Francis, St., quoted, 345, 614
Franco, General Francisco, 288, 432
Frankfurter, Felix, 201, 212; letters to, 201, 284
Franklin, Benjamin, 467
Franks, Sir Oliver, 578
Frederick, Pauline, interviews AES on *Meet the Press*, 796–797, 800
Fredericks, Wayne, 46
Frederika, queen of Greece, 388
Freedman, Max, quoted on AES, viii–ix
Freedom of Information Act, xix

Free Speech Movement (Berkeley, California), 567n
Frei Montalva, Eduardo, 630; letter to, 673
French Revolution, 416, 811
Freud, Sigmund, 418
Friedel, Samuel N., letter to, 626–627
Friendly, Alfred, quoted on AES speech, 615n
Friendly, Fred W., 834n
Frigerio, Rogelio, 86; letter to, 87
Fritchey, Clayton, 3, 53, 100, 101, 229, 355, 397, 545, 601, 650; and AES speeches, xxi, 232, 235, 351, 403, 521–522, 731–732; quoted on AES, 350, 443, 805–806; unpublished letter of, defending AES's Colby speech, 576–577; letters and memos to, 404–405, 578, 650, (on speeches and speechwriting) 232, 235, 403, 500–501, 521–522, 577, 731–732, (on resignation demands) 808–809
Frondizi, Arturo, 76, 83, 86, 87
Frost, Robert, AES speech at dinner honoring, 230, 372
Frye, William, 720, 721; interviews AES on *Meet the Press*, 794–795, 799
Fulbright, J. William, 29, 583; quoted, xiv, 618, 830; denounces Bay of Pigs plan, 52; AES support of, quoted, 579n; letter to, 111

Gaitskell, Mrs. Hugh, letter to, 374–375
Galbraith, John Kenneth, 113, 175, 231; quoted, 54–55, 119, 175; letters to, 58, 113, 231
Gallup Poll, on AES as ambassador to UN, 366n
Gandhi, Indira, 260n
Gandhi, Mohandas K., 176
Garaventa, Norma, 3
Gardner, Ava, 546, 547, 548, 549
Gardner, Richard N., 3, 43, 446, 644; quoted, 453, 646, (on AES) 681n
Garrison, Lloyd, 402, 540; quoted on AES's planned departure from UN, 541n
Gates, Paul W., letter to, 727
Gavin, Lieutenant General James M., letter to, 108
Gaza Strip, UNEF in, 143n, 185, 224, 693, 789. *See also* Israel
Gellhorn, Martha. *See* Matthews, Martha Gellhorn
General Agreement on Tariffs and Trade (GATT), 713, 818
General Motors Corporation, 256

Truce Supervisory Organization (UN-TSO), 242. *See also* United Nations finances (Article 19)

United States: and UN finances, 13 (*see also* United Nations finances [Article 19]); relations with USSR, 17 (*see also* Union of Soviet Socialist Republics); and Portugal, 21n, 41, 48, 89, 174, 175, 179, 424, 433n, 435; position of, on Congo, 33–41 *passim*, 427, 449n (*see also* Congo); and Bay of Pigs, 52 (*see also* Bay of Pigs invasion); and Latin America, 79–83 (*see also* Latin America); embargo against Cuba, 82n, 297, 317, 386, 600; and Berlin, 88; AES on economic development of, 93–97, 252–257, 773–774, 778–779; joint test ban proposal with UK, 105, 131, 186, 265; and Puerto Rico, 112; and resumption of nuclear testing, 116n, 128–133, 145, (signs, ratifies test ban treaty) 442–443, 450 (*see also* nuclear weapons and testing); position of, on Suez, 143n; and "Food for Development" program, 148–150; and Chinese representation at UN, 169n; AES on "image" of, 171–172, 227–228, 250–257, 747; disarmament program of, 186, 203–207, 212 (*see also* disarmament); criticism of UN in, 213, 259, 460, 463, 464, 484, 499, 515, 629–630; AES speech on role of, in UN, 213–226; and enlargement of UN Security Council, 223, 449n, 489, 493; as "pagan" nation, 227–228; and use of veto in UN, 235, 408, 696, 801, 814; USSR accusations against, 263, 297, 326, 330, 470, 553–554, 596, 597, 707, 746n, 760–761; USSR destroys plane of, 263; and missile crisis, 297–307, 309–335 (*see also* Cuba); signs Austrian Treaty, 304n; foreign intervention by troops of, 422, 750, 762, 807, 811, 833n; "under fire" in UN, 425–427, 470; and nuclear weapons in orbit, 480n; position of, on Cyprus, 518, 519–520; official position of, in Vietnam (May, 1964), 553n, 554–562 (*see also* Vietnam; Vietnam War); supports Israel, 626–627; -Belgian intervention in Congo, 648–656, 693, 762; intervention in Dominican Republic, 661, 760–761 (*see also* Dominican Republic, U.S. intervention and crisis in); troop casualties of, since World War II, 811, 831, 837. *See also* defense; foreign policy, U.S.; Pentagon, the; State, U.S.

Department of; United States Mission to the United Nations (USUN)

United States Committee for the United Nations, 469

United States Information Agency (USIA), 806

United States Mission to the United Nations (USUN), 84, 431, 617; AES as head of, xii (*see also* Stevenson, Adlai E.: AND AMBASSADORSHIP TO UN); and policy decisions, xix, 22; abstains from voting, 46, 67n, 110n, 435n, 489; and Bay of Pigs, 53 (*see also* Bay of Pigs invasion); and domestic finances, 71–73, 342, 410–411; and China in UN, 103, 118–119; and change in delegation, 114; State Department vis-à-vis, 154 (*see also* State, U.S. Department of); colonial policy of, 175 (*see also* colonialism); presents award to AES, 407; Public Affairs Section, AES letter to ("my dear friends on the second floor"), 690

U.S. News & World Report, 576

United World Federalists, AES speech at dinner of, 640–643

Universal Copyrights Convention, USSR policy and, 86, 459

Universal Declaration of Human Rights, AES speech commemorating 15th anniversary of, 476–479

University of British Columbia, 403, 410

University of California (Berkeley), AES speaks at, 526n, 527

University of Chicago, 101

University of Illinois: AES speaks at Honors Day Convocation of, 508, 543, 545–546; awards AES honorary degree, 546

University of Mississippi, 383

University of Toronto, AES speaks at, 763, 764, 766, 767, 769

University of West Indies, AES speech at, 671, 689, 707–717, 728

Uppsala University, AES speaks at, 551, 552, 574

"Urgent Need for a Treaty to Ban Nuclear Weapons Tests . . . , The" (AES speech, September, 1961), 117n

Urquhart, Clara, letter to, 169–170

Uruguay: AES visit to and report on, 73, 76, 80, 81; Conference, 79–83 *passim*, 87, 100

Vakil, Mehdi, 673

Valenti, Jack J., 689; letter to, 672–673

Van Buren, Martin, 511